the BIG selection 2012

over 1000 independent reviews

alan rogers

CW01676778

alan rogers publishing
experts in camping for over 40 years

Compiled by: Alan Rogers Guides Ltd

Designed by: Vine Design Ltd

Additional photography: T Lambelin, www.lambelin.com
Maps created by Customised Mapping (01769 540044)
contain background data provided by GisDATA Ltd

Published by: Alan Rogers Guides Ltd,
Spelmonden Old Oast, Goudhurst, Kent TN17 1HE
www.alanrogers.com Tel: 01580 214000

British Library Cataloguing-in-Publication Data:
A catalogue record for this book is available
from the British Library.

ISBN 978-1-906215-79-8

Printed in Great Britain by Stephens & George Print Group

Contents

Alan Rogers in search of 'the best'

Alan Rogers Guides were first published over 40 years ago. Since Alan Rogers published the first campsite guide that bore his name, the range has expanded and now covers 27 countries in six separate guides. No fewer than 20 of the campsites selected by Alan for the first guide are still featured in our 2012 editions.

There are many thousands of campsites in Europe of varying quality: this guide contains impartially written reports on 1,000, including many of the very finest, in no less than 22 countries. Each one is individually inspected and selected. This guide does not include sites in Britain and Ireland, for which we publish a separate guide, and it contains only a limited selection of sites in France, Italy and Spain & Portugal as we also publish separate guides for these destinations. We aim to provide you with a selection of the best, rather than information on all – in short, a more selective, qualitative approach. New, improved maps and indexes are also included, designed to help you find the choice of campsite that's right for you. We hope you enjoy some happy and safe travels – and some pleasurable 'armchair touring' in the meantime!

How do we find the best?

The criteria we use when inspecting and selecting campsites are numerous, but the most important by far is the question of good quality. People want different things from their choice of site so we try to include a range of campsite 'styles' to cater for a wide variety of preferences: from those seeking a small peaceful campsite in the heart of the countryside, to visitors looking for an 'all singing, all dancing' site in a popular seaside resort. Those with more specific interests, such as sporting facilities, cultural events or historical attractions, are also catered for.

The size of the site, whether it's part of a chain or privately owned, makes no difference in terms of it being required to meet our exacting standards in respect of its quality and it being 'fit for purpose'. In other words, irrespective of the size of the site, or the number of facilities it offers, we consider and evaluate the welcome, the pitches, the sanitary facilities, the cleanliness, the general maintenance and even the location.

> "...the campsites included in this book have been chosen entirelon merit, and no payment of any sort is made by them for their inclusion."
>
> Alan Rogers, 1968

Expert opinions

We rely on our dedicated team of Site Assessors, all of whom are experienced campers, caravanners or motorcaravanners, to visit and recommend campsites. Each year they travel some 100,000 miles around Europe inspecting new campsites for the guide and re-inspecting the existing ones. Our thanks are due to them for their enthusiastic efforts, their diligence and integrity.

We rely on our dedicated team of Site Assessors, all of whom are experienced campers, caravanners or motorcaravanners, to visit and recommend campsites. Each year they travel some 100,000 miles around Europe inspecting new campsites for the guide and re-inspecting the existing ones. Our thanks are due to them for their enthusiastic efforts, their diligence and integrity.

We also appreciate the feedback we receive from many of our readers and we always make a point of following up complaints, suggestions or recommendations for possible new campsites. Of course we get a few grumbles too – but it really is a few, and those we do receive usually relate to overcrowding or to poor maintenance during the peak school holiday period. Please bear in mind that, although we are interested to hear about any complaints, we have no contractual relationship with the campsites featured in our guides and are therefore not in a position to intervene in any dispute between a reader and a campsite.

Independent and honest

Whilst the content and scope of the Alan Rogers guides have expanded considerably since the early editions, our selection of campsites still employs exactly the same philosophy and criteria as defined by Alan Rogers in 1968.

'telling it how it is'

Firstly, and most importantly, our selection is based entirely on our own rigorous and independent inspection and selection process. Campsites cannot buy their way into our guides – indeed the extensive Site Report which is written by us, not by the site owner, is provided free of charge so we are free to say what we think and to provide an honest, 'warts and all' description. This is written in plain English and without the use of confusing icons or symbols.

Looking for the best

Highly respected by site owners and readers alike, there is no better guide when it comes to forming an independent view of a campsite's quality. When you need to be confident in your choice of campsite, you need the Alan Rogers Guide.

- Sites only included on merit
- Sites cannot pay to be included
- Independently inspected, rigorously assessed
- Impartial reviews
- Over 40 years of expertise

Using the Big Selection

Written in plain English, our guides are exceptionally easy to use, but a few words of explanation regarding the layout and content may be helpful. This guide is divided firstly by country, subsequently (in the case of larger countries) by region. For a particular area the town index at the back provides more direct access.

Maps, campsite listings and indexes

For this 2012 guide we have changed the way in which we list our campsites and also the way in which we help you locate the sites within each region.

We have changed the maps at the back of the guide to show the towns near which one or more of our featured campsites are located.

Within each country section of the guide, we list these towns and the site(s) in that vicinity in alphabetical order.

You will certainly need more detailed maps for navigation, for example the Michelin atlas. We provide GPS coordinates for each site to assist you. Our three indexes will also help you to find a site by its reference number and name, by region and site name, or by the town where the site is situated.

Country

Index town

Site name

Postal address (including region) T: telephone number. E: email address

alanrogers.com web address (including Alan Rogers reference number)

A description of the site in which we try to give an idea of its general features – its size, its situation, its strengths and its weaknesses. This section should provide a picture of the site itself with reference to the facilities that are provided and if they impact on its appearance or character. We include details on pitch numbers, electricity (with amperage), hardstandings etc. in this section as pitch design, planning and terracing affects the site's overall appearance. Similarly we include reference to pitches used for caravan holiday homes, chalets, and the like. Importantly at the end of this column we indicate if there are any restrictions, e.g. no tents, no children, naturist sites.

Facilities
Lists more specific information on the site's facilities and amenities and, where available, the dates when these facilities are open (if not for the whole season). Off site: here we give distances to various local amenities, for example, local shops, the nearest beach, plus our featured activities (bicycle hire, fishing, horse riding, boat launching). Where we have space we list suggestions for activities and local tourist attractions.

Open: Site opening dates.

Directions
Separated from the main text in order that they may be read and assimilated more easily by a navigator en-route. Bear in mind that road improvement schemes can result in road numbers being altered.

GPS: references are provided in decimal format. All latitudes are North. Longitudes are East unless preceeded by a minus sign e.g. 48.71695 is North, 0.31254 is East and -0.31254 is West.

Charges guide (or a general guide)

Understanding the entries

Facilities

Toilet blocks: We assume that toilet blocks will be equipped with WCs, washbasins with hot and cold water and hot showers with dividers or curtains, and will have all necessary shelves, hooks, plugs and mirrors. We also assume that there will be an identified chemical toilet disposal point, and that the campsite will provide water and waste water drainage points and bin areas. If not the case, we comment. We do mention certain features that some readers find important: washbasins in cubicles, facilities for babies, facilities for those with disabilities and motorcaravan service points. Readers with disabilities are advised to contact the site of their choice to ensure that facilities are appropriate to their needs.

Shop: Basic or fully supplied, and opening dates.

Bars, restaurants, takeaway facilities and entertainment: We try hard to supply opening and closing dates (if other than the campsite opening dates) and to identify if there are discos or other entertainment.

Children's play areas: Fenced and with safety surface (e.g. sand, bark or pea-gravel).

Swimming pools: If particularly special, we cover in detail in our main campsite description but reference is always included under our Facilities listings. We will also indicate the existence of water slides, sunbathing areas and other features. Opening dates, charges and levels of supervision are provided where we have been notified. There is a regulation whereby Bermuda shorts may not be worn in swimming pools (for health and hygiene reasons). It is worth ensuring that you do take 'proper' swimming trunks with you.

Leisure facilities: For example, playing fields, bicycle hire, organised activities and entertainment.

Dogs: If dogs are not accepted or restrictions apply, we state it here. Check the quick reference list at the back of the guide.

Off site: This briefly covers leisure facilities, tourist attractions, restaurants etc. nearby.

Charges

These are the latest provided to us by the sites. In those cases where 2012 prices have not been provided to us by the sites, we try to give a general guide.

Reservations

Necessary for high season (roughly mid-July to mid-August) in popular holiday areas (i.e. beach resorts). You can reserve many sites via our own Alan Rogers Travel Service or through other tour operators. Or be wholly independent and contact the campsite(s) of your choice direct, using the phone or e-mail numbers shown in the site reports, but please bear in mind that many sites are closed all winter.

Telephone Numbers: The numbers given assume you are actually IN the country concerned. If you are phoning from the UK remember that the first '0' is usually disregarded and replaced by the appropriate country code. For the latest details you should refer to an up-to-date telephone directory.

Opening dates

These are advised to us during the early autumn of the previous year – sites can, and sometimes do, alter these dates before the start of the following season, often for good reasons. If you intend to visit shortly after a published opening date, or shortly before the closing date, it is wise to check that it will actually be open at the time required. Similarly some sites operate a restricted service during the low season, only opening some of their facilities (e.g. swimming pools) during the main season; where we know about this, and have the relevant dates, we indicate it – again if you are at all doubtful it is wise to check.

Sometimes, campsite amenities may be dependent on there being enough customers on site to justify their opening and, for this reason, actual opening dates may vary from those indicated.

Some campsite owners are very relaxed when it comes to opening and closing dates. They may not be fully ready by their stated opening dates – grass and hedges may not all be cut or perhaps only limited sanitary facilities open. At the end of the season they also tend to close down some facilities and generally wind down prior to the closing date. Bear this in mind if you are travelling early or late in the season – it is worth phoning ahead.

The Camping Cheque low season touring system goes some way to addressing this in that many participating campsites will have all key facilities open and running by the opening date and these will remain fully operational until the closing date.

You're on your way!

Whether you're an 'old hand' in terms of camping and caravanning or are contemplating your first trip, a regular reader of our Guides or a new 'convert', we wish you well in your travels and hope we have been able to help in some way.

We are, of course, also out and about ourselves, visiting sites, talking to owners and readers, and generally checking on standards and new developments.

We wish all our readers thoroughly enjoyable Camping and Caravanning in 2012 – favoured by good weather of course!

The Alan Rogers Team

Countries of Europe

The Alan Rogers awards

The Alan Rogers Campsite Awards were launched in 2004 and have proved a great success. Our awards have a broad scope and before committing to our winners, we carefully consider more than 2,000 campsites featured in our guides, taking into account comments from our site assessors, our head office team and, of course, our readers.

Our award winners come from the four corners of Europe, from southern Portugalto Slovenia, and this year we are making awards to campsites in 10 different countries.

Needless to say, it's an extremely difficult task to choose our eventual winners, but we believe that we have identified a number of campsites with truly outstanding characteristics.

In each case, we have selected an outright winner, along with two highly commended runners-up. Listed below are full details of each of our award categories and our winners for 2011.

Alan Rogers Progress Award 2011

This award reflects the hard work and commitment undertaken by particular site owners to improve and upgrade their site.

Winner	IT62290	Camping Lago di Levico	Italy
Runners-up	ES87430	Marjal Camping & Bungalows Resort	Spain
	CR6731	Naturist Camping Valalta	Croatia

Alan Rogers Welcome Award 2011

This award takes account of sites offering a particularly friendly welcome and maintaining a friendly ambience throughout readers' holidays.

Winner	ES80500	Camping Aquarius	Spain
Runners-up	DE3670	Camping Hopfensee	Germany
	IR9650	Woodlands Park Touring Caravan & Camping Park	Ireland

Alan Rogers Active Holiday Award 2011

This award reflects sites in outstanding locations which are ideally suited for active holidays, notably walking or cycling, but which could extend to include such activities as winter sports or watersports.

Winner	FR24060	Camping le Paradis	France
Runners-up	ES86250	Kiko Park Rural	Spain
	IT62030	Caravan Park Sexten	Italy

Alan Rogers Innovation Award 2011

Our new Innovation Award acknowledges campsites with creative and original concepts, possibly with features which are unique, and cannot therefore be found elsewhere. We have identified innovation both in campsite amenities and also in rentable accommodation.

Winner	AU0265	Park Grubhof	Austria
Runners-up	IT60370	Camping Jesolo International	Italy
	SV4200	Camping Bled	Slovenia

Alan Rogers Small Campsite Award 2011

This new award acknowledges excellent small campsites (less than 75 pitches) which offer a friendly welcome and top quality amenities throughout the season to their guests.

Winner	FR38040	Camping à la Rencontre du Soleil	France
Runners-up	UK0065	Wayfarers Camping & Caravan Park	England
	DE3750	Camping Schloss Issigau	Germany

Alan Rogers Seaside Award 2011

This award is made for sites which we feel are outstandingly suitable for a really excellent seaside holiday.

Winner	IT60200	Camping Union Lido Vacanze	Italy
Runners-up	NL6948	Camping Strandpark De Zeeuwse Kust	Netherlands
	FR66560	Camping la Sirène	France

Alan Rogers Country Award 2011

This award contrasts with our former award and acknowledges sites which are attractively located in delightful, rural locations.

Winner	FR37140	Huttopia Rillé	France
Runners-up	UK3430	Kelling Heath Holiday Park	England
	FR19200	Les Hameaux de Miel	France

Alan Rogers Family Site Award 2011

Many sites claim to be child friendly but this award acknowledges the sites we feel to be the very best in this respect.

Winner	NL5985	Vrijetijdspark Beerze Bulten	Netherlands
Runners-up	IT60450	Camping Marina di Venezia	Italy
	FR40060	Club Camping International Eurosol	France

Alan Rogers Readers' Award 2011

We believe our Readers' Award to be the most important. We simply invite our readers (by means of an on-line poll at www.alanrogers.com) to nominate the site they enjoyed most.
The outright winner for 2011 is:

Winner	FR17010	Camping Bois Soleil	France

Our warmest congratulations to all our award winners and our commiserations to all those not having won an award on this occasion.

The Alan Rogers Team

Book with us for the best holidays
on the best campsites

The Alan Rogers Travel Service was originally set up to provide a low cost booking service for readers. We pride ourselves on being able to put together a bespoke holiday, taking advantage of our experience, knowledge and contacts. We can even arrange low cost ferry crossings – ask us about our famous Ferry Deals!

FREE 2012 Brochure

call 01580 214000

Over 100 campsites in France, Italy and Spain hand picked for you

www.alanrogers.com/travel

alan rogers travel

The aims of the Travel Service are simple

- **To provide convenience - a one-stop shop to make life easier.**
- **To provide peace of mind - when you need it most.**
- **To provide a friendly, knowledgeable, efficient service – when this can be hard to find.**
- **To provide a low cost means of organising your holiday – when prices can be so complicated.**

When you book with us, you will be allocated an experienced Personal Travel Consultant to provide you with personal advice and manage every stage of your booking. Our Personal Travel Consultants have first-hand experience of many of our campsites and access to a wealth of information. They can check availability, provide a competitive price and tailor your holiday arrangements to your specific needs.

- Discuss your holiday plans with a friendly person with first-hand experience
- Let us reassure you that your holiday arrangements really are taken care of
- Tell us about your special requests and allow us to pass these on
- Benefit from advice which will save you money – the latest ferry deals and more
- Remember, our offices are in Kent not overseas and we do NOT operate a queuing system!

Call us for advice or an instant quote

01580 214000 or visit
www.alanrogers.com/travel

Look for a campsite entry like this to indicate which campsites we can book for you.

The list is growing so please call for up to the minute information.

alan rogers travel

Getting the most from **off peak touring**

There are many reasons to avoid high season, if you can. Queues are shorter, there's less traffic, a calmer atmosphere and prices are cheaper. And it's usually still nice and sunny!

And when you use Camping Cheques you'll find great quality facilities that are actually open and a welcoming conviviality.

Did you know?

Camping Cheques can be used right into mid-July and from late August on many sites. Over 90 campsites in France alone accept Camping Cheques from 20th August.

Camping Cheque

Save up to 60% with Camping Cheques

Camping Cheque is a fixed price scheme allowing you to go as you please, staying on over 600 campsites across Europe, always paying the same rate and saving you up to 60% on regular pitch fees. One Cheque gives you one night for 2 people + unit on a standard pitch, with electricity. It's as simple as that.

Special offers mean you can stay extra nights free (eg 7 nights for 6 Cheques) or even a month free for a month paid! Especially popular in Spain during the winter, these longer-term offers can effectively halve the nightly rate. See Site Directory for details.

Andorra

The tiny independent principality of Andorra is situated high in the Pyrénées between France and Spain. With a diverse landscape of mountains, valleys, forests, lakes and hot springs, it is probably best known for skiing and duty-free shopping.

Shopping and skiing aside, Andorra has plenty to offer the visitor in terms of leisure activities. One of the most unspoilt areas of the country is the hamlet of Llorts. Set amidst fields of tobacco overlooked by mountains, it's a great place for hiking. The enormous spa complex in Caldea offers the perfect place to relax. Fed by natural thermal springs, it houses lots of pools, hot tubs and saunas. Village festivals are a popular event with many Andorran towns and hamlets celebrating their heritage with music, dancing, wine and feasts. Most fall in the high season.

Administratively, Andorra is divided up into seven parishes: Canillo, Encamp, Ordino, La Massana, Andorra la Vella, Sant Julià de Lòria and Escaldes-Engordany. The Principality of Andorra can be accessed by road from France through Pas de la Casa and the Envalira Pass and from Spain via Sant Julià de Lòria. The nearest main cities are Barcelona (185 km) and Lleida (151 km) on the Spanish side and Toulouse (187 km) and Perpignan (169 km) on the French side.

CAPITAL: **Andorra La Vella**

Tourist Office

Embassy of the Principality of Andorra
63 Westover Road, London SW18 2RF
Tel/Fax: 020 8874 4806 (visits by appointment only)
Internet: www.andorra.com

Population

82,000

Climate

The climate is temperate, with cold winters with a lot of snow and warm summers. The country's mountain peaks often remain snowcapped until July.

Language

The official language is Catalan, with French and Spanish widely spoken.

Telephone

The country code is 00 376.

Money

Currency: The Euro
Banks: Mon-Fri 09.00-13.00 and 15.00-17.00, Sat 09.00-12.00.

Shops

Mon-Sat 09.00-20.00, Sun 09.00-19.00.

Public Holidays

New Year's Day; Epiphany; Constitution Day, Mar 14; Holy Thursday to Easter Monday; Labour Day; Ascension; Whit Sunday; Whit Monday; St. John's Day Jun 24; Assumption Aug 15; National Day Sep 8; All Saints' Day Nov 1; St. Charles' Day Nov 4; Immaculate Conception Dec 8; Christmas Dec 24-26; New Year's Eve.

Motoring

There are no motorways in Andorra. Main roads are prefixed 'N' and side roads 'V'. Certain mountain passes may prove difficult in winter and heavy snowfalls could cause road closures. Expect traffic queues in the summer, with a high volume of motorists coming to and from France.

Andorra la Vella

Camping Valira

Avenida Salou s/n, AD500 Andorra la Vella T: 722 384. E: campvalira@andorra.ad

alanrogers.com/AN7145

This small and unusual site is named after the river in the town of Andorra la Vella. It has a steep curving entrance which can become congested at peak times. You pass the pleasant restaurant and bar and the heated indoor pool as you enter the site. Maximum use has been made of space here and it is worth looking at the picture of the site in reception as it was in 1969. The 150 medium sized pitches are mostly level on terraces with some shading. All pitches have access to electricity, although some may need long leads, and there are drinking water points around the site.

Facilities

The facilities are modern and spotless, with provision for disabled campers, plus separate room with toddlers' toilet and good baby room. Two washing machines and dryer. The two blocks can be heated in winter. Bar/restaurant with good menu at realistic prices. Well stocked small shop. Small heated indoor pool. Paddling pool. Jacuzzi. Play area. Table tennis. Pétanque. Picnic area. WiFi. Barbecue. Barrier closed 23.00-07.00. Off site: Town shops 10 minutes walk.

Open: All year.

Directions

Site is on the south side of Andorra la Vella, on left travelling south behind sports stadium. It is well signed off the N145. Watch signs carefully – an error with a diversion round town will cost you dear at rush hour. GPS: 42.50249, 1.51493

Charges guide

Per unit incl. 2 persons and electricity	€ 26.90 - € 29.40
extra person	€ 5.85
child (1-10 yrs)	€ 4.85
dog	€ 2.00

La Massana

Camping Xixerella

Ctra de Pals, Xixerella, AD400 La Massana T: 836 613. E: c-xixerella@campingxixerella.com

alanrogers.com/AN7143

Andorra is a country of narrow valleys and pine- and birch-forested mountains. Xixerella is attractively situated in just such a valley below towering mountains and beside a river. The site is made up of several sections of gently sloping grass, accessed by tarmac or gravel roads which lead to informal pitching. Electricity (3/6A) is available for most of the 150 places. There are barbecues and a picnic area with bridge access to walks in the woods. A pleasant bar and restaurant have a poolside terrace. The site can be very busy from mid July to mid August, but otherwise it is usually quite peaceful.

Facilities

The satisfactory main sanitary building is fully equipped, including British style WCs (no paper), some washbasins in cabins, showers with curtains. Laundry facilities. Further modern facilities in novel round building by the pool. Small shop, bar and restaurant (closed Oct). Swimming and paddling pools (15/6-15/9). Play area. Minigolf. Electronic games. Disco in season. Torch useful. Off site: Riding 3 km. Skiing at Arinsal (5 km) and Pal (6 km).

Open: All year excl. October.

Directions

Site is 8 km. from Andorra la Vella on the road to Pal (this road can only be accessed on the north side of town), via La Massana. GPS: 42.55324, 1.48884

Charges guide

Per person	€ 5.00
child	€ 4.80
pitch	€ 9.80
electricity (3A)	€ 5.00

Austria

Austria is primarily known for two contrasting attractions: the capital Vienna with its fading Imperial glories, and the variety of its Alpine hinterland. It is an ideal place to visit year round, whether you want to admire the spectacular scenery and participate in winter sports or to visit historical sites and cultural attractions.

Perhaps the best known area and the most easily accessible part of the country is the Tirol in the west. A charming region with picturesque valleys to explore, you'll be able to enjoy folklore entertainment all year round. Situated in the centre are the Lake District, and Salzburg with its ancient castles, curative spas and salt mines; it also has plenty of music, art and drama festivals to enjoy. Vienna, too, offers plenty of cultural pursuits with its museums, opera and famous choirs. The neighbouring provinces of Lower Austria, Burgenland and Styria, land of vineyards, mountains and farmland, are off the tourist routes, but provide good walking territory. Further south, in the Carinthia region, lakes and mountains dominate the landscape. The beautiful scenery and rural way of life offers a quieter retreat. There are a few large towns to explore, lots of pleasant villages and good, often uncrowded roads.

CAPITAL: Vienna

Tourist Office

Austrian National Tourist Office
9-11 Richmond Buildings, London W1D 3HF
Tel: 020 7440 3830
Fax: 020 7440 3848
Email: holiday@austria.info
Internet: www.austria.info/uk

Population
8.4 million

Climate
Temperate, with moderately hot summers, cold winters and snow in the mountains.

Language
German

Telephone
The country code is 00 43.

Money
Currency: The Euro
Banks: Mon, Tues, Wed and Fri 08.00-12.30 and 13.30-15.00. Thurs 08.00-12.30 and 13.30-17.30.

Shops
Mon-Fri 08.00-18.30, some close 12.00-14.00; Sat 08.00-17.00.

Public Holidays
New Year; Epiphany; Easter Mon; Labour Day; Ascension; Whit Mon; Corpus Christi; Assumption 15 Aug; National Day 26 Oct; All Saints 1 Nov; Immaculate Conception 8 Dec; Christmas 25, 26 Dec.

Motoring
Visitors using Austrian motorways and 'A' roads must display a Motorway Vignette on their vehicle as they enter Austria. Failure to have one will mean a heavy, on-the-spot fine. Vignettes are obtained at all major border crossings into Austria and at larger petrol stations. All vehicles above 3.5 tonnes maximum permitted laden weight are required to use a small device called the 'GO-Box' - visit the website at http://www.austria.info

see campsite map 4

Abtenau

Oberwötzlhof Camp

Erlfeld 37, A-5441 Abtenau (Salzburg) T: **062 432 698**. E: **oberwoetzlhof@sbg.at**

alanrogers.com/AU0262

High up in the Lammertal Valley is this small, hilltop farm site with attractive views of the surrounding mountains. Part of a working farm, it has a total of 70 pitches, of which 40 are for tourers. All are serviced with electricity (10A), water and drainage. The site is quiet at night, and dark so a torch would be useful. The small, fenced swimming pool (10x5 m) is unheated, and has paved surrounds. The site has new, attractive sanitary facilities, completed in 2010, and together with its rural location and a friendly atmosphere is a good site for those seeking some peace and quiet.

Facilities

New sanitary building. Laundry facilities and drying room. Solarium. Swimming pool. Internet. WiFi throughout (free). Charcoal barbecvues not permitted. Off site: Abtenau 2.5 km. (about 25 minutes walk). Skiing 2.5 km. Riding 8 km. Hallstättersee and salt mines 30 km. The Panorama Strasse.

Open: All year.

Directions

Abtenau is 34 km. southeast of Salzburg. From A10 exit 28 (Golling), take B162 east for 14 km. and site is signed to the left about 2.5 km. before Abtenau (sat nav is unreliable). GPS: 47.585704, 13.324635

Charges guide

Per unit incl. 2 persons (electricity on meter)	€ 21.20 - € 28.00
extra person	€ 6.00 - € 7.50

No credit cards.

Aschau im Zillertal

Erlebnis-Comfort-Camping Aufenfeld

Aufenfeldweg 10, A-6274 Aschau im Zillertal (Tirol) T: **052 822 9160**. E: **info@camping-zillertal.at**

alanrogers.com/AU0120

This attractive site is situated in a mountain region with fine views and first-class facilities. The main area of the site itself is flat with pitches of 100 sq.m. on grass between hard access roads, with further pitches on terraces at the rear. There are 350 pitches (240 for touring units with 6A electricity) including 40 with individual sanitary cubicles. The site can become full mid July until mid August and at Christmas. A splendid indoor swimming pool has been added and there is a heated outdoor pool, paddling pool, and a tennis court, as well as a new attractive playhouse. A member of Leading Campings Group.

Facilities

Five well kept, heated sanitary blocks of excellent quality and size, each with a few washbasins in cabins for each sex, baby rooms and nine units for disabled visitors. Forty private cabins for luxury pitches, and family bathrooms for rent. Laundry and drying room. Ski room. Motorcaravan services. Supermarket. Restaurant. TV. Indoor pool, sauna and sunbeds. Wellness centre. Outdoor pool. Playground. Multisports court. Tennis. Riding. Skateboard and rollerblade facilities. Trampolines. Bicycle hire. WiFi (charged). ATM. Western village. Entertainment in high season. Off site: Walking and cycling in the Zillertall valley.

Open: All year excl. 3 November - 8 December.

Directions

From A12 Inntal motorway, take the Zillertal exit 39, 32 km. northeast of Innsbruck. Follow road no. 169 to village of Aschau from which site is well signed. GPS: 47.263333, 11.899333

Charges guide

Per unit incl. 2 persons, electricity on meter	€ 19.60 - € 33.90
incl. private sanitary cabin	€ 27.50 - € 44.80
extra person	€ 6.20 - € 11.30

Winter prices are higher.

Bairisch Kölldorf

Camping Im Thermenland

Bairisch Kölldorf 240, A-8344 Bairisch Kölldorf (Steiermark) T: **031 593 941**. E: **camping.bk@aon.at**

alanrogers.com/AU0502

Camping in Thermenland is tucked quietly away in the hills of eastern Steiermark, 45 kilometres south east of Graz and close to the borders of Slovenia and Hungary. It is a modern, well maintained site with 70 level touring pitches, with some hedge separation, all with electricity (16A), water and drainage. As the name suggests, the site is situated close to numerous spas and thermal baths including Bad Gleichenberg, which dates back to Roman times. Nearby Bairisch Kölldorf is a town of only 1,000 inhabitants; it does however boast the world's largest fire engine!

Facilities

Excellent toilet facilities are clean, well maintained and include free showers. Facilities for disabled visitors. Dog shower. Washing machine and dryer. Restaurant with terrace adjoining small children's play area. Unheated outdoor, but covered, swimming pool (May-Sept). Off site: Fishing 100 m. Small shop with essential and local produce 500 m. Golf 3 km. Styrassic Park 4 km.

Open: All year.

Directions

Southeast of Graz, but you're unlikely to find Bairisch Kolldorf on any map. Leave A2 at exit 157, and head towards Feldbach on the 68. Continue on the 66 to Bad Gleichenberg, go straight over first roundabout and turn left at the second (supermarket). After 2.8 km. (just past fire station) turn left by a chapel and right towards. GPS: 46.875583, 15.93445

Charges guide

Per unit incl. 2 persons and electricity	€ 21.90
extra person	€ 7.20

Camping Cheques accepted.

Bruck

Sportcamp Woferlgut

Kroessenbach 40, A-5671 Bruck (Salzburg) T: 065 457 3030. E: info@sportcamp.at

alanrogers.com/AU0180

The village of Bruck lies at the junction of the B311 and the Grossglocknerstrasse in the Hohe Tauern National Park. Sportcamp Woferlgut, a family run site, is one of the best in Austria. Surrounded by mountains, the site is quite flat with pleasant views. The 350 level, grass pitches are marked out by shrubs (300 for touring units) and each has electricity (16A Europlug), water, drainage, cable TV socket and gas point. A high grass bank separates the site and the road. The site's own lake, used for swimming and fishing, is surrounded by a landscaped sunbathing area. The fitness centre has a fully equipped gym, whilst another building contains a sauna and cold dip, Turkish bath, solarium (all free) massage (charged) and a bar. In summer there is a free activity programme, evenings with live music, club for children, weekly barbecues and guided cycle and mountain tours. In winter a cross country skiing trail and toboggan run lead from the site and a free bus service is provided to nearby skiing facilities. With Salzburg to the north and Innsbruck to the northwest, the management is pleased to advise on local attractions and tours, making this a splendid base for a family holiday. Good English is spoken. Used by tour operators (45 pitches).

Facilities

Three modern sanitary blocks (the newest in a class of its own) have excellent facilities, including private cabins, underfloor heating and music. Washing machines and dryers. Facilities for disabled visitors. Family bathrooms for hire. Motorcaravan services. Well stocked shop. Bar, restaurant and takeaway. Small, heated outdoor pool and children's pool (1/5-30/9). Fitness centre. Two playgrounds, indoor play room and children's cinema. Tennis. Bicycle hire. Fishing. Watersports and lake swimming. Collection of small animals with pony rides for young children. WiFi throughout (charged). New, large mini-golf facility. Off site: ATM 500 m. Riding 1.5 km. Skiing 2.5 km. Golf 3 km. Boat launching and sailing 3.5 km. Hiking and skiing (all year) nearby.

Open: All year.

Directions

Site is southwest of Bruck. From road B311, Bruck bypass, take southern exit (Grossglockner) and site is signed from the junction of B311 and B107 roads (small signs). GPS: 47.2838, 12.81694

Charges 2012

Per unit incl. 2 persons and electricity (plus meter)	€ 23.00 - € 32.80
extra person	€ 5.40 - € 8.70
child (2-10 yrs)	€ 4.30 - € 6.40
dog	€ 3.30 - € 4.50

Special offers for low season, longer stays.

Döbriach

Camping Brunner am See

Glanzerstrasse 108, A-9873 Döbriach (Carinthia) T: 042 46 7189. E: office@camping-brunner.at

alanrogers.com/AU0475

This well appointed site at the eastern end of the Millstätter See is the only site in the area with its own private beach directly accessible from the site. Consisting of fairly coarse sand, it is regularly cleaned. The 240 marked pitches (60-95 sq.m), all for touring units, are nearly all serviced with water, drainage and electric hook-ups (6A), and are in rows on level grass, with tarmac access roads. The site is fairly open with some shade from bushes and trees. The site owns land on the opposite side of the road, which includes forest walks, a dog walk, a parking area and one of the playgrounds.

Facilities

Well appointed sanitary unit behind reception with good facilities for disabled campers, especially disabled children, plus a children's room etc. Family bathrooms (some for rent), some washbasins in cubicles. Laundry facilities. Motorcaravan service point. Supermarket adjacent (May-Oct). Communal barbecue. New indoor playground for children (up to 10 yrs). Internet access. WiFi. Fishing. Watersports. Off site: Several restaurants (some open all year). Tennis 100 m. Bicycle hire 300 m. with access to cycle route around Millstätter See. Riding 1.5 km. Golf 10 km. Skiing area 11 km.

Open: All year.

Directions

Döbriach is at the eastern end of the Millstätter See, about 15 km. southwest of Spittal. Leave A10, exit 139 (Spittal, Millstätter), then proceed alongside northern shore of lake through Millstatt towards Döbriach. Just before Döbriach turn right and after 1.5 km. turn right at roundabout. Site is on right after 100 m. GPS: 46.76768, 13.64850

Charges guide

Per unit incl. 2 persons and electricity	€ 23.60 - € 41.90
extra person	€ 8.90 - € 10.90
child (4-18 yrs)	€ 5.00 - € 8.50

Eberndorf

Rutar Lido FKK Naturist See-Camping

A-9141 Eberndorf (Carinthia) T: 042 362 2620. E: fkkurlaub@rutarlido.at

alanrogers.com/AU0360

This site is affiliated to the International Naturist Federation (INF) and is in a peaceful location adjacent to both open countryside and forested hills. The 365 pitches (300 for touring units) are either on an open area of grass marked out by low hedges or in a more established area of pine trees. There are electrical connections throughout (10A) and some pitches have their own water supply and waste point. One area is set aside for those with dogs. There are three lakes within the site, one for swimming and dinghies, whilst the other two provide pleasure for those who enjoy fishing.

Facilities

Four sanitary blocks with some private cabins and free controllable showers. Facilities for disabled visitors. Laundry facilities. Small supermarket (1/4-30/9). Two bar/restaurants (one all year). Outdoor pools (1/4-30/9). Indoor pools (all year). Two saunas. Play area, club and activities for children (July/Aug). Fitness room. Disco. Bowling alley. Live music evenings and dances (high season). Fishing. WiFi (charged). Off site: Eberndorf is 20 minutes walk. Riding 2 km. Bicycle hire 4 km.

Open: All year.

Directions

From A2 (Graz - Klagenfurt) road, take B82 south at Volkermarkt to roundabout at Eberndorf and follow signs to site. GPS: 46.588, 14.627

Charges guide

Per unit incl. 2 persons and electricity	€ 18.60 - € 29.20
extra person	€ 5.40 - € 7.70
child (3-12 yrs)	€ 3.70 - € 5.40
dog	€ 2.70 - € 4.00

Ehrwald

Ferienanlage Tiroler Zugspitze

Obermoos 1, A-6632 Ehrwald (Tirol) T: 056 732 309. E: welcome@zugspitze-resort.at

alanrogers.com/AU0040

Although Ehrwald is in Austria, it is from the entrance of Tiroler Zugspitze that a cable car runs to the summit of Germany's highest mountain. Standing at 1,200 feet above sea level at the foot of the mountain, the 200 pitches (120 for touring), mainly of stones over grass, are on flat terraces with fine panoramic views in parts. All have electricity connections (16A). The modern reception building at the entrance also houses a fine restaurant with a terrace which is open to those using the cable car, as well as those staying on the site. There are 30 pitches outside the barrier for late arrivals and overnighters.

Facilities

A good sanitary block provides some washbasins in cabins and 20 private bathrooms for rent. Separate baby and toddler unit. Facilities for disabled visitors. Laundry facilities. Drying rooms. Motorcaravan service point. Shop. Bar. Restaurant. Indoor pool with sauna, whirlpool and fitness centre. Outdoor pool and children's pool with slide. Internet access. Bicycle loan and motor scooters for hire. Play area. Organised activities in season. Off site: Hotel, souvenir shop and cable car station 100 m.

Open: 1 January - Easter, 28 May - 31 October, plus mid - end December.

Directions

Follow signs in Ehrwald to Tiroler Zugspitzbahn and then signs to site. GPS: 47.42521, 10.93809

Charges guide

Per person	€ 10.00 - € 12.00
child (4-15 yrs)	€ 7.50 - € 8.50
pitch	€ 6.00 - € 8.00
electricity per kWh.	€ 0.80
dog	€ 4.00

Special seasonal weekly offers.
Mastercard accepted.

Döbriach

Komfort-Campingpark Burgstaller

Seefeldstrasse 16, A-9873 Döbriach (Carinthia) T: 042 467 774. E: info@burgstaller.co.at

alanrogers.com/AU0480

This is one of Austria's top sites in a beautiful location and with all the amenities you could want. You can always tell a true family run site by the attention to detail and this site oozes perfection. This is an excellent family site with a very friendly atmosphere, particularly in the restaurant in the evenings. Good English is spoken. The 600 pitches (560 for tourists) are on flat, well drained grass, backing onto hedges on either side of access roads. All fully serviced (including WiFi), they vary in size (45-120 sq.m) and there are special pitches for motorcaravans. One pitch actually rotates and follows the sun during the course of the day! The latest sanitary block warrants an architectural award; all toilets have a TV and a pirate ship on the first floor of the children's area sounds its guns every hour. The site entrance is directly opposite the park leading to the bathing lido, to which campers have free access. There is also a heated swimming pool. Much activity is organised here, including games and competitions for children and there are special Easter and autumn events.

Facilities

Three exceptionally good quality toilet blocks include washbasins in cabins, facilities for children and disabled visitors, dishwashers and underfloor heating for cool weather. Seven private rooms for rent (3 with jacuzzi baths). Motorcaravan services. Bar. Good restaurant with terrace (May-Oct). Shop (May-Sept). Bowling alley. Disco (July/Aug). TV room. Sauna and solarium. Two play areas (one for under 6s, the other for 6-12 yrs). Bathing and boating on lake. Special entrance rate for lake attractions. Fishing. Bicycle hire. Mountain bike area. Riding. Comprehensive entertainment programmes. Covered stage and outdoor arena for church services (Protestant and Catholic, in German) and folk and modern music concerts. Off site: Mountain walks, climbing and farm visits all in local area.

Open: 4 April - 5 November.

Directions

Döbriach is at the eastern end of the Millstätter See, about 15 km. southeast of Spittal. Leave A10 at exit 139 (Spittal, Millstätter) then proceed alongside northern shore of lake through Millstätter towards Döbriach. Just before Döbriach turn right and after 1 km. site is on left. GPS: 46.77151, 13.64918

Charges guide

Per unit incl. 2 persons and electricity	€ 19.10 - € 34.00
extra person	€ 7.00 - € 10.00
child (4-14 yrs)	€ 5.00 - € 8.00
dog	€ 3.00 - € 4.00

Discounts for retired people in low season.

Faak am See

Camping Arneitz

Seeuferlandesstrasse 53, A-9583 Faak am See (Carinthia) T: **042 542 137.** E: **camping@arneitz.at**

alanrogers.com/AU0400

Directly on Faakersee, Camping Arneitz is one of the best sites in this area, central for the attractions of the region, watersports and walking. Family run, Arneitz led the way with good quality and comprehensive facilities. A newly built reception building at the entrance reflects the quality of the site and apart from reception facilities, has a good collection of tourist literature and two desks with computers for guests to use. The 400 level, marked pitches are mainly of gravel, off hard roads, with electricity available (6, 10, 16A), some with TV, water and waste water connections also. Some have good shade from mature trees. There is a delightfully appointed restaurant at the entrance where there is entertainment in high season. Day trips can be made to Venice and many other parts of northern Italy.

Facilities

Splendid family washroom, large, heated and airy, with family cubicles, washbasins at child height in a circle with a working carousel in the middle. Extra, small toilet block nearer the lake. Laundry facilities. Motorcaravan services. Supermarket. Self-service restaurant, bar and terrace. TV room. Small cinema for children's films. Beauty salon. Indoor playground. Fishing. Dogs are not accepted in July/Aug. WiFi throughout (charged). Off site: Riding 3 km.

Open: 26 April - 30 September.

Directions

Site is southeast of Villach, southwest of Velden. Follow signs for Faakersee and Egg rather than for Faak village. From A11 take exit 3 and head towards Egg, turn left at T-junction and go through Egg village. Just after leaving village, site is on right. GPS: 46.57768, 13.93775

Charges guide

Per unit incl. 2 persons and electricity	€ 26.10 - € 45.00

Fieberbrunn

Tirol Camp

Lindau 20, A-6391 Fieberbrunn (Tirol) T: **053 545 6666.** E: **office@tirol-camp.at**

alanrogers.com/AU0110

This is one of many Tirol campsites that cater equally for summer and winter (here seemingly more for winter, when reservation is essential and prices are 50% higher). Tirol Camp is in a quiet and attractive mountain situation and has 240 touring pitches all on wide flat terraces, set on a gentle slope, plus 24 de-luxe pitches with their own bathroom at the pitch. Marked out mainly by the electricity boxes or low hedges, they are 80-100 sq.m. and all have electricity (10A), gas, water/drainage, TV and telephone connections. There is a fitness centre, a wellness centre (free to campers) with indoor/outdoor pool complex, sauna, steam room, solarium and aromatherapy massage.

Facilities

The original refurbished toilet block is excellent with some washbasins in cabins and some private bathrooms on payment. A modern heated block at the top of the site has spacious showers and washbasins in cabins. Facilities for disabled campers. Washing machines, dryers and drying room. Motorcaravan services. Self-service shop and snacks. Restaurant (closed Oct, Nov and May). Outdoor swimming pool (12x8 m). Indoor pool and wellness centre. Sauna. Outdoor chess. Playground. Entertainment and activity programmes (July/Aug). WiFi.

Open: 14 May - 4 November and 7 December - 7 April.

Directions

Site is on the east side of Fieberbrunn, which is on the B164 St Johann - Saalfelden road. Turn south off the B164, 2 km. east of Fieberbrunn, large sign Bergbahn site entrance is 200 m. on the left. GPS: 47.468368, 12.554739

Charges 2012

Per unit incl. 2 persons (electricity on meter)	€ 27.00 - € 41.00
with individual sanitary facility	€ 42.00 - € 60.00
extra person (summer/winter)	€ 9.00 - € 14.00

Winter charges higher. No credit cards.

Fügen

Camping Zillertal

Gageringer Str 1, A-6263 Fügen (Tirol) T: **052 886 2203.** E: **info@zillertal-camping.at**

alanrogers.com/AU0090

The village of Fügen lies about six kilometres from the A12 autobahn at the start of the Zillertal, so is well placed for exploring the valley and the area around Schwaz. Easy to reach, Camping Zillertal-Hell is an attractive small site with excellent facilities and 170 marked pitches (140 for touring units) on flat grass. All have electricity (16A), water and drainage and there are some hardstandings for motorcaravans. The site is ideal for stopovers and longer stays but, being on a main road, there is a little daytime road noise.

Facilities

New modern, attractive heated sanitary block has some washbasins in cabins, a children's wash room, and private bathrooms for hire. Unit for disabled campers. Laundry facilities. Drive-over motorcaravan service point. Bar and small restaurant. Small shop. Heated swimming pool (20x10 m, 1/5-15/10). Solarium, sauna and steam room. Games room with TV. Children's activity room. Playground. Internet point. Organised activities and entertainment. Bicycle hire. Off site: Amenities in the village 800 m. .

Open: All year.

Directions

Site is 30 km. east of Innsbruck. From the A12 motorway take exit 39 and turn south on B169 towards Mayrhofen for 5 km. 1 km. north of Fügen turn right, signed Gagering and immediately left to campsite. GPS: 47.3596, 11.8521

Charges 2012

Per unit incl. 2 persons and electricity	€ 36.00 - € 56.00
extra person	€ 5.50 - € 8.00

Fussach am Bodensee

Camping Salzmann Rohrspitz

Rohrspitz Yachting Salzmann GmbH, Rohr 1, A-6972 Fussach am Bodensee (Vorarlberg) T: 055 787 5708.
: office@salzmann.at **alanrogers.com/AU0005**

Camping Salzmann is a part of the large Rohrspitz holiday and leisure complex on Lake Constance's southern bank. There are 45 grassy touring pitches here, of varying sizes each with an electrical connection. The complex comprises many leisure facilities and a club card system enables campers to use these. The same card is also used for access to the washblocks and to pay for warm water. The lakeside restaurant has fine views across the lake to the distant mountains of the Vorarlberg, and is a far cry from the humble kiosk which was the origin of the complex back in 1954. The Salzmann harbour is at the heart of the complex and has moorings for 190 boats, as well as good maintenance facilities.

Facilities

Sanitary facilities include those for disabled visitors. Washing machine. Shop. Snack bar (kiosk). Playground. Games room. Restaurant. Bar. Bicycle hire. Direct beach access. Canoe hire. Watersports courses. Activity and entertainment programme. WiFi and internet corner.
Off site: Cycle and walking routes. Sailing. Boat trips on the MS Elisa.

Open: 1 April - 15 October.

Directions

Approaching from the north and Germany (A96) leave at the Bregenz exit. From here head west on the B202 as far as Höchst and the site is well signed from here. GPS: 47.49722, 9.63083

Charges guide

Per unit incl. 2 persons and electricity	€ 15.00 - € 35.00
extra person	€ 4.00
child (under 14 yrs)	€ 2.00

Grän

Comfort Camp Grän

Engetalstrasse 13, A-6673 Grän (Tirol) T: 056 756 570. E: comfortcamp@aon.at
alanrogers.com/AU0227

In a village location in the Tannheimer Tal, with panoramic mountain scenery, Comfort Camp Grän is a family run site with excellent heated sanitary facilities and a stylish modern indoor pool complex. It makes a good base for exploring this border region of Austria and Germany. The site has 210 pitches of 80-100 sq.m. (160 for touring units) all with 16A electricity, water (only for summer use) and waste water on fairly level grass, over gravel terrain with some shallow terraces. There are 14 private sanitary cabins for rent. The main services are grouped at the entrance.

Facilities

The main sanitary unit is has superb facilities: controllable hot showers, washbasins in cubicles, a children's section in the ladies, a baby room and family bathrooms for rent. A second smaller unit is equally good. Indoor pool complex (access with key card) with relaxation areas, sauna and steam room. Solarium. Shop. Restaurant and bar. Small playground plus indoor playroom for under 12s. WiFi. Teenagers' room. Dogs are not accepted in high season, contact site first. Off site: Lake beach 2 km.

Open: 25 May - 2 November, 15 December - 25 April.

Directions

From Germany on the autobahn A7, turn off at exit 137, and turn south on road 310 to Oberjoch, then take road 308 (road 199 in Austria) east to Grän. At eastern end of village turn north signed Pfronten, and site is 1.5 km. on left. GPS: 47.5023, 10.5535

Charges guide

Per person	€ 7.50 - € 11.00
pitch (electricity on meter)	€ 8.50 - € 13.00
electricity	€ 0.70

Graz

Camping Central

Martinhofstrasse 3, A-8054 Graz (Steiermark) T: 067 637 85102. E: office@campingcentral.at
alanrogers.com/AU0330

Although not as well known as Vienna, Salzburg and Innsbruck, Graz in the southern province of Styria, is Austria's second largest city. Camping Central is a quiet site, which makes a good night stop when travelling between Klagenfurt and Vienna or as a base from which to explore the region. The site's name is misleading as it is situated in the southwest of the town in the Strassgang district, some 6 km. from the centre. The 60 level touring pitches are either in regular rows either side of tarmac roads under a cover of tall trees or on an open meadow where they are not marked out. All have electricity (6A). There is a bus every 15 minutes to the city centre.

Facilities

The new, well built toilet block is of good quality and the other two blocks have been refurbished. Each can be heated in cool weather. Facilities for disabled visitors. Washing machines and dryer. Swimming pool with facilities including a special entry to the water for disabled people. Small restaurant at the pool. Tennis. Playground. Jogging track. Limited animation during high season.
Off site: Two restaurants within 300 m. Good shop 400 m.

Open: 1 April - 31 October.

Directions

From the west take Graz-west exit, from Salzburg the Graz-sud exit and follow signs to Central and Strassgang and turn right just past traffic lights for site (signed). GPS: 47.02045, 15.39253

Charges guide

Per unit incl. 2 persons and electricity	€ 24.00 - € 28.00
extra person	€ 8.00
child (4-15 yrs)	€ 5.00

No credit cards.

Hermagor

Naturpark Schluga Seecamping

A-9620 Hermagor (Carinthia) T: **042 822 051**. E: **camping@schluga.com**

alanrogers.com/AU0450

This site is pleasantly situated on natural wooded hillside. It is about 300 m. from a small lake with clean water, where the site has a beach of coarse sand and a large grassy meadow where inflatable boats can be kept. There is also a small bar and a sunbathing area for naturists although this is not a naturist site. The 250 pitches for touring units are on individual, level terraces, many with light shade and all with electricity (8-16A). 154 pitches also have water, drainage and satellite TV and a further 47 pitches are occupied by a tour operator. English is spoken.

Facilities

Four heated modern toilet blocks have some washbasins in cabins and family washrooms for rent. Facilities for disabled campers. Washing machines and dryer. Motorcaravan services. Shop (20/5-10/9). Restaurant/bar and takeaway (20/5-10/9). Playground. Room for young people and children. Films. Kiosk and bar with terrace at beach. Surf school. Pedalo and canoe hire. Aqua jump and Iceberg. Pony rides. Bicycle hire. Activity programme with mountain walks and climbs (weekly). Internet. WiFi throughout (charged). Off site: Fishing and sailing 200 m.

Open: 10 May - 20 September.

Directions

Site is on the B111 road (Villach - Hermagor) 6 km. east of Hermagor town. GPS: 46.63184, 13.44654

Charges guide

Per unit incl. 2 persons and electricity	€ 18.10 - € 33.75
extra person	€ 5.60 - € 8.85
child (5-14 yrs)	€ 4.00 - € 6.00
dog	€ 3.00 - € 3.90

Camping Cheques accepted.

Hermagor-Pressegger See

Schluga Camping Hermagor

Vellach 15, A-9620 Hermagor-Pressegger See (Carinthia) T: **042 822 051**. E: **camping@schluga.com**

alanrogers.com/AU0440

Schluga Camping is under the same ownership as Schluga Seecamping, some 4 km. to the west of that site in a flat valley with views of the surrounding mountains. The 219 touring pitches are of varying size, 133 with water, drainage and satellite TV connections. Electricity connections are available throughout (10-16A). Mainly on grass covered gravel on either side of tarmac surfaced access roads, they are divided by shrubs and hedges. The site is open all year, to include the winter sports season, and has a well kept tidy appearance, although it may be busy in high season. English is spoken. The site reports a new artificial swimming lake and 23 new pitches for motorcaravans.

Facilities

Four sanitary blocks are heated in cold weather. Most washbasins are in cabins and good showers. Family washrooms for rent. Baby rooms and suite for disabled visitors. Washing machines and dryers. Drying rooms and ski rooms. Motorcaravan services. Well stocked shop (1/5-30/9). Bar/restaurant with terrace (closed Nov). Heated swimming pool (12x7 m; 1/5-30/9). New natural swimming pond (500 sq.m). Playground. Games room. Bicycle hire. Sauna. Solarium. Steam bath. Fitness centre. TV room. Internet point. Kindergarten programme. WiFi throughout (charged). Off site: Fishing and sailing 4 km.

Open: All year.

Directions

Site is on the B111 Villach - Hermagor road (which is better quality than it appears on most maps) just east of Hermagor town. GPS: 46.63141, 13.39598

Charges guide

Per unit incl. 2 persons and electricity	€ 22.20 - € 37.25
extra person	€ 5.60 - € 8.95
child (5-14 yrs)	€ 4.00 - € 0.00
dog	€ 3.00 - € 3.90

Innsbruck

Camping Innsbruck Kranebitterhof

Kranebitterallee 216, A-6020 Innsbruck (Tirol) T: **051 227 9558**. E: **info@camping-kranebitterhof.at**

alanrogers.com/AU0165

Opened in 2009, this site, set on steep terraces, is easily reached from the A12 and being only 5 km. west of Innsbruck is good for overnight stays, as well as a base from which to visit the city. The 70 level pitches are 80 to 120 sq.m. and all have 16A electricity, water and waste water connections and their terracing and southerly aspect make most use of the sunshine, allowing unobstructed views of the valley and mountains. A large sanitary block at the top of the site is on two levels and below are reception, the Italian bar/restaurant and shop, all housed in a modern building with large glass windows.

Facilities

Two new heated sanitary facilities, large block at top of site and smaller one in reception building. Free hot showers, three family shower rooms, one with bath. Facilities for disabled visitors, kitchen with hotplates, dishwashing, laundry and chemical disposal point. Small shop (bread can be ordered). Italian restaurant, bar. Children's play area. WiFi throughout (free). Bicycle hire. Off site: Skiing in winter 5 km. Innsbruck 5 km.

Open: All year.

Directions

Leave A12, Arlberg tunnel - Innsbruck Autobahn at exit 83 (Innsbruck Kranebitten). Follow signs for airport/Kranebitten. After a few hundred metres keep left under main road then very sharp right onto the N171 Kranebitter Allee. Site is a few hundred metres on the right. GPS: 47.262513, 11.328334

Charges 2012

Per unit incl. 2 persons, electricity, water and waste water	€ 25.00 - € 30.00

Itter bei Hopfgarten

Terrassen-Camping Schlossberg Itter

Brixentaler Strasse 11, A-6305 Itter bei Hopfgarten (Tirol) T: 053 352 181. E: info@camping-itter.at

alanrogers.com/AU0130

This well kept site with 200 pitches and good facilities is suitable as a base for longer stays and also for overnight stops, as it lies right by a main road west of Kitzbühel. It is on a slight slope but most of the 200 numbered pitches are on level terraces. Some pitches are individual and divided by hedges and have electricity (8/10A) and cable TV connections, 150 have water and drainage. Space is usually available. There is a toboggan run from the site in winter. Good walks and a wealth of excursions by car are available nearby. There is some road and rail noise.

Facilities

The main sanitary facilities are heated and have a large room with private cubicles. Some have vanity style washbasins, others have baths, one a 'body wash' type brush or showers. Two slightly larger units for families, with baby baths. Facilities for disabled visitors. Washing machines and dryers. Motorcaravan services. Cooking facilities. Fridge. Small shop, bar/restaurant (both closed Nov). Heated swimming pool (16x8 m) and paddling pool (1/5-30/9). Sauna and solarium. Playground and indoor playroom for wet weather. Youth room. Entertainment programme. WiFi. Ski and drying rooms. English spoken.

Open: All year excl. 16-30 November.

Directions

From A12 exit 17 Wörgl Ost direction Brixental and after ca. 4km at the roundabout turn right direction Brixental on B170. Site is 2 km. before Hopfgarten on left. Satnav unreliable. GPS: 47.4663, 12.13972

Charges guide

Per unit incl. 2 persons and electricity (meter in winter)	€ 21.80 - € 30.80
extra person	€ 5.50 - € 7.50

Prices higher in winter. No credit cards.

Jerzens

Mountain Camp Pitztal

Niederhof 206, A-6474 Jerzens (Tirol) T: 054 148 7571. E: info@mountain-camp.at

alanrogers.com/AU0085

This is a small attractive family run site set among mountains in the Pitztal and is an ideal base for walks in the Tiroler Mountains and for mountain bike tours on the numerous paths through the woods and on the Schotterpiste and Wildspitze, the highest mountain in Tirol. Being a new site, the pitches are rather open; all 38 have 13A electricity, water, waste water and gas supplies. The pitches are laid out on level, rectangular fields on a grass and gravel base, with gravel access roads. There are beautiful views on the Tiroler mountains.

Facilities

One new, centrally located toilet block (heated) with toilets, washbasins (open style and in cabins) and free, controllable hot showers. Bathroom. Washing machine. Dryer. Restaurant with bar and covered terrace. WiFi. Fishing. Skate ramp. Swimming pond with small beach. Full activity programme for all in high season.
Off site: Riding 2 km. Golf 25 km.

Open: All year.

Directions

From the A12, take exit 132 at Imst and continue south to Arzl and Wenns; continue toward St. Leonhard. Site is signposted to the right about 5 km south of Wenns. (Important - set sat nav to Wenns not Jerzens). GPS: 47.14253, 10.746483

Charges guide

Per unit incl. 2 persons and electricity	€ 22.00 - € 26.00
extra person	€ 6.50 - € 7.00

Keutschach am See

FKK Kärntner Lichtbund Turkwiese

Dobeinitz 32, A-9074 Seental Keutschach (Carinthia) T: 042 732 838. E: klb.turkwiese@aon.at

alanrogers.com/AU0416

Turkwiese is a tranquil naturist campsite, attractively located on the southern banks of the Keutschacher See, with its own secluded beach. There are 116 pitches here, around 56 of which are available for tourers. Many of these have views across the lake. Pitches are grassy and generally well shaded by mature trees. The site's bar/restaurant is a convivial place for a drink or meal, and there are many other cafés and restaurants in the vicinity. Other amenities include a children's playground and sports field, as well as a giant chess board. The lake offers some excellent opportunities for watersports including sailing, canoeing and windsurfing.

Facilities

Bar/restaurant. Takeaway food. Lake beach. Fishing. Children's play area. Giant chess. Sports field. Tourist information. Please note that this is a naturist site. Dogs are not accepted. Off site: Walking and mountain biking in the Carinthian mountains. Golf. Watersports.

Open: 1 June - 30 September.

Directions

Approaching on A10 motorway (from Salzburg), leave at exit to Villach and continue east on A2 towards Klagenfurt. Follow signs to Keutschach on southern side of Wörther See. At Keutschach, head west on L97 to Keutschacher See, from where the site is well signposted. GPS: 46.5836, 14.1679

Charges guide

Per unit incl. 2 persons and electricity	€ 19.30 - € 21.30
extra person	€ 6.00 - € 7.00

Keutschach am See

Strandcamping Brückler Süd

Keutschach am See, A-9074 Keutschach (Carinthia) T: 042 732 773.
E: info@strandcampingbruecklersued.at alanrogers.com/AU0418

This is a pleasant, family owned site in a secluded area on the edge of the lake. Out of season it is quiet but can be very crowded in the high season. Pitches are level, grassy and well defined, but rather small, with a large proportion of plots being taken up by seasonal units. The toilet block is adequate but in need of some decoration. The site facilities are housed in a split-level building at the entrance. Sanitary areas are at low level and a small restaurant/bar with terrace overlooking the lake, are on top. Basic meals are available.

Facilities

Bar/restaurant (open to general public). Washing machine and dryer. Swimming in lake. Children's play area. Minigolf. Lake fishing (with permit). Lake sailing. Off site: Riding, golf and tennis in the area.

Open: 1 May - 30 September.

Directions

From A10 take road in direction of Veldon and follow signs to Keutschacher See lake. At traffic lights (by Gasthof Brückler and Strandcamping Nord), turn right and site is at end of road.
GPS: 46.58456, 14.172041

Charges guide

Per unit incl. 2 persons and electricity	€ 19.60 - € 24.30
extra person	€ 6.00 - € 7.80

Keutschach am See

Sabotnik Naturist Camping

Dobein 9, A-9074 Keutschach (Carinthia) T: 042 732 509. E: info@fkk-sabotnik.at
alanrogers.com/AU0419

Sabotnik is a very large and extremely well managed naturist site. It is situated on the banks of the Keutschacher See lake and caters specially for families. A separate area is designated for visitors with dogs. It is a very private site with 480 of the 750 pitches set aside for touring. All have 12A, Continental, two-pin electrical supply. The grass pitches are well defined and in orderly rows but there is very little shade. Free WiFi connection is accessible from all parts of the site. The four toilet blocks have all been recently refurbished to a good standard. There is a very good restaurant with a welcoming bar and a well stocked shop is open all season.

Facilities

Four toilet blocks have WCs, private showers with communal changing area, washbasins. Washing machines and dryers. Shop, bar and separate restaurant (open all season). Swimming pool with separate children's pool. Bicycle hire. Accomodation to rent. Off site: Riding 500 m. Boat Hire and launching 3 km. Golf 6 km.

Open: 1 May - 30 September.

Directions

From A2 motorway take exit 335 (Velden). Follow signs for Keutschach. About 4 km. after village of Schiefling, turn right at signs for FKK Centre. Site is on left, just after Camping Müllerhof.
GPS: 46.577997, 14.151893

Charges guide

Per unit incl. 2 persons and electricity	€ 17.00 - € 20.00
extra person	€ 5.50 - € 6.50

Keutschach am See

FKK Naturist Camping Müllerhof

Dobein 10, A-9074 Keutschach-am-See (Carinthia) T: 042 732 517. E: muellerhof@fkk-camping.at
alanrogers.com/AU0420

Müllerhof is an excellent naturist site, very well run with families in mind by its owners, the Safron family. Backed by a pine forest, on the southern side of the Keutschacher lake in Carinthia, the gently sloping site of almost 6 ha. provides for 270 touring units, all with electricity (6A Europlug). Manicured grass with neat rows of varied, mature trees, light coloured compacted gravel access roads and a security barrier at the entrance indicates that this is a well maintained site. Three grass sunbathing areas (one large, two small), each have direct access to the crystal clear waters of the lake which are edged with flowering lilies and rushes.

Facilities

Two large, fully equipped toilet blocks are kept very clean. Washing machines, dryer and ironing facilities. The block at the centre of the site has a high quality baby room. Sauna and massage. Small shop. Restaurant with waiter service and comprehensive menu, also provides takeaway food (May-Sept). Large play room and well appointed play area. Off site: Minimundus model village on the western approach to Klagnefurt. Pyramidenkogel Observation tower (alt. 905 m) with breathtaking views.

Open: 15 April - 30 September.

Directions

From A2 motorway take exit 335 signed Velden. Follow signs for Keutschach (or Keutschacher See). About 4 km. after village of Schiefling, turn right at signs for FKK Centre. Site is on left in just over 1 km.
GPS: 46.57795, 14.150583

Charges guide

Per unit incl. 2 persons and electricity	€ 22.00 - € 26.60
extra person	€ 8.00 - € 9.25

No credit cards.

Keutschach am See

Camping Hafnersee

Plescherken 5, A-9074 Keutschach (Carinthia) T: 042 732 375. E: info@hafnersee.at

alanrogers.com/AU0421

Set within the very well maintained grounds of the hotel of the same name, Camping Hafnersee combines the best of a rural lakeside campsite with the facilities of a very well appointed hotel. The 212 pitches, mostly on level grass, are well defined in rows separated by low hedges, with 88 currently available for touring units (6A electricity). The others are used by seasonal units. The site is set on the gently sloping grass banks of the lake and there are pontoons for swimming and boating. There is some shade from mature trees around the site.

Facilities

Two traditional toilet blocks have very good WCs, washbasins and showers and ample hot water. Drinking water points. Washing machine, dryer. Hotel bar and separate restaurant (all season). Indoor swimming pool with separate children's pool and a sauna. Internet at hotel. Fishing (with permit). Off site: Riding 1 km. Bicycle hire 2 km. Golf 5km.

Open: 1 May - 30 September.

Directions

From A2 motorway take exit 335 signed Velden. Follow signs for Keutschach. Just past village of Schiefling look for sign to Seehotel Hafnersee and Camping. GPS: 46.588966, 14.136808

Charges guide

Per unit incl. 2 persons and electricity	€ 20.70 - € 31.70
extra person	€ 6.40 - € 7.90
child (6-15 yrs)	€ 3.50 - € 4.50
dog	€ 2.00

Keutschach am See

Camping Reichmann

Reauz 5, A-9074 Keutschach (Carinthia) T: 046 328 1452. E: info@camping-reichmann.at

alanrogers.com/AU0422

This is a very basic, rural site at the eastern end of the Rauschelesee lake. The 170 pitches are all on grass, some close to the lake and some on a gentle slope. All have 16A electric supply available (long cables may be required). There is a very pleasant restaurant and bar with outside terrace, where traditional local meals can be sampled at reasonable prices. Very little English is spoken, but the owner and his staff are keen to ensure that all visitors have an enjoyable stay.

Facilities

One large block, built on a slope, houses the restaurant and bar at the higher level with the toilets and other facilities on the lower level. Water points at toilet blocks. Washing machine, dryer. Bar, restaurant and take away open all season. Swimming in lake. Fishing with permit. Off site: Riding 1 km. Bicycle hire 2 km. Boat launching 3 km. Golf 10 km.

Open: 1 May - 30 September.

Directions

From A10 take road towards Veldon and follow signs to Keutschach am See. Continue past the Keutschachersee lake for about 7 km. to Rauschelelsee. At eastern end of lake turn right into Reauz. Site is on right. GPS: 46.58296, 14.228384

Charges guide

Per unit incl. 2 persons and electricity	€ 22.50
extra person	€ 7.00
child (4-14 yrs)	€ 4.00

Kössen

Euro Camp Wilder Kaiser

Kranebittau 18, A-6345 Kössen (Tirol) T: 053 756 444. E: info@eurocamp-koessen.com

alanrogers.com/AU0140

This well run site lies near the A8 and A12 autobahns, which offer easy access to this attractive location. The site sits at the foot of the Unterberg with views of the Kaisergebirge (the Emperor's mountains) and surrounded by forests. Being about 2 km. south of the village, it is a quiet location away from main roads. About 130 of the 190 pitches (grass over gravel) are available for touring units, plus an area for tents and a new area for motorcaravans. Good English is spoken.

Facilities

The heated, central sanitary block is of good quality with spacious showers, some washbasins in cubicles and a baby room. Washing machines and dryers. Motorcaravan services. Shop. Large restaurant/bar (closed 18/10-15/11). Snack bar (high season). Club room with TV and play station. Heated swimming pool (May-Sept). Youth room. Sauna and solarium. Tennis. Large imaginative adventure playground. Club for children and other activities for all (high season). Covered play area. Off site: Paragliding, bicycle hire 1 km. Golf 2 km. Fishing and Riding 4 km. Beach and boat launching 6 km.

Open: All year excl. 7 November - 5 December.

Directions

Site is 18 km. NE of Kufstein. From A8 (München - Salzburg), take Grabenstatt exit 109 and go south on B307/B176 to Kössen. Cross the river and at roundabout follow signs for Bergbahnen and Euro Camp. After 600 m. follow signs to site. From A93 (Rosenheim - Kufstein) take Oberaudorf exit and go east on B172 to Walchsee and Kössen. GPS: 47.65388, 12.41544

Charges 2012

Per unit incl. 2 persons and electricity (plus meter)	€ 23.05 - € 27.05
extra person	€ 6.70 - € 7.70
child (5-14 yrs)	€ 3.50 - € 5.50
dog	€ 3.80 - € 4.80

Kötschach Mauthen

Alpencamp Kärnten

Kötschach 284, A 9640 Kötschach Mauthen (Carinthia) T: 047 154 29. E: info@alpencamp.at

alanrogers.com/AU0445

Materials hundreds of millions of years old, centuries old crafts and practices, together with the very latest technology have been combined in the construction of this environmental award winning site. Four years in the planning, Alpencamp is a showplace of how using techniques available today, comfortable, attractive and environmentally friendly accommodation can be realised. Set against an impressive panorama of mountains in the beautiful Lesactal, this quiet family run site has 85 pitches all with electricity; they are level, on grass with some tree shade. The main building and the sites five rentable chalets were constructed using local materials and were built to strict ecological/allergy free standards.

Facilities

Modern well maintained sanitary facilities. Free hot showers, washbasins in cabins. Laundry. Motorcaravan service point. Shop with fresh bread daily. Comfortable and bright restaurant with bar. Playground and playroom for children. Free internet terminal in reception, WiFi over site. Off site: Walking, cycling, mountain bike trails, climbing, riding, geological trails to follow. Free entry to Aquarena, swimming pool, wellness centre. Golf 20 km.

Open: All year excl. 1 November - 14 December.

Directions

From Villach on the 111, in town at the junction with the 110 turn left then after 200 m. turn right and continue along the 111 towards Lesachtal. Site is to the left after 500 m. GPS: 46.6698184, 12.9909468

Charges guide

Per unit incl. 2 persons and electricity	€ 19.50 - € 29.20
extra person	€ 4.70 - € 7.40
child (3-13 yrs)	€ 2.90 - € 4.60

Kramsach

Camping Seeblick Toni

Reintalersee, Moosen 46, A-6233 Kramsach (Tirol) T: 053 376 3544. E: info@camping-seeblick.at

alanrogers.com/AU0100

Austria has some of the finest sites in Europe and Seeblick Toni is one of them. In a quiet, rural situation on the edge of the small Reintaler See lake, it is well worth considering for holidays in the Tirol with many excursions possible. The surrounding mountains give scenic views and the campsite has a neat and tidy appearance. The 243 level pitches (215 for touring units) are in regular rows off hard access roads and are of good size with grass and hardstanding. All pitches have electricity (10A), 150 are fully serviced including cable TV and phone connections.

Facilities

Two outstanding sanitary blocks (heated in cool weather). One includes en-suite toilet/basin/shower rooms, the other also has individual bathrooms to rent. Facilities for disabled visitors. New facilities for children. Baby room. Laundry facilities. Drying rooms. Freezer. Motorcaravan services. Restaurant. Bar. Snack kiosk. Shop. Fitness centre. Playground. New indoor play area. 'Topi' club, kindergarten and organised activities for children in high season. Youth room. Fishing. Bicycle hire. Riding. Internet. Off site: Kramsach 3 km.

Open: All year.

Directions

Take exit 32 for Kramsach from A12 autobahn and turn right at roundabout, then immediately left following signs 'Zu den Seen' in village. After 3 km. turn right at site sign. Note: there are two sites side by side at the lake; Seeblick Toni is the furthest one. Do not rely on sat nav. GPS: 47.46104, 11.90676

Charges guide

Per unit incl. 2 persons and electricity	€ 22.50 - € 30.50
extra person	€ 5.50 - € 8.00

Camping Cheques accepted.

Kramsach

Seen Camping Stadlerhof

Seebühel 14, A-6233 Kramsach (Tirol) T: 053 376 3371. E: camping.stadlerhof@chello.at

alanrogers.com/AU0102

This child friendly, family run site is in a beautiful location near the Krummsee. There are 130 sensibly sized pitches (99 for touring units) all with electricity (10A Europlug). Many are individual and divided by hedges and shrubs, and some mature trees offer shade in parts. Fifty multi-serviced pitches are available. The site has a heated outdoor pool complex with café and wellness centre in addition to a small lake and a dog walk. Some English is spoken. A 'quickstop' facility with grassy pitches and electric hook-up for overnighting is also offered.

Facilities

Spacious sanitary facilities include showers, some washbasins in cubicles, and five family bathrooms for rent. Laundry facilities. No dedicated facilities for disabled visitors. Small restaurant and bar. Basic provisions available. Wellness centre. Outdoor heated stainless steel swimming pool (12.5x6 m; open in winter) with spa pool and children's pool, and a café. WiFi over site (charged). Playground. TV room. Drying room, ski room. Off site: Reintaler See 500 m. Kramsach 2 km. Riding 3 km.

Open: All year.

Directions

Kramsach is about mid-way between Innsbruck and Kufstein. From A12 exit 32 turn right at roundabout and immediately left following signs for 'Zu den Seen' in village. Site is just outside village on left. GPS: 47.4567, 11.88084

Charges 2012

Per unit incl. 2 persons and electricity	€ 16.00 - € 28.50
extra person	€ 4.70 - € 6.30

No credit cards.

Kramsach

Camping Seehof

Reintalersee, Moosen 42, A-6233 Kramsach (Tirol) T: **053 376 3541**. E: **info@camping-seehof.com**

alanrogers.com/AU0065

Camping Seehof is a family run site and excellent in every respect. It is situated in a marvellous, sunny and peaceful location on the eastern shores of the Reintalersee lake. The site's comfortable restaurant has a terrace with lake and mountain views and serves local dishes as well as homemade cakes and ice cream. The site is in two areas: a small one next to the lake is ideal for sunbathing, the other larger one adjoins the excellent sanitary block. There are 170 pitches, 130 of which are for touring (20 tent pitches), are served by good access roads and have electricity (16A Europlug) and TV points; 80 pitches are fully serviced. Seehof provides an ideal starting point for walking, cycling and riding (with a riding stable nearby) and skiing in winter. The Alpbachtal Seeland card is available without cost at reception and allows free bus transport and free daily entry to many worthwhile attractions in the region. With easy access from the Autobahn A12 the site is also a useful overnight stop. Bread available each morning from 0700 without pre-ordering.

Facilities

The sanitary facilities are first class and include ten bathrooms to rent for private use. Baby room. Facilities for disabled visitors. Dog shower. Washing machine and dryer. Ski room. Motorcaravan service point. Small shop. Good restaurant. Playground. WiFi throughout (charged). Bicycle hire. Fishing. Apartments to rent. Renovated fitness and play rooms. Off site: Tiroler farmhouse museum 1 km. Kramsach 3 km. Rottenberg 4 km. Swarovski Kristallwelten.

Open: All year.

Directions

From the A12 take Kramsach exit and follow the signs 'Zu den Seen' past Camping Krummsee and northern shore of lake, then right at the crossroads. Camping Seehof (300 m) is the first campsite you reach. Park on left, reception is on the right, follow campsite directions. GPS: 47.46188, 11.90734

Charges 2012

Per unit incl. 2 persons and electricity	€ 17.30 - € 26.30
extra person	€ 4.60 - € 6.90
child (2-14 yrs)	€ 3.00 - € 4.50
dog	€ 3.00

Landeck

Camping Riffler

Bruggenfeldstrasse 2, A-6500 Landeck (Tirol) T: **054 426 4898**. E: **lorenz.schimpfoessl@aon.at**

alanrogers.com/AU0150

This attractive 35 pitch site has easy access from the A12/E60 Arlberg-Innsbruck autobahn and being in a small town with numerous supermarkets, restaurants and bars makes it a good stopover point as well as a comfortable base from which to tour this interesting region through which the Via Claudia Augusta, the Roman route linking Venice with Germany, once passed. The pitches are grassed, accessed by hard roads and 25 have 10A electricity. The Tyrol West Card is available free at reception and permits free bus travel as well as free entry to, and reductions on, many of the region's attractions.

Facilities

The small toilet block has been rebuilt to a good standard. Washing machine and dryer. Basic motorcaravan services. Small general room with TV. Fishing. Off site: Bicycle hire and swimming pool 500 m. Reschen and Arlberg mountain passes within easy driving distance. Lots of Walking. Mountain biking. Paragliding. Rafting (including family rafting on the quieter stretches). Canyoning.

Open: All year excl. May.

Directions

Site is at the western end of Landeck. Take exit for Landeck-West from the A12 and turn right towards Landeck. Site is on the left after the roundabout. It is situated beside a shopping area.
GPS: 47.14315, 10.56441

Charges 2012

Per unit incl. 2 persons and electricity	€ 24.90 - € 31.10
extra person	€ 5.30 - € 7.80

Winter prices slightly higher. No credit cards.

Längenfeld

Camping Ötztal Längenfeld

Unterlangenfeld 220, A-6444 Längenfeld (Tirol) T: 052 535 348. E: info@camping-oetztal.com

alanrogers.com/AU0045

Camping Ötztal Längenfeld, a family run site, is situated some 400 metres from the pretty village of Längenfeld, at the edge of a forest. Next door are the local sports centre and swimming pool and a restaurant. In summer the campsite is ideal for walking and cycling, as well as mountaineering tours. In the winter you can enjoy cross-country skiing right from the doorstep and a free bus shuttle operates to the Ötztal Ski arena. The site provides 200 level grass pitches of which 150 are for tourers. All pitches have electricity and 100 also have gas, water, drainage and a TV point.

Facilities

Excellent sanitary facilities include four bathrooms to rent for private use. Baby room. Facilities for disabled visitors. Female hairdressing room. Dog shower. Washing machines and dryer. Ski room. Motorcaravan service point. Restaurant serves breakfast and takeaway. Sauna and solarium. WiFi. Off site: Sports centre and swimming pool adjacent (reduced prices for campers). Längenfeld and Aqua Dome thermal spa facility. Bicycle hire 0.5 km.

Open: All year.

Directions

From the A12 take exit 123 and follow the 186 along the Ötztal Valley towards Sölden for about 20 km. On entering Längenfeld, continue up hill into town and shortly after tourist information office on the right there are signs for the site. Enter through yard and follow lane past sports centre to site entrance. GPS: 47.07229, 10.96431

Charges guide

Per unit incl. 2 persons and electricity (plus meter)	€ 19.50 - € 27.00
extra person	€ 5.90 - € 6.90

No credit cards.

Leibnitz

Camping Leibnitz

Rudolf Hans Bartsch-Gasse 33, A-8430 Leibnitz (Steiermark) T: 034 528 2463. E: camping@leibnitz.at

alanrogers.com/AU0505

Near the Slovenian border, close to the small town of Leibnitz, this site is set in the rolling wine-growing countryside of southeast Austria. A small site with only 61 pitches, it is set in a lovely park area and close to an excellent swimming pool complex (some noise can be heard), which is available for campers' use (with access arrangements for disabled visitors). A sports centre and facilities for minigolf and tennis are nearby. All the pitches are of a good size, level and with 16A electricity connections, and most have some shade. The town has shops and restaurants with weekly events held, for example, at the Jazz Club. There are marked footpaths and cycleways to allow you to explore.

Facilities

Excellent toilet facilities are clean and well maintained with free showers. Facilities for disabled visitors. Washing machine. Small restaurant (15/5-31/8) but many more within walking distance. Small play area. Off site: Leibnitz 500 m. Leisure centre with two heated outdoor swimming pools 100 m. (15/5-15/9).

Open: 1 May - 15 October.

Directions

From the A9 take exit for Leibnitz, go straight over two roundabouts (through factory outlet centre), over traffic lights and after 300 m. turn left (site signed). Go straight over roundabout and enter Leibnitz, turn right and site is 500 m. on the left, set in the park next to the pool complex. GPS: 46.77888, 15.52900

Charges guide

Per person	€ 4.50
child (6-14 yrs)	€ 2.00
pitch incl. car	€ 6.50
electricity	€ 1.80

Less 10% for stays over 10 days.

Lienz

Campingplatz Seewiese

Tristachersee 2, A-9900 Lienz (Tirol) T: **048 526 9767**. E: **seewiese@hotmail.com**

alanrogers.com/AU0185

High above the village of Tristach and 5 km. from Lienz, this is a perfect location for a good campsite. When we arrived the owner said, 'This is a green paradise at the gateway to the Dolomites' – it did not take us long to agree totally with his assessment. The 110 pitches all have 6A electricity (long leads may be necessary) and the 11 pitches for motorcaravans near reception each have electricity, water and internet access. Caravans are sited on a gently sloping field which has level areas although pitches are unmarked and unnumbered. At the bottom of this field is a small lake which can be used for swimming.

Facilities

Toilet facilities are clean, heated and modern with free showers. Washing machine and dryer. Motorcaravan service point. Excellent restaurant/bar (1/6-1/9). Small play area. WiFi (charged). Swimming in adjoining lake. Off site: Lienz 5 km.

Open: 11 May - 25 September.

Directions

Site is 5 km. east of Lienz. In Lienz initially follow signs for Spittal and at traffic lights turn right towards Tristach. Go under the railway and over a small bridge then turn sharp left, still towards Tristach and Tristacher See. Go through village of Tristach and after 1.5 km. turn right up to the site, which is at the top of a 1 km, 1:10 climb.
GPS: 46.80601, 12.80307

Charges guide

Per unit incl. 2 persons and electricity	€ 28.00 - € 32.30
extra person	€ 7.00
child (4-15 yrs)	€ 4.50
dog	€ 3.00

No credit cards. Camping Cheques accepted.

Lienz Amlach

Dolomiten-Camping Amlacher Hof

Amlach 5, A-9900 Lienz Amlach (Tirol) T: **048 526 2317**. E: **info@amlacherhof.at**

alanrogers.com/AU0186

The small hamlet of Amlach is south of the busy town of Lienz in the western Tirol and surrounded by mountain peaks. Dolomiten Camping is located around the old Amlacher Hof and both the site and the villa are in need of some maintenance. Whilst this is a good location with potentially good amenities, the grounds and sporting facilities were very unkempt when we visited in early July. There are 84 level and numbered pitches, all with 16A electricity. A kitchen and toilets for disabled visitors are behind the villa in a modern building, with all other facilities in the basement of what was presumably a good hotel in its day. A small swimming pool is unfenced. Those wishing to play tennis will have to find the nets and spend a good time clearing the high weeds before the game can start so come prepared.

Facilities

Modern sanitary facilities with ample and clean toilets, hot showers and washbasins. Washing machines and dryers. Kitchen facilities. Chemical toilet disposal point. Motorcaravan service point. Small swimming pool. Play areas. Minigolf. Games room. Tennis. Internet access. Riding stables. Bicycle hire. Off site: Fishing and skiing 1 km. Golf 5 km.

Open: 15 December - 26 October.

Directions

The small hamlet of Amlach is just 2 km. south of Lienz. You need to turn south at the traffic lights near the railway station, go under the railway and over the river then straight on to the site.
GPS: 46.813483, 12.764016

Charges guide

Per unit incl. 2 persons and electricity	€ 17.50 - € 21.70

Malta

Terrassen Camping Maltatal

Malta 6, A-9854 Malta (Carinthia) T: 047 332 34. E: info@maltacamp.at

alanrogers.com/AU0490

Situated between two national parks in a valley between the mountains, this four hectare site offers spectacular views over the surrounding area especially from the pool which is over 300 sq.m. with a grassy sunbathing area and is open to all (free for campers). There are 220 grass pitches on narrow terraces (70-100 sq.m) and mostly in rows on either side of narrow access roads. Numbered and marked, some separated with low hedges, all have electricity and 160 have water and drainage (the electric boxes are often inconveniently located on the next terrace). The Kärnten-card is available to purchase from the site which gives free travel on public transport and free entry to many attractions.

Facilities

Two toilet blocks, one new for 2011, have about half the washbasins in cabins and ten family wash cabins. Facilities for babies and children. Laundry facilities. Motorcaravan services. Shop, restaurant, bar (from 16/4). Heated outdoor swimming pool (1/6-1/9). Sauna. Playground. Bicycle hire. Entertainment programme and many walks and excursions. WiFi throughout (free). Gas. Electric barbecues are not permitted. Off site: Village 500 m. Fishing and golf 6 km. Riding 10 km. Malta High alpine road, Reisseck mountain railways and The Porsche Museum in Gmund are all nearby.

Open: 31 March - 31 October.

Directions

Site is 15 km. north of Spittal. Leave A10 at exit 130 Gmund. Pass through Gmund towards Malta. Site is on right 6 km. from autobahn exit. GPS: 46.949724, 13.509606

Charges 2012

Per unit incl. 2 persons and electricity	€ 18.30 - € 26.10
extra person	€ 5.30 - € 7.70
child (2-14 yrs)	€ 3.50 - € 5.20
dog	€ 2.50 - € 3.50

Electricity included. Less for longer stays. Camping Cheques accepted.

Mondsee

Camp Mond See Land

Punz Au 21, A-5310 Mondsee, Tiefgraben (Upper Austria) T: 062 322 600. E: austria@campmondsee.at

alanrogers.com/AU0350

Mond See Land is a well established campsite that first opened in 1970. It is set in a delightful location and offers excellent facilities in a pleasant part of Austria, to the east of Salzburg, between the lakes of Mondsee and Irrsee. There are 60 good sized, level touring pitches (80 long stay), set amongst the trees at a lower level and on terraces, each with water, waste water and 16A electricity. The heated swimming pool is covered and has a sunbathing terrace. There is a small fishing lake (unfenced) and a small children's playground. During summer, there is an entertainment programme for children. Good English is spoken.

Facilities

The sanitary facilities are in the reception and pool complex and offer first class facilities including some washbasins in cabins and a suite for disabled visitors. Laundry with washing machines and dryer. Kitchen with cooking and dishwashing. Motorcaravan service point. Shop and restaurant. Swimming pool (free). Playground. Fishing and riding. The adjoining restaurant offers local and other dishes served in a traditional setting.
Off site: Mondsee is a popular large lake with many sporting opportunities. Golf 5 km.

Open: 15 April - 15 October.

Directions

From A1/E55 exit 265 (signed Straßwalchen) turn north onto B154. In 1.5 m. turn left at crossroads (by glassworks) and then 2 km. to site (signed). Note: Signs can be difficult to spot. GPS: 47.86655, 13.30657

Charges guide

Per unit incl. 2 persons and electricity	€ 20.70 - € 23.00
extra person	€ 5.30 - € 5.90
child (6-15 yrs)	€ 3.80 - € 4.10
dog	€ 2.50

Nenzing

Alpencamping Nenzing

Garfrenga 1, A-6710 Nenzing (Vorarlberg) T: 055 256 2491. E: office@alpencamping.at

alanrogers.com/AU0010

Only a short drive from the A14 autobahn, Alpencamping is a well run and comfortable, all-year-round site, set in a natural bowl from which there are splendid mountain views. All 160 level pitches are for touring with 16A electricity; 120 also have fresh and waste water, gas, TV and telephone connections. Most are set on neat terraces. At the centre of the site is the well appointed restaurant, built in a traditional style with lots of atmosphere and its tables lit by lamps hanging on meter long ropes attached to beams in the massive wooden roof. The restaurant with its bar and terrace understandably attracts a lot of local custom and can be quite busy at weekends.

Facilities

The newer facilities are 'state of the art' and contain 20 private bathrooms (some free, others for rent). Two older blocks remain and provide good facilities. Excellent children's washroom. Baby room. Facilities for disabled visitors. Motorcaravan service point. Small shop. Bar. Restaurant with terrace. New heated indoor and outdoor swimming complex (all year). Paddling pool. Small play area with another larger one on the top terrace. Practice climbing wall. Sauna, solarium, massage and relax room. Internet corner and WiFi. Off site: Trips arranged for the Berlina Express. Bicycle hire, riding, tennis and fishing.

Open: All year excl. week after Easter - 1 May.

Directions

Site is 15 km. southeast of Feldkirk. From the E60, A12/14 Bregenz - Innsbruck motorway take exit 50 for Nenzing on B190 road and then follow small 'Camping' signs which have the site logo, a butterfly. GPS: 47.18333, 9.69997

Charges guide

Per unit incl. 2 persons	€ 19.00 - € 33.90
extra person	€ 6.50 - € 9.50
child (acc. to age)	€ 3.90 - € 7.00
electricity per kWh	€ 0.65

Nussdorf am Attersee

Seecamping Gruber

Dorfstrasse 63, A-4865 Nussdorf am Attersee (Upper Austria) T: 076 668 0450. E: office@camping-gruber.at

alanrogers.com/AU0345

The Attersee is the largest of a group of lakes just to the east of Salzburg in the very attractive Salzkammergut area. Seecamping Gruber is a small, often crowded site halfway up the western side of the lake. There are 150 individual pitches, with an increasing number of seasonal units taking the larger pitches. There are some 70 pitches for tourers, all with 16A electricity and many with shade. Pitches tend to be small to medium size and the access roads are narrow making entrance and exit difficult.

Facilities

Modern sanitary facilities, now with a children's area, offer some private cabins, washing machine and dryer, good unit for disabled visitors, and baby room. Bar, restaurant, shop and takeaway (all 15/4-15/10). Play area. Swimming, paddling pools, sauna, solarium and gym (all 1/5-30/9). Fishing. WiFi (charged). Off site: Windsurfing and sailing. Mountain bikes, diving and balloon rides. Tennis, golf, rambling, cycling and mountain bike tracks.

Open: 15 April - 15 October.

Directions

From the A1/E55/E60 between Salzburg and Linz, take exit 243 to Attersee and then south on the B151 to Nußdorf. Site is on the southern edge of the village. GPS: 47.87905, 13.52444

Charges guide

Per unit incl. 2 persons and electricity	€ 26.60 - € 32.60
extra person	€ 6.50 - € 7.50
child (6-14 yrs)	€ 3.50 - € 5.00

Nüziders

Terrassencamping Sonnenberg

Hinteroferst 12, A-6714 Nüziders bei Bludenz (Vorarlberg) T: 055 526 4035. E: sonnencamp@aon.at

alanrogers.com/AU0232

A friendly welcome awaits at this well equipped, family run site delightfully located at the junction of five Alpine valleys. From this hillside site there are magnificent, ever-changing views along and across the mountains. Very easily reached from the A14 autobahn and located on the outskirts of a large village with all facilities, the site is not only ideal as a stopover but also as a base from which to tour in this spectacular alpine region. All of the 120 generously sized, terraced pitches have 13A electricity, 60 are fully serviced and there are eight motorcaravan hardstandings.

Facilities

A superb new building contains high quality facilities. On the lower floor are WCs, spacious hot showers, and washbasins (some in cubicles), and a baby room. Drying room, laundry and dishwashing room upstairs. Motorcaravan service point. Gas stocked. TV and cinema room. Shop. Baker calls daily in July/Aug. Playground. Only one dog per unit is allowed. Internet access and WiFi. Two chalets to rent. Max. 1 dog. Off site: Free entrance to large outdoor swimming pool (3 km). Village with shops and ATM 500 m. Fishing 3 km.

Open: 30 April - 3 October.

Directions

Nüziders is about 25 km. southeast of Feldkirch. From A14 exit 57 (Bludenz - Nüziders) turn north on road 190 and left at roundabout into village. Follow camping signs through village. Turn right at church, then fork left to site. GPS: 47.170147, 9.807677

Charges guide

Per unit incl. 2 persons and electricity	€ 20.60 - € 27.60
extra person	€ 5.00 - € 6.00

No credit cards.

Natters

Ferienparadies Natterer See

Natterer See 1, A-6161 Natters (Tirol) T: 051 254 6732. E: info@natterersee.com

alanrogers.com/AU0060

In a quiet location arranged around two lakes and set amid beautiful alpine scenery, this site founded in 1930 is renowned as one of Austria's top sites. Over the last few years many improvements have been carried out and pride of place goes to the innovative, award-winning, multifunctional building at the entrance to the site. This contains all of the sanitary facilities expected of a top site, including a special children's section, private bathrooms to rent and also a dog bath. The reception, shop, café/bar/bistro and cinema are on the ground floor, and on the upper floor is a panorama lounge where the owner has assembled the largest collection of model camping cars and caravans in Europe. Almost all of the 235 pitches are for tourers. They are terraced, set on gravel/grass, all have electricity and most offer a splendid view of the mountains. The site's lakeside restaurant with bar and large terrace has a good menu and is the ideal place to spend the evening. With a bus every hour and the city centre only 19 minutes away this is also a good site from which to visit Innsbruck. The Innsbruck Card is available at reception and allows free bus transport in the city, including sightseeing tour, free entry to museums and one cable car trip.

Facilities

The large sanitary block has underfloor heating, some private cabins, plus excellent facilities for babies, children and disabled visitors. Laundry facilities. Motorcaravan services. Fridge box hire. Bar. Restaurant and takeaway with at least one open all year. Pizzeria. Good shop. Playgrounds. Children's activity programme. Child minding (day nursery) in high season. Sports field. Archery. Youth room with games, pool and billiards. TV room with Sky. Open air cinema. Mountain bike hire. Aquapark (1/5-30/9). Surf bikes and pedalos. Canoes and mini sailboats for rent. Fishing. Extensive daily entertainment programme (mid May-mid Oct). Dogs are not accepted in high season (July/Aug). WiFi (charged). Off site: Tennis and minigolf nearby. Riding 6 km. Golf 12 km.

Open: All year.

Directions

From Inntal autobahn (A12) take Brenner autobahn (A13) as far as Innsbruck-sud/Natters exit (no. 3). Turn left by Shell petrol station onto the B182 to Natters. At roundabout take first exit and immediately right again and follow signs to site 4 km. Do not use sat nav for final approach to site, follow camping signs. GPS: 47.23755, 11.34201

Charges guide

Per unit incl. 2 persons and electricity	€ 23.40 - € 34.60
extra person	€ 5.90 - € 8.30
child (under 13 yrs)	€ 4.60 - € 6.10
dog (excl. July/Aug)	€ 4.00 - € 4.00

Camping Cheques accepted.

Obertraun

Camping am See

Winkl 77, A-4831 Obertraun (Upper Austria) T: 061 312 65. E: camping.am.see@chello.at

alanrogers.com/AU0340

It is unusual to locate a campsite so deep in the heart of spectacular mountain scenery, yet with such easy access. Directly on the shores of Halstattersee, near Obertraun and the Dachstein mountains, this 2.5 hectare, flat site, with 70 pitches is an excellent, peaceful holiday base which has been upgraded. The grass site is basically divided into two, with tents in a more shady area, whilst caravans and motorcaravans are more in the open. There are no specific pitches although the owners, within reason, control where you place your unit. At the time of our visit there were only 36 electricity hook-ups.

Facilities

Completely refurbished, fully equipped and modern, the toilet block includes a baby room. Washing machine. Open barn style area with barbecues, seating and tables. Bar and limited restaurant with hot meals and fine wines to order. Basic daily provisions such as bread and milk. Small playground. Off site: Activities include walking, birdwatching, fishing, mountain biking, rock climbing and scuba diving. For naturists, 100 m. from the site there is a delightful popular area designated as an FKK beach.

Open: 1 May - 30 September.

Directions

Due south from Bad Ischl on road B145, take road B166 to Hallstatt. After single carriageway tunnel, site is 4 km. on left on entering village of Winkl. Note: Road is a little narrow in places so care is needed. GPS: 47.54897, 13.67422

Charges guide

Per unit incl. 2 persons and electricity	€ 29.90 - € 31.10
extra person	€ 7.80

No credit cards.

Ossiach

Terrassen Camping Ossiacher See

Ostriach 67, A-9570 Ossiach (Carinthia) T: 042 434 36. E: martinz@camping.at

alanrogers.com/AU0460

This gently terraced site is protected by rising hills and enjoys lovely views across the lake to the mountains beyond. Trees, flowers, hedges and bushes abound, adding atmosphere to this neat, tidy site. The 530 level pitches, all with electricity, are in rows on the level grass terraces, separated by hard roads and some divided by hedges. A separate area (25 pitches only) is provided for campers with dogs. Used by tour operators (28 pitches). Good English is spoken.

Facilities

Five well maintained sanitary blocks, one new in 2011, are heated in cool weather, and some with washbasins in cabins. Ten family washrooms (charged), baby rooms and facilities for disabled campers. Laundry facilities. Motorcaravan services. Restaurant (15/5-15/9). Well stocked supermarket. ATM. High season entertainment programme. Beach volleyball. Trampoline. Playgrounds, games rooms and disco courtyard. Waterskiing and windsurfing schools and boats for hire. Tennis. Bicycle and moped hire. Fishing. Riding. Off site: Cycle path around lake. Hang-gliding possibilities in the area.

Open: 1 May - 30 September.

Directions

Site is directly on the lake shore, 1.5 km. southwest of Ossiach village. Leave the A10 at exit 178 for Ossiacher See, turn left on road B94 towards Feldkirchen and shortly right to Ossiach Sud. Site is shortly before Ossiach. GPS: 46.66371, 13.9748

Charges guide

Per unit incl. 2 persons and electricity	€ 18.45 - € 33.15
extra person	€ 5.80 - € 8.70
child (3-12 yrs)	free - € 5.80
dog	€ 3.00

Barrier card deposit € 20.

Peterdorf

Camping Bella Austria

Peterdorf 100, A-8842 St Peter am Kammersberg (Steiermark) T: 035 367 3902.

E: info@camping-bellaustria.com alanrogers.com/AU0515

The small, quiet campsite with only 48 pitches is ideally located for exploring southwest Styria and the beautiful Mur valley, and the Niedere Tauern alps (highest point Greimberg 2,472 m). To the north, snowcapped Greimberg sits high above the site whilst in other directions you can see pine clad slopes and alpine pastures. Not too far away is Turracher Hohe, the small ski resort that nestles at an altitude of 1,700 m. in the Nocky mountains, one of Austria's most scenic Alpine ranges between Styria and Carinthia. Walks and cycle routes abound or you can just sit and watch the countryside at work from your pitch. The level, unmarked pitches all have access to 6A electricity.

Facilities

The modern sanitary block provides ample and clean facilities including toilets, hot showers and washbasins. Washing machine. Kitchen facilities.

Open: All year.

Directions

From the Murau - Scheifling no. 96 road, turn north towards Katsch just west of Frojach. Follow this road up the valley towards and through Peterdorf to the site on the right set back from the road but clearly signed. GPS: 47.1808, 14.2157

Charges guide

Per unit incl. 2 persons and electricity	€ 15.00 - € 20.00
extra person	€ 3.00 - € 8.00

Pettneu am Arlberg

Arlberg Panorama Camping

Dorfstrasse 58c, A-6574 Pettneu am Arlberg (Tirol) T: 054 488 352. E: info@arlberg-panoramacamping.at

alanrogers.com/AU0025

Owned and run by the Grobner family, this informal little site nestles between wooded mountains with wonderful views along the valley. A crystal clear mountain stream runs down along one side. There are 40 touring pitches on a level terrace overlooking grassy meadows. They vary in size, all have electricity and easy access to water (heated in winter) and five also have drainage and TV points. The main services can be found on the upper terrace, but due to the steep access, it is not suitable for disabled visitors. A ski and boot hire centre is attached to the site, making it a very popular winter destination.

Facilities

Heated sanitary facilities in the main block are clean and well maintained. Showers token operated. Indoor sinks for dishwashing. Washing machine and dryer. No shop but bread, milk and essentials available to order. Cosy bar with limited menu, snacks and takeaway. Large drying room for ski clothing and equipment. Ski and boot hire and maintainence. Games room and TV room with library and children's games. Large indoor caravan storage garage. Water supply to pitches is heated in winter. WiFi throughout site (small charge).

Open: All year.

Directions

From the A12/S16 take the L68 for 6.5 km. towards Pettneu. On arriving at the village, keep left at the chapel. The entrance to the site is signposted in 100 m. on the left, by the fire station. GPS: 47.14802, 10.34646

Charges guide

Per unit incl. 2 persons and electricity (plus meter)	€ 14.00 - € 24.00
extra person	€ 4.00 - € 7.00

No credit cards.

Pettneu am Arlberg

Camping Arlberg

A-6574 Pettneu am Arlberg (Tirol) T: **054 482 22660.** E: **info@camping-arlberg.at**

alanrogers.com/AU0055

This is an unusual site, located alongside, and lower than, the S16 autobahn, just a few kilometres to the east of the 13 km. long Arlberg tunnel. Inevitably there is some traffic noise. The site is unusual because it offers 145 pitches (out of 185) that are provided with an on-pitch wooden cabin housing the sanitary facilities, TV connection and 16A electricity. The grass and hardcore pitches are of medium size, fairly level and offer some views of the surrounding mountains. The other 40 pitches are near the reception building and offer electricity with a prepayment meter only (€ 1 coins).

Facilities

145 private bathrooms in wooden cabins, electrically heated with WC, washbasin and shower (electricity is metered). Motorcaravan service point. Shop. Bar. Restaurant. Indoor pool. Play area. Fishing. Bicycle hire. Off site: Pettneu, swimming pool and the Tirol. Skiing; ski bus operates in the season.

Open: 4 December - 30 April and 10 June - 15 October.

Directions

From S16 (B316) take exit to Pettneu (not St Anton). Just at the end of the slip road between a swimming complex and a play area is the site entrance. If travelling to Pettneu on the L68, access is best from the marked turning to the west of the village. GPS: 47.14495, 10.3388

Charges guide

Per unit incl. 2 persons and electricity	€ 25.00 - € 37.00

No credit cards.

Prutz

Aktiv-Camping Prutz Tirol

Pontlatzstrasse 22, A-6522 Prutz (Tirol) T: **054 722 648.** E: **info@aktiv-camping.at**

alanrogers.com/AU0155

Aktiv-Camping is a long site which lies beside, and is fenced off from, the River Inn. Most of the 100 individual level pitches are for touring and 80 sq.m. They all have 6A electrical connections and in the larger area fit together sideways and back to back. As a result, the site can sometimes have the appearance of being quite crowded. There is a separate overnight area for motorcaravans. This is an attractive area with many activities in both summer and winter for all age groups. You may well consider using this site not just as an overnight stop, but also for a longer stay.

Facilities

The sanitary facilities are of a high standard, with private cabins and good facilities for disabled visitors. Baby room. Washing machine. Dog shower. Small shop (all year). Bar (15/5-15/9). Takeaway (15/5-15/9). Play room. Ski room. Skating rink. Children's entertainment. Guided walks, skiing (free shuttle service). WiFi over site. Off site: Riding 1 km. Indoor pool at Feichten, Pilgrim's Church at Kaltenbrunn. Kaunertaler Glacier.

Open: All year.

Directions

Travelling west from Innsbruck on the E60/A12 for about 65 km. Exit at Landeck and follow the B315 (direction Reschenpass) turn south onto the B180 signed Bregenz, Arlberg, Innsbruck and Fernpass for 11 km. to Prutz. Site is signed to the right from the B180 over the bridge. GPS: 47.08833, 10.65831

Charges 2012

Per unit incl. 2 persons and electricity	€ 16.00 - € 25.90
extra person	€ 4.00 - € 7.20
child (5-14 yrs)	€ 2.50 - € 4.00

Raggal

Camping Grosswalsertal

Plazera 21, A-6741 Raggal (Vorarlberg) T: **055 532 09.** E: **info@camping-austria.info**

alanrogers.com/AU0015

As we climbed up to this site we seemed to be above the clouds. We then descended into a beautiful green valley and saw the site on a flat plateau below. From almost every pitch there are the most fantastic views down the valley. On open grass, there are 55 slightly sloping, unnumbered and unmarked pitches all with 16A electricity. Plenty of sporting activities are available locally and many places to visit, as well as walks and bike rides in the immediate area. Alternatively, just rest on the site and watch the clouds roll by. The site is very popular with Dutch visitors.

Facilities

The modern sanitary block has ample and clean toilets, hot showers and washbasins. Washing machine and dryer. Small shop with essential supplies. Swimming pool (1/6-15/9). Play area. Bicycle hire. WiFi. Off site: Fishing and riding 2 km. Golf 14 km.

Open: 1 May - 30 September.

Directions

From the A14 take exit 50 for Nenzing and Gr. Walsertal and proceed to Bludesch. Turn left toward Raggal where you take the left fork, pass a Spar supermarket and 2 km. downhill to the site. GPS: 47.21585, 9.8537

Charges guide

Per unit incl. 2 persons and electricity	€ 18.50 - € 21.50
extra person	€ 5.00
child (0-13 yrs)	€ 2.00 - € 3.50

No credit cards.

Rennweg

Sommer & Winter Camping Ramsbacher

Gries 53, A-9863 Rennweg (Carinthia) T: 047 346 63. E: camp.ram@utanet.at

alanrogers.com/AU0405

This is a beautiful small site set in a high alpine valley with great views in every direction. With 72 touring pitches, all with electricity, this is a great site for those seeking peace and quiet and the opportunity to explore the local area either by bike or on foot. The site is well placed in the Katschberg Mountains and close to the Pölital nature reserve. Cars are not allowed in the national park in the summer so entry is via a small 'train'. In winter, of course, the site is very well placed for local skiing.

Facilities

Toilet facilities are clean, heated and modern with free showers but a communal changing area. Washing machine, dryer and drying area. Attractive restaurant/bar. Small play area. WiFi (charged). Off site: Swimming pool, minigolf, tennis, rollerskating and play area 25 m. Winter skiing with free shuttle bus.

Open: All year.

Directions

From A10 take exit 113 (south of the Katschberg toll tunnel) and turn towards Rennweg. Turn right a little later into village, then right again towards Oberdorf where site is well signed. GPS: 47.01499, 13.61498

Charges guide

Per unit incl. 2 person and electricity	€ 24.40 - € 25.30
extra person	€ 5.80 - € 6.00

Saint Martin bei Lofer

alan rogers Winner 2011 Awards

Park Grubhof

Nr. 39, A-5092 Saint Martin bei Lofer (Salzburg) T: 065 888 237. E: home@grubhof.com

alanrogers.com/AU0265

Park Grubhof is a well organised, spacious site in a very scenic riverside location. The 200 pitches all with 12A electricity, have been carefully divided into separate areas for different types of visitor – dog owners, young people, families and groups, and a quiet area. There are 150 very large pitches, all with electricity, water and drainage, along the bank of the Saalach river. Although new, the central building housing reception, a cosy inn, a shop with caféteria, as well as a super sauna and wellness area and some of the site's sanitary facilities, has been built in traditional Tirolean style using, in part, materials hundreds of years old reclaimed from old farmhouses. The result is most attractive. Some areas are wooded with plenty of shade, others are more open and there are some very attractive log cabins which have been rescued from the old logging camps. Many of the possible activities are based around the river, where you will find barbecue areas, canoeing and white water rafting, fishing and swimming (when the river level reduces). The ski resort of Lofer Alm is only 2 km. away (free ski shuttle). A cross-county track is 300 m. away and snow cleared winter walks start directly from the site. Bordering the National Park of Berchtesgaden, the area is renowned for hiking, mountain climbing and cycling (the site is on the Tauernradweg cycling trail). Excellent English is spoken.

Facilities

Two attractive, modern sanitary units built with plenty of glass and wood, give a good provision of all facilities. Large showers. Some washbasins in cubicles. Saunas, steam bath, massage, fitness room. Separate facilities for canoeists. Motorcaravan service point. Shop, restaurant and bar. WiFi (free). Playground. Games room. Children's playroom. Watersports. Cabins to rent. Hotel and B&B accommodation. Off site: Cross-country track 300 m. Swimming pools at Lofer (open all day in summer) 1 km. Skiing at Lofer Alm 2 km. Gorges and caves 5-7 km. Salzburg 40 minutes drive. Many marked walking and cycling trails. Mountain climbing.

Open: All year excl. November.

Directions

From A12 exit 17 (south of Kufstein) take B178 east to St Johann in Tyrol, then continue on the B178 to Lofer, then south on B311 towards Zell am See. Site is 200 m. after the Lagerhaus filling station on the left. GPS: 47.57498, 12.70497

Charges guide

Per unit incl. 2 persons and electricity	€ 20.00 - € 29.00
extra person	€ 5.70 - € 7.20
child (under 14 yrs)	€ 3.70 - € 4.50
dog	€ 3.00

No credit cards.

For latest campsite news, availability and prices visit
alanrogers.com

Saint Primus

Strandcamping Turnersee Breznik

A-9123 Saint Primus (Carinthia) T: **042 392 350.** E: **info@breznik.at**

alanrogers.com/AU0410

This neat and tidy site is situated in a valley with views of the surrounding mountains. The 225 marked and numbered pitches for touring units vary in size, on level grass terraces. Although there are many trees, not all parts have shade. All pitches have electricity (6A) and 55 also have water, drainage, TV and phone connections. At the lakeside is a large, well kept grass area for sunbathing, with a wooden deck area right next to the water providing steps for swimming in the lake. It is very much a site for families where children really are catered for and it has a pleasant atmosphere.

Facilities

Four sanitary blocks renovated in 2010 include provision for young children and babies in the largest block. Facilities for disabled visitors. Large, central building housing well stocked shop (24/4-18/9). Pleasant restaurant with terrace, takeaway (9/5-12/9) and play room for small children. Good play areas and small zoo with goats and rabbits. 'Topi' club and organised activities for adults and children. Games room. Bicycle hire. Watersports. Internet access. Off site: Golf 1.5 km. Fishing and riding 3 km. Boat launching 5 km.

Open: 17 April - 3 October.

Directions

Site is 20 km. east-southeast of Klagenfurt. Leave A2 motorway at exit 298 signed Grafenstien. Go east on road 70 for 5 km. and turn right for Tainach and St Kanzian. In St Kanzian keep bearing to the right, St Primas is signed. Site is on left before St Primus. GPS: 46.58569, 14.56598

Charges guide

Per unit incl. 2 persons and electricity	€ 20.58 - € 33.98
extra person	€ 8.34 - € 9.54

Camping Cheques accepted.

Saint Wolfgang

Camping Appesbach

Au 99, A-5360 Saint Wolfgang (Upper Austria) T: **061 382 206.** E: **camping@appesbach.at**

alanrogers.com/AU0240

St Wolfgang, a pretty little village on the lake of the same name which was made famous by the operetta, White Horse Inn, is ringed by hills in a delightful situation. Camping Appesbach has an attractive lakeside location with a small boat jetty and offers views over this most attractive lake. The site has 170 pitches, with 100 for touring units (including 20 tent pitches) with some in regular rows and the rest on open meadows that could become full in high season. Pitches near the lakeside have higher charges. All have electricity (10A) with a mix of German and European sockets.

Facilities

The two toilet blocks have been combined into one, extended and refurbished to a good standard. Motorcaravan service point. Good shop. Bar (1/5-31/8). Restaurant with TV (Easter-30/9). Snack bar with terrace (Easter-30/9). Small playground. WIFI. Off site: Tennis nearby. Village 1 km. Many excursions possible including Salzburg 50 km.

Open: Easter - 31 October.

Directions

Site is 30 km. ESE of Salzburg. From B158 Salzburg - Bad Ischl road, just east of Stobl turn north to St Wolfgang. Site is on the left 1 km. before St Wolfgang. GPS: 47.73254, 13.463756

Charges guide

Per person	€ 5.00 - € 7.00
pitch acc. to position and unit size	€ 6.00 - € 15.00
electricity	€ 3.00

Salzburg

Panoramacamping Stadtblick

Rauchenbichl, Rauchenbichler Strasse 21, A-5020 Salzburg (Salzburg) T: **066 245 0652.**

E: **info@panorama-camping.at** **alanrogers.com/AU0212**

Salzburg and Panoramacamping Stadtblick are a superb combination. From this 70 pitch site with excellent new sanitary facilities, there are views over the city to Salzburg's hilltop castle beyond. The city is easily reached, either from a bus stop only a few minutes walk away, or tours can be arranged departing directly from the site. All the 70 level pitches are on grass-gravel with 6A electricity and are arranged on shallow terraces with a separate area for tents. The site's restaurant is extremely good value. Mornings (from 08.00) fresh bread and breakfast are available and evenings (18.00-21.00) there is a comprehensive menu; do try the regional specialities.

Facilities

Excellent sanitary facilities include six spacious wash rooms with shower and washbasin. Facilities for disabled visitors. Laundry. Dishwashing. Motorcaravan service point. Shop for basic supplies, gas and souvenirs. Restaurant (May-Sept). TV lounge. Small playground. WiFi (charged). Off site: Bus stop to city centre five mins. walk away, bus every ten minutes. Many tours available by bus and ship, i.e. Mozart, The Sound of Music. Lots of sweet specialities to try out. Bicycle hire 3 km. Swimming pool 3 km. Golf 3 km. and 10 km.

Open: 20 March - 5 November; 5-15 December and 28 December - 10 January.

Directions

From A1 exit 288 (Salzburg-Nord) turn south towards city. Approaching the first set of traffic lights get into the right hand lane, turn right here on a minor road (site signed) and continue to top of hill, and follow site signs. GPS: 47.81664, 13.05232

Charges guide

Per unit incl. 2 persons and electricity	€ 24.00 - € 28.00
extra person	€ 8.00
child (2-14 yrs)	€ 5.00
dog	€ 2.00

Sankt Margareten im Rosental

Camping Rosental Roz

Gotschuchen 34, A-9173 Sankt Margareten im Rosental (Carinthia) T: **042 268 1000**.

E: **camping.rosental@roz.at** **alanrogers.com/AU0415**

In the picturesque Drau valley, southeast of Flagenfurt, Rosental Roz has magnificent views along the valley and of the cliffs that form the Austrian southern border with Slovakia. The site is also close to Italy. With 430 pitches (all for touring) and 16 mobile homes to rent around a small swimming lake with water slide. All pitches have 16A electricity and 50 pitches also have water and drainage. An active children's club provides lots to occupy the youngsters and guided walks for adults are organised from the site.

Facilities

Toilet facilities are clean and modern with free showers, ten family washrooms and a large shower facility with fun mirrors for young children. Washing machine and dryer. Facilities for disabled visitors. Restaurant/bar (1/5-30/9). Shop (1/6-15/9). Children's club (1/6-30/8). Playgrounds and large games area. WiFi. Spring drinking water. Dog exercise area. Off site: Fishing 1 km. Riding 2 km. Many walks to suit all levels of fitness. Cycle tracks.

Open: Easter - 15 October.

Directions

Site is southeast of Klagenfurt. From the 91 road turn onto the 85 towards Feriach. Before St Margareten, in the centre of the small hamlet of Gotschuchen turn left towards site. It is 1.5 km. but well signed (watch the overhanging gutters especially when passing another vehicle).
GPS: 46.54363, 14.39088

Charges guide

Per unit incl. 2 persons and electricity	€ 24.52 - € 29.50
extra person	€ 8.30

Schönbühel

Camping Stumpfer

A-3392 Schönbühel (Lower Austria) T: **027 528 510**. E: **office@stumpfer.com**

alanrogers.com/AU0280

This small, well appointed site with just 60 pitches is directly on the River Danube, near the small town of Schönbühel, and is a convenient night stop being near the Salzburg - Vienna autobahn. The 50 unmarked pitches for touring units, all with electricity (16A), are on flat grass and the site is lit at night. There is shade in most parts and a landing stage for boat trips on the Danube. The main building also houses a Gasthof, with a bar/restaurant of the same name. This is very much a family run site. The Danube cycle track runs past the site.

Facilities

Part of the main building, the toilet block is of good quality with hot water on payment. Facilities for disabled visitors include ramps by the side of steps up to the block. Washing machine and dryer. Motorcaravan services. Small shop. Playground. Fishing. WiFi. Off site: Swimming pool, bicycle hire and riding within 5 km. Golf 25 km. Day trips to Vienna.

Open: 1 April - 31 October.

Directions

Leave Salzburg - Vienna autobahn at Melk exit. Drive towards Melk, but continue towards Melk Nord. Just before bridge turn right (Schönbühel and St Polten), at T-junction turn right again and continue down hill. Turn right just before BP filling station (signed Schönbühel) and site is 3 km. on left with narrow entrance, next to the Gasthof Stumpfer.
GPS: 48.254, 15.37106

Charges guide

Per unit incl. 2 persons and electricity	€ 22.90
extra person	€ 6.70

Schwaz

Alpencamping Mark

Bundesstrasse 12, Maholmhof, A-6114 Weer bei Schwaz (Tirol) T: **052 246 8146**. E: **alpcamp.mark@aon.at**

alanrogers.com/AU0250

This pleasant Tirol site is neat and friendly with family owners who offer a warm welcome and a variety of outdoor activities. Formerly a farm, they now breed horses, giving free horse and carriage rides to youngsters as well as organising mountain treks. Herr Mark junior (a certified alpine ski guide and ski instructor) runs courses for individuals or groups in climbing (there are practice climbing walls on site), rafting, mountain biking, trekking, hiking, etc. Set in the Inn valley, with wonderful mountain views, the site has 96 flat, plush, grass pitches, all with 10A electrical connections. Site is close to the Inn valley cycle track.

Facilities

Good quality, modern, heated sanitary facilities are provided in the old farm buildings. Washing machines and dryer. Freezer. Motorcaravan services. Small, cheerful bar/restaurant and shop (1/6-1/9). Small heated pool (5/5-15/9). Activity programme with instruction. Bicycle hire. Riding (free for children). Glacier tours. Large play area. Barn for use by children in wet weather. WiFi. Off site: Swarovski Kristallwelten.

Open: 1 April - 31 October.

Directions

Site is 20 km. east of Innsbruck. (If using A12, take exit 61 from west or 53 from east). Site is 200 m. east of the village of Weer, on Wattens - Schwaz road no. B171. GPS: 47.30647, 11.65091

Charges 2012

Per unit incl. 2 persons and electricity	€ 17.70 - € 23.70
extra person	€ 4.50 - € 6.50

Camping Cheques accepted.

Seefeld

Camp Alpin Seefeld

Leutascherstrasse 810, A-6100 Seefeld (Tirol) T: 052 124 848. E: info@camp-alpin.at

alanrogers.com/AU0035

Camp Alpin Seefeld is a beautifully laid out, modern campsite with first class facilities in an attractive setting some 1,200 metres above sea level. With excellent views of the surrounding mountains and forests there are 140 large, individual pitches mainly on flat grass (plus a few hardstandings). All have 16A electricity, gas and TV connections (metered), with ten well placed water points. Some pitches at the back and edge of the site are terraced. This is a good base for both summer and winter activity, whether you wish to take a gentle stroll or participate in something more demanding, including skiing direct from the site.

Facilities

Excellent heated sanitary facilities include nine private bathrooms for hire, some private cabins. Washing machines and dryer. Sauna, Turkish bath and solarium. Sunbed cabin. Shop. Bar. Cosy restaurant with a limited menu and takeaway. Play area. Bicycle hire. Apartments to rent. Off site: Sports centre with heated indoor and outdoor pools and restaurant are nearby. The popular Tirolean village of Seefeld 1 km. Golf 1.5 km. Free shuttle to town centre.

Open: All year.

Directions

From the A12 motorway, take the 67 (87) exit to the B177, signed Seefeld (steep climb). Take slip road on right, signed Seefeld and Alpin Camping. Follow green signs through village to site.
GPS: 47.33735, 11.1786

Charges guide

Per unit incl. 2 persons and electricity	€ 15.80 - € 36.60
extra person	€ 4.00 - € 9.90
child (3-14 yrs)	€ 3.00 - € 7.90
dog	€ 3.00 - € 4.80

Tulln

Donaupark Camping Tulln

Donaulande 76, A-3430 Tulln (Lower Austria) T: 022 726 5200. E: camptulln@oeamtc.at

alanrogers.com/AU0290

Donaupark Camping, owned and run by the Austrian Motor Club (OAMTC), is imaginatively laid out village style with unmarked grass pitches grouped around six circular gravel areas. Further pitches are to the side of the hard road which links the circles and these include some with grill facilities for tents; 100 of the 120 touring pitches have electricity (3/6A) and cable TV sockets. Tall trees surrounding the site offer shade in parts. Tucked neatly away at the back of the site are 120 long stay caravans. Activities are organised in high season with guided tours around Tulln on foot, by bike and on the river by canoe.

Facilities

Three identical, modern, octagonal sanitary blocks can be heated. One is at reception (next to the touring area), the other two are at the far end of the site. Facilities for disabled visitors. Washing machines and dryers. Cooking rings. Gas supplies. Bar and restaurant (1/5-15/9). Shop (1/5-30/9). Play areas. Tennis. Bicycle and canoe hire. Excursion programme. Internet access. Off site: Lake swimming in adjacent park (entry free for campers). Fishing 500 m. Bus service into Vienna (May-Sept). Train service to Vienna. Steamer excursions.

Open: 15 April - 15 October.

Directions

From Vienna follow south bank of the Danube on B14; from the west, leave the A1 autobahn at either St Christophen or Altenbach exits and go north on B19 to Tulln. Site is on the east side of Tulln and well signed. GPS: 48.33239, 16.07275

Charges guide

Per unit incl. 2 persons and electricity	€ 27.26 - € 31.76
extra person	€ 7.00
child (5-14 yrs)	€ 3.50

Camping Cheques accepted.

Umhausen

Ötztal Arena Camp Krismer

Mühlweg 32, A-6441 Umhausen (Tirol) T: 052 555 390. E: info@oetztal-camping.at

alanrogers.com/AU0220

This is a delightful site with lovely views, in the beautiful Ötz valley, on the edge of the village of Umhausen. Situated on a gentle slope in an open valley, it has an air of peace and tranquillity and makes an excellent base for mountain walking in spring and autumn, skiing in winter or a relaxing holiday. The 98 pitches, some on individual terraces, are all marked and numbered and have electrical connections (12A); charges relate to the area available, long leads may be necessary. The reception building houses an attractive bar/restaurant, a TV room and a new, fully equipped sauna.

Facilities

With underfloor heating, open washbasins, hairdressing room and showers on payment, the toilet facilities are of good quality. A small toilet/wash block at the far end of the site is used in summer. Baby room. Washing machine and dryer, drying room. Basic motorcaravan services. Bar/restaurant (May-Sept, Dec-April). No shop, but bread can be ordered at reception. Sauna. TV room. Ski room. Fishing. Bicycle hire. Playground. WiFi. Off site: Swimming pool and tennis 100 m. Shops in village 200 m. Play area 300 m. Boat launching 6 km. Riding 10 km. Golf 20 km.

Open: All year.

Directions

Site is 60 km. west of Innsbruck. Take Ötztal valley exit 123 from Imst - Innsbruck A12 motorway, and Umhausen is 13 km. towards Solden on the B186; site is well signed to south of village (follow campings signs not sat nav). GPS: 47.13452, 10.93147

Charges guide

Per unit incl. 2 persons	€ 17.20 - € 20.00
electricity (per kWh)	€ 0.75
extra person	€ 7.40

No credit cards.

Velden - Auen

Camping Weisses Rössl

Auenstrasse 47, A-9220 Velden - Auen (Carinthia) T: 042 742 898. E: weisses.roessl@aon.at

alanrogers.com/AU0423

This small site is part of the Stingler family-owned Weisses Rössl Gasthof - Pension House and is located on a hillside overlooking the south side of Worthersee lake. The campsite is run as a supplement to the guesthouse and has only basic facilities. There is space for up to 150 touring units. All are undefined and on grassy terraces on the open hillside. Electricity (6A) is available for 80 units. Some areas have views of the lake and there is some shade in places. A small reception hut is open in high season. At other times register at the guesthouse.

Facilities

One old toilet block, in need of decoration, has WCs, washbasins and hot showers. Shop, small restaurant and bar in guesthouse (open to public). Lake swimming. Off site: Lake fishing (with permit). Boat launching 3 km. Bicycle hire and riding 5 km. Golf 15 km.

Open: 1 May - 30 September.

Directions

From A2 motorway take exit 335 to Velden. Follow signs for Auen and Worthersee Sud. Site is well signed on right. GPS: 46.618996, 14.105319

Charges 2012

Contact the site for details. -

No credit cards.

Villach Landskron

Seecamping Berghof

Ossiachersee Süduferstrasse 241, A-9523 Villach Landskron (Carinthia) T: 042 424 1133.
E: office@seecamping-berghof.at **alanrogers.com/AU0425**

This surely must be the ultimate camping experience: a perfect location, excellent facilities, great pitches and a welcome to match. The Ertl family and their staff manage this 460 pitch site to perfection. Use of the natural topography means that you actually think you are in a small site wherever you camp. With lovely lake views from almost every spot, this is a great site to stop for a short or long stay. Constant improvements mean that the number of pitches slowly reduces as larger and more equipped places are provided. There are 190 pitches with water, electricity and drainage and all pitches have WiFi.

Facilities

Five modern toilet blocks spread around the site, provide the usual facilities including special provision for young children and babies in two blocks. Facilities for disabled visitors. Well stocked supermarket. Pleasant restaurant with terrace, takeaway and games room for older children. TV room. Good play area and daily club for 4-11 year olds. Car hire. Bicycle hire. Watersports including boat and canoe hire and windsurfing school. Minigolf. Swimming possible in the lake. Skateboard park. Tennis. Volleyball. WiFi. Fishing with permit. Off site: Shops, bars and restaurants in Villach 5 km.

Open: Easter - mid October.

Directions

From A10 take exit 178, which travelling south is just after the tunnel. Head towards Ossiacher See and after 1 km. turn right towards Ossiacher See Sud. At traffic lights turn left and site is 3.5 km. on the left just after entering hamlet of Heiligengestade. GPS: 46.64997, 13.91663

Charges guide

Per unit incl. 2 persons and electricity	€ 18.80 - € 28.30
extra person	€ 5.40 - € 8.40
child (2-13 yrs)	€ 3.80 - € 7.40

Volders

Schloss-Camping

A-6111 Volders (Tirol) T: 052 245 2333. E: campingvolders@utanet.at

alanrogers.com/AU0080

The Inn valley is a very beautiful and popular part of Austria. Volders, some 15 km. from Innsbruck, is one of the little villages on the banks of the Inn river and is perhaps best known for its 17th-century Baroque Servite Church and monastery. Conveniently situated here is the very pleasant Schloss-Camping, dominated by the castle from which it gets its name, and which towers at the back of the site with views of the mountains across the Inn valley. The 160 numbered grass pitches are on level or slightly sloping ground. Electricity connections throughout (16A, long leads may be necessary).

Facilities

New modern, attractive sanitary block to left of entance, washbasins in cabins. Laundry room with washing machines and iron. Motorcaravan service point. New attractive bar/restaurant. Snack bar with terrace. Shop for basics (all May-end Sept). Fenced and heated swimming pool (mid May-mid Sept). Playground. Car wash. Games and entertainment for children in high season. Off site: Supermarket 400 m. Bicycle hire 500 m. Golf and riding 7 km.

Open: 15 April - 15 October.

Directions

From A12 motorway, travelling east, leave at exit 68 for Hall, going west, take exit 61 for Wattens and follow the B171 and signs for Volders where site is signed. GPS: 47.28714, 11.57259

Charges guide

Per person	€ 5.10 - € 7.00
child (2-14 yrs)	€ 3.80 - € 4.60
pitch incl. car and electricity	€ 10.50 - € 11.90
dog	€ 2.00 - € 2.50

Credit cards accepted for stays of over 5 nights.

Weisskirchen

50plus Campingpark Fisching

Fisching 9, A-8741 Weisskirchen (Steiermark) T: 035 778 2284. E: campingpark@fisching.at

alanrogers.com/AU0525

This small site is unusual in that it only accepts clients over 50 years of age. It is a high quality site with an attractive setting in the Steiermark region, east of Graz. There are 50 large, level pitches (100-130 sq.m), all equipped with electricity (6A), water, drainage and cable TV connections. Most pitches are on hardstanding. A number of chalets and holiday apartments are also available for rent. There is a small swimming lake which is surrounded by an attractive garden and sunbathing area. The site's bar/snack bar is inviting with a selection of homemade dishes on offer (1/4-30/10).

Facilities

Two excellent modern toilet blocks were very clean, with free controllable showers. No facilities for children or disabled visitors. Dishwashing. Laundry room. Bar, snack bar and shop (all open 1/4-30/10). Swimming lake. Tennis. Bicycle hire. Activity programme. Chalets and apartments for rent. WiFi (charged). Off site: Walking and cycle tracks. Fishing 1 km. Riding 2 km. Golf (Murtal) 8 km. Graz 70 km.

Open: 1 April - 30 October.

Directions

From the north (A9), head for Graz and join the westbound S36 at Sant Michael in Obersteiermark. Continue on this road as far as Aichdorf and then head south on B78 to Weisskirchen and then follow signs to Fisching, from where site is clearly signed. GPS: 47.163189, 14.738281

Charges guide

Per unit incl. 2 persons and electricity	€ 22.00 - € 25.50
extra person	€ 7.50

Wien

Camping Rodaun

Breitenfurter Strasse 487, An der Au 2, A-1230 Wien-Südwest-Rodaun (Vienna) T: 018 884 154.

alanrogers.com/AU0300

It is difficult to believe that this quiet family run site is only 9 kilometres from Vienna. It is within the city boundary and is a pleasant base for visiting this old, interesting and world famous city. From the site, there is an excellent public transport system for visiting Vienna nd visitors are well advised to use it since car parking is almost impossible within the city. Situated in a southern suburb, it has space for about 40 units on flat grass pitches or on concrete bases and an additional area for about 20 tents. With little shade, the pitches are not numbered or marked, either in the centre or outside the circular tarmac road running round the camping area, with electricity provided (6A).

Facilities

The toilet block has some washbasins in cabins and hot showers for which a token is needed (purchased at reception). Laundry service provided by Frau Deihs. Off site: Supermarket and restaurant within 250 m. Swimming pool 2 km. Golf and riding 3 km.

Open: 1 July - 20 October.

Directions

Take Pressbaum exit from Westautobahn or Vosendorf exit from Sudautobahn and follow signs. Site is at An der Au 2, which is a small side street leading off from Breitenfurter Strasse (a 16 km. long road). An der Au is opposite house number 487 Breitenfurter Strasse. GPS: 48.1166, 16.2833

Charges guide

Per unit incl. 2 persons	€ 21.80 - € 22.30
extra person	€ 6.90
electricity per kWh	€ 0.80

Wien

Camping Wien West

Hüttelbergstrasse 80, A-1140 Wien (Vienna) T: **019 142 314**. E: **west@campingwien.at**

alanrogers.com/AU0306

Opera, classical music, museums, shopping and the Danube; whatever it is you want in Vienna you are spoilt for choice. Wien West is an all year round site with good transport links to the city centre. It is the parent site of Wien Sud and Neue Donau and is inevitably busier. The site is located on the edge of the Vienna Woods with direct access to walking and mountain bike trails. There are 202 level and numbered pitches, all with 13A electricity. Buses to the metro stop right outside the gates and you can be in the centre in 35 minutes. For somewhere different try the 'Black Camel' for a light lunch – it is easy to find from Stephensplatz – or perhaps the Danube cruise that will introduce you to the architecture of Freiderreich Hundertwasser. Whatever you do it will be a memorable visit to the Austrian capital.

Facilities

Three modern toilet blocks provide ample and clean toilets, hot showers and washbasins. Washing machine and dryer. Kitchen facilities. Motorcaravan services. Small shop for essentials, bar and restaurant (all 15/4-1/10). Games room. Playground. Bicycle hire. WiFi (free) and internet point. Off site: Vienna centre 8 km. Schönbrunn palace. Bicycle and walking trails. Tennis.

Open: All year excl. February.

Directions

From the city centre follow signs to autobahn west and Linz. Site is well signed from the main roads. Coming from the A1 (Salzburg - Vienna) drive over the Bergmillergasse (bridge). Stay on this road to Huttelbergstraße after the first traffic lights.
GPS: 48.21433, 16.25018

Charges guide

Per unit incl. 2 persons and electricity	€ 25.10 - € 28.60
extra person	€ 6.30 - € 7.30
child (5-14 yrs)	€ 4.50
dog	€ 4.50

Wien

Aktiv Camping Wien Neue Donau

Am Kaisermuhlendamm 119, A-1220 Wien-Ost (Vienna) T: **012 024 010**. E: **neuedonau@campingwien.at**

alanrogers.com/AU0302

This is a very good site from which to visit Vienna. It is easily accessable from the autobahn system and the city centre is quickly reached from the site by the efficient Vienna U-Bahn system, line U2; tickets for which can be purchased at reception. There is some traffic and train noise as is found on most city sites. With 254 level touring pitches with electricity and a further 12 with water and drainage, the site has a large and changing population. The site is close to the 'Donauinsel', a popular recreation area. The Neue Donau (New Danube), a 20 km. long artificial side arm of the Danube provides swimming, sports and play areas, while the Danube bicycle trail runs past the site. This is a useful location for an overnight stop or a short break to visit old Vienna and the Danube.

Facilities

Modern toilet facilities are clean, and well maintained with free showers. Facilities for disabled visitors. Washing machines and dryers. Motorcaravan service point. Campers' kitchen with cooking, fridges, freezers and TV. Shop. Small restaurant. Play area. Barbecue areas. Bicycle hire and free guided bicycle tours. WiFi.
Off site: Vienna city centre 5 km. Prater Park 1 km.

Open: Easter - 15 September.

Directions

Site is close to the A23 and A22. From A23 heading east turn off at first exit after crossing the Donau (signed Lobau). At first traffic lights, near Shell station, turn left and after 200 m. turn right into site.
GPS: 48.20848, 16.44733

Charges guide

Per unit incl. 2 persons and electricity	€ 25.10 - € 31.10
extra person	€ 6.30 - € 7.30
child (5-14 yrs)	€ 4.00 - € 5.00
dog	€ 4.50

Wien

Camping Wien-Sud

Breitenfursterstrasse 269, A-1230 Wien-Atzgersdorf (Vienna) T: **018 673 649**. E: **sued@campingwien.at**

alanrogers.com/AU0304

This site, which is in a former Palace park and was closed for some years, reopened in 2003 with new facilities and new management. It is now probably the best site in the greater Vienna area, with good public transport links to the city centre and a friendly and welcoming atmosphere. With 154 touring pitches with electricity (16A) and 42 with water and drainage, the site provides a good base for city sightseeing. With many mature trees and some shade you will find this a peaceful and quiet site. Walking and cycling are popular in the nearby Vienna woods.

Facilities

Excellent modern toilet facilities are clean and well maintained with free showers. Facilities for disabled visitors. Washing machine and dryer. Some cooking facilities. Motorcaravan service point. Small play area. Tickets for Schloss Schönbrunn and other attractions sold at reception. Off site: Vienna 6 km.

Open: 1 June - 31 August.

Directions

From the A2 turn onto A21 towards Linz (if heading north the slip is just past IKEA). Turn off A21 at first exit (Brunn am Gebirge) and go north. Keep going on this road to site (well signed) on the right in Atzgersdorf. GPS: 48.14973, 16.3004

Charges guide

Per unit incl. 2 persons and electricity	€ 25.10 - € 31.10
extra person	€ 6.30 - € 7.30

Zell-am-See

Seecamp Zell am See

Thumersbacherstrasse 34, A-5700 Zell-am-See (Salzburg) T: **065 427 2115**. E: **zell@seecamp.at**

alanrogers.com/AU0160

The Zeller See, delightfully situated in the south of Salzburg province and near the start of the Grossglocknerstrasse, is ideally placed for enjoying the splendid southern Austrian countryside. Seecamp is right by the water about three kilometres from the town of Zell and with fine views to the south end of the lake. One is immediately struck by the order and neat appearance of the site, with 176 good level, mainly grass-on-gravel pitches of average size, all with electricity (10/16A). About half have water, drainage and TV connections. Units can be close together in peak season. Good English is spoken.

Facilities

Excellent, heated sanitary facilities include facilities for disabled visitors and a baby room. Washing machines, dryers and irons. Motorcaravan services. Bar. Restaurant (15/12-30/9). Shop (1/7-31/8 and 15/12-6/1). Play area. Play room. Fishing. Bicycle hire. Topi Club and summer entertainment for children. Activity programme. Winter ski packages and free ski bus. Glacier skiing possible in summer. WiFi. Off site: Free entry to nearby lake beach, indoor pool and ice skating rink. Skiing 1.8 km. Golf 2 km.

Open: All year.

Directions

Approaching from the north on the B311 take the Thumersbach exit just before tunnel entrance (2 km. north of Zell-am-See town). After 500 m. turn left and site entrance is 750 m. on the right. GPS: 47.339925, 12.809141

Charges 2012

Per unit incl. 2 persons	€ 26.10 - € 32.30
extra person	€ 7.00 - € 8.80
child (5-14 yrs)	€ 4.50 - € 5.60
electricity (plus meter)	€ 2.50

Zell-am-Ziller

Campingdorf Hofer

Gerlosstrasse 33, A-6280 Zell-am-Ziller (Tirol) T: **052 822 248**. E: **info@campingdorf.at**

alanrogers.com/AU0070

Zell-am-Ziller is in the heart of the Zillertal valley at the junction of the B169 and B165 Gerlos Pass road and nestles round an unusual 18th-century church noted for its paintings. Campingdorf Hofer, owned by the same family for over 50 years, is on the edge of the village just five minutes walk from the centre on a quiet side road. The 100 pitches, all with electricity (6/10A; long leads may be needed) are grass on gravel. A few trees decorate the site and offer some shade. A pleasant development provides a bar/restaurant and terrace, sun deck, games and TV room, and a small heated pool, which can be covered.

Facilities

Good quality, heated sanitary provision is on the ground floor of the apartment building and has some washbasins in cabins. Baby room. Washing machines and dryers. Gas supplies. Motorcaravan services. Restaurant with bar (closed 1/11-10/12 and 30/4-31/5), offers special themed weeks with international dishes. Shop opposite. Swimming pool (1/4-31/10). WiFi (charged). Free organised entertainment and activities in high season. Guided walks, cycle tours, barbecues, biking, skiing. Ski room. Youth room. Apartments to rent. Off site: Town and supermarket within walking distance. Gerlos passroad.

Open: All year.

Directions

Site is well signed from the main B169 road at Zell-am-Ziller. Site is at southern end of town close to the junction of the B169 and B165. GPS: 47.22862, 11.88603

Charges guide

Per unit incl. 2 persons and electricity (plus meter in winter)	€ 21.80 - € 32.00
extra person	€ 6.00 - € 8.70

No credit cards (debit cards accepted). Camping Cheques accepted.

Belgium

A small country divided into three regions, Flanders in the north, Wallonia in the south and Brussels the capital. Belgium is rich in scenic countryside, culture and history, notably the great forest of Ardennes, the historic cities of Bruges and Gent and the western coastline with its sandy beaches.

Brussels is at the very heart of Europe and doubles as the capital of the European Union. A multi-cultural and multi-lingual city full of remarkable monuments, interesting museums and highly acclaimed restaurants. In the French speaking region of Wallonia lies the mountainous Ardennes, an area famous for its forests, lakes, streams and grottoes, making it a popular holiday destination, especially for those who like nature and walking.

The safe, sandy beaches on the west coast run for forty miles. Here lies Ostend, a popular seaside resort with an eight kilometre long beach and a promenade coupled with a bustling harbour and shops. Bruges is Europe's best preserved medieval city and is certainly one of the most attractive, whether you want to relax on a boat trip along the canals, explore the narrow streets or visit one of the many churches and art museums.

CAPITAL: Brussels

Tourist Office

Belgian Tourist Office Brussels & Wallonia,
217 Marsh Wall, London E14 9FJ
Tel: 020 7537 1132 Fax: 020 7531 0393
Email: info@belgiumtheplaceto.be
Internet: www.belgiumtheplaceto.be

Tourism Flanders-Brussels,
Flanders House, 1a Cavendish Square,
London W1G 0LD
Tel: 020 7307 7738
Email: info@visitflanders.co.uk

Population

10.6 million

Climate

Temperate climate similar to Britain.

Language

There are three official languages. French is spoken in the south, Flemish in the north, and German is the predominant language in the eastern provinces.

Telephone

The country code is 00 32.

Money

Currency: The Euro
Banks: Mon-Fri 09.00-15.30
Some banks open Sat 09.00-12.00.

Shops

Mon-Sat 09.00-17.30/18.00 – later on Thurs/Fri; closed Sundays.

Public Holidays

New Year's Day; Easter Mon; Labour Day; Ascension; Whit Monday; Flemish Day 11 July; National Day 21 July; Assumption 15 Aug; French Day 27 Sept; All Saints 1, 2 Nov; Armistice Day 11 Nov; King's Birthday 15 Nov; Christmas 25, 26 Dec.

Motoring

For cars with a caravan or trailer, motorways are toll free except for the Liefenshoek Tunnel in Antwerp. Maximum permitted overall length of vehicle/trailer or caravan combination is 18 m. Blue Zone parking areas exist in Brussels, Ostend, Bruges, Liège, Antwerp and Gent. Parking discs can be obtained from police stations, garages, and some shops.

see campsite map 1

Amberloup

Camping Tonny

Tonny 35, B-6680 Amberloup (Luxembourg) T: 061 688 285. E: camping.tonny@skynet.be

alanrogers.com/BE0720

The new Dutch owners here are rightly proud of their site. With a friendly atmosphere, it is an attractive, small campsite in a pleasant valley by the River Ourthe. A family site, there are 75 grass touring pitches, with wooden chalet buildings giving a Tirolean feel. The pitches (80-100 sq.m.) are separated by small shrubs and fir trees, electricity (4/6A) is available. Cars are parked away from the units and there is a separate meadow for tents. Surrounded by natural woodland, Camping Tonny is an ideal base for outdoor activities.

Facilities

Two fully equipped sanitary units (both heated in cool weather) include showers on payment. Baby area and laundry. Freezer for campers use. Small shop. TV lounge and library. Sports field. Boules. Games room. Playgrounds. Bowling alley. Bicycle hire. Fishing. Cross-country skiing. WiFi (charged).

Open: 15 March - 15 November.

Directions

From N4 take exit for Libramont at km. 131 (N826), then to Amberloup (4 km) where site is signed just outside of the southwest town boundary. GPS: 50.02657, 5.51283

Charges guide

Per unit incl. 2 persons and electricity	€ 20.00 - € 22.00
extra person	€ 3.60 - € 4.00
child (0-12 yrs)	€ 2.25 - € 2.50

Attert

Camping Sud

Voie de la Liberté 75, B-6717 Attert (Luxembourg) T: 063 223 715. E: info@campingsudattert.com

alanrogers.com/BE0680

This is a pleasant family run site which would make a good base for a short stay and is also well sited for use as an overnight halt. The 86 touring pitches are on level grass, all with (6A Europlug) and are arranged around an oval loop access road. There are 11 drive-through pitches especially for stopovers, plus four hardstandings for motorcaravans and a tent area. The far end of the site is close to the N4 and may suffer from some road noise. On-site facilities include a small restaurant/bar with takeaway facility and a shop for basics. An outdoor swimming pool (12x6 m) has a separate paddling pool and there is an open sports field at the far end of the site.

Facilities

A single building provides modern sanitary facilities including some washbasins in cubicles and baby areas. Showers are free in low season (€ 0.50 July/Aug). No facilities for disabled campers. Small bar/restaurant and takeaway (1/4-15/10). TV in bar. Swimming pool (1/6-1/9). Small playground. Children's entertainment (4-12 yrs; July/Aug). Dogs are not accepted. Off site: Attert village has two churches and a museum. Supermarket and riding 5 km. Internet café and Roman Museum in Arlon 8 km. Golf 8 km. Fishing 10 km. Bicycle hire 12 km.

Open: 1 April - 15 October.

Directions

Attert is 8 km. north of Arlon. From N4 take Attert exit, continue east for 1 km. to Attert village, site entrance is immediately on your left as you join the main street. GPS: 49.74833, 5.78698

Charges guide

Per unit incl. 2 persons and electricity	€ 14.50 - € 20.50
extra person	€ 4.50
child (2-11 yrs)	€ 2.25

No credit cards.

Auby-sur-Semois

Camping Maka

Route du Maka 100, B-6880 Auby sûr Semois (Luxembourg) T: 061 411 148. E: info@campingmaka.be

alanrogers.com/BE0716

Camping Maka is a delightful, rural site on the banks of the River Semois, reputedly Belgium's cleanest river. Forty touring pitches are sited close to the water, but allowing everyone access to the river and its banks. Thirty have electricity and water, while the remainder are more suitable for tents. Private mobile homes are hidden on two higher terraces. Two fully equipped wooden cabins and two tents are for rent. The river is popular for swimming, fishing and canoeing. Canadian canoes, mountain bikes, barbecues and outdoor cooking equipment are available for hire. Facilities include a bar with a terrace overlooking the water and a shop.

Facilities

A modern, heated toilet block includes facilities for babies and for campers with disabilities (key access). Pub/café with terrace. Shop. Play area. Fishing. Games area. Direct river access. Campfire area. Canoe and mountain bike hire. Occasional activities and entertainment. Tents and cabins for rent. WiFi. Off site: Walking and cycle tracks. Golf. Mountain biking. Canoeing. Bouillon, Bertrix.

Open: 1 April - 1 November.

Directions

Approaching from the east on N89, leave at N853 exit and follow signs to Bertrix. Before reaching the centre of Bertrix, follow signs to Auby-sur-Semois to the southwest, and then signs to site. GPS: 49.808842, 5.164824

Charges guide

Per unit incl. 2 persons and electricity	€ 25.50
child (under 14 yrs)	€ 4.00
dog	€ 2.50

Bertrix

Ardennen Camping Bertrix

Route de Mortehan, B-6880 Bertrix (Luxembourg) T: **061 412 281**. E: **info@campingbertrix.be**

alanrogers.com/BE0711

Bertrix is located at the heart of the Belgian Ardennes, between the towns of Bastogne and Bouillon and overlooking the hills of the Semois valley. There are 498 terraced pitches, giving an open aspect and views for everyone, of which 303 level touring pitches, all with electricity (10A), are scattered amongst a variety of seasonal caravans and there is a friendly feel to the area. The activities, particularly for children, are of a high standard and well supervised. A visit to the nearby ruined castle at Bouillon is a must as well as experiencing the many Belgian beers. The war memorial and excellent museum at Bastogne commemorate the Battle of the Bulge.

Facilities

Five well appointed toilet blocks, one with facilities for disabled visitors. The central one has a large laundry and a unit for children, with baby baths in cubicles. Motorcaravan service point. Shop for basics and bread. Excellent restaurant and bar (closed in low season on Tues. and Thurs), with satellite TV and Internet access and a terrace overlooking pool. Heated swimming and paddling pools (27/4-16/9, supervised high season). Tennis. Bicycle hire. Children's games room. Chalets and holiday homes for rent. Off site: Canoeing. Fishing. Shops, banks and restaurants in Bertrix.

Open: 23 March - 12 November.

Directions

Take exit 25 from the E411 motorway and join the N89 towards Bertrix. After 6.5 km. join the N884 to Bertrix and upon arrival in the town, follow yellow signs to site. GPS: 49.83861, 5.25122

Charges guide

Per unit incl. 2 persons	€ 20.00 - € 33.40
extra person (over 2 yrs)	€ 4.00 - € 5.50
dog	€ 4.00 - € 5.00

Camping Cheques accepted.

Bocholt

Goolderheide Vakantiepark

Bosstraat 1, B-3950 Bocholt (Limburg) T: **089 469 640**. E: **info@goolderheide.be**

alanrogers.com/BE0760

A large family holiday site with 900 individual pitches, Goolderheide has been owned and operated by the same family for many years and has an excellent pool complex and playgrounds. There are many seasonal and rental units, plus around 300 tourist pitches with 4/6A electricity, all in a forest setting. The pitches are of variable size and access roads are quite narrow. The outdoor pool complex has two large pools (one of Olympic size), a slide and a paddling pool. There is also a fishing lake, and a lake with a small sandy beach. An enormous area is devoted to a comprehensive play area with a vast range of equipment. During the main season there is also a weekly supervised assault course with aerial ropeways etc, a soundproofed over-16s disco, plus a younger kids' disco and a wide programme of activities to keep children and adults occupied. There are no extra charges for most of these activities.

Facilities

Four sanitary buildings provide an ample supply of WCs and washbasins, but rather fewer showers. Baby areas. Laundry facilities. Two suites for disabled visitors. Bar. Shop (daily in July/Aug, w/ends and public holidays in low season). Takeaway. Swimming pools. Tennis. Fishing. Boules. Minigolf. Play area and assault course. Children's discos. Programme of activities. Night security staff (main season). Off site: Bicycle hire 1 km.

Open: 1 April - 30 September.

Directions

From A13 (E313, Antwerp - Liege) take exit 25 and N141 to Leopoldsburg, then N73 through Peer, to outskirts of Bree (35 km). Take N76 north for 3 km, turn left at large roundabout into Bocholt, and towards Kaulille. Site road is on left towards edge of town. GPS: 51.17343, 5.53902

Charges guide

Per unit incl. 2 persons and electricity	€ 31.20
extra person	€ 5.80
child (under 12 yrs)	€ 3.30 - € 5.00
dog	€ 5.00

No credit cards.

De Haan

Camping Ter Duinen

Wenduinsesteenweg 143, B-8421 De Haan (West Flanders) T: **050 413 593.**

E: **infolawrence.sansens@scarlet.com** **alanrogers.com/BE0578**

Ter Duinen is a large, seaside holiday site with 120 touring pitches and over 700 privately owned static holiday caravans. The pitches are laid out in straight lines with tarmac access roads and the site has three immaculate toilet blocks. Other than a bar and a playing field, the site has little else to offer, but it is only a 400 m. walk to the sea and next door to the site is a large sports complex with a sub-tropical pool and several sporting facilities. Opportunities for riding and golf (18-hole course) are close by. It is possible to hire bicycles in the town. The best places to visit for a day trip are Ostend with the Atlantic Wall from WWII, Knokke (which holds many summer festivals) and Bruges.

Facilities

Three modern toilet blocks have good fittings, washbasins in cubicles (hot and cold water) and showers (€ 1.20). Baby bath. Facilities for disabled visitors. Laundry facilities with two washing machines and a dryer, irons and ironing boards. Motorcaravan service point. Shop. Snack bar and takeaway. WiFi (charged). Off site: Bicycle hire and sea with sandy beach 400 m. Riding 1 km. Golf 3 km. Boat launching 6 km. A bus for Bruges stops 200 m. from the site, a tram for the coast 400 m.

Open: 16 March - 15 October.

Directions

On E40 in either direction take exit for De Haan/Jabbeke. About 3 km. south of De Haan, turn at signs for campsites. GPS: 51.28318, 3.05753

Charges guide

Per unit incl. 2 persons and electricity	€ 17.00 - € 24.00
extra person	€ 2.50
child (under 10 yrs)	€ 2.00
dog	€ 3.00

Camping Cheques accepted.

Deinze

Camping Groeneveld

Groenevelddreef 14, Bachte-Maria-Leerne, B-9800 Deinze (East Flanders) T: **093 801 014.**

E: **info@campinggroeneveld.be** **alanrogers.com/BE0600**

Quiet and clean is how Rene Kuys describes his campsite. Groeneveld is a traditional site in a small village within easy reach of Gent. It has a friendly atmosphere and is also open over a long season. Although this site has 98 pitches, there are a fair number of seasonal units, leaving around 50 large touring pitches with electricity (10A). Hedges and borders divide the grassy area, access roads are gravel and there is an area for tents. Family entertainment and activities organised in high season include themed, musical evenings, barbecues, pétanque matches, etc.

Facilities

Two fully updated toilet blocks provide British style WCs, washbasins and free hot showers. Motorcaravan services. Freezer (free). Bar (July/Aug. and weekends) with comprehensive range of speciality and local beers. Small coarse fishing lake. Floodlit pétanque court. Adventure style play area. TV room. Internet access (at reception) and WiFi (free). Bicycles on loan from reception (free). Max. 1 dog. Off site: Shops and restaurants nearby. Golf 3 km. Swimming pool and kayaking 5 km.

Open: 1 April - 30 September.

Directions

From A10 (E40) exit 13, turn south on N466. After 3 km. continue straight on at roundabout and site is on left on entering village (opposite large factory). Yellow signs are very small. GPS: 51.00509, 3.57229

Charges 2012

Per unit incl. 2 persons and electricity	€ 20.00 - € 23.00
extra person	€ 3.00 - € 5.00
child (0-13 yrs)	€ 2.00 - € 3.00

No credit cards.

Dochamps

Panoramacamping Petite Suisse

Al Bounire 27, B-6960 Dochamps (Luxembourg) T: 084 444 030. E: info@petitesuisse.be

alanrogers.com/BE0735

This quiet site is set in the picturesque countryside of the Belgium Ardennes, a region in which rivers flow through valleys bordered by vast forests where horses are still usefully employed. Set on a southerly slope, the site is mostly open and offers wide views of the surrounding countryside. The 193 touring pitches, all with 10A electricity, are either on open sloping ground or in terraced rows with hedges in between, and trees providing some separation. Gravel roads provide access around the site. To the right of the entrance barrier a large wooden building houses reception, a bar and a restaurant. Close by is an attractive, heated outdoor swimming pool with wide terraces surrounded by grass. Behind this is a large play area adjoining a small terrace. Although the site has many activities on offer, the opportunity should not be missed to make excursions into the countryside with its hills and forests. The villages are filled with houses built from the local stone and small inviting bars and restaurants just waiting to be visited.

Facilities

All the facilities that one would expect of a large site are available. Showers are free, washbasins both open and in cabins. Baby room. Laundry with washing machines and dryers. Shop, restaurant, bar and takeaway (2/4-5/11). Heated outdoor swimming pool (1/5-1/9), paddling pool and slide. Sports field. Tennis. Bicycle hire. Playground and club for children. Entertainment programme during school holidays. Varied activity programme, including archery, canoeing, climbing, abseiling and walking. WiFi (charged). Off site: La Roche en Ardennes and Baraque de Fraiture (ski resort) 10 km. Golf 20 km.

Open: All year.

Directions

From E25/A26 autoroute (Liège - Luxembourg) take exit 50 then the N89 southwest towards La Roche. After 8 km. turn right (north) on N841 to Dochamps where site is signed. GPS: 50.23127, 5.62583

Charges guide

Per unit incl. 2 persons and electricity	€ 21.20 - € 42.20
extra person (over 4 yrs)	€ 4.25 - € 7.25
dog (high season max. 1)	€ 2.00 - € 5.00

Camping Cheques accepted.

Erezée

Camping Le Val de l'Aisne

Rue du TTA 1 A, B-6997 Erezée (Luxembourg) T: 086 470 067. E: info@levaldelaisne.be

alanrogers.com/BE0725

From a nearby hill, Château de Blier overlooks Camping Le Val de l'Aisne, a large site attractively laid out around a 1.5 hectare lake in the Belgium Ardennes. The site has 450 grass pitches with 150 for touring units, on level ground and with 16A electricity. Tarmac roads circle the site providing easy access. Trees provide some shade although the site is fairly open allowing views of the surrounding hills and the château. Activities play a large part on this site, from quiet fishing in the lake to hectic quad bike tours in the surrounding hills. A building by the entrance houses reception and the bar/restaurant.

Facilities

Three toilet blocks provide showers (paid for by token) and mainly open washbasins. Facilities for disabled visitors. Baby room. Washing machines and dryers. Motorcaravan service point. Bar/restaurant and snack bar with takeaway. Bread can be ordered in reception. On the lake: fishing, swimming, kayaks (to hire). Quad bike hire and tours arranged. Mountain bike hire. Play area. Entertainment programme (summer). Activities team arrange a range of adventure activities including paintball, canyoning, etc. Off site: Riding, cycle and walking routes in the Ardennes forest.

Open: All year.

Directions

From E411/A4 (Brussels - Luxembourg) motorway take exit 18 (Courière, Marche en Famenne), then southeast on the N4 to Marche. At Marche head northeast on N86 to Hotton, crossing bridge over the river. In Hotton follow signs for Soy and Erezée. West of Erezée at roundabout follow signs for La Roche. Site is 900 m. on left. GPS: 50.2815, 5.5505

Charges guide

Per unit incl. 2 persons and car	€ 18.00
extra person (over 3 yrs)	€ 3.00
electricity (3A)	€ 3.00

No credit cards.

Gent

Camping Blaarmeersen

Zuiderlaan 12, B-9000 Gent (East Flanders) T: 092 668 160. E: camping.blaarmeersen@gent.be

alanrogers.com/BE0610

Blaarmeersen is a comfortable, well managed municipal site in the west of the city. It adjoins a sports complex and a fair sized lake which together provide facilities for a variety of watersports, tennis, squash, minigolf, football, athletics track, roller skating and a playground. There are 238 pitches for touring units, these are flat, grassy, individually separated by tall hedges and mostly arranged in circular groups, all with electricity. There are 40 hardstandings for motorcaravans, plus a separate area for tents with barbecue facilities. There is some noise from the nearby city ring road.

Facilities

Five sanitary units of a decent standard vary in size. Showers and toilets for disabled visitors. Laundry. Motorcaravan services. Shop, café/bar (both daily March-Oct). Takeaway. Sports facilities. Playground. Fishing on site in winter, otherwise 500 m. Lake swimming. Communal barbecue. Off site: Bicycle hire 5 km. Riding and golf 10 km.

Open: 15 March - 1 November.

Directions

From E40 take exit 13 (Gent-West) and follow dual carriageway for 5 km. Cross second bridge and look for Blaarmeersen sign, turning sharp right and following signs to leisure complex. In city avoid overpasses - most signs are on the lower levels. GPS: 51.04722, 3.68333

Charges guide

Per unit incl. 2 persons and electricity (plus meter)	€ 15.75 - € 19.75
extra person	€ 4.50 - € 5.50

Geraardsbergen

Camping De Gavers

Onkerzelestraat 280, B-9500 Geraardsbergen (East Flanders) T: 054 416 324.

E: gavers@oost-vlaanderen.be **alanrogers.com/BE0590**

Camping De Gavers is a modern, well organised holiday site in a peaceful location adjacent to a large sports complex, about 5 km. outside Geraardsbergen. A busy site in season, there is good security and a card operated barrier. Most of the 448 grassy, level pitches are taken by seasonal units but about 80 are left for touring units. Pitches are arranged on either side of surfaced access roads with some hedges and a few trees to provide shade in parts, with electricity available to most. The site offers an extensive range of sporting activities and a full entertainment programme over a long season.

Facilities

Six modern, heated sanitary buildings have hot showers on payment (€ 0.50). Modern rooms for disabled visitors and babies. Launderette. Shop (July/Aug). Restaurant and takeaway. Caféteria and bars (daily 1/4-30/9, otherwise weekends). Heated indoor pool (all year). Outdoor pool (1/5-31/8). Playground. Tennis. Boules. Minigolf. Fishing. Sailing. Canoes, windsurfers, pedaloes, yachts and rowing boats for hire. Bicycle hire. Tourist train. Beach area at lake. WiFi in bar area. Off site: Restaurants within 1.5 km.

Open: All year.

Directions

From E429/A8 exit 26 towards Edingen, take N255 and N495 to Geraardsbergen. Down a steep hill, then left at site sign towards Onkerzele, through village and turn north to site. From E40/A10 take exit 17 on N42, turn left on to N495 and follow as above. GPS: 50.79098, 3.92370

Charges guide

Per unit incl. up to 6 persons and electricity	€ 13.00 - € 25.00
extra person	€ 5.00 - € 7.00

Gierle

Camping De Lilse Bergen

Strandweg 6, Gierle, B-2275 Lille (Antwerp) T: **014 557 901**. E: **info@lilsebergen.be**

alanrogers.com/BE0655

This attractive, quietly located holiday site has 513 shady pitches, of which 238 (all with 10A Europlug electricity) are for touring units. Set on sandy soil among pine trees and rhododendrons and arranged around a large lake, the site has a Mediterranean feel. It is well fenced, with a night guard and comprehensive, well labelled, fire-fighting equipment. Cars are parked away from units. The site is really child-friendly with each access road labelled with a different animal symbol to enable children to find their own unit easily. An entertainment programme is organised in high season. The lake has marked swimming and diving areas (for adults), a sandy beach, an area for watersports, plus a separate children's pool complex (depth 50 cm) with a most imaginative playground. There are lifeguards and the water meets Blue Flag standards. There are picnic areas and lakeside and woodland walks.

Facilities

Five of the six main toilet blocks have been fully refitted to a good standard and can be heated. Some washbasins in cubicles and good hot showers (on payment). Well equipped baby rooms. Facilities for disabled campers. Laundry. Barrier keys can be charged up with units for operating showers, washing machine etc. Motorcaravan service point. Restaurant (all year, weekends only in winter), takeaway and well stocked shop (Easter-30/9; weekends only outside July/Aug). Tennis. Minigolf. Boules. Climbing wall. New Playground (2011), trampolines and skateboard ramp. Pedaloes, kayaks and bicycles for hire. Children's electric cars and pedal kart tracks (charged for). Off site: Golf 1 km.

Open: All year.

Directions

From E34 Antwerp - Eindhoven take exit 22. On the roundabout take exit for Lilse Bergen, follow forest road to site entrance. GPS: 51.28908, 4.85508

Charges guide

Per unit incl. 4 persons and electricity	€ 20.00 - € 26.50
dog	€ 4.50

Grimbergen

Camping Grimbergen

Veldkantstraat 64, B-1850 Grimbergen (Brabant) T: **022 709 597**. E: **camping.grimbergen@telenet.be**

alanrogers.com/BE0630

A popular little site with a friendly atmosphere, Camping Grimbergen has 90 pitches on fairly level grass, of which around 50 have electricity (10A). The site is not really suitable for large units, although some hardstandings for motorcaravans have been added. The municipal sports facilities are adjacent and the site is well placed for visiting Brussels. The bus station is by the traffic lights at the junction of N202 and N211 and buses run into the city centre every 15 minutes, as well as every hour from the campsite. In Grimbergen itself visit Norbertine Abbey, St Servaas church, and the Sunday morning market.

Facilities

Immaculate new sanitary facilities are heated in colder months. Separate facilities for disabled visitors. Motorcaravan services. Off site: Restaurant 100 m. Fishing 2 km. Riding 5 km.

Open: 1 April - 25 October.

Directions

From Brussels ring road take exit 7 (N202) to Grimbergen. After 2.5 km, turn right at traffic lights on N211 towards Vilvoorde (site signed), then left at second set of lights (slightly oblique turn). Site entrance is on right in 500 m. (watch for blue and white sign 'Lammekenshoeve).
GPS: 50.93486, 4.38257

Charges 2012

Per unit incl. 2 persons and electricity	€ 21.00
extra person	€ 5.00

No credit cards.

Hechtel

Vakantiecentrum De Lage Kempen

Kiefhoekstraat 19, B-3941 Hechtel-Eksel (Limburg) T: 011 402 243. E: info@lagekempen.be

alanrogers.com/BE0796

This is a small, good quality site of which the owners are rightly proud. There are 100 pitches with 62 available for touring units. The pitches are large, all with electricity (6/10A) and are laid out in rows. A swimming pool complex has three heated pools, two for children and one with a large slide, and they are supervised in high season. A traditional bar also provides a limited menu and serves as a popular meeting point for relaxation. Entertainment is provided daily in high season. This is a pleasant site with a good atmosphere. The owners have found the right balance of entertainment and time for relaxation.

Facilities

Single, high quality toilet block providing very good facilities including hot showers, washbasins in cabins and good facilities for babies and disabled visitors. Laundry facilities. Motorcaravan services. Bar/restaurant. Takeaway. Outdoor heated pool complex (May-Sept). Large adventure playground. Bicycle hire. Max. 1 dog. Off site: Riding 3 km. Fishing 5 km.

Open: Easter - 30 October.

Directions

From the E314/A2 motorway take exit for Houthalen and follow signs to Hechtel. Shortly after passing through Hechtel look for campsite signs on the left. GPS: 51.16092, 5.31433

Charges guide

Per unit incl. 2 persons and electricity	€ 23.00
extra person	€ 5.00
child (0-2 yrs)	free
dog (max. 1)	€ 2.00

Houthalen

Oostappen Vakantiepark Hengelhoef

Tulpenstraat 141, B-3530 Houthalen-Helchteren (Limburg) T: 089 382 500. E: info@hengelhoef.nl

alanrogers.com/BE0788

This attractive and well cared for site would suit families with younger children. Situated in a forest it has 478 pitches of which 368 are for touring units. The pitches are large and laid out in avenues with plenty of shade and all have electricity (10A), water and drainage. At the centre of the site is a large, man-made lake surrounded by sand which is safe for children. A good sub-tropical style pool complex offers a range of slides and water based activities. With a range of activities on offer there is little need to leave the site. There is a large supermarket and a good restaurant and bars.

Facilities

Several good quality toilet blocks throughout the site provide very good facilities including hot showers, washbasins in cabins and good facilities for babies and disabled visitors. Laundry facilities. Motorcaravan services. Supermarket. Restaurant. Bar. Takeaway. Lake with beach. Indoor pool complex. Multisports court. Max. 1 dog, accepted in certain areas. Off site: Bicycle hire 1 km. Riding 3 km.

Open: All year.

Directions

From the E314/A2 motorway take exit towards Houthalen Centrum Zuid. The site is well signed from the centre. GPS: 51.01439, 5.46655

Charges guide

Per unit incl. 3-4 persons and electricity	€ 14.00 - € 39.00
extra person	€ 5.00 - € 7.50
child (4-15 yrs)	€ 2.50 - € 5.00
dog	free

Houthalen

Camping De Binnenvaart

Binnenvaartstraat 49, B-3530 Houthalen-Helchteren (Limburg) T: 011 526 720. E: info@debinnenvaart.be

alanrogers.com/BE0793

De Binnenvaart is a well equipped family site north of Hasselt, open all year. This is a very well equipped holiday centre with a good range of leisure amenities including minigolf and a sports field. The site has been developed alongside a small lake, with its own sandy beach, and is surrounded by woodland. Of the 165 pitches, 34 are for touring, all are of a good size and equipped with electricity (10A Europlug). Many pitches here are reserved all year. The site is part of the same group as BE0792 and BE0780, both of which are nearby, and guests are able to use amenities at these sites too.

Facilities

There is a heated sanitary block with disabled facilities. Caféteria and bar. Lake (swimming, fishing and windsurfing) with sandy beach. Tennis. Sports field. Minigolf. Childrens play area. Animal park. Tourist information. Activity and entertainment programme. Motorcaravan service point. WiFi. No charcoal barbecues. Off site: Walking and cycle routes. Riding. Paintball. Hot-air ballooning. Golf 5 km.

Open: All year.

Directions

Leave the A2 motorway at the Houthalen – Helchteren exit (number 29) and join the northbound N715 to the town. The site is clearly signed from here. GPS: 51.032158, 5.415949

Charges guide

Per unit incl. 2 persons and electricity	€ 24.00
extra person	€ 7.00
child	€ 4.00
dog	€ 4.00

Jabbeke

Recreatiepark Klein Strand

Varsenareweg 29, B-8490 Jabbeke (West Flanders) T: 050 811 440. E: info@kleinstrand.be

alanrogers.com/BE0555

In a convenient location just off the A10 motorway and close to Bruges, this site is in two distinct areas divided by an access road. The touring section has 137 large pitches on flat grass separated by well trimmed hedges; all have electricity and access to water and drainage. Though surrounded by mobile homes and seasonal caravans, this is a surprisingly relaxing area and the ambience should have been further enhanced in 2011 when a small park was created at its centre. Some children's leisure facilities are provided here, and there is a spacious bar and a snack bar with takeaway.

Facilities

A single modern, heated, toilet block provides the usual facilities including good sized showers (charged) and open washbasins. Baby room. Basic facilities for disabled campers. Washing machines and dryer. Dishwashing outside. Motorcaravan service point. Bar and snack bar. Children's playground. Fun pool for small children. In main park: European and Chinese restaurants, bar and snack bar, takeaways. Shop (Easter-end Aug). Tennis courts and sports field. Waterski school. Bicycle hire. Cable TV point (incl) and WiFi (charged, first hour free) on all pitches. Off site: Riding 5 km. Beach 8 km. Golf and sailing 10 km.

Open: All year.

Directions

Jabbeke is 12 km. southwest of Bruges. From A18/A10 motorways, take exit 6/6B signed Jabbeke. At roundabout take first exit signed for site. In 650 m. on left-hand bend, turn left to site in 600 m. Main reception is on left but in high season continue to touring site on right in 200 m.
GPS: 51.18448, 3.10445

Charges 2012

Per unit incl. up to 4 persons and electricity	€ 20.00 - € 36.00
dog	€ 2.00

La Roche-en-Ardenne

Camping Floréal La Roche

Route de Houffalize 18, B-6980 La Roche-en-Ardenne (Luxembourg) T: 084 219 467.
E: camping.laroche@florealclub.be alanrogers.com/BE0732

Maintained to very high standards, this site is set in a beautiful wooded valley bordering the Ourthe river. Open all year, the site is located on the outskirts of the attractive small town of La Roche-en-Ardenne, in an area understandably popular with tourists. The site is large with 587 grass pitches (min. 100 sq.m), of which 290 are for touring units. The pitches are on level ground and all have 10/16A electricity and water connections. Amenities on site include a well stocked shop, a bar, a restaurant and takeaway food. In the woods and rivers close by, there are plenty of opportunities for walking, mountain biking, rafting and canoeing. For children there is a large adventure playground which is very popular and during the summer entertainment programmes are organised. The Ardennes region is rightly proud of its cuisine in which game taken from the local forests is prominent; for those who really enjoy eating, a visit to a small restaurant should be planned. English, French, Dutch and German are spoken in reception.

Facilities

Six modern, well maintained sanitary blocks provide washbasins (open and in cabins) and free preset showers. Facilities for disabled visitors. Baby room. Washing machines and dryers (token from reception). Motorcaravan service point. Well stocked shop (fresh bread, pastries and newspapers in July/Aug). Bar, restaurant, snack bar and takeaway. At Camping Floreal 2: heated outdoor swimming pool. New wellness facilities with sauna and jacuzzi. Professional entertainment team (during local school holidays). Volleyball. Tennis. Minigolf. Pétanque. WiFi. Mobile homes to rent. Off site: Mountain bike and canoe hire 300 m. Golf, riding and bicycle hire 1 km.

Open: All year.

Directions

From E25/A26 take exit 50 and follow N89 southwest to La Roche. In La Roche follow signs for Houffalize (beside Ourthe river). Floreal Club Camping 1 is 1.5 km. along this road. Note: go to camping 1 not 2. GPS: 50.17600, 5.58600

Charges guide

Per unit incl. 2 persons and electricity	€ 14.45 - € 22.85
extra person	€ 3.60
child (3-11 yrs)	€ 2.60
dog (max. 1)	€ 4.95

La Roche-en-Ardenne

Camping le Vieux Moulin

Petite Strument 62, B-6980 La Roche-en-Ardenne (Luxembourg) T: 084 411 380. E: info@strument.com

alanrogers.com/BE0770

Located in one of the most beautiful valleys in the heart of the Ardennes, le Vieux Moulin has 183 pitches and, although there are 127 long stay units at the far end of the site, the 60 touring pitches do have their own space. Some are separated by hedges, others for tents and smaller units are more open, all are on grass, and there are 50 electric hook-ups (6A). The 19th-century watermill has been owned and operated by the owner's family for many years, but is now a small hotel and a fascinating mill museum.

Facilities

A newly constructed, centrally located toilet block is between the touring and long stay areas. It can be heated in cool weather and provides washbasins in cubicles and controllable hot showers on payment. Washing machine. No facilities for disabled campers. A further older unit is at the end of the mill building. Restaurant and bar with hotel (8 rooms). Mill museum. Off site: Town facilities 800 m.

Open: 1 April - 11 November.

Directions

From town centre take N89 south towards St Hubert, turning right towards Hives where site is signed. Site is 800 m. from the town centre. GPS: 50.17362, 5.57750

Charges guide

Per unit incl. 2 persons and electricity	€ 16.00 - € 18.50
extra person	€ 2.50
dog	€ 2.00

Lichtaart

Camping Floréal Kempen

Herentalsesteenweg 64, B-2460 Lichtaart (Antwerp) T: 014 556 120. E: kempen@florealclub.be

alanrogers.com/BE0665

This is an attractive woodland site and is a member of the Floréal group. It is located close to the well known Purperen Heide, a superb nature reserve with 15 scenic footpaths leading through it. There are 207 pitches, of which only 26 are reserved for touring units. These are of a good size (100 sq.m. or more), all with 10A electricity and most with their own water supply. Several simple cabins are available for hikers, as well as fully equipped mobile homes. There are some good leisure facilities, including tennis and a multisports pitch, as well as a popular bar and restaurant.

Facilities

Toilet facilities are in need of some investment. When we visited cleaning and maintenance needed attention. Motorcaravan services. Shop. Bar. Restaurant. Tennis. Play area. Multisport terrain. Tourist information. Mobile homes for rent. Off site: Walking and cycling tracks. Golf. Antwerp. Bobbejaanlaan amusement park

Open: All year.

Directions

Approaching from Antwerp, head east on the A21 motorway as far as exit 24 (Turnhout). Leave here and head south on N19 to Kasterlee, and then west on N123 to Lichtaart. Follow signs to the site. GPS: 51.21024, 4.90423

Charges guide

Per unit incl. 2 persons	€ 11.00 - € 16.50
extra person	€ 3.25
child (3-11 yrs)	€ 2.50
dog (max. 1)	€ 3.00

Lombardsijde

Camping De Lombarde

Elisabethlaan 4, B-8434 Lombardsijde Middelkerke (West Flanders) T: 058 236 839. E: info@delombarde.be

alanrogers.com/BE0560

De Lombarde is a spacious, good value holiday site between Lombardsijde and the coast. It has a pleasant atmosphere and modern buildings. The 380 pitches are set out in level, grassy bays surrounded by shrubs, all with electricity (16A), long leads may be needed. Vehicles are parked in separate car parks. There are many seasonal units and 22 holiday homes, leaving 180 touring pitches. There is a range of activities and an entertainment programme in season. This is a popular holiday area and the site becomes full at peak times. A pleasant stroll takes you into Lombardsijde. There is a tram service from near the site entrance to the town and the beach.

Facilities

Three heated sanitary units are of an acceptable standard, with some washbasins in cubicles. Facilities for disabled visitors (but not for children). Large laundry. Motorcaravan services. Shop, restaurant/bar and takeaway (July/Aug. plus weekends and holidays 1/4-31/8). Tennis. Boules. Fishing lake. TV lounge. Entertainment programme for children. Playground. Internet access (in the bar). ATM. Torch useful. Max. 1 dog. Off site: Beach 400 m. Riding and golf 500 m. Bicycle hire 1 km.

Open: All year.

Directions

Coming from Westende, follow the tramlines. From traffic lights in Lombardsijde, turn left following tramlines into Zeelaan. Continue following tramlines until crossroads and tram stop, turn left into Elisabethlaan. Site is on right after 200 m. GPS: 51.15644, 2.75329

Charges 2012

Per unit incl. 1-6 persons and electricity	€ 18.00 - € 32.50
dog (max 1)	€ 2.60

No credit cards.

Lommel

Oostappen Vakantiepark Blauwe Meer

Kattenbos 169, B-3920 Lommel (Limburg) T: 011 544 523. E: info@blauwemeer.be

alanrogers.com/BE0785

Surrounded by woodland, and with shade from tall pines, this large site has 976 pitches, of which 277 are for touring units. The touring pitches are attractively arranged around a large man-made lake with a fence surrounding it (safe for children). Each pitch has electricity (10A), water, drainage and television connections. There is a whole range of activities including a disco and a heated outdoor pool with slide. There are two additional small pools for children. A bar offers takeaway food and a good supermarket is on the site. This is a popular and lively site with an extensive entertainment programme which is varied to suit all age groups.

Facilities

Good clean toilet blocks are located throughout the site. Free hot showers, washbasins in cabins. Facilities for babies and children. Good facilities for disabled visitors. Laundry room. Supermarket. Bar. Takeaway. Heated outdoor swimming pool, two smaller ones for children (May-Aug). Several adventure style playgrounds. Children's zoo. Minigolf. WiFi (charged). Max. 1 dog. Off site: Forest Park adjacent for walking and cycling. Riding 7 and 12 km. Golf 10 km.

Open: Easter - 30 October

Directions

Lommel is 35 km. north of Hasselt. From the N71 at Lommel, turn south at traffic lights on N746 (signed Leopoldsburg), for 2 km. to Kattenbos, and site entrance is on southern side of village on left. GPS: 51.19407, 5.30322

Charges guide

Per unit incl. up to 4 persons	€ 25.00 - € 33.00

Minimum stays apply (1 week in high season, 3 or 4 nights on public holidays. American RVs, 12 m. max. in high season, larger at other times).

Lommel

Oostappen Vakantiepark Parelstrand

Luikersteenweg 313A, B-3920 Lommel (Limburg) T: 011 649 349. E: info@parelstrand.be

alanrogers.com/BE0798

This large, attractive site is situated alongside the Bocholt - Herentals canal and the Lommel yacht marina. It has 800 pitches of which 250 are for touring units. Each pitch has electricity (10A), water and drainage. The site fronts onto a large lake with a safe beach and there are two smaller lakes on the site, one of which is used for fishing (well stocked but all fish must be returned). There is an Olympic size, outdoor pool with a large slide and a small pool for children (not supervised). Several good play areas are spread over the site, which is ideal for relaxing or enjoying the canal and other water-based activities.

Facilities

All the facilities that one would expect from a large site are available. Free hot showers, some washbasins in cabins. Facilities for babies and children. Good facilities for disabled visitors. Laundry room. Supermarket. Bar. Takeaway. Outdoor swimming pools, one for children. WiFi (charged). Max. 1 dog per pitch.
Off site: Boat launching 1 km. Riding 5 km.

Open: Easter - 30 October.

Directions

Take the N712 from Lommel and after 3 km. turn left on the N715. After a further 3 km. the site is on the right hand side. It is well signed from Lommel. GPS: 51.2431, 5.3791

Charges guide

Per unit incl. 3-4 persons and electricity	€ 25.00 - € 33.00

Manhay

Domaine Moulin de Malempré

1 Malempré, B-6960 Manhay (Luxembourg) T: 086 455 504. E: info@camping-malempre.be

alanrogers.com/BE0730

This pleasant countryside site, very close to the E25, is well worth a visit and the Dutch owners will make you very welcome (English is spoken). The reception building houses the office and a small shop, above which is an attractive bar and restaurant with open fireplace. The 140 marked touring pitches are separated by small shrubs and gravel roads on sloping terrain. All have electricity (10A), 40 have water and drainage as well and the site is well lit. There is a little traffic noise from the nearby E25 (not too intrusive).

Facilities

Modern toilet facilities include some washbasins in cubicles and family bathrooms on payment. The unisex unit can be heated and has a family shower room. Unit for disabled visitors. Baby room. Laundry. Motorcaravan services. Shop for basic provisions (15/5-31/8). Baker calls daily 08.30-09.15. Restaurant and bar (both 15/5-15/9 and weekends). Takeaway (15/5-15/9). Heated swimming and children's pools (15/5-15/9). TV. Boules. Playground. Off site: Bicycle hire 3 km. Riding 6 km. Fishing 10 km. Places to visit include the Hotton Grottoes, one of the prettiest Belgian caves (daily April-Oct).

Open: 1 April - 31 October.

Directions

From E25/A26 (Liege - Bastogne) exit 49. Turn onto N651 (southwest) towards Manhay. After 220 m. turn sharp left (east) towards Lierneux. Follow signs for Malempré and site. GPS: 50.29498, 5.72317

Charges guide

Per unit incl. 2 persons	€ 18.50 - € 22.00
extra person	€ 4.00
child (3-12 yrs)	€ 2.75
electricity	€ 2.85
dog	€ 2.85

Less 20% in low season.

Mons

Camping du Waux-Hall

Avenue Saint-Pierre 17, B-7000 Mons (Hainaut) T: 065 337 923. E: ot1@ville.mons.be

alanrogers.com/BE0530

Waux-Hall is a useful and convenient site for a longer look at historic Mons and the surrounding area. It is a well laid out municipal site, close to the town centre and E42 motorway. The 50 pitches, most with electricity (10A), are arranged on either side of an oval road, on grass and divided by beds of small shrubs; the landscape maintenance is excellent. The pitches vary in size from average to small, so manoeuvring could be difficult for larger units. A large public park is adjacent with a refreshment bar, tennis, a playground and a lake. There is direct access from the site when the gate is unlocked.

Facilities

A single, heated toilet block is of older style, basic but clean, with most washbasins in cubicles for ladies.
No facilities for disabled visitors or children. Washing machine and dryer. Soft drinks machine and ice cream. Playground. Passport identity is required on arrival.
Off site: Public park adjacent. Town centre shops and restaurants within easy walking distance. Fishing 300 m. Riding 2 km. Golf 4 km.

Open: All year.

Directions

From Mons inner ring road, follow signs for Charleroi, La Louviere, Binche, Beaumont. When turning off the ring road (at the Hotel St James), keep to right hand lane, turning for site is immediately first right (signed Waux-Hall and camping). Site is on the left in 200 m. GPS: 50.45138, 3.96296

Charges guide

Per unit incl. 2 persons	€ 12.00
extra person	€ 5.00
child (0-12 yrs)	€ 2.90
electricity per kWh	€ 0.30

No credit cards.

Neufchâteau

Camping Spineuse

Rue de Malome 7, B-6840 Neufchâteau (Luxembourg) T: 061 277 320. E: info@camping-spineuse.be

alanrogers.com/BE0675

This Dutch-owned site lies about 2 km. from the town centre. It is on low lying, level grass, bordered by a river, with trees and shrubs dotted around the 87 pitches. The main gravel access road can be dusty in dry weather. Seasonal units take 25 pitches leaving 62 for touring units, all with 10/15A electricity. There is also a separate area for tents. Parents of small children should be aware that there is unfenced water on site and a footbridge over the river with no guard rails. Reception is in the main building and basic food items are kept here in July/August.

Facilities

Toilet facilities are in the central building and are looking dated with some cubicles rather small. Preset showers and open washbasins. However the building can be heated and was reasonably clean when seen. No facilities for disabled campers. Washing machine and dryer. Extra facilities are in a portacabin (July/Aug). Motorcaravan service point. Bistro/bar (1/4-31/10). Small inflatable children's pool (1/6-30/9). Tennis. Boules. Small playground. Fishing. Off site: Riding 10 km. Golf 30 km.

Open: All year.

Directions

Site is 2 km. southwest of Neufchâteau on the N15 towards Florenville. There are three sites fairly close together, this is the last one on the left hand side. GPS: 49.83287, 5.41743

Charges guide

Per unit incl. 2 persons and electricity	€ 17.40 - € 19.00
extra person	€ 3.15 - € 3.50
child (0-6 yrs)	€ 1.80 - € 2.00
dog	€ 1.25

Nieuwpoort

Kompas Camping Nieuwpoort

Brugsesteenweg 49, B-8620 Nieuwpoort (West Flanders) T: 058 236 037.

E: nieuwpoort@kompascamping.be **alanrogers.com/BE0550**

Near Ostend and convenient for the A18 motorway, this large, well equipped and well run site with 952 pitches caters particularly for families. There are many amenities including a heated pool complex, a range of sporting activities, and a children's farm. The 469 touring pitches, all with electricity (10A), are in regular rows on flat grass in various parts of the site; 120 also have a water point and waste water drain. With many seasonal units and caravan holiday homes, the site becomes full during Belgian holidays and in July and August.

Facilities

Seven modern, clean and well maintained toilet blocks include washbasins in cubicles, controllable showers and excellent facilities for families, children and disabled visitors. Dishwashing and laundry rooms. Washing machines and dryers. Motorcaravan service point. Supermarket, bakery, restaurant, takeaway and café/bar (July/Aug). Swimming pools (heated and supervised) with slide, children's pool and pool games (16/5-13/9). Bicycle hire. Tennis. Extensive adventure playgrounds. Multisport court. Minigolf. Entertainment programme in July/Aug. WiFi. Largest unit accepted 2.5x8 m. Off site: Fishing within 500 m. Nearest village is 2 km. Riding 3 km. Beach 4 km. Golf driving range 5 km.

Open: 23 March - 12 November.

Directions

Nieuwpoort is 19 km southwest of Ostende. From east on A18 (E40) take exit 4 (Middelkerke). Turn north towards Diksmuide on D369; in 2 km. turn right on N367 towards Nieuwpoort. Pass through Sint-Joris and the site is on the right. From west on A18 take exit 3 (Nieuwpoort) and at roundabout take third exit N356a (Westende Bad). At T junction, turn right on N367 to camspite on left. GPS: 51.12965, 2.77222

Charges guide

Per unit incl. 4 persons and electricity	€ 24.70 - € 37.70
dog	€ 2.70

Less 10% with camping carnet.
Camping Cheques accepted.

Opglabbeek

Family Camping Wilhelm Tell

Hoeverweg 87, B-3660 Opglabbeek (Limburg) T: 089 810 014. E: receptie@wilhelmtell.com

alanrogers.com/BE0780

Wilhelm Tell is a family run site that caters particularly well for children with its indoor and outdoor pools and lots of entertainment throughout the season. There are 128 pitches with 70 available for touring units, some separated, others on open fields and 60 electricity connections (10A). The super bar/restaurant has access for wheelchair users. M. Lode Nulmans has a very special attitude towards his customers and tries to ensure they leave satisfied and want to return. For example, in his restaurant he says 'it serves until you are full'. The Limburg region is a relaxing area with much to do, including shopping or touring the historic towns with a very enjoyable choice of food and drink!

Facilities

Toilet facilities are adequate. Facilities around the pool supplement at busy times. Baby room in reception area. Two en-suite units for disabled visitors. Laundry facilities. Motorcaravan service point. Fridge hire. Bar/restaurant and snack bar (times vary acc. to season). Outdoor heated pool with slide and wave machine (1/7-31/8) and indoor pool (all year), both well supervised. Play area. WiFi. No charcoal barbecues.

Open: All year.

Directions

From E314 take exit 32 for Maaseik and follow the 730 road towards As. From As follow the signs to Opglabbeek. In Opglabbeek take the first right at roundabout (Weg van Niel) then first left (Kasterstraat) to site. GPS: 51.02852, 5.59813

Charges guide

Per unit incl. 2 persons and electricity	€ 32.00
extra person	€ 8.00
child (0-12)	€ 4.00
dog	€ 4.00

Less 30% in low season.
Camping Cheques accepted.

Opoeteren

Camping Zavelbos

Kattebeekstraat 1, B-3680 Opoeteren (Limburg) T: 089 758 146. E: receptie@zavelbos.com

alanrogers.com/BE0792

Camping Zavelbos lies between woodland and moorland in a nature park of 2,000 hectares. It is a pleasant spot for nature lovers and those who love peace and quiet. There are many cycling and walking routes to enjoy in this beautiful region, alternatively you can simply relax in the peaceful campsite grounds complete with a fishpond. There is no swimming pool here but guests have free use of the pool complex at Wilhelm Tell Holiday Park (6 km). The 45 touring pitches (80-100 sq.m) all have electricity (16A Europlug) and water. Bungalows and chalets are available to rent.

Facilities

New sanitary facilities include family bathrooms, baths with jacuzzi and jetstream. Bar and snack bar. Tavern. Fishpond. Playground. Boules. WiFi. No charcoal barbecues. Off site: Shops. Cycling and walking routes. National Park Hoge Kempen. Bobbejaanland. Maastricht. Hasselt. Genk.

Open: All year.

Directions

Take the Maaseik exit from the A2 (Eindhoven - Maastricht) motorway and drive via Neerpoeteren to Opoeteren. The site is on the right heading to Opglabbeek. GPS: 51.0583, 5.6288

Charges guide

Per unit incl. 2 persons and electricity	€ 30.00
extra person	€ 8.00
child (under 12 yrs)	€ 4.00
dog	€ 4.00

Oteppe

Camping l'Hirondelle

Rue de la Burdinale 76a, B-4210 Oteppe (Liège) T: **085 711 131**. E: **info@lhirondelle.be**

alanrogers.com/BE0705

This site is set in 20 hectares of woodland in the grounds of a castle that dates back to the 14th century. From the entrance one gets a glimpse of the restaurant in one part of the castle. There are 800 pitches with 300 for touring units, all with 6A electricity. The pitches are arranged around a huge playground, basketball court and a building housing a games room, a supermarket and a bar. In high season the site is bustling and lively, offering a full programme of entertainment with sports tournaments, discos and contests. This site has a lot to offer for families with children and teenagers. The large open-air pool (15x25 m) will accommodate all ages. A video circuit in all the buildings advertises and informs about the activity programmes.

Facilities

The two toilet blocks for touring units provide some washbasins in cabins, showers on payment, children's toilets and basins and a unisex baby room. Washing machine and dryer. Good provision for disabled visitors. These facilities will be very pressed to cope in high season. Shop. Bar. Restaurant. Swimming pool (15x25 m). Huge adventure type playground. Boules. Playing field. Entertainment (10/7-22/8). Games room. WiFi (free).

Open: 1 April - 31 October.

Directions

From Namen on the E42 take exit 10 towards Biewart then continue on the 80 to Burdinne. In Burdinne follow signs for Oteppe. The site is signed just before entering Oteppe.
GPS: 50.56758, 5.11718

Charges guide

Per unit incl. 2 persons and electricity	€ 13.75 - € 21.00
extra person (over 3 yrs)	€ 2.75 - € 4.00
dog	€ 5.00

Rendeux

Camping Floréal le Festival

89 route de la Roche, B-6987 Rendeux (Luxembourg) T: **084 477 371**. E: **camping.festival@florealclub.be**

alanrogers.com/BE0733

Floréal le Festival is a member of the Floréal group, attractively located in the wide wooded valley of the River Ourthe. There are 390 pitches here and the site is open all year. Pitches are of a good size and each is surrounded by hedges. Most have electrical connections. On-site amenities include a small supermarket, a bar (which also provides takeaway meals) and a restaurant. Sports amenities are good and include a football field, volleyball and tennis. Furthermore, the region is ideal for walking and mountain biking, and the site's managers will be pleased to recommend routes.

Facilities

Three traditional toilet blocks have washbasins (open style and in cabins), free showers, baby bath and facilities for disabled visitors. Washing machines and dryers. Supermarket. Bar. Takeaway meals. Restaurant. Play area. Tennis. Volleyball. Football. Tourist information. Mobile homes for rent. WiFi. Off site: Walking and cycle tracks. Riding 0.5 km. Bicycle hire 1 km. Grottes de Hotton. La Roche en Ardennes.

Open: All year.

Directions

Approaching from Namur, head south on N4 as far as Marche-en-Famenne. Here, join the westbound N86 to Hotton and then the southbound N822 to Rendeux. From here follow signs to the site.
GPS: 50.22469, 5.52603

Charges guide

Per unit incl. 2 persons and electricity	€ 14.45 - € 22.85
extra person	€ 3.60
child (3-11 yrs)	€ 2.60
dog	€ 3.00

Sart-lez-Spa

Camping Spa d'Or

Stockay 17, B-4845 Sart-lez-Spa (Liège) T: 087 474 400. E: info@campingspador.be

alanrogers.com/BE0700

Camping Spa d'Or is set in a beautiful area of woodlands and picturesque villages, 4 km. from the town of Spa (the 'Pearl of the Ardennes'). The site is on the banks of a small river and is an ideal starting point for walks and bicycle trips through the forests. With 310 pitches in total, 240 are for touring (40 places are reserved for tents). The touring pitches have an open aspect, most are slightly sloping and all have 10A electricity connections. The remainder are used for site owned mobile homes and tents.

Facilities

One new large, bright and cheerful sanitary block and one new smaller block (Portacabin) both with all the usual facilities. Room for visitors with disabilities. Laundry. Shop (6/4-24/10). Bar, restaurant and takeaway (6/4-24/10). Outdoor heated swimming pool (1/5-15/9). Play area with good equipment. TV in bar. Goal posts and two boules courts. Entertainment during July/Aug. WiFi (on payment). Off site: Fishing 2 km. Golf and riding 5 km. Spa 4 km. Maps for cycling and walking on sale at reception.

Open: 1 April - 7 November.

Directions

From E42 take exit 9 and follow the signs to Spa d'Or. GPS: 50.50758, 5.91952

Charges guide

Per unit incl. 2 persons and electricity	€ 15.00 - € 24.50

Camping Cheques accepted.

Sint Job in't Goor

Camping Floréal-Club Het Veen

Eekhoornlaan 1, B-2960 Sint Job in't Goor (Antwerp) T: 036 361 327. E: het.veen@florealclub.be

alanrogers.com/BE0650

Floréal Het Veen can be found 20 km. north of Antwerp in a woodland area, and with many sports facilities. There are 345 marked pitches (60 for tourists) on level grass, most with some shade and electricity (10A, long leads in some places) and also seven hardstandings. Amenities include an indoor sports hall (charged by the hour), and courts for tennis, football, basketball and softball are outside. Good cycling and walking opportunities exist in the area. English is spoken.

Facilities

Four spacious toilet blocks include a few washbasins in cubicles (only two are close to touring pitches). Facilities for disabled visitors. Laundry facilities. Motorcaravan services. Shop. Restaurant, bar, café and takeaway (daily July/Aug. weekends only at other times). Tennis. Badminton. Boules. Playgrounds and children's entertainment in season. Fishing. Canoeing. Bicycle hire. Wooden chalets for rent. Off site: Riding and golf 8 km.

Open: 1 March - 31 October.

Directions

Sint Job in't Goor is northeast of Antwerp. From the A1 (E19) exit 4, turn southeast towards Sint Job in't Goor, straight on at traffic lights and, immediately after canal bridge, turn left at campsite sign. Continue straight on for about 1.5 km. to site. GPS: 51.30513, 4.58622

Charges guide

Per person	€ 3.80
child (3-11 yrs)	€ 2.80
pitch incl. electricity	€ 9.40
hiker/cyclist and tent	€ 5.70

Stavelot

Camping l'Eau Rouge

Cheneux 25, B-4970 Stavelot (Liège) T: 080 863 075. E: fb220447@skynet.be

alanrogers.com/BE0740

A popular, lively and attractively situated site, l'Eau Rouge is in a sheltered valley close to Spa and the Grand Prix circuit. There are 180 grassy pitches of 110 sq.m. on sloping ground either side of a central road (speed bumps) – 60 are taken by permanent units and 120 for touring units. The main building houses the busy reception, shop, bar and the main sanitary facilities. There are plenty of sporting activities in the area including skiing and luge in winter. The site is close to the motor race circuit at Spa Francorchamps and is within walking distance for the fit. The site's Dutch owners have embarked on a five year programme upgrading the infrastructure and have other ideas in the pipeline.

Facilities

A main block and a smaller unit serving the touring area. Good numbers of British WCs, mostly open washbasins, but rather fewer hot showers (free) which may be stretched at times. Additional facilities should be available in the near future. Shop. Baker calls daily at 08.30 (in season). Takeaway (in summer). Bar. Boules. Archery (free lessons in high season). Playground. Entertainment in season. Max. 2 dogs. Off site: Bicycle hire 6 km. Riding 10 km. Spa Francorchamps motor racing circuit.

Open: All year.

Directions

Site is 1 km. east of Stavelot on the road to the race circuit. Leave E42 exit 11 Malmédy, at roundabout follow signs for Stavelot. At end of road at T-junction turn right, then first right. GPS: 50.41203, 5.95317

Charges guide

Per unit incl. 2 persons and electricity	€ 17.50 - € 20.00
extra person	€ 2.25 - € 3.00
child (4-15 yrs)	€ 2.00 - € 2.50
dog	€ 1.00

Tellin

Camping Parc La Clusure

Chemin de la Clusure 30, B-6927 Bure-Tellin (Luxembourg) T: 084 360 050. E: info@parclaclusure.be

alanrogers.com/BE0670

A friendly and very well run site, Parc La Clusure is highly recommended. Set in a river valley in the lovely wooded uplands of the Ardennes, known as the l'Homme Valley touring area, the site has 438 large marked, grassy pitches (350 for touring). All have access to electricity, cable TV and water taps and are mostly in avenues off a central, tarmac road. There is some noise from the nearby railway. There is a very pleasant riverside walk; the river is shallow in summer and popular with children (caution in winter). The site's heated swimming pool and children's pool have a pool-side bar and terrace.

Facilities

Three excellent sanitary units, one new and one heated in winter, include some washbasins in cubicles, facilities for babies and family bathrooms. Facilities for disabled campers. Motorcaravan services. Well stocked shop, bar, restaurant, snack bar and takeaway (all 27/4-1/11). Swimming pools (25/4-13/9). Bicycle hire. Tennis. New playgrounds. Organised activity programme including canoeing, archery, abseiling, mountain biking and climbing (summer). Caving. Fishing (licence essential). WiFi free to all areas. Barrier card deposit (€ 20). Off site: Riding 7 km.

Open: All year.

Directions

Site is signed north at the roundabout off the N803 Rochefort - St Hubert road at Bure, 8 km. southeast of Rochefort with a narrow, fairly steep, winding descent to site. GPS: 50.09647, 5.2857

Charges guide

Per unit incl. 2 persons and electricity	€ 20.00 - € 36.00
extra person (over 2 yrs)	€ 4.00 - € 6.00
dog (max. 1 in July/Aug)	€ 4.00 - € 5.00

Camping Cheques accepted.

Turnhout

Camping Baalse Hei

Roodhuisstraat 10, B-2300 Turnhout (Antwerp) T: 014 448 470. E: info@baalsehei.be

alanrogers.com/BE0660

The Campine is an area covering three quarters of the Province of Antwerp, noted for its nature reserves, pine forests, meadows and streams and is ideal for walking and cycling, while Turnhout itself is an interesting old town. Baalse Hei, a long established, friendly site, is a recent Green Key ecolabel award winner. It has 459 pitches including a separate touring area of 71 large pitches (all with 16A electricity, TV connections and shared water point) on a large grass field, thoughtfully developed with trees and bushes. Cars are parked away from the pitches. Large motorcaravans can be accommodated (phone first to check availability). There is also accommodation to rent. It is 100 m. from the edge of the field to the modern, heated, sanitary building. There is a small lake for swimming with a beach, a boating lake and a large fishing lake (on payment). Entertainment and activities are organised in July and August. Walk in the woods and you will undoubtedly come across some of the many red squirrels or take the pleasant 1.5 km. riverside walk to the next village.

Facilities

The toilet block provides hot showers on payment (€ 0.50), some washbasins in cabins and facilities for disabled visitors. Dishwashing (hot water € 0.20), Launderette. Motorcaravan services. Café/restaurant (daily 1/4-31/10, w/ends only other times, closed 16/11-25/1). Breakfast served in high season. Shop (high season). Club/TV room. Lake swimming. Fishing. Tennis. Boules. Adventure play area. Bicycle hire. English is spoken. Overnight pitches for vehicles under 3.5t. In low season reception opens for limited hours (14.00-17.00). Only charcoal barbecues permitted. WiFi throughout (free). Off site: Riding 1.5 km.

Open: 16 January - 15 December.

Directions

Site is northeast of Turnhout off the N119. From Antwerp on E34/A12 take Turnhout ring road to the end (not a complete ring) and turn right. There is a small site sign to right in 1.5 km. then a country lane. GPS: 51.35467, 4.95500

Charges 2012

Per unit incl. 2 persons and electricity	€ 19.00 - € 26.00

Visa cards accepted.

Tintigny

Camping De Chênefleur

Norulle 16, B-6730 Tintigny (Luxembourg) T: 063 444 078. E: info@chenefleur.be

alanrogers.com/BE0715

This is a comfortable site with 223 pitches (196 for tourers), set beside the Semois river, close to Luxembourg and France. All pitches have 6A electricity and are separated by young trees. On the whole the site is open but there is some shade. One of the guests we spoke to, a first time visitor, was very pleased with the spacious pitches and the peace and quiet on site. The site is still being developed, but Fred, the owner, is very enthusiastic and hard working. It has a swimming pool (also used by the locals) and in high season, entertainment is organised.

Facilities

Two new fully refurbished sanitary blocks, one with facilities for children. Washing machine and dryer. Shop. Bar. Restaurant. Heated outdoor swimming pool (30/4-15/9). Two new play areas. Full entertainment programme in season. Bicycle hire. Max. 2 dogs. Off site: Riding 4 km. Luxembourg City 40 km.

Open: 1 April - 1 October.

Directions

From Luik follow E25 towards Luxembourg and continue on E411. Take exit 29 Habay-La-Neuve and continue to Etalle. From Etalle follow N83 to Florenville. Drive through Tintigny and follow site signs. GPS: 49.68497, 5.52050

Charges guide

Per unit incl. 2 persons and electricity	€ 18.50 - € 31.00
extra person (over 3 yrs)	€ 4.30 - € 5.40
dog	€ 4.00 - € 5.00

Virton

Camping Colline de Rabais

Rue de Bonlieu, B-6760 Virton (Luxembourg) T: 063 571 195. E: info@collinederabais.be

alanrogers.com/BE0710

Colline de Rabais is a large site with an unusual layout. This comprises a circular road with smaller roads leading to circular pads with wedge shaped pitches. In a hill top setting, the site is surrounded by forest. The present Dutch owners took over in 1997 and are slowly revamping the site. There are around 250 pitches for touring units, all with 16A electricity (some long leads needed), plus 43 mobile homes and bungalows for rent and 22 tour operator tents. Various activities are organised during the season.

Facilities

Three toilet blocks, one modernised with shower/washbasin cubicles and an en-suite room for disabled visitors. Cleaning and maintenance can be variable and not all blocks are open in low season. Washing machines and dryers. Motorcaravan service point. Bar/restaurant and shop (opening times vary). Small outdoor swimming pool (1/5-1/10) with sunbathing area. Bicycle hire. Off site: Fishing 1 km. Riding 3 km.

Open: All year.

Directions

From E25/E411 take exit 29 towards Etalle and Virton. Follow signs for Vallée de Rabais. Turn right at sports complex. At crossroads (with phone box) turn right and uphill to site at end of road. GPS: 49.58015, 5.54773

Charges guide

Per unit incl. 2 persons	€ 17.50 - € 23.00
extra person (over 2 yrs)	€ 4.00 - € 4.50
electricity (16A)	€ 3.00
dog	€ 4.00 - € 5.00

Zonhoven

Camping Holsteenbron

Hengelhoefseweg 9, B-3520 Zonhoven (Limburg) T: 011 817 140. E: camping.holsteenbron@telenet.be

alanrogers.com/BE0786

Situated in the heart of the Park Midden-Limburg, this is a delightful site. There are 91 pitches with 60 for touring units, numbered and arranged in rows that are separated by hedges. All have easy access and electricity (6A). Water is provided by a single supply at the toilet block, but being such a small site, this is not a problem. A pretty lake is at the centre of the site and is well stocked with fish for the exclusive use of the camping guests. The site is situated only 500 m. from the start of a network of cycle tracks that stretches for 1,600 km. throughout the National Park. The site is highly recommended.

Facilities

One single well equipped toilet block with large token operated showers. Laundry room. Excellent bar and restaurant with limited but good menu (all season). Playground. Sports field. Fishing. TV in bar. Off site: Riding 3 km.

Open: 1 April - 11 November.

Directions

Site is situated on the N29 Eindhoven - Hasselt road and is well signed from Zonhoven. GPS: 50.99826, 5.42451

Charges guide

Per unit incl. electricity	€ 17.00 - € 22.00
dog	€ 1.00

Westende

Kompas Camping Westende

Bassevillestraat 141, B-8434 Westende (West Flanders) T: 058 223 025. E: westende@kompascamping.be

alanrogers.com/BE0565

Camping Westende is a large holiday site near the sea. Of the 370 pitches, half are taken by seasonal caravans plus 43 rental units, leaving about 100 touring pitches on grass and with 10A electricity, plus a group of 24 serviced pitches with water, waste water drain and electricity. The site seems reasonably well cared for, but on a previous visit, some pitches were looking rather worn, perhaps partly because of the rigid pitching policy which dictates that caravans have to be placed on a specific side of the pitch. All the main services are grouped around reception which can be a fair walk from the more remote pitches. One end of the site is now leased to a firm providing rental accommodation in mobile homes. Adjacent are a large Kompas holiday rental complex and an automated motorcaravan park. Ostend is only 15 km. away and offers a wide variety of activities. Day trips could include Ypres and the First World War battlefields, Bruges and even Ghent. Alternatively, the beach is only a short walk away.

Facilities

Four toilet blocks were well cared for when we visited, but reportedly have suffered from heavy use and variable maintenance and cleaning in high season. One block renovated in 2010. Good facilities for children and disabled visitors in furthest block but access was very difficult at time of visit. Shop, bar, restaurant and takeaway (Easter-November, but weekends only outside July/Aug. and certain public holidays). Adventure playground. Tennis. Boules. Children's entertainment and activities programme (July/Aug). Bicycle hire. Max. 2 dogs. Off site: Fishing 20 m. Golf 100 m. Beach 800 m. Shops, bars and restaurants 1 km. Riding and sailing 2 km. Markets in Nieuwpoort Fri, Middelkerke Thurs.

Open: 23 March - 12 November.

Directions

Westende is 15 km. southwest of Ostende. From the E40 take exit 4 to Middelkerke. At the church turn left to Westende. After Westende church take the fourth turn right to the site. GPS: 51.15787, 2.7606

Charges 2012

Per unit incl. 4 persons and electricity	€ 24.70 - € 37.70
dog	€ 2.70

Camping Cheques accepted.

Zutendaal

Vakantiepark Mooi Zutendaal

Roelerweg 13, B-3690 Zutendaal (Limburg) T: 089 715 527. E: info@mooi-zutendaal.be

alanrogers.com/BE0778

This family site in Belgian Limburg is situated at the edge of the National Park Hoge Kempen which offers 6,000 hectares of nature. The beautiful landscape of valleys, moors and pine forests provides an ideal opportunity for walking or cycling tours. There are 130 serviced pitches available for touring on flat grass and separated by good hedges. A wide range of bungalows (6-12 persons) are available to rent. Swimming is possible all year as there are both outdoor and indoor pools. The interesting Dutch towns of Valkenburg and Maastricht are close by, as is the friendly Belgian town of Hasselt.

Facilities

The modern toilet block includes facilities for disabled visitors. Laundry. Supermarket. Restaurant. Café/bar. Snack bar. Takeaway. Outdoor and indoor swimming pools. Paddling pool. Entertainment programmes. Indoor playground. Play areas. Sports field. Boules. Bicycle and go-kart hire. Off site: National Park Hoge Kempen with many walking and cycle paths. Cities of Hasselt, Maastricht and Valkenburg.

Open: 27 March - 8 November.

Directions

From A2 take exit for Lanaken at Stein and follow direction Lanaken. Turn right at roundabout Rekem, after 6 km. at T-junction turn right and immediately left. Site is 1 km. and well signed. GPS: 50.91385, 5.59739

Charges guide

Per unit incl. up to 6 persons and electricity and water	€ 16.00 - € 29.00
extra person	€ 6.00
dog	€ 3.00

Croatia

Croatia has thrown off old communist attitudes and blossomed into a lively and friendly place to visit. A country steeped in history, it boasts some of the finest Roman ruins in Europe and you'll find plenty of traditional coastal towns, clusters of tiny islands and medieval villages to explore.

The heart-shaped peninsula of Istria, located in the north, is among the most developed tourist regions in Croatia. Here you can visit the preserved Roman amphitheatre in Pula, the beautiful town of Rovinj with its cobbled streets and wooded hills, and the resort of Umag, well known for its recreational activities, most notably tennis. Islands are studded all around the coast, making it ideal for sailing and diving enthusiasts. Istria also has the highest concentration of campsites.

Further south, in the province of Dalmatia, Split is the largest city on the Adriatic coast and home to the impressive Diolectian's Palace. From here the islands of Brac, Hvar, Vis and Korcula, renowned for their lively fishing villages and pristine beaches, are easily accessible by ferry. The old walled city of Dubrovnik is 150 km. south. At over 2 km. long and 25 m. high, with 16 towers, a walk along the city walls affords spectacular views.

CAPITAL: Zagreb

Tourist Office

Croatian National Tourist Office
2 The Lanchesters
162-164 Fulham Palace Road
London W6 9ER
Tel: 020 8563 7979 Fax: 020 8563 2616
Email: info@cnto.freeserve.co.uk
Internet: www.croatia.hr

Population

4.4 million

Climate

Predominantly warm and hot in summer with temperatures of up to 40°C

Language

Croat

Telephone

The country code is 00 385.

Money

Currency: Kuna (Kn)
Banks: Mon-Fri 08.00-19.00.

Shops

Mainly Mon-Sat 08.00-20.00, although some close on Monday.

Public Holidays

New Year's Day; Epiphany 6 Jan; Good Friday; Easter Monday; Labour Day 1 May; Parliament Day 30 May; Day of Anti-Fascist Victory 22 June; Statehood Day 25 June; Thanksgiving Day 5 Aug; Assumption 15 Aug; Independence Day 8 Oct; All Saints 1 Nov, Christmas 25, 26 Dec.

Motoring

Croatia is proceeding with a vast road improvement programme. There are still some roads which leave a lot to be desired but things have improved dramatically. Roads along the coast can become heavily congested in summer and queues are possible at border crossings. Tolls: some motorways, bridges and tunnels. Cars towing a caravan or trailer must carry two warning triangles. It is illegal to overtake military convoys.

see campsite map 9

Cres

Camping Kovacine

Melin I/20, HR-51557 Cres (Kvarner) T: 051 573 150. E: campkovacine@kovacine.com

alanrogers.com/CR6765

Camping Kovacine is located on a peninsula on the beautiful Kvarner island of Cres, just 2 km. from the town of the same name. The site has 750 numbered, mostly level pitches, of which 632 are for tourers (300 with 12A electricity). On sloping ground, partially shaded by mature olive and pine trees, pitching is on the large, open spaces between the trees. Some places have views of the Valun lagoon. Kovacine is partly an FKK (naturist) site, which is quite common in Croatia, and has a pleasant atmosphere. Here one can enjoy local live music on a stage close to the pebble beach (Blue Flag), where there is also a restaurant and bar. The site has its own beach, part concrete, part pebbles, and a jetty for mooring boats and fishing. It is close to the historic town of Cres, the main town on the island, which offers a rich history of fishing, shipyards and authentic Kvarner-style houses. There are also several bars, restaurants and shops.

Facilities

Modern, comfortable toilet blocks (two refurbished) offer British style toilets, equipped with solar power, open plan washbasins (some cabins for ladies) and hot showers. Private family bathroom for hire. Facilities for disabled visitors plus facilities for children. Laundry sinks and washing machine. Fridge box hire. Motorcaravan service point. Car wash. Mini-marina and boat crane. Supermarket. Bar, restaurant and pizzeria. Playground. Daily children's club. Evening shows with live music. Boat launching. Fishing. Diving centre. Motorboat hire. WiFi (free). Airport transfers. Off site: Wellness and fitness centre 0.5 km. Historic town of Cres with bars, restaurants and shops 2 km.

Open: 31 March - 15 October.

Directions

From Rijeka take no. 2 road south towards Labin and take ferry to Cres at Brestova. Continue to Cres and follow site signs. GPS: 44.96188, 14.39650

Charges 2012

Per unit incl. 2 persons and electricity	€ 16.90 - € 34.40
extra person	€ 5.70 - € 11.60
child (3-12 yrs)	€ 2.70 - € 4.80
dog	free - € 3.00

Dubrovnik

Camping Solitudo

Vatroslava Lisinskog 17, HR-20000 Dubrovnik (Dalmatia) T: 020 448 686.
E: camping-dubrovnik@valamar.com **alanrogers.com/CR6890**

Solitudo is located on the north side of Dubrovnik. There are 238 pitches, all for touring units, all with 12A electricity and 30 with water, arranged on four large fields that are opened according to demand. Field D is mainly used for tents and pitches here are small. Field A has pitches of up to 120 sq.m. and takes many motorcaravans (long leads required). From some pitches here there are beautiful views of the mountains and the impressive Dr. Franjo Tudman Bridge. All pitches are numbered, some are on terraces and most are shaded by a variety of mature trees.

Facilities

Attractively decorated, clean and modern toilet blocks have British style toilets, open washbasins and controllable, hot showers. Good facilities for disabled visitors. Laundry. Motorcaravan service point. Shop. Attached restaurant/bar. Snack bar. Tennis. Minigolf. Fishing. Bicycle hire. Beach with pedalo, beach chair, kayak and jet ski hire. Excursions organised to the Elafiti Islands. WiFi. Off site: Outdoor pool, bar, disco and restaurant 500 m.

Open: 1 April - 1 November.

Directions

From Split follow no. 8 road south towards Dubrovnik. Site is very well signed, starting 110 km. before reaching Dubrovnik, and throughout the city. GPS: 42.661883, 18.07135

Charges guide

Per person	€ 3.74 - € 7.00
child (4-10 yrs)	free - € 4.90
pitch with services	€ 9.63 - € 15.30
dog	€ 2.92 - € 4.73

Camping Cheques accepted.

CROATIA
KVARNER
CAMP KOVAČINE
CRES-CHERSO
A crystal clear sea, beautiful beaches and pine and olive trees which provide plenty of shade, make Kovacine a unique holiday destination. The campsite is situated on the Cres peninsula and is close to the village with the same name. There are 850 pitches which offer all the comfort you might wish. Room (with breakfast), direct on the beach with sea view.
New mobile homes (for 2 and 4–6 persons) – the freedom of camping with all the comforts of home.
We offer you a range of facilities:
• New, modern sanitary facilities (solar energy)
• Bar, buffet, restaurant, self service shop
• Mini-marina and boat crane
• First aid service
• Animation for children
• Sport facilities
• Diving and diving school
• Free WiFi
• Ferry costs refunded for 10 or 18 nights stay
• Special offers in low season: 7=6, 14=12 nights
NEW: Shuttle service/ Airport-transfer: Airport Rijeka – Cres and back: only € 30,–/person
Camping »Kovačine« Cres • HR-51557 Cres • Tel. 00-385/51/573-150
Fax 00-385/51/571-086 • campkovacine@kovacine.com • www.camp-kovacine.com

Fazana

Camping Bi-Village

Dragonja 115, HR-52212 Fazana (Istria) T: 052 300 300. E: info@bivillage.com

alanrogers.com/CR6745

Camping Bi-Village is a large holiday village in an attractive location close to the historic town of Pula and opposite the islands of the Brioni National Park. From the beach superb sunsets can be observed as the sun sinks below the sea's horizon. The site is landscaped with many flowers, shrubs and rock walls and offers over 1,000 pitches for touring units (the remainder taken by bungalows and chalets). The campsite is separated from the holiday bungalows by the main site road which runs from the entrance to the beach. Pitches are set in long rows accessed by gravel lanes, slightly sloping towards the sea, with only the bottom rows having shade from mature trees and good views over the Adriatic. The pitches are separated by young trees and shrubs. Bi-Village has 800 m. of pebble beach, but also offers three attractive swimming pools, one heated, with a fun pool, slides and flumes. At the top end of the site is a commercial centre with a supermarket, shops, restaurants and bars. During the high season a 30-strong team provides entertainment and activities.

Facilities

Four modern toilet blocks with toilets, open plan washbasins and controllable hot showers. Child-size washbasins. Baby room. Facilities for disabled visitors. Washing machine. Shopping centre (1/5-11/10). Bars (1/5-30/9) and restaurants. Bazaar. Gelateria. Pastry shop. Three swimming pools. Playground on gravel. Playing field. Trampolines. Motorboats and pedaloes for hire. Boat launching. Games hall. Sports tournaments and entertainment organised. Massage. Internet point. WiFi in some areas (charged). Dogs are not permitted on the beach. Off site: Historic towns of Pula and Rovinj are close. Fishing 3 km. Riding 15 km.

Open: 31 March - 10 November.

Directions

Follow no. 2 road south from Rijeka to Pula. In Pula follow site signs. Site is close to Fazana. GPS: 44.91717, 13.81105

Charges 2012

Per unit incl. 2 persons and electricity	€ 14.00 - € 40.00
extra person	€ 4.00 - € 10.00
dog	€ 3.00 - € 6.00
child (7-14 yrs)	€ 3.50 - € 7.00

Camping Cheques accepted.

Funtana

Naturist Camping Istra

Grgeti 35, HR-52452 Funtana (Istria) T: 052 465 010. E: camping@valamar.com

alanrogers.com/CR6726

Located in the tiny and picturesque village of Funtana, this peaceful site is part of the Camping on the Adriatic group. Istra has a fine array of facilities and, although there is no pool, it is surrounded by sparkling sea water on three sides. The formally marked pitches ring the peninsula and some are directly at the water's edge giving great views of the island off to the south (early booking is advised). There are 1,000 pitches on site with 745 for touring, most with ample shade and varying in size from about 60-120 sq.m. The ground is undulating and some areas have been cut into low terraces.

Facilities

Three old and three new sanitary buildings provide toilets, washbasins, showers (hot and cold), hair dryers and some facilities for disabled campers. Laundry facilities. Small supermarket. Restaurant and bars. Play areas. Entertainment for children in high season. Organised sport. Minigolf. Tennis. Massage. WiFi near reception. Dogs are allowed in some areas. Off site: Fishing. Shops and restaurants in Funtana, a short walk from the gate. Riding 1 km. Porec 7 km. with regular bus service from the village.

Open: 1 April - 8 October.

Directions

Site is signed off the Porec - Vrsar road 6 km. south of Porec in Funtana. Access for large units could be difficult when turning off the main road from the direction of Porec. If so, go past signed turning and turn around in nightclub car park a few metres further on. GPS: 45.17464, 13.59869

Charges guide

Per unit incl. 2 persons and electricity	€ 15.70 - € 29.50
incl. full services	€ 17.10 - € 31.50
extra person	€ 3.80 - € 7.20

Krk

Camping Jezevac

HR-51500 Krk (Kvarner) T: 051 221 081. E: jezevac@valamar.com

alanrogers.com/CR6757

Camping Jezevac is an excellent and well maintained seaside site, close to the pretty town of Krk. It is a large site extending to over 11 hectares and is built on a hillside at the western side of the town. The 584 pitches, all for touring are mainly on level terraces with plenty of shade and some enjoy views of the bay below. All have 10A electricity, 120 are fully serviced. Some premium beach side pitches are available, with water and electricity, but waste water from these plots has to be taken to drainage points further up the site, which can be a problem. The toilet blocks were completely modernised and decorated to a high standard for 2010.

Facilities

Heated toilet block with hot showers. Washing machines. Shops (1/4-15/10). Restaurants (1/5-1/10) and bars. Takeaway (1/5-30/9). Tennis. Playground. Activity and entertainment programmes and a children's club (May-Sept). Fishing. Bicycle hire. Boat launching and sailing. Max. 1 dog. Off site: Sports centre 300 m. Shops, bars and restaurants in Krk.

Open: Easter - 15 October.

Directions

From the toll bridge onto Krk, follow signs to Krk town and the town centre. Take the second right turn and continue ahead for 2.2 km. At the first roundabout take the second exit. Continue for 600 m. following signs to Camp Jezevac. GPS: 45.01964, 14.57072

Charges guide

Per unit incl. 2 persons and electricity	€ 21.20 - € 35.60
extra person	€ 5.00 - € 6.90

Krk

Naturist Camping Politin

Politin bb, HR-51500 Krk (Kvarner) T: 051 221 351. E: camping@valamar.com

alanrogers.com/CR6758

Politin is an attractive naturist site in a secluded hillside setting on the wooded peninsula of Prniba, quite close to the centre of Krk. On arrival you are assured of a good welcome from the staff, who speak good English. There are 247 clearly defined and well spaced out touring pitches, mostly on level sandy terraces, all with 10A electricity, and ranging in size from 70-110 sq.m. Of these, 130 plots are fully serviced and include 96 with satellite TV connection. There are also 55 seasonal pitches that do not impinge on the touring units.

Facilities

Restaurant, bar and shop (all 1/5-30/9). Tennis. Playground. Children's activity programme (May-Sept). Fishing. Boat launching. Sailing. Free WiFi to most of site. Five mobile homes for rent. Payphones at reception. Off site: Fitness centre 1.5 km. Sports centre 2 km. Krk town. Buses from Krk serve other towns on the island.

Open: 22 April - 2 October.

Directions

Cross toll bridge from mainland to the island of Krk, head for the island's capital, Krk (around 28 km). On arrival head to first traffic junction and turn right. After 500 m. turn left (beyond petrol station). Continue on this road for 800 m. to site. Site is well signed. GPS: 45.02440, 14.59280

Charges guide

Per unit incl. 2 persons and electricity	€ 20.40 - € 37.70
extra person	€ 4.80 - € 6.90

Labin

Camping Marina

Sveta Marina bb, HR-52220 Labin (Istria) T: 052 879 058. E: camping@valamar.com

alanrogers.com/CR6747

Camping Marina is a very quiet site with a somewhat steep approach. Overlooked by high, tree clad hills and adjoining a small bay, there are views of the rocky coast and the island of Cres. The 293 pitches are of all types, from those in the central area on level marked areas with electricity and water, to the cliff top pitches on the outskirts of the site. The particularly clear wate,r where there are shipwrecks and caves to explore, has made Marina a haven for divers and the campsite diving club, which has a diving school, is a past winner of Croatia's best diving club award.

Facilities

The single toilet block houses British style toilets, free controllable showers and washbasins. Baby room, Facilities for disabled campers. Washing machine and ironing area. Motorcaravan service point and points for washing diving/snorkelling equipment. Restaurant/bar. Play area. WiFi. Dog shower and garden. Off site: Well stocked supermarket at start of entrance road to site. Places to visit are Lapin, the old town. Rabac, a seaside resort popular during the time of Tito, with hotels, restaurants, bars and a small harbour.

Open: 4 April - 4 October.

Directions

Site is 10 km. south/southeast of Labin. From the E751/21 Pula - Opatija road turn off to Lapin and follow signs towards Rabac. On outskirts of Labin site is signed sharp right and up a climbing cobbled road. Follow signs for Marina SV. Turn off the country road for the site and Marina SV is well signed to the left. GPS: 45.033391, 14.157976

Charges guide

Per person	€ 3.80 - € 5.70
child (4-10 yrs)	free - € 3.30
pitch	€ 5.80 - € 18.90

Nin

Zaton Holiday Resort - Camp

Draznikova ulica 76 t, HR-23232 Nin (Dalmatia) T: 023 280 215. E: camping@zaton.hr

alanrogers.com/CR6782

Zaton Holiday Resort is a newly built, family holiday park, close to the historic town of Nin and just a few kilometres from the ancient city of Zadar. This park itself is more like a large village and has every amenity one can think of for a holiday on the Dalmatian north coast. The village is divided into two areas separated by a shopping centre and a large parking area, one for campers close to the sea, the other for a complex with holiday bungalows. Zaton has 1,030 mostly level pitches for tourers, all with electricity, water and waste water.

Facilities

Five modern and one refurbished toilet blocks have British and Turkish style toilets, washbasins (some in cabins) and controllable hot showers. Facilities for disabled visitors. Campers' kitchen. Motorcaravan service point. Car wash. Shopping centre. Restaurants, bars (all season) and kiosks. Water play area for older children. Heated swimming pool. Mini-car track. Riding. Trim track. Scuba diving. Professional entertainment team (high season). Teen club. Games hall. Internet point. Live shows on stage by the beach. Off site: Historic towns of Zadar and Nin.

Open: 1 May - 30 September.

Directions

From Rijeka take no. 2 road south and leave at exit for Zadar. Drive north towards Nin and Zaton Holiday Resort is signed a few kilometres before Nin. GPS: 44.234767, 15.164367

Charges 2012

Per unit incl. 2 persons and electricity	€ 20.80 - € 60.50
extra person	€ 5.40 - € 11.10
child (1-11 yrs acc. to age)	€ 3.10 - € 8.80
dog	€ 4.70 - € 9.30

Novigrad

Camping Mareda

Mareda, HR-52466 Novigrad (Istria) T: 052 735 291. E: camping@laguna-novigrad.hr

alanrogers.com/CR6713

Backed by oak woods and acres of vineyards, Camping Mareda is located on the coast just north of the small picturesque town of Novigrad. The site is on hilly ground with 800 sloping grass and gravel pitches, most with shade from mature trees and some with views of the sea. There are 600 pitches for touring units, all with 16A electricity and 28 with electricity, water and drainage. Some are marked and numbered in two areas near the sea, the remainder are for free camping in other areas of the site where it may be difficult to find space in high season.

Facilities

Four modern toilet blocks with British and Turkish style toilets, open plan washbasins and hot showers. Child-size toilets and basins. Laundry with sinks and washing machine. Motorcaravan service point. Supermarket. Coffee bar and bar with terrace. Restaurant. Play area. Tennis. Fishing. Boats, kayaks, canoes and pedaloes for hire. Games hall with video games. Organised entertainment. WiFi. Off site: Bicycle hire 4 km. Golf 10 km.

Open: 1 May - 30 September.

Directions

From Novigrad travel north towards Umag. After 4 km. the site is signed to the left. GPS: 45.34363, 13.54815

Charges guide

Per person	€ 4.00 - € 6.90
child (5-9 yrs)	free - € 3.80
pitch	€ 3.00 - € 11.50
electricity	€ 3.00

Plitvicka Jezera

Autocamp Korana

HR-47246 Dreznik Grad (Central) T: 053 751 888. E: info@np-plitvicka-jezera.hr

alanrogers.com/CR6650

This is an excellent site for a visit to the famous Plitvice Lakes National Park, in the far eastern part of the country and is only 6 km. from Entrance Gate no. 1. Within the large, park-like environment there are 540 unmarked pitches, and caravans and motorcaravans have a choice of using tarmac hardstandings close to the entrance, or pitching on grass plots with spectacular views at the back of the site. All plots have 16A electricity. The toilets and showers are adequate and clean but there are no other facilities available – no washing machines, fridges, Internet, swimming pools, sport or other forms of entertainment. Most people stay here for only one or two nights, so every morning and afternoon there can be queues at reception.

Facilities

The toilet blocks include facilities for disabled visitors. Chemical disposal and motorcaravan service point. Large restaurant. Shop is opened in the morning and afternoon and a dedicated information office with details about the National Park is open all day. WiFi in the information office area. 47 furnished cabins for hire. Off site: The wonderful National Park with its spectacular lakes and waterfalls (1- and 2-day visitors' tickets available). Walking. Cycling.

Open: 1 April - 15 October.

Directions

Take road from Karlovac to Plitvicka. Camp Korana is on the left, just past village of Grabovac. Site is north of the park area just before the village of Seliste and is signed. GPS: 44.95043, 15.64114

Charges guide

Per person	€ 7.00 - € 9.00
child (7-12 yrs)	€ 4.90 - € 6.30
pitch incl. electricity	€ 6.00

Camping Cheques accepted.

Porec

Camping Lanterna

Lanterna 1, Tar-Vabriga, HR-52465 Porec (Istria) T: **052 465 010**. E: **camping@valamar.com**

alanrogers.com/CR6716

This is a well organised site and one of the largest in Croatia with high standards and an amazing selection of activities, and is part of the Camping on the Adriatic group. Set in 80 hectares with over 3 km. of beach, there are 2,851 pitches, of which 1,887 are for touring units. All have electricity (10A) and fresh water, and 225 also have waste water drainage. Pitches are 80-120 sq.m. with some superb locations right on the sea, although these tend to be taken first so it is advisable to book ahead. Some of the better pitches are in a 'reserved booking' area. There are wonderful coastal views from some of the well shaded terraced pitches.

Facilities

The sixteen sanitary blocks are clean and of good quality. Children's facilities and babycare areas, some Turkish style WCs, hot showers, and some blocks with facilities for disabled campers. Three supermarkets. Fresh fish shop. Four restaurants, bars and snack bars and fast food outlets. Swimming pool and two paddling pools. Sandpit and play areas. Entertainment (high season). Tennis. Bicycle hire. Watersports. Boat hire. Minigolf. Riding. Internet café. Jetty and ramp for boats. WiFi (free). Mobile homes for rent. Dogs are accepted in certain areas. Off site: Hourly bus service. Fishing. Riding 500 m.

Open: 1 April - 10 October.

Directions

The turn to Lanterna is well signed off the Novigrad to Porec road about 8 km. south of Novigrad. Continue for about 2 km. along the turn off road towards the coast and the campsite is on the right hand side. GPS: 45.29672, 13.59442

Charges guide

Per unit incl. 2 persons and electricity	€ 16.90 - € 31.00
with full services	€ 18.30 - € 32.60

Prices for pitches by the sea are higher.

Porec

Naturist Resort Solaris

Lanterna bb, HR-52440 Porec (Istria) T: **052 465 110**. E: **camping-porec@valamar.com**

alanrogers.com/CR6718

This naturist site is part of the Camping on the Adriatic group and has a most pleasant atmosphere. When we visited in high season there were lots of happy people having fun. A pretty cove and lots of beach frontage with cool pitches under trees makes the site very attractive. Of the 1,333 pitches, 550 are available for touring, with 600 long stay units. There are 145 fully serviced pitches (100 sq.m) available on a 'first come, first served' basis, with an ample supply of electricity hook-ups (10-16A) and plentiful water points. As this is a naturist site, there are certain rules that must be followed.

Facilities

Eleven excellent, fully equipped toilet blocks provide toilets, washbasins and showers. Some blocks have facilities for disabled visitors. Washing machines and ironing facilities. Restaurants, grills and fast food, and supermarkets. Swimming pool. Tennis. Bicycle hire. Riding. Play areas. Boat launching. Car wash. Entertainment. WiFi (free). Dogs allowed in certain areas, but not on beach. Off site: Excursions. Riding and fishing.

Open: 1 April - 10 October.

Directions

Site is 8 km. south of Novigrad on the Novigrad - Porec road. Turn towards the coast signed Lanterna. Continue straight on down this road and after passing the security barrier, turn left to Solaris. GPS: 45.29126, 13.5848

Charges guide

Per unit incl. 2 persons and electricity	€ 15.60 - € 27.20
extra person	€ 4.10 - € 7.10

Porec

Autokamp Zelena Laguna

HR-52440 Porec (Istria) T: **052 410 101**. E: **mail@plavalaguna.hr**

alanrogers.com/CR6722

Zelena Laguna (green lagoon) is a well run and long established site with 540 touring pitches, all with 10A electricity, 42 being fully serviced. Access to the pitches is by hard surfaced roads with gravel side roads. There are many mature trees providing plenty of shade and hedges separate most pitches. Part of the site is on a peninsular with terraced pitches and the remainder are either on level or slightly sloping ground. A path circles the peninsular below which are paved waterside sunbathing areas. Those to the right of the site are within easy reach of the cocktail bar. Further to the right is a small harbour, attractive restaurant and swimming pool.

Facilities

Six modern and well maintained sanitary blocks with free controllable hot showers. Toilets are mostly British style. Facilities for disabled campers. Supermarket and shop. Several restaurants and snack bars. Swimming pool. Tennis (tuition available). Bicycle hire. Boat hire and launching. Riding. Entertainment. Off site: Small market and parade of shops selling beach wares, souvenirs etc. immediately outside site. Road train into Porec.

Open: One week before Easter - 7 October.

Directions

Site entrance is 2 km. south of Porec on the Vrsar - Porec coastal road. It is very well signed and part of a large multiple hotel complex. GPS: 45.19529, 13.58927

Charges guide

Per unit incl. 2 persons and electricity	€ 15.30 - € 30.20
extra person	€ 4.10 - € 7.80

Primosten

Camp Adriatic

Huljerat bb, HR-22202 Primosten (Dalmatia) T: 022 571 223. E: info@camp-adriatic.hr

alanrogers.com/CR6845

As we drove south down the Dalmatian coast road, we looked across a clear turquoise bay and saw a few tents, caravans and motorcaravans camped under some trees. A short distance later we were at the entrance of Camp Adriatic. With 530 pitches that slope down to the sea, the site is deceptive and enjoys a one kilometre beach frontage which is ideal for snorkelling and diving. Most pitches are level and have shade from pine trees. There are 212 numbered pitches and 288 unnumbered, all with 10/16A electricity. Close to the delightful town of Primosten (with a taxi boat service in high season) the site boasts good modern amenities and a fantastic location.

Facilities

Four modern sanitary blocks provide clean toilets, hot showers and washbasins. Facilities for disabled visitors. Bathroom for children. Washing machine and dryer. Kitchen facilities. Small supermarket (15/5-30/9). Restaurant, bar and takeaway (all season). Sports centre. Miniclub. Beach. Diving school. Sailing school and boat hire. Entertainment programme in July/Aug. WiFi in reception area (charged). Off site: Primosten 2.5 km. Riding 15 km. Sibenic 25 km.

Open: 1 May - 15 October.

Directions

Take the A1 motorway south and leave at the Sibenik exit. Follow the 33 road into Sibenik and then go south along the coast road (no. 8), signed Primosten. Site is 2.5 km. north of Primosten. GPS: 43.606517, 15.92095

Charges guide

Per person	Kn 34.00 - 60.00
child (3-12 yrs)	Kn 25.00 - 45.00
pitch incl. car and electricity	Kn 54.00 - 105.00
dog	Kn 18.00 - 32.00

Camping Cheques accepted.

Porec

Camping Bijela Uvala

Bijela Uvala, Zelena Laguna, HR-52440 Porec (Istria) T: 052 410 551. E: mail@plavalaguna.hr

alanrogers.com/CR6724

Bijela Uvala is a large friendly campsite with an attractive waterside location and an extensive range of facilities. The direct sea access makes the site very popular in high season. The 2,000 pitches, 1,476 for touring, are compact and due to the terrain some have excellent sea views and breezes, however as usual these are the most sought after, so book early. They range from 60-120 sq.m. and all have electricity and water connections. Some are formal with hedging, some are terraced and most have good shade from established trees or wooded areas. There are also very informal areas where unmarked pitches are on generally uneven ground.

Facilities

Eight sanitary blocks are clean and well equipped with mainly British style WCs. Free hot showers. Washing machines. Facilities for disabled visitors. Motorcaravan service point. Gas. Fridge boxes. Three restaurants, three fast food cafés, two bars and a bakery. Large well equipped supermarket and a shop. Two swimming pool complexes, one with a medium size pool and the other a larger lagoon style with fountains. Tennis. Playground. Amusements. TV room. Entertainment centre for active children. WiFi (charged). Off site: Zelena Laguna campsite facilities. Sports complex 100 m. Naturist beach 25 m.

Open: 19 March - 7 October.

Directions

The site adjoins Zelena Laguna. From the main Porec to Vrsar coast road turn off towards coast and the town of Zelena Laguna about 4 km. south of Porec and follow campsite signs.
GPS: 45.19149, 13.59686

Charges guide

Per unit incl. 2 persons and electricity	€ 15.30 - € 30.20
extra person	€ 4.10 - € 7.80
child (4-10 yrs)	free - € 5.40
dog	€ 3.20 - € 6.00

Pula

Camping Brioni

Puntizela 155, HR-52100 Pula (Istria) T: 052 517 490. E: camping@valamar.com

alanrogers.com/CR6744

Situated on a small peninsula overlooking the Brioni archipelago (a National Park comprising 14 islands) and within easy reach of Pula, Camping Brioni is a quiet and useful base from which to tour in a scenically attractive and historically interesting region. The site has 420 touring pitches under ample shade, all with 10A electricity and 272 with fresh water taps. On mainly level grass and gravel, the pitches are numbered with some terracing. Part of the site is devoted to a youth hostel which shares the campsites facilities. A diving club is based on the site, the sea water being clear; ideal for snorkelling.

Facilities

Three sanitary blocks, one with facilities for disabled visitors. Cleaning and maintenance needed some attention when we visited. Baby room. Laundry room. Small supermarket and kiosk selling fruit, vegetables and bread. Restaurant. Beachside snack bar. Play area. Boat rental. Internet access. Off site: Pula, Brioni National Park.

Open: All year.

Directions

Site is 7 km. northwest of Pula. Heading north on the road running alongside the harbour in Pula (Trscanska ulinka) turn left at the roundabout towards Rijeka. After 800 m. site is signed to the left (west).
GPS: 44.89812, 13.80833

Charges guide

Per unit incl. 2 persons and electricity	€ 13.60 - € 32.70
extra person	€ 5.10 - € 11.00
child (6-11 yrs)	free - € 5.50

Rovinj

Camping Amarin

Monsena bb, HR-52210 Rovinj (Istria) T: 052 802 000. E: ac-amarin@maistra.hr

alanrogers.com/CR6730

Situated 4 km. from the centre of the lovely old port town of Rovinj, this site has much to offer. The complex is part of the Maistra group. It has 12.6 hectares of land and is adjacent to the Amarin bungalow complex. Campers can take advantage of the facilities afforded by both areas. There are 670 pitches for touring units on various types of ground, all between 80-120 sq.m. Most are separated by foliage, 10A electricity is available. A rocky beach backed by a grassy sunbathing area is very popular, but the site has its own superb, supervised round pool with corkscrew slide plus a splash pool for children. Boat owners have a mooring area and launching ramp and a breakwater is popular with sunbathers. The port of Rovinj contains many delights, particularly if you are able to contend with the hundreds of steps which lead to the church above the town from where the views are well worth the climb.

Facilities

Thirteen respectable toilet blocks have a mixture of British style and Turkish toilets. Half the washbasins have hot water. Some showers have hot water, the rest have cold and are outside. Some blocks have a unit for disabled visitors. Fridge box hire. Laundry service. Motorcaravan service point. Supermarket. Market. Two restaurants, taverna, pizzeria and terrace grill. Swimming pool. Flume and splash pool. Watersports. Bicycle hire. Fishing (permit). Daily entertainment. Hairdresser. Massage. Barbecues are not permitted. Dogs are not allowed on beach. WiFi in some areas (charged). Off site: Minibus service to Rovinj. Excursions from site including Venice.

Open: 25 April - 27 September.

Directions

Follow signs towards Rovinj and if approaching from the north turn off about 2 km. before the town towards Amarin and Valalta. Then follow signs to Amarin and the campsite. Watch for a left turn after about 3 km. where signs are difficult to see.
GPS: 45.10876, 13.61988

Charges guide

Per unit incl. 2 persons and electricity	€ 15.50 - € 31.30
extra person	€ 4.60 - € 8.40
child (5-11 yrs)	€ 3.00 - € 5.20

For stays less than 3 nights in high season add 10%.

Rovinj

Naturist Camping Valalta

alan rogers Runner up 2011 Awards

Cesta za Valaltu - Lim 7, HR-52210 Rovinj (Istria) T: 052 804 800. E: valalta@valalta.hr

alanrogers.com/CR6731

This is a most impressive site for up to 6,000 naturist campers, which has a pleasant, open feel. The passage through reception is efficient and this feeling is maintained around the well organised site. A friendly, family atmosphere is to be found here as Valalta is a family oriented campsite. All pitches are the same price with 16A electricity, although they vary in size and surroundings. The variations include shade, views, sand, grass, sea frontage, level ground, slopes and terracing. It is not possible to reserve a particular pitch and campers do move pitches at will. The impressive pool is in lagoon style with water features and cascades.

Facilities

Twenty high quality new or refurbished sanitary blocks of which four are smaller units of plastic 'pod' construction. Hot showers (coin operated). Facilities for disabled campers. Washing machines and dryers. Supermarket. Four restaurants (one specialising in seafood). Pizzeria. Two bars. Large lagoon style pool complex. Beauty salon. Fitness club. Massage. Minigolf. Tennis. Sailing. Play area. Bicycle hire. Beach volleyball. Marina with full services. Internet. Entertainment all season. Kindergarten. Dogs are not accepted. Off site: Riding 7 km.

Open: 25 April - 26 September.

Directions

Site is on the coast 8 km. north of Rovinj. Approaching from the north turn inland (follow signs to Rovinj) to drive around the Limski Kanal. Then follow signs towards Valalta about 2 km. east of Rovinj. Site is at the end of the road and is well signed. GPS: 45.12235, 13.632083

Charges 2012

Per unit incl. 2 persons and electricity	€ 18.70 - € 42.00
extra person	€ 5.10 - € 11.00

Rovinj

Camping Polari

Polari bb, HR-52210 Rovinj (Istria) T: 052 801 501. E: polari@maistra.hr

alanrogers.com/CR6732

This 60-hectare site has excellent facilities for both textile and naturist campers, the latter in an area of 12 hectares to the left of the main site. There is shade here from a good covering of trees. In all, the site has 1,650 pitches for touring units which are level with some shade. All have access to 10A electricity. There is something for everyone to enjoy here or you might prefer to just relax in this quiet location. An impressive swimming pool complex is child friendly with large paddling areas. The ancient town of Rovinj is well worth a visit, although parking is difficult. It is best reached via the 4.5 km. coastal cycle path or by bus from the campsite. Part of the Maistra group, a massive improvement programme has been undertaken and the result makes it a very attractive option. Enjoy a meal on the huge restaurant terrace with panoramic views of the sea.

Facilities

All the sanitary facilities have been renovated to a high standard with plenty of hot water and good showers. Washing machines and dryers. Laundry service including ironing. Motorcaravan service point. Two shops, one large and one small, one restaurant and snack bar. Tennis. Minigolf. Children's entertainment with all major European languages spoken. Bicycle hire. Watersports. Sailing school. Off site: Riding 1 km. Five buses daily to and from Rovinj 3 km. Golf 30 km.

Open: 1 April - 2 October.

Directions

From any access road to Rovinj look for red signs to AC Polari (amongst other destinations). The site is about 3 km. south of Rovinj.
GPS: 45.06286, 13.67489

Charges guide

Per unit incl. 2 persons and electricity	€ 18.00 - € 36.10
extra person (18-64 yrs)	€ 5.00 - € 9.30
child (5-17 yrs)	€ 4.00 - € 7.50
dog	€ 3.10 - € 6.50

For stays less than 3 nights in high season add 20%.

Rovinj

Camping Vestar

Vestar bb, HR-52210 Rovinj (Istria) T: 052 829 150. E: vestar@maistra.hr

alanrogers.com/CR6733

Camping Vestar, just 5 km. from the historic harbour town of Rovinj, is one of the rare sites in Croatia with a partly sandy beach. Right behind the beach is a large area, attractively landscaped with young trees and shrubs, with grass for sunbathing. The site has 650 large pitches, of which 500 are for tourers, all with 6/10A electricity (the rest being taken by seasonal units and 60 pitches for tour operators). It is largely wooded with good shade and from the bottom row of pitches there are views of the sea. Pitching is on two separate fields, one for free camping, the other with numbered pitches. The pitches at the beach are in a half circle around the shallow bay, making it safe for children to swim. Vestar has a small marina and a jetty for mooring small boats and excursions to the islands are arranged. There is a miniclub and live music with dancing at one of the two bar/restaurants in the evenings. The restaurants all have open-air terraces, one covered with vines to protect you from the hot sun.

Facilities

Six modern and one refurbished toilet blocks with British style toilets, open washbasins and controllable hot showers. Child size facilities. Baby rooms. Family bathroom. Facilities for disabled visitors. Laundry service. Fridge box hire. Motorcaravan services. Shop. Two bar/restaurants. Large swimming pool. Playground. Fishing. Boat and pedalo hire. Miniclub (5-11 yrs). Excursions. Internet access in reception. WiFi.

Open: 23 April - 1 October.

Directions

Site is on the coast 4 km. southeast of Rovinj. From Rovinj travel south in the direction of Pula. After 4 km. turn right following campsite signs.
GPS: 45.05432, 13.68568

Charges guide

Per person	€ 5.00 - € 9.90
child (5-18 yrs)	free - € 7.90
pitch incl. electricity	€ 7.00 - € 25.00
dog	€ 3.10 - € 6.50

For latest campsite news, availability and prices visit
alanrogers.com

Rovinj

Camping Valdaliso

Monsena bb, HR-52210 Rovinj (Istria) T: **052 805 505**. E: **info@rovinjturist.hr**

alanrogers.com/CR6736

Camping Valdaliso has its affiliated hotel in the centre of the site. The pitches are mostly flat with shade from pine trees and the site is divided into three sections all with 16A electricity. The choice of formal numbered pitches, informal camping or proximity to the sea impacts on the prices. The kilometre plus of pebble beach has crystal clear water. The entertainment programme is extremely professional and there is a lot to do at Valdaliso, which is aimed primarily at families. The variety of activities here and the bonus of the use of the hotel make this a great choice for campers. The fine Barabiga restaurant within the hotel offers superb Istrian and fish cuisine and the pool is also within the hotel. You are close to the beautiful old town of Rovinj and parts of this site enjoy views of the town. A water taxi makes exploring Rovinj very easy, compared with the impossible parking for private cars. A bus service is also provided but this involves considerable walking. Alternatively it is a 3 km. cycle ride.

Facilities

Two large, clean sanitary blocks have hot showers. The north-eastern block has facilities for disabled campers. Hotel facilities. Shop. Pizzeria. Restaurant. Tennis. Fitness centre. Bicycle hire. Games room. Children's games. Summer painting courses. Exchange. Boat rental. Watersports. Boat launching. Fishing. Diving school. Internet in both receptions. WiFi (charged). Water taxi. Bus service. Dogs are not accepted. Off site: Town 1 km.

Open: 16 April - 8 October.

Directions

Site is 7 km. north of Rovinj on the local road between Rovinj and Monsena.
GPS: 45.104267, 13.625183

Charges guide

Per unit incl. 2 persons and electricity	€ 15.50 - € 33.00
extra person	€ 4.50 - € 8.50
child (5-12 yrs)	free - € 5.20

Savudrija

Autocamp Pineta

Istarska bb, HR-52475 Savudrija (Istria) T: **052 709 550.** E: **camp.pineta@istraturist.hr**

alanrogers.com/CR6711

This pleasant, quiet site is set under tall pines and has direct access to the sea over fairly level rocks. It is of medium size (17 hectares) and gets its name from its setting amongst a forest of fully mature pine trees around two sides of a coastal bay. There are 460 pitches of which 160 are occupied on a long stay basis. Pitches are numbered and are 50-120 sq.m. all having access to electricity (10A). This is a site for those who prefer cooler situations as the dense pines provide abundant shade. Those who like the peaceful life will enjoy this site. Sea bathing is easy from the site and sunbathing areas are on the rocks the whole length of the site.

Facilities

Toilet blocks have been refurbished to a high standard. Hot and cold showers. Mostly British style WCs and a few Turkish style. Excellent facilities for disabled campers. Fresh water at toilet blocks only. Motorcaravan service point. Supermarket. Six bars, three restaurants and snack bar. Tennis. Fishing (permit). Bicycle hire. Boat launching. Activities centre. Evening music. WiFi in some areas (charged). Off site: Gas is available in local garage 500 m. from site entrance. Riding 6 km. Sailing 9 km. Golf 12 km.

Open: 22 April - 25 September.

Directions

Site is 6 km. north of Umag. From Umag travel north following signs for Savundrija signs. In the village of Basanija, at the tourist office, turn left. Reception is 500 m. on the left. GPS: 45.48674, 13.49246

Charges guide

Per unit incl. 2 persons and electricity	€ 15.50 - € 30.20
extra person	€ 4.30 - € 7.70
child (5-11 yrs)	€ 2.10 - € 4.20

For stays less than 3 nights in high season add 10%.

Umag

Camping Stella Maris

Savudrijska cesta bb, HR-52470 Umag (Istria) T: **052 710 900.** E: **camp.stella.maris@istraturist.hr**

alanrogers.com/CR6712

This extremely large, sprawling site of 4.5 hectares is split by the Umag - Savudrija road. The camping site and reception is to the east of the road and the amazing Sol Stella Maris leisure complex, where the Croatian open tennis tournament is held (amongst other competitions), is to the west and borders the sea. Located some 2 km. from the centre of Umag, the site comprises some 575 pitches of which 60 are seasonal and 20 are for tour operators. They are arranged in rows on gently sloping ground, some are shaded. The pitches all have 10A electricity. The site's real strength is its attachment to the leisure complex, with numerous facilities available to campers.

Facilities

Three sanitary blocks of a very high standard. Hot water throughout. Excellent facilities for disabled visitors. Large supermarket. Huge range of restaurants, bars and snack bars. International tennis centre with pools and beach area. Watersports. Fishing (permit required from Umag). Entertainment programme for children. Communal barbecue areas. Excursions organised. Off site: Land train every 15 minutes into Umag and a local bus service to towns further along the coast. Riding 0.5 km. Golf 1 km.

Open: 23 April - 26 September.

Directions

Site is 2.5 km. north of Umag. On entering Umag look for signs on the main coast road to all campsites and follow the Stella Maris signs. GPS: 45.450417, 13.5222

Charges guide

Per unit incl. 2 persons and electricity	€ 11.50 - € 33.20
extra person	€ 3.50 - € 8.20
child (5-12 yrs)	€ 2.10 - € 4.40

For stays less than 3 nights in high season add 10%.

Umag

Camping Finida

Krizine 55a, HR-52470 Umag (Istria) T: **052 725 950.** E: **camp.finida@istraturist.hr**

alanrogers.com/CR6714

Finida is a small, fairly quiet and friendly site with good sanitary facilities and with easy access from the Umag-Novigrad road. The sea runs the length of the site and offers places to swim, either from a concrete jetty or from a small beach. The site is heavily wooded affording abundant shade and from the terrace of the bar/restaurant there are views over the sea. There are 285 marked pitches (80-100 sq.m), all with 10A electricity, 103 also have water and TV connection. Finida will appeal to those who prefer the cosiness of a smaller, friendly site.

Facilities

Three new toilet blocks contain mostly British style WCs and a few Turkish style. Facilities for disabled campers. Washing machines. Motorcaravan service point (a bit tight to drive onto). Small supermarket. Bar, snack bar and restaurant. Minigolf. Fishing (permit). Boats may be moored off the beach. Pedalos. Bicycle hire. Communal barbecue areas. WiFi in some areas (charged).
Off site: Buses into Umag and Novigrad. Riding 3 km.

Open: 23 April - 26 September.

Directions

Site is on the right off the Umag-Novigrad road, 4 km. south of Umag. GPS: 45.39263, 13.54196

Charges guide

Per unit incl. 2 persons and electricity	€ 16.00 - € 32.20
extra person	€ 4.30 - € 8.20
child (5-12 yrs)	€ 2.10 - € 4.40
dog	€ 2.10 - € 3.60

Umag

Camping Park Umag

Karigador bb, HR-52470 Umag (Istria) T: **052 725 040**. E: **camp.park.umag@istraturist.hr**

alanrogers.com/CR6715

This extremely large site is very well planned in that just 60% of the 127 hectares is used for the pitches, resulting in lots of open space around the pitch area. It is the largest of the Istraturist group of sites. Of the 2,090 pitches, 1,800 are for touring units, all with 10A electricity. Some pitches have shade. There are around 300 mobile homes, 70 for rent. Some noise is transmitted from the road alongside the site. The site is very popular with Dutch campers and a friendly and happy atmosphere prevails, even in the busiest times. The very long curved beach is of rock and shingle with grassy sunbathing areas. There are watersports on offer and a new swimming pool complex has four pools, cascades and fountains.

Facilities

Ten toilet blocks include two bathrooms with deep tubs. Two blocks have children's WCs and there are facilities for disabled campers. The site has plans to update these facilities. Fresh water and waste water points only at toilet blocks. Motorcaravan service point. Range of shops and supermarket. Bars, snack bars and restaurant (musical entertainment some evenings) all open early morning to midnight (one until the small hours). Swimming pool complex. Tennis. Fishing (permit from Umag). Minigolf. Watersports. WiFi (free in some areas). Off site: Bus service to Umag and Novigrad. Riding 3 km. Golf 20 km.

Open: 23 April - 26 September.

Directions

Site is on the Umag-Novigrad road about 6 km. south of Umag. Look for large signs.
GPS: 45.36707, 13.54716

Charges guide

Per unit incl. 2 persons and electricity	€ 19.00 - € 48.40
extra person	€ 4.90 - € 9.40
child (5-12 yrs)	€ 2.60 - € 5.20
dog	€ 2.10 - € 4.20

For stays less than 5 nights in high season add 20%.

Vrsar

Camping Porto Sole

Petalon 1, HR-52450 Vrsar (Istria) T: **052 426 500**. E: **petalon-portosole@maistra.hr**

alanrogers.com/CR6725

Located near the pretty town of Vrsar and its charming marina, Porto Sole is a large campsite with 800 pitches and is part of the Maistra group. The pitches vary; some are in the open with semi shade and are fairly flat, others are under a heavy canopy of pines on undulating land. There is some terracing near the small number of waterfront pitches. The site could be described as almost a clover leaf shape with one area for rental accommodation and natural woods, another for sporting facilities and the other two for pitches. There is a large water frontage and two tiny bays provide delightful sheltered rocky swimming areas. In peak season the site is buzzing with activity and the hub of the site is the pool and shopping arcade area where there is also a pub and both formal and informal eating areas. The food available is varied but simple with a tiny terrace restaurant by the water.

Facilities

The five toilet blocks with mostly British style WCs are kept very clean and well maintained. Facilities for disabled visitors and children. Washing machines and dryers. Large well stocked supermarket (1/5-15/9). Small shopping centre. Pub. Pizzeria. Formal and informal restaurants. Swimming pools (1/5-29/9). Play area (alongside beach). Boules. Tennis. Minigolf. Massage. Entertainment in season. Miniclub. Scuba-diving courses. Boat launching. Off site: Vrsar 500 m. Marina and sailing 1 km. Riding 3 km.

Open: 25 April - 3 October.

Directions

Follow signs towards Vrsar and take turn for Koversada, then follow campsite signs.
GPS: 45.142117, 13.602267

Charges guide

Per unit incl. 2 persons and electricity	€ 17.50 - € 42.50
extra person	€ 5.00 - € 8.00
child (5-12 yrs)	free - € 5.00
dog	€ 3.10 - € 6.50

Vrsar

Camping Valkanela

Valkanela, HR-52450 Vrsar (Istria) T: **052 445 216**. E: **valkanela@maistra.hr**

alanrogers.com/CR6727

Camping Valkanela is located in a beautiful green bay, right on the Adriatic Sea, between the villages of Vrsar and Funtana. It offers 1,300 pitches, all with 10A electricity. Pitches near the beach are numbered, have shade from mature trees and are slightly sloping towards the sea. Those towards the back of the site are on open fields without much shade and are not marked or numbered. Unfortunately, the number of pitches has increased dramatically over the years, many are occupied by seasonal campers and statics of every description, and these parts of the site are not very attractive. Most numbered pitches have water points close by, but the back pitches have to go to the toilet blocks for water. Access roads are gravel. For those who like activity, Valkanela has four gravel tennis courts, beach volleyball and opportunities for diving, water skiing and boat rental. There is a little marina for mooring small boats and a long rock and pebble private beach, with some grass lawns for sunbathing. It is a short stroll to the surrounding villages with their bars, restaurants and shops. There may be some noise nuisance from the disco outside the entrance and during high season the site can become very crowded.

Facilities

Fifteen toilet blocks of varying styles and ages have toilets, open style washbasins and controllable hot showers. Child-size toilets, basins and showers. Bathroom (free). Facilities for disabled visitors. Laundry with sinks and washing machines. Two supermarkets. Souvenir shops and newspaper kiosk. Bars and restaurants with dance floor and stage. Patisserie. Tennis. Minigolf. Fishing (with permit). Bicycle hire. Games room. Marina with boat launching. Boat and pedalo hire. Disco outside entrance. Daily entertainment programme for children up to 12 yrs. Excursions organised. Off site: Riding 2 km.

Open: 25 April - 3 October.

Directions

Site is 2 km. north of Vrsar. Follow campsite signs from Vrsar. GPS: 45.16522, 13.60723

Charges guide

Per person	€ 4.50 - € 7.00
child (5-18 yrs)	free - € 5.30
pitch incl. electricity	€ 5.50 - € 18.50
dog	€ 2.50 - € 6.00

Vrsar

Camping Orsera

Sv. Martin 2/1, HR-52450 Vrsar (Istria) T: **052 465 010**. E: **camping@valamar.com**

alanrogers.com/CR6728

This is a very attractive site with a 900 m. shoreline from which there are stunning views over the sea to the islands and very often there are spectacular sunsets. This 30-hectare site with direct access to the old fishing port of Vrsar has 575 pitches of which 433 are available to touring units. Marked and numbered, the pitches vary in size with 90 sq.m. being the average. There is some terracing but the pitches to the north of the site are on level ground and offer better views. Ample shade is provided by mature pines and oak trees. All pitches have 10/16A electricity.

Facilities

The modern and well maintained sanitary blocks have mainly British style WCs. Free showers, hot and cold water to washbasins. Some have facilities for disabled visitors. Facilities for babies and children. Motorcaravan service point. Laundry. Supermarket (1/5-15/9). Bar/restaurant and takeaway (1/5-15/9). Sports centre. Cinema. Bicycle hire. Fishing. Watersports (no jet skis). Only electric barbecues are permitted. Free WiFi over site. Off site: Shops in Vrsar (large shopping centre at Porec).

Open: 1 April - 8 October.

Directions

Site is on the main Porec (7 km) - Vrsar (1 km) road, well signed. GPS: 45.15548, 13.61032

Charges guide

Per unit incl. 2 persons and electricity	Kn 122.10 - 231.70
extra person	Kn 30.00 - 57.00
child (4-9 yrs)	free - Kn 40.90
dog	Kn 27.00 - 40.20

Prices for pitches by the sea are higher.

Vrsar

Naturist Park Koversada

Koversada, HR-52450 Vrsar (Istria) T: 052 441 378. E: koversada-camp@maistra.hr

alanrogers.com/CR6729

According to history, the first naturist on Koversada was the famous adventurer Casanova. Today Koversada is an enclosed holiday park for naturists with bungalows, 1,700 pitches (all with 10/16A electricity), a shopping centre and its own island. The main attraction of this site is the Koversada island, connected to the mainland by a small bridge. It is only suitable for tents, but has a restaurant and two toilet blocks. Between the island and the mainland is an enclosed, shallow section of water for swimming and, on the other side of the bridge, an area for mooring small boats. The pitches are of average size on grass and gravel ground and slightly sloping. Pitches on the mainland are numbered and partly terraced under mature pine and olive trees. Pitching on the island is haphazard, but there is also shade from mature trees. The bottom row of pitches on the mainland has views over the island and the sea. The site is surrounded by a long beach, part sand, part paved.

Facilities

Seventeen toilet blocks provide British and Turkish style toilets, washbasins and controllable hot showers. Child-size toilets and basins. Family bathroom (free). Facilities for disabled visitors. Laundry service. Motorcaravan service point. Supermarket. Kiosks with newspapers and tobacco. Several bars and restaurants. Tennis. Minigolf. Boats, surf boards, canoes and kayaks for hire. Tweety Club for children. Live music. Sports tournaments. Internet access in reception and WiFi on part of site (charged). Off site: Riding 2 km.

Open: 23 April - 24 September.

Directions

Site is just south of Vrsar. From Vrsar, follow site signs. GPS: 45.14288, 13.60527

Charges guide

Per unit incl. 2 persons and electricity	€ 18.00 - € 36.00
extra person	€ 5.00 - € 8.50
child (5-18 yrs)	free - € 6.00
dog	€ 3.10 - € 6.00

Czech Republic

The Czech Republic is a land full of fascinating castles, romantic lakes and valleys, picturesque medieval squares and famous spas. It is divided into two main regions, Bohemia to the west and Moravia in the east.

Although small, the Czech Republic is crammed with attractive places to explore. Indeed, since the new country first appeared on the map in 1993, Prague has become one the most popular cities to visit in Europe. Steeped in history with museums, architectural sights, art galleries and theatres, it is an enchanting place. The beautiful region of Bohemia, known for its Giant Mountains, is popular for hiking, skiing and other sports. The town of Karlovy Vary, world famous for its regenerative waters, is Bohemia's oldest spa town, with 12 hot springs containing elements that are said to treat digestive and metabolic ailments. It also has many picturesque streets to meander through and peaceful riverside walks. Moravia is quieter, the most favoured area of Brno and from here it is easy to explore historical towns such as Olomouc and Kromeriz. North of Brno is the Moravian Karst, with around 400 caves created by the underground Punkya River. Some caves are open to the public, with boat trips along the river and out of the caves.

CAPITAL: **Prague**

Tourist Office

Czech Tourist Authority
13 Harley Street, London W1G 9QG
Tel: 020 7631 0427 Fax: 020 7631 0419
Email: info-uk@czechtourism.com
Internet: www.visitczech.cz

Population
10.6 million

Climate
Temperate, continental climate with four distinct seasons. Warm in summer with cold, snowy winters.

Language
The official language is Czech.

Telephone
The country code is 00 420.

Money
Currency: The Koruna
Banks: Mon-Fri 08.30-16.30.

Shops
Mon-Fri 08.00-18.00, some close at lunchtime.
Sat 09.00 until midday.

Public Holidays
New Year; Easter Mon; May Day; Prague Uprising 5 May; National Day 8 May; Saints Day 5 July; Festival (John Huss) Day 6 July; Independence Day 28 Oct; Democracy Day 17 Nov; Christmas 24-26 Dec.

Motoring
There is a good and well signposted road network throughout the Republic and, although stretches of cobbles still exist, surfaces are generally good. An annual road tax is levied on all vehicles using Czech motorways and express roads, and a disc can be purchased at border crossings, post offices and filling stations. Do not drink any alcohol before driving. Dipped headlights are compulsory throughout winter months. Always give way to trams and buses.

see campsite map 8

Benesov u Prahy

Autocamping Konopiste

CZ-25601 Benesov u Prahy (Stredocesky) T: 317 722 732. E: konopiste@amberholtels.cz

alanrogers.com/CZ4780

Benesov's chief claim to fame is the Konopiste Palace, the last home of Archduke Franz Ferdinand whose assassination in Sarajevo sparked off the First World War in 1914. Autocamp Konopiste, now under new ownership, is part of a motel complex with excellent facilities situated in a very quiet, tranquil location south of Prague. On a hillside, rows of terraces separated by hedges provide 65 grassy pitches of average size, 50 with electricity (10A). Konopiste has many different varieties of trees and much to offer. A fitness centre and heated swimming pool are shared with motel guests.

Facilities

The good quality sanitary block is central to the caravan pitches. Washing machine and irons. Kitchen. Site's own bar/buffet (high season) with simple meals and basic food items. Motel bar and two restaurants (all year). Swimming pool (1/6-31/8). Tennis. Minigolf. Bicycle hire. Badminton. Fitness centre. Playground. Club room with TV. Château and park. WiFi. Off site: Shop 200 m. Fishing 1.5 km. Riding 5 km. Beach and boat launching 15 km. Prague 48 km. (public transport available).

Open: 1 May - 30 September.

Directions

Site is signed near the village of Benesov on the main Prague - Ceske Budejovic road no. 3/E55. GPS: 49.776, 14.669

Charges guide

Per person	CZK 70
child (6-15 yrs)	CZK 50
pitch	CZK 150

Electricity included.

Bojkovice

Eurocamping Bojkovice S.R.O.

Stefanikova ATC, CZ-68771 Bojkovice (Jihomoravsky) T: 604 236 631. E: eurocamping@iol.cz

alanrogers.com/CZ4890

This family site in Bojkovice, close to the Slovak border, is one of the better Czech sites. It is on hilly ground with tarmac access roads connecting the 40 pitches. These are all for touring units on grassy fields taking six or eight units, but the manager will try to fit you in wherever possible. Mostly on terraces in the shade of mature birch trees, all have 6A electricity. A footpath connects the three toilet blocks which offer a more than adequate provision and are cleaned twice daily. It also leads to the bar/restaurant and the centrally located outdoor pool. This is a good, well run site.

Facilities

Three toilet blocks (one refurbished) are good, clean provisions, including British style toilets, open washbasins and controllable hot showers (free). Washing machine. Campers' kitchen. Bar/restaurant with open-air terrace (breakfast and dinner served). Outdoor swimming pool (15x8 m, unfenced). Fishing. Bicycle hire. Off site: Riding 3 km.

Open: 1 May - 30 September.

Directions

From Brno take E50 road southeast towards the Slovakian border. Exit onto the 495 road towards Uhersky Brod and follow signs for Bojkovice. In town, turn left uphill and follow the green signs. GPS: 49.0398, 17.79993

Charges guide

Per unit incl. 2 persons and electricity	€ 12.00 - € 16.15
extra person	€ 2.50 - € 3.05

Ceské Budejovice

Camping Dlouhá Louka

Stromovka 8, CZ-37001 Ceské Budejovice (Jihocesky) T: 387 203 601. E: motel@dlouhalouka.cz

alanrogers.com/CZ4770

The medieval city of Ceské Budejovice is the home of Budweiser beer and is also an industrial centre. It lies on the River Vltava with mountains and pleasant scenery nearby. Dlouhá Louka is a motel and camping complex two kilometres south of the town on the Ceské Budejovice - Cesky Krumlov road. The camping part is a flat, rectangular meadow surrounded by trees which give some shade around the edges. There are some marked, hedged pitches and hardstanding, but many of the grass pitches are not marked or numbered so pitching can be rather haphazard. In total, 100 units are taken and there are 50 electricity connections (10A) and 10 with electricity and waste water.

Facilities

The single sanitary block, with British style WCs, is at one end making a fair walk for some. Washing machine and irons. Kitchen with electric rings. Playground. Tennis. Volleyball. Football. Bicycle hire. Off site: Shops 200 m. Bicycle hire 2 km. Fishing and golf 10 km.

Open: All year.

Directions

From town follow signs for Cesky Krumlov. After leaving ring road, turn right at motel sign. Take this small road and turn right 60 m. before Camp Stromovky. Campsite name cannot be seen from the entrance - only the word 'Motel'. GPS: 48.96640, 14.46050

Charges guide

Per unit incl. 2 persons and electricity	CZK 450
extra person	CZK 100

No credit cards.

Cheb

Camping Václav

Jesenická prehrada, CZ-35002 Cheb - Podhrad (Zapadocesky) T: **354 435 653**. E: **info@kempvaclav.cz**

alanrogers.com/CZ4645

Camping Václav is situated close to the German border on the banks of the Jesenice Lake. The site is on two levels - the lower one, which is slightly sloping, has beautiful views over the lake; the upper level, which is newer and has an excellent new toilet block, offers less shade. The 150 touring pitches are generous (80-150 sq.m), all have 6 or 10A electricity and ten also have water and drainage. Václav is in the 'spa triangle', giving visitors a choice of three different spas - Karlovy Vary, Mariánské Lázné or Frantiskovy Lázné. Guests at Camping Václav can take advantage of discounts for Frantiskovy Lázné.

Facilities

Excellent modern toilet block with open style basins, controllable hot showers and facilities for disabled visitors. Washing machine and dryer. Motorcaravan services. Bar/restaurant. Small shop for drinks and ice creams. Internet. Football field. Tennis. Fishing. Play area. Lake for swimming and boating. WiFi (free). Off site: Sailing 1 km. Bicycle hire 4 km. Riding 7 km. Golf 10 km.

Open: 27 April - 15 September.

Directions

Coming from the west on the 21 road, follow the signs Centrum - Cheb and then Podhrad. From there follow the signs 'Kemp Václav'. On the motorway take exit 146 Podhrad. GPS: 50.04997, 12.41183

Charges 2012

Per unit incl. 2 persons and electricity	CZK 470 - 645
extra person	CZK 80 - 115

No credit cards.

Dolni Brezany

Camping Oase Praha

Libenska, CZ-25241 Zlatniky (Prague) T: **241 932 044**. E: **info@campingoase.cz**

alanrogers.com/CZ4840

Camping Oase Praha is an exceptional site, only five kilometres from Prague and with easy access. You can take the bus (from outside the site) or drive to the underground stop (10 minutes). The site has 110 pitches, all around 100 sq.m, with 6/10A electricity and 55 with water and drainage, on level, well kept fields. The site is very well kept and has just about everything one may expect, including a new Western style toilet block, a well maintained outdoor and new indoor swimming pool with separate paddling pool, a restaurant and a bar.

Facilities

An outstanding, new toilet block includes washbasins, controllable showers and child sized toilets. Facilities for disabled visitors. Family showers. Jacuzzi with sauna and massage (30/4-15/9). Laundry facilities. Campers' kitchen. Motorcaravan services. Restaurant and bar. Shop sells basic groceries. Outdoor pool (9x15 m; open 1/7-31/8), indoor pool (10x4 m; all season). Paddling pool. New adventure style playgrounds. Miniclub. Football. Minigolf. Trampolines. WiFi. TV and video. Off site: Fishing 2 km. Riding 3 km. Bicycle hire 8 km. Golf 10 km.

Open: 20 April - 15 September.

Directions

Go south from Prague on the R1 (Prazsky okruh) and take exit 82 to Jesenice. At Jesenice turn left, following camping signs to the site in Zlatniky where you turn left at the roundabout. Site is 700 m. after the village. GPS: 49.95145, 14.47517

Charges guide

Per unit incl. 2 persons and electricity	CZK 450 - 650
extra person	CZK 120 - 140
child (under 11 yrs)	CZK 60 - 80
dog	CZK 50

Frymburk

Camping Frymburk

Frymburk 184, CZ-38279 Frymburk (Jihocesky) T: **380 735 284**. E: **info@campingfrymburk.cz**

alanrogers.com/CZ4720

Camping Frymburk is beautifully located on the Lipno lake in southern Bohemia and is an ideal site. From this site, activities could include walking, cycling, swimming, sailing, canoeing or rowing and afterwards you could relax in the small, cosy bar/restaurant. The site has 170 level pitches on terraces (all with 6A electricity, some with hardstanding and 4 have private sanitary units) and from the lower terraces on the edge of the lake there are lovely views over the water to the woods on the opposite side. A ferry crosses the lake from Frymburk where one can walk or cycle in the woods.

Facilities

Three immaculate toilet blocks with toilets, washbasins, preset showers on payment and an en-suite bathroom with toilet, basin and shower. Facilities for disabled visitors. Launderette. Restaurant and bar (10/5-15/9). Motorcaravan services. Playground. Canoe, bicycle, pedalos, rowing boat and surfboard hire. Kidstown. Volleyball competitions. Rafting. Bus trips to Prague. Torches useful. Internet access and WiFi. Off site: Shops and restaurants in the village 900 m. from reception. Golf 7 km. Riding 20 km.

Open: 29 April - 1 October.

Directions

Take exit 114 at Passau in Germany (near Austrian border) towards Freyung in the Czech Republic. Continue until Philipsreut. Then follow no. 4 road (Vimperk). Turn right a few kilometres after border (Volary, no. 141 road). From Volary follow no. 163 road (Horni Plana, Cerna, Frymburk). Site on the 163 road, right after village. GPS: 48.655947, 14.170239

Charges guide

Per unit incl. 2 persons and electricity	CZK 460 - 810
extra person	CZK 80 - 130

No credit cards.

Hluboke Masuvky

Camping Country

Hluboke Masuvky 257, CZ-67152 Hluboke Masuvky (Jihomoravsky) T: **515 255 249.**

E: **camping-country@cbox.cz** **alanrogers.com/CZ4896**

Camping Country is a well cared for and attractively landscaped site close to the historical town of Znojmo. It is a rural location, near to a national park and the Austrian border, making it ideal either as a stopover on your way south or for a longer stay to enjoy the new cycling routes which have been set out in the national park. Camping Country has 60 pitches (all for tourers), 30 with 6A electricity, on two fields – one behind the main house taking six or eight units, the other one larger with a gravel access road. The fields are connected by two wooden bridges (one is only fenced on one side).

Facilities

Modern and comfortable toilet facilities provide British style toilets, open washbasins (cold water only) and free, controllable hot showers. Campers' kitchen. Bar/restaurant with one meal served daily. Play area. Tennis. Minigolf. Riding. Some live music nights in high season. Internet and WiFi (charged). Only gas and electric barbecues allowed. Tours to Vienna, Brno and wine cellars organised. Torch useful. Off site: Fishing and boat launching 2 km. Beach 10 km.

Open: 1 May - 31 October.

Directions

Coming from the northwest on the E59 road exit to the east at Kasarna onto the 408 road and continue north on the 361 road towards Hluboke Masuvky. Site is well signed. GPS: 48.9192, 16.0256

Charges guide

Per unit incl. 2 persons and electricity	CZK 440 - 490
extra person	CZK 120
child (3-12 yrs)	CZK 60 - 170
dog	CZK 50

Januv Dul

Camping 2000

Janov Dul 15, CZ-46352 Januv Dul (Severocesky) T: **485 179 621.** E: **camping2000@wanadoo.nl**

alanrogers.com/CZ4695

Created from pleasant farm buildings and the fields behind them, Camping 2000 is especially popular with Dutch visitors. It is a good base for exploring Northern Bohemia with Prague (90 km) and the Krkonose mountains (50 km) from a pleasant, rural location. Most of the pitches are of average size (up to 100 sq.m) and numbered, all with 6A electricity. There is little shade and cars parked on the pitches make the curved rows feel a bit crowded during high season. Further off, however, there are a few larger pitches catering for larger units.

Facilities

Until an extra new block is built, in high season Portacabin units are used next to the main toilet block. Facilities for disabled visitors. Washing machine and dryer. Bar and takeaway. Swimming and paddling pools. Bicycle hire. TV room. Five wooden cottages (fully equipped) for hire. Off site: Liberec 15 km.

Open: 15 April - 30 September.

Directions

From E65/E442 (Prague - Liberec) motorway take exit 35 for Hodkovicevia Ceske Dub and on to Osecna, then to Januv Dul hamlet where site is signed. GPS: 50.7043, 14.93898

Charges guide

Per unit incl. 2 adults, 2 children (under 18 yrs) and electricity	€ 25.50 - € 28.50
dog	€ 3.00

Litomerice

Slavoj Autocamp Litomerice

Strerelecky Ostrov, CZ-41201 Litomerice (Severocesky) T: **416 734 481.** E: **kemp.litomerice@post.cz**

alanrogers.com/CZ4685

Slavoj is a pleasant, small site with a friendly atmosphere and welcoming people. The site was totally destroyed during the flood of 2002 and has been rebuilt with help from many camp guests from all over Europe. For example, an American visitor painted the little landscape on the restaurant. Located centrally, the bar/restaurant is the main focus on the site and here you can enjoy a good value breakfast, as well as lunch and dinner. The site is on level ground, with 50 unmarked pitches, all for tourers. Some look out over the river Laba which is well fenced. Around 24 electricity connections (8/16A) are available. In high season the site can become rather crowded.

Facilities

The basic but clean toilet block has British style toilets, open washbasins and free, controllable hot showers. Laundry facilities. Kitchen. Motorcaravan service point. Basics from restaurant. Bar/restaurant with covered and open-air terrace. River fishing. Canoeing. WiFi. Off site: Tennis adjacent. Boat launching 500 m.

Open: 1 May - 30 September.

Directions

On E55 from either direction, take exit 45 towards Litomerice. Cross the river, the railway bridge and turn left. Take first left and go left again. Cross under railway bridge and continue to site. GPS: 50.532, 14.13867

Charges guide

Per unit incl. 2 persons and electricity	CZK 320 - 445
extra person	CZK 80 - 85
child (6-12 yrs)	CZK 50 - 55
dog	CZK 30

Lodenice

Caravan Camp Valek

Chrustenice 155, CZ-26712 Lodenice (Stredocesky) T: **311 672 147**. E: **info@campvalek.cz**

alanrogers.com/CZ4820

Only 2.5 km. from the E50 motorway, this well maintained, family owned site creates a peaceful, friendly base enjoyed by families. Surrounded by delightful countryside, it is possible to visit Prague even though it is about 28 km. from the city centre. The medium sized, gently sloping grass site is divided in two by a row of well established trees, offering some shade, and the toilet block. Most of the 50 pitches are relatively flat, in the open and not specifically marked. However this does not appear to cause overcrowding and generally there is plenty of space. Electricity (10A) is available to all.

Facilities

The single clean toilet block has limited numbers of toilets and showers, but during our visit in high season coped well. Small shop with fresh rolls daily. Restaurant with terrace. Natural swimming pool (20x60 m; June-Sept) with constantly changing water checked regularly by the authorities to ensure its purity. Games room with arcade machines and Internet. Live musical nights on Saturdays. Tennis. Off site: Prague 28 km. Plzen 69 km.

Open: 1 May - 30 September.

Directions

From E50 (D5) motorway take exit 10 for Lodenice. Follow camping signs and for Chrustenice. Site is 300 m. on right on leaving Chrustenice.
GPS: 50.03333, 14.18333

Charges guide

Per unit incl. 2 persons and electricity	CZK 495 - 570
extra person	CZK 115
child (6-14 yrs)	CZK 55

Nové Straseci

Camping Bucek

Tratice 170, CZ-27101 Nové Straseci (Stredocesky) T: **313 564 212**. E: **info@campingbucek.cz**

alanrogers.com/CZ4825

Camping Bucek is a pleasant, Dutch owned site 40 km. west of Prague. Its proprietors also own Camping Frymburk (CZ4720). Bucek is located on the edge of woodland and has direct access to a small lake – canoes and rowing boats are available for hire, as well as sun loungers on the site's private beach. There are 100 pitches here, many with pleasant views over the lake, and all with electrical connections (6A). Shade is quite limited. Nearby, Revnicov is a pleasant small town with a range of shops and restaurants. The castles of Karlstejn and Krivoklát are also within easy reach, along with Karlovy Vary and Prague itself.

Facilities

Renovated toilet blocks with free hot showers. Washing and drying machine. Direct lake access. Swimming pool. Pedaloes, canoes, lounger hire. Minigolf. Play area.
Off site: Revnicov 2 km. with shops, a supermarket, bars and restaurants. Karlovy Vary 10 km. Prague 40 km. Koniprusy caves.

Open: 24 April - 15 September.

Directions

From the west, take no. 6/E48 express road towards Prague. Site is close to this road, about 3 km. after the Revnicov exit and is clearly signed from this point. Coming from the east, ignore other camping signs and continue until Bucek is signed (to the north). GPS: 50.1728, 13.8348

Charges guide

Per unit incl. 2 persons and electricity	CZK 450 - 590
extra person	CZK 75 - 95
child (under 12 yrs)	CZK 50 - 60

No credit cards.

Praha

Camp Drusus

K Reporyjim 4, CZ-15500 Praha 5 Trebonice (Prague) T: **235 514 391**. E: **drusus@drusus.com**

alanrogers.com/CZ4785

Camp Drusus is a friendly, family site on the western edge of Prague. It provides a good base from which to explore this beautiful city with the metro station only 15 minutes walk away. The site has 70 level pitches (all for tourers), with 16A electricity and varying in size (60-90 sq.m), with access off a circular, grass and gravel road. There is no shop here but basics can be ordered at reception and one of the biggest shopping areas in Prague is only 2 km. You could enjoy a real Czech breakfast in the restaurant which also opens for dinner and serves as a bar. This is a pleasant, well kept and quiet site with good connections to the Czech capital.

Facilities

Modern sanitary facilities. Laundry. Kitchen. Motorcaravan service point. No shop, but basics to order at reception. Bar/restaurant. Small fitness centre. Playground. Games room with billiards. WiFi throughout (free). Off site: Bus 200 m. Shops 2 km. Metro station for Prague (15 minutes). Golf 12 km.

Open: 1 April - 5 October.

Directions

The site is not far from the junction of the D5 and the Prague ring road R1/E48/E50 (prazsky okruh) to the west of the city. From the Ring road take exit 21 and follow signs to Trebonice and the camp for approx. 2 km. GPS: 50.044083, 14.284217

Charges guide

Per unit incl. 2 persons and electricity	CZK 450 - 580
extra person	CZK 100 - 120
child (6-14 yrs)	CZK 60 - 70

Praha

Camping Busek Praha

U parku 6, CZ-18200 Praha 8 Brezineves (Prague) T: **283 910 254**. E: **campbusekprag@volny.cz**

alanrogers.com/CZ4845

No trip to the Czech Republic would be complete without a visit to the capital, Prague. At this site you can do just that without getting tangled up with the city traffic. Just about 8 km. from the centre, there is an excellent bus link from the site to the new metro station at Ladvi that is a part of the new integrated transport system. The site is part of a small motel complex and provides 20 level and unnumbered pitches, all with 10A electricity. It is on the edge of a small, rural village, which offers peace and quiet at the end of a long day's sightseeing. Some road noise can be heard.

Facilities

Older style sanitary block with clean toilets, hot showers and washbasins. Washing machine and dryer. Kitchen and dishwashing facilities. Small restaurant (all year). WiFi (free). Off site: Prague city centre only a bus and metro ride away. Outdoor swimming pool.

Open: All year.

Directions

From the Prague - Teplice (Dresden) motorway, the D8/E55, take exit to Brezineves and head towards the village. The site is 200 m. after the village sign on the right. Turn towards the small fire station and the site is on the right. GPS: 50.164716, 14.485578

Charges guide

Per unit incl. 2 persons and electricity	CZK 520 - 560
extra person	CZK 120
child (5-15 yrs)	CZK 70

No credit cards.

Praha

Camp Sokol Troja

Trojská 171A, CZ-17100 Praha (Prague) T: **233 542 908**. E: **info@camp-sokol-troja.cz**

alanrogers.com/CZ4850

This site is very close to the Vltava river although you cannot see it. It was subject to heavy flooding in 2002 and some of the facilities were washed away. There are 75 touring pitches (10 with 16A electricity). The pitches are small (80-90 sq.m) and about half are on hardstanding. The grass pitches can become muddy with rain. The access road is narrow and manoeuvring space is limited so the site may be less suitable for large caravans and motorcaravans. Nevertheless, it is only a 15 or 20 minute journey to the centre of the city by bus. There is a bus stop in front of the site or a tram (no. 17) a 300 m. walk away.

Facilities

The single, refurbished toilet block has toilets, washbasins with hot and cold water and preset showers in cabins without curtain or door. Cleaning can be variable. Facilities for disabled visitors. Motorcaravan services. Campers' kitchen with hob. Good restaurant. Off site: Fishing 1 km.

Open: All year.

Directions

From Dresden or Teplice, follow signs to the centre and turn right before the first bridge over the Moldau into the Kozlovka Pátkova, in the Troja district. Site is well signed from here. GPS: 50.11683, 14.42500

Charges guide

Per person	CZK 110 - 130
child (under 18 yrs)	CZK 80 - 90
caravan	CZK 120 - 190
motorcaravan	CZK 200 - 250
electricity	CZK 150

Praha

Camping Zizkov Prague

Nad Ohradou 17, CZ-13000 Praha 3 (Prague) T: **775 102 808**. E: **camp.zizkov@gmail.com**

alanrogers.com/CZ4855

Camping Zizkov is a small site in the centre of Prague, within the grounds of a 'pension'. It has 35 pitches on level grass in a circular area and all have 6A electricity. Pitches are rather small, as is the entrance, but the site does take large units. There is a nice ambience here and it is close to the river where you can take a stroll. Adjacent is a large sports centre with an open-air pool, tennis courts and basketball. All necessary amenities are available on site, including a bar in high season, but one should be aware that the pension in high season is mostly populated with youngsters.

Facilities

Toilet block in the pension with communal showers. Washing machine. Basic kitchen. Open air bar with terrace. Trampoline. Basketball. Beach volleyball. WiFi. Off site: Open-air pool, tennis and basketball 200 m.

Open: 15 June - 15 September.

Directions

From the centre of Prague, follow the Konevovo main road east and turn left at the Prazacka sports complex with hotel. Follow the small road to the left for 150 m. to the entrance.
GPS: 50.09194, 14.47305

Charges guide

Per unit incl. 2 persons and electricity	CZK 730 - 800
extra person	CZK 150

No credit cards.

Roznov pod Radhostem

Camping Roznov

Horni Paseky 940, CZ-75661 Roznov pod Radhostem (Severomoravsky) T: **571 648 001**.

E: info@camproznov.cz **alanrogers.com/CZ4880**

Roznov pod Radhostem is halfway up the Roznovska Becva valley amidst the Beskydy hills which extend from North Moravia into Poland, in the extreme east of the Republic. It is a busy tourist centre which attracts visitors to the Wallachian open-air museum and those who enjoy hill walking. There are 300 pitches (200 for touring units), some of which are rather small, although there are some new landscaped pitches of 90-100 sq.m. Arranged on flat grass and set amidst a variety of fruit and other trees, there are 120 electrical connections (16A) and shade in some parts.

Facilities

The good quality central toilet block has hot water in showers, washbasins and sinks. This block also has a large TV lounge/meeting room. A further well equipped toilet block has washbasins and WCs en-suite for ladies and a washing machine. Only very basic food items in the shop (not always open). Swimming pool (25 m. open July/Aug). Tennis. Trampolines. Off site: Restaurant/snack bar and night club at the Europlan Hotel some 300 m. towards the town. Fishing and golf 1 km. Riding 4 km.

Open: All year.

Directions

Site is at eastern end of Roznov on the main 35/E442 Zilina - Olomouc road opposite sports stadium. GPS: 49.46628, 18.16400

Charges guide

Per person	CZK 55 - 90
child (3-15 yrs)	CZK 45 - 70
pitch	CZK 95 - 175
electricity	CZK 60 - 80

Camping Cheques accepted.

Veverska Bityska

Camping Hana

Dlouha 135, CZ-66471 Veverska Bityska (Jihomoravsky) T: **607 905 801**. E: **camping.hana@seznam.cz**

alanrogers.com/CZ4895

The caves of the Moravian Karst, the site of the battle of Austerlitz and the castles of Veveri, Pertstejn and Spillberk are all within easy reach of this pleasant, small and quiet campsite. Hana Musilova runs the site to very high standards, speaks excellent English and Dutch and is keen to provide lots of local information. There are 55 level, numbered pitches with 10A electricity. Brno, the capital of Moravia and the Czech Republic's second largest city, is a short boat or bus ride away and the village of Veverska Bityska has shops, restaurants, bars and an ATM plus a reasonable, small supermarket.

Facilities

The modernised sanitary block provides ample and clean toilets, hot showers (token, 1st free per person then CZK 5), washbasins and baby changing. Washing machine and dryer. Kitchen and dishwashing facilities. Small shop with essential supplies. Free WiFi throughout. Charcoal and gas barbecues allowed. Off site: Boat cruise to Brno 500 m. Veverska Bityska village and fishing 1 km. Riding 4 km. Golf 10 km.

Open: 1 May - 30 September.

Directions

From the D1 Prague - Brno autoroute, turn off at Ostrovacice and head towards Tisnov. The site is at Veverska Bityska on the road to Chudcice. From the 43 turn off south of Lipuvka towards Kurim and then follow the signs to Veverska Bityska where the site is on the right before entering the village.
GPS: 49.276567, 16.452633

Charges guide

Per unit incl. 2 persons and electricity	CZK 370 - 410
extra person	CZK 80

Vrchlabi

Holiday Park Lisci Farma

Dolni Branna 350, CZ-54362 Vrchlabi (Vychodocesky) T: **499 421 473**. E: **info@liscifarma.cz**

alanrogers.com/CZ4590

This is truly an excellent site that could be in Western Europe considering its amenities, pitches and welcome. However, Lisci Farma retains a pleasant Czech atmosphere. In the winter months, when local skiing is available, snow chains are essential. The 260 pitches are fairly flat, although the terrain is slightly sloping and some pitches are terraced. There is shade and some pitches have hardstanding. The site is well equipped for the whole family with its adventure playground, archery, beach volleyball, Russian bowling and an outdoor bowling court. A beautiful sandy, lakeside beach is 800 m. from the entrance.

Facilities

Two good sanitary blocks near the entrance and another modern block next to the hotel, both include toilets, washbasins and spacious, controllable showers (on payment). Child size toilets and baby room. Toilet for disabled visitors. Sauna and massage. Launderette. Shop (15/6-15/9). Bar/snack bar with pool table. Games room. Swimming pool (6x12 m). Adventure style playground on grass with climbing wall. Trampolines. Tennis. Minigolf. Archery. Russian bowling. Paragliding. Rock climbing. Bicycle hire. Entertainment. Excursions to Prague.
Off site: Fishing and beach 800 m. Riding 2 km. Golf 5 km.

Open: All year.

Directions

Follow road no. 14 from Liberec to Vrchlabi. At the roundabout turn in the direction of Prague and site is about 1.5 km. on the right.
GPS: 50.61036, 15.60264

Charges guide

Per unit incl. 2 persons and electricity	CZK 294 - 390
extra person	CZK 55 - 65
child (4-15 yrs)	CZK 38 - 45
dog	CZK 45 - 50

Various discounts available in low season.

Denmark

Denmark offers a diverse landscape all within a relatively short distance. The countryside is green and varied with flat plains, rolling hills, fertile farmland, many lakes and fjords, wild moors and long beaches, interrupted by pretty villages and towns.

Denmark is the easiest of the Scandinavian countries to visit, both in terms of cost and distance. There are many small islands but the main land masses that make up the country are the islands of Zeeland and Funen and the peninsula of Jutland, which extends northwards from the German border. Zeeland is the most visited region, its main draw being the capital, Copenhagen. This vibrant city has a beautiful old centre, an array of museums and art galleries, plus a boisterous nightlife. Funen is the smaller of the two main islands and is known as the Garden of Denmark, with its neat green fields and fruit and vegetable plots. Sandy beaches and quaint villages can be found here. Jutland has the most varied landscape ranging from heather-clad moors to dense forests to plunging gorges. It's also home to one of the most popular attractions in Denmark, Legoland, and the oldest town in Scandinavia, Ribe.

CAPITAL: **Copenhagen**

Tourist Office

Danish Tourist Board
55 Sloane Street, London SW1X 9SY
Tel: 020 7259 5958
Fax: 020 7259 5955
Email: london@visitdenmark.com
Internet: www.visitdenmark.com

Population

5.4 million

Climate

Generally mild although changeable throughout the year.

Language

Danish, but English is widely spoken.

Telephone

The country code is 00 45.

Money

Currency: Danish Krone (DKK).
Banks: Mon-Wed & Fri 09.30-16.00, Thurs to 18.00. Closed Sat. In the provinces opening hours vary.

Shops

Hours may vary in the main cities.
Regular openings are Mon-Thu 09.00-17.30, Fri 09.00-19.00/20.00, and Sat 09.00-13.00/14.00.

Public Holidays

New Year's Day; Three Kings Day 6 Jan; April Fools Day 1 April, Maundy Thursday, Good Friday; Easter Monday; Queen's Birthday 16 April; Flag Day 18 April; Ascension; Whit Mon; Constitution Day 5 Jun; Valdemars 15 June; Mortens Day 11 Nov; Christmas 24-26 Dec; New Year's Eve

Motoring

Driving is much easier than at home as roads are much quieter. Driving is on the right. Do not drink and drive. Dipped headlights are compulsory at all times. Strong measures are taken against unauthorised parking on beaches, with on-the-spot fines.

see campsite map 2

Aalbæk

Skiveren Camping

Niels Skiverenrej 5-7, DK-9982 Skiveren/Aalbæk (Nordjylland) T: 98 93 22 00. E: info@skiveren.dk

alanrogers.com/DK2165

This friendly, family run seaside site, a member of the Danish TopCamp organisation, is adjacent to a beautiful, long sandy beach. Skiveren Camping has 595 pitches (496 for tourers), all with 10/16A electricity and generally separated into named areas. Around the site are different varieties of low spruce and fir which give the site a pleasing appearance and atmosphere. There is an excellent indoor play area as well as many outdoor amenities. A horse and cart can take campers for rides.

Facilities

Three toilet blocks include free family showers and private facilities with shower, toilet and basin for rent (DKK 40-70). Facilities for disabled visitors. Laundry. Campers' kitchens. Motorcaravan services. Supermarket. Strand Café for meals, drinks and takeaway (20/4-18/9). Outdoor pool (21/5-30/9) with whirlpool and sauna. Playground with area for toddlers. Excellent new large indoor play hall. Multisports court. Tennis. Games room with machines and wide screen TV. Bicycle hire. Minigolf (charged). Fishing. Horse and cart rides. Children's club daily (from 16). Live music and dancing. Off site: Golf 7 km. Riding 10 km.

Open: Weekend before Easter - 30 September.

Directions

From the 40 road going north from Ålbæk, turn left at sign for 'Skiveren'. Follow this road all the way to the end. GPS: 57.61611, 10.27908

Charges guide

Per unit incl. 2 persons and electricity	DKK 210 - 340
extra person	DKK 60 - 80
child (0-11 yrs)	DKK 40 - 60
dog	DKK 10

Credit cards 2.75% surcharge.
Low season discount 10-30%.

Blavand

Hvidbjerg Strand Camping

Hvidbjerg Strandvej 27, DK-6857 Blavand (Ribe) T: 75 27 90 40. E: info@hvidbjerg.dk

alanrogers.com/DK2010

A family owned TopCamp holiday site, Hvidbjerg Strand is on the west coast near Blåvands Huk, 43 km. from Esbjerg. It is a high quality, seaside site with a wide range of amenities. Most of the 570 pitches have electricity (6/10A) and the 130 'comfort' pitches also have water, drainage and satellite TV. To the rear of the site, 70 new, fully serviced pitches have been developed, some up to 250 sq.m. and 16 with private sanitary facilities. Most pitches are individual and divided by hedges, in rows on flat sandy grass, with areas also divided by small trees and hedges. A member of Leading Campings group.

Facilities

Five superb toilet units include washbasins (many in cubicles), roomy showers, spa baths, suites for disabled visitors, family bathrooms, kitchens and laundry facilities. The most recent units include a children's bathroom decorated with dinosaurs and Disney characters, and racing car baby baths. Motorcaravan services. Supermarket. Café/restaurant. TV rooms. Pool complex, solarium and sauna. Play areas. Supervised play rooms (09.00-16.00 daily). Barbecue areas. Minigolf. Riding (Western style). Fishing. Dog showers. ATM machine. Off site: Legoland 70 km.

Open: 18 March - 23 October.

Directions

From Varde take roads 181/431 to Blåvand. Site is signed left on entering the town (mind speed bump on town boundary). GPS: 55.54600, 8.13507

Charges guide

Per unit incl. 2 persons and electricity	DKK 239 - 404
extra person	DKK 77
child (0-11 yrs)	DKK 57
dog	DKK 27

Broager

Gammelmark Strand Camping

Gammelmark 20, DK-6310 Broager (Sønderjylland) T: 74 44 17 42. E: info@gammelmark.dk

alanrogers.com/DK2036

The Siegers, a Danish/Dutch couple, have owned this site since 2001 and are proud to be the first Scandinavian site to achieve Ecocamp status, showing commitment to the environment. Gammelmark has 289 level, grass pitches (200 for tourers), all with 13A electricity. Many have great views of the Flensburger Förde. This site combines Danish hospitality with historical interest and family activities are available, many involving nature and the history of the area when war was waged over the Flensburger Förd. It is useful as a stopover on your way north, but is also a good choice for active campers.

Facilities

Modern, heated sanitary facilities include toilets, washbasins (open and in cabins), controllable showers. Facilities for children and disabled visitors. Baby room. Private facilities to rent. Laundry facilities. Motorcaravan services. Shop. Snacks (high season). Heated swimming pool. Play area. Children's farm. Fishing. Riding. Sailing and boat launching. Diving. Beach. Daily activities (high season). TV room. WiFi (charged). Torches advised. Off site: Restaurant 2 km. Bicycle hire 6 km. Golf 10 km.

Open: Easter - 22 October.

Directions

From Flensburg take 7 road north and at exit 75 turn east towards Sønderborg. Take exit Dynt and follow site signs. Do not turn into house at 16 Gammelmark, but continue 200 m. down small road to reception. GPS: 54.88545, 9.72876

Charges guide

Per person	€ 11.80
child (1-11 yrs)	€ 6.95
pitch (high season)	€ 8.35
electricity per kWh	€ 0.55

Charlottenlund

Camping Charlottenlund Fort

Strandvejen 144B, DK-2920 Charlottenlund (Sjælland) T: 39 62 36 88. E: info@campingcopenhagen.dk

alanrogers.com/DK2265

On the northern outskirts of Copenhagen, this unique site is within the walls of an old fort which still retains its main armament of twelve 29 cm. howitzers (disabled, of course). There are 100 pitches on grass, all with 10A electricity. The obvious limitation on the space available means that pitches are relatively close together, but many are quite deep. The site is very popular and is usually full every night, so we suggest that you either reserve or arrive well before midday. The site is only 6 km. from the centre of Copenhagen, with a regular bus service from just outside the site.

Facilities

Sanitary facilities located in the old armoury are newly rebuilt, well maintained and heated. Free showers. Kitchen facilities include gas hobs and a dining area. Laundry. Motorcaravan service point. Small shop in reception. Bicycle hire. WiFi. Beach. Off site: Riding 1.5 km. Golf 2 km. Copenhagen town centre 20 minutes by bus.

Open: 1 May - 14 September.

Directions

Leave E47/E55 at exit 17, and turn southeast on Jægersborgvej. After a short distance turn left (east) on Jægersborg Allé, following signs for Charlottenlund (5 km) and follow all the way to the end. Finally turn right (south) on to Strandvejen, and site entrance is on left after 500 m.
GPS: 55.74480, 12.58538

Charges guide

Per person	DKK 80
pitch	DKK 25 - 45
electricity	DKK 5

Ebberup

Helnæs Camping

Strandbakken 21, Helnæs, DK-5631 Ebberup (Fyn) T: 64 77 13 39. E: info@helnaes-camping.dk

alanrogers.com/DK2220

Helnæs Camping is on the remote Helnæs peninsula to the southeast of Fyn, connected to the mainland by a small road. The site is adjacent to a nature reserve making it ideal for walkers, cyclists and birdwatchers, or for those who enjoy sea fishing (this is a great location for sea trout). The road to the site takes you through a breathtaking environment with colourful flowerbeds on the Bobakkerne Wall to the north and large outer marches in the south. Helnæs Camping has 160 pitches, some terraced, on grassy fields sloping down towards to the sea. Almost all the pitches have beautiful views of Helnæs Bugt and the site is only 300 m. from the beach.

Facilities

Two toilet blocks, one brand new, with washbasins in cabins and controllable showers. Baby room (heated). Facilities for disabled visitors. Laundry with washing machines and dryers. Campers' kitchen. Shop. Takeaway. Adventure type playground. Minigolf. Bicycle hire. Canoe hire. Watersports. In high season small circus for children. TV lounge. Internet access. Covered barbecue area. Off site: Sea fishing.

Open: 15 March - 1 September.

Directions

From Nørre Åby follow 313 road south to Ebberup. In Ebberup turn south to Helnæs and follow signs for Helnæs Strand. GPS: 55.13254, 10.03622

Charges guide

Per person	DKK 55 - 67
electricity	DKK 25

No credit cards.

Camping Cheques accepted.

Ebeltoft

Blushoj Camping

Elsegårdevej 55, DK-8400 Ebeltoft (Århus) T: 86 34 12 38. E: blushoj@mail.dk

alanrogers.com/DK2100

This is a traditional type of site where the owners are making a conscious effort to keep mainly to touring units – there are only six seasonal units and four rental cabins. The site has 250 pitches on levelled grassy terraces surrounded by mature hedging and shrubs. Some have glorious views of the Kattegat and others overlook peaceful rural countryside. Most pitches have electricity (10A), but long leads may be required. There is a heated and fenced swimming pool (14x7 m) with a slide and a terrace. The beach below the site provides opportunities for swimming, windsurfing and sea fishing.

Facilities

One toilet unit includes washbasins with dividers and showers with divider and seat (on payment). The other unit has a new kitchen with electric hobs, sinks, dining/TV room, laundry and baby facilities. A heated extension provides six very smart family bathrooms, and additional WCs and washbasins. Motorcaravan service point. Well stocked shop. Swimming pool (20/5-20/8). Minigolf. Play area. Games room. Beach. Fishing. Internet access. WiFi (charged). Off site: Riding, bicycle hire, boat launching and golf all 5 km.

Open: 1 April - 15 September.

Directions

From road 21 northwest of Ebeltoft turn off at junction where several sites are signed towards Dråby. Follow signs through the outskirts of Ebeltoft turning southeast to Elsegårde village. Turn left for Blushøj and follow site signs.
GPS: 56.16773, 10.73067

Charges guide

Per unit incl. 2 persons and electricity	DKK 178 - 200
extra person	DKK 74 - 85

No credit cards.

Esbjerg

Ådalens Camping

Gudenåvej 20, DK-6710 Esbjerg V-Sædding (Ribe) T: 75 15 88 22. E: info@adal.dk

alanrogers.com/DK2015

Owned and run by Britta and Peter Andersen, this superb site is in the northeast of Esbjerg and is a great starting point from which to tour the city with its harbour, museums and sea water aquarium. It is also convenient for those arriving on the ferry from Harwich (16 hours). From the tree lined drive, gravel lanes lead to large fields with well mown grass and good services. Ådalens has 193 pitches for touring visitors and 30 seasonal places. The pitches are split into groups of five or ten by mature trees that provide some shade. Everything on this site is in pristine order, with amenities that will ensure a pleasant stay.

Facilities

Two modern toilet blocks with free hot showers. Children's section and family shower rooms (for rent). Facilities for disabled visitors. Baby room. Laundry. Campers' kitchen. Motorcaravan services. Basics from reception (bread to order). Outdoor pool (15x10 m) with slide, waterfall, flume and paddling pool (1/6-1/9). Two new playgrounds. Animal farm. Giant chess. Minigolf. WiFi Internet access. TV room with library. Off site: Fishing, golf, bicycle hire and boat launching 5 km. City centre 5 km.

Open: All year.

Directions

From Esbjerg, take the 447 road northeast and continue along the coast. Turn right at sign for site and follow the signs. GPS: 55.51302, 8.38778

Charges 2012

Per unit incl. 2 persons and electricity	€ 28.30 - € 32.40
extra person	€ 10.50
child (1-11 yrs)	€ 6.67
dog	€ 1.36

Fåborg

Bøjden Strand Ferie Park

Bøjden Landevej 12, Bøjden, DK-5600 Fåborg (Fyn) T: 63 60 63 60. E: info@bojden.dk

alanrogers.com/DK2200

Bøjden is located in one of the most beautiful corners of southwest Fyn (Funen in English), known as the Garden of Denmark. This is a well equipped site, with just a hedge separating it from the beach. It is suitable for an entire holiday, while remaining a very good centre for excursions. Arranged in rows on mainly level, grassy terraces and divided into groups by hedges and some trees, many pitches have sea views as the site slopes gently down from the road. The 295 pitches (210 for touring) all have electricity (10A) and include 65 new, fully serviced pitches (water, drainage and TV aerial point).

Facilities

Superb quality, central toilet block includes washbasins in cubicles, controllable showers, family bathrooms, baby room and excellent facilities for disabled visitors. Kitchen. Laundry. A new unit serves a recent extension to the site. An older unit provides extra facilities. Motorcaravan services. Supermarket. Licensed restaurant. Takeaway. Indoor and outdoor swimming pools. Solarium. Fenced toddler play area. Adventure playground. TV and games rooms. Internet café and WiFi. Barbecue area. Fishing. Minigolf. Off site: Beach adjacent. Bicycle hire and riding 10 km. Golf 12 km.

Open: 14 March - 20 October.

Directions

From Fåborg follow 8 road to Bøjden and site is on right 500 m. before ferry terminal (from Fynshav). GPS: 55.105289, 10.107808

Charges guide

Per person	DKK 67
child (0-11 yrs)	DKK 45
pitch	DKK 10 - 100
electricity	DKK 31

Credit cards accepted with 5% surcharge.

Faxe

TopCamp Feddet

Feddet 12, DK-4640 Faxe (Sjælland) T: 56 72 52 06. E: info@feddetcamping.dk

alanrogers.com/DK2255

This interesting, spacious site with ecological principles is located on the Baltic coast. It has a fine, white, sandy beach (Blue Flag) which runs the full length of one side, with the Præstø fjord on the opposite side of the peninsula. There are 413 pitches for touring, generally on sandy grass, with mature pine trees giving adequate shade. All have 10A electricity and 20 are fully serviced (water, electricity, drainage and sewerage). Two recently constructed sanitary buildings which have been specially designed, are clad with larch panels from sustainable local trees and are insulated with flax mats.

Facilities

Both sanitary buildings are equipped to a very high standard. Family bathrooms (with twin showers), suites for small children and babies. Facilities for disabled visitors. Laundry. Kitchens, dining room and TV lounge. Excellent motorcaravan service point. Well stocked licensed shop. Licensed bistro and takeaway (1/5-20/10 but weekends only outside peak season). Minigolf. Games room. Indoor playroom and several playgrounds for all ages. Event camp for children. Pet zoo. WiFi. Massage. Watersports. Fishing. Off site: Abseiling and pool. Amusement park.

Open: All year.

Directions

From south on E47/55 take exit 38 towards Præsto. Turn north on 209 road towards Faxe and from Vindbyholt follow site signs. From the north on E47/55 take exit 37 east towards Faxe. Just before Faxe turn south on 209 road and from Vindbyholt, site signs. GPS: 55.17497, 12.10203

Charges guide

Per unit incl. 2 persons and electricity	DKK 250 - 323
extra person	DKK 72
child (0-11 yrs)	DKK 50 - 105

Fjerritslev

Klim Strand Camping

Havvejen 167, Klim Strand, DK-9690 Fjerritslev (Nordjylland) T: 98 22 53 40. E: ksc@klim-strand.dk

alanrogers.com/DK2170

A large family holiday site right beside the sea, Klim Strand is a paradise for children. It is a privately owned TopCamp site with a full complement of quality facilities, including its own fire engine and trained staff. The site has 460 numbered touring pitches, all with electricity (10A), laid out in rows, many divided by trees and hedges, with shade in parts. Some 220 of these are fully serviced with electricity, water, drainage and TV hook-up. On-site activities include an outdoor water slide complex, an indoor pool, tennis and pony riding. A wellness spa centre is a recent addition. A member of Leading Campings group.

Facilities

Two good, large, heated toilet blocks with spacious showers and some washbasins in cubicles. Children's room. Baby rooms. Bathrooms for families (some charged) and disabled visitors. Two further smaller units. Laundry. Kitchens and barbecue areas. TV lounges. Motorcaravan services. Pizzeria. Supermarket, restaurant and bar. Pool complex. Sauna, solariums, whirlpool bath, hairdressing rooms, fitness room. Wellness centre. Internet café. TV rental. Play areas. Crèche. Bicycle hire. Cabins to rent. WiFi (charged). Off site: Golf 10 km. Boat launching 25 km.

Open: 30 March - 21 October.

Directions

Turn off Thisted - Fjerritslev 11 road to Klim from where site is signed. GPS: 57.133333, 9.166667

Charges 2012

Per unit incl. 2 persons and electricity	DKK 255 - 365
extra person	DKK 80
child (1-11 yrs)	DKK 60
dog	DKK 25

Føllenslev

Vesterlyng Camping

Ravnholtvej 3, DK-4591 Føllenslev (Sjælland) T: 59 20 00 66. E: info@vesterlyng-camping.dk

alanrogers.com/DK2257

Vesterlyng is a pleasant, quiet site, close to Føllenslev and Havnsø on Sjælland. The ground slopes towards the sea and there are good views from some pitches. It is an open site but some mature trees provide shade. Vesterlyng has 181 mostly level touring pitches, 150 with 6/13A electricity. A further 100 pitches are used by mostly elderly, seasonal units. The pitches are on long, grassy meadows each taking 16-20 units, off tarmac access roads. Facilities on this site are basic, but clean. The local beaches are ideal for swimming and a relaxing beach holiday.

Facilities

Two traditional style toilet blocks include washbasins (open style and in cabins) and controllable hot showers. Family shower rooms. Basic facilities for disabled visitors. Washing machine and dryer. Small shop. Bar. Swimming pool complex. Minigolf. Riding. Bicycle hire. Watersports. WiFi. Boules. Animal enclosure. Live music nights. Off site: Fishing and boat launching 1 km. Golf 15 km.

Open: 22 March - 21 October.

Directions

From Kalundborg follow 23 road east and exit on 155 road towards Svinninge. At Snertinge, continue north on 255 road for 2 km. Follow signs to site (6 km). From the west exit on 255 road towards Snertinge and follow signs after 2 km. GPS: 55.7417, 11.309

Charges guide

Per person	DKK 67
pitch	DKK 10 - 40
electricity	DKK 27

No credit cards.

Fredericia

Mycamp Trelde Næs

Trelde Næsvej 297, Trelde, DK-7000 Fredericia (Vejle) T: 75 95 71 83. E: trelde@mycamp.dk

alanrogers.com/DK2046

Trelde Næs is a busy and lively site next to a beach. It is one of Denmark's larger sites with 500 level and numbered pitches. The 350 touring pitches all have 10A electricity and there are 37 fully serviced pitches with electricity, water, drainage and Internet access. Seasonal units take up the remaining pitches. Pitches are mainly in rows off tarmac access roads on well kept, grassy fields with some shade from bushes. At the front of the site is a heated, open-air, fun pool with slide, jacuzzi and play island. Here there is also a room with a sauna, Turkish baths and massage chairs, with play stations for children.

Facilities

Four traditional toilet blocks have washbasins in cabins and controllable hot showers (card operated). Child sized toilets and basins. Family shower room. Baby room. Laundry. Fun pool (10x20 m) with island and slide. Turkish bath, solarium and sauna. Shop. Takeaway. Playgrounds. Minigolf. Fishing. Bicycle hire. Watersports. Entertainment for children (high season). TV room. WiFi (charged). Cabins and rooms to rent. Off site: Riding 1 km. Golf 6 km. Boat launching and sailing 7 km.

Open: 1 April - 23 October.

Directions

From Fredericia follow road 28 north and take Trelde exit. Follow signs for Trelde and Trelde Næs. GPS: 55.62489, 9.83333

Charges guide

Per unit incl. 2 persons and electricity	DKK 175 - 245
extra person	DKK 60
child (3-11 yrs)	DKK 35
dog	DKK 20

Frederikshaven

Nordstrand Camping

Apholmenvej 40, DK-9900 Frederikshaven (Nordjylland) T: 98 42 93 50. E: info@nordstrand-camping.dk

alanrogers.com/DK2180

An excellently positioned site, Nordstrand is 2 km. from Frederikshaven and the ferries to Sweden and Norway. It is a TopCamp site and provides very good facilities with all the attractions of the nearby beach, town and port. The 440 large pitches, of which 350 are for tourers, mostly with electricity (10/13A), are attractively arranged in small enclosures of 9-13 units surrounded by hedges and trees. Many hedges are of flowering shrubs and this makes for a very pleasant atmosphere. A major attraction for families is the modern fun house with many indoor activities.

Facilities

Centrally located toilet blocks provide spacious showers (on payment) and washbasins in cubicles. Some family bathrooms, rooms for disabled visitors and babies. All are spotlessly clean. Laundry. Good kitchens at each block and some covered terraces. Motorcaravan services. Supermarket (1/4-15/9). Café and pizza service. Indoor swimming pool. Sauna. Solarium. 'Short' golf course. Minigolf. Tennis. Bicycle hire. Play areas. WiFi (charged). Fun house (charged). Off site: Beach and fishing 200 m. Shops in Frederikshaven 2 km. Golf 2 km. Riding 20 km.

Open: 1 April - 2 October.

Directions

Turn off the main 40 road 2 km. north of Frederikshaven at roundabout just north of railway bridge. Site is signed. GPS: 57.46422, 10.52755

Charges guide

Per unit incl. 2 persons and electricity	DKK 198 - 280
extra person	DKK 80
child (1-12 yrs)	DKK 58 - 64
dog	DKK 12

Give

TopCamp Riis Feriepark

Osterhovedvej 43, DK-7323 Give (Vejle) T: 75 73 14 33. E: info@topcampriis.dk

alanrogers.com/DK2040

TopCamp Riis is a good quality touring site ideal for visiting Legoland and Lalandia Billund (18 km), and Givskov Zoo (3 km). It is a friendly, family run site with 150 large touring pitches on sheltered, gently sloping, well tended lawns surrounded by trees and shrubs. Electricity (13A) is available to all pitches, and 15 comfort pitches also have water and drainage. The outdoor heated pool and water slide complex, and the bar that serves beer, ice cream, soft drinks and snacks, are only open in the main season. There is a small, well stocked shop. The excellent indoor kitchen facilities and an attractive covered barbecue area are very useful.

Facilities

Two excellent sanitary units (the older one now refurbished) include washbasins with divider/curtain and controllable showers (on payment). Suites for babies and disabled visitors, family bathrooms (one with whirlpool bath, on payment) and solarium. Excellent new kitchen. Large sitting room with TV, plus new barbecue grill house. Laundry. Motorcaravan services. Shop (all season). Pool complex (2/6-4/9). Café/bar (25/5-11/8). Minigolf. New playground. Train ride for children. Animal farm. Bicycle hire. WiFi. Off site: Fishing and golf 4 km. Beach 35 km.

Open: 31 March - 30 September.

Directions

Turn onto Osterhovedvej southeast of Give town centre (near Shell garage) at sign to Riis and site. After 4 km. turn left into tarmac drive which runs through the forest to the site. Alternatively, turn off the 442 Brande-Jelling road at Riis village north of Givskud. GPS: 55.83116, 9.30076

Charges guide

Per unit incl. 2 persons and electricity	DKK 235 - 285
extra person	DKK 80
child (0-11 yrs)	DKK 55

Grenå

Fornæs Camping

Stensmarkvej 36, DK-8500 Grenå (Århus) T: 86 33 23 30. E: fornaes@1031.inord.dk

alanrogers.com/DK2070

In the grounds of a former farm, Fornæs Camping is about 5 km. from Grenå. From reception, a wide gravel access road descends through a large grassy field to the sea. Pitches to the left are mostly level, to the right slightly sloping with some terracing and views of the Kattegat. The rows of pitches are divided into separate areas by colourful bushes and each row is marked by a concrete tub containing a young tree and colourful flowers. Fornæs has 320 pitches of which 240 are for tourers, the others being used for seasonal visitors. All touring pitches have 10A electricity.

Facilities

Two toilet blocks include washbasins in cabins and controllable hot showers (on payment). Child sized toilets. Family shower rooms. Baby room. Facilities for disabled campers. Laundry. Campers' kitchen. Motorcaravan service point. Shop. Café/grill with bar and takeaway (evenings). Swimming pool (80 sq.m) with paddling pool. Sauna and solarium. Play area and adventure playground. Games room with satellite TV. Minigolf. Fishing. Watersports. Off site: Golf and riding 5 km.

Open: 15 March - 20 September.

Directions

From Århus follow the 15 road towards Grenå and then the 16 road towards town centre. Turn north and follow signs for Fornæs and the site. GPS: 56.45602, 10.94107

Charges guide

Per person	DKK 67 - 75
child (1-12 yrs)	DKK 38 - 42
electricity (10A)	DKK 28

Credit cards 5% surcharge.

Haderslev

Vikær Diernæs Strand Camping

Dundelum 29, Diernæs, DK-6100 Haderslev (Sønderjylland) T: 74 57 54 64. E: info@vikaercamp.dk

alanrogers.com/DK2022

Vikær Diernæs Strand Camping in Southern Jutland lies in beautiful surroundings, right on the Diernæs Bugt beaches – ideal for both active campers and relaxation seekers. There are 390 grass pitches (210 for touring units), all with electricity and separated by low hedges. Access is from long, gravel lanes. Forty newly developed, fully serviced pitches have electricity, water, drainage, TV aerial point and Internet. From these, and from the front pitches on the lower fields, there are marvellous views over the Diernæs Bugt. There are several routes for walking and cycling and sea fishing trips are possible.

Facilities

Three modern toilet blocks with washbasins in cabins and controllable hot showers. Family shower rooms. Children's section. Baby room. En-suite facilities for disabled visitors. Laundry. Campers' kitchen. Motorcaravan services. Shop (July/Aug, then weekends only). Playground. Minigolf. Fishing. Archery. Watersports. Boat launching. Pétanque. TV room. Play house with Lego and Play Station. Daily activities for children in high season. WiFi (charged). Torch useful. Off site: Golf 8 km. Bicycle hire 15 km.

Open: Week before Easter - 30 October.

Directions

From German/Danish border follow E45 north. Take exit 69 and follow to Hoptrup. From Hoptrup follow to Diernæs and Diernæs Strand.
GPS: 55.15029, 9.4969

Charges guide

Per person	DKK 69
child (under 12 yrs)	DKK 46
pitch	DKK 40 - 70
electricity (10/16A)	DKK 35

Haderslev

Sandersvig Camping & Tropeland

Espagervej 15-17, DK-6100 Haderslev (Sønderjylland) T: 74 56 62 25. E: sandersvig@dk-camp.dk

alanrogers.com/DK2030

An attractively laid out, family run site, Sandersvig offers the very best of modern facilities in a peaceful and beautiful countryside location, 300 metres from the beach. The 470 very large grassy pitches (270 for tourers) are divided by hedges, shrubs and small trees into small enclosures, many housing only four units, most with electricity (10A). The site is well lit, very quiet at night and there are water taps close to most pitches. The playground boasts Denmark's largest bouncing cushion! 500 m. from the site a seven hectare park has a thriving herd of red deer.

Facilities

Four heated sanitary blocks offer some washbasins in cubicles and roomy showers (on payment). Suites for disabled visitors, 14 family bathrooms and baby rooms. Excellent kitchens. Very good laundry. Fish cleaning area. Motorcaravan services. Supermarket. Fast food service, with dining room (Easter-13/9). Takeaway (15/6-15/8). Indoor heated pool with sauna, solarium, jacuzzi, whirlpool and slide. Solarium. Playground. Games room. TV lounge. Tennis. Boat launching. WiFi throughout (charged). Off site. Riding 4 km. Bicycle hire 6 km. Fishing 7 km.

Open: 30 March - 16 September.

Directions

Leave E45 at exit 66 and turn towards Christianfeld. Turn right at roundabout onto 170 and follow signs for Fjelstrup and Knud village, turning right 1 km. east of the village from where site is signed.
GPS: 55.33424, 9.63152

Charges guide

Per unit incl. 2 persons and electricity	DKK 198 - 228
extra person	DKK 74
child (0-11 yrs)	DKK 42

Hampen

Hampen Sø Camping

Hovedgaden 31, DK-7362 Hampen (Vejle) T: 75 77 52 55. E: info@hampen-soe-camping.dk

alanrogers.com/DK2044

Hampen Sø Camping is well placed for visits to Legoland, the Lion Park and Silkeborg. It is in a natural setting close to lakes and moors and there is good cycling and walking in this very pleasant area. There are 230 pitches in total, with 80 seasonal units plus 34 cabins. The pitches are arranged in large grassy bays taking around 15 units, and there are 10A electric hook-ups (long leads may be needed). The site would benefit from improved maintenance, but some aspects, such as the free kitchens and well stocked shop, are extremely good.

Facilities

Three toilet blocks, one basic near the entrance, one central on the site with new laundry, new children's room and new kitchen, and one to far end with two family shower rooms. En-suite facilities for disabled visitors. Laundry. Good supermarket. Bar, restaurant and takeaway (weekends only outside high season; restaurant open to the general public). Games and TV rooms. Very small outdoor pool (15/6-1/9). Covered minigolf. Trampolines and new play equipment. Race track for mini cars. WiFi (charged). Off site: Riding 500 m. Fishing 3 km. Golf and boat launching 10 km.

Open: All year.

Directions

Site lies on road 176, 500 m. southwest of its junction with road 13 between Vejle and Viborg (around 50 km. south of Viborg). Look for Spar supermarket and camping signs.
GPS: 56.01425, 9.36427

Charges guide

Per person	DKK 72
child (0-11 yrs)	DKK 35
electricity	DKK 30

No credit cards.
Camping Cheques accepted.

Hårby

Løgismosestrand Camping

Løgismoseskov 7, DK-5683 Hårby (Fyn) T: 64 77 12 50. E: info@logismose.dk

alanrogers.com/DK2205

A countryside site with its own beach and pool, Løgismosestrand is surrounded by picturesque villages and the owners are a friendly young couple. The pitches here are arranged in rows and groups divided by hedges and small trees which provide a little shade. All the 221 pitches for touring units have 6/10A electricity points. A barbecue area has been developed with gas grills and there are swimming (8x14 m) and paddling pools for which there is a small charge. Recent additions include an Asian restaurant, a new football pitch and ten cabins to rent.

Facilities

Heated toilet units, kept very clean, include washbasins in cubicles, roomy showers (on payment), baby room, bathrooms for families and disabled visitors. Good laundry with washing machine and dryer. Excellent fully fitted kitchen (cooking charged). Motorcaravan services. Well stocked shop. Asian restaurant. Takeaway (high season). Swimming pool (1/6-1/9). Minigolf. Bicycle and boat hire. Adventure playground. Large undercover games room. Play field. Off site: Riding 2 km. Golf 8 km.

Open: 20 March - 22 September.

Directions

Southwest of Hårby via Sarup and Nellemose to Løgismoseskov, site is well signed. Lanes are narrow, large units should take care.
GPS: 55.17938, 10.07390

Charges guide

Per person	DKK 59
child (0-11 yrs)	DKK 35
pitch	free - DKK 40
electricity	DKK 26

Credit cards accepted with 4% surcharge.

Hesselager

Bøsøre Strand Feriepark

Bøsørevej 16, DK-5874 Hesselager (Fyn) T: 62 25 11 45. E: info@bosore.dk

alanrogers.com/DK2210

A themed holiday site on the eastern coast of Fyn, the tales of Hans Christian Andersen are evident in the design of the indoor pool complex and the main outdoor play area. The former has two pools on different levels, two hot tubs and a sauna, and features characters from the stories; the latter has a fairytale castle with a moat as its centrepiece. There are 300 pitches in total, and with only 25 seasonal units there should always be room for touring units out of the main season. All have 10A electricity, there are 124 multi-serviced pitches and 20 hardstandings.

Facilities

Sanitary facilities are in one central block and a smaller unit close to reception. Some family bathrooms, special children's section, baby rooms, facilities for disabled visitors. They could be stretched in high season. Laundry. Motorcaravan service point. Shop, bar/restaurant, pizzeria, takeaway. Kitchen (water charged). Solarium. Indoor pool complex. Games and TV rooms. Playground with moat. Animal farm. Internet access and WiFi (charged). Bicycle hire. Entertainment (main season). Boat launching with jetty. Communal barbecue. Off site: Golf 10 km.

Open: Easter - 22 October.

Directions

Site is on the coast about midway between Nyborg and Svendborg. From 163 road just north of Hesselager, turn towards coast signed Bøsøre Strand (5 km). GPS: 55.19287, 10.80530

Charges guide

Per unit incl. 2 persons and electricity	DKK 214 - 274
extra person	DKK 79
child (0-11 yrs)	DKK 53 - 70
dog	DKK 20

Hillerød

Hillerød Camping

Blytækkervej 18, DK-3400 Hillerød (Sjælland) T: 48 26 48 54. E: info@hillerodcamping.dk

alanrogers.com/DK2250

The northernmost corner of Sjælland is packed with interest, based not only on fascinating periods of Denmark's history but also its attractive scenery. Hillerød is also a fine base for visiting Copenhagen and is only 25 km. from the ferries at Helsingør and the crossing to Sweden. Centrally situated, the town is a hub of main roads from all directions, with this neat campsite clearly signed. It has a park-like setting in a residential area with five acres of well kept grass and some attractive trees. There are 100 pitches, of which 70 have electricity (10A) and these are marked.

Facilities

The bright, airy toilet block is older in style and includes washbasins with partitions and curtains. Facilities for babies can be used by disabled guests. Campers' kitchen adjoins the club room and includes free new electric hot plates and coffee making machine. Laundry room (free iron). Motorcaravan services. Small shop. Comfortable club room with TV. Play area. Bicycle hire. Off site: Tennis and indoor pool 1 km. Riding 2 km. Golf 3 km. Excellent electric train service every 10 minutes (20 minutes walk) to Copenhagen. The site sells the Copenhagen card.

Open: Easter - 16 September.

Directions

Follow road no. 6 bypassing road to south until sign for Hillerød S. Turn towards town at sign for 'Centrum' on Roskildvej road no. 233 and site is signed to the right. GPS: 55.924144, 12.294522

Charges guide

Per person	DKK 60 - 67
child (2-11 yrs)	DKK 30 - 35
electricity	DKK 25 - 30
dog	free

Hobro

Hobro Camping Gattenborg

Skivevej 35, DK-9500 Hobro (Nordjylland) T: 98 52 32 88. E: hobro@dk-camp.dk

alanrogers.com/DK2130

This neat and very well tended municipal site is imaginatively landscaped and has 139 pitches on terraces arranged around a bowl shaped central activity area. Most pitches (100 for touring units) have electricity (10A) and there are many trees and shrubs. Footpaths connect the various terraces and activity areas. There are 30 seasonal units and ten cabins. The reception building, with a small shop, has a covered picnic terrace behind and houses a large TV lounge. The small, heated, outdoor swimming pool with water slide is free to campers and open in high season, weather permitting.

Facilities

The main heated sanitary building includes washbasins in cubicles and hot showers (on payment). Two family bathrooms. Facilities for disabled visitors. Baby room. Kitchen (free herbs). Laundry facilities. Tiny unit in the centre of the site has two unisex WCs and basins (cold water only) and a small kitchen. Motorcaravan services. Shop (order bread before 9 pm). Swimming pool (high season). Play areas. Minigolf. TV lounge with board games and library. Bicycle hire. Internet access. Off site: Town 500 m. Beach 1 km. Fishing 7 km. Golf 25 km.

Open: 4 April - 27 September.

Directions

From E45 exit 35, take road 579 towards Hobro Centrum. Site is well signed to the right, just after railway bridge. GPS: 56.635875, 9.781308

Charges guide

Per person	DKK 65
child (0-11 yrs)	DKK 35
electricity	DKK 28
dog	DKK 10

Jelling

Fårup Sø Camping

Fårupvej 58, DK-7300 Jelling (Vejle) T: 75 87 13 44. E: faarup-soe@dk-camp.dk

alanrogers.com/DK2048

Fårup Sø Camping is a friendly and welcoming family run site next to the beautiful Fårup Lake and in a good location for visiting some of Denmark's best known attractions such as Legoland and the Lion Park. There are 250 grassy pitches, mostly on terraces (from top to bottom the height difference is 53 m). Some have beautiful views of the Fårup Lake. There are 200 pitches for touring units, all with 16A electricity, and some tent pitches without electricity. A heated swimming pool (min. 25 degrees Celsius), a whirlpool (free of charge) and an indoor play area for children are popular, as are the available activities, many associated with the lake.

Facilities

One modern and one older toilet block include open style washbasins and controllable hot showers. Family shower rooms. Baby room. Facilities for disabled visitors. Laundry. Campers' kitchen. Motorcaravan services. Shop (bread to order). Heated swimming pool and whirlpool. Indoor play area. Playgrounds. Games room. Lake with fishing. Viking ship. Watersports. Three play areas. Activities for children (high season). WiFi (charged). Off site: Golf and riding 2 km. Lion Park 8 km. Boat launching 10 km.

Open: 1 April - 9 September.

Directions

From Vejle take the 28 road towards Billund. In Skibet turn right towards Fårup Sø, Jennum and Jelling and follow the signs to Fårup Sø. GPS: 55.73614, 9.41777

Charges guide

Per unit incl. 2 persons and electricity	DKK 181 - 226
extra person	DKK 73
child (1-11 yrs)	DKK 43

Nibe

Sølyst Camping

Logstorvej 2, DK-9240 Nibe (Nordjylland) T: 98 35 10 62. E: soelyst@dk-camp.dk

alanrogers.com/DK2150

Sølyst Camping is a family run site with welcoming, enthusiastic and hardworking owners. It is next to the peaceful waters of Limfjord and a 15 minute walk from the old town centre of Nibe. There are 170 numbered pitches, of which 120 are for tourers. All have electricity (13A) and are arranged in rows separated by hedges. The pitches are spacious (100-140 sq.m), and those next to the fjord have uninterrupted views. There are watersports and swimming in the fjord. The site has a heated swimming pool (8x16 m), slide and splash pool, a children's pool, all with paved sunbathing area.

Facilities

New sanitary block. Second central sanitary unit includes washbasins in cubicles, four family bathrooms, a baby room and facilities for disabled visitors. Kitchen and small dining area. Laundry. Hot water (except in washbasins) is charged for. Motorcaravan services. Shop. Café/takeaway (main season). Swimming pool (June-Aug). Solarium. Play area. Minigolf. Boules. TV room. Games room. Fishing. Bicycle hire. Boat launching. Beach. Communal barbecue area. WiFi (charged). Off site: Riding and boat launching 1 km. Nibe 1 km. Golf 4 km.

Open: All year.

Directions

Site is clearly signed from the 187 road west of Nibe town, with a wide entrance. GPS: 56.9722, 9.6245

Charges guide

Per person	DKK 68 - 75
child (under 12 yrs)	DKK 43
pitch	DKK 10 - 40
electricity	DKK 35

Nykobing Mors

Jesperhus Feriecenter & Camping

Legindvej 30, DK-7900 Nykobing Mors (Viborg) T: 96 70 14 00. E: jesperhus@jesperhus.dk

alanrogers.com/DK2140

Jesperhus is an extensive, well organised and busy site with many leisure activities, adjacent to Blomsterpark (Northern Europe's largest flower park). This TopCamp site has 662 numbered pitches, mostly in rows with some terracing, divided by shrubs and trees and with shade in parts. Many pitches are taken by seasonal, tour operator or rental units, so advance booking is advised for peak periods. Electricity (6A) is available on all pitches and water points are in all areas. With all the activities at this site an entire holiday could be spent here, although Jesperhus is also an excellent centre for touring.

Facilities

Four good sanitary units are cleaned three times daily. Facilities include washbasins in cubicles or with divider/curtain, family and whirlpool bathrooms (on payment), suites for babies and disabled visitors. Sauna. Superb kitchens and laundry. Supermarket (1/4-1/11). Restaurant. Bar. Café, takeaway. Pool complex with spa facilities. Bowling. Minigolf. Tennis. Go-karts and other outdoor sports. Children's 'playworld'. Playgrounds. Pets corner. Golf. Fishing pond. Practice golf (3 holes). Off site: Beach and riding 2 km. Bicycle hire 6 km.

Open: All year.

Directions

From south or north, take road 26 to Salling Sund bridge, site is signed Jesperhus, just north of the bridge. GPS: 56.75082, 8.81580

Charges guide

Per person	DKK 75
child (1-11 yrs)	DKK 55
pitch	free - DKK 50
electricity	DKK 40

Odense

DCU Camping Odense

Odensevej 102, DK-5260 Odense (Fyn) T: 66 11 47 02. E: odense@dcu.dk

alanrogers.com/DK2215

Although within the confines of the city, this site is hidden away amongst mature trees and is therefore fairly quiet and an ideal base from which to explore the fairytale city of Odense. The 225 pitches, of which 200 have electricity (10A), are on level grass with small hedges and shrubs dividing the area into bays. There are a number of seasonal units on site, together with 13 cabins. A good network of cycle paths lead into the city. The Odense Adventure Pass (available at the site) allows unrestricted free travel on public transport within the city limits.

Facilities

Large sanitary unit provides modern facilities including washbasins in cubicles, family bathrooms, baby room and excellent suite for disabled visitors. Well equipped kitchen with gas hobs. Laundry with washing machines and dryer. Motorcaravan services. Shop. Small swimming and paddling pools. Games marquee. TV room. Large playground. Minigolf. WiFi. Off site: Cycle track through the zoo to city centre. Hans Christian Andersen's house. Bicycle hire 700 m. Golf 4 km. Fishing 10 km.

Open: All year.

Directions

From E20 exit 50, turn towards Odense Centrum, site entrance is 3 km. on left immediately beside the Hydro-Texaco garage. GPS: 55.3697, 10.3929

Charges guide

Per person	DKK 65 - 68
child (0-11 yrs)	DKK 33 - 34
pitch	DKK 20 - 40
electricity	DKK 25 - 30

Ry

Holmens Camping

Klostervej 148, DK-8680 Ry (Århus) T: 86 89 17 62. E: info@holmens-camping.dk

alanrogers.com/DK2080

A warm welcome awaits you at Holmens Camping, which lies between Silkeborg and Skanderborg in a very beautiful part of Denmark. The site is close to the waters of the Gudensø and Rye Møllesø lakes which are used for boating and canoeing, and fishing is a speciality of the site. Walking and cycling are also popular activities. Holmens has 225 grass touring pitches, partly terraced and divided by young trees and shrubs. The site itself is surrounded by mature trees. Almost all the pitches have 6A electricity and vary in size between 70-100 sq.m. The lake is suitable for swimming but the site also has an attractive pool complex (charged).

Facilities

One traditional and one modern toilet block have washbasins (open and in cabins) and controllable hot showers (on payment). En-suite facilities with toilet, basin, shower. Baby room. Facilities for disabled visitors. Laundry. Campers' kitchen. Shop. Covered pool with jet stream. Paddling pool. Wellness facilities (charged). Pool bar. Games room. Playground. Pétanque. Pony rides. Minigolf. Fishing. Bicycle hire. Boat rental. Some activities incur a charge. WiFi (charged). Off site: Riding 2 km. Golf 14 km.

Open: 1 April - 30 September.

Directions

Going north on E45, take exit 52 at Skanderborg turning west on 445 road towards Ry. In Ry follow the site signs. GPS: 56.07607, 9.76549

Charges guide

Per person	DKK 69 - 79
child (3-11 yrs)	DKK 38 - 44
pitch	DKK 26
electricity (6A)	DKK 29 - 38

Sakskøbing

Sakskøbing Camping

Saxes Allé 15, DK-4990 Sakskøbing (Lolland) T: 54 70 47 57. E: info@saxcamping.dk

alanrogers.com/DK2235

This small, traditional style site provides a useful stopover on the route from Germany to Sweden, within easy reach of the Puttgarden - Rødby ferry. There are 100 level grass pitches (90 for tourers), most with electricity (10A Europlug) and, although there are a fair number of seasonal units, one can usually find space. There is a pool at a nearby sports centre. The site has a well stocked shop, which is open long hours, but the town centre is semi-pedestrianised, and has a good range of shops and a supermarket. The town is noted for its unusual 'smiling' water tower, which you pass on the way to the site.

Facilities

Two sanitary units provide basic, older style facilities, including pushbutton free hot showers, some curtained washbasin cubicles and a baby room. Cooking and laundry facilities. Motorcaravan services. Shop. New play area. Bicycle hire. WiFi throughout (charged). Off site: Town and fishing 100 m. Golf and riding 10 km.

Open: 1 April - 30 September.

Directions

From E47, exit 46, turn towards town on no. 9 road. Turn right at crossroads towards town centre (site is signed), cross railway and then turn right again, and site entrance is 250 m. on left.
GPS: 54.79842, 11.64093

Charges guide

Per unit incl. 2 persons and electricity	DKK 170
extra person	DKK 70

Silkeborg

Terrassen Camping

Himmelbjergvej 9A, Laven, DK-8600 Silkeborg (Århus) T: 86 84 13 01. E: info@terrassen.dk

alanrogers.com/DK2050

Terrassen Camping is a family run site arranged on terraces, overlooking the lovely Lake Julso and the countryside. It is open and spacious, and when we visited was lively with people enjoying themselves. There are 235 touring pitches with good views, all with electricity (10/16A). The solar heated swimming pool has a paved terrace and is well fenced. This is a comfortable base from which to explore this area of Denmark where a warm welcome, real enthusiasm for making your holiday enjoyable, and good English will greet you. The area has much to offer including a trip on Lake Julso.

Facilities

The main modern sanitary unit is heated and includes many washbasins in cubicles. Controllable showers (on payment). Family bathrooms. Baby room. Facilities for disabled visitors. Kitchen. An older refurbished unit contains another kitchen, plus four further showers with external access. Motorcaravan services. Well stocked shop. Takeaways from town (by arrangement). Swimming pool (8x16 m; 12/5-31/8). Games/TV rooms with Internet. Adventure playground. Indoor play room. Pets corner. Covered barbecue area. Canoe hire. Bicycle hire. Electric bikes to order. Riding. WiFi (charged). Off site: Fishing 200 m. Golf, sailing and boat launching 5 km.

Open: 30 March - 23 September.

Directions

From the harbour in the centre of Silkeborg follow signs and minor road towards Sejs (5 km) and Ry (20 km). Site lies on the northern side of the road at village of Laven (13 km). Height restriction of 3 m. on railway bridge over this road.
GPS: 56.12409, 9.71037

Charges guide

Per unit incl. 2 persons and electricity	DKK 243 - 318
extra person	DKK 80
child	DKK 55
dog	DKK 25

Tønder

Møgeltønder Camping

Sonderstregsvej 2, Møgeltønder, DK-6270 Tønder (Sønderjylland) T: 74 73 84 60.
E: info@mogeltondercamping.dk **alanrogers.com/DK2020**

This site is only five minutes walk from one of Denmark's oldest villages and ten minutes drive from Tønder with its well preserved old buildings and interesting pedestrian shopping street. A quiet family site, Møgeltønder is well maintained with 285 large, level, numbered pitches on grass, with electricity (10A), of which 250 are for tourers. They are divided up by shrubs and hedges. The site has an excellent outdoor heated swimming pool and children's pool, a good playground with bouncy cushion and a range of trolleys, carts and tricycles. There are two good free kitchens for campers' use, and fishing is available next to the site. The new owners, Linda and Paul, are friendly and welcoming.

Facilities

Two heated sanitary units include roomy showers (on payment), washbasins with either divider/curtain or in private cubicles, plus bathrooms for families and disabled visitors. Baby room. Two kitchens with hobs (free). Laundry. Motorcaravan services. Well stocked shop (bread ordered daily, 1/4-1/10). Swimming pool (10x5 m) with chute and paddling pool. Minigolf. Playground. TV and games rooms. WiFi (charged). Off site: Fishing 200 m. Golf and bicycle hire 10 km.

Open: All year.

Directions

Turn left off no. 419 Tønder - Højer road, 4 km. from Tønder. Drive through Møgeltønder village and past the church where site is signed. The main street is cobbled so drive slowly. GPS: 54.93826, 8.7994

Charges guide

Per person	DKK 65
child (0-12 yrs)	DKK 35
electricity	DKK 30
dog	DKK 10

Finland

Situated in the far north, Finland is a long and mainly flat country, dominated by huge dense forests and glorious lakes. The unspoilt wilderness of Finland makes it a perfect place for relaxing in natural, peaceful surroundings.

There is a considerable difference in the landscape between north and south, with the gently rolling, rural landscape of the south giving way to the hills and vast forests of the north and treeless fells and peat-lands of Lapland, where reindeer and moose run free. Forests of spruce, pine and birch cover three quarters of the country's surface and are inhabited by hares, elk and occasional wolves and bears.

The other outstanding feature of Finland is its thousands of post-glacial lakes and islands. The main Lake District is centred on the beautiful Lake Saimaa in the south east, where you can swim, sail and fish. In the south, the capital, Helsinki, retains a small town feel, with open-air cafés, green parks, waterways and a busy market square surrounded by 19th-century architecture and museums. The flat western coastal regions include Turku and the Åland islands, ideal for sailing and fishing.

CAPITAL: Helsinki

Tourist Office

Finnish Tourist Board
PO Box 33213, London W6 8JX
Tel: 020 7365 2512
Fax: 020 8600 5681
Email: finlandinfo.lon@mek.fi
Internet: www.visitfinland.com

Population
5.3 million

Climate
Temperate climate, but with considerable variations. Summer is warm, winter is very cold.

Language
Finnish

Telephone
The country code is 00 358.

Money
Currency: The Euro
Banks: Mon-Fri 09.15-16.15
(regional variations may occur).

Shops
Mon-Fri 09.00-17.00/18.00.
Sat 09.00-14.00/15.00, department stores usually remain open to 18.00. Supermarkets are usually open to 20.00 Mon-Fri.

Public Holidays
New Year; Epiphany; Saints Day 16 Mar; Language Day 9 April; Good Friday; Easter Mon; May Day 30 Apr/1 May; All Saints Day 1 Nov; Independence Day 6 Dec; Christmas 25, 26 Dec.

Motoring
Main roads are excellent and relatively uncrowded outside city limits. Traffic drives on the right. Horn blowing is frowned upon. There are many road signs warning motorists of the danger of elk dashing out on the road. If you are unfortunate enough to hit one, it must be reported to police. Do not drink and drive, penalties are severe if any alcohol is detected.

see campsite map 3

Helsinki

Rastila Camping

Karavaanikatu 4, FIN-00980 Helsinki (Uusimaa) T: 093 107 8517. E: rastilacamping@hel.fi

alanrogers.com/FI2850

No trip to Finland would be complete without a few days stay in Helsinki, the capital since 1812. This all year round site has exceptional transport links, with the metro only five minutes walk from the campsite gates. It provides 165 pitches with electrical hook-ups, plus an additional small field for tent campers. Shrubs have been planted between the tarmac and grass pitches. All visitors will want to spend time in the capital and a 24-hour bus, tram and metro pass can be bought at the metro station. Once on the metro, you are in the city centre within 20 minutes on this regular, fast train service.

Facilities

Four sanitary blocks (two heated) provide toilets and showers. Kitchens with cooking rings and sinks. Facilities for disabled visitors and babies. Laundry room. Saunas. Motorcaravan service point. Fully licensed restaurant. Playground. Games and TV room. Bicycles for hire. Off site: Small beach adjacent. Golf 5 km. Tallinn the capital of Estonia is only 90 minutes away from Helsinki by fast Jetliner ferry.

Open: All year.

Directions

Well signed from 170 or Ring I. From the 170, turn at Itakeskus shopping complex towards Vuosaari. After crossing bridge go up slip road to Rastila. At top of road turn left. Site is directly ahead.
GPS: 60.206667, 25.121111

Charges guide

Per unit incl. 2 persons and electricity	€ 20.00 - € 29.50
extra person	€ 5.00
child (0-15 yrs)	€ 1.00

Discounts for weekly or monthly bookings.

Iisalmi

Koljonvirta Camping

Ylemmäisentie 6, FIN-74160 Iisalmi (Kuopio) T: 017 825 252. E: koljonvirta@koljonvirta.fi

alanrogers.com/FI2960

Koljonvirta Camping is a large but quiet site located about five kilometres from the centre of Iisalmi. There are 200 marked grass pitches, 120 with electricity (16A). The site adjoins a lake and has a small beach and facilities for boating and fishing. Iisalmi town itself is on the northern edge of the Finnish Lake District and provides a good variety of shops, including some factory outlets, and an interesting variety of events during June, July and August. These vary from the world famous 'Wife Carrying' World Championships to the Lapinlahti 'Cattle Calling' Competition and the International Midnight Marathon.

Facilities

The sanitary blocks provide showers, toilets and a sauna in one block. Launderette. Shop. Snack bar. Fully licensed restaurant. Motorcaravan service point. Lake and small beach with facilities for boating and fishing. The site exhibits large wooden sculptures of animals, plus they now have a new beach, volley field and minigolf.
Off site: Riding 100 m. Golf 5 km.

Open: May - September.

Directions

From road 5 turn onto the 88 (towards Oulu) just north of Iisalmi. Go straight over the roundabout and the site is about 1 km. on the left. Follow signs.
GPS: 63.59462, 27.16084

Charges guide

Per unit incl. 2 persons and electricity	€ 25.00

Ivalo

Ukonjärvi Camping

Ukonjärventi 141, FIN-99801 Ivalo (Lapland) T: 016 667 501. E: nuttu@ukolo.fi

alanrogers.com/FI2995

Ukonjärvi Camping lies on the banks of Lake Inari, situated in a forested area alongside a nature reserve. It is a quiet, peaceful site, ideal for rest and relaxation. Thirty touring pitches have electricity and are surrounded by pine and beech trees. Cottages are available to rent. A bar and restaurant are located at reception; a range of local dishes are produced including reindeer casserole. There is also a barbecue hut, located in the centre of the site, if you prefer to cook your own food. A climb up to the nearby viewpoint offers spectacular views over the lake – you can even see over to Russia. The lake also provides plenty of opportunities for boating and fishing.

Facilities

Sanitary block includes toilets and showers. Laundry and campers' kitchen. Lakeside sauna (charged). Bar and restaurant. Charcoal barbecues are not permitted. Barbecue hut with logs. Small beach. Fishing and boating on lake. TV room. WiFi. Off site: Tankavaaran Kansainvalinen Kulamuseo, a gold mining experience where you can try gold panning, keeping what you find! The Northern Lapland Centre and the Sami Museum, displaying cultural and natural history exhibitions.

Open: 15 May - 15 September.

Directions

Ukonjärvi Camping is 11 km. north of Ivalo on road 4. Look for signs to Lake Inari viewpoint; site is about 1 km. down a narrow road (signed).
GPS: 68.73687, 27.47687

Charges 2012

Per unit incl. 2 persons and electricity	€ 3.50
extra person	€ 4.00
child	€ 2.50

Karigasniemi

Camping Tenorinne

Ylatenontie 55, FIN-99950 Karigasniemi (Lapland) T: **016 676 113**. E: **camping@tenorinne.com**

alanrogers.com/FI2990

This is probably the most northerly campsite in Finland and makes an excellent stopover en route to North Cape. This is a small site with space for 30 units, on three levels with a small access road sloping down to the river. Electricity points (16A) are available throughout the site but the pitches are unmarked. This area is still largely unpopulated, scattered with only small Sami communities and herds of reindeer. Karigasniemi is a slightly larger town as it is a border post with Norway and is close to both the Kevo Nature reserve and the Lemmenjoki National Park.

Facilities

Sanitary block includes showers, toilets and sauna. Launderette. Kitchen. Reception with TV.

Open: 5 June - 15 September.

Directions

If travelling south on the 970, site is on right as you enter town. If travelling west on the 92, turn right immediately before Norwegian customs point. Site is shortly on left past petrol station. Entrance is quite steep. GPS: 69.40033, 25.84450

Charges guide

Per unit incl. 2 persons and electricity	€ 21.00 - € 23.00
extra person	€ 3.00

Manamansalo

Manamansalo Camping

Teeriniemientie 156, FIN-88340 Manamansalo (Oulu) T: **088 741 38**. E: **manamansalo@kainuunmatkailu.fi**

alanrogers.com/FI2975

Manamansalo is a top class, 'wild north' tourist centre on the island of Manamansalo in Lake Oulojärvi. You come by ferry or via a bridge from the mainland. This site is a real find if you are looking for peace and quiet and is also very good for families. It has 200 pitches, 140 with electricity, very attractively laid out in the forest with natural dividers of pine trees. The site stretches along the lake and has a long, narrow sandy beach. Nature lovers will appreciate the network of trails in the pine forest. Choose between walking and cycling or even skiing in spring.

Facilities

Three toilet blocks have toilets, washbasins and showers in cubicles with free hot water. Washing machines and dryers. Kitchen with sinks, cooking rings and ovens. Motorcaravan service point. Fully licensed restaurant and small shop (from May). Playground. Canoes, pedaloes and rowing boats for hire. Fishing. WiFi.

Open: 1 March - 30 September.

Directions

Coming from the south on road 5/E63 turn at Mainau on road 28. At Vuottolahti turn on road 879 and follow signs to Manamansalo and site. From road 22 turn at Liminpuro or Melaillahti and follow signs. GPS: 64.389417, 27.026083

Charges guide

Per unit incl. 2 persons and electricity	€ 28.50
extra person	€ 4.50
child (0-15 yrs)	€ 1.00

Oulu

Nallikari Camping

Leiritie 10, FIN-90510 Oulu (Oulu) T: **044 703 1353**. E: **nallikari.camping@ouka.fi**

alanrogers.com/FI2970

This is probably one of the best sites in Scandinavia, set in a recreational wooded area alongside a sandy beach on the banks of the Baltic Sea, with the added bonus of the adjacent Eden Spa complex. Nallikari provides 200 pitches, 176 with 16A electricity (7 also have water supply and drainage), plus an additional 78 cottages to rent, 28 of which are suitable for winter occupation. Oulu is a modern town, about 100 miles south of the Arctic Circle, that enjoys long, sunny and dry summer days. The Baltic however is frozen for many weeks in the winter and then the sun barely rises for two months. In early June the days are very long with the sun setting at about 23.30 and rising at 01.30!

Facilities

The modern shower/WC blocks also provide male and female saunas, kitchen and launderette facilities. Facilities for disabled visitors. Motorcaravan service point. Playground. Reception with café/restaurant (June-Aug), souvenir and grocery shop. TV room. Free WiFi over site. Bicycle hire. Communal barbecues only. Off site: The adjacent Eden Centre provides excellent modern spa facilities where you can enjoy a day under the glass-roofed pool with its jacuzzis, saunas, Turkish baths and an Irish bath. Riding 2 km. Fishing 5 km. Golf 15 km.

Open: All year.

Directions

Leave road 4/E75 at junction with road 20 and head west down Kiertotie. Site well signed, Nallikari Eden, but continue on, just after traffic lights, cross a bridge and take the second on the right. Just before the Eden Centre turn right towards Leiritie and reception. GPS: 65.02973, 25.41793

Charges guide

Per unit incl. 2 persons	€ 13.00 - € 26.00
extra person	€ 4.00
child (under 15 yrs)	€ 2.00
electricity	€ 4.50 - € 6.50

Rovaniemi

Ounaskoski Camping

Jäämerentie 1, FIN-96200 Rovaniemi (Lapland) T: 016 345 304. E: ounaskoski-camping@windowslive.com

alanrogers.com/FI2980

Ounaskoski Camping is situated almost exactly on the Arctic Circle, 66 degrees north and just 8 km. south of the Santa Claus post office and village, on the banks of the Kemijoki River. The site has 153 marked touring pitches, 72 with electricity, plus a further small area for tents. Rovaniemi attracts many visitors each year, especially in the weeks leading up to Christmas, who fly direct to the local airport and pay Santa Claus a visit. The town has much to offer with a good selection of shops and some restaurants. Reindeer meat is well worth trying!

Facilities

There are two sanitary buildings each providing toilets, showers, laundry and kitchen. One also houses a sauna. Facilities for disabled visitors. Motorcaravan service point. Café. Small shop. Playground. Fishing. Organised coach trips. Off site: Ranua Zoo. The Kemijoki, Finland's largest river, offers numerous opportunities for sightseeing by boat. Santa Claus village and Santa Park.

Open: 21 May - 15 September.

Directions

Ounaskoski Camping is on the banks of the Kemijoki River in the middle of Rovaniemi. From the 4/E75 go via the centre across the river and turn right. Site is between the Jatkankynttilasilta Bridge and the Rautatiesilta Bridge. GPS: 66.49748, 25.743504

Charges guide

Per unit incl. 2 persons and electricity	€ 29.00 - € 31.00

Ruovesi

Camping Haapasaaren Lomakylä

Haapasaarentie 5, FIN-34600 Ruovesi (Häme) T: 044 080 0290. E: lomakyla@haapasaari.fi

alanrogers.com/FI2840

Haapasaaren is located on Lake Näsijärvi, around 70 km. north of Tampere in south western Finland. This is a well equipped site with a café and restaurant, a traditional Finnish outside dancing area and, of course, plenty of saunas! Rowing boats, canoes, cycles and, during the winter months, sleds are all available for rent. Fishing is very popular here. Pitches are grassy and of a good size. There is also a good range of accommodation to rent, including holiday cottages with saunas. The cosy restaurant, Jätkäinkämppä, has an attractive terrace and fine views across the lake. Alternatively, the site's café, Portinpieli, offers a range of snacks as well as Internet access. Haapasaaren's friendly owners organise a series of guided tours throughout the year. These include hiking and nature treks, berry and mushroom picking, and, during the winter, ice fishing and cross-country skiing. Helvetinjärvi National Park is one of the most dramatic areas of western Finland, and is made up of deep gorges and dense forests. There is a rich population of birds and occasionally even brown bears and lynx can be seen here.

Facilities

Café. Restaurant. Direct lake access. Saunas. Fishing. Minigolf. Boat and canoe hire. Bicycle hire. Guided tours. Play area. Tourist information. Chalets for rent. Off site: Walking and cycle routes. Boat trips. Helvetinjärvi National Park.

Open: All year.

Directions

From Helsinki, head north on the E12 motorway to Tampere and then northeast on N63-9 to Orivesi. Then, continue north on route 66 to Ruovesi and follow signs to the site. GPS: 61.99413, 24.069843

Charges guide

Per unit incl. 2 persons and electricity	€ 25.00
extra person	€ 4.00
child (under 15 yrs)	€ 2.00

For latest campsite news, availability and prices visit
alanrogers.com

Sodankylä

Camping Sodankylä Nilimella

Kelukoskentie 4, FIN-99600 Sodankylä (Lapland) T: 016 612 181. E: antti.rintala@naturex-ventures.fi

alanrogers.com/FI2985

Camping Sodankylä Nilimella is a small, quiet site situated alongside the Kitinen River, just one kilometre from the centre of Sodankylä. The site is split into two areas by a small, relatively quiet, public road. The good sized pitches (80 in total) are clearly marked with hedges and 40 have 16A electricity. The reception area also serves drinks and snacks. Sodankylä town itself, at the junction of routes 4 and 5, is home to a small Sami community and is an important trading post, so you will find a variety of shops including supermarkets. The town is also home to the Geophysical Observatory, which constantly surveys the earth's magnetic field and measures earthquakes using seismic recordings.

Facilities

Two good sanitary blocks with toilets, hot showers and saunas. Facilities for disabled visitors. Campers' kitchen. Motorcaravan service point. Playground. Bicycle hire. River swimming, canoeing and water skiing. WiFi.
Off site: Shops and supermarkets in Sodankylä town.

Open: 1 June - 30 September.

Directions

Turn off road 4 onto road 5. Site is on the left just after crossing the river. It is well signed and easy to find. GPS: 67.41755, 26.60803

Charges guide

Per unit incl. 2 persons and electricity	€ 17.00 - € 22.00
extra person	€ 3.00 - € 4.00
child	€ 1.00 - € 2.00

Tampere

Tampere Camping Härmälä

Leirintäkatu 8, FIN-33900 Tampere (Häme) T: 020 719 9777. E: harmala@fontana.fi

alanrogers.com/FI2820

Härmälä is a lively campsite near Lake Pyhäjärvi. It is situated only 4 km. from Tampere city centre. You can chose from a large, unspecified number of unmarked pitches (about 180). The site has 111 cabins of various sizes and facilities. Amenities include a beach, saunas, playgrounds for children, a small shop and a pizzeria. The site seems a little run down but is acceptable for a couple of nights. Tampere is beautifully situated beside Lake Näsijärvi. A stroll along the harbour with its yachts and through the parks is a pleasant experience. Another must is the Sänkänniemi Adventure Park with its 168 m. high tower and revolving restaurant, children's zoo, aquarium and amusements.

Facilities

There are four sanitary blocks, one is new, three are rather basic. Washbasins and showers have free hot water. Facilities for disabled visitors. Laundry room. Campers' kitchen with cooking rings, microwave. Motorcaravan service point. Small shop. Pizzeria. Off site: Golf and riding 5 km.

Open: 15 May - 30 August.

Directions

Turn off the E12 and follow signs.
GPS: 61.471967, 23.73945

Charges guide

Per unit incl. 2 persons and electricity	€ 26.00
extra person	€ 4.00
child (4-14 yrs)	€ 2.00
child (0-3 yrs)	free

Virrat

Camping Lakari

Lakarintie 405, FIN-34800 Virrat (Häme) T: 034 758 639. E: lakari@virtainmatkailu.fi

alanrogers.com/FI2830

The peace and tranquillity of the beautiful natural surroundings are the main attractions at this vast campsite (18 hectares), which is located on a narrow piece of land between two lakes. This site is a must if you want to get away from it all. There are a variety of cabins to rent, some with their own beach and jetty! Marked pitches for tents and caravans are beside the beach or in little meadows in the forest. You pick your own place. Site amenities include a café and a beach sauna. This is a spectacular landscape with deep gorges and steep lakeside cliffs.

Facilities

Two toilet blocks, basic but clean and well kept, include toilets, washbasins and showers. Free hot water. Chemical disposal and motorcaravan service point. Covered campers' kitchen with fridge, cooking rings and oven. Washing machine. Small shop and caféteria. TV. Fishing. Bicycle hire. Off site: Golf 1 km. Riding 5 km.

Open: 1 May - 30 September.

Directions

Site is 7 km. south of Virrat on road 66. Follow signs.
GPS: 62.209817, 23.837767

Charges guide

Per unit incl. 2 persons and electricity	€ 22.00
extra person	€ 3.00
child	€ 1.50

France

From the hot sunny climate of the Mediterranean to the more northerly and cooler regions of Normandy and Brittany, with the Châteaux of the Loire and the lush valleys of the Dordogne, France offers holidaymakers a huge choice of destinations to suit all tastes.

France boasts every type of landscape imaginable, ranging from the wooded valleys of the Dordogne to the volcanic uplands of the Massif Central, the rocky coast of Brittany to the lavender-covered hills of Provence and snow-capped peaks of the Alps. Each region is different and this is reflected in the local customs, cuisine, architecture and dialect. Many rural villages hold festivals to celebrate the local saints and you can also find museums devoted to the rural arts and crafts of the regions.

France has a rich architectural heritage with a huge variety of Gothic cathedrals, châteaux, Roman remains, fortresses and Romanesque churches to visit. Given the varied landscape and climate, there is also great scope for outdoor pursuits with plenty of hiking and cycling opportunities across the country, and rock climbing and skiing in the mountains. And of course a trip to France wouldn't be complete without sampling the local food and wine.

CAPITAL: Paris

Tourist Office

French Government Tourist Office
Maison de la France
178 Piccadilly, London W1J 9AL
Tel: 020 7399 3520
Fax: 020 7493 6594
Email: info.uk@franceguide.com
Internet: www.franceguide.com

Population
63 million

Climate
France has a temperate climate but this varies considerably from region to region.

Language
French

Telephone
The country code is 00 33.

Money
Currency: The Euro
Banks: Mon-Fri 09.00-12.00 and 14.00-16.00.

Shops
Mon-Sat 09.00-18.30. Some are closed between 12.00-14.30. Food shops are open 07.00-18.30/19.30. Some food shops (particularly bakers) are open Sunday mornings. Many shops close Mondays.

Public Holidays
New Year; Easter Mon; Labour Day; VE Day 8 May; Ascension; Whit Mon; Bastille Day 14 July; Assumption 15 Aug; All Saints 1 Nov; Armistice Day 11 Nov; Christmas Day.

Motoring
France has a comprehensive road system from motorways (Autoroutes), Routes Nationales (N roads), Routes Départmentales (D roads) down to purely local C class roads. Tolls are payable on the autoroute network which is extensive but expensive, and also on certain bridges.

see campsite map 5

Agay

Camping Caravaning Esterel

Avenue des Golf, Agay, F-83530 Saint Raphaël (Var) T: 04 94 82 03 28. E: contact@esterel-caravaning.fr

alanrogers.com/FR83020

Esterel is a quality, award-winning caravan site east of St Raphaël, set among the hills beyond Agay. The site is 3.5 km. from the sandy beach at Agay where parking is perhaps a little easier than at most places on this coast, but a shuttle runs from the site to and from the beach several times daily in July and August (€1). It has 164 touring pitches for caravans but not tents; all have electricity (10A) and a water tap, 18 special ones have their own en-suite washroom adjoining whilst others also have a washing machine, dishwasher, jacuzzi,16A electricty and free WiFi. Pitches are on shallow terraces, attractively landscaped with good shade and a variety of flowers, giving a feeling of spaciousness.

Facilities

Excellent refurbished, heated toilet blocks. Individual toilet units on 18 pitches. Facilities for disabled visitors. Laundry room. Motorcaravan services. Shop. Gift shop. Takeaway. Bar/restaurant. Five circular swimming pools (two heated). Spa with sauna etc. Disco. Archery. Minigolf. Tennis. Pony rides. Pétanque. Squash. Playground. Nursery. Bicycle hire. Internet access. Events in season. No barbecues. WiFi throughout. Baby club. Off site: Trekking (foot, bicycle or pony) in L'Esterel forest park. Fishing and beach 3 km.

Open: 31 March - 29 September.

Directions

From A8, exit Fréjus, follow signs for Valescure, then for Agay, site is on left. The road from Agay is the easiest to follow but it is possible to approach from St Raphaël via Valescure. Look carefully for site sign, which is difficult to see. GPS: 43.453775, 6.832817

Charges guide

Per unit incl. 2 persons and electricity	€ 18.00 - € 83.00
extra person	€ 9.00 - € 11.00

Aléria

Riva Bella Nature Resort & Spa

B.P. 21, F-20270 Aléria (Haute-Corse) T: 04 95 38 81 10. E: rivabella.corsica@gmail.com

alanrogers.com/FR20040

This is a relaxed, informal, spacious site alongside an extremely long and beautiful beach. Riva Bella is naturist from 16 May to 19 September only. It offers a variety of pitches situated in beautiful countryside and seaside. The site is divided into several areas with 200 pitches (133 for touring with 6A electricity), some of which are alongside the sandy beach with little shade. Others are in a shady wooded glade on the hillside. The huge fish-laden lakes are a fine feature of this site and a superb balnéotherapy centre offers the very latest beauty and relaxation treatments (men and women) based on marine techniques.

Facilities

High standard toilet facilities. Provision for disabled visitors, children and babies. Laundry. Large shop (15/5-15/10). Fridge hire. Two restaurants with sea and lake views. Excellent beach restaurant/bar. Watersports, sailing school, pedaloes, fishing. Balnéotherapy centre. Sauna. Aerobics. Giant chess. Archery. Fishing. Riding. Mountain bike hire. Half-court tennis. Walking with llamas. Internet. WiFi (charged). Professional evening entertainment. Off site: Tours of the island. Walking. Riding 7 km. Scuba diving 10 km. Paragliding.

Open: All year (naturist 16/5-19/9).

Directions

Site is 12 km. north of Aleria on N198 (Bastia) road. Watch for large signs and unmade road to site and follow for 4 km. GPS: 42.16151, 9.55269

Charges guide

Per unit incl. 2 persons and electricity	€ 23.30 - € 40.30
extra person	€ 5.00 - € 9.00
child (3-8 yrs)	€ 2.00 - € 6.00
dog	€ 2.00 - € 3.50

Camping Cheques accepted.

Allés-sur-Dordogne

Camping le Port de Limeuil

F-24480 Allés-sur-Dordogne (Dordogne) T: 05 53 63 29 76. E: didierbonvallet@aol.com

alanrogers.com/FR24170

At the confluence of Dordogne and Vézère rivers, opposite the picturesque village of Limeuil, this delightful family site exudes a peaceful and relaxed ambience. There are 75 marked touring pitches on grass, some spacious and all with electricity (5/10A). The buildings are in traditional Périgourdine style and surrounded by flowers and shrubs. A sports area on a large, open, grassy space between the river bank and the main camping area adds to the feeling of space and provides an additional recreation and picnic area (there are additional unmarked pitches for tents and camper vans along the bank here).

Facilities

Two clean, modern toilet blocks provide excellent facilities. Bar/restaurant with snacks and takeaway (all 20/5-5/9). Small shop. Swimming pool with jacuzzi, paddling pool and children's slide (1/5-30/9). Badminton. Tennis. Volleyball. Football. Boules. Trampoline. Mountain bike hire. Canoe hire, launched from the site's own pebble beach. WiFi in bar area (free). Off site: The pretty medieval village of Limeuil 200 m. Riding 1 km. Golf 10 km.

Open: 1 May - 30 September.

Directions

Site is 7 km. south of Le Bugue. From D51/D31E Le Buisson to Le Bugue road turn west towards Limeuil. Just before bridge into Limeuil, turn left (site signed), across another bridge. Site shortly on the right. GPS: 44.87977, 0.88587

Charges guide

Per unit incl. 2 persons and electricity	€ 16.50 - € 30.00
extra person	€ 4.50 - € 6.50

Andelys

Camping de l'Ile des Trois Rois

1 rue Gilles Nicolle, F-27700 Andelys (Eure) T: 02 32 54 23 79. E: campingtroisrois@aol.com

alanrogers.com/FR27070

One hour from Paris, on the banks of the Seine and overlooked by the impressive remains of Château Gaillard (Richard Coeur de Lion), this attractive and very spacious, ten-hectare site will appeal to everyone. There is easy access to the 108 touring pitches on level grass, in a well landscaped setting and all with electricity (6A), although some long leads may be required. Many of these back onto the River Seine where you can watch the barges, and most have views of the château. Of the 80 mobile homes on site, there are five to let, leaving lots of space to enjoy the surroundings, including the large lake full of perch and bream for those eager fishermen. Others can try their luck in the Seine. A nearby station will whisk you to Paris for the day, or a short drive will bring the delights of Monet's house and garden. A Medieval Festival is held in Les Andelys in the last weekend of June. Walk along the banks of the Seine and watch the huge passenger boats cruising there, or stroll into the main town for shopping and restaurants.

Facilities

Four small, unheated toilet blocks have British style toilets (no seats), showers and washbasins, all in cubicles; dishwashing and laundry sinks. One has facilities for disabled visitors, another has a laundry facility. Motorcaravan service point. Heated swimming and paddling pools (15/5-30/9). Bar and restaurant (1/4-30/9). Fenced play area. Evening entertainment (4/7-30/8). Bicycles and barbecues for hire. Satellite TV. Internet access and WiFi (charged). Adult open-air exercise area. Off site: Cycling and walking trails. Riding 5 km. Golf 9 km. Giverny 20 km. Rouen 40 km.

Open: 15 March - 15 November.

Directions

Les Andelys is 40 km. southeast of Rouen. From the town centre, continue on D125 and follow signs until roundabout by bridge where second exit leads directly into site. GPS: 49.23564, 1.40005

Charges guide

Per unit incl. 2 persons and electricity	€ 21.00
extra person	€ 5.50
child (under 3 yrs)	free
dog	€ 2.00

Low season promotion (15/3-20/6)
€ 16.00 for 2 persons incl. electricity.

Argelès-Gazost

Kawan Village du Lavedan

Lau-Balagnas, 44 Route des Vallees, F-65400 Argelès-Gazost (Hautes-Pyrénées) T: 05 62 97 18 84.

E: contact@lavedan.com alanrogers.com/FR65080

Camping du Lavedan is an old established, family owned site set in the Argelès-Gazost valley south of the Lourdes, where a warm welcome and an impressive mountain view await you. There are 60 level touring pitches, all with electricity (2-10A) and most have shade from trees. They are set away from the 48 mobile homes, of which 12 are to rent. Landscaping has been carefully considered. The large well-designed restaurant and bar area is the scene of some lively evening entertainment in the summer. There is some noise from the road. Lourdes is an important pilgrimage town and a bus goes from outside the campsite. It is beside the main road so there is some daytime road noise.

Facilities

Recent, well maintained toilet block. Baby room. Facilities for disabled visitors. Washing machines and dryer in separate block heated in winter. Restaurant with terrace, pizzeria and snacks (1/5-15/9). Bar. TV. No shop, bread delivery (1/5-15/9). Swimming pool (with cover), paddling pool. Play area. WiFi (charged). Boules. Off site: Trout fishing, bicycle hire 1 km. Supermarket 2 km. Riding 5 km. Golf 15 km. Nearby is La Voie Verte, a 17 km. traffic-free cycle path from Lourdes south to Soulom.

Open: All year.

Directions

From Lourdes take the N21 (Voie rapide) south. This becomes the N821/N821A. Take exit 3 (Argelès-Gazost). Take D921 then D921B to Lau-Balagnas. Site on right, southern edge of town. GPS: 42.98822, -0.089

Charges guide

Per unit incl. 2 persons	€ 15.00 - € 24.00
electricity (10A max)	€ 1.00

Camping Cheques accepted.

Argelès-sur-Mer

Camping la Sirène

Route de Taxo à la Mer, F-66702 Argelès-sur-Mer (Pyrénées-Orientales) T: 04 68 81 04 61.
E: contact@camping-lasirene.fr **alanrogers.com/FR66560**

alan rogers Runner up 2011 Awards

From the moment you step into the hotel-like reception area you realise that this large site offers the holiday maker everything they could want in a well managed and convenient location close to Argelès-sur-Mer and the beaches. The 740 mobile homes and chalets vary in standard but all are less than five years old, very clean, comfortable and located on neat tidy pitches. There are also some touring pitches. In the summer there are 170 staff on duty to ensure your stay is as enjoyable as they can make it. All the shops and amenities are near reception making the accommodation areas quite peaceful and relaxing. There are many things to do and summer visitors have the option of using the free bus service to the beach where the site has its own club where you can even go windsurfing at no charge.

Facilities
Restaurant, bar and takeaway. Large shop (all season). Large aqua park, paddling pools, slides, jacuzzi. Games room. Multisports field, tennis, archery, minigolf, football. Theatre, evening entertainment, discos, show time spectacular. Riding. Bicycle hire. Off site: Resort of Argelès-sur-Mer with beaches, karting, 10-pin bowling, amusement park and the site's private Emeraude Beach Club, all 2 km. Interesting old town of Collioure close by. Fishing 4 km. Golf 7 km.

Open: 17 April - 26 September.

Directions
Leave A9 motorway at exit 42, take D114, towards Argelès. Leave D114, exit 10 and follow signs for Plage Nord. Site signed after first roundabout and is on right 2 km. after last roundabout.
GPS: 42.57093, 3.02906

Charges guide

Per unit incl. 1-3 persons and electricity	€ 26.00 - € 43.00
extra person	€ 6.00 - € 9.00
child (under 5 yrs)	€ 4.00 - € 6.00

Argelès-sur-Mer

Camping l'Hippocampe

Route de Taxo à la Mer, F-66702 Argelès-sur-Mer (Pyrénées-Orientales) T: 04 68 81 04 61.
E: contact@camping-lasirene.fr **alanrogers.com/FR66570**

A sister site to la Sirène just opposite, this site has some touring pitches along with 170 mobile home and chalet pitches and is aimed at families with young children and adults looking for a quieter site. The mobile homes and chalets are all modern, well maintained and have space around them to provide privacy. The pool on site is dedicated to the smaller children and is a great place for them to gain confidence in the water whilst still being able to play. Entertainment, shops, bars and the full range of activities offered by la Sirène, just across the road. Visitors here also have free access to the beach club Emeraude which offers free transport to Plage Nord where the club is situated.

Facilities
Pool and laundry. Shop, small bar (all season). All other facilities are at la Sirène just across the road. Riding. Bicycle hire. Off site: Karting, 10-pin bowling, amusement park within 1 km. Beach at Argelès-sur-Mer within 2 km. Fishing 4 km. Golf 7 km.

Open: 17 April - 26 September.

Directions
Leave A9 at exit 42. Take D114, Argelès road. Leave D114 at exit 10, follow signs for Plage Nord. Site signed after the first roundabout, on left 2 km. after last roundabout. GPS: 42.5705, 3.03065

Charges guide

Per unit incl. 1-3 persons and electricity	€ 26.00 - € 43.00
extra person	€ 6.00 - € 9.00
child (under 5 yrs)	€ 4.00 - € 6.00

Argelès-sur-Mer

Camping le Bois du Valmarie

F-66702 Argelès-sur-Mer (Pyrénées-Orientales) T: 04 68 81 09 92. E: contact@camping-lasirene.fr
alanrogers.com/FR66590

Pitches here are exclusively for mobile home and chalet accommodation. Le Bois du Valmarie is a member of the same group of sites as la Sirène (FR66560) and l'Hippocampe (FR66570). The site has 181 pitches, the majority of which are available for booking (none available for touring) and is located south of the port beside Racou beach. The site has a pleasant woodland location and a range of amenities including a large swimming pool complex with waterslides and a separate children's pool. The sea is just 50 m. from the site entrance with a sandy beach and within easy walking distance. The site has its own bar and a good restaurant but visitors are welcome at la Sirène to enjoy the entertainment and activities on offer. Popular with tour operators.

Facilities
Supermarket. Restaurant. Bar. Beach shop. Takeaway food. Swimming pool with waterslides and separate children's pool. Play area. Mobile homes for rent.
Off site: Argelès town centre 3 km. Diving club. Blue Bear activity club. Emeraude Beach Club. Fishing 2 km. Riding 4 km. Golf 7 km.

Open: 7 April - 28 September.

Directions
Leave autoroute at Perpignan Sud exit and join the N114 southbound toward Argelès. Take exit 13 and follow signs to Le Racou. Site is well signed from here. GPS: 42.53784, 3.05445

Charges guide
Contact the site for details.

Ascou

Camping Ascou la Forge

F-09110 Ascou (Ariège) T: 05 61 64 60 03. E: info@ascou-la-forge.fr

alanrogers.com/FR09120

The Dutch owners of Ascou la Forge will give you a warm, friendly welcome at their oasis in the mountains of the Pyrenees, close to the borders of Andorra and Spain. The site is 3,500 feet above sea level but is easily accessible for motorcaravans and caravans. Lying alongside the Lauze river, there are 50 pitches. In low season, 44 mainly level, grass touring pitches with electricity are available, but this number reduces to 20 in July and August to allow more room for the large influx of campers with tents. There are also three chalets, two bungalows and one apartment available to rent. The site is quite open but a few trees scattered around provide some shade.

Facilities

Modern, bright, sanitary block is fully equipped including facilities for disabled visitors which double as a family shower room with a baby bath. Shop. Bar with large screen for major sports events and films about the local flora/fauna. Play area. Maps and walking routes. Free WiFi. Off site: Restaurant next door to site (all year). Restaurants, bars and shops in Ax-les-Thermes 7 km.

Open: All year.

Directions

From Ax-Les-Thermes take D613 signed Quérigat, Quillan and Ascou-Pailhéres. After 3.6 km. turn right on D25 to site on right after 3.4 km.
GPS: 42.72444, 1.89274

Charges guide

Per unit incl. 2 persons and electricity	€ 15.00 - € 23.00
extra person	€ 3.50 - € 5.00

Autrans

Kawan Village Au Joyeux Réveil

Le Château, F-38880 Autrans (Isère) T: 04 76 95 33 44. E: camping-au-joyeux-reveil@wanadoo.fr

alanrogers.com/FR38080

The superb site is run by a very friendly family (English is spoken). It is on the outskirts of Autrans, high on a plateau (1,050 m) in the Vercors region close to a ski jump and short lift. There are 101 pitches with 70 for touring, electricity (6A). They are mainly on gently sloping grass, in a sunny location with fantastic views over the surrounding wooded mountains with small trees giving just a little shade. There is a new swimming pool area with two pools, one covered, a river and slide plus a separate paddling pool. This site is ideally situated for many of the activities that this area has to offer with magnificent scenery.

Facilities

The spotless toilet block is very well appointed, with underfloor heating and all the expected facilities. Another chalet-style building houses a bar with terrace, snack bar/takeaway (July/Aug). Two pools, one covered, toboggan for children, sunbathing area and a separate paddling pool. Small play area. TV room. Internet point and WiFi (free). Family entertainment (July/Aug).
Off site: Fishing 200 m. Riding 300 m. Autrans with a few shops 500 m. Bicycle hire 500 m. Villard de Lans, supermarket, shops, restaurants, bars, ice rink and many other activities 16 km. Bus to Villard de Lans and Grenoble. Golf 20 km.

Open: 1 May - 30 September.

Directions

Leave A48, northwest of Grenoble, exit 13 (going south) or 3A (north). Follow N532 to Sassenage, turn west at roundabout, D531 to Lans-en-Vercors. At roundabout turn right, D106 Autrans. At roundabout in Autrans turn right (site signed) and very shortly right again. Site is on the left. This is the only route recommended for caravans and motorcaravans.
GPS: 45.17517, 5.54762

Charges 2012

Per unit incl. 2 persons and electricity	€ 24.00 - € 39.00
extra person	€ 5.00

Camping Cheques accepted.

Avrillé

Castel Camping Domaine des Forges

Rue des Forges, F-85440 Avrillé (Vendée) T: 02 51 22 38 85.
E: contact@campingdomainedesforges.com **alanrogers.com/FR85930**

Le Domaine des Forges was acquired by Cathy and Thierry Pacteau a few years ago, and since then they have undertaken a vast improvement programme with huge investments made to improve the site's infrastructure. Arranged in the beautiful grounds of a 16th-century manor house, the 295 touring pitches are very generous in size (170-300 sq.m) and fully serviced, including 32A electricity, Internet access and cable TV. The owners' aim is to develop a prestige campsite with the highest quality of services and they have made a very good start. An extension to the site was opened for the first time in 2011.

Facilities

Four brand new toilet blocks including facilities for disabled visitors and babies. Laundry facilities. Shop (15/6-31/8). Restaurant (15/6-31/8). Bar and takeaway (15/6-15/9). Heated outdoor pool (15/5-15/9). Heated indoor pool (15/3-31/10). Tennis. Minigolf. Fishing lake. Internet (charged). One dog per pitch. Off site: Village 400 m. Vendée beaches 7 km. Golf de la Domangère and Golf Port Bourgenay (with discount) 10 km. Riding 10 km. Les Sables d'Olonne 25 km.

Open: All year.

Directions

Travel south from La Roche-sur-Yon on the D747 for about 21 km. At the D19, turn right for Avrille (about 6 km). At junction with the D949 turn right and first right again into rue des Forges. Site at the end of the road. GPS: 46.47609, -1.49454

Charges guide

Per unit incl. 2 persons, electricity, water and waste water	€ 16.00 - € 38.40
extra person	€ 2.00 - € 6.00
child (2-6 yrs)	free - € 4.00

Baguer-Pican

Camping le Vieux Chêne

Baguer-Pican, F-35120 Dol-de-Bretagne (Ille-et-Vilaine) T: 02 99 48 09 55.
E: vieux.chene@wanadoo.fr alanrogers.com/FR35000

to book this site call 01580 214000 ...we arrange everything — the travel service

This attractive, family owned site is situated between Saint-Malo and Mont Saint Michel. Developed in the grounds of a country farmhouse dating from 1638, its young and enthusiastic owner has created a really pleasant, traditional atmosphere. In spacious, rural surroundings it offers 199 good sized pitches on gently sloping grass, most with 10A electricity, water tap and a light. They are separated by bushes and flowers, with mature trees for shade. A very attractive tenting area (without electricity) is in the orchard. The site is used by a Dutch tour operator (20 pitches). There are three lakes in the grounds and centrally located leisure facilities include a restaurant with a terrace overlooking an attractive pool complex. Some entertainment is provided in high season, which is free for children. A Sites et Paysages member.

Facilities

Three very good, unisex toilet blocks, which can be heated, include washbasins in cabins, a baby room and facilities for disabled visitors. Small laundry. Motorcaravan services. Shop, bar, takeaway and restaurant (1/6-4/9). Heated swimming pool, paddling pool, slides (17/5-11/9; lifeguard July/Aug). TV room (satellite). Games room. Tennis. Minigolf. Giant chess. Play area. Riding in July/Aug. Fishing. WiFi (charged). Off site: Supermarket in Dol 3 km. Riding 2 km. Bicycle hire 4 km. Golf 15 km. Beach 20 km.

Open: 17 May - 25 September.

Directions

Site is by the D576 Dol-de-Bretagne - Pontorson road, just east of Baguer-Pican. It can be reached from the new N176 taking exit for Dol-Est and Baguer-Pican. GPS: 48.54924, -1.684

Charges guide

Per unit incl. 2 persons and electricity	€ 19.00 - € 33.00
extra person	€ 4.50 - € 6.00
child (4-13 yrs)	€ 2.50 - € 3.90
dog	€ 3.00

Bédoin

Domaine Naturiste de Bélézy

F-84410 Bédoin (Vaucluse) T: 04 90 65 60 18. E: info@belezy.com
alanrogers.com/FR84020

At the foot of Mont Ventoux, surrounded by beautiful scenery, Bélézy is an excellent naturist site with many amenities and activities and the ambience is relaxed and comfortable. The 320 pitches, 248 for touring (12A electricity, long leads required) are set amongst many varieties of trees and shrubs giving space and privacy. The attractive bar/restaurant and terrace overlook the swimming pool area and have superb views over the large recreational area and hills beyond. The site has an ecological theme with a small farm, fishpond and a vegetable garden especially for the children. Only gas and electric barbecues are permitted. Pets are not accepted.

Facilities

Four toilet blocks with very good facilities for campers with disabilities – newer ones are excellent, some have hot showers in the open air. Superb children's section. Shop. Bar. Excellent restaurant/takeaway (all 31/3-30/9). Swimming pools. Sauna. Tennis. Adventure play area. Activities all season. Archery. Guided walks. Children's club. Hydrotherapy centre (31/3-30/9). Only gas barbecues are allowed. Off site: Bédoin with shops and restaurants 1.5 km. Discover the riches of Provence with its many interesting old market towns and villages. Superb area for walking and cycling with the challenge of Mont Ventoux.

Open: 31 March - 5 October.

Directions

From A7 autoroute (exit 22) or RN7, south of Orange, take D950 southeast to Carpentras, then D974 northeast to Bédoin. In Bédoin turn right at roundabout, site signed, site in 2 km. GPS: 44.13352, 5.18745

Charges 2012

Per unit incl. 2 persons and electricity	€ 15.00 - € 40.20
extra person	€ 6.00 - € 9.40
child (3-8 yrs)	free - € 9.30

Camping Cheques accepted.

Belvès

RCN le Moulin de la Pique

F-24170 Belvès (Dordogne) T: 05 53 29 01 15. E: moulin@rcn.fr

alanrogers.com/FR24350

This high quality campsite set in the heart of the Dordogne has fine views looking up to the fortified town of Belvès. It is a splendid rural estate where there is plenty of space and a good mixture of trees and shrubs. Set in the grounds of a former mill, the superb traditional buildings date back to the 18th century. There are 200 level pitches with 154 for touring units, all with 6A electricity, a water point and drainage. The remainder are used for mobile homes to rent. The site is ideally suited for families with young and teenage children as there is so much to do, both on site and in the surrounding area. Moulin de Pique boasts four swimming pools, two heated, and with three water slides – a water paradise. There is also a lake which can be used for boating and fishing. Large motorhomes are catered for and access is good. Activities are organised daily and are a feature of this campsite.

Facilities

Three modern sanitary blocks include facilities for disabled visitors. Launderette. Shop, bar, restaurant, snack bar and takeaway. Swimming pools (two heated). Recreational lake. Playgrounds. Library. Fossil field. Sports field. Tennis. Minigolf. Boules. Satellite TV. Games room. Bicycle hire. Internet facilities. WiFi (charged). Off site: Bars, restaurants and shops in the village of Belvès 2 km. Canoeing 2 km. Riding 5 km. Golf 7 km.

Open: 9 April - 1 October.

Directions

Site is 35 km. southwest of Sarlat on the D710, about 7 km. south of Siorac-en-Périgord. GPS: 44.76228, 1.01412

Charges guide

Per unit incl. 2 persons, electricity and water	€ 19.90 - € 43.90
extra person (over 3 yrs)	€ 2.50 - € 4.90
dog (max. 1)	€ 6.00

Camping Cheques accepted.

Bénodet

Camping du Letty

F-29950 Bénodet (Finistère) T: 02 98 57 04 69. E: reception@campingduletty.com

alanrogers.com/FR29030

The Guyader family have ensured that this excellent and attractive site has plenty to offer for all the family. With a charming ambience, the site on the outskirts of the popular resort of Bénodet spreads over 22 acres with 493 pitches, all for touring units. Groups of four to eight pitches are set in cul-de-sacs with mature hedging and trees to divide each group. All pitches have electricity, water and drainage. As well as direct access to a small sandy beach, with a floating pontoon (safe bathing depends on the tides). The site has recently built a grand aquatic parc, with heated open air and indoor pools including children's pools, jacuzzi, and slides.

Facilities

Six well placed toilet blocks are of good quality and include mixed style WCs, washbasins in large cabins and controllable hot showers (charged). One block includes a separate laundry and dog washing enclosures. Baby rooms. Separate facility for disabled visitors. Launderette. Hairdressing room. Motorcaravan service points. Well stocked shop. Extensive snack bar and takeaway. Bar with games room and night club. Library/reading room with four computer stations. Entertainment room with satellite TV. New pool complex with indoor and outdoor pools, children's pool, jacuzzi and slide. Fitness centre (no charge). Saunas, jacuzzi and solarium (all charged). Tennis and squash (charged). Boules. Archery. Well equipped play area. Entertainment and activities (July/Aug). WiFi in reception. Off site: Sailing, fishing, riding and golf all nearby. Bénodet and Quimper.

Open: 11 June - 6 September.

Directions

From N165 take D70 Concarneau exit. At first roundabout take D44 to Fouesnant. Turn right at T-junction. After 2 km. turn left to Fouesnant (still D44). Continue through La Forêt Fouesnant and Fouesnant, picking up signs for Bénodet. Shortly before Bénodet at roundabout turn left (signed Le Letty). Turn right at next mini-roundabout and site is 500 m. on left. GPS: 47.86700, -4.08783

Charges guide

Per unit incl. 2 persons and electricity	€ 20.50 - € 36.00
extra person	€ 4.00 - € 7.50
child (1-6 yrs)	€ 2.00 - € 3.75
dog	€ 2.30

Bidart

Camping le Pavillon Royal

Avenue du Prince de Galles, F-64210 Bidart (Pyrénées-Atlantiques)

T: 05 59 23 00 54. E: info@pavillon-royal.com alanrogers.com/FR64060

Le Pavillon Royal has an excellent situation on raised ground overlooking the sea, with good views along the coast to the south and to the north coast of Spain beyond. There is a large heated swimming pool and sunbathing area in the centre of the site. The camping area is divided up into 303 marked, level pitches, many of a good size. About 50 are reserved for tents and are only accessible on foot. The remainder are connected by asphalt roads. All have electricity and most are fully serviced. Much of the campsite is in full sun, although the area for tents is shaded. Beneath the site – and only a very short walk down – stretches a wide sandy beach where the Atlantic rollers provide ideal conditions for surfing. A central, marked-out section of the beach is supervised by lifeguards (from mid June). There is also a section with rocks and pools. Reservation in high season is advisable.

Facilities

Good quality toilet blocks with baby baths and two units for disabled visitors. Washing facilities (only two open at night). Washing machines, dryers. Motorcaravan services. Shop (including gas). Restaurant and takeaway (from 1/6). Bar (all season). Heated swimming and paddling pools. Playground. General room, TV room, games room, films. Fishing. Surf school. Fitness room. Wellness facilities (1/6-25/9). Dogs are not accepted. WiFi (charged). Off site: Golf 500 m. Bicycle hire 2 km. Riding 3 km. Sailing 5 km. New oceanographic centre at Biarritz.

Open: 14 May - 30 September.

Directions

From A63 exit 4, take the N10 south towards Bidart. At roundabout after the 'Intermarché' supermarket turn right (signed for Biarritz). After 600 m. turn left at site sign. GPS: 43.45458, -1.57649

Charges 2012

Per unit incl. 2 persons, electricity and water	€ 32.00 - € 55.00
tent pitch	€ 26.00 - € 45.00
extra person (over 4 yrs)	€ 8.00 - € 12.00

Biscarrosse

Camping du Domaine de la Rive

Route de Bordeaux, F-40600 Biscarrosse (Landes) T: 05 58 78 12 33.
E: info@larive.fr **alanrogers.com/FR40100**

Surrounded by pine woods, la Rive has a superb beach-side location on Lac de Sanguinet. It provides 250 mostly level, numbered and clearly defined touring pitches of 100 sq.m. all with electricity connections (10A). The swimming pool complex is wonderful with pools linked by water channels and bridges. There is also a jacuzzi, paddling pool and two large swimming pools all surrounded by sunbathing areas and decorated with palm trees. This is a friendly site with a good mix of nationalities. The latest additions are a super children's aquapark with various games, and a top quality bar/restaurant complex where regular entertainment is organised. The beach is excellent, shelving gently to provide safe bathing for all ages. There are windsurfers and small craft can be launched from the site's slipway.

Facilities

Five good clean toilet blocks have washbasins in cabins and mainly British style toilets. Facilities for disabled visitors. Baby baths. Motorcaravan service point. Shop with gas. New bar/restaurant complex with entertainment. Swimming pool complex (supervised July/Aug). Games room. Play area. Tennis. Bicycle hire. Boules. Archery. Fishing. Waterskiing. Watersports equipment hire. Tournaments (June-Aug). Skateboard park. Trampolines. Miniclub. No charcoal barbecues on pitches. WiFi (charged). Off site: Riding 2 km. Golf 8 km. Beach 17 km.

Open: 6 April - 9 September.

Directions

Take D652 from Sanguinet to Biscarrosse and site is signed on the right in about 6 km. Turn right and follow tarmac road for 2 km.
GPS: 44.46052, -1.13065

Charges guide

Per unit incl. 2 persons and electricity	€ 24.50 - € 47.00
extra person	€ 3.80 - € 8.50
child (3-7 yrs)	€ 2.50 - € 7.00

Camping Cheques accepted.

Bourdeaux

Camping les Bois du Chatelas

Route de Dieulefit, F-26460 Bourdeaux (Drôme) T: 04 75 00 60 80. E: contact@chatelas.com
alanrogers.com/FR26210

Located at the heart of the Drôme Provençale, les Bois du Chatelas is a quality, family run site just 1.5 km. from the delightful village of Bourdeaux which offers some shops, cafés, etc. There are 138 level, good sized, terraced pitches, 70 for touring. They all have electricity, water and drainage. There is a superb swimming pool complex with indoor and outdoor pools, toboggan, paddling pool, fitness room, jacuzzi and sauna. Overlooking the pool area is a restaurant with superb views over the valley and hills beyond. Les Bois du Chatelas is a good choice for those seeking an active holiday. The long distance GR9 footpath passes through the site and there are very many walking and cycling routes close at hand. A popular aquagym is organised in the large outdoor pool in peak season. In the high season, there is a lively entertainment programme. A member of Sites et Paysages.

Facilities

Two excellent toilet blocks (one heated), on upper and lower levels, with facilities for babies and disabled visitors (though not ideal for those with mobility problems). Shop. Bar. Restaurant/takeaway/pizzeria. Indoor pool. Outdoor pool with water slide, waterfall, sauna, aquagym and jacuzzi. Sports pitch. Archery. Play area. Bicycle hire. Entertainment and excursions (July/Aug). WiFi everywhere. Off site: Fishing 1 km. Bourdeaux 1.5 km. Riding 5 km. Dieulefit with a wider range of shops 12 km. Rafting and canoe trips. Walking and mountain biking opportunities. Vercors mountain range. Many stunning medieval villages.

Open: 6 April - 16 September.

Directions

Leave A7 Autoroute, exit 16 Loriol. Take D104 east to Crest. Leave Crest bypass at traffic lights, take D538 south to Bourdeaux and continue towards Dieulefit for 1.5 km. Site is on the left (well signed).
GPS: 44.57825, 5.12795

Charges 2012

Per unit incl. 2 persons and electricity	€ 21.70 - € 38.50
extra person	€ 4.90 - € 8.30
child (2-7 yrs)	€ 3.90 - € 5.20
dog	€ 2.20 - € 5.20

Bourg-Saint-Maurice

Camping Caravaneige le Versoyen

Route des Arcs, F-73700 Bourg-Saint-Maurice (Savoie) T: 04 79 07 03 45. E: leversoyen@wanadoo.fr
alanrogers.com/FR73020

Bourg-St-Maurice is on a small, level plain at an altitude of 830 m. on the River Isère, surrounded by mountains. Le Versoyen attracts visitors all year round (except for a short time when they close). The site's 205 unseparated, flat pitches (180 for touring) are marked by numbers on the tarmac roads and all have electrical connections (4/6/10A). Most are on grass but some are on tarmac hardstanding making them ideal for use by motorcaravans or in winter. Trees give shade in some parts, although most pitches have almost none. Duckboards are provided for snow and wet weather.

Facilities

Two acceptable toilet blocks can be heated, although the provision may be hard pressed in high season. British and Turkish style WCs. Laundry. Motorcaravan service facilities. Outdoor and covered pools (July/Aug). Heated rest room with TV. Small bar with takeaway in summer. Off site: Cross-country ski track just behind the site. Fishing and bicycle hire 200 m. Tennis and swimming pool 500 m. Riding 1 km. Golf 15 km.

Open: All year excl. 7/11-14/12 and 2/5-25/5.

Directions

Site is 1.5 km. east of Bourg-Saint-Maurice on the CD119 Les Arcs road. GPS: 45.62248, 6.78475

Charges guide

Per unit incl. 2 persons and electricity	€ 17.40 - € 20.40
extra person	€ 4.30 - € 5.10
child (4-13 yrs)	€ 2.00 - € 4.80
dog	€ 0.50 - € 1.00

Brem-sur-Mer

Camping Caravaning le Chaponnet

Rue du Chaponnet (N16), F-85470 Brem-sur-Mer (Vendée) T: 02 51 90 55 56.
E: campingchaponnet@wanadoo.fr alanrogers.com/FR85480

This well established, family run site is within five minutes' walk of Brem village and 1.5 km. from a sandy beach. The 81 touring pitches are level with varying amounts of grass, some with shade from mature trees. Pitches are separated by tall hedges and serviced by tarmac or gravel roads and have frequent water and electricity points (long leads may be required). Tour operators have mobile homes and tents on 100 pitches and there are 146 other mobile homes and chalets, over half available for rent. The swimming pool complex includes a jacuzzi, sauna and fitness centre, slides and a children's pool.

Facilities

The five sanitary blocks are well maintained with washbasins in cubicles, and some showers and basins with controllable water temperature. Facilities for babies and disabled visitors. Laundry facilities. Bar, restaurant, snack bar and pizzeria (early June-late Aug). Indoor and outdoor heated pools. Waterslide, jacuzzi and sauna. Play area. Tennis. Bicycle hire. Games room. WiFi in bar/pool area (charged). Children's club. Activities and entertainment (July/Aug). Free bus to beach (July-Aug). Off site: Shops 200 m. Beach 1.5 km. Fishing 2 km. Riding 4 km. Golf 12 km. Les Sables d'Olonne 15 km.

Open: 2 April - 30 September.

Directions

Brem is 35 km. west of La Roche-sur-Yon and is on the D38 St Gilles - Les Sables d'Olonne road. From A87 at La Roche continue on D160 towards Les Sables d'Olonne. Take exit for La Mothe-Achard and Brétignolles-sur-Mer. Follow D54 to Brem-sur-Mer. Site is clearly signed, just off the one-way system in centre of village. GPS: 46.60433, -1.83244

Charges guide

Per unit incl. 2 persons and electricity	€ 21.60 - € 30.80
extra person	€ 4.90 - € 6.90

Brignogan-Plages

Camping de la Côte des Légendes

B.P. 36 Keravezan, F-29890 Brignogan-Plages (Finistère) T: 02 98 83 41 65.
E: camping-cote-des-legendes@wanadoo.fr alanrogers.com/FR29340

With direct access to a safe, sandy beach on the Baie de Brignogan and adjacent to a Centre Nautique (sailing, windsurfing, kayaking), this site could be ideal for a family seaside holiday in high season. It is very quiet in low season. There are 102 level touring pitches arranged in rows and protected by hedges, together with 31 privately-owned mobile homes and 14 for rent. A shop, bar and takeaway are open in July and August when activities are arranged for adults and children by the helpful manager Manuelle; she and her assistant Pierre both speak good English.

Facilities

Main toilet facilities (open only in July/Aug) are at the rear of the site in a large block that provides washbasins in cubicles, laundry room, baby baths and facilities for disabled visitors. The upper floor provides a games room with sea views. At other times the only facilities are in the snack bar building and are fairly basic. Motorcaravan service point. Bar, small shop and takeaway (July/Aug). Playground and playing field. WiFi available in most areas. Off site: Watersports centre adjacent. Village services 700 m. Bicycle hire 1 km. Riding 6 km. Golf 35 km.

Open: Easter - 1 November.

Directions

Brignonan-Plages is 35 km. west of Roscoff. From ferry terminal take the D58 (Morlaix) and after 6 km. turn right on the D10 (Plouescat then Plouguerneau). Turn right on the D770 to Brignogan-Plages. At top of main street bear left following signs (NOT satnav!) for site and Club Nautique. From N12 Morlaix-Brest road, turn north on D770 to Lesneven and Brignonan. GPS: 48.67278, -4.32929

Charges guide

Per unit incl. 2 persons	€ 11.90 - € 13.90
extra person	€ 3.35 - € 4.20
electricity (5/10A)	€ 2.50 - € 3.50

Boussac-Bourg

Castel Camping le Château de Poinsouze

Rte de la Châtre, B.P. 12, F-23600 Boussac-Bourg (Creuse) T: **05 55 65 02 21.**

E: **info.camping-de.poinsouze@orange.fr** **alanrogers.com/FR23010**

to book this site call **01580 214000** ...we arrange everything — the travel service

Le Château de Poinsouze is a well established site arranged on the open, gently sloping, grassy park with views over the small lake and château. It is an attractive, well maintained, high quality site situated in the unspoilt Limousin region. The 118 touring pitches, some with lake frontage, all have electricity (6-20A Europlug), water and drainage and 68 have sewerage connections. The site has a friendly family atmosphere with many organised activities in main season including dances, children's games and crafts. There are marked walks around the park and woods. All facilities are open all season. This great site should ensure a stress-free, enjoyable holiday for all the family. Exceptionally well restored outbuildings on the opposite side of the drive house a shop, bar and a new restaurant serving excellent cuisine. The pool complex has a new superb water play area for children with many fun fountains. The château is not open to the public.

Facilities

High quality, sanitary unit, washing machines, dryer, ironing, suites for disabled visitors. Motorcaravan services. Well stocked shop. Takeaway. Bar, internet and WiFi, two satellite TVs, library. Restaurant with new mini-bar for low season. Heated swimming pool, slide, children's pool and new water play area with fountains. Fenced playground. Petanque. Bicycle hire. Free fishing in the lake, boats and lifejackets can be hired. Sports facilities. No dogs in high season (14/7-18/8). Off site: Boussac (2.5 km) has a market every Thursday morning. The massive 12th-/15th-century fortress, Château de Boussac, is open daily all year.

Open: 1 June - 1 September.

Directions

Boussac lies 35 km. west of Montluçon, between the A20 and A71 autoroutes. Site is 2.5 km. north of Boussac on D917 (towards La Châtre). GPS: 46.37243, 2.20268

Charges guide

Per unit incl. 2 persons and full services	€ 19.00 - € 35.00
extra person	€ 3.00 - € 6.00
child (2-7 yrs)	€ 2.00 - € 5.00
dog	€ 3.00

Candé-sur-Beuvron

Kawan Village la Grande Tortue

3 rte de Pontlevoy, F-41120 Candé-sur-Beuvron (Loir-et-Cher) T: **02 54 44 15 20.**

E: **grandetortue@wanadoo.fr** **alanrogers.com/FR41070**

to book this site call **01580 214000** ...we arrange everything — the travel service

In the region that the Kings of France chose to build their most beautiful residences, this pleasant, shady site has been developed in the surroundings of an old 800-hectare forest, just 1 km. from the banks of the Loire river. For those seeking a relaxing holiday, it provides 169 touring pitches (the majority of more than 100 sq.m), all with 10A electricity and includes 58 fully serviced pitches. The friendly family owners continue to develop the site with a new multisport court and an attractive swimming pool complex. During July and August, they organise a programme of trips including canoeing and horse riding excursions, as well as twice weekly concerts and shows. La Grande Tortue is very well placed for visiting the châteaux of the Loire or the cities of Orléans and Tours. It is located on the long distance 'Loire à Vélo' cycle track and this leads from the site to Chaumont, Blois and Chambord, with over 300 km. of marked cycle tracks in the surrounding area. There are a number of good restaurants close at hand, although the site restaurant is also recommended with a range of good-value meals in a pleasant environment.

Facilities

Three sanitary blocks offer British style WCs, washbasins in cabins and pushbutton showers. Facilities for disabled visitors in one block. Laundry facilities. Motorcaravan service point. Shop, terraced bar and restaurant with reasonably priced food and drink plus a takeaway service (all 2/4-15/9). Covered, heated swimming pool (2/4-15/9) and two shallower pools for children (15/5-30/9). Trampolines, a ball crawl with slide and climbing wall, two bouncy inflatables. Club for children (July/Aug). Multisport court. Bicycle hire. Off site: Walking and cycling. Fishing 500 m. Golf 10 km. Châteaux at Blois 10 km, Chambord 20 km. and Chenonceau 20 km. Riding 12 km.

Open: 2 April - 25 September.

Directions

Site is just outside Candé-sur-Beuvron on the D751, between Amboise and Blois. From Amboise, turn right just before Candé, then left into site. GPS: 47.4900069, 1.2583208

Charges guide

Per unit incl. 2 persons and electricity	€ 22.00 - € 32.50
extra person	€ 6.75 - € 9.00
child (3-9 yrs)	€ 3.75 - € 5.75
dog	€ 3.70

Camping Cheques accepted.

Canet-en-Roussillon

Yelloh! Village le Brasilia

B.P. 204, F-66141 Canet-en-Roussillon (Pyrénées-Orientales) T: 04 68 80 23 82. E: info@lebrasilia.fr

alanrogers.com/FR66070

Situated across the yacht harbour from the upmarket resort of Canet-Plage, le Brasilia is an impressive, well managed family site directly beside the beach. It is pretty, neat and well kept with an amazingly wide range of facilities – indeed, it is camping at its best. There are 428 neatly hedged touring pitches, all with electricity (6/10A) and 315 with water and drainage. They vary in size from 80 to 120 sq.m. and some of the longer pitches are suitable for two families together. With a range of shade from pines and flowering shrubs, less on pitches near the beach, there are neat access roads (sometimes narrow for large units). There are also 161 pitches with mobile homes and chalets to rent (the new ones have their own gardens). The sandy beach here is busy, with a beach club (you can hire windsurfing boards) and a naturist section is on the beach to the west of the site. A completely new pool complex is planned with pools catering for all ages and hydrotherapy facilities for adults and all overlooked by its own snack bar and restaurant. The village area of the site offers a range of shops, a busy restaurant and bar, entertainment (including a night club) and clubs for children of all ages. In fact you do not need to stir from the site which is almost a resort in itself. It does have a nice, lively atmosphere but is orderly and well run. If you would like to visit Canet-Plage, a free tourist train runs in summer and a small ferry crosses the harbour. A member of Yelloh! Village and Leading Campings Group.

Facilities

Ten modern sanitary blocks are very well equipped and maintained, with British style WCs (some Turkish) and washbasins in cabins. Good facilities for children and for disabled visitors. Laundry room. Motorcaravan services. Range of shops. Gas supplies. Bars and restaurant. New pool complex (heated). Play areas. Sports field. Tennis. Sporting activities. Library, games and video room. Hairdresser. Internet café and WiFi. Daily entertainment programme. Bicycle hire. Fishing. ATM. Exchange facilities. Post office. Weather forecasts. Only gas or electric barbecues are allowed. Off site: Boat launching and sailing 500 m. Riding 5 km. Golf 12 km.

Open: 21 April - 20 September.

Directions

From A9 exit 41 (Perpignan Centre, Rivesaltes) follow signs for Le Barcarès and Canet on D83 for 10 km. then for Canet (D81). At first Canet roundabout, turn fully back on yourself (Sainte-Marie) and watch for Brasilia sign almost immediately on right.
GPS: 42.70467, 3.03483

Charges guide

Per unit incl. 2 persons and electricity (6A)	€ 23.00 - € 55.00
extra person	€ 6.00 - € 9.00
child (3-6 yrs)	free - € 8.50
dog (max. 2)	€ 4.00

Castellane

Castel Camping le Domaine du Verdon

Camp du Verdon, F-04120 Castellane (Alpes-de-Haute-Provence) T: 04 92 83 61 29.
E: contact@camp-du-verdon.com alanrogers.com/FR04020

Close to the Route des Alpes and the Gorges du Verdon. Two heated swimming pools and numerous on-site activities during high season help to keep non-canoeists here. Du Verdon is a large level site, part meadow, part wooded, with 500 partly shaded, rather stony pitches (390 for tourists). Numbered and separated by bushes, they vary in size, have 6A electricity, and 125 also have water and waste water. They are mostly separate from the mobile homes (60) and pitches used by tour operators (110). Some overlook the unfenced river Verdon, so watch the children. This is a very popular holiday area, the gorge, canoeing and rafting being the main attractions, ideal for active families. One can walk to Castellane without using the main road where there are numerous shops, cafés and restaurants. Dances and discos in July and August suit all age groups. The latest finishing time is around 23.00, after which time patrols make sure that the site is quiet. The site is popular and very busy in July and August.

Facilities

Refurbished toilet blocks include facilities for disabled visitors. Washing machines. Motorcaravan services. Babysitting service. Restaurant, terrace, log fire for cooler evenings. New supermarket. Pizzeria/crêperie. Takeaway. Heated swimming pools, paddling pool with 'mushroom' fountain (all open all season). Fitness equipment. Organised entertainment (July/Aug). Play areas. Minigolf. Archery. Organised walks. Bicycle hire. Riding. Small fishing lake. Room for games and TV. Internet access and WiFi (free). Off site: Bus stop outside main entrance (only one bus each day). Castellane and the Verdon Gorge 1 km. Riding 2 km. Boat launching 4.5 km. Golf 20 km. Watersports.

Open: 15 May - 15 September.

Directions

From Castellane take the D952 westwards towards Gorges du Verdon and Moustiers. Site is 1 km. on the left. GPS: 43.83921, 6.49396

Charges guide

Per unit (low season 2 or high season 3 persons) and electricity	€ 25.00 - € 42.00
extra person (over 4 yrs)	€ 8.00 - € 13.00
dog	€ 3.00

Cavalaire-sur-Mer

Kawan Village Cros de Mouton

B.P. 116, F-83240 Cavalaire-sur-Mer (Var) T: 04 94 64 10 87. E: campingcrosdemouton@wanadoo.fr

alanrogers.com/FR83220

Cros de Mouton is a reasonably priced campsite in a popular area. High on a steep hillside, about 2 km. from Cavalaire and its popular beaches, the site is a calm oasis away from the coast. There are stunning views of the bay but, due to the nature of the terrain, some of the site roads are very steep – the higher pitches with the best views are especially so. There are 199 large, terraced pitches (electricity 10A) under cork trees with 73 suitable only for tents with parking close by, and 80 for touring caravans. A range of languages is spoken by the welcoming and helpful owners. The terrace of the restaurant and the pool area share the wonderful view of Cavalaire and the bay. Olivier and Andre are happy to take your caravan up with their 4 x 4 Jeep if you are worried, and they will help you set up if necessary – all part of the service.

Facilities

Clean, well maintained toilet blocks have all the usual facilities including those for disabled customers (although site is perhaps a little steep in places for wheelchairs). Washing machine. Shop. Bar/restaurant with reasonably priced meals and takeaway. Swimming and paddling pools with many sun beds on the terrace and small bar for snacks and cold drinks. Small play area. Games room. Off site: Beach and bicycle hire 1.5 km. Riding 3 km. Golf 15 km.

Open: 15 March - 9 November.

Directions

Take the D559 to Cavaliare-sur-Mer (not Cavalière 4 km. away). Site is about 1.5 km. north of Cavaliare-sur-Mer, very well signed from the approach to the town.
GPS: 43.18247, 6.5161

Charges guide

Per unit incl. 2 persons and electricity	€ 24.00 - € 29.10
extra person	€ 6.50 - € 8.20
child (under 7 yrs)	€ 4.10 - € 4.50
dog	free - € 2.00

Camping Cheques accepted.

Châlon-sur-Saône

Camping du Pont de Bourgogne

Rue Julien Leneveu, Saint-Marcel, F-71380 Châlon-sur-Saône (Saône-et-Loire) T: **03 85 48 26 86.**
E: campingchalon71@wanadoo.fr **alanrogers.com/FR71140**

This is a well presented and cared for site, useful for an overnight stop or for a longer stay to explore the local area. It is close to the A6 autoroute, and the interesting market town of Châlon-sur-Saône is only 2 km. There are 100 slightly sloping pitches (90 sq.m) all with 10A electricity, most on grass, but 30 have a gravel surface. They are separated by beech hedging, and a variety of mature trees gives varying amounts of shade. Many pitches overlook the river, a good spot to watch the passing boats. Access is easy for large outfits.

Facilities

Three toilet blocks, two traditional in style and fittings. The third is a superb modern building, including a children's bathroom, disabled bathroom and family shower. Motorcaravan services. Dishwashing facilities, laundry. No shop but essentials kept in the bar (bread to order). Modern bar/restaurant (July/Aug). Simple play area. Bicycle hire arranged. WiFi. Off site: Fishing and boat ramp 200 m. Municipal swimming pool 300 m. Golf, sailing 1 km. Riding 10 km. Châlon-sur-Saône with many shops, bars, banks etc.

Open: 1 April - 30 September.

Directions

From A6 exit 26 (Châlon-Sud), take N80 (signed Dôle) to second roundabout. Take fourth exit (signed Roseraie) and fork right (Les Chavannes). At traffic lights turn right (signed Roseraie) under bridge to site entrance 500 m. GPS: 46.78448, 4.87295

Charges guide

Per unit incl. 2 persons and electricity	€ 19.40 - € 26.10
extra person	€ 4.70 - € 6.30
child (under 7 yrs)	€ 3.30 - € 4.80

Camping Cheques accepted.

Châtellerault

Camping le Relais du Miel

Route d'Antran, F-86100 Châtellerault (Vienne) T: **06 07 52 04 74.** E: **camping@lerelaisdumiel.com**
alanrogers.com/FR86030

This is a good site situated halfway between Poiters and Tours and with very easy access to the A10 and N10 roads. The site is set in the ten-acre grounds of a grand house dating from Napoleonic times, beside the River Vienne. Divided by trees and bushes that provide plenty of shade, there are 80 level pitches with 10A electricity and 13 also with water and drainage. One of the two old barns which form the sides of the courtyard behind the house has been converted to provide 19 apartments and these provide additional accommodation to rent.

Facilities

Excellent toilet facilities include washbasins in cabins. Facilities for disabled visitors. Laundry facilities. Shop with basic essentials (July/Aug). Bar (all season) and restaurant (July/Aug). Pizzas (from local pizzeria). Takeaway. Snack bar (evenings July/Aug). Swimming and paddling pools with terrace. Playground. Tennis. Bicycle hire. Boules. Games room. Fishing. Internet access. Torch useful. Off site: Supermarket 400 m. Riding 5 km. Golf 11 km. Futuroscope 16 km.

Open: 15 May - 2 September.

Directions

Châtellerault is between Tours and Poitiers. Site is north of town close to A10 autoroute. Take exit 26 (Châtellerault-Nord) and site is signed just off roundabout. From N10 follow signs for motorway (Tours - Péage) and at roundabout take exit for Antran. GPS: 46.83858, 0.53441

Charges guide

Per unit incl. 2 persons and electricity	€ 20.00 - € 25.00
extra person over 5 yrs	€ 3.00 - € 5.00

Concarneau

Flower Camping le Cabellou Plage

Avenue du Cabellou, F-29185 Concarneau (Finistère) T: **02 98 97 37 41.** E: **info@le-cabellou-plage.com**
alanrogers.com/FR29520

Le Cabellou Plage is a very pleasant, well maintained site located close to Concarneau. The large, grassy pitches are divided by young hedges, all have 10A electricity and some also have water and drainage. Many have fine views to the nearby beach and the old walled town beyond. The enthusiastic owner has tastefully landscaped many areas of the site with a profusion of shrubs and flowers. A large swimming pool on site is overlooked by a terrace and bar and the beach is just 25 m. away. La Cabellou is ideally situated for those wishing to visit Concarneau with its twice weekly market, Pont Aven and the cathedral city of Quimper.

Facilities

One modern toilet block is bright and cheerful and provides mainly open style washbasins and preset showers. Baby room. Facilities for disabled visitors. Laundry room. Shop. Bar with television and Internet access. Outdoor heated swimming pool (all season). Scuba lessons and water gymnastics. Bicycle hire. Off site: Bus stop outside site. Supermarkets, shops and restaurants in Concarneau 4 km. Tennis 3 km. Riding 7 km. Golf 10 km.

Open: 7 April - 15 September.

Directions

Site is just south of Concarneau. Take the D783 towards Tregunc. Turn right onto Avenue Cabellou. Site is well signed from here. GPS: 47.85516, -3.90521

Charges guide

Per unit incl. 2 persons and electricity	€ 15.00 - € 29.00
extra person	€ 3.00 - € 5.50
child (2-7 yrs)	free - € 4.00
pet	€ 2.00

Crespian

Kawan Village le Mas de Reilhe

Chemin du Mas de Reilhe, F-30260 Crespian (Gard) T: **04 66 77 82 12**. E: **info@camping-mas-de-reilhe.fr**

alanrogers.com/FR30080

This is a pleasant family site in the heart of the Gard region with a favourable climate. There are 95 pitches, 70 for tourers, 57 have electricity (6/10A), 25 also have water and waste water and some of the upper ones may require long leads. The large lower pitches are separated by tall poplar trees and hedges, close to the main facilities but may experience some road noise. The large terraced pitches on the hillside are scattered under mature pine trees, some with good views, more suited to tents and trailer tents but with their own modern sanitary facilities.

Facilities

Excellent, very clean toilet facilities with facilities for campers with disabilities. Laundry facilities. Reception. Limited shop (bread to order). Bar, takeaway, restaurant (1/5-16/9). Small play area on grass. Pétanque. Heated swimming pool (27/4-16/9). Internet. WiFi throughout (charged). Only gas or electric barbecues on pitches; new communal barbecue. Bicycle hire. Motorcaravan services. Off site: Tennis 500 m. Fishing 3 km. Riding 5 km. Golf 25 km. The sea and the gorges are about 30 km.

Open: 14 April - 16 September.

Directions

From the A9 take exit 25, Nimes-ouest signed Alès, then D999 towards Le Vigan (about 23 km). Turn north on the D6110, site shortly on right at southern edge of Crespian. GPS: 43.87931, 4.09637

Charges guide

Per unit incl. 2 persons and electricity	€ 20.00 - € 26.00
extra person	€ 5.00 - € 6.00

Camping Cheques accepted.

Crèvecoeur-en-Brie

Caravaning des 4 Vents

Rue de Beauregard, F-77610 Crèvecoeur-en-Brie (Seine-et-Marne) T: **01 64 07 41 11**. E: **f.george@free.fr**

alanrogers.com/FR77040

This peaceful, pleasant site has been owned and run by the same family for over 35 years. There are around 200 pitches, with many permanent or seasonal units, however, there are 140 spacious grassy pitches for tourists, well separated by good hedges, all with 6A electricity and a water tap shared between two pitches. The whole site is well landscaped with flowers and trees everywhere. This is a great family site with pool and games facilities located at the top end of the site so that campers are not disturbed. Central Paris is just a 40 minute train ride from the nearest railway station (8 km).

Facilities

Three modern sanitary units (heated in cooler weather) provide British style WCs, washbasins (mainly in cubicles) and pushbutton showers. Facilities for disabled visitors. Laundry facilities. Motorcaravan service point. In high season (July/Aug) a mobile snack bar and pizzeria (open 16.00-23.00), and a baker (07.30-11.00). Swimming pool (16 m. diameter; May to Sept). Playground, games room, volleyball and boules court. Riding (high season). WiFi. Off site: La Houssaye 1 km. Fontenay Tresigny 5 km.

Open: 15 March - 1 November.

Directions

Crèvecoeur is just off the D231 between A4 exit 13 and Provins. From north, pass obelisk and turn right onto the C3 in 3 km. From south 19 km. after junction with N4, turn left at signs to village. Follow site signs. GPS: 48.75060, 2.89714

Charges guide

Per unit incl. 2 persons and electricity	€ 27.00
extra person (over 5 yrs)	€ 6.00
dog	€ 3.00

Darbres

Camping les Lavandes

Le Village, F-07170 Darbres (Ardèche) T: **04 75 94 20 65**. E: **sarl.leslavandes@online.fr**

alanrogers.com/FR07140

Situated northeast of Aubenas, in a quieter part of this region, les Lavandes is surrounded by magnificent countryside, vineyards and orchards. The welcoming French owners, who speak English well, run their site in the heart of the tiny village of Darbres with dedication and enthusiasm. The 70 pitches (58 for touring) are arranged on low terraces separated by a variety of trees and shrubs that give welcome shade in summer. Electricity 6/10A is available to all. Visit at the end of May to see the trees laden with luscious cherries. Organised activities include jazz and piano musical evenings and children's games. The village, with a quaint boulangerie, is just a stroll away.

Facilities

Well maintained facilities, baby room and excellent facilities for disabled visitors. Washing machine. Small shop (1/7-31/8). Bar, terrace (1/6-31/8). Restaurant (15/6-31/8). Takeaway (15/4-31/8). Excellent swimming pool, paddling pool and sunbathing areas. Three small play areas. Games room. Outdoor chess. Electric barbecues are not permitted, but gas and, unusually, charcoal barbecues are allowed. Off site: Fishing 1 km. Riding 3 km. Tennis 5 km. Bicycle hire 15 km. Canoeing, walking, cycling, riding, karting nearby.

Open: 15 April - 30 September.

Directions

Site is best approached from the south. From Montélimar take N102 towards Aubenas. After Villeneuve, in Lavilledieu, turn right at traffic lights on D224 to Darbres (10 km). In Darbres turn sharp left by post office (care needed) and follow site signs. GPS: 44.64788, 4.50338

Charges guide

Per unit incl. 2 persons and electricity	€ 16.00 - € 23.40
extra person	€ 2.80 - € 3.90

Doucier

Camping Domaine de Chalain

F-39130 Doucier (Jura) T: 03 84 25 78 78. E: chalain@chalain.com

alanrogers.com/FR39030

Doucier lies 25 km. east of Lons-le-Saunier among the wooded hills of the Jura and rather away from the main routes. This large, spacious site is in a parkland setting beside Lac de Chalain and is surrounded by woods and cliffs. Large areas are left for sports and recreation. The lake shelves gently but then becomes deep quite suddenly. The site also has an attractive, well equipped pool complex. There are 800 good-sized, level pitches with 462 for touring units. Most have electricity (7A) and there are varying amounts of shade. Booking is obligatory for caravans and motorcaravans over 7 m.

Facilities

Nine sanitary blocks with facilities for babies and disabled visitors. Shops (some high season only). Restaurant, takeaway and bar. Swimming pool complex with heated indoor pool (all season), outdoor pools (1/6-15/9) with slide, sauna and spa (one entrance per day). Play areas. Fishing. Pedalo and bicycle hire. Activities include rock climbing, archery, aquagym. Disco. Entertainment. TV room. Dogs not permitted on lake beach. Off site: Signed walk starts at edge of site. Riding 2 km. Golf 25 km.

Open: 27 April - 18 September.

Directions

Doucier is 25 km. east of Lons-le-Saunier. In village turn left off D39, site signed, entrance in 3 km. GPS: 46.66435, 5.81315

Charges guide

Per unit incl. 3 persons and electricity	€ 21.00 - € 37.00
extra person	€ 4.00 - € 6.00
child (4-15 yrs)	€ 3.00 - € 5.00
dog	€ 2.00

Duras

Le Cabri Holiday Village

Route de Savignac, F-47120 Duras (Lot-et-Garonne) T: 05 53 83 81 03. E: holidays@lecabri.eu.com

alanrogers.com/FR47110

This countryside site of 5.5 hectares is divided into three areas: camping, chalets and open fields. It is on the border of the Dordogne and the Lot-et-Garonne departments. Le Cabri Holiday Village is an English owned and run, small holiday complex. The owners, Peter and Eileen Marston who are keen caravanners themselves, have developed 24 new spacious pitches (generally 150 sq.m), all with electricity (4/16A) and water. The open, level pitches are all on hardstandings surrounded by grass and separated by young trees, so with limited shade. Access for large motorhomes using the rear entrance is possible as this was considered when the site was planned.

Facilities

A recently refurbished, central sanitary block is heated in low season and includes three new private cabins. Separate cabin for disabled visitors. Laundry facilities. Shop selling basics including bread. Restaurant with occasional entertainment. Internet access. Swimming pool (June-Sept). Large play area. Boules. Fishing pond. WiFi (charged). Off site: Riding and tennis 1 km. Golf 10 km. Watersports 7 km. Canoeing 8 km. Aquatic park.

Open: All year.

Directions

In Duras, look for the D203 and follow signs for site. It is less than 1 km. away. GPS: 44.68296, 0.18615

Charges guide

Per unit incl. 2 persons and 10A electricity	€ 18.00 - € 23.00
extra person	€ 4.00 - € 5.00
child (under 12 yrs)	€ 2.00 - € 3.00
dog	€ 2.00

Eperlecques

Kawan Village Château du Gandspette

133 rue de Gandspette, F-62910 Eperlecques (Pas-de-Calais) T: 03 21 93 43 93.
E: contact@chateau-gandspette.com **alanrogers.com/FR62030**

This spacious family run site, in the grounds of a 19th-century château, conveniently situated for the Channel ports and tunnel, provides overnight accommodation together with a range of facilities for longer stays. There are 110 touring pitches, all with electric hook-ups, intermingled with 20 privately owned mobile homes and caravans, with a further 18 for hire. Pitches are delineated by trees and hedging. Mature trees form the perimeter of the site, through which there is access to woodland walks.

Facilities

Two sanitary blocks with a mixture of open and cubicled washbasins. Good facilities for disabled visitors and babies. Laundry facilities. Motorcaravan service point. Bar, grill restaurant and takeaway (all 1/5-15/9). Swimming pools (15/5-15/9). Playground. Multisport court. Tennis. Pétanque. Children's room. Entertainment in season. WiFi in bar area (charged). Off site: Supermarket 1 km. Fishing 3 km. Riding and golf 5 km. Beach 30 km.

Open: 1 April - 30 September.

Directions

From Calais follow D943 (St Omer) for 25 km. Southeast of Nordausques take D221 (east). Follow site signs for 5-6 km. From St Omer follow D943 to roundabout at junction with D300. Turn right on D300 (Dunkirk). After 5 km. turn left on D221. Site is 1.5 km. on right. From Dunkirk ferry follow signs for St Omer D300. At Watten roundabout exit right (Gandspette). Follow signs. GPS: 50.81924, 2.17753

Charges guide

Per unit incl. 2 persons and electricity (6A)	€ 18.00 - € 28.00
extra person	€ 5.00 - € 6.00

Camping Cheques accepted.

Estaing

Camping Pyrénées Natura

Route du Lac, F-65400 Estaing (Hautes-Pyrénées) T: **05 62 97 45 44.**
E: **info@camping-pyrenees-natura.com** **alanrogers.com/FR65060**

Pyrénées Natura, at an altitude of 1,000 m. on the edge of the national park is the perfect site for lovers of nature. The 66 pitches (51 for touring units), all with electricity (3-10A), are in a landscaped area with 75 varieties of trees and shrubs – but they do not spoil the fantastic views. A traditional style building houses the reception, bar and indoor games/reading room. There is a small, well-stocked shop in the former water-mill. Prices are very reasonable and home-made bread can be purchased. Children will love the animals, including the unusual hens, the guinea pigs, goat and donkey. On the river there is a small beach belonging to the site for supervised water play.

Facilities

First class toilet blocks. Facilities for disabled visitors and babies. Washing machine and airers (no lines allowed). Motorcaravan services. Bar, small shop and takeaway (1/5-15/9). Lounge, library, TV. Upstairs games/reading room. Bird watching is a speciality of the site and equipment is available. Sauna, solarium and jacuzzi (free between 12.00-17.00). Music room. Play area for the very young. Small beach beside river. Boules. Giant chess. Weekly evening meal in May, June and Sept. Internet. Walks. Off site: Village with two restaurants. Bicycle hire and riding 4 km. Walking and hiking.

Open: 1 May - 20 September.

Directions

At Argelès-Gazost, take D918 towards Aucun. After 8 km. turn left on D13 to Bun, cross the river, then right on D103 to site (5.5 km). Narrow road, few passing places. GPS: 42.94152, -0.17726

Charges guide

Per unit incl. 2 persons and electricity (3A)	€ 17.50 - € 42.00
extra person	€ 5.75
child (under 8 yrs)	€ 3.75
dog	€ 3.00

Less in low season.

Figeac

Camping les Rives du Célé

Domaine du Surgié, F-46100 Figeac (Lot) T: **05 61 64 88 54.** E: **contact@marc-montmija.com**
alanrogers.com/FR46320

Very conveniently placed, this rural site is only 2 km. from the centre of the interesting old town of Figeac. There are 163 pitches, of which 103 are for touring, the remaining 60 for mobile homes and gîtes, all of which are for rent. The grass pitches are level, with a mixture of shade and sun and all have 10A electricity. Access is easy for large outfits. The site is split into different areas with the aquatic centre next to the camping area. There are many organised activities on site and in the surrounding area making it an ideal choice for an active family including teenagers. The thoughtful positioning of many of the amenities works very well and tends to keep the camping area quieter. Canoes can be hired on the river, a short walk away from the site. There is a varied programme of organised activities and entertainment laid on, together with a daily children's club. There are many places of interest to visit in this area, most notably the ancient towns and vineyards which offer many different types of fine wine.

Facilities

Three modern toilet blocks include facilities for babies and disabled visitors. Laundry. Shop, bar, restaurant and takeaway. Swimming pool complex adjacent (15/5-15/9, open to the public). Sports competitions and party nights with themed dining. Children's clubs. Canoeing. Fishing. Minigolf. Boules. Bicycle hire. WiFi near reception (charged). Off site: Riding 2 km. Figeac with shops, bars, restaurants and museums 2 km.

Open: 1 April - 30 September.

Directions

From the west, enter Figeac on the D802 and then turn right across river, signed Base de Loisirs. Shortly turn left at small roundabout and then, at traffic lights, branch left uphill to site. Well signed from the centre of Figeac. GPS: 44.60989, 2.05015

Charges guide

Per unit incl. 2 persons and electricity	€ 14.00 - € 22.00
extra person	€ 4.00 - € 6.80
child (3-12 yrs)	€ 2.50 - € 4.00
dog	€ 1.50 - € 2.50

Forcalquier

Camping le Moulin de Ventre

Niozelles, F-04300 Forcalquier (Alpes-de-Haute-Provence) T: **04 92 78 63 31**. E: **moulindeventre@aol.com**

alanrogers.com/FR04030

This is a friendly, family run site in the heart of Haute-Provence, near Forcalquier, a bustling small French market town. Attractively located beside a small lake and 28 acres of wooded, hilly land, which is available for walking. Herbs of Provence can be found growing wild and flowers, birds and butterflies abound – a nature lovers' delight. The 124 level, grassy pitches for tourists are separated by a variety of trees and small shrubs, 114 of them having electricity (6A; long leads may be necessary). Some pitches are particularly attractive, bordering a small river which runs through the site. English is spoken. Fishing is possible on the lake and pedalos are available to hire. Mobile homes and chalets are available for rent. The site is well situated to visit Mont Ventoux, the Luberon National Park, the Gorges du Verdon and a wide range of ancient hill villages with their markets and museums etc. A Sites et Paysages member.

Facilities

Refurbished toilet block. Facilities for disabled visitors. Baby bath. Washing, drying machines. Fridge hire. Bread. Bar/restaurant, takeaway (all season), themed evenings (high season). Pizzeria. Swimming pools (15/5-30/9). New playground. Bouncy castle. Fishing, boules. Some activities organised in high season. No discos. Only electric or gas barbecues. Internet access and free WiFi. Off site: Shops, local market, doctor, tennis 2 km. Supermarket, chemist, riding, bicycle hire 5 km. Golf 20 km. Walking, cycling.

Open: 9 April - 30 September.

Directions

From A51 motorway take exit 19 (Brillanne). Turn right on N96 then turn left on N100 westwards (signed Forcalquier) for about 3 km. Site is signed on left, just after a bridge 3 km. southeast of Niozelles. GPS: 43.93364, 5.86815

Charges guide

Per unit incl. 2 persons and electricity	€ 20.00 - € 29.00
extra person (over 4 yrs)	€ 4.20 - € 6.00
child (2-4 yrs)	€ 2.50 - € 4.00
dog	€ 3.00

No credit cards.

Font-Romeu

Huttopia Font-Romeu

Route de Mont-Louis, F-66120 Font-Romeu (Pyrénées-Orientales)

T: 04 68 30 09 32. E: font-romeu@huttopia.com alanrogers.com/FR66250

to book this site call **01580 214000** ...we arrange everything — the travel service

This is a large, open site of some seven hectares, with 125 touring pitches (100 with 10A electricity), nestling on the side of the mountain at the entrance to Font-Romeu. This part of the Pyrenees offers some staggering views and the famous Mont Louis is close by. An ideal base for climbing, hiking or cycling, it would also provide a good stopover for a night or so whilst travelling between Spain and France, or to and from Andorra into France. The terraced pitches are easily accessed, with those dedicated to caravans and motorcaravans at the top of the site, whilst tents go on the lower slopes.

Facilities

Two toilet blocks are bright and clean. Toilet for children and excellent facilities for disabled visitors. Shop (25/5-16/9). Bar, restaurant and takeaway (all July/Aug). Outdoor heated swimming pool (25/5-16/9). Laundry facilities. Large games hall. Electric barbecues only. Max. 1 dog. Off site: Opportunities for walking and climbing are close by as are golf, riding, fishing, cycling and tennis. The small town of Font-Romeu is very near with all the usual shops and banking facilities. Beach 8 km.

Open: 3 December - 10 April, 21 June - 10 September.

Directions

Font-Romeu is on the D118, some 12 km. after it branches off the N116 heading west, just after Mont Louis. The site is just before the town, on the left and accessed off the car park. GPS: 42.51511, 2.05183

Charges guide

Per unit with 2 persons and electricity	€ 19.70 - € 29.70
extra person	€ 5.20 - € 6.60
child (2-7 yrs)	€ 3.00 - € 4.50
dog	€ 4.00

Forcalquier

Camping Indigo Forcalquier

Rte de Sigonce, F-04300 Forcalquier (Alpes-Haute-Provence) T: 04 92 75 27 94.

: forcalquier@camping-indigo.com alanrogers.com/FR04120

to book this site call **01580 214000** ...we arrange everything — the travel service

Although Camping Indigo is an urban site, there are extensive views over the surrounding countryside where there are some excellent walks. The pitches are on grass and are of a good size, all with electricity, six fully serviced. The site is secure, with an electronic barrier (card deposit required) and there is no entry between 22.30 and 07.00. Local guides lead tours of the historic town and areas. This is an excellent base for visiting Forcalquier and the Monday market (the best in Haute-Provence). Since Camping Indigo acquired this site, an extensive modernisation programme has been put into effect.

Facilities

Two refurbished toilet blocks with washbasins in cubicles and excellent facilities for disabled visitors. Bar. Snack bar and takeaway (July and August). Play area. Heated swimming and paddling pools. Range of activities in high season, often involving local people, including astrology sessions, food tasting and storytelling. Free Internet access. Max. 1 dog. Off site: All shops, banks etc. in town centre 200 m. Riding 5 km. Fishing 15 km. Golf 20 km.

Open: 27 April -7 October.

Directions

From town centre, follow D16 signed to Montlaux and Sigonce. Site is approx. 500 m. on the right. Well signed from town. GPS: 43.96206, 5.78743

Charges guide

Per unit incl. 2 persons and electricity	€ 19.70 - € 27.10
extra person	€ 4.90 - € 5.90

Camping Cheques accepted.

Francueil-Chenonceau

Camping le Moulin Fort

F-37150 Francueil-Chenonceau (Indre-et-Loire) T: 02 47 23 86 22.

E: lemoulinfort@wanadoo.fr alanrogers.com/FR37030

to book this site call **01580 214000** ...we arrange everything — the travel service

Camping Le Moulin Fort is a tranquil, riverside site with British owners, John and Sarah Scarratt. The 130 pitches are enhanced by trees and shrubs offering plenty of shade and 110 pitches have electricity (6A). From the snack bar terrace, adjacent to the restored mill building, a timber walkway over the mill race leads to the unheated swimming pool and paddling pools. The site is ideal for couples and families with young children, although the river is unfenced. There is occasional noise from trains passing on the opposite bank of the river.

Facilities

Two toilet blocks are of a good standard and include washbasins in cubicles, baby baths and facilities for disabled visitors. Motorcaravan service point. Shop, bar (limited hours), restaurant and takeaway (all 25/5-16/9). Swimming pool (25/5-16/9). Excellent play area. Minigolf. Pétanque. Games room and TV. Library. Fishing. Bicycle and canoe hire. In high season family entertainment including wine tasting, quiz evenings, activities for children, games tournaments and live music events. WiFi (charged). Off site: Trains to Tours 1.5 km. Boat launching 2 km. River beach 4 km. Riding 12 km. Golf 20 km.

Open: 1 April - 30 September.

Directions

Site is 35 km. east of Tours off the D976 Vierzon road. From A85 at exit 11 take D31 towards Bléré and turn east on D976 (Vierzon) for 7 km. then turn north on D80 (Chenonceau) to site. From north bank of Cher (D140/D40) turn south on D80 to cross river between Chenonceau and Chisseaux. Site on left just after bridge. GPS: 47.32735, 1.08936

Charges 2012

Per unit incl. 2 persons and electricity	€ 19.00 - € 27.00
extra person	€ 4.00 - € 5.00
child (4-12 yrs)	€ 3.00 - € 4.00

Fréjus

Camping Resort la Baume – la Palmeraie

3775 rue des Combattants d'Afrique du Nord, F-83618 Fréjus (Var) T: 04 94 19 88 88.
E: reception@labaume-lapalmeraie.com alanrogers.com/FR83060

La Baume is a large, busy site about 5.5 km. from the long sandy beach of Fréjus-Plage, although with its fine and varied selection of swimming pools many people do not bother to make the trip. The pools with their palm trees are remarkable for their size and variety (water slides, etc) – the very large feature pool being a highlight. There is also an aquatic play area and two indoor pools with a slide and a spa area. The site has nearly 250 adequately sized, fully serviced pitches with some separators and most have shade. Although tents are accepted, the site concentrates mainly on caravanning. It becomes full in season. Adjoining la Baume is its sister site, la Palmeraie, providing self-catering accommodation, its own landscaped pool and some entertainment to supplement that at la Baume. There are 500 large pitches with mains sewerage for mobile homes. La Baume's convenient location has its downside as there is traffic noise on some pitches from the nearby autoroute – somewhat obtrusive at first but we soon failed to notice it. It is a popular site with tour operators.

Facilities

Five toilet blocks. Supermarket, several shops. Two bars, terrace overlooking pools, TV. Restaurant, takeaway. Six swimming pools (heated all season, two covered, plus steam room and jacuzzi). Fitness centre. Tennis. Archery (July/Aug). Skateboard park. Organised events, daytime and evening entertainment, some in English. Amphitheatre. Discos all season. Children's club (all season, 4-11 yrs). 2 play areas renovated. Off site: Bus to Fréjus passes gate. Riding 2 km. Fishing 3 km. Golf and beach 5 km.

Open: 31 March - 29 September (with full services).

Directions

From west, A8, exit Fréjus, take N7 southwest (Fréjus). After 4 km, turn left on D4 and site is 3 km. From east, A8, exit 38 Fréjus and follow signs for Cais. Site is signed. GPS: 43.45998, 6.72048

Charges guide

Per unit incl. 2 persons, electricity, water and drainage	€ 19.00 - € 47.00
extra person	€ 5.00 - € 13.00
child (under 7 yrs)	free - € 7.00
dog	€ 5.00

Min. stay for motorcaravans 2 nights.
Large units should book.

Fréjus

Camping Caravaning les Pins Parasols

3360 rue des Combattants d'Afrique du Nord, F-83600 Fréjus (Var) T: 04 94 40 88 43.
E: lespinsparasols@wanadoo.fr alanrogers.com/FR83010

Les Pins Parasols with its 189 pitches is a comfortably sized site, which is quite easy to walk around. It is family owned and run. Although on very slightly undulating ground, virtually all the pitches (all have electricity 6A) are levelled or terraced and separated by hedges or bushes with pine trees for shade. There are 48 pitches equipped with their own fully enclosed, sanitary unit, with WC, washbasin, hot shower and dishwashing sink. These pitches naturally cost more but may well be of interest to those seeking a little bit of extra comfort. The nearest beach is Fréjus-Plage with its new marina, adjoining St Raphaël. The site is used by tour operators (10%).

Facilities

Good quality toilet blocks (one heated) providing facilities for disabled visitors. Small shop with reasonable stock, restaurant, takeaway (15/4-20/9). Heated swimming pool with attractive rock backdrop, separate long slide with landing pool and small paddling pool. Half-court tennis. General room, TV. Volleyball. Basketball court. Children's play area. Internet in reception and WiFi (charged). Off site: Bicycle hire and riding 2 km. Bus from the gate into Fréjus 5 km. Beach and fishing 6 km. Golf 10 km.

Open: 7 April - 29 September.

Directions

From A8 take exit 38 for Fréjus Est. Turn right immediately on leaving pay booths on a small road which leads across to D4, then right again and under 1 km. to site. GPS: 43.46290, 6.72570

Charges guide

Per unit incl. 2 persons and electricity	€ 18.40 - € 28.45
pitch with sanitary unit	€ 23.15 - € 35.48
extra person	€ 4.60 - € 6.58
child (under 7 yrs)	€ 3.05 - € 3.97
dog	€ 1.90 - € 2.85

La Baume ★★★★ La Palmeraie ★★

Camping Resort ★★★★ Résidence de Tourisme ★★

www.labaume-lapalmeraie.com

Fréjus Côte d'Azur

from April to September :
On going entertainment- Cabaret - Show
Disco - Children's club

Le Sud Grandeur Nature

Heated sanitary blocks,
marked-out pitches,
6 swimming pools including
2 covered and heated,
6 water-slides and jacuzzi.
5 kilometers from the sandy
beaches of Fréjus
and Saint Raphaël.

E.S.E COMMUNICATION - Draguignan Tel : 04 94 67 06

Bastidons for rent
1or 2 bedrooms - 4/6 persons
or 3 bedrooms - 6/8 persons
Mobil-homes 4/6 persons
Mobil-homes 6 persons
3 rooms - air conditioning
Appartment
6 or 10 persons

3775, Rue des Combattants d'Afrique du Nord 83618 FREJUS Cedex
Tel: +33(0)4 94 19 88 88 - Fax:+33(0)4 94 19 83 50
E-mail : reception@labaume-lapalmeraie.com

Gigny-sur-Saône

Kawan Village Château de l'Epervière

Rue du Château, F-71240 Gigny-sur-Saône (Saône-et-Loire) T: 03 85 94 16 90.
E: domaine-de-leperviere@wanadoo.fr alanrogers.com/FR71070

This popular and high quality site is peacefully situated in the wooded grounds of a 16th-century château, close to the A6 and near the village of Gigny-sur-Saône. It is within walking distance of the river where you can watch the cruise boats on their way to and from Châlon-sur-Saône. There are 160 pitches in two separate areas, of which 100 are used for touring, all with 6A electricity. Some are on hardstanding and 30 are fully serviced. Some pitches close to the château and fishing lake are hedged and have shade from mature trees; another area has a more open aspect. Red squirrels, ducks and the occasional heron can be found on the campsite and the pitches around the periphery are good for birdwatchers. The château's main restaurant serves regional dishes and there is a good range of takeaway meals. Gert-Jan, François and their team enthusiastically organise many activities, mainly for children, but including wine tasting in the cellars of the château. Don't forget, here you are in the Maconnais and Châlonnaise wine regions, so arrange some visits to the local caves.

Facilities

Two well equipped, very clean toilet blocks with all necessary facilities including those for babies and campers with disabilities. Washing machine/dryer. Basic shop (1/5-30/9). Restaurant with good menu and takeaway (1/4-30/9). Cellar with wine tasting. Converted barn with bar, large TV. Unheated outdoor swimming pool (1/5-30/9) partly enclosed by old stone walls. Smaller indoor heated pool, jacuzzi, sauna (1/4-30/9). Play areas with paddling pool. Fishing. Bicycle hire. Motorcaravan services. WiFi (free) in bar area. Off site: Boat launching 500 m. Riding 15 km. Golf 20 km. Historic towns of Châlon and Tournus, both 20 km. The Monday market of Louhans, to see the famous Bresse chickens 26 km.

Open: 30 March - 30 September.

Directions

From A6 heading south, take exit 26 Châlon-Sud, or from A6 heading north take exit 27 Tournus. Then N6 to Sennecey-le-Grand, turn east D18, signed Gigny. Follow site signs to site (6.5 km).
GPS: 46.65485, 4.94463

Charges 2012

Per unit incl. 2 persons and electricity	€ 24.30 - € 35.10
extra person	€ 5.90 - € 8.50
child (under 7 yrs)	€ 3.60 - € 5.80
dog	€ 2.40 - € 3.00

Camping Cheques accepted.

Gien

Kawan Village les Bois du Bardelet

Route de Bourges, Le Petit Bardelet, F-45500 Gien (Loiret) T: 02 38 67 47 39. E: contact@bardelet.com
alanrogers.com/FR45010

This attractive, high quality and lively site, ideal for families with young children, is in a rural setting and well situated for exploring the less well known eastern part of the Loire Valley. Two lakes (one for boating, one for fishing) and a pool complex have been attractively landscaped in 12 hectares of former farmland, blending old and new with natural wooded areas and more open field areas with rural views. There are 260 large, level grass pitches with 130 for touring units. All have 8A or 16A electricity, 20 have water and waste water and some have hardstanding. A weekly family club card can be purchased to make use of the many activities on a daily basis (some high season only).

Facilities

Two toilet blocks include facilities for disabled visitors and babies. Washing machines, dryers. Minimart (3/4-16/9). Bar and takeaway (3/4-16/9). Full restaurant (high season and weekends). Heated outdoor pool (1/5-31/8). Heated indoor pool and children's pool. Aquagym, fitness and jacuzzi room. Games area. Archery. Canoeing and fishing. Tennis. Minigolf. Boules. Volleyball. Pétanque. Children's playground with trampoline. Sports tournaments (July/Aug). Bicycle hire. WiFi in bar area (charged). Off site: Supermarket 5 km. Riding 7 km. Golf 25 km. Walking and cycling routes.

Open: 1 April - 30 September.

Directions

Leave A77 autoroute at exit 19 (Gien). Take D940 (signed Bourges) to Gien, cross river Loire, continue D940 for 5 km. At junction with D53 (site signed) turn right and right again to cross D940 (no left turn). Follow signs for 1.5 km. to site.
GPS: 47.64152, 2.61528

Charges 2012

Per unit incl. 2 persons and electricity	€ 19.80 - € 33.00
extra person	€ 5.00 - € 6.80
child (2-5 yrs)	free - € 6.80
dog	€ 4.00

Camping Cheques accepted.

3 campsites in the heart of southern burgundy
www.campings-bourgogne.com
Holiday in château park
Domaine du Château de l'Epervière
Camping Caravaning - Locations
Bourgogne du Sud
www.domaine-eperviere.com
Discover Tournus
N° 27
Camping de Tournus
Bourgogne du Sud
www.camping-tournus.com
City campsite
Camping du Pont de Bourgogne
Chalon sur Saône
Bourgogne du Sud
www.camping-chalon.com
Bourgondië

Graveson-en-Provence

Camping les Micocouliers

445 route de Cassoulen, F-13690 Graveson-en-Provence (Bouches du Rhône) T: 04 90 95 81 49.

E: micocou@free.fr alanrogers.com/FR13060

M. et Mme. Riehl started work on les Micocouliers in 1997 and they have developed a comfortable site. On the outskirts of the town, the site is only some 10 km. from St Rémy and Avignon. Purpose built, terracotta 'houses' in a raised position provide all the facilities at present. The 75 pitches radiate out from here with the pool and entrance to one side. The pitches are on level grass, separated by small bushes, and shade is developing well. Electricity connections are possible (4-13A). There are also a few mobile homes. The popular swimming pool is a welcome addition. Bread can be ordered and in July and August a simple snack kiosk operates.

Facilities

Unisex facilities in one unit provide toilets and facilities for disabled visitors (by key), another showers and washbasins in cabins and another dishwashing and laundry facilities. Another block is planned. Reception and limited shop (July/Aug) are in another. Swimming pool (12x8 m; 5/5-15/9). Paddling pool (1/7-31/8). Play area. Gas and electric barbecues permitted. WiFi (charged). Off site: Riding next door. Bicycle hire 1 km. Golf and fishing 5 km. Beach 60 km. at Ste Marie-de-la-Mer.

Open: 15 March - 15 October.

Directions

Site is southeast of Graveson. From the N570 at new roundabout take D5 towards Saint Rémy and Maillane and site is 500 m. on the left.
GPS: 43.84397, 4.78131

Charges guide

Per unit incl. 2 persons and electricity	€ 19.00 - € 25.00
extra person	€ 5.00 - € 7.00
child (1-10 yrs)	€ 3.40 - € 4.90
dog	€ 2.00

Camping Cheques accepted.

Grimaud

Domaine des Naïades

Quartier Cros d'Entassi, Saint Pons-les-Mûres, F-83310 Grimaud (Var) T: 04 94 55 67 80.

E: info@lesnaiades.com alanrogers.com/FR83640

Les Naïades is a well equipped site with an enviable setting close to the modern resort of Port Grimaud and the Gulf of St Tropez. The 454 pitches (219 are mobile homes for rent) are of a good size and well shaded, most have electricity (10A). The site boasts an Olympic sized pool and 2 water slides, as well as a separate children's pool. The restaurant specialises in Mediterranean cuisine and local wines. Les Naïades becomes lively in high season with a full activity and entertainment programme, as well as a miniclub for children. Port Grimaud is a stylish resort, built in the 1960s in the marshy delta of the Giscle. It is modelled on Venice and is a car-free environment. Most property owners are able to moor their boats on the many canals which criss-cross the resort. Grimaud, in contrast, is a hilltop village dominated by its partially restored 11th century castle. St Tropez needs little introduction and, although very busy in the summer months, it resumes a rather more sedate character in the low season.

Facilities

Four basic but adequate toilet blocks. Facilities for disabled visitors, but access can be difficult. Laundry facilities. Covered dishwashing area. New supermarket for 2011. Bar. Restaurant. Swimming pool with water slides. Play area. Tourist information. Motorcaravan services. Mobile homes for rent. Off site: Port Grimaud. St Tropez. Fishing. Watersports. Walking and cycle routes in the Massif des Maures.

Open: 31 March - 21 October.

Directions

The site is located slightly to the north of Port Grimaud. From D98 head north to the N98, Pons-les-Mûres and the site is clearly signed.
GPS: 43.285278, 6.579722

Charges guide

Per unit incl. 3 persons and electricity	€ 25.00 - € 52.00
extra person (over 7 yrs)	€ 5.00 - € 8.00
dog	€ 5.00

Guérande

Le Domaine de Léveno

Route de Sandun, F-44350 Guérande (Loire-Atlantique) T: 02 40 24 79 30. E: domaine.leveno@wanadoo.fr

alanrogers.com/FR44220

There have been many changes to this extensive site over the past years and considerable investment has been made to provide some excellent new facilities. The number of mobile homes and chalets has increased considerably, leaving just 38 touring pitches. However, these are mainly grouped at the far end of the site and are rather worn with little grass. Pitches are divided by hedges and trees which offer a good deal of shade and all have electricity (10A). Access is tricky to some and the site is not recommended for larger units. Twin axle caravans and American motorhomes are not accepted. Roads and paths tend to be busy, so a close watch on younger children is required.

Facilities

Main refurbished toilet block offers preset showers, washbasins in cubicles and facilities for disabled visitors. Laundry facilities. Small shop selling basics and takeaway snacks. Restaurant. Bar with TV and games. Indoor pool. Heated outdoor pool complex with water slides and a flume, paddling pool (15/5-30/9). Fitness room. Play area. Multisport court and crazy golf. Activities and events (high season). Electric barbecues are not permitted. WiFi in bar. Off site: Large hypermarket 1 km. Fishing 2 km. Beach, golf and riding all 5 km. Boat launching 7 km.

Open: 4 April - 30 September.

Directions

Site is less than 3 km. from the centre of Guérande. From D774 and from D99/N171 take D99E Guérande by-pass. Turn east following signs for Villejames and Leclerc hypermarket and continue on D247 to site on right. GPS: 47.33352, -2.3906

Charges guide

Per unit incl. 2 persons, electricity and water	€ 22.00 - € 42.00
extra person	€ 5.00 - € 9.00
child (under 7 yrs)	€ 3.00 - € 7.00
dog	€ 3.00 - € 6.00

Jablines

International de Jablines

Base de Loisirs, F-77450 Jablines (Seine-et-Marne) T: 01 60 26 09 37. E: welcome@camping-jablines.com

alanrogers.com/FR77030

Jablines is a modern site which, with the leisure facilities of the adjacent Espace Loisirs, offers an interesting, if a little impersonal, alternative to other sites in the region. Man-made lakes provide opportunities for many water-based activities. The Grand Lac is said to have the largest beach on the Ile-de-France. The site itself has 150 pitches, of which 141 are for touring units. Most are of a good size, often slightly sloping, with gravel hardstanding and grass, accessed by tarmac roads and marked by young trees. All have 10A electrical connections, 60 with water and waste connections also. Whilst staying on the campsite admission to the Base de Loisirs is free. Water activities include catamaran sailing, windsurfing, water boarding, canoeing, fishing and supervised bathing, plus a large equestrian centre, an orienteering course, a multisport court and mountain bike trails. In high season, activities at the leisure complex are supplemented by a bar/restaurant and some very French style group activities.

Facilities

Two toilet blocks, heated in cool weather, include pushbutton showers, some washbasins in cubicles. Dishwashing and laundry facilities. Motorcaravan service point (charged). Shop (all season). Play area. Internet point in reception. Ticket sales for Disneyland and Parc Astérix. Mobile homes for rent. Off site: Bar/restaurant adjacent (500 m) at Base de Loisirs with watersports, riding, tennis and minigolf. Fishing, horse riding, bicycle hire, beach, boat launching all 500 m. Golf 15 km.

Open: 31 March - 29 September.

Directions

From A4 Paris - Rouen turn north on A104. Take exit 8 on D404 Meaux/Base de Loisirs Jablines. From A1 going south, follow signs for Marne-la-Vallée using A104. Take exit 6A Clay-Souilly on the N3 (Meaux). After 6 km. turn south on D404 and follow signs. At park entry keep left for campsite. GPS: 48.91378, 2.73451

Charges 2012

Per unit incl. 2 persons and electricity	€ 25.00 - € 28.00
extra person	€ 6.50 - € 7.50

Camping Cheques accepted.

Hourtin-Plage

Airotel Camping de la Côte d'Argent

to book this site call **01580 214000** ...we arrange everything — the travel service

F-33990 Hourtin-Plage (Gironde) T: 05 56 09 10 25. E: info@cca33.com

alanrogers.com/FR33110

Côte d'Argent is a large, well equipped site for leisurely family holidays. It makes an ideal base for walkers and cyclists with over 100 km. of cycle lanes in the area. Hourtin-Plage is a pleasant invigorating resort on the Atlantic coast and a popular location for watersports enthusiasts. The site's top attraction is its pool complex, where wooden bridges connect the pools and islands and there are sunbathing and play areas plus an indoor heated pool. The site has 588 touring pitches (all with 10A electricity), not always clearly defined, arranged under trees with some on sand. High quality entertainment takes place at the impressive bar/restaurant near the entrance. Spread over 20 hectares of undulating sand-based terrain and in the midst of a pine forest. The site is well organised and ideal for children.

Facilities

Very clean sanitary blocks include provision for disabled visitors. Washing machines. Motorcaravan service points. Large supermarket, restaurant, takeaway, pizzeria, bar (all open 1/6-15/9). Four outdoor pools with slides and flumes (1/6-19/9). Indoor pool (all season). Fitness room. Massage (Institut de Beauté). Tennis. Play areas. Miniclub, organised entertainment in season. Bicycle hire. WiFi (charged). ATM. Charcoal barbecues are not permitted. Hotel (12 rooms). Off site: Path to the beach 300 m. Fishing and riding. Golf 30 km.

Open: 14 May - 18 September.

Directions

Turn off D101 Hourtin-Soulac road 3 km. north of Hourtin. Then join D101E signed Hourtin-Plage. Site is 300 m. from the beach. GPS: 45.22297, -1.16465

Charges guide

Per unit incl. 2 persons and electricity	€ 26.00 - € 48.00
extra person	€ 4.00 - € 8.00
child (3-9 yrs)	€ 3.00 - € 7.00
dog	€ 2.00 - € 6.00

Camping Cheques accepted.

Jard-sur-Mer

Camping les Ecureuils

to book this site call **01580 214000** ...we arrange everything — the travel service

Route des Goffineaux, F-85520 Jard-sur-Mer (Vendée) T: 02 51 33 42 74.

E: ecureuils@franceloc.fr **alanrogers.com/FR85210**

Les Ecureuils is a wooded site in a quieter part of the southern Vendée. It is undoubtedly one of the prettiest sites on this stretch of coast, with an elegant reception area, attractive vegetation and large pitches separated by low hedges with plenty of shade. Of the 278 pitches, some 128 are for touring units, each with water and drainage, as well as easy access to 10A electricity. This site is popular with tour operators (54 pitches). Jard is rated among the most pleasant and least hectic of Vendée towns. The harbour is home to some fishing boats and rather more pleasure craft. There is a public slipway for those bringing their own boats.

Facilities

Two toilet blocks are kept very clean and include baby baths, and laundry rooms. Small shop (bread baked on site). Snack bar and takeaway (1/6-30/8). Bar with snacks and ice creams. Good sized L-shaped swimming pool and separate paddling pool (30/5-15/9). New large flume into separate pool. Indoor pool and fitness centre (all season). New, imaginative play area for ages 3-10. Minigolf. Boules. Multisports pitch. Bouncy castle. Club for children (5-10 yrs, July/Aug). Games room. Bicycle hire. Internet access and WiFi (free). Only gas barbecues are allowed. Dogs are not accepted. Off site: Beach, fishing 400 m. Marina and town.

Open: 9 April - 25 September.

Directions

From Les Sables d'Olonne take the N949 towards Talmont-St Hilaire. Keep right in the centre (D21 towards Jard). From la Roche-sur-Yon follow the D474 and the D49 towards Jard-sur-Mer. Do not use sat nav for final approach. From the village follow the signs 'Autres campings' or Camping les Ecureuils. Site is on the left. GPS: 46.4113, -1.5896

Charges guide

Per unit incl. 2 persons, and electricity	€ 16.00 - € 32.00
extra person	€ 4.70 - € 7.00
child (0-7 yrs)	€ 3.50 - € 4.50

La Bastide-de-Sérou

Camping l'Arize

Lieu-dit Bourtol, F-09240 La Bastide-de-Sérou (Ariège) T: 05 61 65 81 51. E: camparize@aol.com

alanrogers.com/FR09020

The site sits in a delightful, tranquil valley among the foothills of the Pyrenees and is just east of the interesting village of La Bastide-de-Sérou beside the River Arize (good trout fishing). The river is fenced for the safety of children on the site, but may be accessed just outside the gate. The 70 large pitches are neatly laid out on level grass within the spacious site. All have 3/6A electricity and are separated into bays by hedges and young trees. An extension to the site gives 24 large, fully serviced pitches (10A) and a small toilet block. Discounts have been negotiated for several of the local attractions.

Facilities

Toilet block includes facilities for babies and disabled visitors. Laundry room. Motorcaravan services. New shop and restaurant. Small swimming pool and sunbathing area. Entertainment in high season. Weekly barbecues and welcome drinks on Sundays. Fishing, riding and bicycle hire. WiFi. Off site: Several restaurants and shops within a few minutes drive. The nearest restaurant is located at the national stud for the famous Merens horses just 200 m. away and will deliver takeaway meals to your pitch. Golf 5 km.

Open: 12 March - 10 November.

Directions

Site is southeast of the village La Bastide-de-Sérou. Take the D15 towards Nescus and site is on right after about 1 km. GPS: 43.00182, 1.44538

Charges guide

Per unit incl. 2 persons and electricity	€ 16.40 - € 28.30
extra person	€ 4.20 - € 5.80
child (2-12 yrs)	€ 2.80 - € 4.90
dog	€ 1.20 - € 2.20

Discounts for longer stays in mid and low season.

La Flotte-en-Ré

Camping la Grainetière

Route de Saint-Martin, F-17630 La Flotte-en-Ré (Charente-Maritime) T: 05 46 09 68 86.

E: la-grainetiere@orange.fr alanrogers.com/FR17280

A truly friendly welcome awaits you from the owners, Isabelle and Eric, at la Grainetière. It is a peaceful campsite set in almost three hectares of pine trees which provide some shade for the 88 touring pitches of various shapes and sizes. There are also 50 well spaced chalets for rent. Some pitches are suitable for units up to seven metres (these should be booked in advance). There are no hedges for privacy and the pitches are sandy with some grass. Ample new water points and electricity (10A) hook-ups (Euro plugs) serve the camping area. The site is well lit.

Facilities

The unisex sanitary block is first class, with washbasins in cubicles, showers, British style WCs, facilities for children and campers with disabilities. Shop. Takeaway. Swimming pool (heated all season) and jacuzzi. Bicycle hire. Fridge hire. TV room. Charcoal barbecues are not permitted. WiFi (charged). Off site: Beach, fishing, boat launching and sailing 2 km. Bar and restaurant 2 km. Riding 3 km. Golf 10 km.

Open: 1 April - 30 September.

Directions

Follow camping signs from La Flotte, 1 km. from the village. GPS: 46.18755, -1.344933

Charges guide

Per unit incl. 2 persons and electricity	€ 19.50 - € 34.50
extra person	€ 5.00 - € 8.00
child (0-7 yrs)	€ 3.00 - € 4.00
dog	€ 2.50 - € 4.00

La Plaine-sur-Mer

Camping la Tabardière

F-44770 La Plaine-sur-Mer (Loire-Atlantique) T: 02 40 21 58 83.

E: info@camping-la-tabardiere.com alanrogers.com/FR44150

Owned and managed by the Barré family, this campsite is pleasant, peaceful and immaculate. It will suit those who want to enjoy the local coast and towns but return to an 'oasis' for relaxation. However, it still provides activities and fun for those with energy remaining. The pitches are mostly terraced and care needs to be taken in manoeuvring caravans into position – although the effort is well worth it. The pitches have access to electricity and water taps are conveniently situated nearby. The site is probably not suitable for people using wheelchairs. A Sites et Paysages member.

Facilities

Two good, clean toilet blocks are well equipped and include laundry facilities. Motorcaravan service point. Shop, bar, snacks and takeaway (high season). Good sized covered swimming pool, paddling pool and slides (supervised). Playground. Minigolf. Volleyball and basketball. Half size tennis courts. Boules. Fitness programme. Bicycle hire (July/Aug). Overnight area for motorcaravans (€ 14 per night). Off site: Beach and sea fishing 3 km. Golf, riding and bicycle hire all 5 km.

Open: 16 April - 25 September.

Directions

Site is well signed, situated inland off the D13 Pornic - La Plaine-sur-Mer road. GPS: 47.140767, -2.15052

Charges guide

Per unit incl. 2 persons	€ 15.50 - € 28.60
extra person	€ 3.00 - € 6.90
child (2-9 yrs)	€ 3.00 - € 4.75
dog	€ 3.40
electricity (3/10A)	€ 3.50 - € 6.00

Camping Cheques accepted.

La Romieu

Kawan Village le Camp de Florence

Route Astaffort, F-32480 La Romieu (Gers) T: 05 62 28 15 58.

E: info@lecampdeflorence.com **alanrogers.com/FR32010**

to book this site call **01580 214000** ...we arrange everything – the travel service

Camp de Florence is an attractive and very well equipped site on the edge of an historic village in pleasantly undulating Gers countryside. The 183 large, part terraced pitches (100 for tourers) all have electricity (10A), 20 with hardstanding and 16 fully serviced. They are arranged around a large field with rural views, giving a feeling of spaciousness. The 13th-century village of La Romieu is on the Santiago de Compostela pilgrim route. The Pyrénées are a two hour drive, the Atlantic coast a similar distance. The site has been developed by the friendly Mynsbergen family who are Dutch (although Susan is English). They have sympathetically converted the old farmhouse buildings to provide facilities for the site. The collegiate church, visible from the site, is well worth a visit (the views are magnificent from the top of the tower), as is the local arboretum, the biggest collection of trees in the Midi-Pyrénées.

Facilities

Three toilet blocks (one completely rebuilt for 2009), provide all the necessary facilities. Washing machines and dryers. Motorcaravan services. Restaurant (1/5-30/9, also open to the public). Takeaway. Bread. Swimming pool area with water slide. Jacuzzi, protected children's pool (open to public in afternoons). New playgrounds, games and animal park. Bouncy castle, trampoline. Outdoor fitness machines. Games room. Tennis. Pétanque. Bicycle hire. Discos, picnics, musical evenings. Excursions. WiFi (charged). Max. 2 dogs. Off site: Shop 500 m. in village. Fishing 5 km. Riding 10 km. Walking tours, excursions and wine tasting arranged.

Open: 1 April - 10 October.

Directions

Site signed from D931 Agen - Condom road. Small units turn left at Ligardes (signed), follow D36 for 1 km, turn right La Romieu (signed). Or continue until outskirts of Condom and take D41 left to La Romieu, through village to site. GPS: 43.98299, 0.50183

Charges guide

Per unit incl. 2 persons and electricity	€ 17.50 - € 34.90
extra person	€ 3.60 - € 7.40
child (4-9 yrs)	€ 3.50 - € 5.30
dog (max. 2)	€ 1.50 - € 2.30

Special prices for groups, rallies, etc.
Camping Cheques accepted.

La Tranche-sur-Mer

Camping du Jard

123 bvd Maréchal de Lattre de Tassigny, F-85360 La Tranche-sur-Mer (Vendée)

T: 02 51 27 43 79. E: info@campingdujard.fr **alanrogers.com/FR85020**

to book this site call **01580 214000** ...we arrange everything – the travel service

Camping du Jard is a well maintained site between La Rochelle and Les Sables d'Olonne. First impressions are good, with a friendly welcome from M. Marton and his staff. The 160 touring pitches, all with electricity and 60 also with water and drainage, are level and grassy; many are hedged by bushes and a large variety of trees provide shade in places. An impressive pool complex has a heated outdoor pool with toboggan and paddling pool, plus an indoor pool with jacuzzi. The site is 700 m. from a sandy beach with many shops and restaurants nearby.

Facilities

Three toilet blocks (only one open in low season) provide basic facilities for babies and disabled visitors. Controllable showers in one block and others to come; some washbasins in cabins. Laundry facilities. Motorcaravan service point. Shop (1/6-10/9), restaurant and bar (25/5-10/9). Heated outdoor pool (from 25/5); heated indoor pool (all season). Sauna, solarium and fitness room. Tennis. Minigolf. Bicycle hire. Play area. Games and TV rooms. WiFi around bar. American motorhomes not accepted. No pets. Off site: Beach 700 m. Fishing 1 km. Sailing 3 km. Riding 10 km.

Open: 26 April - 15 September.

Directions

La Tranche-sur-Mer is 40 km. southeast of Les Sables d'Olonne. From A87 Cholet/La Roche-sur-Yon leave at exit 32 for La Tranche-sur-Mer and take D747 to La Tranche. Turn east following signs for La Faute-sur-Mer along bypass. Take exit for La Grière and then turn east to site. GPS: 46.34836, -1.38738

Charges guide

Per unit incl. 2 persons and electricity	€ 23.50 - € 32.00
extra person	€ 5.00 - € 6.00
child (under 5 yrs)	€ 3.50 - € 4.50

La Tour-du-Meix

Camping de Surchauffant

Le Pont de la Pyle, F-39270 La Tour-du-Meix (Jura) T: **03 84 25 41 08**. E: **info@camping-surchauffant.fr**

alanrogers.com/FR39020

With only 200 pitches, this site may appeal to those who prefer a more informal atmosphere, however it can be lively in high season. It is pleasantly situated above the beaches bordering the Lac de Vouglans, which can be reached quickly on foot directly from the site. The 157 touring pitches are of a reasonable size and are informally arranged, some are fully serviced and most have electricity (10A). They are divided by hedges and there is some shade. The lake offers a variety of watersports activities, boat trips, etc. and is used for fishing and swimming (guarded in high season as it shelves steeply). Two signposted walks start from within 100 m. of the site entrance. English is spoken.

Facilities

The sanitary facilities are older in style and adequate rather than luxurious, but reasonably well maintained and clean when we visited. They include some washbasins in private cabins. Laundry. Heated swimming pool (200 sq.m), paddling pool and surround (15/6-15/9). Three playgrounds. Entertainment (July/Aug). Safety deposit boxes. Off site: Bicycle hire and riding 5 km. Restaurant, takeaway and shops adjacent.

Open: 20 April - 17 September.

Directions

From A39 take exit 7 and N1082 to Lons-le-Saunier. Continue south on D52 for about 20 km. to Orgelet. Site is by the D470, at La Tour-du-Meix, about 4 km. east of Orgelet. GPS: 46.5231, 5.67401

Charges guide

Per unit incl. 2 persons and electricity	€ 15.00 - € 23.50
extra person (over 4 yrs)	€ 2.50 - € 4.70
dog	€ 1.00 - € 1.60

Lacanau-Océan

Yelloh! Village les Grands Pins

Plage Nord, F-33680 Lacanau-Océan (Gironde) T: **05 56 03 20 77**. E: **reception@lesgrandspins.com**

alanrogers.com/FR33130

This Atlantic coast holiday site with direct access to a fine sandy beach, is on undulating terrain amongst tall pine trees. A large site with 576 pitches, there are 370 of varying sizes for touring units all with electricity (12A). One half of the site is a traffic free zone (except for arrival or departure day, caravans are placed on the pitch, with separate areas outside for parking). There is a good number of tent pitches, those in the centre of the site having some of the best views. This popular site has an excellent range of facilities available for the whole season. The large sandy beach is a 350 m. stroll from the site.

Facilities

Four well equipped toilet blocks, one heated, including baby room and facilities for disabled visitors. Launderette. Motorcaravan services. Supermarket. Bar, restaurant and takeaway plus heated swimming pool complex (800 sq.m; lifeguard in July/Aug) with sunbathing surround and jacuzzi (all season). Fitness activities (charged) and fitness suite. Games room. Tennis. Two playgrounds. Adventure playground. Bicycle hire. Organised activities. WiFi in the bar (on payment). Only gas barbecues are permitted. Off site: Fishing, golf, riding and bicycle hire 5 km.

Open: 16 April - 24 September.

Directions

From Bordeaux take the N125/D6 west to Lacanau-Océan. At second roundabout, take the second exit: Plage Nord, follow signs to 'campings'. Les Grand Pins signed to right at the far end of road. GPS: 45.01107, -1.19337

Charges guide

Per unit incl. 2 persons and electricity	€ 15.00 - € 47.00
extra person	€ 5.00 - € 9.00
child (3-12 yrs)	free - € 5.00
dog	€ 4.00

Half-board arrangements available.

Lagorce

Castel Domaine de Sévenier

F-07150 Lagorce (Ardèche) T: 04 75 88 29 44. E: domainedesevenier@orange.fr

alanrogers.com/FR07660

Le Domaine de Sévenier is a modern, high quality chalet complex enjoying a hilltop location with fine panoramic views over the surrounding garrigue, a unique mix of oak trees, juniper, rosemary and thyme. Located 4 km. from Vallon-Pont-d'Arc and 800 m. from the pretty village of Lagorce, the domaine is an old winery which has been sensitively converted and offers accommodation in well appointed wooden chalets, serving the needs of different sized families. Rest and relaxation is the theme here and the restaurant has a good reputation.

Facilities

Restaurant. Bar. Shop. Swimming pool. Children's pool. Activity programme. Play area. Minigolf. Tourist information. Fully equipped chalets for rent. No touring pitches. Off site: Lagorce 800 m. (shops and cafés). Cycle and walking tracks. Riding. Vallon Pont d'Arc 5 km.

Open: 13 March - 15 November.

Directions

Head north from Vallon-Pont-d'Arc (at western end of the Ardèche gorges) on D1 and upon reaching Lagorce, follow signs to the site.
GPS: 44.434151, 4.410989

Charges guide

Contact the site for details.

Langres

Kawan Village Lac de la Liez

Peigney, F-52200 Langres (Haute-Marne) T: 03 25 90 27 79.

E: campingliez@free.fr alanrogers.com/FR52030

Managed by the enthusiastic Baude family, this excellent lakeside site is near the city of Langres. Only ten minutes from the A5, Camping Lac de la Liez provides an ideal spot for an overnight stop en route to the south of France. There is also a lot on offer for a longer stay. The site provides 131 fully serviced pitches, some with panoramic views of the 250 hectare lake with its sandy beach and small harbour where boats and pedalos may be hired. Ideal for swimming and watersports, access to the lake is down steps and across quite a fast road (in total 150 m).

Facilities

Two toilet blocks have all facilities in cabins (only one is open in low season). Facilities for disabled visitors and babies. Laundry facilities. Motorcaravan services. Shop, bar and restaurant (with takeaway food). Indoor pool complex with spa and sauna. Heated outdoor pool (15/6-15/9). Games room. Playground. Extensive games area. Tennis (free in low season). WiFi. Off site: Lake with beach. Boat and bicycle hire and cycle tracks around lake. Fishing 100 m. Riding 5 km. Golf 40 km.

Open: 1 April - 15 October.

Directions

From Langres take the N19 towards Vesoul. After 3 km. turn right, straight after the large river bridge, then follow site signs. GPS: 47.87022, 5.37627

Charges guide

Per unit incl. 2 persons and electricity	€ 22.00 - € 31.00
extra person	€ 6.00 - € 8.00
child (2-12 yrs)	€ 3.00 - € 4.50
dog	€ 3.00

Camping Cheques accepted.

Le Château-d'Oléron

Airotel Oléron

F-17480 Le Château-d'Oléron (Charente-Maritime) T: 05 46 47 61 82.

E: info@camping-airotel-oleron.com alanrogers.com/FR17060

This family run site on the outskirts of Le Château-d'Oléron has very good facilities, including a superb equestrian centre, a full range of sporting activities and an attractive heated pool complex. This is a mature site with 272 pitches of a good size, with varying degrees of shade provided by trees and attractive shrubs. It is well laid out and most of the 133 touring pitches have electricity (10A), 4 with individual water and drainage. The remaining pitches are used for mobile homes of which 30 are for rent. A full entertainment programme is provided in high season. Visitors can enjoy exploring the island with its fine sandy beaches on the Atlantic coast.

Facilities

Two modern toilet blocks with facilities for disabled visitors and babies. Washing machine and dryer. Motorcaravan service point. Shop. Bar, restaurant and takeaway (15/6-15/9). Heated swimming and paddling pools. Equestrian centre. Playground. Multisport court. Tennis. Minigolf. Fishing. Canoe hire. Bicycle hire. TV and games room. Internet access. WiFi (charged).
Off site: Supermarket. Local markets. Zoo. Aquarium.

Open: Easter - 30 September.

Directions

Cross the bridge onto the island and continue on D26. At second roundabout turn right, marked Dolus and Le Château. Proceed 500 m. and take first right, marked Campings. Site is 1 km. on the right.
GPS: 45.88207, -1.20648

Charges guide

Per unit incl. 2 persons and electricity	€ 17.90 - € 26.90
extra person	€ 4.00 - € 6.90
dog	€ 3.50

Le Croisic

Camping de l'Océan

15 route de la Maison Rouge, F-44490 Le Croisic (Loire-Atlantique) T: 02 40 23 07 69.
E: camping-ocean@wanadoo.fr **alanrogers.com/FR44210**

Camping de l'Océan is situated on the Le Croisic peninsula, an attractive part of the Brittany coastline. Out of a total of 400 pitches, 60 are available for tourers with the remainder being taken by mobile homes, either privately owned or for rent. The pitches are level and 80-100 sq.m. in size (they were rather worn when we visited). The leisure facilities, which include a restaurant, bar and pool complex, are of an excellent standard. This site, probably more suitable for families with young teenagers, can be very lively in high season with a wealth of activities and entertainment for all ages. Sports are well catered for and there are tournaments in high season. After an excellent meal in the restaurant you can enjoy different entertainment on most evenings in July and August. The site is within walking distance of the Atlantic Ocean and white sandy beaches just 150 m. away.

Facilities

Three adequate toilet blocks, however there are no facilities for disabled visitors. Washing machines and dryers. Good restaurant and bar. Takeaway. Shop. Motorcaravan service point. Swimming pool complex comprising an indoor pool, outdoor pool and paddling pool, hammam, sauna and balnéo. Volleyball. Football. Basketball. Tennis. Bicycle hire. Charcoal barbecues are permitted. WiFi throughout (charged; free in bar area). Off site: Market (most days). Le Croisic for shops, bars and restaurants. Sailing, riding and golf.

Open: 6 April - 30 September.

Directions

From Le Pouliguen, travel west on N171 to Le Croisic. Site is well signed from here and found in about 1.5 km. GPS: 47.29752, -2.53593

Charges 2012

Per unit incl. 2 persons and electricity	€ 25.00 - € 52.00
extra person	€ 6.00 - € 9.00
child (2-7 yrs)	€ 4.00 - € 7.00
dog	€ 5.00 - € 7.00

Le Grand-Bornand

Camping Caravaning l'Escale

Route de la Patinoire, F-74450 Le Grand-Bornand (Haute-Savoie) T: 04 50 02 20 69.

E: contact@campinglescale.com alanrogers.com/FR74070

You are assured a good welcome in English from the Baur family at this beautifully maintained and picturesque site, situated at the foot of the Aravis mountain range. There are 149 pitches with 122 for touring. Of average size, part grass, part gravel they are separated by trees and shrubs that give a little shade. All pitches have electricity (2-10A) and 86 are fully serviced. Rock pegs are essential. A 200-year-old building houses a bar/restaurant decorated in traditional style and offering regional dishes in a delightful, warm ambience. The village is 200 m. away and has all the facilities of a resort with activities for both summer and winter holidays.

Facilities

Good toilet blocks are heated in winter. Drying room for skis, clothing and boots. Superb pool complex with interconnected indoor (all season) and outdoor pools and paddling pools (15/6-29/8), jacuzzi and water jets. Cosy bar/restaurant and takeaway. Play area. Tennis. WiFi. Activities for all. Video games. Discounts on organised walks and visits to Chamonix-Mont Blanc. Off site: Village (5 minutes walk), shops, bars, restaurants, archery, paragliding, golf, minigolf. 150 km. of signed walks. Ice skating, snow shoes in winter. Bicycle hire 200 m. Riding and golf 3 km. Free bus to cable car (500 m).

Open: 15 December - 25 April, 1 June - 25 September.

Directions

From Annecy follow D16 and D909 towards La Clusaz. At St Jean-de-Sixt, turn left at roundabout D4 signed Grand-Bornand. Just before village fork right signed Vallée de Bouchet and camping. Site entrance is on right at roundabout in 1.2 km. GPS: 45.94036, 6.42842

Charges guide

Per unit incl. 2 persons and electricity	€ 20.30 - € 34.40
extra person (over 2 yrs)	€ 5.00 - € 5.90
dog	€ 2.30

Le Pouldu

to book this site call **01580 214000** ...we arrange everything — the travel service

Camping les Embruns

Le Pouldu Plages, F-29360 Clohars-Carnoët (Finistère) T: 02 98 39 91 07.

E: camping-les-embruns@orange.fr alanrogers.com/FR29180

This site is unusual in that it is located in the heart of a village, yet is only 250 metres from a sandy cove. The entrance with its code operated barrier and wonderful floral displays, is the first indication that this is a well tended and well organised site, and the owners have won numerous regional and national awards for its superb presentation. The 180 pitches (100 occupied by mobile homes) are separated by trees, shrubs and bushes, and most have electricity (16A Europlug), water and drainage. There is a covered, heated swimming pool, a circular paddling pool and a water play pool and slide. It is only a short walk to the village centre with all its attractions and services. It is also close to beautiful countryside and the Carnoët Forest which are good for walking and cycling.

Facilities

Two modern sanitary blocks, recently completely renewed and heated in winter, include mainly British style toilets, some washbasins in cubicles, baby baths and good facilities for disabled visitors. Family bathrooms. Laundry facilities. Motorcaravan service point. Shop. Restaurant by entrance, bar and terrace, takeaway (6/4-15/9). Covered, heated swimming and paddling pools. Large games hall. Play area. Football field. Minigolf. Communal barbecue area. Daily activities for children and adults organised in July/Aug. Bicycle hire. Internet access and WiFi in reception area (charged). Off site: Nearby sea and river fishing and watersports. Beach 250 m. Riding 2 km.

Open: 6 April - 22 September.

Directions

From N165 take either 'Kervidanou, Quimperlé Ouest' exit or 'Kergostiou, Quimperlé Centre, Clohars Carnoët' exit and follow D16 to Clohars Carnoët. Then take D24 for Le Pouldu and follow site signs in village. GPS: 47.76867, -3.54508

Charges 2012

Per unit incl. 2 persons and electricity	€ 10.50 - € 31.50
extra person	€ 3.95 - € 5.90
child (under 7 yrs)	€ 2.80 - € 3.80
dog	€ 2.70

Use of motorcaravan services € 4.

Locunolé

Castel Camping le Ty Nadan

Route d'Arzano, F-29310 Locunolé (Finistère) T: 02 98 71 75 47.
E: infos@camping-ty-nadan.fr alanrogers.com/FR29010

Camping le Ty Nadan is a well organised site set amongst wooded countryside along the bank of the River Elle. There are 183 grassy pitches for touring units, many with shade and 99 fully serviced. The pool complex with slides and paddling pool is very popular as are the large indoor pool complex and indoor games area with a climbing wall. There is also an adventure play park and a minikids park for 5-8 year olds, not to mention tennis courts, table tennis, pool tables, archery and trampolines. This is a wonderful site for families with children. An exciting and varied programme of activities is offered throughout the season – canoeing and sea kayaking expeditions, rock climbing, mountain biking, aquagym, paintball, riding and walking – all supervised by qualified staff. A full programme of entertainment for all ages is provided in high season including concerts, Breton evenings with pig roasts, dancing, etc. (be warned, you will be actively encouraged to join in!). Several tour operators use the site.

Facilities

Two older, split-level toilet blocks are of fair quality and include washbasins in cabins and baby rooms. A newer block provides easier access for disabled campers. Washing machines and dryers. Restaurant, takeaway, bar and well stocked shop. Heated outdoor pool (17x8 m). Indoor pool. Small river beach (unfenced). Indoor badminton and rock climbing facility. Activity and entertainment programmes (all season). Horse riding centre. Bicycle hire. Boat hire. Canoe trips. Fishing. Internet access and WiFi (charged). Off site: Beaches 20 minutes by car. Golf 12 km.

Open: 27 March - 2 September.

Directions

Make for Arzano which is northeast of Quimperlé on the Pontivy road and turn off D22 just west of village at site sign. Site is about 3 km.
GPS: 47.90468, -3.47477

Charges guide

Per unit incl. 2 persons and electricity	€ 20.10 - € 46.00
extra person	€ 4.30 - € 8.80
child (2-6 yrs)	€ 2.00 - € 5.40
dog	€ 2.10 - € 5.80

Camping Cheques accepted.

Longeville-sur-Mer

Camping les Brunelles

Le Bouil, F-85560 Longeville-sur-Mer (Vendée) T: 02 51 33 17 00.

E: camping@les-brunelles.com alanrogers.com/FR85440

to book this site call **01580 214000** ...we arrange everything — the travel service

This is a well managed site with a wide range of facilities and a varied programme of high season entertainment for all the family. In 2007, les Brunelles was combined with an adjacent campsite to provide 600 pitches of which 200 are for touring units; all have electricity (10A) and 20 of the new touring pitches also have water and a drain. All are in excess of 100 sq.m. to allow easier access for larger units. On the original les Brunelles site, the touring pitches are all level on sandy grass and separated by hedges, away from most of the mobile homes.

Facilities

Four well maintained and modernised toilet blocks have British and Turkish style toilets and washbasins, both open style and in cabins. Laundry facilities. Shop, takeaway and large modern, airy bar (all season). Covered pool with jacuzzi (all season). Outdoor pool with slides and paddling pools (21/5-24/9). Tennis. Bicycle hire. Max. 1 dog. Off site: Riding 3 km. Supervised, sandy beach 900 m. St Vincent-sur-Jard 2 km. Golf 20 km.

Open: 2 April - 24 September.

Directions

From D21 (Talmont-Longeville), between St Vincent and Longeville, site signed south from main road towards coast. Turn left in Le Bouil (site is signed). Site is 800 m. on left. GPS: 46.41330, -1.52313

Charges guide

Per unit incl. 2 persons and electricity	€ 21.00 - € 35.00
extra person	€ 5.00 - € 9.00

Camping Cheques accepted.

Maisons-Laffitte

Camping Caravaning International

1 rue Johnson, F-78600 Maisons-Laffitte (Yvelines) T: 01 39 12 21 91.

E: ci.mlaffitte@wanadoo.fr alanrogers.com/FR78010

to book this site call **01580 214000** ...we arrange everything — the travel service

This site on the banks of the Seine is consistently busy, has multilingual, friendly reception staff and occupies a grassy, tree covered area bordering the river. There are 317 pitches, 107 occupied by mobile homes and tour operators, plus two areas dedicated to tents. Most pitches are separated by hedges, are of a good size with some overlooking the Seine (unfenced access), and all 210 touring pitches have electricity hook-ups (6A). The roads leading to the site are a little narrow so large vehicles need to take care. Train noise can be expected.

Facilities

Three sanitary blocks, two insulated for winter use and one more open (only used in July/Aug). Facilities are clean with constant supervision necessary, due to volume of visitors. Provision for disabled visitors. Laundry and dishwashing areas. Motorcaravan service point. Shop. Restaurant/bar. Takeaway food and pizzeria. TV in restaurant, table tennis, football area. Fishing possible with licence. Internet point. WiFi (charged). Off site: Sports complex adjoining. Riding 500 m. Bicycle hire 5 km.

Open: 1 week before Easter - 3 November.

Directions

Best approached from A13 or A15 autoroute. From A13 take exit 7 (Poissy) and follow D153 (Poissy), the D308 (Maisons-Laffitte), then site signs on right before town centre. From A15 exit 7 take the D184 towards St Germain, after 11 km. turn left on D308 (Maisons-Laffitte). Follow site signs. From the A1 take the A86, then at exit 2 (Bezons) take the D308 (Maisons-Laffitte). Follow signs to site on left. GPS: 48.9399, 2.14589

Charges guide

Per unit incl. 2 persons and electricity	€ 26.70 - € 32.20
extra person	€ 5.70 - € 6.40

Malbuisson

Camping les Fuvettes

24 route de la Plage et des Perrières, F-25160 Malbuisson (Doubs) T: 03 81 69 31 50.

E: les-fuvettes@wanadoo.fr alanrogers.com/FR25080

High in the Jura and close to the Swiss border, les Fuvettes is a well established family site beside Lac Saint Point. The 320 reasonably sized grass pitches are separated by hedges and small trees with varying degrees of shade and many are slightly sloping. There are 250 for touring with 200 having electricity (6A). Only a few have views over the lake. The swimming pool complex is impressive with water slides and a children's pool. The site's bar/snack bar offers panoramic views across the lake.

Facilities

Three toilet blocks include facilities for babies and disabled visitors. Shop. Bar and snack bar. Swimming pool with water slides, jacuzzi and paddling pool (from June). Play area. Minigolf. Archery. Bicycle hire. Sports pitch. Fishing (permit needed). Boat and pedalo hire. Games room. TV room. Children's club in peak season. Entertainment and excursions (July/Aug). Mobile homes and chalets for rent. Gas and charcoal barbecues only. WiFi (charged). Off site: Lakeside beach. Sailing school. Tennis. Riding 1 km. Bicycle hire 3 km. Cycling and walking trails. Restaurants, cafés and shops in Malbuisson.

Open: 1 April - 30 September.

Directions

From Besançon, head south on the N57 to just beyond Pontarlier. Take the D437 signed Lac St Point and Mouthe. The road skirts the lake and through Malbuisson. Site is on right at the end of the village. GPS: 46.79197, 6.29334

Charges guide

Per unit incl. 2 persons and electricity	€ 18.90 - € 24.90
extra person	€ 3.80 - € 5.00
child (2-7 yrs)	€ 1.80 - € 3.00
dog	free - € 1.50

Mandelieu-la-Napoule

Camping Caravaning les Cigales

505 ave. de la Mer, F-06210 Mandelieu-la-Napoule (Alpes-Maritimes)
T: 04 93 49 23 53. E: campingcigales@wanadoo.fr alanrogers.com/FR06080

It is hard to imagine that such a quiet, peaceful site could be in the middle of such a busy town and so near Cannes. The entrance (easily missed) has large electronic gates that ensure that the site is very secure. There are only 115 pitches (42 mobile homes) so this is quite a small, personal site. There are three pitch sizes, from small ones for tents to pitches for larger units and all have electricity (6A), some fully serviced. All are level with much needed shade in summer, although the sun will get through in winter when it is needed. The site is alongside the Canal de Siagne and for a fee, small boats can be launched at La Napoule, then moored outside the campsite's side gate. Les Cigales is open all year so it is useful for the Monte Carlo Rally, the Cannes Film Festival and the Mimosa Festival, all held out of the main season. English is spoken.

Facilities

Well appointed, clean, heated toilet blocks. Excellent facilities for babies and disabled visitors. Laundry area. Motorcaravan services. Restaurant and takeaway (May-Oct). Attractive swimming pool, heated according according to the weather conditions and large sunbathing area (April-Oct). New play area. River fishing. WiFi (free). Only gas barbecues allowed. Max 1 dog per pitch.
Off site: Beach 800 m. The town is an easy walk. Two golf courses within 1 km. Railway station 1 km. for trains to Cannes, Nice, Antibes, Monte Carlo. Hypermarket 2 km. Bus stop 30 m.

Open: All year.

Directions

From A8, exit 40, bear right. Remain in right hand lane, continue right signed Plages-Ports, Creche-Campings. Casino supermarket on right. Continue under motorway to T-junction. Turn left, site is 60 m. on left opposite Chinese restaurant. Some other approaches have a 3.3 m. height restriction.
GPS: 43.5391, 6.94275

Charges 2012

Per unit incl. 2 persons and electricity	€ 41.50 - € 55.00
extra person	€ 8.00
child (under 5 yrs)	€ 4.00

Martres-Tolosane

Camping le Moulin

Lieu-dit le Moulin, F-31220 Martres-Tolosane (Haute-Garonne) T: 05 61 98 86 40.
E: info@campinglemoulin.com alanrogers.com/FR31000

With attractive shaded pitches and many activities, this family-run campsite has 12 hectares of woods and fields beside the River Garonne. It is close to Martres-Tolosane, an interesting medieval village. Some of the 60 level and grassy pitches are 'supersize' and all have electricity (6/10A). There are 24 chalets to rent. Summer brings opportunities for guided canoeing, archery and walking. A large sports field is available all season, with tennis, volleyball, basketball, boules and birdwatching on site. Facilities for visitors with disabilities are very good, although the sanitary block is a little dated. Some road noise. Large grounds for dog walking. A member of Sites et Paysages.

Facilities

Large sanitary block with separate ladies' and gents WCs. Communal area with showers and washbasins in cubicles. Separate heated area for disabled visitors. Baby bath. Laundry facilities. Motorcaravan services. Outdoor bar with WiFi. Restaurant (1/7-20/8). Snack bar and takeaway (1/6-15/9). Daily bakers van (except Monday). Heated swimming and paddling pools (1/6-15/9). Fishing. Tennis. Canoeing. Archery. BMX track. Playground. Games room. Bouncy castle. Entertainment and children's club (high season). Massage by arrangement (charged).
Off site: Martres-Tolosane 1.5 km. Riding 4 km. Golf 12 km.

Open: 1 April - 30 September.

Directions

From the A64 motorway (Toulouse-Tarbes) take exit 21 (Boussens) or exit 22 (Martres-Tolosane) and follow signs to Martres-Tolosane. Site is well signed from village. GPS: 43.19048, 1.01788

Charges guide

Per unit incl. 2 persons and electricity	€ 18.50 - € 26.90
extra person	€ 4.50 - € 6.00
child (under 7 yrs)	€ 2.50 - € 3.00
dog	€ 2.00 - € 2.50

Less 20% outside July/Aug.

Messanges

Airotel le Vieux Port

Plage Sud, F-40660 Messanges (Landes) T: **01 76 76 70 00.**
E: **contact@levieuxport.com** **alanrogers.com/FR40180**

A well established destination appealing particularly to families with teenage children, this lively site has 1,546 pitches of mixed sizes, most with electricity (6A). The camping area is well shaded by pines and pitches are generally of a good size, attractively grouped around the toilet blocks. There are many tour operators here and well over a third of the site is taken up with mobile homes and chalets. An enormous 7,000 sq.m. aquatic park is now open, and is the largest on any French campsite. This heated complex is exceptional, boasting five outdoor pools, three large water slides plus waves and a heated spa. There is also a heated indoor pool. The area to the north of Bayonne is heavily forested and a number of very large campsites are attractively located close to the superb Atlantic beaches. Le Vieux Port is probably the largest, and certainly one of the most impressive, of these. At the back of the site a path leads across the dunes to a good beach (400 m). Other recent innovations include an outdoor fitness area and a superb riding centre. All in all, this is a lively site with a great deal to offer an active family.

Facilities

Nine well appointed, recently renovated toilet blocks with facilities for disabled visitors. Motorcaravan services. Good supermarket and various smaller shops in high season. Several restaurants, takeaway and three bars (all open all season). Large pool complex (no Bermuda shorts; open all season) including new covered pool and Polynesian themed bar. Tennis. Multisport pitch. Minigolf. Outdoor fitness area. Fishing. Bicycle hire. Riding centre. Organised activities in high season including frequent discos and karaoke evenings. Only communal barbecues are allowed. WiFi (charged). Off site: Beach 400 m. Sailing 2 km. Golf 8 km.

Open: 31 March - 30 September.

Directions

Leave RN10 at Magescq exit heading for Soustons. Pass through Soustons following signs for Vieux-Boucau. Bypass this town and site is clearly signed to the left at second roundabout.
GPS: 43.79778, -1.40111

Charges 2012

Per unit incl. 2 persons and electricity	€ 21.30 - € 61.00
extra person	€ 4.80 - € 9.00
child (under 13 yrs)	€ 3.80 - € 6.20
dog	€ 3.10 - € 5.80

Camping Cheques accepted.

Matafelon-Granges

Camping des Gorges de l'Oignin

Rue du Lac, F-01580 Matafelon-Granges (Ain) T: 04 74 76 80 97.
E: camping.lesgorgesdeloignin@wanadoo.fr **alanrogers.com/FR01050**

This family run, terraced site (English spoken) offers lovely views across the lake to the hills beyond. There are 132 good sized pitches, 102 for touring, separated by young trees and flowering shrubs and with a choice of grass or hardstanding. About half have their own water point and all have 10A electricity. Twin axle caravans are not accepted. The reception, bar/restaurant and the pool complex are at the top of the site with a steep road down to the terraces and the rest of the campsite. At the bottom of the site is a large grassy area next to the lake for sunbathing and activities.

Facilities

Two modern, well equipped and clean toilet blocks with all the usual facilities except facilities for disabled visitors. Bar/restaurant, takeaway and TV room (July/Aug). Swimming pool, paddling pool and new 'lazy river' (1/6-30/9). Playground and sports area. Swimming, fishing and boating on the lake (no motorboats). Off site: Matafelon 800 m. Golf and riding 2 km. Thoirette 6 km. Oyonnax with range of shops, market, bar/restaurants 10 km.

Open: 1 April - 30 September.

Directions

Matafelon is 40 km. east of Bourg-en-Bresse. Leave autoroute A404 at Oyonnax, exit 11 and head west on D13 to Matafelon (10 km). On entering village and opposite the Mairie turn left, signed camping, and descend to site (800 m). GPS: 46.25535, 5.55717

Charges guide

Per unit incl. 2 persons and electricity	€ 17.00 - € 26.20
extra person	€ 3.60 - € 5.80
child (3-10 yrs)	€ 2.40 - € 4.20
dog	€ 1.20 - € 2.40

Moliets-Plage

Le Saint-Martin Camping

Avenue de l'Océan, F-40660 Moliets-Plage (Landes) T: 05 58 48 52 30. E: contact@camping-saint-martin.fr
alanrogers.com/FR40190

A family site aimed mainly at couples and young families, le Saint-Martin is a welcome change from most of the sites in this area in that it has only a relatively small number of mobile homes (127) compared to the number of touring pitches (383). First impressions are of a neat, tidy, well cared for site and the direct access to a wonderful fine sandy beach is an added bonus. The pitches are mainly typically French in style with low hedges separating them, and with some shade. Electricity hook ups are 10/15A and a number of pitches also have water and drainage. Entertainment in high season is low key (with the emphasis on quiet nights) – daytime competitions and a miniclub, plus the occasional evening entertainment, well away from the pitches and with no discos or karaoke. With pleasant chalets and mobile homes to rent, a top-class pool complex and an 18-hole golf course 700 m. away (special rates negotiated), this would be an ideal destination for a golfing weekend or longer stay.

Facilities

Seven toilet blocks of a high standard and very well maintained, have washbasins in cabins, large showers, baby rooms and facilities for disabled visitors. Washing machines and dryers. Motorcaravan service point. Fridge rental. Supermarket. Bars, restaurants and takeaways. Indoor pool, jacuzzi and sauna (charged July/Aug). Outdoor pool area with jacuzzi and paddling pool (15/6-15/9). Multisport pitch. Play area. Bicycle hire. Beach access. Internet access. Electric barbecues only. Off site: Fishing and beach 300 m. Golf and tennis 700 m. Sailing 6 km. Riding 8 km.

Open: 4 April - 7 November.

Directions

From the N10 take D142 to Lèon, then D652 to Moliets-et-Mar. Follow signs to Moliets-Plage, site is well signed. GPS: 43.85242, -1.38732

Charges guide

Per unit incl. 2 persons and electricity	€ 22.70 - € 48.60
extra person	€ 6.00 - € 7.50
child (under 10 yrs)	€ 4.00 - € 5.30
dog	free - € 5.00

Prices are for reserved pitches.

For latest campsite news, availability and prices visit
alanrogers.com

Miannay

to book this site call 01580 214000 ...we arrange everything
the travel service

Camping le Clos Cacheleux

Route de Bouillancourt, F-80132 Miannay (Somme) T: 03 22 19 17 47.
E: raphael@camping-lecloscacheleux.fr alanrogers.com/FR80210

Le Clos Cacheleux is a well situated campsite of eight hectares bordering woodland in the park of the Château Bouillancourt which dates from the 18th century. The site was first opened in July 2008. It is 11 km. from the Bay of the Somme, regarded as being amongst the most beautiful bays in France. There are 100 very large, grassy pitches (200 sq.m) and all have electricity (10A Europlug). The aim of the owners is to make your stay as enjoyable as possible by providing high quality services and activities. Visitors have access to the swimming pool, bar and children's club of the sister site – le Val de Trie (20 m). Ask at reception for free walking and cycling tours. A Sites et Paysages member.

Facilities

The single sanitary block is clean and well maintained. Facilities for disabled visitors. Baby room. Laundry facilities. Motorcaravan service point. At the sister site: shop, bar with terrace (22/4-10/9), library and TV room, restaurant and takeaway (27/4-2/9). Play area. Boules. Picnic tables. Barbecue hire. Bicycle hire. Fishing pond. Caravan storage. Covered pool (15/4-30/9) on the sister site and a second sanitary block with family showers plus children's facilities. WiFi (free). Off site: Village 1 km. Hypermarket in Abbéville. Riding 4 km. Golf 9 km. Sandy beaches of the Picardy coast 12 km. Riding 14 km.

Open: 15 March - 15 October.

Directions

From the A28 at Abbéville take the D925 towards Eu and Le Tréport; do not go towards Moyenville. Turn left in Miannay village on the D86 towards Toeufles. The road to Bouillancourt-sous-Miannay is on the left after 2 km. and site is signed in the village.
GPS: 50.08352, 1.71343

Charges guide

Per unit incl. 2 persons and electricity	€ 18.50 - € 25.80
extra person	€ 3.10 - € 5.30
child (under 7 yrs)	€ 1.90 - € 3.30
dog	€ 1.80 - € 2.00

Montpezat de Quercy

Camping le Faillal

F-82270 Montpezat de Quercy (Tarn-et-Garonne) T: 05 63 02 07 08. E: contact@revea-vacances.com
alanrogers.com/FR82050

Le Faillal is located at Montpézat de Quercy, around 35 km. north of Montauban. There are 69 pitches here, all of a good size and each has its own electricity (4/6A), water and light. The surrounding trees and hedges give shade and some privacy. The site forms a part of the Parc de Loisirs de Faillal and includes a swimming pool, tennis court and minigolf, all of which are free for campers. There is no bar, restaurant or snack provision. These amenities are available in the town, a short walk away. Le Faillal provides some activities for children in high season and some entertainment for families, including barbecues and karaoke evenings. There are many excellent cycle tracks through the rolling countryside of the Quercy and the site managers will be pleased to recommend routes. Cahors and its world renowned vineyards are just 25 km. distant and the Aveyron gorges are around 30 km. away. Le Faillal is open for a long season and is a tranquil spot for a holiday, particularly outside the peak holiday period.

Facilities

One sanitary block with no facilities for disabled campers. Washing machines and irons. Municipal swimming pool, tennis court, basketball and mini-golf (all open to public). Very small play area. Tourist information and limited WiFi in reception. Service for motorcaravans. Gîtes for rent. Communal barbecue area, no others allowed. Max. 1 dog. Torch useful. Off site: Village centre 800 m. Fishing 6 km. Riding 18 km. Golf 25 km.

Open: 4 April - 10 October.

Directions

Approaching from the north, leave A20 autoroute at exit 58 and head west on D19 and then south on D820 as far as La Baraque. Then head southwest on D20 to Montpézat de Quercy and follow signs to the site. GPS: 44.243139, 1.47764

Charges guide

Per unit incl. 2 persons and electricity	€ 16.50 - € 19.50
extra person	€ 3.20 - € 3.90
child (2-7 yrs)	free - € 2.00

Camping Cheques accepted.

Moyenneville

Camping le Val de Trie

Rue des Sources, Bouillancourt, F-80870 Moyenneville (Somme)

T: 03 22 31 48 88. E: raphael@camping-levaldetrie.fr alanrogers.com/FR80060

to book this site call
01580 214000
...we arrange everything
the travel service

Le Val de Trie is a natural countryside site in woodland, near a small village. The 80 numbered, grassy touring pitches are of a good size, divided by hedges and shrubs with mature trees providing good shade in most areas, and all have electricity (6A) and water. It can be very quiet in April, June, September and October. If there is no-one on site, just choose a pitch or call at the farm to book in. This is maturing into a well managed site with modern facilities and a friendly, relaxed atmosphere. It is well situated for the coast and also the cities of Amiens and Abbeville. There are five new wooden chalets (including one for people with disabilities). There are good walks around the area and a notice board keeps campers up to date with local market, shopping and activity news. English is spoken. The owners of le Val de Trie have recently opened a new campsite nearby, le Clos Cacheleux (FR80210), where larger units can be accommodated.

Facilities

Two clean, recently renovated sanitary buildings include washbasins in cubicles, units for disabled visitors, babies and children. Laundry facilities. Microwave. Shop (all season), bread to order and butcher visits in season. Bar with TV (23/4-4/9), snack bar with takeaway (27/4-2/9). Room above bar for children. Covered heated swimming pool with jacuzzi (14/4-30/9). Outdoor pool for children (26/4-10/9). WiFi in bar area (free). Electric barbecues are not permitted. Off site: Riding 4 km. Golf 10 km. Beach 12 km.

Open: 1 April - 15 October.

Directions

From A28 take exit 2 near Abbeville and D925 to Miannay. Turn left on D86 to Bouillancourt-sous-Miannay: site is signed in village.
GPS: 50.08539, 1.71499

Charges 2012

Per unit incl. 2 persons and electricity	€ 18.90 - € 25.90
extra person	€ 3.10 - € 5.30
child (under 7 yrs)	€ 2.00 - € 3.40
dog	€ 1.80 - € 2.00

Camping Cheques accepted.

Nampont-Saint Martin

Kawan Village la Ferme des Aulnes

1 rue du Marais, Fresne-sur-Authie, F-80120 Nampont-Saint Martin (Somme)

T: 03 22 29 22 69. E: contact@fermedesaulnes.com alanrogers.com/FR80070

This peaceful site, with 120 pitches, has been developed on the meadows of a small, 17th-century farm on the edge of Fresne and is lovingly cared for by its new enthusiastic owners, Marie and Denis Lefort and their hard working team. Restored outbuildings house reception and the facilities, around a central courtyard that boasts a fine heated swimming pool. A new development includes a bar and entertainment room. Outside, facing the main gate, are 20 large level grass pitches for touring. There is also an area for tents. The remaining 22 touring pitches are in the main complex, hedged and fairly level. Activities are organised for children and there are indoor facilities for poor weather. From here you can visit Crécy, Agincourt, St Valéry and Montreuil (where Victor Hugo wrote Les Misérables). The nearby Bay of the Somme has wonderful sandy beaches and many watersports.

Facilities

Both sanitary areas are heated and include washbasins in cubicles with a large cubicle for disabled visitors. Dishwashing and laundry sinks. Shop. Piano bar and restaurant. Motorcaravan service point. TV room. Swimming pool (16x9 m; heated and with cover for cooler weather). Jacuzzi and sauna. Fitness room. Aquagym and balnéotherapy. Playground. Boules. Archery. Rooms with PlayStations and videos. Internet café. WiFi (free). Shuttle service to stations and airports. Off site: Private lake fishing (free) 2 minutes away. River fishing 100 m. Golf 1 km. Riding 8 km.

Open: 1 April - 1 November.

Directions

From Calais, take A16 to exit 25 and turn for Arras for 2 km. and then towards Abbeville on N1. At Nampont-St Martin turn west on D485 and site will be found in 2 km. GPS: 50.33645, 1.71285

Charges guide

Per unit incl. 2 persons and electricity	€ 27.00 - € 33.00
extra person	€ 7.00
child (under 7 yrs)	€ 4.00
dog	€ 4.00

Camping Cheques accepted.

Narbonne

Yelloh! Village les Mimosas

Chaussée de Mandirac, F-11100 Narbonne (Aude) T: 04 68 49 03 72. E: info@lesmimosas.com

alanrogers.com/FR11070

Six kilometres inland from the beaches of Narbonne and Gruissan, this site benefits from a less hectic situation than others by the sea. The site is lively with plenty to amuse and entertain the younger generation whilst offering facilities for the whole family. A free club card is available in July/August for use of the children's club, gym, sauna, tennis, minigolf, billiards etc. There are 250 pitches, 150 for touring, many in a circular layout of a very good size, most with 6A electricity. There are a few 'grand confort', with reasonable shade, mostly from two metre high hedges. There is also a number of mobile homes and chalets to rent. This could be a very useful site offering many possibilities to meet a variety of needs, on-site entertainment (including an evening on Cathar history), and easy access to popular beaches. Nearby Gruissan is a fascinating village with its wooden houses on stilts, beaches, ruined castle, port and salt beds. Narbonne has Roman remains and inland Cathar castles are to be found perched on rugged hill tops.

Facilities

Sanitary buildings refurbished to a high standard include a baby room. Washing machines. Shop and 'Auberge' restaurant (open all season). Takeaway. Bar. Small lounge, amusements (July/Aug). Landscaped heated pool with slides and islands (open 1/5), plus the original pool and children's pool (high season). Play area. Minigolf. Mountain bike hire. Tennis. Sauna and new gym. Children's activities, sports, entertainment (high season). Bicycle hire. Multisports ground. WiFi. Off site: Lagoon with boating and fishing via footpath 200 m. Riding and windsurfing/sailing school 300 m. Gruissan's beach 10 minutes.

Open: 28 March - 1 November.

Directions

From A9 exit 38 (Narbonne Sud) take last exit on roundabout, back over the autoroute (site signed from here). Follow signs La Nautique and then Mandirac and site (6 km. from autoroute). Also signed from Narbonne centre.
GPS: 43.13662, 3.02562

Charges guide

Per unit incl. 2 persons and electricity	€ 17.50 - € 36.00
extra person	€ 4.10 - € 8.00
child (2-7 yrs)	free - € 6.00
dog	€ 1.50 - € 3.50

Narbonne

Camping la Nautique

La Nautique, F-11100 Narbonne (Aude) T: 04 68 90 48 19.

E: info@campinglanautique.com **alanrogers.com/FR11080**

to book this site call **01580 214000** ...we arrange everything — the travel service

Owned and run by a very welcoming Dutch family, this well established site has pitches each with an individual sanitary unit. It is an extremely spacious site situated on the Etang de Bages, where flat water combined with strong winds make it one of the best windsurfing areas in France. La Nautique has 390 huge, level pitches, 270 for touring, all with 10A electricity and water. Six or seven overnight pitches with electricity are in a separate area. A range of mobile homes are available to hire. The flowering shrubs and trees give a pleasant feel. Each pitch is separated by hedges making some quite private and providing shade. Entertainment is organised for adults and children from Easter to September (increasing in high season), plus windsurfing, sailing, rafting, walking, pedalos and canoeing (some activities are charged for). The unspoilt surrounding countryside is excellent for walking and cycling (reception has a booklet with routes), and locally there is horse riding and fishing. This site caters for families with children including teenagers and is fenced off from the water for the protection of children. Windsurfers can have a key for the gate (with deposit) that leads to launching points on the lake.

Facilities

Each pitch has its own fully equipped sanitary unit. Specially equipped facilities for disabled visitors. Laundry. Shop. Bar/restaurant, terrace, TV. Takeaway. All 1/5-30/9. Snack bar 1/7-31/8. Swimming pool, water slide, paddling pool (1/5-30/9). Play areas. Tennis. Minigolf. Pétanque. Miniclub (high season). Games room. WiFi (charged). Only electric barbecues are permitted. Torch useful. Off site: Narbonne is only 4 km. Sandy beaches at Gruissan (12 km) and Narbonne Plage (20 km). Kite surfing. Canoeing, sailing and windsurfing on the Etang.

Open: 15 February - 15 November.

Directions

From A9 take exit 38 (Narbonne Sud). Go around roundabout to last exit and follow signs for La Nautique and site, then further site signs to site on right in 2.5 km. GPS: 43.14696, 3.00439

Charges guide

Per unit incl. 2 persons, electricity, water and sanitary unit	€ 19.50 - € 42.00
extra person	€ 5.00 - € 8.00
child (2-7 yrs)	€ 3.00 - € 6.00
dog	€ 2.50 - € 4.00

Noirmoutier-en-l'Ile

Camping Indigo Noirmoutier

23 allée des Sableaux, Bois de la Chaize, F-85330 Noirmoutier-en-l'Ile (Vendée)

T: 02 51 39 06 24. E: noirmoutier@camping-indigo.com **alanrogers.com/FR85720**

to book this site call **01580 214000** ...we arrange everything — the travel service

Located in woodland and on dunes along a two kilometre stretch of sandy beach, just east of the attractive little town of Noirmoutier on the island of the same name, this could be paradise for those who enjoy a simple campsite in a natural setting. On land belonging to France's forestry commission, this site is operated by Huttopia whose aim is to adapt to the environment rather than take it over. The 398 touring pitches, all with electricity (10A), are situated among the pine trees and accessed along tracks. Those on the sand dunes have fantastic views across the Baie de Bourgneuf.

Facilities

Five sanitary blocks currently provide basic facilities including preset showers and some washbasins in cubicles. The central one is larger and more modern, and another has been refurbished with controllable showers and washbasins. Facilities for babies and disabled visitors. Washing machines and dryers. Basic motorcaravan services point. Play area. Bicycle hire. Free Internet point in reception. Only electric barbecues allowed. Off site: Noirmoutier-en-l'Ile 2 km. with shops, bars and restaurants. Riding 4 km. Sailing 5 km. Golf 25 km.

Open: 30 March - 7 October.

Directions

At La Barre-de-Monts, take D38 across bridge to island. Continue 20 km. to Noirmoutier-en-l'Ile. Go through town past three sets of traffic lights and at roundabout turn right following blue signs to 'Campings'. Site is ahead at roundabout in about 2 km. GPS: 46.9969, -2.2201

Charges guide

Per unit incl. 2 persons and electricity	€ 18.80 - € 25.80
extra person	€ 3.40 - € 5.00

Camping Cheques accepted.

Névez

Camping le Raguénès-Plage

19 rue des Iles, F-29920 Névez (Finistère) T: 02 98 06 80 69.
E: info@camping-le-raguenes-plage.com **alanrogers.com/FR29090**

Mme. Guyader and her family will ensure you receive a warm welcome on arrival at this well kept and pleasant site. Le Raguénès-Plage is an attractive and well laid out campsite with many shrubs and trees. The 287 pitches are a good size, flat and grassy, separated by trees and hedges. All have electricity, water and drainage. The site is used by two tour operators (15 pitches), and has 61 mobile homes of its own. A pool complex complete with new heated indoor pool and water toboggan is a key feature and is close to the friendly bar, restaurant, shop and takeaway. From the far end of the campsite a delightful five minute walk along a path and through a cornfield takes you down to a pleasant, sandy beach looking out towards the Ile Verte and the Presqu'île de Raguénès.

Facilities

Two clean, well maintained sanitary blocks include mixed style toilets, washbasins in cabins, baby baths and facilities for disabled visitors. Laundry room. Motorcaravan service point. Small shop (from 15/5). Bar and restaurant (from 1/6) with outside terrace and takeaway. Reading and TV room, Internet access. Heated indoor and outdoor pools with sun terrace and paddling pool. Sauna (charged). Play areas. Games room. Various activities are organised in July/Aug. WiFi (charged). Off site: Beach, fishing and watersports 300 m. Supermarket 3 km. Riding 4 km.

Open: 1 April - 30 September.

Directions

From N165 take D24 Kerampaou exit. After 3 km. turn right towards Nizon and bear right at church in village following signs to Névez (D77). Continue through Névez, following signs to Raguénès. Continue for 3 km. to site entrance on left (entrance is quite small and easy to miss).
GPS: 47.79337, -3.80049

Charges 2012

Per unit incl. 2 persons and electricity	€ 20.30 - € 39.70
extra person	€ 4.40 - € 6.00
child (under 7 yrs)	free - € 3.90
dog	€ 1.50 - € 3.20

Palinges

Camping du Lac

Le Fourneau, F-71430 Palinges (Saône-et-Loire) T: 03 85 88 14 49. E: camping.palinges@hotmail.fr
alanrogers.com/FR71110

Camping du Lac is a very special campsite and it is all due to M. Labille, the owner, who thinks of the campsite as his home and every visitor as his guest. The campsite has 40 pitches in total, 16 of which have 10A electricity and 16 are fully serviced. There are seven chalets to rent. The site is adjacent to a lake with a beach and safe bathing. Set in the countryside yet within easy reach of many tourist attractions, especially Cluny, the local Château Digoin and Mont Saint Vincent with distant views of Mont Blanc on a clear day.

Facilities

The central sanitary block provides all necessary facilities including those for campers with disabilities. This site is particularly well adapted for disabled visitors. Motorcaravan services. Washing machine and fridge. Bread and croissants to order. Boules. Play area. TV room. Sports field, lake beach and swimming adjacent. WiFi. Off site: Bar/snack bar outside entrance (1/7-31/8). Palinges is within walking distance, cycle and walking routes, museums, cruises on canals, châteaux, 'museographical' complex. Riding 8 km.

Open: 1 April - 30 October.

Directions

Palinges is midway between Montceau les Mines and Paray le Monial. From Montceau take N70, then turn left onto D92 to Palinges. Follow campsite signs. The site is also well signed from the D985 Toulon-sur-Arroux to Charolles road.
GPS: 46.56095, 4.22492

Charges guide

Per unit incl. 2 persons and electricity	€ 20.00
extra person	€ 3.50

No credit cards.

Périgueux

Camping le Grand Dague

Route du Grand Dague, Atur, F-24750 Périgueux (Dordogne) T: 05 53 04 21 01. E: info@legranddague.fr

alanrogers.com/FR24160

This is a beautifully situated campsite in the centre of a wooded area in an ideal location from which to discover the area of the Dordogne. The village of Atur is closest to the site and the town of Perigueux, the capital of the region, is just a few kilometres away. The site was bought by the present owners in 2009 and many changes have been made. There are now 242 pitches, 121 for mobile homes and 71 for touring units. A tour operator has 50 frame tents on the site. There is a new swimming pool complex with a lagoon style pool and a pirate ship. There is also a separate paddling pool and water slide.

Facilities

Excellent, part heated sanitary facilities include a baby room and facilities for campers with disabilities. Launderette. Small shop and bar (all season). Attractive restaurant with appetising menu (May-Sept) and takeaway (June-Aug). Swimming pool, water slide and paddling pool (all season). Covered play area. Pétanque. Minigolf. Play area. Fishing. Off site: Paintball outside gate. Riding and fishing 5 km. Bicycle hire 8 km. Golf 10 km.

Open: 29 May - 26 September.

Directions

From the Bordeaux - Brive inner ring road in Périgueux take D2 south, signed Atur. Campsite signed. Turn east at roundabout just before entering Atur. Site is in 3 km. GPS: 45.14833, 0.77817

Charges guide

Per unit incl. 2 persons and electricity	€ 14.00 - € 29.00
extra person	€ 4.00 - € 6.75

Camping Cheques accepted.

Pierrefitte-sur-Sauldre

Leading Camping les Alicourts

Domaine des Alicourts, F-41300 Pierrefitte-sur-Sauldre (Loir-et-Cher) T: 02 54 88 63 34.
E: info@lesalicourts.com **alanrogers.com/FR41030**

A secluded holiday village set in the heart of the forest, with many sporting facilities and a super spa centre, Camping les Alicourts is midway between Orléans and Bourges, to the east of the A71. There are 490 pitches, 150 for touring and the remainder occupied by mobile homes and chalets. All pitches have electricity connections (6A) and good provision for water, and most are 150 sq.m. (min. 100 sq.m). Locations vary, from wooded to more open areas, thus giving a choice of amount of shade. All facilities are open all season and the leisure amenities are exceptional. A member of Leading Campings Group.

Facilities

Three modern sanitary blocks include some washbasins in cabins and baby bathrooms. Laundry facilities. Facilities for disabled visitors. Motorcaravan services. Shop. Restaurant. Takeaway in bar with terrace. Pool complex. Spa centre. 7-hectare lake (fishing, bathing, canoes, pedaloes). 9-hole golf course. Adventure play area. Tennis. Minigolf. Boules. Roller skating/skateboarding (bring own equipment). Bicycle hire. Internet access. WiFi (charged).

Open: 29 April - 9 September.

Directions

From A71, take Lamotte Beuvron exit (no 3) or from N20 Orléans to Vierzon turn left on to D923 towards Aubigny. After 14 km. turn right at camping sign on to D24E. Site signed in 4 km. GPS: 47.54398, 2.19193

Charges guide

Per unit incl. 2 persons and electricity	€ 20.00 - € 44.00
extra person	€ 7.00 - € 10.00
child (1-17 yrs)	free - € 0.00

Plouha

Castel Camping Domaine de Keravel

La Trinité, F-22580 Plouha (Côtes d'Armor) T: 02 96 22 49 13. E: keravel@wanadoo.fr

alanrogers.com/FR22400

This site is in the grounds of a manor house that has a rather faded grandeur. The setting is spectacular, the site being on the tree-clad slopes below the house from where there are glimpses of the sea in the distance. However, when we visited at the very start of their season, the site had not opened on schedule and the pitches had not been prepared. There are 90 grass touring pitches among the trees, all with electricity and 40 with water and a drain. Agnes and Gilles Pierre have plans to improve their site and we wish them well. There is a good beach nearby and this is an excellent area for walking and cycling enthusiasts.

Facilities

Large but rather drably-furnished toilet block with washbasins in cubicles and controllable showers. Baby room. Facilities for disabled visitors. Laundry room with washing machine and dryer. Motorcaravan service point. Heated swimming pool (15/6-15/9). Tennis court. There is a shop, restaurant (with drinks licence) and takeaway (all 30/6-1/9), but no bar. Gas barbecues are not permitted. WiFi. Off site: Beach 1 km. Bicycle hire 2 km. Shops, bars and restaurants in village 2 km. Riding, sailing and boat launching all 3 km. Golf 4 km.

Open: 1 June - 15 September.

Directions

Plouha is 30 km. northwest of Saint Brieuc and 100 km. from both Roscoff and Saint Malo. From N12 Saint Brieuc by-pass take D786 Paimpol (par la Côte). On reaching Plouha turn east at second roundabout to town centre and follow signs to campsite in 2 km. GPS: 48.68968, -2.90848

Charges 2012

Per unit incl. 2 persons and electricity	€ 30.50
extra person	€ 7.40
child (0-7 yrs)	€ 3.60
dog	€ 3.00

Pommeuse

Camping le Chêne Gris

24 place de la Gare de Faremoutiers, F-77515 Pommeuse (Seine-et-Marne) T: 01 64 04 21 80.
E: info@lechenegris.com alanrogers.com/FR77020

This site is being progressively developed by a Dutch holiday company. A principal building houses reception on the ground floor and also an airy restaurant/bar plus a takeaway. Of the 350 pitches, 53 are for touring, many of which are on aggregate stone, the rest (higher up the hill on which the site is built) being occupied by over 217 mobile homes and 80 tents belonging to a Dutch tour operator. The pitches are not suitable for larger units (over 7 m). Terraces look out onto the heated leisure pool complex and an outdoor adventure-type play area for over-fives.

Facilities

One toilet block with pushbutton showers, washbasins in cubicles and a dishwashing/laundry area. At busy times these facilities may be under pressure. Facilities for disabled visitors and children. Bar, restaurant, takeaway and swimming pool complex (from Easter weekend). Indoor and outdoor play areas. WiFi (charged).
Off site: Shops, bars and restaurants within walking distance. Fishing and riding 2 km.

Open: 20 April - 8 November.

Directions

From A4 at exit 16 take N34 towards Coulommiers. In 10 km. turn south for 2 km. on D25 to Pommeuse; site on right after level-crossing. Also signed from south on D402 Guignes - Coulommiers road, taking D25 to Faremoutiers. GPS: 48.808213, 2.993935

Charges guide

Per unit incl. 2 persons and electricity	€ 25.00 - € 44.00
extra person	€ 2.50 - € 5.00

Camping Cheques accepted.

Pontchâteau

Kawan Village du Deffay

B.P. 18 Le Deffay, Sainte Reine, F-44160 Pontchâteau (Loire-Atlantique)
T: 02 40 88 00 57. E: campingdudeffay@wanadoo.fr alanrogers.com/FR44090

A family managed site, Château du Deffay is a refreshing departure from the usual formula in that it is not over organised or supervised and has no tour operator units. The 170 good sized, fairly level pitches have pleasant views and are either on open grass, on shallow terraces divided by hedges, or informally arranged in a central, slightly sloping wooded area. Most have electricity (6/10A). The bar, restaurant and covered pool are located within the old courtyard area of the smaller château that dates from before 1400. A significant attraction of the site is the large, unfenced lake which is well stocked for fishermen.

Facilities

The main toilet block is well maintained, if a little dated, and includes washbasins in cabins, provision for disabled visitors, and a baby bathroom. Laundry facilities. Shop. Bar and small restaurant with takeaway (1/5-15/9). Covered and heated swimming pool and paddling pool. Play area. TV. Entertainment in season including miniclub. Fishing and pedalos on the lake. Torches useful. WiFi (charged). Off site: Golf 7 km. Riding 10 km. Beach 25 km.

Open: 1 May - 30 September.

Directions

Site is signed from D33 Pontchâteau - Herbignac road near Sainte Reine. Also signed from the D773 and N165-E60 (exit 13). GPS: 47.44106, -2.15981

Charges guide

Per unit incl. 2 persons and electricity	€ 18.30 - € 28.20
extra person	€ 3.35 - € 5.60

Camping Cheques accepted.

Pontorson

Kawan Village Haliotis

Chemin des Soupirs, F-50170 Pontorson (Manche) T: 02 33 68 11 59.
E: camping.haliotis@wanadoo.fr alanrogers.com/FR50080

The whole staff at this beautiful campsite offer a warm welcome to visitors. Situated on the edge of the little town of Pontorson, the site has 152 pitches, including 118 for touring units. Most have electricity (16A) and 34 really large ones also have water and drainage. Excellent private sanitary facilities are available on 12 'luxury' pitches. The site is attractively laid out and includes a Japanese garden. Haliotis (which takes its name from a large shell) is next to the river Couesnon and it is possible to walk, cycle or canoe along the river to Mont Saint-Michel, 9 km. away.

Facilities

Well equipped heated toilet block with controllable showers and washbasins in cubicles. Good facilities for disabled visitors incorporating baby room. Laundry facilities. Bar where breakfast is served. Bread to order. Outdoor heated swimming pool (1/5-30/9) with jacuzzi and separate paddling pool. Sauna and solarium. Play areas. Trampoline. Pétanque. Archery. Games room. Tennis. Golf practice range. Multisport court. Outdoor fitness equipment. Bicycle hire. River fishing. Japanese garden and animal park. Club for children. Internet in bar. WiFi throughout. Off site: Supermarket, restaurants and bars in Pontorson (an easy walk). Riding 3 km. Bay 10 km.

Open: 16 March - 11 November.

Directions

Pontorson is 22 km. southwest of Avranches and is by-passed by the N176 which links with D137 from Saint Malo to the west and (via N175) with A84 (Caen - Rennes) to the east. Site is 300 m. north of the town centre and is well signed. NB. Entrance is on rue du Général Patton. Sat nav users should follow signs! GPS: 48.55836, -1.51429

Charges 2012

Per unit incl. 2 persons and electricity	€ 19.50 - € 25.50
with individual sanitary facility	€ 25.00 - € 31.00
extra person	€ 5.00 - € 6.00

Camping Cheques accepted.

Pordic

Camping les Madières

Le Vau Madec, F-22590 Pordic (Côtes d'Armor) T: 02 96 79 02 48. E: campinglesmadieres@wanadoo.fr

alanrogers.com/FR22110

Les Madières is well placed for exploring the Goëlo coast with its seaside resorts of St Quay-Portrieux, Binic and Etables-sur-Mer, ports used in the past by fishing schooners and now a haven for pleasure boats though a few coastal fishing boats remain. The young and enthusiastic owners are always on hand to ensure the smooth running of this quiet, friendly campsite. The 93 pitches (11 with mobile homes for rent) are mainly set among trees and separated by hedges. An open area without electrical connections is available for campers. Only 800 m. away is the Vau Madec beach, ideal for collecting shellfish.

Facilities

Two traditional heated toilet blocks include washbasins in cubicles and pushbutton showers. Facilities for disabled visitors. Laundry facilities. Simple shop. Bar, restaurant and takeaway (all season). Swimming pool (1/6-20/9). Games room. New play area. Some entertainment (high season). Off site: Bus service 400 m. Beach 800 m. Shops, bars and restaurants in village 2 km. Riding 2.5 km. Sailing 3 km. Bicycle hire and boat launching 4 km.

Open: 1 April - 30 October.

Directions

Pordic is 10 km. northwest of Saint Brieuc and 80 km. west of Saint Malo. From St Brieuc ring-road (N12), turn north on D786 signed Paimpol (par la côte). In 3 km. follow 'campings' signs through Pordic. Site is 2 km. northeast of village (well signed). GPS: 48.58240, -2.80480

Charges guide

Per unit incl. 2 persons and electricity	€ 17.00 - € 21.50
extra person	€ 5.00

Pornic

Camping le Patisseau

29 rue du Patisseau, F-44210 Pornic (Loire-Atlantique) T: 02 40 82 10 39. E: contact@lepatisseau.com

alanrogers.com/FR44100

Le Patisseau is situated in the countryside just a short drive from the fishing village of Pornic. It is a relaxed site with a large number of mobile homes and chalets and is popular with young families and teenagers. The 102 touring pitches, all with electrical connections (6A), are divided between the attractive 'forest' area with plenty of shade from mature trees and the more open 'prairie' area. Some are on a slight slope and access to others might be tricky for larger units. A railway runs along the bottom half of the site with trains several times a day (but none overnight and the noise is minimal).

Facilities

The modern heated toilet block is very spacious and well fitted; most washbasins are open style, but the controllable showers are all in large cubicles which have washbasins. Also good facilities for disabled visitors and babies. Laundry rooms. Shop (1/7-30/8). Bar, restaurant and takeaway (all season). Indoor heated pool with sauna, jacuzzi and spa (all season). Small heated outdoor pools and water slides (1/6-30/9). Play area. Multisport court. Bicycle hire. WiFi in bar area. Off site: Fishing and beach 2.5 km. Riding, golf, sailing and boat launching all 5 km.

Open: 3 April - 11 November.

Directions

Pornic is 19 km. south of the St Nazaire bridge. Access to site is at junction of D751 Nantes - Pornic road with the D213 St Nazaire - Noirmoutier Route Bleue. From north take exit for D751 Nantes. From south follow D751 Clion-sur-Mer. At roundabout north of D213 take exit for le Patisseau and follow signs to site. Avoid Pornic town centre. GPS: 47.118833, -2.072833

Charges guide

Per unit incl. 2 persons and electricity (6A)	€ 25.00 - € 41.00
extra person	€ 4.00 - € 8.00

Pornic

Camping de la Boutinardière

Rue de la Plage de la Boutinardière 23, F-44210 Pornic (Loire-Atlantique) T: 02 40 82 05 68.

E: info@laboutinardiere.com **alanrogers.com/FR44180**

This is truly a holiday site to suit all the family, whatever their ages, just 200 m. from the beach. It has 250 individual good sized pitches, 100-120 sq.m. in size, many bordered by three metre high, well maintained hedges for shade and privacy. All pitches have electricity available. It is a family owned site and English is spoken by the helpful, obliging reception staff. Beside reception is the excellent site shop and across the road is a complex of indoor and outdoor pools, paddling pool and a twin toboggan water slide. On site there are sports and entertainment areas.

Facilities

Toilet facilities are in three good blocks, one large and centrally situated and two supporting blocks. Washbasins are in cabins. Laundry facilities. Shop. New complex of bar, restaurant, terraces. Three heated swimming pools, one indoor (April-Sept), a paddling pool and water slides (15/5-22/9). Games room. Sports and activity area. Playground. Minigolf. Fitness equipment and sauna. Off site: Sandy cove 200 m. Golf, riding, sea fishing, restaurants, cafés, fishing harbour, boat trips, sailing and windsurfing, all within 5 km.

Open: 3 April - 28 September.

Directions

From north or south on the D213, take the Nantes D751 exit. At roundabout (with McDonalds) take the D13 signed Bemarie-en-Retz. After 4 km. site is signed to right. Note: do NOT exit from D213 at Pornic Ouest or Centre. GPS: 47.09150, -2.05133

Charges guide

Per unit incl. 2 persons and electricity	€ 22.00 - € 48.20
extra person	€ 4.00 - € 8.00
child (under 8 yrs)	€ 3.00 - € 6.00
dog	€ 4.00 - € 5.50

Port Leucate

Camping Rives des Corbières

Avenue du Languedoc, F-11370 Port Leucate (Aude) T: 04 68 40 90 31. E: rivescamping@wanadoo.fr

alanrogers.com/FR11050

Port Leucate is part of the major Languedoc development which took place during the sixties and seventies and it is now a thriving resort. The campsite is situated on the old coast road into Port Leucate between the Etang de Salas and the beach, 800 m. from the centre of the town and port and only 150 m. from the beach. A mixture of tall poplars and pine trees provide reasonable shade for the 305 pitches, on good-sized sandy plots, all with 6A electricity connections. About 90 are used for mobile homes. With no tour operators this should be a good value site, now under new management. A pleasant pool area with a jacuzzi is open when the site is open with other facilities only in high season (July and August) when family entertainment is arranged. This is a good base from which to enjoy this stretch of coast with its various 'étangs', which are very popular for watersports, particularly windsurfing.

Facilities

Four toilet blocks opened as required. Two have mainly Turkish toilets. Facilities for disabled visitors. Laundry room. Small supermarket, bar and takeaway (July/Aug). Swimming pools. Play area. Daytime games and tournaments and in the evening, live music, karaoke and dancing. WiFi. Off site: Beach 150 m. (lifeguards July/Aug). Port 800 m. Available in Port Leucate: watersports, tennis, riding and water park. African wildlife reserve at Sigean Fort at Salses.

Open: 1 April - 30 September.

Directions

From the A9 take exit 40 and follow signs for Port Leucate on D627 (passing Leucate village) for 14 km. Exit the D627 which is like a bypass into Port Leucate village. Go right at roundabout into Avenue du Languedoc and site is on right after 800 m. GPS: 42.84932, 3.04083

Charges guide

Per unit incl. 2 persons and electricity	€ 14.00 - € 26.70
extra person	€ 2.90 - € 5.90
child (0-4 yrs)	free - € 3.50
dog	€ 2.60 - € 3.20

Port-en-Bessin

Sunêlia Port'land

Chemin du Castel, F-14520 Port-en-Bessin (Calvados) T: 02 31 51 07 06.
E: campingportland@wanadoo.fr **alanrogers.com/FR14150**

The Gerardin family will make you most welcome at Port'land, now a mature site lying 700 m. to the east of the little resort of Port-en-Bessin, one of Normandy's busiest fishing ports. The 300 pitches are large and grassy with 202 available for touring units, including 128 with 15A electricity. There is a separate area for tents without electricity. The camping area has been imaginatively divided into zones, some overlooking small fishing ponds and another radiating out from a central barbecue area. An attractive modern building houses reception and the good amenities which include a shop and a bar/restaurant with fine views over the Normandy coastline. A member of the Sunelia Group.

Facilities

The two sanitary blocks are modern and well maintained. Special disabled facilities. Heated swimming pool (covered in low season) and paddling pool. Bar, restaurant, takeaway (all open all season). Large TV and games room. Multisports pitch. Fishing. Play area. WiFi. Off site: 27-hole Omaha Beach International Golf Course adjacent. Fishing 600 m. Nearest beach 4 km. Bicycle hire and riding 10 km. D-Day beaches. Colleville American war Cemetery. Bayeux.

Open: 1 April - 3 November.

Directions

Site is clearly signed off the D514, 4 km. west of Port-en-Bessin. GPS: 49.3463, -0.7732

Charges guide

Per unit incl. 2 persons and electricity	€ 20.50 - € 32.00
extra person	€ 5.00 - € 8.00
child (2-10 yrs)	€ 3.00 - € 5.00
dog	€ 3.00

Reductions for stays over 7 nights.

Quimper

Castel Camping l'Orangerie de Lanniron

Château de Lanniron, F-29336 Quimper (Finistère) T: 02 98 90 62 02.
E: camping@lanniron.com alanrogers.com/FR29050

L'Orangerie is a beautiful and peaceful family site set in ten acres of a 17th-century, 38-hectare country estate on the banks of the Odet river, formerly the home of the Bishops of Quimper. The site has 199 grassy pitches (156 for touring units) of three types, varying in size and services. They are on flat ground, laid out in rows alongside access roads with shrubs and bushes providing pleasant pitches. All have electricity and 88 have three services. The original outbuildings have been attractively converted around a walled courtyard. Used by tour operators (30 pitches). There are lovely walks within the grounds and in spring the rhododendrons and azaleas are magnificent – the gardens and the restaurant are both open to the public. The site is just to the south of Quimper and about 15 km. from the sea and beaches at Bénodet. The restoration of the park, including the original canal, fountains, ornamental 'bassin de Neptune', the boathouse and gardens, is now complete. In addition to the golf course (9 holes) and driving range, a training bunker and pitching area have been created along with a second putting green. The aqua-park has a new waterfall and exotic plants; it provides in excess of 600 sq.m. of heated water and includes balneotherapy, spa, jacuzzi, fountains, slides and games.

Facilities

Excellent heated block in the courtyard and second modern block serving the top areas of the site. Facilities for disabled visitors and babies. Washing machines and dryers. Motorcaravan services. Shop (15/5-9/9). Gas supplies. Bar, snacks and takeaway. New restaurant (open daily). Swimming and paddling pools. Aqua-park with waterfall, balneo, spa, jacuzzi, fountains, water slides and games. Small play area. Tennis. Minigolf. Golf course (9 holes), driving range, two putting greens, training bunker and pitching area (weekly green fee package available). Fishing. Archery. Bicycle hire. General reading, games and billiards rooms. TV/video room. Karaoke. Outdoor activities. Large room for indoor activities. Pony rides and tree climbing (high season). Internet access and WiFi throughout (charged). Off site: Two hypermarkets 1 km. Historic town of Quimper under 3 km. Activities in the area include golf, cycling, walking, fishing, canoeing, surfing and sailing. Beach 15 km.

Open: 15 May - 15 September.

Directions

From Quimper follow Quimper Sud signs, then 'Toutes Directions' and general camping signs, finally signs for Lanniron. GPS: 47.97685, -4.11102

Charges 2012

Per unit incl. 2 persons and electricity	€ 23.20 - € 41.00
extra person	€ 4.50 - € 7.90
child (2-9 yrs)	€ 3.00 - € 5.10
dog	€ 3.20 - € 4.70

Less 15% outside July/Aug.

Rambouillet

Huttopia Rambouillet

Rue du Château d'Eau, F-78120 Rambouillet (Yvelines) T: 01 30 41 07 34.
E: rambouillet@huttopia.com alanrogers.com/FR78040

This pleasant site is now part of the Huttopia group whose philosophy is to 'rediscover the camping spirit'. It is in a peaceful forest location beside a lake, with good tarmac access roads and site lighting. The 141 touring pitches, 100 with electrical connections (10A), are set among the trees and in clearings. As a result, shade is plentiful and grass sparse. The main area is kept traffic-free but there is a section for motorcaravans and those who need or prefer to have their car with them. The result is a safe, child-friendly site. There is an 'espace nature' with 40 huge pitches for campers.

Facilities
The brand new sanitary block has controllable showers, some washbasins in cubicles and a number of family cubicles. Facilities for disabled visitors. Laundry facilities. Three outlying 'rondavels' each with two family rooms. Motorcaravan service point. Small shop selling basics. Bar/restaurant with terrace (weekends in low season and daily in July and August). Games room with TV. Play area. Natural swimming pool (June-Sept, earlier if possible). Bicycle hire. Fishing. Activities (July-Aug). Off site: Riding 5 km. Golf and lake with beach 15 km. Sailing 20 km.

Open: 30 March - 7 November.

Directions
Rambouillet is 52 km. southwest of Paris. Site is southeast of town: from N10 southbound take Rambouillet/Les Eveuses exit, northbound take Rambouillet centre exit, loop round (site signed) and rejoin N10 southbound, taking next exit. Pass under N10, following signs to site in 1.7 km. GPS: 48.62638, 1.84375

Charges guide

Per unit incl. 2 persons and electricity	€ 23.00 - € 32.20
extra person	€ 5.50 - € 7.10

Ravenoville-Plage

Kawan Village le Cormoran

2 le Cormoran, F-50480 Ravenoville Plage (Manche) T: 02 33 41 33 94.
E: lecormoran@wanadoo.fr alanrogers.com/FR50050

This welcoming, environmentally friendly, family run site, close to Cherbourg and Caen, is situated just across the road from a long sandy beach. It is also close to Utah beach and is ideally located for those wishing to visit the many museums, landing beaches and remembrance gardens of WW2. On flat, quite open ground, the site has 110 good sized pitches on level grass, all with 6/10A electricity (Europlug). Some extra large pitches are available. The well kept pitches are separated by mature hedges and the site is decorated with shrubs. A covered pool, a sauna and a gym are among recent improvements.

Facilities
Four toilet blocks, three heated, are of varying styles and ages but all are maintained to a good standard. Laundry facilities. Shop. Bar and terrace. Snacks and takeaway. Outdoor pool (1/6-15/9, unsupervised). New covered pool, sauna and gym (all season). Play areas. Tennis. Boules. Entertainment, TV and games room. Billiard golf. Playing field with archery (July/Aug). Hairdresser and masseuse. Bicycle hire. Riding (July/Aug). Communal barbecues. BMX park. WiFi (charged). Off site: Beach 20 m. Sand yachting. Golf 3 km. Ste-Mère-Eglise 9 km.

Open: 7 April - 29 September.

Directions
From N13 take Ste Mère-Eglise exit and in centre of town take road to Ravenoville (6 km), then Ravenoville-Plage (3 km). Just before beach turn right and site is 500 m. GPS: 49.46643, -1.23533

Charges 2012

Per unit incl. 2 persons and electricity	€ 21.00 - € 33.00
extra person	€ 4.00 - € 7.90

Advanced booking advised in peak season.
Camping Cheques accepted.

Rillé

Huttopia Rillé

Lac de Rillé, F-37340 Rillé (Indre-et-Loire) T: 02 47 24 62 97.
E: rille@huttopia.com alanrogers.com/FR37140

Huttopia Rillé is a rural site ideal for tent campers seeking a more natural, environmentally friendly, peaceful campsite close to a lake. Cars are parked outside the barrier but allowed on site to unload and load. The 146 slightly uneven and sloping pitches, 80 for touring, are scattered between the pine trees. All have 10A electricity (very long leads needed) and 24 are fully serviced. They vary in size and are numbered but not marked. This site is designed for those with tents, though small caravans and motorcaravans (special area) are accepted. It is not ideal for those with walking difficulties.

Facilities
Modern toilet block with family rooms and facilities for disabled visitors (no ramps and difficult access for wheelchairs). A smaller block has separate showers, washbasins and facilities for disabled visitors. Motorcaravan service point. Small heated swimming pool with paddling area (21/4-30/9). Play area. Fishing. Canoes on lake. Communal barbecue areas (no charcoal barbecues). Max. 1 dog. Off site: Small steam train passes site. Châteaux to visit. Marked walks. Cycle tracks. Nature reserve at the lake. Riding 6 km. Golf 15 km.

Open: 21 April - 7 November.

Directions
Rillé is 40 km. west of Tours. Leave the D766 Angers - Blois road at Château la Vallière take the D749 southwest. In Rillé turn west on D49. Site is on right in 2 km. GPS: 47.45811, 0.2192

Charges guide

Per unit incl. 2 persons and electricity	€ 20.20 - € 31.90
extra person	€ 5.30 - € 7.10
child (2-7 yrs)	€ 3.20 - € 4.75
dog	€ 4.00

Roquebrune-sur-Argens

Camping Caravaning Leï Suves

Quartier du Blavet, F-83520 Roquebrune-sur-Argens (Var) T: 04 94 45 43 95.

E: camping.lei.suves@wanadoo.fr alanrogers.com/FR83030

This quiet, pretty site is a few kilometres inland from the coast, 2 km. north of the N7. Close to the unusual Roquebrune rock, it is within easy reach of St Tropez, Ste Maxime, St Raphaël and Cannes. The site entrance is appealing – wide and spacious, with a large bank of well tended flowers. Mainly on a gently sloping hillside, the 310 pitches are terraced with shade provided by the many cork trees which give the site its name. All pitches have electricity and access to water. A pleasant pool area is beside the bar/restaurant and entertainment area. Please note that reception is closed on Sundays. It is possible to walk in the surrounding woods. There are 150 mobile homes available to rent.

Facilities

Modern, well kept toilet blocks include facilities for disabled visitors, washing machines and dryers. Shop. Good sized swimming pool, paddling pool. Bar, terrace, snack bar, takeaway (all 31/3-15/10). Outdoor stage near the bar for evening entertainment in high season. Excellent play area. Table tennis, tennis, sports area. WiFi over whole site. Only gas barbecues are permitted. Off site: Bus stop at site entrance. Riding 1 km. Fishing 3 km. Bicycle hire 5 km. Golf 7 km. Beach at St Aygulf 15 km.

Open: 2 April - 15 October.

Directions

Leave autoroute at Le Muy and take the N7 towards St Raphaël. Turn left at roundabout onto D7 heading north signed La Bouverie (site also signed). Site on right in 2 km. GPS: 43.47793, 6.63881

Charges 2012

Per unit incl. 2 persons	
and electricity	€ 26.50 - € 46.50
incl. 3 persons	€ 28.50 - € 49.70
extra person	€ 5.25 - € 9.90
child (under / yrs)	€ 3.25 - € 6.80
dog	€ 2.00 - € 3.50

Roquebrune-sur-Argens

Camping Domaine de la Bergerie

Vallée du Fournel, route du Col-du-Bougnon, F-83520 Roquebrune-sur-Argens (Var) T: 04 98 11 45 45.

E: info@domainelabergerie.com alanrogers.com/FR83170

This excellent site near the Côte d'Azur will take you away from all the bustle of the Mediterranean to total relaxation amongst the cork, oak, pine and mimosa in its woodland setting. The 60 hectare site is quite spread out with semi-landscaped areas for mobile homes and 200 separated pitches for touring caravans and tents. All pitches average over 80 sq.m. and have electricity, with those in one area also having water and drainage. The restaurant/bar, a converted farm building, is surrounded by shady patios, whilst inside it oozes character with high beams and archways leading to intimate corners.

Facilities

Four toilet blocks are kept clean and include washbasins in cubicles, facilities for disabled visitors and babies. Supermarket. Bar/restaurant. Takeaway. Pool complex with indoor pool and fitness centre. Tennis. Archery. Roller skating. Minigolf. Children's club. Mini-farm. Fishing. Internet. WiFi. Only gas barbecues are permitted. Off site: Riding and golf 2 km. Bicycle hire 7 km. Beach, St Aygulf and Ste Maxime 7 km. Water skiing nearby.

Open: 28 April - 30 September (mobile homes 1 March - 15 November).

Directions

Leave A8 at Le Muy exit on N7 towards Roquebrune. Proceed for 9 km. then right onto the D7 signed St Aygulf. Continue for 8 km. and then right at roundabout on D8; site is on the right. GPS: 43.4091, 6.6747

Charges 2012

Per unit incl. 2 persons and electricity	€ 19.00 - € 45.00
incl. water and drainage	€ 23.00 - € 50.50
extra person	€ 5.50 - € 10.00

Roquebrune-sur-Argens

Camping les Pêcheurs

F-83520 Roquebrune-sur-Argens (Var) T: 04 94 45 71 25.

E: info@camping-les-pecheurs.com alanrogers.com/FR83200

Les Pêcheurs will appeal to families who appreciate natural surroundings together with many activities, both cultural and sporting. Interspersed with mobile homes, the 123 good sized touring pitches (10A electricity) are separated by trees or flowering bushes. The Provençal style buildings are delightful, especially the bar, restaurant and games room, with its terrace down to the river and the site's own canoe station (locked gate). Across the road is a lake used exclusively for waterskiing with a sandy beach and restaurant.

Facilities

Modern, refurbished, well designed toilet blocks, baby baths, facilities for disabled visitors. Washing machines. Shop. Bar and restaurant. Heated outdoor swimming pool. Separate paddling pool (lifeguard in high season), ice cream bar. Games room. Spa facilities. Playing field. Fishing. Canoeing. Waterskiing. Rafting and diving schools. Mini-golf. Activities for children and adults (high season), visits to local wine caves. Only electric barbecues allowed. WiFi in reception, bar/restaurant and pool area. Off site: Bicycle hire 1 km. Riding and golf 5 km.

Open: 31 March - 30 September.

Directions

From A8 take Le Muy exit, follow N7 towards Fréjus for 13 km. bypassing Le Muy. After crossing A8, turn right at roundabout towards Roquebrune-sur-Argens. Site is on left after 1 km. just before bridge over river. GPS: 43.450783, 6.6335

Charges guide

Per unit incl. 2 persons and electricity	€ 23.00 - € 46.50
extra person	€ 4.00 - € 8.80
child (acc. to age)	free - € 6.75

Roquebrune-sur-Argens

Camping Caravaning Moulin des Iscles

Chemin du Moulin des Iscles, F-83520 Roquebrune-sur-Argens (Var) T: 04 94 45 70 74.

E: moulin.iscles@wanadoo.fr alanrogers.com/FR83240

Moulin des Iscles is a small, pretty site beside the river Argens with access to the river in places for fishing, canoeing and swimming, with some sought after pitches overlooking the river. The 80 grassy, level pitches have water and electricity (6A). A nice mixture of deciduous trees provides natural shade and colour and the old mill house is near the entrance, which has the security barrier closed at night. This is a quiet site with little on-site entertainment, but with a pleasant restaurant. Visitors with disabilities are made very welcome. It is a real campsite, not a 'camping village'.

Facilities

Fully equipped toilet block, plus small block near entrance, ramped access for disabled visitors. Some Turkish style toilets. Washbasins have cold water. Baby bath and changing facilities. Washing machine. Restaurant. Shop. Library with some English books. TV, pool table, table tennis. Play area, minigolf, boules all outside the barrier. Internet and WiFi. Canoeing possible. Off site: Excursions organised during the high season include rock climbing, visits to châteaux and olive oil mills. Roquebrune-sur-Argens is close by with shops and restaurants. Bicycle hire 1 km. Riding and golf 4 km. Beach 9 km.

Open: 1 April - 30 September.

Directions

From A8, exit Le Muy, follow N7 towards Fréjus for 13 km. Cross over A8 and turn right at roundabout through Roquebrune-sur-Argens towards St Aygulf for 1 km. Site signed on left. Follow private unmade road for 500 m. GPS: 43.44513, 6.65783

Charges guide

Per unit incl. 2 persons and electricity	€ 18.30 - € 24.20
extra person	€ 2.60 - € 3.30

Camping Cheques accepted.

Saint Avit-de-Vialard

Castel Camping Caravaning Saint-Avit Loisirs

Le Bugue, F-24260 Saint Avit-de-Vialard (Dordogne) T: **05 53 02 64 00.** E: **contact@saint-avit-loisirs.com**

alanrogers.com/FR24180

Although Saint-Avit Loisirs is set amidst rolling countryside, far from the hustle and bustle of the main tourist areas of the Dordogne, the facilities are first class, providing virtually everything you could possibly want without the need to leave the site. The site is in two sections. One part is dedicated to chalets and mobile homes which are available to rent, whilst the main section of the site contains 199 flat and mainly grassy, good sized pitches, 99 for touring, with electricity (6/10A). With a choice of sun or shade, they are arranged in cul-de-sacs off a main access road and are easily accessible.

Facilities

Three modern unisex toilet blocks provide high quality facilities, but could become overstretched in high season. Shop, bar, good quality restaurant, caféteria. Outdoor swimming pool, children's pool, water slide, 'crazy river', heated indoor pool with jacuzzi. Fitness room. Minigolf. Soundproofed disco. Boules. BMX track. Tennis. Quad bikes. Play area. Bicycle hire. Canoe trips on the Dordogne and other sports. Walks and cycle routes. Additional charge for some activities. Off site: Boulangerie, supermarket, Tuesday market, Birdland at Le Bugue 6 km. Sarlat 20 km. Canoeing, golf, riding, fishing nearby.

Open: 2 April - 18 September.

Directions

Site is 6 km. north of Le Bugue. From D710 Le Bugue-Périgueux road, turn west on narrow and bumpy C201 towards St Avit-de-Vialard. Follow road through St Avit, bearing right and site is 1.5 km. GPS: 44.95161, 0.85042

Charges guide

Per unit incl. 2 persons and electricity	€ 18.10 - € 44.00
extra person	€ 3.60 - € 10.20
child (under 4 yrs)	free
dog	€ 2.00 - € 4.00

Saint Brévin-les-Pins

to book this site call **01580 214000** ...we arrange everything | the travel service

Camping le Fief

57 chemin du Fief, F-44250 Saint Brévin-les-Pins (Loire-Atlantique)

T: **02 40 27 23 86.** E: **camping@lefief.com** **alanrogers.com/FR44190**

If you are a family with young children or lively teenagers, this could be the campsite for you. Le Fief is a well established site only 800 m. from sandy beaches on the southern Brittany coast. It has a magnificent aquapark with outdoor and covered swimming pools, paddling pools, slides, river rapids, fountains, jets and more. The site has 174 pitches for touring units (out of 405). Whilst these all have 5A electricity, they vary in size and many are worn and may be untidy. There are also 183 mobile homes and chalets to rent and 48 privately-owned units.

Facilities

One excellent new toilet block and three others of a lower standard. Laundry facilities. Shop (1/6-31/8). Bar, restaurant and takeaway (3/4-26/9) with terrace. Outdoor pools, etc. (1/5-15/9). Covered pool (all season). Wellness centre. Play area. Tennis. Pétanque. Archery. Games room. Internet access. Entertainment and activities (weekends April/June, daily July/Aug). Bicycle hire. WiFi throughout (charged). Off site: Beach 800 m. Riding 1 km. Golf 15 km. Planète Sauvage safari park.

Open: 3 April - 3 October.

Directions

From the St Nazaire bridge take the fourth exit from the D213 signed St Brévin-l'Océan. Continue over first roundabout and bear right at the second to join Chemin du Fief. The site is on the right, well signed. GPS: 47.23486, -2.16757

Charges guide

Per unit incl. 2 persons and electricity	€ 22.00 - € 45.00
extra person	€ 5.00 - € 10.00

No credit cards.

Saint Cast-le-Guildo

to book this site call **01580 214000** ...we arrange everything | the travel service

Castel Camping le Château de Galinée

La Galinée, F-22380 Saint Cast-le-Guildo (Côtes d'Armor) T: **02 96 41 10 56.**

E: **chateaugalinee@wanadoo.fr** **alanrogers.com/FR22090**

Situated a few kilometres back from Saint Cast and owned and managed by the Vervel family, Galinée is in a parkland setting on level grass with numerous and varied mature trees. It has 273 pitches, all with electricity, water and drainage and separated by many mature shrubs and bushes. The top section is mostly for mobile homes. An attractive outdoor pool complex has swimming and paddling pools and two pools with a water slide and a 'magic stream'. A new indoor complex has now also been added and includes a swimming pool, bar, restaurant and large entertainment hall.

Facilities

The large modern sanitary block includes washbasins in private cabins, facilities for babies and a good unit for disabled visitors. Laundry room. Shop for basics, bar and takeaway menu (all 25/5-4/9). Heated pool complex (indoor 16/4 and outdoor 14/5-10/9) with swimming and paddling pools. New covered complex with heated swimming pool, bar, restaurant, entertainment hall and Internet access. Outside terrace with play area. Tennis. Fishing. Off site: Beach and golf 3.5 km. Riding 6 km.

Open: 14 May - 10 September.

Directions

From D168 Ploubalay - Plancoet road turn onto D786 towards Matignon and St Cast. Site is very well signed 1 km. after leaving Notre Dame de Guildo. GPS: 48.58475, -2.25656

Charges guide

Per unit incl. 2 persons and electricity	€ 21.70 - € 41.30
extra person	€ 4.00 - € 6.80
child (under 7 yrs)	€ 2.50 - € 4.80

Camping Cheques accepted.

Saint Georges-de-Didonne

Camping Bois Soleil

2 avenue de Suzac, F-17110 Saint Georges-de-Didonne (Charente-Maritime) T: 05 46 05 05 94.
E: camping.bois.soleil@wanadoo.fr **alanrogers.com/FR17010**

alan rogers Winner 2011 Awards

Close to the sea, Bois Soleil is a large site in three parts, with 165 serviced pitches for touring units and a few for tents. All the touring pitches are hedged and have electricity, with water and drainage between two. The main part, Les Pins, is attractive with trees and shrubs providing shade. Opposite is La Mer with direct access to the beach, some areas with less shade and an area for tents. The third part, La Forêt, is for caravan holiday homes. It is best to book your preferred area as it can be full mid June to late August. Excellent private sanitary facilities are available to rent, either on your pitch or at a block (subject to availability). There are a few pitches with lockable gates. The areas are all well tended and are cleared and raked between visitors. This lively site offers something for everyone, whether it be a beach-side spot or a traditional pitch, plenty of activities or the quiet life. Recent additions include a new toilet block and some accommodation to rent with sea views. The wide sandy beach is popular with children and provides a pleasant walk to the pretty town of Saint Georges-de-Didonne.

Facilities
Each area has one large and one small sanitary block. Heated block near reception. Cleaned twice daily, they include facilities for disabled visitors and babies. Launderette. Supermarket, bakery, beach shop (all 15/4-15/9). Restaurant, bar and takeaway (all 15/4-15/9). Swimming pool (heated 15/6-15/9). Steam room. Tennis. Bicycle hire. Play area. TV room and library. Internet terminal and WiFi. Charcoal barbecues are not permitted. Dogs are not accepted 26/6-5/9. Off site: Fishing, riding 500 m. Golf 20 km.

Open: 2 April - 9 October.

Directions
From Royan centre take coast road (D25) along the seafront of St Georges-de-Didonne towards Meschers. Site is signed at roundabout at end of the main beach. GPS: 45.583583, -0.986533

Charges guide

Per unit incl. 3 persons and electricity	€ 26.00 - € 50.00
extra person	€ 3.00 - € 8.50
child (3-7 yrs)	free - € 6.50
dog (not 26/6-5/9)	€ 3.00 - € 4.00

Less 20% outside July/Aug.
Camping Cheques accepted.

Saint Emilion

Yelloh! Village Saint Emilion

Route de Montagne, D122, F-33330 Saint Emilion (Gironde) T: 05 57 24 75 80. E: barbanne@wanadoo.fr
alanrogers.com/FR33080

Yelloh! Village Saint Emilion (formerly La Barbanne) is a pleasant site in the heart of the Bordeaux wine region, only 2.5 km. from the famous town of St Emilion. It became part of the Yelloh! group in 2010. With 175 pitches, most for touring, the owners have created a carefully maintained, well equipped site. The large, level and grassy pitches have dividing hedges and electricity (long leads necessary). The original parts of the site bordering the lake have mature trees, good shade and pleasant surroundings, whilst in the newer area the trees have yet to provide full shade and it can be hot in summer. Twelve pitches for motorcaravans are on tarmac surrounded by grass.

Facilities
Two modern, fully equipped toilet blocks include facilities for children and for campers with disabilities. Motorcaravan services. Well stocked shop. Bar, terrace, takeaway, restaurant. Breakfast service. Two swimming pools, one heated with water slide. Enclosed play area with seats for parents. Children's club. Tennis. Boules. Volleyball. Fishing. Minigolf. Bicycle hire. Evening entertainment. WiFi (charged). Max. 1 dog. Off site: St Emilion and shops 2.5 km. Riding 8 km.

Open: 14 April - 22 September.

Directions
Site is 2.5 km. north of St Emilion. Caravans and motorcaravans are forbidden in the village of St Emilion and they must approach the site from Libourne on D243 or from Castillon leave D936 and take D130/D243. GPS: 44.91679, -0.14148

Charges guide

Per unit incl. 2 persons and electricity	€ 17.00 - € 39.00
extra person	€ 6.00 - € 8.00
child (3-12 yrs)	free - € 6.00
dog	€ 4.00

Bois Soleil

Camping ★★★★

Charente-Maritime

Surrounded by pine trees and a sandy beach on the Atlantic Coast, with one direct access to the beach, Bois Soleil proposes to you many attractions like tennis, tabletennis, children playgrounds and entertainment. Shops, take-away and snack-bar with big TV screen.

Campings-Caravanings Les pieds dans l'eau

Camping Chèque

Spring and Summer

2, avenue de Suzac - 17110 ST GEORGES DE DIDONNE
Tel: 0033 546 05 05 94 - Fax: 0033 546 06 27 43
www.bois-soleil.com / e-mail: camping.bois.soleil@wanadoo.fr

Saint Georges-les-Baillargeaux

Kawan Village le Futuriste

F-86130 Saint Georges-les-Baillargeaux (Vienne) T: 05 49 52 47 52. E: camping-le-futuriste@wanadoo.fr

alanrogers.com/FR86040

Le Futuriste is a neat, modern site, open all year and close to Futuroscope. Its location is very convenient for the A10 and N10 motorway network. There are 112 individual, level, grassy pitches of a generous size and divided by flowering hedges. Eighty two have electricity (6A) and 30 also have water and waste water connections. Pitches are mostly open although some do have the benefit of shade from trees. All are accessed via tarmac roads. There are lovely panoramic views from this site and the popular attraction of Futuroscope can be clearly seen. Large units are accepted by prior arrangement. There is a pleasant restaurant on site offering good food at reasonable prices. Entertainment takes place in the daytime rather than in the evenings. This site is ideal for a short stay to visit Futuroscope which is only 2 km. away but it is equally good for longer stays to see the region.

Facilities

Excellent, clean sanitary facilities in two heated blocks. Good facilities for disabled visitors and babies. Laundry facilities. Shop (1/5-30/9, bread to order). Bar/restaurant snack bar and takeaway (1/7-31/8). Heated outdoor pool with slide and paddling pool (1/7-31/8). Covered pool. Games room. TV. Boules. Multisports area. Lake fishing. Daily activities in season. Youth groups not accepted. Only gas and electric barbecues allowed. Off site: Bicycle hire 500 m. Hypermarket 600 m. Futuroscope 2 km. Golf 5 km. Riding 10 km.

Open: All year.

Directions

From either A10 autoroute or N10, take Futuroscope exit. Site is east of both roads, off D20 (St Georges-les-Baillargeaux). Follow signs to St Georges. Site on hill; turn by water tower and site is on left.
GPS: 46.66447, 0.394564

Charges 2012

Per unit incl. 3 persons and electricity	€ 20.60 - € 27.80
extra person	€ 2.30 - € 3.20
dog	€ 2.20

Camping Cheques accepted.

Saint Geniès-en-Périgord

Camping Caravaning la Bouquerie

F-24590 Saint Geniès-en-Périgord (Dordogne) T: 05 53 28 98 22. E: labouquerie@wanadoo.fr

alanrogers.com/FR24310

La Bouquerie is situated within easy reach of the main road network in the Dordogne, but without any associated traffic noise. Recent new owners here are investing in new amenities. The main complex is based around some beautifully restored traditional Périgord buildings. There is a bar and restaurant that overlook the pool complex with a large outdoor terrace for fine weather. Of the 185 pitches, 58 are used for touring units and these are of varying size (80-120 sq.m), flat and grassy, some with shade, and all with 10A electrical connections. The majority of the remainder are for mobile homes and chalets for rent.

Facilities

Three toilet blocks with facilities for disabled visitors and baby rooms. Shop (15/5-15/9). New bar and restaurant (12/5-15/9). Takeaway. Heated swimming pool complex including water slides, paddling pool and sunbathing areas. Carp fishing in lake. Multisport area. Boules. Gym. Paint ball. WiFi (charged). Off site: Shops, restaurants and market in St Geniès. The prehistoric caves at Lascaus. Museum and animal park at Le Thot.

Open: 7 April - 15 September.

Directions

Site is signed on east side D704 Sarlat - Montignac, about 500 m. north of junction with D64 St Geniès road. Turn off D704 at campsite sign and take first left turn signed La Bouquerie - site is straight ahead. GPS: 44.99865, 1.24549

Charges guide

Per unit incl. 2 persons and electricity	€ 19.00 - € 25.50
extra person	€ 4.60 - € 6.50

Saint Jean-de-Monts

Camping la Yole

Chemin des Bosses, Orouet, F-85160 Saint Jean-de-Monts (Vendée)

T: 02 51 58 67 17. E: contact@la-yole.com **alanrogers.com/FR85150**

La Yole is an attractive and well run site, two kilometres from a sandy beach. It offers 369 pitches, some of which are occupied by tour operators and mobile homes to rent. There are 180 touring pitches, most with shade and separated by bushes and trees. A newer area at the rear of the site is a little more open. All the pitches are of at least 100 sq.m. and have electricity (10A), water and drainage. The pool complex includes an attractive outdoor pool, a paddling pool, slide and an indoor heated pool with jacuzzi.

Facilities

Two toilet blocks include washbasins in cabins and facilities for disabled visitors and babies. A third block has a baby room. Laundry facilities. Shop (15/5-5/9). Bar, restaurant and takeaway (1/5-15/9). Outdoor pool and paddling pool. Indoor heated pool with jacuzzi (all season, no shorts). New gym centre. Play area. Club room. Tennis. Games room. Entertainment in high season. WiFi (charged). Gas barbecues only. Max. 1 dog. Off site: Beach, bus service, bicycle hire 2 km. Riding 3 km. Fishing, golf and watersports 6 km.

Open: 2 April - 21 September.

Directions

Site is signed off the D38, 6 km. south of St Jean-de-Monts in the village of Orouet. Coming from St Jean-de-Monts turn right at l'Oasis restaurant towards Mouette and follow signs to site. GPS: 46.75659, -2.00792

Charges guide

Per unit incl. 2 persons and electricity	€ 16.00 - € 31.00
extra person	€ 3.70 - € 6.80

Camping Cheques accepted.

Saint Jean-de-Monts

Camping les Places Dorées

Route de Notre-Dame-de-Monts, F-85160 Saint Jean-de-Monts (Vendée)

T: 02 51 59 02 93. E: contact@placesdorees.com **alanrogers.com/FR85280**

Les Places Dorées is, in high season, a busy, popular site with a lively programme of activities and entertainment. At other times it is quieter, but still has plenty to offer. There are 288 grassy pitches, of which just 60 are available for touring units, the quietest being towards the back of the site. Those nearer the leisure complex can be noisy in high season with the bar and disco closing late. Pitches are separated by hedges and there is some shade from maturing trees. A 20 minute walk will take you to a long sandy beach.

Facilities

Three traditional toilet blocks are beginning to show their age, but seem to be kept clean. Preset showers and washbasins in cubicles. Facilities for disabled visitors. Laundry facilities. Bread to order. Bar/restaurant (July/Aug and busy weekends) with themed evenings in high season; also snack bar and takeaway. Outdoor pool complex with slides, jacuzzi and waterfall. Covered, heated pool, spa facilities, gym. Multisport pitch. Entertainment and activities. Children's club (July/Aug). Bicycle hire arranged. WiFi in bar area (charged). Facilities at l'Abri des Pins (opposite, same owners) may be used. Max. 1 small dog. Off site: Fishing 500 m. Beach 800 m (2 km. by road). Riding 1 km. Golf, sailing 3 km. St Jean-de-Monts 4 km.

Open: 11 June - 11 September.

Directions

Saint Jean-de-Monts is 55 km. northwest of La Roche-sur-Yon. Site is 4 km. north of St Jean-de-Monts on the D38 St Jean-de-Monts - Notre Dames-de-Monts road on the eastern side, almost opposite L'Abri des Pins. GPS: 46.80993, -2.10992

Charges guide

Per unit incl. 3 persons and electricity	€ 24.20 - € 36.20
extra person	€ 3.90 - € 6.70
child (under 5 yrs)	€ 2.70 - € 4.50
dog	free - € 3.50

No credit cards.

Saint Martin-de-Seignanx

Camping Caravaning Lou P'tit Poun

110 avenue du Quartier Neuf, F-40390 Saint Martin-de-Seignanx (Landes)

T: 05 59 56 55 79. E: contact@louptitpoun.com alanrogers.com/FR40140

The manicured grounds surrounding Lou P'tit Poun give it a well kept appearance, a theme carried out throughout this very pleasing site which celebrated its 20th anniversary in 2009. It is only after arriving at the car park that you feel confident it is not a private estate. Beyond this point an abundance of shrubs and trees is revealed. Behind a central sloping flower bed lies the open plan reception area. The avenues around the site are wide and the 168 pitches (142 for touring) are spacious. All have 10A electricity, many also have water and drainage and some are separated by low hedges. The jovial owners not only make their guests welcome, but extend their enthusiasm to organising weekly entertainment (at the café/restaurant) for young and old during high season. A Sites et Paysages member.

Facilities

Two unisex sanitary blocks, maintained to a high standard and kept clean, include washbasins in cabins, a baby bath and provision for disabled visitors. Laundry facilities with washing machine and dryer. Motorcaravan service point. Small shop (1/7-31/8). Café/restaurant (1/7-31/8). Swimming pool (1/6-15/9). Play area. Games room, TV. Half-court tennis. Off site: Bayonne 6 km. Fishing and riding 7 km. Golf 10 km. Sandy beaches of Basque coast ten minute drive. Trips to the Pyrénées.

Open: 2 June - 12 September.

Directions

Leave A63 at exit 6 and join D817 in the direction of Pau. Site is signed at Leclerc supermarket. Continue for 3.5 km. and site is clearly signed on right.
GPS: 43.52406, -1.41196

Charges guide

Per unit incl. 2 persons and electricity	€ 22.65 - € 33.80
extra person	€ 7.40 - € 7.80
child (under 7 yrs)	€ 5.55 - € 6.05
dog	€ 4.00 - € 5.00

Sainte Pierre-Lafeuille

Camping Quercy Vacances

Mas de la Combe, F-46090 Sainte Pierre-Lafeuille (Lot) T: 05 65 36 87 15. E: quercy-vacances@wanadoo.fr
alanrogers.com/FR46240

This clean and well run site is owned by a young, English speaking, French couple keen to improve the facilities and ambiance. It is only 4.5 km. from the A20 and is an ideal stopover site for holidaymakers travelling to and from Spain but is also good for longer stays. It has 80 large, unmarked and slightly sloping grass pitches, some with shade from maturing trees. There are 52 pitches for touring units and most have 10A electricity. Access is good for larger outfits. The site facilities include a rustic bar and restaurant with hand painted murals on the walls.

Facilities

Clean, modern toilet block with all necessary facilities, including those for disabled visitors in a separate building. Small basic shop. Bar and takeaway. Restaurant serving specials like couscous and paella once a week (July/Aug). Large round swimming pool (20/6-15/9), children's pool. Live music, dancing (July/Aug). Small play area. WiFi near entrance. Off site: Riding 5 km. Bicycle hire, fishing 10 km. Cahors with many shops and bars etc. 10 km. Many ancient towns and villages. Ancient caves.

Open: 1 April - 30 September.

Directions

Leave A20 exit 57 (Cahors). Shortly turn left on the N20 and then turn right on small un-named road (site signed) before reaching St Pierre-Lafeuille (about 4.5 km. from the A20). Site on right in about 600 m.
GPS: 44.53136, 1.45926

Charges guide

Per unit incl. 2 persons and electricity	€ 18.70 - € 22.50
extra person	€ 3.80 - € 5.00
child (3-9 yrs)	€ 3.00 - € 4.00

Saint Pardoux la Riviere

Kawan Village Château le Verdoyer

Champs Romain, F-24470 Saint Pardoux la Riviere (Dordogne)

T: 05 53 56 94 64. E: chateau@verdoyer.fr **alanrogers.com/FR24010**

to book this site call **01580 214000** ...we arrange everything — the travel service

This 26-hectare estate has three lakes, two for fishing and one with a sandy beach and safe swimming area. There are 135 good sized touring pitches, level, terraced and hedged. With a choice of wooded area or open field, all have electricity (5/10A) and most share a water supply between four pitches. There is a swimming pool complex and high season activities are organised for children (5-13 yrs), but there is no disco. This site is well adapted for those with disabilities, with two fully adapted chalets, wheelchair access to all facilities and even a lift into the pool. Château le Verdoyer has been developed in the park of a restored château and is owned by a Dutch family. We particularly like this site for its beautiful buildings and lovely surroundings. It is situated in the lesser known area of the Dordogne sometimes referred to as the Périgord Vert, with its green forests and small lakes. The courtyard area between reception and the bar is home to evening activities, and provides a pleasant place to enjoy drinks and relax. The château itself has rooms to let and its lakeside restaurant is also open to the public. There are Dutch tour operators on site with pre-erected tents for hire that occupy some of the touring pitches.

Facilities

Well appointed toilet blocks include facilities for disabled visitors and baby baths. Serviced launderette. Motorcaravan services. Fridge rental. Shop with gas (from 1/5). Bar, snacks, takeaway and restaurant (from 1/5). Bistro (July/Aug). Two pools, the smaller covered in low season, slide, paddling pool. Play areas. Tennis. Minigolf. Bicycle hire. Fishing. Small library. WiFi (charged). Internet access. Off site: Riding 5 km. Golf 33 km. 'Circuit des Orchidées' (22 species of orchid). Vélo-rail at Bussière Galant. Market at Saint Pardoux 12 km.

Open: 28 April - 30 September.

Directions

Site is 2 km. from the Limoges (N21) - Chalus (D6bis-D85) - Nontron road, 20 km. south of Chalus and is well signed from main road. Site on the D96 about 4 km. north of village of Champs Romain. GPS: 45.55035, 0.7947

Charges guide

Per unit incl. 2 persons and electricity	€ 21.00 - € 38.50
extra person	€ 5.00 - € 6.50
child (6-11 yrs)	€ 4.00 - € 5.00

Camping Cheques accepted.

Sanchey

Kawan Village Lac de Bouzey

19 rue du Lac, F-88390 Sanchey (Vosges) T: 03 29 82 49 41. E: lacdebouzey@orange.fr

alanrogers.com/FR88040

Open all year, Camping Lac de Bouzey is 8 km. west of Épinal, at the start of the Vosges Massif. The 147 reasonably level grass pitches are separated by very tall trees and some hedging giving varying amounts of shade. There are 107 for touring, all with electricity (6/10A) and 100 fully serviced. They are on a gently sloping hillside above the lake and there are views over the lake and its sandy beaches. In high season there is entertainment for all ages, especially teenagers, and the site will be very lively. English is spoken.

Facilities

The refurbished toilet block includes a baby room and one for disabled visitors (there are some gradients). Small, heated section in the main building with toilet, washbasin and shower is used in winter. Laundry facilities. Motorcaravan service point. Shop and bar (all year), restaurant and takeaway (1/3-1/11). Heated pool (1/5-30/9). Fishing. Riding. Games room. Archery. Bicycle hire. Internet access. Soundproofed room for cinema shows and discos (high season). Lake beach, bathing and boating. WiFi. Off site: Golf 8 km.

Open: All year.

Directions

Site is 8 km. west of Épinal on the D460. From Épinal follow signs for Lac de Bouzey and Sanchey. At western end of Sanchey turn south, site signed. GPS: 48.16692, 6.35990

Charges guide

Per unit incl. 2 persons and electricity	€ 23.00 - € 34.00
extra person	€ 6.00 - € 10.00
child (4-10 yrs)	free - € 7.00
dog	free - € 4.00

Camping Cheques accepted.

France

Sanguinet

Camping les Grands Pins

1039 avenue de Losa, F-40460 Sanguinet (Landes) T: 05 58 78 61 74. E: info@campinglesgrandspins.com

alanrogers.com/FR40250

Approached by a road alongside the lake, this Airotel group site is surrounded by tall trees. Of the 345 pitches, the 80 sand/gravel pitches are of average size, mostly level with varying degrees of shade. Low hedges and young trees divide those available for tourers and most are set away from the mobile homes and chalets. An impressive central pool complex includes a covered heated indoor pool, an outdoor pool, water slide and flume, children's pool and jacuzzi. There are plenty of walks, cycle rides and the lake to enjoy. The poolside bar, restaurant and shops are open in July and August when the site becomes busier, offering watersports, minigolf, a children's club, boat trips and organised activities. Volleyball, tennis and boules are available all season. Fishing is also available. The charming small village of Sanguinet is 2 km. away with supermarket and shops, bank, bars and restaurants.

Facilities

Four toilet blocks include washbasins in cabins, showers and British style toilets (not all open in low seasons). Baby bath and provision for disabled visitors. Laundry facilities. Motorcaravan service point. Shop, bar, restaurant and takeaway (1/7-31/8). Indoor pool (all season). Outdoor pool complex with jacuzzi (1/4-15/9). Play area. Games room and TV in bar. Tennis, volleyball, boules. Sports equipment available to hire. Bicycle hire. Children's club. WiFi (charged). Dogs are not accepted in July/Aug. Barbecues allowed in dedicated areas provided.
Off site: Fishing 200 m. Boat launching 1 km. Golf and riding 15 km. Beach and windsurfing 18 km.

Open: 1 April - 30 September.

Directions

Enter Sanguinet from the north on the D46. At one way system turn right. Do not continue on one way system but go straight ahead toward lake (signed) on rue de Lac. Site is 2 km. on left.
GPS: 44.48396, -1.089716

Charges guide

Per unit incl. 2 persons and electricity	€ 18.00 - € 41.00
extra person	€ 5.50 - € 9.00
child (3-7 yrs)	€ 4.50 - € 6.50
dog	€ 3.00

Sarlat-la-Canéda

Camping les Grottes de Roffy

Sainte Nathalène, F-24200 Sarlat-la-Canéda (Dordogne) T: 05 53 59 15 61.
E: contact@roffy.fr alanrogers.com/FR24130

About 5 km. east of Sarlat, Les Grottes de Roffy is a pleasantly laid out, family site. There are 162 clearly marked pitches, some very large, set on very well kept grass terraces. They have easy access and good views across an attractive valley. Some have plentiful shade, although others are more open, and all have 6A electricity. Those with very large units are advised to check availability in advance. The reception, bar, restaurant and shop are located within converted farm buildings surrounding a semi-courtyard. The site shop is well stocked with a variety of goods and a tempting épicerie. A good heated outdoor pool complex is open all season and popular with visitors.

Facilities

Two toilet blocks with modern facilities are more than adequate. Well stocked shop. Bar and gastronomic restaurant with imaginative and sensibly priced menu. Takeaway. Good swimming pool complex comprising two deep pools (one heated), a fountain, paddling pool and heated jacuzzi. All amenities are available all season. Tennis. Games room. Room for teenagers. Play area. Bicycle hire. Entertainment and activities for all ages. Internet access. WiFi in courtyard area (free).
Off site: Fishing 2 km. Riding 10 km. Golf 15 km.

Open: 18 April - 21 September.

Directions

Take D47 east from Sarlat to Ste Nathalène. Just before Ste Nathalène the site is signed on the right hand side of the road. Turn here and the site is about 800 m. along the lane.
GPS: 44.90404, 1.2821

Charges guide

Per pitch incl. 1-6 persons and electricity	€ 9.30 - € 21.40
with full services	€ 11.30 - € 23.40

Les Grands Pins
CAMPING CARAVANING ★★★★
Club Airotel
Sanguinet
Lac de Biscarrosse
Chalets and mobile homes for rent
Camping Caravaning les Grands Pins
Avenue de Losa (route du lac) 40460 SANGUINET
Tél : 00 33 (0)5 58 78 61 74 - Fax : 00 33 (0)5 58 78 69 15
info@campinglesgrandspins.com www.campingaquitaine.com
Situated
at the lakeside
Aquatic Parc
The best place to enjoy t
the Les Landes Sun!
www.campinglesgrandspins.com

Sarlat-la-Canéda

Domaine de Soleil Plage

Caudon par Montfort, Vitrac, F-24200 Sarlat-la-Canéda (Dordogne) T: 05 53 28 33 33. E: info@soleilplage.fr

alanrogers.com/FR24090

This site is in one of the most attractive sections of the Dordogne valley, with a riverside location. There are 199 pitches, in three sections, with 100 for touring units. Additionally there are 47 mobile homes and 27 chalets for rent. The site offers river swimming from a sizeable sandy bank or there is a very impressive heated pool complex. All pitches are bounded by hedges and are of adequate size with 16A electricity, water and a drain. Most pitches have some shade. If you like a holiday with lots going on, you will enjoy this site. Various activities are organised during high season including walks and sports tournaments, and daily canoe hire is available from the site. Once a week in July and August there is a 'soirée' (charged for) usually involving a barbecue or paella, with a band and lots of free wine – worth catching! The site is busy and reservation is advisable. English is spoken. The site is quite expensive in high season and you also pay more for a riverside pitch, but these have fine river views. There is some tour operator presence.

Facilities

Toilet facilities are in three modern unisex blocks. One has been completely renovated to a high standard with heating and family shower rooms. Washing machines and dryer. Motorcaravan service point. Well stocked shop, pleasant bar with TV and attractive, newly refurbished restaurant with local menus and a pleasant terrace (all from 1/5). Picnics available to order. Very impressive heated main pool, paddling pool, spa pool and two slides. Tennis. Minigolf. Three play areas. Fishing. Canoe and kayak hire. Bicycle hire. Currency exchange. Small library. WiFi throughout (charged). Activities and social events (high season). Off site: Golf 1 km. Riding 5 km. Many attractions of the Dordogne are within easy reach.

Open: Easter - 30 September.

Directions

Site is 6 km. south of Sarlat. From A20 take exit 55 (Souillac) towards Sarlat. Follow the D703 to Carsac and on to Montfort. At Montfort castle site is signed on left. Continue for 2 km. down to the river and site. GPS: 44.825, 1.25388

Charges guide

Per unit incl. 2 persons	
and electricity	€ 21.00 - € 35.50
incl. full services	€ 24.50 - € 50.50
extra person	€ 5.00 - € 7.50
child (2-8 yrs)	€ 3.00 - € 4.50
dog	€ 2.50 - € 3.50

Camping Cheques accepted.

Saumur

Camping de Chantepie

Saint Hilaire-Saint Florent, F-49400 Saumur (Maine-et-Loire) T: 02 41 67 95 34.
E: info@campingchantepie.com **alanrogers.com/FR49020**

On arriving at Camping de Chantepie with its colourful, floral entrance, a friendly greeting awaits at reception, set beside a restored farmhouse. The site is owned by a charitable organisation which provides employment for local people with disabilities. Linked by gravel roads (which can be dusty), the 150 grass touring pitches are level and spacious, with some new larger ones (200 sq.m. at extra cost – state preference when booking). All pitches have electricity and are separated by low hedges of flowers and trees which offer some shade. This is a good site for families. A Sites et Paysages member.

Facilities

The toilet block is clean and facilities are good with washbasins in cubicles, new showers (men and women separately) and facilities for disabled visitors. Baby area. Laundry facilities. Shop, bar, terraced café and takeaway (all 15/6-31/8). Covered and heated pool, outdoor pool and paddling pool. Play area with apparatus. Terraced minigolf, TV. Video games. Pony rides. Bicycle hire. WiFi (charged). Off site: Fishing 500 m. Golf, riding 2 km. Sailing 7 km.

Open: 15 May - 15 September.

Directions

St Hilaire-St Florent is 2 km. west of Saumur. Take D751 (Gennes). Right at roundabout in St Hilaire-St Florent and on until Le Poitrineau and campsite sign, then turn left. Continue for 3 km. then turn right into site road. GPS: 47.29381, -0.14264

Charges guide

Per unit incl. 2 persons and electricity (6/10A)	€ 18.50 - € 30.60
extra person	€ 4.00 - € 6.00

Camping Cheques accepted.

Sauveterre-la-Lemance

Flower Camping Moulin du Périé

F-47500 Sauveterre-la-Lemance (Lot-et-Garonne) T: 05 53 40 67 26. E: moulinduperie@wanadoo.fr
alanrogers.com/FR47010

Set in a quiet area and surrounded by woodlands this peaceful little site is well away from much of the tourist bustle. It has 95 reasonably sized, grassy touring pitches, all with 6A electricity, divided by mixed trees and bushes with most having good shade. All are extremely well kept, as indeed is the entire site. The attractive front courtyard is complemented by an equally pleasant terrace at the rear. Two small, clean swimming pools overlook a shallow, spring water lake, ideal for inflatable boats and paddling, and bordering the lake, a large grass field is popular for games.

Facilities

Two clean, modern and well maintained toilet blocks include facilities for disabled visitors. Motorcaravan services. Fridge, barbecue. Basic shop. Bar/reception, restaurant and takeaway. Two small swimming pools (no Bermuda-style shorts). Boules. Outdoor chess. Playground. Small indoor play area. Bicycle hire. Activities in high season include canoeing, riding, wine tasting visits, sightseeing trips and barbecues. Winter caravan storage. Internet access should be available using cable connection to your own equipment. Off site: Fishing 1 km. Riding 7 km. Small shop in village with larger stores in Fumel.

Open: 12 May - 18 September.

Directions

From D710, Fumel - Périgueux, turn southeast into Sauveterre-la-Lemance. Turn left (northeast) at far end on C201 signed Château Sauveterre and Loubejec (site also signed). Site is 3 km. on right. GPS: 44.59016, 1.04761

Charges guide

Per unit incl. 2 persons and electricity	€ 18.15 - € 27.65
extra person	€ 4.50 - € 7.00
child (2-7 yrs)	€ 1.90 - € 3.70
dog	€ 2.30 - € 4.40

Camping Cheques accepted.

Séez

Camping le Reclus

F-73700 Séez (Savoie) T: 04 79 41 01 05. E: contact@campinglereclus.com
alanrogers.com/FR73100

Bordering a fast flowing but well-fenced stream, this small mountain campsite, set in the hills above Bourg-St-Maurice in the Vanoise National Park, is enthusiastically run by Mélanie Bonato. The 90 sunny pitches, most with electricity (4-10A), are on terraces. The village of Séez is a few minutes' walk away. Winter sports enthusiasts are well catered for here, with a drying room and ski-shoe heating, plus discounts on ski passes and other activities. There is a free shuttle to Les Arcs and La Rosière and it is centrally situated for the Tarentaise ski lifts. This site is not recommended for larger units.

Facilities

Two sanitary blocks have been renovated, the central one more modern. Small shower cubicles with preset hot water and open style washbasins. Laundry facilities. Restaurant and takeaway (1/7-5/9). Small play area. Bread, drinks and ice cream for sale. Bicycle hire. TV room. Off site: Shops and bars in the village of Séez. Riding 1 km. Access to the ski resort of Les Arcs via the funicular railway in Bourg-St-Maurice 2 km. Swimming pools 2 km. Golf 15 km.

Open: All year.

Directions

From A43 Lyon-Chambéry-Grenoble motorway take A430 to Albertville and RN90 to Moutiers and Bourg-St-Maurice. Drive through town, at third roundabout follow signs for Tignes and Val d'Isère. Site is 2 km. up the hill on the right on entering village of Séez. GPS: 45.625844, 6.792794

Charges guide

Per unit incl. 2 persons and electricity	€ 16.50 - € 18.80
extra person	€ 4.20 - € 4.70

Sérignan-Plage

Yelloh! Village le Sérignan-Plage

Le Sérignan Plage, F-34410 Sérignan-Plage (Hérault) T: 04 67 32 35 33. E: info@leserignanplage.com

alanrogers.com/FR34070

With direct access onto a superb 600 m. sandy beach (including a naturist section) and with three swimming pools, this is a must for a Mediterranean holiday. It is a busy, friendly, family orientated site with a very comprehensive range of amenities. Having recently acquired an adjacent site complete with a small lake, there are now over 1,100 pitches with 278 available for touring units. These vary in size and in terms of shade. They are mainly on sandy soil and all have 6A electricity. The collection of spa pools (balnéo) built in Romanesque style with colourful terracing and columns, overlooked by a very smart restaurant, Le Villa, is still the 'pièce de résistance' and available to use in the afternoons (used by the adjacent naturist site in the mornings). The enthusiastic owners, Jean-Guy and Catherine, continually surprise us with their unique style and new developments – this year a most dramatic play area featuring Hensel and Gretal style wooden play houses has been added. There are over 300 mobile homes and chalets to let, plus some 400 privately owned units. The heart of the site developed in the local Catalonian style is some distance from reception and is a busy and informal area with shops, another good restaurant, the Au Pas d'Oc, an indoor pool and a super roof-top bar. There is a range of sporting activites, children's clubs and evening entertainment, indeed something for all the family – a good holiday choice.

Facilities

Seven modern blocks of individual design with good facilities including showers with washbasin and WC. Facilities for disabled visitors. Baby bathroom. Launderette. Motorcaravan services. Supermarket, bakery and newsagent (all season). Other shops (21/4-2/10). ATM. Restaurants, bar and takeaway. Hairdresser. Balnéo spa (afternoons). Gym. Heated indoor pool. Outdoor pools (21/4-2/10). Tennis courts. Multisports courts. Play areas. Trampolines. Children's clubs. Evening entertainment. Sporting activities. Bicycle hire. Bus to Sérignan village July/Aug. Beach (lifeguards 15/6-15/9). WiFi (charged). Gas barbecues only. Off site: Riding 2 km. Golf 10 km. Sailing and windsurfing school on beach.

Open: 26 April - 2 October.

Directions

From A9 take exit 35 (Béziers Est) towards Sérignan, the D64 (9 km). Before Sérignan, turn left, Sérignan-Plage (4 km). At small sign (blue) turn right. At T-junction turn left over road bridge and after left hand bend. Site is 100 m. GPS: 43.26308, 3.31976

Charges guide

Per unit incl. 2 persons and electricity	€ 15.00 - € 52.00
extra person	€ 5.00 - € 8.50
child (3-7 yrs)	free - € 8.50
dog	€ 4.00

Low season offers.
Discounts in low season for children under 7 yrs.

Sérignan-Plage

Camping le Sérignan Plage Nature

Route de l'Orpellière, F-34410 Sérignan-Plage (Hérault) T: 04 67 32 09 61. E: info@leserignannature.com

alanrogers.com/FR34080

Sérignan-Plage Nature benefits from the same 600 m. of white, sandy beach as its sister site next door. Being a naturist site, it actually abuts the naturist section of the beach with direct access to it. It also has the use of the Sérignan-Plage balnéotherapy pool in the mornings, an excellent facility with spa and jacuzzi pools in a Romanesque style setting. The site has 286 good sized pitches on level sandy grass of which 99 are available for touring (6A electricity). There is plenty of shade except on the pitches beside the beach. Eighty-three mobile homes and chalets are available to rent. A friendly bar and shop serve the site although visitors may use the facilities at le Sérignan-Plage. In recent years both Sérignan-Plage and Sérignan-Plage Nature have been developed by Jean-Guy and Catherine. The original work was done by Jean-Guy's father who loved his Romanesque columns, arches and pillars which give both sites a degree of individuality. It was his foresight that masterminded the award-winning, environmentally friendly irrigation system that reuses waste water which serves both this site and Camping Sérignan-Plage. This allows colourful shrubs and trees to grow providing shade and a very pleasant environment ensuring a comfortable site suitable for young and old. After crossing the Orb by a ferry boat, it is possible to cycle a round trip taking in Valras and Sérignan, and even Béziers and the 'Neuf Ecluses' (nine locks) via the towpath of the Canal du Midi.

Facilities

Two toilet blocks of differing designs (one refurbished to a very modern design) offer modern facilities with some washbasins in cabins. All clean and well maintained. Washing machines. Supermarket, fresh fruit and vegetables, newsagent/souvenir shop and ice cream kiosk. Small bar/café. Evening entertainment. Play area, miniclub and disco for children. Facilities and pools at Serignan-Plage. Only gas barbecues are permitted. WiFi throughout (charged). Off site: Bicycle hire 200 m. Fishing 500 m. Riding 800 km. Golf 2 km.

Open: 26 April - 6 October.

Directions

From A9 exit 35 (Béziers Est) towards Sérignan, D64 (9 km). Before Sérignan, take road to Sérignan-Plage. At small sign (blue) turn right for 500 m. At T-junction turn left over bridge, site is 75 m. immediately after left hand bend (the second naturist site). GPS: 43.263409, 3.320148

Charges 2012

Per unit incl. 2 persons and electricity	€ 17.00 - € 53.00
extra person	€ 6.00 - € 10.00
child (1-7 yrs)	free - € 10.00
dog	€ 5.00

Camping Cheques accepted.

Seignosse

Camping les Deux Etangs

1379 route de l'Etang Blanc, F-40510 Seignosse (Landes) T: 05 58 41 66 99. E: info@les2etangs.com

alanrogers.com/FR40750

Located in the Landes forest this site consists mainly of mobile homes and chalets of various designs with just a few touring pitches. The owner wishes to create a peaceful village for holidaymakers away from the hectic Atlantic coastal resorts whilst still being within thirty minutes drive of surfing and sailing attractions. The 12 touring pitches are on soft sand with shade provided by tall pines. Access is difficult for large units. The mobile homes are all new and furnished to a high standard. Evening entertainment is available for adults but there are no organised activities for children.

Facilities

One adequate toilet block. Laundry facilities. Basic shop, small bar, restaurant and takeaway (all 1/6-30/9). Basic swimming pool (July-Sept). Wellness centre (sauna, steam room, shower and therapy beds). Play area. Boules. Volleyball. Bicycle hire. Games room. Communal barbecues only. WiFi (charged). Off site: Basque Country. Fishing 250 m. Golf 3 km. Riding 5 km. Sea beach 5 km. Boat launching 8 km. Walks and cycling in the forest.

Open: All year.

Directions

Located 2 km. north of Seignosse town. From autoroute A63 take exit 8 on D112 signed Seignosse. Turn right signed Tosse and turn left onto Route de l'Etangs. Site is on right within 4 km. GPS: 43.70047, -1.37273

Charges guide

Per unit incl. 2 persons and electricity	€ 18.00 - € 23.00
extra person	€ 4.00

Sonzay

Camping l'Arada Parc

Rue de la Baratière, F-37360 Sonzay (Indre-et-Loire) T: 02 47 24 72 69. E: info@laradaparc.com

alanrogers.com/FR37060

A good, well maintained site in a quiet location, easy to find from the motorway and popular as an overnight stop. Camping l'Arada Parc is an attractive family site nestling in the heart of the Touranelle countryside between the Loire and Loir valleys. The 73 grass touring pitches all have electricity and 19 have water and drainage. The clearly marked pitches, some slightly sloping, are separated by trees and shrubs, some of which are now providing a degree of shade. This is a new site with modern facilities which include a superb new covered pool and fitness room.

Facilities

Two modern toilet blocks provide unisex toilets, showers and washbasins in cubicles. Baby room. Facilities for disabled visitors (wheelchair users may find the gravel access difficult). Laundry facilities. Shop, bar, restaurant and takeaway. Motorcaravan service point. Outdoor swimming pool (no Bermuda-style shorts; 1/5-15/9). Heated, covered pool (all season). Fitness room. Play area. Games area. Boules. TV room. Bicycle hire. Internet. WiFi throughout site. Footpath to village. Off site: Tennis 200 m. Fishing 500 m. Golf 12 km. Riding 14 km.

Open: 26 March - 1 November.

Directions

Sonzay is northwest of Tours. From the new A28 north of Tours take the exit to Neuillé-Pont-Pierre which is on the N138 Le Mans - Tours road. Then take D766 towards Château la Vallière and turn southwest to Sonzay. Follow campsite signs. GPS: 47.625963, 0.452843

Charges guide

Per unit incl. 2 persons and electricity (10A)	€ 19.00 - € 25.10
extra person	€ 4.00 - € 5.30

Camping Cheques accepted.

Souillac

Castel Camping le Domaine de la Paille Basse

F-46200 Souillac-sur-Dordogne (Lot) T: 05 65 37 85 48. E: info@lapaillebasse.com

alanrogers.com/FR46010

Set in a rural location some 8 km. from Souillac, this family owned site is easily accessible from the A20 and well placed to take advantage of excursions into the Dordogne. It is part of a large domain of 80 hectares, all available to campers for walks and recreation. The site is quite high up and there are excellent views over the surrounding countryside. The 262 pitches are in two main areas – one is level in cleared woodland with good shade, and the other on grass with limited shade. Numbered and marked, the pitches are a minimum 100 sq.m. and often considerably more. All have electricity (10A) with 80 fully serviced. If you like a livelier type of site, you will enjoy la Paille Basse.

Facilities

Three main toilet blocks all have modern equipment and are kept very clean. Laundry. Small shop with a large selection of wine. Restaurant, bar (open until 2 a.m. in high season), terrace, pizza takeaway. Crêperie. Main swimming pool, a smaller one, paddling pool (unheated), water slides. Sun terrace. Soundproofed disco (three times weekly in season). TV. Cinema below the pool area. Tennis. Play area. Library. WiFi in office/bar area (charged). Mini-farm. Animation (July-August). Off site: Golf 4 km.

Open: 15 May - 15 September.

Directions

From Souillac take D15 and then D62 roads leading northwest towards Salignac-Eyvignes and after 6 km. turn right at site sign and follow steep and narrow approach road for 2 km. GPS: 44.94728, 1.43924

Charges guide

Per person	€ 5.40 - € 7.50
pitch	€ 7.80 - € 10.80
incl. water and drainage	€ 9.80 - € 13.00

Camping Cheques accepted.

Telgruc-sur-Mer

Camping le Panoramic

to book this site call **01580 214000** ...we arrange everything — the travel service

Rte de la Plage-Penker, F-29560 Telgruc-sur-Mer (Finistère) T: 02 98 27 78 41.
E: info@camping-panoramic.com **alanrogers.com/FR29080**

This medium sized, traditional site is situated on quite a steep, ten-acre hillside with fine views. It is personally run by M. Jacq and his family who all speak good English. The 200 pitches are arranged on flat, shady terraces, in small groups with hedges and flowering shrubs, and 20 pitches have services for motorcaravans. Divided into two parts, the main upper site is where most of the facilities are located, with the swimming pool, its terrace and a playground located with the lower pitches across the road. Some up-and-down walking is therefore necessary, but this is a small price to pay for such pleasant and comfortable surroundings. This area provides lovely coastal footpaths. The sandy beach and a sailing school at Trez-Bellec-Plage are a 700 m. walk. A Sites et Paysages member.

Facilities

The main site has two well kept toilet blocks with another very good block opened for main season across the road. All three include British and Turkish style WCs, washbasins in cubicles, facilities for disabled visitors, baby baths, plus laundry facilities. Motorcaravan services. Small shop (1/7-31/8). Refurbished bar/restaurant with takeaway (1/7-31/8). Barbecue area. Heated pool, paddling pool and jacuzzi (1/6-15/9). Playground. Games and TV rooms. Tennis. Bicycle hire. WiFi. Off site: Beach and fishing 700 m. Riding 6 km. Golf 14 km. Sailing school nearby.

Open: 1 May - 15 September.

Directions

Site is just south of Telgruc-sur-Mer. On D887 pass through Ste Marie du Ménez Horn. Turn left on D208 signed Telgruc-sur-Mer. Continue straight on through town and site is on right within 1 km. GPS: 48.22409, -4.37186

Charges guide

Per unit incl. 2 persons and electricity (10A)	€ 26.50
extra person	€ 5.00
child (under 7 yrs)	€ 3.00
dog	€ 2.00

Less 20% outside July/Aug.

Tournus

Camping de Tournus

14 rue des Canes, F-71700 Tournus (Saône-et-Loire) T: 03 85 51 16 58. E: info@camping-tournus.com
alanrogers.com/FR71190

This very well maintained, pleasant site is just a few minutes from the A6 autoroute, 200 metres from the River Saône and close to the interesting old market town of Tournus. It is ideal for a night halt but deserving of a longer stay. The new owners have made some hardstanding pitches to complement the fairly level grassy pitches. All 90 pitches are for touring and 70 have 6A electricity. A few trees give some pitches varying amounts of shade. Access is very easy for large units. A municipal outdoor swimming pool is adjacent to the site and open for the high season.

Facilities

Two clean toilet blocks near the entrance provide all necessary facilities, including those for disabled visitors. Motorcaravan services. Small bar and shop in the reception area where bread can be ordered daily and light snacks purchased. Small play area. Internet terminal. Bicycle hire. WiFi. Off site: Municipal pool next door. Fishing 100 m. Tournus, Saturday market, shops, bars, cafés, banks etc. short walk/cycle ride along river.

Open: 1 April - 30 September.

Directions

From the A6 take exit 12 for Tournus and the N6 south for just over 1 km. In Tournus (opposite railway station), turn left signed camping and follow signs to site, about 1 km. GPS: 46.57372, 4.909349

Charges guide

Per unit incl. 2 persons and electricity	€ 19.10 - € 24.50
extra person	€ 4.20 - € 5.60
child (under 7 yrs)	€ 2.60 - € 3.70

Camping Cheques accepted.

Vallon-Pont-d'Arc

Castel Camping Nature Parc l'Ardéchois

Route touristique des Gorges, F-07150 Vallon-Pont-d'Arc (Ardèche) T: **04 75 88 06 63.**

E: **ardecamp@bigfoot.com** **alanrogers.com/FR07120**

This very high quality, family run site is within walking distance of Vallon-Pont-d'Arc. It borders the River Ardèche and canoe trips are run, professionally, direct from the site. This campsite is ideal for families with younger children seeking an active holiday. The facilities are comprehensive and the central toilet unit is of an extremely high standard. Of the 244 pitches, there are 225 for tourers, separated by trees and individual shrubs. All have electrical connections (6/10A) and 125 have full services. Forming a focal point are the bar and restaurant (good menus), with a terrace and stage overlooking the attractive heated pool. There is also a large paddling pool and sunbathing terrace. For children, there is a well thought out play area plus plenty of other space for youngsters to play, both on the site and along the river. Activities are organised throughout the season; these are family based – no discos. Patrols at night ensure a good night's sleep. Access to the site is easy and suitable for large outfits. The campsite is ideally situated near the Pont-d'Arc, a huge arch of limestone in the Ardèche Gorge. The local tourist centre of Vallon-Pont-d'Arc which is within comfortable walking distance. A worthwhile trip down the gorge by car passes a number of spectacular viewpoints with good parking. Member of Leading Campings Group.

Facilities

Two well equipped toilet blocks, one superb with everything working automatically. Facilities are of the highest standard, very clean and include good facilities for babies, those with disabilities, washing up and laundry. Four private bathrooms to hire. Washing machines. Well stocked shop. Swimming pool and paddling pool (no Bermuda shorts). Tennis. Very good play area. Organised activities, canoe trips. Only gas barbecues are permitted. Communal barbecue area. Internet access. WiFi (charged). Off site: Canoeing, rafting, walking, riding, mountain biking, golf, rock climbing, bowling, wine tasting and dining. Vallon-Pont-d'Arc 800 m. Explore the real Ardèche on the minor roads and visit Labaume, Balazuc and Largentière (market Tuesday).

Open: 15 April - 30 September.

Directions

From Vallon-Pont-d'Arc (western end of the Ardèche Gorge) at a roundabout go east on the D290. Site entrance is shortly on the right. GPS: 44.39804, 4.39878

Charges guide

Per unit incl. 2 persons and electricity	€ 30.00 - € 55.00
extra person	€ 5.90 - € 9.80
child (0-13 yrs)	€ 4.30 - € 7.60
dog	€ 3.50 - € 7.50

Urrugne

Sunêlia Col d'Ibardin

F-64122 Urrugne (Pyrénées-Atlantiques) T: **05 59 54 31 21.** E: **info@col-ibardin.com**

alanrogers.com/FR64110

This family owned site at the foot of the Basque Pyrénées is highly recommended and deserves praise. It is well run with emphasis on personal attention, the friendly family and their staff ensuring that all are made welcome, and it is attractively set in the middle of an oak wood with a mountain stream cascading through it. Behind the forecourt, with its brightly coloured shrubs and modern reception area, various roadways lead to the 203 pitches. These are individual, spacious and enjoy the benefit of the shade (if preferred a more open aspect can be found). There are electricity hook-ups (6/10A) and adequate water points. A very attractive chalet 'village' has been added. From this site you can enjoy the mountain scenery, be on the beach in 7-10 km. or cross the border into Spain in about 14 km.

Facilities

Two toilet blocks, one rebuilt to a high specification, are kept very clean. WC for disabled visitors. Laundry facilities. Motorcaravan service point. Shop for basics and bread orders (1/6-15/9). Restaurant, takeaway service and bar (1/6-15/9). Heated swimming pool and paddling pool (with water games). Playground and club (adult supervision). Tennis. Boules. Video games. Bicycle hire. Multisport area. WiFi (charged). Not suitable for American motorhomes. Off site: Supermarket and shopping centre 5 km. Fishing, boat launching, sailing and golf 7 km. Riding 20 km.

Open: 1 April - 30 September.

Directions

Leave A63 at St Jean-de-Luz sud, exit no. 2 and join RN10 in direction of Urrugne. Turn left at roundabout (Col d'Ibardin) on D4. Site on right after 5 km. Do not turn off to the Col itself, carry on towards Ascain. GPS: 43.33376, -1.68458

Charges guide

Per unit incl. 2 persons and electricity	€ 17.50 - € 38.50
extra person	€ 3.50 - € 6.50
child (2-7 yrs)	€ 2.50 - € 4.00
dog	€ 2.80

Trogues

Camping du Château de la Rolandière

F-37220 Trogues (Indre-et-Loire) T: 02 47 58 53 71. E: contact@larolandiere.com

alanrogers.com/FR37090

This is a charming site set in the grounds of a château and you are assured of a very warm welcome here. There are 50 medium sized, level or gently sloping pitches, separated by hedges with a variety of trees giving some shade. Most have 6A electricity (long leads advised) with water taps nearby. There is a large chalet and mobile homes for hire and bed and breakfast is also available. The site has a pleasant swimming pool, paddling pool, fitness room and games/TV room. This is a delightfully peaceful spot from which to visit the châteaux at Chinon, Loches, Villandry and Azay-le-Rideau and the villages of Richelieu and Crissay-sur-Manse. A Sites et Paysages member.

Facilities

The older style toilet block has been refurbished to provide good facilities with modern showers, washbasin and laundry areas. Provision for disabled visitors. Small shop for basics. Bar with terrace. Snacks and takeaway (July/Aug). Swimming pool (15/5-30/9). Minigolf. Play area. Fitness room. TV lounge. WiFi. Off site: Fishing 1 km. on River Vienne. River beach and boat launching 4 km. Restaurant 4 km. Bicycle hire and shops 6 km. St Maure 7 km. Golf 15 km.

Open: 23 April - 24 September.

Directions

Trogues is 40 km. southwest of Tours on the D760 Loches - Chinon road. Site is on D760, midway between Trogues and A10 (exit 25). Entrance is signed and marked by a model of the château. GPS: 47.10767, 0.51052

Charges guide

Per unit incl. 2 persons and electricity	€ 20.90 - € 28.90
extra person	€ 4.50 - € 6.00

No credit cards.

Vielle-Saint-Girons

Camping Club International Eurosol

Rte de la Plage, F-40560 Vielle-St-Girons (Landes) T: 05 58 47 90 14.
E: contact@camping-eurosol.com alanrogers.com/FR40060

Eurosol is an attractive, friendly and well maintained site extending over 15 hectares of undulating ground amongst mature pine trees giving good shade. Of the 356 touring pitches, 209 have electricity (10A) with 120 fully serviced. A wide range of mobile homes and chalets are available for rent too. This is very much a family site with multilingual entertainers. Many games and tournaments are organised and a beach volleyball competition is held regularly in front of the bar. An excellent sandy beach 700 metres from the site has supervised bathing in high season, and is ideal for surfing.

Facilities

Four main toilet blocks and two smaller blocks are comfortable and clean with facilities for babies and disabled visitors. Motorcaravan services. Fridge rental. Well stocked shop and bar. Restaurant, takeaway (2/6-8/9). Stage for live shows arranged in July/Aug. Outdoor swimming pool, paddling pool (all season) and heated covered pool (low season). Tennis. Multisports court. Bicycle hire. WiFi (charged). Charcoal barbecues are not permitted. Off site: Riding (July/Aug) 200 m. Surf school 500 m. Beach and fishing 700 m. Golf 18 km.

Open: 19 May - 15 September.

Directions

Turn off D652 at St Girons on D42 towards St Girons-Plage. Site is on left before coming to beach (4.5 km). GPS: 43.95166, -1.35212

Charges guide

Per unit incl. 2 persons and electricity	€ 18.00 - € 35.00
extra person (over 4 yrs)	€ 5.00
dog	€ 4.00

Vieux-Mareuil

Camping de l'Etang Bleu

F-24340 Vieux-Mareuil (Dordogne) T: 05 53 60 92 70. E: letangbleu@orange.fr

alanrogers.com/FR24330

The English owners at this site, Marc and Jo Finch, are warm and friendly and work hard to maintain high standards. Set in 42 acres, there are only 98 pitches, with 3 used for mobile homes for rent. All are generously sized and level, enjoying a mixture of sun and shade. Electricity is available (10A). The site's best features are the lake where anglers can fish for carp, the bistro which offers great food, reasonably priced, and the sparkling clean swimming pool. This site is spacious, tranquil and relaxing. A gym and a spa are planned. Entertainment is limited but there are sporting facilities and themed nights.

Facilities

Modern well maintained toilet block provides facilities for babies and disabled visitors. Laundry. Bar with terrace (all season). Bistro. Takeaway. Small shop. Swimming pool, sun terrace. Playground, paddling pool. Boules. Badminton. Entertainment, sporting activities, excursions in high season. WiFi (charged). Off site: Restaurant 'Auberge de l'Etang Bleu' adjacent to campsite, small supermarket, post office etc. in Mareuil 7 km. Riding and bicycle hire 5 km. Golf 40 km.

Open: Easter/1 April - 21 October.

Directions

Site is between Angoulême and Périgueux. Leave D939 in Vieux Mareuil, take D93, and follow narrow road. Just after leaving village site signed on right, just past Auberge de l'Etang Bleu. Turn right, follow signs to site. GPS: 45.44614, 0.50859

Charges guide

Per unit incl. 2 persons and electricity	€ 17.25 - € 23.00
extra person	€ 3.75 - € 5.50
child (2-7 yrs)	€ 1.25 - € 2.00

Villers-sur-Authie

Kawan Village Caravaning le Val d'Authie

20 route de Vercourt, F-80120 Villers-sur-Authie (Somme) T: 03 22 29 92 47. E: camping@valdauthie.fr

alanrogers.com/FR80090

In a village location, this well organised site is fairly close to several beaches, but also has its own excellent pool complex, small restaurant and bar. The owner has carefully controlled the size of the site, leaving space for a leisure area with an indoor pool complex. There are 170 pitches in total, but with many holiday homes and chalets, there are only 60 for touring units. These are on grass, some are divided by small hedges, with 6/10A electric hook-ups, and ten have full services. The site has a fitness trail and running track, mountain bike circuit, and plenty of good paths for evening strolls.

Facilities

Good toilet facilities, some unisex, include shower and washbasin units, washbasins in cubicles, and limited facilities for disabled visitors and babies. Shop (not October). Bar/restaurant (5/4-12/10; hours vary). Swimming and paddling pools with lifeguards in July/Aug). Playground, club room with TV. Weekend entertainment in season. Multisport court, beach volleyball, football, boules and tennis court. Trampoline. Internet room. Fitness room including sauna (charged). WiFi throughout (charged). Off site: Shops, banks and restaurants in Rue 6 km.

Open: 1 April - 10 October.

Directions

Villers-sur-Authie is about 25 km. NNW of Abbéville. From A16 exit 24 take N1 to Vron, then left on the D175 to Villers-sur-Authie. Or use D85 from Rue, or D485 from Nampont St Martin. Site is at southern end of village at road junction.
GPS: 50.31357, 1.69488

Charges guide

Per unit incl. 2 persons and electricity	€ 24.00 - € 33.00
extra person	€ 6.00
child (2-6 yrs)	€ 3.00
dog	€ 1.50

Camping Cheques accepted.

Volonne

Sunêlia Hippocampe

Route de Napoléon, F-04290 Volonne (Alpes-de-Haute-Provence) T: 04 92 33 50 00.
E: camping@l-hippocampe.com **alanrogers.com/FR04010**

Hippocampe is a friendly, family run, 'all action' lakeside site, with families in mind, situated in a beautiful area of France. The perfumes of thyme, lavender and wild herbs are everywhere and the higher hills of Haute-Provence are not too far away. There are 447 level, numbered pitches (177 for touring units), medium to very large (130 sq.m) in size. All have electricity (10A) and 140 have water and drainage, most are separated by bushes and cherry trees. Some of the best pitches border the lake. The restaurant, bar, takeaway and shop have all been completely renewed. Games, aerobics, competitions, entertainment and shows, plus a daily club for younger family members are organised in July/August. This is a very good site for an active or restful holiday and is suitable for outfits of all sizes. English is spoken.

Facilities

Toilet blocks vary from old to modern, all with good clean facilities that include washbasins in cabins. Washing machines. Motorcaravan service point. Bread available (from 7/5). Shop, bar, restaurant and pizzeria (7/5-11/9). Large, heated pool complex (23/4-30/9) with five waterslides, (second pool 1/6-30/9). Tennis. Fishing. Canoeing. Boules. Bicycle hire. Several sports facilities (some with free instruction). Charcoal barbecues are not permitted. WiFi (charged). Off site: Village of Volonne 600 m (market on Fridays). Riding 12 km. Various sporting opportunities.

Open: 16 April - 30 September.

Directions

Approaching from the north turn off N85 across river bridge to Volonne, then right to site. From the south right on D4, 1 km. before Château Arnoux.
GPS: 44.10462, 6.01688

Charges guide

Per unit incl. 2 persons and electricity	€ 16.00 - € 33.00
with full services	€ 16.00 - € 43.00
extra person (over 4 yrs)	€ 3.00 - € 7.00
dog	free - € 2.00

Camping Cheques accepted.

Germany

With its wealth of scenic and cultural interests, Germany is a land of contrasts. From the flat lands of the north to the mountains in the south, with forests in the east and west, regional characteristics are a strong feature of German life, and present a rich variety of folklore and customs.

Each region in Germany differs greatly from the next. Home of lederhosen, beer and sausages is Bavaria in the south, full of charming forest villages, beautiful lakes, and towering mountains dotted with castles. In the southwest, Baden Württemberg is famous for its ancient Black Forest, with dense woodlands, medieval towns and scenic lakes, this region is a walkers' paradise. Further west is the stunningly beautiful Rhine Valley, full of romantic castles, wine villages, woodland walks and river trails. Eastern Germany is studded with lakes and rivers, and undulating lowlands that give way to mountains. The north has its lively ports such as Bremen and Hamburg and picturesque coastal towns, where watersports are a popular pastime in the North Sea. The capital city of Berlin, situated in the northeast of the country, is an increasingly popular tourist destination, with its blend of old and modern architecture and huge variety of entertainment on offer.

CAPITAL: **Berlin**

Tourist Office

German National Tourist Office
PO Box 2695, London W1A 3TN
Tel: 020 7317 0908
Fax: 020 7317 0917
Email: gntolon@d-z-t.com
Internet: www.germany-tourism.co.uk

Population

82.2 million

Climate

Temperate climate. In general, winters are a little colder and summers a little warmer than in the UK.

Language

German

Telephone

The country code is 00 49.

Money

Currency: The Euro
Banks: Mon-Fri 08.30-12.30 and 14.00-16.00. Late opening on Thurs until 18.00.

Shops

Mon-Fri 08.30/09.00 to 18.00/18.30.

Public Holidays

New Year's Day; Good Fri; Easter Mon; Labour Day; Ascension; Whit Mon; Unification Day 3 Oct; Christmas, 25, 26 Dec. In some areas: Epiphany 6 Jan; Corpus Christi 22 Jun; Assumption 15 Aug; Reformation 31 Oct; All Saints 1 Nov (plus other regional days).

Motoring

An excellent network of (toll-free) motorways (autobahns) exists in the West and the traffic moves fast. Remember in the East a lot of road building is going on, amongst other works, so allow plenty of time when travelling and be prepared for poor road surfaces.

see campsite map 2

Aitrang

Camping Elbsee

Am Elbsee 3, D-87648 Aitrang (Bavaria (S)) T: 083 432 48. E: camping@elbsee.de

alanrogers.com/DE3672

This attractive site, with its associated hotel and restaurant about 200 m. away, lies on land sloping down to a lake. This is not an area well known to tourists, although the towns of Marktoberdorf (14 km), Kaufbeuren (16 km) and Kempten (21 km) merit a visit. With this in mind, the owners have set about providing good facilities and a developing programme of interesting activities. All the 120 touring pitches have access to electricity (16A) and 78 also have their own water supply and waste water outlet. Some of the pitches (those restricted to tents) slope slightly.

Facilities

Two well appointed, well maintained heated sanitary blocks include free showers, washbasins all in cabins, a children's bathroom area and family bathrooms to rent. Facilities for disabled visitors. Dog shower. Motorcaravan service point. Shop (order bread for following day). New playground, indoor play area and activity rooms. TV, games and meeting rooms. Sports field. Fishing. Bicycle hire. Riding. Boat launching. Activity programme (20/7-31/8). WiFi in reception area. Off site: At hotel, good restaurant, takeaway and bar. Shop and ATM point 2 km. Golf 12 km. Cycling. Rambling. Cross-country skiing.

Open: All year.

Directions

Site is 36 km. NNW of Fussen. From centre of Marktoberdorf, take minor road northwest to Ruderatshofen and from there take minor road west towards Aitrang/Elbsee. Just south of Aitrang, site is signed to south of the road. The road to the site (2 km) is winding and narrow in places. GPS: 47.80277, 10.55343

Charges 2012

Per unit incl. 2 persons	€ 22.40 - € 26.00
extra person	€ 6.40
electricity (per kWh)	€ 0.65

Camping Cheques accepted.

Amtsberg

Waldcamping Erzgebirgsblick

An der Dittersdorfer Höhe, D-09439 Amtsberg (Saxony) T: 037 177 50833.

E: info@waldcamping-erzgebirge.de alanrogers.com/DE3836

The Scheibner family first thought of opening a campsite when touring Canada in 1998, so it is not surprising to find reminders of their trip appearing in the site's buildings with pictures and Canadian names. They found their spot on land once belonging to the Stasi, the East German secret police, and turned it into a well kept and welcoming campsite. It has 90 touring pitches, either under mature pine trees in the woods or on open ground, partly separated by low bushes and shrubs. All have 16A electricity and there are 12 with electricity, water, drainage and hardstanding.

Facilities

Excellent sanitary facilities with British style toilets, free, controllable hot showers and washbasins (1 cabin each for men and women). Washbasin and toilet for children. Baby room. Bathroom for rent. Laundry facilities. Fully equipped kitchen. Small shop in reception (bread to order). Takeaway food. Lounge with dining table, TV and library. Playground. Bicycle hire. Riding. Off site: Riding 2 km. Fishing and golf 5 km.

Open: All year.

Directions

Site is 11 km. southeast of Chemnitz. From A72/E41 autobahn exit 14 for Chemnitz Sud, take the B174 southeast (Gornau, Marienberg, then Prag). Signed in Amtsberg, off B174. GPS: 50.76600, 13.01448

Charges guide

Per person	€ 6.00
pitch	€ 4.00 - € 13.00
electricity (per kWh)	€ 0.65

No credit cards.

Asbacherhütte

Camping Harfenmühle

An der Deutschen Edelsteinstrasse, D-55758 Asbacherhütte (Rhineland Palatinate) T: 067 867 076.

E: mail@harfenmuehle.de alanrogers.com/DE3254

Harfenmühle is a quiet, family run and family orientated site set in a wooded valley on the Edelsteinstrasse (precious stone route) between the wine regions Mosel and Nahe and is a site well suited to those interested in an active outdoor holiday. Besides on-site activities for children, such as searching for gems in the gemstone river (10.15 daily) or 'gold' washing offsite, there are many interesting places to visit and things to do, such as stone breaking in search of gemstones at a nearby quarry. The 100 touring pitches are arranged in several separate areas, level, on grass and all with electricity.

Facilities

Two sanitary blocks include shower cubicles (on payment), facilities for babies and disabled visitors. Launderette. Kiosk with fresh bread daily. Takeaway. Wine cellar/bar. Restaurant with terrace serving international cuisine with a French flavour (open daily). Sauna and solarium. Swimming lake. Children's playgrounds. Bicycle hire. Playing field. Water play area. Rental accommodation. WiFi. Off site: Walking paths directly from site. Naturpark Saar-Hunsrück. Riding 3 km. and 4.5 km. Bicycle hire and golf 10 km. Heated outdoor and indoor pools 12 km.

Open: All year.

Directions

Site is 12 km. north of Idar-Oberstein. From the B41 Saarbrücken - Bad Kreuznach, exit north at Fischbach signed towards Herrstein and then on through Morschied to Asbacherhütte, with site entrance on right. GPS: 49.80362, 7.26945

Charges guide

Per unit incl. 2 persons and electricity	€ 19.50
extra person	€ 5.00
child (2-15 yrs)	€ 3.00

No credit cards.

Augsburg

Lech Camping

Seeweg 6, D-86444 Affing-Mühlhausen bei Augsburg (Bavaria (S)) T: 082 072 200. E: info@lech-camping.de

alanrogers.com/DE3642

Situated just north of Augsburg, this beautifully run site is a pleasure to stay on. Gabi Ryssel, the owner, spends her long days working very hard to cater for every wish of her guests – from the moment you arrive and are given the key to one of the cleanest toilet blocks we have seen, and plenty of tourist information, you are in very capable hands. The 50 level, grass and gravel pitches are roomy and have shade from pine trees. Electricity connections are available (10/16A). This is an immaculate site with a separate area for disabled visitors to park near the special facilities provided.

Facilities

The new toilet block (cleaned several times daily) provides British style WCs and good showers with seating area and non-slip flooring. Baby room. Family bathroom for rent. Five star facilities for disabled visitors. Separate room with laundry facilities. Motorcaravan service point. Small shop. Restaurant. Small playground (partially fenced). Bicycle hire. WiFi. Trampolines. Pedal boats and rowing boats (free). Charcoal barbecues are not permitted.
Off site: Football field 300 m. Bus service to city. Legoland 25 minute drive. Fishing 4 km. Golf 10 km. Riding 15 km.

Open: 1 April - 17 September.

Directions

Site is 8 km. NNE of Augsburg at the border of Mühlhausen. Leave E52/A8 (Munich - Stuttgart) at exit 73 and follow signs to Neuburg/Pöttmes. After 3 km. (pass airport on right) on U49 you will see the Mühlhausen sign. Lech Camping is on right.
GPS: 48.43759, 10.92937

Charges guide

Per unit incl. 2 persons and electricity	€ 24.80 - € 25.80
extra person	€ 6.00 - € 6.50
child (2-13 yrs)	€ 3.00

Bad Birnbach

Kur-Gutshof-Camping Arterhof

Hauptstrasse 3, Lengham, D-84364 Bad Birnbach (Bavaria (S)) T: 085 639 6130. E: info@arterhof.de

alanrogers.com/DE3696

Based around a Bavarian farmstead, Arterhof combines the charm of the old together with the comfort of the new. An attractive courtyard at the front of the site houses reception, a farm shop and a café with a flower decked terrace. To the rear is a tropical indoor pool containing soft water at a comfortable 30°C as well as a sauna, solarium, fitness room and much more. The 190 touring pitches with some hedge separation, on grass or pebble standing, all have TV, electricity, fresh and waste water connections, and 12 have their own pitch-side sanitary facilities. For winter camping, 50 of the pitches have a gas supply. Opposite the site entrance is Inattura, a spacious flower-filled meadow with a large, natural pool, scented garden and lots of lawn; ideal for quiet relaxation and sunbathing in the open Bavarian countryside. This is very much a site with facilities for those who feel they have earned a well deserved break. There are numerous fitness programmes to cure one's present aches and pains, as well as preventative programmes. With ample provision for children, both outdoor and traditional indoor restaurants, this is a site to suit the whole family.

Facilities

Modern, attractive, well maintained sanitary blocks with heated floor, free showers, washbasins in cabins, hairdryers and bathrooms to rent. Hairdressing salon, cosmetic studio. Laundry facilities. Motorcaravan service point. Restaurant serving southern Bavarian dishes with meat from the farm's own Aberdeen Angus cattle. Playground. Live music Fridays. WiFi. Off site: Rottal Thermal baths in Bad Birnbach (free bus from site). Cycle and mountain bike tracks. Nordic walking. Golf.

Open: All year.

Directions

Site is 12 km. east of Pfarrkirchen. Leave autobahn 3 at exit 106 and head south on B20 to Eggenfelden then east on B20 past Pfarrkirchen to Bad Birnbach where site is signposted to the right opposite supermarket. GPS: 48.435176, 13.109415

Charges guide

Per unit incl. 2 persons and electricity (plus meter)	€ 21.90
extra person	€ 6.30
child (2-14 yrs)	€ 3.50

Bad Dürkheim

Knaus Campingpark Bad Dürkheim

In den Almen 3, D-67098 Bad Dürkheim (Rhineland Palatinate) T: **063 226 1356.**

E: **badduerkheim@knauscamp.de** **alanrogers.com/DE3260**

This is a large, comfortable site with almost 600 pitches, half of which are for touring. Being situated in Bad Dürkheim, which claims to have the world's largest wine festival, it can understandably become quite full in high season. The site is arranged either side of a long, central arcade of growing vines and along one side of the site there is a lake. Growing trees provide some shade and electrical connections are available throughout (16A). There is some noise from light aircraft, especially at weekends. Bathing is possible in the lake, which has a mostly sandy floor. There is a little beach and non-powered boats can be launched. This is essentially a wine growing region with lots of attractive villages to visit and an almost endless variety of wines to try out.

Facilities

Three large sanitary blocks are spaced out along the central avenue. They are of a high standard (private cabins, automatic taps etc) and are heated in cool weather. Laundry facilities. Gas supplies. Motorcaravan services. Cooking facilities. Shop (all year). Restaurant. Sports programme. Tennis. Playground. Sauna. Swimming and non-powered boats on lake. Activity programme (guided tours, biking, canoeing and climbing). WiFi.

Open: All year (reduced facilities in November).

Directions

Bad Dürkheim is 18 km. west of Ludwigshafen. Site is signposted on the 37 (Ludwigshafen) road on the eastern outskirts of Bad Dürkheim at the traffic lights. GPS: 49.47380, 8.19170

Charges guide

Per person	€ 5.00 - € 6.80
child (4-14 yrs)	€ 2.00 - € 3.00
pitch incl. electricity (plus meter)	€ 9.60 - € 19.40
dog	€ 2.00 - € 2.50

No credit cards.

Bad Griesbach

Kur & Feriencamping Dreiquellenbad

Singham 40, D-94086 Bad Griesbach (Bavaria (S)) T: **085 329 6130.** E: **info@camping-bad-griesbach.de**

alanrogers.com/DE3697

This site is to the southwest of Passau, a town which dates back to Roman times and lies on a peninsula between the rivers Danube and Inn. Dreiquellenbad is an exceptional site in a quiet, rural area with 200 pitches, all of which are used for touring units. All pitches have electricity, water, waste water and TV points. English is spoken at reception, which also houses a shop and good tourist information. A luxury leisure complex includes indoor and outdoor thermal pools, a sauna, Turkish bath and jacuzzi (the use of which is free to campers). An adjoining building provides various beauty and complementary health treatments. A member of Leading Campings group.

Facilities

Excellent sanitary facilities include private cabins and free showers, facilities for disabled visitors, special child facilities and a dog shower. Two private bathrooms for rent. Laundry facilities. Bar/restaurant. Motorcaravan services. Shop. Gym. Luxury leisure complex (heated outdoor pool 1/3-15/11, indoor pool and wellness all year). Play area. Bicycle hire. Fishing. Internet. WiFi. No charcoal barbecues. Off site: Golf 2 km. Spa facilities of Bad Griesbach within walking distance.

Open: All year.

Directions

Site is 15 km. from the A3. Take exit 118 and follow signs for Pocking. After 2 km. turn right on B388. Site is in the hamlet of Singham - turn right into Karpfhan then left towards site. GPS: 48.42001, 13.19261

Charges 2012

Per unit incl. 2 persons and electricity	€ 19.00 - € 27.00
extra person	€ 7.60
child (0-14 yrs)	€ 4.80
dog	€ 2.50

Bad Wildbad

Camping Kleinenzhof

Kleinenzhof 1, D-75323 Bad Wildbad (Baden-Württemberg) T: **070 813 435**. E: **info@kleinenzhof.de**

alanrogers.com/DE3406

In the northern Black Forest, popular with walkers and cyclists alike, this large and busy site runs along the bank of a small but safe stream in a dramatic wooded valley. Of the 300 or so pitches, some 120 are for tourers, all with 16A electricity and water, and most with drainage. The four shower blocks are of the highest quality. In the middle of the site is a hotel/bar/restaurant complex which incorporates indoor and outdoor pools available free to campers. A full programme of activities is arranged, including walks, other outings, visits to the site's own distillery, films and communal barbecues at weekends, and a children's club every afternoon from May to September. A free bus runs four times a day in season to Calmbach.

Facilities

Four excellent sanitary blocks, all heated, are clean with many washbasins in cabins and showers. Facilities for disabled visitors. Baby changing. Children's bathroom. 12 free family bathrooms (for rental). Dog shower. Laundry facilities and dishwasher. Motorcaravan service point. Gas. Shop. Bar and restaurant (at hotel). Indoor pool. Outdoor pool (May-Sept) and paddling pool. Impressive new indoor sports/games hall with toddler annexe. TV and games room. Internet and WiFi. Bicycle and go kart hire. Off site: Fishing 3 km. Riding 8 km. Golf 25 km.

Open: All year.

Directions

Whether approaching from Pforzheim in the north or Freudenstadt in the south, stay on the 294. Do not go to Bad Wildbad. The site is on the main road just south of Calmbach, and is clearly signposted. If coming from the south, the turning into the site is very sharp. GPS: 48.73807, 8.57710

Charges guide

Per unit incl. 2 persons and electricity (plus meter)	€ 21.80 - € 22.90
extra person	€ 6.70 - € 7.00
child (1-12 yrs)	€ 4.20 - € 4.40
dog	€ 2.10 - € 2.30

Badenweiler

Kur & Feriencamping Badenweiler

Weilertalstrasse 73, D-79410 Badenweiler (Baden-Württemberg) T: **076 321 550**.

E: **info@camping-badenweiler.de** **alanrogers.com/DE3454**

Badenweiler is an attractive spa centre on the edge of the southern Black Forest, and is the site of the largest Roman baths north of the Alps. It is easily accessed from the A5 or B3, but far enough from them to be peaceful. This well kept, family run campsite with pleasant open views is on a hillside close to Badenweiler and the cure facilities. There are four terraces with 100 large, individual grass pitches, 96 for touring and all with electricity (16A), water and drainage. Reception is part of a building which also houses a bar/café with takeaway snacks in the evenings in high season. Here too is a small shop and a children's room downstairs. Limited facilities on-site for children so it may not suit all families.

Facilities

Top quality sanitary facilities are contained in two fully tiled buildings, one with toilets and the other with free, controllable hot showers with full glass dividers and washbasins (cabins and vanity style). Family washrooms, facilities for babies and disabled visitors. Washing machines and dryers. Motorcaravan services. Gas supplies. Shop for basics. Play area. Games room. Internet point and WiFi access throughout site. No charcoal barbecues. Off site: Municipal outdoor, heated swimming pool (free to campers, 15/5-15/9) 200 m. Restaurants 200 m. Shop 300 m. Golf 12 km.

Open: All year excl. 14 December - 16 January.

Directions

From the A5 about midway between Freiburg and Basel take exit 65 onto the B378 to Müllheim, then the L131 signed to Badenweiler-Ost from where site is well signed. GPS: 47.809961, 7.676954

Charges guide

Per unit incl. 2 persons	€ 29.10
extra person	€ 8.20
child (2-15 yrs)	€ 3.75 - € 5.25
electricity (per kWh)	€ 0.60
dog	€ 3.00

Credit cards accepted but 2% discount given if paying in cash.

Barntrup

Ferienpark Teutoburger Wald

4 Bade-Anstalts-Weg, D-32683 Barntrup (North Rhine-Westphalia) T: 052 632 221.
E: info@ferienparkteutoburgerwald.de alanrogers.com/DE3182

Under Dutch ownership, this site has 110 touring pitches, all with 16A electricity. Just outside the main gate there are nine fully serviced hardstanding pitches with charcoal grills designed with motorcaravans in mind. Although the site is sloping, the pitches are 110-250 sq.m. on mainly level grassy areas with some shade. Energy saving equipment has been installed in the toilet block for the production of hot water and the site is actively promoting good environmental practices. The famous fairytale town of Hameln (20 km) is worth a visit, especially on a Sunday for the Rattenfangerspiel.

Facilities

Excellent toilet block with underfloor heating, roomy showers and open washbasins. Children's section. Family showers. Dog shower. Laundry facilities. Key system for use of hot water. Motorcaravan service point. Games room with TV. WiFi. Play area. Electric scooters for hire. Off site: Walking in the adjacent woods. Outdoor pool next door. Bicycle hire and golf 10 km. Spa town of Bad Pyrmont 12 km. Riding and fishing 20 km.

Open: 1 April - 1 November.

Directions

From Hanover, take the A2 west towards Osnabrück. At exit 35 continue on B83 road towards Hameln. In Hameln take the B1 road south towards Barntrup and follow signs. GPS: 51.98681, 9.10842

Charges guide

Per unit incl. 2 persons and electricity	€ 19.00 - € 27.00
extra person	€ 5.50
child (2-15 yrs)	€ 3.00

Berchtesgaden

Camping Allweglehen

Allweggasse 4, D-83471 Berchtesgaden (Bavaria (S)) T: 086 522 396. E: urlaub@allweglehen.de
alanrogers.com/DE3685

This spacious and well maintained all-year site occupies a hillside position, with spectacular mountain views. The site access road is steep in places (14%) with a sharp, steep bend about halfway up, but the proprietor will use his tractor to tow caravans if requested, especially during snowy weather. There are 130 pitches (122 for touring), all arranged on a series of level, gravel terraces, separated by hedges or fir trees and all with good views and electrical connections (16A). There is a separate area on a sloping meadow for tents. The traditional restaurant offers Bavarian specialities at reasonable prices.

Facilities

Two adjacent older style toilet blocks near the restaurant (heated in winter). Another small unit serves the lowest terrace, but will be replaced in 2011 by a new luxury block providing modern facilities. Bathroom. Baby room. Washing machines, dryers and iron. Motorcaravan services. Gas supplies. Restaurant/bar/takeaway. Small shop for essentials (all year). Play area. Small heated pool. Solarium. Minigolf. Fishing. Excursions in high season. WiFi. Off site: Winter sports nearby. Walks. Riding 2 km. Bicycle hire 3 km. Golf 5 km.

Open: All year.

Directions

Easiest access is via the Austrian autobahn A10 (vignette necessary), Salzburg Sud and follow the B160 (Berchtesgaden) for 4 km. when it then becomes the B305. Site is on left after another 8 km. Or take the B305 from Ruhpolding (Alpenstrasse – winding and with 4 m. height limit), or the B20 from Bad Reichenhall. Site is 4 km. northeast of Berchtesgaden. GPS: 47.64489, 13.05086

Charges guide

Per unit incl. 2 persons and electricity	€ 23.15 - € 24.15
extra person	€ 6.75

Bremen

Camping am Stadtwaldsee

Hochschulring 1, D-28359 Bremen (Bremen) T: 042 184 10748. E: contact@camping-stadtwaldsee.de
alanrogers.com/DE3021

This well designed and purpose built campsite overlooking a lake is ideally placed for those travelling to northern Europe and for people wishing to visit Bremen and places within the region. There is a bus stop outside the site. Of the 220 level pitches 168 are for touring units, standing on grass with openwork reinforcements at the entrances. All have electricity (16A), water and drainage. The pitches are positioned around the spacious grass-roofed sanitary block and are laid out in areas separated by young trees and hedges. A restaurant/caféteria overlooks the lake.

Facilities

Modern sanitary block with free hot showers, facilities for disabled visitors, five private bathrooms for rental. Laundry facilities. Modern kitchen. Sitting/dining room with LCD projector facilities. Small supermarket (1/3-31/12). Lakeside café/restaurant with terrace. Play room. Play area. Lake swimming, windsurfing, fishing and scuba diving. Tents for hire. WiFi (charged). Bicycle and go-kart hire. Motorcaravan services. Off site: Naturist beach and general beach nearby. Health centre with fitness courses. Swimming pool 1 km. Riding 8 km. Golf 10 km.

Open: All year.

Directions

From A27 northeast of Bremen take exit 19 for 'Universitat' and follow signs for university and camping. Site is on the left, 1 km. after leaving the university area. GPS: 53.114833, 8.832467

Charges guide

Per unit incl. 2 persons and electricity (plus meter)	€ 28.00 - € 31.00
extra person	€ 9.00 - € 10.00
child (3-14 yrs)	€ 4.00 - € 5.00
dog	€ 3.00 - € 4.00

Bühl

Camping Adam

Campingstrasse 1, D-77815 Bühl (Baden-Württemberg) T: 072 232 3194. E: info@campingplatz-adam.de

alanrogers.com/DE3415

This very convenient lakeside site is by the A5 Karlsruhe - Basel autobahn near Baden-Baden, easily accessed from exit 52 Bühl (also from the French autoroute A35 just northeast of Strasbourg). It is also a useful base for the Black Forest. Most of the touring pitches (160 from 490 total) have electricity connections (10A Europlug), many with waste water outlets too. Tents are positioned along the outer area of the lake. At very busy times, units staying overnight only may be placed close together on a lakeside area of hardstanding. The site has a well tended look and good English is spoken. The lake is divided into separate areas for bathing or boating and windsurfing, with a long slide. The public are admitted to this on payment and it attracts many people on fine weekends. The shop and restaurant/bar remain open virtually all year (not Monday or Tuesday in low season), so this is a useful site to use out of season.

Facilities

Three heated sanitary buildings. Private cabins in the new block, hot showers on payment. Facilities for babies and disabled visitors. Washing machine and dryer. Gas supplies. Motorcaravan services. Shop (1/4-31/10). Restaurant (1/3-30/10). Takeaway (1/5-31/8). Playground. Bicycle hire. Fishing. WiFi in reception (charged). Off site: Riding and golf 5 km.

Open: All year (mobile homes 1/4-31/9 only).

Directions

Take A5/E35-52, exit 52 (Bühl), turn towards Lichtenau, go through Oberbruch and left to site. From French autoroute A35 take exits 52 or 56 onto D2 and D4 respectively then turn onto A5 as above. GPS: 48.72650, 8.08500

Charges guide

Per unit incl. 2 persons and electricity	€ 16.30 - € 26.30
extra person	€ 4.50 - € 8.00
child (3-15 yrs)	€ 2.50 - € 5.00
dog	€ 2.50

Clausthal-Zellerfeld

Camping Prahljust

An den Langen Brüchen 4, D-38678 Clausthal-Zellerfeld (Lower Saxony) T: **053 231 300.**

E: **camping@prahljust.de** **alanrogers.com/DE3055**

In a woodland setting, 600 metres high and well away from main roads, Camping Prahljust is a quiet site providing plenty of fresh air in an attractive location. The site slopes gently down to a lake which is used for swimming, boating, windsurfing and fishing, and in winter, ice skating. Of the 800 plus pitches 500 are reserved for tourists. These are arranged in larger open, grass areas separated by hedges with plenty of tree cover and all have electrical connections. The Oberharz is a winter sports region and January and February are the busiest months, with cross-country skiing from the site.

Facilities

Three modern, heated toilet blocks are well maintained and hold all the usual facilities. Showers are free. Facilities for disabled visitors. Baby room. Washing machines, dryers, drying room and kitchen. Motorcaravan service point. Shop, restaurant and bar (closed Nov). Indoor, heated swimming pool (12x9 m; no shallow end). Sauna and solarium. Clubroom. Lake trail. Beer garden. Bicycle and kayak hire. There is also a small library with books (also in English) in reception. WiFi. Off site: Bus service 1 km. Riding 5 km. Downhill skiing 20 km.

Open: All year.

Directions

Leave Clausthal-Zellerfeld on the B242 towards Braunlage. After 1 km. site is signed. Turn south and site is a further 1 km. GPS: 51.78330, 10.38332

Charges guide

Per person	€ 5.70 - € 6.30
child (2-14 yrs)	€ 3.60 - € 3.80
pitch	€ 5.40 - € 6.00
electricity (per kWh)	€ 0.55

Winter charges higher.
Camping Cheques accepted.

Creglingen

Camping Romantische Strasse

Munster 67, D-97993 Creglingen-Münster (Baden-Württemberg) T: **079 332 0289.**

E: **camping.hausotter@web.de** **alanrogers.com/DE3602**

This popular tourist area can become very busy during the summer when this site would be much appreciated for its peaceful situation in a wooded valley just outside the small village of Münster. There are 100 grass touring pitches (out of 140), many level, others with a small degree of slope. They are not hedged or fenced to keep the natural appearance of the woodland. All the pitches have electricity (6A), some shade, and are situated either side of a stream (fenced off from a weir at the top of the site). Good English is spoken by the friendly owners, who also own the restaurant. They have long term plans to further develop this attractive site, having already built a new reception, renovated the pool, sauna, solarium and changing rooms and made an open air chess and boules area.

Facilities

The main sanitary facilities are of good quality with free hot water. A small unit further into the site is not of the same quality. Launderette. Motorcaravan services. Small shop. Gas supplies. Large, pleasant bar/restaurant at the entrance (1/4-1/11, closed Mondays). Barbecue and covered sitting area. Heated indoor swimming pool (caps required) and sauna. Minigolf. Play area. Bicycle hire. Rooms to let. WiFi (charged). Off site: Bus service 200 m. Large lakes for swimming 100 m. and fishing 500 m. Riding 3.5 km.

Open: 15 March - 15 November.

Directions

From the Romantische Strasse between Rothenburg and Bad Mergentheim, exit at Creglingen to Münster (3 km). Site is just beyond this village. GPS: 49.43928, 10.04200

Charges 2012

Per unit incl. 2 persons and electricity	€ 19.60 - € 23.10
extra person	€ 5.50 - € 6.50
child (3-14 yrs)	€ 3.50 - € 4.00
dog	€ 1.00

No credit cards.
Camping Cheques accepted.

Drage

Camping Stover Strand International

Stover Strand 10, D-21423 Drage (Lower Saxony) T: **04177 430**. E: **info@stover-strand.de**

alanrogers.com/DE2899

This is a large site, part of which directly borders the river Elbe. The main part of the site is located behind a dyke and contains reception and the principal sanitary facilities. Pitches bordering and overlooking The Elbe are serviced by small movable sanitary units that are relocated in winter; they contain toilets and washbasins. Along the Elbe's banks there are sandy areas useful for playing and sunbathing in summer. Next to the site's main building there is a further area set aside for touring units and this has easy access to the main sanitary facilities, the bar and restaurant and children's playground. With its location some 20 km. southeast of Hamburg, Stover Strand is a useful site from which to visit the city and the many attractions that it has to offer, which include the world famous Reeperbahn; another popular tourist attraction is the fish market. To the south of the site is the old town of Lüneburg, the Lüneburger Heide and other attractive towns.

Facilities

Modern sanitary facility with washing machines and dryer, facilities for disabled visitors, and a baby changing room. Dishwashing room. Kitchen with cooking facilities. Motorcaravan service point. Supermarket. Bar. Restaurant. Children's playgrounds. Bicycle hire. Fishing. Sport boat harbour with 100 moorings. Boat slipway. WiFi (charged). Off site: Boat trips on The Elbe. Golf 8 km. Hamburg and other interesting towns and cities to visit.

Open: All year.

Directions

Site is 20 km. south east of Hamburg on the southern banks of the River Elbe. Leave A250 at exit 3 Winsen West and travel north east on the L217 though Winsen and Drage. Site entrance is signposted to the left 4 km. north east of Drage. Stover Strand is the last campsite at the end of the entrance road. GPS: 53.424383, 10.294977

Charges guide

Per unit incl. 2 persons and electricity	€ 14.00 - € 20.00
extra person	€ 4.00 - € 5.00
child (2-12 yrs)	€ 2.50 - € 3.00
dog	€ 2.00

Camping Cheques accepted.

Dresden

Camping Dresden-Mockritz

Boderitzer Str 30, D-01217 Dresden (Saxony) T: **035 147 15250**. E: **camping-dresden@t-online.de**

alanrogers.com/DE3834

Within 15 minutes of the city centre and with a bus every 20 minutes, this family run site is ideally located for visiting one of Europe's most attractive and interesting cities. Very good English is spoken in the well organised reception, where bus tickets and plenty of tourist information are readily available. The site has 180 pitches in three areas: the main short stay section has grass pitches in rows with concrete entry roads. Here the units are packed next to each other under mature trees. For longer stays there is a fairly open grass section and adjoining is a grass area for tents.

Facilities

Three heated sanitary blocks with controllable showers (token required) and washbasins in cabins (crowded at peak periods). Facilities for disabled visitors. Laundry room. Motorcaravan service point. Bar. Restaurant with terrace. Small shop with essentials and camping goods. Play area. Accommodation to rent. Off site: Dresden, with large open squares, the newly rebuilt Frauen Kirche and its visitors centre. Boat trips along The Elbe. Schloss Pilnitz and park. Meissen porcelain works and cathedral.

Open: All year excl. 20 December - 5 January.

Directions

Site is 4 km. south of the city centre. Leave the A4 at Dreieck Dresden West and travel east on the A17 for 11 km. Leave the A17 at exit 3 (Anschlusstelle, Dresden, Südvorstatdt) just after two fairly long tunnels. Head north on the 170 towards city centre. After 1.5 km. site is signed to the right, just after an orange Dresden city sign. GPS: 51.01452, 13.74766

Charges guide

Per unit incl. 2 persons and electricity	€ 20.20
extra person	€ 6.00

Dresden

Camping & Freizeitpark LuxOase

Arnsdorfer Strasse 1, Kleinröhrsdorf, D-01900 Dresden (Saxony) T: **035 952 56666**. E: **info@luxoase.de**
alanrogers.com/DE3833

This is a well organised and quiet site located just north of Dresden with easy access from the autobahn. The site has very good facilities and is arranged on grassland beside a lake. There is access from the site to the lake through a gate. Although the site is fairly open, trees do provide shade in some areas. There are 138 large touring pitches (plus 50 seasonal in a separate area), marked by bushes or posts on generally flat or slightly sloping grass. All have 10/16A electricity and 100 have water and drainage. At the entrance is an area of hardstanding (with electricity) for late arrivals. The main entrance building houses the amenities and in front of the building is some very modern play equipment on bark. You may swim, fish or use inflatables in the lake. A wide entertainment programme is organised for children in high season. There are many interesting places to visit apart from Dresden and Meissen, with the fascinating National Park Sächsische Schweiz (Saxon Switzerland) on the border with the Czech Republic offering some spectacular scenery. Boat trips on The Elbe can be taken from the tourist centres of Königstein and Bad Schandau and Saxony is also famous for its many old castles, including Colditz, for which an English language guide is available. Bus trips are organised to Prague and Dresden. A member of Leading Campings group.

Facilities

A well equipped building provides modern, heated facilities with private cabins, a family room, baby room, units for disabled visitors and two bathrooms for hire. Jacuzzi. Kitchen. Gas supplies. Motorcaravan services. Shop and bar (1/3-31/12) plus restaurant (15/3-31/12). Bicycle hire. Lake swimming. Sports field. Fishing. Play area. Sauna. Train, bus and theatre tickets from reception. Internet point. WiFi. Minigolf. Fitness room. Regular guided bus trips to Dresden, Prague etc. Off site: Riding next door (lessons available). Public transport to Dresden 1 km. Golf 7.5 km. Nearby dinosaur park, zoo and indoor karting etc.

Open: 1 March - 31 December.

Directions

Site is 17 km. northeast of Dresden. From the A4 (Dresden - Görlitz) take exit 85 (Pulnitz) and travel south towards Radeberg. Pass through Leppersdorf and site is signed to the left. Follow signs for Kleinröhrsdorf and camping. Site is 4 km. from the autobahn exit. GPS: 51.120401, 13.980103

Charges guide

Per unit incl. 2 persons and electricity	€ 20.10 - € 29.50
extra person	€ 5.00 - € 7.80
child (3-15 yrs)	€ 2.50 - € 4.50

Various special offers in low season.

Eggelstetten

Camping Donau-Lech

Campingweg 1, D-86698 Eggelstetten (Bavaria (S)) T: **090 904 046**. E: **info@donau-lech-camping.de**
alanrogers.com/DE3630

The Haas family have developed this friendly site just off the attractive Romantische Strasse very well and run it very much as a family site, providing a useful information sheet in English for their guests. The lake provides swimming and wildlife for children and adults to enjoy. Alongside it are 50 marked touring pitches with 16A electrical connections, on flat grass arranged in rows either side of a tarmac access road. With an average of 120 sq.m. per unit, it is a comfortable site with an open feeling and developing shade. There are three flat, grass areas with unmarked pitches by the entrance, for people with tents.

Facilities

All amenities are housed in the main building at the entrance with reception. Sanitary facilities are downstairs with free showers and washbasins (no cabins), all of a good standard. Sauna. Washing machine and dryer. Motorcaravan services. Large bar area with terrace. Small shop for basics, bread to order (1/4-31/10). General room. Youth room. Play area. Health studio with massage, manicure and pedicure. Lake for swimming (at own risk). Off site: Golf course and driving range 300 m. Larger lake used for sailboarding 400 m. Fishing 3 km. Restaurants and other amenities a short drive.

Open: All year.

Directions

Turn off main B2 road about 5 km. south of Donauwörth (site signed) at signs for Asbach, Bäumenheim Nord towards Eggelstetten, then follow signs for over 1 km. to site.
GPS: 48.67590, 10.84083

Charges guide

Per unit incl. 2 persons and electricity	€ 18.00 - € 19.50
extra person	€ 5.50
child (2-15 yrs)	€ 3.00
dog	€ 2.20

Erlangen

Camping Rangau

Campingstrasse 44, D-91056 Erlangen-Dechsendorf (Bavaria (N)) T: 091 358 866.
E: infos@camping-rangau.de **alanrogers.com/DE3605**

This pleasant, but basic site makes a convenient stopover and is quickly and easily reached from either the A3 Würzburg - Nürnberg or the A73 Bamberg - Nürnberg autobahns. It has 110 pitches on flat ground which are mainly for tourists. All are numbered and partly marked but mainly between 50-70 sq.m. so it can look very cramped when busy. There are also 60 permanent units. There is usually space available, but in peak season overnight visitors can often be put on the adjacent football pitch. A large lake with access from the site through a gate, can be used for sailing or windsurfing and boats are available to hire. There is no fishing at present.

Facilities

A satisfactory sanitary block, heated when cold, has well spaced washbasins (some cabins for ladies) and showers. Good facilities for disabled visitors. A new facility provides washbasins in cabins and WCs. Laundry facilities. Gas supplies. Purpose-built dog shower. Motorcaravan services. Pleasant restaurant with terrace for meals or drinks. Order bread from reception. Playground. Club/TV room. Off site: Swimming 200 m. Erlangen centre 5 km.

Open: 1 April - 30 September.

Directions

Take exit for Erlangen-West from A3 autobahn, turn towards Erlangen but after less than 1 km. at Dechsendorf turn left and follow signs to site. GPS: 49.62690, 10.94100

Charges guide

Per unit incl. 2 persons and electricity	€ 19.00
extra person	€ 5.50
child (6-12 yrs)	€ 3.50
dog	€ 2.50

Ettenheim

Terrassen-Camping Oase

Mühlenweg 34, D-77955 Ettenheim (Baden-Württemberg) T: 078 224 45918. E: info@campingpark-oase.de
alanrogers.com/DE3428

This pleasant well run site lies on wooded land on the western edge of the Black Forest, a very good region for walking and cycling. The level area near the entrance holds the main facilities and 190 touring pitches, all with 5A electricity. Pitches for tents are on grass and there is grass or hardstanding for caravans and motorcaravans. On sloping land further away are 95 terraced seasonal pitches. Just outside the entrance is the family hotel/restaurant, which also has a playground, all open to campers. Europa Park is 7 km. away, and the city of Freiburg is 40 km. to the south.

Facilities

Two sanitary blocks are heated, clean and well maintained. Many washbasins are in cabins. Showers are coin operated. Facilities for wheelchair users. Baby room, children's bathroom. Motorcaravan services. Gas supplies. Shop. Restaurant and takeaway (at hotel). TV and club room. Off site: Municipal pool and leisure centre adjacent (weekly family membership available). Tennis, riding and bicycle hire within 1 km. Fishing 2 km. Golf 5 km.

Open: Week before Easter - 4 October.

Directions

From A5/E35, exit 57A (Ettenheim), follow L103 road southeast to Ettenheim (about 2.5 km). From here site is signed, and is a further 1 km. along the same road. GPS: 48.24770, 7.82753

Charges guide

Per unit incl. 2 persons and electricity	€ 22.50 - € 25.50
extra person	€ 7.00
child (1-15 yrs)	€ 3.50 - € 9.00
dog	€ 2.50

Fehmarn

Strandcamping Wallnau

Wallnau 1, D-23769 Fehmarn (Schleswig-Holstein) T: 043 729 456. E: wallnau@strandcamping.de
alanrogers.com/DE3007

With direct beach access and protected from the wind by a dyke, this family site is on Germany's second largest island (since 1963 joined to the Baltic sea coast by a bridge). This is a quiet location on the western part of Fehmarn Island in close proximity to a large bird sanctuary. Of the 800 pitches, 400 are for touring, all with electricity and on level grass areas arranged in alleys and separated by hedges. The island is low lying, ideal for leisurely walking or cycle riding, especially along the track that runs along the top of the dyke. The beach is a mixture of sand and pebbles and in summer lifeguards are on duty. The southern part is a naturist area.

Facilities

Heated sanitary blocks (cleaning variable) provide free showers. Child-size toilets and showers. Baby rooms. Facilities for disabled visitors. Laundry facilities. Motorcaravan service points. Shop. Bar, restaurant and snack bar. Open-air stage and soundproofed disco. Health/cure centre, solarium and sauna. Archery. Watersports. Minigolf. Internet café. Beach fishing. Riding. WiFi (charged). Off site: Boat launching 6 km. Golf 15 km.

Open: 27 March - 25 October.

Directions

After crossing bridge follow road to Landkirchen and Petersdorf. From Petersdorf site is signed. It is 4 km. northwest of the town. GPS: 54.48761, 11.0186

Charges guide

Per unit incl. 2 persons and electricity	€ 18.00 - € 35.30
child (under 17 yrs)	€ 2.00 - € 6.30
extra person	€ 4.00 - € 7.40

No credit cards.
Camping Cheques accepted.

Flessenow

Seecamping Flessenow

Am Schweriner See 1A, D-19067 Flessenow (Mecklenburg-West Pomerania) T: 038 668 1491.
E: info@seecamping.de **alanrogers.com/DE3812**

Seecamping Flessenow is owned and run by an enthusiastic, young Dutch couple. It is on the banks of the Schwerinner See and makes an ideal base for a quiet holiday or for an active holiday on the water. There are 250 pitches (170 for touring units), arranged on two rectangular fields to one side of a hardcore access lane and on a newer field to the rear of the site. Some pitches have views over the lake and these have some shade from mature trees. All have 10A electricity, 45 with electricity, water and drainage.

Facilities

Three toilet blocks (one older style) with open washbasins and controllable hot showers (token from reception). Baby room with shower. Washing machine and dryer. Motorcaravan services. Bar, kiosk and takeaway (all season; bread to order). Playground. TV room. Lake with beach. Fishing. Watersports. Bicycle hire. Boat launching. Sailing. WiFi. Off site: Riding 1.5 km. Golf 20 km.

Open: April - October.

Directions

Site is 14 km. north-northeast of Schwerin. From 8 km. east of Schwerin, take the A14 (formerly the 241) north along the east side of the lake. At Schwerin Nord take exit 4 and turn west towards Rampe, then north on minor road through Retgendorf to Flessenow. Site is signed from there. GPS: 53.75175, 11.49628

Charges guide

Per unit incl. 2 persons and electricity	€ 17.50 - € 26.50
extra person	€ 4.00

Frankenhain

Oberhof Camping

Am Stausee 09, D-99330 Frankenhain (Thuringia) T: 493 620 576518. E: info@oberhofcamping.de
alanrogers.com/DE3855

Beside a lake, at an altitude of 700 metres and quietly hidden in the middle of the Thüringer forest, Oberhof Camping has seen many changes since the departure of its former owners, the East German secret police. There are 150 touring pitches, all with electricity (10A Europlug) and 52 with water and drainage. From this fairly open site there are views of the surrounding forests and of the lake which is bordered by wide grass areas ideal for a picnic or for just lazing around and enjoying the view. The site is very quiet and has direct access to marked routes for rambling and cycling in the forest.

Facilities

New heated sanitary block with all usual facilities including free hot water, plus 15 bathrooms to rent. Facilities for disabled visitors. Baby room. Laundry. Motorcaravan services. Gas sales. Modern reception building with shop and attractive restaurant serving traditional dishes. Shop. TV room. Children's club room. Play area. On the lake: fishing (licence required), swimming and boating.
Off site: Over 100 km. of waymarked paths from the site. Bus service 1.5 km. Riding 5 km.

Open: All year.

Directions

Site is 25 km. south of Gotha. From the A4 between Eisenach and Dresden take exit 42 (Gotha). Travel south on the B247 to Ohrdruf then the B88 to Crawinkel then Frankenhain. In Frankenhain follow Lütsche Stausee and Campingpark signs.
GPS: 50.73367, 10.75667

Charges guide

Per unit incl. 2 persons and electricity	€ 21.00
extra person	€ 6.50
child (1-13 yrs)	€ 4.00

Camping Cheques accepted.

Freiburg

Camping am Möslepark

Waldseestrasse 77, D-79117 Freiburg (Baden-Württemberg) T: 076 176 79333.
E: information@camping-freiburg.com **alanrogers.com/DE3438**

This is a small, quiet, family run site in the suburbs of Freiburg. Its grass pitches, set on small terraces, are shaded by many mature trees. Most of the 70 pitches are for touring units and have electricity (10/16A Europlug) . On the upper part of the site is a long established and very attractive restaurant. Open in the evenings, the restaurant specialises in dishes freshly prepared from organic ingredients; vegetarian and local specialities are also part of the menu. Additionally a small bar and bistro is part of a wellness centre which adjoins the site. The site is well placed for visiting the Black Forest region.

Facilities

Well maintained sanitary facilities provide some washbasins in cabins and showers with free hot water. Space for baby changing. Small dining room with metered hotplate and kettle. Motorcaravan service area. Small shop. Play area. Bicycle hire. WiFi (charged). The adjoining wellness centre has sauna, steam bath, massage and jacuzzi plus a small swimming pool (reduced rate entrance for campers). Accommodation to rent. Off site: Old university city of Freiburg. Good base from which to visit the Black Forest. Some walking and cycle riding locally from site.

Open: 1 April - 6 November.

Directions

Site is 2 km. southeast of Freiburg. Leave autobahn 5 at exit 62 (Freiburg Mitte) and take B31A southeast, following signs for Titisee, Neustadt. After 7 km. travelling through Freiburg keep left and do not descend into tunnel. After 300 m. turn right (Stadthalle), keep straight on then bear left at sign Waldsee. Continue bearing left, and site is signed to the left. GPS: 47.98064, 7.88153

Charges guide

Per unit incl. 2 persons and electricity	€ 22.10 - € 22.60
extra person	€ 3.00

Freiburg

Hirzberg Camping Freiburg

Kartäuserstrasse 99, D-79104 Freiburg (Baden-Württemberg) T: 076 135 054.

E: hirzberg@freiburg-camping.de **alanrogers.com/DE3439**

Hirzberg Camping is a quiet city site backing onto meadows and wooded hills, yet within easy reach of Freiburg's old town quarter. To the right of the entrance is reception, a shop, the sanitary facilities and a children's room with a play area outside. Opposite is a large convenient overnight parking area. The main part of the site is reached by a short climb passing a small reading room and flower decked sitting area. The upper part has 76 pitches, 60 for tourists, almost all with 10A electricity connections. Hardcore roads lead to open grass pitches, many under mature trees.

Facilities

Modern, heated sanitary block provides free hot water, roomy adjustable showers and some washbasins in cabins. Washing machines and dryer. Kitchen with fridge, microwave and cooking rings on payment. Small shop with essential supplies. Play room and play area. Reading room with daily weather report. Bicycle hire. WiFi over whole site (charged). Off site: Bus service at entrance, tram 300 m. Golf 6 km. Riding 8 km.

Open: All year.

Directions

Site is in the eastern part of the city. To reach it without having to drive through the city, from the B31 take exit Freiberg Kappel (F. Kappel) which is well to the east of the city and follow camping signs. GPS: 47.992047, 7.873356

Charges guide

Per unit incl. 2 persons and electricity	€ 20.00 - € 24.00
extra person	€ 6.50 - € 7.50
child (0-13 yrs)	€ 2.00 - € 3.00

Frickenhausen

Knaus Campingpark Frickenhausen

Ochsenfurter Strasse 49, D-97252 Frickenhausen (Bavaria (N)) T: 093 313 171.

E: frickenhausen@knauscamp.de **alanrogers.com/DE3625**

This is a pleasant riverside site with good facilities just south of Würzburg, situated towards the northern end of the Romantische Strasse and not far from the A3 Frankfurt to Nürnberg. There are 125 fair sized, numbered touring pitches on generally flat grass, arranged in sections leading from tarmac access roads with flowers around. Most have 16A electricity connections. About 80 long stay places are mostly separate nearer the river. All the amenities are in a long block opposite reception. Upstairs is a little shop and a restaurant with a terrace for candlelit meals.

Facilities

Modernised, heated, sanitary facilities have washbasins (some private cabins), and dishwashing sinks. Soap and paper towels are provided for the toilets. Washing machine and dryer. Cooking facilities. Gas supplies. Restaurant and shop (1/12-31/10). Bread to order. Club room. Large screen TV. Small, free swimming pool (1/5-31/10). Play area on river island. Open-air theatre. Bicycle hire. Fishing. Boat marina. WiFi. Off site: Public swimming pool 300 m. Riding 1 km. Golf and boat launching 15 km.

Open: All year.

Directions

From the A3 at Würzburg, take exit 71 (Ochsenfurt) and continue on the B13 towards Ochsenfurt and Ansbach. Just before main bridge (which is sharp right) continue straight on towards Frickenhausen site is 200 m. on the right. GPS: 49.66914, 10.07453

Charges guide

Per unit incl. 2 persons and electricity	€ 16.60 - € 28.50
extra person	€ 5.00 - € 6.70
child (4-14 yrs)	€ 2.00 - € 3.00

Füssen im Allgäu

alan rogers Runner up 2011 Awards

Camping Hopfensee

Fischerbichl 17, D-87629 Füssen im Allgäu (Bavaria (S)) T: 083 629 17710.

E: info@camping-hopfensee.com **alanrogers.com/DE3670**

This exceptional, family run site is situated beside a lake in the beautiful Bavarian Alps, not far from the fairytale castle of Neuschwanstein. Although one can appreciate the mountain scenery from the 376 level, fully serviced pitches, it is more comfortably viewed whilst swimming in the 31 degree swimming pool on the first floor of the wellness complex. The wellness complex, which offers a full spa programme, and the sanitary facilities are arranged around a large courtyard adorned with cascading flowers. The site has an excellent restaurant and bar with views over the lake.

Facilities

The exceptionally good, heated sanitary facilities provide free hot water in washbasins (some in cabins) and large showers. Separate baby and children's washrooms. Private units for rent. Motorcaravan services. Takeaway. Shop. Supervised courses of water treatments, aromatherapy, massage, etc. Sauna, solarium and steam bath. Playground and kindergarten. Large games room. Bicycle hire. Tennis. Fishing. Ski safari in winter. Small golf academy and discounts for two local courses. No tents taken. Off site: Riding and boat launching 1 km.

Open: 16 December - 4 November.

Directions

Site is 4 km. north of Füssen. Turn off B16 to Hopfen and site is on the left through a car park. If approaching from the west on B310, turn towards Füssen at T-junction with the B16 and immediately right again for the road to Hopfen. GPS: 47.60572, 10.68052

Charges 2012

Per unit incl. 2 persons and electricity (plus meter)	€ 30.05 - € 33.80
extra person	€ 8.70 - € 9.90
child (2-18 yrs acc. to age)	€ 5.30 - € 6.20

Gemünden

Spessart-Camping Schönrain

Schönrainstrasse 4-18, D-97737 Gemünden-Hofstetten (Bavaria (N)) T: **093 518 645.**

E: **info@spessart-camping.de** **alanrogers.com/DE3735**

Situated 4 km. west of the town of Gemünden, with views of forested hills bordering the Main river, this is a very friendly, well organised, family run site, with excellent facilities. Frau Endres welcomes British guests and speaks a little English. There are 100 pitches, 70 of which are for touring. They vary in size (70-150 sq.m) and all have 10A electricity, 20 also with water. Another area has been developed for tents. The site has a pleasant bar with a terrace. Meals can be ordered from local restaurants for delivery or the site's bus will provide transport. This is a good area for cycling and walking.

Facilities

A superb new sanitary building has card-operated entry – the card is prepaid and operates the showers, washing machines and dryers, gas cooker, baby bathroom, jacuzzi etc. Two private bathrooms (complete with wine and balcony!) for rent. Motorcaravan services. General room with play area for very young children, games and a TV. Library. Internet café. Fitness room and solarium. Bar. Shop. Swimming pool. Playground. Bicycle hire. Beauty and wellness. Off site: Bus service 200 m. Fishing 400 m. Canoeing, cycling and walking.

Open: 1 April - 30 September.

Directions

From Frankfurt - Würzburg autobahn, take Weibersbrunn-Lohr exit and then B26 to Gemünden. Turn over Main river bridge to Hofstetten and follow official town camping signs. From Kassel - Würzburg autobahn, leave at Hammelburg and take B27 to Gemünden, and as above. GPS: 50.05144, 9.65684

Charges 2012

Per unit incl. 2 persons and electricity (plus meter)	€ 21.75 - € 26.35
extra person	€ 6.20
child (under 14 yrs)	€ 3.60

Gera

Camping Strandbad Aga

Reichenbacherstrasse 14, D-07554 Gera-Aga (Thuringia) T: **036 695 20209.**

E: **info@campingplatz-strandbad-aga.de** **alanrogers.com/DE3850**

Strandbad Aga is a useful night stop near the A4/A9 and is within reach of Dresden, Leipzig and Meissen. It is situated in open countryside on the edge of a small lake, with 200 individual, fenced pitches, mostly fairly level, without shade. The 70 touring pitches all have 16A electricity – for stays of more than a couple of days, over-nighters being placed on an open area. The lake is used for swimming, boating and fishing (very popular with day visitors at weekends and with a separate naturist area) and there is a small playground on one side (close to a deep part).

Facilities

The sanitary building, which has been completely renovated and now includes some family rooms, is at one side, with some washbasins in cabins and hot showers on payment. Large room for wheelchair users. Washing machines and dryers. Motorcaravan services. Modern restaurant/bar open long hours. Kiosk for drinks, ice creams, etc. (high season). Playground. Small lake used for inflatables, fishing, swimming and watersports. Entertainment (high season). Off site: Football 200 m. Shop in village 1 km. Riding and tennis 1 km.

Open: 1 April - 31 October.

Directions

Site is 8 km. north of Gera. From A4/E40 Chemnitz - Erfurt autobahn take exit 58A for Gera and Landenberg, then the B2 towards Zeitz, following Bad Köstritz signs at first, then Reichenbach and site signs. Site is on left 1 km. after passing through Reichenbach. GPS: 50.95387, 12.08683

Charges guide

Per unit incl. 2 persons and electricity	€ 15.50 - € 16.00
extra person	€ 4.00

No credit cards.

Hamburg

Knaus Camping Hamburg

Wunderbrunnen 2, D-22457 Hamburg (Hamburg) T: **040 559 4225.** E: **hamburg@knauscamp.de**

alanrogers.com/DE3005

Situated some 15 km. from the centre of Hamburg on the northern edge of the town, this is a suitable base either for visiting this famous German city, or as a night stop before catching the Harwich ferry or travelling to Denmark. There is some traffic noise because the autobahn runs alongside (despite efforts to screen it out) and also some aircraft noise. However, the proximity of the A7 (E45) does make it easy to find. The 145 pitches for short-term touring are of about 100 sq.m, on grass with access from gravel roads. All have 6A electricity and are marked out with small trees and hedges.

Facilities

A deposit is required for the key to the single sanitary block, a well constructed modern building with good quality facilities and heated in cool weather. Good facilities for disabled visitors, with special pitches close to the block. Washing machines and dryers. Motorcaravan service point (for site guests only). Shop (basics only). Playground. Dogs are not accepted. Off site: Bus service, restaurants and shops 10 minutes walk. Swimming pool, tennis courts, golf and fishing nearby.

Open: 1 April - 31 October.

Directions

From A7 autobahn take Schnelsen Nord exit. Stay in outside lane as you will soon need to turn back left; follow signs for Ikea store and site signs. GPS: 53.65015, 9.92927

Charges guide

Per person	€ 6.00
child (3-13 yrs)	€ 3.50
pitch	€ 7.20 - € 11.50
electricity (6A)	€ 2.50

Herbolzheim

Terrassen Campingplatz Herbolzheim

Im Laue, D-79336 Herbolzheim (Baden-Württemberg) T: **076 431 460.** E: **s.hugoschmidt@t-online.de**

alanrogers.com/DE3442

This well equipped campsite is in a quiet location on a wooded slope to the north of Freiburg. There are 70 touring pitches, all with electricity (16A) and grass surfaces, on terraces linked by hard access roads with a little shade for some. Many pitches are used by a tour operator and for long-term occupancy. This is good walking country and with only occasional entertainment, this is a very pleasant place in which to relax between daily activities. It is useful as a night stop when travelling between Frankfurt and Basel, and is just 5 km. from Europa Park, only a short way from the A5 autobahn.

Facilities

The main toilet facilities are modern, with new facilities for babies and disabled visitors. Laundry facilities (charged). Motorcaravan services. Bar/restaurant (Easter-Sept). Two play areas. WiFi (charged). Dogs are not accepted 15/7-15/8. Off site: Large open-air heated municipal swimming pool complex adjacent (1/5-15/9). Restaurants and shops in the village 3 km. Riding and bicycle hire 5 km. Local market Fri mornings.

Open: 1 April - 7 October.

Directions

From A5 Frankfurt - Basel autobahn take exit 57, 58 or 59 and follow signs to Herbolzheim. Site is signed on south side of town near swimming pool. Go through pool car park and about 350 m. past the pool entrance. GPS: 48.21610, 7.78857

Charges guide

Per unit incl. 2 persons and electricity	€ 22.00 - € 25.00
extra person	€ 7.00
child (0-15 yrs)	€ 3.00

Hohenstadt

Camping Waldpark Hohenstadt

Waldpark 1, D-73345 Hohenstadt (Baden-Württemberg) T: **073 356 754.**

E: **camping@waldpark-hohenstadt.de** **alanrogers.com/DE3408**

Situated on a wooded hillside close to the A8 autoroute, this neat and tidy site is open all year and is an ideal stopover between Stuttgart and Ulm. The 45 good sized plots for touring units each have water and 16A electric supply and are positioned on terraces at the front of the site, with little shade. The rear of the site is used for seasonal units. The restaurant/bar provides a good selection of local food and is open every evening. For a longer stay, the towns of Ulm and Blaubeuren are worth a visit and a tour of the Laichingen Pothole (the deepest show cave in Germany) should not be missed.

Facilities

A large modern toilet block is centrally situated, containing WCs, hot showers (free tokens for tourers), washbasins and facilities for disabled visitors. A smaller modern block in the touring area provides WCs and washbasins. Laundry facilities. Motorcaravan services. Small shop in reception for basics (bread to order). Restaurant/bar (evenings). Swimming pool (15/5-30/9). Children's play area. Activity programme (5-10 yrs; high season). Electric bicycle hire. Nordic skiing in winter. WiFi. Off site: Nordic skiing from site. Riding 200 m. Fishing 10 km. Golf 15 km.

Open: All year.

Directions

From A8/E52 Stuttgart – Ulm, exit at junction 60, signed Behelfsausfahrt and follow signs to Hohenstadt and the site.
GPS: 48.548009, 9.667245

Charges guide

Per unit incl. 2 persons and electricity	€ 18.40 - € 19.60
extra person	€ 4.70 - € 5.10
child (4-14 yrs)	€ 3.00 - € 3.50
dog	€ 1.00

Irring bei Passau

Dreiflüsse Camping

Am Sonnenhang 8, Donautat, D-94113 Irring bei Passau (Bavaria (S)) T: **085 466 33.**

E: **dreifluessecamping@t-online.de** **alanrogers.com/DE3695**

Although the site overlooks the Danube, it is in fact some 9 km. from the confluence of the Danube, Inn and Ilz. Dreiflüsse Camping occupies a hillside position, well above high water level, to the west of Passau with pitches, flat or with a little slope, on several rows of terraces. The 180 places for touring units are not all numbered or marked, although 16A electricity connection boxes determine where units pitch, and half have water and drainage. Trees and low banks separate the terraces which are of gravel with a thin covering of grass. There is some road and rail noise (24 hrs).

Facilities

The sanitary facilities are acceptable, if a little old, with two private cabins for women, one for men. Laundry. Motorcaravan services. Gas supplies. Shop (all season). Pleasant, modern Gasthof restaurant with terrace at site entrance, where the reception, shop and sanitary buildings are also located. Small heated indoor swimming pool (1/5-15/9 on payment). Play area. Bicycle hire. New 'Aquakur' w-ellness centre added in 2008. Off site: Bus service for Passau (4 daily) from outside site, or from Schalding 1.5 km. Riding 3 km. Passau 9 km. Golf 10 km.

Open: 1 April - 31 October.

Directions

From autobahn A3, take exit 115 (Passau-Nord) from where site is signed. Follow signs from Passau on road to west of city and north bank of Danube towards Windorf and Irring.
GPS: 48.60647, 13.34602

Charges 2012

Per unit incl. 2 persons and electricity	€ 21.00
extra person	€ 5.50
child (4-14 yrs)	€ 4.00
dog	€ 2.00

No credit cards.

Isny

Waldbad Camping Isny

Lohbauerstrasse 61-69, D-88316 Isny (Baden-Württemberg) T: 075 622 389.
E: info@waldbad-camping-isny.de alanrogers.com/DE3467

Isny is a delightful spot for families and for others looking for a peaceful stay in a very well managed environment. The site has been developed to a high standard and lies just south of the village in a wood, by a lake. In an open area there are 50 individual 100 sq.m. hardstanding pitches (all with 16A electricity) with a circular access road. A further area is on a terrace just above. A café with light snacks during the week and meals at the weekends is open long hours in high season. It has a terrace that overlooks the lake, which is used for swimming (unsupervised).

Facilities

The main sanitary unit is first class and has automatic toilet seat cleaning. There are cabins as well as vanity style washbasins, large controllable showers, with full curtain, token operated. Further facilities near reception house showers, WCs, washbasins, and a good unit for disabled visitors. Laundry. Basic motorcaravan services. Café/bar. Reception keeps a few basic supplies. Bicycles to borrow. Off site: Tennis club. Recreation and play areas. Barbecue area. Restaurant and supermarket 1.5 km.

Open: 1 January - 31 December.

Directions

From the B12 between Lindau and Kempten, exit Isny - Mitte (new road) and follow signs.
GPS: 47.67828, 10.03035

Charges guide

Per unit incl. 2 persons (electricity on meter)	€ 22.50
extra person	€ 6.50
child per year of age	€ 0.40
dog	€ 2.00

Special rates for senior citizens (low season).

Issigau

alan rogers Runner up 2011 Awards

Camping Schloss Issigau

Schloss Issigau, altes Schloss 3, D-95188 Issigau (Bavaria (N)) T: 092 937 173.
E: info@schloss-issigau.de alanrogers.com/DE3750

This family run site is small, attractive and well run. On the left of the entrance courtyard, the small Schloss (c.1398) houses reception, a display of armour, a comfortable breakfast room and a restaurant serving regional and international dishes. Home made cakes and drinks are served on the small terrace in front of the Schloss. There are 40 level pitches, all with 16A electricity and five with fresh water and drainage. They are on grass with some terracing and in places, trees offer some shade. To the rear of the site, beside a pond, is a large grass sloping area for tents.

Facilities

Modern heated sanitary facilities are housed in an attractively renovated old building. Showers are controllable and free, some washbasins in cabins, Laundry facilities. Baby room. The building also houses a games room and upstairs, a sauna, solarium, fitness studio, children's play room, and a reading room. Delightful café/bar and restaurant. Bicycle hire. Playground. Hotel accommodation. Off site: Bus service and small supermarket 300 m. Riding 1.5 km. Fishing 6 km. Golf 10 km.

Open: 15 March - 31 October, 18 December - 9 January.

Directions

The village of Issigau is between Holle and Berg. From A9 (Berlin - Nuremberg) take exit 31 Berg/Bad Steben. Turn left and follow signs for Berg and then continue straight on towards Holle. Site is signed in Issigau. Go down a small slope and to the right.
GPS: 50.37418, 11.72122

Charges guide

Per unit incl. 2 persons	€ 16.50 - € 17.50
extra person	€ 5.00
child (4-14 yrs)	€ 3.00
electricity (plus meter)	€ 1.00

Kipfenberg

Azur Camping Altmühltal

Campingstrasse 1, D-85110 Kipfenberg (Bavaria (N)) T: 084 659 05167. E: kipfenberg@azur-camping.de
alanrogers.com/DE3632

In the beautiful Altmühltal river valley, this Azur site is in pretty woodland, with lots of shade for much of it. On flat grassland with direct access to the river, one looks from the entrance across to the old Schloss on the hill. Outside the main entrance is a large, flat, grass/gravel field for 60 overnight tourers (with electricity). The main site has 277 pitches, of which 178 are for touring, plus two small areas for tents and one large one (at the end in an open area). Ranging in size up to 90 sq.m. they are generally in small groups marked by trees or bushes.

Facilities

The main sanitary facilities are good, with free hot water (no private cabins), baby room, unit for disabled visitors. Launderette. Kitchen. These facilities are mostly duplicated portacabin style at the other end of the site (toilets only in low season). Motorcaravan services. Shop combined with reception and vending machine for drinks. Beer garden with campfire and serving snacks in July/Aug. Play area. Fishing. WiFi. Off site: Supermarket 100 m. Outdoor pool 200 m. Two restaurants within 300 m. Bicycle, electric scooter and canoe hire in town.

Open: 1 April - 31 October.

Directions

From the A9/E45 (Munich - Nürnberg), take exit 59 Denkendorf or 58 Eichstätt and follow the signs to Kipfenberg. Site is signed in Kipfenberg and is opposite a supermarket. GPS: 48.94840, 11.38933

Charges guide

Per unit incl. 2 persons and electricity	€ 19.80 - € 26.80
extra person	€ 6.00 - € 8.00
child (2-12 yrs)	€ 3.00 - € 4.50
dog	€ 3.50

Kirchzarten

Camping Kirchzarten

Dietenbacher Strasse 17, D-79199 Kirchzarten (Baden-Württemberg) T: **076 619 040910.**

E: **info@camping-kirchzarten.de** **alanrogers.com/DE3440**

There are pleasant views of the Black Forest from this municipal site which is within easy reach by car of Titisee, Feldberg and Todtnau, and 8 km. from the large town of Freiburg in Breisgau. It is divided into 496 numbered pitches, 380 of which are for touring, all with electricity (16A Europlug). Most pitches, which are side by side on gently sloping ground, are of quite reasonable size and clearly marked out, though there is nothing to separate them. There are some hardstanding pitches suitable for large motorcaravans and RVs. From about late June to mid August it does become full. The fine swimming pool complex adjoining the site is free to campers and is a great attraction, with pools for diving, water games, swimming and a separate children's pool, surrounded by spacious grassy sunbathing areas and a play area on sand. It is only a short stroll from the site to the village centre, which has supermarkets, restaurants, etc.

Facilities

The splendid main sanitary building includes a large, central section for children, private cabins (some for hire) and a laundry room. The sanitary block at the entrance was modernised in 2011. Cooking stoves. Laundry facilities (all on payment by meter). There is a new restaurant/bar. Shop. Swimming pool complex (15/5-15/9). TV room. Play room. Youth room. Large playground. Bicycle hire (electric). WiFi (charged). Children's activities in season. Off site: Tennis (covered court, can be booked from site). Adventure playground, fitness track, tennis and minigolf. Riding 2 km. Golf 4 km.

Open: All year.

Directions

From Freiburg take B31 road signed Donaueschingen to Kirchzarten where site is signed (it is south of the village). GPS: 47.96042, 7.95083

Charges guide

Per unit incl. 2 persons and electricity (plus meter)	€ 24.60 - € 32.80
extra person	€ 7.30 - € 10.50
child (4-15 yrs)	€ 3.80 - € 5.50
dog	€ 2.00

Every 15th day free.

Klein Rönnau

Klüthseecamp Seeblick

Klüthseehof 2, D-23795 Klein Rönnau (Schleswig-Holstein) T: **045 518 2368.** E: **info@kluethseecamp.de**

alanrogers.com/DE3008

Klüthseecamp Seeblick is a modern, family run site situated on a small hill between two lakes. It is an ideal location for a family holiday with activities on site for all ages and a useful base to explore the region. The large, open grass, touring part of the site has sunny, shaded and semi-shaded areas on offer. There are 120 touring pitches on fairly level ground, all with electricity (10/16A) and 30 with water and drainage, and pitches for tents in natural surroundings. Klüthseecamp offers wellness, a swimming pool, food and drink, organised entertainment for young and old, and a sandy lakeside beach.

Facilities

Two modern, heated sanitary blocks, some washbasins in cabins, five bathrooms to rent and free showers. Facilities for disabled visitors including electric vehicle. Baby room. Gas. Laundry. Wellness. Sauna, steam bath, massage. Bar and café in main building, additional beer garden and restaurant by the lake. Play room/kindergarten. Bouncy castle. Three small play areas. Electronic games, table football, table tennis and large LCD projected TV. Bicycle hire. Go-kart hire. Minigolf. Way-marked paths around lake. Motorcaravan services. Kids' and teenagers' clubs including weekly disco. Off site: Golf 6 km. Beach 25 km.

Open: All year.

Directions

Site is 26 km. west-northwest of Lübeck. Leave A1 at exit 27 and travel north towards Kiel on the A21 to exit 13 (Bad Segeberg Sud). Follow B432 (Hamburger Strasse) into Bad Segeberg and at T-junction with Ziegelstrasse turn left (north) and continue on B432. 300 m. after Klein Rönnau turn right into Stripsdorferweg. Site is signed. GPS: 53.96142, 10.33737

Charges guide

Per unit incl. 2 persons and electricity	€ 26.30
extra person	€ 7.50

Camping Cheques accepted.

Koblenz

Camping Gülser Moselbogen

Am Gülser Moselbogen 20, Güls, D-56072 Koblenz (Rhineland Palatinate) T: 026 144 474.
E: info@moselbogen.de alanrogers.com/DE3222

This site is set well above the river and has a pleasant outlook to the forested valley slopes. A large proportion of the 16-acre site is taken up by privately owned bungalows, but the touring section of 125 large individual pitches is self contained and accessed by gravel paths leading off the main tiled roads. Some pitches have little or no shade, but all have 11/16A electricity and there are water points in each section. An area of gravel hardstanding has been developed and RVs are accepted.

Facilities
Entry to the excellent, heated sanitary building is by a coded card that also operates the hot water to the showers (free to the washbasins, many of which are in cabins). Unit for disabled visitors. Baby room. Cooking rings (charged). Laundry. Gas supplies. Motorcaravan services. Shop, bar/café/takeaway (1/4-31/10). Play area. Bicycle hire. Off site: Fishing and special area for swimming in the Mosel 200 m. Restaurant 500 m. Güls village 1.5 km. Riding 3 km. Cycling.

Open: All year.

Directions
Site is about 6 km. west of Koblenz. From A61 take exit 38 in direction Winningen. After 1 km. right at roundabout and then straight on towards Winningen (do not follow Güls/camping sign to the left) then left on the B416 towards Koblenz. Site is on the right after 3.5 km. GPS: 50.33257, 7.55308

Charges guide

Per unit incl. 2 persons and electricity	€ 21.50 - € 22.00
extra person	€ 6.00

Köln-Poll

Campingplatz der Stadt Köln

Weidenweg 35, D-51105 Köln-Poll (North Rhine-Westphalia) T: 022 183 1966.
E: die-eckardts@netcologne.de alanrogers.com/DE3205

The ancient city of Cologne offers much for the visitor. This wooded park is pleasantly situated along the river bank, with wide grass areas on either side of narrow tarmac access roads with low wire mesh fencing separating it from the public park and riverside walks. Of 140 unmarked, level or slightly undulating touring pitches, 50 have 10A electricity and there is shade for some from various mature trees. Tents have their own large area. Because of its position close to the autobahn bridge over the Rhine, there is road and river noise.

Facilities
The toilet block, which has been totally renovated, is heated with free hot water (06.00-12.00, 17.00-23.00) in washbasins and by 50 cent coin in the showers. New facilities for disabled visitors. Large open-fronted room for cooking and eating with microwave oven. Washing machine and dryer. Small shop for bread and basic supplies (mid May-Sept). Evening snacks (March-Oct). Fishing. Bicycle hire. Drinks machine. WiFi (charged). Off site: Bar/café by entrance. Trams and buses to city centre 1 km. across the bridge. Golf 5 km. Riding 15 km.

Open: 1 April - 16 October.

Directions
Leave A4 at exit 13 for Köln-Poll (just to west off intersection of A3 and A4). Turn left at first traffic lights and follow international site signs through a sometimes fairly narrow one-way system to the riverside, back towards the motorway bridge. GPS: 50.90438, 6.99188

Charges guide

Per unit incl. 2 persons and electricity	€ 19.00 - € 21.50
extra person	€ 6.00
child (4-12 yrs)	€ 3.00

Krün-Obb

Alpen-Caravanpark Tennsee

Am Tennsee 1, D-82494 Krün-Obb (Bavaria (S)) T: 088 251 70. E: info@camping-tennsee.de
alanrogers.com/DE3680

Tennsee is an excellent, friendly site in truly beautiful surroundings high up (1,000 m) in the Karwendel Alps with super mountain views, and close to many famous places of which Innsbruck (44 km) and Oberammergau (26 km) are two. Mountain walks are plentiful, with several lifts close by. It is an attractive site with good facilities including 164 serviced pitches with individual connections for electricity (up to 16A and two connections), gas, TV, radio, telephone, water and waste water. The other 80 pitches all have electricity and some of these are available for overnight guests at a reduced rate.

Facilities
The first class toilet block has underfloor heating, washbasins in cabins and private units with WC, shower, basin and bidet for rent. Unit for disabled guests. Baby bath, dog bathroom and a heated room for ski equipment (with lockers). Laundry facilities. Motorcaravan services. Gas supplies. Cooking facilities. Shop. Restaurants and takeaway. Bar. Youth room. Solarium. Bicycle hire. Playground. WiFi (charged). Activities and excursions. Bus service to ski slopes in winter. Off site: Fishing 400 m. Riding and golf 3 km. Alpspitz-Wellenbad in Garmisch -Partenkirchen and Karwendel Bad in Mittenwald.

Open: All year excl. 6 November - 15 December.

Directions
Site is just off main Garmisch-Partenkirchen - Innsbruck road no. 2 between Klais and Krün, 15 km. from Garmisch watch for small sign 'Tennsee & Barmsee' and turn right there for site. GPS: 47.49066, 11.25396

Charges 2012

Per unit incl. 2 persons	€ 23.00 - € 26.00
extra person	€ 7.50 - € 8.00
child (6-16 yrs)	€ 3.00 - € 4.00
electricity (per kWh)	€ 0.70
dog	€ 3.30

Senior citizens special rates (not winter).

Lahnstein

Camping Burg Lahneck

Ortsteil Oberlahnstein, D-56112 Lahnstein (Rhineland Palatinate) T: 026 212 765

alanrogers.com/DE3220

The location of this site is splendid, high up overlooking the Rhine valley and the town of Lahnstein – many of the pitches have their own super views. It consists partly of terraces and partly of open grassy areas, has a cared for look and all is very neat and tidy. One can usually find a space here, though from early July to mid August it can become full. There are 100 individual touring pitches marked but not separated and mostly level, all with electricity (16A). Campers are sited by the management. Reception staff at the site are friendly and charges reasonable.

Facilities

The single central, heated toilet block is of a good standard, and very well maintained. There are some cabins for both sexes. Showers are on payment. Washing machine and dryer. Restaurant with terrace. Motorcaravan services. Gas supplies. Small shop. Small playground. Off site: Café/restaurant adjoining site; meals also in Burg Lahneck restaurant. Town swimming pool (15/5-31/8). Tennis nearby. Riding 500 m. Bicycle hire 2 km. Fishing 3 km. Bad Ems thermal baths 12 km.

Open: Easter/1 April - 31 October.

Directions

From B42 road bypassing Lahnstein, take Oberlahnstein exit and follow signs 'Kurcentrum' and Burg Lahneck. GPS: 50.30832, 7.61664

Charges guide

Per unit incl. 2 persons and electricity (plus meter)	€ 20.00 - € 22.00
extra person	€ 6.00
child (3-14 yrs)	€ 3.00
dog	€ 1.00

No credit cards.

Leipzig

Campingplatz Auensee

Gustav-Esche Strasse 5, D-04159 Leipzig (Saxony) T: 034 146 51600. E: info@camping-auensee.de

alanrogers.com/DE3847

It is unusual to find a good site in a city, but this large, neat and tidy site is one. It is far enough away from roads and the airport to be reasonably peaceful during the day and very quiet overnight and has 168 pitches, all for short-term tourers. It is set in a mainly open area with tall trees and attractive flower beds, with some chalets and 'trekker' cabins for rent in the adjoining woodland, home to shoe-stealing foxes. The individual, numbered, flat grassy pitches are large (at least 100 sq.m), all with electricity and five on hardstanding, arranged in several sections. There is a separate area for young people with tents.

Facilities

Five central sanitary buildings with WCs, washbasins in cabins and showers. Well equipped rooms for babies and disabled visitors (key access). Kitchen and laundry rooms. Motorcaravan service point. Bar/restaurant and snack bar (all year). Entertainment rooms. Multisport court. Several play areas. Barbecue area. English usually spoken. Off site: Public transport to the city centre every 15 mins. from just outside the site (tickets from reception). Supermarkets 15-20 minutes walk.

Open: All year.

Directions

Site (not well signed) is in an area called Wahren. Best approached from A9 exit 17, turning towards Leipzig on B181 Merseberger Str. After 8 km. turn left on Ludwig Hupfeld. At T-junction, turn left across a railway and immediately right. After crossing two canals, site is on left in 100 m. GPS: 51.36975, 12.31400

Charges guide

Per person	€ 5.00 - € 6.00
pitch	€ 3.00 - € 9.00
electricity (16A)	€ 2.00

Leiwen

Landal Sonnenberg

D-54340 Leiwen (Rhineland Palatinate) T: 065 079 3690. E: info@landal.de

alanrogers.com/DE3245

Sonnenberg is a pleasant hilltop site reached from the attractive riverside wine village of Leiwen by a 4 km. twisty climb from which there are wonderful views of the Mosel valley. It has a splendid free leisure centre incorporating an indoor activity pool with paddling pool, whirlpool, cascade and slides. Also in this building are ten-pin bowling, sauna, solarium and fitness room, tennis and badminton, plus a snack bar. Combining a bungalow complex (separate) with camping, the site has 140 large, individual and numbered grass/gravel pitches on terraces with electricity (6A) and TV connections.

Facilities

The single toilet block has underfloor heating, washbasins in cabins (all for women, a couple for men). It is stretched in busy times. Separate suite for disabled visitors. Large laundry. Indoor dishwashing. Motorcaravan services. Shop. Restaurant, bistro, bar and snacks. Indoor leisure centre with activity pool, climbing wall, 10-pin bowling, tennis and badminton. Minigolf. Playground. Bicycle hire (high season). Disco, entertainment and excursions at various busy times. Deer park. Off site: Fishing 5 km. Riding and golf 12 km.

Open: 23 March - 1 November.

Directions

From A48/A1 (Trier - Koblenz) take new exit 128 for Bekond, Föhren, Hetzerath and Leiwen. Follow signs for Leiwen and in town follow signs for Ferienpark, Sonnenberg or Freibad. GPS: 49.80378, 6.89257

Charges guide

Per unit incl. 2 persons and electricity	€ 22.40 - € 37.00
extra person	€ 5.20
dog	€ 3.00

No credit cards. Special 5, 8 or 10 day rates.

Limburg an der Lahn

Lahn Camping

Schleusenweg 16, D-65549 Limburg an der Lahn (Hessen) T: 064 312 2610. E: info@lahncamping.de

alanrogers.com/DE3265

Pleasantly situated directly on the bank of the river Lahn between the autobahn and the town of Limburg, the site is a useful overnight stop for travellers along the Köln-Frankfurt stretch of the A3. The site is on level grass with 200 touring pitches, each approximately 50-60 sq.m. One hundred an forty have 6A electricity, but may need long cables. There are some trees giving a degree of shade, but it is mainly open. The site is very popular with many nationalities and can become very crowded at peak times, so arrive early. There is some road and rail noise day and night. No arrivals between 13.00-15.00.

Facilities

The main sanitary block is old and facilities are rather tired. A better quality, heated block is at the far end of the site. Showers (by token). Laundry facilities. Cookers. Gas supplies. Motorcaravan services. Bar/restaurant (evenings and Sundays) and takeaway. Small shop (not Sunday p.m). Fishing (permit on payment). Play area. WiFi.
Off site: Swimming pool opposite. Supermarkets, shops and restaurants in town. Pleasure cruises. Riding 5 km.

Open: 5 April - 28 October.

Directions

Leave A3 autobahn at Limburg-Nord exit and follow road towards town. Turn left at traffic lights just before the bridge over River Lahn into Schleusenweg. Site is on right, just past the swimming pool. GPS: 50.38897, 8.07388

Charges 2012

Per unit incl. 2 persons and electricity	€ 20.60
extra person	€ 4.80

No credit cards.

Lindau

Camping Gitzenweiler Hof

Gitzenweiler 88, D-88131 Lindau-Gitzenweiler (Bavaria (S)) T: 083 829 4940. E: info@gitzenweiler-hof.de

alanrogers.com/DE3650

Gitzenweiler Hof is a really well equipped, first-class site with quality amenities. Set in the countryside with 620 pitches, 320 for touring units arranged in rows with access roads, all are numbered and have 6/16A electricity. A separate open area is for tents, with 30 electrical connections; 56 of the pitches have water, drainage and TV connections. A large outdoor swimming pool has attractive surrounds. This is a friendly, well run site with lots of activities for children. A member of Leading Campings group.

Facilities

The toilet blocks have been beautifully renovated and include some washbasins in cabins, a children's bathroom and baby bath. Laundry facilities. Motorcaravan services. Shop (limited hours in low season). Two restaurants with takeaway. Large swimming pool in summer (33x25 m). Three playgrounds, one with water, and play room with entertainment during the holidays. Organised activities. Small animals and ponies for children. Fishing in lake. Minigolf. Cinema. Club room with arcade games, library and WiFi. American motorhomes accepted up to ten tons. Overnight parking for motorcaravans outside all year.

Open: 15 April - 6 November.

Directions

Site is signed from the B12 4 km. north of Lindau. Also from A96 exit 3 (Weißensberg), and from in and around Lindau. GPS: 47.58331, 9.68331

Charges guide

Per unit incl. 2 persons and electricity	€ 26.50 - € 32.00
extra person	€ 7.00
child (3-15 yrs)	€ 2.50 - € 4.50
dog	€ 2.50

Overnight hardstanding with electricity outside barrier € 15.80.

Lorch

Naturpark Camping Suleika

Im Bodental 2, D-65391 Lorch am Rhein (Hessen) T: 067 269 464. E: suleika-camping@t-online.de

alanrogers.com/DE3225

On a steep hillside in the Rhine-Taunus Nature Park and approached by a narrow and steep system of lanes through the vineyards, this site is steeply arranged on small terraces up the side of the wooded hill with a stream flowing through – the water supply is direct from springs. The surroundings are most attractive, with views over the vineyards to the river below. Of the 100 pitches, 50 are available for touring units. These are mostly on the lower terraces, in groups of up to four units. All have electricity (16A Europlugs) and there are water points. Cars are parked away from the pitches near the entrance.

Facilities

The excellent toilet block is heated in cool weather and provides some washbasins in cabins for each sex and a nicely furnished baby washroom, with WC, shower and bath. Laundry service. Motorcaravan services. Gas supplies. Restaurant (closed Mon. and Thurs). Small shop (bread to order). Playground. Some entertainment in season. Off site: The Rheinsteig footpath passes above the site. Fishing 300 m. Riding 4 km. Bicycle hire 8 km. Touring and wine tasting in the Rhine valley.

Open: 15 March - 31 October.

Directions

Site is 8 km. NW of Rudesheim. Direct entrance road from B42 (cars only), between Rudesheim and Lorch, with height limit of 2.25 m. under railway bridge. Higher vehicles will find the site signed on the south side of Lorch where it is reached via a one-way system (one-way for caravans and motorcaravans only - tractors/cars in the opposite direction). Follow signs. GPS: 50.02146, 7.84579

Charges guide

Per unit incl. 2 persons and electricity	€ 19.20
extra person	€ 5.60

No credit cards.

Markdorf

Camping Wirthshof

Steibensteg 12, D-88677 Markdorf (Baden-Württemberg) T: 075 449 6270. E: info@wirthshof.de

alanrogers.com/DE3465

Lying 7 km. back from the Bodensee, 12 km. from Friedrichshafen, this friendly site with excellent facilities will be of interest to Britons with young children as well as those seeking a tranquil holiday in a delightful region. The 280 individual touring pitches have electrical connections (6-12A) and are of about 80 sq.m. on well tended flat grass, adjoining access roads. There are 78 larger (120 sq.m) pitches with water, waste water and electricity and 30 hardstandings for motorcaravans. Dogs are only accepted by prior arrangement, on pitches in a reserved area.

Facilities

The three heated toilet blocks provide washbasins in cubicles, a unit for disabled visitors and two children's bathrooms. Cosmetic studio. New beauty spa. Laundry facilities. Gas. Motorcaravan services. Restaurant/bar with takeaway. Shop. Swimming pool (25x12.5 m; 10/5-10/9). Sports field. Adventure playgrounds. Bicycle and electric bike hire. Minigolf and 'pit-pat'. Activities. Crafts room. WiFi (charged). Dogs are not accepted in July/Aug. Off site: Tennis. Riding 8 km. Golf and fishing 10 km.

Open: 15 March - 30 October.

Directions

Site is on eastern edge of Markdorf, turn south off B33 Ravensburg road. The site is signed (but not named) from Markdorf, immediately off the main B33. GPS: 47.71459, 9.40924

Charges guide

Per unit incl. 2 persons and electricity	€ 24.50 - € 27.70
extra person	€ 6.50 - € 7.60
child (1-14 yrs)	€ 3.80 - € 4.80

No credit cards.

Mesenich

Family Camping

Wiesenweg 25, D-56820 Mesenich bei Cochem (Rhineland Palatinate) T: 026 734 556.

E: info@familycamping.de alanrogers.com/DE3232

Situated beside the River Mosel with views of forest and vineyard, this attractive (Dutch/German) family run site is on a stretch of the river. Most of the 100 touring pitches are separated by vines, they are mainly level, with electricity hook-ups (6/10A), and some have shade. There are 25 pitches with their own water tap and 27 tents available for rent. The site roads are relatively narrow and are not suitable for larger units especially American RVs or twin-axle caravans. On arrival you must stop in the layby on the approach road while booking in at reception. Good English is spoken.

Facilities

Well equipped, heated toilet facilities provide good sized showers (€ 0.50), washbasins mainly in cubicles or curtained. Good baby room. Laundry facilities. Shop, bar. Takeaway (1/5-15/9). Swimming pools (1/6-15/9, weather dependant). Play area. Disco evenings and wine tours in July/Aug. River fishing (with permit). Internet access. Dogs are not accepted in July/Aug. Off site: Bicycle hire 300 m. Golf 7 km. Riding 10 km. Wine museum. Cochem with its castle and leisure centre 15 km. Cycle paths. Wine tasting. Touring the Mosel.

Open: 21 April - 3 October.

Directions

Site is 40 km. SW of Koblenz on the eastern banks of the Mosel river. It is signposted in the village of Mesenich. GPS: 50.10151, 7.19391

Charges guide

Per unit incl. 2 persons	€ 12.00 - € 15.00
extra person	€ 4.00

No credit cards.

München

Camping München-Obermenzing

Lochhausenerstrasse 59, D-81247 München (Bavaria (S)) T: 089 811 2235.

E: campingplatz-obermenzing@t-online.de alanrogers.com/DE3635

On the northwest edge of Munich, this site makes a good stopover for those wishing to see the city or spend the night. The flat terrain is mostly covered by mature trees, giving shade to most pitches. Caravan owners have a special section of 130 individual drive-through pitches, mainly separated from each other by high hedges and opening off the hard site roads with easy access. These have 10A electricity connections and 15 have water and drainage also. About 200 tents and motorcaravans are taken on quite large, level grass areas, with an overflow section, so space is usually available.

Facilities

The central sanitary block is large, having been extended, and together with a new Portacabin style unit, the provision should now be adequate. Cleaning is satisfactory. Heating in low season. Hot showers require tokens, as do some washbasins. Cooking facilities on payment. Washing machine and dryers. Gas supplies. Motorcaravan services. Shop (from May). Bar (from July). TV room. No charcoal barbecues. Off site: Baker and café nearby. Riding and golf 5 km. Bicycle hire 8 km. Public transport services to the city from very close by.

Open: 15 March - 31 October.

Directions

Site is 5 km. northwest of the city centre. From Stuttgart, Nürnberg, Deggendorf or Salzburg, leave A99 at Kreuz-West, exit 8 for München-Lochhausen and turn left into Lochhausener Strasse (site signed). The site is a further 1.5 km. GPS: 48.18055, 11.44032

Charges guide

Per unit incl. 2 persons	€ 18.50 - € 21.50
extra person	€ 5.00
electricity (per kWh)	€ 0.50

No credit cards.

München

Camping Municipal München-Thalkirchen

Zentralländstrasse 49, D-81379 München (Bavaria (S)) T: 089 723 1707.

E: munichtouristoffice@compuserve.com **alanrogers.com/DE3640**

This well cared for municipal site is pleasantly and quietly situated on the southern side of Munich in parkland formed by the River Isar conservation area, 4 km. southwest of the city centre (there are subway and bus links) and tall trees offer shade in parts. The large city of Munich has much to offer and the Thalkirchen site becomes quite crowded during the season. There are 550 touring pitches, all with 10A electricity and shared water and waste water. The pitches are of various sizes (some quite small), marked by metal or wooden posts and rails. The site is very busy (and noisy) during the Beer Festival (mid September - early October), but is well maintained and kept clean.

Facilities

There are five refurbished toilet blocks, two of which can be heated, with seatless toilets, washbasins with shelf, mirror and cold water. Hot water for showers and sinks is on payment. Facilities for disabled visitors. Washing machines and dryers. Shop. Snack bar with covered terrace. Drinks machine (incl. beer). General room with TV, pool and games. Good small playground. Bicycle hire. Dormitory accommodation for groups. Office hours 07.00-23.00. Maximum stay 14 days. Off site: Restaurant 200 m. Adjacent parkland and Munich zoo.

Open: 15 March - end October.

Directions

From autobahns follow 'Mittel' ring road to southeast of the city centre where site is signed; also follow signs for Thalkirchen or the Zoo and site is close. Well signed now from all over the City. GPS: 48.08333, 11.51665

Charges guide

Per person	€ 4.70 - € 8.30
child (2-14 yrs)	€ 1.54
pitch	€ 8.00 - € 11.50
electricity	€ 2.00

Credit cards only accepted for souvenirs.

Münster

Campingplatz Münster

Laerer Werseufer 7, Wolbecker Strasse, D-48157 Münster (North Rhine-Westphalia) T: 025 131 1982.

E: campingplatz-muenster@t-online.de **alanrogers.com/DE3185**

This is a first class site on the outskirts of Münster. Of a total of 570 pitches, 120 are for touring units, each with electricity, water, drainage and TV socket. The pitches are level, most with partial hardstanding and others are separated into groups by mature hedges and a number of trees provide shade. The university city of Münster with its many historical buildings and over 500 bars and restaurants, many offering local traditional dishes, is only 5 km. from the site. The city is the main attraction in this region and well worth visiting, especially on market days (Wednesdays and Saturdays). In the campsite reception there is a large range of tourist brochures, many in English, full of useful tips.

Facilities

The two toilet blocks are well designed, modern and maintained to the highest standards. Controllable showers are token operated. Two units for disabled campers. Baby room. Cooking facilities. Washing machine, dryer and ironing facilities. Sauna. Hairdressing salon. Motorcaravan service point. Shop. Bar/restaurant. Minigolf. Play area. Beach volleyball. Chess. Tennis. Playroom for children under 8 yrs. Bicycle hire. Security barrier card deposit € 10. Off site: Public open-air swimming pool adjacent. Canoeing and fishing. Bus stop 100 m.

Open: All year.

Directions

Site is 5 km. southeast of Münster city centre. Leave A1 autobahn at exit 78 (Münster Süd) and take B51 towards Münster. After 2 km. stay on the B51 in the direction of Bielefeld/Warendorf. After 5 km. turn south (right) towards Wolbeck. Follow site signs. GPS: 51.94645, 7.68908

Charges guide

Per unit incl. 2 persons and electricity	€ 26.00
extra person	€ 6.00
child (4-11 yrs)	€ 4.00
dog	€ 3.00

Various out of season reduction from 10%-20%.

Münstertal

Ferien-Campingplatz Münstertal

Dietzelbachstrasse 6, D-79244 Münstertal (Baden-Württemberg) T: **076 367 080.**

E: **info@camping-muenstertal.de** **alanrogers.com/DE3450**

Münstertal is an impressive site pleasantly situated in a valley on the western edge of the Black Forest. It has been one of the top graded sites in Germany for 20 years, and first time visitors will soon realise why when they see the standard of the facilities here. There are 305 individual pitches in two areas, either side of the entrance road on flat gravel, their size varying from 70-100 sq.m. All have electricity (16A) and 200 have drains, many also with water, TV and radio connections. The large indoor pool with sauna and solarium, and the outdoor pool, are both heated and free. There is a large, grass sunbathing area. The health and fitness centre provides a range of treatments, massages, etc. Children are very well catered for here with a play area and play equipment, tennis courts, minigolf, a games room with table tennis, table football and pool table and fishing. Riding is popular and the site has its own stables. The latest addition is an ice rink for skating and ice hockey in winter. There are 250 km. of walks, with some guided ones organised, and winter sports with cross-country skiing directly from the site (there are courses in winter for both children and adults, and ski hire). Visitors wanting a quiet holiday are thoughtfully pitched on one side of the site, whilst more active families and children are pitched nearer the games and sports areas. The site becomes full in season and reservations, especially in July, are necessary. A member of Leading Campings Group.

Facilities

Three toilet blocks are of truly first class quality, with washbasins, all in cabins, showers with full glass dividers, baby bath, a unit for disabled visitors and individual bathrooms, some for hire. Dishwashers in two blocks. Laundry. Drying room. Motorcaravan services. Well stocked shop (all year). Restaurant, particularly good (closed Nov). Heated swimming pools, indoor all year, outdoor (with children's area). New health and fitness centre. Sauna and solarium. Games room. Bicycle hire. Tennis courses in summer. Riding. Ice rink (in winter). WiFi throughout (charged). Off site: Village amenities and train station next to site entrance. Golf 15 km. Freiburg and Basel easy driving distances for day trips.

Open: All year.

Directions

Münstertal is south of Freiburg. From A5 autobahn take exit 64, turn southeast via Bad Krozingen and Staufen and continue 5 km. to the start of Münstertal, where site is signed from the main road on the left. GPS: 47.85973, 7.76375

Charges guide

Per unit incl. 2 persons and services	€ 24.30 - € 30.30
extra person	€ 6.80 - € 8.30
child (2-10 yrs)	€ 4.50 - € 5.20
dog	€ 3.50

Maestro cards accepted.

Neuerburg

Camping In der Enz

In der Enz 25, D-54673 Neuerburg (Rhineland Palatinate) T: 065 642 660. E: info@camping-inderenz.com

alanrogers.com/DE3237

This site is just outside the town, next to the municipal swimming pool complex, and the enthusiastic Dutch owners give a very warm welcome which makes this a very pleasant place to stay. The site is bisected by the unfenced River Enz which is little more than a stream at this point. The section nearest the road is occupied by 50 long stay units. The other half, on the other side of the river with its own access road, is solely for tourers. This has 66 very large, open grass pitches, all with electricity (16A), of which 32 are multi-service with water and drainage.

Facilities

New sanitary block of very high quality with the usual facilities and provision for disabled visitors. Baby room. Kitchen and laundry. Family sauna room (extra charge). Play area. Bicycle hire. WiFi. Site is not suitable for American RVs. Off site: Swimming pool complex (May-Sept) and all-year restaurant and bar, both adjacent. Fishing, riding and tennis within walking distance. Golf 13 km.

Open: 15 January - 15 December.

Directions

Site is 15 km. northwest of Bitburg. From A60 (E29) take exit 6 and head south to Bitburg, then take road 50 west to Sinspelt. Finally turn north for 6 km. to Neuerburg, pass through town and follow camping signs to site 1.5 km. north of the town. GPS: 50.02852, 6.27266

Charges guide

Per unit incl. 2 persons	€ 19.50
extra person	€ 5.00
child (3-15 yrs)	€ 4.00
electricity (per kWh)	€ 0.50
dog	€ 2.00

Nürnberg

Knaus Campingpark Nürnberg

Hans Kalb Strasse 56, D-90471 Nürnberg (Bavaria (N)) T: 091 198 12717. E: nuernberg@knauscamp.de

alanrogers.com/DE3610

This is an ideal site for visiting the fascinating and historically important city of Nürnberg (Nuremberg). There are 160 shaded pitches, 118 with 10A electrical connections and with water taps in groups. On mainly flat grass among the tall trees, some pitches are marked out with 'ranch' style boards, others still attractively 'wild', some others with hardstanding. There is sufficient space for them to be quite big and many have the advantage of being drive through. When there is an event at the Stadion there is a lot of noise and road diversions are in place. It is well worth checking before planning an arrival.

Facilities

A brand new heated sanitary building offers first class facilities including free showers. Washing machines and dryers. Cooking facilities. Unit for disabled visitors. Gas supplies. Motorcaravan services. Shop. Bar/bistro area with terrace and light meals served. Play area in woodland. Off site: Swimming pool (free entry for campers) and football stadium 200 m. Boat launching 2 km. City centre 4 km. (a 20 minute walk following signs takes you to the underground station).

Open: All year.

Directions

Site is 4 km. southeast of the city centre. From the A9 (München - Bayreuth) east of Nürnberg, take exit 52 (Nürnberg-Fischbach). Proceed 5 km. on dual carriageway towards city turning left at first traffic lights (Burger King) under two bridges and follow road around to the left and the site. GPS: 49.42318, 11.12154

Charges guide

Per person	€ 6.70
child (3-14 yrs)	€ 3.00
pitch	€ 12.30
electricity	€ 2.50
dog	€ 2.00

No credit cards.

Neuenburg

Gugel's Dreiländer Camping

Oberer Wald 3, D-79395 Neuenburg-am-Rhein (Baden-Württemberg) T: 076 317 719.
E: info@camping-gugel.de alanrogers.com/DE3455

Set in natural heath and woodland, Gugel's is an attractive site with 220 touring pitches, either in small clearings in the trees, in open areas or on a hardstanding section used for overnight stays. All have electricity (16A), and some also have water, waste water and satellite TV connections. Opposite is a meadow where late arrivals and early departures may spend the night. There may be some road noise near the entrance. The site may become very busy in high season and on bank holidays but you should always find room. The excellent pool and wellness complex add to the attraction of this all year site. There is a social room with satellite TV where guests are welcomed with a glass of wine and a slide presentation of the attractions of the area. The Rhine is within walking distance. Neuenburg is ideally placed not only for enjoying and exploring the south of the Black Forest, but also for night stops when travelling from Frankfurt to Basel on the A5 autobahn. The permanent caravans, set away from the tourist area with their well-tended gardens, enhance rather than detract from the natural beauty.

Facilities

Three good quality, heated sanitary blocks include some washbasins in cabins. Baby room. Facilities for disabled visitors. Laundry facilities. Motorcaravan services. Shop. Excellent restaurant. Takeaway (weekends and daily in high season). Wellness centre. Indoor/outdoor pool. Boules. Tennis. Fishing. Minigolf. Barbecue. Beach bar. Bicycle hire. Community room with TV. Activity programme (high season). Play areas. Off site: Riding 1.5 km. Golf 5 km. Neuenburg, Breisach, Freiburg, Basel and the Black Forest.

Open: All year.

Directions

From autobahn A5 take Neuenburg exit, turn left, then almost immediately left at traffic lights, left at next junction and follow signs for 2 km. to site (called 'Neuenburg' on most signs). GPS: 47.79693, 7.55

Charges 2012

Per unit incl. 2 persons and electricity	€ 26.50
extra person	€ 6.50
child (2-15 yrs)	€ 3.00
dog	€ 3.00

Discount every 10th night.

Olpe

Feriencamp Biggesee - Vier Jarheszeiten

Am Sonderner Kopf 3, D-57462 Olpe-Sondern (North Rhine-Westphalia) T: 027 619 44111.
E: info@biggesee-sondern.com alanrogers.com/DE3210

Situated on a gentle, south facing, slope that leads down to the water's edge of the Biggesee, Feriencamp Biggesee blends in well with its wooded surroundings. The 250 touring pitches, all with electricity, are arranged in circles at the top part of the site and on a series of wide terraces lower down. They are grassy with some hardstanding. From the lower part of the site there is access to a large open meadow that ends at the water's edge where swimming is permitted. The attractive Biggesee, with arms branching out into the surrounding hills, is a watersports paradise.

Facilities
Excellent heated sanitary facilities are in two areas. New building with cabins to hire. Washbasins in cabins and special showers for children. Facilities for babies and disabled visitors. Laundry. Motorcaravan services. Cooking facilities. Shop. Restaurant. Bistro (including breakfast). Playroom. Playground. Grill hut. Fishing. Bicycle hire. Solarium and sauna. Entertainment and excursions. Dog shower. Off site: Restaurant and snacks 300 m. (Easter-31/10). Tennis. Riding 8 km. Golf 12 km.

Open: All year.

Directions
From A45 (Siegen - Hagen) autobahn, take exit 18 to Olpe (N), and turn towards Attendorn. After 6 km. turn right signed 'Erholungsanlage', then after 100 m. turn right and follow site signs.
GPS: 51.07529, 7.85323

Charges guide

Per unit incl. 2 persons and electricity	€ 20.70 - € 24.00
extra person	€ 4.10 - € 4.70

No credit cards.

Pfalzfeld

Country Camping Schinderhannes

D-56291 Hausbay-Pfalzfeld (Rhineland Palatinate) T: 06746 80280. E: info@countrycamping.de
alanrogers.com/DE3242

About 30 km. south of Koblenz, between Rhine and Mosel, this site is set in a 'bowl' of land which catches the sun all day. With trees and parkland all around, it is a peaceful and picturesque setting. There are 150 permanent caravans in a separate area from 90 short stay touring pitches on hardstanding. For longer stays, an area around the lake has a further 160 numbered pitches. These are of over 100 sq.m. on grass, some with hardstanding and all with 8A electricity. You can position yourself for shade or sun. The lake is used for swimming and fishing. Some breeds of dog not admitted.

Facilities
The sanitary buildings, which can be heated, are of a high standard with one section in the reception/shop building for the overnight pitches, and the remainder close to the longer stay places. Laundry. Bar. Restaurant with takeaway. TV area. Skittle alley. Shop (all amenities 1/3-31/10 and Xmas). Tennis. Fishing. Play area. Rallies welcome. Torches useful. WiFi in restaurant and reception areas. Off site: Boat trips. Walking. Cycle paths.

Open: All year.

Directions
Site is 28 km. south of Koblenz. From A61 Koblenz - Ludwigshafen road, take exit 43 Pfalzfeld and on to Hausbay where site is signed. If using sat nav enter Hausbayer Strasse in Pfalzfeld.
GPS: 50.10597, 7.56822

Charges guide

Per unit incl. 2 persons and electricity	€ 17.00 - € 23.00
extra person	€ 7.00

Pielenhofen

Internationaler Campingplatz Naabtal

Distelhausen 2, D-93188 Pielenhofen (Bavaria (S)) T: 094 093 73. E: camping.pielenhofen@t-online.de
alanrogers.com/DE3720

International Camping Naabtal is an attractive riverside site in a beautiful tree-covered valley and makes an excellent base for exploring the ancient city of Regensburg on the Danube and other areas of this interesting part of Germany. It is also a good overnight site for those wishing to visit or pass through Austria or the Czech Republic. The best 100 of the 270 pitches, all with electricity, are reserved for touring units. They are mainly located on the banks of the river on flat or gently sloping ground under willow and other trees. This is good walking and mountain biking country with many marked trails.

Facilities
Two original, heated toilet blocks (one renovated in 2010) are part of larger buildings and there is a newer block for the tent area. Some washbasins are in cabins, showers are on payment. First class unit for disabled campers. Washing machines and dryers. Gas supplies. Motorcaravan services. Sauna and solarium. Bar/restaurant (1/4-31/10 plus Xmas/New Year). Small shop (Easter-end Sept). Playground with imaginative apparatus. Large meeting room. Tennis. Bicycle hire. Fishing (permit required). Small boats on river. (Electric barbecues are not permitted). WiFi (free). Off site: Shop and bus service in the village 1.5 km. Golf 15 km.

Open: All year.

Directions
Site is 15 km. northwest of Regensburg. From A3 (Nürnberg - Regensburg) take exit 97 (Nittendorf). Follow road to Pielenhofen and pass under the arch (Camping Naabtal is signed from exit). Cross river and turn right to site. Site is 11 km. from autobahn exit. From A93 exit 39 onto B8 towards Nittendorf, then at Etterzhausen turn towards Pielenhofen.
GPS: 49.06959, 11.96204

Charges 2012

Per unit incl. 2 persons and electricity (plus meter)	€ 20.10
extra person	€ 5.65

No credit cards.

Prien am Chiemsee

Panorama Camping Harras

Harrasser Strasse 135, D-83209 Prien am Chiemsee (Bavaria (S)) T: 080 519 04613.
E: info@camping-harras.de alanrogers.com/DE3688

Panorama Harras is a popular, friendly site on a small, wooded peninsula by the Chiemsee, with good views to the mountains across the lake. With some near the lake, the pitches vary in size (40-70 sq.m) and most have electricity (6A). There are 80 numbered pitches marked by trees, but with no hedges, the site can look and feel crowded at busy times. A separate, all numbered section of gravel hardstanding is provided for motorcaravans and an area for tents on grass and gravel. Sailing and windsurfing are very popular here and you can swim from the shingle beach.

Facilities

Toilet facilities include family shower rooms with washbasin and toilet (no paper). Pushbutton showers need a token. Baby room. Launderette. Good unit for disabled campers. Well stocked shop. Restaurant with bar and takeaway (all open for the whole season). Beach and boat launch access from site. Off site: Bus services 1 km. in town. Boat trips on the lake. Bicycle hire 2 km. Golf and riding 5 km. Automobile museum 20 km.

Open: 5 April - 30 October.

Directions

The Chiemsee is north of the A8 (E52, E60) between Munich and Salzburg. Take exit 106 (Bernau) then north towards Prien. After 3 km, at the roundabout, turn east towards Harras (and Kreiskrankenhaus) following site signs. GPS: 47.84083, 12.37150

Charges guide

Per unit incl. 2 persons and electricity	€ 18.60 - € 21.60
extra person	€ 5.50 - € 6.80

Camping Cheques accepted.

Rabenkirchen

Camping Park Schlei-Karschau

Karschau 56, D-24407 Rabenkirchen-Faulück (Schleswig-Holstein) T: 046 429 20820.
E: info@campingpark-schlei.de alanrogers.com/DE3002

Schlei-Karschau is a pleasant, quiet site on the only Baltic Sea fjord in Germany. All you will hear is the wind from the sea and the calls of the birds. This site is ideal if you enjoy fishing or sailing, or you could visit one of the beaches on this coast, just 10 km. to the north east. The site has 160 open pitches, 60 for touring units, all with at least 6A electricity. There is no shop as yet, but bread can be ordered from a kiosk and a restaurant, with a bar and takeaway, is open in high season.

Facilities

The single sanitary block includes controllable hot showers in cabins with washbasin, child-size toilets and washbasins and facilities for disabled visitors. Washing machines and dryers. Campers' kitchen with fridge. Motorcaravan services. Shop. Restaurant and bar (daily in high season). New playground. Sports field. Children's activity programme six days a week in high season. River fishing (permits from reception). Bicycle hire. Motor boat hire. Off site: Golf 4 km. Riding 6 km.

Open: All year

Directions

Follow the A7 from Hamburg north to Flensburg and take exit Schleswig - Schuby. Take the B201 road towards Kappeln. Drive through Süderbrarup and turn right 5 km. after village to Faulück. Follow signs to site. GPS: 54.61960, 9.88415

Charges guide

Per unit incl. 2 persons and electricity	€ 19.80 - € 24.10
extra person	€ 4.30 - € 5.30
child (1-16 yrs)	€ 2.20 - € 3.20
dog	€ 2.00

Camping Cheques accepted.

Reinsfeld

Azur Camping Hunsrück

Parkstrasse 1, D-54421 Reinsfeld (Rhineland Palatinate) T: 065 039 5123. E: reinsfeld@azur-camping.de
alanrogers.com/DE3256

This quiet countryside site, spread over 20 hectares, is situated close to the French and Luxembourg borders. With 980 pitches (600 for touring units), the site is constructed with 29 circular grassed areas, each surrounded by trees, and containing no more than 25 pitches. This creates the impression that you are staying on a small site, although you do have the facilities provided by a larger one. A spacious central meadow opposite a lake is used for caravans and tents, and is separated from a playing field by a tree-lined stream. This is a quiet and relatively unknown corner of Germany.

Facilities

Six heated sanitary buildings with free hot showers, washbasins in cabins and family bathrooms to rent. Baby rooms. Facilities for disabled visitors. Laundry facilities. Motorcaravan service point. Gas and camping supplies. Comfortable restaurant/bar with takeaway. Swimming pool (heated June-Sept). Tennis. Large play area, new water play area and children's activities.

Open: All year.

Directions

Site is 20 km. southeast of Trier. Leave A1 at exit 132 (Reinsfeld) and follow sign for Reinsfeld. Continue through village and site is signed on the left just before leaving village.
GPS: 49.687053, 6.869502

Charges guide

Per unit incl. 2 persons and electricity	€ 20.00 - € 25.50
extra person	€ 5.50 - € 7.50
child (2-12 yrs)	€ 3.00 - € 4.50
dog	€ 3.00

Remagen

Camping Goldene Meile

Simrockweg 9-13, D-53424 Remagen (Rhineland Palatinate) T: **026 422 2222.**
E: **info@camping-goldene-meile.de** **alanrogers.com/DE3215**

This site is on the banks of the Rhine between Bonn and Koblenz. Although there is an emphasis on permanent caravans, there are about 200 pitches for tourers (out of 500), most with 6A electricity and 100 with water and drainage. They are either in the central, more mature area or in a newer area where the numbered pitches of 80-100 sq.m. are arranged around an attractively landscaped, small fishing lake. Just five are by the busy river and there may be some noise from the trains that run on the other side. Access to the river bank is through a locked gate. Adjacent to the site is a large complex of open-air public swimming pools (campers pay the normal entrance fee). They claim always to find space for odd nights, except perhaps at Bank Holidays. This site is in a popular area and, although busy at weekends and in high season, appears to be well run.

Facilities

The main toilet block is heated and clean, with some washbasins in cabins, showers and facilities for wheelchair users. A smaller block serves the newer pitches (no showers). Laundry and cooking facilities. Motorcaravan services. Gas. Shop, bar, restaurant and takeaway (all 1/4-30/10 and some weekends). Play areas. Entertainment for children (July/Aug). Bicycle hire. Main gate locked at 22.00 (also 13.00-15.00).
Off site: Swimming pool complex (May-Sept). Riding 1 km. Cycling and walking in the Ahr valley. Remagen, Bonn and Cologne. Boat trips on the Rhine and Mosel.

Open: All year.

Directions

Remagen is 20 km. south south east of Bonn. Site is beside the Rhine and is signposted on the N9 road just south of Remagen. GPS: 50.57428, 7.25189

Charges guide

Per unit incl. 2 persons and electricity	€ 22.80 - € 24.40
extra person	€ 6.00
child (6-16 yrs)	€ 5.00
dog	€ 1.70

Eurocards accepted.

Rheinmunster

Freizeitcenter Oberrhein

D-77836 Rheinmunster (Baden-Württemberg) T: **072 272 500.** E: **info@freizeitcenter-oberrhein.de**
alanrogers.com/DE3420

This large, well equipped holiday site provides much to do and is also a good base for visiting the Black Forest. To the left of reception are a touring area and a section of hardstanding for motorcaravans. The 285 touring pitches (out of 700 overall) all have electricity connections (mostly 16A, 3 pin, a few with 2 pin), and include 230 with water and drainage, but little shade. Two of the site's lakes are used for swimming, with roped-off areas for toddlers, and non-powered boating (the water was very clean when we visited), the third small one is for fishing. Occasional live music is organised until late and it may be noisy and rather crowded in high season.

Facilities

Seven top quality, heated toilet buildings have free hot water and very smart fittings. Some have special rooms for children, babies and families. Excellent dog shower! Family wash cabins to rent. Motorcaravan services. Gas supplies. Shop (1/4-31/10). Two restaurants (one at the lakeside), two snack bars, two terraced beer gardens and a takeaway (1/4-31-10). Play areas on sand. Small zoo. Tennis. Bicycle hire. Minigolf. Windsurf school. Swimming and boating lakes. Fishing (charged). Three small cars for hire (for those with motorcaravans to explore locally).
Off site: Supermarket 3 km. Riding 4 km. Golf 5 km.

Open: All year.

Directions

Leave A5/E35-52 at exit 51 and travel west in direction of Iffezheim. Turn south onto B36 passing through Hügelsheim to Stollhoffen where at the roundabout site is signed. GPS: 48.77243, 8.04150

Charges guide

Per unit incl. 2 persons and electricity	€ 18.50 - € 28.00
extra person	€ 5.00 - € 8.50
child (2-16 yrs)	€ 2.50 - € 6.00
dog	€ 2.50 - € 4.50

Rieste

Alfsee Ferien & Erholungspark

Am Campingpark 10, D-49597 Rieste (Lower Saxony) T: 054 649 2120. E: info@alfsee.com

alanrogers.com/DE3025

Alfsee has plenty to offer for the active family and children of all ages. It is a really good base for enjoying the many watersports activities available here on the two lakes. The smaller one has a 780 m. water-ski 'tug' ski lift style (on payment) and there is also a separate swimming area here with a sandy beach. Improvements to this already well equipped site continue. There are now over 800 pitches (many long stay but with 400 for tourers) on flat grass, all with electricity, with some shade for those in the original area. A new camping area provides 290 large, serviced pitches. A member of Leading Campings group.

Facilities

Three excellent sanitary blocks serve the original area with two new first class, heated buildings with family bathrooms (to rent), baby rooms and laundry facilities. Cooking facilities. Motorcaravan services. Gas. Shop, restaurants and takeaway (high season). Watersports. Playground, new indoor play centre and entertainment for children. Entertainment hall. Tennis. Trampoline. Minigolf. Go-kart track. Games room. Fishing. Bicycle hire. Riding. WiFi (charged). Off site: Bus service 500 m. Golf 10 km.

Open: All year.

Directions

From A1 autobahn north of Osnabrück take exit 67 for Neuenkirchen and follow signs for Rieste, Alfsee and site. GPS: 52.48597, 7.99215

Charges guide

Per unit incl. 2 persons and electricity (16A)	€ 16.90 - € 29.90
extra person	€ 3.50 - € 4.50
child (2-17 yrs)	€ 2.00 - € 3.50
dog	€ 2.00 - € 3.00

Saarburg

Landal Warsberg

In den Urlaub 1, D-54439 Saarburg (Rhineland Palatinate) T: 065 819 1460. E: info@landal.de

alanrogers.com/DE3250

From the valley a series of hairpin bends leads to this attractive hilltop site. From the site and approach road there are wonderful panoramic views of the Saar valley and the surrounding region. A large, well organised site, there are 461 numbered touring pitches of quite reasonable size on flat or slightly sloping ground, separated in small groups by trees and shrubs, with electrical connections (16A) available in most places. There are some tour operator pitches and a separate area with holiday bungalows to rent. This is a site which should appeal to all age groups. July and August are very busy.

Facilities

Three toilet blocks of very good quality provide washbasins (many in private cabins) and a unit for disabled visitors. Large launderette by reception. Motorcaravan services. Gas supplies. Shop. Restaurant and takeaway, games rooms adjacent. WiFi (charged). Swimming pool (all year). Tennis. Minigolf. Bicycle hire. Large playground. Entertainment in season for all ages. Off site: 530 m. 'Rodelbahn' toboggan and cable chair lift to the valley 300 m. Riding and fishing 5 km.

Open: 30 March - 4 November.

Directions

From Trier on road 51 site is well signed in the northwest outskirts of Saarburg off the Trierstrasse (signs also for 'Ferienzentrum') and from all round town. Follow signs up hill for 3 km. GPS: 49.61992, 6.54348

Charges guide

Per unit incl. 2 persons and electricity	€ 16.00 - € 35.00
extra person	€ 4.50 - € 5.50
dog	€ 3.00 - € 4.75

Senheim

Campingplatz Holländischer Hof

Am Campingplatz 1, D-56820 Senheim (Rhineland Palatinate) T: 026 734 660. E: holl.hof@t-online.de

alanrogers.com/DE3233

Senheim, an attractive village dominated by a church, lies along a bend of the river Moselle, surrounded on three sides by hills, and on the other by the river. An arm of the river intrudes here and a harbour for small boats has been made. A road bridge to the south of the village passes over the very last pitches at one end of the site, but this did not seem to generate any noise nuisance. The site caters mostly for tourists. All 195 touring pitches have electricity points (6/10A). Dogs are not allowed on the site, but there are a dozen pitches outside the barrier for those who have dogs.

Facilities

The main sanitary block includes washbasins (some in cubicles) and showers (by token € 0.85). Unit for disabled visitors. Laundry facilities. Other toilet facilities in a portacabin unit. Motorcaravan service point. Shop. Gas. Restaurant, snack bar, pizzeria and takeaway (with children's menu) and terrace. Playground. TV room. Games room. Sports field. River fishing. WiFi.
Off site: Cycle tracks direct from site. Tennis 300 m. Bicycle hire and ATM point 2 km. Golf 4 km. Wine tasting. Wine festivals. Boat trips.

Open: 15 April - 1 November.

Directions

Site is 42 km. SW of Koblenz on the eastern bank of the Mosel River. When travelling south on the B49 after passing Senheim, site entrance is just before the bridge, on the right. GPS: 50.08218, 7.20868

Charges guide

Per unit incl. 2 persons and electricity	€ 17.59 - € 19.40
extra person	€ 4.85
child (3-10 yrs)	€ 3.55

No credit cards.

Seelbach

Ferienparadies Schwarzwälder Hof

Tretenhofstrasse 76, D-77960 Seelbach (Baden-Württemberg) T: 078 239 60950.
E: info@campingplatz-schwarzwaelder-hof.de **alanrogers.com/DE3427**

This site lies in a wooded valley, just south of the pleasant village of Seelbach in the Black Forest. The old buildings have been replaced by very attractive ones built in the old traditional style, but containing very modern facilities. There are 180 well drained touring pitches, either grass or hardstanding, all with electricity (10A Europlug), water supply and waste water outlet. There is also space for groups in tents. Just at the entrance is the family hotel with a restaurant. Besides a comprehensive general menu, there are also menus for children and older people with smaller appetites. A short walk from the site is a well equipped municipal swimming pool and surrounding grass area. A new on-site health spa and swimming pools were under construction when we visited (May 2010). In July and August a good range of activities are organised for all ages, including a children's club. Fishing is possible in the stream which runs along the bottom of the site. The surrounding countryside is good for walking and cycling, and Europa Park is 30 km.

Facilities

Two good sanitary blocks, all heated, clean and well maintained, include many washbasins in cabins and free showers. Facilities for wheelchair users. Family rooms (free). Baby room, superb children's bathroom, child sized toilets and washbasins. Laundry facilities. Motorcaravan services. Gas supplies. Small shop (31/3-4/11). Restaurant, snacks and takeaway. New spa centre and swimming pools (outdoor 12/5-9/9, heated indoor all year). TV and club room. Playground. Sauna (free after two night stay). Children's club. Fishing. Riding. Off site: Swimming 150 m. Fishing 1 km. ATM in Seelbach 1 km. Riding 1.5 km. Golf 5 km.

Open: All year.

Directions

From A5/E35 autobahn, leave at exit 56 (Lahr). Follow road east through Lahr, until turn south to Seelbach. Go through Seelbach and the site is about 1 km. south. GPS: 48.29972, 7.94422

Charges guide

Per unit incl. 2 persons and electricity	€ 29.70 - € 32.90
extra person	€ 10.20
child (3-12 yrs)	€ 7.50
dog	€ 3.50

No credit cards.

Soltau

Röders' Park

Ebsmoor 8, D-29614 Soltau (Lower Saxony) T: 051 912 141. E: info@roeders-park.de

alanrogers.com/DE3010

Röders' Park is a most attractive site near Soltau centre (1.5 km), in a peaceful location, ideal for visits to the famous Luneburg Heath or as a stop en-route to Denmark. The site is run by the third generation of the Röders family who make their visitors most welcome (each guest receives a local information pack) and speak excellent English. There are 120 pitches (90 touring), all with 6-10A electricity and 85 with water and drainage. All pitches have satellite TV connections and WiFi. Most have hardstanding and there is reasonable privacy between pitches. The central feature of this wooded site is a small lake crossed by a wooden bridge.

Facilities

Two modern, very clean sanitary blocks (both with underfloor heating and a wood burning stove) contain all necessary facilities. Excellent, separate unit (including shower) for wheelchair users. Private bathrooms for rent. Laundry room. Motorcaravan services. Gas supplies. Simple shop. Restaurant and takeaway (all Easter-Oct). Play area. Bicycle hire. Internet (free), WiFi (on payment). Off site: Thermal swimming pool 1 km. Fishing and riding 1.5 km. Golf 3 km. 999 km. of cycle paths. Bremen and Hamburg are within a 75 km. radius.

Open: All year.

Directions

From the A7 Exit Soltau Sud then on the B3 to Soltau. In Soltau travelling in the direction of Hamburg, directly after the town's end, at the traffic island turn left into Ebsmoor Strasse. GPS: 53.00222, 9.83862

Charges guide

Per unit incl. 2 persons and electricity (plus meter)	€ 26.50
extra person	€ 6.50
child (4-13 yrs)	€ 4.00
dog	€ 2.00

Sommerach am Main

Camping Katzenkopf

Am See, D-97334 Sommerach am Main (Bavaria (N)) T: 093 819 215

alanrogers.com/DE3739

This is an excellent family run site on the banks of the Main, to the east of Wurzburg. For peace and quiet this site is likely to be at the top of the list. There are 242 pitches with some 142 for touring units. All pitches have electricity (6-16A Europlug), and 25 provide electricity, water, and drainage. Reception also houses a shop and good tourist information. Wurzburg is an important commercial and cultural centre that was substantially destroyed by bombing and has risen again from the ashes. The town is the home of the excellent Franconian wine. The village of Sommerach, a few minutes walk from the site, is surrounded by vineyards which produce a special local vintage.

Facilities

Excellent, modern toilet blocks include private cabins, free showers and facilities for disabled campers and children. Laundry facilities. Motorcaravan service point. Shop, restaurant, bar and takeaway (all open all season). Fishing. Boat launching. Sailing courses. Dogs accepted in part of the site only. Off site: Sailing. Shops and vineyards.

Open: 1 April - 23 October.

Directions

From the A3 take Kitzingen exit and turn towards Schweinfurt. After 4 km. turn right towards Sommerach. Just before the village turn left and site is well signed. GPS: 49.84163, 10.20833

Charges guide

Per unit incl. 2 persons and electricity	€ 19.90 - € 20.70
extra person	€ 5.90

No credit cards.

Stadtkyll

Landal Wirfttal

Wirftstrasse, D-54589 Stadtkyll (Rhineland Palatinate) T: 065 979 2920. E: info@landal.de

alanrogers.com/DE3212

Peacefully and attractively set in a small valley in the northern Eifel, Wirfttal is a good all-round family site with 250 numbered pitches of which 150 are for tourers. They mostly back onto fences, hedges etc. on fairly flat ground. The pitches (many on gravel) are 80 sq.m. or more, and all have electricity (8A) and TV aerial points. Five individual pitches have water and waste water points. Also part of the site, but separate from the camping, is a large holiday bungalow complex. This is a good base for rambling or mountain biking in the surrounding hills.

Facilities

One main toilet block, and two small units, all heated, some washbasins in cabins. Two indoor play areas. New shop. Restaurant and snacks. Swimming pool complex (discount for campers). Indoor pool (free) and sauna and solarium (on payment). Tennis. Minigolf. Fishing. Bicycle hire. Large adventure playground. Sports centre adjacent with squash hall. Winter sports. Bicycle and sledge hire. WiFi in restaurant. Entertainment in season.
Off site: Riding 1 km. Rambling trails.

Open: All year.

Directions

Site is 1.5 km. south of Stadtkyll on road towards Schüller. Follow signs in Stadtkyll for Haus an der See. GPS: 50.33877, 6.53753

Charges guide

Per unit incl. 2 persons and electricity	€ 15.00 - € 33.00
extra person	€ 5.20
dog	€ 4.00

Stadtsteinach

Camping Stadtsteinach

Badstrasse 5, D-95346 Stadtsteinach (Bavaria (N)) T: 092 258 00394. E: info@camping-stadtsteinach.de

alanrogers.com/DE3615

Stadtsteinach is well placed for exploring this region with its interesting towns, forest walks and the Fichtel Mountains nearby and this is a comfortable base. Occupying a quiet position in gently undulating countryside with tree-clad hills rising to the east, there are 80 static caravans and space for 100 tourers. Brick main roads give way to hard access roads with pitches on either side, all of which have electricity (16A). The site is on a gentle slope, pitches having been terraced where necessary and there are some hardstandings for motorcaravans. High hedges and trees separate pitches or groups of pitches in some areas giving the effect of camping in small clearings.

Facilities

The sanitary area is part of the administration and restaurant building, heated and of good quality. It has free hot water and some washbasins in cabins. Facilities for campers with disabilities. Motorcaravan services. Cooking rings on payment. Laundry facilities. Gas supplies. Restaurant (all year). Bread and papers from reception. Solar heated swimming pool near the entrance is free to campers (high season). Play area. Tennis. TV. Bicycle hire. Off site: Walking. Local shops 800 m. Riding 2 km.

Open: All year.

Directions

Stadtsteinach is 22 km. north of Bayreuth. Take exit 39 from the A9/E51 Nürnberg - Berlin autobahn and travel north on road 303 to Stadsteinach. Site is well signed. GPS: 50.16666, 11.51664

Charges guide

Per unit incl. 2 persons and electricity	€ 19.70 - € 22.80
extra person	€ 5.20 - € 5.70
child (4-16 yrs)	€ 2.10 - € 3.70
dog	€ 2.00

No credit cards.

Staufen

Camping Belchenblick

Münstertälerstrasse 43, D-79219 Staufen (Baden-Württemberg) T: 076 337 045.
E: info@camping-belchenblick.de alanrogers.com/DE3445

This site stands at the gateway, so to speak, to the Black Forest. Not very high up itself, it is just at the start of the long road climb which leads to the top of Belchen, one of the highest summits of the forest. The site has 230 pitches (182 for touring units), all with electrical connections (10/16A) and TV (100 also have water). On site is a small heated indoor swimming pool and adjacent is a municipal sports complex, including an outdoor pool and tennis courts. Reservation is necessary from early June to late August at this popular site. Charges include free hot water and use of the indoor pool. A little tractor will site your caravan if required. It is well situated for excursions by car to the best areas of the forest, for example the Feldberg-Titisee-Höllental circuit, and many excellent walks are possible nearby. Staufen is a pleasant little place with character. A local train runs past the site during the day.

Facilities

Three sanitary blocks are heated and have free hot water, individual washbasins (six in private cabins), plus 21 family cabins with WC, basin and shower (some on payment per night for exclusive use). Washing machine. Gas supplies. Motorcaravan services. Shop (1/3-31/10). Bar (all year). Snacks and takeaway (1/3-31/10). Indoor pool. Sauna and solarium. Tennis. Playground with barbecue area. Bicycle, funbike and skate hire. WiFi (charged). Off site: Restaurant nearby. Riding 2 km. Fishing 20 Km.

Open: All year.

Directions

Take autobahn exit for Bad Krozingen, south of Freiburg, and continue to Staufen. Site is southeast of the town and signed, across an unmanned local railway crossing near the entrance. GPS: 47.87178, 7.73667

Charges guide

Per unit incl. 2 persons and electricity	€ 21.60 - € 24.60
extra person	€ 6.00 - € 7.50
child (2-12 yrs)	€ 4.00
dog	€ 2.50

No credit cards.

Suderburg

Campingplatz am Hardausee

D-29556 Suderburg-Hösseringen (Lower Saxony) T: 058 267 676. E: info@camping-hardausee.de

alanrogers.com/DE3080

The Hardausee site is evolving from a 'seasonal only' site into a site for touring units. When we visited, there were 80 touring pitches, all with fresh water connections and 16A electricity, and 270 seasonal units, but as soon as a seasonal guest leaves, the pitch will be re-allocated for touring. Hardausee is on sloping ground although the grassy, marked pitches are mostly level. Some pitches are numbered and most are 100 sq.m or larger. The newer pitches have hardly any shade, but mature trees surround the older field. There are 45 serviced pitches with 16A electricity, fresh water and drainage.

Facilities

Three heated toilet blocks provide washbasins in cabins and free, controllable hot showers. Washing machines and dryer. Motorcaravan services. Shop (for basics). Bar, restaurant and takeaway (April-Oct, closed Mon). Large adventure playground. Cycling tours and excursions in the woods. Fishing. Lakeside beach. Off site: Bus service 200 m. Bicycle hire 300 m. Riding 1 km.

Open: 1 March - 31 October.

Directions

From Uelzen, follow 4/191 road south towards Braunschweig. Take exit for Suderburg and follow signs for Hösseringen. Site signed on right 2 km. before Hösseringen. GPS: 52.86430, 10.420414

Charges guide

Per unit incl. 2 persons and electricity	€ 20.00 - € 45.00
extra person	€ 6.00

No credit cards.

Sulzburg

Terrassen-Camping Alte Sägemühle

Badstrasse 57, D-79295 Sulzburg (Baden-Württemberg) T: 076 345 51181.

E: info@camping-alte-saegemuehle.de alanrogers.com/DE3452

This delightful site celebrated its 50th anniversary in 2005 and has erected a stone weighing several tons to commemorate the event. Situated beside a peaceful road leading only to a natural swimming pool (formerly the mill pond) and a small hotel, the site lies just beyond the picturesque old town of Sulzburg with its narrow streets. This attractive location is perfect for those seeking peace and quiet. Set in a tree -covered valley with a stream running through the centre, the site has been kept as natural as possible. It is divided into terraced areas, each surrounded by high hedges and trees. Electrical connections (16A) are available on 42 of the 45 large touring pitches, although long leads may be needed.

Facilities

In the main building, facilities are of good quality with two private cabins, separate toilets, dishwashing, washing machine and dryer. Small shop for basics, beer and local wines (all year). Torch may be useful. New room for tent guests and motorcaravan service point. Free bus and train travel in the Black Forest for guests. Off site: Natural, unheated swimming pool adjacent (June-Aug) with discount to campers. Public transport, restaurants and other shops in Sulzburg 1.5 km. Bicycle hire in Sulzburg. Riding 3 km. Fishing 8 km. Golf 12 km. Europa Park is less than an hour away.

Open: All year.

Directions

Site is easily reached (25 minutes) from autobahn A5/E35. Take exit 64 for Bad Krozingen just south of Freiburg onto the B3 south to Heitersheim, then on and up through Sulzburg, or if coming from the south, exit 65 through Müllheim, Heitersheim and Sulzburg. Reception is to the left of the road. Note: the arch in Sulzburg has only 3.1 m. height clearance. GPS: 47.83548, 7.72337

Charges guide

Per unit incl. 2 persons and electricity (plus meter)	€ 18.50 - € 21.00
extra person	€ 6.50

Tecklenburg

Regenbogen-Camp Tecklenburg

Grafenstrasse 31, D-49545 Tecklenburg-Leeden (North Rhine-Westphalia) T: 054 051 007.

E: tecklenburg@regenbogen-camp.de alanrogers.com/DE3030

This is a well designed and attractive countryside site with lots of trees and hedges where modern buildings have been built in keeping with the traditional, half timbered style of the region. There are 500 grass touring pitches arranged on large, open areas divided by tall hedges. Trees provide good shade and all pitches have electrical connections. Access from the A30 autobahn is convenient, although this is offset by the fact that some noise from the autobahn is evident in the touring pitch area. Facilities on this site are really good, from the modern pool complex, to the half timbered bar/restaurant with its wooden beams and adjoining beer garden.

Facilities

Four modern, heated toilet blocks have free showers and provision for disabled visitors. Family shower rooms to rent. Laundry facilities. Cooking facilities. Motorcaravan service point. Shop. Large traditional, timbered bar and restaurant (Easter-end Oct and Christmas). Heated pool complex with slide and paddling pool. Sauna, wellness, massage and cosmetic studio (charged). Play area. Minigolf. Off site: Riding 3 km. Golf 5 km. Fishing 6 km.

Open: 15 December - 5 November.

Directions

Leave A30/E30 autobahn at exit 13 towards Tecklenburg. Between the autobahn exit and Tecklenburg, the site is signed at a roundabout. Leeden is a village to the east of Tecklenburg, site is 2 km. from the village. GPS: 52.22947, 7.89019

Charges guide

Per unit incl. 2 persons and electricity	€ 16.90 - € 30.10
extra person	€ 4.50 - € 7.90

Tengen

Hegau Familien Camping

An der Sonnenhalde 1, D-78250 Tengen (Baden-Württemberg) T: **077 369 2470**. E: **info@hegau-camping.de**

alanrogers.com/DE3490

Located in the sunny southwest corner of Germany, this site must be one of the best we have seen. It is ultra modern in design and exceptionally high standards are maintained. Located in meadowland in a quiet rural valley close to the Swiss border, it provides excellent opportunities for walking, cycling and sightseeing. All 140 touring pitches (out of a total of 170) have electricity (16A), water and drainage, although water points are shared. The pitches are grassy and level and of a good size.

Facilities

New heated sanitary facilities include private cabins, showers, facilities for disabled visitors and for children. Three family shower rooms for rent (two also have a bath). Laundry facilities. Motorcaravan service point. Good value restaurant, small shop and bar. Indoor swimming pool, sauna and Turkish bath (charged). Games rooms with TV and computer. Play areas and new indoor play room with bouncy castle, trampoline and go-kart style track. Minigolf. Communal barbecue pit. Free WiFi throughout. Off site: Golf 20 km. Skiing for children possible in the adjoining meadows. Supermarket less than 1 km.

Open: All year.

Directions

From A81 take exit 42 on to B314. At roundabout in Tengen follow international camping signs. Turn right at supermarket on edge of village. From Kommingen follow camp signs turning left towards site at supermarket on edge of village.
GPS: 47.8244, 8.65323

Charges guide

Per unit incl. 2 persons	€ 35.00
extra person	€ 9.00
child (over 4 yrs)	€ 6.00
electricity (per kWh)	€ 0.50
dog	€ 4.00

Titisee

Camping Bankenhof

Bruderhalde 31a, D-79822 Titisee (Baden-Württemberg) T: **076 521 351**. E: **info@camping-bankenhof.de**

alanrogers.com/DE3436

This peacefully located, fairly informal woodland site, with a friendly atmosphere, is situated just beyond the western end of Lake Titisee. The 180 pitches are on sparse grass and gravel, with some shade from a variety of trees, and 30 are occupied by seasonal units. The site is generally level, although there is a separate grassy area for tents which does have a slight slope. All pitches have electric hook-ups (16A), with gravel roads, and water taps for each area. Although there is some site lighting a torch might be useful for the darker areas under the trees.

Facilities

Two sets of quality, heated sanitary facilities plus three family bath/shower rooms for rent. They include controllable hot showers and some washbasins in cubicles. A separate building houses facilities for disabled campers, and a unit for children (under 10 yrs). Kitchen (on payment). Laundry. Motorcaravan service point. Shop. Bar. Restaurant. Fitness room. TV and cinema room. Adventure play area. Youth room. Bicycle, go-kart and buggy hire. WiFi. Fishing. Off site: Golf, riding and boat launching within 3 km. Germany's highest waterfall at Triberg both around 50 km.

Open: All year.

Directions

From Freiburg take road B31 east to Titisee. Pass through the town centre and continue for 2.5 km. following camping signs. The entrance to Bankenhof is on the left. GPS: 47.88598, 8.13070

Charges guide

Per unit incl 2 persons	€ 21.00 - € 26.00
extra person	€ 7.50 - € 9.00
child (3-15 yrs)	€ 3.00 - € 3.50
electricity per kWh	€ 0.50
dog	€ 2.00

Todtnau

Camping Hochschwarzwald

Oberhäuserstrasse 6, D-79674 Todtnau-Muggenbrunn (Baden-Württemberg) T: **076 711 288**.

E: **camping.hochschwarzwald@web.de** **alanrogers.com/DE3437**

Hochschwarzwald is a small, peaceful, quality site in an attractive wooded valley high up in the Black Forest. Of 85 marked pitches (some with shade), 50 are for tourers (all with 10A electricity) on level terraces of grass and gravel. There is an area at the entrance for overnight stays in high season. This is an extremely popular area, with many summer visitors enjoying walking and cycling, but it is also ideal for winter stays, with skiing from the site. At the back of the site, as well as being able to walk in the woods, you can paddle in a flat area of the stream, which tumbles down the hill.

Facilities

The modern, heated sanitary building has good facilities with a few private cabins, a family room and a unit for disabled campers. Washing machine and dryer. Small shop for essentials. Restaurant/bar (closed Mon). Bicycle, motorbike and ski washing facilities. Off site: Walking and skiing directly from the site. Bus to Freiburg 50 m. Heated indoor pool, tennis court and ski school in Muggenbrunn. Todtnau waterfalls 3 km. Bicycle hire 5 km. Fishing 6 km. Riding 12 km. Golf 14 km. Freiburg and Titisee 25 km.

Open: All year.

Directions

Site is about 1 km. beyond Muggenbrunn on the road from Todtnau towards Freiburg.
GPS: 47.86557, 7.91617

Charges guide

Per unit incl. 2 persons and electricity	€ 18.00
extra person	€ 5.60
child (3-12 yrs)	€ 3.20
electricity (per kWh)	€ 0.50

No credit cards.

Trippstadt

Camping - Freizeitzentrum Sägmühle

D-67705 Trippstadt (Rhineland Palatinate) T: **063 069 2190**. E: **info@saegmuehle.de**

alanrogers.com/DE3258

Camping Sägmühle has been in the same family since 1950, during which time it has undergone several major developments which have turned it into a first class site. It is peacefully situated beside a lake, in a wooded valley in the heart of the Palatinate Nature Park, and there are many kilometres of walks to enjoy, as well as castles to explore. The 200 touring pitches (half the total) are at least 80 sq.m. or more on flat grass, each with electricity (4/16A) and TV connections, with plenty of water points around. There are three separate areas of pitches. One area is close to the lake and it is a pleasant change to find a site that keeps the lakeside pitches for touring units. A first class restaurant offers local and international dishes and fine local wines, and there is plenty for younger children to enjoy with fishing, swimming and boating in the lake (pedaloes for hire), a fort, minigolf and tennis.

Facilities

Each area has its own sanitary facilities, which feature private cabins, baby bathroom, facilities for disabled visitors, launderette. Motorcaravan services. Restaurant serving local specialities and takeaway (lunchtime and evening). Bread available in high season. Solarium. Tennis. Play areas. Mountain bike hire. Boules. Minigolf. Lake fishing. Beach volleyball. Entertainment daily in high season. Guided tours for ramblers and mountainbikers. Off site: Shops and bus service 10 minutes walk in Trippstadt. Wilenstein Castle (12th-century ruin) and the famous romantic Karls Valley Gorge are nearby. Riding 4 km. Golf 25 km.

Open: All year excl. 1 November - 16 December.

Directions

Site is 14 km. SSE of Kaiserslautern. From the A6, take exit 15 (Kaiserslautern West) onto B270 towards Pirmasens. Turn left after 9 km. towards Karlstal/Trippstadt and follow site signs. GPS: 49.35174, 7.78066

Charges 2012

Per unit incl. 2 persons and electricity	€ 21.10 - € 27.70
extra person	€ 6.80 - € 7.90
child (2-14 yrs)	€ 2.80 - € 3.60
dog	€ 2.20 - € 2.80

Camping Cheques accepted.

Vlotho

Camping Sonnenwiese

Borlefzen 1, D-32602 Vlotho (North Rhine-Westphalia) T: **057 338 217**. E: **info@sonnenwiese.com**

alanrogers.com/DE3180

Sonnenwiese is a first class, family run campsite where care has been taken to make everyone feel at home – there is even an insect hotel! The site is tastefully landscaped with lots of flowers, an ornamental pond crossed by a wooden bridge and large grass areas extending to the river. Situated between wooded hills to the north and bordering the Weser river to the south, this 400 pitch site offers 100 touring pitches, all with electricity and most also having water and drainage. In addition, there are special pitches with a private shower, toilet and washbasin unit. The site is particularly orientated towards families with children.

Facilities

The toilet block is modern and maintained to the highest standard. Showers are token operated. Baby room. Washing machines, dryer and ironing board. Cooking facilities. Supermarket. Panorama restaurant with good choice of dishes. Snack bar. Sauna, solarium and fitness room. Club room and room used for children's entertainment. Large adventure play area. Grass bordered lake for swimming. Fishing. Bicycle hire. WiFi (charged). Off site: Bus service from gate. Golf 4 km. Riding 5 km.

Open: All year.

Directions

Leave A2 autobahn at exit 31, 32 or 33 and head for Vlotho. In Vlotho, cross the Weser river bridge and turn right towards Rinteln and after 3 km. on the right are the entrances to two campsites. Sonnenwiese is on the left hand side at the end of the entrance road. GPS: 52.17083, 8.904

Charges guide

Per unit incl. 2 persons and electricity	€ 23.30
extra person	€ 5.40
child (5-14 yrs)	€ 3.80

No credit cards.

Userin

Camping & Ferienpark Havelberge am Woblitzsee

An den Havelbergen 1, Userin, D-17237 Gross Quassow (Mecklenburg-West Pomerania) T: 039 812 4790.
E: info@haveltourist.de **alanrogers.com/DE3820**

The Müritz National Park is a very large area of lakes and marshes, popular for birdwatching as well as watersports, and Havelberge is a large, well equipped site to use as a base for enjoying the area. It is quite steep in places with many terraces, most with shade, less in newer areas, and views over the lake. There are 400 pitches in total with 330 good sized, numbered touring pitches (most with 16A Europlug electrical connections) and 230 pitches on a newly developed area to the rear of the site with water and drainage. Pitches on the new field are level and separated by low hedges and bushes but have no shade. Over 170 seasonal pitches with a number of attractive chalets and an equal number of mobile homes in a separate area. In the high season this is a busy park with lots going on to entertain family members of all ages, whilst in the low seasons this is a peaceful base for exploring an unspoilt area of nature. A member of Leading Campings group.

Facilities

Four sanitary buildings (one new and of a very high standard) provide very good facilities, with private cabins, showers on payment and large section for children. Fully equipped kitchen and laundry. Motorcaravan service point. Small shop, modern restaurant, bar, takeaway and wellness (all 1/4-31/10). The lake provides fishing, swimming from a small beach and boats can be launched (over 5 hp requires a German boat licence). Canoes, rowing boats, windsurfers and bikes can be hired. Play areas and entertainment in high season. Internet access. Off site: Riding 1.5 km.

Open: All year.

Directions

From A19 Rostock - Berlin road take exit 18 and follow B198 to Wesenberg and go left to Klein Quassow and follow site signs.
GPS: 53.30517, 13.00133

Charges 2012

Per unit incl. 2 persons and electricity	€ 15.90 - € 31.50
extra person	€ 4.30 - € 6.80
child (2-14 yrs)	€ 1.60 - € 4.60
dog	€ 1.00 - € 4.60

Vöhl

Camping & Ferienpark Teichmann

Zum Träumen 1A, D-34516 Vöhl-Herzhausen (Hessen) T: 056 352 45. E: info@camping-teichmann.de

alanrogers.com/DE3280

Situated near the eastern end of the 27 km. long Edersee and the National Park Kellerwald-Edersee, this attractively set site is surrounded by wooded hills and encircles a six-hectare lake, which has separate areas for swimming, fishing and boating. Of the 460 pitches, 250 are for touring; all have 10A electricity and 50 have fresh and waste water connections. The pitches are on level grass, some having an area of hardstanding, and are separated by hedges and mature trees. At the opposite side of the lake from the entrance, there is a separate area for tents with its own sanitary block. The adjoining national park, a popular leisure attraction, offers a wealth of holiday/sporting activities including walking, cycling (there are two passenger ferries that take cycles), boat trips, cable car and much more. Full details are available at the friendly reception. For winter sports lovers, the ski centre at Winterberg is only 30 km. away from this all year round site. With a wide range of facilities for children, this is an ideal family site, as well as being suited to country lovers who can enjoy the forest, lakeside walks and cycle tracks in the park.

Facilities

Three good quality sanitary blocks can be heated and have free showers, washbasins (open and in cabins), baby rooms and facilities for wheelchair users. Laundry. Motorcaravan services. Café and shop (both summer only). Restaurant by entrance open all day (closed Feb). Watersports. Boat and bicycle hire. Lake swimming. Fishing. Minigolf. Tennis. Playground. Sauna. Solarium. Disco (high season). Internet access. Off site: New national park opposite site entrance. Riding 500 m. Golf 25 km. Cable car (bicycles accepted). Aquapark. Boat trips on the Edersee.

Open: All year.

Directions

Site is 45 km. from Kassel. From A44 Oberhausen - Kassel autobahn, take exit 64 for Diemelstadt and head south for Korbach. Site is between Korbach and Frankenberg on the B252 road, 1 km. to the south of Herzhausen at the pedestrian traffic lights. GPS: 51.17550, 8.89067

Charges guide

Per unit incl. 2 persons and electricity	€ 25.00 - € 29.00

Waging am See

Strandcamping Waging am See

Am See 1, D-83329 Waging-am-See (Bavaria (S)) T: 086 815 52. E: info@strandcamp.de

alanrogers.com/DE3686

This is an exceptionally big site on the banks of a large lake fed by clear alpine streams. There are some 700 pitches for touring units out of a total of over 1,200. All the grass, level touring pitches have electricity (16A) with 150 also providing water and drainage and some new 150 sq.m. super comfort pitches. As you would expect with a site of this kind, there is a considerable range of sports facilities and an extensive games and entertainment programme during July and August. A small sandy beach offers facilities for swimming in the lake (lifeguards are in attendance in the high season). A helicopter pad is next to the well staffed reception! A member of Leading Campings group.

Facilities

Good sanitary facilities include private cabins and free showers. Facilities for disabled visitors and children in the four modern blocks. 11 private bathrooms for rent. Laundry facilities. Motorcaravan service point. Shop and Internet access at reception. Restaurant and bar. Lake beach. Windsurfing. Tennis. Archery. Minigolf. Fishing. Bicycle hire. WiFi. A new 200 sq.m. indoor children's play area and a young people's games room and trampoline have been added. Off site: Golf 1 km.

Open: 1 March - 31 October.

Directions

From A8 take exit 112 and head towards Traunstein. Turn right on road no. 304 then left towards Waging. Just before bridge turn right and then right towards site. GPS: 47.9434, 12.7475

Charges guide

Per unit incl. 2 persons and electricity	€ 20.70 - € 34.70
extra person	€ 5.90 - € 7.90
child (3-15 yrs)	€ 3.50 - € 5.90
dog	€ 3.00

Wesel

Erholungszentrum Grav-Insel

Grav-Insel 1, D-46487 Wesel (North Rhine-Westphalia) T: 028 197 2830. E: info@grav-insel.com

alanrogers.com/DE3202

Grav-Insel claims to be the largest family camping site in Germany, providing entertainment and activities to match, with over 2,000 permanent units. A section for 500 touring units runs beside the water to the left of the entrance and this area has been completely renewed. These pitches, all with 10A electricity, are flat, grassy, mostly without shade and of about 100 sq.m. A walk through the site takes you past a nature reserve and to the Rhine. Despite its size, this site is very well maintained, calm, clean and spacious and this is down to the family which started it 40 years ago.

Facilities

Excellent sanitary facilities, all housed in a modern building above which is the bar/restaurant. Touring area augmented by Portacabin units to be renewed. Facilities for disabled visitors. Baby room. Launderette. Motorcaravan service point. Large supermarket. Entertainment area with satellite TV. WiFi. Solarium. Large play area on sand plus wet weather indoor area. Boat park. Sailing. Fishing. Swimming. Football (international coaching in high season). Entertainment in high season. Off site: Bus service 500 m. The town of Xanten 23 km. Nord Park Duisburg (leisure complex) 25 km.

Open: All year.

Directions

Site is 5 km. northwest of Wesel. From the A3 take exit 6 and B58 towards Wesel, then right towards Rees. Turn left at sign for Flüren, through Flüren and left to site after 1.5 km. If approaching Wesel from the west (B58), cross the Rhine, turn left at first traffic lights and follow signs Grav-Insel and Flüren. GPS: 51.67062, 6.55600

Charges guide

Per person	€ 2.00 - € 3.00
child (under 12 yrs)	€ 1.00 - € 1.50
pitch	€ 3.00 - € 6.50

Wietzendorf

Südsee-Camp

Südsee-Camp 1, D-29649 Wietzendorf (Lower Saxony) T: 051 969 80116. E: info104@suedseecamp.de

alanrogers.com/DE3070

Südsee-Camp in the Lüneburger Heide is a large well organised holiday centre where children are especially well catered for. Südsee has its own brochures that include walking, cycling and car tours. There are 497 touring pitches of varying types and sizes, all with electricity and fresh water, drainage and TV connection. Modern sanitary blocks are well maintained and contain all necessary facilities, including some areas specially built for children. Although centred around a large sandy shored lake, complete with shipwreck, the main swimming attraction is the South See Tropical swimming pool. A member of Leading Campings group.

Facilities

Twelve modern, well maintained sanitary blocks with all the expected facilities, including those for disabled visitors and private bathrooms to rent. Hot showers need a token. Special areas for children. Facilities for babies. Laundry rooms. Kitchens. Bars, restaurants and snack bars. Pool complex (on payment). Soundproofed disco. Fitness room. Bicycle and pedal car hire. Games room. Internet. Climbing wall. Jungle golf. Overnight parking outside site. Off site: Riding adjacent. Fishing 2 km. Golf 12 km.

Open: All year.

Directions

From A7 autobahn take exit 45 towards Bergen and Celle on the B3 (campsite is signed). After 6 km. turn left (site again signed). GPS: 52.931639, 9.965254

Charges guide

Per unit incl. 2 persons and electricity	€ 24.10 - € 38.00
extra person	€ 4.00 - € 5.00
child (2-18 yrs)	€ 2.50 - € 4.00
dog	€ 2.50 - € 3.50

Wolfach

Trendcamping Wolfach

Schiltacher Strasse 80, D-77709 Wolfach-Halbmeil (Baden-Württemberg) T: 078 348 59309.

E: info@trendcamping.de alanrogers.com/DE3432

This site is set in a quiet position on the side of an attractive valley in the Black Forest. If you would like to dine or wake up to beautiful views across an alpine valley and watch herds of wild deer graze in the meadows opposite, then this is the site for you. Terraced but with little shade as yet, the site has 80 fairly level touring pitches, most with electricity (10A), water and drainage, and an area which is used for tents. In front of the main building is an area of hardstanding for overnight visitors, also with electricity connections. Local attractions include the excellent waterfalls near Triberg.

Facilities

One main block has been refurbished to a very high standard and provides first class sanitary facilities including private cabins and large free showers. It also houses reception with a small shop and a restaurant (open daily). Excellent facilities for disabled visitors. Laundry facilities. Bicycle hire. Play area. WiFi (charged). No charcoal barbecues. Off site: Wolfach 2 km. Outdoor swimming pool 5 km. Golf 20 km.

Open: Week before Easter - 31 October.

Directions

From A5 Karlsruhe - Freiburg, take exit 55 Offenburg on B33/E531 to Haslach, then on 33/294 through Hausach and soon after left on 294 to Wolfach. Go through tunnel, stay on 294 for 3 km. to Halbmeil. Site on left at end of village. GPS: 48.2911, 8.2781

Charges guide

Per unit incl. 2 persons	€ 19.50 - € 23.00
child (3-14 yrs)	€ 4.50
electricity (plus € 0.60 kWh)	€ 1.50

Wulfen

Camping Wulfener Hals

Wulfener Hals Weg, D-23769 Wulfen auf Fehmarn (Schleswig-Holstein) T: 043 718 6280.

E: camping@wulfenerhals.de **alanrogers.com/DE3003**

This is a top class, all year round site suitable as a stopover or as a base for a longer stay. Attractively situated by the sea, it is a large, mature site (34 hectares) and is well maintained. It has over 800 individual pitches (half for touring) of up to 160 sq.m. in glades. Some are separated by bushes providing shade in the older parts, less so in the newer areas nearer the sea. There are many hardstandings and all pitches have electricity, water and drainage. A separate area has been developed for motorcaravans. It provides 60 extra large pitches, all with electricity, water and drainage, and some with TV aerial points, together with a new toilet block. There is much to do for young and old alike at Wulfener Hals, with a new heated outdoor pool and paddling pool (unsupervised), although the sea is naturally popular as well. The site also has many sporting facilities including its own golf courses and schools for watersports. A member of Leading Campings group.

Facilities

Five heated sanitary buildings have first class facilities including showers and both open washbasins and private cabins. Family bathrooms for rent. Facilities for children and disabled campers. Beauty, wellness and cosmetic facilities. Laundry. Motorcaravan services. Shop, bar, restaurants and takeaway (April-Oct). Swimming pool (May-Oct). Sauna. Solarium. Jacuzzi. Sailing, catamaran, windsurfing and diving schools. Boat slipway. Golf courses (18 holes, par 72 and 9 holes, par 27). Riding. Fishing. Archery. Well organised and varied entertainment programmes for children of all ages. Bicycle hire. Catamaran hire. Off site: Naturist beach 500 m. Village mini-market 2 km.

Open: All year.

Directions

From Hamburg take A1/E47 north direction Puttgarden, after crossing the bridge to Fehmarn first exit to the right to Avendorf. In Avendorf turn left and follow the signs for Wulfen and the site. GPS: 54.40805, 11.17374

Charges guide

Per unit incl. 2 persons and electricity	€ 14.60 - € 42.11
extra person	€ 4.10 - € 8.60
child (2-13 yrs)	€ 2.30 - € 2.80
child (14-18 yrs)	€ 3.60 - € 7.40
dog	€ 1.00 - € 7.50

Plus surcharges for larger pitches.
Many discounts available and special family prices.

Wolfstein

Camping am Königsberg

Am Schwimmbad 1, D-67752 Wolfstein (Rhineland Palatinate) T: 063 044 143. E: info@campingwolfstein.de

alanrogers.com/DE3255

Situated in an area between the Rhine and Mosel rivers in a nature area at the foot of the Königsberg, this is a small attractive, well maintained site with plenty of facilities. Of the 100 pitches, 70 are reserved for tourists, all with electricity, most with fresh and waste water connections. The level, grass, mainly open pitches are easily reached by tarmac site roads. A large separate meadow is for tents and has a paddling pool, communal grill and covered eating area. Trees and hedges provide some shade and division of the site. A local railway with one train an hour, passes unobtrusively close to the site. The site's Dutch managers speak very good English and obviously enjoy running the site together with its restaurant and friendly bar.

Facilities

Modern comfortable, heated sanitary block with all usual facilities including showers, free hot water and private cabins. Facilities for campers with disabilities. Laundry room. Fridge rental. Shop. Bar/restaurant (all year). Takeaway. Play cabin, play area and games room for children with entertainment daily in summer. Minigolf. Bicycle hire. Fishing. WiFi throughout (charged). Off site: Large swimming pool complex next to site (free to campers). Shops and other facilities in the village 300 m. Riding 2 km.

Open: All year.

Directions

Wolfstein is 20 km. northwest of Kaiserslautern on the B270. From A6 (Ludwigshafen - Saarbrücken) take exit 15 for Kaiserslauten West and head north towards Lauterecken. In Erfenbach left on B270 towards Lauterecken and Idar-Oberstein. Stay on the B270. Site is signed 300 m. south of the village of Wolfstein. GPS: 49.58034, 7.61883

Charges guide

Per unit incl. 2 persons and electricity	€ 21.00 - € 25.00
extra person	€ 5.50 - € 7.00
child (2-12 yrs)	€ 4.50 - € 5.00

Zwiesel

Ferienpark Arber

Waldesruhweg 34, D-94227 Zwiesel (Bavaria (N)) T: 099 228 02595. E: info@ferienpark-arber.de

alanrogers.com/DE3710

Ferienpark Arber is a large site on the edge of town with views to the hills and a stream running through it. Pleasantly situated nearly 2,000 feet up (it can be cool at night) on a slight slope, there are 300 pitches, 200 of which are individual numbered ones for tourers (some new comfort pitches), with partial shade. There are various areas, with motorcaravans taken on a flat open, grassy section, whilst for caravans there are some flat and many sloping or undulating pitches, all with electricity (some 10A Euro, most 16A German) and water points along the central roadway. One side of the park is for dog owners and there is an overnight area of hardstanding just outside the entrance.

Facilities

The two tiled sanitary blocks (one partly modernised) have some private cabins. Facilities for disabled visitors. Baby room. Laundry facilities. Mini-market. Pleasant restaurant/bar (closed November). Bicycle hire. Fishing. WiFi (charged). Off site: Indoor and outdoor pools adjacent. Ski lifts nearby.

Open: All year.

Directions

Site is on north side of Zwiesel. From A3 autobahn (Regensburg-Passau), take Deggendorf exit and then B11 to Regen, then Zwiesel. Site is signed left over a bridge on the outskirts of Zwiesel, from the B11 going to Bayerisch-Esenstein. GPS: 49.02550, 13.22067

Charges guide

Per person	€ 6.00 - € 9.00
child (2-12 yrs)	€ 3.60 - € 4.60
pitch	€ 5.50 - € 7.50
dog	€ 3.00
electricity	€ 2.80

No credit cards.

Greece

The country's coastline offers huge variety – sheltered bays and coves, golden stretches of sand with dunes, pebbly beaches, coastal caves with steep rocks and volcanic black sand and coastal wetlands.

Stretching from the Balkans in the north to the south Aegean, Greece shares borders with Albania, Macedonia, Bulgaria and Turkey.

It is above all a mountainous country – the Pindus range forms the backbone of mainland Greece, extending through central Greece into the Peloponnese and Crete. The majority of islands throughout the Aegean are in fact the mountain peaks of the now submerged landmass of Aegeis, which was once the link between mainland Greece and Asia Minor. Mount Olympus in the north of the country, known from Greek mythology as the abode of the gods, is the highest mountain (2,917 m).

Six thousand islands are scattered in the Aegean and Ionian Seas, a unique phenomenon on the continent of Europe; of these islands, only 227 are inhabited.

CAPITAL: **Athens**

Tourist Office

Greek National Tourism Organisation
4 Conduit Street, London W1S 2DJ
Tel: 020 7495 9300
Fax: 020 7287 1369
Email: info@gnto.co.uk
Internet: www.gnto.co.uk

Population

10.7 million

Climate

Greece has a Mediterranean climate with plenty of sunshine, mild temperatures and a limited amount of rainfall.

Language

Greek, but most of the people connected to tourism and the younger generations currently practise English and sometimes German, Italian or French.

Telephone

The country code is 00 30.

Currency

The Euro

Time

GMT + 2 (GMT + 3 from last Sunday in March to last Sunday in October).

Public Holidays

New Year's Day 1 Jan; Epiphany 6 Jan; Shrove Monday Orth. Easter; Independence Day 25 Mar; Easter: Good Friday, Easter Sunday and Easter Monday (Orthodox); Labour Day 1 May; Whit Sunday and Monday (Orthodox); Assumption Day 15 Aug; Ochi Day (National Fest) 28 Oct; Christmas 25/26 Dec.

Motoring

Speed limits are 100-120 km/h on highways unless otherwise posted; 50 km/h in residential areas unless otherwise marked. An international driver's licence is required. Road signs are written in Greek and repeated phonetically in English. Road tolls exist on two highways in Greece, one leading to Northern Greece and the other to the Peloponnese.

see campsite map 10

Athens

Camping Athens

198-200 Leoforos Athinon, GR-12136 Athens- Peristeri (Attica) T: **210 581 4114.**

E: **info@campingathens.com.gr** **alanrogers.com/GR8590**

Camping Athens is an all-year site, located to the west of the city and convenient for visiting Athens. The site prides itself on friendly Greek hospitality and offers 66 touring pitches most of which have 16A electricity connections. The pitches are of a reasonable size and are generally well shaded. Smaller pitches are available for tents. The two toilet blocks are of modern design and well maintained. To visit the city, there is a bus stop opposite the site entrance. The site's restaurant is most welcoming after a day's sightseeing, and a selection of Greek starters, helped along by cool wine, can be thoroughly recommended. Before coming to Athens, be sure to plan your visit programme in advance; the city is hot in summer, very busy and the traffic extremely heavy. The public transport system (bus/metro) works well, so don't plan to drive into the city yourself.

Facilities

Two modern toilet blocks. Washing machines. Shop. Bar. Takeaway food and restaurant (all May-Oct). Free WiFi over site. Excursions can be arranged. Barbecues and open fires are forbidden. Off site: Bus stop opposite site entrance with frequent service to the bus terminus at main railway station where you descend into the metro station (just in front of the bus stop) for journey to the city sites. Full travel information, including bus tickets, from reception staff (remember to validate on the bus). Bicycle hire 7 km. Beach 12 km. Golf 20 km.

Open: All year.

Directions

From the north (Thessaloniki/Lamia) E75 signed Athina - Pireas, turn right for second exit towards Korinthos E94 (old N8 road). Site is on right after 2.2 km. and well signed. From the south (Peloponissos) take Nr 8 road (Athina-Pireas). Continue towards Athens, site is 4 km. after Dafni Monastery. Keep to the right-hand lane and make a U-turn in about 1.2 km. GPS: 38.008883, 23.6721

Charges 2012

Per unit incl. 2 persons and electricity	€ 30.00
extra person	€ 8.50
child	€ 6.00

Corfu

Camping Dionysus

Dassia Kerkyra, GR-49100 Corfu (Ionian Islands) T: **266 109 1417.** E: **laskari7@otenet.gr**

alanrogers.com/GR8370

The Ionian island of Corfu is known by most as a popular tourist destination but perhaps not considered by many for camping. The hourly ferry from Igoumenitsa, takes 90 minutes to cross to Kerkyra. Many ferries from Italian ports now stop here en-route to either Igoumenitsa or Patras so it is possible to break your journey to mainland Greece. The north of the island now has some good campsites and Dionysus is amongst them, with its 107 pitches of which 55 are suitable for caravans and motorcaravans. The site, south of Dassia, slightly slopes and has been terraced in part to provide grassy pitches under old olive trees which offer some shade.

Facilities

Two excellent toilet blocks include showers, WCs and washbasins. Sinks for dishwashing. Washing machine. Chemical disposal. Small shop, bar and restaurant (all 1/6-1/10). Swimming pool (1/6-1/10). Bicycle hire. Off site: Beach, boat launch and fishing 600 m. Kerkyra 9 km. Golf 15 km.

Open: 1 April - 15 October (depending on the weather).

Directions

Most people will arrive in Corfu on one of the many ferries from either Igoumenitsa or one of the Italian ports. So, from the ferry terminal turn right initially signed Paleokastritsa. After 8 km. turn right at traffic lights signed Dassia. Site is on the right after 1 km. GPS: 39.66440, 19.84430

Charges guide

Per unit incl. 2 persons and electricity	€ 22.20 - € 26.90
extra person	€ 5.60 - € 6.50
child (4-10 yrs)	€ 3.10 - € 4.00

Corfu

Camping Karda Beach

Dassia, P.O. Box 225, GR-49100 Corfu (Ionian Islands) T: 266 109 3595. E: campco@otenet.gr

alanrogers.com/GR8375

The popular holiday island of Corfu offers many sporting and leisure activities and access to it is easy, and comparatively cheap, via one of the many ferries from either Igoumenitsa or one of the Italian ports serving the Greek mainland. Camping Karda Beach offers a quiet low season site with excellent facilities, close to the beach and the island's main town, Kerkyra. It also offers a popular high season site for families and those looking for good weather, good beaches and lots of activities close at hand. It has 127 good grassy pitches (70 for touring units) under tall trees.

Facilities

Three excellent toilet blocks include showers, WCs and washbasins. Facilities for disabled visitors. Fridges. Laundry. Chemical disposal. Bar, small shop and restaurant (open all day). Swimming pool with sunbeds. Internet access. Play area and pool. Bungalows to rent. Off site: Beach 50 m. Dassia 1-2 km. Kerkyra 12 km.

Open: 20 April - 30 October.

Directions

From the ferry terminal turn right initially signed Paleokastritsa. After 8 km. turn right at traffic lights signed Dassia. Go through Dassia and site is on the right after 1 km. just after a right hand bend. GPS: 39.685777, 19.838331

Charges guide

Per person	€ 5.80 - € 6.30
child (4-10 yrs)	€ 3.30 - € 3.50
pitch incl. car	€ 7.00 - € 10.70
electricity	€ 4.00

Delphi

Camping Delphi

Delphi-Itea km 4, GR-33054 Delphi (Central Greece) T: 226 508 2209. E: info@delphicamping.com

alanrogers.com/GR8520

Camping Delphi enjoys a stunning location on the slopes of Mount Parnassus, just four kilometres from ancient Delphi. There are some truly outstanding views over valleys of olive groves across to the Gulf of Corinth. The site's 80 fairly level pitches all offer electrical connections (6A) and some benefit from the great views. This is a well managed and well equipped site with an attractive pool and a friendly bar featuring an exhibition of paintings by Avyeris Kanatas, a former owner of the site. The prevailing ambience here is geared towards a peaceful, relaxing stay.

Facilities

Two toilet blocks, one modern and one refurbished. Facilities for disabled visitors. Washing machine. Motorcaravan service point. Shop, bar, restaurant, takeaway food (all April-Oct). Swimming pool. Tennis. Play area. Max. 1 dog. Off site: Bus stop opposite site entrance with regular service to Athens and other places of interest. Beach 13 km. Walking trails to Delphi and Chrisso.

Open: 1 April - 20 October.

Directions

From Delphi take the road towards Itea. Just after a bridge, 4 km. from Delphi, site is signed to the right. Site is 500 m. on the right. GPS: 38.478533, 22.474733

Charges guide

Per unit incl. 2 persons and electricity	€ 23.80 - € 26.30
extra person	€ 6.20 - € 6.70
child (4-10 yrs)	€ 3.95 - € 4.60

Delphi

Chrissa Camping

GR-33054 Delphi (Central Greece) T: 226 508 2050. E: info@chrissacamping.gr

alanrogers.com/GR8525

From this well kept site a free road train takes guests to Delphi which was once sacred to the god Apollo and is now the setting for some of the most important monuments of ancient Greek civilisation. The site's situation on a hill ensures stunning views across a vast olive grove to the Gulf of Corinth beyond. There are 60 pitches with electricity connections (16A). They are well shaded and mostly terraced, which means that everyone can enjoy the views. The site is attractively landscapes, with lots of flowers and round wooden cabins to rent blend in very well with the natural environment. An evening meal on the restaurant's terrace is a must.

Facilities

Modern, well maintained toilet block with British style WCs, open washbasins and controllable showers. Family shower rooms. Motorcaravan service point. Chemical disposal. Laundry room with sinks, washing machine and dryer. Dishwashing room. Shop (1/4-30/10). Bar, restaurant and takeaway (weekends only in winter). Outdoor pool and paddling pool. Barbecues are not allowed. Internet point. WiFi (charged). Off site: Distance to fishing and sailing 7 km. Beach 8 km. Skiing 18 km. Trekking opportunities close to the site include the historic E4 trekking path.

Open: All year.

Directions

Site is half way between Itea and Delphi (6 km. from each) on the E65. It is well signposted and entry is via a 300 m. lane. GPS: 38.472433, 22.45915

Charges 2012

Per unit incl. 2 persons and electricity	€ 22.50 - € 25.50

Camping Cheques accepted.

Epidavros

Camping Bekas

Gialasi, GR-21052 Ancient Epidavros (Peloponnese) T: 275 309 9930. E: info@bekas.gr

alanrogers.com/GR8625

Just 60 kilometres south of Corinth you will find the town of Ancient Epidavros, and just south of that is Camping Bekas. With 150 pitches (120 for touring) set amongst the trees you will find shade and a quiet atmosphere. Arranged along a small sand and shingle beach, the site offers opportunities for swimming, sailing and fishing. The Argolid region of the Peloponnese has much to offer the inquisitive tourist. About 12 km. south is the sanctuary of Asclepios. On a hillside lies the theatre, the most famous and best preserved of all the ancient theatres in Greece.

Facilities

Three toilet blocks include the usual facilities including two shower rooms for disabled visitors. Laundry with washing machine. Shop. Bar. Restaurant (15/5-15/9). Internet access. TV room. Sand and shingle beach. Apartments to rent. Off site: Theatre of Epidavros 12 km.

Open: 1 April - 20 October.

Directions

To avoid driving right through the town of Ancient Epidavros take the southern exit towards the town. Turn inland here down a slip road, then turn under the main road above towards the town. On entering the town turn right towards Gialasi and site is 1.6 km. on the left. GPS: 37.61855, 23.15639

Charges guide

Per person	€ 5.00 - € 5.50
child (4-10 yrs)	€ 3.20 - € 3.80
pitch incl. electricity	€ 10.00 - € 15.00

Finikounda

Camping Anemomilos

GR-24006 Finikounda (Peloponnese) T: 272 307 1120

alanrogers.com/GR8690

Small friendly site situated directly on a beautiful sandy beach, with turquoise sea and the quayside fish restaurants in the nearby village. Many German campers come here for the windsurfing, sailing and beach life generally. The site offers 80 level pitches with good shade and great views. The small picturesque village, just a few minutes walk away, is at the back of the bay. Caiques and fishing boats are drawn up all along the sandy shore, while tavernas serve their fresh catch along the water's edge.

Facilities

Two good toilet blocks include showers, WCs and washbasins. Facilities for disabled visitors. Laundry with washing machines and ironing boards. Two kitchens with sinks, electric hobs, fridges and ice machines. Bar and small shop (1/5-31/10). Beach. Off site: Restaurant opposite. Riding. Finikounda and the Inouse Islands. Tractor rides around the local villages!

Open: 1 March - 31 November.

Directions

Site is just 5 minutes walk from the centre of Finikounda. From the village head west and turn left at the end of the wide pavement. The site is 300 m. ahead. GPS: 36.8054, 21.8018

Charges guide

Per unit incl. 2 persons and electricity	€ 24.00

Finikounda

Camping Finikes

GR-24006 Finikounda (Peloponnese) T: 272 302 8524. E: camping-finikes@otenet.gr

alanrogers.com/GR8695

This site offers 80 level pitches with good shade and great views. It also has 16 apartments to rent. Some pitches have high reed screens that give good protection from the blazing Greek sun and the turquoise sea is great for swimming, windsurfing and sailing. The site is at the western corner of Finikounda Bay and has direct access to the sandy beach by crossing small natural dunes. The facilities are excellent and in low season, when there are 18 or less campers, each camper is given the keys to a WC and shower for their own personal use.

Facilities

The good toilet block includes showers, WCs and washbasins. Facilities for disabled visitors. Kitchen includes sinks, electric hobs and fridges. Laundry. Chemical disposal. Bar, small shop and restaurant. Accommodation to rent. Off site: Finikounda and the Inouse Islands. Distance to boat launching and sailing 3 km. Bicycle hire 25 km.

Open: All year.

Directions

Site is 3 km. from the centre of Finikounda. From the village head west and turn left into the site. GPS: 36.802817, 21.78105

Charges 2012

Per unit incl. 2 persons and electricity	€ 21.00 - € 24.00

No credit cards.

Gythion

Camping Gythion Bay

Mavrovouni Gythion, GR-23200 Gythion (Peloponnese) T: 273 302 2522. E: info@gythiocamping.gr

alanrogers.com/GR8685

Camping Gythion Bay has 71 unmarked pitches set amongst orange, fig, olive and pine trees and all with electricity. Some trees limit access but the owner Mr Zafirakos is dealing with this to improve the site. Indeed he has also been busy refurbishing the toilets, showers and other facilities. With a good beach alongside the site, there are good opportunities for windsurfing and storage for boards is available. This is a good starting point for excursions to the Caves of Diros and for wider exploration of Lakonia and especially Inner and Outer Mani and Sparta.

Facilities

Four toilet blocks (totally renovated) include the usual facilities plus those for disabled visitors. Sinks for dishwashing. Laundry with washing machines. Chemical disposal. Small shop (1/5-30/9) including gas. Bar (1/5-30/9). Restaurant (10/6-17/9). Play area. Fishing, windsurfing and limited boat launching. Small beach. Off site: Gythion 4 km. Bicycle hire 4 km. Riding and waterskiing 10 km.

Open: All year.

Directions

Site is about 4 km. south of the fishing port of Gythion on the road to Aeropoli. It is between two petrol stations on the left and has a wide entrance. GPS: 36.72817, 22.54614

Charges guide

Per unit incl. 2 persons and electricity	€ 23.00 - € 24.50
extra person	€ 5.50 - € 6.00
child (4-10 yrs)	€ 4.00 - € 4.50
dog	free

Igoumenitsa

Camping Kalami Beach

Plataria, GR-46100 Igoumenitsa (Epirus) T: 266 507 1211. E: info@campingkalamibeach.gr

alanrogers.com/GR8235

Set in a bay, this is a colourful, attractive family run site that leads down to a beach and the crystal clear waters of the Ionian Sea. Colour comes mainly from the beautiful bougainvillea plants that clad many site buildings, and ample shade for the 75 level, terraced pitches, all with 10A electricity, is provided mainly by olive and eucalyptus trees. From the lower pitches there are panoramic views of the island of Corfu from which, at night, lights reflect across the open water. The construction of the site with natural stone paving and a generous display of plants is totally in keeping with its well chosen setting.

Facilities

One sanitary block with British style WCs, washbasins and large showers. Second block has showers and washbasins in cabins. Chemical disposal. Dishwashing. Laundry room with sinks and washing machines and dryer (token operated). Shop. Bar and restaurant, takeaway. Beach.

Open: 20 March - 20 October.

Directions

Site is 6 km. south of Igoumenista on the E55 coastal road to Preveza. From port follow signs for Preveza. From A2 motorway keep to the left at the end and take Exit Preveza. Site is signposted towards the bottom of an incline. Entrance is very sharp right. GPS: 39.473783, 20.240817

Charges guide

Per unit incl. 2 persons and electricity	€ 25.00
extra person	€ 5.50

Discounts. 15% for low season and 10% for stays over 10 nights in high season. Credit cards accepted.

Kato Gatzea

Camping Sikia

GR-38500 Kato Gatzea (Thessaly) T: 242 302 2279. E: info@camping-sikia.gr

alanrogers.com/GR8280

Camping Sikia is an attractive, well maintained site enthusiastically run by the Pandelfi family. The site offers 80 pitches of varying sizes all with 16A electricity. They are arranged on terraces and may become quite dusty during the dry season, but most are well shaded by olive trees. There are superb views from many pitches – the sea to the south and the mountains to the north. There are also 17 apartments to rent. The calm sea and golden beaches of the Pagasitikos Gulf make this a perfect spot for family holidays. The site is just 100 m. from a sand and shingle beach on the edge of a rocky bay.

Facilities

Two modern and one refurbished sanitary blocks with British style WCs, open washbasins and preset showers. Facilities for disabled visitors are planned. Chemical disposal. Laundry area with sinks, washing machines and ironing facilities. Shop. Bar. TV room. Internet corner. Restaurant. Communal barbecue areas. Fishing. Dogs are not allowed on the beach. Off site: Bicycle hire 1 km. Riding and sailing 2 km. Pelion steam railway, boat trips to Skiathos.

Open: 1 April - 31 October.

Directions

Follow E75 south towards Lamia, turn left at sign for Volos onto E92. Follow coastal road towards Argalasti for 18 km. Site is off the coastal road on the right at Kato Gatzea immediately past Camping Hellas. GPS: 39.310267, 23.109783

Charges guide

Per unit incl. 2 persons and electricity	€ 22.90 - € 26.10
extra person	€ 7.90 - € 8.50
child (4-16 yrs)	€ 4.00

Kato Alissos

Camping Kato Alissos

GR-25002 Kato Alissos (Western Greece) T: 269 307 1249. E: demiris-cmp@otenet.gr

alanrogers.com/GR8315

Kato Alissos can be found 21 km. west of Patras, the capital of the Peloponnese and has direct access to a long beach. This is an attractive site with lemon, orange and olive trees providing a pleasant camping environment. At the heart of the site, the bar/restaurant specialises in traditional Greek cuisine and has welcome shade from a giant olive tree, said to be over 1,000 years old. There is another bar which has fine panoramic views across Patraikos Bay. Pitches here are well shaded and all are equipped with electrical connections. Various activities are organised throughout the season, including Greek folk music and dancing. Patras is Greece's third largest city and worth a visit. The city is home to St Andrew's church, the largest in the Balkans. Further afield, ancient Olympia is one of the great sites of Greek antiquity and highly recommended. Alternatively, Kalavrita is a delightful hilltop town, renowned for the monasteries of Mega Spileo and St Lavra, and best visited by the scenic Odontotos railway.

Facilities

Restaurant. Bar. Takeaway food. Shop. Playground. Tourist information. Activity and entertainment programme. Direct beach access. Off site: Fishing. Walking and cycle tracks. Riding. Patras 21 km. Kalavrita 80 km. Olympia 90 km.

Open: 1 April - 25 October.

Directions

From Patras, head west on E55 to Kato Alissos. Cross the old national road here and then follow signs to the site. GPS: 38.150092, 21.577111

Charges guide

Per unit incl. 2 persons and electricity	€ 22.10 - € 24.80
extra person	€ 5.80 - € 6.00
child (4-10 yrs)	€ 3.00 - € 3.50

Killinis

Camping Fournia Beach

Kastro, GR-27050 Killinis (Western Greece) T: 262 309 5095. E: fournia-beach@acn.gr

alanrogers.com/GR8325

The village of Kastros and the Chlemoutsi castle that towers above it can be seen for miles across the flat landscape towards the coast. Camping Fournia Beach is owned by the four Lefkaditis brothers, and their wives have ensured that this new site is awash with flowering shrubs. The site offers 90 first class pitches and modern facilities, and the bar and restaurant sit in a landscaped area high above the beach with spectacular views across the sea to Zakinthos. Steps to the beach provide private access to the sandy cove below. The brothers plan to install a swimming pool.

Facilities

Two modern toilet blocks include showers, WCs and washbasins and good facilities for disabled visitors. Laundry with washing machines, sinks and hot water. Kitchen with hobs, fridge and freezer. Shop. Restaurant and bar overlooking the sea and the island of Zakinthos. Accommodation for rent. Off site: Chlemoutsi castle.

Open: 1 April - 30 October.

Directions

Travel 61 km. south of Patras on the main road to Pyrgos. At traffic lights, turn west signed Killinis and Zakinthos. Site is well signed from here, 15 km. and past village of Kastros. Descend towards the thermal springs and go straight ahead on a left hand hairpin bend towards the beach. GPS: 37.8992, 21.1165

Charges guide

Per unit incl. 2 persons and electricity	€ 17.60 - € 21.60
extra person	€ 4.60 - € 5.40
child	€ 2.50 - € 3.10

Camping Cheques accepted.

Nafplio

Camping New Triton

Plaka Drepano, GR-21060 Nafplio (Peloponnese) T: 275 209 2128

alanrogers.com/GR8635

What do we look for in a good campsite in Greece? Given the excellent Greek weather, the answer is probably a good, flat pitch with some shade, excellent toilets and showers that are spotlessly clean, a small shop and proximity to a beach and local tavernas. Well, here you have it all! Under the control of the owners, Mr. and Mrs. George Christopoulous, this is an exceptional site with 40 good sized touring pitches under high screens, just across the road from Drepano beach. Local tavernas are within strolling distance and the town's shops are about a mile away.

Facilities

Excellent refurbished toilet blocks include showers, WCs and washbasins. Baby bath. Facilities for disabled visitors. Chemical disposal. Laundry with washing machines and ironing board. Electric hobs for cooking. Fridge and freezer. Small shop (1/6-30/9). Off site: Drepano beach, local tavernas and bars. Assini.

Open: 1 April - 30 October.

Directions

From Nafplio follow the main road west and then turn right towards Drepano. In the town follow the signs Plaka Drepano and turn left towards the coast. At the beach turn right and site is just ahead. GPS: 37.53202, 22.89165

Charges guide

Per unit incl. 2 persons and electricity € 23.00

Nea Kifissia

Camping Nea Kifissia

Potamou 60 & Dimitsanas str., Adames, GR-14564 Nea Kifissia (Attica) T: 210 807 5579. E: camping@hol.gr

alanrogers.com/GR8595

Many visitors to Greece will want to spend some time in Athens, the capital. Camping Nea Kifissia offers one of the best opportunities to do that, being in a quiet location with easy access. A small site, run personally by the Komianidou family, there are 66 level pitches, some with shade, in well kept grounds. A regular bus service runs to the Kifissia metro station for fast and regular transport to all the sights. The Acropolis, Parthenon and the Porch of Caryatids are essential viewing, as are the many museums. Athens' shops and the flea market near Monastiraki also have much to offer.

Facilities

A centrally positioned toilet block includes showers, WCs and washbasins. Chemical disposal. Washing machine. Bar and coffee shop (1/6-20/9). Swimming pool (1/6-20/9). WiFi over site. Communal barbecue area. English spoken in reception. Off site: Riding 4 km. Athens 16 km. (45 minutes by bus/metro).

Open: All year.

Directions

From Athens - Thessaloniki motorway travelling north take Kifissa exit. At roundabout, site is signposted. Under motorway, straight ahead site is again signposted to right. Travelling south, just before Mercedes garage, turn right and immediately right again. Follow camping signs. GPS: 38.09943, 23.79175

Charges guide

Per unit incl. 2 persons and electricity € 31.00

Neos Marmaras

Camping Areti

GR-63081 Neos Marmaras (Central Macedonia) T: 237 507 1430. E: info@areti-chalkidiki.gr

alanrogers.com/GR8145

If you imagine a typical Greek campsite as being set immediately behind a small sandy beach in a quiet cove with pitches amongst pine and olive trees which stretch a long way back to the small coast road, then you have found your ideal site. Camping Areti is beautifully located just off the beaten track on the peninsula of Sithonia. It has 130 pitches for touring units. The olive groves at the rear provide hidden parking spaces for caravans and boats, and small boats can be launched from the beach. The Charalambidi family maintain their site to very high standards and this is a site where visitors will not be disappointed.

Facilities

Three excellent toilet blocks include showers, WCs and washbasins. Kitchen with sinks, electric hobs and fridges. Laundry with washing machines. Chemical disposal. Small shop and restaurant. Sandy beach. Bungalows to rent. Fishing, sailing and swimming. Communal barbecues. Free WiFi over part of site. Dogs are not allowed on the beach. Off site: Riding, golf and bicycle hire 10 km. Sithonia, Mount Athos and the nearby Spalathronisia islands.

Open: 1 May - 31 October.

Directions

Although the postal address is Neos Marmaras the site is 12 km. south. So stay on the main coast road, past the casino resort at Porto Carras and 5 km. further on turn right towards the site (signed). Then turn right again down to the coast and turn left and on for 1.5 km. Turn right into site access road. Reception is 700 m. GPS: 40.024183, 23.81595

Charges guide

Per unit incl. 2 persons and electricity € 34.20 - € 38.00

No credit cards.

Olympia

Camping Alphios

GR-27065 Olympia (Western Greece) T: 262 402 2951. E: alphios@otenet.gr

alanrogers.com/GR8340

High above ancient and modern Olympia, this site enjoys spectacular views, both across the adjoining countryside and to the coast at Pyrgos. It provides 97 pitches, all have 16A electricity and many have high reed screens that provide shade. Olympia is a popular tourist destination with dozens of coaches each day bringing tourists from around the world to this small town and the adjoining archaeological sites. However, the area also offers opportunities for walking and cycling amidst some wonderful scenery and this site provides a good base for visiting the surrounding northern Peloponnese countryside.

Facilities

Two toilet blocks include showers, WCs and washbasins. Two kitchens with sinks for dishwashing, electric hobs and fridges. Laundry with washing machines. Small shop. Bar and restaurant. Small swimming pool. Off site: Ancient Olympia. Town centre within walking distance.

Open: 1 April - 15 October.

Directions

Site is at a height of 400 m. to the west of the town, about 1.5 km. from the centre. Go through the town and past the station. Turn right, then at back of the town follow signs up the hill to the site.
GPS: 37.64317, 21.61975

Charges guide

Per unit incl. 2 persons and electricity	€ 22.00

Parga

Camping Valtos

Valtos Beach, GR-48060 Parga (Epirus) T: 268 403 1287. E: info@campingvaltos.gr

alanrogers.com/GR8220

Valtos Camping lies two kilometres west of the picturesque village of Parga and just 60 m. from the beautiful sandy beach at Valtos. This is a small, friendly site with a shop, bar and restaurant. The 92 touring pitches here are of various sizes, all with electrical connections (16A). There is little grass but good shade is supplied by mulberry, lemon and olive trees. Access to the site is quite narrow and owners of larger motorcaravans will need to be careful. The 35-minute walk up over the castle hill and the steep descent through the narrow, shop-lined alleys of Parga yields magnificent views, especially from the castle walls.

Facilities

Two toilet blocks – one modern and one refurbished. Washing machine. Motorcaravan service point. Shop, bar, takeaway food and restaurant (all May-Sept). Caravans for rent. Off site: Beach, sailing, fishing and boat launching 60 m. Water taxi to Parga beach. Bicycle hire 2 km. Boat trips to the Ionian islands. Walking trails.

Open: 1 May - 30 September.

Directions

From Igoumenitsa head south towards Preveza (E55). Turn right to Parga, in Parga keep right and continue on the coastal road towards Anthousa. Watch out for Valdos sign to the left and descend to Valdos beach. At the end of the beach (Tango Club) right; site is 50 m. GPS: 39.28555, 20.389833

Charges guide

Per unit incl. 2 persons and electricity	€ 27.00

Parga

Camping Enjoy-Lichnos

Lichnos, GR-48060 Parga (Epirus) T: 268 403 1171. E: holidays@enjoy-lichnos.net

alanrogers.com/GR8225

This is a quiet campsite with attractive views of the Ionian Sea and the coastlines towards Preveza and Parga. The site has been created on a steep incline with wide terraces and pitches under constructed shade, all with electricity. The ground levels out in front of the beach and pitches here have sea views. The site has 180 touring pitches and a large area for tents under the shade of the 500-year-old olive trees. The sandy beach is the site's main attraction and various water-based activities are available.

Facilities

Unisex toilet blocks in small units are situated on each terrace with washbasins (cold water only) and solar -heated showers. Main sanitary facilities at base of site, two blocks, one of which has wheelchair access. Washing machine and ironing. Chemical disposal. Shop. Bar and beach bar. Restaurant with discount for campsite visitors and children's menu. English is spoken. Off site: Parga, ruins of Nekromanteio, island of Lefkada.

Open: 1 May - 31 October.

Directions

From Igoumenitsa head south (E55) towards Preveza. At sign for Parga turn right and follow road for 7 km. At Lichnos village turn left at Lichnos Camping and Apartments. Campsite entrance is 500 m. down steep slope.
GPS: 39.281717, 20.43395

Charges guide

Per person	€ 6.50 - € 7.00
child	€ 3.80 - € 4.00
pitch	€ 7.50 - € 8.50
electricity	€ 4.00

Pylos

Camping Navarino Beach

Gialova, GR-24001 Pylos (Peloponnese) T: 272 302 2973. E: info@navarino-beach.gr

alanrogers.com/GR8705

There are 150 pitches, most facing the beach, with 30 being directly situated alongside. All have electricity (10A) and most have good shade. The pitches are arranged in rows to ensure that all have beach access. The facilities are adequate and cleaned regularly. The staff are friendly and efficient, and there is a very good restaurant with a terrace directly by the beach. The light wind in the morning which strengthens on some afternoons makes it a great windsurfing location and boats can be moored by the beach. This site is highly recommended.

Facilities

The five toilet blocks are well situated and, even in high season, were kept very clean and never became overcrowded. There are open washbasins, hot water to showers, and communal refrigerators and freezers. A small shop sells basic provisions. Other shops within walking distance. Dogs are accepted but must be kept on a lead and out of the sea. Off site: Within walking distance of Gialova with its promenade restaurants. Pylos 6 km. Nestors Palace 12 km. Numerous places to visit.

Open: All year, full facilities Easter - October.

Directions

Directly on the National Road Pylos Kyparissia 300 m. from the village of Gialova.
GPS: 36.94764, 21.70618

Charges guide

Per unit incl. 2 persons and electricity	€ 23.00 - € 25.00
extra person	€ 6.00
child	€ 3.00

Vartholomio Ilias

Camping Ionion Beach

Glifa, GR-27050 Vartholomio Ilias (Western Greece) T: 262 309 6395. E: ioniongr@otenet.gr

alanrogers.com/GR8330

This is a very attractive and well kept site in a beautiful location by the Ionian Sea, created from former farmland by the Fligos family. Much has changed since they welcomed their first guests in 1982, when they still left plenty of space for growing potatoes. Now it is a modern site with a large pool and a paddling pool and two blocks of apartments to rent. Separated by a variety of trees and oleander bushes, there are 235 pitches with 16A electricity and of between 80 and 100 sq.m. Those at the front of the site have a view over the sea and the island of Zakynthos.

Facilities

Three excellent sanitary blocks with British style WCs and showers with washbasins in cabins. Motorcaravan service point. Turkish style chemical disposal point. Laundry room. Shop, bar, restaurant (15/4-15/11). Internet access. Swimming pool (no depth markings) and paddling pool (15/4-15/11). Excellent new play area. Off site: Ferries to Zakynthos from Kilini, ancient city of Olympia, Frankish fortress of Chlemoutsi.

Open: All year.

Directions

From Patra head south on E55 towards Pyrgos. At sign for Vartholomio, turn right in town centre, then right at sign for Glyfa and Ionion Beach. In 15 km. campsite sign is on right. Coming from the north of Greece, there is a toll for the Korinthian Gulf bridge.
GPS: 37.836617, 21.1338

Charges guide

Per unit incl. 2 persons and electricity	€ 25.90 - € 27.40
extra person	€ 5.60 - € 6.10
child (4-11 yrs)	€ 3.50 - € 4.00

Volos

Camping Hellas International

GR-38500 Kato Gatzea (Thessaly) T: 242 302 2267. E: info@campinghellas.gr

alanrogers.com/GR8285

There is a warm welcome from the English-speaking brother and sister team who own and run Camping Hellas. The campsite has been in the family since the sixties, when tourists first asked if they could camp overnight and use the facilities of the taverna. It is in a beautiful setting in a 500 year old olive grove, right next to the beach and the calm blue waters of the Pagasitikos gulf. There are around 100 pitches all with 16A electricity. Pitch sizes vary and some parts are more level than others, but shade is plentiful thanks to the olive trees.

Facilities

One modern and one old sanitary block, both very clean with British style toilets and open washbasins. Very good facilities for disabled visitors. Laundry room with sinks and washing machines, ironing facilities. Shop, bar, restaurant and takeaway from 1 May. TV room. Dogs are not allowed on the beach. Off site: Sailing 5 km. Riding and bicycle hire 18 km. Pelion steam railway, boat trips to Skiathos.

Open: 1 April - 31 October.

Directions

From the north follow the E75 towards Lamia. Turn left at sign for Volos onto E92. Follow coastal road south towards Argalasti for 18 km. Site is off coastal road on right at Kato Gatzea.
GPS: 39.310833, 23.1091

Charges guide

Per unit incl. 2 persons and electricity	€ 23.80 - € 27.50
extra person	€ 6.00 - € 7.00
child (4-16 yrs)	€ 3.50 - € 5.50

Hungary

Centrally located in Europe, Hungary comprises mountain ranges, hilly regions and flat plains, with the River Danube running along its length. The country also has over one thousand lakes, an abundance of thermal baths, Europe's largest cave system and several notable wine regions.

An increasingly popular destination, Budapest is divided into two parts by the Danube, the hilly side of Buda on the western bank and the flat plain of Pest on the eastern bank. A cruise along the river will enable you to appreciate this picturesque city with its grand buildings, romantic bridges, museums and art galleries. It also has plenty of spas to tempt you. North of the city, the Danube Bend is one of the grandest stretches of the river, along the banks of which you'll find historic towns and ruins. Further afield in the north-eastern hills, the caves at Aggtelek are another firm favourite.

One of the largest in Europe, Lake Balaton covers an area of nearly 600 square miles and is great for swimming, sailing, windsurfing and waterskiing. It has two distinct shores, the bustling south with its string of hotels, restaurants and beaches, and the north offering a quieter pace with beautiful scenery and sights.

CAPITAL: **Budapest**

Tourist Office

Hungarian National Tourist Office
46 Eaton Place, London SW1X 8AL
Tel: 00 800 36 000 000
Fax: 020 7823 1459
Email: info@gotohungary.co.uk
Internet: www.gotohungary.co.uk

Population

9.9 million

Climate

There are four fairly distinct seasons – hot in summer, mild spring and autumn, very cold winter with snow.

Language

The official language is Magyar, but German is widely spoken.

Telephone

The country code is 00 36.

Money

Currency: Hungarian Forints (HUF).
Banks: Mon-Fri 09.00-14.00, Sat 09.00-12.00.

Shops

Mon-Fri 10.00-18.00, Sat 10.00-14.00.
Food shops open Mon-Fri 07.00-19.00,
Sat 07.00-14.00.

Public Holidays

New Year; Revolution Day 15 March; Easter Mon; Labour Day; Whitsun; Constitution Day 20 Aug; Republic Day 23 Oct; All Saints Day 1 Nov; Christmas 25, 26 Dec.

Motoring

Dipped headlights are compulsory at all times but main beams should not be used in towns. Motorway stickers must be purchased for the M1 to Budapest, the M7 from Budapest to Lake Balaton and also on the M3 eastward. Also the full length of the M5 (Budapest - Kiskunfelegyhaza). Give way to trams and buses at junctions. Carrying spare fuel in a can is not permitted.

see campsite map 8

Abádszálok

Camping Füzes

Strand út 2, H-5241 Abádszálok (Jász-Nagkyun-Szolnok County) T: 59 535 345. E: info@fuzescamping.hu

alanrogers.com/HU5245

Füzes Camping is beside the beaches of one of the most popular holiday resorts in Eastern Hungary. The site is arranged with grass pitches in the shade of mature füz trees, which provide a cooler environment in the heat of the Hungarian summer. There are around 200 pitches (all for touring units) on both sides of a long tarmac access lane, including 40 with 16A electricity. The popular beaches of Abádszalók are only 200 m. away and here there are many possibilities for watersports, plus restaurants and bars to enjoy the Hungarian lifestyle.

Facilities

One basic toilet block with toilets, controllable hot showers and open style washbasins. Bar and restaurant (all season). Tisza lake with sandy beaches. Fishing. Watersports. Torch useful. German is spoken.
Off site: Fishing and beach 200 m. Boat launching 20 km.

Open: May - September.

Directions

From the M3 motorway from Budapest to the east, take the exit for Tiszafüred and continue south after passing Tiszafüred towards Abádszálok. On entering town, turn right towards the beaches and the site.
GPS: 47.47949, 20.59014

Charges guide

Per person	HUF 1400
child (under 14 yrs)	HUF 1100
pitch incl. electricity	HUF 1400

Balatonfüred

Balatontourist Camping & Bungalows Füred

Széchenyi út 24., H-8230 Balatonfüred (Veszprem County) T: 87 580 241. E: fured@balatontourist.hu

alanrogers.com/HU5090

This is a large international holiday village rather than just a campsite. Pleasantly decorated with flowers and shrubs, it offers a very wide range of facilities and sporting activities. All that one could want for a family holiday can be found here. The 890 individual pitches (60-120 sq.m), all with electricity (6/10A), are on either side of hard access roads on which pitch numbers are painted. Many bungalows are for rent. Mature trees cover about two thirds of the site giving shade, with the remaining area being in the open. Directly on the lake with 800 m. of access for boats and bathing, there is a large, grassy area for relaxation, a small beach area for children and a variety of watersports.

Facilities

Five fully equipped toilet blocks include hot water for dishwashing and laundry (cleaning and maintenance variable). Private cabins for rent. Laundry service. Numerous bars, restaurants, cafés, food bars and supermarket (15/5-15/9). Excellent swimming pool (1/6-31/8). Sandy beach. Large free water chute. Entertainment for children. Sports activities for adults. Sauna. Fishing. Water-ski lift. Windsurf school. Sailing. Pedalos. Play area. Bicycle hire. Tennis. Minigolf. Video games. WiFi (charged). Dogs are not accepted.
Off site: Riding and golf 10 km.

Open: 27 April - 30 September.

Directions

Site is just south of Balatonfüred, at the traffic circle on Balatonfüred - Tihany road is well signed. Gates closed 13.00-15.00 except at weekends.
GPS: 46.94565, 17.87709

Charges guide

Per unit incl. 2 persons and electricity	HUF 3600 - 9200
extra person	HUF 800 - 1600
child (2-14 yrs)	HUF 500 - 1200

Camping Cheques accepted.

Balatonszemes

Balatontourist Camping & Bungalows Vadvirág

Lellei u. 1-2., H-8636 Balatonszemes (Somogy County) T: 84 360 114. E: vadvirag@balatontourist.hu

alanrogers.com/HU5000

This large Balatontourist site (seven hectares) on the southern shore of Lake Balaton has a grassy beach almost 600 metres long, which is also used by day visitors. On flat grass, the 308 touring pitches are individual ones with electricity connections (10/16A). Shade is provided by a variety of trees. Windsurfing and excellent swimming are possible in the lake and there are pedaloes for hire. There is a small pool on the site. There are many sporting activities available and children's entertainment. A train line runs along the back of the site.

Facilities

Two sanitary blocks with some washbasins in cabins, six private bathrooms for hire and facilities for disabled visitors. Launderette. Motorcaravan services. Shop and bar (15/5-31/8). Takeaway. Small pool (15/5-31/8). Playground. Lake swimming with water slide. Beach volleyball. Paddle boats. Three tennis courts. Minigolf. Bicycle hire. Boat launching. Fishing. Entertainment for children. WiFi throughout (charged). Off site: Restaurants and gift shop nearby. Riding 2 km.

Open: 27 April - 16 September.

Directions

On the M7 coming from the North, take the exit for Balatonöszöd and then continue towards the no. 7 road. Turn towards the lake at km. 132, over the railway. GPS: 46.80092, 17.74019

Charges guide

Per unit incl. 2 persons and electricity	HUF 2900 - 5900
extra person	HUF 700 - 1100
child (2-14 yrs)	HUF 500 - 750
dog	HUF 500 - 750

Balatonszepezd

Balatontourist Camping Venus

Halász u. 1., H-8252 Balatonszepezd (Veszprem County) T: 87 568 061. E: venus@balatontourist.hu

alanrogers.com/HU5380

For those who want to be directly beside Lake Balaton and would like a reasonably quiet location, Camping Venus would be a good choice. Apart from the rather noisy train that regularly passes the site, this is a quiet setting with views of the lake from almost all the pitches. From the front row of pitches you could almost dangle your feet from your caravan in the warm water of the lake. There are 88 flat pitches all with at least 4/10A electricity. Varying in size (70-100 sq.m), almost all have shade.

Facilities

Two good sanitary blocks provide toilets, washbasins (open style and in cabins) with hot and cold water and preset showers. Facilities for disabled campers. Child size toilets and basins. Launderette. Motorcaravan services. Shop for basics. Bar. Restaurant. Snack bar. Playground. Daily activity programme with pottery, fairy tale reading, horse shows, tournaments in Sümeg, trips over the lake and to Budapest. Pedalo and rowing boats for hire. WiFi. Off site: Riding 3 km. Golf 14 km.

Open: 14 May - 5 September.

Directions

On the 71 road between Balatonfüred and Keszthely, site is in Balatonszepezd on the lake side of the road. GPS: 46.861051, 17.673368

Charges guide

Per unit incl. 2 persons and electricity	HUF 2750 - 6000
extra person	HUF 700 - 950
child (2-14 yrs)	HUF 550 - 750
dog	HUF 550 - 750

Budapest

Zugligeti Niche Camping

Zugligeti út 101, H-1121 Budapest (Budapest City) T: 36 12 00 83 46. E: camping.niche@t-online.hu

alanrogers.com/HU5165

Zugligeti Niche is in the Buda Hills on the starting point of the former 58 tramline, of which the main building now houses the reception, bar and restaurant. There are 80 pitches in one long row, all for tourers, mainly suitable for camper vans and caravans, and a few pitches for tents off a tarmac and gravel access road. After a sharp right turn, a sandy road takes you further uphill where there are pitches mostly for tents, varying in size from 20-40 sq.m. To the front of the site are two old tram carriages; one functions as reception and the other is a restaurant. Zugligeti Niche is popular with Italians, who park their camper vans here to enjoy a few days sightseeing in Budapest. By bus it is an easy 20 minutes to the first metro station at Moszkva Tér. From here you can visit the parliament and the royal palace and enjoy the great views on the Danube from Castle Hill (UNESCO World Heritage).

Facilities

There are two good refurbished toilet blocks with free, controllable hot showers, toilets and open style basins. Scattered around the site are several toilet blocks which include British style toilets, open washbasins and controllable showers (free). Basic shower for disabled visitors. Laundry with sinks and washing machine. Campers' kitchen. Bar/restaurant with good value meals. Torch useful. Free breakfast and free WiFi. Off site: Cable track. Budapest city centre 30 minutes by public transport.

Open: All year.

Directions

Site is in the Budapest district 12. Coming from the north follow signs for M1 and M7 motorway. Site is well signed from Moszkva Tér. GPS: 47.516383, 18.974617

Charges guide

Per unit incl. 2 persons and electricity	HUF 7500 - 8200
extra person	HUF 1800
child	HUF 900
dog	free

Budapest

Római Camping

Szentendrei út 189, H-1031 Budapest (Budapest City) T: 13 887 167. E: romaicamping@message.hu

alanrogers.com/HU5155

Római Camping is a large, but basic site with 2,000 pitches within the boundaries of Budapest, next to the Római Fürdö Aqualand centre. There are about 500 touring pitches on level, grassy fields, 180 with 4A electricity. Pitches are under mature trees that provide useful shade with access off tarmac roads. A small buffet on site provides drinks, ice cream, fruit and basics. At the Római pool complex is a good restaurant. The site is an easy half hour by public transport (first stop ten minutes walk) to the bustling and interesting city centre of Budapest.

Facilities

Basic toilet facilities (cleaned twice daily) provide British and Turkish style toilets, open washbasins and controllable, hot showers (free). Laundry with sinks, washing machine and dryer. Motorcaravan service point. Playground. Torch useful. Off site: Római open-air pool 100 m. Budapest centre 30 minutes by public transport.

Open: All year.

Directions

Coming into town from the north via main road 11, turn left at OMV petrol station. Keep right at the end and continue to keep right until Csalina utca. Turn left at crossing and take first right. Go past swimming pool and turn right again. Coming out of town, take sharp right bend 100 m. after camping sign. GPS: 47.574667, 19.051717

Charges guide

Per unit incl. 2 persons and electricity	€ 22.40 - € 27.43

No credit cards.

Cserszegtomaj

Panoráma Camping

Panoráma Köz 1, H-8372 Cserszegtomaj (Zala County) T: 83 330 215. E: matuska78@freemail.hu

alanrogers.com/HU5030

Campsites around Lake Balaton generally have the disadvantage of being close to the main road and/or the railway, as well as being extremely busy in high season. Panoráma is popular too, but is essentially a quiet site inland from the western end of the lake. It also has the benefit of extensive views from the flat, grass terraces. Only the young or very fit are advised to take the higher levels with the best views of all. The original 50 pitches vary in size from fairly small to quite large (100 sq.m), all with 10A electricity, with the lower terraces having fairly easy access. The lower part of the site is a suntrap, but the top part is shaded by mature trees. This site is for those who prefer a quiet holiday, yet still being close to the major attractions.

Facilities

A new sanitary block, with the original block, are heated and very satisfactory, with large, curtained, controllable showers (communal changing). Washing machine. Ladies' hairdresser. Massage. Small swimming pool. Off site: Many walking and cycling opportunities. Riding, bicycle hire and tennis 3 km. Fishing and boat launching 6 km. Lake Balaton 7 km. Héviz is the famous, large, thermal lake and there are castles to visit.

Open: 1 April - 31 October.

Directions

Site is 2 km. north of Héviz. From the 71 road initially follow the signs for Helvi, then take road to Sümeg. Entering Cserszegtomaj, site is off to the left via a long, hard access road with a large sign. GPS: 46.80803, 17.21248

Charges guide

Per unit incl. 2 persons	€ 12.00 - € 13.30
tent (2 persons)	€ 9.00 - € 10.00

No credit cards.

Dömös

Dömös Camping

Duna-Part, H-2027 Dömös (Komarom-Esztergom County) T: 33 482 319. E: info@domoscamping.hu

alanrogers.com/HU5110

The area of the Danube Bend is a major tourist attraction and here at Dömös is a lovely, modern, well maintained and presented, friendly, peaceful site with large pitches and easy access. There are 107 quite large pitches, of which 80 have 6A electricity, in sections on flat grass, numbered and divided by small plants and some with little shade. At the top of the site is an inviting open air swimming pool with a grass lying out area and tiny children's pool with a large bar with pool tables alongside. Sightseeing tours to Budapest, Esztergom and Szentendre are arranged. The Danube is just over 50 m. away and quite fast flowing.

Facilities

The modern sanitary building is tiled and includes large, preset hot showers with individual changing, and good facilities for children and disabled visitors. Cooking area. Laundry with washing machines and dryer. Motorcaravan services. Bar. Restaurant. Small café with terrace. Swimming pool (20x10 m, all season). WiFi. Small play area on grass. English is spoken. Off site: Fishing 50 m. Village facilities 300 m. Riding 2 km. Bicycle hire 8 km.

Open: 1 May - 15 September.

Directions

Site is between the village and the Danube, off road 11 Esztergom - Visegrad - Szentendre. GPS: 47.76545, 18.91440

Charges guide

Per unit incl. 2 persons and electricity	HUF 4440 - 5500
extra person	HUF 800 - 1300

No credit cards (cash only).

Dunaföldvár

Kék-Duna Camping

Hösök Tere 23, H-7020 Dunaföldvár (Tolna County) T: **75 541 107.**

E: **postmaster@camping_gyogyfurdo.axelero.net** **alanrogers.com/HU5300**

Dunaföldvár is a most attractive town of 10,000 people and you are in the heart of it in just two or three minutes on foot from this site, easily reached via the wide towpath on the west bank of the Danube. For a town site, Kék-Duna is remarkably peaceful. This is a pleasant small site on the banks of the Danube, fenced all round and locked at night, with flat concrete access roads to 50 pitches. All have electricity (16A), the first half being open, the remainder well shaded. Apart from the obvious attractions of the river, with a large island opposite and pleasant walks possible, the ancient town has an interesting museum.

Facilities

Older style, tiled and clean sanitary building with nicely decorated ladies' section offers curtained showers with communal changing. Dishwashing outside with cold water. Washing machine. Shop and café (from mid June), town shops nearby. Bicycle hire. Excursion information. Off site: Tennis 50 m. Thermal swimming pool 200 m. (under the same ownership). Riding 5 km.

Open: All year.

Directions

From the roundabout south of Dunaföldvár turn towards the town centre. At the traffic lights turn right and go down as far as the Danube then turn left, under the green bridge and follow the towpath about 300 m. to the site. GPS: 46.812, 18.927

Charges guide

Per unit incl. 2 persons and electricity	HUF 3400 - 3500

Eger

Öko-Park Camping

Borsod út 9, H-3323 Eger-Szarvaskö (Heves County) T: **36 352 201.** E: **info@oko-park.hu**

alanrogers.com/HU5205

Öko-Park Camping is close to the Baroque style town of Eger, on the edge of the protected Bükk National Park. Buildings on the site are all made of natural materials and there is a well used for watering the plants. Öko-Park has 45 pitches off a single gravel access lane that runs to the back of the site. The grass pitches are level, marked and numbered. All have 16A electricity and are in the shade of mature trees. There is a small adventure park on site with climbing wall, tree path and waterfall. The disadvantages are a road running alongside, a railway to the back and pitches which may be small for larger units.

Facilities

One good toilet block to the front provides toilets, open style washbasins and preset hot showers. Baby bath and changing mat. Basic facilities for disabled visitors. Washing machine and spin dryer. Campers' kitchen. Restaurant with bar for breakfast and dinner (all year). Climbing wall. Playground on gravel. Eco tours, walks and wine cave visits organised. Riding. Bicycle hire. WiFi (free). Off site: Shop nearby. Fishing 7 km. Eger 9 km.

Open: All year.

Directions

From Budapest, follow M3 motorway east and take exit for Eger. Follow to Eger and, from there, the 25 road north towards Szarvaskö. It is the second site on the right. GPS: 47.988283, 20.331017

Charges guide

Per unit incl. 2 persons and electricity	€ 20.00
extra person	€ 4.50
child (3-15 yrs)	€ 3.00
dog	€ 3.00

Györ

Gasthof Camping Pihenö

I-es föút, H-9011 Györszentivan-Kertváros (Györ-Moson-Sopron County) T: **96 523 008.**

E: **piheno@piheno.hu** **alanrogers.com/HU5120**

This privately owned site makes an excellent night stop when travelling to and from Hungary as it lies close to the M1 motorway to the east of Györ. It is set amidst pine trees with pitches which are not numbered, but marked out by small shrubs, in a small clearing or between the trees (firm pegs needed). With space for about 40 touring units, all with electrical connections (6A), and eight simple, one roomed bungalows and four en-suite rooms. On one side of the site, fronting the road, is the reception and bar (hot food available for camp guests; menu in English).

Facilities

A single, small, basic toilet block has just two showers for each sex (on payment) and curtained, communal dressing space. Baby room. Room for washing clothes and dishes with small cooking facility. Washing machine. Order bread at reception the previous evening. Bar. Restaurant with good menu and reasonable prices. Solar heated swimming pool and children's pool (10x5 m, June-Sept). Some road noise can be heard. Off site: Györ with shops and swimming pool.

Open: 1 April - 30 October.

Directions

Coming from Austria via the M1 motorway, take the exit for Györ and continue on the no. 1 road towards Budapest. Site is 3 km to the East of Györ on the left. GPS: 47.71664, 17.69997

Charges guide

Per person	€ 4.40
pitch	€ 3.40
dog	€ 0.87
electricity	€ 1.50

Less 10% for stays over 4 days, 20% after 8.

Kemeneskápolna

Vulkán Resort Camping

Szabadság út 023/2 hrsz., H-9553 Kemeneskápolna (Vas) T: **95 466 070**. E: **info@vulkanresort.com**

alanrogers.com/HU5095

Vulkán Resort has been recently developed as Hungary's first campsite built according to the five feng shui principles. The theme here is therefore one of relaxation and the site boasts an indoor and outdoor swimming pool and wellness centre with three different kinds of sauna. The surrounding Sar Hegy National Park, lying at the western end of the Kette Zeugenberger mountain range, is a popular environment for hiking and cycling. There are 50 level pitches here, all equipped with electricity (16A) and water, and several also have drainage and TV and Internet connections. The site's toilet block is modern and well maintained. Various activities are possible in the area, including hunting and fishing, and the nearby spa towns of Sárvár and Celldömölk have a good selection of shops and restaurants. A free shuttle service to the nearby spa towns is available to motorcaravan users. Unusually, the site offers stabling facilities for campers with horses and special excursions are organised for riders.

Facilities

Modern and well maintained sanitary facilities (small shower cabins). Indoor and outdoor swimming pool. Wellness centre with saunas, solarium and massage. Play area. Football field. Tennis. Stables and riding. Mobile homes for rent. Internet access. Free shuttle service for motorcaravanners. Off site: Village centre with shops and restaurants. Sárvár health resort 11 km. Lake Balaton 50 km.

Open: All year.

Directions

Heading south from Sopron on road 84 continue to Sárvár. Shortly beyond here follow signs to Gercé and Vásárosmiske and finally Kemeneskápolna from where the site is well signed.
GPS: 47.21466, 17.10043

Charges guide

Per unit incl. 2 persons and electricity	€ 18.50
extra person	€ 4.00
child (4-15 yrs)	€ 2.50
dog	free

Camping Cheques accepted.

Keszthely

Castrum Camping Keszthely

Mora Ferenc út 48, H-8360 Keszthely (Zala County) T: **83 312 120**. E: **info@castrum.eu**

alanrogers.com/HU5035

Castrum Keszthely is a large site on the southwest corner of Lake Balaton. Although it is next to the main road and a railway and there is a disco nearby, we found it surprisingly quiet at night. It is a real family site with 176 pitches, all for tourers and with electricity (6/12A). The level pitches of up to 90 sq.m. are numbered on a grass and gravel surface (firm tent pegs necessary) and are separated by hedges with shade from a variety of mature trees. It is on the wrong side of the railway that runs along the north side of Lake Balaton and therefore has no direct access to the lake or the beach. However, this is compensated for by a large, well kept outdoor pool in the centre of the site, which includes a paddling pool and sunbathing area.

Facilities

Traditional toilet blocks with British style toilets, open washbasins and preset, hot showers (free, hot water variable). Washing machine and spin dryer. Small shop for basics. Bar/restaurant. Swimming pool (25x10 m) with oval paddling pool (daily charge). Tennis. Minigolf. Daily activity programme for children in high season. Bus service to Thermal Spa. Bicycle hire. Off site: Riding, fishing and Lake Balaton 1 km. Golf 10 km.

Open: 15 April - 15 October.

Directions

Follow no. 71 road along Lake Balaton into Keszthely and then follow signs 'Castrum 2,900 metres'. Continue straight on for exactly 2,900 metres and turn right towards site.
GPS: 46.768117, 17.25955

Charges 2012

Per unit incl. 2 persons and electricity	HUF 4200 - 6500

Camping Cheques accepted.

Kiskunmajsa

Jonathermál Motel-Camping

Kökút 26, H-6120 Kiskunmajsa (Bacs-Kiskun County) T: 77 481 855. E: jonathermal@mail.datanet.hu

alanrogers.com/HU5260

Situated three kilometres to the north of the town of Kiskunmajsa, a few kilometres west of road 5 (E75) from Budapest (140 km) to Szeged (35 km) this is one of the best Hungarian campsites. The camping area is large, reached by tarmac access roads, with 250 unmarked pitches in several areas around the motel and sanitary buildings. Some shade is available and more trees are growing. All the 205 large touring pitches have electricity (6A) and are set on flat grass. Entrance to the impressive pool complex is charged (daily or weekly tickets are available - 40 per cent reduction for campsite guests).

Facilities

A heated sanitary block provides first class facilities including washbasins in cabins and a unit for disabled visitors. Second new block to the back with showers and toilets. Launderette. Gas supplies. Kiosk on site for bread and basics. etc. Smart bar and rest room. Restaurant by pool complex. Large swimming and thermal complex with other facilities (1/5-1/10). Massage (charged). New playground. Tennis. Minigolf. Fishing lake (day permits). Bicycle hire. Riding. WiFi. German spoken. Accommodation to rent. Off site: Restaurants nearby. Riding 100 m. Shop opposite entrance 120 m.

Open: All year.

Directions

From M5 motorway Budapest - Szeged, take Kiskunmajsa exit and site is well signed 3 km. north of the town on road 5402.
GPS: 46.52133, 19.74687

Charges guide

Per unit incl. 2 persons and electricity	HUF 2720 - 3200
extra person	HUF 660 - 800
child (6-14 yrs)	HUF 300 - 350
dog	HUF 350 - 500

Less 5-10% for longer stays. No credit cards.

Lenti

Castrum Thermal Camping Lenti

Tancsics M. u. 18-20, H-8960 Lenti (Zala County) T: 92 351 368. E: lenti@castrum.eu

alanrogers.com/HU5024

Camping Lenti is one of a series of thermal spa campsites in the Hungarian-Slovenian-Austrian border region. It is a well established, well kept site with friendly management, ideal for those seeking peace and quiet in combination with the healing thermal waters of the Lenti spa. There are 146 numbered and fenced pitches (40-80 sq.m) with 6A electricity connections. Pitching is in rows, off gravel access roads mostly in the shade of mature trees.

Facilities

The modern, heated toilet block is clean and well equipped with open style basins and hot showers. Washing machine and spin dryer. Restaurant and rooms housed in a modern main building. WiFi and Internet in reception. Off site: Thermal baths. Bars, takeaways and restaurants available inside the thermal bath complex. Shop 500 m.

Open: All year.

Directions

From roundabout in centre of Lenti, go west towards Rédics for a little under 1 km. Site is on the left (big blue sign) just before the railway station.
GPS: 46.61764, 16.53155

Charges guide

Per unit incl. 2 persons and electricity	HUF 3800 - 5500
extra person	HUF 900 - 1200
child (2-10 yrs)	HUF 700 - 900
dog	HUF 700 - 900

Magyaregregy

Máré Vára Camping

Várvölgy utca 2, H-7332 Magyaregregy (Baranya) T: 72 420 126. E: info@camping-marevara.com

alanrogers.com/HU5320

Máré Vára takes its name from an ancient castle situated a few kilometres down the road where the German noble family of Mariën once lived. The site is on archaeological ground: where the main house stands now, there used to be a monastery and centuries before that there was an ancient Roman settlement. Some 62 pitches (36 with 10A electricity) are on slightly sloping, well kept fields. On site is a small swimming pool (7x3 m) and across the road is a new larger pool. Modern toilet facilities are in an old barn and here in the walls one can see remains of the former monastery.

Facilities

Modern and clean toilet facilities (in a former barn) with British style toilets, open washbasins and controllable showers (free, hot water variable). Washing machine. No shop, but bread to order. Small bar with terrace for drinks and ice cream, restaurant and takeaway (1/5-30/9). Swimming pool (7x3 m) on site and larger one across the road. Playground. Social events organised. TV room with satellite, DVD and video. WiFi throughout (free). Off site: Máré Vára Castle 2.5 km. Riding 3 km.

Open: 30 April - end September.

Directions

Magyaregregy is northeast of Pécs. Site is just outside Magyaregregy on the left and well signed.
GPS: 46.233611, 18.308333

Charges 2012

Per unit incl. 2 persons and electricity	HUF 4800
extra person	HUF 1010
child (under 12 yrs)	HUF 750
dog	HUF 375

No credit cards.

Magyarhertelend

Camping Forras

Bokréta u. 105, H-7394 Magyarhertelend (Baranya) T: 72 521 110. E: bojtheforras@freemail.hu

alanrogers.com/HU5315

This well established site is close to the historic city of Pécs, in a part of Hungary with a Mediterranean style climate. Camping Forras, or 'Bij Balázc' as it is called by some Dutch guests, is also close to the Mescék National Park, where there are many marked walking routes. The site has 120 pitches, all for tourers, off gravel and grass access roads. Of these, 80 are marked and have 6A electricity connections. The remaining pitches are used mainly for tents. The whole site looks well cared for with many different varieties of trees giving a pleasant atmosphere and providing useful shade in summer.

Facilities

The traditional toilet block provides acceptable facilities with British style toilets, open washbasins and controllable showers (free). Washing machine and spin dryer. Bar with library. Basic playground. Minigolf. Torch useful.
Off site: Fishing 3 km. City of Pécs is nearby.

Open: 7 May - 30 September.

Directions

From Pécs, take no. 66 road north towards Sásd. Turn left in Magyarszék towards Magyarhertelend and follow signs. Site is just outside the village on the left. GPS: 46.190883, 18.141767

Charges guide

Per unit incl. 2 persons and electricity	HUF 3200

No credit cards.

Martfü

Martfü Health & Recreation Centre

Tüzép út, H-5435 Martfü (Jász-Nagkyun-Szolnok County) T: 56 580 531. E: martfu@camping.hu

alanrogers.com/HU5255

The Martfü campsite is a modern site with 61 touring pitches on grassy terrain with rubber hardstandings. Each is around 90 sq.m. and separated by young bushes and trees. All have electricity (16/25A), waste water drainage, cable and satellite TV. There is a water tap per two pitches. There is no shade as yet, which may cause the site to become a real suntrap in summer, when temperatures may rise up to 34 degrees. A small lake and its beach on the site will cool you off. The main attraction at this site is the thermal spa, which is said to aid people with skin and rheumatic problems.

Facilities

Two modern, heated toilet blocks with British style toilets, open style washbasins, and free, controllable hot showers. Children's toilet and shower. Heated baby room. En-suite facilities for disabled visitors. Laundry. Kitchen with cooking rings. Motorcaravan services. Shop for basics. Takeaway for bread and drinks. Welcoming bar with satellite TV and WiFi. Indoor and outdoor swimming pools. Bowling. Library. Sauna. Jacuzzi. Playing field. Tennis. Minigolf. Fishing. Bicycle hire. Watersports. English is spoken. Off site: Fishing 50 m. Boat launching 1.5 km. Riding 5 km.

Open: All year.

Directions

Driving into Martfü from the north on the 442 road, take the first exit at the roundabout (site is signed). Continue for about 800 m. and site is signed on the right. GPS: 47.019933, 20.268517

Charges guide

Per person	HUF 1200
child (6-14 yrs)	HUF 600
pitch	HUF 900 - 1200

No credit cards.

Pannonhalma

Panorama Camping

Fenyvesalja 4/A, H-9090 Pannonhalma (Györ-Moson-Sopron County) T: 96 471 240.
E: info@borbirodalum.hu **alanrogers.com/HU5130**

In 1982 this became the first private enterprise campsite in Hungary. It offers a very pleasant outlook and peaceful stay at the start or end of your visit to this country, situated just 20 km. southeast of Györ, on a hillside with views across the valley to the Sokoro hills. The 70 numbered and hedged touring pitches (50 with 16A electricity, long leads necessary) are on terraces, generally fairly level but reached by fairly steep concrete access roads, with many trees and plants around. Some small hardstandings are provided. There are benches provided and a small, grass terrace below reception from where you can purchase beer, local wine and soft drinks, etc.

Facilities

Good sanitary facilities are in a small building near reception and a larger unit halfway up the site. Curtained, hot showers with curtained communal changing. Hot water for dishwashing and laundry. Cooking facilities. Bar and meals (1/6-31/8). Shop. Recreation room with TV and games. Small play area and small pool (cleaned once a week). No charcoal barbecues. No English is spoken. Off site: Hourly bus service to Györ. Shop for essentials 150 m. Good value restaurant 400 m. away in the village. Riding 3 km. Fishing 4 km.

Open: 1 May - 31 August.

Directions

From no. 82 Györ - Veszprém road turn to Pannonhalma at Ecs. Site is well signed – the final approach road is fairly steep.
GPS: 47.54915, 17.7578

Charges guide

Per unit incl. 2 persons and electricity	HUF 4900
extra person	HUF 1000
child (2-14 yrs)	HUF 500
dog	HUF 450

No credit cards.

Révfülöp

Balatontourist Camping Napfény

Halász u. 5, H-8253 Révfülöp (Veszprem County) T: 87 563 031. E: napfeny@balatontourist.hu

alanrogers.com/HU5370

Camping Napfény, an exceptionally good site, is designed for families with children of all ages looking for an active holiday, and has a 200 m. frontage on Lake Balaton. The site's 370 pitches vary in size (60-110 sq.m) and almost all have shade – very welcome during the hot Hungarian summers – and 6-10A electricity. As with most of the sites on Lake Balaton, a train line runs just outside the site boundary. There are steps to get into the lake and canoes, boats and pedaloes for hire. An extensive entertainment programme is designed for all ages and there are several bars and restaurants.

Facilities

The three excellent sanitary blocks have toilets, washbasins (open style and in cabins) with hot and cold water, spacious showers (both preset and controllable), child size toilets and basins, and two bathrooms (hourly charge). Heated baby room. Facilities for disabled campers. Launderette. Dog shower. Motorcaravan services. Supermarket. Several bars, restaurants and souvenir shop. Children's pool. Sports field. Minigolf. Fishing. Bicycle hire. Canoe, rowing boats and pedalo hire. Extensive entertainment programme for all ages. WiFi throughout (charged). Off site: Tennis 300 m. Riding 3 km.

Open: 27 April - 30 September.

Directions

Follow road 71 from Veszprém southeast to Keszthely. Site is in Révfülöp.
GPS: 46.829469, 17.640164

Charges 2012

Per unit incl. 2 persons and electricity	HUF 3600 - 7150
extra person	HUF 850 - 1200
child (2-14 yrs)	HUF 550 - 950
dog	HUF 550 - 950

Camping Cheques accepted.

Sárvár

Thermal Camping Sárvár

Vadkert u. 1, H-9600 Sárvár (Vas) T: 95 320 292. E: info@thermalcamping.com

alanrogers.com/HU5094

Thermal Camping Sárvár opened in 2006 and is the municipal site next to the impressive thermal spa. There are 89 pitches off of tarmac access lanes on hardstandings, all with 16A electricity, water, waste water and TV connections. To the back of the site there are additional pitches on well kept grassy fields. The main attraction of this site is of course the renovated spa and if staying here, access to the spa is included in the price (some activities are charged extra). You can also enjoy a ten per cent discount on meals in the restaurant. Those looking to enjoy a wellness holiday will be in the right place in Sárvár.

Facilities

Two adequate, heated toilet blocks with washbasins in cabins, controllable hot showers, baby room and facilities for disabled visitors. Washing machines. Campers' kitchen. Motorcaravan services. Shop. Playground. Bicycle hire. Gym. Off site: Wellness centre with indoor and outdoor pools, sauna, jacuzzi, massage and a restaurant. Centre of Sárvár 200 m.

Open: All year.

Directions

Site is in the centre of Sárvár. From the north, follow the 84 road around town and exit towards Sótony. Drive towards Sárvár and to the pool. Site is directly next to the pool. GPS: 47.246717, 16.9473

Charges guide

Per unit incl. 2 persons and electricity	€ 28.30 - € 36.00
extra person	€ 11.00
child (6-16 yrs)	€ 7.00

Camping Cheques accepted.

Szilvásvárad

Diófaház Accommodations

Ady Endre út 12, H-3348 Szilvásvárad (Heves County) T: 36 816 168. E: info@diofahaz.hu

alanrogers.com/HU5210

Diófaház is an ideal base in northeast Hungary for exploring this wooded part of the country, to visit the stud farm of the famous Lipizzaner horses (one of only five in the world) or to visit the town of Eger, world famous for its culture and red wine. The site is in private grounds on the edge of the village and provides a maximum of four pitches, all with electricity, which makes it quiet and peaceful. Gyöngyi Pap, the owner provides a warm welcome and if you're lucky you may arrive for the weekly barbecue or the home made Hungarian goulash soup. English is spoken.

Facilities

The single, freshly painted toilet block includes washbasins in cabins with hot and cold water, controllable hot showers and sinks with free hot water. There are several little shops in the village where you can buy your groceries. WiFi Internet access. 10% discount at three restaurants in the village if you show the Diófaház Accommodation discount card. Off site: Bicycle hire 500 m. Riding 2 km. Fishing 6 km.

Open: All year.

Directions

Take the no. 25 road from Eger north to Szilvásvárad. Site is signed when entering the village.
GPS: 48.09816, 20.384

Charges guide

Per unit incl. 2 persons	€ 9.00 - € 10.00
extra person	€ 4.00
child (0-6 yrs)	free - € 2.80
electricity per kWh	€ 0.18

Tiszaújváros

Termál Camping

Szederkényi út 53, H-3580 Tiszaújváros (Borsod-Abauj-Zemplen) T: 49 542 210. E: camping@tujvaros.hu

alanrogers.com/HU5197

Termál Camping was opened in 2004 and is on the outskirts of Tiszaújváros (the former Lenin City) and not far from the River Tisza in eastern Hungary. The site has some 166 grass pitches (all for touring units), of which 16 have 25A electricity. To one end of the site are eight holiday homes and centrally located is a well equipped toilet block. The trees and bushes have not yet fully developed and the site can become a suntrap in the hot Hungarian summer. The site is next to a tributary of the River Tisza, and the area offers good opportunities for walking, cycling, boating and fishing.

Facilities

One central, modern toilet block with toilets, preset hot showers, basins and facilities for disabled visitors (out of order when we visited). Laundry with washing machines. Kitchen with cooking rings, oven and fridge. Communal barbecue areas. Small buffet/bar. Fishing. Bicycle hire. Torch useful. Some English is spoken. Off site: Thermal spa. Supermarket and swimming pool 300 m.

Open: All year.

Directions

From M3 motorway from Budapest to the east, take exit for Debrecen and then to Tiszaújváros. On entering town follow the signs to the Thermal Spa bath and the site. GPS: 47.9318, 21.0465

Charges guide

Per unit incl. 2 persons and electricity	HUF 5500 - 6000
extra person	HUF 1500

Törökbálint

Fortuna Camping

Dózsa György út 164, H-2045 Törökbálint (Pest County) T: 23 335 364. E: info@fortunacamping.hu

alanrogers.com/HU5150

This good site lies at the foot of a hill with views of the vineyards, but Budapest is only 25 minutes away by bus. Concrete and gravel access roads lead to terraces where there are 170 individual pitches most bordered with hedges, all with electricity (up to 16A, long leads needed), and 14 with water, on slightly sloping ground. The site is surrounded by mature trees and Mr Szücs, the owner, will proudly name the 150 varieties of bushes and shrubs that edge the pitches. An open-air swimming pool with flume will help you to cool off in summer with an indoor pool for cooler weather.

Facilities

One fully equipped sanitary block and two smaller blocks. Good facilities for disabled campers. Dishwashing facilities, plus cookers in sheltered area. Washing machine and dryer. Gas supplies. Motorcaravan services. Bar (all year). Snack bar. Essentials from reception (order bread previous day). Outdoor swimming pool with slide (15/5-15/9). Indoor pool. Small play area. WiFi over site (charged). Excursions organised. English spoken. Off site: Restaurant (for camp guests - check with reception). Close to bus terminal for city centre 1 km.

Open: All year.

Directions

From M1 (Györ - Budapest) take exit for Törökbálint following signs for town and then site. Also accessible from M7 Budapest - Balaton road. GPS: 47.43203, 18.90110

Charges guide

Per person	€ 6.00
child (4-14 yrs)	€ 4.00
pitch	€ 6.00
electricity	€ 2.00

No credit cards.

Üröm

Jumbo Camping

Budakalászi út 23-25, H-2096 Üröm (Pest County) T: 26 351 251. E: jumbo@campingbudapest.com

alanrogers.com/HU5180

Jumbo Camping is a modern, thoughtfully developed, terraced site in the northern outskirts of Budapest. The concrete and gravel access roads lead shortly to 55 terraced pitches of varying sizes, a little on the small size for large units, and some slightly sloping. Hardstanding for cars and caravan wheels, as well as large hardstandings for motorcaravans. There is a steep incline to some pitches and use of the site's 4x4 may be required. All pitches have 6A electricity (may require long leads) and there are eight caravan pitches with water and drainage. They are mostly divided by small hedges and the whole area is fenced.

Facilities

Sanitary facilities are excellent, with large showers (communal changing). Washing machine, iron and cooking facilities (charged). Motorcaravan services. Café (bread orders taken), milk and butter available. Small, attractive swimming pool (1/7-31/8). Playground with covered area for wet weather. Barbecue area. WiFi and TV in reception. English spoken and information sheet provided in English. Off site: Shop and restaurant 500 m. The Old Swabian Wine-Cellar, said to serve extremely good food. Bus to city 500 m. every 30 minutes. Fishing 8 km.

Open: 1 April - 31 October.

Directions

Site signed on roads to Budapest - 11 from Szentendre and 10 from Komarom. If approaching from Budapest use 11 (site sign appears very quickly after sharp right bend; signs and entry are clearer if using road 10). Can also approach via Györ on M1/E60 and Lake Balaton on M7/E71. Turn into site is quite acute and uphill. GPS: 47.60178, 19.01967

Charges guide

Per unit incl. 2 persons and electricity	€ 12.80 - € 18.90
extra person	€ 4.20 - € 5.00

No credit cards (cash only).

Visegrad

Blue Danube Camping

Föut 70, H-2025 Visegrad (Pest County) T: 26 398 120. E: info@hotelhonti.hu

alanrogers.com/HU5175

Just opposite a road that runs alongside the beautiful Danube river, this small site has only 40 pitches (all for tourers and with 4A electricity) and two static units. It is owned by the Honti Hotel 50 m. down the road and this is where reception is located. It is attractively landscaped with low trees, shrubs and flowers. The good sized pitches are arranged on well kept, grassy lawns, separated by hedges in the middle field. From some there are good views of Visegrád Castle, once the home of King Mátyás Corvinus. Some road noise can be heard from the main road that runs to Budapest.

Facilities

Adequate Portacabin toilet block with British style toilets, open washbasins and controllable showers (free). Basic kitchen with electric cookers and fridge. Bar/restaurant to the front of the site. Fishing. Canoe hire.
Off site: Restaurants nearby. Riding 6 km. Golf 7 km.

Open: 1 May - 30 September.

Directions

Site is on the right of the no. 11 road running to Budapest at km. 43. GPS: 47.783083, 18.8339

Charges guide

Per person	HUF 1100
pitch incl. car	HUF 1700
electricity	HUF 850
dog	HUF 500

No credit cards.

Zalakaros

Balatontourist Camping Termál

Gyógyfürdo 6, H-8749 Zalakaros (Zala County) T: 93 340 105. E: termal@balatontourist.hu

alanrogers.com/HU5025

Balatontourist Camping Termál in Zalakaros has 280 attractively laid out, level pitches, all with 10A electricity and varying in size from 50-100 sq.m. (the larger pitches need to be reserved). There are 280 for touring units on grass and gravel (firm tent pegs may be needed), with around ten hardstandings for larger units and motorcaravans. Mature trees provide useful shade and access roads are gravel. Zalatour attracts many elderly people who spend their days at the thermal spa 200 m. down the road – the waters are reputedly good for rheumatism and other joint problems.

Facilities

Comfortable toilet facilities with British style toilets, open washbasins and controllable, hot showers (free). Facilities for disabled visitors. Full service laundry including ironing. Campers' kitchen. Motorcaravan service point and car wash. Shop and restaurant (1/4-30/9). Small playground. WiFi throughout (charged). Massage, acupuncture and pedicure. Sauna. Hairdresser. Bicycle hire. Off site: Golf 500 m. Riding 2 km. Fishing and beach 3 km.

Open: 1 April - 31 October.

Directions

On the M7/E71 travelling southwest, take exit 191 for Zalakomár and then Zalakaros. Follow good site signs in Zalakaros. GPS: 46.552267, 17.125933

Charges 2012

Per person	HUF 1050 - 1200

Zamardi

Balatontourist Camping Autós

Szent István út, H-8621 Zamárdi (Somogy County) T: 84 348 931. E: autos@balatontourist.hu

alanrogers.com/HU5040

If you have young children or non-swimmers in your party, then the southern shores of the lake where this Balatontourist site is situated are ideal as you can walk out for nearly a kilometre before the water rises to more than a metre in depth. It is a large site with its own direct access to the lake, offering 456 touring pitches with 10A electricity. There are many tall trees and the more attractive pitches are near the lakeside, including some unshaded ones alongside the water with views on the Tihany peninsula.

Facilities

Three modern, tiled sanitary buildings. Three en-suite private bathrooms can be rented including bath and shower. Warm water to washbasins. Showers with private changing area. Facilities for disabled visitors. Laundry facilities. Restaurant with excellent menu. Snack bar with terrace (from June). Lake swimming. Fishing. Minigolf. Wooden play equipment on sandy grass by the lake. Bicycle hire. Free guided walks in summer. Accommodation for hire. Off site: Restaurant and gift shop nearby. Riding 4 km.

Open: 7 May - 12 September.

Directions

Exit road no. 7/E71 between Balatonföldvár and Siófok towards Tihany, and the site is well signed. GPS: 46.88065, 17.91556

Charges guide

Per unit incl. 2 persons and electricity	HUF 3300 - 6100
extra person	HUF 800 - 1050
child (2-14 yrs)	HUF 550 - 800
dog	HUF 550 - 800

Camping Cheques accepted.

Italy

Whether you want to explore historic cities, stroll around medieval hill towns, relax on sandy beaches or simply indulge in opera, good food and wine, Italy has it all. Roman ruins, Renaissance art and beautiful churches abound. The Italian Alps are a haven for winter sports enthusiasts and also offer good hiking trails.

photo Brian Leslie

Italy only became a unified state in 1861, hence the regional nature of the country today. With 20 distinct regions, each one has retained its own individualism which is evident in the cuisine and local dialects.

In the north, the vibrant city of Milan is great for shopping and home to the famous opera house, La Scala, as well as Leonardo's Last Supper fresco. It is also a good starting-off point for the Alps; the Italian Lake District, incorporating Lake Garda, Lake Como and Lake Maggiore; the canals of Venice and the lovely town of Verona. Central Italy probably represents the most commonly perceived image of the country and Tuscany, with its classic rolling countryside and the historical towns of Florence, Siena, San Gimignano and Pisa, is one of the most visited areas. Further south is the historic capital of Rome and the city of Naples. Close to some of Italy's ancient sites such as Pompeii, Naples is within easy distance of Sorrento and the Amalfi coast.

CAPITAL: Rome

Tourist Office

Italian State Tourist Office (ENIT)
1 Princes Street, London W1B 2AY
Tel: 020 7408 1254
Fax: 020 7399 3567
Email: italy@italiantouristboard.co.uk
Internet: www.enit.it

Population

58 million

Climate

The south enjoys extremely hot summers and mild, dry winters, whilst the mountainous regions of the north are cooler with heavy snowfalls in winter.

Language

Italian. There are several dialect forms and some German is spoken near the Austrian border.

Telephone

The country code is 00 39.

Money

Currency: The Euro.
Banks: Mon-Fri 08.30-13.00 and 15.00-16.00.

Shops

Mon-Sat 08.30/09.00-13.00 and 15.30/16.00-19.30/20.00, with some variations in larger cities.

Public Holidays

New Year; Easter Mon; Liberation Day 25 Apr; Labour Day; Republic Day 2 June; Assumption 15 Aug; All Saints 1 Nov; Unity Day 4 Nov; Immaculate Conception 8 Dec; Christmas 25, 26 Dec; plus some special local feast days.

Motoring

Tolls are payable on the autostrada network. If travelling distances, save time by purchasing a 'Viacard' from pay booths or service areas. An overhanging load, e.g. a bicycle rack, must be indicated by a large red/white hatched warning square. Failure to do so will result in a fine.

see campsite map 7

Aglientu

Camping Baia Blu La Tortuga

Pineta di Vignola Mare, I-07020 Aglientu (Sardinia) T: 079 602 200. E: info@baiablu.com

alanrogers.com/IT69550

Tortuga is named after the giant turtle-like rock off the site's beautiful beach, and is a large, professionally run campsite. The 450 sizeable touring pitches (all with 3/10A electricity) are on grass and coarse-grained sand and shaded by tall pines with banks of colourful oleanders and wide boulevards providing easy access. This is a busy, bustling site with plenty to do, with its attractive bars and restaurants by the beach, which shelves rather steeply. The excellent play areas are cleverly placed to allow parents a break and the entertainment is first class. We were impressed by this quality family site.

Facilities

Four excellent sanitary blocks (most with solar panels for hot water) with free hot showers. Facilities for disabled campers. Private cabins for rent. Washing machines and dryers. Motorcaravan services. Supermarket, beachside restaurant and bars, self-service restaurant, snack bar and takeaway (open all season). Gas. Gym. Hairdresser. Doctor's surgery. Playground. Tennis. Games and TV rooms. Windsurfing and diving schools. WiFi area. Massage centre (July/Aug). Entertainment and sports activities (mid May-Sept). Excursions. Barbecue area (not permitted on pitches). Two specially adapted mobile homes are available for family members with disabilities. Off site: Disco 50 m. Riding 18 km. Ferry to Corsica.

Open: 1 April - 14 October.

Directions

Site is on the north coast road (SP 90) between the towns of Costa Paradiso and S. Teresa di Gallura (18 km) at Pineta di Vignola Mare and is well signed around the 47 km. marker. GPS: 41.12436, 9.067594

Charges 2012

Per unit incl. 2 persons, water and electricity	€ 16.00 - € 51.00
extra person	€ 5.40 - € 13.50
child (3-9 yrs)	€ 3.40 - € 11.50
dog	€ 3.50 - € 8.00

Alghero

Camping Mariposa

Via Lido 22, I-07041 Alghero (Sardinia) T: 079 950 360. E: info@lamariposa.it

alanrogers.com/IT69960

Mariposa is a sprawling beachside site with its own access to a fine sand beach, and it has a comfortable feel. The pitches are of various sizes (50-80 sq.m); those on uneven ground are best suited for tents, while those on gravel are for caravans and motorcaravans (some alongside the sea). Some pitches have shade but all have 6A electrical connections. Cars must be parked away from the pitches. There is an entertainment programme in high season. The amenities are by the site entrance and include a pizzeria, bar and restaurant with TV. The small shop is also here. The beach has soft sand and is safe, with umbrellas and loungers for hire. The range of sports available here is excellent for active young visitors. The town with all the usual facilities is very close by. Alghero (1.5 km) is interesting to explore as it still has a strong Catalan flavour from its 400-year occupation by the Spanish.

Facilities

The brightly coloured, open plan sanitary facilities are clean, with cold water to washbasins. Dishwashing and laundry sinks. Hot showers (€ 0,50 token). Washing machines and dryer. Motorcaravan service point. Shop. Restaurant and bar. Bicycle hire. Kite surfing. Diving. Windsurfing. Stand-up paddling. Sailing. Surfing. Paragliding. (Courses available at extra charge). Communal barbecue. Dogs are not accepted in August. Off site: Site-owned restaurant in town ('The Kings') offers 10% discount to campers. Neptune Caves.

Open: 1 April - 15 October.

Directions

Alghero is on the northwest coast, about 35 km. southwest of Sassari. Mariposa is at the north end of the town. Follow the signs on the beach road, but watch for one-way systems which you have to navigate. GPS: 40.57885, 8.31253

Charges guide

Per unit incl. 2 persons and electricity	€ 23.00 - € 44.00
extra person	€ 10.00 - € 13.00
child (3-12 yrs)	€ 5.00 - € 9.00

Albinia

Camping International Argentario

Localitá Torre Saline, I-58010 Albinia (Tuscany) T: 056 487 0302. E: info@argentariocampingvillage.com

alanrogers.com/IT66710

Argentario is really two separate campsites with a large holiday villa complex, all sharing the common facilities. The pools, entertainment area and bar area, like the villa complex are new and elegantly designed. The large irregularly shaped pool and smaller circular paddling pool are very inviting. Entertainment is organised daily by the team where there is something for everyone, young and old. The 806 pitches with 300 for tourers are small but mostly flat and on a surface of dark sand and pine needles, all are shaded by tall pines. The area is quite dusty and many of the pitches are a very long way from the amenities. Motorcaravans are parked in a large separate open square.

Facilities

Three mature blocks have mostly Turkish style toilets, a few cramped showers (stretched at peak periods) with hot water, and cold water to sinks. Facilities for disabled campers but sandy surface and remote facilities make it unsuitable. Washing machines. Motorcaravan service point. Shop. Restaurant, bar and takeaway. Swimming pools. Tennis. Boat hire. Minigolf. ATM. Cars are parked in a separate car park in high season. Torches useful. Dogs are not accepted. Off site: Bar and restaurant on beach.

Open: 1 April - 18 September.

Directions

Site is south of Grosseto, off the SS1 at the 150 km. mark, signed Porto S. Stefano. Ignore the first 'combined' campsite sign and proceed 300 m. to the main entrance. GPS: 42.49623, 11.19413

Charges guide

Per unit incl. 2 persons and electricity	€ 24.00 - € 42.00
extra person	€ 8.00 - € 14.00
child (1-6 yrs)	€ 4.00 - € 7.00

Ameglia

Camping River

Localitá Armezzone, I-19031 Ameglia (Ligúria) T: 018 765 920. E: info@campingriver.com

alanrogers.com/IT64190

Ameglia, near La Spezia, is just south of the A12 autrostada and Camping River is just 5 km. from the Sarzana exit. On the banks of the Magna river, this popular site provides 100 level 75-100 sq.m. touring pitches with an umbrella of tall trees to provide much welcome shade on hot days. The touring pitches are mostly separated from the equal number of long stay pitches. The site has its own small marina and swimming pool complex. Alongside the pool is a terrace which overlooks the river, providing a great atmosphere for a drink or an 'al fresco' meal. The site provides an ideal location for a short stop to enjoy some boating or fishing, or for a longer stay to explore Ligúria. It is possible to launch your boat into the Magra river from the campsite and there are good fishing opportunities further up river. A busy entertainment programme is provided at Camping River from mid June until September. Camping River has something for all the family; we saw fishermen setting off for the afternoon, families playing in the pool and small children enjoying the large play area while their parents relaxed with a cup of coffee on the terrace. This is a wonderful area to explore with the Cinque Terre nearby, its beautiful coastline and interesting hilltop villages. Liguria is also a well known wine growing area.

Facilities

Two sanitary blocks provide toilets (some Turkish style), washbasins and unisex showers. Facilities for disabled campers. Motorcaravan service point. Restaurant and bar. Shop. Pizzeria. Swimming pool and sun deck. Boat launching. Fishing. Mobile homes and bungalows to rent. Off site: Tennis and riding 200 m. Archery. Sailing. Scuba diving. La Spezia. Le Cinque Terre.

Open: 1 April - 30 September.

Directions

Take Sarzana exit on the A12 (Genoa - Livorno) and follow the signs initially towards Lerici. After 3 km. follow signs to Bocca di Magra and Ameglia where the site is well signed off to the left. The final access road is narrow and has a tight bend. GPS: 44.07556, 9.96972

Charges guide

Per person	€ 4.50 - € 10.00
child (2-10 yrs)	€ 2.00 - € 7.00
pitch	€ 17.00 - € 49.00

Aquileia

Camping Aquileia

Via Gemina10, I-33051 Aquileia (Friuli - Venézia Giúlia) T: 043 191 042. E: info@campingaquileia.it

alanrogers.com/IT60020

Situated in former parkland under mature trees, Camping Aquileia, with 121 level and grass touring pitches, is a quiet site 10 km. away from the bustling coastal beaches. The pitches, all with 4/6A electricity, are separated from the entrance, swimming pool and play areas by tall hedges, and the more peaceful part of the site with the newer sanitary block is at the rear of the site. The now small town of Aquileia, founded in 181 BC, became one of the most important Roman military and trading posts and is now a UNESCO World Heritage Site. In the basilica, only a short walk from the campsite, along the former harbour, lays one of the world's most magnificent mosaics. The campsite is popular with families and for those who seek a quiet base from which to visit the beaches or tour this interesting region. From reception, tours can be organised with the town's tourist office to the region's archaeological sites, and not surprisingly a weekly mosaic course is also on offer.

Facilities

Two sanitary blocks with free hot water, controllable showers and washbasins in cabins. Facilities for disabled visitors. Folding baby changing bench. Laundry facilities. Motorcaravan service point. Restaurant, bar and automat for drinks and ice cream. Large playing field with playground. Swimming and paddling pools. Bicycle hire. Mobile homes and chalets for rent. Off site: Supermarket opposite entrance. Riding 12 km. The historic towns of Trieste, Gorizia and the beach resort of Grado.

Open: 21 April - 15 September.

Directions

Site is 30 km. west northwest of Trieste. From the A4 (Venice - Trieste) take exit for Palmanova and travel south for 20 km. towards Grado. Just after entering Aquileia turn left at traffic lights, signed Trieste and Goriza and site is 400 m. on the right. GPS: 45.77585, 13.37084

Charges guide

Per unit incl. 2 persons and electricity	€ 21.00 - € 38.00
extra person	€ 5.00 - € 9.00
child (3-12 yrs)	€ 3.00 - € 5.50
dog	€ 3.00 - € 4.50

Baia Domizia

Baia Domizia Villaggio Camping

I-81030 Baia Domizia (Campania) T: 082 393 0164. E: info@baiadomizia.it

alanrogers.com/IT68200

This large, beautifully maintained seaside site is about 70 kilometres northwest of Naples, and is within a pine forest, cleverly left in its natural state. Although it does not feel like it, there are 750 touring pitches in clearings, either of grass and sand or on hardstanding, all with electricity. Finding a pitch may take time as there are so many good ones to choose from, but staff will help in season. Most pitches are well shaded, however there are some in the sun for cooler periods. The central complex is superb with well designed buildings providing for all needs (the site is some distance from the town). A member of Leading Campings Group.

Facilities

Seven new toilet blocks have hot water in washbasins (many cabins) and showers. Good access and facilities for disabled campers. Washing machines, spin dryers. Motorcaravan services. Gas supplies. Supermarket and general shop. Large bar. Restaurants, pizzeria and takeaway. Ice cream parlour. Swimming pool complex. Playground. Tennis. Windsurfing hire and school. Disco. Excursions. Torches required in some areas. Dogs are not accepted. Off site: Bicycle hire 100 m. Fishing 3 km.

Open: 5 May - 18 September.

Directions

The turn to Baia Domizia leads off the Formia - Naples road 23 km. from Formia. From Rome - Naples autostrada, take Cassino exit to Formia. Site is to the north of Baia Domizia and well signed. Site is off the coastal road that runs parallel to the SS7. GPS: 41.207222, 13.791389

Charges guide

Per unit incl. 2 persons and electricity	€ 22.80 - € 47.80
extra person	€ 5.90 - € 11.90
child (1-11 yrs)	€ 2.40 - € 8.90

Bardolino

Camping Serenella

Localitá Mezzariva 19, I-37011 Bardolino (Lake Garda) T: **045 721 1333**. E: **serenella@camping-serenella.it**

alanrogers.com/IT63590

Situated alongside Lake Garda, Serenella has 300 average sized pitches, some with good lake views. Movement around the site may prove difficult for large units (look for the wider roads). The pitches are shaded and have 10A electricity. A long promenade with brilliant views of the mountains and lake runs the length of the campsite. It is dotted with grassy relaxation areas and beach bars where snacks are served and the atmosphere is charming. The pleasant pool complex is near an older style taverna where delicious, sensibly priced food is served. There is some road noise at some of the amenities and the pool. There is an entertainment programme from May to September, with a miniclub for the children. A small market selling a variety of goods and newspapers, and a stall selling fresh fruit and vegetables. Serenella is popular with Italians and international guests. Gardaland is nearby. Professional coaches are available for many watersports and courses may be taken.

Facilities

Five clean, well equipped sanitary blocks, include three that are more modern with laundry facilities. British style toilets, free hot water throughout. Facilities for disabled visitors. Infirmary. Washing machines and dryer. Freezer. Bar/restaurant, takeaway and shop (all season). Watersports. Outdoor swimming pool (1/5-18/9). Entertainment and sporting programme for all in high season. Play area. Bicycle hire. Boat launching. Minigolf. Tennis. Satellite TV. Internet and WiFi (charged). Dogs are not accepted. Off site: Beach with fishing and watersports. Town and golf 3 km. Riding 3.5 km. Verona 35 km. Gardaland.

Open: 24 March - 21 October.

Directions

From E70/A4 Milan - Venice autostrada take the Pescheria exit and follow signs to Bardolino. Site is on lakeside between Bardolino and Garda, about 4 km. south of Garda. GPS: 45.55939, 10.71657

Charges guide

Per unit incl. 2 persons and electricity	€ 18.50 - € 39.00
per person	€ 4.50 - € 10.00
child (0-5 yrs)	free - € 4.40

No credit cards.

Bardolino

La Rocca Camp

Localitâ San Pietro, I-37011 Bardolino (Lake Garda) T: **045 721 1111**. E: **info@campinglarocca.com**

alanrogers.com/IT63600

This site was one of the first to operate on the lake and the family has a background of wine and olive oil production. La Rocca is in two areas, each side of the busy A249, the upper part being used mostly for bungalows, although some touring pitches are here and these have great lake views. The remaining touring pitches are on the lower part of the site, along with the main facilities. There is access between the two parts via a tunnel. The 445 pitches are mostly on terraces with shade, 6A electricity and access from narrow tarmac roads.

Facilities

Four toilet blocks with two on each side of the site. WCs are mixed British and Turkish style and showers are controllable. Facilities for disabled visitors but many steps to pool. Children's facilities and baby baths. Washing machines. Motorcaravan services. Shop and bakery. Restaurant, bar and takeaway. Swimming and paddling pools (lifeguard). Whirlpool. Pool bar. Play area. Miniclub. Entertainment programme in season. Internet point. Bicycle hire. WiFi (charged). Torches useful. Off site: Public transport at gate. Boat launching 20 m. Bicycle hire 1 km.

Open: 1 April - 30 September.

Directions

Site is on the east side of Lake Garda, on the lake ring road 249. From the A4 take Pescheria exit and the 249 north for Garda (there are many signs for Gardaland). Site is well signed approaching village of Bardolino. GPS: 45.5645, 10.7129

Charges guide

Per unit incl. 2 persons and electricity	€ 19.00 - € 42.00
extra person	€ 5.00 - € 9.50
child (3-11 yrs)	€ 4.00 - € 6.50
dog	€ 2.00 - € 5.00

Bari Sardo

Camping L'Ultima Spiaggia

Localitá Planargia, I-08042 Bari Sardo (Sardinia) T: 078 229 363. E: info@campingultimaspiaggia.it

alanrogers.com/IT69720

L'Ultima Spiaggia (the ultimate beach) is an apt name as the beach really is extremely pleasant, although coarse grained. There are four great paddling and swimming pools, and the facilities have bright, colourful decor. The 252 pitches all have electricity (3/6A), are terraced on sand and some enjoy limited sea views. The ambitious entertainment programme can be enjoyed from the terrace of the restaurant, which offers a variety of good food, including local seafood specialities.

Facilities

Two modernised toilet units include facilities for babies and disabled campers, but are some way from the lower pitches. Washing machines and dryers. Motorcaravan service point. Small supermarket. Restaurant and snack bar. Play areas. Domestic animal area with donkeys. Windsurfing, diving and sailing. Aerobics. Riding. Tennis. Minigolf. Canoeing. Bicycle hire. Miniclub. Multisports area. Entertainment. WiFi (charged). Excursions. Torches useful. Off site: Restaurants, bars and shops. Fishing. Boat launching. Kite surfing. Free-climbing.

Open: 20 April - 30 September.

Directions

Site is on east coast of Sardinia, well signed from the main coast road, the SS125 in the village of Bari Sardo. GPS: 39.819003, 9.670484

Charges guide

Per unit incl. 2 persons and electricity	€ 19.50 - € 59.50
extra person	€ 6.80 - € 15.00
child (1-12 yrs)	€ 4.00 - € 12.00
dog	€ 4.00 - € 6.50

Baveno

Camping Tranquilla

Via Cave-Oltrefiume 2, I-28831 Baveno (Piedmont) T: 032 392 3452. E: info@tranquilla.com

alanrogers.com/IT62470

Tranquilla is a family run site on the western slopes above Baveno, close to Lake Maggiore. The site is in two terraced sections, both with electricity connections (6A). The 55 touring pitches vary in size with trees offering plenty of shade. There is a very pleasant swimming pool with an attractive paddling pool. Reception is housed in an attractive old railway carriage from where the Cagiada family will welcome you. Excellent English is spoken. The site is an ideal base from which to explore this very attractive area. Tourist information is available and reception will book any of the local activities and facilities including watersports. The lakeside town of Baveno is about 1.5 km. away, down a fairly steep hill. About half way down are bus stops and there is a weekly market on Mondays. Boat trips to three islands are available from the quay.

Facilities

The sanitary block offers the usual facilities including those for disabled visitors. All are kept very clean. British and Turkish style WCs. Laundry. Motorcaravan services. Pizza ordering service. Drinks machine. Swimming pool (10/5-30/9). Aquarium. Play area. Excursions. Free WiFi. Off site: Restaurant 300 m. Fishing and bus service 800 m. Sailing 1.5 km. Golf, bicycle hire and riding 3 km. Shops nearby.

Open: 15 March - 15 October.

Directions

Baveno is 90 km. northwest of Milan on the western shore of Lake Maggiore, and is on the SS33 road between Arona and Verbania. Site is well signed to the west in the northern part of the town. GPS: 45.91172, 8.49071

Charges guide

Per unit incl. 2 persons and electricity	€ 20.40 - € 29.30
extra person	€ 5.30 - € 7.50
child (1-12 yrs)	free - € 5.30

Special discounts for campers with the latest Alan Rogers guide. No credit cards, but travellers cheques and British currency accepted.

Bibione

Camping Lido

Via dei Ginepri 115, I-30020 Bibione-Pineda (Veneto) T: 043 143 8480. E: lido@bibionemare.com

alanrogers.com/IT60130

Camping Village Lido is a quiet, green site with direct access to the seafront in the centre of the town of Bibione-Pineda. Of 730 pitches, 388 are for touring units. Mostly shaded, there are three sizes, all with 6A electricity. There is convenient access to the long white sandy beach with its slowly shelving water, ideal for swimming. There are 261 high quality mobile homes available for campers who choose to fly to the site (car hire is available in a package deal). This is a simple site with good sporting and children's facilities, and an uncomplicated bar and restaurant.

Facilities

Six sanitary blocks are conveniently located and of a high standard. Car wash and motorcaravan service point. Bar, restaurant, supermarket and bazaar. Archery. Canoeing. Children's play park. Table tennis. Football. Tennis and windsurfing schools. Boat mooring. Internet access and WiFi. Dogs and other animals are not accepted. Off site: Town of Bibione-Pineda. Marina. Excursions to Venice. Parking for late arrivals with electricity.

Open: 13 May - 18 September.

Directions

Bibione is 80 km. east of Venice. Leave the E55 at Latisana exit and take the 354 for Bibione. Site is well signed from afar on approach roads. 1 km. before Bibione turn right towards Bibione-Pineda and follow site signs. GPS: 45.63222, 13.00132

Charges guide

Per unit incl. 2 persons and electricity	€ 17.00 - € 37.80
extra person	€ 4.50 - € 9.90
child (1-11 yrs)	free - € 6.50

Bibione

Camping Capalonga

Via della Laguna 16, I-30020 Bibione-Pineda (Veneto) T: 043 143 8351. E: capalonga@bibionemare.com

alanrogers.com/IT60100

A quality site right beside the sea, Capalonga is a large site with 832 shaded touring pitches (70-90 sq.m) with 4/10A electricity, 35 fully serviced. The site is pleasantly laid out and permanent pitches are unobtrusive. The new (2010) additional lagoon swimming pool is excellent. Alternatively, the wide, sand beach is very safe. Quality entertainment adds to the enjoyment here and the site has something for everyone. It is roomy and bicycles are a real boon here. The site has a great location between the sea and a large lagoon. Boating (motor or sail) can be undertaken; a landing stage, crane and moorings are available. Security is handled well and all staff are cheerful and attentive. Capalonga is an excellent site, with comprehensive facilities.

Facilities

Nine toilet blocks are of a high standard and frequently cleaned. There are facilities for disabled visitors, and great children's rooms. British and Turkish style toilets, some washbasins in private cabins. Launderette. Dishwashers (€ 1.00). Motorcaravan services. Large supermarket. General shop. Self-service restaurant and separate bar (open all season). Two swimming pools. Boating (170 moorings). Fishing (sea or lagoon). Bicycle hire. Playground. Entertainment programme. Internet access and WiFi. Late arrival parking with electricity. Dogs are not accepted. Off site: Bus by entrance. Riding 2 km. Golf 10 km. Touring and excursions. Boat hire.

Open: 28 April - 30 September.

Directions

Bibione is about 80 km. east of Venice, well signed from afar on approach roads. 1 km. before Bibione turn right towards Bibione-Pineda and follow site signs. GPS: 45.63050, 12.99358

Charges guide

Per unit incl. 2 persons and electricity	€ 25.80 - € 51.20
extra person	€ 6.90 - € 11.60
child (1-11 yrs)	free - € 9.50

Bibione

Camping Residence Il Tridente

Via Baseleghe 12, I-30020 Bibione-Pineda (Veneto) T: 043 143 9600. E: tridente@bibionemare.com

alanrogers.com/IT60150

This is an unusual site in that it has huge open spaces. Formerly a holiday centre for deprived children, it occupies a large area of woodland stretching from the main road to the sea. It is divided into two parts by the apartment block of first class rooms which are for rent. The 206 tourist pitches (6/10A) are located among tall, shading pines in the area between the entrance and the Residence. From here to the sea is a pleasant open area used for many sports facilities and two swimming pools.

Facilities

Three sanitary blocks, two in the main camping area and one near the sea, are of excellent quality. Mixed British and Turkish style WCs in cabins with washbasins and facilities for disabled visitors. Washing machines and dryers. Motorcaravan services. The Residence includes an excellent restaurant and bar. Huge new supermarket. Swimming pools. Playground. Tennis. Gym. Fishing. Internet access and WiFi. Animation programme in high season. Late arrival parking with electricity. Dogs are not accepted. Off site: Bus service outside site. Bicycle hire 1 km. Riding and boat launching 2 km. Golf 10 km.

Open: 6 May - 18 September.

Directions

From A4 Venice - Trieste autostrada, take Latisana exit and follow signs to Bibione and then Bibione-Pineda and site signs. GPS: 45.63330, 13.06666

Charges guide

Per unit incl. 2 persons and electricity	€ 23.00 - € 44.00
extra person	€ 6.00 - € 11.00
child (1-11 yrs)	free - € 7.50

BIBIONE
BIBIONE PINEDA IS A PEACEFUL AND RELAXING SEASIDE RESORT LOCATED BETWEEN VENICE AND TRIESTE. ITS SILKY SAND BEACH STRETCHES ALONG THE COASTLINE FOR MORE THAN 3 KM AND IT IS 150 METERS WIDE. ITS MARINA, THE RESTAURANTS, CAFÉS, SHOPS, SPORT FACILITIES AND NIGHT CLUBS, ALL THIS IN A FANTASTIC PINE WOOD SETTING MAKES IT A PARTICULARLY DELIGHTFUL DESTINATION.
EMAS
Capalonga CAMPING
CAMPING Lido
CAMPING RESIDENCE IL TRIDENTE
1
2
3
THE ONLY CAMPING SITE IN EUROPE WITH MOORING FACILITIES FOR 170 BOATS.
Viale della Laguna, 16
I-30020 BIBIONE PINEDA (VE)
Information/Reservation
Tel. +39-0431-438351
Fax +39-0431-438370
Telephone in winter: +39-0431-447190
+39-0431-447198
Facsimile in winter: +39-0431-438986
www.capalonga.com
e-mail: capalonga@bibionemare.com
IDEAL FOR PEOPLE WHO LOVE NATURE WHILE BEING A STONE'S THROW FROM THE TOWN CENTRE.
Viale dei Ginepri, 115
I-30020 BIBIONE PINEDA (VE)
Information/Reservation
Tel. +39-0431-438480
Fax +39-0431-439292
Telephone in winter: +39-0431-447386
Facsimile in winter: +39-0431-439193
www.campinglido.com
e-mail: lido@bibionemare.com
ESPECIALLY THOUGHT TO SATISFY THE NEEDS OF FAMILIES WITH YOUNG CHILDREN
Via Baseleghe, 12
I-30020 BIBIONE PINEDA (VE)
Information/Reservation
Tel. +39-0431-439600
Fax +39-0431-446245
Telephone in winter: +39-0431-447393
Facsimile in winter: +39-0431-439193
www.iltridente.com
e-mail: tridente@bibionemare.com
www.bibionemare.com
3
2
2011
Private transfert from airports Venice, Trieste, Treviso
Bibione PINEDA
Venezia - Italia
1
New Swimming-Pool 1.500 m²
Suite Caravans
Chalet Mobil
DISCOVER A NEW WAY OF HOLIDAYING...
Veneto
Tra la terra e il cielo
Climate control system
Heating
New "Golden Suite" with dishwasher
Safe
Barbeque
Bicycle
Private beach
Facilities for the disables

Bibione

Villaggio Turistico Internazionale

Via Colonie 2, I-30020 Bibione (Veneto) T: 043 144 2611. E: info@vti.it

alanrogers.com/IT60140

This is a large, professionally run tourist village which offers all a holidaymaker could want. The Granzotto family have owned the site since the sixties and the results of their continuous improvements are impressive. There are 330 clean pitches with electricity (10/16A), fully serviced, including TV connections, shaded by mature trees and mostly on flat ground. The site's large sandy beach is excellent (umbrellas and loungers available for a small charge), as are all the facilities within the campsite where English speaking, uniformed assistants will help when you arrive. The tourist village is split by a main road (bridge for pedestrians) with the main restaurant, gym, laundry, disco, cinema and children's club on the very smart chalet side.

Facilities

Four modern toilet blocks house excellent facilities with mainly British style toilets. Excellent facilities for children and disabled campers. Private bathrooms € 10. Washing machines and dryers. Motorcaravan service point. Supermarket. Two good quality restaurants. Snack bar. Pool complex with two large pools and a fun pool. Fitness centre. Disco. TV. Cinema and theatre. WiFi over site (charged). Play areas. Tennis. Off site: Bicycle hire 1 km.

Open: 2 April - 30 September.

Directions

Leave A4 east of Venice at Latisana exit on Latisana road. Then take road 354 towards Lignano, after 12 km. turn right to Bevazzana and then left to Bibione. Site is well signed on entering town. GPS: 45.6351, 13.0374

Charges 2012

Per unit incl. 2 persons and electricity	€ 20.50 - € 61.00
extra person	€ 5.50 - € 12.00

Bracciano

Camping Roma Flash

Via Settevene Palo km 19,800, I-00062 Bracciano (Lazio) T: 069 980 5458. E: info@romaflash.it

alanrogers.com/IT68120

This excellent site is in a superb location with magnificent views over Lake Bracciano, the source of Rome's drinking water. When we visited, although it was busy, it was still peaceful and relaxing. There are 275 pitches in total and facilities include a restaurant with a large terrace and small indoor area both overlooking the lake where you can enjoy a good menu and excellent pizzas. The owners Elide and Eduardo speak excellent English and happily go out of their way to ensure guests enjoy their holiday. Many of the visitors told us that they return year after year and some stay for 8 to 12 weeks at a time, enjoying all that the Lazio region has to offer.

Facilities

Two new large toilet blocks are very well appointed. Free hot water throughout and fully adjustable showers. Facilities for disabled visitors and children. Laundry facilities. Gas supplies. Bar/pizzeria. Small shop. Swimming pool (caps compulsory). Play area. Watersports. Games room. Animation for children in high season. Excursions. Private bus daily to Roma S. Pietro and return. New sports area. Off site: Rome (40 minutes).

Open: 1 April - 30 September.

Directions

From E35/E45 north of Rome, take Settebagni exit. Follow GRA orbital road west to Cassia exit. Follow sign for Lago Bracciano to town of Bracciano. Site is well signed southeast of town on the SP4A. GPS: 42.130113, 12.173527

Charges guide

Per unit incl. 2 persons and electricity	€ 16.00 - € 32.00

Camping Cheques accepted.

Bracciano

Camping Porticciolo

Via Porticciolo, I-00062 Bracciano (Lazio) T: 069 980 3060. E: info@porticciolo.it

alanrogers.com/IT68130

This small family run site, useful for visiting Rome, has its own private beach on the southwest side of Lake Bracciano. A pleasant feature is that the site is overlooked by the impressive castle in the village of Bracciano. There are 170 pitches (160 for tourers) split into two sections, some with lake views and 120 having electricity. Pitches are of average size and shaded by very green trees that are continuously watered in summer by a neat overhead watering system. The friendly bar has two large terraces, shared by the trattoria which opens for lunch and the pizzeria with its wood fired oven in the evenings.

Facilities

Three rustic, but clean, sanitary units with children's toilet and showers. Hot showers (token). Laundry facilities. Motorcaravan services. Gas supplies. Shop (basics). Bar. Trattoria/pizzeria (15/5-5/9). Tennis. Play area. Bicycle hire. Fishing. Internet point and free WiFi. Torches required in some areas. Excursions 'Rome By Night' and nearby nature parks. For dogs, contact site first. Off site: Bus service from outside site to central Rome. Train service from Bracciano (1.5 km) into the city – site runs connecting bus. (09.00 daily). Riding 2 km.

Open: 1 April - 30 September.

Directions

From Rome ring road (GRA) northwest side take Cassia exit to Bracciano S493 (not Cassia bis). 2 km. before Bracciano village, just after going under bridge follow site signs and turn along lake away from Anguillara. Site is 1 km. on the SP1f and has a steep entrance. GPS: 42.10582, 12.18928

Charges guide

Per person	€ 5.00 - € 7.00
tent, caravan or motorcaravan and electricity	€ 5.00 - € 8.00
car	€ 2.50 - € 4.00

Calceranica al Lago

Camping Punta Lago

Via Lungo Lago 42, I-38050 Calceranica al Lago (Trentino - Alto Adige) T: 046 172 3229.

E: info@campingpuntalago.com **alanrogers.com/IT62260**

Camping Punta Lago is in a beautiful setting on Lago di Caldonazzo. This attractive family run campsite, with easy lake access across a small road, has 140 level, shaded pitches on grass. Of a good size, all have electricity (3/6A) and 50 are serviced with water and drainage. The campsite first opened 45 years ago and brothers Gino and Mauro continue the friendly family tradition of ensuring you enjoy your holiday. As President of 'Consortia Trentino Outdoors', Gino knows all about the range of activities available locally including fishing, lake swimming, windsurfing, sailing and canoeing. There are excellent restaurants within 50 m. of the gate. The site itself has a large terraced snack bar with wonderful views of the lake and the most amazing ice cream (gelato), yogurt and fruit concoctions.

Facilities

One central sanitary block has superb facilities with hot water throughout. Well designed bathroom and washbasin area. Excellent facilities for disabled visitors and babies. Private units for rent, some with massage baths. Washing machines and dryer. Freezer. Shop. Bar/snack bar. Fishing (with permit). Modern comprehensive play area. Entertainment programme (July/Aug). Internet access. WiFi over site (charged). Cinema. TV. Off site: Bicycle hire, town and ATM 1 km. Watersports. Riding 3 km. Golf 20 km. Train 1 km. to Venice and other cities.

Open: 1 May - 15 September.

Directions

From A22 Bolzano - Trento autostrada take the SS47 towards Padova and then after about 15 km. turn for Lago di Caldonazzo and Calceranica al Lago. Approaching town from the west beside the railway, continue along Via Donegani, turn left at Esso petrol station into Via al Lago and right at lakeside into Via Lungo Lago. Site is on the right. Coming from the east follow Calceranica then turn right just before the Esso petrol station. Do not try to cut across before this as you will enter a one-way system with no through road to site. GPS: 46.00230, 11.25450

Charges guide

Per unit incl. 2 persons and electricity	€ 16.00 - € 40.00
extra person	€ 5.00 - € 9.00
child (2-12 yrs)	€ 4.00 - € 7.00
dog	€ 3.00

Caldonazzo

Camping Mario

Via Lungolago, 4, I-38052 Caldonazzo (Trentino - Alto Adige) T: 046 172 3341.

E: direzione@campingmario.com **alanrogers.com/IT62255**

Camping Mario is a family site, across a small road from Lake Caldonazzo, one of the most attractive small Italian lakes where swimming, fishing and other activities can be enjoyed. The 116 grassy pitches (80–100 sq.m) have 6A electricity and a further 52 also have water and drainage. Mobile homes are also available for rent. There is a large swimming pool with a new bar/pizzeria/restaurant adjacent and new play areas for children. There is also a well stocked mini-market. This region is popular for mountain sports, particularly mountain biking, trekking and rafting.

Facilities

Two well maintained toilet blocks provide all the usual facilities including an area for children and two rooms for disabled visitors (key access). Laundry facilities. Motorcaravan service point. Shop selling fresh bread. Bar. Restaurant/pizzeria. Large swimming pool with children's pool. New play areas. Miniclub, teenage club and evening entertainment for adults (high season). Tourist information. Mobile homes to rent. WiFi over site (free in low season). Off site: Bicycle hire 1.5 km. Riding 5 km. Golf 10 km.

Open: 29 April - 12 September.

Directions

Leave A22 motorway at Trento Nord, follow the SS47 towards Padova. After passing Pergine and Valsugana, follow signs to Calceranica/Caldonazzo. After Caldonazzo railway station turn left and after level crossing, turn left again towards the lake and site is well signposted. GPS: 46.004662, 11.260619

Charges guide

Per unit incl. 2 persons and electricity	€ 19.00 - € 67.00
extra person	€ 6.00 - € 10.00

Caorle

Centro Vacanze Pra' Delle Torri

P.O. Box 176, Via Altanea 201, I-30021 Caorle (Veneto) T: **042 129 9063**. E: **info@pradelletorri.it**

alanrogers.com/IT60030

Pra' Delle Torri is a superb Italian Adriatic site which has just about everything! Pitches for camping, hotel, accommodation to rent and two very large, well equipped pool complexes, which may be rated among the best in the country. There is also a full size golf course. Of the 1,500 pitches, 888 are available for touring and are arranged in zones, with 5/10A electricity and shade. There is an amazing choice of good restaurants, bars and shops arranged around an attractive square. Although a large site, there is a great atmosphere here that families will enjoy. The fabulous lagoon pool complex with islands, slides and sunbathing areas is the site's crowning glory plus indoor (Olympic size) and outdoor laned pools. Other super amenities include a large grass area for ball games, a good playground, a children's car track, and a whole range of sports, fitness and entertainment programmes, along with a medical centre, skin care and other therapies. The site has its own sandy beach and Porto Santa, Margherita and Caorle are nearby. One could quite happily spend a whole holiday here without leaving the site but the attractions of Venice, Verona, etc. might well tempt one to explore the area.

Facilities

Sixteen high quality toilet blocks with excellent facilities including very attractive 'junior stations'. Units for disabled visitors. Laundry facilities. Motorcaravan service point. Large supermarket and wide range of shops, restaurants, bars and takeaways. Indoor and outdoor pools. Tennis. Minigolf. Fishing. Watersports. Archery. Diving. Fitness programmes and keep fit track. Crèche and supervised play area. Bowls. Mountain bike track. Wide range of organised sports and entertainment. Road train to town in high season. Dogs are not accepted. Off site: Riding 3 km. Beach fishing. Tours and excursions.

Open: 21 April - 30 September.

Directions

From A4 Venice - Trieste motorway leave at exit for Sto Stino di Livenze and follow signs to Caorle then Sta Margherita and signs to site.
GPS: 45.57312, 12.81248

Charges guide

Per unit incl. 2 persons and electricity	€ 16.40 - € 62.80
extra person	€ 4.20 - € 9.90
child (2-5 yrs)	free - € 7.00
child (6-12 yrs)	€ 1.00 - € 8.20

Min. stay 2 nights.

Caorle

Camping San Francesco

Porto Santa Margherita, I-30020 Caorle (Veneto) T: 042 129 82. E: info@villaggiosfrancesco.com

alanrogers.com/IT60110

Camping San Francesco is a large, family site with direct access to a broad sandy beach. This site has been recommended by our Italian agent and we plan to undertake a full inspection in 2012. It is a well equipped site with five swimming pools dispersed around the site and including an aquapark. The site boasts extensive shopping and catering amenities including three restaurants. There are 687 pitches, all offering electrical connections (up to 10A). The camping area is well shaded and pitches are generally of a good size. A lively entertainment and activity programme is organised here including a children's club and beach activities.

Facilities

Bars, restaurants, pizzeria and ice cream parlour. Shopping centre. Swimming pools, paddling pool and hydromassage centre. Diving school. Aquapark with waterslides. Tennis. Playground. Games room. Entertainment and activity programme, children's club. Excursions. Mobile homes and chalets for rent.
Off site: Sailing and diving. Venice.

Open: 22 April - 23 September.

Directions

From A4 motorway (Venice - Trieste) take exit to Ste Stino di Livenza and follow signs to Caorle joining the P59. Site is signed from Caorle on the continuation of this road to Porto Santa Margherita.
GPS: 45.56709, 12.7943

Charges guide

Per person	€ 3.10 - € 9.80
child (3-6 yrs)	free - € 7.70
pitch incl. electricity	€ 7.20 - € 24.70

Camping Cheques accepted.

Castiglione del Lago

Camping Listro

Via Lungolago, I-06061 Castiglione del Lago (Umbria) T: **075 951 193**. E: **listro@listro.it**

alanrogers.com/IT66530

This is a simple, pleasant, flat site with the best beach on Lake Trasimeno. Listro provides 110 pitches, all with electricity, 70% of which enjoy the shade of mature trees. Younger campers are in a separate area of the site, ensuring no noise disturbance and some motorcaravan pitches are right on the lakeside giving stunning views out of your windows. Facilities are fairly limited with a small shop, bar and snack bar, and there is no organised entertainment. English is spoken and British guests are particularly welcome. If you enjoy the simple life and peace and quiet in camping terms then this site is for you. The campsite's beach is private and the lake has very gradually sloping beaches making it very safe for children to play and swim. This also results in very warm water, which is kept clean as fishing and tourism are the major industries hereabouts. Camping Listro is a few hundred yards north of the historic town of Castiglione and the attractive town can be seen rising up the hillside from the site.

Facilities

Two screened sanitary facilities are very clean with British and Turkish style WCs. Facilities for disabled visitors. Washing machine. Motorcaravan services. Bar. Shop. Snack bar. Play area. Fishing. Bicycle hire. Private beach. Off site: Bars and restaurants nearby. Good swimming pool and tennis courts (discounts using the campsite card). Town 800 m.

Open: 1 April - 30 September.

Directions

From A1/E35 Florence - Rome autostrada take Val di Chiana exit and join the Perugia (75 bis) superstrada. After 24 km. take Castiglione exit and follow town signs. Site is clearly signed just before the town. GPS: 43.1341, 12.0448

Charges guide

Per unit incl. 2 persons and electricity	€ 9.70 - € 16.70
extra person	€ 4.10 - € 4.90
motorcycle	€ 1.10 - € 1.50

Less 10% for stays over 8 days in low season.

Castiglione della Pescaia

Camping Maremma Sans Souci

I-58043 Castiglione della Pescaia (Tuscany) T: **056 493 3765**. E: **info@maremmasanssouci.it**

alanrogers.com/IT66600

This delightful seaside site is owned and run by the Perduca family and sits in natural woodland on the coast road between Follonica and Grosseto. The minimum amount of undergrowth has been cleared to provide 370 individually marked and hedged, flat pitches for camping enthusiasts. This offers considerable privacy in individual settings. There are 6A electrical connections for all caravan and motorcaravan pitches and 40 have a satellite TV point. Some are small and cars may not remain with tents or caravans but must go to a shaded and secure car park near the entrance. There is a wide road for motorcaravans but other roads are mostly narrow and bordered by trees (this is a protected area, and they cannot fell the trees).

Facilities

Five small, very clean, older style toilet blocks are well situated around the site. Free showers, plus lots of extras such as hairdryers, soap dispensers etc. Three blocks have private cabins, each with WC, basin and shower. Separate facilities for disabled campers. Motorcaravan services. Laundry. Shop. Restaurant. Bar with snacks. Bicycle hire. ATM. WiFi (charged). Torches needed in some areas. Dogs are not accepted 16/6-31/8. Off site: Excursions to Elba and Rome. Sailing school.

Open: 1 April - 31 October.

Directions

Site is 2.5 km. northwest of Castiglione on road to Follonica on the S322. GPS: 42.77343, 10.84392

Charges guide

Per unit incl. 2 persons and electricity	€ 24.00 - € 43.00
extra person	€ 7.00 - € 13.00
child (3-5 yrs)	free - € 7.00
dog	€ 3.00

Camping Cheques accepted.

Catania

Camping Jonio

Via Villini a Mare 2, Ognina, I-95126 Catania (Sicily) T: 095 491 139. E: info@campingjonio.com

alanrogers.com/IT69230

This is a small, uncomplicated and tranquil city site with the advantage of being on top of a cliff at the water's edge. The 70 level touring pitches are on gravel with shade from some tall trees and artificial bamboo screens. There are some clean high quality sanitary facilities (also some private facilities for hire). There is no pool but the views of the water compensate and there are delightful rock pools in the sea just a few steps from the campsite. A new attractive restaurant offers food in the summer high season. Camping Jonio is ideal for a short stay to unwind. You could bask in the sun on the rocky platforms and dive into the clear waters, or take advantage of the many excursions to the local historical sites. Excellent winter rates are available for long stay visitors. Five languages including English are spoken and access to the site is good.

Facilities

Sanitary facilities are modern and clean in two blocks, one small block for men and another for women. Laundry with roof top drying area. Motorcaravan services. Shop. Bar and restaurant. Basic old style playground (supervision recommended). Entertainment (high season). Diving school. Access to small gravel beach. Excursions. Dogs are not accepted in July/Aug. Off site: Large town of Catania, many historical sites and Mount Etna.

Open: All year.

Directions

From A18 Catania exit follow signs to the coast road (SS114) in the direction of Ognina. Site is off the SS114 (signed) on the northeast outskirts of town. Access to site is off the small one way system and via the site's separate car park.
GPS: 37.53232, 15.12012

Charges guide

Per person	€ 7.00 - € 10.00
pitch	€ 7.00 - € 14.00
car	€ 4.00 - € 6.00
electricity	€ 3.00

Cavallino-Treporti

Residence Village

Via F Baracca 47, I-30013 Cavallino-Treporti (Veneto) T: 041 968 027. E: info@residencevillage.com

alanrogers.com/IT60250

Camping Residence is a stylish site with a sandy beach directly on the Adriatic. It is well kept and has many floral displays. A medium sized site (for this region), the 265 touring pitches are marked out with small fences or pines, and some give excellent shade. The pitches are in regular rows on level sand and vary in size (55-80 sq.m). All have 6A electricity connections. There are strict rules regarding noise (no radios or dogs, quiet periods and no unaccompanied under 18s). A pleasant restaurant offering fine food is located in an impressive building. The beach runs the whole length of the site and shelves gradually into the sea making it safe for children.

Facilities

Three large toilet blocks, plus a smaller one near the beach, are very clean with good facilities including British style WCs. Supermarket, separate shops for fruit and other goods. Well appointed restaurant with separate bar. Takeaway. Swimming pools with sunbathing areas. Playground. Tennis. Fitness programme. Games room. Entertainment programme. Miniclub. Bicycle hire. WiFi (charged). Dogs are not accepted. Mobile homes and chalets to rent. Off site: Boat moorings for hire at nearby marina. Fishing 1 km. Golf and riding 3 km.

Open: 7 May - 18 September.

Directions

From A4 Venice - Trieste autostrada take exit for airport or Quarto d'Altino. Follow signs for Jesolo, then Punta Sabbioni. Take first left after Cavallino bridge and site is 800 m. on the left.
GPS: 45.48002, 12.57395

Charges guide

Per unit incl. 2 persons and electricity	€ 19.60 - € 42.70
extra person	€ 5.00 - € 9.70
child (3-10 yrs)	free - € 7.60

Less 10% on pitch fee for over 60s.

Cavallino-Treporti

Camping Union Lido Vacanze

Via Fausta 258, I-30013 Cavallino-Treporti (Veneto) T: 041 257 5111. E: info@unionlido.com

alanrogers.com/IT60200

This amazing site is very large, offering everything a camper could wish for. It is extremely well organised and it has been said to set the standard that others follow. It lies right beside the sea with direct access to a 1.2 km. long, broad sandy beach which shelves very gradually and provides very safe bathing (there are lifeguards). The site itself is regularly laid out with parallel access roads under a covering of poplars, pine and other trees providing good shade. There are 2,222 pitches for touring units, all with 6/10A electricity and 1,777 also have water and drainage. Because of the size of the site there is an internal road train and amenities are repeated across the site (cycling is not permitted and cars are parked away from the pitches). You really would not need to leave this site – everything is here, including a sophisticated wellness centre. Overnight parking is provided outside the gate with electricity, toilets and showers for those arriving after 21.00. There are two aqua parks, one with fine sandy beaches (a first in Europe) and both with swimming pools, lagoon pools for children, a heated whirlpool and a slow flowing 160 m. 'river'. A heated pool for hotel and apartment guests is open to others on payment. A huge selection of sports is offered, along with luxury amenities too numerous to list. Entertainment and fitness programmes are organised in season. The golf academy (with a professional) has a driving range, pitching green, putting green and practice bunker, and a diving centre offers lessons and open water diving. Union Lido is above all an orderly and clean site, which is achieved by reasonable regulations to ensure quiet, comfortable camping, and by good management. A member of Leading Campings Group.

Facilities

Fourteen well kept, fully equipped toilet blocks which open and close progressively during the season; 11 have facilities for disabled visitors. Launderette. Motorcaravan service points. Gas supplies. Comprehensive shopping areas set around a pleasant piazza (all open till late). Eight restaurants each with a different style plus 11 pleasant and lively bars (all services open all season). Impressive aqua parks (all season). Tennis. Riding. Minigolf. Skating. Bicycle hire. Archery. Two fitness tracks in 4 ha. natural park with play area and supervised play for children. Golf academy. Diving centre and school. Windsurfing school in season. Boat excursions. Recreational events. Church service in English in July/Aug. Hairdressers. Internet cafés. ATM. Dogs are not accepted. Off site: Boat launching 3.5 km. Aqualandia (special rates).

Open: 22 April - 25 September (with all services).

Directions

From Venice - Trieste autostrada leave at exit for airport or Quarto d'Altino and follow signs first for Jesolo and then Punta Sabbioni, and site will be seen just after Cavallino on the left.
GPS: 45.467883, 12.530367

Charges guide

Per unit incl. 2 persons	
and electricity	€ 25.40 - € 47.50
with services	€ 28.50 - € 63.90
extra person	€ 6.60 - € 11.20
child (1-11 yrs)	€ 3.70 - € 9.30

Three different seasons: (i) high season 29/6-31/8; (ii) mid-season 18/5-29/6 and 31/8-14/9, and (iii) off-season, outside these dates.

Cavallino-Treporti

Italy Camping Village

Via Fausta 272, I-30013 Cavallino-Treporti (Veneto) T: 041 968 090. E: info@campingitaly.it

alanrogers.com/IT60210

Italy Camping Village, under the same ownership as the better known Union Lido which it adjoins, is suggested for those who prefer a smaller, more compact site. The 180 touring pitches are on either side of sand tracks off hard access roads under a cover of trees. All have 6A electricity connections and 73 are fully serviced. Pitches are between 50-70 sq.m. but access is impossible for large units, particularly in high season when cars are parked everywhere. Units for rental take 55 plots, with 26 being used by tour operators. There is direct access to a gently sloping sandy beach. A pleasant, heated, swimming pool has a slide and a whirlpool at one end, but for those who want a greater choice of activities, guests can use the facilities at Union Lido for a small additional charge. Strict regulations regarding undue noise here make this a relatively peaceful site and with lower charges than some in the area, this would be a good choice for families with young children. Advance booking is possible.

Facilities

Two good quality, fully equipped sanitary blocks include facilities for disabled visitors. Washing machines. Shop. Restaurant with TV. Bar beside beach. Heated swimming pool (17x7 m). Small playground, miniclub and children's disco. Bicycle hire. WiFi (charged). Only gas barbecues permitted on individual pitches; charcoal only permitted in the designated area. Dogs are not accepted. Off site: Use of facilites at IT60200 Union Lido (extra charge for pool). Sports centre, golf and riding 500 m.

Open: 21 April - 18 September.

Directions

From Venice - Trieste A4 autostrada leave at exit for airport or Quarto d'Altino and follow signs for Jesolo and Punta Sabbioni. Site well signed on left after Cavallino. GPS: 45.46836, 12.53338

Charges guide

Per unit incl. 2 persons	
and electricity	€ 18.10 - € 38.60
extra person	€ 4.90 - € 8.90
child (1-5 yrs)	free - € 6.50

Three charging seasons.

MANIFESTO TURISTICO AMBIENTALE VENETO CAVALLINO QUALITY CAMPING
MY HOLIDAYS
UNION LIDO Vacanze
PARK & RESORT
CAMPING
LODGING
HOTEL
UNIONLIDO.COM
A variety of offers,
made to measure hospitality!
THE CHANCE TO BOOK LARGE, SHADY PITCHES, BUNGALOWS, CAMPING HOMES AND LUXURY TENTS WITH ALL COMFORTS.
NEWS 2012
New Fun Park, with Adventure Slides & Jungle Golf /
New Camping Home Veranda / New beach play area
For last minute offers and promotions visit
WWW.UNIONLIDO.COM/LASTMINUTE
Union Lido Vacanze is located on the green Cavallino coastline, between the splendid Venice Lagoon and the Adriatic sea.
Open from 21st April to 23rd September 2012.
30013 CAVALLINO VENEZIA ITALIA
Camping Park & Resort Tel. Camping +39 0412575111
Tel. Art&Park Hotel +39 041968043 Fax +39 0415370355
info@unionlido.com booking@unionlido.com
ADAC Super-Platz 2011
UNITER
LeadingCampings
Parco Turistico di Cavallino Treporti
Veneto Between Earth and Sky
REGIONE DEL VENETO
LR. 33/02

Cavallino-Treporti

Camping Vela Blu

Via Radaelli 10, I-30013 Cavallino-Treporti (Veneto) T: 041 968 068. E: info@velablu.it

alanrogers.com/IT60280

Thoughtfully landscaped within a natural wooded coastal environment, the tall pines here give shade, while attractive flowers enhance the setting, and paved roads give easy access to most pitches. The 241 pitches vary in size (55-100 sq.m) and shape, but all have electricity (10A) and 80 have drainage. A sister site to nos. IT60360 and IT60140, Vela Blu is a smaller family style site and a pleasant alternative to the other massive sites on Cavallino. It is a popular destination for Italian families, booking is essential for high season and national holidays. A substantial swimming pool with mini waterpark was added in 2010. A clean, sandy beach runs the length of one side of the site with large stone breakwaters for fun and fishing.

Facilities

Two modern, well maintained toilet blocks include baby rooms and good facilities for disabled visitors. An attendant is on hand to maintain high standards. Laundry facilities. Motorcaravan service point. Medical room. Shop. Bar. Gelateria. Restaurant and takeaway. New swimming pool complex. Games room. Satellite TV room. Pedalos. Windsurfing. Fishing. Bicycle hire. Entertainment. WiFi (charged). Off site: Bars, restaurants and shops.

Open: 16 April - 24 September.

Directions

Leave A4 Venice - Trieste motorway at exit for 'Aeroporto' and follow signs for Jesolo and Punta Sabbioni. Site is signed after village of Cavallino. GPS: 45.45681, 12.5072

Charges guide

Per unit incl. 2 persons and all services	€ 17.20 - € 42.60
extra person	€ 4.20 - € 9.30

Camping Cheques accepted.

Cavallino-Treporti

Camping Village Cavallino

Via delle Batterie 164, I-30013 Cavallino-Treporti (Veneto) T: 041 966 133.
E: info@campingcavallino.com **alanrogers.com/IT60320**

This large, well ordered site is run by a friendly, experienced family. It lies beside the sea with direct access to a superb beach of fine sand, which is very safe and has lifeguards. The site is thoughtfully laid out with the 457 large touring pitches shaded by olives and pines. All pitches have 6/10A electricity. There are 264 further pitches which are mainly occupied by mobile homes and chalets available to rent. For visiting Venice, there is a bus to the ferry at Punta Sabbioni which is 20 minutes away. The charming ferry journey takes 40 mins. and drops you directly at Saint Marco Square.

Facilities

The clean, modern toilet blocks (two with solar panels for hot water) can be heated. They provide a mixture of Turkish and British style WCs with facilities for disabled campers. Dog shower. Launderette. Motorcaravan services. Supermarket. Restaurant with large terrace. Takeaway. Pizzeria. Swimming pools and whirlpool (May-Sept). Minigolf. Playground. Bicycle hire. Fishing. Entertainment programme. ATM. WiFi. Dogs are accepted in certain areas. Mobile homes to rent. Off site: Golf 1 km.

Open: 24 March - 31 October.

Directions

From Venice - Trieste autostrada leave at exit for airport or Quarto d'Altino. Follow signs first forJesolo, then Punta Sabbioni. Site signs will be seen just after Cavallino on left. GPS: 45.45666, 12.50055

Charges 2012

Per unit incl. 2 persons and electricity	€ 19.00 - € 47.00
extra person	€ 5.40 - € 12.50

Min. stay in high season one week.

Cavallino-Treporti

Camping Ca'Pasquali

Via A Poerio 33, I-30013 Cavallino-Treporti (Veneto) T: 041 966 110. E: info@capasquali.it

alanrogers.com/IT60360

Situated on the attractive natural woodland coast of Cavallino with its wide, safe, sandy beach, Ca'Pasquali is a good quality holiday resort with easy access to magnificent Venice. This is an ideal place for a holiday interspersed with excursions to Verona, Padova, the glassmakers of Murano, the local water park, pretty villages and many other cultural attractions. This is a large site affiliated with nos. IT60280 and IT60140. Detail is important here; there are superb pools, a fitness area, an arena for an ambitious entertainment programme and a beachside restaurant. The 400 pitches are shaded and flat (80-120 sq.m), and some have spectacular sea views.

Facilities

Three spotless modern units have excellent facilities with superb amenities for disabled campers and babies. Washing machines and dryers. Motorcaravan services. Restaurant. Pizzeria. Crêperie. Cocktail bar. Snack bar. Supermarket. Superb pool complex (all services open all season). Fitness centre. Play areas. Bicycle hire. Canoe hire and lessons. Excellent entertainment. Amphitheatre. Miniclub. Internet. Excursion service. Caravan storage. Dogs are not accepted. Off site: Golf and riding 5 km.

Open: 21 April - 24 September.

Directions

Leave autostrada A4 at Noventa exit in San Doná di Piave and head towards Jesolo and to Cavallino - Treporti. Site is well signed shortly after town of Cavallino. GPS: 45.45237, 12.48905

Charges guide

Per unit incl. 2 persons and electricity	€ 16.90 - € 48.40
extra person	€ 4.50 - € 10.20

No credit cards.

Cavallino-Treporti

Camping Village Garden Paradiso

Via Baracca 55, I-30013 Cavallino-Treporti (Veneto) T: 041 968 075. E: info@gardenparadiso.it

alanrogers.com/IT60400

There are many sites in this area and there is much competition in providing a range of facilities. Garden Paradiso is a good seaside site which also provides three excellent, centrally situated pools, a fitness centre, minigolf, a train to the market and other activities for children. Compared with other sites here, this one is of medium size with 752 pitches. All have electricity (6/10A), tv-sat, water and drainage points and all are marked and numbered with hard access roads, under a good cover of trees. Many flowers and shrubs give a pleasant and peaceful appearance and a new reception provides a professional welcome. The restaurant, with self-service at lunch time and waiter service at night, is near the beach with a bar/snack bar in the centre of the site. The site is directly on the sea with a beach of fine sand. A community bus service runs daily to the local markets. Used by tour operators (35 pitches).

Facilities

Four brick toilet blocks are tiled and fully equipped with a mix of British and Turkish style toilets. Facilities for babies. Washing machines and dryers. Motorcaravan services. Shopping complex. Restaurant, snack bar and takeaway (all season). 'Aqualandia' pool complex (charged). Fitness centre. Tennis. Minigolf. Play area. Organised entertainment and excursions (high season). Bicycle hire. WiFi throughout (charged). Dogs are not accepted. Off site: Riding 2 km. Fishing 2.5 km.

Open: 21 April - 30 September.

Directions

Leave Venice - Trieste autostrada either by taking airport or Quarto d'Altino exits; follow signs to Jesolo and Punta Sabbioni. Take first road left after Cavallino roundabout and site is a little way on the right. GPS: 45.47897, 12.56359

Charges guide

Per unit incl. 2 persons, electricity, water and drainage	€ 20.50 - € 48.50
extra person	€ 4.90 - € 10.70
child (6-12 yrs) or senior (over 61 yrs)	€ 3.40 - € 8.20
child (3-5 yrs)	€ 1.90 - € 7.00

Less 10% for stays over 30 days (early), or 20 days (late) season.

Cavallino-Treporti

Sant'Angelo Village

Via F Baracca 63, I-30013 Cavallino-Treporti (Veneto) T: 041 968 882. E: info@santangelo.it

alanrogers.com/IT60390

Sant'Angelo Village is aptly named. It is a large site, built around a central square where a restaurant, shops, bar and an information centre with booking service for excursions can be found. The site is well planned and includes a beach bar servicing the sports areas and a fine sandy beach with lifeguards. There are 600 mostly shaded, level pitches, but a large proportion are taken by seasonal units and tour operators. Those for tourers are mainly around the perimeter of the site, necessitating a long walk to the centre. Although large, the site has a friendly atmosphere and is ideal for families with young children and campers with mobility problems. The staff here are fluent in several languages including English.

Facilities

Five modern toilet blocks provide excellent facilities with mainly British toilets and very good facilities for disabled campers and babies. Washing machines. Restaurant and snack bar. Supermarket. Great pool complex with water slide, pool bar and fun pool. Aerobics. Fitness centre. Play areas. Games room. Tennis. Bicycle and boat hire. Small boat launching. Miniclub, entertainment and excursion service. WiFi (charged). Fridge box hire. Dogs and other animals are not accepted. Accommodation to rent.
Off site: Sailing 1.5 km. Golf and riding 5 km. Theme parks.

Open: 8 May - 20 September.

Directions

Leave autostrada A4 at San Doná Noventa exit and head for San Doná di Piave, Jesolo and on to peninsula of Cavallino and Punta Sabbioni. Site is well signed shortly after town of Cavallino.
GPS: 45.47681, 12.55509

Charges guide

Per unit incl. 2 persons, electricity and water	€ 19.40 - € 44.30
extra person	€ 4.95 - € 10.30
child (3-10 yrs)	free - € 7.80
senior (over 61 yrs)	€ 2.90 - € 7.80

Cavallino-Treporti

Camping Village Europa

Via Fausta 332, I-30013 Cavallino-Treporti (Veneto) T: 041 968 069. E: info@campingeuropa.com

alanrogers.com/IT60410

Europa is a large site in a great position with direct access to a fine, sandy, Blue Flag beach with lifeguards. There are 500 touring pitches, 450 of which have 8A electricity, water, drainage and satellite TV connections. There is a separate area for campers with dogs and some smaller pitches are available for those with tents. The site is kept beautifully clean and neat and there is an impressive array of restaurants, bars, shops and leisure amenities. These are cleverly laid out along an avenue and include a jeweller's, a doctor's surgery, Internet services and much more. Leisure facilities are arranged around the site. The touring area is surprisingly peaceful for a site of this size. A professional team provides entertainment and regular themed summer events. Some restaurant tables have pleasant sea views. Venice is easily accessible by bus and then ferry from Punta Sabbioni.

Facilities

Three superb toilet blocks are kept pristine and have hot water throughout. Facilities for disabled visitors. Washing machines. Large supermarket and shopping centre, bars, restaurants, cafés and pizzeria (all season; takeaway service 15/5-30/9). Excellent pool complex with slide and spa centre (9/4-25/9). Tennis. Games room. Playground. Children's clubs. Entertainment programme. WiFi (charged). Direct access to the beach. Windsurf and pedalo hire. Mobile homes, chalets and 14 eco apartments for rent. Off site: ATM 500 m. Riding and boat launching 1 km. Golf and fishing 4 km. Walking and cycling trails. Excursions to Venice.

Open: 31 March - 30 September.

Directions

From A4 autostrada (approaching from Milan) take Mestre exit and follow signs initially for Venice airport and then Jesolo. From Jesolo, follow signs to Cavallino from where site is well signed. GPS: 45.47380, 12.54903

Charges guide

Per unit incl. 2 persons and electricity	€ 20.00 - € 48.00
extra person	€ 5.00 - € 10.50
child (2-5 yrs)	€ 3.35 - € 9.30
dog	€ 2.65 - € 5.60

Cavallino-Treporti

Camping Scarpiland

Via A Poerio 14, I-30010 Cavallino-Treporti (Veneto) T: 041 966 488. E: info@scarpiland.com

alanrogers.com/IT60470

Scarpiland faces the Adriatic and has a fine sandy beach. This campsite is a most peculiar shape in that it is dissected by rows of accommodation to rent belonging to the site with long separating fences. This forces campers in the touring area to have long walks to the single beach access. It is a large site with the informal touring pitches under the shade of mature pines. Pitches vary in size (50-80 sq.m) all with 6A electricity. The irregular tree placing will challenge some units and larger units are not suitable here. The site has an attractive woodland setting but there is a very long walk to the two sanitary blocks. The first very small block is unisex and has all Turkish toilets, we envisage problems here at peak periods. The larger block is even further away but has British style toilets and hot showers. The only chemical disposal site is in this block. Few activities are on offer but much is available outside the site. The site's entertainment team organise activities for the children in a small staged area. All other amenities are worryingly situated on the main road which serves the site. All are open fronted and the games area and some shops are across the road so children must be carefully supervised. There is a selection of shops plus a bar and restaurant all open to the public.

Facilities

Two sanitary blocks, one large and one very small with Turkish style toilets only. Dated facilities for babies in the large block and one unit for disabled visitors. Restaurant/pizzeria. Ice cream parlour. Newsagent. Supermarket. Butcher. Souvenir shop. Greengrocer and local produce (all on the main site road). Bicycle hire. WiFi (charged). Off site: Golf and riding 3.4 km. Boat launching 5 km.

Open: 20 April - 25 September.

Directions

From Milan, take A4 autostrada to Venice and continue towards Trieste as far as the A27 junction, then follow signs to the airport. At the end of the bypass, follow signs to Jesolo then Cavallino and Punta Sabbioni. From here the site is clearly signed. GPS: 45.45507, 12.48874

Charges guide

Per unit incl. 2 persons and electricity	€ 15.70 - € 34.30
extra person	€ 4.10 - € 7.90
child (1-5 yrs)	free - € 4.90

MANIFESTO Turistico Ambientale VENETO

www.cavallinoqualitycamping.com

qualitycamping.com

VENETO ENVIRONMENTAL TOURISM MANIFESTO CAVALLINO QUALITY CAMPING

The sensitivity of operators in the tourism sector towards the unique and precious environment in their Region has led to the development of the "Veneto Environmental Tourism Manifesto", which is today the most concrete example of eco-compatible tourism in Europe.

Cavallino-Treporti

Camping Miramare

Punta Sabbioni, I-30010 Cavallino-Treporti (Veneto) T: 041 966 150. E: info@camping-miramare.it

alanrogers.com/IT60460

This small family owned site is well located, being the closest site to the Punta Sabbione ferry. However, it currently lacks a swimming pool and has no direct access to a beach, so the site provides a free bus service to the ferry and to the local beach. It has an unusually long season compared with other sites in the area. Miramare is ideally located for exploring Venice and its islands, as well as the Lido di Venezia. There are 100 level pitches here, all with 6A electricity. The shop is superb for a small site and the restaurant, 50 m. out of the gate, is renowned for its excellent regional meals. The restaurant has an Internet terminal and WiFi is available over part of the site. Everywhere is kept clean and most pitches have shade from mature trees and are level. Ask about the campsite logo – the 'Venetian iron' – very interesting, and about the local flamingos, which from time to time appear in winter!

Facilities

Two toilet blocks (one heated in low season) with facilities for disabled campers and babies. Motorcaravan service point. Excellent supermarket/shop. Bar, restaurant and pizzas from the oven in the restaurant. Takeaway. Play area. Internet point. Bicycle hire. Dogs are only accepted on 15 specific pitches. Free shuttle bus to Punta Sabbioni square (departure point for trips to Venice and the islands) and to the nearest beach (free sun umbrellas). Barbecues on pitches not permitted. Off site: Boat launching 1.5 km. Beach 1.8 km. Fishing 2 km. Riding 8 km. Golf 15 km.

Open: 31 March - 4 November.

Directions

Leave the A4 autostrada at exit for Venezia Mestre and follow signs to Jesolo and Punta Sabbioni, where the site is clearly signed.
GPS: 45.44035, 12.42110

Charges guide

Per unit incl. 2 persons and electricity	€ 22.50 - € 34.00
extra person	€ 5.00 - € 7.80
child (1-10 yrs)	€ 3.30 - € 5.80

Ceriale

Camping Baciccia

Via Torino 19, I-17023 Ceriale (Ligúria) T: 018 299 0743. E: info@campingbaciccia.it

alanrogers.com/IT64030

This friendly, family run site is a popular holiday destination. Baciccia was the nickname of the present owner's grandfather who grew fruit trees and tomatoes on the site. Tall eucalyptus trees shade the 106 flat pitches which encircle the central facilities block. The pitches are on flat ground and all have electricity. There is always a family member by the gate to greet you, and Vincenzina and Giovanni, along with their daughter and son, Laura and Mauro, work tirelessly to ensure that you enjoy your stay. The pool has a giant elephant slide and there is a vibrant play area for children. The informal restaurant serves delightful seasonal Italian dishes and overlooks a large swimming pool. There is a free shuttle to the site's private beach and the town has the usual seaside attractions. This site will suit campers looking for a family atmosphere with none of the brashness of large seaside sites. If you have forgotten anything by way of camping equipment just ask and the family will lend it to you.

Facilities

Two clean and modern sanitary blocks by reception have British and Turkish style WCs and hot water throughout. Laundry. Motorcaravan services. Restaurant/bar. Shop. Pizzeria and takeaway. A swimming pool and paddling pool (1/4-31/10) and private beach. Tennis. Bowls. Excellent new play area. Bicycle hire. Wood-burning stove and barbecue. WiFi. Fishing. Diving. Entertainment for children and adults in high season. Excursions. Off site: Department store 150 m. Bus 200 m. Aquapark 500 m. Riding and golf 2 km. Ancient town of Albenga (2,000 years old) 3 km. Parachuting school 10 km.

Open: 20 March - 3 November, 4 December - 10 January.

Directions

From the A10 between Imperia and Savona, take Albenga exit. Follow signs Ceriale/Savona and Aquapark Caravelle (which is 500 m. from site) and then site signs. Site is just south of Savona.
GPS: 44.08165, 8.21763

Charges guide

Per unit incl. up to 3 persons (over 2 yrs) and electricity	€ 26.50 - € 49.00
extra person	€ 6.50 - € 11.00
half pitch incl. 2 persons, no car	€ 16.00 - € 35.00
dog	€ 2.50 - € 5.00

Discounts for stays in excess of 7 days.
Discount for readers 10% in low season.

Cecina Mare

Camping Mareblu

Localitá Mazzanta, I-57023 Cecina Mare (Tuscany) T: 058 662 9191. E: info@campingmareblu.com

alanrogers.com/IT66310

Mareblu is a well equipped family site with an impressive range of amenities, including a large swimming pool with an attractive terraced surround, and a shopping complex incorporating a greengrocer, hairdressing salon, newsagent and Internet centre. There is also a sandy beach 300 m. away, accessed through a pine forest. The pitches at Mareblu are well shaded and all have electrical connections (6A). A communal barbecue area is provided as they are not allowed on individual pitches. Parking for all cars is in a dedicated area at the front of the site which ensures a pleasant, traffic-free ambience. The site is close to Cecina Mare, a popular resort with easy access to some of Tuscany's great cities, and the island of Elba.

Facilities

Five modern toilet blocks include facilities for disabled visitors. Shopping centre. Bar, restaurant and self-service caféteria, pizzeria and takeaway. Swimming and paddling pools. Play area. Games field. Boules. Bicycle hire. Entertainment. Miniclub. Internet access. Direct access to beach. Windsurfing and subaqua diving organised. Internet access and WiFi. Dogs are not accepted in July/Aug. Off site: Boat launching 300 m. Bus 400 m. Riding 2 km. Watersports and diving. Tennis. Excursions.

Open: 26 March - 15 October.

Directions

Site is south of Livorno. From north, take A12 to Rosignano and then join the E80 to Vada, then to La Mazzanta. From here site is well signed. GPS: 43.31848, 10.47407

Charges guide

Per person	€ 4.50 - € 9.00
child (0-8 yrs)	€ 3.20 - € 7.00
pitch incl. electricity	€ 7.20 - € 19.00

No credit cards.
Camping Cheques accepted.

Chioggia

Villaggio Turistico Isamar

Isolaverde, via Isamar 9, I-30010 Chioggia (Veneto) T: 041 553 5811. E: info@villaggioisamar.com

alanrogers.com/IT60550

This is a very large site with many shops, restaurants and leisure facilities. The camping area, with different pitch sizes, is under pine trees and grouped around the pool complex and covered entertainment centre. The pool complex comprises an Olympic size, saltwater swimming pool, a paddling pool and several new leisure pools. The pitches are arranged on either side of hard access roads and all have 6A electrical connections. There are many other areas containing well constructed chalets and holiday bungalows. The site is right beside the sea, with its own sandy beach.

Facilities

Four large modern sanitary blocks, are arranged around the main camping area. Fully equipped and of good quality with facilities for children and disabled visitors. Laundry. Motorcaravan services. Gas supplies. Hairdresser. Supermarket and general shopping centre. Large bar/pizzeria and self-service restaurant. Swimming pools. Tennis. Playground. Disco. Games room. Riding. Bicycle hire. Extensive entertainment and fitness programme. Supervised play for children over 4 yrs old. WiFi (charged). Dogs are not accepted. Off site: Fishing and boat launching 500 m.

Open: Second Friday in May - 14 September.

Directions

Turn off the main 309 road towards sea just south of Adige river about 10 km. south of Chioggia, and proceed 5 km. to site. GPS: 45.16236, 12.32477

Charges guide

Per unit incl. 2 persons and electricity	€ 16.00 - € 47.00
extra person	€ 4.00 - € 11.00
child (2-12 yrs)	free - € 11.00

Cisano di Bardolino

Campings Cisano & San Vito

Via Peschiera 48, I-37011 Cisano di Bardolino (Lake Garda) T: **045 622 9098**. E: **cisano@camping-cisano.it**

alanrogers.com/IT63570

This is a combination of two sites, each with its own reception. Some of the 700 touring pitches have superb locations along the 1 km. of shaded lakeside contained in Cisano. Some are on sloping ground and most are shaded but the San Vito pitches have no lake views. Both sites have a family orientation and considerable effort has been taken in the landscaping to provide maximum comfort even for the largest units. San Vito is the smaller and more peaceful location, which shares many of the facilities of Cisano. A security fence separates the pitches from the beach, so access involves a short walk. The facilities are constantly upgraded, although visitors with disabilities should select their pitch carefully to ensure an area appropriate to all their needs (there are some slopes in Cisano). On the San Vito site there is a pleasant family style restaurant (some road noise) which also sells takeaway food. San Vito is accessed through a tunnel under the road. Excellent pools and play equipment, along with a children's club and entertainment in high season are all here. The friendly, efficient staff at both sites speak English.

Facilities

Plentiful, good quality sanitary facilities are provided in both sites (nine blocks at Cisano and two at San Vito). Facilities for disabled visitors. Baby room. Washing machines. Fridge hire. Shop, two bar/restaurants and takeaway (all season). Swimming pool (May-Sept). Whirlpool. Play area. Fishing and sailing. Free windsurfing and canoeing. Archery. Football. Minigolf. Boat launching. WiFi (charged). Car wash. Dogs are not accepted (cats are). Motorcycles not allowed on site (parking provided). Off site: Indoor pool, bicycle hire and tennis 2 km. Riding 15 km. Golf 20 km.

Open: 1 April - 8 October.

Directions

Leave A4 autoroute at Pescheria exit and head north towards Garda on lakeside road. Pass Lazise and site is signed (small sign) on left halfway to Bardolina. Site is 12 km. beyond the Gardaland theme park. GPS: 45.52290, 10.72760

Charges guide

Per unit incl. 2 persons and electricity	€ 18.50 - € 45.00
extra person	€ 4.50 - € 11.00
child (2-5 yrs)	free - € 4.30
motorboat	€ 10.00 - € 18.00

Camping Cheques accepted.

Cortina d'Ampezzo

Camping Rocchetta

Via Campo 1, I-32043 Cortina d'Ampezzo (Veneto) T: **043 650 63**. E: **camping@sunrise.it**

alanrogers.com/IT62055

Cortina d'Ampezzo is well known as one of Europe's most exclusive and smartest winter resorts. However, this is an enchanting area at any time and Camping Rocchetta has been recommended to us by our Italian agent. We plan to undertake a full inspection in 2008. The site lies 20 minutes walk from the centre of Cortina and is the closest to the town. Pitches are generally flat and some offer shade. Electrical connections are available on most pitches. The site enjoys fine views of the surrounding mountains and the bar has a pleasant sun terrace. Rocchetta is open for a winter season as well as the summer, and has a heated toilet block and drying room. Although on-site amenities are limited, Cortina offers a very wide range of shops and restaurants, and also hosts many festivals and exhibitions. Winter sports facilities are excellent with 30 chairlifts, with many of these also available in the summer months for exploration of the Dolomites.

Facilities

Heated toilet block and drying room. Play area. Shop. Bar. Motorcaravan services (all year). Minigolf. Off site: Cortina 1.5 km. (bus stop at site entrance). Winter sports. Ampezzo Valley and the Dolomite mountains. Walking and cycle trails.

Open: All year.

Directions

From the south (Venice), take the northbound A27. Beyond Belluno, take the exit towards Cadore and Cortina, joining the SS51. Continue on this road until you reach Cortina (passing the Olympic ski jump). Drive through the town and follow signs for the campsite to the left. The site can be found after a further 500 m. and is well indicated.
GPS: 46.52262, 12.13406

Charges guide

Per person	€ 5.50 - € 8.25
child (1-6 yrs)	€ 2.50 - € 4.00
pitch	€ 7.00 - € 10.00
dog	free

Deiva Marina

Villaggio Camping Valdeiva

Localitá Ronco, I-19013 Deiva Marina (Ligúria) T: **018 782 4174**. E: **camping@valdeiva.it**

alanrogers.com/IT64120

A mature and cheerful site, 3 km. from the sea between the famous Cinque Terre and Portofino, Valdeiva is open all year. The 40 touring pitches, with 3A electricity, are in a square at the bottom of the site, some with shade and views, and cars may be required to park in a separate area depending on the pitch and season. There are 100 permanent pitches on the upper reaches of the site. Camping Valdeiva does have a small swimming pool, which is very welcome if you do not wish to take the free bus to the beach. A small busy bar/restaurant offers food at realistic prices. There was late night noise from residents when we stayed in high season. The beach is pleasant and the surrounding village has several bars and restaurants. There are very pleasant walks and treks in the unspoilt woods of Liguria nearby or the most interesting tourist option is a visit to Cinque Terre, five villages, some of which can only be reached by rail, boat or by cliff footpath. Their history is one of fishing but now they also specialise in wines. Unusually, some of the vineyards can only be reached by boat. This is a great site for short stays to visit the Cinque Terre.

Facilities

The toilet block nearest the touring pitches provides cramped facilities. A new block is in the centre of the site. WCs are mainly Turkish, but there are some of British style. Washing machines and dryers. Shop (15/6-10/9). Bar/restaurant and takeaway with reasonable menu and pizzas cooked in a traditional oven (15/6-10/9). Small swimming pool. Play area. Excursions. Free bus to the beach. Torches required. Bicycle hire. Camping gas. Internet access. WiFi. Off site: Beach, fishing and boat launching 3 km. Tours and excursions.

Open: All year excl. 10/1-10/2 and 5/11-5/12.

Directions

Leave A12 at Deiva Marina exit and follow signs to Deiva Marina. Site signs are clear at the first junction and site is on left 3 km. down this road.
GPS: 44.22470, 9.55168

Charges guide

Per unit incl. 2 persons and electricity	€ 19.00 - € 35.00
extra person (over 6 yrs)	€ 6.00

Dormelletto

Camping Village Lago Maggiore

Via Leonardo da Vinci 7, I-28040 Dormelletto (Piedmont) T: 032 249 7193. E: info@lagomag.com

alanrogers.com/IT62435

This lively and happy site can be found on the southwestern shores of Lake Maggiore, close to the pretty town of Arona. There are 290 pitches here, of which around 60 are available for tourers. Pitches are all equipped with electrical connections (6A) and have reasonable shade. A number of mobile homes, apartments and bungalows are available for rent. The site has direct access to the lake and a sandy beach. On-site amenities include a well stocked shop and a bar/restaurant and there are many opportunities for sports and organised activities.

Facilities

Five toilet blocks in total, of which two are for tourers and a mix of Turkish and British style (a small charge is made for hot water and showers). Private family bathrooms for rent. Motorcaravan services. Bar, restaurant/pizzeria. Shop. Games room. Adventure and play areas. Swimming pools. Beach bar. Children's pool. Sports field. Entertainment and activity programme (high season). Direct access to lake. Mobile homes and chalets for rent. WiFi. Off site: Supermarket across road from site. Arona 3 km. Walking and cycle routes. Watersports. Fishing.

Open: 1 April - 30 September.

Directions

Leave the A26 motorway at the Sesto Calende exit and join the northbound SS33 as far as Dormelletto. The campsite is clearly signed from the village. GPS: 45.73333, 8.57722

Charges guide

Per unit incl. 2 persons and electricity	€ 23.00 - € 41.00
extra person	€ 5.00 - € 9.00
child (2-6 yrs)	€ 3.00 - € 5.00
dog	€ 5.00 - € 6.00

No credit cards.

Feriolo di Baveno

Camping Orchidea

Via 42 Martiri 20, I-28831 Feriolo di Baveno (Piedmont) T: 032 328 257. E: info@campingorchidea.it

alanrogers.com/IT62465

Camping Orchidea can be found on the western bank of Lake Maggiore, 35 km. south of the Swiss border and 5 km. from Stresa. This site has direct access to the lake, the banks of the river Sarentto and has a sandy beach. Orchidea has a good range of modern amenities, including a shop, bar and restaurant. Watersports are understandably popular here and pedaloes and kayaks can be rented on site. Pitches are grassy and generally well shaded, all with electrical connections (6A). Some pitches are available facing the lake (a supplement is charged in peak season). There are apartments and mobile homes available for rent. Stresa, nearby, is an important town with 5,000 inhabitants and has a harbour with regular boat trips to the Borromean islands, and also a cable car to the summit of Monte Mottarone, passing the stunning Giardino Botanico Alpinia, world-renowned mountain gardens. This site would suit families who prefer a simple and peaceful holiday.

Facilities

Three toilet blocks are kept clean and have hot and cold water throughout. Shop. Restaurant. Bar. Takeaway. Direct lake access. Pedalo and kayak hire. Fishing. Playground. Children's club. Mobile homes and caravans for rent. Bicycle hire. WiFi (charged). Off site: Walking and cycle trails. Tennis. Golf 3 km. Stresa 5 km. Riding 15 km. Excursions.

Open: 16 March - 6 October.

Directions

Take Baveno/Stresa exit from the A26 (autostrada dei Trafori) and head north on the Via Sempione. In Feriolo follow signs to the campsite. GPS: 45.9334, 8.4812

Charges guide

Per unit incl. 2 persons and electricity	€ 17.50 - € 41.50
extra person	€ 4.80 - € 8.00
child (2-12 yrs)	€ 3.40 - € 5.80
dog	€ 2.60 - € 5.50

Feriolo di Baveno

Camping Conca d'Oro

Via 42 Martiri 26, I-28835 Feriolo di Baveno (Piedmont) T: 032 328 116. E: info@concadoro.it

alanrogers.com/IT62485

Conca d'Oro is a delightful site with spectacular views across Lake Maggiore to the distant mountains. The first impression is one of spaciousness and colour. There are just a dozen mobile homes for rent, the rest of the 210 grass plots provide good sized touring pitches. All have 6A electrical connections, some have shade and many have spectacular views especially at night. The land slopes gently down to a fine sandy beach. An attractive terraced restaurant serves a range of regional dishes and there is a pleasant bar and pizzeria plus a well stocked shop. The owners Maurizio and Alessandra are sure to give you a warm welcome. The site is close to the lakeside town of Baveno from where boat trips are available to the three small islands on this part of Lake Maggiore. Fishing and boat launching are possible from the beach at the site, with sailing and other watersports available. There are nature reserves nearby and drives out into the surrounding mountains provide opportunities for walkers, cyclists and climbers.

Facilities

Three toilet blocks provide all necessary facilities kept in immaculate condition, including controllable showers and open style washbasins; some toilets with washbasins. En-suite unit for disabled visitors. Laundry room. Motorcaravan service point. Bar, restaurant, pizzeria and shop (all season). Swimming, fishing and boat launching from beach. Bicycle hire. Dogs must be prebooked and are not allowed 3/7-21/8. Off site: Shops, bars and restaurants nearby. Riding 700 m. Golf 1 km. Sailing 7 km. Excursions to nearby attractions.

Open: 1 April - 30 September.

Directions

Baveno is 90 km. northwest of Milan on the western shore of Lake Maggiore. Site is off the SS33 road between Baveno and Fondotoce di Verbania, 1 km. south of the junction with the SS34 and is well signed. GPS: 45.93611, 8.48583

Charges guide

Per unit incl. 2 persons and electricity	€ 19.50 - € 42.00
extra person	€ 5.00 - € 8.00
child (2-13 yrs)	€ 3.50 - € 6.50
dog	€ 3.50 - € 4.50

Feriolo di Baveno

Camping Miralago

Via 42 Martiri 24, I-28831 Feriolo di Baveno (Piedmont) T: 032 328 226. E: miralago@miralago-holiday.com

alanrogers.com/IT62464

Miralago is located on the western banks of Lake Maggiore and the bank of the Stronetta river where it runs into the lake, offering many waterfront pitches. It is very close to the little resort of Feriolo which can be accessed via a cycle track. There are 74 neat and easily accessed touring pitches here, all of which have 6A electricity connections. On-site amenities include a restaurant/bar with terrace and a simple play area for children. Miralago is a simple site and would suit those who prefer a quiet and peaceful holiday without all the entertainment and activities of the larger sites.

Facilities

A single sanitary block provides a mix of British and Turkish style toilets and facilities for disabled visitors. Shop. Bar/restaurant (serving pizzas) with terrace (all season). Play area. Tourist information. Direct access to lake and sandy beach. Boat launching ramp. WiFi. Off site: Feriolo and riding 500 m. Golf and bicycle hire 2 km. Baveno 3 km. Stresa 7 km. Walking and cycle routes. Watersports. Fishing.

Open: 1 April - 3 October.

Directions

Leave the A26 motorway at the Casale exit and join the eastbound S33 as far as Feriolo. Site is clearly signed from the village. GPS: 45.93388, 8.48471

Charges guide

Per unit incl. 2 persons and electricity	€ 21.50 - € 34.50
extra person	€ 5.00 - € 7.50
child (3-12 yrs)	€ 4.50 - € 6.00
dog	€ 4.50 - € 5.50

Low season discounts.

Fiesole

Camping Panoramico Fiesole

Via Peramonda 1, I-50014 Fiesole (Tuscany) T: 055 599 069. E: panoramico@florencecamping.com

alanrogers.com/IT66100

This is a mature but pleasant site in a fine hilltop situation offering wonderful views over Florence in the distance – on some evenings you can hear music from the nearby Roman amphitheatre famous for its classical entertainment in summer. It can become crowded in the main season and a very steep final access can be very difficult for larger units although the site will assist with a jeep. The 120 pitches, all with electricity (5A), are on terraces and steep walks to and from the various facilities could cause problems for guests with mobility problems. There is shade in many parts. Pitches are separated, motorcaravans and caravans in the upper area and tents on the lower terraces. The last approach to the site takes you through the charming village of Fiesole but there are some challenging turns and tight squeezes (look for the helpful wall mounted mirrors). Fiesole itself is interesting, its history predating that of Florence. It was founded in the 7th century BC when the Estruscan colony here was a powerful force in Italy. The site is appreciably fresher and quieter than nearer the very busy city. A shuttle bus service operates one way from the site to the centre of town (08.30-11.45 and 14.00-16.45 on request) to connect with the service to Florence (tickets from site office). However, it is an extremely long uphill walk back to the campsite from the town and thus the local bus (to within 300 m) or taxi may be essential.

Facilities

Two tastefully refurbished toilet blocks have mainly British style WCs, free hot water in washbasins and good showers. Washing machines and dryers. Fridges, freezer, microwaves, irons and little cookers for campers' use. Shop (1/4-31/10). Bar and restaurant (1/4-31/10). Swimming pool (1/6-30/9). Play area. Nursery. Torches required in some parts. English is spoken. Free shuttle service to Fiesole. WiFi (charged). Off site: Riding 9 km.

Open: 15 March - 31 December.

Directions

From A1 take Firenze-Sud exit and follow signs to Fiesole (NNE of central Firenze). From Fiesole centre follow SP54 and camping signs out of town for 1 km; the roads are very narrow both through the town and the final steep access is difficult. Site is signed on the right from Fiesole. Do not try to enter from the north as the left turn is extremely difficult.
GPS: 43.8065, 11.3051

Charges guide

Per unit incl. 2 persons and electricity	€ 30.00 - € 35.00
extra person	€ 9.00 - € 10.00
child (3-12 yrs)	€ 4.00 - € 5.00
dog	free

Firenze

Camping Internazionale

Via San Cristofano 2, Bottai, I-50029 Firenze (Tuscany) T: 055 237 4704.
E: internazionale@florencecamping.com alanrogers.com/IT66090

Camping Internazionale is set in the hills about 5 km. south of Florence, and 8 km. from the Duomo with its wonderful dome by Brunelleschi. There is an 800 m. walk to a bus stop which will take you into Florence. This is a well shaded, terraced site with 240 touring pitches set around the top of a hill. These all have electricity, with water obtained from the laundry and kitchen areas or the motorcaravan service point only. The site is often lively at night with young people from tour groups enjoying themselves, however this area is located well away from the touring pitches. Although it is a very green site, the camping area is somewhat more open with two electricity pylons at the top of the hill and some noise from the busy motorway which is below and next to the site. The two toilet blocks are clean and well equipped with many washing machines and dryers. Although showers are a little small they are fully adjustable with free hot water. There is a kitchen area stocked with pots, pans etc, gas hobs and free use of refrigerators. Two good sized pools, one for children, are fenced with a nice playground adjacent. The inviting restaurant with its open bar area has a good menu. This site offers an easily accessible location to explore Florence, and of the city sites is probably the most family friendly.

Facilities

Two toilet blocks include free hot showers. Laundry. Kitchen facilities. Motorcaravan service point. Shop. New bar and restaurant at the lower level. Evening entertainment. Two swimming pools. Playground. WiFi over part of site. Gas barbecues only. Off site: Florence 5 km.

Open: 1 April - 31 October.

Directions

From A1 take Firenza Certosa exit towards Florence. The turn to the site is just outside Bottai – turn left if coming from this direction (if you reach Galluzzo you have gone too far). From Florence take Via Senese (S2) through Galluzzo, turn right at site sign just before entering Bottai. Continue 500 m. to site.
GPS: 43.72187, 11.22058

Charges guide

Per unit incl. 2 persons and electricity	€ 29.00 - € 34.00
extra person	€ 9.00 - € 10.00
child (3-12 yrs)	€ 4.00 - € 5.00

Fondotoce di Verbania

Camping Continental Lido

Via 42 Martiri 156, I-28924 Fondotoce di Verbania (Piedmont) T: 032 349 6300.
E: info@campingcontinental.com **alanrogers.com/IT62490**

Continental Lido is a large, bustling site situated on the shore of the charming little Lake Mergozzo, about one kilometre from the better known Lake Maggiore. The 405 average sized touring pitches are back to back in rows on grass and although a little close together, the rest of the site has a more open feel. All have electricity (6A) and there is some shade. There are also 233 mobile homes available to rent. There is an impressive pool complex and a small sandy beach slopes gently into the lake where swimming and watersports can also be enjoyed (no powered craft may be used). A bustling entertainment programme is provided, centred around a very large amphitheatre. Pine-clad mountains and a pretty village directly opposite the beach provide a pleasing, scenic background. An unusual feature here is the nine-hole golf course. There is a busy programme of activities from May to September. Under the same ownership as Isolino Camping Village, this site is managed by the son, Gian Paolo, who speaks good English.

Facilities

Five high standard toilet blocks have free hot water. Facilities for disabled visitors. Washing machines and dryers. Mini-fridges. Well stocked shop and bar/restaurant with terrace and takeaway. Swimming pool complex (21/4-26/9) with slides, rapids and waves, plus free sun loungers and parasols. Snack bars by pool and lake. Large amphitheatre. TV. Tennis. Golf course (9 holes). Playground. Fishing. Windsurfing, pedaloes, canoes, kayaks. Games room. Bicycle hire. Entertainment and activities (mid June-mid Sept). Bus on request to Verbania. Internet access and WiFi. Off site: Riding 1 km. Sailing 5 km. 18-hole golf 12 km. Excursions.

Open: 30 March - 24 September.

Directions

Verbania is 100 km. northwest of Milan, on the western shore of Lake Maggiore. Site is off the SS34 road between Fondotoce and Gravellona, 200 m. west of junction with the SS33.
GPS: 45.94960, 8.48058

Charges guide

Per unit incl. 3 persons and electricity	€ 23.20 - € 45.75
extra person	€ 4.75 - € 8.00
child (6-11 yrs)	€ 3.45 - € 6.60

No credit cards.

Fondotoce di Verbania

Camping Village Isolino

Via per Feriolo 25, I-28924 Fondotoce di Verbania (Piedmont) T: 032 349 6080. E: info@isolino.com
alanrogers.com/IT62460

Lake Maggiore is one of the most attractive Italian lakes and Isolino is an impressive site and one of the largest in the region. Most of the 531 touring pitches have shade from a variety of trees. They vary in size, all have electrical connections (6A), 182 are fully serviced and some have lake views. The bar and restaurant terraces overlook the very large, lagoon style swimming pool with its island sun deck area, water games and a 'canyon river' and stunning views across the lake to the fir-clad mountains beyond. Often the social life of the campsite is centred around the large bar/terrace which has a small stage inside, sometimes used for musical entertainment. A huge and impressive amphitheatre is where an extensive programme of activities and entertainment takes place throughout the season. The large poolside terrace outside the bar provides an ideal casual eating area for pizzas and ice cream. In the restaurant on the floor above you can enjoy an excellent menu and the magnificent views across the lake. The site is well situated for visiting the many attractions of the region which include the famous gardens on the islands in the lake and at the Villa Taranto, Verbania. The site is owned by the friendly Manoni family who also own Camping Continental Lido at nearby Lake Mergozzo.

Facilities

Six well built toilet blocks have hot water for showers and washbasins but cold for dishwashing and laundry. Good baby room. Laundry facilities. Motorcaravan services. Supermarket, bar and takeaway (all season). Boutique. Gelateria. Swimming pool (30/4-19/9). Amphitheatre. Fishing. Watersports. Boat launching. Bicycle hire and guided mountain bike tours. Long beach. Internet access and WiFi. Good English is spoken. Dogs must be prebooked in high season. Off site: Golf 2 km. Sailing 5 km. Riding 12 km. Swiss mountains and resort of Locarno.

Open: 30 March - 24 September.

Directions

Verbania is 100 km. northwest of Milan on the western shore of Lake Maggiore. From the A26 motorway, leave at exit for Stresa/Baveno, turn left towards Fondotoce. Site is well signed off the SS33 north of Baveno and 300 m. south of the junction with the SS34 at Fondotoce.
GPS: 45.93835, 8.50008

Charges guide

Per unit incl. 3 persons and electricity	€ 23.20 - € 44.10
extra person	€ 4.75 - € 8.00
child (3-11 yrs)	free - € 6.60
dog	€ 3.45 - € 8.00

Continental camping village

REGIONE PIEMONTE

The campsite is situated on the picturesque **Lake Mergozzo**, the cleanest lake of Europe, only 1 km far from **Lake Maggiore**. The sandy beach, long and quiet is ideal for children. Bar, bar on the beach, pool bar, restaurant, shop, free hot showers, Beachvolleyball, children's playground, football field, 2 soccer fields with synthetic grass, 1 tenniscourt with synthetic gras (free), spinning, table tennis, **animation, internet point. We rent**: bicycles, canoes and pedalò. Both mobile homes and rooms available for renting. **How to reach us:** from Verbania direction Fondotoce. At the cross road direction Gravellona, straight ahead for 100 mt. 1.200 m2 **SWIMMING POOL** for adults and children with slides, wave pool with whirlpool and lazy river, free deckchairs and sunshade parasols, watergames "La Botte". Maxicaravan for disabled. Covered Arena.

CHILDREN GRATIS
0-2 all the season long.
3-5 years till 07.07.
and from 17.08.12

OPEN:
30.03.
24.09.12

Special Offer
Discount for 5 and 7 nights,
excl. highseason

ANIMATION from **28.04.** to **09.09.12**
SWIMMING POOL from **28.04.** to **09.09.12**

REGIONE PIEMONTE

ISOLINO camping village

Sandy beach which slightly goes deeper into the water ideal for children. • Bungalows, mobile homes and chalets for rent. • Animation 28.04-09.09.2012 swimmingpools 28.04-16.09.2012 • Large covered arena.

New!
New swimmigpool with watergames and canyon river. • Concrete insideroads and mainroad to the campsite • Spinning area.

Finale di Pollina

Camping Rais Gerbi

Ctra Rais Gerbi, SS113 km 172.9, I-90010 Finale di Pollina (Sicily) T: 092 142 6570. E: camping@raisgerbi.it

alanrogers.com/IT69350

Rais Gerbi provides very good quality camping with excellent facilities on the beautiful Tyrrhenian coast not far from Cefalu. This attractive terraced campsite is shaded by well established trees and the good sized pitches vary from informal areas under the trees near the sea to gravel terraces and hardstandings. Most have stunning views, many with their own sinks and with some artificial shade to supplement the trees. From the mobile homes to the unusual white igloos, everything here is being established to a high quality. The large pool with its entertainment area and the restaurant, like so much of the site, overlook the beautiful rocky coastline and aquamarine sea. Vincenzo Cerrito who speaks excellent English has been developing the site for many years and is continually upgrading and improving the resort style facilities. A frequently used rail line in a cutting, then a tunnel, divides part of the site. The cutting is well fenced and lined with trees but has some impact and one is unaware of the tunnel under the site. Budget airlines fly into a nearby airport and it is possible to rent tents and other accommodation at the site. Packages are available to tour the island and use other campsites near major attractions in Sicily (reception staff will advise). This is a central location from which to explore many of the island's attractions, although it may prove difficult to leave the glorious coastline. Try to visit in spring and autumn when the weather is usually perfect and the site is less busy.

Facilities

Excellent new sanitary blocks with British style toilets, free hot showers in generous cubicles. Small shop. Casual summer terrace and indoor (winter) restaurant. Communal barbecue. Entertainment area and pool near the sea. Tennis. WiFi over site (charged). High quality accommodation and tents for rent. Rocky beach at site. Dogs are not accepted in August. Off site: Small village of Finale 500 m. Larger historic town of Cefalu 12 km.

Open: All year.

Directions

Site is on the SS113 running along the east - north coast of the island, km. 172.9 just west of the village of Finale (turn into site at end of bridge on outskirts of the village). It is 12 km. east of Cefalu and 11 km. north of Pollina. GPS: 38.02278, 14.15389

Charges guide

Per unit incl. 2 persons	€ 23.50 - € 45.00
extra person (over 3 yrs)	€ 5.00 - € 10.00

Fondotoce di Verbania

Camping La Quiete

Via Turati 72, I-28040 Fondotoce di Verbania (Piedmont) T: 032 349 6013. E: info@campinglaquiete.it

alanrogers.com/IT62495

La Quiete is a small site, attractively located on the shore of Lake Mergozzo, a small lake to the west of the much larger Lake Maggiore. There are 180 pitches here, mostly well shaded and with electrical connections (6A), many of which have fine views across the lake. A number of mobile homes are available for rent. On-site amenities include a shop and bar/restaurant, as well as a sports field and volleyball court. This is excellent mountain biking and walking country and the site owners will be pleased to recommend possible routes.

Facilities

The clean and modern sanitary facilities are well placed along the length of the site. Washing machines. Bar/restaurant. Shop. Sports field. Games room. Play area. Direct access to Lake Mergozzo. Off site: Verbania. Golf and riding 1 km. Bicycle hire 5 km. Lake Maggiore. Watersports. Fishing. Motorboats are not allowed on the lake. Walking and cycle routes.

Open: 1 May - 20 September.

Directions

Leave the A26 motorway at the Casale exit and join the eastbound S34 as far as Fondotoce. Head north here on SP54 and the campsite is clearly signed. GPS: 45.9535, 8.47745

Charges guide

Per unit incl. 2 persons and electricity	€ 20.00 - € 33.00
extra person	€ 5.00 - € 7.50

No credit cards.

Fusina

Camping Fusina

Via Moranzani 79, I-30030 Fusina (Veneto) T: 041 547 0055. E: info@camping-fusina.com

alanrogers.com/IT60530

This is one of those sites that take one by surprise. This is old fashioned camping, but what fun, and we met English-speaking people who have been coming here for 30 years. Choose from 500 well shaded, flat and grassy informal pitches or a position with views over the lagoon to the towers in Saint Mark's Square. With water on three sides there are welcoming cool breezes and fortunately many trees hide the industrial area close by. Those who don't wish to be disturbed by the lively bar can choose from the many superb informal waterside pitches at the far end of the site. The site owns a large ferry car park and a 700-boat marina which accepts and launches all manner of craft. A deep water channel carries huge ships close by and the water views are never boring. Fusina offers a very easy and comfortable, 20 minute ferry connection to the cultural heart of Venice, Accademia. Several site buildings, including some of the showers and toilets, were designed by the famous modern architect Scarpa. These are heritage listed and are visited by design students, although this listing makes development and improvement difficult. Many of the staff are mature Australian/New Zealand people and English is used everywhere. This is a fantastic touring site with much to offer.

Facilities

Modern, well equipped facilities include units for disabled visitors, and some existing older units. Washing machines and dryers. Motorcaravan service point. Shop (15/3-31/10). Charming restaurant (no credit cards). Pizzeria and beer garden. Lively bar entertainment. Satellite TV. Playground. Boat hire. Marina with cranes, moorings, and maintenance facilities. Air-conditioned London Cyber bus (really!) and another 'Info bus' for information and ticket sales. WiFi. Bicycle hire. ATM. Torches useful. Off site: Public transport and ferry connections to Venice and Alberono beach.

Open: All year.

Directions

From SSII Padua - Venice road follow site signs on road east of Mira, turning right as signed. Site is in Fusina at end of peninsula and is well signed (also as 'Fusina parking'). With the road system undergoing much modernisation, keep a keen watch for brown camping signs for Fusina and Serenisima. GPS: 45.4195, 12.2563

Charges guide

Per unit incl. 2 persons and electricity	€ 31.00 - € 33.00
extra person	€ 8.50 - € 9.50

Gavorrano

Camping La Finoria

Via Monticello 66, I-58023 Gavorrano (Tuscany) T: 056 684 4381. E: info@campeggiolafinoria.it

alanrogers.com/IT66670

An unusual site, primarily for tents, La Finoria is set high in the mountains with incredible views. It is a rugged site with a focus on nature. Italian school children attend education programmes here. The three motorcaravan pitches are at the top of the site for those who enjoy a challenge, with a dozen caravan pitches on lower terraces accessed by a steep gravel track. Under huge chestnut trees there is a very pretty terraced area for tents. These have a private natural feel which some might say is what camping is all about. Electricity (3A) is available to all pitches, although long leads may be needed.

Facilities

Two blocks provide British and Turkish style toilets, hot showers and cold water at washbasins and sinks. Facilities for disabled campers. Washing machines and dryer. Quaint, small shop (closed Jan/Feb). Good restaurant and bar (closed Jan/Feb). Swimming pool (May-Sept). Tennis. Lessons on the environment. Excursions. Torches essential. Off site: Riding 2 km. Tennis and village 3 km. Bicycle hire 6 km. Golf 8 km. Site's private beach for relaxing and fishing 12 km.

Open: All year.

Directions

From SS1 (Follonica - Grosseto) take Gavorrano exit, then Finoria road. This is a steady, steep climb for some 10 minutes. Start to descend and at junction (the only one), look left (difficult turn) downhill for a large white sign to site. Access to this site is only possible for small units. GPS: 42.9225, 10.91233

Charges guide

Per person	€ 3.00 - € 10.00
child (1-6 yrs)	€ 2.00 - € 5.00
pitch	€ 4.00 - € 13.00

Grado

Camping Tenuta Primero

Via Monfalcone 14, I-34073 Grado (Friuli - Venézia Giúlia) T: 043 189 6900. E: info@tenuta-primero.com

alanrogers.com/IT60065

Tenuta Primero is a large, attractive, well run, family owned site with direct access to its own private beach via a pathway on top of a low banm. Apart from the beach – an ideal place to enjoy the view, sunbathe or take a dip in the Adriatic – the site offers a wealth of facilities and activities catering for all members of the family. The 740 pitches are all level, with 6A electricity, some separating hedges and ample tree shade, and many are reached by branch roads from an attractive palm tree-lined avenue. The site has several restaurants and bars conveniently tucked around the site; the large flower decked Terrazza Mare overlooking the sea is particularly attractive. As well as the many activities that the site has to offer, its location makes it a useful base to visit many of the historically interesting towns and sites in the region. In addition, it's a good point to stop over, relax and stock up on the way down to Croatia or Slovenia. However, be prepared to spend a bit more time than planned so as to fully enjoy the facilities that the site has to offer. The site does not accept dogs.

Facilities

Nine well maintained sanitary blocks, seven with facilities for disabled visitors. Washing machines and dryers. Chemical disposal. Motorcaravan service point. Swimming pools and paddling pool. Shop. Bars and restaurants, pizzeria (all April-Sept), takeaway (May-Sept). Beauty salon. Aerobics. Water gymnastics. Football pitch. Tennis courts. Children's playgrounds. Windsurfing. Marina, sailing, boat launching and boat hire. Bicycle hire. Children's and family entertainment. Live music, disco, dancing. Private beach with sunshades, deck chairs and jetty. Internet corner and WiFi (charged). Off site: 18-hole golf course opposite entrance. Grado 5 km. Riding 7 km. Venice. Palmanova. Aquileia with wonderful mosaic floors.

Open: 1 April - 3 October.

Directions

Leave the A4 autostrada at the Palmanova exit and head towards Grado. In Grado, after crossing the causeway turn left towards Monfalcone on the SP19. Site is on the right after 5 km. opposite a large golf course. GPS: 45.7051, 13.4640

Charges guide

Per unit incl. 2 persons and electricity	€ 19.00 - € 49.00
extra person	€ 6.00 - € 12.00
child (0-15 yrs)	free - € 10.00

Grado

Villaggio Turistico Camping Europa

Via Monfalcone 12, I-34073 Grado (Friuli - Venézia Giúlia) T: 043 180 877. E: info@villaggioeuropa.com

alanrogers.com/IT60050

This large, flat, good quality site is beside the sea and has 500 pitches, with 400 for touring units. They are all neat, clean and marked, most with shade and 6/10A electricity, 300 are fully serviced. The terrain is undulating and sandy in the areas nearer the sea, where cars have to be left in parking places. An impressive, large new Aquatic Park covers 1,500 sq.m. with two slides (100 m. and 60 m. long) and many other features. With many shallow areas it is very popular with children and there are lifeguards. A new pool bar is an attractive feature. There is direct access to the beach. The water recedes up to 200 m. from the beach, but leaves a natural paddling pool which is enjoyed by children when it is hot. A narrow wooden jetty gives access to deeper water. This is a neat, well managed site which is probably the best in the area.

Facilities

Five excellent, refurbished toilet blocks are well designed and very clean. Free hot water in all facilities, mostly British style WCs and excellent facilities for disabled visitors. Baby showers and baths. Washing machines. Motorcaravan services. Large supermarket, small general shop (all season). Large bar and restaurant with takeaway (all season). Swimming pools (15/5-15/9). Tennis. Fishing. Bicycle hire. Playground. Full entertainment programme in season. Internet access. Dogs are restricted to specific areas and not allowed on the beach. Off site: Golf 500 m. Riding 10 km.

Open: 21 April - 24 September.

Directions

Site is 4 km. east of Grado on the road to Monfalcone. Venice - Trieste motorway exit at Reipuglia-Monfalcone, first roundabout take second exit, direction airport and follow Grado signs for 13 km. Site is on the left opposite a golf course. GPS: 45.69649, 13.45595

Charges guide

Per unit incl. 2 persons and electricity	€ 19.00 - € 45.00
extra person	€ 5.50 - € 10.50
child (3-16 yrs)	€ 3.50 - € 9.50
dog	€ 3.00 - € 6.00

Less 10% for longer stays out of season.

Iseo

Camping del Sole

Via per Rovato 26, I-25049 Iseo (Lombardy) T: 030 980 288. E: info@campingdelsole.it

alanrogers.com/IT62610

Camping del Sole lies on the southern edge of Lake Iseo, just outside the pretty lakeside town of Iseo. The site has 306 pitches, many taken up with chalets and mobile homes. The 180 touring pitches all have 3A electricity and some have fine views of the surrounding mountains and lake. Pitches are generally flat and of a reasonable size, but cars must park in the carpark. The site has a wide range of excellent leisure amenities, including a large swimming pool. There is a bar and restaurant with a pizzeria near the pool and an entertainment area and a second bar by the lake.

Facilities

Sanitary facilities are modern and well maintained, including special facilities for disabled visitors. Washing machines and dryers. Bar, restaurant, pizzeria, snack bar and supermarket (all open all season). Motorcaravan service point. Bicycle hire. Swimming pool with children's pool (21/5-10/9). Canoe and pedal boat hire. Tennis. WiFi. Dog exercise area. Entertainment in high season. Off site: Golf 5 km. Riding 6 km.

Open: 16 April - 25 September.

Directions

Lake Iseo is 50 km. west of Lake Garda. Leave from A4 Milan - Venice autostrada take Rovato exit and at roundabout go north on SPX1 following signs for Lago d'Iseo for 12 km. Site is well signed to left at large roundabout. From Brescia on SS510, turn north before Iseo towards Rovato and turn right to site. GPS: 45.65708, 10.03740

Charges guide

Per unit incl. 2 persons and electricity	€ 19.80 - € 42.90
extra person	€ 5.90 - € 10.10

Camping Cheques accepted.

Laces-Latsch

Camping Latsch an der Etsch

Reichstrasse 4, via Nazionale 4, I-39021 Laces-Latsch (Trentino - Alto Adige) T: 047 362 3217.

E: info@camping-latsch.com **alanrogers.com/IT62120**

Gasthof Camping Latsch is 640 m. above sea level between a main road and the river, with splendid views across to the surrounding mountains. About 20 of the 100 touring pitches are on a terrace by reception with the remainder alongside the river. They are in regular rows which are separated by hedges with thin grass on gravel which can look quite dry. All have 6A electricity and 47 also have water and drainage. Trees provide some shade. An underground car park (for 35 cars) protects vehicles from winter snow and summer sun and, if used, gives a reduction in pitch charges. Mountain walkers will be in their element here and several chairlifts give access to higher slopes.

Facilities

The traditional but well maintained sanitary block is on two floors (to serve each section), has all the usual facilities and is heated in cool weather. Excellent private bathrooms (20 with basin, shower, toilet) for hire. Facilities for disabled visitors. Washing machine and dryer. Motorcaravan service point. Shop, bar and pleasant restaurant. Small heated indoor pool, sauna, solarium and fitness room. Larger, irregularly shaped outdoor pool with marble surrounds. Playground. Off site: Fishing 50 m (an international fishing permit is required prior to obtaining a licence). Bicycle hire 1 km. Skiing 6 km. Riding 7 km.

Open: 6 December - 10 November.

Directions

Latsch/Laces is 28 km. west of Merano on the SS38 Bolzano-Silandro road. Site entrance by the Hotel Vermoi (keep on main road, do not turn off to village). GPS: 46.622592, 10.864921

Charges guide

Per unit incl. 2 persons and electricity	€ 27.60 - € 33.60
extra person	€ 7.20 - € 8.20
child (2-12 yrs)	€ 6.00 - € 7.20
dog	€ 3.90 - € 5.20

Reduction on pitch fee if underground car park used.

Laives - Leifers

Camping-Park Steiner

J.F. Kennedy Strasse 32, I-39055 Laives - Leifers (Trentino - Alto Adige) T: 047 195 0105.

E: info@campingsteiner.com **alanrogers.com/IT62100**

The welcoming Camping Steiner is very central for touring with the whole of the Dolomite region within easy reach. With much on-site activity, one could spend an enjoyable holiday here, especially now the SS12 by which it stands has a motorway alternative. The 180 individual touring pitches, mostly with good shade and hardstanding, are in rows with easy access and all have electricity (6A). There are also 30 chalets available to rent. There is a family style pizzeria/restaurant, and indoor and outdoor pools. The Steiner Park Hotel provides another restaurant, café and full hotel facilities. This friendly, family run site has a long tradition of providing a happy camping experience in the more traditional style – the owner remembers Alan Rogers who stayed here on many occasions. We met a Danish couple during our visit who were staying for five weeks as it is so easy to get to different parts of the Dolomites and is ideal for walking.

Facilities

The two sanitary blocks are equipped to a high standard, one having been completely refurbished. They can be heated in cool weather. Shop. Bar/pizzeria/restaurant with takeaway (April-Oct). Outdoor pool, with paddling pool, and a smaller covered heated pool (all season, except July/Aug). Playground. Bicycle hire. Dogs are not accepted in July/Aug. Off site: Fishing 2.5 km. Riding 12 km. Golf and skiing 28 km.

Open: 24 March - 31 October.

Directions

Site is by SS12 on northern edge of Leifers, 8 km. south of Bolzano. From north, at the Bolzano-Süd exit from A22 Brenner-Modena motorway follow Trento signs for 7 km. From south on motorway take Ora exit, then north on SS12 towards Bolzano for 14 km. GPS: 46.42955, 11.34380

Charges guide

Per unit incl. 2 persons and electricity	€ 26.00 - € 32.00
extra person	€ 7.00 - € 9.00
child (under 9 yrs)	€ 3.00 - € 5.00

Lazise

Camping du Parc

I-37017 Lazise sul Garda (Lake Garda) T: 045 758 0127. E: duparc@camping.it

alanrogers.com/IT62535

Camping du Parc is a very pleasant, family owned site which resembles a Tardis, in that it extends and extends as you progress further through the site. Olive groves are interspersed with the pitch areas which gives an open and green feel. The site is set on a slope which goes down to the lakeside beach of soft sand. The 150 pitches are terraced, and all have 6A electricity. Units above 10 m. long will be challenged by some of the corners here. Pitches are separated by trimmed hedges and some have shade, others have fine views of the lake. The restaurant is on the lower level with a terrace to catch the sunsets and the pizzeria also has a patio with sea views. Relax by the beach bar or in the pool whilst the children enjoy the slides and paddling pool. This is a very good site for those who prefer peace and quiet to the noisier atmosphere of the larger sites hereabouts. Buses stop by the gate to take you to Gardaland and other tourist attractions. As a site which caters for families, there is no disco or excessive noise and when we visited there were many happy customers. Entertainment takes place in the lower sports areas and is aimed mainly at children. All facilities are open the whole season. The beach, accessed through a security gate, is safe for swimming and there is a lifeguard.

Facilities

Four modern sanitary blocks are well placed and have free hot water throughout. Three blocks have facilities for disabled campers, one for children and babies. Washing machines and dryers. Motorcaravan services. Well stocked mini-market. Restaurant. Pizzeria with terrace. Takeaway. Beach bar. Pool bar. Swimming pool. Large paddling pool with slides. Children's entertainment programme. Baby club. Play area. Tennis. Fitness suite. Multisports court. Fishing. WiFi. Off site: Bicycle hire 500 m.

Open: 15 March - 30 September.

Directions

Leave A4 Venice - Milan autostrada by taking the Brennero exit to Lake Garda and then on to Lazise. At the lakeside in town turn left and follow signs for site. GPS: 45.49833, 10.7375

Charges guide

extra person	€ 5.60 - € 10.00
child (2-6 yrs)	€ 1.50 - € 5.10
pitch	€ 10.90 - € 22.00
dog	€ 1.50 - € 5.80

Lazise

Camping Piani di Clodia

Via Fossalta 42, I-37017 Lazise (Lake Garda) T: 045 759 0456. E: info@pianidiclodia.it

alanrogers.com/IT62530

Piani di Clodia is one of the largest sites on Lake Garda and it has a positive impression of space and cleanliness. It is located on a slope between Lazise and Peschiera in the southeast corner of the lake, with lovely views across the water to Sirmione's peninsula and the mountains beyond. The site slopes down to the water's edge and has 950 pitches, 920 with electricity (6/16A), 290 with electricity, water and drainage, terraced where necessary and back to back from hard access roads. There is some shade from mature and young trees. The pool complex is truly wonderful with a range of pools, a pleasant sunbathing area and a bar. A member of Leading Campings Group.

Facilities

Seven modern, immaculate sanitary blocks have British and Turkish style WCs. All have facilities for disabled visitors and one has a baby room. Washing machines, dryers and laundry service. Motorcaravan services. Shopping complex. Two bars. Self-service restaurant with takeaway. Pizzeria. Ice cream parlour. Swimming pools. Tennis. Gymnastics. Fishing. Bicycle hire. Playground. Outdoor theatre with entertainment programme. WiFi. Dog area and shower. Off site: Riding 6 km. Golf 12 km.

Open: 20 March - 10 October.

Directions

Lazise is on the southeast side of Lake Garda about 30 km. west of Verona. From north on Trento - Verona A22 autostrada take Affi exit then follow signs for Lazise and site. From south on A4 Brescia - Venice motorway take Peschiera exit and site is 6 km. towards Lazise and Garda on SS249. GPS: 45.48272, 10.72932

Charges guide

Per unit incl. 2 persons and electricity	€ 19.40 - € 52.50

Lazise

Camping La Quercia

I-37017 Lazise sul Garda (Lake Garda) T: 045 647 0577. E: laquercia@laquercia.it

alanrogers.com/IT62550

La Quercia is a spacious, popular site on a slight slope leading down to Lake Garda and is decorated by palm trees and elegantly trimmed hedges. Accommodating up to 850 touring units, pitches are mostly in regular double rows between access roads, all with electricity (6A). Most are shaded by mature trees, although those furthest from the lake are more open to the sun. Much of the activity centres around the impressive pool complex with its fantastic slides and the terrace bar, restaurant and pizzeria which overlook the entertainment stage. The daytime activities and evening entertainment are very professional with the young team working hard to involve everyone (some courses require enrolment on a Sunday). La Quercia has a fine sandy beach on the lake, with diving jetties and a roped off section for launching boats or windsurfing (high season). A second restaurant serving traditional Italian food is located closer to the beach. The site is a short distance from the delightful lakeside towns of Lazise and Peschiera, which have a wide choice of restaurants, and is a short drive from Verona, one of Italy's finest cultural centres.

Facilities

Six toilet blocks are perfectly sufficient and are of a very high standard. Laundry. Supermarket. General shop. Bar, restaurant, self-service restaurant and pizzeria. Swimming pools (small charge). Tennis. Aerobics, judo and yoga. Scuba club. Playground with water play. Organised events (sports competitions, games, etc.) and free courses (e.g. swimming, surfboarding). Canoeing. Roller-blading. Archery. Minigolf. Evening entertainment or dancing. Baby sitting service. WiFi (charged). ATM. Free weekly excursion. Dogs accepted (max. 2). Off site: Gardaland, Movieland and Caneva Aqua Park nearby. Bicycle hire 300 m. Golf 10 km. Riding 15 km.

Open: 29 March - 30 September.

Directions

Lazise is on the southeast side of Lake Garda about 30 km. west of Verona. From north on Trento - Verona A22 autostrada take Affi exit then follow signs for Lazise and site. From south on the A4 Brescia - Venice motorway, take Peschiera exit and site is 7 km. towards Lazise and Garda on SS249. GPS: 45.49318, 10.73337

Charges guide

Per unit incl. 2 persons and electricity	€ 21.10 - € 59.00
extra person	€ 5.40 - € 12.85
child (5-7 yrs)	€ 3.15 - € 8.40
dog	€ 4.80 - € 8.00

Low season discount for pensioners.

Lazise

Camping Park Delle Rose

Strada San Gaetano 20, I-37017 Lazise (Lake Garda) T: 045 647 1181. E: info@campingparkdellerose.it

alanrogers.com/IT63580

An orderly, well designed site with a feeling of spaciousness, Delle Rose is on the east side of Lake Garda, three kilometres from the attractive waterside village of Peschiera. The 455 pitches are of average size, most with grass and shade and laid out in 30 short, terraced avenues. The ratio of recreational area to pitches is unusually high, particularly for sites at Lake Garda. Unusually, reception is located one third of the way into the site. On approach one sees the attractive restaurant, gardens and comprehensive sporting facilities including the pool complex with its stylish terraced bar and animation area close by.

Facilities

Five very clean, modern sanitary blocks provide hot water throughout. British style toilets, some in cabins with washbasins. Private bathrooms for hire. Good baby rooms. Facilities for disabled visitors. Washing machines. Motorcaravan service point. Fridge hire. Bar/restaurant, takeaway and pool bar serving snacks. Shops. New swimming pool with flumes (mid April-Sept). Tennis. Archery. Minigolf. Play area and miniclub for children. Fishing (with permit). Beach at site. Watersports. Kayaking. Windsurfing. Daily medical services. Entertainment programme in high season. Excursions. Dogs and motorbikes are not accepted. Torches useful. WiFi. Off site: Peschiera with ATM and usual town amenities 2 km. Golf 6 km. Riding 8 km. Gardaland close by.

Open: 21 April - 30 September.

Directions

From A4 Milan - Venice autostrada take exit for Perschiera, west of Verona. Travel north towards Lazise. The campsite is on the southeastern lakeside about 2.5 km. north of Peschiera and well signed. GPS: 45.48300, 10.73183

Charges guide

Per person	€ 5.00 - € 10.00
child (4-9 yrs)	€ 2.00 - € 5.00
pitch	€ 11.00 - € 22.00

COMPANY WITH ENVIRONMENTAL MANAGEMENT SYSTEM CERTIFIED BY DNV
ISO 14001
COMPANY WITH QUALITY SYSTEM CERTIFIED BY DNV
ISO 9002
The Camping No. 1 of Lake Garda!
Your front line seat on Lake Garda!
VR.2012
CAMPING LA QUERCIA, YOUR HOLIDAY FILM
Shady emplacements - Heated toilet bloks for both grown-up's and children - 24 hours Warm water - Restaurant - Pizzeria - Cocktail Bar - Funny Bar on the beach - Swimmingpools with slides - Whirlpool - Full-comfort maxicaravans and bungalows for 4-5 persons with sight on the lake - The widest sand beach on the lake - Theatre - Supermarket - Butcher's shop - Pastry- and bakers shop - Typical products of the lake - Fresh fruit and vegetables every days - Tobacconist's shop - International newspaper kiosk - Rent a car service - Fax service - Professional animators - Animation for children and teenagers - Tennis - Canoe - Archery - Surfing - Judo - Football - Fitness gym - Spinning - Horse-riding.
6500 SQUARE METRES OF CLEAN AND SAFE PRIVATE BEACH, JUST A FEW METRES AWAY FROM ALL THE AMENITIES.
900 SHADY SPOTS IN BEAUTIFULLY-TENDED GROUNDS.
18 AREAS WITH FACILITIES FOR SPORTS AND LEISURE ACTIVITIES.
CAMPING LAQUERCIA ... more than a camping!
Information and booking:
+ 39.045.6470577
laquercia@laquercia.it
www.laquercia.it
LAZISE SUL GARDA • VERONA • ITALY

Levico Terme

Camping Lago di Levico

Loc. Pleina 5, I-38056 Levico Terme (Trentino - Alto Adige) T: 046 170 6491.
E: info@lagolevico.com alanrogers.com/IT62290

Camping Lago di Levico, by a pretty lakeside in the mountains, is the merger of two popular sites, Camping Levico and Camping Jolly. Brothers Andrea and Geno Antoniolli are making great improvements, already there is an impressive new reception and further developments of the lakeside and swimming areas are planned. The lakeside pitches are quite special. There are 430 mostly grassy and shaded pitches (70-120 sq.m) with 6A electricity, 150 also have water and drainage and 12 have private facilities. Staff are welcoming and fluent in English. The swimming pool complex is popular, as is the summer family entertainment. There is a small supermarket on site and it is a short distance to the local village. The restaurant, bar, pizzeria and takeaway are open all season. The beautiful grass shores of the lake are ideal for sunbathing and the crystal clear water is ideal for enjoying (non-motorised) water activities. This is a site where the natural beauty of an Italian lake can be enjoyed without being overwhelmed by commercial tourism.

Facilities

Four modern sanitary blocks provide hot water for showers, washbasins and washing. Mostly British style toilets. Single locked unit for disabled visitors. Laundry facilities. Freezer. Motorcaravan service point. Good shop. Bar/restaurant and takeaway. Outdoor swimming pool. Play area. Miniclub and entertainment (high season). Fishing. Satellite TV and cartoon cinema. Internet access (free in low season). Kayak hire. Tennis. Torches useful. Off site: Boat launching 500 m. Bicycle hire and bicycle track 1.5 km. Town with all the usual facilities and ATM 2 km. Riding 3 km. Golf 6 km.

Open: 15 April - 9 October.

Directions

From A22 Verona - Bolzano road take turn for Trento on S47 to Levico Terme where campsite is very well signed. GPS: 46.00799, 11.28454

Charges guide

Per unit incl. 2 persons and electricity	€ 9.50 - € 38.00
extra person	€ 3.00 - € 14.25
child (3-11 yrs)	free - € 6.50
dog	free - € 5.00

Lido degli Scacchi

Kawan Village Florenz

Viale Alpi Centrali 199, I-44020 Lido degli Scacchi (Emília-Romagna) T: 053 338 0193.
E: info@campingflorenz.com alanrogers.com/IT60750

Popular with Italian families for over 30 years, Camping Florenz has many loyal campers who stay for the whole season. The area which is most sought after by tourers is over the sand dunes along the seafront where there are good sized, shaded and level pitches with views of the water. The gently shelving beach has fine grey sand and lots of chairs and umbrellas. Away from the beach area there is heavy shade cover from pine trees. The pitches are mostly a mixture of sand and grass, of a good size and level, all with electricity (3A). A large restaurant with a terrace area overlooks the lively entertainment area where lots of families were enjoying themselves when we visited.

Facilities

Six mixed mostly old sanitary blocks with half British, half Turkish style toilets and preset showers. Some unisex showers at beach. Good facilities for disabled campers. Motorcaravan service point. Good supermarket. Restaurant and bar with TV. Large outdoor pool. Activities and children's club in season. Good play area. Excellent beach for swimming and boat launching. Beach bar. Bicycle hire. WiFi. Off site: Small town with restaurants and shops 1 km.

Open: 4 April - 27 September.

Directions

Site is at Lido degli Scacchi just off the S309 running between Chioggia and Ravenna. Both Lido degli Scacchi and site are well signed from the S309. GPS: 44.70111, 12.23806

Charges guide

Per person	€ 4.40 - € 9.00
child (3-10 yrs)	free - € 5.60
pitch	€ 10.00 - € 25.60
dog	€ 2.70 - € 5.30

Camping Cheques accepted.

Lido delle Nazioni

Camping Bungalow Park Tahiti Village

Viale Libia 133, I-44020 Lido delle Nazioni (Emília-Romagna) T: **053 337 9500**. E: **info@campingtahiti.com**

alanrogers.com/IT60650

Tahiti is an excellent, extremely well run site, thoughtfully laid out less than 1 km. from the sea (a continuous, fun road-train link is provided). Flowers, shrubs, ponds and attractive wooden structures enhance its appearance and, unlike many campsites of this size, it is family owned and run. The 469 pitches are of varying size, back to back from hard roads and defined by trees with shade in most areas. There are 30 pitches with a private unit containing a WC and washbasin. Electricity is available throughout and 100 pitches also have water and drainage. Several languages, including English, are spoken by the friendly management team, although the British have not yet really discovered this site, which is popular with other European campers.

Facilities

All toilet blocks are of a very high standard. British and Turkish style WCs. Baby room. Large supermarket. Two waiter service restaurants. Bar. Pizzeria. Takeaway. Swimming pools. Fitness and beauty centre. Several playgrounds and miniclub. Gym. Tennis. Floodlit sports area. Minigolf. Bicycle hire. Entertainment and excursions (high season). 'Disco-pub'. ATM. Internet. Free transport to the beach. Torches needed in some areas. Dogs are not accepted. Off site: Fishing 300 m. Riding 500 m.

Open: 18 April - 23 September.

Directions

Turn off SS309 35 km. north of Ravenna to Lido delle Nazioni (north of Lido di Pomposa) and follow site signs. GPS: 44.73179, 12.22718

Charges guide

Per unit incl. 2 persons and electricity	€ 21.70 - € 49.70
extra person	€ 5.90 - € 9.90
child (2-8 yrs)	free - € 7.60

Lignano Sabbiadoro

Camping Sabbiadoro

Via Sabbiadoro 8, I-33054 Lignano Sabbiadoro (Friuli - Venézia Giúlia) T: **043 171 455**.

E: **campsab@lignano.it** **alanrogers.com/IT60080**

Sabbiadoro is a large, good quality site in two parts with separate entrances and efficient receptions. It has 1,215 pitches and is ideal for families who like all their amenities to be close by. Quite tightly packed, the pitches vary in size, are shaded by attractive trees and have electricity, TV and Internet connections. You may wish to cover your car and unit to prevent sap covering it over time. The facilities are all in excellent condition and well thought out, especially the pool complex, and everything here is very modern, safe and clean. Open in high season, the smaller and quieter part of the site with entrance from Viale Central, is only a few metres away from the main site entrance in Via Sabbiadoro. This has four new sanitary blocks, 41 fixed pitches for touring units, an area for tents and a section of mobile homes to rent. The site's private beach (with 24 hour guard) is only 250 m. away. Shopping and nightlife can be found in the town of Sabbiadoro itself, more so in Pineta about 1.5 km. away.

Facilities

Well equipped sanitary facilities with free showers includes superb facilities for disabled visitors. Laundry facilities. Motorcaravan service point. Huge supermarket. Bazaar. Good restaurant (15/5-6/9), snack bar and takeaway (15/5-28/9). Heated outdoor pool complex with separate fun pool area, slides and fountains (all season). Heated indoor children's pool. Disco. TV room. Internet. Play areas. Tennis. Fitness centre. Boat launching. Range of entertainment in the main season. WiFi. Bicycle hire. Off site: Shops. Restaurants. Bars. Riding, sailing and golf.

Open: 31 March - 7 October.

Directions

Leave A4 at Latisana exit, west of Trieste. From Latisana follow road to Lignano, then Sabbiadoro. Site is well signed as you approach the town. GPS: 45.68198, 13.12577

Charges guide

Per unit incl. 2 persons and electricity	€ 21.60 - € 39.10
extra person	€ 5.70 - € 10.30
child (3-12 yrs)	€ 3.50 - € 5.80
dog	free - € 2.50

Lido di Jesolo

Camping Jesolo International

Viale A da Giussano, I-30016 Lido di Jesolo (Veneto) T: 042 197 1826.
E: info@jesolointernational.it **alanrogers.com/IT60370**

alan rogers Runner up 2011 Awards

At this brilliant family resort style site with a focus on sporting activities, you can plan the cost of your holiday with confidence. The amazing array of on-site activities is included in the price and there are large discounts for some off-site attractions. Jesolo International is located on a beautiful promontory with 700 m. of uncrowded white sandy beach and slowly shelving waters for safe swimming. As the site is narrow, all the pitches are close to the sea. There is a choice of two types of pitch, all flat, well shaded and with 10/20A electricity, water and drainage, WiFi and satellite TV connection. Each 'ultra' pitch has a private bathroom. Chalet accommodation is excellent. This is said to be the first carbon neutral campsite worldwide. The superb pool complex, where an excellent entertainment programme is presented each night, is centrally located and very spacious. The dynamic director Sergio Comino works long hours to maintain and improve this high quality, family orientated site, to combine a unique holiday experience for guests, with real value for money. As the site is community owned, profits are returned to the guests in the form of facilities, sporting opportunities and entertainment. Cleanliness and security are high priorities, as are environmental issues. Electronic tags are given to guests to gain entrance and exit to the beach gates and this, combined with video surveillance of these key locations, allows guests to feel secure. Children's passes exclude them from accessing the beach or the hydro massage whirlpools reserved for adults alone. A ferry service to Venice leaves from the marina adjoining the campsite and takes just 40 minutes to reach St Mark's Square in the heart of the city.

Facilities

Sanitary facilities include 72 modern, continually cleaned bathroom units (shower, toilet and basin), private bathrooms (extra cost) and baby rooms. Washing machines and dryers. Fridge boxes. Motorcaravan service point. Supermarket. Family style restaurant. Beach bar with snacks. Pool bar serving light lunches. Sports centre. Children's club. Indoor gym. Tennis courts (free lessons). Golf (lessons and fees all free). Sailing with tuition. Introductory scuba diving lesson. Large grassy play area with adventure style equipment. WiFi. Sailing, banana boat, canoes, pedal boats, loungers and sunshades (all free). Doctor on site (free). Scuba diving (free). Language course (free). Pony riding (free). Pirates ship (free). Large dogs are not accepted. Off site: Ferry to Venice and Murano 200 m. Jesolo promenade with shops, restaurants and bars 500 m. Aqualandia 1.5 km. (free). Golf 2 km. (free lesson and use of 18-hole course). Go-kart racing (free) and riding 4 km. Clay target shooting and archery 10 km. (free lesson and equipment).

Open: 28 April - 30 September.

Directions

From A4 Venice - Trieste autostrada take Dona di Piave exit and follow signs to Jesolo then Punta Sabbioni. Turn off to Lido di Jesolo just before the Cavallino bridge where the site is well signed. GPS: 45.48395, 12.58763

Charges guide

Per unit incl. 2 persons and electricity	€ 27.00 - € 55.00
extra person	€ 6.00 - € 13.00
child (1-5 yrs)	free - € 5.50

Manerba del Garda

Camping Belvedere

Via Cavalle 5, I-25080 Manerba del Garda (Lake Garda) T: 036 555 1175. E: info@camping-belvedere.it
alanrogers.com/IT62840

Situated along a promontory reaching into Lake Garda, this friendly, traditional campsite has been terraced to give many of the 85 touring pitches wonderful views. They are mostly shaded, on gravel with 6A electricity. There is a long beach and pleasant lakeside pitches; swimming and boat launching is easy. The restaurant and bar with pretty flowers is under shady trees at the water's edge. The facilities are of a high standard, although there are none for disabled visitors, and the site prices are reasonable compared with others in the area. Overall, the site has a pleasant, open feel and we enjoyed it here. Italian villages with lots of atmosphere are close by as are the huge theme parks the area is known for.

Facilities

Five traditional sanitary blocks are well maintained and kept clean. Washing machine. Motorcaravan service point. Shop selling basics. Restaurant, bar and takeaway are all open most of the season. Play area. Tennis. Music and TV in bar. Fishing. WiFi (charged). Torches useful. Mobile homes to rent. Off site: Watersports nearby. Bars and restaurant a short walk away. Golf and bicycle hire 2 km. Riding 4 km. Theme parks.

Open: 4 April - 4 October.

Directions

Manerba is on western shore of Lake Garda at the southern end. From A4 Milan - Venice autostrada take Desenzano exit and head north on the SS572 towards Saló for about 11 km. and look for site signs. Turn right off main road, then right again along Via Belvedere. GPS: 45.56207, 10.56315

Charges guide

Per unit incl. 2 persons and electricity	€ 18.00 - € 34.00
extra person	€ 5.00 - € 8.00
child (3-11 yrs)	€ 3.50 - € 5.60
dog	€ 2.00 - € 4.00

Club Camping

JESOLO INTERNATIONAL

The best location on the Adriatic at the boulevard of Jesolo, opposite the ferry to Venice, pitches with a average distance of just 60 mt. from the beach.
Unbeatable price/service quality through countless inclusive Services: Wi-fi, banana boat, sunny beds and umbrellas on the beach and the pool, free entry of Aqualandia, the best water park in Italy (well-known, 2 Km), free entrance at Adventure Mini Golf, go fing on the 18 hole course of Jesolo (3 km), diving, pedal boats, canoes, pony rides, heated spa, tennis, pirate ship, clay pigeon shooting, go-kart race at the race track in Jesolo (4 km), top fitness center, large child center, animation.

Excellent surveillance system. Europe exemplary environmental concept. World-wide first climate neutral campsite.

Camping own luxury mobile homes very well equipped and top service.
Camping at it's best: new Ultra pitches. 170-250 sqm with private bathroom.

www.jesolointernational.it / info@jesolointernational.it DIRECT RESERVATIONS BY TELEPHONE 0039.0421.971826 OPEN: 28 APRIL - 30 SEPTEMBER

Limite Sull'Arno

Camping Village San Giusto

Via Castra, 71, I-50050 Limite Sull'Arno (Tuscany) T: 055 871 2304. E: info@campingsangiusto.it

alanrogers.com/IT66075

Camping San Giusto can be found around 25 km. from Florence, within the Montalbano National Park. Pitches here are well shaded and are mostly equipped with electricity. Some have superb views over the Tuscan countryside. A number of mobile homes and chalets are available for rent. Amenities include a café, a trattoria specialising in Tuscan cuisine and a small shop. Vehicle access to pitches is restricted to arrival and departure, with a large car park at the front of the site. A daily shuttle bus service is provided to Empoli railway station, with regular services to destinations throughout Tuscany. This site is a good base for exploring Tuscany. The beautiful small town of Vinci, best known as Leonardo's birthplace can be reached within 20 minutes. Florence, the cradle of the Renaissance, can be reached within 30 minutes. A little further afield, Pisa and Volterra, are also highly recommended. The Montalbano National Park has a great wealth of walking and mountain biking tracks, and the site's owners will be pleased to recommend routes.

Facilities

Bar and snack bar. Trattoria. Shop. Playground. Games room. Shuttle bus service. Mobile homes and chalets for rent. Off site: Walking and cycling. Swimming pool 1 km. Florence, Siena and Vinci.

Open: 1 April - 5 November.

Directions

Approaching from Milan and Rome, leave the A1 motorway at Firenze Scandicci exit and then take the Firenze/Pisa/Livorno road towards Pisa. Leave this road at Montelupo and head towards Limite sull' Arno. From there head towards Carmignano for 5.5 km. to the site. GPS: 43.783251, 10.988329

Charges guide

Per unit incl. 2 persons and electricity	€ 20.00 - € 25.50

Manerba del Garda

Camping Baia Verde

Via del Edera 19, I-25080 Manerba del Garda (Lake Garda) T: 036 565 1753. E: info@campingbaiaverde.com

alanrogers.com/IT62860

Baia Verde is a smart, luxurious and peaceful campsite located in the southwestern corner of Lake Garda. The 89 touring pitches are in regular rows on flat, open ground where the young trees are giving some shade. The pitches are all fully serviced, and 12 have superb private facilities. The excellent restaurant block and the building housing the other facilities are architect designed and it shows. Swimming/paddling pools and the rooftop spa with its great views are attractively designed and incorporate a wellness centre and elevated TV room. A great deal of thought and loving care has gone into Baia Verde. We were impressed!

Facilities

Full range of high quality sanitary facilities in an impressive three storey building in the style of an Italian villa. Baby and children's rooms. Superb facilities for disabled visitors. Washing machines and dryers. TV lounge. Rooftop sunbathing area with jacuzzi. Entertainment and activity programme (high season). Bicycle hire. WiFi. Only some breeds of dog accepted. Off site: Beach with fishing, swimming and boat launching 400 m. Manerba del Garda 1 km. Golf and riding 2 km. Cycle and walking trails. Excursions.

Open: 1 April - 30 September.

Directions

Manerba is on western shore of Lake Garda at the southern end. From A4 Milan - Venice autostrada take Desenzano exit and head north on the SS572 towards Saló for about 12 km; then turn right following signs to site. GPS: 45.56155, 10.55352

Charges guide

Per unit incl. 2 persons and electricity	€ 19.00 - € 46.00
extra person	€ 4.50 - € 10.50
child (3-11 yrs)	free - € 8.00
dog	€ 3.00 - € 8.00

Massa Lubrense

Camping Nettuno

Via A Vespucci 39, Marina del Cantone, I-80061 Massa Lubrense (Campania) T: 081 808 1051.
E: info@villaggionettuno.it **alanrogers.com/IT68380**

Camping Nettuno is owned and run by the friendly Mauro family, who speak excellent English. Nestled in the bay of Marina del Cantone, it is situated in the protected area of Punta Campanella, away from the busiest tourist spots. As a result the approach roads are difficult and narrow. This tiny campsite of only 42 pitches (4A) is spread over three levels above the pebbly beach. Up several steps and across the road are the amenities, reception, shop, and dive centre and then above this is a restaurant with views over the bay. Pitches are informally arranged, some with a fabulous sea view (extra charge) and most with shade. Because the site is tucked into the hillside pitches are small and close together.

Facilities

The single central sanitary block includes facilities for disabled campers (and access via a ramp to the beach). Washing machine. Basic motorcaravan service point. Gas supplies. Small shop. Delightful restaurant with sea views. Bar (lively at night). Dive centre. Excursions. TV in bar area. Small play area. Free tennis arranged at court next door. Fishing. Off site: Small beach (pebbles) 5 m. from bottom of site. Excellent restaurant 100 m. Amalfi Coast, Capri, nature parks, walking etc.

Open: 20 March - 2 November.

Directions

From A3 motorway (Naples - Salerno), take Castellamare di Stabia exit onto S145. Pass Castellamare, follow signs to Meta di Sorrento through Vico Equense bypass tunnel and turn off towards Positano in Meta. After 5 km. turn to S. Agata dei due Golfi (6.5 km). Follow signs to Nerano then Marina del Cantone. Entrance is 50 m. past entrance to reception. Go on for 100 m. to turn round in order to enter site with its steep and narrow entrance. GPS: 40.58389, 14.35194

Charges guide

Per unit incl. 2 persons and electricity	€ 23.00 - € 36.50
extra person	€ 6.50 - € 10.00

Mazara del Vallo

Sporting Club Village & Camping

Ctra Bocca Arena, I-91026 Mazara del Vallo (Sicily) T: 092 394 7230. E: info@sportingclubvillage.com
alanrogers.com/IT69160

Mazara del Vallo can be found on Sicily's southwestern coast. As the crow flies, Tunisia is not far, and the town has a distinct Arabic influence in its winding streets. The site is 2.5 km. from Mazara and boasts some good amenities including a large swimming pool, surrounded by tall palm trees. Pitches here are grassy and generally well shaded. This is a lively site in high season with a wide range of activities and a regular entertainment programme. The nearest beach is 350 m. away.

Facilities

Good sports club with swimming pool, gymnasium, floodlit football pitches, tennis and volleyball. Restaurant, bar and large reception/function room. Off site: Beach 350 m. Mazara 2.5 km. Various excursions organised by the site, for example to the Acropolis at Selinunte (25 km) and the island of Mozia.

Open: 1 April - 5 October.

Directions

From the A29 take the Mazara del Vallo exit and head towards the town. Go straight over the first roundabout and after about 1.5 km. turn right at the traffic lights toward the beach. At the roundabout exit left and go straight ahead to the site, not over the bridge. GPS: 37.63647, 12.61631

Charges guide

Per unit incl. 2 persons and electricity	€ 20.50 - € 41.80
extra person	€ 4.50 - € 7.90

Numana

Numana Blu Camping Village

Via Costaverde 37, I-60026 Numana (Marche) T: 071 739 0993. E: info@numanablu.it
alanrogers.com/IT66190

Numana Blu lies on the Cónero Riviera, south of Ancona, just 300 metres from the sea, and close to the town of Marcelli. Beneath the site's 12,000 trees there are 380 shady pitches, most offering electrical connections. Separate areas have a range of rentable accommodation, including chalets and bungalows. There's plenty to do here but the site retains a relaxed atmosphere. In peak season there are several children's clubs catering for different ages. The site also boasts an impressive array of leisure amenities including a large swimming pool, a restaurant/pizzeria and supermarket.

Facilities

Supermarket. Bar, restaurant/pizzeria and takeaway meals. Swimming pool and children's pool. Playground. Bicycle hire. Football pitch. Tennis. Children's clubs. Entertainment programme in high season. Off site: Beach 300 m. Riding 1 km. Golf 6 km. Cónero Riviera, Monte Cónero (at 572 m. the highest peak in the area) and Ancona. Cycle and walking trails.

Open: 24 April - 30 September.

Directions

Take the Loreto Porto Recanati exit from the A14 autostrada and follow signs to Numana. Site is south of Numana, 1.5 km. from the small town of Marcelli. GPS: 43.49806, 13.62306

Charges guide

Per unit incl. 2 persons and electricity	€ 22.50 - € 45.40
extra person	€ 4.50 - € 9.50

Oliveri

Camping Villaggio Marinello

Via del Sol 17, I-98060 Oliveri (Sicily) T: 094 131 3000. E: marinello@camping.it

alanrogers.com/IT69300

Camping Marinello is located alongside the sea with direct access to a lovely uncrowded sandy beach with an informal marina at one end and natural pool areas with a spot of sand at the other. The 220 gravel touring pitches here are shaded by tall trees. We enjoyed a delicious traditional meal in the excellent terraced restaurant with its lovely sea views. Tours are arranged to major sightseeing destinations such as Mount Etna, Taormina and the nearby Aeolian Islands. The Greco family have been here for over 30 years and work hard to ensure that their guests enjoy a pleasant stay. There is some noise from the coastal rail line which runs along the length of the site.

Facilities

Two sanitary blocks with free hot showers, one is not currently used and is awaiting a much needed refurbishment and heating. Washing machines. Bazaar, market and supermarket. Bar with sea views. Restaurant and terraced eating area also with views. Electronic games. Piano bar in high season. Dogs are not accepted in July/Aug. Off site: Seaside resort style town of Oliveri.

Open: All year.

Directions

From A20 motorway take Falcone exit and follow signs to Oliveri. At the town turn north towards the beach (site sign), then turn west along the beach and continue 1 km. to site. You will need to make a right turn immediately before a small narrow bridge (2.2 m. high and 2.5 m. wide).
GPS: 38.13246, 15.05452

Charges guide

Per person (over 3 yrs)	€ 4.50 - € 9.00
pitch incl. electricity	€ 13.00 - € 21.00
tent	€ 4.50 - € 12.00
car	€ 3.00 - € 5.00

Oriago

Camping Della Serenissima

Via Padana 334/a, I-30034 Oriago (Veneto) T: 041 921 850. E: info@campingserenissima.it

alanrogers.com/IT60500

This is a delightful little site of some 155 pitches (all with 16A electricity) where one could stay for a number of days whilst visiting Venice (12 km), Padova (24 km), Lake Garda (135 km) or the Dolomites. There is a good service by bus to Venice and the site is situated on the Riviera del Brenta, at a section with some very large old villas. A long, narrow and flat site, numbered pitches are on each side of a central road. There is good shade in most parts with many trees, plants and grass. The management is friendly and good English is spoken.

Facilities

Sanitary facilities are of a good standard and include those for disabled visitors. New additional toilet facilities next to restaurant. Motorcaravan services. Gas supplies. Shop (all season). Bar. Restaurant and takeaway (1/6-31/10). Play area. Fishing. Bicycle hire. Reduced price bus ticket to Venice if staying for 3 days. No organised entertainment but local markets, etc. all well publicised. Off site: Golf and riding 3 km.

Open: Easter - 10 November.

Directions

Approaching Venice on the A4 take exite for Oriago-Mira then signs for Ravenna, Padova (SS11) to Oriago. On A27 or SS309 take exit for Venezia-Mestre then signs for Ravenna, Padova and Milano. After Padova-Riviera del Brenta follow signs to Oriago. Site is well signed.
GPS: 45.451769, 12.183784

Charges guide

Per unit incl. 2 persons and electricity	€ 27.00 - € 32.00
extra person	€ 7.00 - € 9.00
child (3-12 yrs)	€ 4.00 - € 5.50

Orta San Giulio

Camping Orta

Via Domodossola 28, I-28016 Orta San Giulio (Piedmont) T: 032 290 267. E: info@campingorta.it

alanrogers.com/IT62420

Lake Orta is a delightful, less visited small lake just west of Lake Maggiore. The site is on a considerable slope, and most of the 90 touring pitches (all with 4A electricity) are on the top grass terrace with spectacular views across the lake to the mountains beyond. There are some superb lakeside pitches across the main road (linked by a pedestrian underpass) although there is some traffic noise here. Amenities include a large games and entertainment room and a traditional Italian bar and restaurant serving good value family meals. Some English is spoken by the Guarnori family, who take pride in maintaining their uncomplicated site to a high standard. Book ahead to enjoy the lakeside pitches. If you are anxious about towing a large caravan to the top terraces, the owner will help out with his tractor!

Facilities

Three modern sanitary blocks are clean and well maintained providing mainly British style toilets, coin operated showers and an excellent unit for disabled visitors. Laundry facilities. Motorcaravan services. Good quality shop. Bar and restaurant with basic menu serving good value Italian family meals. Playground. Large games/TV room. WiFi in reception/bar area. Fishing. Bicycle hire. Boat launching. Lake swimming and watersports. Off site: Riding, golf and sailing within 10 km.

Open: 1 March - 31 December.

Directions

Lake Orta is 85 km. northwest of Milan and just west of Lake Maggiore. Site is on the SR229 between Borgomanero and Omega, 600 m. north of the turn to Orta San Giulio. There is a parking area for arrivals on the lake side of the road, but reception and main entrance are on the opposite side.
GPS: 45.80188, 8.42047

Charges guide

Per person	€ 5.50 - € 7.50
child (2-11 yrs)	€ 4.00 - € 5.00
pitch	€ 9.00 - € 18.00
electricity	€ 2.50

No credit cards. Low season discounts.

Pacengo

Camping Lido

Via Peschiera 2, I-37017 Pacengo (Lake Garda) T: 045 759 0611. E: info@campinglido.it

alanrogers.com/IT62540

Camping Lido is one of the largest and amongst the best of the 120 campsites around Lake Garda and is situated at the southeast corner of the lake. There is quite a slope from the entrance down to the lake so many of the 683 grass touring pitches are on terraces which give lovely views across the lake. They are of varying sizes, separated by hedges, all have electrical connections and 57 are fully serviced. This is a most attractive site with tall, neatly trimmed trees standing like sentinels on either side of the broad avenue which runs from the entrance right down to the lake.

Facilities

Seven modern toilet blocks (three heated) include provision for disabled visitors and three family rooms. Washing machines and dryer. Fridge rental. Restaurant, bars, pizzeria, takeaway and well stocked supermarket. Swimming pool, paddling pool and slides. Superb fitness centre. Playground. Tennis. Bicycle hire. Watersports. Fishing. Activity programme (high season). Shingle beach with landing stage and mooring for boats. Dogs are not accepted in high season (5/7-15/8). Off site: Bus service 200 m. Gardaland theme park.

Open: 20 March - 11 October.

Directions

Leave A4 Milan - Venice motorway at exit for Peschiera. Head north on east side of lake on the SS249. Site entrance on left after Gardaland theme park. GPS: 45.46996, 10.72042

Charges guide

Per person	€ 4.50 - € 7.00
child (3-5 yrs)	€ 3.00 - € 4.10
pitch incl. services	€ 8.60 - € 17.00

Pacengo

Eurocamping Pacengo

Via Porto 13, I-37010 Pacengo di Lazise (Lake Garda) T: 045 759 0012. E: info@eurocampingpacengo.it

alanrogers.com/IT63010

Eurocamping is at the southeast corner of Lake Garda, with direct lake access and a pleasant beach. It is a good site for launching boats as there is a little harbour/marina area adjacent. This is the best part of the site, where a pleasant restaurant terrace overlooks the lake and boats. Pacengo includes a large area of mobile homes. Most pitches, although quite small, have very good shade and all have electrical connections (4A). The swimming pool incorporates a jacuzzi and separate children's pool. Although a little untidy, Eurocamping's lower prices may suit some campers.

Facilities

The sanitary blocks, although quite old, are kept reasonably clean. Supermarket. Bar, restaurant and pizzeria (closed Tues in low season). Swimming pools. Second bar at the poolside. Large play area. Tennis. Fishing. Boat launching. Organised entertainment (July/Aug). Off site: Theme parks within 1.5 km. Riding 2 km. Bicycle hire 5 km. Golf 7 km. Sailing 8 km.

Open: 1 April - 24 September.

Directions

Pacengo is on the SS249 between Peschiera and Lazise, 30 km. west of Verona. From north on the A22 (Trento - Verona) autostrada take Affi exit then follow signs for Lazise and site. From the south on the A4 (Brescia - Venice) take Peschiera exit and follow signs for Lazise and Garda. At traffic lights in Pacengo, turn towards lake and follow road for 500 m. GPS: 45.46772, 10.71654

Charges guide

Per person	€ 3.70 - € 6.50
pitch	€ 8.70 - € 14.50

Passignano sul Trasimeno

Camping La Spiaggia

Via Europa 22, I-06065 Passignano sul Trasimeno (Umbria) T: 075 827 246. E: info@campinglaspiaggia.it

alanrogers.com/IT66460

This site has its own beach and is pleasantly covered with pine and oak trees providing shade to most pitches. The 50 spacious touring pitches with 6A electricity are clearly defined and some are separated by dwarf hedges. This is an attractive, compact site which is well managed and cared for and still being developed. A small café/restaurant has a terrace overlooking the lake and a small shop provides fresh bread to order. All sorts of activities are possible on the lake including canoeing, sailing and windsurfing and there are numerous possibilities for hiking and mountain biking in the surrounding hills.

Facilities

The new toilet block is very clean and modern with free hot water. It includes facilities for disabled visitors and a baby room. Separate laundry room. Small shop for basics, bar/restaurant with terrace and takeaway (April - Sept). Lake swimming. Heated outdoor swimming pool (1/6-15/9). Play area. Bicycle and canoe hire. WiFi throughout (free). Off site: Restaurant across road from campsite. Tours and excursions.

Open: 31 March - 7 October.

Directions

From A1 (Firenze - Roma) take Beltolle exit towards Perugia (S326). Follow this to Passignano exit (30 km. from the A1). Take the exit and go towards town (site signed). GPS: 43.1837, 12.1492

Charges guide

Per unit incl. 2 persons and electricity	€ 22.50 - € 28.00
extra person	€ 7.00 - € 8.50
child (2-9 yrs)	€ 4.50 - € 6.50
dog	€ 2.00

Peschici

Centro Turistico San Nicola

Localitá San Nicola, I-71010 Peschici (Puglia) T: 088 496 4024. E: sannicola@sannicola.it

alanrogers.com/IT68450

This is a really splendid site occupying a hillside position, sloping down to a cove with a 500 metre beach of fine sand – a special feature is an attractive grotto at the eastern end. Hard access roads lead to spacious, well constructed, grassy pitches, under shade from mature trees. Scores of pitches are on the beach fringes (no extra charge) and there is a separate area for campers with animals. There are 800 pitches of varying size, all with electricity. Cars may have to be parked away from the pitches in high season. There are no static caravans, but some bungalows are on site.

Facilities

Six modern toilet blocks, two in the beach part, the others around the site, are excellent with British and Turkish style toilets, hot water in the washbasins (some with toilets in private cabins) and showers. Laundry facilities. Supermarket. Two beach bars (from 1/5; some evening noise until 22.30). Large bar/restaurant with terraces and pizzeria. Tennis. Watersports. Playground. Organised activities and entertainment (July/Aug). Dogs are not accepted in high season. Off site: Coach and boat excursions. Gargano National Park.

Open: 1 April - 15 October.

Directions

Leave autostrada A14 at exit for Poggio Imperiale, and proceed towards Peschici and Vieste. Just as you enter Peschici, follow Vieste signs. At T-junction turn left towards Peschici and at top of hill turn right towards San Nicola. It will take at least 1.5 hrs from the motorway. GPS: 41.94291, 16.03493

Charges guide

Per unit incl. 2 persons and 16A electricity	€ 27.50 - € 47.40
extra person	€ 6.60 - € 13.00
child (3-7 yrs)	€ 3.80 - € 7.90

Pietra Ligure

Camping Piandei Boschi

Viale Riviera 114, I-17027 Pietra Ligure (Ligúria) T: 0196 254 25. E: info@piandeiboschi.it

alanrogers.com/IT64107

Camping Piandei Boschi can be found on the Ligurian Riviera, 700 m. from the sea, close to the resort of Pietra Ligure. Pitches are well shaded and most have electrical connections. A number of mobile homes are available for rent, as well as apartments (for 4-6 people). There is a large swimming pool surrounded by a wide sun terrace, with a paddling pool adjacent. The campsite restaurant includes a wood-fired pizza oven, and offers an enticing range of Mediterranean cuisine. Other on-site amenities include a tennis court and sports field. An entertainment and activity programme is organised in peak season, and includes evening entertainment. Pietra Ligure is a pleasant seaside resort and is well located for exploring the Ligurian coast. San Remo is delightful, with a wide promenade fringed with palm trees. The town also hosts an important music festival. Savona, to the north, is the regional centre, and home to Colombus. There is much of interest here, including a fine cathedral and the unfinished Palazzo delle Rovere.

Facilities

Shop. Bar/restaurant/pizzeria. Takeaway food. Swimming pool. Paddling pool. Children's play area. Tennis. Sports field. Entertainment and activity programme. Tourist information. Mobile homes and apartments for rent. Off site: Nearest beach 700 m. Shops and restaurants in Pietra Ligure. Golf. Watersports.

Open: All year.

Directions

Approaching from France (Menton) on the A10 motorway, leave at the exit to Pietra Ligure and head south on Viale Riviera towards the town centre, from where the site is well signed.
GPS: 44.14906, 8.26856

Charges guide

Per unit incl. 3 persons and electricity	€ 27.00 - € 42.00
extra person (over 2 yrs)	€ 5.00 - € 8.00
dog	€ 2.00 - € 3.50

Pozza di Fassa

Camping Vidor-Family & Wellness Resort

Strada de Ruf de Ruacia 15, I-38036 Pozza di Fassa (Trentino - Alto Adige) T: 046 276 0022.
E: info@campingvidor.it **alanrogers.com/IT62090**

This family run site is in a beautiful mountainous setting two kilometres from the town of Pozza. The pitches are of average size with 1-16A electricity, water, hardstanding and drainage. There are some slopes so chocks are advisable. Vidor has excellent facilities including a new reception, camping shop, restaurant and pizzeria (serving local cuisine with special menus for children), and café with terrace and lounge. There is an indoor heated swimming pool (with whirlpool etc) and a superb beauty and wellness centre offering a large variety of treatments and a fitness room.

Facilities

Two excellent hotel standard sanitary blocks provide hot water throughout and good showers with private bathrooms for hire. Facilities for disabled visitors. Washing machines, drying room and dryer. Bar/restaurant, takeaway and shop. Beauty and wellness centre, heated indoor pool and gym (all season). TV room and cinema. Indoor playrooms and miniclub. WiFi over whole site. Entertainment programme. Off site: Fishing 500 m. Ski lift 1 km. Town 2 km. with usual facilities. Golf 8 km. Many excursions to places of interest.

Open: All year except November.

Directions

From A22 Trento - Bolzano road take S48 to Pozza di Fassa. In the centre of the town, at the roundabout take the first exit towards Meida and Valle San Nicolo. Site is well signed in 2 km.
GPS: 46.41987, 11.70754

Charges guide

Per unit incl. 2 persons and electricity	€ 19.00 - € 41.00
extra person	€ 6.00 - € 11.00
child (2-15 yrs)	€ 4.50 - € 9.00
dog	€ 3.00 - € 5.00

Peschiera del Garda

Camping Bella Italia

Via Bella Italia 2, I-37019 Peschiera del Garda (Lake Garda) T: 045 640 0688. E: info@camping-bellaitalia.it

alanrogers.com/IT62630

Peschiera is a picturesque village on the southern shore of Lake Garda and Camping Bella Italia is a very attractive, large, well organised and very busy site in the grounds of a former farm, just west from the centre of the village. Half of the 1,100 pitches are occupied by the site's own mobile homes and chalets and by tour operators; there are some 400 touring pitches, most towards the lakeside and reasonably level on grass under trees. All have electricity (16A), water and waste water and are separated by shrubs. There are some fine views across the lake to the mountains beyond. A superb promenade allows direct access to the town. Bella Italia collaborates with Cisano/San Vito (IT63570) and Butterfly (IT62520). The site slopes gently down to the lake with access to the water for watersports and swimming. A feature of the site is the group of pools of varying shapes and sizes with an entertainment area and varied sports provision nearby. A range of supervised activities is organised. Regulations are in place to ensure that the site is peaceful. English and Dutch are spoken by the friendly staff. Although large, this site has not lost its personal touch, and their sixty years of experience has been wisely used.

Facilities

Six modern toilet blocks have British style toilets, washbasins and showers. Baby rooms and facilities for disabled visitors. Washing machines. Motorcaravan services. Infirmary. Shops. Gelateria. Bars. Waiter service restaurant and terrace and two other restaurants (one in the old farm building). Swimming pools (all season). Tennis. Archery. Playgrounds (small). Games room. Watersports. Fishing. Bicycle hire. Organised activities and entertainment. Mini club. WiFi (charged). ATMs. Dogs are not accepted. Off site: Fishing 1 km. Golf 2.5 km. Riding 3 km. Gardaland, Italy's most popular theme park, is about 2 km. east of Peschiera, with others nearby. Verona 40 mins.

Open: 24 March - 28 October.

Directions

Peschiera is 32 km. west of Verona. From the A4 take exit for Peschiera del Garda and follow the SS11 towards Brescia. Site is at the large junction at the western entrance to the village.
GPS: 45.44165, 10.67920

Charges guide

Per unit incl. 2 persons and electricity	€ 26.30 - € 51.80
extra person	€ 6.40 - € 13.40
child (3-5 yrs)	free - € 5.30

Four charging seasons.
No credit/debit cards.
Camping Cheques accepted.

Punta Sabbioni

alan rogers Runner up 2011 Awards

Camping Marina di Venezia

Via Montello 6, I-30013 Punta Sabbioni (Veneto) T: 041 530 2511.
E: camping@marinadivenezia.it **alanrogers.com/IT60450**

This is a very large site (2,853 pitches) with much the same atmosphere as many other large sites along this appealing stretch of coastline. Marina di Venezia, however, has the advantage of being within walking distance of the ferry to Venice. It will appeal particularly to those who enjoy an extensive range of entertainment and activities, and a lively atmosphere. Individual pitches are marked out on sandy or grassy ground, most separated by trees or hedges. They are of an average size for the region (around 80 sq.m) and all are equipped with electricity and water. The site's excellent sandy beach is one of the widest along this stretch of coast and has five pleasant beach bars. The main pool is Olympic size and there is also a very large children's pool adjacent. The magnificent Aqua Marina Park swimming pool complex is now open and offers amazing amenities (free to all campers). This is a well run site with committed management and staff.

Facilities

Ten modern toilet blocks (two recently replaced by a new one) are maintained to a high standard with good hot showers and a reasonable proportion of British style toilets. Good provision for disabled visitors. Washing machines and dryers. Range of shops. Several bars, restaurants and takeaways. Swimming pool complex with slides and flumes. Several play areas. Tennis. Windsurf and catamaran hire. Kite hire. Wide range of organised entertainment. WiFi Internet access in all bars and cafés. Church. Special area and facilities for dog owners.

Open: 16 April - 30 September.

Directions

From A4 motorway, take Jesolo exit. After Jesolo continue towards Punta Sabbioni. Site is clearly signed to the left towards the end of this road, close to the Venice ferries. GPS: 45.43750, 12.43805

Charges guide

Per unit incl. 2 persons and electricity	€ 19.80 - € 48.90
extra person	€ 4.40 - € 9.90
child or senior (2-5 and over 60)	€ 3.70 - € 8.00
dog	€ 1.10 - € 3.50

Bella Italia
SINCERT
SINCERT
ADAC
Super-Platz 2011

Pisa

Camping Torre Pendente

Viale delle Cascine 86, I-56122 Pisa (Tuscany) T: 050 561 704. E: info@campingtorrependente.com

alanrogers.com/IT66080

Torre Pendente is a most friendly site, well run by the Signorini family who speak good English and make everyone feel welcome. It is amazingly close to the famous leaning tower of Pisa and obviously its position means it is busy throughout the main season. It is a medium sized site, on level, grassy ground with some shade from trees and lots of artificial shade. There are 220 touring pitches, all with electricity. All site facilities are near the entrance including a most pleasant restaurant, swimming pool complex with pool bar and a large terrace. Here you can relax after hot days in the city and enjoy drinks and snacks or find more formal fare in the restaurant with a reasonable á la carte menu. This is a very busy site in high season with many nationalities discovering the delights of Pisa. It is ideal for exploring the fascinating leaning tower and other attractions. It is very close to the railway stations for travel to Lucca and Florence.

Facilities

Three new toilet blocks are very clean and smart with British style toilets and good facilities for disabled campers. Private cabins for hire. Hot water at sinks. Washing machines. Motorcaravan services. Well stocked supermarket. Pleasant restaurant, bar and takeaway. Swimming pool with pool bar, paddling pool and spa. Playground. Boules. Entertainment in high season. WiFi. Accommodation. Off site: Bicycle hire. Bus 100 m. Railway station 300 m. ATM 400 m. Riding 3 km. Fishing 10 km. Golf 15 km.

Open: 1 April - 15 October.

Directions

From A12, exit at Pisa Nord and follow for 5 km. to Pisa. Do not take first sign to town centre. Site is well signed at a later left turn (Viale delle Cascine). GPS: 43.7252, 10.3819

Charges guide

Per person	€ 8.00 - € 9.50
child (3-10 yrs)	€ 4.50 - € 6.00
pitch	€ 10.00 - € 15.00
dog	€ 1.60

No credit cards.

Rapallo

Camping Miraflores

Via Savagna 10, I-16035 Rapallo (Ligúria) T: 018 526 3000. E: camping.miraflores@libero.it

alanrogers.com/IT64110

Camping Miraflores is located on the Ligurian coast, close to the famous resort of Portofino and the Cinque Terre. It is a small, uncomplicated site with a tiny restaurant and bar offering pizzas and a reasonable menu of the day. The 87 pitches are fairly flat and arranged around the lower levels of the site with separate terraced areas for tents (small pitches) and caravans or motorcaravans with electricity (6A Europlug). There are eight mobile homes on higher terraces. A small swimming pool is free to campers (hats required) and showers are now free. Rapallo is an attractive resort in its own right with an interesting old town centre. The A12 motorway is very close to the site and from its very visible, elevated position there is road noise. The many tours and activities in the local area can be organised by reception and there are protected sea and land areas to explore. Subaqua diving packages are organised and a visit to the Rapallo funicular is worthwhile. The site is run by the friendly James family and good English is spoken. The single central sanitary block has been renovated and now offers a basic standard of facilities. The site charges reasonable pitch prices.

Facilities

Single central traditional sanitary block with a small number of toilets (some Turkish style). Showers. Washing machine. Shop. Restaurant/pizzeria and takeaway meals. Basic games room. Playground. Swimming pool (hats compulsory). WiFi (free). Mobile homes for rent. Tours and visits booked by reception. Off site: Golf 500 m. Tennis and riding 1 km. Nearest beach, fishing and boat launching 1.5 km. Rapallo centre 1.5 km.

Open: All year.

Directions

Site is located extremely close to the Rapallo exit from the A12 motorway. From this point, follow signs to Rapallo town and immediately around a roundabout to the left for the site entrance, which is well signed. GPS: 44.35772, 9.20964

Charges guide

Per unit incl. 2 persons and electricity	€ 25.50 - € 29.50
extra person	€ 6.50 - € 7.00
child (under 9 yrs)	€ 3.50 - € 4.00
dog	free

No credit cards.

Rasen

Camping Corones

I-39030 Rasen (Trentino - Alto Adige) T: 047 449 6490. E: info@corones.com

alanrogers.com/IT61990

Situated in a pine forest clearing at the foot of the attractive Antholz valley in the heart of German-speaking Südtirol, Corones is ideally situated both for winter sports enthusiasts and for walkers, cyclists, mountain bikers and those who prefer to explore the valleys and mountain roads of the Dolomites by car. There are 135 level pitches, all with electricity (16A) and many also with water, drainage and satellite TV. The Residence offers luxury apartments and there are authentic Canadian log cabins for hire. The bar/restaurant and small shop are open all season. From the site you can see slopes which in winter become highly rated skiing pistes. A short drive up the broad Antholz/Anterselva valley takes you to an internationally important biathlon centre. An excellent day trip would be to drive up the valley and over the pass into Austria and then back via another pass. Back on site, a small pool and paddling pool could be very welcome. There is a regular programme of free excursions and occasional evening events are organised. Children's entertainment is provided in July and August.

Facilities

The central toilet block is traditional but well maintained and clean. Additional facilities below the Residence are of the highest quality including individual shower rooms with washbasins, washbasins with all WCs, a delightful children's unit and an excellent facility for disabled visitors. Fully equipped private shower rooms for hire. Luxurious wellness centre with saunas, solarium, jacuzzis, massage, therapy pools and heat benches. Heated outdoor swimming and paddling pools. Play area. Internet facilities. Off site: Tennis 800 m. Bicycle hire 1 km. Riding and fishing 3 km. Golf (9 holes) 10 km. Canoeing/kayaking 15 km.

Open: 6 December - 30 March, 31 May - 31 October.

Directions

Rasen/Rasun is 85 km. northeast of Bolzano. From Bressanone/Brixen exit on A22 Brenner - Modena motorway, go east on SS49 for 50 km. then turn north (signed Rasen/Antholz). Turn immediately west at roundabout in Niederrasen/Rasun di Sotto to site on left in 100 m. GPS: 46.7758, 12.0367

Charges guide

Per unit incl. 2 persons, electricity on meter	€ 19.70 - € 28.80
extra person	€ 4.60 - € 7.80
child (3-15 yrs)	€ 3.00 - € 7.20

Ribera

Camping Kamemi

Loc. Seccágrande, I-92016 Ribera (Sicily) T: 092 569 212. E: info@kamemivillage.com

alanrogers.com/IT69170

Camping Kamemi can be found close to Ribera in Sicily's southwestern corner, just 300 m. from the sea. There are 160 pitches here – all are shaded, but some make use of artificial screening. A number of mobile homes are available for rent. There is a typically Sicilian restaurant (with some excellent local fish cuisine) and a pizzeria. A snack bar incorporates an ice cream parlour, with typical Sicilian ice creams. Other on-site amenities include two swimming pools, a tennis court and a football pitch. In high season, a lively activity and entertainment programme is on offer, including Latin American music and a summer carnival. The city of Agrigento is a worthwhile day trip. Agrigento is renowned as the site of the ancient Greek city of Akragas, one of the richest and most famous colonies. Much of the site remains unexcavated but a stunning complex of seven monumental Greek temples is widely considered one of the best preserved Greek sites outside Greece itself, and has been classed a World Heritage site by UNESCO.

Facilities

Restaurant. Pizzeria. Snack bar. Takeaway. Bar. Shop. Swimming pools. Tennis. Football pitch. Playground. Tourist information. Activity and entertainment programme. Mobile homes for rent. Off site: Nearest beach 300 m. Fishing. Ribera. Agrigento.

Open: All year.

Directions

From Agrigento, head up the coast towards Ribera on SS115. Before reaching Ribera, turn off to Secca Grande, and then follow signs to the site. GPS: 37.438304, 13.245145

Charges guide

Per unit incl. 2 persons and electricity	€ 18.00 - € 42.00

Rivoltella

Camping San Francesco

Strada Vicinale, I-25015 Rivoltella (Lake Garda) T: 030 911 0245. E: moreinfo@campingsanfrancesco.com

alanrogers.com/IT62520

San Francesco is a large, very well organised site situated to the west of the Simione peninsula on the south east shores of Lake Garda. The 323 touring pitches are generally on flat gravel and sand and enjoy shade from mature trees. There are three choices of pitch of different sizes with 6A electricity; 76 are fully serviced. They are marked by stones but there is no division between them. A wooded beach area of about 400 m. on the lake is used for watersports and there is a jetty for boating. There are delightful lake views from the restaurant and terrace. There is also an excellent shopping centre with a games area, bazaar and takeaway. The comprehensive sports centre, great pools with own bar, and entertainment area are all located across a busy road away from the pitches and safely accessed by a tunnel. As with most sites in Italy, reception closes for siesta, but there is a waiting area with electricity. This is a high quality site which is great for families and for campers with disabilities, as there are ten adapted mobile homes.

Facilities

Sanitary facilities are in two large, modern, centrally located buildings. Spotlessly clean and well equipped. Excellent facilities for disabled campers. Shop (sells gluten-free products). Restaurant. Bar. Pool bar. Pizzeria. Takeaway and snacks. In a separate area across the road: swimming pools (1/5-19/9; disability hoist) and jacuzzi, sports centre and tennis. Playground. Entertainment programme, organised activities and excursions. Bicycle hire arranged. Torches required in some areas. WiFi (charged). Off site: Riding 5 km. Golf 10 km.

Open: 1 April - 30 September.

Directions

From autostrada A4, between Brescia and Verona, exit towards Simione and follow signs to Simione and site. GPS: 45.46565, 10.59443

Charges guide

Per unit incl. 2 persons and electricity	€ 25.00 - € 54.00
extra person	€ 6.50 - € 12.00
child (0-10 yrs)	free - € 8.50
dog	free

Camping Cheques accepted.

Roma

Camping Tiber

Via Tiberina km 1,400, I-00188 Roma (Lazio) T: 063 361 0733. E: info@campingtiber.com

alanrogers.com/IT68090

An excellent city site with extensive facilities, which also caters for backpackers. Although a lively site, the thoughtful layout and the division of different areas with flowering shrubs makes it surprisingly peaceful. It is ideally located for visiting Rome with a free shuttle bus every 30 minutes to the station and then an easy train service to Rome (20 minutes), with trams operating late at night. The 350 tourist pitches (with electricity) are mostly shaded under very tall trees and many have very pleasant views over the river Tiber. This mighty river winds around two sides of the site boundary (safely fenced) providing a cooling effect for campers. There is a new section with some shade, and bungalows to rent are in a separate area. A small but pleasant outdoor pool with a bar awaits after a busy day in the city. The excellent main bar, beer garden and restaurant all have terraces and, along with the takeaway, give good value. The site is extremely well run with friendly and helpful staff and especially good for campers with disabilities.

Facilities

Fully equipped, very smart sanitary facilities include hot water everywhere, private cabins, a baby room and very good facilities for disabled campers. Laundry facilities. Motorcaravan service point. Shop. Bar, restaurant, pizzeria and takeaway. Swimming pool (hat required) and bar. Play area. Internet access. Free shuttle bus to the underground station every 15 or 30 minutes according to season. Torches useful. WiFi. Off site: Local bars, restaurants and shops. Golf and riding 20 km.

Open: 25 March - 20 October.

Directions

From Florence, exit at Rome Nord Fiano on A1 and turn south onto Via Tiberina and site is signed. From other directions on Rome ring road (GRA) take exit 6 northbound on S3 Via Flaminia following signs to Tiberina. GPS: 42.0095, 12.50233

Charges guide

Per person	€ 9.50 - € 10.00
child (3-12 yrs)	€ 6.50 - € 7.00
motorcaravan	€ 10.50 - € 12.60
caravan and car	€ 12.00 - € 14.30

Roma

Happy Village & Camping

Via del Prato della Corte, 1915, I-00123 Roma (Lazio) T: 063 362 6401. E: info@happycamping.net

alanrogers.com/IT68095

This is a friendly all-year site, located on the Riviera Romagnola, between Rimini and Ravenna. Happy Village faces the Adriatic, with its own private beach (equipped with parasols and sun loungers). There are 160 good sized pitches, generally well shaded and all equipped with electricity (max 16A). A number of mobile homes are available for rent and a small hotel is also located within the site. Leisure amenities here include tennis courts and a swimming pool (with hydro massage). The site restaurant is appealing and offers a good range of menu choices, including pizzas. There is also a large, well stocked supermarket. Reservations are recommended in peak season (minimum 3 nights accepted).

Facilities

Restaurant/bar. Pizzeria. Takeaway food. Shop. Swimming pool with hydro massage. TV and games room. Play area. Direct beach access. Tourist information. Excursions. Activity and entertainment programme. Mobile homes and chalets for rent. Off site: Cycle and walking tracks. Water sports. Bellaria and Rimini.

Open: 1 March - 6 January.

Directions

From the A14 motorway, take the Rimini Nord exit. Head towards Ravenna on SS16. Leave at exit for San Mauro Mare. In the village, immediately after the railway crossing, turn right. Happy Village is 400 m. GPS: 42.003242, 12.452724

Charges guide

Per unit incl. 2 persons and electricity	€ 23.80 - € 36.00
extra person	€ 7.50 - € 11.00

Roma

Camping Seven Hills Village

Via Cassia 1216, I-00189 Roma (Lazio) T: 063 031 0826. E: info@sevenhills.it

alanrogers.com/IT68100

Close to Rome, this site provides a quieter, garden setting in some areas, but has a very lively, busy atmosphere in others. It is situated in a delightful valley, flanked by two of the seven hills of Rome and is just off the autostrada ring road (GRA) to the north of the city. The site runs a bus shuttle service every 30 minutes in the mornings to the local station and one return bus to Rome each day (08.00-12.00 and 16.30-20.30). The 250 pitches for touring units (3A electricity to some) are not marked, but the management supervise in busy periods.

Facilities

Three soundly constructed sanitary blocks are well situated around the site, with open plan washbasins, and hot water in the average sized showers. Facilities for disabled campers. Well stocked shop. Bar/restaurant and terrace. Money exchange. Swimming pool at the bottom of the site with bar/snack bar and a room where the younger element tends to congregate (separate pool charge). Disco. Excursions. Bungalows to rent. WiFi. Off site: Golf 4 km.

Open: 15 March - 1 November.

Directions

From autostrada ring road exit 3 take Via Cassia (signed SS2 Viterbo, NOT Via Cassia Bis) and look for site signs. Turn right after 1 km. and follow small road, Via Italo Piccagli for 1 km. to site. This narrow twisting road is heavily parked on during the day so access can be interesting. GPS: 41.993, 12.41685

Charges guide

Per unit incl. 2 persons and car	€ 18.00 - € 21.00
extra person	€ 8.00 - € 9.50
child (5-12 yrs)	€ 6.00 - € 7.50

Roseto degli Abruzzi

Camping Village Eurcamping

Lungomare Trieste Sud, I-64026 Roseto degli Abruzzi (Abruzzo) T: 085 899 3179.

E: eurcamping@camping.it **alanrogers.com/IT68040**

Eurcamping is about 2 km. south of the small town of Roseto degli Abruzzi, at the end of the coastal road which runs parallel to the SS16. This is a relatively quiet site, situated beside the sea, but with no direct access to it. There are 265 well defined pitches, many under green screens, and all with electricity (3/6A). Accessing the site is not difficult, but you have to pass under the coastal railway line so must use the bridge with 4 m. headroom. There is some road noise but little from the railway. There is a small harbour and yacht club nearby and a small sandy section of the beach, about 75 m.

Facilities

Three sanitary blocks with free hot showers. Facilities for disabled visitors. Motorcaravan services. Laundry. Bar. Restaurant. Takeaway. Pizzeria. Shop. Swimming pools (hats must be worn) with solarium terrace. Play area and sports ground. Tennis. Bowling. WiFi (charged). Bicycle hire. Entertainment in high season. Clubs for children and teenagers. Pets are allowed only on assigned pitches. Bungalows to rent. Off site: Beach. Canoe and pedalo hire.

Open: 1 May - 31 October.

Directions

From north or south on A14 motorway, take exit for Roseto degli Abruzzi. Turn on SS150 to Roseto degli Abruzzi. Pass under 4 m. bridge below railway at south end of town and turn right onto coast road. From Rome and L'Aquila on A24 motorway take exit for Villa Vomano-Teramo, onto SS150 (Roseto degli Abruzzi). GPS: 42.6577, 14.0353

Charges guide

Per unit incl. 2 persons and electricity	€ 18.00 - € 42.50
extra person	€ 4.50 - € 11.00

Camping Cheques accepted.

San Baronto di Lamporecchio

Camping Barco Reale

Via Nardini 11, I-51035 San Baronto di Lamporecchio (Tuscany) T: 057 388 332. E: info@barcoreale.com

alanrogers.com/IT66000

Just forty minutes from Florence and an hour from Pisa, this site is beautifully situated high in the Tuscan hills close to the fascinating town of Pistoia. Part of an old walled estate, there are impressive views of the surrounding countryside. It is a quiet site of 15 hectares with 250 pitches with good shade from mature pines and oaks. Some pitches are huge with great views and others are very private. Most are for tourers, but some have difficult access (site provides tractor assistance). All 187 touring pitches have electricity and 40 have water and drainage. The site has an attractive bar, a smart restaurant with terraces (try the brilliant traditional dishes) and a leased shop. The pools have really stunning views to the west (on a clear day you may see the island of Capraia). Pleasant walks are available in the grounds of the estate. This most attractive and popular site, will appeal to those who prefer a quiet site but with plenty to do for all age groups. In high season an information kiosk supplies tourist information, makes bookings and helps generally. Used by tour operators. A member of Leading Campings Group.

Facilities

Three modern sanitary blocks are kept very clean. Good facilities for disabled visitors (dedicated pitches close by). Baby room. Laundry facilities. Motorcaravan services. Dog shower. Shop. Restaurant. Bar. Supervised and enlarged swimming pool (caps required; 1/5-30/9). Ice cream shop (1/6-31/8). Playgrounds. Bowls. Bicycle hire. Internet point. WiFi. Disco. Entertainment. Cooking lessons for Tuscan style food. Excursions. No charcoal fires.
Off site: Village and shops 1 km. Fishing 8 km. Golf 15 km.

Open: 1 April - 30 September.

Directions

From Pistoia take Vinci - Empoli - Lamporecchio signs to San Baronto. From Empoli signs to Vinci and San Baronto. Final approach involves a sharp bend and a steep slope. GPS: 43.84190, 10.91130

Charges guide

Per unit incl. 2 persons and electricity	€ 24.20 - € 37.80
extra person	€ 7.10 - € 10.50
child (3-11 yrs)	€ 4.00 - € 6.50
dog	free - € 1.50

San Croce Camerina

Camping Scarabeo

I-97017 San Croce Camerina (Sicily) T: 093 291 8096. E: info@scarabeocamping.it

alanrogers.com/IT69190

Camping Scarabeo is a beautiful site located in Punta Braccetto, a little fishing port in Sicily's southeastern corner. It is a perfect location with exceptional facilities to match. Split into two separate sites (just 50 m. apart) with a total of 80 pitches, it is being constantly improved with care by Angela di Modica. All pitches are well shaded, some naturally and others with an artificial cane roof, and have 3/6A electricity. Scarabeo lies adjacent to a sandy beach and the little village is close by. The site layout resembles a Sicilian farm courtyard and is divided into four principal areas. The ancient Greek ruins of Kamerina and Caucana are just a few kilometres from the site and their ruins can be reached by bicycle. The Riserva Naturale at the mouth of the River Irminio is also a popular excursion.

Facilities

Exceptional sanitary blocks provide personal WC compartments (personal key access). Ample hot showers (free low season). Facilities for disabled visitors. Washing machine. Direct access to beach. Playground. Entertainment programme in high season. WiFi over site (charged). Mobile homes for rent. Off site: Restaurant/café 500 m. Riding 3 km. Supermarket 4 km. Golf 6 km. Cycling and walking trails.

Open: All year.

Directions

Site is 20 km. southwest of Ragusa. From Catania, take S194 towards Ragusa and, at Comiso, follow signs to S. Croce Camerina, then Punta Braccetto, from where site is well signed. Use second entrance for reception. GPS: 36.81645, 14.46964

Charges guide

Per person	€ 4.00 - € 8.50
pitch	€ 4.00 - € 11.00

Camping Cheques accepted.

San Felice del Benaco

Camping Europa Silvella

Via Silvella 10, I-25010 San Felice del Benaco (Lake Garda) T: **036 565 1095**. E: **info@europasilvella.it**

alanrogers.com/IT62600

This large, traditional, lakeside site is a slightly confusing merger of two different sites with the result that the 345 pitches (about 108 for tourers) appear randomly dispersed around the site. However, those alongside the lake are in small groups and close together; the main bar, restaurant and shop are also located at the lower level. The main area is at the top of a steepish hill on slightly sloping or terraced grass and has slightly larger pitches. There is reasonable shade in many parts and all pitches have 4A electricity. An attractive swimming pool complex also has a daytime bar and a restaurant which serves lunch and is the hub of the evening entertainment programme in high season. There is a considerable tour operator presence (160 pitches) and there are 50 bungalows, mobile homes and log cabins to rent. The site has steep slopes to the lake, so is unsuitable for campers with disabilities. The beach is suitable for swimming and has a jetty and moorings. A choice of watersports is available.

Facilities

Toilet blocks include washbasins in cabins, facilities for disabled visitors and a superb children's room with small showers. Laundry. Shop. Restaurant/Pizzeria. Swimming pools (hats required) with bar. Tennis. Five-a-side soccer. Volleyball. Playground. Bowling alley. Entertainment (every night in July/Aug). Disco for children. Tournaments. Fishing and boat launching. First aid room. WiFi (charged). Off site: Golf and bicycle hire 5 km. Sailing 10 km. Riding 12 km. Theme parks.

Open: 21 April - 24 September.

Directions

San Felice is on the western shore of Lake Garda at the southern end. From A4 Milan - Venice autostrada take Desenzano exit and head north on SS572 towards Saló for 14 km, turn right towards San Felice and follow brown tourist signs with site name (about 3 km). GPS: 45.574474, 10.54857

Charges guide

Per unit incl. 2 persons and electricity	€ 19.00 - € 49.00
child (3-9 yrs)	free - € 8.50
extra person	€ 6.00 - € 10.50
dog	free - € 4.00

San Felice del Benaco

Camping Villaggio Weekend

Via Vallone della Selva 2, I-25010 San Felice del Benaco (Lake Garda) T: **036 543 712**. E: **info@weekend.it**

alanrogers.com/IT62800

Created among the olive groves and terraced vineyards of the Château Villa Louisa, which overlooks it, this modern well equipped site enjoys some superb views over the small bay which forms this part of Lake Garda. On reaching the site you will pass through a most impressive pair of gates. There are 230 pitches, all with electricity, of which about 30 per cent are taken by tour operators and statics. The touring pitches are in several different areas, and many enjoy superb views. Some pitches for larger units are set in the upper terraces on steep slopes, manoeuvring can be challenging and low olive branches may cause problems for long or high units.

Facilities

Three sanitary blocks, one below the restaurant/shop, are modern and well maintained. Mainly British style WCs, a few washbasins in cabins and facilities for disabled visitors in one. Baby room. Laundry. Bar/restaurant (waiter service). Takeaway. Shop. Supervised swimming pool and paddling pool. Entertainment programme all season. TV. Barbecues. All facilities are open throughout the season. Two playgrounds. English spoken. WiFi (charged). Off site: Windsurfing, water skiing and tennis nearby. Fishing 2 km. Golf 6 km. Riding 8 km.

Open: 17 April - 25 September.

Directions

Approach from Saló (easier when towing) and follow site signs. From Milan - Venice autostrada take Desenzano exit towards Saló and Localita Cisano - S. Felice. Watch for narrow right fork after Cunettone roundabout. Pass petrol station on left, then turn right towards San Felice for 1 km. Site is next left. GPS: 45.59318, 10.53088

Charges guide

Per unit incl. 2 persons and electricity	€ 17.00 - € 60.50
extra person	€ 4.00 - € 10.50

San Gimignano

Camping Boschetto di Piemma

Localitá Santa Lucia 38/C, I-53037 San Gimignano (Tuscany) T: **057 794 0352.**

E: **info@boschettodipiemma.it** **alanrogers.com/IT66270**

The medieval Manhattan of San Gimignano is one of Tuscany's most popular sites. This new site lies just 2 km. from the town and there are 100 small pitches here, all with electrical connections (10A). The site is in a wood surrounded by olive groves and vineyards and has been developed with much care for the environment, using rain water for irrigation, for example. San Gimignano has been classified by UNESCO as a world heritage site and is best known for its towers, built by rival families, and which date back to the 11th century. An hourly bus service connects the site with the town.

Facilities

Excellent sanitary block and facilities for disabled visitors. Restaurant/pizzeria and bar. Shop (specialising in local produce). Swimming pool (15/5-15/9, small charge). Tennis (lessons available). Sports pitch. Playground. Entertainment and activity programme in high season. Apartments for rent. Off site: San Gimignano 2 km. Cycle and walking trails. Riding. Golf.

Open: All year.

Directions

Take the Poggibonsi Nord exit from the Florence - Siena superstrada. Then follow signs to San Gimignano. At first roundabout follow signs to Volterra and then take first road to the left, signed Santa Lucia. Site is located close to the sports area. GPS: 43.4533, 11.0536

Charges guide

Per unit incl. 2 persons and electricity	€ 20.30 - € 33.50
extra person	€ 6.70 - € 10.10
child (3-11 yrs)	€ 4.30 - € 5.40

San Piero a Sieve

Camping Mugello Verde

Via Massorondinaio 39, I-50037 San Piero a Sieve (Tuscany) T: **055 848 511.**

E: **mugelloverde@florencecamping.com** **alanrogers.com/IT66050**

Mugello Verde is a country hillside site with long curving terraces and one tarmac access road. Some pitches offer good views. English is spoken at reception where much tourist information is available – ask for the limited dates of the Ferrari team practices and the racing on the nearby international Mugello racing track! There are 200 good sized pitches for motorcaravans and caravans with smaller areas for tents. All pitches have electricity (6A) and mature trees provide shade. We met British campers who liked the site's charm and loved the proximity to the Ferrari race track, but found the facilities a little rustic and the pitches somewhat unkempt.

Facilities

Two toilet blocks on the terraces have been refurbished to a good standard and facilities are clean and relatively modern with mixed British and Turkish style WCs. Most washbasins have hot water. Comprehensive facilities for disabled campers. Laundry facilities. Shop. Restaurant/bar and pizzeria (all season). Swimming pool (1/6-18/9; no paddling pool). Play area. Tennis. Off site: Riding, golf, bicycle hire and fishing all within 5 km.

Open: All year.

Directions

From A1 autostrada take Barberino del Mugello exit and follow SS65 towards San Piero a Sieve and before town, turn left and just past Tamoil garage turn right to site. GPS: 43.96148, 11.31030

Charges guide

Per unit incl. 2 persons and electricity	€ 22.00 - € 30.00
extra person	€ 6.00 - € 8.00
child (3-12 yrs)	€ 3.00 - € 5.50

San Remo

Camping Villaggio dei Fiori

Via Tiro a Volo 3, I-18038 San Remo (Ligúria) T: 018 466 0635.

E: info@villaggiodeifiori.it **alanrogers.com/IT64010**

Open all year round, this open and spacious site is a member of the Senelia group and maintains very high standards. It is ideal for exploring the Italian and French Rivieras or for just relaxing by the enjoyable, filtered sea water pools or on the private beach. Unusually, all of the pitch areas at the site are totally paved, with some extremely large pitches for large units (ask reception to open another gate for entry). Electricity (3/6A) is available (at extra cost) to all 107 pitches; 20 also have water and drainage, and there is an outside sink and cold water for every four pitches. There is ample shade from mature trees and shrubs, which are constantly watered and cared for in summer. The 'gold' pitches and some wonderful tent pitches are along the seafront with great views. There is a path to a secluded and pleasant beach with sparkling waters, overlooked by a large patio area. The rocky surrounds are excellent for snorkelling and fishing, with ladder access to the water. The friendly management speak excellent English and will supply detailed touring plans. Activities and entertainment are organised throughout the year for adults and children. A good range of excursions are offered (extra cost) in the site's eight-seater bus along the Italian Riviera dei Fiori and the French Côte d'Azur, including night excursions to Nice and Monte Carlo. Buses run from outside the site to Monte Carlo, Nice, Cannes and Eze. This is a very good site for visiting all the attractions in the local area.

Facilities

Four clean and modern toilet blocks have British and Turkish style WCs and hot water throughout. Controllable showers. Baby rooms. Facilities for disabled campers. Laundry facilities. Motorcaravan services. Gas. Bar sells limited essential supplies. Large restaurant. Pizzeria and takeaway (all year; prepaid card system). Sea water swimming pools (small extra charge in high season) and heated whirlpool spa (June-Sept). Tennis. Excellent play area. Fishing. Satellite TV. Internet access. WiFi (charged). Bicycle hire. Dogs are not accepted. Off site: Bus at gate. Supermarket 100 m. Shop 150 m. Riding and golf 2 km. Very safe cycle route to the city and a further 24 km. along coastal path.

Open: All year.

Directions

From SS1 (Ventimiglia-Imperia), site is on right just before San Remo. There is a very sharp right turn into site if approaching from the west. From autostrada A10 take San Remo exit. Site is well signed. GPS: 43.80117, 7.74867

Charges guide

Per unit incl. 4 persons and electricity	€ 35.00 - € 72.00

Some charges must be paid on arrival.

Discounts for low season and long stays. Special discount for Alan Rogers customers in low season.

San Vincenzo

Camping Park Albatros

Pineta di Torre Nuova, I-57027 San Vincenzo (Tuscany) T: **056 570 1018.** E: **parkalbatros@ecvacanze.it**

alanrogers.com/IT66380

Camping Albatros is situated on the historic Costa Degli Etruschi where natural parks abound. There is a theme of circles throughout the site in the form of round buildings and the placing of mobile homes in curves. Of the 1000 pitches, the 300 for touring are in a separate area on flat ground. All have water, drainage, 10A electricity and shade. The pools at this ultra modern site are outstanding and the facilities are superb. A great site for family holidays. The top quality facilities and entertainment provided here are so good that you need not leave the site for your entire holiday.

Facilities

Two superb toilet blocks and brilliant children's room. Good showers. Facilities for disabled visitors. Washing machines. Huge air-conditioned supermarket. Bazaar. Lagoon complex with 5 amazing pools (one covered and heated). 2 bars, 2 restaurants and pizzeria with large terrace. Takeaway. Daily entertainment in season. Disco. Miniclub (4-12 yrs). Play areas. Diving organised. Bicycle hire. No barbecues allowed. Internet points and WiFi. Train around site in high season. Off site: Beach 800 m. Riding 15 km. Excursions and walks.

Open: 16 April - 25 October.

Directions

Site is northwest of Grossetto and south of Livorno on the coast. From the SS1 take San Vincenzo exit. Site is well signed in San Vincenzo and is 6 km. south of village along the beach road.
GPS: 43.04972, 10.55861

Charges guide

Per unit incl. 2 persons and electricity	€ 26.50 - € 50.70
extra person	€ 7.50 - € 14.90
child (2-12 yrs)	free - € 11.90

San Vito Lo Capo

El Bahira Camping Village

Ctra da Makari - Localitá Salinella, I-91010 San Vito Lo Capo (Sicily) T: **092 397 2577.** E: **info@elbahira.it**

alanrogers.com/IT69140

El Bahira is a popular site in quite a remote area overlooking the Gulf of Makari toward Monte Cofano. The views are outstanding and the location is good as it is near the sea, nature reserves and ancient cities such as Segtesta and Selinunte. Partners Maurizio, Maceri, Sugameli and Michele, who speak good English, have chosen this area to develop a campsite of a high standard. The 200 fairly small pitches are on sloping gravel (chocks required), most are shady and all have electricity. There are also numerous statics which unfortunately rather spoil the look of the site. There is a separate area for tents.

Facilities

Three well placed sanitary blocks, showers are by token (€ 4 for 8 showers), these are unisex, in tiny cabins. Motorcaravan service point. Supermarket. Restaurant and pizzoria. Swimming pool. Two entertainment areas. Tennis. Sub-aqua facilities. Boat launching at rocky beach on site. Off site: Popular resort village of San Vito Lo Capo 3 km.

Open: 1 April - 4 October.

Directions

From the east follow the A19 motorway and take Castellammare del Golfo exit then follow the S187 towards Trapani. After about 16 km. turn right and follow signs to San Vito Lo Capo and site is well signed off the road approaching the town.
GPS: 38.150707, 12.73191

Charges guide

Per unit incl. 2 persons and electricity	€ 24.90 - € 35.40

Sant Arcangelo

Camping Villaggio Italgest

Via Martiri di Cefalonia, I-06063 Sant Arcangelo-Magione (Umbria)

T: **075 848 238.** E: **camping@italgest.com** **alanrogers.com/IT66520**

Villaggio Italgest is a mature but pleasant site with 208 touring pitches (with 6A electricity) on level grass and plenty of shade. Cars are parked away from the pitches and the site offers a wide variety of activities with tours organised daily. The pools and restaurant are dated, but enjoyable. Directly on the shore on the south side of Lake Trasimeno, Sant Arcangelo is ideally placed for exploring Umbria and Tuscany. The area around the lake is fairly flat but has views of the distant hills and can become very hot during summer. There is some entertainment in high season, including Italian courses.

Facilities

One large and two smaller sanitary blocks have mainly British style WCs, washbasins and showers. Children's toilets. Baby room. Facilities for disabled visitors. Motorcaravan services. Laundry facilities. Campers' kitchen. Bar, restaurant, pizzeria and takeaway. Shop. Recently enlarged swimming pool with flume. Paddling pool. Spa. Tennis. Play area. TV and games rooms. Disco. Films. Watersports. Motorboat hire. Lake swimming. Fishing. Barbecues. Picnic area by pond. Mountain bike and scooter hire. WiFi. Activities and entertainment. Off site: Golf, parachuting, riding, canoeing and sailing.

Open: 1 April - 30 September.

Directions

Site is on the southern shore of Lake Trasimeno. Take Magione exit from the Perugia spur of the Florence - Rome autostrada, proceed southwest round the lake to S. Arcangelo where site is signed.
GPS: 43.0881, 12.1561

Charges guide

Per unit incl. 2 persons and electricity	€ 20.50 - € 31.00
extra person	€ 6.00 - € 8.50
child (3-9 yrs)	€ 4.00 - € 6.50
dog	€ 2.00 - € 2.50

Camping Cheques accepted.

Sarteano

Parco Delle Piscine

Via del Bagno Santo 29, I-53047 Sarteano (Tuscany) T: 057 826 971. E: info@parcodellepiscine.it

alanrogers.com/IT66450

On the spur of Monte Cetona, Sarteano is a spa, and this large, smart site utilises that spa in its very open environs. The site is well run with an excellent infrastructure and there is a friendly welcome from the English speaking staff. The 500 individual, flat pitches, are all 90 to 100 sq. m. with electricity (6/10A) and fully marked with high neat hedges giving real privacy. The novel features here are the three unique swimming pools fed by the natural thermo-mineral springs. These springs have been known since antiquity as 'del Bagno Santo' which flows at a constant temperature of about 24°. Two of these pools (the largest is superb with water cascade and hydro-massage, and the other large shallow pool is just for children) are set in a huge park-like ground with many picnic tables.

Facilities

Two heated toilet blocks are of high quality with mainly British style WCs, many cubicles also with bidet and numerous sinks for laundry and dishwashing (with hot water). Gas supplies. Motorcaravan services. Restaurant/pizzeria with bar. Takeaway. Coffee bar. Swimming pools (one all season). Satellite TV room and mini-cinema with 100 seats and very large screen. Tennis. Exchange facilities. Free guided cultural tours. Internet. Dogs are not accepted. Off site: Bicycle hire 100 m. Riding 3 km.

Open: 1 April - 30 September.

Directions

From autostrada A1 take Chiusi/Chianciano exit, from where Sarteano is well signed (6 km). In Sarteano follow camping/piscine signs to site (entrance sign reads Piscine di Sarteano). GPS: 42.9885, 11.8639

Charges guide

Per unit incl. 2 persons and electricity	€ 32.00 - € 58.00
extra person	€ 9.00 - € 15.50
child (3-10 yrs)	€ 6.00 - € 10.00

Savignano Mare

Camping Villaggio Rubicone

Via Matrice Destra 1, I-47039 Savignano Mare (Emilia-Romagna) T: 054 134 6377.
E: info@campingrubicone.com alanrogers.com/IT66240

This is a sophisticated, professionally run site where the friendly owners, Sandro and Paolo Grotti are keen to fulfill your every need. Rubicone covers over 30 acres of thoughtfully landscaped, level ground by the sea. There is an amazing array of amenities on offer. The 457 touring pitches vary in size (up to 100 sq.m) and are arranged in back to back, double rows. In some areas the central pitches are a little tight for manoeuvring larger units. All the pitches are kept very neat with hedges and all have electricity, 150 with water and drainage and 20 with private sanitary facilities. Some are shaded by poplar trees. There are many bars around the site, from beach bars to night club bars and the restaurant offers excellent food and efficient service at very reasonable prices.

Facilities

Modern heated toilet blocks have hot water for showers and washbasins (half in private cabins), mainly British style toilets, baby rooms and two excellent units for disabled visitors. Washing machines. Motorcaravan services. An excellent shop and bars (21/5-18/9) plus a restaurant and snack bar (28/5-11/9). Pizzeria. Swimming pools (caps mandatory; open 21/5-18/9). Games room with Internet access. Golf (lessons available). Tennis. Solarium. Jacuzzi. Beach with lifeguard. Fishing. Sailing and windsurfing schools. Dogs are not accepted. Off site: Bicycle hire 500 m. Riding 2 km. Golf 15 km. Cesenatico 5 km. Rimini 15 km. Riccione 25 km. True architectural pearls and world famous art cities in the area count Ravenna (28 km) and Republic of San Marino (30 km).

Open: 21 May - 18 September.

Directions

Site is 15 km. northwest of Rimini. From Bologna (Autostrada A14) exit Rimini Nord. Continue on the SS16 'Adriatica' direction Ravenna, then exit Savignano Mare. At the roundabout go straight through to San Mauro Mare and turn left immediately after the railway. At the end of the street turn right and you have arrived at Camping Rubicone. GPS: 44.16475, 12.441117

Charges guide

Per unit incl. 2 persons and electricity	€ 22.90 - € 41.90
extra person	€ 5.20 - € 10.30
child (2-8 yrs)	€ 4.00 - € 8.20

No credit cards.

Sexten

Caravan Park Sexten

Saint Josef Strasse 54, I-39030 Sexten (Trentino - Alto Adige) T: 047 471 0444.
E: info@caravanparksexten.it alanrogers.com/IT62030

Caravan Park Sexten is 1,520 metres above sea level and has 268 pitches, some very large and all with electricity (16A), TV connections and water and drainage in summer and winter (underground heating stops pipes freezing). Some pitches are in the open to catch the sun, others are tucked in forest clearings by the river. They are mostly gravelled to provide an ideal all-year surface. It is the facilities that make this a truly remarkable site; no expense or effort has been spared to create a luxurious environment that matches that of any top class hotel. The health spa has every type of sauna, Turkish and Roman baths, sunbeds, herbal and hay baths, hairdressing and beauty treatment salons, relaxation and massage rooms and a remarkable indoor pool with children's pool, Kneipp therapy pool and whirlpools. The timber of the buildings is from 400-year-old farmhouses and is blended with top quality modern materials to create amazing interiors and (mainly) authentic Tyrolean exteriors. The restaurant, bars and taverna are of equally high quality. Sexten is in the Dolomites, in the German-speaking Südtirol, where the scenery is spectacular and there is a wide variety of leisure activities on offer from gentle walking to extreme summer and winter sports. A member of Leading Campings Group.

Facilities

The three main toilet blocks are remarkable in design, fixtures and fittings. Heated floors. Controllable showers. Hairdryers. Luxurious private facilities to rent. Children and baby rooms. En-suite facilities for disabled visitors. Laundry and drying room. Motorcaravan services. Shop. Bars and restaurants with entertainment 2-3 nights a week. Indoor pool. Heated outdoor pool (1/6-30/9). High quality health spa. New outdoor play area for children. Good range of activities for all. Tennis. Bicycle hire. Climbing wall. Fishing. Adventure activity packages. Internet access and WiFi (whole site). Off site: Skiing in winter (free bus to 2 ski lifts within 5 km). Walking, cycling and climbing. Fishing. Riding and golf nearby.

Open: All year.

Directions

Sexten/Sesto is 110 km. northeast of Bolzano. From Bressanone/Brixen exit on A22 Brenner - Modena motorway follow the SS49 east for about 60 km. Turn south on SS52 at Innichen/San Candido and follow signs to Sexten. Site is 5 km. past village (signed). GPS: 46.66727, 12.40221

Charges guide

Per unit incl. 2 persons	€ 22.00 - € 49.00
extra person	€ 8.00 - € 13.00
child (2-14 yrs)	€ 4.50 - € 11.00
electricity per kWh (16A)	€ 0.70
dog	€ 3.00 - € 6.00

Siena

Camping Colleverde

Strada Scacciapensieri 47, I-53100 Siena (Tuscany) T: 057 733 2545. E: info@sienacamping.com

alanrogers.com/IT66245

Camping Colleverde enjoys a panoramic setting overlooking the beautiful Tuscan city of Siena and the surrounding Chianti hills. The proprietor Andrea Sassolini and his family are on hand to ensure you have an enjoyable stay. Open for a long season, this is a great base for visiting Siena and the Chianti region. A bus stop is just 100 m. away and the railway station is 1.5 km. There are 221 pitches arranged on terraces, many with hardstanding and 97 with 10A electricity. On-site facilities include a swimming pool, a pizzeria/restaurant, bar and a shop, all newly built in 2009. There are 25 mobile homes, which can be reserved for short stays. Bicycle hire and bus tours to major attractions can be arranged by the site.

Facilities

Three new top quality sanitary facilities include those for disabled visitors. Laundry. Motorcaravan services. Shop, bar, restaurant/pizzeria (all March-Oct). Swimming and paddling pools (June-Sept). Play area. WiFi over site (charged). Mobile homes for rent. Bicycle hire. Bus tours to major attractions arranged. Off site: Railway station 1.5 km. City centre 2 km. Bicycle hire 3 km. Riding 10 km. Chianti countryside. Cycle and walking tracks.

Open: 1 March - 31 December.

Directions

Site is north of the city. Approaching from the north, leave RA3 superstrada (Florence - Siena) at Siena Nord exit. Turn right and follow signs for Hospital (Ospedale) and Camping. Site is 1 km. from the hospital, well signed and is the only campsite here so all signs refer to Colleverde.
GPS: 43.33771, 11.33048

Charges guide

Per unit incl. 2 persons and electricity	€ 31.50 - € 35.00
extra person	€ 9.50 - € 10.50
child (3-12 yrs)	€ 4.50 - € 5.50

Solcio di Lesa

Camping Solcio

Via al Campeggio, I-28040 Solcio di Lesa (Piedmont) T: 032 274 97. E: info@campingsolcio.com

alanrogers.com/IT62440

Camping Solcio is a family-run site on the lakeside and has lovely views over the lakes and the surrounding green hills. The 105 neat touring pitches are 60-90 sq.m. with 6A electricity and mostly shaded by trees. A very pleasant restaurant and a bar back onto a large building alongside the site, and there are some views of the lake from the terraces. All manner of watersports are available here and the beach is of coarse sand. The lake is fine for safe swimming. An ambitious entertainment programme is arranged for children in high season, and there is adventure sport for the over tens. This is a pleasant site with modest facilities and it may suit those who do not seek the luxuries of the larger sites. English and Dutch are spoken and the site is very popular with Dutch campers.

Facilities

One main central toilet block is smart and clean. Toilets here are British style. An older block nearer reception has mixed Turkish and British style toilets. Facilities for disabled visitors. Baby room. Washing machine and dryer. Restaurant and bar with terrace. Basic shop. Full entertainment programme in season. Play areas. Baby club. Bicycle hire. Internet. WiFi in restaurant. Torches useful. Dogs are not accepted. Off site: Public transport 50 m. Town facilities 1 km. ATM 2 km. Riding 5 km. Golf 10 km.

Open: 7 March - 30 September.

Directions

Site is on the west side of Lake Maggiore. From A4 (Milan - Torino) take the A8 to Castelletto Sticino. Then north on SS33 towards Stresa and look for site sign at km. 57 marker at town of Lesa. Take the narrow access road to the site.
GPS: 45.81586, 8.54962

Charges guide

Per unit incl. 2 persons and electricity	€ 19.50 - € 42.00
extra person	€ 5.20 - € 8.00
child (3-13 yrs)	€ 3.70 - € 6.20

Low season discounts.

Silvi

to book this site call
01580 214000
...we arrange everything
the travel service

Camping Europe Garden

Contrada Vallescura n. 10, I-64028 Silvi (Abruzzo) T: 085 930 137.
E: info@europegarden.it alanrogers.com/IT68000

This site is 13 kilometres northwest of Pescara and, lying just back from the coast approximately 2 km. up a very steep hill from where it has pleasant views over the sea. The site predominantly consists of bungalows and chalets for hire, with around 40 spaces at the top of the site available for smaller touring units and tents. These are mainly on level terraces, but access to some may be difficult. All have 6A electricity. If installation of caravans is a problem a tractor is available to help. Cars remain with units on some of the pitches or in nearby parking spaces for the remainder. Most pitches are shaded. This site has very steep slopes and is not suitable for disabled or infirm campers.

Facilities

The toilet block provides a mixture of British and Turkish style WCs. Hot showers. Washing machines. Restaurant. Bar. Swimming pool (300 sq.m; caps compulsory), small paddling pool and jacuzzi. Tennis. Playground. Entertainment. Free weekly excursions (15/6-8/9). Free shuttle bus (18/5-7/9) to site's own private beach. WiFi. Dogs are not accepted. No barbecues on pitches.

Open: 24 April - 18 September.

Directions

Turn inland off SS16 coast road at km. 433 for Silvi Alta and follow site signs. From autostrada A14 take Pineto exit from north or Pescara Nord exit from the south. GPS: 42.56738, 14.09247

Charges guide

Per unit incl. 2 persons and electricity	€ 23.50 - € 42.50
extra person	€ 5.00 - € 11.00

Sottomarina di Chioggia

Camping Miramare

Via Barbarigo 103, I-30015 Sottomarina di Chioggia (Veneto) T: 041 490 610. E: campmir@tin.it
alanrogers.com/IT60560

Camping Miramare is a pleasant, fairly shady site with beach access, a good swimming pool and entertainment programme. The site is divided by a road and reception is on the beach side, along with most of the amenities. The other side is very peaceful with just sports amenities and a sanitary block. The 230 touring pitches are separated from the permanent units. All have 6A electricity and some have water and drainage. The beach is of soft sand and there is a lifeguard. You can hire sunshades and loungers. The restaurant offers traditional food and a plethora of pizzas which can be enjoyed on the terraces. Children have several play areas and there is entertainment all season. The separated swimming pool is excellent, with two diving boards and a lifeguard. The site lies close to the ancient city of Chioggia, famous for its fishing and Venice like construction. It is well worth a visit on a bicycle as it has an amazing history. An excursion to Venice naturally holds a strong appeal, but other stunning cities are also close at hand, notably Padova, Vicenza, Treviso and, a little further afield, Verona. This is a pleasant, family oriented site which has a distinct Italian feel. English is spoken.

Facilities

Three modern and clean blocks, one of which is in the area of the permanent campers. Push button hot showers and primarily Turkish style toilets. Facilities for disabled guests. Baby room. Laundry rooms. Motorcaravan service point. Bar, restaurant, pizzeria and takeaway. Smart shop. Excellent swimming pool and separate paddling pool (14/5-19/9). Several great play areas. Multisport court. Bicycle hire. Entertainment and children's activities in high season. WiFi throughout (charged). Mobile homes to rent. Dogs are not accepted in high season. Off site: Fishing and sailing 1 km. Riding 6 km. Golf 20 km. Visits to Chioggia. Excursions to Venice and other cities.

Open: 4 April - 23 September.

Directions

Site is off the S309 south of Chioggia. Follow signs to Sottomarina, crossing the Laguna del Lusenzo, then look for site signs. Site is off Viale Mediterranneo road to the right. Site is the second of many along this narrow road.
GPS: 45.19018, 12.30341

Charges guide

Per unit incl. 2 persons and electricity	€ 20.00 - € 33.90
extra person	€ 4.75 - € 8.20
child (1-6 yrs)	€ 2.50 - € 4.00

Tabiano di Salsomaggiore Terme

Camping Arizona

Via Tabiano 42/A, I-43039 Tabiano di Salsomaggiore Terme (Emilia-Romagna) T: 052 456 5648.
E: info@camping-arizona.it alanrogers.com/IT60900

Tabiano and Salsomaggiore Terme are thermal springs dating back to the Roman era and the beneficial waters have given rise to attractive inland resort towns. The focus on water is continued within this family-run site by a complex of four large pools, long water slides, a jacuzzi and play area, all set in open landscaped grounds with superb views (open to the public). Camping Arizona is an expanding 'green' site set on steep slopes and is 500 m. from the pretty town of Tabiano. The 300 level pitches with electricity (3A generated on site) vary from 50-90 sq.m. Those on terraces enjoy shade from mature trees, others have no shade. Cars must be parked in the large adjacent car park in shade, under the solar panel array and trollies are provided. Sporting facilities include the water park area, tennis, volleyball and basketball courts and a five-a-side football pitch on synthetic grass. Younger children will be entertained by the large, supervised play centre and other indoor and outdoor games.

Facilities

Sanitary facilities in two new blocks provide modern facilities including those for disabled visitors. Solar-heated water. Washing machines and dryers. Small well stocked shop (all facilities from 1/4). Restaurant/bar with patio. Swimming pools, slides and jacuzzi (18/5-15/9, also open to the public but free for campers). Tennis. Boules. Large play centre. Mountain bike hire. WiFi (charged). Off site: Restaurant outside gate. Riding 2 km. Fishing 4 km. Golf 6 km. Fidenza shopping village with designer outlets 8 km.

Open: 1 April - 15 October.

Directions

From autostrada A1 take exit for Fidenza and follow signs for Tabiano. The site is on left 500 m. after Tabiano town centre. GPS: 44.80621, 10.0098

Charges guide

Per unit incl. 2 persons and electricity	€ 20.00 - € 32.00
extra person	€ 6.00 - € 9.00
child (2-9 yrs)	€ 4.00 - € 6.50
dog	€ 3.00

No credit cards.

Toblach

Camping Olympia

Camping 1, I-39034 Toblach (Trentino - Alto Adige) T: 047 497 2147. E: info@camping-olympia.com

alanrogers.com/IT62000

In the Dolomite mountains, Camping Olympia continues to maintain its high standards. The 314 pitches are set out in a regular pattern and the tall pine trees, shrubs and hedges make this a very pleasant and attractive site. There are tree-clad hills on either side and craggy mountains beyond. The 238 touring pitches all have electricity (6A) and a TV point. There are 21 fully serviced pitches with water, waste water, gas, telephone and satellite TV points. Some accommodation is available for rent, and there are 62 seasonal caravans which are mainly grouped at one end of the site. The site is an ideal base from which to explore this part of German-speaking Südtirol on foot, by bicycle (a track is just outside the campsite) or by car – and Austria is just up the road!

Facilities

The toilet block is of a very high standard. Rooms with WC, washbasin and shower to rent. Baby room. Facilities for disabled visitors. Two small blocks provide further WCs and showers. Motorcaravan service point. Shop. Attractive bar, restaurant and pizzeria (all year). Second bar with grill and terrace by pool (10/6-30/9; 20/12-Easter). Heated swimming pool (20/5-15/9). Sauna, solarium, steam bath and whirlpools. Massage and Kneipp treatments. Fishing. Bicycle hire. Play area. WiFi throughout (charged). Programme of activities and excursions. Entertainment in high season. Off site: Tennis and minigolf nearby. Riding and golf 3 km.

Open: All year.

Directions

Toblach/Dobbiaco is about 100 km. northeast of Bolzano. Site is west of the town. From the A22 Innsbruck-Bolzano autostrada, take exit for Bressanone/Brixen and travel east on SS49 for 60 km. Site signed to left just after a short tunnel. From Cortina take SS48 and SS51 northwards then turn west on SS49 for 1.5 km.
GPS: 46.734449, 12.194266

Charges guide

Per unit incl. 2 persons and electricity	€ 25.00 - € 34.50
extra person	€ 8.50 - € 11.00
child (3-12 yrs)	€ 4.50 - € 8.00
dog	€ 2.00 - € 4.50

Torre del Lago

Camping Europa

Viale dei Tigli, casella postale 115, I-55049 Torre del Lago Puccini (Tuscany) T: 058 435 0707.
E: info@europacamp.it **alanrogers.com/IT66060**

Europa is a large, flat, rectangular site with roads on all four sides of the site. There are 400 pitches in 17 rows, with the 200 touring pitches occupying six rows at the far end of the site. To reach these, you need to pass rows of very close together, well established permanent pitches and bungalows available for rent. The site's facilities including a bar, shop and air conditioned restaurant, are in rows five and six. The touring pitches are flat, very sandy and close together (55-70 sq.m). Some have shade from small trees or artificial cover and electricity (6A) is available to most. The site has been owned by the Morescalchi family since 1967 and they are very keen that you have an enjoyable stay. The pool (free) and its separate paddling pool are near the site entrance and a jacuzzi is built into one end. The beach is a brisk 20 minute walk through a forest 1 km. away; a bicycle would be useful. However, there is a site minibus service to the beach and once there the sand is soft and the beach shelves gently into the water. Europa is conveniently situated for visiting many of the interesting places around such as Lucca, Pisa, Florence and the wealth of Puccini related historical items.

Facilities

Two sanitary blocks provide hot and cold showers (€ 0.50 token from reception). Toilets are mixed Turkish and British style. Facilities for disabled visitors. Laundry facilities. Cleaning goes on non-stop here. Motorcaravan service point outside gate. Bar/restaurant (air-conditioned), takeaway, small shop (all open all season). Good swimming pool (1/5-23/9, caps required). Large play area. Entertainment. Miniclub. Bicycle hire. Satellite TV. Internet access. Dogs are not accepted 30/6-24/8. Torches useful. Off site: Beach 1 km. Fishing. Riding 2 km. Golf 17 km.

Open: 1 April - 12 October.

Directions

From A11-12 to Pisa Nord take Marina di Torre del Lago exit following the sign 'mare' towards the sea for Marina di Torre Lago Puccini. Follow clear signs for site. GPS: 43.83083, 10.27055

Charges 2012

Per unit incl. 2 persons and electricity	€ 18.00 - € 41.00
extra person	€ 4.50 - € 9.50
child (2-11 yrs)	€ 2.50 - € 4.50

Torre Grande

Camping Village Spinnaker

Strada Provinciale, Oristano, I-09170 Torre Grande (Sardinia) T: **078 322 074**.

E: **info@spinnakervacanze.com** **alanrogers.com/IT69900**

Set on the undulating foreshore under tall pines, with beach frontage to the camping area, Spinnaker Village is a smart, purpose built, modern beach site. The 143 pitches are sandy, with 43 suitable for caravans and motorcaravans, the remainder for tents. All pitches have 6A electricity and there are plenty of water taps. Tent pitches are large and clearly marked, each with a tree to provide shade. Cars must be parked in a car park outside the site. There are many neat, white buildings on site – the restaurant, a café and the swimming pool are set around a large square, where activities for families take place. Transponders are provided for showers and for use around the site in lieu of cash. The pool is very inviting, surrounded by sunshades and with a separated shallow end for children. Whilst there are no views of the sea from the pitches, it is an easy 60 metre stroll to the beach of fine white sand where there are free sun loungers and parasols. It is a pleasant and easy walk along the beach to the resort of Marina Torre Grande. Excursions from the site could include a visit to the marine reserve of Sinis Isola di Maladentre or the ruins of Tharros and S. Christina – a Nuraghe village. English is spoken on the site.

Facilities

Toilet blocks are modern and very clean with British style toilets and facilities for disabled campers. Showers are transponder operated (€ 0.50 per shower). Washing machine. Motorcaravan service point. Small shop. Restaurant and small snack bar. Swimming pool and pool bar. Play area. Bicycle hire. Small boat launching. Miniclub and entertainment in high season. Excursions. Torches essential. Off site: Riding 2 km. Golf 23 km.

Open: All year.

Directions

Take SS131 Cagliari - Oristano road then minor road to Cabras and Torre Grande. Just before Torre Grande village by large water tower take angled left turn back on yourself to site (signed).
GPS: 39.903, 8.5301

Charges guide

Per unit incl. 2 persons and electricity	€ 23.00 - € 45.00
extra person	€ 8.00 - € 18.00
child (3-12 yrs)	€ 4.50 - € 11.00
dog	€ 2.00 - € 3.50

Camping Cheques accepted.

Trevignano Romano

Camping Internazionale Lago di Bracciano

Via del Pianoro 4, I-00069 Trevignano Romano (Lazio) T: **069 985 032**. E: **camping.village@gmail.com**

alanrogers.com/IT67850

Lago di Bracciano, just 45 km. north of Rome, is of a size that provides excellent opportunities for watersports and is inevitably very popular with windsurfers. With some pitches alongside a little beach, the site provides 110 pitches of which about 50 are for tourers. Our pitch had a full view of the lake and the gentle breeze made the temperature at the end of June quite bearable. Some shade is provided by large trees. A bar and restaurant near the entrance are behind the site's small swimming pool and play area. The local bus has a regular service to Rome.

Facilities

The single toilet block is well equipped. Facilities for disabled visitors. Washing machine. Motorcaravan service point. Small shop. Bar and restaurant/pizzeria. Small swimming pool (15/5-15/9). Play area. Barbecue area (not allowed on pitches). WiFi and Internet access. Mobile homes and bungalows to rent. Off site: Lago di Bracciano.

Open: 1 April - 30 September.

Directions

From the Rome GRA take exit 5 on SS2 towards Cassia. Turn left at Trevignano exit (km. 35) and follow SP4a towards the lake where you will find the site on the left. The access road and gate are max. 2.6 m. wide. GPS: 42.144717, 12.26865

Charges guide

Per unit incl. 2 persons and electricity	€ 23.00 - € 28.00
per person	€ 6.00 - € 7.00

Troghi

Camping Il Poggetto

Via Il Poggetto 143 - SP1 Strada provinciale, I-50067 Troghi (Tuscany) T: 055 830 7323.
E: info@campingilpoggetto.com alanrogers.com/IT66110

This superb site has a lot to offer. It benefits from a wonderful panorama of the Colli Fiorentini hills with acres of the Zecchi family vineyards to the east adding to its appeal and is just 15 km. from Florence. The charming and hard working owners Marcello and Daniella have a wine producing background and you can purchase their fine wines at the site's shop. Their aim is to provide an enjoyable and peaceful atmosphere for families. All 106 pitches are of a good size and have electricity and larger units are welcome. On arrival you are escorted to view available pitches then assisted in taking up your chosen pitch. The restaurant offers excellent Tuscan fare including pizzas, pastas and delicate 'cucina casalinga' (home cooking). The locals also come here to eat. An attractive flower-bedecked terrace overlooks the two pools. Enjoy the typically Tuscan views and revel in the choice of Chianti from the region. A regular bus service runs directly from the site to the city. English is spoken at this delightful family site.

Facilities

Two spotless sanitary blocks with a mix of British and Turkish style WCs are a pleasure to use. Three private sanitary units for hire. Five very well equipped units for disabled campers. Separate facilities for children and baby room. Laundry facilities. Motorcaravan services. Gas supplies. Shop. Bar. Restaurant. Takeaway. Swimming pools and jacuzzi (1/5-30/9). Fitness room. Bicycle and scooter hire. Playground and entertainment for children all season. Excursions and organised trekking. Internet point. Off site: Tennis 100 m. Fishing 2 km. Golf 12 km. Bus service to the centre of Florence.

Open: 1 April - 15 October.

Directions

Exit A1 at Incisa southeast of Florence and turn right onto the SS69. After about 4 km. turn left following 'Pian dell Isola'. At next crossing turn right towards Firenze and follow the site signs. Do not use your satellite navigation here as you may be taken into the steep and narrow streets of the nearby village. GPS: 43.701415, 11.405262

Charges guide

Per unit incl. 2 persons and electricity	€ 28.50 - € 38.00
extra person	€ 7.50 - € 9.50
child (2-10 yrs)	€ 5.00 - € 6.50

Tuoro sul Trasimeno

Camping Punta Navaccia

I-06069 Tuoro sul Trasimeno (Umbria) T: 075 826 357. E: info@puntanavaccia.it
alanrogers.com/IT66490

Situated on the north side of Lake Trasimeno and run by friendly and welcoming owners, this is a large site with over 70,000 sq.m. and 400 touring pitches (200 with 6/9A electricity) and all with shade. The campsite has a long (stony) beach with facilities for mooring and launching your boat. There are 75 mobile homes with air-conditioning for rent. The site is ideally located for exploring Umbria and its famous cities, such as Assisi and Perugia. Tuscany and its cities of Siena and Florence are also within easy reach and it is even possible to visit Rome for a day trip.

Facilities

Sanitary block with British style WCs, showers and some private cabins. Washing machine and dryer. Motorcaravan service point. Heated swimming and paddling pools (1/5-30/9). Shop and bar (15/3-30/9). Restaurant and takeaway (1/4-30/9). Play area. Tennis. Large covered amphitheatre. Disco. Cinema screen. Miniclub. Entertainment in high season (in Italian, English, German and Dutch). Boat launching. Daily boat trip around island (free). Fitness room. Fishing. Bicycle hire. Off site: Sandy beach, windsurfing, sailing and canoeing 200 m.

Open: 15 March - 31 October.

Directions

Going south on the A1 (Florence/Firenze - Rome), take exit for Val di Chiana to Perugia near Bettolle. After 15 km. take Tuoro sul Trasimeno exit. Site is well signed. GPS: 43.19191, 12.07665

Charges guide

Per unit incl. 2 persons and electricity	€ 19.00 - € 28.50
extra person	€ 6.00 - € 8.50
child (2-9 yrs)	€ 4.00 - € 6.00
dog	free

Ugento

Camping Riva di Ugento

Litoranea Gallipoli, Santa Maria di Leuca, I-73059 Ugento (Puglia) T: 083 393 3600. E: info@rivadiugento.it

alanrogers.com/IT68650

There are some campsites where you can be comfortable, have all the amenities at hand and still feel you are connecting with nature. Under the pine and eucalyptus trees of the Bay of Taranto foreshore is Camping Riva di Ugento. Its 900 pitches are nestled in and around the sand dunes and the foreshore area. They have space and trees around them and the sizes differ as the environment dictates the shape of most. The sea is only a short walk from most pitches and some are at the water's edge. The site buildings resemble huge wooden umbrellas and are in sympathy with the environment. There are swimming and paddling pools, although these are expensive to use in high season. A free cinema shows special events via satellite TV near the main bar and restaurant area. The area is sandy but well shaded, and the sea breezes scented with pine give the site a cool, fresh feel. This site has an isolated, natural ambiance that defies its size. Cycling along the kilometre of beach, we enjoyed the tranquillity of the amazing pitches – shaded, private and inviting. We were sorry to leave the site which was by far the best we found in the area.

Facilities

Twenty toilet blocks all with WCs, showers and washbasins. New bathrooms. Bar. Restaurant and takeaway. Swimming and paddling pools. Tennis. Bicycle hire. Watersports incl. windsurfing school. Cinema. TV in bar. WiFi. Entertainment for children. Dogs are not accepted. A new play area for children has been added. Beach volleyball. Off site: Fishing. Riding 500 m. Boat launching 4 km. Golf 40 km.

Open: 15 May - 30 September.

Directions

From Bari take the Brindisi road to Lecce, then SS101 to Gallipoli, followed by the SR274 towards Sta Maria di Leuca, drive until exit called Felline and continue in direction of Torre San Giovanni, following the indications for Riva di Ugento. Site is well signed and turn right at traffic lights on SS19. Bumpy approach road. GPS: 39.87475, 18.141117

Charges guide

Per unit incl. 2 persons, 1 child and electricity	€ 21.00 - € 45.00
extra person (over 2 yrs)	€ 5.00 - € 12.00

Camping Cheques accepted.

Vada

Camping Tripesce

Via Cavalleggeri 88, I-57016 Vada (Tuscany) T: 058 678 8167. E: info@campingtripesce.it

alanrogers.com/IT66290

Neat and tidy, this family owned and run site has the great advantage of direct beach access through three gates (CCTV). The beach is of fine sand with very gentle shelving – super for children, with watersports and a lifeguard in season. This great beach makes up for the lack of a pool on the site and the fairly small size of the 230 pitches. All have 4A electricity and 60 are serviced with water and drainage with some shade provided by young trees and artificial shade. The site is contained within a rectangle and bungalows for rent are discreetly placed near reception.

Facilities

Three clean, fresh toilet blocks provide hot and cold showers (water is solar heated and free). British and Turkish style toilets. Facility for disabled visitors. Washing machines. Motorcaravan service points. Bar/restaurant and takeaway. Shop. Excellent beach. Aquarobics and aerobics (high season). Play area (supervision required). Miniclub (high season). Internet and WiFi. Fishing. Dogs are not accepted 23/5-4/9. Off site: Bus service 300 m. Seaside town and ATM 1 km. Riding 5 km.

Open: 1 April - 16 October.

Directions

From S1 autostrada (free) between Livorno and Grosetto head south and take Vada exit. Site is well signed along with lots of others as you approach the town. GPS: 43.34301, 10.45825

Charges guide

Per person	€ 5.00 - € 8.00
child (0-7 yrs)	€ 3.00 - € 5.00
pitch incl. car and electricity	€ 10.00 - € 23.00

No credit cards.

Vieste

Punta Lunga Camping Village

CP339, localitá Defensola, I-71019 Vieste (Puglia) T: **088 470 6031**. E: **puntalunga@puntalunga.com**

alanrogers.com/IT68480

Punta Lunga is located in the spectacularly beautiful Gargano region, a huge National Park. The coast here has an ambience of its own; the scent of pine mingles with the cool Adriatic breezes inviting you to relax. This site nestles into a bay with easy access to a second beach in the next cove. The 320 pitches are flat on a mixture of sand and grass and are of a reasonable size. Some are shaded by trees, others by artificial shade, and most are on steep terraces. Camping along the shore is less formal and in some cases less shaded, but some pitches have spectacular views. This is a delightful place to relax by the sea and to explore the dramatic wilderness of the Gargano peninsula.

Facilities

Two toilet blocks consist of a mixture of unisex showers and dedicated toilets. The facilities are clean and fresh. Single, good central unit for disabled campers. Laundry facilities. Hairdresser. Small shop. Gas. Excellent restaurant with pleasant views. Beach bar with snacks. Children's clubs (high season). Small play area. Bicycle hire. Windsurfing school. Dogs are not accepted.
Off site: Restaurants, bars and shops. Boat launching 3 km. Riding 10 km.

Open: 15 May - 25 September.

Directions

From north take A14 exit for Poggio Imperiale, then to Vico Gargano and Vieste. From south take A14 exit Foggia, then towards Manfredonia, Mattinata and Vieste. GPS: 41.89798, 16.15047

Charges guide

Per unit incl. 2 persons and electricity	€ 17.00 - € 43.50
extra person	€ 4.50 - € 12.50
child (2-8 yrs)	free - € 7.00

Villalago

Camping I Lupi

Riviera di Villalago, Lago di Scanno, I-67030 Villalago (Abruzzo) T: **086 474 0100**. E: **campingilupi@libero.it**

alanrogers.com/IT67930

I Lupi is a large, friendly, all year site in a beautiful location within the Abruzzo National Park. The site is located in a valley on the banks of the Lago di Scanno. Pitches are generally large and many have fine views of the surrounding mountain scenery. Around 500 pitches have electrical connections (10A) and some hardstandings are available. This is a large site and at night torches may be useful. Amenities on site are limited – there is a small shop and snack bar/takeaway but no restaurant. However, a number of restaurants are available within easy walking distance. The Abruzzo National Park offers very many opportunities for walking, cycling and riding, and Il Lupi is particularly well located for these activities.

Facilities

Two well appointed toilet blocks with upgraded facilities including private cabins. Motorcaravan services. Bar, snack bar. Supermarket. Play area. Children's club in peak season. Tourist information. Games room. Sports field. Direct access to lake. Chalets for rent. Off site: Riding. Tennis. Mountain biking and walking throughout the National Park. Fishing.

Open: All year.

Directions

From the A25 motorway (Rome - Pescara) take the Cocullo exit and join the SP60 towards Anversa Degli Abruzzi. At this town, join the SR479 towards Scanno and you will reach the Lago di Scanno and the site shortly after passing Villalago.
GPS: 41.92009, 13.859081

Charges guide

Per person	€ 6.00
child (2-6 yrs)	€ 5.80
pitch	€ 8.20 - € 10.20
electricity	€ 2.70

Villanova d'Albenga

Camping C'era una Volta

Localitá Fasceti, I-17038 Villanova d'Albenga (Ligúria) T: **018 258 0461**. E: **info@villaggioceraunavolta.it**

alanrogers.com/IT64050

An attractive campsite, C'era una Volta is about 6 km. back from the sea, situated on a hillside with panoramic views. Pitches are on terraces in different sections of the site. Varying in size, most have shade from the young trees which harbour crickets with their distinctive noise. Some of the upper pitches have good views. Cars are required to park in separate areas at busy times. There are electricity connections, with water and drainage close by. Charges are high in season but the site has an enjoyable atmosphere and is a good choice for families.

Facilities

The main toilet block is above average. Four additional smaller blocks. Maintenance can be variable. Shop. Bar and pizzeria (15/5-10/9). Restaurant. Takeaway (evenings only 1/4-30/9). Disco (July/Aug). Swimming pools (15/5-20/9). Gym. Fitness track. Miniclub. Health centre with Finnish sauna. Hydromassage bath/shower. Turkish bath. Hydrojet massage bed. Tennis. Boules. Adventure playground. Internet. Satellite TV. Communal barbecue. Off site: Riding 500 m. Golf 2 km. Lake fishing 4 km.

Open: 1 April - 30 September.

Directions

Leave A10 at Albenga, turn left and left again at roundabout for the SS453 for Villanova. At T-junction turn left (Garlenda), turn right in 200 m. and follow signs up a long winding narrow road beyond the Stadium. GPS: 44.04433, 8.1137

Charges guide

Per unit incl. up to 3 persons	€ 25.00 - € 49.00
tent pitch	€ 20.00 - € 38.00
extra person	€ 7.00 - € 12.00

Electricity included. No credit cards.

Völs am Schlern

Camping Seiser Alm

Saint Konstantin 16, I-39050 Völs am Schlern (Trentino - Alto Adige) T: **047 170 6459**.
E: **info@camping-seiseralm.com** **alanrogers.com/IT62040**

What an amazing experience awaits you at Seiser Alm! Elisabeth and Erhard Mahlknecht have created a superb site in the magnificent Südtirol region of the Dolomite mountains. Towering peaks provide a magnificent backdrop when you dine in the charming, traditional style restaurant on the upper terrace. Here you will also find the bar, shop and reception. The 150 touring pitches are of a very high standard with 16A electricity supply, 120 with gas, water, drainage and satellite connections. Guests were delighted with the site when we visited, many coming to walk or cycle, some just to enjoy the surroundings. There are countless things to see and do here. Enjoy the grand 18-hole golf course alongside the site or join the organised excursions and activities. Local buses and cable cars provide an excellent service for summer visitors and skiers alike. Elisabeth's designs incorporating Grimm fairy tales are tastefully developed in the superb children's bathrooms that are in a magic forest setting. A family play park with an enclosure of tame rabbits is at the lower part of the site where goats also roam. If you wish for quiet, quality camping in a crystal clean environment, then visit this immaculate site.

Facilities

One luxury underground block. 16 private units are available. Excellent facilities for disabled visitors. Facilities for children. Infrared sensors, underfloor heating and gently curved floors to prevent slippery surfaces. Constant fresh air ventilation. Laundry facilities. Supermarket. Quality restaurant and bar with terrace. Entertainment. Miniclub. Adventure park. Play room. Sauna. Rooms for ski equipment. Torches useful. WiFi (charged). Apartments and mobile homes for rent. Off site: Riding alongside site. 18-hole golf course (discounts) and fishing 1 km. Bicycle hire and lake swimming 2 km. ATM 3 km. Skiing in winter.

Open: All year excl. 2 November - 20 December.

Directions

Site is east of Bolzano. From A22-E45 take Bolzano Nord exit. Take road for Prato Isarco/Blumau, then road for Fie/Völs. Take care as the split in the road is sudden and if you miss the left fork as you enter a tunnel (Altopiano dello Sciliar/Schlerngebiet) you will pay a heavy price in extra kilometres. Enjoy the climb to Völs am Schlern and site is well signed. GPS: 46.53344, 11.53335

Charges guide

Per unit incl. 2 persons	€ 17.30 - € 43.50
extra person	€ 6.90 - € 9.50
electricity (per kWh)	€ 0.60

The independent Principality of Liechtenstein is the fourth smallest country in the world. Nestled between Switzerland and Austria, it has a total area of 157 square kilometres (61 square miles).

If you like clean mountain air and peaceful surroundings, then a visit to Liechtenstein would be worthwhile. The little town of Vaduz (the Capital) is where you will find most points of interest, including the world famous art collection (Kunstmuseum), which holds paintings by Rembrandt and other world famous artists. Above the town of Vaduz is the restored twelfth-century castle, now owned by the prince of Liechtenstein (not open to the public). Take a walk up to the top of the hill, you can view Vaduz and the mountains stretched out below. Situated on a terrace above Vaduz is Triesenberg village, blessed with panoramic views over the Rhine Valley, a pretty village with vineyards and ancient chapels. Malbun is Liechtenstein's premier mountain resort, popular in both winter and summer, for either skiing or walking.

Triesen

Camping Mittagspitze

Sägastrasse 29, FL 9495 Triesen T: 392 3677. E: info@campingtriesen.li

alanrogers.com/FL7580

Camping Mittagspitze is attractively and quietly situated for visiting the Principality. Probably the best site in the region, it is on a hillside and has all the scenic views that one could wish for. Extensive broad, level terraces on the steep slope provide unmarked pitches (a reader tells us that spacing causes problems in high season) and electricity connections are available. There are some shady pitches in high season. Of the 240 spaces, 120 are used by seasonal caravans. Liechtenstein's capital, Vaduz, is 7 km. away, Austria is 20 km. and Switzerland 3 km.

Facilities

Two good quality sanitary blocks provide all the usual facilities. Washing machine, dryer and ironing. Room where one can sit or eat with cooking facilities. Shop (1/6-31/8). Restaurant (all year). Small swimming pool (15/6-15/8), not heated but very popular in summer. Playground. TV room. Accommodation for hire. Off site: Tennis and indoor pool nearby. Riding and bicycle hire 5 km.

Open: All year.

Directions

From A3 take Trübbach exit 10 and follow road towards Balzers. Then head towards Vaduz and site is 2 km. south of Triesen on the right. Site is signed. GPS: 47.0857, 9.5259

Charges guide

Per unit incl. 2 persons and electricity € 35,00 - € 38,00

Luxembourg

The Grand Duchy of Luxembourg is a sovereign state, lying between Belgium, France and Germany. Divided into two areas: the spectacular Ardennes region in the north and the rolling farmlands and woodland in the south, bordered on the east by the wine growing area of the Moselle Valley.

From wherever you are in Luxembourg you are always within easy reach of the capital, Luxembourg-Ville, home to about one fifth of the population. The city was built upon a rocky outcrop, and has superb views of the Alzette and Petrusse Valleys. Those who love the great outdoors must make a visit to the Ardennes, with its hiking trails, footpaths and cycle routes that take you through beautiful winding valleys and across deep rivers, a very popular region for visitors. If wine tasting takes your fancy, then head for the Moselle Valley, particularly if you like sweet, fruity wines. From late spring to early autumn, wine tasting tours take place in cellars and caves. The Mullerthal region, known as 'Little Switzerland', lies on the banks of the river Sûre. The earth is mostly made up of soft sandstone, so through the ages many fascinating gorges, caves and formations have emerged.

CAPITAL: Luxembourg City

Tourist Office

Luxembourg Tourist Office
Suite 4.1, Sicilian House, Sicilian Ave,
London WC1A 2QR
Tel: 020 7434 2800
Fax: 020 7734 1205
Email: tourism@luxembourg.co.uk
Internet: www.luxembourg.co.uk

Population

497,500

Climate

A temperate climate prevails, the summer often extending from May to late October.

Language

Letzeburgesch is the national language, with French and German also being official languages.

Telephone

The country code is 00 352.

Money

Currency: The Euro
Banks: Mon-Fri 08.30/09.00-12.00 and 13.30-16.30.

Shops

Mon 14.00-18.30. Tues to Sat 08.30-12.00 and 14.00-18.30 (grocers and butchers at 15.00 on Sat).

Public Holidays

New Year; Carnival Day mid-Feb; Easter Mon; May Day; Ascension; Whit Mon; National Day 23 June; Assumption 15 Aug; Kermesse 1 Sept; All Saints; All Souls; Christmas 25, 26 Dec.

Motoring

Many holidaymakers travel through Luxembourg to take advantage of the lower fuel prices, thus creating traffic congestion at petrol stations, especially in summer. A Blue Zone area exists in Luxembourg City and various parts of the country (discs from tourist offices) but meters are also used.

see campsite map 1

Eisenbach

Camping Kohnenhof

Kounenhaff 1, L-9838 Eisenbach (Luxembourg) T: 929 464. E: kohnenhof@pt.lu

alanrogers.com/LU7680

Nestling in a valley with the River Our running through it, Camping Kohnenhof offers a very agreeable location for a relaxing family holiday. From the minute you stop at the reception you are assured of a warm and friendly welcome. There are 105 pitches, 80 for touring, all with 6/16A electricity. Numerous paths cross through the wooded hillside so this could be a haven for walkers. A little bridge crosses the small river over the border to Germany. The river is shallow and safe for children (parental supervision essential). A large sports field and play area with a selection of equipment caters for younger campers. During the high season, an entertainment programme is organised for parents and children. The owner organises special golf weeks with games on different courses and discounts have been agreed at several local courses (contact the site for details). The restaurant is part of an old farmhouse and offers a wonderful ambience to enjoy a meal.

Facilities

Heated sanitary block with showers and washbasins in cabins. Motorcaravan service point. Laundry. Bar, restaurant, takeaway (open all season). Baker calls daily. Games/TV room. Sports field with play equipment. Boules. Bicycle hire. Golf weeks. Discounts on six local 18-hole golf courses. WiFi over site. Apartments to rent. Off site: Bus to Clervaux and Vianden stops (4 times daily) outside site entrance. Riding 5 km. Castle at Vianden 14 km. Monastery at Clervaux 14 km. Golf 15 km.

Open: 30 March - 4 November.

Directions

Take N7 north from Diekirch. At Hosingen, turn right onto the narrow and winding CR324 signed Eisenbach. Follow site signs from Eisenbach or Obereisenbach. GPS: 50.01602, 6.13600

Charges guide

Per unit incl. 2 persons and electricity	€ 19.90 - € 28.00
extra person	€ 5.00
dog	€ 3.00

Enscherange

Camping Val d'Or

Um Gaertchen 2, L-9747 Enscherange (Luxembourg) T: 920 691. E: valdor@pt.lu

alanrogers.com/LU7770

Camping Val d'Or is one of those small family-run countryside sites where you easily find yourself staying longer than planned. Set on lush meadowland under a scattering of trees, the site is divided into two by the tree-lined Clerve river as it winds its way slowly through the site. A footbridge goes some way to joining the site together and there are two entrances for vehicles. There are 76 marked, level grass touring pitches, all with electricity (4A) and with some tree shade. There are open views of the surrounding countryside with its wooded hills. The site's Dutch owners speak good English.

Facilities

Next to the reception is a heated sanitary block where some facilities are found, others including some showers are located under cover, outside. Showers are token operated, washbasins open style. Facilities may be stretched in high season. Laundry room. Gas supplies. Bar (all day in high season). Takeaway (high season except Sundays). Swimming and paddling in river. Three play areas (one with waterways, waterwheel and small pool). Bicycle hire. WiFi (1st hour free). Max. 1 dog. Off site: Fishing and golf 10 km.

Open: 1 April - 1 November.

Directions

From A26/E25 (Liège - Luxembourg) exit 54 travel to Bastogne. From Bastogne take N84/N15 towards Diekirch for 15 km. At crossroads turn left (northeast) towards Wiltz following signs for Clervaux. Pass through Wiltz and entering Weidingen there is a VW garage on the right; 500 m. after the garage turn right on the Wilderwiltz road. In Wilderwiltz follow signs for small village of Enscherange where site is signed. GPS: 50.00017, 5.99106

Charges 2012

Per unit incl. 2 persons and electricity	€ 16.00 - € 22.00
extra person	€ 5.00
child (0-15 yrs)	€ 2.00
dog (max. 1)	€ 5.00

No credit cards.

Ermsdorf

Camping Neumuhle

Reisdorferstrasse 27, L-9366 Ermsdorf (Luxembourg) T: 879 391. E: info@camping-neumuhle.lu

alanrogers.com/LU7810

Camping Neumuhle is located at Ermsdorf, at the heart of Luxembourg close to Diekirch. It is surrounded by the Mullerthal and some delightful countryside, known as Little Switzerland. Pitches here are spacious and all have electricity. This is great walking country and the long-distance hiking track GR5 (North Sea-Riviera) passes close to the site. Walking maps are available for loan at reception. There are 85 touring pitches all with 4/6A electricity and 20 chalets to rent. The site is terraced with level grass pitches separated by small hedges. The restaurant and covered terrace overlook the swimming pool and a small shop sells all basic provisions. Other on-site amenities include a large adventure playground.

Facilities

The central sanitary block is modern and clean. No facilities for disabled visitors. Restaurant with covered terrace and snack bar. Takeaway. Shop. Swimming pool. Boules. Adventure play area. Entertainment and activity programme. Children's club (high season). Bicycle hire. Mobile homes to rent. WiFi (charged). Off site: Diekirch. Luxembourg City. Walking and cycling tracks. Riding 4 km. Golf 6 km. Fishing 10 km.

Open: 1 March - 15 November.

Directions

Ermsdorf can be found northeast of the city of Luxembourg. From Diekirch, head south on the CR356 and the site is well signed from Ermsdorf. From Reisdorf follow Ermsdorf road (4 km). Site is on right before village. GPS: 49.8391, 6.225

Charges guide

Per unit incl. 2 persons and electricity	€ 18.50
extra person	€ 5.50
child (1-14 yrs)	€ 3.50
dog	€ 2.00

No credit cards.

Heiderscheid

Camping Fuussekaul

4 Fuussekaul, L-9156 Heiderscheid (Luxembourg) T: 268 8881. E: info@fuussekaul.lu

alanrogers.com/LU7850

The camp site lies in the rolling wooded hills of central Luxemburg, not far from the lakes of the Sûre River dam. Of the 370 pitches, 220 of varying sizes are for touring units, all with a 6A electricity connection. There are some super pitches with private electricity and water. The site consists of winding roads, some sloping, along which the pitches are set in shaded areas. The touring area (separate from the chalets and seasonal pitches) is well endowed with modern facilities, although there is no provision for visitors with disabilities.

Facilities

Four excellent sanitary blocks provide showers (token € 0.75), washbasins (in cabins and communal) and children and baby rooms with small toilets, washbasins and showers. Laundry. Parking and service area for motorcaravans. Well stocked shop. Bar. Restaurant and takeaway. Swimming pools. Suite with sauna and sun beds. Beauty salon. Playgrounds. Cross-country skiing when snow permits. Bicycle hire. Children's club. Bowling centre. WiFi (charged). Off site: Castles, museums and walks all within a reasonable distance. Bus stops outside site entrance. Riding 500 m. Fishing 3 km. Supermarket and shops in Ettelbruckt 7 km.

Open: All year.

Directions

Take N15 from Diekirch to Heiderscheid. Site is on left at top of hill just before reaching the village. Motorcaravan service area is signed on the right. GPS: 49.87750, 5.99283

Charges guide

Per unit incl. 2 persons and electricity	€ 18.50 € 38.00
extra person	€ 3.00
child	€ 1.00 - € 2.00
dog	€ 2.00

Hosingen

Camping des Ardennes

10 op der Héi, L-9809 Hosingen (Luxembourg) T: 921 911.

alanrogers.com/LU7670

A small municipal site, Camping Ardennes is located on the edge of this attractive, small town with an easy level walk to all amenities and parks and some floral arrangements to admire during the summer season. The 48 touring pitches are level, open and grassy. All have electricity (10A) and are arranged on either side of surfaced roads, with a few trees providing a little shade in places. Adjacent sports complex with tennis and football, etc. This site is useful as a stopover if travelling along the N7.

Facilities

The single well appointed, modern, clean sanitary block can be heated in winter and includes separate men's and women's facilities. Laundry facilities. Café/bar (opening variable). Barbecue. Playground. Skis and winter sports equipment for hire. Rooms for rent (B&B). English spoken.

Open: All year.

Directions

Hosingen is on the N7 21 km. north of Diekirch. Site and sports complex are signed in the village. 20 m. after leaving the main road turn right. Site is 100 m. on the left. GPS: 50.00772, 6.09017

Charges guide

Per unit incl. 2 persons and electricity	€ 15.00

No credit cards.

Larochette

Camping Birkelt

1 Um Birkelt, L-7633 Larochette (Luxembourg) T: 879 040. E: info@camping-birkelt.lu

alanrogers.com/LU7610

This is very much a family site, with a great range of facilities provided. It is well organised and well laid out, set in an elevated position in attractive, undulating countryside. A tarmac road runs around the site with 427 large grass pitches, some slightly sloping, many with a fair amount of shade, on either side of gravel access roads in straight rows and circles. Serviced pitches have 16A electricity, the rest 10A. An all weather swimming pool complex is beside the site entrance (free for campers) and entertainment for children is arranged in high season. The site is very popular with tour operators (140 pitches). The main activities take place adjacent to the large circular all-weather family pool. This is an outdoor pool in high season and covered and heated in cooler weather. Several play areas are dotted all over the site. The entrance to the site has been made vehicle-free (vehicle entrance is on a separate road) and provides a pleasant terrace and shopping area. Seven serviced overnight motorcaravan pitches are provided in the car park area. Throughout the site, all signage is in four languages including English.

Facilities

Three modern heated sanitary buildings well situated around the site include mostly open washbasins (6 cabins in one block). Baby baths. Facilities (including accommodation to rent) for wheelchair users. Washing machines and dryers. Motorcaravan service point. Shops. Coffee bar. Restaurant with terrace. Outdoor swimming pool (covered and heated in cooler weather). Outdoor pool for toddlers. Sauna. Play areas. Trampolines. Volleyball. Minigolf. Tennis. Bicycle hire. Riding. Balloon flights. Internet points. WiFi. Off site: Golf 5 km. Fishing and kayaking 10 km.

Open: 24 March - 4 November.

Directions

From N7 (Diekirch - Luxembourg City), turn onto the N8 (CR118) at Berschblach (just past Mersch) towards Larochette. Site is signed on the right 1.5 km. from Larochette. Approach road is fairly steep and narrow. GPS: 49.78508, 6.21033

Charges guide

Per unit incl. 2 persons	
and electricity	€ 19.50 - € 25.00
with water and drainage	€ 22.50 - € 38.00
extra person	€ 4.00
dog	€ 2.50

Larochette

Camping Auf Kengert

L-7633 Larochette-Medernach (Luxembourg) T: 837186. E: info@kengert.lu

alanrogers.com/LU7640

A friendly welcome awaits you at this peacefully situated, family run site, 2 km. from Larochette, which is 24 km. northeast of Luxembourg City, providing 180 individual pitches, all with 16A electricity (Europlug). Some in a very shaded woodland setting, on a slight slope with fairly narrow access roads. There are also eight hardened pitches for motorcaravans on a flat area of grass, complete with motorcaravan service facilities. Further tent pitches are in an adjacent and more open meadow area. There are also site owned wooden chalets for rent. This site is popular in season, so early arrival is advisable, or you can reserve.

Facilities

The well maintained sanitary block in two parts includes a modern, heated unit with some washbasins in cubicles, and excellent, fully equipped cubicles for disabled visitors. The showers, facilities for babies, additional WCs and washbasins, plus laundry room are located below the central building which houses the shop, bar and restaurant. Motorcaravan services. Gas supplies. Indoor and outdoor play areas. Solar heated swimming pool (Easter-30/9). Paddling pool. WiFi (free). Off site: Bicycle hire. Golf, fishing and riding 8 km.

Open: 1 March - 8 November.

Directions

From Larochette take the CR118/N8 (towards Mersch) and just outside town turn right on the CR119 towards Schrondweiler, site is 2 km. on right. GPS: 49.79992, 6.19817

Charges 2012

Per unit incl. 2 persons	
and electricity	€ 22.00 - € 32.00
extra person	€ 10.00 - € 15.00
child (4-17 yrs)	€ 5.00 - € 7.00
dog	€ 1.50

20% reduction for students, walkers and cyclists.

Lieler

Camping Trois Frontières

Hauptstrooss 12, L-9972 Lieler (Luxembourg) T: 998 608. E: camp.3front@cmdnet.lu

alanrogers.com/LU7880

On a clear day, it is possible to see Belgium, Germany and Luxembourg from the campsite swimming pool, hence its name: Les Trois Frontières. Martin and Esther Van Aalst own and manage the site themselves and all visitors receive a personal welcome and immediately become part of a large happy family. There are 112 touring pitches on slightly sloping fields divided by pine trees which give some shade. Most of the facilities are close to the entrance, leaving the camping area quiet, except for the play area. The restaurant/takeaway provides good quality food at reasonable prices, served either inside or on the pleasant terrace with flower borders and overlooking the pool which is covered and heated. The site is ideally situated for visits to Bitburg, Germany and spa towns in Belgium. A member of the TOP Camp Group.

Facilities

The modern toilet block includes a suite for visitors with disabilities, plus baby bath and changing station, and family bathroom. More WCs in second building (down some steps). Laundry. Covered, heated swimming pool (1/4-31/10). Play area. Boules. Games room. Bicycle hire. WiFi (charged). Off site: Shops 2.3 km. Golf and riding 12 km. Clervaux 12 km.

Open: All year.

Directions

Take N7 northward from Diekirch. 3 km. south of Weiswampach turn right onto CR338 to Lieler (site signed here). Site is on right as you enter the village. GPS: 50.12340, 6.10517

Charges guide

Per unit incl. 2 persons	€ 17.90 - € 23.30
extra person	€ 7.35 - € 7.90
child (under 12 yrs)	€ 4.00 - € 4.50
electricity (4A)	€ 2.75
dog	€ 2.20

Luxembourg

Camping Kockelscheuer

22 route de Bettembourg, L-1899 Luxembourg (Luxembourg) T: 471 815. E: caravani@pt.lu

alanrogers.com/LU7660

Camping Kockelscheuer is 4 km. from the centre of Luxembourg city and quietly situated (although there can be some aircraft noise at times). On a slight slope, there are 161 individual pitches of good size, either on flat ground at the bottom of the site or on wide flat terraces with easy access, all with 16A electricity. There is also a special area for tents, with picnic tables and, in the reception building, a tent campers' lounge. For children there is a large area with modern play equipment on safety tiles and next door to the site is a sports centre. There is a friendly welcome, charges are reasonable and English is spoken. Visit Luxembourg City by bus. Here, there are shops, museums and the Grand Duke's Palace. Explore some of the 23 km. of defensive tunnels built in the Middle Ages under the city. The area south of the campsite has several old mining towns, many of which have excellent museums and walks to discover the old workings. Nearby there are two large parks – the one at Bettembourg is a fairy tale park.

Facilities

Two fully equipped, identical sanitary buildings, both very clean. Washing machines. Motorcaravan services. Shop (order bread the previous day). Snack bar. Restaurant in adjacent sports centre also with minigolf, tennis, squash etc. Rest room. No entry or exit for vehicles (reception closed) 12.00-14.00. Off site: Bus 200 m. every 10 mins. to Luxembourg. Swimming pool and bicycle hire 5 km. Fishing 20 km.

Open: Easter - 31 October.

Directions

Site is SSW of Luxembourg City on the N31 to Bettembourg. From the south, exit A4 at junction signed Kockelscheuer onto N4. In 2 km. turn right (Kockelscheuer and campsite) and continue to follow the signs. GPS: 49.57180, 6.10900

Charges guide

Per unit incl. 2 persons and electricity	€ 15.50
extra person	€ 4.00
child (3-14 yrs)	€ 2.00

No credit cards.

Maulusmühle

Camping Woltzdal

Maison 12, L-9974 Maulusmühle (Luxembourg) T: 998 938. E: info@woltzdal-camping.lu

alanrogers.com/LU7780

Set by a stream in a valley, Camping Woltzdal is one of the many delightful sites in the Ardennes, a region of wooded hills and river valleys that crosses the borders of Belgium, France and Luxembourg. The site has 79 flat touring pitches, set on grass amongst fir trees; all with 4A electricity and 20 of which also have water and waste water. They are fairly open and have views of the surrounding wooded hills. A railway passes the site on the far side of the stream, but there are only trains during the day and they are not disturbing. This is a family-run site where in the small, friendly bar/restaurant, one brother cooks, the other serves the guests while their father runs the bar.

Facilities

The site boasts a new state-of-the-art toilet block with solar-powered water heating (access is by smart key (deposit). Large family bathrooms and facilities for disabled visitors. Laundry room. Service points for motorcaravans. Reception and small shop are in the large house at the entrance where there is also a bar and a restaurant/snack bar with terrace. Children's library/activity room. WiFi. Play area. Boules. Mountain bike hire. Entertainment programme for children in high season. Off site: Fishing and golf 6 km. Riding 20 km.

Open: 31 March - 27 October.

Directions

Site is 6 km. north of Clervaux on the CR335 road. Leave Clervaux in the direction of Troisvierge (N18). After 1 km. take right fork to Maulusmühle on CR335. Site is signed on right just before Maulusmühle village. Steep turn onto campsite road. GPS: 50.091283, 6.027833

Charges guide

Per unit incl. 2 persons and electricity	€ 20.00 - € 23.20
extra person	€ 7.00
child (4-12 yrs)	€ 3.50
dog	€ 4.00

Reisdorf

Camping de la Sûre

23 route de la Sûre, L-9390 Reisdorf (Luxembourg) T: 836 246. E: hientgen@pt.lu

alanrogers.com/LU7650

Camping de la Sûre is on the banks of the river that separates Luxembourg and Germany. It is a pleasant site close to Reisdorf with 180 numbered pitches (120 with 10A electricity). These are not separated but are marked with lovely beech and willow trees that provide some shade. There are caravan holiday homes in a fenced area towards the back of the site, leaving the prime pitches for touring units. The site is surrounded by trees on the hillsides and from Reisdorf visits can be made to Vianden Castle or Trier (oldest German city) just across the border.

Facilities

Modern, clean sanitary facilities which are in the process of being refitted and extended, including some washbasins in cubicles. Laundry. Small shop. Bar and restaurant. Takeaway. Playground. Minigolf. Sports field. Canoeing. Fishing. WiFi throughout (charged). Off site: Town centre within easy walking distance. Cycle ways abound. Bicycle hire 200 m. Riding 5 km. Golf 8 km.

Open: 1 April - 30 October.

Directions

From the river bridge in Reisdorf, take the road to Echternach, de la Sûre is the second campsite on the left. GPS: 49.87003, 6.26750

Charges guide

Per unit incl. 2 persons and electricity	€ 19.50
extra person	€ 5.00
child (under 14 yrs)	€ 2.50
dog	€ 2.50

15% reduction in low season. No credit cards.

Nommern

Europacamping Nommerlayen

Rue Nommerlayen, L-7465 Nommern (Luxembourg) T: 878 078. E: nommerlayen@vo.lu

alanrogers.com/LU7620

Situated at the end of its own road, in the lovely wooded hills of central Luxembourg, this is a top quality site with fees to match, but it has everything! A large, central building housing most of the services and amenities opens onto a terrace around an excellent swimming pool complex with a large fun pool and an imaginative water playground. The 367 individual pitches (100 sq.m) are on grassy terraces, all have access to electricity (2/16A) and water taps. Pitches are grouped beside age-appropriate play areas and the facilities throughout the campsite reflect the attention given to families in particular. Interestingly enough the superb new sanitary block is called Badtemple (having been built in the style of a Greek temple). Entry to the sauna and hot water for washbasins, showers and sinks is by a pre-paid smart key. Sports facilities are varied and cater for all ages. There is organised entertainment for children and families in high season, and beyond the site walking and cycle paths abound. Adults can enjoy spa and beauty treatments. Day visits to Luxembourg, Vianden castle and the Mosel Valley are easy from here. A member of Leading Campings Group.

Facilities

A large, high quality, modern sanitary unit provides some washbasins in cubicles, facilities for disabled visitors, and family and baby washrooms. The new block also includes a sauna. Twelve private bathrooms for hire. Laundry. Motorcaravan service point. Supermarket. Restaurant. Snack bar. Bar (all 4/4-8/11). Excellent swimming pool complex (1/5-15/9) and new covered and heated pool (Easter-1/11). Solarium. Fitness programmes. Bowling. Playground. Large screen TV. Entertainment in season. WiFi (charged). Off site: Riding 1 km. Fishing and golf 5 km.

Open: 1 February - 1 December.

Directions

Take the 118 road between Mersch and Larochette. Site is signed 3 km. north of Larochette towards the village of Nommern on the 346 road.
GPS: 49.78472, 6.16519

Charges guide

Per unit incl. 2 persons and 2A electricity, acc. to pitch and facilities	€ 21.00 - € 38.00
extra adult	€ 5.00
child (under 18 yrs)	€ 3.50
dog	€ 2.85
electricity (16A) plus	€ 3.75

No credit cards.

Netherlands

With vast areas of the Netherlands reclaimed from the sea, nearly half of the country lies at or below sea level. The result is a flat, fertile landscape, criss-crossed with rivers and canals. Famous for its windmills and bulb fields, it also boasts some of the most impressive coastal dunes in Europe.

There is more to the Netherlands than Amsterdam and the bulb fields. Granted, both are top attractions and no visitor should miss the city of Amsterdam with its delightful bridges, canals, museums and listed buildings or miss seeing the springtime riot of colour that adorns the fields and gardens of South Holland. This is a country with a variety of holiday venues ranging from lively seaside resorts to picturesque villages, idyllic old fishing ports and areas where nature rules.

The Vecht valley is an area of natural beauty which centres around the town of Ommen. Giethoorn is justly dubbed the 'Venice of the North'. The Alblasserwaard polder offers time to discover the famed windmills of Kinderdijk, cheese farms and a stork village. The islands of Zeeland are joined by amazing feats of engineering, particularly the Oosterschelde storm surge barrier. Island hopping introduces lovely old towns such as Middelburg, the provincial capital Zierikzee with its old harbour and the quaint old town of Veere.

CAPITAL: Amsterdam

Tourist Office

Netherlands Board of Tourism
PO Box 30783, London WC2B 6DH
Tel: 020 7539 7958
Fax: 020 7539 7953
Email: info-uk@holland.com
Internet: www.holland.com/uk

Population

16.7 million

Climate

Temperate with mild winters and warm summers.

Language

Dutch. English is very widely spoken, so is German and to some extent French. In Friesland a Germanic language, Frisian, is spoken.

Telephone

The country code is 00 31.

Money

Currency: The Euro
Banks: Mon-Fri 09.00-16.00/1700.

Shops

Mon-Fri 09.00/09.30-17.30/18.00.
Sat to 16.00/17.00. Later closing hours in larger cities.

Public Holidays

New Year; April Fools Day 1 April; Good Fri; Easter Mon; Queen's Birthday 30 April; Labour Day; Remembrance Day 4 May; Liberation Day 5 May; Ascension; Whit Mon; SinterKlaas 5 Dec; Kingdom Day 15 Dec; Christmas 25, 26 Dec.

Motoring

There is a comprehensive motorway system but, due to the high density of population, all main roads can become very busy, particularly in the morning and evening rush hours. There are many bridges which can cause congestion. There are no toll roads but there are a few toll bridges and tunnels notably the Zeeland Bridge, Europe's longest across the Oosterschelde.

see campsite map 1

Amstelveen

Camping Het Amsterdamse Bos

Kleine Noorddijk 1, NL-1187 NZ Amstelveen (Noord-Holland) T: **0206 416 868.**
E: **info@campingamsterdam.com** alanrogers.com/NL5660

Het Amsterdamse Bos is a large park to the southwest of Amsterdam, one corner of which has been specifically laid out as the city's municipal campsite and is now under family ownership. Close to Schiphol Airport (we only noticed a little noise), it is about 12 km. from central Amsterdam. The site is well laid out alongside a canal, with unmarked pitches on separate flat lawns mostly backing onto pleasant hedges and trees, with several areas of paved hardstandings. It takes 400 touring units, with 100 electrical connections (10A) and some with cable TV. An additional area is available for tents and groups.

Facilities

Three new sanitary blocks are light and airy. Facilities for babies and disabled visitors. Laundry facilities. Motorcaravan services. Gas supplies. Small shop with basics. Fresh bread from reception. Cooking and dining area. Play area. Bicycle hire. Internet. Off site: Fishing, boating, pancake restaurant in the park. Riding 5 km.

Open: 15 March - 15 December.

Directions

Amsterdamse Bos and site are west of Amstelveen. From the A9 motorway take exit 6 and follow the N231 to site (second traffic light).
GPS: 52.29357, 4.82297

Charges guide

Per person	€ 5.00
child (4-12 yrs)	€ 2.50
caravan and car	€ 11.00
electricity (10A)	€ 4.50
dog	€ 2.50

Group reductions.

Amsterdam

Camping Zeeburg

Zuider IJdijk 20, NL-1095 KN Amsterdam (Noord-Holland) T: **0206 944 430.** E: **info@campingzeeburg.nl**
alanrogers.com/NL5665

Camping Zeeburg is attractively located to the east of Amsterdam on an island in the IJmeer and, unusually, combines a sense of nature with the advantage of being just 20 minutes from the city centre. In a sense Zeeburg reflects the spirit of Amsterdam, claiming to be 'open, friendly and tolerant'. The site offers 475 larger caravan and motorcaravan pitches and smaller (and cheaper) tent pitches. Most pitches have views over the IJmeer. All 75 caravan and motorcaravan pitches have 10A electrical connections. Tent pitches cannot be booked in advance and the maximum duration allowed on site is 14 days. Zeeburg also offers a number of low cost wooden cabins and wagonettes. The city centre is 5 km. distant and can be easily accessed by cycle (hire available on site). Alternatively, a regular bus service runs close to the site. On-site amenities include a bar/restaurant, a shop including a bakery (which claims to bake Amsterdam's best croissants), a children's farm and a canoe rental service. The wetlands of the IJmeer are well worth exploration, extending to the Diemerpark and new city of IJburg.

Facilities

Shop (all year), bar/restaurant (1/4-11/11). Playground. Games room. Bicycle hire. Motorcaravan services. Children's farm. Canoe hire. Cabins and wagonettes to rent. Off site: Swimming pool. Buses and trains to city centre.

Open: All year.

Directions

Site is on the eastern side of Amsterdam. From the A10 (Amsterdam ring road) take exit S114 to Zeeburg. Then follow signs to the city centre and, before reaching the Piet Hein tunnel turn left and then right into the campsite. The site is well signed from the A10. GPS: 52.36532, 4.95871

Charges guide

Per unit incl. 2 persons and electricity	€ 15.00 - € 26.00
extra person	€ 3.50 - € 5.50
child (2-12 yrs)	€ 2.50 - € 3.50

Reduced rates for tents.

Amsterdam

Camping Vliegenbos

Meeuwenlaan 138, NL-1022 AM Amsterdam (Noord-Holland) T: **0206 368 855.**

alanrogers.com/NL5675

Vliegenbos enjoys an appealing location in the middle of a large wood, but is just ten minutes from the lively centre of Amsterdam. It also has good access to the Waterland region, best known for its open expanses and picturesque towns such as Marken, Edam and Volendam. The site has recently celebrated its 50th anniversary. It extends over an 8.5 acre site and has a good range of amenities including a restaurant, shop and recently renewed toilet blocks with facilities for disabled visitors. Pitches here are grassy and most have electrical connections. A separate, open field is available for tents (without electricity). Several 'trekkers' cabins' can be reserved in advance. The site reception is open from 09.00 until 21.00 throughout the season and is able to offer advice on sightseeing options, as well as exploration of the Waterland by cycle. There is a bus stop 200 m. from the campsite with a good service to the city centre. Alternatively, a ferry operates from Centraal Station to a terminal 15 minutes walk from the site.

Facilities

Renovated toilet blocks include facilities for disabled campers. Motorcaravan services. Restaurant. Shop. Cabins for rent. Reservations are not accepted for touring pitches. Dogs are not accepted. Off site: Bus stop 200 m. Cycle tracks in the surrounding Waterland. Ferry terminal 15 minutes walk.

Open: 1 April - 30 September.

Directions

Leave the A10 Amsterdam ring road at exit S116 and follow signs to Camping Vliegenbos. GPS: 52.39055, 4.928083

Charges guide

Per unit incl. 2 persons and electricity	€ 28.50
extra person	€ 8.00
child (2-14 yrs)	€ 5.00

Amsterdam

Gaasper Camping Amsterdam

Loosdrechtdreef 7, NL-1108 AZ Amsterdam (Noord-Holland) T: **0206 967 326**

alanrogers.com/NL5670

Amsterdam is probably the most popular destination for visits in the Netherlands, and Gaasper Camping is on the southeast side, a short walk from a Metro station with a direct 20 minute service to the centre. The site is well kept and neatly laid out on flat grass with attractive trees and shrubs. There are 350 touring pitches in two main areas – one more open and grassy, mainly for tents (30 pitches with 10A connections), the other more formal with numbered pitches mainly divided by shallow ditches or good hedges. Areas of hardstanding are available and all caravan pitches have electrical connections.

Facilities

Three modern, clean toilet blocks (one unisex) for the tourist sections are an adequate provision. Nine new cabins with basin and shower. Hot water for showers and some dishwashing sinks on payment. Facilities for babies. Washing machine and dryer. Motorcaravan services. Gas supplies. Supermarket (1/4-1/11), café/bar/restaurant plus takeaway (1/6-1/9). Play area on grass. Off site: Riding 200 m. Fishing 1 km. Golf 4 km.

Open: 15 March - 1 November.

Directions

Take exit 1 for Gaasperplas-Weesp (S113) from the section of A9 motorway which is on the east side of the A2. Note: do not take the Gaasperdam exit (S112) which comes first if approaching from the west. GPS: 52.312222, 4.991389

Charges guide

Per unit incl. 2 persons and electricity	€ 23.50 - € 27.50
extra person	€ 4.75 - € 5.50
child (4-11 yrs)	€ 2.25 - € 2.75
dog	€ 2.50 - € 3.00

Assen

Vakantiepark Witterzomer

Witterzomer 7, NL-9405 VE Assen (Drenthe) T: 0592 393 535. E: info@witterzomer.nl

alanrogers.com/NL6153

Attractively located in a century old area of woodland and fields in the province of the Hunebedden, this is an attractive, large and well organised site. The Hunebedden are prehistoric monuments, built of enormous granite boulders and older than Stonehenge. The 600 touring pitches at Witterzomer are on grass with a woodland setting, with varying degrees of shade and 4/10A electricity. Most also have water, a drain and TV connections and some have private sanitary facilities. All the amenities here are of excellent quality and are particularly targeted at families. Amenities include a well stocked shop and a bar/restaurant with a good menu and takeaway meals.

Facilities

Good heated toilet blocks include separate facilities for babies and disabled visitors, as well as family bathrooms. Laundry. Shop (1/4-30/9). Restaurant/bar and takeaway (1/4-28/10). Heated outdoor swimming pool (17/5-2/9). Sports field and games room. Tennis. Bicycle hire. Minigolf. Lake with beach and fishing. Internet and WiFi (charged). Off site: Several nature parks. Assen 4 km. Golf 6 km. Groningen 30 km.

Open: All year.

Directions

Site is 4 km. southwest of Assen. From A28 exit 33 follow N371 (Balkenweg) to Assen. After 200 m. turn right (Europaweg) and again after 200 m. to the right onto Witterhoofdweg. Follow this road for around 2 km. (underneath A28) to the site (well signed). GPS: 52.9802, 6.5053

Charges guide

Per unit incl. 2 persons and electricity	€ 18.00 - € 26.00
extra person	€ 4.00
dog (max. 2)	€ 4.00

Barendrecht

Camping De Oude Maas

Achterzeedijk 1A, NL-2991 SB Barendrecht (Zuid-Holland) T: 0786 772 445. E: info@campingdeoudemaas.nl

alanrogers.com/NL5610

This site is easily accessed from the A15 southern Rotterdam ring road and is situated right by the river, so it is well worth considering if you are visiting the city or want a peaceful stop. The entrance is protected by a barrier and you have to drive up close in order to activate the intercom. Once through this, you pass a long strip of private chalets to an area of mixed seasonal and 75 touring pitches. There is a pleasant separate touring area for seven motorcaravans with electricity, water and waste water connections in a hedged group near the marina and river.

Facilities

One toilet block provides all necessary facilities including a unit for disabled visitors, a baby room and dishwashing. Launderette. Fishing. Good play area with swings, slides and climbing frames for all ages. Basketball net, badminton/volleyball area. Bar and small restaurant with caféteria service. WiFi (charged). Motorcaravan service point. Max. 1 dog. Off site: Swimming pool near. Bicycle hire 5 km. Riding 8 km. Golf 10 km. Rotterdam city centre reached by bicycle or train from Barendecht Station 4 km.

Open: 1 March - 15 October.

Directions

Best approached from the Hook/Rotterdam and then the A29 Rotterdam - Bergen op Zoom motorway. Leave A29 at exit 20 (Barendrecht) and follow signs for Heerjansdam and site. GPS: 51.83361, 4.55236

Charges guide

Per unit incl. 2 persons and electricity	€ 20.00
extra person	€ 4.00
child (0-12 yrs)	€ 2.50
dog	€ 2.50

Beilen

Camping Vorrelveen

Vorrelveen 10, NL-9411 VP Beilen (Drenthe) T: 0593 527 261. E: info@campingvorrelveen.nl

alanrogers.com/NL6134

In comparison with the larger (and justifiably popular) campsites in Drenthe, Camping Vorrelveen is a small, farm based site which reflects the pleasant countryside. The site is located on a working farm and enjoys beautiful views of the surrounding country. There are just 30 spacious pitches, all with 6A electricity, and the owners do their best to ensure a very personal, tranquil atmosphere. For example, your bread for breakfast will be delivered to your pitch and, in the evening, you can order home made pizzas and other dishes prepared in the farm kitchen! This is a prime example of a small, uncomplicated rural campsite.

Facilities

Toilet block including a family shower. The same building houses a large room for meals and socialising. Essential supplies kept at the farmhouse. Motorcaravan services (with pitches on hardstanding). Play area with cable track and children's fort. Pétanque. Bicycle hire. Tents (incl. breakfast) for rent. Off site: Fishing 800 m. The museum villages of Orvelte and Kabouterland (Pixieland).

Open: April - October.

Directions

Take exit 30 from A28 following signs to Smilde. Turn right at third bridge towards Hijken, then immediately turn left towards Vorrelveen. After a further 3 km. the site is on the left. GPS: 52.88000, 6.44200

Charges guide

Per person	€ 3.50
child (2-12 yrs)	€ 3.00
pitch	€ 4.50
electricity	€ 2.50

Bergeijk

Camping De Paal

Paaldreef 14, NL-5571 TN Bergeijk (Noord-Brabant) T: **0497 571 977**. E: **info@depaal.nl**

alanrogers.com/NL5970

A really first-class family run campsite, De Paal is especially suitable for families with children up to ten years old, and in low season those seeking a high quality, peaceful site. Situated in 42 hectares of woodland, with 580 touring pitches of up to 150 sq.m. the pitches are numbered and in meadows, separated by trees, with cars parked mainly on dedicated parking areas. All have 6A electricity, TV, water, drainage and a bin. There are 60 pitches with private sanitary facilities some of which are partly underground and attractively covered with grass and flowers. New for 2011 were 16 pitches with kitchen, sleeping accommodation and sanitary facilities, again partly underground. Each group of pitches has a small play area; additionally, there is a large adventure playground.

Facilities

High quality sanitary facilities are ultra modern, including wash cabins, family rooms and baby baths. Facilities for disabled visitors. Launderette. Motorcaravan services. Underground supermarket. Restaurant (high season), bar and snack bar (all season). Indoor pool (all season, supervised in high season). Outdoor pool (May-Sept). Bicycle hire. Tennis. Play areas. Theatre. WiFi (charged). Pet zoo. Off site: Tennis complex with indoor and outdoor courts (Sept-May) and pleasant lounge bar. Riding and covered wagons for hire 500 m. Fishing 4 km.

Open: Easter/1 April - 31 October.

Directions

From E34 Antwerpen-Eindhoven road take exit 32 (Eersel) and follow signs for Bergeijk and site (2 km. from town). GPS: 51.33635, 5.35552

Charges guide

Per unit incl. 2 persons and services	€ 30.00 - € 47.50
extra person	€ 4.00 - € 5.00
dog	€ 5.00

Discounts outside 5/7-16/8, daily 30%, over 7 days 35%, (over 55s 45% for more than 7 days).

Biddinghuizen

Rivièra Parc

Spijkweg 15, NL-8256 RJ Biddinghuizen (Flevoland) T: **0321 331 344**. E: **info@riviera.nl**

alanrogers.com/NL6195

This Dutch Rivièra at the Veluwe Lake actually comprises two campsites with some shared amenities. Camping Rivièra Beach lies beyond the dikes, close to the water and the beach, while the bigger Rivièra Parc can be found within the dikes, with 1,195 pitches, 850 reserved for touring, all on grass and all with 4/10A electricity. There are also 450 serviced pitches (large with water, drainage and TV connection). The site boasts a very impressive range of facilities. In 2012, Snow Village will be replaced by an exciting indoor laser game centre. Other amenities are targeted at families with children up to 14 years, such as the covered play area and indoor swimming pool.

Facilities

Good heated toilet blocks with separate facilities for babies and disabled visitors. Family rooms. Restaurants. Café. Snack bar. Takeaway food. Supermarket. Swimming pool with slide. Covered play area. Laser games. Bowling. Bicycle and go-kart hire. Fishing. Amusement arcade. Internet access. Around 54 mobile homes and bungalows for hire. Off site: Riding. Watersports. Walibi World theme park 2 km. Golf 10 km.

Open: 30 March - 28 October.

Directions

Site is 2 km. southwest of Elburg. From A28 take exit to Elburg (N309). At Elburg follow signs for Dronten. Cross bridge over Veluwe Lake and immediately turn left (N306). Site is signed from here and on the left after 2 km. GPS: 52.44671, 5.79223

Charges 2012

Per unit incl. up to 4 persons and 4A electricity	€ 29.00 - € 44.00
extra person	€ 6.25
dog	€ 5.25

Bloemendaal

Kennemer Duincamping De Lakens

Zeeweg 60, NL-2051 EC Bloemendaal aan Zee (Noord-Holland) T: **0235 411 570**.

E: **delakens@kennemerduincampings.nl** **alanrogers.com/NL6870**

De Lakens is part of de Kennemer Duincampings Group and is beautifully located in the dunes at Bloemendaal aan Zee. This site has 940 reasonably large, flat pitches with a hardstanding of shells. There are 410 for tourers (235 with 16A electricity) and the sunny pitches are separated by low hedging. This site is a true oasis of peace in a part of the Netherlands usually bustling with activity. From this site it is possible to walk straight through the dunes to the North Sea.

Facilities

The six toilet blocks for tourers (two brand new) include controllable showers, washbasins (open style and in cabins), facilities for disabled visitors and a baby room. Launderette. Two motorcaravan service points. Bar/restaurant and snack bar. Supermarket. Adventure playgrounds. Bicycle hire. Entertainment programme in high season for all. Dogs are not accepted. Off site: Beach and riding 1 km. Golf 10 km.

Open: 20 March - 1 November.

Directions

From Amsterdam go west to Haarlem and follow the N200 from Haarlem towards Bloemendaal aan Zee. Site is on the N200, on the right hand side. GPS: 52.40563, 4.58652

Charges guide

Per unit incl. 4 persons	€ 14.10 - € 27.45
incl. electricity	€ 18.40 - € 28.70
extra person	€ 4.20

Bourtange

Camping 't Plathuis

Bourtangerkanaal Noord 1, NL-9545 VJ Bourtange (Groningen) T: 0599 354 383. E: info@plathuis.nl

alanrogers.com/NL6110

Camping 't Plathuis is beautifully located in the fortified village of Bourtange. This small town dates back to the times of the invasion of the Bishop of Münster in the 1600s. The site has 92 touring pitches, most on well established, grass fields with shade from the mature trees that surround the site. On the newest area at the back of the site there are 22 serviced pitches with 6-16A electricity, water and drainage, including 14 with cable TV. There are four hardstandings available for motorcaravans. There are plans to further extend the site. To the front of the site is a lake for swimming and fishing with a sandy beach.

Facilities

Single older style, but neat and adequate, heated toilet block with toilets, washbasins (open style and in cabins) and coin-operated, controllable, hot showers. Second Portacabin block in the new field. Family shower rooms. Baby room. Facilities for disabled visitors. Laundry facilities. Shopping service for basics. Bread to order. Bar. Snack bar. Lake for swimming and fishing. Canoe hire. Playground. WiFi (charged). Off site: Village of Bourtange.

Open: 1 April - 31 October.

Directions

From A7 take exit 47 for Winschoten and continue on N367 towards Vlagtwedde. In Vlagtwedde turn on N368 towards Bourtange. Site is on the right 200 m. after entering the village. GPS: 53.0093, 7.1844

Charges guide

Per unit incl. 2 persons	€ 17.50
incl. water and drainage	€ 20.50
electricity (6A)	€ 2.75

Breskens

Camping Schoneveld

Schoneveld 1, NL-4511 HR Breskens (Zeeland) T: 0117 383 220. E: info@droomparkschoneveld.nl

alanrogers.com/NL6930

This site is well situated within walking distance of Breskens and it has direct access to sand dunes. It has around 200 touring pitches and has many static vans, although these are kept apart. The touring pitches are behind reception, laid out in fields which are entered from long avenues that run through the site. There are also twelve car parking bays. One ultra modern and very clean toilet block serves this area. The complex at the site entrance houses reception, a restaurant and a recreation room. Also near the entrance are the indoor pool, tennis courts and a football field. A member of the Tulip Parc Group.

Facilities

One large sanitary block provides showers, wash cubicles, child sized toilets and washbasins, baby room, en-suite unit for disabled visitors. Motorcaravan service point. Restaurant. Fun Food Plaza and takeaway (5/4-31/10). Bowling. Indoor pool. Tennis. Football field. Play area. Organised entertainment in July/Aug. Bicycle hire. WiFi. Off site: Fishing 200 m. Boat launching 3 km. Golf and riding 10 km.

Open: All year.

Directions

From Breskens port follow N58 south for about 1 km. and turn right at camping sign. Site is 500 m. GPS: 51.40107, 3.53475

Charges guide

Per unit incl. 2 persons	€ 19.50 - € 33.00
incl. 3 persons	€ 22.50 - € 36.00
incl. 5 persons	€ 28.50 - € 42.00
tent pitch incl. 1 or 2 persons	€ 15.00
extra person	€ 3.00

Camping Cheques accepted.

Brielle

Camping De Krabbeplaat

Oude Veerdam 4, NL-3231 NC Brielle (Zuid-Holland) T: 0181 412 363. E: info@krabbeplaat.nl

alanrogers.com/NL6980

Camping de Krabbeplaat is a family run site situated near the ferry port in a wooded, recreation area next to the Brielse Meer lake. There are 510 spacious pitches, with 100 for touring units, 68 with electricity (10A), cable connections and a water supply nearby. A separate field is used for groups of up to 450 guests. A nature conservation plan exists to ensure the site fits into its natural environment. The lake and its beaches provide the perfect spot for watersports and relaxation and the site has its own harbour where you can moor your own boat. The beach is 7 km. away for those who prefer the sea.

Facilities

One large and two smaller heated toilet blocks in traditional style provide separate toilets, showers and washing cabins. High standards of cleanliness, a dedicated unit for disabled campers and provision for babies. Warm water is free of charge. Launderette. Motorcaravan services. Supermarket, snack bar restaurant and takeaway (all season). Recreation room. Youth centre. Tennis. Playground and play field. Animal farm. Bicycle and children's pedal hire. Canoe, surf, pedal boat and boat hire. Fishing. WiFi (charged). Two cottages for hikers. No dogs allowed.

Open: 31 March - 30 September.

Directions

From the Amsterdam direction take the A4 road (Europoort), then the A15 (Europoort). Take exit for Brielle on N57 and, just before Brielle, site is signed. GPS: 51.9097, 4.18536

Charges guide

Per unit incl. 2 persons and electricity	€ 17.00 - € 23.50
extra person	€ 3.20
child (under 12 yrs)	€ 2.70

Buren

Recreatieoord Klein Vaarwater

Klein Vaarwaterweg 114, NL-9163 ME Buren (Friesland) T: 0519 542 156. E: info@kleinvaarwater.nl

alanrogers.com/NL6030

Recreatieoord Klein Vaarwater is a bustling family holiday park on the interesting island of Ameland. The site is 1 km. from the North Sea beaches and has its own indoor pool, with bars, restaurants, supermarket and party centre. Klein Vaarwater has 190 touring pitches (all with 16A electricity), of which 130 also have water, waste water and cable. Pitching is off hardcore access lanes, close to nature, on fields taking 6-10 units, on a grass and sand underground. There is some shade to the back from trees and bushes and level pitches are numbered and partly separated by young trees. Some of the pitches enjoy good views over the countryside.

Facilities

Three heated toilet blocks have open style washbasins, hot showers and facilities for disabled campers. Washing machines and dryers. Supermarket. Bar, restaurant, snack bar. Boutique. Indoor pools (25x15 m) with waterslide and fun paddling pool. Fitness centre. Playing field. Boules pitch. Bowling alley. Minigolf. Entertainment programme for young and old (in the holidays). WiFi (charged). No charcoal barbecues. Off site: Bicycle hire and the village of Buren 500 m. Beach 1 km. Boat launching, fishing and horse riding 1 km. Golf 10 km.

Open: January - December.

Directions

From Leeuwarden, follow N357 all the way north to Holwerd and take the ferry to Ameland (car reservations necessary in high season). On the island, follow the signs for Buren and then site signs. GPS: 53.45339, 5.80476

Charges guide

Per unit incl. 2 persons and electricity	€ 19.00
extra person	€ 4.75
car	€ 4.00

Camping Cheques accepted.

Callantsoog

Camping Tempelhof

Westerweg 2, NL-1759 JD Callantsoog (Noord-Holland) T: 0224 581 522. E: info@tempelhof.nl

alanrogers.com/NL5735

This first class site on the Dutch coast has 500 pitches with 250 for touring units, the remainder used by seasonal campers and a number of static units (mostly privately owned). All touring pitches have electricity (10/16A), water, drain and TV aerial point (40-90 sq.m. but car free). Two pitches have private sanitary facilities. The grass pitches are arranged in long rows which are separated by hedges and shrubs, with access from hardcore roads. There is hardly any shade. There are facilities for many activities, including a heated indoor pool, a fitness room and tennis courts. Tempelhof is close to the North Sea beaches (1 km). Member of Leading Campings Group.

Facilities

Two modern toilet blocks include washbasins (open style and in cabins) and controllable hot showers (SEP key). Children's section and baby room. Private bathroom (€ 50 p/w). Facilities for disabled visitors. Laundry. Motorcaravan services. Shop, restaurant, takeaway and bar (1/4-1/11). Swimming pool with paddling pool. Fitness room (€ 2,50). Climbing wall. Tennis. Trim court. Play area. Entertainment (high season). WiFi. Bicycle hire. Max. 2 dogs. Off site: Fishing 500 m. Boat launching 1 km.

Open: All year.

Directions

From Alkmaar take N9 road north towards Den Helder. Turn left towards Callantsoog on N503 road and follow site signs. GPS: 52.846644, 4.715506

Charges guide

Per unit incl. 2 persons and electricity (plus meter)	€ 17,00 - € 39,00
extra person	€ 4.50
electricity per kWh	€ 0.35

Castricum

Kennemer Duincamping Geversduin

Beverwijkerstraatweg 205, NL-1901 NH Castricum (Noord-Holland) T: 0251 661 095.

E: geversduin@kennemerduincampings.nl alanrogers.com/NL6862

The comfortable, family site of Gerversduin lies in an area of forests and sand dunes. The site offers 614 pitches of which 221 are for touring units and 14 for accommodation to rent. With good shade and privacy, most of the pitches have 4/16A electricity connections. The pitches without electricity have a unique location and cars must be parked elsewhere. In high season, many activities are organised for youngsters including the unusual opportunity to join a forestry worker for the day. The beach is only 4 km. away and is easily accessible by bike or on foot.

Facilities

Four sanitary blocks with WCs, open style basins, preset hot showers, family shower rooms and baby room. Facilities for disabled visitors. Laundry. Supermarket. Snack bar and café for meals with large terrace. Recreation area. Sports pitch. Play area. Bicycle hire. Internet. Safes. Only gas barbecues are permitted. Dogs only accepted in designated areas. Off site: Riding 500 m. Beach and fishing 4 km. Golf 9 km. Sailing 6 km.

Open: 26 March - 31 October.

Directions

On the A9 (Amsterdam - Alkmaar) take exit for the N203 and continue north towards Castricum. In Castricum follow signs to the station and from there drive south towards Heemskerk via the Beverwijkse straatweg. Site is south of Castricum and signed on the Beverwijkse straatweg. GPS: 52.53038, 4.64839

Charges guide

Per unit incl. 4 persons and electricity	€ 26.50 - € 38.95

Castricum

Kennemer Duincamping Bakkum

Zeeweg 31, NL-1901 NZ Castricum aan Zee (Noord-Holland) T: 0251 661 091.
E: bakkum@kennemerduincampings.nl alanrogers.com/NL6872

Kennemer Duincamping Bakkum lies in a wooded area in the centre of a protected dune reserve. There are 1,800 pitches of which 400 are used for touring units. These pitches are spacious and 300 are equipped with electricity (10A Europlug). Mobile homes and seasonal units use the remaining pitches in separate areas of the site. For safety and tranquillity the majority of the site is kept free of cars. Family activities and special entertainment for children are arranged in high season. The dunes are accessible from the site and offer plenty of opportunities for walking and cycling with the beach a walk of only 25 minutes.

Facilities

Three toilet blocks for tourers with toilets, washbasins in cabins, free, controllable showers and family shower rooms. Facilities for disabled visitors. Laundry area. Excellent supermarket, baker, fish shop and chicken shop. Snack bar and restaurant. Gas supplies. Play area. Sports pitch. Tennis. Bicycle hire. Activities for children and teens. Motorbikes and dogs are not accepted. Off site: Beach and fishing 1 km. Supermarket, bar, restaurant, swimming pool 2 km. Riding 4 km. Golf 7 km.

Open: 25 March - 29 October.

Directions

On the A9 between Alkmaar and Amsterdam take exit west onto the N203. Turn left onto the Zeeweg (N513) and after a few kilometres the site is on the right. GPS: 52.5614, 4.6331

Charges 2012

Per unit incl. 4 persons and electricity	€ 31.70 - € 52.90
extra person (over 2 yrs)	€ 4.85

Dalfsen

Vechtdalcamping Het Tolhuis

Het Lageveld 8, NL-7722 HV Dalfsen (Overijssel) T: 0529 458 383. E: tolhuis@gmx.net
alanrogers.com/NL6000

Vechtdalcamping Het Tolhuis is a pleasant, well established site with 145 pitches. Of these, 70 are for tourers, arranged on well kept, grassy lawns off paved and gravel access roads. All touring pitches have 4/10A electricity, water, waste water, cable and WiFi. Some are shaded by mature trees and bushes, others are more in the open. The touring pitches are located apart from static units. To the rear of the site is an open air pool (25x8 m. and heated by solar power) with a small paddling pool for toddlers. Along the lane running from reception to the back of the site is a takeaway for drinks and snacks.

Facilities

Two heated toilet blocks, an immaculate new one to the front, an older one to the back, with toilets, washbasins (open style and in cabins) and controllable hot showers (key). Children's section. Family shower rooms. Baby room. Laundry. Small shop (bread to order). Café for snacks and drinks. Open-air pool with paddling pool. Playing field. Playground and trampoline. Entertainment team for children (high season). ATM point. WiFi. Dogs are not accepted in high season. Off site: Restaurant 2 km.

Open: 1 April - 1 October.

Directions

From the A28 take exit 21 and continue east towards Dalfsen. Site is signed in Dalfsen. GPS: 52.50228, 6.3224

Charges guide

Per unit incl. 2 persons and electricity	€ 20.00 - € 32.25
extra person	€ 4.00
dog (not high season)	€ 3.00

Delft

Recreatiecentrum Delftse Hout

Korftlaan 5, NL-2616 LJ Delft (Zuid-Holland) T: 0152 130 040. E: info@delftsehout.nl
alanrogers.com/NL5600

Pleasantly situated in Delft's park and forest area on the eastern edge of the city, this well run, modern site is part of the Koningshof Group. It has 160 tourist pitches quite formally arranged in groups of four to six and surrounded by attractive trees and hedges. All have sufficient space and electrical connections (10A). Modern buildings near the entrance house the site amenities. A good sized first floor restaurant serves snacks and full meals and has an outdoor terrace overlooking the swimming pool and pitches. Walking and cycling tours are organised and there is a recreation programme in high season.

Facilities

Modern, heated toilet facilities include a spacious family room and children's section. Facilities for disabled visitors. Laundry. Motorcaravan services. Shop for basic food and camping items (1/4-1/11). Restaurant and bar (1/4-1/10). Small outdoor swimming pool (15/5-15/9). Adventure playground. Recreation room. Internet access. Bicycle hire. Gas supplies. Max. 1 dog. Off site: Fishing 1 km. Riding and golf 5 km. Regular bus service to Delft centre.

Open: All year.

Directions

Site is 1 km. east of Delft. From A13 motorway take Delft (exit 9), turn towards Delft Centre and then right at first traffic lights, following camping signs through suburbs and park to site. GPS: 52.01767, 4.37908

Charges guide

Per unit incl. 2 persons and electricity	€ 15.00 - € 32.50
extra person (3 yrs and older)	€ 3.00
dog (max. 1)	€ 3.00

Camping Cheques accepted.

Den Haag

Vakantiecentrum Kijkduinpark

Machiel Vrijenhoeklaan 450, NL-2555 NW Den Haag (Zuid-Holland) T: **0704 482 100.** E: **info@kijkduinpark.nl**

alanrogers.com/NL5640

This is an ultra-modern, all year round centre and family park with many cabins, villas and bungalows for rent and a large indoor swimming pool complex. The wooded touring area is immediately to the left of the entrance, with 330 pitches in shady glades of bark-covered sand. All pitches have electricity (10A), water, waste water and cable TV connections. In a paved central area are a supermarket, a snack bar and a restaurant. The main attraction here is the Meeresstrand, 500 m. from the site entrance. This is a long, wide sandy beach with flags to denote suitability for swimming. Windsurfing is popular.

Facilities

There are five modern sanitary blocks (key entry, € 20 deposit). Four private cabins for rent. Launderette. Snack bar. Shop. Restaurant. Supermarket. Indoor pool. Sun beds. Tennis. Bicycle hire. Special golfing breaks. Entertainment and activities organised in summer. Internet. Off site: Beach, golf and fishing 500 m. Riding 5 km.

Open: All year.

Directions

Site is southwest of Den Haag on the coast and Kijkduin is well signed as an area from all round Den Haag. GPS: 52.05968, 4.21118

Charges guide

Per unit incl. 5 persons and electricity	€ 19.00 - € 37.00
incl. electricity, water and drainage	€ 20.00 - € 48.25
extra person	€ 4.00

Discounts for young families and over 55s.

Denekamp

Camping De Papillon

Kanaalweg 30, NL-7591 NH Denekamp (Overijssel) T: **0541 351 670.** E: **info@depapillon.nl**

alanrogers.com/NL6470

De Papillon is perhaps one of the best campsites in The Netherlands. The site is well thought out with an eye for detail and for nature and the environment. For example, at the toilet blocks, waste water from the showers is used to flush the toilets, all buildings are heated by solar energy and all rubbish is separated for recycling. The 245 touring pitches are spacious, averaging 120-160 sq.m. and all have electricity (4/10/16A) and an extra 120 'comfort' pitches have been created. Arranged in small grassy fields surrounded by hedges and trees, each field provides a small play area. For more fun, children can visit a large adventure style play area, located adjacent to the (covered) heated pool and not far from reception.

Facilities

Two large sanitary buildings with showers, toilets, washbasins in cabins, facilities for babies and for disabled visitors. This building is designed in the shape of a butterfly. Laundry room. Spacious reception area with supermarket, restaurant, bar and takeaway. Heated pool with children's pool and sliding roof. Lake swimming with sandy beach. New modern adventure play area and smaller play areas. Pétanque. Bicycle hire. Fishing pond. Tennis. Pets to stroke. Max. 1 dog. Luxury bungalows to rent (good views). New Water Spray Park for children up to 13 yrs.

Open: 1 April - 1 October.

Directions

From the A1 take exit 32 (Oldenzaal - Denekamp) and continue to Denekamp. Pass Denekamp and turn right at village of Noord-Deurningen and follow signs to site. GPS: 52.39200, 7.04900

Charges guide

Per unit incl. 2 persons and 4A electricity	€ 27.00
incl. full services, plus	€ 30.25
extra person	€ 4.00

Eersel

Recreatiepark TerSpegelt

Postelseweg 88, NL-5521 RD Eersel (Noord-Brabant) T: **0497 512 016**. E: **info@terspegelt.nl**

alanrogers.com/NL6630

Camping TerSpegelt is a real delight. There are three large lakes, one for swimming, one for boating and the other for fishing and diving. The site has 855 pitches, with 481 for touring units and tents, and 65 mobile homes for rent. The remaining pitches are used by seasonal units. All touring pitches have electricity (6-16A Europlug), and 347 also have water and drainage, and with a little luck, a view over the lakes. We can recommend this site to people who like to participate in activities (organised with a variety of sports and outdoor activities, campfires and themed dinners) and to families with children. Starbeach is the new covered playground with a beautiful in-house beach and spectacular play equipment such as an eight metre high castle – ideal for playing and swimming if the weather is poor. For relaxing activities, there are facilities for golf and horse riding near the campsite. You can enjoy an evening meal at the beachside restaurant, De Wijde Blick, and relax with a drink in the bar, along with plenty of evening entertainment.

Facilities

Six toilet blocks, four heated by solar panels, provide toilets, washbasins (open and in cubicles) and showers. Washbasins for children. Heated baby rooms with changing mat and bath. Facilities for disabled visitors. Laundry. Motorcaravan services. Supermarket, restaurant, bar and snack bar, swimming pools (all open as site). Entertainment and activities. Watersports and diving. Minigolf. Bicycle hire. Tennis. Dogs are not accepted. WiFi throughout (charged). Off site: Riding 2 km. Golf 7 km.

Open: 30 March - 28 October.

Directions

From Utrecht follow the A2 south towards Eindhoven, then Maastricht. Take exit for Antwerpen and follow signs for Eersel. From Eersel follow site signs. GPS: 51.33623, 5.29373

Charges guide

Per unit incl. 2 persons and electricity	€ 26.00 - € 69.50

Erichem

Camping De Vergarde

Erichemseweg 84, NL-4117 GL Erichem (Gelderland) T: **0344 572 017**. E: **info@devergarde.nl**

alanrogers.com/NL5870

Situated north of 's Hertogenbosch and west of Nijmegen and Arnhem, De Vergarde has been developed on a former orchard with a beautiful old farmhouse at its entrance. The site is in two sections on either side of a lake. Static holiday caravans are on the left, with the 225 touring pitches to the right. About a third of these are taken by seasonal units. Arranged in sections, each named after a fruit tree, access is good. The pitches are numbered on flat grass and include electricity (10/16A), water, drainage and TV connections. There are trees all around the perimeter (but not much shade on the pitches).

Facilities

Good sanitary facilities in three blocks include family showers and baby bathrooms. Most, but not all, hot water is on payment. Washing machines. Motorcaravan services. Heated swimming pool and attractive paddling pool (1/5-1/9). Shop (1/5-1/10). Restaurant (1/5-1/10). Various play areas, large indoor games room. A small football field plus a children's theatre. Pony riding. Pets corner. Minigolf. Bicycle hire. Games room. Fishing.
Off site: Close to the historic town of Buren. The area is well suited for cycling.

Open: 1 April - 1 October.

Directions

From A15 Dordrecht - Nijmegen road exit at Tiel West (also McDonald's) and follow signs to site. GPS: 51.89898, 5.36077

Charges guide

Per unit incl. 2 persons and electricity	€ 19.00 - € 29.00
extra person (over 2 yrs)	€ 4.00
dog (max. 1)	€ 4.00

Special weekly rates. Low season less 20%.

Emst-Gortel

Camping De Wildhoeve

Hanendorperweg 102, NL-8166 JJ Emst-Gortel (Gelderland) T: **0578 661 324**. E: **info@wildhoeve.nl**

alanrogers.com/NL6285

Camping De Wildhoeve is a welcoming, privately owned site with many amenities of the type one would normally find on larger holiday camps. The well maintained site is located in woodland and has 400 pitches with 330 for tourers. Pitching is in several areas, mostly in the shade of mature conifers. Partly separated by trees and bushes, the level pitches are numbered and all have 6/10A electricity, water and drainage. Behind reception is an octagonally shaped sub-tropical pool with a large water slide and fun paddling pool. Next to reception is a water adventure playground. To the front of the site are tennis courts and next to that is an open-air pool with a large slide. Here also are a shop plus a grand café/restaurant. Many activities are organised for children, including open-air theatre. The toilet facilities on this site are excellent and include one block that has a special children's section with an area for children with disabilities.

Facilities

Four well placed, heated blocks with toilets, washbasins (open style and in cabins) and free, preset hot showers. Special children's section with showers, basins and toilets. Baby room. Family shower room. Facilities for disabled children. Laundry facilities. Shop, grand café/restaurant. Snack bar. Indoor and outdoor pools with slides and paddling pool. Water adventure playground. WiFi. Internet. Bicycle hire. Tennis. Open-air theatre. Dogs are not accepted.

Open: April - September.

Directions

From the A28, take exit 15 (Epe/Nunspeet). Continue east towards Epe and at traffic lights, turn south towards Emst. Continue straight ahead at roundabout in Emst. Turn right at church, into Hanendorperweg. Site is on the right after 3.5 km. GPS: 52.31369, 5.92707

Charges guide

Per unit incl. 2 persons and electricity	€ 21.00 - € 37.75
extra person	€ 5.00

Camping Cheques accepted.

Groede

Camping Groede

Zeeweg 1, NL-4503 PA Groede (Zeeland) T: **0117 371 384**. E: **info@campinggroede.nl**

alanrogers.com/NL5510

Camping Groede is a friendly, fair-sized site by the same stretch of sandy beach as no. NL5500. Family run, it aims to cater for the individual needs of visitors and to provide a good all-round holiday. Campers are sited as far as possible according to taste – in family areas, in larger groups or on more private pitches for those who prefer peace and quiet. In total, there are 500 pitches for tourists (plus 380 seasonal units), all with electrical connections (4-10A) and 300 with water and drainage connections. A new field has been added with 63 fully serviced large pitches.

Facilities

Toilet facilities are excellent with a high standard of cleanliness, including some wash cabins, baby baths, a family room and a dedicated unit for visitors with disabilities. Motorcaravan services. Gas supplies. Shop, restaurant and snack bar (all weekends only in low seasons). Recreation room. Internet access. Sports area. Several play areas (bark base). Plenty of activities for children in peak season. Bicycle hire. Fishing.
Off site: Riding 1 km. Golf 11 km.

Open: 24 March - 31 December.

Directions

From Breskens take the coast road for 5 km. to site. Alternatively, the site is signed from Groede village on the more inland Breskens - Sluis road. GPS: 51.39582, 3.48772

Charges guide

Per unit incl. 2 persons	€ 17.00 - € 30.00

No credit cards.

Groningen

Camping Stadspark

Campinglaan 6, NL-9727 KH Groningen (Groningen) T: 0505 251 624. E: info@campingstadspark.nl

alanrogers.com/NL5770

The Stadspark is a large park to the southwest of the city, well signed and with easy access. The campsite is within a park with many trees and surrounded by water. It has 200 pitches with 150 for touring units, of which 75 have 6A electricity and 30 are fully serviced with electricity, water and drainage. Several hardstandings are available for large units and motorcaravans. The separate tent area is supervised directly by the manager. Buses for the city leave from right outside and timetables and maps are provided at reception. Groningen is a very lively city with lots to do.

Facilities

Two sanitary blocks, one refurbished, the other in need of renovation provide hot showers, washbasins and toilets. Family shower and baby room. Motorcaravan service point. Shop (15/3-15/10). Restaurant, café, bar and takeaway (1/4-15/9). Internet access in reception. Bicycle hire. Fishing. Canoeing. Off site: Riding and golf 5 km. Boat launching 6 km.

Open: 15 March - 15 October.

Directions

From Assen on A28 turn left on the A7 towards Drachten. Follow signs for Stadspark and the campsite. GPS: 53.20090, 6.53570

Charges guide

Per unit incl. 2 persons and electricity	€ 23.70
extra person	€ 4.35
child (2-12 yrs)	€ 2.30

No credit cards.

Gulpen

Terrassencamping Gulperberg Panorama

Berghem 1, NL-6271 NP Gulpen (Limburg) T: 0434 502 330. E: info@gulperberg.nl

alanrogers.com/NL6530

Gulperberg Panorama is just three kilometres from the attractive village of Gulpen, midway between the interesting cities of Maastricht and Aachen. The 350 touring pitches are large and flat on terraces overlooking the village on one side and open countryside on the other. Many have full services. English is spoken in reception, although all written information is in Dutch (ask if you require a translation). Gulperberg Panorama is a haven for children. During the high season there is a weekly entertainment programme to keep them occupied. The site is not suitable for visitors with disabilities. Dogs are restricted to one section of the campsite. Visitors are assured of a warm welcome and if arriving (or leaving) on a Saturday are welcomed (or bade farewell) by the 'Aartje Twinkle'.

Facilities

Four modern sanitary blocks have excellent facilities. Family shower room and baby room. Laundry. Shop (27/4-31/8). Bar. Takeaway. New restaurant with terrace. Swimming pool (29/4-15/9). Three play areas. Bouncy cushion. TV and games room. Extensive entertainment programme for children plus family entertainment. WiFi over site (charged). Off site: Golf and bicycle hire 3 km. Fishing 4 km. Riding 5 km. Further afield are caves, museums and Maastricht. Beach 15 km.

Open: Easter - 31 October.

Directions

Gulpen is east of Maastricht. Take N278 Maastricht - Aachen. Site is signed just as you enter Gulpen at the traffic lights. Turn right and follow camping signs for about 3 km. GPS: 50.80673, 5.89413

Charges guide

Per unit incl. 2 persons and electricity	€ 17.60 - € 23.60
extra person (over 2 yrs)	€ 2.40 - € 3.50

Camping Cheques accepted.

Gulpen

Camping Osebos

Reymerstokker dorpsstraat 1, NL-6271 PP Gulpen (Limburg) T: 0434 501 611. E: info@osebos.nl

alanrogers.com/NL6590

Family run, Camping Osebos is a quiet, attractive and well kept terraced site with a southerly aspect in the Dutch 'mountains'. There are 215 touring pitches, all with electricity and 90 with fresh and waste water connections in addition, plus TV. They are level, grassed and set in rows on terraces or in groups of four surrounded by hedges, on the lower part of the site. From the pitches there are extensive views of the surrounding countryside with its rolling, partially tree clad hills. There is walking and cycling directly from the site and many picturesque villages to visit in this attractive, less well known southern part of Holland closely bordering Belgium and Germany.

Facilities

Three heated sanitary blocks contain free showers, washbasins (open and in cabins), family showers and baby rooms. Laundry facilities, washing machine, dryer plus ironing. Motorcaravan service point. Shop, bar/restaurant, takeaway (22/4-31/10). Outdoor swimming pool with paddling pool (15/5-30/9). Play areas. Children's entertainment in summer. Sports pitch. Bicycle hire. Max. 1 dog. Off site: Fishing 2 km. Golf and riding 7 km.

Open: 1 April - 28 November.

Directions

Site is between Maastricht and Aachen, just south of N278. Leave the E25/A2 motorway at exit 54 (Europaplein), head east towards Aachen on N278. In 3.5 km. after passing through Margraten, on the descent to Gulpen, turn south towards Beutenaken. After 400 m. at the bottom of the hill, the site is to the right. GPS: 50.80669, 5.87078

Charges guide

Per unit incl. 2 persons and electricity	€ 13.00 - € 18.00
extra person	€ 1.95 - € 2.80

Hardenberg

Camping De Vechtstreek

Grote Beltenweg 17, NL-7794 RA Rheeze-Hardenberg (Overijssel) T: **0523 261 369.**

E: **info@sprookjescamping.nl** **alanrogers.com/NL5990**

It would be difficult for any child (or adult) to pass this site and not be curiously drawn to the oversized open story book which marks its entrance. From here young children turn the pages and enter the exciting world of Hannah and Bumpie, two of the nine characters around which this site's fairy tale theme has been created. There are 270 touring pitches (all with 6/12A electricity) mostly laid out in bays which accommodate around 12 units. In the centre of each is a small play area. The area at the back of the site has been upgraded with new electricity connections, a gravel road and attractive lighting.

Facilities

Three modern, well equipped and heated toilet blocks include a baby room, separate child sections and family showers. Excellent laundry room. Sauna, solarium and jacuzzi. Well stocked supermarket, restaurant, snack bar and takeaway (all season). Play areas. Fairytale water play park (heated). Daily activity club. Internet access. Football field. Theatre. Access to a fishing, swimming and boating recreation area at rear of site (200 m).

Open: 5 April - 30 September.

Directions

From Ommen take N34 Hardenberg road for 9 km. Turn right on N36 and proceed south for 3.5 km. Turn left at first crossroads and after 200 m. left again on local road towards Rheeze. Site is clearly signed to the left in 2 km. Follow signs for 'Sprookjescamping'. GPS: 52.54614, 6.57103

Charges guide

Per unit incl. 2 persons and electricity	€ 26.25 - € 44.00
extra person	€ 3.30 - € 4.75

Hardenberg

Vakantiepark Het Stoetenslagh

Elfde Wijk 42, NL-7797 HH Rheezerveen-Hardenberg (Overijssel) T: **0523 638 260.** E: **info@stoetenslagh.nl**

alanrogers.com/NL6004

Arriving at Het Stoetenslagh and passing reception, you reach the pride of the campsite; a large natural lake with several little beaches. Many hours can be spent swimming, canoeing or sailing a dinghy here. There are 258 spacious grass touring pitches (120 sq.m) divided between several fields and arranged around clean sanitary buildings. Each field also has a small volleyball area and climbing frames. You may choose between 'nature' pitches, standard pitches or serviced pitches with water, drainage, 6/10A electricity and cable connection. There are climbing frames for children, much space for playing, a children's club and, particularly popular with little ones, a small animal farm.

Facilities

Five toilet blocks include private cabins, baby facilities, family showers and facilities for disabled visitors. Shop. Beach shower. Washing machines and dryers. Motorcaravan service point. Restaurant with bar. Snack bar with takeaway. New indoor pool. Natural pool with sandy beaches. Canoeing. Disco, bowling, curling and archery. Play areas. Activities for children and teenagers. Bouncy castle. Off site: Fishing 3 km. Golf 15 km.

Open: 1 April - 30 September.

Directions

On the N34 travel towards Ommen and go through town. At TINQ petrol station a few kilometres outside Ommen follow signs for 'Stoetenslagh' following Het Zwarte Pad. About 3 km. after Rheezerveen, follow site signs right and site is on right after 3 km. GPS: 52.58694, 6.53049

Charges guide

Per serviced pitch incl. 2 persons, electricity, water and waste water	€ 19.00 - € 32.00
extra person	€ 3.00

Harlingen

Camping De Zeehoeve

Westerzeedijk 45, NL-8862 PK Harlingen (Friesland) T: **0517 413 465.** E: **info@zeehoeve.nl**

alanrogers.com/NL6080

Superbly located, directly behind the sea dike of the Wadden Sea and just a kilometre from the harbour of Harlingen, De Zeehoeve is an attractive and spacious site. It has 300 pitches (125 for tourers), all with 16A electricity and 20 with water, drainage and electricity. There are 16 hardstandings for motorcaravans and larger units. Some pitches have views over the Harlingen canal where one can moor small boats. An ideal site for rest and relaxation, for watersports or to visit the attractions of Harlingen and Friesland. After a day of activity, one can wine and dine in the site restaurant or at one of the many pubs in the town.

Facilities

Three sanitary blocks include open style washbasins with cold water only, washbasins in cabins with hot and cold water, controllable showers (on payment). Family showers and baby bath. Facilities for disabled visitors. Cooking hob. Launderette. Motorcaravan services. Bar/restaurant (1/7-31/8). WiFi (charged). Play area. Bicycle hire. Boat launching. Pedalo and canoe hire. Fishing. Extensive entertainment programme (July/Aug). Bed and breakfast. Hikers' cabins and boarding houses. Dog exercise area.

Open: 1 April - 15 October.

Directions

From Leeuwarden take A31 southwest to Harlingen, then follow site signs. GPS: 53.16237, 5.41688

Charges guide

Per unit incl. 2 persons and electricity	€ 17.10 - € 20.60
extra person	€ 4.05
child (4-11 yrs)	€ 3.55
tent (no car) incl. 2 persons	€ 15.10
pet	€ 3.00

Hellevoetsluis

Camping Caravaning 't Weergors

Zuiddijk 2, NL-3221 LJ Hellevoetsluis (Zuid-Holland) T: 0181 312 430. E: weergors@pn.nl

alanrogers.com/NL6970

A rustic style site built around old farm buildings, t'Weergors has a comfortable mature feel. At the front of the site is a well presented farmhouse which houses reception and includes the main site services. The sanitary blocks have been renewed recently as has the farm, accommodating an attractive à la carte restaurant and pancake house. The reception has also been renewed including a new mini-market, where fresh bread can be ordered. There are currently 100 touring pitches (plus seasonal and static places), while a field at the back of the site is being developed to provide a further 70-80 touring pitches.

Facilities

Three sanitary blocks have showers (by key), washbasins, some in cabins, children's showers and toilets plus baby baths. Laundry facilities. Motorcaravan service point. Small shop (1/4-31/10). Restaurant and bar (snacks) and pancakes. Tennis. Internet access. Play area. Paddling pool. Organised entertainment in high season. Fishing pond. Bicycle hire. Rally field.

Open: 1 April - 31 October.

Directions

From Rotterdam join A15 west to Rozenburg exit 12 and join N57 south for 11 km. Turn left on the N497 signed Hellevoetsluis and follow site signs for 4.5 km. to roundabout. Turn right at roundabout to site 1.5 km. on right. GPS: 51.82943, 4.11618

Charges 2012

Per unit incl. 2 persons and electricity	€ 19.65 - € 23.65
extra person	€ 3.50
child (3-12 yrs)	€ 2.00
dog	€ 1.80

Camping Cheques accepted.

Heumen

Rekreatiecentrum Heumens Bos

Vosseneindseweg 46, NL-6582 BR Heumen (Gelderland) T: 0243 581 481. E: info@heumensbos.nl

alanrogers.com/NL5950

The area around Nijmegen, the oldest city in the Netherlands, has large forests for walking or cycling, nature reserves and old towns to explore, as well as being quite close to Arnhem. The site covers 16 hectares and is open over a long season for touring families (no groups of youngsters allowed) and all year for bungalows. It offers 165 level, grass pitches for touring units, all with electricity (6A) and cable TV connections. Numbered but not separated, in glades of ten and one large field, all have easy access with cars parked elsewhere. One small section for motorcaravans has some hardstandings. The restaurant, which offers a good menu and a new terrace, is close to the comfortable bar and snack bar. An open air swimming pool with a small children's pool is maintained at 28 degrees by a system of heat transfer from the air. Mr Van Velzen and his sons took over this site in 2002 and are planning new buildings and an Internet point.

Facilities

The main, high quality sanitary building, plus another new block, are modern and heated, providing showers on payment. Rooms for families and disabled visitors. Smart launderette. Motorcaravan services. Gas supplies. Shop. Bar, restaurant and snack bar. Heated outdoor swimming pool (1/5-30/9). Bicycle hire. Tennis. Boules. Glade area with play equipment on sand and grass. Activity and excursion programme (high season). Large wet weather room. WiFi over site (charged). Off site: Riding 300 m. Fishing 2 km. Golf 6 km.

Open: All year.

Directions

From A73 (Nijmegen - Venlo) take exit 3 (4 km. south of Nijmegen) and follow site signs. GPS: 51.76915, 5.82050

Charges 2012

Per unit incl. 2 persons and electricity	€ 18.00 - € 30.00
extra person (over 3 yrs)	€ 4.00
dog (max. 1)	€ 4.00

Special low season weekends (incl. restaurant meal) and special deal for over 55s.

Hilvarenbeek

Vakantiepark Beekse Bergen/SafariCamp Beekse Bergen

Beekse Bergen 1, NL-5081 NJ Hilvarenbeek (Noord-Brabant) T: 0135 491 100. E: info@libema.nl

alanrogers.com/NL5900

Centred around a large lake, Beekse Bergen campsite is part of a large leisure park complex that offers something for all the family, from the Safari Park containing over 1,000 wild animals to Speelland which caters for children from three to eight years old. The site has 225 touring pitches, all with 4/10A electricity, 100 of which have fresh and waste water connections. They are arranged in small, level, grassy areas surrounded by hedges and mature trees. Several small sandy beaches are to be found around the lake, which can be used amongst other things for swimming, windsurfing and fishing.

Facilities

Sanitary facilities in the touring area include all the usual facilities including some washbasins in cabins and facilities for disabled visitors. Launderette. Supermarket. Restaurants, cafés and takeaway (weekends only in low seasons). Children's playgrounds. Indoor pool. Beaches and lake swimming. Watersports including rowing boats and canoe hire. Amusements. Tennis. Minigolf. Fishing. Recreation programme. Bicycle hire. Riding. Bungalows and tents to rent. WiFi (charged). Off site: Golf 5 km. Efteling amusement park.

Open: 21 March – 6 November.

Directions

From A58/E312 Tilburg - Eindhoven motorway, take exit to Hilvarenbeek on the N269 road. Follow signs Beekse Bergen. GPS: 51.48298, 5.12800

Charges guide

Per unit incl. 2 persons and electricity	€ 15.00 - € 25.00
extra person	€ 7.00
dog	€ 4.00

Discounts for weekly stays. Camping packages available.

Kamperland

Camping De Molenhoek

Molenweg 69a, NL-4493 NC Kamperland (Zeeland) T: 0113 371 202. E: info@demolenhoek.com

alanrogers.com/NL5570

This family run site makes a pleasant contrast to the livelier coastal sites in this popular holiday area. It is rurally situated 3 km. from the Veerse Meer, which is very popular for all sorts of watersports. Catering for 300 permanent or seasonal holiday caravans and 100 touring units, it is neat, tidy and relatively spacious. The marked touring pitches are divided into small groups with surrounding hedges and trees giving privacy and some shade, and electrical connections are available. A large outdoor pool is Molenhoek's latest attraction. Entertainment is organised in season (dance evenings, bingo, etc).

Facilities

Sanitary facilities in one fully refurbished and one newer block, include some washbasins in cabins. Toilet and shower facilities for disabled visitors and for babies. Laundry facilities. Motorcaravan services. Simple bar/restaurant with terrace and TV room. Restaurant/bar. Swimming pool (15/5-15/9). Playground. Bicycle hire. Off site: Tennis and watersports nearby. Riding 1 km. Shop 2 km. Fishing 2.5 km.

Open: 1 April - 28 October.

Directions

Site is west of the village of Kamperland on the 'island' of Noord Beveland. From the N256 Goes - Zierikzee road, exit west onto the N255 Kamperland road. Site is signed south of this road. GPS: 51.57840, 3.69642

Charges guide

Per unit incl. 2 or 3 persons and electricity	€ 21.00 - € 33.50
extra person	€ 3.50 - € 4.50
dog	€ 2.50 - € 3.00

No credit cards.

Katwijk

Recreatiecentrum De Noordduinen

Campingweg 1, NL-2221 EW Katwijk aan Zee (Zuid-Holland) T: 0714 025 295. E: info@noordduinen.nl

alanrogers.com/NL5680

This is a large, well managed site surrounded by dunes and sheltered partly by trees and shrubbery, which also separate the various camping areas. The 200 touring pitches are marked and numbered but not divided. All have electricity (10A) and 75 are fully serviced with electricity, water, drainage and TV connection. There are also seasonal pitches and mobile homes for rent. Entertainment is organised in high season for various age groups. A new complex with indoor and outdoor pools, restaurant, small theatre and recreation hall provides a good addition to the site's facilities. Seasonal pitches and mobile homes are placed mostly away from the touring areas and are unobtrusive.

Facilities

The three sanitary blocks are modern and clean, with washbasins in cabins, a baby room and provision for visitors with disabilities. Laundry. Motorcaravan services. Supermarket with fresh bread daily, bar, restaurant, takeaway (all 1/4-31/10). Recreation room. Swimming pool complex. Play area. Only gas barbecues are permitted. Dogs are not accepted. Off site: Riding 150 m. Beach and fishing 300 m. Golf 6 km.

Open: All year.

Directions

Leave A44 at exit 8 (Leiden - Katwijk) to join N206 to Katwijk. Take Katwijk Noord exit and follow signs to site. GPS: 52.21103, 4.40978

Charges guide

Per unit incl. 2 persons and electricity	€ 28.00 - € 36.00
extra person	€ 4.00

Camping Cheques accepted.

Koudum

Camping De Kuilart

Kuilart 1, NL-8723 CG Koudum (Friesland) T: 0514 522 221. E: info@kuilart.nl

alanrogers.com/NL5760

De Kuilart is a well run, modern and partly car-free site by Friesland's largest lake. With its own marina and private boating facilities, it attracts many watersports enthusiasts. The 495 pitches here are set in groups of ten to 16 on areas of grass surrounded by well established hedges. There are 265 for touring units, 207 with electricity (6/16A), water, waste water, WiFi and TV connections, and 20 new pitches with private sanitary facilities. The restaurant provides good views of the lake and woodland. A children's 'house' is home to the entertainment team and there is an interesting Play Ship on the beach. A member of the Holland Tulip Parcs Group.

Facilities

Four modern, heated sanitary blocks have showers on payment and most washbasins (half in private cabins) have only cold water. Launderette. Motorcaravan services. Gas supplies. Restaurant/bar, supermarket, indoor pool, with 3 sessions daily (all open 30/3-4/11). Sauna and solarium. Sports field. Play areas. Tennis. Bicycle hire. Fishing. Animation team (high season). Internet access. Lake swimming area. Marina (600 berth) with windsurfing, boat hire and boat shop. Garage at harbour. Car hire. WiFi throughout (charged). Off site: Riding and golf 4 km.

Open: All year.

Directions

Site is southeast of Koudum, on the Fluessen lake. Follow the camping sign off the N359 Bolsward - Lemmer road. GPS: 52.90250, 5.46620

Charges 2012

Per unit incl. 2 persons and electricity	€ 17.50 - € 24.50
with own sanitary unit	€ 25.50 - € 37.50
extra person	€ 4.60
dog	€ 3.50

Camping Cheques accepted.

Lauwersoog

Camping Lauwersoog

Strandweg 5, NL-9976 VS Lauwersoog (Groningen) T: 0519 349 133. E: info@lauwersoog.nl

alanrogers.com/NL6090

The focus at Camping Lauwersoog is on the sea and watersports. One can have sailing lessons or hire canoes and, with a new extension, there is direct access to the beach from the site. There are 550 numbered pitches with 300 for tourers. Electricity (10A) is available at 275 large pitches and 125 have water, drainage, electricity and cable connections. They are on level, grassy fields (some by the beach), partly separated by hedges and some with shade from trees. A new building in the marina houses a restaurant, bar, shop and laundry, and also provides beautiful views over the Lauwersmeer.

Facilities

The two toilet blocks for tourers provide washbasins, preset showers and child sized toilets. Facilities for disabled visitors. Laundry. Campers' kitchen. Motorcaravan service. Shop. Restaurant (all year), bar and snack bar including takeaway service (1/4-1/10). New play area with bouncy castle. Minigolf at the beach. Sailing school. Canoe hire. Surfing lessons (July/Aug). Riding. Bicycle and go-kart hire. Boules. WiFi. Entertainment programme in high season. Off site: Golf 8 km.

Open: All year.

Directions

Follow N361 from Groningen north to Lauwersoog and then follow site signs. GPS: 53.40205, 6.21732

Charges guide

Per unit incl. 2 persons and 10A electricity	€ 28.50 - € 31.50
extra person	€ 4.75
dog	€ 4.75

Camping Cheques accepted.

Leeuwarden

Camping De Kleine Wielen

De Groene Ster 14, NL-8926 XE Leeuwarden (Friesland) T: 0511 431 660. E: info@dekleinewielen.nl

alanrogers.com/NL5750

Camping De Kleine Wielen (small wheels) is named after a small lake of the same name that lies in the 1,000 hectare nature and recreation area of De Groene Ster. The campsite is adjacent to the lake – possible activities include boating on the lake or cycling and walking around this beautiful area of forest, grassland and ponds. The site provides 360 pitches, of which 220 are for touring units. The remaining pitches are used for privately owned mobile homes. All the touring pitches have 4A electricity and many have wonderful views over the water and surrounding countryside.

Facilities

Four toilet blocks provide washbasins in cabins and preset showers (coin operated). Maintenance is variable. Facilities for disabled visitors. Motorcaravan service point. Shop (1/5-1/10). Café/restaurant and snack bar (1/4-30/9). Bar and takeaway service (1/4-1/10). Playground. Sports pitch. Minigolf. Lake with beach. Fishing. Rowing boats. Surf boards. Extensive recreation programme in July/Aug. Off site: Golf 1 km. Boat launching 2 km. Riding and bicycle hire 5 km.

Open: 1 April - 1 October.

Directions

From the N355 turn off east towards Leeuwarden and follow campsite signs. GPS: 53.21650, 5.88703

Charges guide

Per unit incl. 2 persons, electricity and car	€ 19.70
extra person	€ 4.45
child (2-12 yrs)	€ 2.70

Lierop

Camping De Somerense Vennen

Philipsbosweg 7, NL-5715 RE Lierop (Noord-Brabant) T: 0492 331 216. E: info@somerensevennen.nl

alanrogers.com/NL6690

De Somerense Vennen is an attractive site which underwent a large scale renovation programme in 2006. A very good range of children's activities are organised here, based around The Twinkle Club, which are suitable for children of all ages. There are 125 touring pitches, and these are of a good size and generally well shaded. Most have electrical connections. A number of mobile homes and chalets are available for rent. There is a convivial bar/restaurant, serving the best pancakes locally! The impressive swimming pool complex (with sliding roof) includes a special children's area and a good range of children's games.

Facilities

Swimming pool complex (can be covered). Bar, snack bar and restaurant. Riding centre. Children's playground. Children's club. Activity and entertainment programme. Tourist information. Mobile homes and chalets for rent. Off site: Walking in North Brabant. Shops, bars and restaurants at Someren-Heide.

Open: 26 March - 30 October.

Directions

Use A67 Eindhoven-Venlo motorway and leave at exit 35 (Someren). In Someren head towards Lierop and then follow signs to the site. GPS: 51.400403, 5.675804

Charges guide

Per unit incl. 2 persons and electricity	€ 19.50 - € 26.50
dog	€ 5.00

Maurik

Camping Eiland van Maurik

Eiland van Maurik 7, NL-4021 GG Maurik (Gelderland) T: 0344 691 502. E: receptie@eilandvanmaurik.nl

alanrogers.com/NL6290

Camping Eiland van Maurik is beside a lake in the centre of an extensive nature and recreation park in the Nederrijn area. These surroundings are ideal for all sorts of activities – swimming, windsurfing, water skiing or para-sailing, relaxing on the beach or fishing. There is even an animal farm for the children. The site has 365 numbered, flat pitches, with 260 for touring units, almost all with 10A electricity and cable TV connections and 64 also with water and drainage. You could enjoy pancakes in the Oudhollandse restaurant with its views over the water. There is direct access from the site to the lakeside beach.

Facilities

The three toilet blocks for tourers include washbasins (open style and in cabins), controllable showers and a baby room. Launderette with iron and board. Shop. Bar/restaurant/pizzeria (all season). Play areas (one indoors). Playing field. Tennis. Minigolf. Bicycle hire. Go-karts. Water-skiing. Sailing and motorboat hire. Para-sailing. Animal farm. Entertainment in high season (incl. riding). Max. 2 dogs. Off site: Golf 1 km.

Open: 1 April - 1 October.

Directions

From the A2 (Utrecht - 's Hertogenbosch) take the Culemborg exit towards Kesteren and follow signs for Eiland Maurik. From the A15 (Rotterdam - Nijmegen) take exit 33 Tiel towards Maurik and follow signs as above. GPS: 51.97656, 5.43013

Charges guide

Per unit incl. 2 persons and electricity	€ 18.00 - € 29.00
extra person	€ 4.00
dog	€ 4.00

No credit cards.
Camping Cheques accepted.

Meerkerk

Camping De Victorie

Broekseweg 75-77, NL-4231 VD Meerkerk (Zuid-Holland) T: 0183 352 741. E: info@campingdevictorie.nl

alanrogers.com/NL5690

Within an hour's drive of the port of Rotterdam you can be pitched on this delightful, spacious site in the green heart of the Netherlands. De Victorie, a working farm and a member of a club of small, 'green' sites, offers an alternative to the bustling seaside sites. A modern building houses reception, an open plan office and a space with tables and chairs, where the friendly owners may well invite you to have a cup of coffee. The 73 grass pitches (100-200 sq.m) are level and have 6A electricity supply. Everything about the site is surprising and contrary to any preconceived ideas.

Facilities

The main sanitary block is kept spotlessly clean, tastefully decorated and fully equipped. Showers are on payment. Laundry room. Additional sanitary facilities are around the site. Farm shop and small bar (once a week). Play area. Trampoline, and play field. Fishing. Riding. WiFi over site (charged). Off site: Bicycle hire 2 km.

Open: 15 March - 31 October.

Directions

From Rotterdam follow A15 to junction with the A27. Proceed 6 km. north on A27 to Noordeloos exit (25) and join N214. Site is signed about 200 m. after roundabout at Noordeloos. GPS: 51.93623, 4.95748

Charges guide

Per unit incl. 2 persons and electricity	€ 12.50
extra person	€ 3.00

No credit cards. Special rates for longer stays. Large units may be charged extra.

Nieuwvliet

Vakantiepark Pannenschuur

Zeedijk 19, NL-4504 PP Nieuwvliet (Zeeland) T: 0117 372 300. E: info@pannenschuur.nl

alanrogers.com/NL5500

This is one of several coastal sites on the narrow strip of The Netherlands between the Belgian frontier near Knokke and the Breskens ferry. Quickly reached from the ports of Ostend, Zeebrugge and Vlissingen, it is useful for overnight stops or for a few days to enjoy the seaside. A short walk across the quiet coast road and steps over the dike bring you to the open, sandy beach. Quite a large site, most of the 595 pitches are taken by permanent or seasonal holiday caravans but there are also 165 pitches for tourists, mostly in their own areas.

Facilities

Four toilet blocks including two new, heated buildings, provide first-class facilities including children's washrooms, baby rooms and some private cabins. Launderette. Motorcaravan services. Gas supplies. Supermarket. Restaurant, snack bar and takeaway. Swimming pool, sauna and solarium. Large games room with soft drinks bar. Internet access. Playground and playing field. Bicycle hire. Organised activities in season. Max. 2 dogs. Off site: Fishing 500 m. Riding 2 km. Golf 5 km.

Open: All year (all amenities closed 14/1-31/1).

Directions

At Nieuwvliet, on the Breskens - Sluis minor road, 8 km. southwest of Breskens, turn towards the sea at sign for Nieuwvliet-Bad and follow signs to site GPS: 51.38355, 3.44052

Charges guide

Per unit (max. 5 persons) incl. electricity	€ 25.00 - € 40.00
extra person	€ 4.00

Rates available for weekly stays.

Noord-Scharwoude

Buitencentrum Molengroet

Molengroet 1, NL-1723 PX Noord-Scharwoude (Noord-Holland) T: 0226 393 444. E: info@molengroet.nl

alanrogers.com/NL5700

Molengroet is a pleasant, modern site, located near a watersports complex and only 40 km. from Amsterdam. It is a good place to stop on the way to the Afsluitdijk (the 32 km. dike across the top of the IJsselmeer) or as an ideal holiday site for watersports enthusiasts. The pitches are grouped according to services provided, ranging from pitches with just 6A electricity and TV connections, to fully serviced pitches with 10A electricity, TV, water and drainage. Other pitches have private sanitary facilities, others are used for chalets. Recent developments to the park's facilities include a play area, a heated swimming pool, a sports field and a children's farm. A member of the Holland Tulip Parcs Group.

Facilities

Modern, heated sanitary facilities. Some private facilities for rent. Motorcaravan services. Gas supplies. Shop. Restaurant/bar. Café and takeaway snacks. Swimming pool. Play area. Children's farm. Sports field. Fishing. Bicycle hire. Surfboards and small boats for hire. Entertainment in high season. Off site: Watersports. Tennis, squash, sauna, and swimming nearby. Riding and golf 5 km.

Open: 1 April - 31 October.

Directions

From Haarlem on A9 to Alkmaar take N245 towards Schagen. Site is southwest of Noord Sharwoude on the N245, signed to west on road to Geestermerambacht GPS: 52.69455, 4.77103

Charges guide

Per unit incl. 2 persons and electricity	€ 19.00 - € 26.00

Reductions in low season and for longer stays. Camping Cheques accepted.

Ommen

Camping De Roos

Beerzerweg 10, NL-7736 PJ Beerze-Ommen (Overijssel) T: 0523 251 234. E: info@campingderoos.nl

alanrogers.com/NL5980

De Roos is a family run site in an area of outstanding natural beauty, truly a nature lover's campsite, immersed in an atmosphere of tranquillity. It is situated in Overijssel's Vecht Valley, a unique region set in a river dune landscape on the River Vecht. The river and its tributary wind their way unhurriedly around and through this spacious campsite. It is a natural setting that the owners of De Roos have carefully preserved. The 285 pitches and necessary amenities have been blended into the landscape with great care. Pitches, most with electricity hook-up (6A Europlug), are naturally sited, some behind blackthorn thickets, in the shadow of an old oak, or in a clearing scattered with wild flowers. For some there are lovely views over the Vecht river. De Roos is a car-free campsite during peak periods – vehicles must be parked at the car park, except on arrival and departure. Swimming, fishing and boating are possible in the river, or from an inlet that runs up into the site where there is a small beach with a protected area for swimming and landing stages with steps. The enthusiastic owners have compiled walking and cycling routes which are written in English and follow the ever-changing countryside of the Vecht Valley.

Facilities

Four well maintained sanitary blocks are kept fresh and clean. The two larger blocks are heated and include baby bath/shower and wash cabins. Launderette. Motorcaravan services. Gas supplies. Health food shop and tea room (1/5-1/9). Bicycle hire. Boules. Several small playgrounds and field for kite flying. River swimming. Fishing. Dogs are not accepted (and cats must be kept on a lead!). Torch useful. Off site: Riding 6 km. Golf 10 km.

Open: 6 April - 1 October.

Directions

Leave A28 at Ommen exit 21 and join N340 for 19 km. to Ommen. Turn right at traffic lights over bridge and immediately left on local road towards Beerze. Site on left after 7 km. just after Beerze village sign. GPS: 52.51078, 6.51537

Charges 2012

Per unit incl. 2 persons and electricity	€ 17.90 - € 20.90
extra person	€ 3.00 - € 3.70
child (under 3 yrs)	free

Discounts in low season and special packages.

Ommen

Vrijetijdspark Beerze Bulten

alan rogers Winner 2011 Awards

Kampweg 1, NL-7736 PK Beerze-Ommen (Overijssel) T: 0523 251 398. E: info@beerzebulten.nl

alanrogers.com/NL5985

Beerze Bulten is a large leisure park with all the amenities one could think of. Beside reception is a large, partly underground 'rabbit hole' providing a large indoor playground for children, a theatre for both indoor and outdoor shows and a buffet. Beerze Bulten has over 500 pitches, mainly for touring units, but also accommodation for hire. In the shade of mature woodland, all the pitches are level and numbered, and all have 10A Europlug electricity, water, drainage and TV connections. To the rear of the site is a large lake area with a sandy beach and adventure play equipment. Centrally located on the site is a full wellness spa centre.

Facilities

Several toilet blocks, well placed around the site, with toilets, washbasins in cabins and hot showers (key). Laundry. Shop. Bar and restaurant with open-air terrace. Snack bar. Heated indoor and outdoor pool complex and spa centre. Multisports court. Bicycle hire. Indoor playground and theatre. Playgrounds. WiFi. Full entertainment team in season and school holidays. Dogs only allowed on some fields.

Open: All year.

Directions

From A28, take exit 21 for Ommen and continue east towards Ommen. From Ommen, follow the N34 northeast and turn south on N36 at crossing. Site is signed from there. GPS: 52.51139, 6.54618

Charges guide

Per unit incl. 2 persons and full service pitch	€ 22.50 - € 44.40
extra person	€ 4.00 - € 5.10
dog	€ 3.50

Ommen

Camping De Koeksebelt

Zwolseweg 13, NL-7731 BC Ommen (Overijssel) T: **0529 451 378.** E: **info@koeksebelt.nl**

alanrogers.com/NL6466

Camping De Koeksebelt is a well maintained, green site with 250 fully serviced, spacious touring pitches. All are equipped with 10A electricity, water, drainage and TV cable connections and are accessed off paved roads. Some hardstandings are available. Many of the pitches are on the banks of the river and are ideal for anglers as they can fish from their pitch. Good play areas will appeal to both children and their parents. The sanitary facilities are modern and very well maintained. The site borders a large wooded area and is within walking distance of the town Ommen where the amenities include a swimming pool. Member of the Ardoer Group.

Facilities

Three modern toilet blocks with toilets, washbasins in cabins and controllable hot showers. Free bathroom. Baby room. Toilet for disabled visitors. Laundry with washing machines, dryers, spin dryer, iron and board. Small shop for basics. Canteen for drinks and light meals. Playing field. Tennis. Fishing. Watersports. Boules. Free boats for fishing. Internet access and WiFi. Max. 2 dogs per pitch. Off site: Bicycle hire 1.5 km. Golf 8 km. Riding 25 km.

Open: 31 March - 31 October.

Directions

From the A28 take exit for Ommen and continue east towards Ommen on the N340. In Ommen, go right at traffic lights to cross the Vecht River. After 300 m. turn right at exit r102 and site is on the right after 500 m. GPS: 52.51668, 6.41395

Charges guide

Per unit incl. 2 persons and electricity	€ 23.00 - € 30.50
extra person	€ 4.50

No credit cards.

Oosterhout

Camping De Katjeskelder

Katjeskelder 1, NL-4904 SG Oosterhout (Noord-Brabant) T: **0162 453 539.** E: **kkinfo@katjeskelder.nl**

alanrogers.com/NL5540

This site is to be found in a wooded setting in a delightful area of Noord-Brabant. It is well established and offers extensive facilities with a new and impressive ultra-modern reception area. Around the 25 hectare site there are many bungalows and 102 touring pitches, all with electricity and water, plus 13 fully serviced pitches. Motorcaravans are now accepted (on hardstandings near the entrance), as well as tents and caravans. The site has a cat theme, hence the cat names including that of the restaurant, the Gelaarsde Kat (Puss in Boots) which is situated in the Tropikat complex.

Facilities

One modern, heated sanitary block (may be stretched in high season) provides facilities including a family shower room, baby room and provision for disabled visitors. Laundry. Supermarket. Restaurant, bar, snack bar, pizzeria and takeaway. Indoor tropical pool. Outdoor swimming pools (all season). Tennis. Bicycle hire. Minigolf. Play areas for small children. Adventure playground. Entertainment for children. Off site: Oosterheide nature park.

Open: All year.

Directions

From A27 Breda - Gorinchem motorway take Oosterhout Zuid exit 17 and follow signs for 7 km. to site. GPS: 51.62998, 4.83210

Charges guide

Per unit incl. up to 5 persons, electricity, water and TV connections	€ 22.00 - € 39.00
extra person	€ 4.00

Opende

Camping 't Strandheem

Parkweg 2, NL-9865 VP Opende (Groningen) T: **0594 659 555.** E: **info@strandheem.nl**

alanrogers.com/NL6120

Camping 't Strandheem has 330 quite large, numbered pitches (110 sq.m) some with hardstanding and suitable for motorcaravans. All with electricity (4 or 10A), there are 180 used for touring units, partly separated by low hedges but without much shade. Of these, 45 pitches have water points, drainage and cable TV connections. The De Bruinewoud family will give you a warm welcome. The reception building houses an attractive bar, a full restaurant, a disco for teenagers and a shop. The site has a lot to offer, especially for youngsters with an entertainment programme in high season with water games in the lake next to the site, a games area and an indoor pool.

Facilities

Two modern toilet buildings have washbasins, controllable showers, child sized toilets and basins, a baby room and fully equipped bathroom. Facilities for disabled campers. Launderette. Motorcaravan service. Shop. Restaurant and bar. Café and snack bar. Covered swimming pool (5x5 m) with separate paddling pool. Playgrounds. New indoor play hall. Minigolf. Fishing. Bicycle hire. Boules. Lake with beach (€ 1 p/p per day). Extensive recreation programme (July/Aug). Film and card nights. Internet. WiFi (free). Off site: Lake with beach 100 m. Riding 6 km. Golf 15 km.

Open: 1 April - 1 October.

Directions

Follow A7 west from Groningen towards Heerenveen and take exit 31. Follow campsite signs from there. GPS: 53.15278, 6.19138

Charges 2012

Per unit incl. 2 persons and electricity	€ 17.50 - € 28.00
extra person	€ 4.50
private sanitary facility	€ 7.50 - € 9.00
dog (max. 2)	€ 3.25 - € 4.50

Camping Cheques accepted.

Otterlo

Droompark De Zanding

Vijverlaan 1, NL-6731 CK Otterlo (Gelderland) T: **0318 596 111**. E: **info@zanding.nl**

alanrogers.com/NL5780

De Zanding is a highly rated, family run site that offers almost every recreational facility, either on site or nearby, that active families or couples might seek. Immediately after the entrance, a lake is to the left where you can swim, fish, sunbathe or try a two-person canoe. There are many sporting options and organised high season programmes for all ages. There are 463 touring pitches spread around the site (all with 4/6/10A electricity), some individual and separated, others in more open spaces shaded by trees. Some serviced pitches are in small groups between long stay units and there is another area for tents. A member of the Holland Tulip Parcs Group.

Facilities

First class sanitary facilities are housed in five modern blocks that are clean, well maintained and well equipped. Good provision for babies and disabled guests. Laundry. Kitchen. Motorcaravan services. Gas supplies. Supermarket. Restaurant/bar (30/3-28/10). Lake swimming. Fishing. Tennis. Minigolf. Boules. Five play areas. Bicycle hire. Organised activities.

Open: 3 April - 31 October.

Directions

Leave A12 Utrecht - Arnhem motorway at Oosterbeek at exit 25 and join N310 to Otterlo. Then follow camping signs to site, watching carefully for entrance. GPS: 52.09310, 5.77757

Charges guide

Per unit incl. 2 persons and electricity	€ 21.00 - € 32.90
extra person	€ 4.70

Camping Cheques accepted.

Ouddorp

Recreatiepark De Klepperstee

Vrijheidsweg 1, NL-3253 ZG Ouddorp (Zuid-Holland) T: **0187 681 511**. E: **info@klepperstee.com**

alanrogers.com/NL6960

De Klepperstee is a good quality family site, peacefully located in tranquil countryside amid renowned nature reserves and just outside the village of Ouddorp in Zuid-Holland. It offers excellent recreation areas that are spread over the centre of the site giving it an attractive open parkland appearance which is enhanced by many shrubs, trees and grass areas. The 338 spacious touring pitches are in named avenues, mostly separated by hedging and spread around the perimeter, together with the seasonal and static caravans. A variety of play equipment ensures hours of non-stop fun for children.

Facilities

One main sanitary block and a number of WC/shower units around the touring area provide free hot showers, washbasins, some in cabins (hot water only), baby bath and shower, child sized toilets and a unit for campers with disabilities. Laundry. Motorcaravan service point. Supermarket. Restaurant, bar and takeaway. Play areas. Tennis. TV, pool and electronic games. Entertainment. No animals are accepted. Off site: Fishing 500 m. Beach 600 m. Riding, bicycle hire 4 km. Golf 10 km.

Open: Easter - 31 October.

Directions

From Rotterdam follow A15 west to Rozenburg exit 12 and join N57 south for 22 km. Take exit for Ouddorp and follow signs for 'Stranden'. Site is on the left after about 3 km. GPS: 51.8161, 3.89958

Charges guide

Per unit incl. up to 4 persons	€ 10.00 - € 29.00
incl. 6A electricity	€ 12.50 - € 31.50
incl. 10A electricity	€ 17.50 - € 34.00
extra person	€ 2.75

Renesse

Camping Strandpark De Zeeuwse Kust

alan rogers Runner up 2011 Awards

Helleweg 8, NL-4326 LJ Noordwelle/Renesse (Zeeland) T: **0111 468 282.**

E: **info@strandparkdezeeuwsekust.nl** **alanrogers.com/NL6948**

Camping De Zeeuwse Kust opened in April 2007. This site is positioned on the island of Schouwen-Duivenland, at the foot of the dunes and just five minutes from the well known seaside resort of Renesse. This site has 168 pitches which are spacious and comfortable. The luxurious sanitary facilities are heated and also provide facilities for disabled visitors. Some pitches have private sanitary provision. The sea offers plenty of opportunities for kite surfing, windsurfing and sailing and there are also plenty of walks possible through the dunes. For those who cannot sail but would like to learn, there is a sailing school where you can have lessons.

Facilities

New, first-class sanitary building providing showers, washbasins, private cabins, family shower rooms and other facilities for children and disabled visitors. Launderette. Cooking facilities. Shop. Fresh bread (May-Sept). Excellent heated swimming pool. Play areas (indoors and outdoors). Entertainment team. Barbecue area. First aid post. WiFi. Off site: Riding 500 m. Golf 7 km. Boat launching 7.5 km.

Open: All year (with most facilities)..

Directions

From the A15 take exit 12 towards Middelburg. Follow the N57 through Ouddorp and then turn right on the N652. Immediately turn left for the N651 and follow to Nordwelle. Site is well signed. GPS: 51.739062, 3.802369

Charges guide

Per unit incl. 2 persons and electricity	€ 19.00 - € 45.00
extra person (over 3 yrs)	€ 5.75

Renesse

Camping De Wijde Blick

Lagezoom 23, NL-4325 CP Renesse (Zeeland) T: **0111 468 888**. E: **wijdeblick@ardoer.com**

alanrogers.com/NL5560

The Van Oost family run this neat campsite in a pleasant and personal way. It is located on the outskirts of the village of Renesse in a quiet rural spot. The beach is only 2 km. away and from May to September a free shuttle bus runs to Renesse and the beach. De Wijde Blick has 316 pitches with 234 for touring units, all with 6/10A electricity and TV connections, and 90-120 sq.m. in area. Of these, 16 have private sanitary facilities and 203 are fully serviced. There are 20 attractively arranged motorcaravan pitches with hardstanding. There are special 'bike and hike' pitches for those touring without a car. Those with cars must park away from the pitch areas.

Facilities

Three modern toilet blocks are first class, heated and with clean facilities including washbasins in cabins, controllable showers and facilities for disabled campers. Microwave and fridge. Bath (on payment). Laundry (with cartoons for children). Gas supplies. Motorcaravan services. Shop. Restaurant/bar (15/3-31/10). Swimming pool (1/5-15/9). WiFi throughout (charged). Good playground. Bicycle hire. Activities for children. Dogs are not accepted 1/7-23/8. Hotel chalets for rent. Off site: Tennis and minigolf. Riding and golf 1.5 km. Beach 2 km. Fishing 2 km.

Open: All year.

Directions

Renesse is on the island of Schouwen (connected to the mainland by a bridge and three dams). On the N57 from Middelburg take the Renesse exit. After 2 km. follow road 106 to the left and then site signs. Site is on the east side of the village.
GPS: 51.71843, 3.76713

Charges guide

Per unit incl. 2 persons	€ 17.00 - € 29.50
extra person	€ 4.50

Renesse

Camping International Renesse

Scharendijkseweg 8, NL-4325 LD Renesse (Zeeland) T: **0111 461 391**. E: **info@camping-international.net**

alanrogers.com/NL6950

Situated 300 m. from the beach at Renesse in Zeeland, this is a friendly, family run site. Its owners have set a high standard, which is demonstrated by the immaculate and tastefully decorated sanitary facilities. There are 200 pitches, all for touring units and with electricity connections (16A). These are a generous size and laid out in bays and avenues surrounded by hedging. Around a courtyard area beyond reception is a supermarket and a bar which is attractively decorated with novel figures and the owner's personal memorabilia. Outside bench seating and umbrellas turns this corner of the site into a popular meeting place.

Facilities

Two luxury sanitary blocks provide showers, washbasins (some in cabins) and a baby room. Laundry room. Motorcaravan service point. Supermarket. Bar. Games room. TV. Play area. Bicycle hire. Entertainment in high season for all. Max. 1 dog.

Open: 1 March - 31 October.

Directions

From Zierikzee follow N59 to Renesse for about 15 km. and turn right at roundabout (before town) onto local road signed R101. Continue for about 1 km. and turn left, then first right to site on right.
GPS: 51.73981, 3.78912

Charges guide

Per unit incl. 2 persons	€ 26.40 - € 38.10
extra person	€ 4.85
child (2-9 yrs)	€ 4.10
electricity per kWh	€ 0.37

Renesse

Camping Julianahoeve

Hoogenboomlaan 42, NL-4325 DM Renesse (Zeeland) T: **0111 461 414**. E: **julianahoeve@ardoer.com**

alanrogers.com/NL6952

A very large site with 1,400 pitches, Camping Julianahoeve has 383 for touring units. You cannot get much closer to the sea in The Netherlands and the site is right beside the beach via a path through the dunes. The island of Schouwen-Duiveland is said to be the sunniest place in The Netherlands, so you will probably be using the beach quite often. The grass pitches vary in size (80-120 sq.m), all have electricity (6/16A) and 140 are fully serviced. They are arranged in areas that are separated by hedging. A member of the Ardoer Group.

Facilities

Several well appointed toilet blocks serve the site with facilities for younger children, babies and disabled visitors. Launderette. Supermarket. Café with terrace. Snack bar. Indoor pool complex. Play areas. Sports pitches. WiFi. Dogs are not accepted. Off site: Fishing 500 m. Golf and riding 1 km. Boat launching 5 km.

Open: 1 April - 6 November.

Directions

From the A5 take exit 12 and follow the N57 through Ouddorp, then follow signs to Renesse. Site is well signed from the town. GPS: 51.72738, 3.75897

Charges guide

Per unit incl. 2 persons and electricity	€ 16.00 - € 30.50
extra person (over 2 yrs)	€ 4.00 - € 5.00

Retranchement

Camping Cassandria-Bad

Strengeweg 4, NL-4525 LW Retranchement (Zeeland) T: **0117 392 300**. E: **info@cassandriabad.nl**

alanrogers.com/NL5502

Cassandria-Bad was established in 1992, and lies very close to the Belgian border and the resort of Cadzand Bad, just less than 2 km. from the nearest North Sea beach. Pitches are grassy and of a reasonable size; some are privately let for the full season. All pitches are equipped with 10A electricity and cable TV connections. Unusually, except for loading and unloading, cars are not allowed in the camping area, and a large parking area is provided at the entrance. On-site amenities include a snack bar, small shop and games room. During the peak season, a variety of activities are organised, including karaoke, bingo and sports tournaments. This part of The Netherlands, south of the Schelde, has strong contacts with Belgium and trips to Bruges and Gent are popular. Retranchement translates as 'bulwarks' and there are still remains of vast earthen sea walls, although now this area is best known as a paradise for nature lovers and walkers.

Facilities

Small shop with daily delivery of fresh bread. Snack bar. Sports field. Games room. Playground. Off site: Nearest beach 1.7 km. Walking and cycle routes. Fishing 5 km.

Open: 1 April- 31 October.

Directions

Approaching from the west and Bruges, use the Belgian N31 and then N376 towards Knokke-Heist and then across the Dutch border to Sluis. Here take the road to Groede and turn left towards Cadzand-Bad at the second crossroads. Site is well signed from here. GPS: 51.36613, 3.38583

Charges guide

Per unit incl. up to 4 persons	€ 28.50
extra person	€ 3.75

Discounts available in low season.

Rijnsburg

Kawan Village Koningshof

Elsgeesterweg 8, NL-2231 NW Rijnsburg (Zuid-Holland) T: **0714 026 051**. E: **info@koningshofholland.nl**

alanrogers.com/NL5630

This popular site is run in a personal and friendly way. The 200 pitches for touring units (some with hardstandings for larger units) are laid out in groups of four or twelve, divided by hedges and trees and all with electrical connections (10A). Cars are mostly parked in areas around the perimeter and 100 static caravans, confined to one section of the site, are entirely unobtrusive. Reception, a pleasant good quality restaurant, bar and a snack bar are grouped around a courtyard style entrance which is decorated with seasonal flowers. The site has a small outdoor, heated pool (13.5x7 m) with a separate paddling pool and imaginative children's play equipment. A member of the Holland Tulip Parcs Group.

Facilities

Three good toilet blocks, two with underfloor heating, with washbasins in cabins and provision for disabled visitors. Laundry facilities. Motorcaravan services. Gas supplies. Shop (1/4-15/10). Bar (1/4-1/11). Restaurant (1/4-10/9). Snacks and takeaway (1/4-1/11). Small outdoor pool (unsupervised; 15/5-15/9). Indoor pool (1/4-1/11). Solarium. Adventure playground and sports area. Tennis. Fishing pond (free). Bicycle hire. Entertainment in high season. Room for shows. Max. 1 dog, accepted in a limited area of the site. WiFi over site. Off site: Sandy beach 5 km. Riding and golf 5 km. Den Haag 15 km. and Amsterdam 30 km.

Open: 16 March - 16 November.

Directions

From N44/A44 Den Haag - Amsterdam motorway, take exit 7 for Oegstgeest and Rijnsburg. Turn towards Rijnsburg and follow site signs. GPS: 52.20012, 4.45623

Charges 2012

Per unit incl. 2 persons and electricity	€ 29.50 - € 32.50

Senior citizen discounts, group rates and special packages.
Camping Cheques accepted.

Roermond

Resort Marina Oolderhuuske

Oolderhuuske 1, NL-6041 TR Roermond (Limburg) T: **0475 588 686**. E: **info@oolderhuuske.nl**

alanrogers.com/NL6515

When staying on this interesting site, which is part of a resort complex, you know you are on holiday. The site is situated at the end of an island, on a low lying spit of land in the River Maas and has 220 pitches, 80 of which are for touring. All have electricity (6/16A) water and drainage, are level, grassed and many are waterside – no pitch lies more than 60 m. from the water. From the campsite beach and jetty there are wide ranging views over large stretches of open water. The easiest connection to the mainland and shopping is via the site passenger/cycle ferry.

Facilities

One floating block and two Portacabin style sanitary units provide toilets, free showers, washbasins and outside sinks. Motorcaravan service point. Shop and bar (weekends and high season), restaurant with terrace (all season), snacks and takeaway. Small indoor swimming pool, gym, sauna, steam bath, solarium. Sport fields. Tennis. Playgrounds. Bicycle hire. Boat launching. High season entertainment. Boating, sailing, swimming and fishing. Barrier deposit € 50. WiFi over site (charged). Off site: Floating houses with their gardens, trees and boat mooring point within walking distance of campsite.

Open: 1 April - 31 October.

Directions

Site is on an island in the Maas west of Roermond. Coming from Maastricht on the A2 (Maastricht - Eindhoven) take exit for Roermond and Maasbracht and continue to Roermond (centrum). In Roermond follow signs for Eindhoven and, just after the Muse river bridge (Maasbrug) turn right to Hatenboer/de Weerd. Follow brown signs to Marina Oolderhuuske. GPS: 51.19195, 5.94942

Charges guide

Per unit incl. up to 4 persons and electricity	€ 24.50 - € 35.50
dog	€ 4.00

Roggel

Recreatiepark De Leistert

Heldensedijk 5, NL-6088 NT Roggel (Limburg) T: **0475 493 030**. E: **info@leistert.nl**

alanrogers.com/NL6550

This large, long-established site in the wooded Limburg province of south Holland provides 1,200 pitches, of which 750 are touring pitches. With its varied amenities, the site would be a good choice for families with small children and teenagers. Most of the pitches are unseparated, arranged in hedged groups with tall, mature trees. They are serviced with electricity (4-10A), cable TV connections, water and drainage. Plenty of activities are possible with indoor and outdoor swimming pools, a lake (with a sandy beach) for boating and fishing, and bicycle hire. A recreation programme is organised for all ages in high season.

Facilities

Six excellent toilet buildings are fully equipped, with good facilities for children. Covered plaza with supermarket, bar, restaurant, snack bar, games and TV room and disco, indoor pool, sauna, gym and massage. Outdoor pool (both pools with lifeguard). Minigolf. Tennis. Play areas. Rowing, fishing and sandy beach. Barber. Bicycle hire with plentiful racks all over the site. Gas refill at supermarket. Recreation programme (high season). Chalets to rent. Dogs are not accepted. Off site: Golf 15 km.

Open: 1 April - 1 November.

Directions

From Eindhoven (A2) take A67 (Venlo) and exit for Asten Meijel. At Roggel roundabout turn left on the N562 (Helden) to site. From Nijmegen take the A73 (Venlo), then N273 (Maastricht). In Neer turn right towards Roggel and on to site. GPS: 51.274105, 5.931971

Charges guide

Per unit incl. 2 persons incl. electricity	€ 17.00 - € 33.50
extra person	€ 5.50

Schipborg

Camping De Vledders

Zeegserweg, NL-9469 PL Schipborg (Drenthe) T: **0504 091 489**. E: **info@devledders.nl**

alanrogers.com/NL6130

Camping De Vledders is set in the centre of one of the most beautiful nature reserves in Holland, between the Drentse Hondsrug and the Drentsche Aa river. This attractive site is landscaped with many varieties of trees and shrubs. There are 130 touring pitches (all with 6A electricity) on rectangular, grassy fields, separated by well kept hedges. The level pitches are around 100 sq.m. in size with some shade provided at the back from mature trees and hedges. Static units and seasonal pitches are on separate fields. In one corner of the site there is an attractive lake with sandy beaches.

Facilities

Two refurbished, heated toilet blocks with washbasins (open style and in cabins) and controllable hot showers. Family shower rooms. Baby room. En-suite facilities for disabled visitors. Shop for basics. Snack bar. TV in reception. Lake with fishing, boating and windsurfing. Football field. Riding. Nordic walking. Playground. Torch useful. Off site: Bicycle hire 2 km. Golf 10 km.

Open: April - October.

Directions

From the A28 take exit 35 and continue towards Zuidlaren. Just before Zuidlaren follow signs for Schipborg and then site signs. GPS: 53.079267, 6.665617

Charges guide

Per unit incl. 2 persons and electricity	€ 19.15 - € 22.95
extra person (over 1 yr)	€ 3.25
dog	€ 2.85

Sellingen

Campingpark De Barkhoorn

Beetserweg 6, NL-9551 VE Sellingen (Groningen) T: 0599 322510. E: info@barkhoorn.nl

alanrogers.com/NL6115

Camping De Barkhoorn is located in the Westerwolde southeast of Groningen. The campsite is surrounded by vast forests and heathland, interspersed with beautiful ponds. A car-free site, there are 152 touring pitches (including 13 'comfort' pitches) and pitches for motorcaravans, 82 permanent pitches and six cabins for rent. Tall trees provide plenty of shade. This is a pleasant family campsite, ideal for families with children. There are spacious green areas and in the holidays a recreation team provides entertainment and activities. There is a large natural recreational lake where you can swim. Adjacent to the site are a heated outdoor pool, an outdoor theatre and tennis courts.

Facilities

Four sanitary buildings including one without hot water. Private facilities to rent. Facilities for disabled visitors. Launderette. Shop. Bar and terrace. Restaurant. Snack bar. Swimming pool with slide and toddlers' pool. Play areas. Recreation lake with beach. Sports field. Minigolf. Tennis. Bowling and other activities. Bicycle hire. Fishing. Canoeing. WiFi. Cabins to rent.

Open: 1 April - 31 October.

Directions

Follow signs from Zwolle, Hoogeveen and Emmen for Ter Apel. Sellingen is on the main road between Ter Apel and Winschoten, 2 km. from the centre of Sellingen. Follow site signs from the village. GPS: 52.946406, 7.131192

Charges guide

Per unit incl. 2 persons and electricity	€ 17.50 - € 22.50
dog	€ 3.00

Sevenum

Recreatiecentrum De Schatberg

Midden Peelweg 5, NL-5975 MZ Sevenum (Limburg) T: 0774 677 777. E: info@schatberg.nl

alanrogers.com/NL6510

In a woodland setting of 96 hectares, this family run campsite is more reminiscent of a holiday village, with a superb range of activities that make it an ideal venue for families. Look out for the deer! A large site with 1,100 pitches and many mobile homes and seasonal or weekend visitors, there are 500 touring pitches. All have electricity (6/10/16A Europlug), cable, water and drainage and average 100-150 sq.m. in size. They are on rough grass terrain, mostly with shade, but not separated. Forty pitches have private sanitary facilities (two with sauna and jacuzzi). Road noise can be heard in some areas of this large campsite. The site is well situated for visits to Germany and Belgium, and easily accessible from the port of Zeebrugge. The surrounding countryside offers the opportunity to enjoy nature, either by cycling or walking. For the more 'stay on site' visitor, the location is excellent with several lakes for fishing, windsurfing and swimming, plus an extensive range of activities and a heated outdoor swimming pool (1/5-31/8). A feature at De Schatberg is the attractive restaurant/bar area and the reception and indoor pool (all year), manned by friendly staff.

Facilities

Five modern, fully equipped toilet blocks, supplemented by three small wooden toilet units to save night-time walks. Family shower rooms, baby baths and en-suite units for disabled visitors. Washing machines and dryers. Motorcaravan service point. Supermarket. Restaurant, bar and takeaway. Pizzeria. Pancake restaurant. Indoor and outdoor pools. Trampoline. Play areas. Fishing. Watersports. Bicycle hire. Games room. Bowling and an underground disco. Indoor playground. Entertainment weekends and high season. New waterski track for 2012. WiFi (charged). Off site: Golf 0.5 km.

Open: All year.

Directions

Site is 15 km. west-northwest of Venlo. Leave the A67 Eindhoven - Venlo motorway at Helden, exit 38. Travel north on the 277 for 500 m. and site is signed at new roundabout. GPS: 51.382964, 5.976147

Charges guide

Per unit incl. 2 persons and electricity	€ 18.16 - € 44.56
incl. up to 4 persons and electricity	€ 22.70 - € 55.70

Camping Cheques accepted.

Sint-Oedenrode

Camping De Kienehoef

Zwembadweg 35-37, NL-5491 TE Sint-Oedenrode (Noord-Brabant) T: 0413 472 877. E: info@kienehoef.nl

alanrogers.com/NL6790

Camping De Kienehoef is at Sint-Oedenrode in Noord-Brabant, which boasts many historical sights, including two castles. This site is well cared for and attractively laid out with reception to the right of the entrance and the site facilities to the left. Behind this area is a heated swimming pool. The generous pitches are mostly laid out in bays and placed between trees and shrubs to the right of a long avenue leading through the site. The touring pitches are on three separate fields amongst pitches used for caravan holiday homes. There are some 40 serviced pitches with electricity, water and drainage.

Facilities

Two modern, clean and well maintained toilet blocks include preset showers and some shower/wash cubicles, also family and baby rooms. Laundry area with iron and board. Motorcaravan services. Shop, restaurant/bar and snacks (all 1/5-15/9). Heated outdoor pool (1/5-15/9). Lake fishing. Bicycle hire. Sports field. Tennis. Dogs are not accepted. Off site: Golf 1 km. Riding 15 km.

Open: 28 March - 28 October.

Directions

Leave A2 's Hertogenbosh - Eindhoven motorway at exit 27 and follow signs to Sint-Oedenrode. Site is well signed from village. GPS: 51.57755, 5.44682

Charges guide

Per unit incl. 2 persons and electricity	€ 24.00 - € 29.00

Camping Cheques accepted.

Sumar

Recreatiecentrum Bergumermeer

Solcamastraat 30, NL-9262 ND Sumar (Friesland) T: 0511 461 385. E: info@bergumermeer.nl

alanrogers.com/NL6040

Recreatiecentrum Bergumermeer's location beside the Bergum lake, makes it ideal for lovers of watersports, with sailing, surfing and canoeing available, as well as swimming from two sandy beaches. There is also a large, heated indoor swimming pool with fun paddling pool and an indoor play hall. The site provides 300 good sized, flat touring pitches for both caravans and tents, some having attractive views over the Prinses Margrietkanaal and the surrounding countryside, others with views over the lake. All pitches are fully serviced with 10A electricity, water and drainage, and there are ten large hardstandings.

Facilities

Three sanitary buildings offer private cabins, children's toilets, baby bath and facilities for disabled visitors. Children's section in one block. Launderette. Freezer. Shop. Bar/restaurant. Pancake restaurant. Heated indoor pool. Solarium. Play area. Children's farm. Tennis. Minigolf. Fishing. Sailing dinghies, motorboats and canoes for hire. Entertainment programme in high season. Club space with disco. Bicycle hire. Boat launching. Beach. Off site: Riding 5 km. Golf 19 km.

Open: 27 March - 31 October.

Directions

Either go north from Amsterdam via A7/E22 through Leeuwarden towards Drachten, or east from Amsterdam via A6, onto A7 (Leeuwarden, Groningen), then onto N31 (De Haven/Drachten) and in either case onto N356 towards Bergum following site signs. GPS: 53.19127, 6.12428

Charges guide

Per unit incl. 2 persons and electricity	€ 20.00 - € 29.00
extra person	€ 4.75
dog	€ 5.00

Uitdam

Camping Jachthaven Uitdam

Zeedijk 2, NL-1154 PP Uitdam (Noord-Holland) T: 0204 031 433. E: info@campinguitdam.nl

alanrogers.com/NL5720

Situated beside the Markermeer, which is used extensively for watersports, this large site has its own private yachting marina (300 yachts and boats). It has 200 seasonal and permanent pitches, but also offers 200 marked tourist pitches (140 with 4/16A electricity) on open, grassy ground overlooking the water and 32 mobile homes to rent. There is a special area for campers with bicycles. Very much dominated by the marina, this site will appeal to watersports enthusiasts, with opportunities for sailing, windsurfing and swimming, or for fishing, but it is also on a pretty stretch of coast. Much construction was underway when we visited, but this was mainly in the seasonal areas. All the touring pitches have been upgraded with new drainage and there are new cabins for rent. Uitdam is 15 km. northeast of Amsterdam and is close to the ancient, small towns of Marken, Volendam and Monnickendam, which are well worth a visit. The views over the IJsselmeer from both ends of the touring fields are wonderful and this alone makes this site well worth visiting.

Facilities

Two good toilet blocks and one rather basic one with toilets only. Good facilities include hot showers on payment, toilets, washbasins and a baby room. Motorcaravan services. Gas supplies. Shop (1/4-1/10). Bar/restaurant (weekends and high season). TV room. Tennis. Playground and paddling pool. Bicycle hire. Fishing. Yacht marina (with fuel) and slipway. Watersports. Entertainment in high season. WiFi. Off site: Riding 4 km.

Open: 1 March - 1 November.

Directions

From A10, take exit S116 onto the N247 towards Volendam. Then take Monnickendam exit south in direction of Marken on N518, then Uitdam. Site is just outside Uitdam. GPS: 52.42780, 5.07347

Charges 2012

Per unit incl. 2 persons and electricity	€ 19.60 - € 24.20
extra person (over 3 yrs)	€ 2.40 - € 3.00
boat on trailer	€ 6.15 - € 7.70

Vaals

Camping Rozenhof

Camerig 12, NL-6294 NB Vijlen-Vaals (Limburg) T: 0434 551 611. E: info@campingrozenhof.nl

alanrogers.com/NL6540

Camping Rozenhof is a friendly, family run site and its hillside location offers views over a valley that has won awards for its natural beauty. This partially wooded, hilly region is popular with countryside lovers, ramblers and cyclists. Rozenhof has 101 pitches arranged on a series of small terraced, hedged meadows. There are 82 for touring units, level and mainly on grass and all with electricity (4A). A number of mature trees afford some shade. A rustic restaurant, which can become overstretched in high season, is to the left of the wide entrance. There is a large terrace and, as the site's name suggests, roses and plants are much in evidence.

Facilities

To the rear of reception, the heated modern sanitary unit houses all the usual facilities including controllable showers (tokens), washbasins (open and in cabins). Facilities for disabled visitors. Baby room and family shower room. Washing machines and dryers. Shop. Restaurant/bar and takeaway. Gas supplies. Playground, play room and pets' corner for children. Riding. Bicycle hire. WiFi (free). Off site: Fishing 5 km. Riding 7 km. Golf 9 km.

Open: All year.

Directions

Leave A76/E314 at Knooppunt Bochtolz (not exit for Bocholtz town) and follow N281 southwest towards Vaals for 3 km. to T-junction with N278. Turn left, then first right (Mamelisserweg) to Vijlen. In Vijlen second road to the right (Vijlen Berg) and straight on for 4 km. to T-junction at the other side of the forest. Turn right and continue for 300 m. the site is to the right. GPS: 50.76982, 5.92842

Charges guide

Per unit incl. 2 persons and electricity	€ 15.00 - € 23.00
extra person (over 3 yrs)	€ 3.00
dog	€ 1.50

Vinkel

Vakantiepark Dierenbos

Vinkeloord 1, NL-5382 JX Vinkel (Noord-Brabant) T: **0735 343 536.** E: **info@libema.nl**

alanrogers.com/NL5880

Run by the same group as Beekse Bergen (NL5900), Dierenbos is a large site, with motel accommodation and a bungalow park in addition to its 500 camping pitches. These are divided into several grassy areas, many in an attractive wooded setting. There are 381 for touring units, all with electrical connections (4-10A) and some with full services (water and TV connection). A small, landscaped lake has sandy beaches and is overlooked by a large, modern play area. Some of the touring pitches also overlook the water. Campers are entitled to free entry to several attractions. The varied amenities are located in and around a modern, central complex. They include heated outdoor swimming pools, an indoor sub-tropical pool with slide and jetstream, and ten-pin bowling alley.

Facilities

Eight toilet blocks are well situated with clean and simple facilities (some unisex), some warm water for washing and some individual washbasins. Baby room. Supermarket. Bar. Modern restaurant. Snack bar/takeaway (high season). Free outdoor heated swimming pools (1/6-1/9). Indoor pool (on payment). Ten-pin bowling. Tennis. Minigolf. Boules. Sports field. Bicycle hire. Pedaloes. Fishing. Barbecue area. Play areas on sand. Organised activities in season. Conference facilities. Max. 1 dog.

Open: 21 March - 26 October.

Directions

Site is signed from the N50/A50 road between 's Hertogenbosch and Nijmegen, about 10 km. east of 's Hertogenbosch at Vinkel.
GPS: 51.70798, 5.43298

Charges guide

Per unit incl. 2 persons and electricity	€ 13.00 - € 28.00

Wanroij

Vakantiepark De Bergen

Campinglaan 1, NL-5446 PW Wanroij (Noord-Brabant) T: **0485 335 450.** E: **info@debergen.nl**

alanrogers.com/NL6635

Brabant is an attractive holiday region, within easy access of large cities such as Den Bosch and Nijmegen. This is a well equipped site with direct access to a lake beach. There are four grades of pitch, ranging from the relatively simple 'standard' pitch to 'top of the range' comfort pitches with 10A electricity, cable TV connections, water and drainage. Twin-axle caravans and units over 7.75 m. are not accepted. A range of chalets and mobile homes are available to rent. Several snack bars and restaurants can be found around the park, including Festina, a pleasant spot to watch the sun go down.

Facilities

Snack bars and restaurants. Fishing. Pedaloes. Bicycle hire. Adventure playground. Bowling. Pony rides. Children's playground. Sports field. Activity and entertainment programme. Tourist information. Mobile homes and chalets for rent. Direct lake access (suitable for swimming). Off site: Overloon zoo and Liberty park 14 km. Grave (pretty market town) 14 km. Nijmegen (oldest city in The Netherlands) 36 km.

Open: 1 April - 31 October.

Directions

Head south from Nijmegen on A73. Take the exit to Boxmeer and follow signs to St Anthonis. Here, head north on D602 to Wanroj, from where the site is clearly indicated. GPS: 51.64029, 5.81053

Charges guide

Per unit incl. 2 persons	€ 17.00 - € 28.00
electricity per kWh	€ 0.40
dog	€ 3.50

Wassenaar

Vakantiepark Duinrell

Duinrell 1, NL-2242 JP Wassenaar (Zuid-Holland) T: **0705 155 255.** E: **info@duinrell.nl**

alanrogers.com/NL5620

A very large site, Duinrell's name means 'well in the dunes' and the water theme is continued in the adjoining amusement park and in the extensive indoor pool complex. The campsite itself is very large with 900 tourist places on several flat grassy areas (80-100 sq.m) and it can become very busy in high season. As part of a continuing improvement programme, 850 marked pitches have electricity, water and drainage connections and some have cable TV. Amenities shared with the park include restaurants, a pizzeria and pancake house, supermarket and a theatre. Entry to the popular pleasure park is free for campers – indeed the camping areas surround and open out from the park.

Facilities

Six heated toilet blocks serve the touring areas. Laundry facilities. Amusement park and Tiki tropical pool complex. Restaurant, cafés, pizzeria and takeaways (weekends only in winter). Supermarket. Entertainment and theatre with shows in high season. Rope Challenge trail and Forest Frisbee trail. Bicycle hire. Mini-bowling. Diving experience package. All activities have extra charges. Off site: Beach 4 km. Riding 5 km. Golf 10 km.

Open: All year.

Directions

Site is signed from the N44/A44 (Den Haag - Amsterdam), but from the south the turning is 5 km. after passing sign for start of Wassenaar town – then follow site signs. GPS: 52.14642, 4.38737

Charges guide

Per unit incl. 2 persons and electricity	€ 28.40 - € 37.40

Special package offers. Overnight stays between 17.00-10.00 (when amusement park closed) less 25%.

Weidum

Camping WeidumerHout

Dekemawei 9, NL-9024 BE Weidum (Friesland) T: **0582 519 888**. E: **welkom@weidumerhout.nl**

alanrogers.com/NL5715

Camping WeidumerHout is a member of the Kleine Groene Campings group, literally 'small green campsites'. It has a beautiful rural location, close to the historic village of Weidum. There are 48 well spaced pitches (150 sq.m) with 10A electricity and two with hardstanding. The owner makes sure that all visitors can enjoy the great views over either the countryside or the river that runs past the site. The site has been developed on a farm that dates back to 1867 and has a tranquil, historic atmosphere. The site's fully equipped sauna (on payment) will add to your relaxation – owner Eddy de Boer will describe the benefits of a good sauna.

Facilities

Heated sanitary block with toilets, showers and basins. Baby room. Washing machine and dryer. Bar and restaurant. Sauna. Solarium. Library. Bicycle hire. Beach access plus fishing and boat launching. Canoe hire. WiFi (free). Fitness equipment. Torch useful. Off site: Shop and bus stop 800 m. Riding 5 km. Sailing 8km. Golf 12 km.

Open: All year, excl. Christmas - 1 January.

Directions

From Leeuwarden head south on the A32 and follow signs for Weidum. Just before entering the village, the site is on the right. GPS: 53.14906, 5.76166

Charges guide

Per unit incl. 2 persons and electricity	€ 21.25
extra person (over 2 yrs)	€ 5.75
dog	€ 2.00

Wezuperbrug

Rekreatiepark 't Kuierpadtien

Oranjekanaal NZ 10, NL-7853 TA Wezuperbrug (Drenthe) T: **0591 381 415**. E: **info@kuierpad.nl**

alanrogers.com/NL5790

Professionally run, this all year round site is suitable as a night stop, or for longer if you wish to participate in all the activities offered in July and August. The site itself is in a woodland setting on the edge of the village. The 525 flat and grassy pitches for touring units (with 653 in total) are of reasonable size. All have 4/6/10A electricity and 32 are fully serviced with electricity, TV aerial point, water and drainage. On-site activities include canoeing, windsurfing, water chutes and the dry ski slope, which is also open during the winter so that the locals can practice before going en-masse to Austria. A member of the Holland Tulip Parcs Group.

Facilities

Eight acceptable sanitary blocks, including a new one, with hot showers (07.30-10.00 in July/Aug). Facilities for disabled visitors. Laundry. Motorcaravan services. Supermarket (1/4-15/9) but bread all year. Restaurant and bar with TV. Takeaway. Indoor pool. Outdoor heated pool (1/5-15/9). Sauna, solarium and whirlpool. Dry ski slope. Play areas. Minigolf. Lake with beach. Boat rental. New High Rope Adventure Parc with 517 m. Zipwire. WiFi. Off site: Fishing 500 m. Riding 1 km. Golf 1.5 km.

Open: All year.

Directions

From N34 Groningen - Emmen road exit near Emmen onto N31 towards Beilen. Turn right into Schoonord where left to Wezuperbrug. Site is at beginning of village on the right. GPS: 52.84005, 6.72593

Charges 2012

Per unit incl. 2 persons and electricity	€ 20.00 - € 36.20
serviced pitch	€ 6.00

No credit cards.
Camping Cheques accepted.

Wijlre

Recreatieterrein De Gronselenput

Haasstad 3, NL-6321 PK Wijlre (Limburg) T: **0434 591 645**. E: **gronselenput@paasheuvelgroep.nl**

alanrogers.com/NL6580

Camping Gronselenput is a small, quiet, countryside site located at the end of a tree-lined lane. It is one of five sites run by the Paasheuvel Group in Holland. Family run, it has 60 grassy level pitches, 55 of which are for tourers, 40 having 6A electricity. With a peaceful location between a wooded hill and the river Geul (fishing allowed with permit), it is popular with visitors with younger children and those seeking a quiet site. Cars are parked separately from the camping area, thus ensuring vehicle-free space. The site is set out in a series of small hedged meadows with pitches tending to be located around the edges. Three gravel pitches are reserved for motorcaravans.

Facilities

In the sanitary block hot water for showers is free. Entry to the toilets is directly from outside. Two baby areas. Washing machines and spin dryer. Gas supplies. Shop (excellent English spoken). Bar selling pizzas with a partly covered terrace facing one of the playgrounds. Large room used for organised children's activities. WiFi over site (charged). Off site: Fishing 1 km. Bicycle hire 5 km. Riding 15 km. Golf 25 km.

Open: 2 April - 1 November.

Directions

Site is near village of Wijlre, 10 km. northwest of Aachen. Leave A4/E314/A76 at Knooppunt Bocholtz 2 km. northwest of the German border (not exit for Bocholtz town). Follow N281 southwest for 5 km. and at junction turn right (northwest) to Wittem on the N278. In Wittem, at traffic lights turn right on N595 to Wijlre. Just after entering Wijlre site is signed to the left. GPS: 50.842167, 5.877483

Charges guide

Per unit incl. 2 persons and electricity	€ 16.95 - € 24.80
extra person	€ 2.60

Winterswijk

Camping 't Hilgelomeer

Waliensestraat 137, NL-7103 EA Winterswijk (Gelderland) T: 0543 517 548. E: info@hilgelomeer.nl

alanrogers.com/NL6415

Camping 't Hilgelomeer enjoys a pleasant, quiet lakeside location close to a wooded area and the town of Winterswijk. Pitches here are generally grassy, open and of a good size and all with electric hook-ups (6/10A). Two sanitary units are satisfactory and the smaller one is found beside a number of fully equipped mobile homes and chalets, which are available for rent. The large lake has good fishing and swimming with an attractive sandy beach on the opposite bank. The surrounding countryside of the Achterhoek offers some fine walking and cycling opportunities. On-site amenities include a children's playground and a small area for ball games.

Facilities

Two sanitary units with basic facilities including showers (charged). One larger unit has laundry facilities and hot water (charged). Both have outside dishwashing areas. No shop, but bread to order daily. Motorcaravan service point. Multi-purpose room with TV and activities for all ages. Direct lake access. Fishing. Children's playground. Small games area. Managed waste area. Tourist information. Mobile homes and chalets for rent. Bicycle hire by arrangement. WiFi (charged). Off site: Riding 1.5 km. Swimming pool 2 km. Golf 5 km.

Open: 25 March - 16 October.

Directions

Site is north of Winterswijk. Approaching from the west (Arnhem) use A18 and N18 to Groenlo and then head south on N319 to Winterswijk. From here follow signs to the campsite.
GPS: 51.989493, 6.723029

Charges guide

Per unit incl. 2 persons and electricity	€ 16.30

Winterswijk

Vakantiepark De Twee Bruggen

Meenkmolenweg 13, NL-7109-AH Winterswijk (Gelderland) T: 0543 565 366. E: info@detweebruggen.nl

alanrogers.com/NL6425

De Twee Bruggen is a spacious recreation park set in the countryside. The pitches are divided between several fields of varying sizes. Although the fields are surrounded by tall trees, the ground is open and sunny. Indoor and outdoor swimming pools can be enjoyed by children and adults. At the indoor pool there is a covered terrace and, for relaxation, a sauna and jacuzzi. Adjacent to the pool is a small, openair theatre, where shows are staged in high season. The restaurant at the entrance of the campsite is of high quality and also attracts many outside visitors.

Facilities

Three modern, well maintained sanitary buildings include showers and washbasins in private cabins. Washing machines and dryers. Supermarket. Bar, restaurant and takeaway (all year). Heated outdoor pool (30/4-15/9). Heated indoor pool (all year). Paddling pool. Sauna. Jacuzzi. Supermarket. Tennis courts. Bicycle hire. Minigolf. Bowling. Playground. Bouncy castle. Deer field. Max. 2 dogs. Off site: Distance to fishing and beach 500 m. Riding 2 km. Golf 15 km.

Open: All year.

Directions

Take the A18 towards Varsseveld which will turn onto the N18. In Varsseveld follow signs for Aalten (N318). In Aalten follow signs for Winterswijk. Drive through Aalten and site is signed after about 4 km.
GPS: 51.94961, 6.6477

Charges guide

Per unit incl. 2 persons and electricity	€ 21.00 - € 39.50
extra person	€ 1.00 - € 2.00
dog	€ 3.00

Wolphaartsdijk

Camping De Veerhoeve

Veerweg 48, NL-4471 NC Wolphaartsdijk (Zeeland) T: 0113 581 155. E: info@deveerhoeve.nl

alanrogers.com/NL5580

This is a family run site near the shores of the Veerse Meer, which is ideal for family holidays. It is situated in a popular area for watersports and is well suited for sailing, windsurfing and fishing enthusiasts, with boat launching 100 m. away. A sandy beach and recreation area, ideal for children, is only a five minute walk. As with most sites in this area there are many mature static and seasonal pitches. However, part of the friendly, relaxed site is reserved for touring units with 90 marked pitches on grassy ground, all with electrical connections. A member of the Holland Tulip Parcs Group.

Facilities

Sanitary facilities in three blocks have been well modernised with full tiling. Hot showers are on payment. Laundry facilities. Motorcaravan services. Supermarket (all season). Restaurant and snack bar. TV room. Tennis. Playground and playing field. Games room. Bicycle hire. Fishing. Accommodation for groups. Max. 1 dog. WiFi (charged). Off site: Slipway for launching boats 100 m. Riding 2 km. Golf 5 km.

Open: 1 April - 30 October.

Directions

From N256 Goes - Zierikzee road take Wolphaartsdijk exit. Follow through village and signs to site (be aware – one of the site signs is obscured by other road signs and could be missed).
GPS: 51.54678, 3.81345

Charges guide

Per unit incl. up to 4 persons and electricity	€ 20.00 - € 27.00
dog	€ 4.00

Camping Cheques accepted.

Wolphaartsdijk

Camping Veerse Meer

Veerweg 71, NL-4471 NB Wolphaartsdijk (Zeeland) T: **0113 581 423.** E: **info@campingveersemeer.nl**

alanrogers.com/NL6920

This well cared for, family run site is situated beside the Veerse Meer on the island of Zuid-Beveland in Zeeland. Emphasis at this site is on a neat and tidy appearance, quality facilities and a friendly reception. The site spreads over both sides of the road. One area provides 15 pitches with individual sanitary facilities (some seasonal), fully serviced hardstanding pitches for motorcaravans and a tent field at the far end. There are 40 generous touring pitches in another area, many fully serviced and separated by hedging. Further seasonal and static places are kept apart. A feature of this campsite is a narrow canal crossed by a bridge.

Facilities

The single updated toilet block has showers (token operated), open style wash areas, two wash cabins, child sized WC and a baby bath. Laundry. Motorcaravan service point. Bar. WiFi throughout. Play area. Organised events for all in high season. Bicycle hire. Fishing.

Open: 1 April - 31 October.

Directions

From N256 Goes-Zierikzee road take Wolphaartsdijk exit. Follow through village and signs to site. GPS: 51.54436, 3.81242

Charges guide

Per unit incl. 2 persons and electricity	€ 15.00 - € 22.50
extra person	€ 2.50 - € 3.00

No credit cards.

Workum

Camping It Soal

Suderséleane 27, NL-8711 GX Workum (Friesland) T: **0515 541 443.** E: **info@itsoal.nl**

alanrogers.com/NL5710

This is an attractive, child-friendly site with 800 m. of beach, situated directly beside the IJsselmeer with a canal on one side. It is ideal for those who enjoy watersports as there are many activities on the lake, including windsurfing, sailing, swimming, fishing, or you can launch your own boat. There are 650 pitches here, of which 400 are good sized, individual, flat and grassy for tourers, with 4/6A electrical connections. A few pitches also have water and drainage. In separate areas, the other pitches are taken by seasonal guests and about 50 static units. Dogs are only allowed in one area and cars must be left in a car park.

Facilities

Sanitary facilities are clean and include toilets, washbasins (open and in private cabins) and free controllable showers. Facilities for disabled visitors. Baby room. Laundry facilities. Shop, restaurant and takeaway (1/4-1/10). Play areas. Tennis. Video games room. Skate track. Bicycle hire. Fishing. Boat launching. Beach. Surfboards and sailing boats for hire. Entertainment programme.
Off site: Riding 10 km. Golf 15 km. The surrounding areas are ideal for cycling, walking, skating and fishing.

Open: 1 April - 31 October.

Directions

From Groningen on the A7 (via Drachten, Joure and Sneek), exit just before Bolsward onto the N359 towards Workum, then exit Workum. Pass through village, follow sign (IJsselmeer) and then site signs. GPS: 52.96900, 5.41438

Charges guide

Per unit incl. 1 or 2 persons and electricity	€ 18.50 - € 27.00
extra person	€ 2.50
dog	€ 5.00

Zeewolde

Erkemederstrand Camping Horeca Jachthaven & Dagrecreatie

Erkemederweg 79, NL-3896 LB Zeewolde (Flevoland) T: **0365 228 421.** E: **info@erkemederstrand.nl**

alanrogers.com/NL6200

The Erkemederstrand (the beach of Erkemede) is a leisure park at Flevoland, with direct access to the Nuldernauw, a sandy beach, water and a forest. It provides a campsite for families, a marina, an area for youngsters to camp, a camping area for groups and a recreation area for day visitors. The campsite itself is divided into two areas: one before the dike at the waterfront and one behind the dike. The pitches are spacious (around 125 sq.m) and all have electricity, water and drainage. The focal point of the site and marina is the beach restaurant, De Jutter.

Facilities

Four neat and clean toilet blocks (access by key; exclusively for campers). Washbasins in cabins, showers and family bathrooms (free hot water). Dishwashing and laundry facilities in heated buildings. Shop for basic provisions. Bar, restaurant and takeaway. Several play areas and children's farm. Watersports facilities and lake swimming. Football pitch. Minigolf. Bicycle hire. Extended entertainment programme. Off site: Golf and riding 11 km.

Open: 30 March - 28 October.

Directions

From the A28 (Utrecht - Zwolle) take exit 9 (Nijkerk, Almere) and follow N301 to Zeewolde. Cross the bridge and turn right following signs to site. From Amsterdam/Almere, take exit 5 and follow N27 to Zeewolde; this road changes into the N305. Then take N301 to Nijkerk. From the bridge turn right and follow signs to site. GPS: 52.27021, 5.48871

Charges guide

Per unit incl. 2 persons and electricity	€ 25.75 - € 32.00
extra person	€ 3.00

Norway

A land full of contrasts, from magnificent snow-capped mountains, dramatic fjords, vast plateaux with wild untamed tracts, to huge lakes and rich green countryside. With nearly one quarter of the land above the Arctic Circle, Norway has the lowest population density in Europe.

Norway is made up of five regions. In the heart of the eastern region and the oldest of the Scandinavian capitals, Oslo is situated among green hills and vast forest areas, rich in Viking folklore and traditions. If your main reason for visiting Norway is to see the fjords, then head to the west. They are magnificent, with waterfalls and mountains that plunge straight down into the fjords. Trondheim, the third largest city, is in the heart of central Norway, steeped in history with a mixture of old wooden houses and modern architecture. Southern Norway sees the most sun, a popular holiday destination for the Norwegians, with a coastline ideal for swimming, sailing, scuba diving and fishing. The north is the 'Land of the Midnight Sun', where the sun never sets in summer and in winter it fails to rise. The scenery is diverse with forested valleys, stark mountains and lush valleys, and there are also coastal cities to explore, including Tromsø, which boasts the world's most northerly brewery.

CAPITAL: **Oslo**

Tourist Office

Norwegian Tourist Board
Charles House, 5 Lower Regent Street
London SW1Y 4LR
Tel: 020 7839 2650
Email: infouk@ntr.no
Internet: www.visitnorway.com

Population
4.9 million

Climate
Weather can be unpredictable, although less extreme on the west coast. Some regions have 24 hours of daylight in summer but none in winter.

Language
Norwegian, but English is widely spoken.

Telephone
The country code is 00 47.

Money
Currency: Norwegian Krone
Banks: Mon-Fri 09.00-15.00.

Shops
Mon-Fri 09.00-16.00/17.00, Thu 09.00-18.00/20.00 and Sat 09.00-13.00 /15.00.

Public Holidays
New Year's Day; King's Birthday 21 Feb; Holy Thursday; Good Friday; Easter Monday; May Day; Liberation Day 8 May; Constitution Day 17 May; Ascension; Whit Monday; Queen's Birthday 4 July; Saints Day 19 July; Christmas 25, 26 Dec.

Motoring
Roads are generally uncrowded around Oslo and Bergen but be prepared for tunnels and hairpin bends. Certain roads are forbidden to caravans or best avoided (advisory leaflet from the Norwegian Tourist Office). Vehicles must have sufficient road grip and in winter it may be necessary to use winter tyres with or without chains. Vehicles entering Bergen on weekdays must pay a toll and other tolls are also levied on certain roads.

see campsite map 3

Ålesund

Prinsen Strandcamping

Grønvika 15, N-6015 Ålesund (Møre og Romsdal) T: 70 15 21 90. E: post@prinsencamping.no

alanrogers.com/NO2460

Prinsen is a lively, fjord-side site, five kilometres from the attractive small town of Ålesund. It is a more attractive option than the more crowded sites closer to town, even so, this is mainly a transit and short-stay site. Divided by trees and shrubs, and sloping gently to a small sandy beach with views down Borgundfjord, the site has 100 grassy pitches, 34 cabins and 7 rooms, 110 electricity connections (16A) and 50 cable TV hook-ups. Reception shares space with the kiosk and freshly baked bread can be ordered daily.

Facilities

The sanitary units were renewed in 2009/10 and include family and children's bathrooms and sauna. Kitchen with cooker and dishwashing sinks. Playground and boat hire. Fishing. WiFi. Off site: Supermarket 1 km. Aksla and Fjellstua Viewpoint (418 steps to the point).

Open: All year.

Directions

Turn off E136 at roundabout signed to Hatlane and site. Follow signs to site. GPS: 62.464, 6.255064

Charges guide

Per unit incl. 5 persons and electricity NOK 250

Alta

Solvang Camping

Box 1280, N-9505 Alta (Finnmark) T: 78 43 04 77. E: solvangcamp@hotmail.com

alanrogers.com/NO2435

This is a restful little site with a welcoming atmosphere. It is set well back from the main road, so there is no road noise. The site overlooks the tidal marshes of the Altafjord, which are home to a wide variety of birdlife, providing ornithologists with a grandstand view during the long summer evenings bathed by the Midnight Sun. The 30 pitches are on undulating grass amongst pine trees and shrubs, and are not marked, although there are 16 electric hook-ups (16A). The site is run by a church mission organisation. All of the facilities are brand new.

Facilities

New block with reception and sanitary facilities with underfloor heating, washbasins in cubicles, showers and a family room. Facilities for disabled visitors. Sauna. New kitchen with cooker, sinks and dining area. Washing machine and dryer. Large TV room. Football field. Play area. Off site: Alta Museum. Rock carvings.

Open: 1 June - 10 August.

Directions

Site is signed off the E6, 10 km. north of Alta. GPS: 69.97968, 23.4681

Charges guide

Per unit incl. 2 persons and electricity NOK 210

Alvdal

Gjelten Bru Camping

N-2560 Alvdal (Hedmark) T: 62 48 74 44. E: post@gjeltenbrucamping.no

alanrogers.com/NO2515

Located a few kilometres west of Alvdal, this peaceful little site with its traditional turf roof buildings, makes an excellent base from which to explore the area. The 50 touring pitches are on level, neatly trimmed grass, served by gravel access roads and with electricity (10A) available to all. Some pitches are in the open and others under tall pine trees spread along the river bank. There are also 13 cabins to rent. Across the bridge on the other side of the river and main road, the site owners also operate the local, well stocked supermarket and post office.

Facilities

Heated toilet facilities are clean and housed in two buildings. One unit has been refurbished and is well appointed, the other is of newer construction. There is a mix of conventional washbasins and stainless steel washing troughs, and hot showers on payment. Separate unit with WC, basin, shower and handrails for disabled visitors. Two small kitchens provide dishwashing facilities, hot plates and an oven, all free of charge. Laundry facilities. Shop. TV room. Swings. Fishing. Off site: Supermarket and post office nearby. Bicycle hire 5 km.

Open: All year.

Directions

On the road 29 at Gjelten 3.5 km. west of Alvdal. Turn over the river bridge opposite village store and post office, and site is immediately on right. GPS: 62.13293, 10.57091

Charges guide

Per pitch incl. electricity NOK 220

Åndalsnes

Trollveggen Camping

Horgheimseidet, N-6300 Åndalsnes (Møre og Romsdal) T: 71 22 37 00. E: post@trollveggen.no

alanrogers.com/NO2452

The location of this site provides a unique experience – it is set at the foot of the famous vertical cliff of Trollveggen (the Troll Wall), which is Europe's highest vertical mountain face. The site is pleasantly laid out in terraces with level grass pitches. The facility block, four cabins and reception are all very attractively built with grass roofs. Beside the river is an attractive barbecue area where barbecue parties are sometimes arranged. This site is a must for people who love nature. The site is surrounded by the Troll Peaks and the Romsdalshorn Mountains with the rapid river of Rauma flowing by. Here in the beautiful valley of Romsdalen you have the ideal starting point for trips to many outstanding attractions such as 'The Troll Road' to Geiranger or to the Mardalsfossen waterfalls. In the mountains there are nature trails of various lengths and difficulties. The campsite owners are happy to help you with information. The town of Åndalsnes is 10 km. away and has a long tourism tradition as a place to visit. It is situated in the inner part of the beautiful Romsdal fjord and has a range of shops and restaurants.

Facilities

One heated toilet block provides washbasins, some in cubicles, and showers on payment. Family room with baby bath and changing mat, plus facilities for disabled visitors. Communal kitchen with cooking rings, small ovens, fridge and sinks (free hot water). Laundry facilities. Motorcaravan service point. Barbecue area (covered). Playground. Duck pond. WiFi over site (free).
Off site: Climbing, glacier walking and hiking. Fjord fishing. Sightseeing trips. The Troll Road. Mardalsfossen (waterfall). Geiranger and Åndalsnes.

Open: 10 May - 20 September.

Directions

Site is located on the E136 road, 10 km. south of Åndalsnes. It is signed. GPS: 62.49444, 7.758333

Charges guide

Per unit incl. 2 persons and electricity	NOK 229
extra person (over 4 yrs)	NOK 12

Averoy

Skjerneset Bryggecamping

Ekkilsoya, N-6530 Averoy (Møre og Romsdal) T: 71 51 18 94. E: info@skjerneset.com

alanrogers.com/NO2490

Uniquely centred around a working fishing quay set in an idyllic bay, Skjerneset Camping has been developed by the Otterlei family to give visitors an historical insight into this industry. It steps back in time in all but its facilities and offers 20 boats to hire and organised trips on a real fishing boat. Found on the tiny island of Ekkilsøya off Averøy, there is space for 30 caravans or motorcaravans on gravel hardstandings landscaped into rocks and trees, each individually shaped and sized and all having electricity connections (10/16A). There are grassy areas for tents on the upper terraces and six fully equipped cabins.

Facilities

Unisex sanitary facilities are heated but basic and include washbasins in cubicles. Two new sanitary blocks. Kitchen. Small laundry. Motorcaravan service point. Kiosk for basic packet foods, crisps, ices, sweets, postcards etc. Satellite TV. Motor boat hire. Organised sea fishing and sightseeing trips in the owner's sea-going boat. For non-anglers who want a fish supper, fresh fish are usually available on site.

Open: All year.

Directions

Site is on the little island of Ekkilsøya which is reached via a side road running west from the main Rv 64 road, 1.5 km. south of Bremsnes. GPS: 63.08135, 7.59612

Charges guide

Per person	NOK 150
pitch	NOK 250 - 500
electricity	NOK 25

No credit cards.

Andenes

Andenes Camping

Storgata 53, N-8483 Andenes (Nordland) T: 76 14 14 12. E: camping@whalesafari.no

alanrogers.com/NO2428

Lying on the exposed west coast of Andøy between the quiet main road and white sandy beaches, this site has an exceptional location for the midnight sun. Extremely popular, offering mountain and ocean views, it is only three kilometres from the base of Whalesafari and Andenes town. There is space for an unspecified number of touring units and you park where you like. With only 20 places with 16A electricity connections, it is advisable to arrive by mid-afternoon. Late arrivals may pitch and pay later when reception opens. Level areas of grass with some hardstanding can be found on gently sloping ground. Visitors come to Andenes for the opportunities to see whales at close quarters. Whalesafari is deemed the world's largest, most successful Arctic whale watching operation for the general public. It has an over 90 percent 'chance of seeing the quarry' and a 'whale guarantee' that offers a free second chance or your money back if your first trip fails to locate a whale. It is worth driving north to the site along the road which follows the west coast, a National Tourist road because of the areas outstanding natural beauty it passes through. The nearby white sand beach, Bleikstranda, is the longest in the region.

Facilities

One building houses separate sex sanitary facilities, each providing two toilets, two showers (10 NOK) with curtain and three washbasins. In each, one toilet is suitable for disabled visitors and has a washbasin. The reception building houses a well equipped kitchen, a sitting/dining room, 2 showers, WC and washbasin. Laundry facilities. Motorcaravan service point. Chemical disposal (charged 30 NOK). Picnic tables. Swings for children. WiFi (free). Off site: Well stocked supermarket 250 m. From nearby village of Bleik (8 km), trips are available for deep sea fishing and to Bleiksøya, one of Norway's most famous bird cliffs. Whale safari 3 km. Guided walks. Kayaking.

Open: 1 June - 30 September.

Directions

Either take the scenic roads 946 and 947 on the west side of Andøy north or to the east road 82, site is on left 250 m. from where 947 rejoins the 82, 3 km. before Andenes. The scenic west route is about 9 km. further. GPS: 69.30411, 16.06641

Charges guide

Per pitch incl. electricity	NOK 200
tent pitch	NOK 100
car	NOK 100

Ballangen

PlusCamp Ballangen

N-8540 Ballangen (Nordland) T: 76 92 76 90. E: ballcamp@c2i.net

alanrogers.com/NO2455

Ballangen is a pleasant, lively site conveniently located on the edge of a fjord with a small sandy beach, with direct access off the main E6 road. The 150 marked pitches are mostly on sandy grass, with electricity (10/16A) available to all. There are a few hardstandings, also 54 cabins for rent. A TV room has tourist information, coffee and games machines and there is a heated outdoor pool and waterslide (charged), free fjord fishing, and boat hire. An interesting excursion is to the nearby Martinstollen mine where visitors are guided through the dimly lit Olav Shaft, 500 m. into the mountain.

Facilities

Toilet facilities include some washbasins in cubicles. Facilities for disabled visitors, sauna and solarium. Kitchen with dishwashing sinks, two cookers and covered seating area. Laundry. Motorcaravan services. Well stocked shop. Café and takeaway (main season). TV/games room. Swimming pool and waterslide (charged). Minigolf. Fishing. Golf. Boat and bicycle hire. Pedal car hire. Mini zoo. Playground. Covered barbecue areas. Off site: Riding 2 km. Supermarket and other services in Ballangen 4 km.

Open: 1 March - 31 December.

Directions

Access is off the E6, 4 km. north of Ballangen, 40 km. south of Narvik. GPS: 68.33888, 16.85780

Charges guide

Per unit incl. 2 persons and electricity	NOK 210 - 290

Brekke

Botnen Camping

N-5961 Brekke (Sogn og Fjordane) T: 57 78 54 71. E: joker.brekke@ngbutikk.net

alanrogers.com/NO2370

For those setting forth north on E39 from Bergen there are surprisingly few attractive sites until one reaches the southern shore of the mighty Sognefjord. At Brekke is a well known tourist landmark, the remarkable Breekstranda Fjord Hotel, a traditional turf-roofed complex which tourist coaches are unable to resist. A mile or two beyond the hotel, also on the shore of the fjord, is the family-run Botnen Camping. This simple site slopes steeply towards the fjord, providing wonderful views to distant mountains from individual, mostly level pitches. It has its own jetty and harbour, with motorboats and canoes for hire.

Facilities

Toilet block with washbasins and showers (on payment). Small kitchen with microwave, hotplate and washing machine. Small shop. Play area. Swimming, fishing and boating in fjord. Boats and canoes for hire.
Off site: Hiking, fishing and boating.

Open: 1 June - 31 August.

Directions

Site is on the coast road west of Brekke, 11 km. from E39. GPS: 61.03333, 5.29998

Charges guide

Per person	NOK 15
caravan or motorcaravan	NOK 90
tent	NOK 80
electricity	NOK 20

Byglandsfjord

Neset Camping

N-4741 Byglandsfjord (Aust-Agder) T: 37 93 42 55. E: post@neset.no

alanrogers.com/NO2610

On a semi-promontory on the shores of the 40 km. long Byglandsfjord, Neset is a good centre for activities or as a stop en route north from the ferry port of Kristiansand (from England or Denmark). Neset is situated on well kept grassy meadows by the lake shore, with water on three sides and the road on the fourth, and provides 200 unmarked pitches with electricity and cable TV available. The main building houses reception, a small shop and a restaurant with fine views over the water. This is a well run, friendly site where one could spend an active few days. Byglandsfjord offers good fishing (mainly trout) and the area has marked trails for cycling, riding or walking in an area famous for its minerals.

Facilities

Three modern sanitary blocks which can be heated, all with comfortable hot showers (some on payment), washing up facilities (metered hot water) and a kitchen. Restaurant and takeaway (15/6-15/8). Shop (1/5-1/10). Campers' kitchen. Playground. Lake swimming, boating and fishing. Excellent new barbecue area and hot tub. Bicycle, canoe and pedalo hire. Climbing, rafting and canoeing courses arranged (including trips to see beavers and elk). Cross-country skiing possible in winter.
Off site: Rock climbing wall. Marked forest trails.

Open: All year.

Directions

Site is on route 9, 2.5 km. north of the town of Byglandsfjord on the eastern shores of the lake. GPS: 58.68848, 7.80132

Charges guide

Per unit incl. 2 persons and electricity	NOK 30

Camping Cheques accepted.

Byrkjelo

Byrkjelo Camping

N-6826 Byrkjelo (Sogn og Fjordane) T: 91 73 65 97. E: mail@byrkjelo-camping.no

alanrogers.com/NO2436

This neatly laid out and well equipped small site offers 25 large marked and numbered touring pitches, all with electrical connections (10A) and 15 with gravel hardstandings. It is a good value site in a village location with neatly mown grass, attractive trees and shrubs with a warm welcome from the owners. Fishing is possible in the river adjacent to the site. Reception and a small kiosk selling ices, sweets and soft drinks, are housed in an attractive cabin and there is a bell to summon the owners should they not be on site when you arrive. A garage, mini-market and café are just 100 m. away and the lively town of Sandane is 19 kilometres.

Facilities

The good heated sanitary unit (new in 2010), includes seven shower rooms each with washbasin, on payment. Facilities for families with babies and disabled visitors, incorporating a WC, basin and shower with handrails, etc. Campers' kitchen with dishwashing sinks, hot-plates and dining area. Laundry facilities. Motorcaravan services. Kiosk. Large playground. Fishing. Swimming pool and children's pool (20/6-20/8), both heated (fee charged). WiFi (charged). Off site: Riding 4 km. Golf 15 km. Ideal base for Nordfjord and Jostedalsbreen. Rafting.

Open: 1 May - 1 October.

Directions

Site is beside the E39 in the village of Byrkjelo, 19 km. east of Sandane. GPS: 61.73454, 6.50800

Charges guide

Per unit incl. 2 persons and electricity	NOK 205
extra person	NOK 10

Gaupne

PlusCamp Sandvik

Sandvik Sor, N-6868 Gaupne (Sogn og Fjordane) T: 57 68 11 53. E: sandvik@pluscamp.no

alanrogers.com/NO2385

Sandvik is a compact, small site on the edge of the town of Gaupne close to the Nigardsbreen Glacier. It provides 60 touring pitches, 48 with electrical connections (8/16A), arranged on fairly level grassy terrain either side of a road. A large supermarket, post office, banks, etc. are all within a level 500 m. stroll. A café in the reception building is open in summer for drinks and meals and the small shop sells groceries, ices, soft drinks, sweets, etc. This is a useful site for those using the spectacular Rv 55 high mountain road from Lom to Sogndal or for visiting the Nigardsbreen Glacier and Jostedalsbreen area of Norway.

Facilities

The single, fully equipped, central sanitary unit includes washbasins with dividers and two hot showers per sex (on payment). Multi-purpose unit for families or disabled visitors with facilities for baby changing and a further WC, basin and shower with ramp for access. Small campers' kitchen. Tables, chairs and TV. Laundry. Playground. Boat hire. Fishing. Bicycle hire. Off site: Nigardsbreen (glacier).

Open: All year.

Directions

Signed just off Rv 55 Lom-Sogndal road on eastern outskirts of Gaupne. GPS: 61.40057, 7.3007

Charges guide

Per unit incl. up to 4 persons	NOK 140
electricity	NOK 30

Granvin

Espelandsdalen Camping

N-5736 Granvin (Hordaland) T: 56 52 51 67. E: post@espelandsdalencamping.no

alanrogers.com/NO2350

If one follows Hardangerfjord on the map and considers the mighty glacier which once scooped away the land along its path, it is easy to imagine that it started life in Espelandsdalen. For generations farmers have struggled to make a living out of the narrow strip of land between water and rock. One of these farmers has converted a narrow, sloping field bisected by the road (572) into a modest lakeside campsite taking about 50 units. The grassy meadow pitches below the road run right down to the lake shore. There are 30 electrical hook ups (10A). Campers come here for the fishing and walking, or just to marvel at the views of the valley and its towering mountain sides.

Facilities

A newly refurbished sanitary block consists of a washing trough with hot water, a shower on payment and WCs. Some basic foodstuffs are kept in the office. Swimming, fishing and boating in lake. Boat hire. Off site: Pleasant walk to local waterfall.

Open: 1 May - 31 August.

Directions

The northern loop of the 572 road follows Espelandsdalen and the campsite is on this road, about 6 km. from its junction with route 13 at Granvin. GPS: 60.59754, 6.80095

Charges guide

Per person	NOK 15
pitch	NOK 90
electricity	NOK 35

No credit cards.

Harstad

Harstad Camping

Nesseveien 55, N-9411 Harstad (Troms) T: 77 07 36 62. E: postmaster@harstad-camping.no

alanrogers.com/NO2432

In a delightful setting with fine views, the campsite has space for 120 units as it slopes down to Vågsfjorden with on-site fishing and boating. This well established, popular site near Harstad, provides an excellent base on Hinnøya, the largest island in Norway. Pitches are unmarked but a flat area by the water's edge provides most of the site's 46 electricity hook-ups (16A). These pitches are sought after and a mid-afternoon arrival may gain a level pitch with electricity. Harstad Camping is ideal for those looking for a scenic view and a bustling town nearby with a variety of activities on offer.

Facilities

Two sanitary units, one modern and unisex with showers (10 NOK) and two ensuite WC with basins. Older unit is separate sex, each with showers (10 NOK), toilets and washbasins (some in individual cabins for ladies). Room for disabled visitors with key from reception. Laundry room (tokens required). Kitchen with hot plates, tables and chairs. Reception (08.00-23.00 high season) sells drinks, ices, postcards etc. WiFi (charged). Off site: Grottebadet waterpark 4 km. One of northern Norway's largest shopping centres, including a supermarket and garage within 2 km. Par 68, 9-hole golf course at Harstad 4 km.

Open: All year.

Directions

Travelling north on road 83, site is well signposted on right 3 km. before Harstad. After turning right, turn immediate left and site is 1 km. along tarmac road (site signed from either direction).
GPS: 68.77278, 16.57712

Charges guide

Per pitch (max. 6 persons)	NOK 200
incl. electricity	NOK 225

Jørpeland

Preikestolen Camping

Jørssangvegen 265, Preikestolvegen 97, N-4100 Jørpeland (Sogn og Fjordane) T: 51 74 97 25.
E: info@preikestolencamping.com **alanrogers.com/NO2660**

Taking its name from one of Norway's best known attractions, the Preikestolen (Pulpit Rock) cliff formation, Preikestolen Camping is situated in the beautiful region of Rogaland, surrounded by high mountains and deep fjords. This is a site where you could easily stay a few days to explore the beautiful region. The friendly owners are happy to help with maps and guidance. The site is laid out in a relaxed way with an open, level grass area where trees and bushes create pleasant little 'rooms' for your tent, caravan or motorcaravan. There are 100 pitches, 56 with electricity, water tap and waste water drainage.

Facilities

The modern heated sanitary block has showers, washbasins in cubicles and facilities for disabled visitors. Room with dishwashing sinks but no cookers. Washing machines and dryers. Motorcaravan service point. Small shop (15/5-15/9). Restaurant and takeaway (15/5-15/9). Fishing. Internet (WiFi). Off site: Golf 500 m.

Open: 1 March - 1 December.

Directions

Site is on road 13, 3 km. south of Jørpeland. Follow signs to site. GPS: 58.998883, 6.092167

Charges guide

Per unit incl. 2 persons and electricity	NOK 240
extra person	NOK 30

Kabelvag

Lyngvær Lofoten Bobilcamping

N-8313 Kleppstad (Nordland) T: 76 07 77 78. E: relorent@online.no

alanrogers.com/NO2465

This established site is very popular, with many customers returning for the well maintained facilities and easy access to fishing and boating. In the centre of Lofoten, alongside a tidal fjord with mountains all around, the setting and location is quite idyllic. Large terraces provide fine views for most of the 200 pitches, mainly grass, some with hardstanding, with electricity for 110 (10/16A). Lyngvaer provides a base to absorb the island's scenery and traditions in an area which also offers walking, ornithology and photography.

Facilities

Toilet facilities are spotless and cleaned regularly. Two heated sanitary units include showers in cubicles (NOK 10 for 6 mins). Two communal kitchens with cooking, dishwashing and fish freezer (free). Laundry facilities. Large sitting area with satellite TV. Play areas. Boat hire. Fishing (good fish cleaning area). Well equipped motorcaravan service point. WiFi (free). Off site: Henningsvaer 11 km. Kabelvag Aquarium 11 km. Golf 15 km. Lofotr Viking Museum 36 km.

Open: 1 May - 20 September.

Directions

From Svolvaer turn south west on E10 towards Kabelvag for 5 km. Site is on left in 14 km. from Kabelvag. The site is 110 km. north on E10 from Moskenes on the right. Ferries link mainland from Skutvik to Svolvaer or from Bodø to Moskenes. Ferries can be busy in high season so it is possible to take the long drive to Lofoten via greatly improved roads with new bridges and tunnels.
GPS: 68.224812, 14.216609

Charges guide

Per unit incl. 2 persons and electricity	NOK 165
extra person	NOK 5

Eighth night free. No credit cards.

Kautokeino

Kautokeino Fritidssenter & Camping

Suohpatjavri, N-9520 Kautokeino (Finnmark) T: 78 48 57 33. E: elvabe@gmail.com

alanrogers.com/NO2415

This is a friendly, lakeside site 8 km. south of Kautokeino. The 50 pitches are not marked but are generally on a firm sandy base amongst low-growing birch trees, with 20 electric hook-ups (16A) available. There are also cabins and motel rooms for rent. Although the grass is trying to grow, the ground is frozen from September until May so there are mainly hardstandings with some grass areas. The site is 35 km. north of the Finnish Border and is one day's drive from North Cape. During the season when there are enough guests, the owner arranges an evening campfire around two Sami tents, with talks about the Sami people.

Facilities

The modern sanitary building is heated and well maintained, with two British style WCs, two open washbasins and two showers (on payment) per sex. Small kitchen with cooker, dishwashing sinks and refrigerator. Laundry facilities. Separate bathroom for disabled visitors, also containing baby facilities. Football. Canoes, boats and pedalos for hire. Free fishing in lake. Off site: Kautokeino (Sami Museum), Juhl's Silver Gallery.

Open: 1 June - 30 September.

Directions

Site is 8 km. south of Kautokeino on road Rv 93. GPS: 68.94735, 23.0896

Charges guide

Per pitch	NOK 140
electricity	NOK 40

Kinsarvik

Ringoy Camping

N-5780 Kinsarvik (Hordaland) T: 53 66 39 17. E: torleivr@kinsarvik.net

alanrogers.com/NO2315

Although the village of Ringoy is quiet and peaceful, it occupies a pivotal position, lying not only midway between two principal ferry ports of Upper Hardangerfjord (Kinsarvik and Brimnes), but also near the junction of two key roads (routes 7 and 13). This site is basically a steeply sloping field running down from the road to the tree-lined fjord with two flat terraces and the shore area for camping. The owners, the Raunsgard family, are particularly proud of the site's remarkable shore-side barbecue facilities. On arrival you find a place as there is no reception – someone will call between 8 and 9 pm.

Facilities

The toilet block is small and simple (with metered showers), but well designed, constructed and maintained. It is possibly inadequate during peak holiday weeks in July. Rowing boat (free). Off site: Supermarket, bank and other facilities in Kinsarvik 10 km.

Open: 15 May - 15 September.

Directions

Site is on route 13, midway between Kinsarvik and Brimnes. GPS: 60.44111, 6.77988

Charges guide

Per unit incl. 2 persons and electricity	NOK 150
extra person	NOK 10
child (0-12 yrs)	NOK 5

No credit cards.

Lærdal

Lærdal Ferie & Fritidspark

Grandavegens, N-6886 Lærdal (Sogn og Fjordane) T: 57 66 66 95. E: info@laerdalferiepark.com

alanrogers.com/NO2375

This site is beside the famous Sognefjord, the longest fjord in the world. It is ideally situated if you want to explore the glaciers, fjords and waterfalls of the region. The 100 pitches are level with well trimmed grass, connected by tarmac roads and are suitable for tents, caravans and motorcaravans. There are 80 electrical hook-ups. The fully licensed restaurant serves traditional meals as well as snacks and pizzas. The pretty little village of Laerdal, only 400 m. away, is well worth a visit. A walk among the old, small wooden houses is a pleasant and interesting experience.

Facilities

Two modern and well decorated sanitary blocks with washbasins (some in cubicles), showers on payment, and toilets. Facilities for disabled visitors. Children's room. Washing machine and dryer. Kitchen. Motorcaravan services. Small shop. Bar, restaurant and takeaway (20/5-5/9). TV room. Playground. Motorboats, rowing boats, canoes, bicycles and pedal cars for hire. Bicycle hire. Fishing. WiFi at reception. Off site: Cruises on the Sognefjord 400 m. The Norwegian Wild Salmon Centre 400 m. Riding 500 m. Golf 12 km. The Flåm railway 40 km.

Open: All year, by telephone request 1 Nov - 14 March.

Directions

Site is on road 5 (from the Oslo - Bergen road, E16) 400 m. north of Laerdal village centre. GPS: 61.10037, 7.46986

Charges guide

Per unit incl. 2 persons and electricity	NOK 210
extra person	NOK 50
child (4-15 yrs)	NOK 25

Camping Cheques accepted.

Malmefjorden

Bjolstad Camping

N-6445 Malmefjorden (Møre og Romsdal) T: 71 26 56 56. E: post@bjolstad.no

alanrogers.com/NO2450

This is delightful small, rural site, which slopes down to Malmefjorden, a sheltered arm of Fraenfjorden. Bjølstad has space for just 55 touring units on grassy, fairly level, terraces either side of the tarmac central access road. A delight for children is a large, old masted boat which provides hours of fun playing at pirates or Vikings. At the foot of the site is a waterside barbecue area, a shallow, sandy, paddling area for children and a jetty. Both rowing and motorboats (with life jackets) can be hired, one can swim or fish in the fjord.

Facilities

The very basic, clean, heated sanitary unit includes two showers per sex (on payment), plus washbasins with dividers. Small campers' kitchen with two dishwashing sinks and hot plate. Laundry service at reception. Playground. Boat hire. Fjord fishing and swimming. Dogs are not accepted in cabins. Off site: Riding 9 km. Golf 12 km.

Open: 1 June - 30 September (possibly earlier on request).

Directions

Turn off Rv 64 on northern edge of Malmefjorden village towards village of Lindset (lane is oil bound gravel). Site is 1 km. GPS: 62.81458, 7.22530

Charges guide

Per unit incl. 2 persons and electricity	NOK 100 - 210

Mosjøen

PlusCamp Mosjoen

E6, N-8657 Mosjøen (Nordland) T: 75 17 79 00. E: post@mosjoenhotell.no

alanrogers.com/NO2487

This campsite off the E6 near Mosjøen, allows access to 'The World's Most Beautiful Journey'. The Kystriksveien (RV17) runs north to Bodø or south to Steinkjer, however it offers more to the traveller than a simple stopover or change of route. Complete with six-lane, ten-pin bowling alley, heated outdoor swimming pool with slide, games rooms, food and bar, it has both entertainment and mountain views with forested valley slopes. It has modern, well equipped sanitary facilities. Terraced pitches are level with electricity (10A), some on tarmac and gravel, and others on grass with a separate area for tents.

Facilities

Two heated sanitary units are linked together in the centre of the site. The newer unit offers up-to-date facilities for all, with family rooms and disabled access. Motorcaravan service point (ask at reception). Good sized kitchen and dining area. Laundry. Restaurant, café/bar, Heated outdoor swimming pool with slide. 10-pin bowling alley with bar. Pool table and video games. TV room. WiFi. Access to large ball games area. Autogas/LPG filling station off main car park. Off site: Sports area 500 m. Sjøgata wooden buildings and commercial centre 1 km. Fishing 2 km. Skiing 8 km. Golf 15 km.

Open: All year.

Directions

1 km. south of Mosjøen turning left off the E6 when travelling north from Trondheim. GPS: 65.83417, 13.22025

Charges guide

Per unit incl. electricity	NOK 230

Nå

Eikhamrane Camping

N-5776 Nå (Hordaland) T: 53 66 22 48

alanrogers.com/NO2330

About halfway along the western shore of Sørfjord is Eikhamrane Camping. Arranged on a well landscaped and partly terraced field which slopes alongside the road to a pebbly lakeside beach, it was formerly part of an orchard which still extends on both sides of the site. There is room for 40 units on unmarked, well kept grass with 20 electrical hook ups (10A). There are attractive trees and good gravel roads, with areas of gravel hardstanding for poor weather. Many pitches overlook the fjord where there are also picnic benches.

Facilities

Two small timber toilet blocks, one for toilets with external access, the other for washbasins (open) and showers (on payment). Both are simple but very well kept. Small kitchen with dishwashing facilities (hot water on payment) and two laundry sinks outside, under cover. Some supplies kept at reception office in the old farmhouse, home of the owner (bread and milk to order). Watersports (sailing, canoeing and rowing), and fishing in fjord. Off site: Digranes nature reserve (birdwatching) nearby.

Open: 1 June - 31 August.

Directions

Site is on road 550 about 8 km. south of the village of Nå, on the western shore of Sørfjord, 32 km. south of Utne and 16 km. north of Odda. GPS: 60.1830, 6.5517

Charges guide

Per person	NOK 10
child (4-12 yrs)	NOK 5
pitch	NOK 100
electricity	NOK 25

No credit cards.

Odda

Odda Camping

Borsto, N-5750 Odda (Hordaland) T: **41 32 16 10**. E: **post@oppleve.no**

alanrogers.com/NO2320

Bordered by the Folgefonna glacier to the west and the Hardangervidda plateau to the east and south, Odda is an industrial town with electro-chemical enterprises based on zinc mining and hydro-electric power. This site has been attractively developed on the town's southern outskirts. It is spread over 2.5 acres of flat, mature woodland, which is divided into small clearings by massive boulders. Access is by well tended tarmac roads which wind their way among the trees and boulders. There are 55 tourist pitches including 36 with electricity. The site fills up in the evenings and can be crowded with facilities stretched from the end of June to early August.

Facilities

A single timber building at the entrance houses the reception office and the simple, but clean, sanitary facilities which provide for each sex, two WCs, one hot shower (on payment) and three open washbasins. A new building provides additional unisex toilets, showers and laundry facilities. Small kitchen with dishwashing facilities. Mini shop. Off site: Town facilities close.

Open: All year.

Directions

Site is on the southern outskirts of Odda, signed off road to Buar, with a well marked access. GPS: 60.05320, 6.54380

Charges guide

Per person	NOK 10
tent and car	NOK 110
caravan or motorcaravan	NOK 130
electricity	NOK 40

No credit cards. Camping Cheques accepted.

Oppdal

Magalaupe Camping

Engan, N-7340 Oppdal (Sør Trøndelag) T: **72 42 46 84**. E: **camp@magalaupe.no**

alanrogers.com/NO2505

This friendly, good value, riverside site in a sheltered position in the mountains is easily accessed from the E6. The 52 unmarked and grassy touring pitches (42 with 16A electricity) are in natural surroundings amongst birch trees and rocks and served by gravel access roads. There are also eight attractive and fully equipped site owned cabins. As the site rarely fills up, the facilities should be adequate at most times. There are a host of unusual activities in the surrounding area. These include caving, canyoning, rafting, gold panning, mineral hunting, and musk oxen, reindeer and elk safaris.

Facilities

Small, clean, heated sanitary unit fully equipped and the showers are on payment. Extra WC/washbasin units in reception building. Small kitchen with dishwashing facilities, hot plate, fridge and freezer, plus a combined washing/drying machine. Kiosk for ices, soft drinks, etc. Bar (mid June-Aug). Motorcaravan service point. TV lounge. Fishing. Bicycle hire. Off site: Supermarkets and other services in Oppdal 11 km. Riding and golf 12 km. Organised walking, cycling and car tours.

Open: All year.

Directions

Site is signed on E6, 11 km. south of Oppdal. Height restriction under railway bridge (3.3 m). GPS: 62.49703, 9.58535

Charges guide

Per pitch incl. 4 persons and electricity	NOK 140

No credit cards.

Oyer

PlusCamp Rustberg

Kongsvegen 691, N-2636 Oyer (Oppland) T: **61 27 77 30**. E: **rustberg@online.no**

alanrogers.com/NO2545

Conveniently located beside the E6, 23 km. from the centre of Lillehammer, this attractive terraced site provides a comfortable base for exploring the area. Like all sites along this route it does suffer from road and train noise at times, but the site's facilities and nearby attractions more than compensate for this. There are 70 pitches with 30 available for touring units, most reasonably level and with some gravel hardstandings available for motorcaravans. There are 70 electrical connections (16A). A small open air, heated swimming pool has a water slide.

Facilities

Heated, fully equipped sanitary facilities include washbasins in cubicles, showers on payment and free saunas. Two good family bathrooms. Unit for disabled visitors. Campers' kitchen and dining room with microwave oven and double hob. Laundry. Motorcaravan services. Restaurant. Solarium (on payment). Kiosk for basics. Swimming pool and slide (1/6-31/8, weather permitting). Billiards. Golf. Playground. New reception and café. Off site: Forest walks directly from site. Fishing in the nearby river, day licence from reception. Golf 7 km. Children's farm and pony riding.

Open: All year.

Directions

Site is well signed from the E6, 20 km. north of Lillehammer (North) exit. GPS: 61.28025, 10.36095

Charges guide

Per pitch incl. electricity	NOK 210 - 260

Røros

Håneset Camping

Osloveien, N-7374 Røros (Sør Trøndelag) T: 72 41 06 00

alanrogers.com/NO2510

At first sight Håneset Camping is unpromising, lying between the main road and the railway, with gritty sloping ground because grass has difficulty growing at this altitude. However, it is the best equipped campsite in Røros, ideal to cope with the often cold, wet weather of this 1,000 m. high plateau. You can expect a warm welcome here and in winter, a picture postcard cover of snow. All 50 unmarked touring pitches have access to electricity (10/16A), with most facilities housed in the main building complex. Walk or cycle from the site to join people from all over Europe visiting the remarkably well preserved mining town of Røros.

Facilities

Heated sanitary facilities provide three separate rooms for each sex, fully equipped with showers on payment. Washing machine and two clothes washing sinks. Huge sitting/TV room and two well equipped kitchens which the owners, the Moen family, share fully with their guests, plus nine rooms for rent. Free WiFi throughout site. Off site: Town centre 20 minutes walk. Fishing 200 m. Bicycle hire 2 km. Golf 3 km.

Open: All year.

Directions

Site is on the Rv 30 leading south from Røros to Os, 3 km. from Røros. GPS: 62.5675, 11.351944

Charges guide

Per unit incl. 2 persons and electricity	NOK 200

No credit cards.

Rysstad

Rysstad Feriesenter

N-4748 Rysstad (Aust-Agder) T: 37 93 61 30. E: post@rysstadferie.no

alanrogers.com/NO2600

Setesdal is on the upper reaches of the Otra river which runs north from the southern port of Kristiansand and right up to the southern slopes of Hardangervidda. The small village of Rysstad is named after the family who has developed camping in this area. The site occupies a wide tract of woodland between the road and the river towards which it shelves gently, affording a splendid view of the valley and the towering mountains opposite. The site is in effect divided into two sections; one is divided by trees and hedges into numbered pitches, some occupied by chalets, the other is an adjacent open field and 20 electrical connections are available (six with satellite TV).

Facilities

Sanitary facilities have showers on payment, washbasins in cubicles, dishwashing sinks and a cooker. Laundry facilities. Play area and amusement hut. Sports field. Fishing, swimming and boating (boats for hire). Fitness track. Bicycle hire. Centre includes café, mini shop and restaurant. Handicraft shop. Area on the river's edge for barbecues and entertainment with an arena type setting. New 5 room motel, open all year. Off site: Village within walking distance. Bank, shop, petrol station.

Open: 1 May - 1 October.

Directions

Site is about 1 km. south of junction between route 9 (from Kristiansand) and the extended route 45 (from Stavanger). GPS: 59.09107, 7.54057

Charges guide

Per person	NOK 20
child (4-12 yrs)	NOK 10
caravan or tent	NOK 130
hiker	NOK 00
electricity	NOK 25

Saltstraumen

PlusCamp Saltstraumen

Bok 33, N-8056 Saltstraumen (Nordland) T: 75 58 75 60. E: salcampi@online.no

alanrogers.com/NO2475

On a coastal route, this extremely popular site, in a very scenic location with a magnificent backdrop, is close to the largest Maelstrom in the world. It is an easy short walk to this outstanding phenomenon. As well as 20 cabins, the site has 60 plain touring pitches mostly on level, gravel hardstandings in rows, each with electricity (10A). A few 'softer' pitches are available for tents. The nearby fjord is renowned for the prolific numbers of coalfish and cod caught from the shore. Many 'have a go' to catch their evening meal. You are advised to arrive by late afternoon.

Facilities

Excellent heated sanitary facilities are clean and fully equipped. Unisex with four large cubicles containing WC, shower and washbasin. Others have a WC and washbasin, and one family room provides both adult and child sized WC, washbasin and shower. Full wet room with access for disabled visitors. Kitchen with two cookers. Laundry facilities. Motorcaravan service point. Playground. Minigolf. Fishing. WiFi (free). Off site: Mini supermarket and snack bar outside site entrance. Hotel and cafeteria nearby.

Open: All year.

Directions

Travelling from the south: Before Rognan take Rv 812 signed Saltstraumen. At junction with Rv 17 turn right. Site on left immediately after second bridge. From the north: From Rv 80 (Fauske - Bodø) turn south on Rv 17, site is 12 km. at Saltstraumen on right just before bridge. GPS: 67.2355, 14.62091

Charges guide

Per unit incl. 3 persons and electricity	NOK 230

Skarsvåg

Kirkeporten Camping

Box 22, N-9763 Skarsvåg (Finnmark) T: 78 47 52 33. E: kipo@kirkeporten.no

alanrogers.com/NO2425

This is the most northerly mainland campsite in the world (71¼ 06) and considering the climate and the wild, unspoilt location it has to be one of the best sites in Scandinavia, and also rivals the best in Europe. The 40 pitches, 22 with electricity (16A), are on grass or gravel hardstanding in natural 'tundra' terrain beside a small lake, together with 16 rental cabins and 5 rooms. We advise you pack warm clothing, bedding and maybe propane for this location. Note: Although overnighting at Nordkapp Centre is permitted, it is on the very exposed gravel car park with no electric hook-ups or showers.

Facilities

Excellent modern sanitary installations in two underfloor heated buildings. They include a sauna, two family bathrooms, baby room, and excellent unit for disabled visitors. Laundry. Kitchen with hot plates, sinks and a dining area. Motorcaravan service point. Reception, restaurant and mini shop at the entrance open daily. Off site: North Cape, Kirkeporten.

Open: 15 May - 15 September.

Directions

On the island of Magerøya, from Honningsvåg take the E69 for 20 km. then fork right signed Skarsvåg. Site is on left after 3 km. just as you approach Skarsvåg. GPS: 71.11217, 25.82177

Charges guide

Per unit incl. 2 persons and electricity	NOK 29

Snåsa

Vegset Camping

N-7760 Snåsa (Nord-Trøndelag) T: 93 20 67 54. E: magnar@vegset.no

alanrogers.com/NO2495

Located within forested lakeside slopes, this small, pleasant site is seven kilometres south of Snåsa. Although directly accessible from the E6 road, it is set well back on the banks of Lake Snåsavatn. There are eight site-owned cabins, some static units and space for about 20 touring units on slightly sloping ground. There are 10/16A electricity connections available. For those travelling to or from Northern Norway, Vegset provides a good resting point or night halt. However it is possible to explore Snåsa, the centre for the South Lapp people with their own boarding school, museum and information centre.

Facilities

The heated toilet block provides showers (NOK 10), plus a shower with toilet suitable for disabled visitors. Another small unit has a kitchen with a small oven and double hob, washing machine and drying rack. Reception has a sitting room overlooking the lake and doubles as a TV room with kiosk selling emergency groceries, drinks and confectionery (end June-mid Aug). Swimming, boat hire and fishing (licence from site). WiFi (free). Off site: National Park and museum in Snåsa.

Open: Easter - 10 October.

Directions

Site is just off the E6 road, 7 km. south of Snåsa. GPS: 64.26590, 12.28673

Charges guide

Per pitch	NOK 150
electricity	NOK 30

No credit cards.

Sogndal

Kjørnes Camping

N-6856 Sogndal (Sogn og Fjordane) T: 57 67 45 80. E: camping@kjornes.no

alanrogers.com/NO2390

Kjørnes Camping is idyllically situated on the Sognefjord, 3 km. from the centre of Sogndal. It occupies a long open meadow which is terraced down to the waterside. The site has 100 pitches for camping units (all with electricity), 14 cabins and two apartments for rent. Located at the very centre of the 'fjord kingdom' by the main no. 5 road, this site is the ideal base from which to explore the Sognefjord. You are within a short drive (maximum one hour) from all the major attractions including the Jostedal glacier, the Nærøyfjord, the Flåm Railway, the Urnes Stave Church and Sognefjellet. This site is ideal for those who enjoy peace and quiet, lovely scenery or a spot of fishing. Access is via a narrow lane with passing places, which drops down towards the fjord three kilometres from Sogndal.

Facilities

A high quality sanitary building was added in 2008. Baby room. Facilities for disabled visitors. A new building provides a kitchen with cooking facilities, dishwasher, a dining area overlooking the fjord, and laundry facilities. Small shop (20/6-20/8). Satellite TV, WiFi and Internet. Off site: Hiking, glacier walks, climbing, rafting, walking around Sognefjord. Details from reception. Bicycle hire 3 km.

Open: 1 May - 1 October.

Directions

Site is off the Rv 5, 3 km. east of Sogndal, 8 km. west of Kaupanger. GPS: 61.21164, 7.12108

Charges guide

Per unit incl. 2 persons and electricity	NOK 250
extra person	NOK 30
child (4-16 yrs)	NOK 10

Storforshei

Krokstrand Camping

Krokstrand, Saltfjellveien 1573, N-8630 Storforshei (Nordland) T: 75 16 60 02

alanrogers.com/NO2485

In a stunning location, this site is a popular resting place on the long trek to Nordkapp and is only 18 km. from the Arctic Circle and its Visitor Centre. There are 45 unmarked pitches set amongst birch trees with electrical connections (10A) for 28 units and 15 cabins available for rent. In late spring and early summer the river alongside, headed by rapids, is impressive and there remains the possibility of the surrounding mountains being snow-capped. A reception kiosk is open 08.00-10.00 and 15.00-22.00 in high season, otherwise campers are invited to find a pitch and pay later at the hotel complex opposite.

Facilities

Modern, well maintained and clean, small sanitary unit includes two showers per sex (on payment). Laundry with washing machine and dryer. Small kitchen with double hot plate, microwave and dishwashing sink. Motorcaravan services. Brightly painted play area with trampoline, well maintained. Minigolf. Fishing. Off site: Hotel with café/restaurant just outside site entrance (same ownership as the site) with good meals, snacks and very basic provisions. Souvenir shop 500 m. Caves and glacier 30 km.

Open: 1 June - 20 September.

Directions

Entrance is off E6 at Krokstrand village opposite hotel, 65 km. north of Mo I Rana and 18 km. south of the Arctic Circle. GPS: 66.46108, 15.0952

Charges guide

Per unit incl. 2 persons and electricity	NOK 200
extra person	NOK 15
child (4-12 yrs)	NOK 10

Tinn Austbygd

Sandviken Camping

N-3650 Tinn Austbygd (Telemark) T: 35 09 81 73. E: kontakt@sandviken-camping.no

alanrogers.com/NO2590

Sandviken is a remote, lakeside site in a scenic location, suitable for exploring Hardangervidda. With its own shingle beach, at the head of Tinnsjo Lake, it provides 150 grassy, mostly level, pitches. In addition to 50 seasonal units and 12 cabins, there are 85 numbered tourist pitches, many with electricity (10/16A), plus an area for tents, under trees along the waterfront. The office/reception kiosk also sells sweets, soft drinks, ices etc. and a baker calls daily in July. A 1 km. stroll takes you to the tiny village of Tinn Austbygde which has a mini-market, bakery, café, bank, garage and post office.

Facilities

Tidy, heated sanitary facilities include some washbasins in cubicles, showers on payment, sauna, solarium and a dual-purpose disabled/family bathroom with ramped access and baby changing mat. Kitchen and laundry rooms (hot water on payment). Motorcaravan services. Kiosk (20/6-1/9). Playground. TV and games room. Minigolf. Fishing and watersports. Boat hire.
Off site: Handicraft exhibition 5 km. Riding 15 km. At Rjukan (27 km) industrial museum, cable car, Gausta peak.

Open: All year.

Directions

Easiest access is via the Rv 37 from Gransherad along the western side of the lake.
GPS: 59.98917, 8.81577

Charges guide

Per unit incl. 2 persons and electricity	NOK 210 - 230
extra person	NOK 15
child (4-18 yrs)	NOK 10

Trogstad

Olberg Camping

Sandsveien 4, Olberg, N-1860 Trogstad (Østfold) T: 69 82 86 10. E: froesol@online.no

alanrogers.com/NO2615

Olberg is a delightful small farm site, close to Lake Øyeren and within 70 km. of Oslo. There are 35 large, level pitches and electricity connections (10-16A) are available for 28 units located on neatly tended grassy meadow with trees and shrubs. The reception building also houses a small gallery with paintings, glasswork and other crafts. A short drive down the adjacent lane takes you to the beach on Lake Øyeren, and there are many woodland walks in the surrounding area. Please bear in mind that this is a working farm. In high season fresh bread is available (except Sunday) and coffee, drinks, ices and snacks are provided. The old church and museum at Trøgstad, and Båstad church are worth visiting. Forest and elk 'safaris' are arranged.

Facilities

Excellent, heated sanitary facilities are fully equipped and include a ramp for wheelchair access and one bathroom for families or disabled visitors. Laundry facilities. Small kitchenette with full size cooker and food preparation area. Kiosk. Snacks available. Craft gallery. Playground.
Off site: Fishing 3 km. Golf, tropical pool and spa 18 km.

Open: 1 May - 1 October, other times by arrangement.

Directions

Site is signed on Rv 22, 20 km. north of Mysen on southern edge of Båstad village.
GPS: 59.68837, 11.29286

Charges guide

Per unit incl. 2 persons and electricity	NOK 175

Ulvik

Ulvik Fjord Camping

Eikjeledbakkjen 2, N-5730 Ulvik (Hordaland) T: **56 52 61 70**. E: **post@ulvikfjord.no**

alanrogers.com/NO2360

Ulvik was discovered by tourists 150 years ago when the first liners started operating to the head of Hardangerfjord. This pretty little site is 500 m. from the centre of the town and occupies what must once have been a small orchard running down to the fjord beside a small stream. There is room for about 80 units on undulating ground which slopes towards the fjord, with some flat areas and 32 electrical connections and 6 cabins. Access is by winding roads, either along the side of the fjord or up a steep narrow road behind the town – probably not to be recommended for caravans.

Facilities

Reception is at the hotel opposite and campers are welcome to use the facilities here. On the site, a small wooden building houses the well kept sanitary facilities. For each sex there are two open washbasins, WCs and two modern showers on payment. Kitchen with cooker and dishwashing sink. Washing machine. Boat slipway, fishing and swimming in fjord. Jetty with large barbecue area. Off site: Hotel opposite with breakfast buffet, lounges, bar and TV room. Shops and restaurants in town.

Open: 1 May - 15 September.

Directions

Ulvik is reached by road no. 572; the site is on the southern side of the town, opposite the Ulvikfjord Pension. There is a ferry from road no. 7 at Brimnes. Cars and caravans can also connect with road 7 via a tunnel. GPS: 60.56513, 6.90812

Charges guide

Per unit incl. electricity	NOK 180 - 200

Vangsnes

Tveit Camping

N-6894 Vangsnes (Sogn og Fjordane) T: **57 69 66 00**. E: **tveitca@online.no**

alanrogers.com/NO2380

Located in the district of Vik on the south shore of Sognefjord, 4 km. from the small port of Vangsnes, Tveit Camping is part of a small working farm and it is a charming neat site. Reception and a kiosk open most of the day in high season, with a phone to summon assistance at any time. Three terraces with wonderful views of the fjord provide 35 pitches with 30 electricity connections (10A) and there are also site owned cabins. On the campsite you will find a restored Iron Age burial mound dating from 350-550AD, whilst the statue of 'Fritjov the Intrepid' towers over the landscape at Vangsnes.

Facilities

Modern, heated sanitary facilities provide showers on payment, a unit for disabled visitors, kitchens with facilities for dishwashing and cooking, and laundry facilities (hot water on payment). Motorcaravan services. Kiosk (15/6-15/8). TV rooms. Playground. Harbour for small boats, slipway and boat/canoe hire. Fishing. WiFi is planned. Bicycle hire. Off site: Shop, café and pub by ferry terminal in Vangsnes 4 km. Riding 15 km.

Open: 1 May - mid-October.

Directions

Site is by Rv 13 between Vik and Vangsnes, 4 km. south of Vangsnes. GPS: 61.14466, 6.6218

Charges guide

Per unit incl. 2 persons and electricity	NOK 175 - 185
extra person	NOK 10
child (under 5 yrs)	free

No credit cards.

Vassenden

PlusCamp Jolstraholmen

Postboks 11, N-6847 Vassenden (Sogn og Fjordane) T: 95 29 78 79. E: post@jolstraholmen.no

alanrogers.com/NO2400

This family run site is situated on the E39 between Sognefjord and Nordfjord. It is located between the road and the fast-flowing Jolstra river (renowned for trout fishing), 1.5 kilometres from the lakeside village of Vassenden, behind the Statoil filling station, restaurant and supermarket complex which is also owned by the family. The 30 pitches (some marked) are on grass or gravel hardstanding, all with electricity (16A), five also have water and waste points and some have TV connections. A river tributary runs through the site and forms an island on which some pitches are located, and there are also 22 cabins.

Facilities

The main heated sanitary facilities, fully equipped in rooms below the complex, include showers on payment plus one family bathroom per sex. Site reports a new block with family room and facilities for disabled visitors. Two small kitchens provide dishwashing and cooking facilities (free of charge). Laundry. Supermarket and café. Restaurant. Garage. Covered barbecue area. Playground. Water slide (open summer, weather permitting). Rafting. Fishing. Guided walks. Boat hire. WiFi over site (charged; one area free). Off site: 9-hole golf course 50 m. Ski slopes within 1 km.

Open: All year.

Directions

Site is beside the E39 road, 1.5 km. west of Vassenden, 18 km. east of Førde.
GPS: 61.48787, 6.08432

Charges guide

Per unit incl. 1-4 persons and electricity	NOK 190 - 230

Viggja

Tråsåvika Camping

Orkanger, N-7354 Viggja (Sør Trøndelag) T: 72 86 78 22. E: post@trasavika.no

alanrogers.com/NO2500

On a headland jutting into the Trondheimfjord, some 40 km. from Trondheim, Trasavika commands an attractive position. For many this compensates for the extra distance into town. The 32 pitches with fjord view (some slightly sloping), all with electricity connections (10/16A), are on an open grassy field at the top of the site, or on a series of terraces below. These run down to the small sandy beach, easily accessed via a well designed gravel service road. To one side, on a wooded bluff at the top of the site, are 19 cabins (open all year), many in traditional style.

Facilities

The neat, fully equipped, sanitary unit includes two controllable hot showers per sex (on payment). Water for touring pitches is also accessed from this block. Hot water on payment in kitchen and laundry which have a hot plate, dish and clothes washing sinks, washing machine and dryer. Shop. Café (sells beer, wine and food, 20/6-30/8). TV/sitting room. Play area. Jetty and boat hire. Free fjord fishing with catches of good sized cod from the shore. Free WiFi covering touring pitches. Off site: Shopping in Orkanger 6 km. Løkken Verk for Orkla Industry Museum and Information Centre 21 km. Trondheim 40 km.

Open: 1 May - 10 September.

Directions

Site is to the west of Viggja with direct access from the E39 between Orkanger and Buvik, 21 km. from the E6 and 40 km. west of Trondheim. It is best to use the Børsa exit from the direction of Trondheim off the E39 to save possible toll charges if using Orkanger exit, a 6 km. detour in each direction.
GPS: 63.34686, 9.96234

Charges guide

Per pitch	NOK 190
electricity	NOK 40

Portugal

Portugal is a relatively small country occupying the southwest part of the Iberian peninsula, bordered by Spain in the north and east, with the Atlantic coast in the south and west. In spite of its size, the country offers a tremendous variety in both its way of life and traditions.

Most visitors looking for a beach type holiday head for the busy Algarve, with its long stretches of sheltered sandy beaches, and warm, clear Atlantic waters, great for bathing and watersports. With its monuments and fertile rolling hills, central Portugal adjoins the beautiful Tagus river that winds its way through the capital city of Lisbon, on its way to the Atlantic Ocean. Lisbon city itself has deep rooted cultural traditions, coming alive at night with buzzing cafés, restaurants and discos. Moving southeast of Lisbon the land becomes rather impoverished, consisting of stretches of vast undulating plains, dominated by cork plantations. Consequently, most people head for the walled town of Evora, an area steeped in two thousand years of history. The Portuguese consider the Minho area in the north to be the most beautiful part of their country, with its wooded mountains and wild coastline, a rural and conservative region with picturesque towns.

CAPITAL: **Lisbon**

Tourist Office

Portuguese National Tourist Office
11 Belgrave Square, London SW1X 8PP
Tel: 0845 355 1212
E-mail: info@visitportugal.com
Internet: www.visitportugal.com

Population

10.7 million

Climate

The country enjoys a maritime climate with hot summers and mild winters with comparatively low rainfall in the south, heavy rain in the north.

Language

Portuguese

Telephone

The country code is 00 351.

Money

Currency: The Euro

Banks: Mon-Fri 08.30-11.45 and 13.00-14.45. Some large city banks operate a currency exchange 18.30-23.00.

Shops

Mon-Fri 09.00-13.00 and 15.00-19.00.
Sat 09.00-13.00.

Public Holidays

New Year; Carnival (Shrove Tues); Good Fri; Liberty Day 25 Apr; Labour Day; Corpus Christi; National Day 10 June; Saints Days; Assumption 15 Aug; Republic Day 5 Oct; All Saints 1 Nov; Immaculate Conception 8 Dec; Christmas 24-26 Dec.

Motoring

The standard of roads is very variable, even some of the main roads can be very uneven. Tolls are levied on certain motorways (auto-estradas) out of Lisbon, and upon southbound traffic at the Lisbon end of the giant 25th Abril bridge over the Tagus. Parked vehicles must face the same direction as moving traffic.

see campsite map 6

Albufeira

Parque de Campismo Albufeira

N395 Ferreiras - Albufeira, P-8200-555 Albufeira (Faro) T: **289 587 629**. E: **campingalbufeira@mail.telepac.pt**

alanrogers.com/PO8210

The spacious entrance to this site will accommodate the largest of units (watch for severe speed bumps at the barrier). One of the better sites on the Algarve, it has pitches on fairly flat ground with some terracing, trees and shrubs giving reasonable shade in most parts. There are some marked and numbered pitches of 50-80 sq.m. Winter stays are encouraged with many facilities remaining open including a pool. An attractively designed complex of traditional Portuguese style buildings on the hill, with an unusually shaped pool and two more for children, forms the central area of the site. It has large terraces for sunbathing with pleasant views and is surrounded by a variety of flowers, shrubs and well watered lawns, complete with a fountain. The à la carte restaurant, impressive with its international cuisine, and the very pleasant self-service one; both have views across the three pools. A pizzeria, bars and a soundproofed disco are great for younger campers.

Facilities

Very clean toilet blocks include hot showers. Launderette. Very large supermarket. Tabac (English papers). Waiter and self-service restaurants. Pizzeria. Bars. Satellite TV. Soundproofed disco. Swimming pools. Tennis. Playground. Internet access. First aid post with doctor nearby. Car wash. ATM. Car hire. Off site: Site bus service from gate to Albufeira every 45 minutes (2 km). Theme parks nearby. Beaches.

Open: All year.

Directions

From N125 coast road or N264 (from Lisbon) at new junctions follow N395 to Albufeira. Site is about 2 km. on the left. GPS: 37.10639, -8.25361

Charges guide

Per unit incl. 2 persons	€ 23.50 - € 24.65
extra person	€ 5.50
child (4-10 yrs)	€ 2.70
electricity	€ 3.00

Alvito

Camping Markádia

Barragem de Odivelas, Apartado 17, P-7920-999 Alvito (Beja) T: **284 763 141**. E: **markadia@hotmail.com**

alanrogers.com/PO8350

A tranquil, lakeside site in an unspoilt setting, this will appeal most to those nature lovers who want to 'get away from it all' and to those who enjoy country pursuits such as walking, fishing and riding. There are 130 casual unmarked pitches on undulating grass and sand with ample electricity connections (16A). The site is lit but a torch is required. The friendly Dutch owner has carefully planned the site so each pitch has its own oak tree to provide shade. The open countryside and lake provide excellent views and a very pleasant environment.

Facilities

Four modern, very clean and well equipped toilet blocks are built in traditional Portuguese style with hot water throughout. Washing machines. Motorcaravan services. Bar and restaurant (1/4-30/9). Shop (all year, bread to order). Lounge. Playground. Fishing. Boat hire. Tennis. Riding. Medical post. Car wash. Dogs are not accepted in July/Aug. Facilities and amenities may be reduced outside July/Aug. Off site: Swimming and boating in the lake.

Open: All year.

Directions

From A2 between Setubal and the Algarve take exit 10 on IP8 signed Ferreira and Beja. Take road to Torrao and 13 km. later, 1 km. north of Odivelas, turn right towards Barragem and site is 3 km. after crossing head of reservoir following small signs (400 m. section of poor road).
GPS: 38.1812, -8.10293

Charges guide

Per unit incl. 2 persons and electricity	€ 25.70
extra person	€ 5.80
child (5-10 yrs)	€ 2.90

Discounts of 10-20% outside June - Aug, and for longer stays.
No credit cards.

Arganil

Camping Municipal Arganil

EN17 km 5 Sarzedo, Township Sarzedo, P-3300 Arganil (Coimbra) T: **235 205 706.**

E: **camping@cm-arganil.pt** **alanrogers.com/PO8330**

This peaceful, inland site is attractively located in the hamlet of Sarzedo, some 2 km. from the town of Arganil. A spacious and well planned site, it is of a high quality for a municipal and prices are very reasonable! Delightfully situated among pine trees above the River Alva where one can swim, fish or canoe. The 150 pitches, most with electricity (15A), are of a reasonable size, mainly on flat sandy grass terraces and most shaded by tall trees. The site is kept beautifully clean and neat and access roads are tarmac. An excellent, small restaurant has an unusual attached bar with terrace.

Facilities

Sanitary facilities are clean and well maintained, with Turkish and British style WCs, controllable hot showers, washbasins in semi-private partitioned cabins and a hairdressing area. Ramped entrances make it suitable for disabled visitors. Washing machines. Bar, restaurant and snacks. Shop (July-Sept). TV room. Tennis. Free WiFi over part of site. Off site: Bus service 50 m. River beach and fishing 100 m. Watersports 200 m. Swimming pool in nearby Arganil. Golf 25 km.

Open: All year.

Directions

From Coimbra on the IC2 take exit 8 onto the IP3 towards Viseu. Take exit 13 onto the IP6 (N17) towards Arganil and onto the N324-4 to Sarzedo (site signed). Ignore the first site sign in Avelar as there is better access 500 m. further up the road on the right, also signed. GPS: 40.23333, -8.08333

Charges guide

Per unit incl. 2 persons and electricity	€ 8.30 - € 13.00
extra person	€ 1.60 - € 1.80

Armação de Pera

Parque de Campismo de Armação de Pera

P-8365 Armação de Pera (Faro) T: **282 312 260.** E: **camping_arm_pera@hotmail.com**

alanrogers.com/PO8410

A pleasant site with a wide attractive entrance and a large external parking area, the 1,200 pitches at ths site are in zones on level grassy sand. They are marked by trees that provide some shade, and are easily accessed from tarmac and gravel roads. Electricity is available for most pitches. The facilities are good and the self-service restaurant, bar and well stocked supermarket should cater for most needs. You can relax around the swimming pools. The disco near the entrance and café complex is soundproofed which should ensure a peaceful night for non-revellers. The site is within easy reach of Albufeira and Portimão.

Facilities

Three modern sanitary blocks provide British and Turkish style WCs and showers with hot water on payment. Facilities for disabled campers. A reader reports that maintenance can be variable. Laundry. Supermarket. Self-service restaurant. Three bars (one all year). Swimming and paddling pools (May-Sept; charged per day; no lifeguard). Games and TV rooms. Tennis. Well maintained play area. ATM. Internet access. Off site: Bus to town from gate. Fishing, bicycle hire and watersports.

Open: All year.

Directions

Site is west of Albufeira. Turn off N125/IC4 road in Alcantarilha, taking the EN269-1 towards the coast. Site is the second 'campismo' left on the roundabout just before Armação de Pera. There are further sites with similar names in the area, so be sure to find the right one. GPS: 37.10947, -8.35329

Charges guide

Per person	€ 2.50 - € 5.50
child (4-10 yrs)	€ 1.60 - € 3.20
pitch	€ 3.00 - € 9.50
electricity (6A)	€ 2.50 - € 4.00

Min. stay 3 nights 1/6-31/8.

Aveiro

Orbitur Camping São Jacinto

EN327 km 20, São Jacinto, P-3800-909 Aveiro (Aveiro) T: **234 838 284.** E: **infosjacinto@orbitur.pt**

alanrogers.com/PO8050

This small site is in the São Jacinto Nature Reserve, on a peninsula between the Atlantic and the Barrinha, with views to the mountains beyond. The area is a weekend resort for locals and can be crowded in high season – it may therefore be difficult to find space in July and August, particularly for larger units. This is not a large site, taking 169 units on unmarked pitches, but in most places trees provide natural limits and shade. Swimming and fishing are both possible in the adjacent Ria, or the sea, a 20 minute walk from a guarded back gate.

Facilities

Two toilet blocks, very clean when inspected, contain the usual facilities. Dishwashing and laundry sinks. Washing machine and ironing board in a separate part of the toilet block. Motorcaravan services. Shop. Restaurant, bar and snack bar (Easter, June-Oct). Attractive new playground. Five bungalows to rent. Off site: Bus service 20 m. Fishing 200 m. Bicycle hire 10 km.

Open: 30 December - 16 October.

Directions

Turn off N109 at Estarreja to N109-5 to cross bridge over Ria da Gosta Nova and on to Torreira and São Jacinto. From Porto go south N1/09, turn for Ovar on the N327 which leads to São Jacinto.
GPS: 40.67497, -8.72295

Charges guide

Per person	€ 4.30
child (5-10 yrs)	€ 2.20
pitch	€ 11.40
electricity	€ 2.90 - € 3.50

Budens

Parque de Campismo Quinta dos Carriços

Praia da Salema, Vila do Bispo, P-8650-196 Budens (Faro) T: **282 695 201.** E: **quintacarrico@oninet.pt**

alanrogers.com/PO8440

This is an attractive and peaceful, valley site with a separate naturist area. A traditional tiled Portuguese style entrance leads you down a steep incline into this excellent and well maintained site which has a village atmosphere. With continuing improvements, the site has been developed over the years by the Dutch owner. It is spread over two valleys (which are real sun traps), with the 300 partially terraced pitches marked and divided by trees and shrubs (oleanders and roses). A small stream (dry when seen) meanders through the site. The most remote part, 250 m. from the main site, is dedicated to naturists.

Facilities

Four modern, spacious sanitary blocks, well tiled with quality fittings, are spotlessly clean. Washbasins with cold water, hot showers on payment. Washing machine. Excellent facility for disabled visitors. Gas supplies. Well stocked shop. Restaurant (1/3-15/10). Bar (daily in season, once weekly 1/3-15/10). TV (cable). WiFi. Games room. Bicycle, scooter, moped and motorcycle hire. Off site: Fishing, golf and beach 1 km. Riding 8 km.

Open: All year.

Directions

Turn off RN125 (Lagos - Sagres) road at junction to Figuere and Salema (17 km. from Lagos); site is signed. GPS: 37.075427, -8.831338

Charges guide

Per person	€ 5.65
child	€ 2.60
pitch and electricity	€ 12.15 - € 15.75
dog	€ 2.50

Discounts for long winter stays.

Caminha

Orbitur Camping Caminha

EN13 km 90, Mata do Camarido, P-4910-180 Caminha (Viana do Costelo) T: **258 921 295.**

E: **infocaminha@orbitur.pt** **alanrogers.com/PO8010**

In northern Portugal, close to the Spanish border, this pleasant site is just 200 m. from the beach. It has an attractive and peaceful setting in woods alongside the river estuary that marks the border with Spain and is on the edge of the little town of Caminha. The site is shaded by tall pines with other small trees planted to mark large sandy pitches. The main site road is surfaced but elsewhere take care not to get trapped in soft sand. Pitching and parking can be haphazard. Static units are grouped together on one side of the site.

Facilities

The clean, well maintained toilet block has British style toilets, washbasins (cold water) and hot showers, plus beach showers, extra dishwashing and laundry sinks (cold water). Laundry. Motorcaravan services. Supermarket. Small restaurant/bar with snacks (all Easter and 1/6-15/9). Bicycle hire. Off site: Beach and fishing 200 m. Bus service 800 m.

Open: All year.

Directions

From the north, turn off the main coast road (N13-E50) just after camping sign at end of embankment alongside estuary, about 1.5 km. south of ferry. From the south on N13 turn left at Hotel Faz de Minho at start of estuary and follow for 1 km. through woods to site. GPS: 41.86635, -8.85844

Charges guide

Per person	€ 2.50 - € 4.50
caravan and car	€ 5.60 - € 10.20
electricity	€ 2.50 - € 3.10

Campo do Gerês

Parque de Campismo de Cerdeira

Rua de Cerdeira 400, P-4840 Campo do Gerês (Braga) T: **253 351 005.** E: **info@parquecerdeira.com**

alanrogers.com/PO8370

Located in the national park of Peneda-Gerês, amidst spectacular mountain scenery, this excellent site offers modern facilities in a truly natural area. The national park is home to all manner of flora, fauna and wildlife, including the roebuck, wolf and wild boar. The well fenced, professional and peaceful site has some 600 good sized, unmarked, mostly level, grassy pitches in a shady woodland setting. Electricity is available for most pitches, though some long leads may be required. A very large timber complex, tastefully designed with the use of noble materials – granite and wood – provides a superb restaurant with a comprehensive menu.

Facilities

Four very clean sanitary blocks provide mixed style WCs, controllable showers and hot water. Laundry. Gas supplies. Shop. Restaurant/bar (1/4- 6/10, plus weekends and holidays). Playground. Bicycle hire. TV room (satellite). Medical post. Good tennis courts. Minigolf. Car wash. Barbecue area. Torches useful. English spoken. Attractive bungalows to rent. Dogs are not accepted June-Aug. Off site: Fishing and riding 800 m.

Open: All year.

Directions

From north, N103 (Braga - Chaves), turn left at the N205 (7.5 km. north of Braga). Follow N205 to Caldelas Terras de Bouro and Covide where site is clearly marked to Campo do Gerês. An eastern approach from the N103 is for the adventurous but will be rewarded by magnificent views over mountains and lakes. GPS: 41.7631, -8.1905

Charges guide

Per unit incl. 2 persons and electricity	€ 15.75 - € 24.45
extra person	€ 3.20 - € 4.60

Cascais

Orbitur Camping Guincho

EN247, Lugar da Areia - Guincho, P-2750-053 Cascais (Lisbon) T: 214 870 450. E: infoguincho@orbitur.pt

alanrogers.com/PO8130

Although this is a popular site for permanent Portuguese units with 1,295 pitches, it is nevertheless quite attractively laid out among low pine trees and with the A5 autostrada connection to Lisbon (30 km), it provides a useful alternative to sites nearer the city. This is viewed as an alternative for visiting Lisbon, not a holiday site. There is a choice of pitches (small – mainly about 50 sq.m), mostly with electricity, although siting amongst the trees may be tricky, particularly when the site is full. Located behind sand dunes and a wide, sandy beach, the site offers a wide range of facilities.

Facilities

Three sanitary blocks, one refurbished, are in the older style but are clean and tidy. Washbasins with cold water but hot showers. Facilities for disabled visitors. Washing machines and dryers. Motorcaravan services. Gas. Supermarket. Restaurant, bar and terrace. General room with TV. Tennis. Playground. Entertainment in summer. WiFi. Chalets to rent. Off site: Bus service from gate. Excursions. Riding 500 m. Beach 800 m. Fishing 1 km. Golf 3 km.

Open: All year.

Directions

Approach from either direction on N247. Turn inland 6.5 km. west of Cascais at site sign. Travelling direct from Lisbon, the site is well signed as you leave the A5 at exit 12 and follow directions for Birre. GPS: 38.72117, -9.46667

Charges guide

Per person	€ 5.10
child (5-10 yrs)	€ 2.60
pitch	€ 10.90 - € 11.90
electricity	€ 2.90 - € 3.50

Costa da Caparica

Orbitur Camping Costa da Caparica

Avenida Alfonso de Albuquerque, Quinta de Ste Antonio, P-2825-450 Costa da Caparica (Setubal)

T: 212 901 366. E: infocaparica@orbitur.pt **alanrogers.com/PO8150**

This site has relatively easy access to Lisbon (just under 20 km) via the motorway, by bus or even by bus and ferry if you wish. It is situated near a small resort, favoured by the Portuguese themselves, which has all the usual amenities plus a good sandy beach (200 m. from the site) and promenade walks. An area for touring units includes some larger pitches for motorcaravans. There are 240 pitches with electricity connections (long electricity leads may be needed). In addition, there are 140 permanent caravans. We see this very much as a site to visit Lisbon rather than for prolonged stays.

Facilities

The three toilet blocks have mostly British style toilets, washbasins with cold water and some hot showers – they come under pressure when the site is full. Facilities for disabled visitors. Washing machine. Motorcaravan services. Supermarket. Large bar/restaurant (not Nov). TV room (satellite). Playground. Gas. Off site: Bus service from site gate. Fishing 1 km. Riding 4 km. Golf 5 km.

Open: All year.

Directions

Cross the Tagus bridge (toll) on A2 motorway going south from Lisbon, immediately take the turning for Caparica and Trafaria. At 7 km. marker on IC20 turn right (no sign) – the site is at the second roundabout. GPS: 38.65595, -9.24107

Charges guide

Per person	€ 5.10
child (5-10 yrs)	€ 2.60
pitch	€ 10.90 - € 11.90
electricity	€ 2.90 - € 3.50

Darque

Orbitur Camping Viana do Castelo

Rua Diogo Alvares, Cabadelo, P-4900-161 Darque (Viana do Costelo) T: 258 322 167.

E: infoviana@orbitur.pt **alanrogers.com/PO8020**

This site in northern Portugal is worth considering as it has the advantage of direct access, via a gate in the fence (locked at night), to a large and excellent soft sand beach (400 m.) which is popular for windsurfing. There are 225 pitches on undulating sand, most with good shade from pine trees and with electricity in all areas (long leads may be needed). Some flat good sized pitches are reserved for caravans and motorcaravans. As usual with Orbitur sites, most pitches are not marked and it could be crowded in July/August. A pleasant restaurant terrace overlooks the pool.

Facilities

Toilet facilities are in two blocks, both with washbasins with cold water and hot showers. Facilities for disabled campers. Laundry. Motorcaravan services. Gas supplies. Supermarket. Small restaurant with terrace and bar (all Easter and 1/6-30/9). Open-air pool (June-Sept). Reading room with TV, video and fireplace. Playground. Tennis. Medical post. Off site: Beach 50 m. Fishing 100 m.

Open: All year.

Directions

On N13 coast road driving north to south drive through Viana do Castelo and over estuary bridge. Turn immediately right off N13 towards Cabedelo and the sea. Site is the third campsite signed, the other two are not recommended. GPS: 41.67866, -8.82637

Charges guide

Per person	€ 2.70 - € 4.80
child (5-10 yrs)	€ 1.40 - € 2.50
caravan and car	€ 6.70 - € 11.30
electricity	€ 2.50 - € 3.10

Évora

Orbitur Camping Évora

Estrada de Alca Covas, Herdade Esphrragosa, P-700-703 Évora (Evora) T: 266 705 190.
E: infoevora@orbitur.pt alanrogers.com/PO8340

Situated some 1.5 km. from the historic former provincial capital, this site is well located for an overnight stop. There is a small swimming pool and a simple small bar where snacks may be served. Most of the 285 sandy and good sized touring pitches have 15A electricity and those in the older part of the site have well developed shade. The ground is probably not suitable for visitors using wheelchairs. The historic walled town and its castle (on the World Heritage list), and the surrounding area with its megalithic monuments, are well worth visiting.

Facilities
Two toilet blocks are just acceptable. Free hot showers and British style WCs. Laundry. Motorcaravan services. Gas supplies. Bar and snacks (May-Oct). Bread to order. Swimming pool (June-Sept). Tennis. Mature play area (supervision necessary). Off site: Bicycle hire 2 km. Riding and golf 5 km. Supermarkets in the town.

Open: All year.

Directions
Site is 1.5 km. southwest of the town on N380 road to Alcácovas. GPS: 38.557294, -7.925863

Charges guide

Per person	€ 5.10
child (5-10 yrs)	€ 2.60
pitch	€ 10.90 - € 11.90
electricity	€ 2.90 - € 3.50

FernFernao Ferroo Ferro

Camping Parque Verde

Avenida do Casal Sapo, Fontainhas, P-2685-065 Fernão Ferro (Setubal) T: 212 108 999.
E: info@parqueverde.pt alanrogers.com/PO8155

This is very much a site for 812 permanent caravans but it has relatively easy access to Lisbon (just under 20 km) via the motorway and the impressive bridge. It is very much favoured by the Portuguese themselves. The site has all the usual amenities and a village-like central bar and restaurant complex. Most of the amenities are open all year round. There is a small area for touring units containing about 18 pitches and some larger pitches for motorcaravans. There are 20 mobile homes for rent. We see this site as useful for visiting Lisbon rather than for prolonged stays.

Facilities
The single toilet block for the touring units provides acceptable facilities. Washing machines. Supermarket. Bar, restaurants and snack bar (all year). Swimming pool and children's pool (1/5-30/9). Fitness facilities. Play area. Disco and other entertainment. Off site: Trains for Lisbon 4 km. Golf 5 km. Riding 12 km. Fishing 15 km.

Open: All year.

Directions
From the A2 toll road take exit 2 onto N378 towards Sesimbra. Pass through Fernão Ferro and at roundabout follow for Coina into Fontainhas. Stay on tarred road meandering through Fontainhas (rua 25 de Abril) and site is on the right.
GPS: 38.55056, -9.07167

Charges guide

Per unit incl. 2 persons and electricity	€ 16.00
extra person	€ 2.00 - € 3.00
child (over 10 yrs)	€ 1.50

Ferreira do Zêzere

Camping Quinta da Cerejeira

P-2240-333 Ferreira do Zêzere (Santarem) T: 249 361 756. E: info@cerejeira.com
alanrogers.com/PO8550

This is a delightful, small, family owned venture run by Gert and Teunie Verheij assisted by Catarina and Rodrigo Santos. It is a converted farm (quinta) and has been coaxed into a very special campsite. The pitches are on flat grass or on long terraces under fruit and olive trees. There are 30 pitches of which 18 have access to 6A electricity (long leads may be needed). There is a some shade and the site is full of rustic charm and craft works. It is very peaceful with views of the surrounding green hills from the charming vine-covered patio above a small swimming pool. You will notice the working well, no longer powered by a donkey but you can see where he used to circle to pump water.

Facilities
The single rustic sanitary building has British style WCs with hot showers. It could be busy at peak periods. Washing machine. No facilities for disabled campers. No shop but just ask and the baker calls daily. Bar with snacks and restaurant. Children's club room. Separate games and rest room with satellite TV. Artistic workshops. Internet terminals and WiFi. Swing for children. Torches useful. Off site: Town with shops, bars and restaurants and bus service 1 km. Fishing and watersports 5 km. Riding 11 km.

Open: 1 February - 30 November.

Directions
From Lisbon take A1/A23 to Torres Novas then IC3 to Tomar and N238 to Ferreira do Zêzere. Take road N348 to Vila de Rei and the site is 1 km. from Ferreira do Zêzere to the eastern side of town (do not go into the town). From Coimbra use N238 road at an earlier exit. GPS: 39.70075, -8.2782

Charges guide

Per unit incl. 2 persons and electricity	€ 16.25 - € 18.25
extra person	€ 3.50 - € 4.00
child (under 11 yrs)	€ 1.50 - € 2.00

Figueira da Foz

Orbitur Camping Gala

EN109 km 4 Gala, P-3080-458 Figueira da Foz (Coimbra) T: 233 431 492. E: infogala@orbitur.pt

alanrogers.com/PO8090

One of the best Orbitur sites, Gala has around 450 pitches on sandy terrain under a canopy of pine trees and is well cared for. Some pitches near the road are rather noisy. One can drive or walk the 300 m. from the back of the site to a private beach; you should swim with caution when it is windy – the warden will advise. The site fills in July/August and units may be very close together, but there should be plenty of room at other times. Besides the beach, Coimbra and the nearby Roman remains are worth visiting.

Facilities

The three toilet blocks have British and Turkish style toilets, individual basins (some with hot water) and free hot showers. Laundry. Motorcaravan services. Gas supplies. Supermarket and restaurant/bar with terrace. Lounge. Open-air pool (June-Sept). Playground. Tennis. TV. WiFi throughout. Doctor visits in season. Car wash area.
Off site: Beach 300 m. Fishing 1 km. Bicycle hire and riding 3 km.

Open: All year.

Directions

Coming from the north, the site is 4 km. south of Figueira da Foz beyond the two rivers; turn off the N109 1 km. from bridge on southern edge of Gala, look for Orbitur sign on roundabout it is then 600 m. to site. GPS: 40.11850, -8.85683

Charges guide

Per person	€ 5.10
child (5-10 yrs)	€ 2.60
pitch	€ 10.90 - € 11.90
electricity	€ 2.90 - € 3.50

Foz do Arelho

Orbitur Camping Foz do Arelho

Rua Maldonado Freitas, P-2500-516 Foz do Arelho (Leiria) T: 262 978 683. E: infofozarelho@orbitur.pt

alanrogers.com/PO8480

This is a large and roomy ex-municipal site and improvements are still taking place. It is 2 km. from the beach and has a new central complex with a most impressive swimming pool and separated children's pool with lifeguard. Pitches are generally sandy with some hardstandings. They vary in size and are unmarked on two main levels with wide tarmac roads. There is some shade and all touring pitches have electricity (5/15A). The large two storey, brick-faced building contains all the site's leisure facilities but has no ramped access.

Facilities

Four identical modern sanitary buildings (solar heating) with seatless British and Turkish style WCs and free showers. Washing machine in one. Facilities for disabled campers at the block near reception. Supermarket. Bar/snacks and restaurant (closed Nov). Bread to order (1/0 30/6). Children's club. Games room. Small new amphitheatre. Playground – supervision needed. Bus service. Doctor's room. Torches useful. Off site: Bus 500 m. Seaside town and fishing 2 km. Three supermarkets in Foz do Arelho.

Open: All year.

Directions

Site is north of Lisbon and west of Caldos la Rainha. From the A8 take N360 to Foz do Arelho. Site is well signed. GPS: 39.43067, -9.20083

Charges guide

Per person	€ 5.10
child (5-10 yrs)	€ 2.60
pitch	€ 10.90 - € 11.90
electricity	€ 2.90 - € 3.50

Idanha-a-Nova

Orbitur Camping Idanha-a-Nova

Barragem Marechal Carmona, P-6060-192 Idanha-a-Nova (Castelo Branco) T: 277 202 793.
E: infoidanha@orbitur.pt **alanrogers.com/PO8360**

This attractive and well laid out site is located in quiet, unspoilt countryside close to a reservoir near the small town of Idanha-a-Nova. The site has around 500 spacious, unmarked pitches on wide grassy terraces and there is a little shade from young trees. Electricity (16A) is included in the price. Amenities include tennis courts with stadium-style spectator seating and a medium sized swimming pool with paddling pool, together with several playgrounds. A good supermarket, restaurant, bar and terrace complex is located centrally on site but these are only open in high season.

Facilities

Four large toilet blocks, built in the traditional Portuguese style, provide quality installations with some washbasins in private cabins, hot showers with dividers, foot baths and facilities for disabled visitors. Laundry. Supermarket (1/7-30/9). Café and bar (1/6-30/9). Restaurant (1/7-20/9). Swimming pool. Tennis. TV room. Vending machines. Medical post. Car wash. Canoe hire. Off site: Small town of Idanha-a-Nova.

Open: All year.

Directions

Using the N240, turn off at Ladoeiro onto the N354 (32 km. east of Castelo Branco) and follow signs to Idanha. After 16 km. follow signs for 'Campismo'. Do not turn towards Idanha-a-Nova or approach via this town. GPS: 39.950485, -7.187011

Charges guide

Per unit incl. 2 persons and electricity	€ 15.60 - € 26.00
extra person	€ 2.58 - € 4.30
child (5-10 yrs)	€ 1.32 - € 2.20
dog	€ 0.78 - € 1.30

Ilhavo

Camping Costa Nova

Quinta dos Patos, Costa Nova do Prado, P-3830 Gafanha da Encarnação - Ilhavo (Aveiro)

T: 234 393 220. E: info@campingcostanova.com **alanrogers.com/PO8060**

Camping Costa Nova is situated between a river (Ria de Aveiro) and the sea in a protected natural reserve. There is direct access to a large sandy beach via a wooden walkway over the dunes. The 300 grassy pitches are provided with electricity hook ups (10A). This site is ideal for those who enjoy watersports and the surroundings offer plenty of sites of interest for exploration. The site boasts a large bar/restaurant and a café with TV and Internet access. English speaking visitors are welcomed and this sheltered site also attracts many for winter stays. Apartments are available for let.

Facilities

Three toilet blocks are well spaced around the site and offer adequate facilities with free hot water. Laundry room. Supermarket. Bar (all season). Restaurant (1/7-31/8). Takeaway. Snack bar. Shop. Games room. Disco. TV. Play area. Football field. Internet access. Off site: Beach 500 m. Fishing. Golf 600 m.

Open: 2 February - 31 December.

Directions

On the IP5 travelling from Aveiro east towards Barra, cross the bridge. At roundabout take third exit and site is well signed. GPS: 40.59972, -8.75139

Charges guide

Per unit incl. 2 persons and electricity	€ 12.70 - € 16.40
extra person	€ 2.50 - € 3.80
child (5-10 yrs)	€ 1.25 - € 1.90
dog	€ 1.50 - € 1.70

Lagos

Orbitur Camping Valverde

Estrada da Praia da Luz, Valverde, P-8600-148 Lagos (Faro) T: 282 789 211. E: infovalverde@orbitur.pt

alanrogers.com/PO8200

A little over a kilometre from the village of Praia da Luz and its beach and about 7 km. from Lagos, this large, well run site is certainly worth considering for your stay in the Algarve. It has 650 numbered pitches, of varying sizes, which are enclosed by hedges. All are on flat ground or broad terraces with good shade in most parts from established trees and shrubs. The site has a swimming pool with a long curling slide and a paddling pool (under tens free, adults charged). This is an excellent site with well maintained facilities and good security.

Facilities

Six large, clean, toilet blocks have some washbasins and sinks with cold water only, and hot showers. Units for disabled campers. Laundry. Motorcaravan services. Supermarket, shops, restaurant and bar complex with both self-service and waiter service in season (closed November). Takeaway. Coffee shop. Swimming pool (Apr-Sept) with slide and paddling pool (June-Sept). Playground. Tennis. Satellite TV in bar. Disco. Pub. WiFi throughout (free). Excursions. Off site: Bus service from site gate. Beach and fishing 1.5 km. Bicycle hire 3 km. Golf 10 km.

Open: All year.

Directions

From Lagos on N125 road, after 7 km. turn south to Praia da Luz. At the town follow signs for 'campismo'. The beach road is narrow and cobbled and is very challenging in a large unit. GPS: 37.09973, -8.71744

Charges guide

Per person	€ 5.80
child (5-10 yrs)	€ 3.00
pitch	€ 11.50 - € 12.50
electricity	€ 2.90 - € 3.50

Lagos

Yelloh! Village Turiscampo

N125, Espiche, Luz, P-8600 Lagos (Faro) T: 282 789 265. E: info@turiscampo.com

alanrogers.com/PO8202

This good quality site has been thoughtfully refurbished and updated since it was purchased by the friendly Coll family, who are known to us from their previous Spanish site. The site provides 206 pitches for touring units, mainly in rows of terraces, all with electricity (6/10A) and some with shade. Twelve pitches have water and waste water. The pitches vary in size (70-120 sq.m). The upper areas of the site are mainly used for bungalow accommodation (and are generally separate from the touring areas). A new, elevated Californian style pool plus a children's pool have been constructed. The supporting structure is a clever water cascade and surround, with a large sun lounger area on astroturf. One side of the pool area is open to the road. The restaurant/bar has been tastefully refurbished and Roberto and his staff are delighted to use their excellent English, providing good fare at most reasonable prices. The restaurant has two patios, one of which is used for live entertainment and discos in season and the other for dining out. The sea is 2 km. away and the city of Lagos 4 km. with all the attractions of the Algarve within easy reach. This is a very good site for families and for 'snowbirds' to over-winter.

Facilities

Four toilet blocks are well located around the site. Two have been refurbished, two are new and contain modern facilities for disabled campers. Hot water throughout. Facilities for children. Washing machines. Shop. Gas supplies. Restaurant/bar. Swimming pool (Mar-Oct) with two terraces. Bicycle hire. Entertainment in high season on the bar terrace. Two children's playgrounds. Adult art workshops. Aqua gymnastics. Miniclub (5-12 yrs) in season. Boules. Archery. Sports field. Cable TV. Internet. WiFi on payment. Bungalows to rent. Off site: Bus to Lagos and other towns from Praia da Luz village 1.5 km.

Open: All year.

Directions

Take exit 1 from the N125 Lagos - Vila do Bispo. The impressive entrance is about 3 km. on the right. GPS: 37.10111, -8.73278

Charges guide

Per unit incl. 2 persons and electricity	€ 16.20 - € 28.83
extra person	€ 3.28 - € 6.56
child (3-10 yrs)	€ 1.77 - € 3.28
dog	€ 1.01

Camping Cheques accepted.

Lisboa

Lisboa Camping-Parque Municipal de Monsanto

Estrada da Circunvalacao, P-1400-061 Lisboa (Lisbon) T: 217 628 200. E: info@lisboacamping.com

alanrogers.com/PO8140

This very large site is professionally operated by many uniformed staff, providing a quality service at a good price. The wide entrance with its ponds, fountains and the trees, lawns and flowering shrubs leading up to the two swimming pools, is a most attractive feature. On sloping ground, the site's many terraces are well shaded by trees and shrubs. The 400 good pitches include 170 serviced pitches on concrete hardstandings. There is a huge separate area for tents, and 70 chalet style bungalows are for hire. Central Lisbon is 8 km. away with two bus routes giving a regular service from the gate.

Facilities

Eight solar-powered toilet blocks contain quality facilities, including those for disabled visitors. Launderette. Motorcaravan service point. Shops, bar and restaurants. Two swimming pools (with lifeguard; May-Sept). Tennis. Minigolf. Sports field. Playgrounds. Roman theatre. Entertainment in high season. General and TV (cable) rooms. Internet. Organised excursions. Off site: Excellent bus service from site gate. Lisbon city. Bicycle hire 2 km. Golf 5 km. Beaches 10 km. Riding 16 km.

Open: All year.

Directions

From Lisbon take A5 motorway towards Estoril and site is signed from junction 4 onto the 1C17 (huge site signs at first exit to Buraca). The site is immediately on the right. Enter to the right of the fountain on the tiled road. GPS: 38.72477, -9.20737

Charges guide

Per unit incl. 2 persons and electricity	€ 20.00 - € 30.00
extra person	€ 5.50 - € 7.00
child (6-12 yrs)	€ 2.50 - € 3.50

Nazaré

Camping Caravaning Vale Paraiso

EN242, P-2450-138 Nazaré (Leiria) T: **262 561 800**. E: **info@valeparaiso.com**

alanrogers.com/PO8460

A pleasant, well managed site, Vale Paraiso improves every year, with the latest additions being new reception buildings and pool areas. The owners are keen to welcome British visitors and English is spoken. The site is by the main N242 road in eight hectares of undulating pine woods. There are 650 shady pitches, many on sandy ground only suitable for tents. For other units there are around 250 individual pitches of varying size on harder ground with electricity available. A large range of sporting and leisure activities includes an excellent outdoor pool and paddling pool with sunbathing areas. The adventure playground is very safe with new equipment. There is a pleasant bar, innovative takeaway selling roasts and a lower level restaurant/bar. Several long beaches of white sand are within 2-15 km. allowing windsurfing, sailing, surfing and body-boarding. Entertainment for children and evening entertainment is organised in season. Nazaré is an old fishing village with narrow streets, a harbour and marina and many outdoor bars and cafés, with a lift to Sitio. There is much of historical interest in the area although the mild Atlantic climate is also conducive to just relaxing.

Facilities

Spotless sanitary facilities have hot water throughout. Nearly all WCs are British style. Modern facilities for disabled visitors. Baby baths. Washing machine and dryers. Motorcaravan services. Supermarket (1/5-30/9). Restaurant (15/5-15/9). Café/bar with satellite TV. Takeaway. Tabac. Swimming and paddling pools (Mar-Sept; free for under 11s). Pétanque. Leisure games. Amusement hall. Bicycle hire. Safety deposit. Gas supplies. Email and fax facilities. WiFi (free). Apartments, tents and mobile homes to rent. Off site: Bus service from gate. Fishing and boat launching 2 km. Riding 6 km.

Open: All year except 19-27 December.

Directions

Site is 2 km. north of Nazaré on the EN242 Marinha Grande road. GPS: 39.62028, -9.05639

Charges guide

Per unit incl. 2 persons and electricity	€ 21.20 - € 26.70
extra person	€ 3.25 - € 4.85
child (3-10 yrs)	€ 1.60 - € 2.40
dog	€ 2.90

Credit cards accepted for amounts over € 150. Camping Cheques accepted.

Nazaré

Orbitur Camping Valado

Rua dos Combatentes do Ultramar 2, Valado, P-2450-148 Nazaré (Leiria) T: **262 561 111**.

E: **infovalado@orbitur.pt** **alanrogers.com/PO8110**

This popular site is close to the old, traditional fishing port of Nazaré which has now become something of a holiday resort and popular with coach parties. The large sandy beach in the town (about 2 km. steeply downhill from the site) is sheltered by headlands and provides good swimming. The campsite is on undulating ground under tall pine trees. There are said to be 503 pitches and, although some smallish individual pitches with electricity and water can be reserved, the bulk of the site is not marked out and units are close together during July/August. About 420 electrical connections are available.

Facilities

The three toilet blocks have British and Turkish style WCs, washbasins (some cold water) and 17 hot showers, all very clean when inspected. Laundry. Motorcaravan services. Gas supplies. Supermarket. Bar, snack bar and restaurant with terrace (Easter and June-Oct). TV/general room. Playground. Tennis. WiFi. Off site: Bus service 20 m. Fishing and bicycle hire 2 km.

Open: 30 December - 16 October.

Directions

Site is on the Nazaré - Alcobaca N8-5 road, 2 km. east of Nazaré. GPS: 39.5934, -9.02783

Charges guide

Per person	€ 4.30
child (5-10 yrs)	€ 2.20
pitch	€ 8.60 - € 9.60
electricity	€ 2.90 - € 3.50

Odemira

Parque de Campismo São Miguel

São Miguel, Odeceixe, P-7630-592 Odemira (Beja) T: **282 947 145**. E: **camping.sao.miguel@mail.telepac.pt**

alanrogers.com/PO8170

Nestled in green hills near two pretty white villages, 4 km. from the beautiful Praia Odeceixe (beach) is the attractive camping park São Miguel. Unusually, the site works on a maximum number of 700 campers, you find your own place (there are no defined pitches) under the tall trees, there are ample electrical points, and the land slopes away gently. Wooden chalet style accommodation to rent is in a separate area, but some mobile homes share the two traditional older style but clean sanitary blocks. The main building with its traditional Portuguese architecture is built around two sides of a large grassy square.

Facilities

Two older style toilet blocks with British style WCs and free hot showers. Washing machines. Toilets and basins for disabled campers but no shower. Shop (June-Sept). Self-service restaurant (Mar-Oct). Bar, snacks and pizzeria (June-Sept). Satellite TV. Playground. Tennis (charged). Swimming pool (charged). Dogs are not accepted. Torches useful. Off site: Bus service from gate. Historic village of Odeceixe 2 km. Beach, fishing and sailing 4 km. Riding 20 km. Site is inside the Alentejo nature park.

Open: All year.

Directions

Between Odemira and Lagos on the N120 just before the village of Odeceixe on the main road well signed. GPS: 37.43868, -8.75568

Charges guide

Per unit incl. 2 persons and electricity	€ 17.40 - € 27.40
extra person	€ 4.20 - € 6.40
child (5-10 yrs)	€ 2.50 - € 3.70

Odemira

Zmar-Eco Camping Resort

Herdade A de Mateus E.N. 393/1, San Salvador, P-7630 Odemira (Beja) T: **707 200 626**. E: **info@zmar.eu**

alanrogers.com/PO8175

Zmar is an exciting new project which should be fully open this year. The site is located near Zambujeira do Mar, on the Alentejo coast. This is a highly ambitious initiative developed along very strict environmental lines. For example, renewable resources such as locally harvested timber and recycled plastic are used wherever possible and solar energy is used whenever practicable. Public indoor spaces have no air-conditioning, but there is adequate cooling through underfloor ventilation and electric fans where possible. Pitches are 100 sq.m. and benefit from artificial shade. Caravans and wood-clad mobile homes are also available for rent.

Facilities

Eight toilet blocks provide comprehensive facilities including those for children and disabled visitors. Bar. Restaurant. Crêperie. Takeaway food. Large supermarket. Swimming pool. Covered pool. Wellness centre. Sports field. Games room. Play area, farm and play house. Tennis. Bicycle hire. Activity and entertainment programme. Mobile homes and caravans for rent. Caravan repair and servicing. The site's own debit card system is used for payment at all facilities. Off site: Vicentina coast and the Alentejo natural park. Sines (birthplace of Vasco de Gama). Cycle and walking tracks. Sea fishing.

Open: All year.

Directions

From the N120 from Odemira to Lagos, at roundabout in the centre of Portas de Transval turn towards Milfontes. Take turn to Cabo Sardão and then Zambujeira do Mar. Site is on the left. GPS: 37.60422, 8.70142

Charges guide

Per unit incl. up to 4 persons and electricity	€ 20.00 - € 50.00
extra person	€ 5.00 - € 10.00
child (4-12 yrs)	€ 5.00

Camping Cheques accepted.

Olhão

Camping Olhão

Pinheiros de Marim, P-8700 Olhão (Faro) T: 289 700 300. E: parque.campismo@sbsi.pt

alanrogers.com/PO8230

This site, with around 800 pitches, is open all year. It has many mature trees providing good shade. The pitches are marked, numbered and in rows divided by shrubs, although levelling will be necessary and the trees make access tricky on some. There is electricity for 102 pitches (6A) and a separate area for tents. Permanent and long stay units take 20% of the pitches, the touring pitches filling up quickly in July and August, so arrive early. There is some noise nuisance from an adjacent railway. The site has a relaxed, casual atmosphere. Amenities include very pleasant swimming pools and tennis courts, a reasonable restaurant/bar and a café/bar with TV and games room. All are very popular with the local Portuguese who pay to use the facilities. The large, sandy beaches in this area are on offshore islands reached by ferry and are, as a result, relatively quiet; some are reserved for naturists. This site can get very busy in peak periods and maintenance can be variable. There was a large, low season British contingent when we visited, enjoying the low prices.

Facilities
Eleven sanitary blocks are adequate, clean when seen, and are specifically sited to be a maximum of 50 m. from any pitch. One block has facilities for disabled visitors. Laundry. Excellent supermarket. Kiosk. Restaurant/bar. Café and general room with cable TV. Playgrounds. Swimming pools (all year) and tennis courts (fees for both). Bicycle hire. Internet at reception. Off site: Bus service to the nearest ferry at Olhão 50 m. from site. Riding 1 km. Indoor pool and fishing 2 km.

Open: All year.

Directions
Just over 1 km. east of Olhão, on EN125, take turn to Pinheiros de Marim. Site is back off the road on the left. Look for very large, white, triangular entry arch as the site name is different on the outside wall. GPS: 37.03528, -7.8225

Charges guide

Per person	€ 2.30 - € 4.70
child (5-12 yrs)	€ 1.30 - € 2.30
pitch	€ 3.45 - € 12.80
electricity	€ 1.80

Less for longer winter stays.

Outeiro do Louriçal

Campismo O Tamanco

Rua do Louriçal 11, Casas Brancas, P-3105-158 Outeiro do Louriçal (Leiria) T: 236 952 551.
E: tamanco@me.com **alanrogers.com/PO8400**

O Tamanco is a peaceful countryside site, with a homely almost farmstead atmosphere; you will have chickens and ducks wandering around and there is a Burro here. The young Dutch owners, Irene and Hans, are sure to give you a warm welcome at this delightful little site. The 65 good sized pitches are separated by cordons of all manner of fruit trees, ornamental trees and flowering shrubs, on level grassy ground. There is electricity (6/16A) to all the pitches and 5 pitches are suitable for large motorhomes. The site is lit and there is nearly always space available.

Facilities
The single toilet block provides very clean and generously sized facilities including washbasins in cabins. No easy access for disabled visitors. As facilities are limited they may be busy in peak periods. Hot water throughout. Washing machine. Bar/restaurant. Roofed patio with fireplace. TV room/lounge (satellite). Internet access. Swimming pool. Yurts for hire. Off site: Bus service 1 km. Lake 2 km. Beach 11 km. Market in nearby Lourical every Sunday. Lake 12 km.

Open: All year.

Directions
From the A17 (Lisboa - Porto), take exit 5 for Carrico, turn right at the roundabout and O Tamanco is on the left. GPS: 39.99455, -8.78584

Charges 2012

Per unit incl. 2 persons and electricity	€ 18.55

Winter discounts up to 40%. No credit cards. Special low season prices for self-contained motorhomes.

Porto Covo

Parque de Campismo Porto Covo

Estrada Municipal 554, P-7520-437 Porto Covo (Setubal) T: **269 905 136**. E: **camping.portocovo@gmail.com**

alanrogers.com/PO8160

This is a site in a popular, small seaside resort where a fairly large proportion of the pitches are occupied by Portuguese units. However, it has a reasonable sense of space as you pass the security barrier to reception which is part of an uncluttered and attractively designed village square area with some well established apartments for rent. The pitches are somewhat small but are hedged, reasonably level, all have electricity (5A), and are shaded. The beaches are a short walk and feature steep cliffs and pleasant sandy shores.

Facilities

The toilet blocks are clean with the usual amenities including hot showers. Motorcaravan services (outside gate). Restaurant (10/6-30/9). Bar with satellite TV. Shop in season. Recreation room with games and a TV. Play area. Swimming pools (10/6-30/9). Tennis. Barbecue areas. Boat trips and fishing trips organised. Off site: The village is a short walk with shops, bars and restaurants. Bus service to Lisbon 300 m. from site. Fishing 500 m. Riding 20 km. Golf 25 km.

Open: All year.

Directions

From E120-1 Cercal - Sines road (the road changes from the E120 at Tanganheira). Turn left (southwest) to Porto Covo and follow site signs. Do not be surprised to be led through a new housing estate. Look for large white-water tower with site logo. GPS: 37.85269, -8.78806

Charges guide

Per person	€ 2.50 - € 3.55
child (5-10 yrs)	€ 1.75
pitch	€ 5.25 - € 10.80
electricity	€ 2.65 - € 3.30

Póvoa de Varzim

Orbitur Camping Rio Alto

EN13 km 13 Rio Alto-Est, Estela, P-4570-275 Póvoa de Varzim (Porto) T: **252 615 699**.

E: **inforioalto@orbitur.pt** **alanrogers.com/PO8030**

This site makes an excellent base for visiting Porto which is some 35 km. south of Estela. It has around 700 pitches on sandy terrain and is next to what is virtually a private beach. There are some hardstandings for caravans and motorcaravans and electrical connections to most pitches (long leads may be required). The area for tents is furthest from the beach and windswept, stunted pines give some shade. There are arrangements for car parking away from camping areas in peak season. There is a quality restaurant, a snack bar and a large swimming pool across the road from reception.

Facilities

Four refurbished and well equipped toilet blocks have hot water. Laundry facilities. Facilities for disabled campers. Gas supplies. Shop (1/6-31/10). Restaurant, bar, snack bar (1/5-31/10). Swimming pool (1/6-30/9). Tennis. Playground. Games room. Surfing. TV. Medical post. Car wash. Evening entertainment twice weekly in season. Off site: Fishing. Golf. Bicycle hire. Riding (all within 5 km).

Open: All year.

Directions

From A28 in direction of Porto, leave at exit 18 signed Fao/Apuila. At roundabout take N13 in direction of Pavoa de Varzim/Porto for 2.5 km. At Hotel Contriz, turn right onto narrow cobblod road. Site well signed in 2 km. GPS: 41.44504, -8.75767

Charges guide

Per person	€ 2.90 - € 5.40
child (5-10 yrs)	€ 1.50 - € 3.00
caravan and car	€ 6.80 - € 12.00
electricity (5/15A)	€ 2.50 - € 3.10

Praia de Mira

Orbitur Camping Mira

Estrada Florestal no 1 km 2, Dunas de Mira, P-3070-792 Praia de Mira (Coimbra) T: **231 471 234**.

E: **infomira@orbitur.pt** **alanrogers.com/PO8070**

A small, peaceful seaside site set in pinewoods, Orbitur Camping Mira is situated to the south of Aveiro and Vagos, in a quieter and less crowded area. It fronts onto a lake at the head of the Ria de Mira, which eventually runs into the Aveiro Ria. A back gate leads directly to the sea and a wide quiet beach 300 m. away. A road runs alongside the site boundary where the restaurant complex is situated resulting in some road noise. The site has around 225 pitches on sand, which are not marked but have trees creating natural divisions. Electricity and water points are plentiful.

Facilities

The modern toilet blocks are clean, with 14 free hot showers and washing machines. Facilities for disabled visitors. Motorcaravan services. Gas supplies. Shop. Restaurant, bar and snack bar (Easter, June-Oct). TV room. Play area. Bicycle hire. WiFi at the bar. Bungalows (7) to rent. Off site: Bus service 150 m. (summer only). Fishing 500 m. Indoor pool, lake swimming and riding at Mira 7 km.

Open: 30 December - 16 October.

Directions

Take the IP5 (A25) southwest to Aveiro then the A17 south to Figuera da Foz. Then take N109 north to Mira and follow signs west to Praia (beach) de Mira. GPS: 40.4533, -8.79902

Charges guide

Per person	€ 4.90
child (5-10 yrs)	€ 2.50
pitch	€ 8.60 - € 11.90
electricity	€ 2.90 - € 3.50

Quarteira

Orbitur Camping Quarteira

Estrada da Fonte Santa, avenida Sá Cameiro, P-8125-618 Quarteira (Faro) T: 289 302 826.

E: infoquarteira@orbitur.pt **alanrogers.com/PO8220**

This is a large, busy, attractive site on undulating ground with some terracing, taking 795 units. On the outskirts of the popular Algarve resort of Quarteira, it is 600 m. from a sandy beach which stretches for a kilometre to the town centre. Many of the unmarked pitches have shade from tall trees and there are a few small individual pitches of 50 sq.m. with electricity and water. There are 659 electrical connections. Like others along this coast, the site encourages long winter stays. There is a large restaurant and supermarket which have a separate entrance for local trade.

Facilities

Five toilet blocks provide British and Turkish style toilets, washbasins with cold water, hot showers plus facilities for disabled visitors. Washing machines. Motorcaravan services. Gas supplies. Supermarket. Self-service restaurant (closed Nov). Separate takeaway (from late May). Swimming pools (Apr-Sept). General room with bar and satellite TV. WiFi. Tennis. Open-air disco (high season). Off site: Bus from gate to Faro. Fishing and bicycle hire (summer) 1 km. Golf 4 km.

Open: All year.

Directions

Turn off N125 for village of Almancil. In the village take road south to Quarteira. Site is on the left 1 km. after large, official town welcome sign. GPS: 37.06666, -8.08333

Charges guide

Per person	€ 5.90
child (5-10 yrs)	€ 3.00
pitch	€ 12.70 - € 13.70
electricity	€ 2.90 - € 3.50

Sagres

Orbitur Camping Sagres

Cerro das Moitas, P-8650-998 Sagres (Faro) T: 282 624 371. E: infosagres@orbitur.pt

alanrogers.com/PO8430

Camping Sagres is a pleasant site at the western tip of the Algarve, not very far from a lighthouse in the relatively unspoilt southwest corner of Portugal. With 960 pitches for tents and 120 for tourers, the sandy pitches, some terraced, are located amongst pine trees that give good shade. There are some hardstandings for motorcaravans and electricity throughout. The fairly bland restaurant, bar and café/grill provide a range of reasonably priced meals. This is a reasonable site for those seeking winter sun, or as a base for exploring this 'Land's End' region of Portugal.

Facilities

Three spacious toilet blocks are showing some signs of wear but provide hot and cold showers and washbasins with cold water. Washing machines. Motorcaravan services. Supermarket. Restaurant/bar and café/grill (all Easter and June-Oct). TV room. Satellite TV in restaurant. Bicycle hire. Barbecue area. Playground. Fishing. Medical post. Car wash. WiFi (free). Off site: Buses from village 1 km. Beach and fishing 2 km. Boat launching 8 km. Golf 12 km.

Open: All year.

Directions

From Sagres, turn off the N268 road west onto the EN268. After about 2 km. the site is signed off to the right. GPS: 37.02278, -8.94583

Charges guide

Per person	€ 4.90
child (5-10 yrs)	€ 2.50
caravan and car	€ 9.90 - € 10.90
electricity (6A)	€ 2.90 - € 3.50

São Pedro de Moel

Orbitur Camping São Pedro de Moel

Rua Volta do Sete, P-2430 São Pedro de Moel (Leiria) T: **244 599 168.** E: **infospedro@orbitur.pt**

alanrogers.com/PO8100

This quiet and very attractive site is situated under tall pines, on the edge of the rather select small resort of São Pedro de Moel. This is a shady site which can be crowded in July and August. The 525 pitches are in blocks and unmarked (cars may be parked separately) with 404 electrical connections. A few pitches are used for permanent units. Although there are areas of soft sand, there should be no problem in finding a firm place. The large restaurant and bar are modern as is the superb swimming pool, paddling pool and flume (there is a lifeguard).

Facilities

Four clean toilet blocks have mainly British style toilets (some with bidets), some washbasins with hot water. Hot showers are mostly in one unisex block. Laundry. Motorcaravan services. Gas supplies. Supermarket. Large restaurant and bar with terrace (closed in November). Swimming pools (1/3-30/9). Satellite TV. Games room. Playground. Tennis. WiFi. Off site: Bus service 100 m. Beach 500 m. Fishing 1 km.

Open: All year.

Directions

Site is 9 km. west of Marinha Grande, on the right as you enter São Pedro de Moel.
GPS: 39.75883, -9.02229

Charges guide

Per person	€ 5.10
child (5-10 yrs)	€ 2.60
pitch	€ 10.90 - € 11.90
electricity	€ 2.90 - € 3.50

Vagos

Orbitur Camping Vagueira

Gafanha da Vagueira, Gafanha da Boa Hora, P-3840-254 Vagos (Aveiro) T: **234 797 526.**
E: **infovagueira@orbitur.pt** **alanrogers.com/PO8040**

This is a large site set 1.5 km. from the beach and 500 m. from the Ria da Gosta Nova river. It is shaded under tall pine trees and has comprehensive facilities and reasonable prices. The 800 pitches are unmarked, on sand and pine needles with a large number of permanent Portuguese units, which are here in high season and weekends at other times. Groups are taken in high season. All touring pitches have electricity (6A). In sympathy with the surroundings, the modern buildings have clean lines and include a restaurant and bar with a disco area outside where music is played at weekends.

Facilities

Seven modern sanitary buildings with British and Turkish style WCs and free showers. Facilities for disabled campers (unlocked). Washing machines. Bar/snacks and separate restaurant (June-Sept). Large supermarket. Children's club. Outdoor disco. Games room. Playground. Tennis (charge). Satellite TV. Internet room and WiFi. Torches useful. Off site: Seaside town has shops, bars and restaurants. Bus 500 m. River fishing 500 m. Golf and riding 1 km. Watersports at beach 1.5 km.

Open: All year.

Directions

Site is south of Aveiro. Take N109 south from Aveiro towards Mira. At Vagos take the N333 right turn towards Vagueira. Site is well signed at this turn and is just off the roundabout you arrive at on the beach road. GPS: 40.55792, -8.74517

Charges guide

Per person	€ 1.83 - € 3.65
child	€ 0.95 - € 1.85
pitch and car	€ 3.25 - € 8.50
electricity	€ 2.00

Camping Cheques accepted.

Slovakia

Slovakia is a small scale country in the heart of Europe, consisting of a narrow strip of land between the spectacular Tatra Mountains and the river Danube. Picturesque, there are historic castles, evergreen forests, rugged mountains, cave formations, and deep lakes and valleys.

Slovakia has much to offer the visitor with an abundance of year round natural beauty. Its terrain varies impressively; the Carpathian Arc Mountains take up nearly half the country and include the Tatra Mountains, with their rugged peaks, deciduous forests and lakes. Southern and eastern Slovakia is mainly a lowland region and home to many thermal springs, with several open to the public for bathing. Many Hungarians have moved to this area and there is a strong Hungarian influence.

Slovakia has over four thousand registered caves, twelve are open to the public and vary from drop stone to glacial; each one claims to have healing benefits for respiratory disorders. The capital, Bratislava is situated on the river Danube and directly below the Carpathian Mountains. Although it may not be as glamorous as Prague, it contains many fascinating buildings from nearly every age and is a lively cheerful city.

CAPITAL: Bratislava

Tourist Office

Czech & Slovak Tourist Centre
16 Frognal Parade,
Finchley Road,
London NW3 5HG
Tel: 020 7794 3263 Fax: 020 7794 3265
E-mail: info@czechtravel.co.uk
Internet: www.slovakiatourism.sk

Population

5.4 million

Climate

Cold winters and mild summers. Hot summers and some rain in the eastern lowlands.

Language

Slovak

Telephone

The country code is 00 421.

Money

Currency: The Koruna
Banks: Mon-Fri 08.00-13.00 and 14.00-17.00.

Shops

Mon-Fri 09.00-12.00 and 14.00-18.00. Some remain open at midday. Sat 09.00-midday.

Public Holidays

New Year; Easter Mon; May Day; Liberation Day 8 May; Saints Day 5 July; Festival Day 5 July; Constitution Day 1 Sept; All Saints 1 Nov; Christmas 24-26 Dec.

Motoring

A full UK driving licence is acceptable. The major route runs from Bratislava via Trencin, Banska, Bystrica, Zilina and Poprad to Presov. A windscreen sticker which is valid for a year must be purchased at the border crossing for use on certain motorways. Vehicles must be parked on the right.

see campsite map 8

Bratislava

Autocamping Zlaté Piesky

Senecka cesta c 2, SK-82104 Bratislava (Bratislava) T: 024 445 0592. E: kempi@netax.sk

alanrogers.com/SK4950

Bratislava undoubtedly has charm, being on the Danube and having a number of interesting buildings and churches in its centre. However, industry around the city, particularly en route to the site from the south, presents an ugly picture and gives no hints of the hidden charms. Zlaté Piesky (golden sands) is part of a large, lakeside sports complex which is also used during the day in summer by local residents. The site is on the northeast edge of the city with 200 touring pitches, 160 with 10A electrical connections, on level grass under tall trees. For a night stop or a short stay, this might suit.

Facilities

Four toilet blocks, two for campers and two for day visitors, are good and clean. Two restaurants, one with waiter service, the other self-service. Many small snack bars. Shops. Lake for swimming and watersports with large beach area. Minigolf. Play areas. Room with billiards and electronic games. Disco. Off site: Tesco supermarket nearby.

Open: 1 May - 15 October.

Directions

From E75 Bratislava - Trencin motorway exit towards Zlaté Piesky just north of the airport. Head towards Bratislava on 61/E571 and immediately after footbridge turn left at traffic lights. Site is a little way ahead on the left. GPS: 48.11310, 17.11137

Charges guide

Per unit incl. 2 persons and electricity	€ 15.00 - € 16.70
extra person	€ 3.50
child (4-15 yrs)	€ 2.00 - € 5.30

No credit cards.

Levoca

Autocamping Levocská Dolina

Kovácová vila 2, SK-05401 Levoca (Presov) T: 053 451 2705. E: rzlevoca@pobox.sk

alanrogers.com/SK4980

According to the owner, Mr Rusnák, this three-hectare campsite is one of the top ten sites in Slovakia and we agree. The site forms part of a restaurant and pension business and the good value restaurant is welcoming. The entrance is attractively landscaped with varieties of shrubs and colourful flowers and the whole site looks well cared for. There are 60 pitches for tourers, 29 with 10A electricity connections. On grassy fields with views of the mountains, there is some terracing. The main road runs steeply uphill and then continues on grass roads. This may cause larger units some difficulty in bad weather.

Facilities

Good, partly refurbished toilet block (hot water variable) with British style toilets, open washbasins and controllable, hot showers (free). Campers' kitchen. Sauna. Whirlpool. Bar/restaurant. Basic playground. WiFi in reception. Torch useful. Off site: Lake with pedalo hire 300 m. Dobsinska Ice Caves and Slovakian Paradise. Town of Levoca.

Open: All year.

Directions

From Liptovsky Mikulás, take the E50 road east towards Levoca. In Levoca follow site signs. Site is 3 km. north of the town. GPS: 49.04984, 20.58723

Charges guide

Per unit incl. 2 persons and electricity	€ 14.30 - € 15.45
extra person	€ 3.10
child	€ 2.00

Liptovsky Trnovec

Mara Camping

SK-03222 Liptovsky Trnovec (Zilina) T: 044 559 8458. E: info@maracamping.sk

alanrogers.com/SK4915

This is a bustling Slovakian site beside the Liptovská Mara reservoir, also close to the Tatra Mountains which are popular for climbing, hiking and mountain biking. The lake can be used for sailing, surfing, boating and pedaloes and some of this equipment may be rented on the site. Bicycles are also available for hire. There are 250 pitches, all used for touring units and with 14A electricity. With tarmac access roads, the level pitches are on a circular, grassy field and as pitching is rather haphazard, the site can become crowded in high season. Mature trees provide some shade, but in general this is an open site. English is spoken.

Facilities

Two good modern toilet blocks have British style toilets, washbasins in cabins and showers. Facilities for disabled visitors. Laundry and kitchen. Motorcaravan service. Bar with covered terrace and takeaway service. Good adventure playground. Minigolf. Fishing. Bicycle hire. Canoe hire, jetski and boat rental. Games room. Beach. WiFi. Off site: Restaurant 300 m. Tatralandia Aqua Park nearby. Walking in the Lower Tatra Mountains, or serious climbing in the Higher Tatra Mountains.

Open: 30 April - 30 October.

Directions

From E50 road take exit for Liptovsky Mikulás and turn left towards Liptovsky Trnovec on 584 road. Continue alongside the lake to site on the left. GPS: 49.111135, 19.545946

Charges guide

Per unit incl. 2 persons and electricity	€ 20.00
extra person	€ 10.00
child (3-15 yrs)	€ 3.50
dog	€ 2.00

Martin

Autocamping Turiec

Kolonia hviezda 92, SK-03608 Martin (Zilina) T: 043 428 4215. E: recepcia@autocampingturiec.sk

alanrogers.com/SK4910

Turiec is situated in northeast Slovakia, 1.5 kilometres from the small village of Vrutky, four kilometres north of Martin, at the foot of the Lucanska Mala Fatra mountains and with castles nearby. This good site has views towards the mountains and is quiet and well maintained. Holiday activities include hiking in summer, skiing in winter, both downhill and cross-country. There is room for about 30 units on slightly sloping grass inside a circular tarmac road with some shade from tall trees. Electrical connections (6A) are available for all pitches. You will receive a friendly welcome from Viktor Matovcik and his wife Lydia.

Facilities

One acceptable sanitary block to the side of the camping area, but in winter the facilities in the bungalow at the entrance are used. Cooking facilities. Badminton. Rest room with TV. Small games room. Covered barbecue. WiFi. Off site: Shop outside entrance. Swimming pool 1.5 km.

Open: All year.

Directions

Site is signed from E18 road (Zilina - Martin) in the village of Vrutky, 3 km. northwest of Martin. Turn south on the bend and follow signs to Martinské Hole. GPS: 49.108492, 18.899467

Charges guide

Per unit incl. 2 persons and electricity	€ 15.20 - € 17.60
extra person	€ 4.30
child (6-10 yrs)	€ 2.60
dog	€ 0.70 - € 1.30

Namestovo

Autocamping Stara Hora

Oravska Priehrada, SK-02901 Namestovo (Zilina) T: 043 552 2223. E: camp.s.hora@stonline.sk

alanrogers.com/SK4905

Stara Hora has a beautiful location on the Orava artificial lake. It is in the northeast of Slovakia in the Tatra Mountains and attracts visitors from all over Europe which creates a happy and sometimes noisy atmosphere. The site has its own pebble beach with a large grass area behind it for sunbathing. Autocamping Stara Hora is on steeply sloping ground with 160 grassy pitches, all for touring units and with 10A electricity. The lower pitches are level and have good views over the lake, pitches at the top are mainly used by tents.

Facilities

The modern toilet block has British style toilets, open washbasins and controllable hot showers (free). It could be pressed in high season and hot water to the showers is only available from 7.00-10.00 and from 19.00-22.00. Shop for basics. Bar and lakeside bar. Small restaurant. Basic playground (new playground planned). Pedalo, canoe and rowing boat hire. Waterskiing. Fishing (with permit). Torch useful. Off site: Slanica Island.

Open: May - September.

Directions

From Ruzomberok take E77 road north towards Trstena. Turn left in Tvrdosin on the 520 road towards Námestovo. Site is on the right. GPS: 49.359333, 19.555

Charges guide

Per person	€ 2.42
child	€ 1.21
pitch incl. car	€ 3.04
electricity	€ 2.73

Trencin

Autocamping Trencin

Na Ostrove, P.O. Box 10, SK-91101 Trencin (Trencin) T: 032 743 4013. E: autocamping.tn@mail.pvt.sk

alanrogers.com/SK4920

Trencin is an interesting town with a long history and dominated by the partly restored castle which towers high above. The small site with room for 30 touring units (all with electricity, ten hardstandings) and rooms to let, stands on an island about one kilometre from the town centre opposite a large sports complex. Pitches occupy a grass and gravel area surrounded by bungalows, although when the site is busy, campers park between and almost on top of the bungalows. The castle is high on one side and woods and hills on the other, with some pitches enjoying good views of the castle. There is some rail noise. This is a neat, tidy, friendly site with German spoken during our visit.

Facilities

Toilet block is old but tiled and clean with hot water to washbasins (in cabins with curtains) and showers (doors and curtains) under cover but not enclosed. Hot water for dishwashing and laundry. Electric cookers, fridge/freezer, tables and chairs. Little shade. Bar in high season. Boating and fishing in river. Off site: Restaurants 200 m. Shops 300 m. Tennis, indoor and outdoor swimming pools within 400 m.

Open: 1 May - 15 September.

Directions

Initially follow signs for 61 Zilina and having crossed the river, bear left. Turn left at first main traffic lights, under the railway and left again. Then turn right after the stadium. Site is over the canal on the left.
GPS: 48.88327, 18.04067

Charges guide

Per unit incl. 2 persons and electricity	€ 21.00
extra person	€ 5.50

No credit cards.

Turany

Autocamping Trusalová

SK-03853 Turany (Zilina) T: 043 429 2636. E: autocampingtrusalova@zoznam.sk

alanrogers.com/SK4900

Autocamping Trusalová is situated right on the southern edge of the Malá Fatra National Park, northeast of the historic town of Martin which has much to offer to tourists. The site is behind reception on a slight slope. Surrounded by trees with a stream rushing along one side, pitches are grass from a hard road with room for about 150 units and there are some bungalows. A quiet, orderly and pleasant campsite. Information on the area is available from reception, and this site is ideal for those wishing to explore this beautiful region.

Facilities

Old, but clean and acceptable, toilet provision including hot water in basins, sinks and showers. Motorcaravan service point. Covered barbecue area. TV lounge. Playground. Volleyball. Football. Outdoor chess board. Bicycle hire. Off site: Bar just outside site. Restaurants 500 m. and 1 km. Shops in the village 3 km.

Open: 1 June - 15 September.

Directions

Turn north between the Auto Alles car dealer and the Restaurica of the same name on road 18/E50 near the village of Turany to campsite.
GPS: 49.13833, 19.05000

Charges guide

Per unit incl. 2 persons and electricity	€ 14.50
extra person	€ 2.50

No credit cards.

Zvolen

Autocamping Neresnica

Neresnická cesta, SK-96001 Zvolen (Banská Bystrica) T: 045 533 2651. E: jurajivan@stonline.sk

alanrogers.com/SK4940

If you are travelling through Slovakia from Hungary to Poland and looking for a night stop or exploring the central Slovak area, Neresnica is well situated, being on the main 66/E77 highway just to the south of the town. There is inevitably some traffic noise but we did not notice this during our one night stay. The glories of Zvolen lie in the past rather than the present; this basic site, under private ownership, is surrounded by trees with a rushing steam along one side. It is level and has room for 65 units with unmarked pitches of grass from tarmac roads and electrical connections (10A) for about 60%. Apart from Slovak, only German is spoken.

Facilities

Two sanitary blocks are basic (cleaning and maintenance variable) with cold water in cabins for washing and hot water for dishes. A few showers have been installed in former WC compartments, but if you are over 5 ft tall, you might have a problem. Special covered areas have barbecue pits with tables and benches. Bar. Restaurant (at entrance) has an extensive menu with good value meals and sometimes provides music from a violin, cello, zither trio. Off site: Shops 200 m. Swimming pool 150 m.

Open: 1 April - 20 October.

Directions

From Zvolen centre take road 66/E77 towards Sahy. Site is signed as Neresnica and/or Camping Salas at junction with 50/E571 road to Lucenec. The site is on the left just beyond the Slovnaft petrol station.
GPS: 48.56447, 19.13415

Charges guide

Per unit incl. 2 persons and electricity	€ 16.00 - € 18.00
extra person	€ 3.00
child	€ 1.50

Slovenia

What Slovenia lacks in size it makes up for in exceptional beauty. Situated between Italy, Austria, Hungary and Croatia, it has a diverse landscape with stunning Alps, rivers, forests and the warm Adriatic coast.

With its snow-capped Julian Alps and the picturesque Triglav National Park that includes the beautiful lakes of Bled and Bohinj, and the peaceful Soca River, it is no wonder that the northwest region of Slovenia is so popular. Stretching from the Alps down to the Adriatic coast is the picturesque Karst region, with pretty olive groves and thousands of spectacular underground caves, including the Postojna and Skocjan caves. Although small, the Adriatic coast has several bustling beach towns such as the Italianised Koper resort and the historic port of Piran, with many opportunities for watersports and sunbathing. The capital Ljubljana is centrally located, with Renaissance, Baroque and Art Nouveau architecture, you will find most points of interest are along the Ljubljana river. Heading eastwards the landscape becomes gently rolling hills, and is largely given over to vines (home of Lutomer Riesling). Savinja with its spectacular Alps is the main area for producing wine.

CAPITAL: Ljubljana

Tourist Office

Slovenian Tourist Board Office
10 Little College Street
London SW1P 3SH
Tel: 0870 225 5305
E-mail: london(at)slovenia.info
Internet: www.slovenia.info

Population

2 million

Climate

Warm summers, cold winters with snow in the Alps.

Language

Slovene, with German often spoken in the north and Italian in the west.

Telephone

The country code is 00 386.

Money

Currency: The Euro. Banks: Mon-Fri 08.30-16.30 with a lunch break 12.30-14.00, plus Saturday mornings 08.30-11.30.

Public Holidays

New Year; Culture Day 8 Feb; Easter Monday; Resistance Day 27 Apr; Labour Day 1-2 May; National Day 25 Jun; People's Day 22 July; Assumption; Reformation Day 31 Oct; All Saints Day; Christmas Day; Independence Day 26 Dec.

Motoring

A small, but expanding network of motorways. A 'vignette' system for motorway travel is in place. The cost is around € 35 (for a six month vignette) and they can be purchased at petrol stations and DARS offices in Slovenia and neighbouring countries near the border. Winter driving equipment (winter tyres or snow chains) is mandatory between 15 Nov and 15 March. By law, you must have your headlights on **at all times**, while driving in Slovenia. You are also required to carry a reflective jacket, a warning triangle and a first aid kit in the vehicle. Do not drink and drive – any trace of alcohol in your system will lead to prosecution.

see campsite map 4

Bled

Camping Bled

Kidriceva 10c SI, SLO-4260 Bled (Slovenia) T: 045 752 000. E: info@camping-bled.com

alanrogers.com/SV4200

On the western tip of Lake Bled is Camping Bled. The waterfront here has a small public beach, immediately behind which runs a gently sloping narrow wooded valley. Pitches at the front, used mainly for overnighters, are now marked, separated by trees and enlarged, bringing the total number to 280. In areas at the back, visitors are free to pitch where they like. There is some noise from trains as they trundle out of a high tunnel overlooking the campsite on the line from Bled to Bohinj. But this is a small price to pay for the pleasure of being in a pleasant site from which the lake, its famous little island, its castle and town can be explored on foot or by boat. Unlike many other Slovenian sites, the number of statics (and semi-statics) here appears to be carefully controlled with touring caravans, motorcaravans and tents predominating.

Facilities

Toilet facilities in five blocks are of a high standard (with free hot showers). Two blocks are heated. Solar energy used. Washing machines and dryers. Motorcaravan services. Gas supplies. Fridge hire. Supermarket. Restaurant. Play area and children's zoo. Games hall. Trampolines. Organised activities in July/Aug including children's club, excursions and sporting activities. Mountain bike tours. Live entertainment. Fishing. Bicycle hire. Internet access and WiFi. Off site: Riding 3 km. Golf 5 km. Within walking distance of waterfront and town. Restaurants nearby.

Open: 1 April - 15 October.

Directions

From the town of Bled drive along south shore of lake to its western extremity (some 2 km) to the site. GPS: 46.36155, 14.08075

Charges guide

Per unit incl. 2 persons and electricity	€ 20.50 - € 28.50
extra person	€ 8.50 - € 12.50
child (7-13 yrs)	€ 5.95 - € 8.75
dog	€ 1.50 - € 2.50

Less 10% for stays over 6 days.

Bohinjska Bistrica

Camping Danica Bohinj

Triglavska 60, SLO-4264 Bohinjska Bistrica (Slovenia) T: 045 721 702. E: info@camp-danica.si

alanrogers.com/SV4250

For those wishing to visit the famous Bohinj valley, which stretches like a fjord right into the heart of the Julian Alps, Danica Bohinj is an ideal site lying in the valley 3 km. downstream of the lake. It is spacious, stretching from the main road to the bank of the newly formed Sava river, on a flat meadow set in natural woodland. This excellent site has 165 pitches, 145 for touring units (all with 16A electricity), and forms an ideal base for the many sporting activities the area has to offer.

Facilities

Two good toilet blocks with open plan washbasins and hot showers. Facilities for disabled visitors. Laundry facilities (expensive). Motorcaravan service point. Small shop. Bar (also used by locals, open until 01.00 and can be noisy). Café. Tennis. Fishing. Badminton. Volleyball. Cross-country skiing from site. Bicycle hire. WiFi. Excursions in the Triglavski National Park. Off site: Four ski resorts. Riding 6 km. Canoeing, kayaking, rafting and numerous walking and mountain bike trails.

Open: All year.

Directions

Driving from Bled to Bohinj, in Bohinjska Bistrica stay on main road (it goes to the right). Site is 200 m. on the right-hand (north) side of the road. GPS: 46.27335, 13.94868

Charges guide

Per person	€ 7.00 - € 11.00
child (7-14 yrs)	€ 5.60 - € 9.00
electricity	€ 3.50
dog	€ 2.50

Less 10% for stays over 7 days.

Bovec

Camping Polovnik

Ledina 8, SLO-5230 Bovec (Slovenia) T: 053 896 007. E: kamp.polovnik@siol.net

alanrogers.com/SV4280

Camping Polovnik is a small site set in a circular field with trees in the centre, providing useful shade, and an open part to one side. There are 50 unmarked pitches (45 for tourers) all with 16A electricity, off a circular, gravel access road. To the back of the site is a separate field for groups. All pitches have good views of the surrounding mountains. This site is useful as a stopover on your way to the Postojna Caves, the Slovenian Riviera or Italy and for touring the local area with kayaking, rafting and canoeing possible.

Facilities

One well maintained toilet block with British style toilets, open style washbasins with cold water only and preset hot showers (€ 0,50 token). Washing machine, dryer. Motorcaravan service point. Off site: Restaurant at entrance. Fishing 1 km. Bovec town.

Open: 1 April - 16 October.

Directions

Bovec is 35 km. NE of Udine (Italy). Site is south of town and well signposted on the main 203 road. GPS: 46.33622, 13.55837

Charges guide

Per person	€ 6.50
child (7-14 yrs)	€ 5.00

Catez ob Savi

Camping Terme Catez

Topliska cesta 35, SLO-8251 Catez ob Savi (Slovenia) T: 074 936 700. E: info@terme-catez.si

alanrogers.com/SV4415

Terme Catez is part of the modern Catez thermal spa, which includes very large and attractive indoor (31°C) and outdoor swimming complexes, both with large slides and waves. The campsite has 450 pitches, with 190 places for tourers, arranged on one large, open field, with some young trees – a real sun trap – and provides level, grass pitches which are numbered by markings on the tarmac access roads. All have 10A electricity connections. Although the site is ideally placed for an overnight stop when travelling on the E70, it is well worthwhile planning to spend some time here to take advantage of the excellent facilities that are included in the overnight camping charges.

Facilities

Two modern toilet blocks with British style toilets, washbasins in cabins, large and controllable hot showers. Child sized washbasins. Facilities for disabled visitors. Dishwashing and laundry facilities. Motorcaravan service point. Supermarket. Kiosks for fruit, newspapers, souvenirs and tobacco. Attractive restaurant with buffet. Bar with terrace. Large indoor and outdoor swimming complexes. Rowing boats. Jogging track. Fishing. Golf. Bicycle hire. Sauna. Solarium. Riding. Organised activities. Video games. WiFi throughout (free). Off site: Golf 7 km.

Open: All year.

Directions

Site is signed from the Ljubljana-Zagreb motorway (E70) 6 km. west of the Slovenia/Croatia border, close to Brezice. GPS: 45.89137, 15.62598

Charges 2012

Per unit incl. 2 persons and electricity	€ 40.30 - € 49.50
dog	€ 4.00
extra person	€ 17.90 - € 22.50
child (4-11 yrs)	€ 8.95 - € 11.25

Kobarid

Lazar Kamp

Gregorciceva, SLO-5222 Kobarid (Slovenia) T: 053 885 333. E: edi.lazar@siol.net

alanrogers.com/SV4265

Lazar Camp is a fairly open site with a relaxed atmosphere, from which there are good views of the surrounding mountains. Located in the countryside 40 m. above the Soca River, popular with wild watersport fans, there are plenty of walking and mountain biking opportunities directly from the site, in this attractive region of Slovenia. The site has 50 open plan grassy pitches, all with 10A electricity, arranged in large sections divided by low openwork wooden fences. The friendly, informal bar/restaurant (08.00-22.00) serves English breakfast, and fresh bread is available.

Facilities

The sanitary block is of a very good standard and includes facilities for disabled visitors. Washing machine. Fridge. Bar. Crêperie and grill with terrace area. Internet corner, WiFi. Ranch style clubroom. Excursions and lots of local sporting activities. Off site: Kozjak Waterfall. Mountain biking, walking, paragliding, touring.

Open: 1 April - 31 October.

Directions

When approaching Kobarid from Tolmin on the 102 just before Kobarid turn right on the 203 towards Bovec, after 100 m. take the descending slip road to the right and keep more or less straight on to Napoleon's bridge (about 500 m) then continue straight on down the gravel road 700 m. to the site (the road is unsuitable for larger units). GPS: 46.25513, 13.58626

Charges guide

Per person	€ 10.00 - € 11.00
child (7-13 yrs)	€ 6.00
electricity	€ 5.00

Kobarid

Kamp Koren Kobarid

Ladra 1b, SLO-5222 Kobarid (Slovenia) T: 053 891 311. E: info@kamp-koren.si

alanrogers.com/SV4270

Superbly run by its owner, Lidija Koren, this peaceful, well shaded site is located above the Soca river gorge in the countryside close to Kobarid. A small site with 90 pitches, it is deservedly very popular with those interested in outdoor sports, including hiking, mountain biking, paragliding, canoeing, canyoning, rafting and fishing. At the same time, its quiet location makes it a good site for those seeking a relaxing break. Six attractive, well equipped chalets are a recent addition (2009). The Julian Alps and in particular the Triglav National Park is a wonderful and under-explored part of Slovenia that has much to offer.

Facilities

Two excellent, attractive and well maintained log-built toilet blocks. Facilities for disabled visitors. Laundry facilities. Motorcaravan services. Shop (March-Nov). Café dispenses light meals, snacks and drinks apparently with flexible closing hours. Sauna. Play area. Bowling. Fishing. Bicycle hire. Canoe hire. Climbing walls for adults. Communal barbecue. WiFi. Off site: Town within walking distance. Riding 5 km. Golf 20 km. Guided tours in the Soca valley and around Slovenia start from the campsite.

Open: All year.

Directions

When approaching Kobarid from Tolmin on the 102, just before Kobarid turn right on 203 towards Bovec and after 100 m. take the descending slip road to the right and keep more or less straight on to Napoléon's bridge (about 500 m). Cross bridge and site is on left, 100 m. GPS: 46.25075, 13.58658

Charges guide

Per unit incl. 2 persons and electricity	€ 23.00 - € 26.00
dog	€ 2.00

Lesce

Camping Sobec

Sobceva cesta 25, SLO-4248 Lesce (Slovenia) T: 045 353 700. E: sobec@siol.net

alanrogers.com/SV4210

Sobec is situated in a valley between the Julian Alps and the Karavanke Mountains, in a pine grove between the Sava Dolinka river and a small lake. It is only 3 km. from Bled and 20 km. from the Karavanke Tunnel. There are 500 unmarked pitches on level, grassy fields off tarmac access roads (450 for touring units), all with 16A electricity. Shade is provided by mature pine trees and younger trees separate some pitches. Camping Sobec is surrounded by water – the Sava river borders it on three sides and on the fourth is a small, artificial lake with grassy fields for sunbathing.

Facilities

Three traditional style toilet blocks (all refurbished) with mainly British style toilets, washbasins in cabins and controllable hot showers. Child sized toilets and basins. Well equipped baby room. Facilities for disabled visitors. Laundry facilities. Motorcaravan service point. Supermarket, bar/restaurant with stage for live performances. Playgrounds. Rafting, canyoning and kayaking organised. Miniclub. Tours to Bled and the Triglav National Park organised. WiFi throughout (free). Off site: Golf and riding 2 km.

Open: 14 April - 30 September.

Directions

Site is off the main road from Lesce to Bled and is well signed just outside Lesce.
GPS: 46.35607, 14.14992

Charges 2012

Per unit incl. 2 persons and electricity	€ 24.70 - € 30.10
extra person	€ 10.60 - € 13.30
child (7-14 yrs)	€ 7.90 - € 9.90
dog	€ 3.50

Ljubljana

Camping Ljubljana Resort

Dunajska Cesta 270, SLO-1000 Ljubljana (Slovenia) T: 015 683 913. E: ljubljana.resort@gpl.si

alanrogers.com/SV4340

Located only five kilometres north of central Ljubljana on the relatively quiet bank of the river Sava, Ljubljana Resort is an ideal city campsite. This relaxed site is attached to – but effectively separated from – the sparkingly modern Laguna swimming pool complex (open 1/6-15/9). The site has 220 pitches, largely situated between mature trees and all with electricity connections (16A). A modern toilet block is operational in summer while a smaller heated block is opened in winter. The main building and the pool complex provide several bars, restaurants and takeaways to cater for campsite guests and day visitors.

Facilities

The modern toilet block includes facilities for disabled campers, a baby room and children's toilet and shower. Motorcaravan service point. Laundry service. Internet access. Airport transfer service. Bicycle hire. New children's play area. Entertainment for children in July/Aug. Off site: Ljubljana centre 5 km.

Open: All year except 1 January - 14 March.

Directions

From either direction on the northern city ring road, take exit no.3 for Ljubljana-Jezica north towards Crnuce for a little over 1 km. Site is signed (blue sign) on the right just before railway crossing and bridge over the river. GPS: 46.09752, 14.5187

Charges guide

Per unit incl. 2 persons and electricity	€ 18.50 - € 30.50
extra person	€ 7.00 - € 13.00

Camping Cheques accepted.

Mojstrana

Camping Kamne

Dovje 9, SLO-4281 Mojstrana (Slovenia) T: 045 891 105. E: campingkamne@telemach.net

alanrogers.com/SV4150

For visitors proceeding down the 202 road, from Italy or the Wurzen Pass towards the prime attractions of the twin lakes of Bled and Bohinj, a delightfully informal, little site is to be found just outside the village of Mojstrana. For those arriving via the Karavanke Tunnel, the diversion along the 202 is very well worth it. Owner Franc Voga opened the site in 1988, on a small terraced orchard. He has steadily developed the facilities, adding a small pool and two tennis courts and improving all other facilities. The little reception doubles as a bar.

Facilities

The small excellent sanitary block is of a high quality and well maintained. New facilities for babies and disabled visitors. Reception/bar. Small swimming pool. Two tennis courts. TV room. Mountain bike hire. Franc's English is good and his daughter Anna is fluent. Twice weekly excursions to the mountains (free) in July/Aug. Two new apartments and bungalows now available to rent.
Off site: Walking trails.

Open: All year.

Directions

Site is well marked on north side of the 202, 4 km. from Jesenice, just to west of exit for Mojstrana. Site is 4 km. from the Karawanken tunnel.
GPS: 46.46453, 13.95787

Charges guide

Per unit incl. 2 persons and electricity	€ 20.12 - € 21.12
extra person	€ 6.20 - € 7.30
child (5-17 yrs)	€ 4.70 - € 5.20
dog	€ 2.00

Moravske Toplice

Camping Terme 3000

Kranjceva ulica 12, SLO-9226 Moravske Toplice (Slovenia) T: 025 121 200.
E: recepcija.camp2@terme3000.si **alanrogers.com/SV4410**

Camping Terme 3000 is a large site with 430 pitches. There are 200 places for touring units (all with 16A electricity), the remaining pitches being taken by seasonal campers. On a grass and gravel surface (hard tent pegs may be needed), the level, numbered pitches are of 50-100 sq.m. There are hardstandings available in the newer area of the site. The site is part of an enormous thermal spa and fun pool complex (free entry to campers) under the same name. Here there are over 5,000 sq.m. of water activities – swimming, jet streams, waterfalls, water massages, four water slides (the longest is 170 m) and thermal baths. The complex also provides bars and restaurants and a large golf course.

Facilities

Modern and clean toilet facilities provide British style toilets, open washbasins and controllable, free hot showers. Laundry facilities. Football field. Tennis. Water gymnastics. Daily activity programme for children. Golf. WiFi (charged).

Open: All year.

Directions

From Maribor, go east to Murska Sobota. From there go north towards Martjanci and then east towards Moravske Toplice. Access to the site is on the right before the bridge. Then go through a park for a further 500 m. GPS: 46.67888, 16.22165

Charges guide

Per unit incl. 2 persons and electricity	€ 36.50 - € 40.00
extra person	€ 16.00 - € 18.00
child (6-14 yrs)	€ 8.00 - € 13.60
dog	€ 4.00

Postojna

Camping Pivka Jama

Veliki Otok 50, SLO-6230 Postojna (Slovenia) T: 057 203 993. E: avtokamp.pivka.jama@siol.net

alanrogers.com/SV4330

Postojna is renowned for its extraordinary limestone caves, which form one of Slovenia's prime tourist attractions. Pivka Jama is a most convenient site for the visitor, being midway between Ljubljana and Piran and only about an hour's pleasant drive from either. The 300 pitches are not clustered together but nicely segregated under trees and in small clearings, all connected by a neat network of paths and slip roads. Some level, gravel hardstandings are provided. The facilities are both excellent and extensive and run with obvious pride by enthusiastic staff.

Facilities

Two toilet blocks with very good facilities. Washing machines. Motorcaravan service point. Campers' kitchen with hobs. Supermarket. Bar/restaurant. Swimming pool and paddling pool. Tennis. Bicycle hire. Daytrips to Postojna Caves and other excursions organised.
Off site: Fishing 5 km. Riding and skiing 10 km. Golf 30 km.

Open: March - October.

Directions

Site is 5 km. north of Postojna. Leave the A1/E61 autobahn at Postojna exit. In Postojna follow signs to Postojna Caves (Postojnska Jama) continue past caves for about 4 km. where site is signed to the right. Follow road through forest 3 km. to site.
GPS: 45.80533, 14.20457

Charges guide

Per person	€ 10.40 - € 11.40
child (7-14 yrs)	€ 7.90 - € 8.90
electricity	€ 3.90

Prebold

Camp Dolina Prebold

Vozlic Tomaz Dolenja vas 147, SLO-3312 Prebold (Slovenia) T: 035 724 378. E: camp@dolina.si

alanrogers.com/SV4400

Prebold is a quiet village about 15 kilometres west of the large historic town of Celje. It is only a few kilometres from the remarkable Roman necropolis at Sempeter. Dolina is an exceptional little site where reception and bar are housed in the beautifully converted 150-year-old stable, taking 50 touring units, 25 with 10A electricity. It belongs to Tomaz and Manja Vozlic who look after the site and its guests with loving care. It has been in existence since 1960 and was one of the first private enterprises in the former Yugoslavia.

Facilities

The small, heated toilet block is immaculately maintained. Washing machine and dryer. Small swimming pool (heated 30-33°C, 1/5-30/9). Children's play area with trampoline. Large wood-fired oven with doors for traditional cooking. Sauna. Bicycle hire. WiFi. Off site: Good supermarket and restaurant 200 m. Tennis and indoor pool within 1 km. Fishing 1.5 km.

Open: All year.

Directions

Leave E57 at Sempeter/Prebold exit. Head south, after 100 m, right at roundabout, over bridge. Follow site signs to the left after 150 m. Upon reaching Prebold, site is signed to the right down a small side street. GPS: 46.24392, 15.09108

Charges guide

Per unit incl. 2 persons and electricity	€ 22.00
extra person	€ 7.36
dog	€ 3.00

No credit cards.

Prebold

Camping Park Plevcak Povse

Latkova vas 227, SLO-3312 Prebold (Slovenia) T: 037 001 986. E: info@campingpark.si

alanrogers.com/SV4402

Park Plevcak is set on a grassy field close to the E57, directly beside the Savinja river. It provides 30 pitches (all for tourers) and is attractively landscaped with flowers and young trees. Pitching is on one large field, with some shade provided by mature trees and the high hedge surrounding the site. Pitches are not separated, but when it is quiet you can take as much space as you need. There are 18 electricity connections. Tennis courts and a riding centre are just 1 km. away.

Facilities

One traditional style toilet block with modern fittings with toilets, open plan washbasins and controllable hot showers. Laundry facilities. Fridge boxes (free). Fishing. Large barbecue area. WiFi (free). Torch useful.
Off site: Riding 1 km. Golf 20 km.

Open: 1 April - 30 October.

Directions

Leave the E57 motorway at the Sempeter/Prebold exit. Head south. At the roundabout just south of the motorway, turn right. Site is 250 m. on left.
GPS: 46.25588, 15.09917

Charges guide

Per unit incl. 2 persons and electricity	€ 19.50
extra person	€ 8.00
dog	€ 2.00

Ptuj

Camping Terme Ptuj

Pot v toplice 9, SLO-2251 Ptuj (Slovenia) T: 027 494 100. E: info@terme-ptuj.si

alanrogers.com/SV4440

Camping Terme Ptuj is close to the river, just outside the interesting town of Ptuj. It is a small site with 100 level pitches, all for tourers and all with 10A electricity. In two areas, the pitches to the left are on part grass and part gravel hardstanding and are mainly used for motorcaravans. The pitches on the right-hand side are on grass under mature trees, off a circular, gravel access road. The main attraction of this site is clearly the adjacent thermal spa and fun pool complex that also attracts many local visitors.

Facilities

Modern toilet block with British style toilets, open washbasins and controllable, hot showers (free).
En-suite facilities for disabled visitors with toilet and basin. Two washing machines. Football field. Torch useful.
Off site: Bar/restaurant and snack bar and large thermal spa 100 m.

Open: All year.

Directions

From Maribor go southeast towards Ptuj or exit the new (2009) A4 motorway at exit for Ptuj. Follow Golf/Therm signs, drive past spa/therm complex, camping is a further 100 m.
GPS: 46.422683, 15.85495

Charges 2012

Per unit incl. 2 persons and electricity	€ 35.00 - € 39.00
extra person	€ 15.50 - € 17.50
child (6-10 yrs)	€ 7.75 - € 8.75
dog	€ 4.00

Camping Cheques accepted.

Recica ob Savinji

Camping Menina

Varpolje 105, SLO-3332 Recica ob Savinji (Slovenia) T: 035 835 027. E: info@campingmenina.com

alanrogers.com/SV4405

Camping Menina is in the heart of the 35 km. long Upper Savinja Valley, surrounded by 2,500 m. high mountains and unspoilt nature. It is being improved every year by the young, enthusiastic owner, Jurij Kolenc and has 200 pitches, all for touring units, on grassy fields under mature trees and with access from gravel roads. All have 6/10A electricity. The Savinja river runs along one side of the site, but if its water is too cold for swimming, the site also has a lake which can be used for swimming. This site is a perfect base for walking or mountain biking in the mountains.

Facilities

Two toilet blocks (one new) have modern fittings with toilets, open plan washbasins and controllable hot showers. Motorcaravan service point. Bar/restaurant with open-air terrace (evenings only) and openair kitchen. Sauna. Playing field. Play area. Fishing. Mountain bike hire. Russian bowling. Excursions (52). Live music and gatherings around the camp fire. Indian village. Hostel. Skiing in winter. Kayaking. Mobile homes to rent. Climbing wall. Rafting. Off site: Fishing 2 km. Recica and other villages with much culture and folklore are close. Indian sauna at Coze.

Open: All year.

Directions

From Ljubljana/Celje on autobahn A1. Exit at Sentupert and turn north towards Mozirje (14 km). At roundabout just before Mozirje hard left staying on the 225 for 6 km. to Nizka then just after the circular automatic petrol station, left where site is signed. GPS: 46.31168, 14.90913

Charges 2012

Per unit incl. 2 persons and electricity	€ 17.80 - € 23.00
extra person (over 16 yrs)	€ 7.50 - € 10.00
child (5-15 yrs)	€ 3.50 - € 6.00
dog	€ 2.50 - € 3.00

Smlednik

Camp Smlednik

Dragocajna 14a, SLO-1216 Smlednik (Slovenia) T: 013 627 002. E: camp@dm-campsmlednik.si

alanrogers.com/SV4360

Camp Smlednik is relatively close to the capital, Ljublijana, yet within striking distance of Lake Bled, the Karawanke mountains and the Julian Alps. It provides a good touring base, set above the Sava river, and also provides a small, separate enclosure for those who enjoy naturism. Situated beside the peaceful tiny village of Dragocajni, in attractive countryside, the site provides 190 places for tourers, each with electricity (6/10A). Although terraced, it is probably better described as a large plateau with tall pines and deciduous trees providing some shade. The naturist area measuring only some 30x100 m. accommodates 15 units adjacent to the river (INF card not required).

Facilities

Three fully equipped sanitary blocks are of varying standards, but it is an adequate and clean provision. In the main camping area a fairly new, solar powered two storey block has free hot showers, the lower half for use within the naturist area. Normally heated showers in the old block are also free. Laundry facilities. Toilet for disabled visitors. Supermarket at entrance. Bar (all year), food 1/5-30/9. Two good quality clay tennis courts (charged). Swings for children. River swimming and fishing. WiFi.

Open: 1 May - 15 October.

Directions

Travelling on road no.1, both Smlednik and the site are well signed. From E61 motorway, Smlednik and site are again well signed at the Vodiice exit 11. (Watch out for sharp right turn to site on a bend just after camping 1 km. sign). GPS: 46.17425, 14.41628

Charges guide

Per person	€ 7.50 - € 8.50
child (7-14 yrs)	€ 3.50 - € 4.00
electricity (6/10A)	€ 3.00 - € 4.00

Soca

Kamp Klin

Lepena 1, SLO-5232 Soca (Slovenia) T: 053 889 513. E: kampklin@siol.net

alanrogers.com/SV4235

With an attractive location surrounded by mountains in the Triglav National Park, Kamp Klin is next to the confluence of the Soca and Lepenca rivers, which makes it an ideal base for fishing, kayaking and rafting. The campsite has 50 pitches, all for tourers and with 7A electricity, on one large, grassy field, connected by a circular, gravel access road. It is attractively landscaped with flowers and young trees, which provide some shade. Some pitches are right on the bank of the river (unfenced) and there are beautiful views of the river and the mountains.

Facilities

One modern toilet block and a Portacabin style unit with toilets and controllable showers. Laundry with sinks. Bar/restaurant. Play field. Fishing (permit required). Torch useful. Off site: Riding 500 m. Bicycle hire 10 km.

Open: March - October.

Directions

Site is on the main Kranjska Gora - Bovec road and is well signed 3 km. east of Soca. Access is via a sharp turn from the main road and over a small bridge. GPS: 46.33007, 13.644

Charges guide

Per person	€ 11.00 - € 13.00
child (7-12 yrs)	€ 5.50 - € 6.50
electricity	€ 3.50

Spain

One of the largest countries in Europe with glorious beaches, a fantastic sunshine record, vibrant towns and laid back sleepy villages, plus a diversity of landscape, culture and artistic traditions, Spain has all the ingredients for a great holiday.

Spain has a huge choice of beach resorts. With charming villages and attractive resorts, the Costa Brava boasts spectacular scenery with towering cliffs and sheltered coves. There are plenty of lively destinations, including Lloret, Tossa and Calella, plus several quieter ones. Further along the east coast, the Costa del Azahar stretches from Vinaròs to Almanzora, with the great port of Valencia in the centre. Orange groves abound. The central section of the coastline, the Costa Blanca, has 170 miles or so of silvery-white beaches. Benidorm is the most popular resort. The Costa del Sol lies in the south, home to more beaches and brilliant sunshine, whilst in the north the Costa Verde is largely unspoiled, with clean water, sandy beaches and rocky coves against a backdrop of mountains.

Beaches and sunshine aside, Spain also has plenty of great cities and towns to explore, including Barcelona, Valencia, Seville, Madrid, Toledo and Bilbao, all offering an array of sights, galleries and museums.

CAPITAL: Madrid

Tourist Office

Spanish Tourist Office
Second Floor, 79 New Cavendish Street
London W1W 6XB
Tel: 020 7486 8077
Fax: 020 7317 2048
Email: info.londres@tourspain.es
Internet: www.spain.info

Population

46.5 million

Climate

Spain has a very varied climate. The north is temperate with most of the rainfall; dry and very hot in the centre; sub-tropical along the Mediterranean.

Language

Castilian Spanish is spoken by most people with Catalan (northeast), Basque (north) and Galician (northwest) used in their respective areas.

Telephone

The country code is 00 34.

Moncy

Currency: The Euro
Banks: Mon-Fri 09.00-14.00. Sat 09.00-13.00.

Shops

Mon-Sat 09.00-13.00/14.00 and 15.00/16.00-19.30/20.00. Many close later.

Public Holidays

New Year; Epiphany; Saint's Day 19 Mar; Maundy Thurs; Good Fri; Easter Mon; Labour Day; Saints Day 25 July; Assumption 15 Aug; National Day 12 Oct; All Saints' Day 1 Nov; Constitution Day 6 Dec; Immaculate Conception 8 Dec; Christmas Day.

Motoring

The surface of the main roads is on the whole good, although secondary roads in some rural areas can be rough and winding. Tolls are payable on certain roads and for the Cadi Tunnel, Vallvidrera Tunnel and the Tunnel de Garraf on the A16.

see campsite map 6

Albanyà

Camping Bassegoda Park

Camí Camp de l'illa, E-17733 Albanya (Girona) T: 972 542 020. E: info@bassegodapark.com

alanrogers.com/ES80640

Surrounded by mountains alongside the Muga river, Bassegoda Park is a place to experience Spain in a natural environment but with a touch of luxury. This totally rebuilt site is just beyond Albanyá on the edge of the Alta Garrotxa National Park in an area of great beauty. In their own area, the 60 touring pitches are level and shaded, all on hardstanding and with access to electricity, water and drainage. Tents are dotted informally in the terraced forest areas. Particular care has been taken in the landscaping, layout and design of the attractive pool, bar and restaurant, the hub of the site. Regional wines and dishes are available in the reasonably priced restaurant.

Facilities

A new spacious and well equipped, main toilet building provides controllable showers and facilities for babies and disabled visitors. Washing machine and dryer. Gas. Supermarket. Bar, restaurant and takeaway (all season). Swimming pool (1/6-15/9). Playground. New leisure area. Minigolf. Activities for adults and children, plus weekend entertainment. Bicycle hire. Barbecue areas. WiFi. Torches useful. Air-conditioned bungalows to rent. Off site: Fishing and river 1 km. Sailing 5 km. Riding 15 km. Golf 20 km.

Open: 1 March - 11 December.

Directions

Site is north of Girona, 23 km. west of Figueres. From Barcelona on AP7/E15, take exit 4 and the N11 towards France, then the GI 510 to Llers and GI 511 to St Llorenc de la Muga and Albanyá. Site is beyond the village (take care with sharp bend), well signed where road ends. GPS: 42.30654, 2.70933

Charges guide

Per unit incl. 2 persons and electricity	€ 29.85 - € 35.40
extra person	€ 5.60 - € 6.85

Albarracin

Camping Ciudad de Albarracin

Junto al Polideportivo, Camino de gea, E-44100 Albarracin (Teruel) T: 978 710 197

alanrogers.com/ES90950

Albarracin, in southern Aragon is set in the Reserva Nacional de los Montes Universales and is a much frequented, fascinating town with a Moorish castle. The old city walls towering above date from its days when it attempted to become a separate country within Spain. This neat and clean family site is set on three levels on a hillside behind the town, with a walk of 1 km. to the centre. It is very modern and has high quality facilities including a superb building for barbecuing (all materials provided). There are 140 pitches (70 for touring units), all with electricity and separated by trees. Some require cars to be parked separately.

Facilities

The two spotless, modern sanitary buildings provide British style WCs, quite large showers and hot water throughout. Baby bath. Washing machines. Bar/restaurant (all season). Essentials from bar. Special room for barbecues with fire and wood provided. Play area. Torches required in some areas. Off site: Municipal swimming pool 100 m. (high season). Town shops, bars and restaurants 500 m. Fishing 1 km.

Open: 1 March - 2 November.

Directions

From Teruel north on the N330 for about 8 km. then west onto A1512 for 30 km. From the A23 use exit 124 then the A1512, from the N235 take exit for Albarracin and the A1512. Site is well signed in the town. GPS: 40.41655, -1.43332

Charges guide

Per unit incl. 2 persons and electricity	€ 18.05 - € 18.75
extra person	€ 3.80

Alcossebre

Camping Playa Tropicana

Playa Tropicana, E-12579 Alcossebre (Castelló) T: 964 412 463. E: info@playatropicana.com

alanrogers.com/ES85600

Playa Tropicana is a unique site which will strike visitors immediately as being very different. It has been given a tropical theme with scores of 'Romanesque' white statues around the site including in the sanitary blocks. The site has 300 marked pitches separated by lines of flowering bushes under mature trees. The pitches vary in size (50-90 sq.m), most are shaded and there are electricity connections throughout (some need long leads). There are 50 pitches with shared water and drainage on their boundaries. The site has a delightful position away from the main hub of tourism, alongside a good sandy beach which shelves gently into the clean waters.

Facilities

Three sanitary blocks are fully equipped and of excellent standard, with washbasins in private cabins. Baby baths and facilities for disabled visitors. Washing machine. Motorcaravan services. Gas supplies. Large supermarket. Superb restaurant. (Easter-late Sept). Swimming pools and children's pool. Playground. Bicycle hire. Children's club. Fishing. Torches necessary in some areas. No TVs allowed in July/Aug. Dogs are accepted in one area. WiFi (charged). Off site: Fishing and watersports on beaches.

Open: All year.

Directions

Alcoceber (or Alcossebre) is between Peñiscola and Oropesa. Turn off N340 at 1018 km. marker towards Alcossebre on CV142. Just before town go through two sets of traffic lights and turn right immediately after second set, follow the road to coast and site is 2.5 km. Avoid alternative route given by GPS (very narrow in places and uneven). GPS: 40.222, 0.267

Charges 2012

Per unit incl. 2 persons and electricity	€ 24.50 - € 48.00

Alcossebre

Camping Ribamar

Partida Ribamar s/n, E-12579 Alcossebre (Castelló) T: 964 761 163. E: info@campingribamar.com

alanrogers.com/ES85610

Camping Ribamar is tucked away within the National Park of the Sierra de Irta, to the north of Alcossebre, and with direct access to a rugged beach. There are two grades of pitches on offer here. A number of 'standard' pitches are available for small tents. These pitches of around 30 sq.m. have electrical connections. The majority of pitches are larger (90-100 sq.m) and are classed 'premium', with electricity and a water supply. A number of chalets (with air-conditioning) are available for rent. Leisure facilities here include a large swimming pool plus delightful children's pool and a paddling pool.

Facilities

One spotlessly clean toilet block with facilities for babies and campers with disabilities. Dishwashing and laundry facilities. Bar. Restaurant. Shop. Swimming pool. Paddling pool. Multisports terrain. Tennis. Five-a-side football. Boules. Paddle court. Bicycle hire. Play area. Social room/library. Tourist information. Chalets for rent. Direct access to rocky beach. Fishing. WiFi. Charcoal barbecues are not allowed. Off site: Beach 2 km. Alcossebre 3 km. Riding 10 km. Golf 35 km. Coastal walks.

Open: All year.

Directions

Leave AP7 motorway at exit 44 and follow signs to Alcossebre using N340 and CV142. The site can be found to the north of the town. Follow signs to Sierra de Irta and then the site, which is 2.5 km. along a dusty, gravel track. GPS: 40.270282, 0.306729

Charges 2012

Per unit incl. 2 persons and electricity	€ 22.20 - € 47.00
extra person	€ 3.70 - € 5.25
child (3-12 yrs)	€ 2.90 - € 4.50

Almeria

Camping La Garrofa

Ctra N340 km 435,4, direccion a Aguadulce via Litoral, E-04002 Almeria (Almer'a) T: 950 235 770.
E: info@lagarrofa.com **alanrogers.com/ES87650**

One of the earliest sites in Spain (dating back to 1957), La Garrofa nestles in a cove with a virtually private beach accessed only by sea or through the campsite. It is rather dramatic with the tall mountain cliffs behind. Many of the rather small 100 flat and sloping sandy pitches are shaded, with some very close to the beach and sea. Eighty have 6/10A electricity. An old fortress looks down on the campsite you can walk to it via a valley at the back of the site and across an old Roman bridge. Other walks directly from the site include a Roman road providing fine coastal views.

Facilities

Sanitary facilities are mature but clean. Facilities for disabled campers. Restaurant/snack bar. Shop. Play area. Fishing. Torches useful. WiFi. Off site: Town close by. Walks. Sub-aqua diving. Bicycle hire 2 km. Golf 8 km. Excursions – tickets to attractions sold. Bus stop nearby to Almeria and Aguadulce.

Open: All year.

Directions

Site is west of Almeria. Take 438 exit from the N340 and follow the Almeria/Puerto signs. Then take the Aguadulce direction, from where site is signed. GPS: 36.8257, -2.5161

Charges guide

Per unit incl. 2 persons and electricity	€ 24.28 - € 27.90
extra person	€ 5.50
child	€ 4.86

Almonte

Camping La Aldea

El Rocio, E-21750 Almonte (Huelva) T: 959 442 677. E: info@campinglaaldea.com

alanrogers.com/ES88730

This impressive site lies just on the edge of the Parque Nacional de Do–ana, southwest of Sevilla on the outskirts of El Rocio. The town hosts a fiesta at the end of May with over one million people attending the local shrine. They travel for days in processions with cow-drawn or motorised vehicles to attend. If you want to stay this weekend book well in advance! The well planned, modern site is well set out and the 246 pitches have natural shade from trees or artificial shade and 10A electricity. There are 52 serviced pitches with water and sewerage.

Facilities

Two sanitary blocks provide excellent facilities including provision for disabled visitors. Motorcaravan service point. Swimming pool (May-Oct). Restaurant and bar in separate new complex. Shop. Internet connection. Playground. Off site: Bus stop 5 minutes walk. Beach 15 km. Huelva and Sevilla are about an hour's drive.

Open: All year.

Directions

From main Huelva - Sevilla road E1/A49 take exit 48 and drive south through Almonte to outskirts of El Rocio. Site is on left just past 25 km. marker. Go down to the roundabout and back up to be on the right side of the road to turn in. GPS: 37.1428, -6.491164

Charges guide

Per unit incl. 2 persons and electricity	€ 23.00 - € 26.00
extra person	€ 5.50
child (0-10 yrs)	€ 4.50
dog	€ 3.00

Altea

Camping Cap Blanch

Playa de Cap Blanch 25, E-03590 Altea (Alacant) T: 965 845 946. E: capblanch@ctv.es

alanrogers.com/ES86870

This small site was untidy when seen, but it has direct access across a small but busy road to the attractive pebble beach and is within a few hundred yards of all Albir's shops and restaurants. The 250 pitches on flat stone and gravel are of a good size with 5/10A electricity (extra charge for 10A). The site tends to be full in winter and is very popular with several nationalities, especially the Dutch, as prices have not risen for four years. For winter stays, it would pay to get there before Christmas as January and February are the peak months. Although it is on the coast, the site is well sheltered and something of a suntrap. However, there is considerable traffic noise from the roads along two sides of the site and it is overlooked by the high-rise flats nearby.

Facilities

The neglected sanitary block can be heated and provides tired facilities including some washbasins in cabins, separate baby facilities and a room for disabled visitors (both these accessed by key). Motorcaravan services. Gas supplies. Laundry. Rustic bar and restaurant on seafront (open to public). Takeaway. Playground. Tennis. Boules. Fitness centre. Organised entertainment and courses. ATM. Off site: Restaurants, shops and commercial centre close. Golf 500 m. Bicycle hire 1 km. Riding 5 km.

Open: All year.

Directions

Site is on the Albir - Altea coast road and can be reached from either end. From N332, north or south, watch for sign Playa del Albir and proceed through Albir to the coast road. Site is on north side of Albir, well signed along one-way system alongside sea. GPS: 38.5777, -0.06461

Charges guide

Per person	€ 3.90 - € 6.00
child (3-12 yrs)	€ 3.25 - € 5.00
pitch incl. car	€ 8.45 - € 13.00
electricity	€ 3.25 - € 5.00

Less 10-35% for low season stays 7-30 days, special rates for long stays.

Ametlla de Mar

Camping Caravanning Ametlla Village Platja

Apdo 240, Paraje Santes Creus, E-43860 Ametlla de Mar (Tarragona) T: 977 267 784.

E: info@campingametlla.com alanrogers.com/ES85360

Occupying a terraced hillside above colourful coves with shingle beaches and two small associated lagoons, this site falls into four areas. The central one with reception and supermarket has a group of 44 touring pitches, below this are chalets for rent and a few touring pitches on ground falling away towards lagoons and the beach. A second larger touring section also has 54 mobile homes owned by tour operators and finally, the bar/restaurant, pool and other leisure facilities take pride of place on the hilltop, with glimpses of the sea through the trees. There is some train noise, especially in the front section. The site is in a protected area and the buildings are in keeping with the environment in materials used and quality of construction.

Facilities

Two large toilet blocks, plus a smaller, simpler one. Controllable showers and open-style washbasins. Some private cabins with WC and washbasin and a few also have a shower. En-suite unit for diabled visitors. Baby rooms with bath for toddlers. Motorcaravan services. Gas supplies. Supermarket (2/4-30/9; small shop incl. bread at other times). Good bar/restaurant with TV and terrace, snack menu and takeaway, new pub/cocktail bar upstairs with balcony and sea views (all 2/4-30/9). Attractive swimming pools (supervised 22/6-15/9). Sub-aqua diving. Kayaking. Fishing. Children's club and play area. Fitness room. Gym. Bicycle hire. Entertainment (July/Aug). Barbecue area. Fishing. WiFi area (charged). Off site: Boat launching 1 km. Village with shops, bars and restaurants 2 km. Riding 3 km. Golf 17 km. Mature reserve and Port Aventura both an easy drive.

Open: All year.

Directions

Ametlla is 50 km. south of Tarragona. From the AP7/E15 (Barcelona-Valencia) at exit 39 (or from N340) follow signs for Ametlla de Mar. Bear right before village following numerous white signs and continue for 2 km. Take care on final steep bend to site. GPS: 40.8645, 0.7788

Charges guide

Per unit incl. 2 persons and electricity	€ 20.70 - € 36.50
extra person	€ 3.40 - € 6.50
child (under 10 yrs)	€ 2.70 - € 5.20

Less for longer stays in low season.

Amposta

Camping Eucaliptus

Platja Eucaliptus s/n, E-43870 Amposta (Tarragona) T: 977 479 046. E: eucaliptus@campingeucaliptus.com

alanrogers.com/ES85550

Ideally situated in the Parc Natural del Delta del Ebro, a unique area of wetland and a World Heritage site, this campsite is close to the golden sands of Platja Eucaliptus. Arriving here is like finding an oasis after the extraordinary drive through miles of flat marshland and rice fields. There are 264 small, level, shady grass pitches, 156 for touring, all with electricity (6A). The site is very well maintained and has a pleasant bar/restaurant which has a terrace that overlooks both the pleasant pool area and the campsite's own lagoon and its variety of wildlife. The pool has an attractive grassy area for sunbathing and the lagoon (fenced) replicates in miniature the habitat of the Delta, with helpful signs identifying flora and fauna. There is access to the beach through a gate at the back of the site where care must be taken with children as there is an open irrigation channel. There are purpose built hides and observation platforms nearby making this site a birdwatchers' paradise. Due to the nature of the Delta, mosquitoes may be encountered and you are advised to take precautions, although the owners take regular action to reduce this nuisance.

Facilities

The single toilet block is kept very clean and includes open style washbasins and good sized shower cubicles. Baby bath. Good facilities for disabled visitors. Laundry facilities. Dog shower. Well stocked shop. Gas supplies. Bar with satellite TV. Good restaurant and snack bar with takeaway (all season). Play area. Swimming pool with paddling pool (1/6-15/9). Bicycle hire. Attractive barbecue area with covered seating. Large units may require two pitches (no extra charge in low season). Off site: Beach and fishing 300 m. Birdwatching. Small town of Sant Jaume, some shops, Friday market 9 km. Sailing.

Open: 23 March - 30 September.

Directions

Site is 20 km. southeast of Amposta. From the AP7 take exit 41 and follow N340 south. Immediately after crossing river Ebro take exit signed Els Muntells and Sant Jaume, then bear right in 4 km. on the TV3405 to Els Muntells. Continue 13.5 km. to site on the right. GPS: 40.65658, 0.77978

Charges guide

Per unit incl. 2 persons and electricity	€ 25.55 - € 33.10
extra person	€ 4.90 - € 6.90
child (3-10 yrs)	€ 3.60 - € 4.95

Aranda de Duero

Camping Costajan

Ctra NI E-5 km 164-165, E-09400 Aranda de Duero (Burgos) T: 947 502 070.
E: costajan@camping-costajan.com **alanrogers.com/ES92500**

This site is well placed as an en route stop for the ferries, being 80 km. south of Burgos. This is the capital of the Ribera del Duero wine region that produces many fine wines competing with the great Riojas. With 225 unmarked pitches, all with electricity available, there are around 100 for all types of tourer. Large units may find access to the 225 unmarked, variably sized pitches a bit tricky among dense olive and pine trees and on the slightly undulating sandy ground but the trees provide good shade. There are 115 electricity connections. The welcome from Juan Carlos is warm and friendly (in any one of seven languages).

Facilities

Good, heated, modern sanitary facilities. Facilities for disabled campers. Washing machine. Gas supplies. Shop with essentials (all year). Bar serving simple meals (all year). Free access to adjacent large swimming pool (June-Sept). Tennis. Minigolf. WiFi throughout (charged). Torch useful. If reception is unmanned, choose a pitch and book in later. Off site: Public transport 1 km. Riding 2 km. Fishing and river beach 3 km. Golf 30 km.

Open: All year.

Directions

From A1/E5 take exit at 164,5 km. and turn south on N1 towards Aranda de Duero. The site is on the right at the 162 km. mark. GPS: 41.702, -3.68803

Charges guide

Per person	€ 5.40 - € 5.60
child	€ 5.10 - € 5.30
pitch	€ 8.90 - € 11.50
electricity	€ 5.00
dog	€ 2.40

Aranjuez

Camping Internacional Aranjuez

Soto del Rebollo, s/n antigua NIV km 46,8, E-28300 Aranjuez (Madrid) T: 918 911 395.

E: info@campingaranjuez.com **alanrogers.com/ES90910**

Aranjuez, supposedly Spain's version of Versailles, is worthy of a visit with its beautiful palaces, leafy squares, avenues and gardens. This useful, popular and unusually well equipped site is therefore excellent for enjoying the unusual attractions or for an en-route stop. It is 47 km. south of Madrid and 46 km. from Toledo. The site is alongside the River Tajo in a park-like situation with mature trees. There are 162 touring pitches, all with electricity (16A), set on flat grass amid tall trees. The site was bought by the owners of La Marina (ES87420) who have worked hard to improve the pitches and the site. Two little tourist road trains run from the site to the palaces daily. You can visit the huge, but slightly decaying, Royal Palace or the Casa del Labrador (translates as farmer's cottage) which is a small neo-classical palace in unusual and differing styles. It has superb gardens commissioned by Charles II. Canoes may be hired from behind the supermarket and there is a lockable moat gate to allow access to the river. There is good security backed up with CCTV around the river perimeter.

Facilities

The largest of three modern, good quality sanitary blocks is heated in winter and well equipped with some washbasins in cabins. Laundry facilities. Gas supplies. Small shop, bar and restaurant (all year) with attractive riverside patio (also open to the public). Takeaway. TV room. Swimming and paddling pools, (renovated in 2009; 1/5-15/10). New play area. Pétanque. Bicycle hire. Canoe hire. WiFi (free). Torch useful. Off site: Within easy walking distance of palace, gardens and museums. Golf 2 km.

Open: All year.

Directions

From the M305 (Madrid - Aranjuez) look for 8 km. marker on the outskirts of town. Then follow campsite signs leading back onto M305 (going north now) and site is signed off right at 300 m. on first left bend. Follow signs down narrow road for 400 m. If coming from south ensure that you have the M305 to Madrid (other roads are signed to Madrid). GPS: 40.0426, -3.5995

Charges 2012

Per unit incl. 2 persons and electricity	€ 25.10 - € 35.10
extra person	€ 4.50 - € 6.00
child (3-10 yrs)	€ 3.25 - € 4.90

Baños de Fortuna

Camping La Fuente

Camino de La Bocamina, E-30626 Baños de Fortuna (Murcia) T: 968 685 125. E: info@campingfuente.com

alanrogers.com/ES87450

Located in an area known for its thermal waters since Roman and Moorish times and with just 87 pitches and 14 bungalows, La Fuente is a gem. Unusually, winter is high season here. The main attraction here is the huge hydrotherapy centre where the water temperature is constant at 36° all year. The pool can be covered in inclement weather. The site is in two sections, one where pitches are in standard rows and the other where they are in circles around blocks. The hard, flat pitches are on shingle (rock pegs advised), have 10A electricity (Europlug) and 53 have their own mini sanitary unit. Some artificial shade has been added on 22 pitches.

Facilities

Some pitches have their own facilities including a unit for disabled campers. Washing machines and dryers. Supermarket. High quality restaurant shared with accommodation guests. Snack bar by pool. Jacuzzi. Bicycle hire. Communal barbecues only. WiFi (free). Off site: Spa town, massage therapies and hot pools 500 m. Fortuna with shops, bars and restaurants 3 km. Golf and riding 20 km.

Open: All year.

Directions

From A7/E15 Alicante - Murcia road take C3223 to Fortuna then follow signs to Baños de Fortuna. The site has yellow walls and is easily seen from the road and is well signed. GPS: 38.20682, -1.10732

Charges 2012

Per unit incl. 2 persons and electricity	€ 16.74
with individual sanitary facility	€ 18.90
extra person	€ 3.51
child (3-12 yrs)	€ 1.35

Bayona

Camping Bayona Playa

Ctra Vigo - Bayona km 19, E-36393 Bayona (Pontevedra) T: 986 350 035.
E: campingbayona@campingbayona.com **alanrogers.com/ES89360**

Situated on a narrow peninsula with the sea and river estuary all around it, this large and well maintained campsite is great for a relaxing break. The 450 pitches, 358 for touring, benefit from the shade of mature trees whilst still maintaining a very open feel. All have 5A electricity and 50 are fully serviced. It is busy here in high season so advance booking is recommended. Sabaris is a short walk away and Bayona is a 20-minute walk along the coast, where you can find a variety of shops, supermarkets, banks, bars and eating places. Maximum unit length is 7.5 m.

Facilities

Three well maintained modern toilet blocks (one open low season), washbasins and shower cubicles. No washing machines but site provides a service wash. Facilities for visitors with disabilities. Large well stocked supermarket and gift shop (June-Sept). Terrace bar, caféteria, restaurant. Excellent pool complex with slide (small charge, redeemable in shop and restaurant). Play area. Organised activities July/Aug. Off site: Fishing 100 m. Bicycle hire 5 km. Riding 8 km. Golf 20 km.

Open: All year.

Directions

From Vigo leave AG57, exit 5 Bayona North. Follow signs to site at Sabaris, 2 km. east of Bayona.
GPS: 42.113978, -8.826013

Charges guide

Per person	€ 6.30
child (3-12 yrs)	€ 3.95
pitch	€ 3.95 - € 13.05
electricity	€ 3.95

Begur

Camping El Maset

Playa de Sa Riera, E-17255 Begur (Girona) T: 972 623 023. E: info@campingelmaset.com
alanrogers.com/ES81030

A delightful little gem of a site in lovely surroundings, El Maset has 107 pitches, of which just 20 are slightly larger for caravans and motorcaravans, the remainder suitable only for tents. The site celebrated its 50th anniversary in 2011 and the owner, Sr Juan Perez is delightful and his staff are very helpful. The site entrance is steep and access to the caravan pitches can be quite tricky. However, the owner's son will tow your caravan to your pitch. Some pitches are shaded and all have electricity, 20 also have water and drainage. Tent pitches are more shaded on attractive, steep, rock-walled terraces on the hillside.

Facilities

Good sanitary facilities in three small blocks are kept very clean. Baby facilities. Washing machines and dryers. Unit for disabled campers but the ground is steep. Bar/restaurant, takeaway and shop (all season). Swimming pool (all season). Solarium. Play area. Area for football and basketball. Excellent games room. Satellite TV. Internet access and free WiFi. Dogs are not accepted. Charcoal barbecues are not permitted. Off site: Fishing and beach 300 m. Golf and bicycle hire 1 km. Riding 8 km.

Open: 13 March - 13 October.

Directions

From the C31 Figueres - Palamos road south of Pals, north of Palafrugell, take GI653 to Begur. Site is 2 km. north of the town; follow signs for Playa de Sa Riera and site (steep entrance).
GPS: 41.96860, 3.21002

Charges 2012

Per unit incl. 2 persons and electricity	€ 27.70 - € 40.50
extra person	€ 6.00 - € 8.50
child (1-10 yrs)	€ 3.40 - € 5.60

Begur

Camping Begur

Ctra d'Esclanya km 2, E-17255 Begur (Girona) T: 972 623 201. E: info@campingbegur.com
alanrogers.com/ES81040

The choice of pitches on this pleasant, wooded site just three kilometres from the coast is remarkable; some are on gently-sloping grassland, others on hillside terraces or on the hilltop itself, and one steep slope has terraced tent pitches. There are 232 pitches with electricity (10A), water and drainage, 30 for tents and various corners are occupied by 45 mobile homes and chalets to rent, and by seasonal caravans. At the centre is a pleasant swimming pool with grassy terrace and a small paddling pool, overlooked by an attractive bar and snack bar. Begur is an attractive village with seven beaches.

Facilities

Two modern toilet blocks are fully equipped. Each has open style washbasins, large showers, a good unit for disabled visitors. Baby room, hot water to sinks and a private bathroom for hire. Washing machines, dryers and ironing table. Motorcaravan services. Bar/snack bar. Swimming and paddling pool. Boules. Gym (free). Play area. Field for children's and family activities (20/6-11/9). Children's 'huerta' (small market garden). Little farm with donkeys, goats, rabbits and chickens. WiFi. Off site: Site's own supermarket just outside gate. Village and riding 2 km. Beaches 3-5 km. Fishing 3 km. Bicycle hire 4 km.

Open: 1 April - 26 September.

Directions

Begur is 45 km. east of Girona. From north on AP7 at exit 6 (Girona) take C66 to La Bisbal; before Palafrugell follow signs for Begur. From south on AP7 at exit 9 follow Palamós, Palafrugell, then Begur. Site is 2 km. south of Begur on minor road to Palafrugell. GPS: 41.940216, 3.200079

Charges guide

Per unit incl. 2 persons and electricity	€ 20.10 - € 41.00
extra person	€ 3.50 - € 6.70

No credit cards.

Bellver de Cerdanya

Camping Solana del Segre

Ctra N260 km 198, E-25720 Bellver de Cerdanya (Lleida) T: 973 510 310. E: sds@solanadelsegre.com

alanrogers.com/ES91420

The Sierra del Cadi offers some spectacular scenery and the Reserva Cerdanya is very popular with Spanish skiers. This site is situated in an open, sunny lower valley beside the River Segre where the far bank is a National Park (unfenced so children will need supervision). The immediate area is ideal for walkers and offers many opportunities for outdoor sports enthusiasts. The site is in two sections, the lower one nearer the river being for tourists, mainly flat and grassy with 200 pitches of 100 sq.m. or more, shaded by trees with 15A electricity. The upper area is taken by permanent units.

Facilities

Modern sanitary facilities are in a central building with extra Portacabin style units (unisex toilets/showers). Facilities for disabled campers are on the upper level (wheelchair users will experience problems). Laundry facilities. Motorcaravan services. Shop, bar and restaurant (1/7-15/9). Swimming and paddling pools (1/7-5/9). Indoor pool. Two play areas. Games room. River fishing. Dance area. Barbecue areas. Internet. Torches are required. Off site: Village with shops bars and restaurants. Riding 2 km. Bicycle hire and golf 10 km. Skiing.

Open: 1 July - 15 September.

Directions

Bellver de Cerdanya is 18 km. southwest of Puigcerdá, which is on the French border opposite Bourg-Madame. Site is on left at the 198 km. marker on the N260 from Puigcerdá to La Seu d'Urgell, well signed just beyond Bellver de Cerdanya. GPS: 42.372697, 1.760484

Charges guide

Per unit incl. 1 person and electricity	€ 28.50
extra person	€ 6.00
child (2-9 yrs)	€ 5.50
dog	€ 4.75

Benicasim

Bonterra Park

Avenida de Barcelona 47, E-12560 Benicasim (Castelló) T: 964 300 007. E: info@bonterrapark.com

alanrogers.com/ES85800

If you are looking for a town site which is not too crowded and has very good facilities, this one may be for you. It is a 300 m. walk to a good beach – and parking is not too difficult. The site has 320 pitches (70-90 sq.m), all with electricity (6/10A) and a variety of bungalows, some attractively built in brick. There are dedicated 'green' pitches for tents. Bonterra has a clean and neat appearance with tarmac roads, gravel covered pitches, palms, grass and a number of trees which give good shade. Overhead sunshades are provided for the more open pitches in summer. There is a little road and rail noise.

Facilities

Four attractive, well maintained sanitary blocks provide some private cabins, some washbasins with hot water, others with cold. Baby and dog showers. Facilities for disabled campers. Laundry. Motorcaravan services. Restaurant/bar. Shop. Swimming pool (heated Sept-June) and paddling pool. Playground (some concrete bases). Tennis. Multisports court. Gym. Disco. Bicycle hire. Miniclub. Satellite TV. Internet access (WiFi). Dogs are not accepted in July/Aug. Off site: Town facilities. Sandy beach and fishing 500 m. Riding 3 km. Boat launching 4 km. Golf 12 km. Nature Park.

Open: All year.

Directions

Site is on the quiet old main road running through Benicasim. From either direction leave the N340 at km. 987. At roundabout turn left and travel for about 1.5 km. to site on the left (white painted walls). Look for two supermarkets, one 200 m. before site and a second directly opposite. Site is well signed. GPS: 40.05708, 0.07432

Charges 2012

Per unit incl. 2 persons and electricity	€ 28.72 - € 52.26
extra person	€ 4.30 - € 6.26
child (0-9 yrs)	€ 3.65 - € 5.10

Benidorm

Camping Villasol

Avenida Bernat de Sarria no. 13., E-03503 Benidorm (Alacant) T: 965 850 422. E: info@camping-villasol.com

alanrogers.com/ES86810

Benidorm is increasingly popular for winter stays and Villasol is a genuinely good, purpose built modern site. Many of the 309 well separated pitches are arranged on wide terraces which afford views of the mountains surrounding Benidorm. All pitches (80-85 sq.m) have electricity and satellite TV connections, with 160 with full services for seasonal use. Shade is mainly artificial. Reservations are only accepted for winter stays of over three months (from 1 October). There is a small indoor pool, heated for winter use, and a very attractive, large outdoor pool complex (summer only) overlooked by the bar/restaurant and attractive, elevated restaurant terrace.

Facilities

Modern toilet blocks provide free, controllable hot water to showers and washbasins and British WCs. Good facilities for disabled campers. Laundry facilities. Good value restaurant. Bar. Shop. Swimming pools, outdoor and indoor. Satellite TV. Playground. Evening entertainment programme. Safes. Dogs not accepted. Off site: Beach, fishing and bicycle hire 1.3 km. Riding 3 km.

Open: All year.

Directions

From autopista exit 65 (Benidorm) and turn left at second set of lights. After 1 km. at another set of lights turn right, then right again at next lights. Site is on right in 400 m. GPS: 38.538, -0.119

Charges guide

Per person	€ 5.50 - € 7.20
pitch incl. car	€ 11.20 - € 26.40
electricity	€ 4.15

Benidorm

Camping Benisol

Avenida de la Comunidad Valenciana s/n, E-03500 Benidorm (Alacant) T: 965 851 673.
E: campingbenisol@yahoo.es **alanrogers.com/ES86830**

Camping Benisol is a well developed and peaceful site with lush, green vegetation and a mountain background. Mature hedges and trees afford privacy to each pitch and some artificial shade is provided where necessary. There are 298 pitches of which around 115 are for touring units (60-80 sq.m). All have electrical hook-ups (4/6A) and 75 have drainage. All the connecting roads are now surfaced with tarmac. Some daytime road noise should be expected. The site has an excellent restaurant serving traditional Spanish food at great prices, with a pretty, shaded terrace overlooking the pool with its palms and thatched pool bar.

Facilities

Modern sanitary facilities, heated in winter and kept very clean, have free, solar heated hot water to washbasins, showers and sinks. Laundry facilities. Gas supplies. Restaurant with terrace and bar (all year, closed 1 day a week). Shop. Swimming pool (Easter-Nov). Small, old style play area. Minigolf. Jogging track. Tennis. Golf driving range. ATM. WiFi. Off site: Riding 1 km. Bicycle hire and sea fishing 3 km. Golf 14 km. Bus route.

Open: All year.

Directions

Site is northeast of Benidorm. Exit N332 at 152 km. marker and take turn signed Playa Levant. Site is 100 m. on left off the main road, well signed.
GPS: 38.559, -0.097

Charges guide

Per person	€ 4.95 - € 5.25
child (1-10 yrs)	€ 4.00 - € 4.40
pitch	€ 13.25 - € 18.10
electricity	€ 2.80

No credit cards.

Blanes

Camping Blanes

Avenida Villa de Madrid 33, Apdo 72, E-17300 Blanes (Girona) T: 972 331 591. E: info@campingblanes.com
alanrogers.com/ES82280

Camping Blanes is the first of the sites which edge the pedestrian promenade here and probably the smallest. Open all year, it is family owned and run and indeed has been in the hands of the Boix family for 40 years. Antonio, the son, runs the site now with pride and care, speaking good English. With only 206 pitches, no bungalows or mobile homes and only five seasonal vans, it has a comfortable family atmosphere. Shade is provided by tall pines and because of this, some of the pitches are a bit irregular in shape and average between 60-80 sq.m. The ground is sandy but access to the pitches is easy. For a small site it is well served with a bar, restaurant and a shop. A fairly small swimming pool and excellent sunbathing terrace is cleverly hidden on the roof above the bar area and is a brilliant suntrap. It makes an ideal family venue with the beach just across the promenade, or an excellent winter choice with all amenities within walking distance.

Facilities

Smart, well equipped sanitary block with provision for disabled visitors (by key). Baby changing unit. Excellent washing machines and dryers. Shop (15/6-15/9). Bar (1/4-12/10). Restaurant (7/7-25/8). Takeaway (7/7-25/8). Swimming pool. Play area. No organised entertainment. Beach alongside site. Car wash. Internet access and WiFi. Off site: All amenities of the town are within walking distance (500 m). Blanes is a fishing port and tourist resort with a range of watersports possible. Golf and riding 5 km.

Open: All year.

Directions

Site is south of the town beside the beach before Camping Bella Terra and El Pinar. Follow signs for 'campings' until individual site signs appear.
GPS: 41.65918, 2.77959

Charges guide

Per unit incl. 2 persons and electricity	€ 25.20 - € 35.90

No credit cards in winter season.

Blanes

Beach Camp El Pinar

Avenida Vila de Madrid 39, E-17300 Blanes (Girona) T: 972 331 083. E: camping@elpinarbeach.com

alanrogers.com/ES82300

A long established campsite, El Pinar enjoys an excellent location on the southern edge of Blanes with direct access to the superb beach. The site is in two halves, arranged on either side of a large road that terminates just past the site entrance gates where it meets the very clean, sandy beach. One side of the site is more modern than the other. The 300 touring pitches are on level sandy grass and all have 6A electricity. There is a degree of shade with younger trees on the newer side while the very old pine trees on the original, older side are impressive and provide a good deal of shade.

Facilities

Sanitary facilities in two large blocks (one refurbished) include some private washbasins. Facilities for disabled visitors. Baby room. Cleaning is continual through the day. Full laundry facilities. Shop (all season). Bar/restaurant and takeaway (all season). Games room. Large swimming pool with adjacent paddling pool on the newer side (1/5-15/9). Multisports area. Bicycle hire. Simple play area. Miniclub (late June-early Sept). WiFi (free). Boat launching can be organised. Beach. Off site: Tourist train into town (10 mins).

Open: 31 March - 30 September.

Directions

From AP7 or C-32 motorways follow signs for Blanes. Site is the last travelling south from Blanes town centre. Follow camping signs in Blanes until you see the El Pinar sign. GPS: 41.6555, 2.77862

Charges 2012

Per unit incl. 2 persons and electricity	€ 28.70 - € 38.70
extra person	€ 5.50 - € 6.60
child (2-10 yrs)	free - € 5.70

Blanes

Camping Bella Terra

Avenida Vila de Madrid 35-40, E-17300 Blanes (Girona) T: 972 348 017. E: info@campingbellaterra.com

alanrogers.com/ES82320

Camping Bella Terra is set in a shady pine grove facing a white sandy beach on the Mediterranean coast. There are 797 pitches with 600 for touring units, the rest taken by bungalows to rent (97) and by Spanish 'residents' (200). All pitches have 5/6A electricity and 134 are fully serviced. The site is in two sections, each with its own reception. The main reception is on the right of the road as you approach, with the swimming and paddling pools and delightful new pool bar and restaurant. The other half with direct access to the beach is the older part of the site which always fills up first. The older area has a supermarket with its own bakery.

Facilities

The newer side of the site has excellent new sanitary blocks with top of the range equipment. The older side has older blocks which are clean, but dated. Provision for disabled visitors and laundry on both sides. The blocks on the newer side have superb facilities for children and a baby room. Shop, restaurant, bar and takeaway. Outdoor swimming and paddling pools (from May). Playground. Fishing. Bicycle hire. Internet café and WiFi. Miniclub. For dogs, contact site first. Off site: Blanes town within walking distance. Road train (high season).

Open: 31 March - 30 September.

Directions

Site is on the southwest side of Blanes. From exit 9 on the AP7 Girona - Barcelona road follow N11 to the B600 towards Blanes. Before entering Blanes turn southwest following site signs at the roundabouts which will direct you avoiding Blanes town which has narrow roads and is best avoided by large units. GPS: 41.6616, 2.77612

Charges guide

Per unit incl. 2 persons and electricity	€ 25.60 - € 56.60
extra person	€ 4.50 - € 6.20

Bocairent

Camping Mariola

Ctra Bocairent - Alcoi km 9, E-46880 Bocairent (Valencia) T: 962 135 160. E: info@campingmariola.com

alanrogers.com/ES86450

Situated high in the Sierra Mariola National Park, in a beautiful rural setting but only 12 km. from the old town of Bocairent, this is a real taste of Spain with hilltop views all around. Used mainly by the Spanish, the site is an undiscovered jewel with 170 slightly sloping pitches. These are well spaced and have shade from a mixture of young and mature trees. An orchard area well away from the main site (with no amenities close by) is used for more casual camping. A traditional, stone built restaurant is slightly elevated with views over the site. Accessed by a few steps, this attractive building is covered in roses.

Facilities

Six identical small toilet blocks offer adequate facilities with British style WCs and showers with shared changing area. Open style washbasins. No facilities for disabled visitors. Washing machine. Motorcaravan services. Small shop (weekends only). Bar/restaurant (weekends only in low season). Satellite TV. Outdoor pool with separate paddling pool (June-Sept). Two multisports pitches. Play area. Communal barbecue area. Children's club and entertainment (Aug. only). Off site: Riding and golf 12 km.

Open: All year.

Directions

From CV40 take exit for Ontinyent and follow CV81. Pass Bocairent heading west and in 2 km. look for camping sign (at textiles factory). Turn south on VV2031 to Alcoy. Turn right at first roundabout and straight on at next through small industrial estate. Continue for about 10 km. and site is a turn to left. GPS: 38.753317, -0.549402

Charges guide

Per person	€ 4.45
pitch	€ 4.45 - € 6.00

Boltaña

Camping Boltaña

Ctra N260 km 442, E-22340 Boltaña (Huesca) T: 974 502 347. E: info@campingboltana.com

alanrogers.com/ES90620

Nestled in the Rio Ara valley, surrounded by the Pyrenees mountains and below a tiny but enchanting, historic, hill top village, is the very pretty, thoughtfully planned Camping Boltaña. Generously sized, 190 grassy pitches (all with 10A electricity) have good shade from a variety of trees and a stream meanders through the campsite. The landscaping includes ten charming rocky water gardens and a covered pergola doubles as an eating and play area. A stone building houses the site's reception, social room and supermarket. Angel Moreno, the owner of the site, is a charming host and has tried to think of everything to make his guests comfortable.

Facilities

Two modern sanitary blocks include facilities for disabled visitors and laundry facilities. Supermarket. Bar, restaurant and takeaway (1/7-31/8). Swimming pools (15/6-15/9). Playground. Entertainment for children (high season). Pétanque. Guided tours, plus hiking, canyoning, rafting, climbing, mountain biking and caving. Bicycle hire. WiFi. No charcoal barbecues. Torches useful in some parts. Off site: Local bus service. Fishing 1 km.

Open: 15 January - 15 December.

Directions

South of the Park Nacional de Ordesa, site is about 50 km. from Jaca near Ainsa. From Ainsa travel northwest on N260 toward Boltaña (near 443 km. marker) and 1 km. from Boltaña turn south toward Margudgued. Site is well signed and is 1 km. along this road. GPS: 42.43018, 0.07882

Charges guide

Per unit incl. 2 persons and electricity	€ 35.40
extra person	€ 6.50

Camping Cheques accepted.

Burgos

Camping Municipal Fuentes Blancas

Ctra Cartuja - Miraflores km 3,5, E-09193 Burgos (Burgos) T: 947 486 016. E: info@campingburgos.com

alanrogers.com/ES90210

Fuentes Blancas is a comfortable municipal site on the edge of the historical town of Burgos and within easy reach of the Santander ferries. There are around 350 marked pitches of 70 sq.m. on flat ground, 250 with electrical connections (6A) and there is good shade in parts. The site has a fair amount of transit trade and reservations are not possible for August, so arrive early. Burgos is an attractive city, ideally placed for an overnight stop en-route to or from the south of Spain. The old part of the city around the cathedral is beautiful and there are pleasant walks along the riverbanks outside the campsite gates.

Facilities

Clean, modern, fully equipped sanitary facilities in five blocks with controllable showers and hot and cold water to sinks (not all are always open). Facilities for babies. Washing machine/dryer. Motorcaravan service point. Small shop (high season). Bar/snack bar and restaurant (high season). Swimming pool (1/7-30/8). Playground. English is spoken. Off site: Fishing and river beach 200 m. Bus service to city or a fairly shaded walk. Golf 30 km.

Open: All year.

Directions

From the north (Santander) continue on the N623 through city centre to km. 0. Follow signs for E5/A1 Madrid. After crossing river take slip road for N120/A231 Leon but then turn left towards Fuentes Blancas and Cartuja de Miraflores for 3 km. Site is well signed on left. GPS: 42.34125, -3.65762

Charges guide

Per person	€ 4.65
child (2-10 yrs)	€ 3.20
pitch incl. electricity	€ 13.30

Cabo de Gata

Camping Cabo de Gata

Ctra Cabo de Gata s/n, E-04150 Cabo de Gata (Almería) T: 950 160 443. E: info@campingcabodegata.com

alanrogers.com/ES87630

Cabo de Gata is situated on the Gulf of Almer'a, a pleasant, all-year campsite offering facilities to a good standard. Popular with British visitors through the winter, and within the Cabo de Gata-Nijar Nature Park and set amongst fruit farms, it is only a 1 km. walk to a fine sandy beach. The 250 gravel pitches are level and of a reasonable size, with 6/16A electricity and limited shade from maturing trees or canopies. There are specific areas for very large units with very high canopies for shade and seven chalets for rent.

Facilities

Two, well maintained, clean toilet blocks provide all the necessary sanitary facilities. including British type WCs, washbasins and free hot showers. Facilities for disabled campers. Restaurant, bar and shop (all year). Swimming pool. Football. Pétanque. Tennis. Small playground. Library. Bicycle hire. English spoken. Entertainment programme. Internet access (charged). WiFi throughout site. Off site: Bus from gate. Nearest beach and fishing 1 km. Golf 10 km. Riding 15 km.

Open: All year.

Directions

From A7-E15 take exit 460 or 467 and follow signs for Retamar via N344 and for Cabo de Gata. Site is on the right before village of Cabo de Gata. The final stretch of road is in a poor state of repair due to restrictions imposed within the natural park. GPS: 36.80188, -2.24471

Charges guide

Per unit incl. 2 persons and electricity	€ 29.45 - € 30.10
extra person	€ 5.95
child (2-10 yrs)	€ 5.40

Calella de la Costa

Camping Botánic Bona Vista Kim

Ctra NII km 665,8, E-08370 Calella de la Costa (Barcelona) T: 937 692 488. E: info@botanic-bonavista.net

alanrogers.com/ES82400

While Calella itself may conjure up visions of mass tourism, this site is set on a very steep hillside some 3 km. out of the town. Any noise from the nearby coast road and railway gets lost as you gain height and it is a quite delightful setting with an abundance of flowers, shrubs and roses (1,700, all planted by the knowledgeable owner Kim, who has won prizes for his roses). The design of the site successfully marries the beautiful botanic surrounds with the wonderful views over the bay. Of the 160 pitches, 130 are for tourers, all with electricity and on flat terraces on the slopes, with some shade.

Facilities

The standard of design in the three sanitary blocks is quite outstanding for a small site (indeed for any site). Some washbasins in cabins in the newest block. Baby room. Washing machines. Motorcaravan services. Bar/restaurant, takeaway and shop (all year). Outdoor pool (1/5-30/9). Large play area. Recreation park. Satellite TV. Internet point. Games room. Barbecue and picnic area. Entertainment (11/7-26/8). No cycling on site. Off site: Fishing 100 m. Bicycle hire 1 km.

Open: All year.

Directions

From N11 coast road, site is signed south of Calella (km. 665), and is on the coastal side of road. The road is busy but site signs give ample warning of the entrance (shared ES82420). Entrance is very steep. From the Barcelona direction you must pass the entrance and turn at the roundabout in some 800 m. GPS: 41.606667, 2.639167

Charges guide

Per unit incl. 2 persons and electricity	€ 38.75 - € 40.65

Calonge

Camping Internacional de Calonge

Ctra San Feliu/Guixols - Palamós km 7.6, E-17251 Calonge (Girona) T: 972 651 233.
E: info@intercalonge.com **alanrogers.com/ES81300**

This spacious, well laid out site has access to a fine beach via a footbridge over the coast road, or you can take the little road train as the site is on very sloping ground. Calonge is a family site with two good sized pools on different levels, a paddling pool and large sunbathing areas. A great restaurant, bar and snack bar are by the pool. The site's 793 pitches are on terraces and all have electricity (5A), with 84 being fully serviced. The pitches are set on attractively landscaped terraces (access to some may be challenging). There is good shade from the tall pine trees and some views of the sea through the foliage.

Facilities

Generous sanitary provision in new and renovated blocks include some washbasins in cabins. No toilet seats. One block is heated in winter. Laundry facilities. Motorcaravan services. Gas supplies. Shop (26/3-30/10). Restaurant (1/2-31/12). Bar, patio bar with pizzas and takeaway (27/3-24/10, weekends for the rest of the year). Swimming pools (26/3-16/10). Playground. Electronic games. Rather noisy disco two nights a week (but not late). Bicycle hire. Tennis. Hairdresser. ATM. WiFi. Torches necessary in some areas. Road train in high season.

Open: All year.

Directions

Site is on the inland side of the coast road between Palamós and Platja d'Aro. Take the C31 south to the 661 at Calonge. At Calonge follow signs to the C253 towards Platja d'Aro and on to site which is well signed. GPS: 41.83333, 3.08417

Charges guide

Per unit incl. 2 persons and electricity	€ 20.25 - € 47.70
extra person	€ 3.70 - € 8.35

No credit cards.

Calonge

Camping Cala Gogo

Avenida Andorra 13, E-17251 Calonge (Girona) T: 972 651 564. E: calagogo@calagogo.es

alanrogers.com/ES81600

Cala Gogo is a large traditional campsite with a pleasant situation on a wooded hillside with mature trees giving shade to most pitches. The 578 shaded touring pitches vary in size and are in terraced rows, some with artificial shade. All have 10A electricity and water, and most have drainage. There may be road noise in eastern parts of the site. Some pitches are now right by the beach, the remainder are up to 800 m. uphill, but the 'Gua gua' tractor train, operating almost all season, takes people between the centre of the site and the beach and adds to the general sense of fun.

Facilities

Seven toilet blocks (one new) are of a high standard and continuously cleaned. Some washbasins in private cabins. Two private cabins for hire. New baby rooms. Facilities for disabled visitors. Laundry room. Motorcaravan services. Gas supplies. Supermarket, shop, restaurants/takeaway and bars, two heated swimming pools (lifeguards) and paddling pool. Playground and crèche. Sports centre. Sports and entertainment. Bicycle hire. Kayaks (free). Fishing. WiFi (free). Medical service. Bus to local disco. Dogs are not accepted in high season.

Open: 28 April - 16 September.

Directions

Sant Antoni de Calonge is southeast of Girona. Leave the AP7/E15 at exit 6. Take the C66 towards Palamós which becomes the C31. Use the C31 (Girona - Palamós) road to avoid Palamós town. Take the C253 coast road. Site is at km. 46.5, which is 4 km. south of Palamós. GPS: 41.83083, 3.08247

Charges 2012

Per unit incl. 2 persons and electricity	€ 22.80 - € 52.00
extra person	€ 3.90 - € 8.30

Cambrils

Camping Playa Cambrils Don Camilo

Ctra Cambrils - Salou km 1,5, Avenida Oleastrum, E-43850 Cambrils (Tarragona) T: 977 361 490.
E: info@playacambrils.com **alanrogers.com/ES84790**

This is a smart, well kept site with a canopy of mature shading trees, 300 m. from the beach across a busy road. The small (60 or 80 sq.m) pitches are on flat ground, divided by hedges. There are many permanent pitches and a quarter of the site is given up to chalet style accommodation, which is generally separate from the touring pitches. Large units are placed in a dedicated area where the trees are higher. The very pleasant pool complex includes a smart glassed restaurant and bar with a distinct Spanish flavour reflected in the menu and tapas available throughout the day.

Facilities

Three smart, attractively tiled modern sanitary buildings, offer sound, clean facilities with British style WCs and showers in separate buildings. Excellent facilities for disabled campers. Laundry facilities. Supermarket (April-Sept). Bar/snacks and separate restaurant (April-Sept). Swimming pools. Playground. Entertainment in high season. Miniclub. Huge electronic games room. Bicycle hire. Torches useful. WiFi (free). Off site: Resort town has a wide range of shops, bars and restaurants. Boat launching 400 m. Fishing and golf 1 km. Riding 1.5 km.

Open: 15 March - 14 October.

Directions

Leave AP7 autopista at exit 37 and head for Cambrils and then to the beach. Turn left along beach road. Site is 1 km. east of Cambrils Playa and is well signed as you leave Cambrils marina. GPS: 41.06487, 1.08368

Charges 2012

Per unit incl. 2 persons and electricity	€ 19.10 - € 55.90
extra person	€ 2.90 - € 5.45
child (under 9 yrs)	€ 2.00 - € 4.10
dog	€ 1.85 - € 4.35

Camping Cheques accepted.

Cambrils

Cambrils Park Resort

Avenida Mas Clariana s/n, E-43850 Cambrils (Tarragona) T: 977 351 031. E: mail@cambrilspark.es
alanrogers.com/ES84810

Close to the wonderful Cambrils beaches, this is a wonderful holiday destination for the whole family. Lawns lined with palm trees and flowers lead to 330 fully equipped chalets (touring units are no longer taken here). The accommodation is divided between three themed areas: the Polynesian Village with Aloha bungalows – 158 authentic wooden chalets in an exotic landscape; the Caribbean Village offering splendid luxury Villa Bonitas – 172 coloured wooden chalets; and the Mediterranean Village, which will be ready for 2013 with 170 new units in the style of a typical Mediterranean coastal town. There are three themed swimming pools with amazing elephants, dragons, slides and a huge pirate ship.

Facilities

Quality indoor and outdoor restaurant. Takeaway. Several themed bars. Huge supermarket, souvenir shop and bakery. Laundry. Themed swimming pools with lifeguards. Minigolf. Tennis. Multisports court. Pétanque. Entertainment all season. Miniclub. WiFi (free). Medical centre. Pets are not accepted. Off site: Fishing and bicycle hire 400 m. Beach 500 m. Riding 3 km. Port Aventura theme park 4 km. Golf 7 km.

Open: 26 March - 12 October.

Directions

On west side of Salou about 1.5 km. from the centre, site is well signed from the coast road to Cambrils and from the other town approaches. Caution as there are many campsites with similar names off this road. GPS: 41.076463, 1.109238

Charges guide

Per person	€ 6.00
child (4-12 yrs)	€ 4.00
pitch incl. electricity	€ 15.00 - € 52.00
incl. water and waste water	€ 17.00 - € 55.00

Campell

Camping Vall de Laguar

Ctra Sant Antonio 24, la Vall de Laguar, E-03791 Campell (Alacant) T: 965 577 490.
E: info@campinglaguar.com **alanrogers.com/ES86750**

Near the pretty mountain-top village of Campell, this new site is perched high on the side of a mountain with breathtaking views of hilltop villages, the surrounding hills and distant sea. With a wholehearted welcome from the owners, the well maintained site promises a real taste of Spain. The pitches, pool, terrace and restaurant all share the views. The 68 average sized, gravel pitches are on terraces and all have electricity and water. Trees and hedges have been planted and now give ample shade. This is a great place to get away from the coastal hustle, bustle and high rise of the beaches.

Facilities
Two new sanitary blocks have excellent clean facilities including some for disabled campers. Washing machines and dryers. Restaurant with pretty terrace (closed Sept). Bar and small pool bar. Swimming pool. Entertainment programme in high season. WiFi over site (free). Charcoal barbecues only (communal area). Torches useful.
Off site: Attractive town close by. Golf and beach 18 km.

Open: All year.

Directions
Site is 20 km. west of Xabia/Javea. From the }A7/E15 exit 62 head to Ondara/Valencia on the N332 and at the roundabout on the Ondara by-pass head to Benidoleig/Orba. At Orba turn right and follow the site signs. GPS: 38.7766, -0.105

Charges guide

Per unit incl. 2 persons and electricity	€ 21.75 - € 24.25
extra person	€ 5.00

Camprodon

Camping Vall de Camprodon

Ctra C38 Ripoll a Camprodon, E-17867 Camprodon (Girona) T: 972 740 507. E: info@valldecamprodon.net
alanrogers.com/ES91225

This large holiday village is attractively situated in a wooded valley with cows grazing to one side, their pleasant bells often to be heard. A stream runs below the site between it and the road. There are 200 grass and gravel pitches, some with shade, others without. Most are occupied by seasonal caravans (some rather scruffy) and private chalets interspersed with just 40 for touring units, all with 4/10A electricity. There are 26 modern chalets for rent. Only 20 km. away is the mountain and ski resort of Vallter 2000 and to the southwest is the historical town of Ripoll. Camprodon is a very pleasant old town with a magnificent ancient bridge at its centre.

Facilities
One centrally placed, fully equipped and well maintained toilet block with controllable showers, washbasins with dividers, and a large en-suite unit for disabled visitors. Baby/toddler baths. Washing machines, dryers and ironing board. Shop and bar/restaurant (July/Aug plus holiday periods and weekends in low season). Swimming and paddling pools (July/Aug). Play area. Adventure play area with zip-wire. Fishing and bathing in river. Tennis. Multisports court. Boules. Miniclub (July/Aug). Riding possible (July/Aug). WiFi over site (free). Motorcaravan park outside entrance (€20-26).

Open: All year.

Directions
Camprodon is 50 km. west of Figueres, 72 km. by road. From south on the AP7 leave at exit 6 (Girona), take C66/A26 to Olot. From north leave AP7 at Figueres, join N11 south and turn west signed Olot to join N260/A26. At exit 84 follow signs for Camprodon on C26 via Valley of Bianya. After the tunnels turn north on C38 to Camprodon. Site is halfway between Sant Pau de Seguries and Camprodon, on the right. GPS: 42.29033, 2.36242

Charges guide

Per unit incl. 2 persons and electricity	€ 35.60
extra person	€ 7.95

Camping Cheques accepted.

Canet de Mar

Camping Globo Rojo

Ctra NII km 660.9, E-08360 Canet de Mar (Barcelona) T: 937 941 143. E: camping@globo-rojo.com
alanrogers.com/ES82430

Camping Globo Rojo is cleverly laid out in a semi-circular fashion. Within the various sectors, permanent campers and touring units stay alongside each other. The restaurant which serves authentic food and tapas, is within a sensitively restored farmhouse and is superb. The site is located on the beach road (N11) so is subject to some traffic noise, but the full shading of mature trees also absorbs the noise. The 170 flat pitches include 100 touring pitches, all with 10A electricity and with an average size of 70 sq.m. An excellent elevated pool and paddling pool are waiting for you to enjoy and the beach is close by.

Facilities
Two sanitary blocks have clean, modern equipment. Baby room. Facilities for disabled campers. Hot water throughout. Washing machines. Motorcaravan service areas. Shop. Bar. Restaurant. Takeaway. Swimming and paddling pools (with lifeguards). Miniclub. WiFi (free) in restaurant area. Playground. Pétanque. Electronic games. Dog bath. Car wash. Safes. Off site: Fishing 100 m. Bus 200 m. Train to Barcelona 600 m. Watersports 2 km. Bicycle hire 5 km.

Open: 1 April - 30 September.

Directions
Site is at 660.9 km. marker on the N11. Leave the C-32 autoroute at exit 20 (AP7 exit 120) and follow signs to Canet de Mar. Site is well signed on both carriageways of the N11. GPS: 41.590903, 2.591951

Charges guide

Per unit incl. 2 persons and electricity	€ 22.50 - € 45.75
extra person	€ 4.50 - € 6.50
child (2-10 yrs)	€ 4.00 - € 6.00

Caravia Alta

Camping Caravaning Arenal de Moris

A8 Salida 337, E-33344 Caravia Alta (Asturias) T: 985 853 097. E: camoris@desdeasturias.com

alanrogers.com/ES89550

This smart, well run site is close to three fine sandy beaches so gets very busy at peak times. It has a backdrop of the mountains in the nature reserve known as the Sueve which is important for a breed of short Asturian horse, the Asturcone. The site has 330 grass pitches (269 for touring) of 40-70 sq.m. and with 200 electricity connections available (10A). There are some shady, terraced pitches while others are on an open, slightly sloping field with limited views of the sea. The restaurant with a terrace serves local dishes and overlooks the pool with hills and woods beyond.

Facilities

Three sanitary blocks provide comfortable, controllable showers (no dividers) and vanity style washbasins, laundry facilities and external dishwashing (cold water). Supermarket. Bar/restaurant. Swimming pool. Tennis. Play area in lemon orchard. English is spoken. WiFi in the restaurant area. Off site: Beach and fishing 200 m. Bus 1 km. from gate. Bar and restaurants in village 2 km. Golf 5 km. Riding, bicycle hire and sailing 10 km.

Open: 1 June - 17 September.

Directions

Caravia Alta is 50 km. east of Gijón. Leave the A8 Santander - Oviedo motorway at km. 337 exit, turn left on N632 towards Colunga and site is signed to right in village. GPS: 43.47248, -5.18332

Charges guide

Per person	€ 5.50
child	€ 4.40
pitch incl. car	€ 9.70 - € 14.00
electricity	€ 4.50

Cartagena

Camping Naturista El Portus

El Portus, E-30394 Cartagena (Murcia) T: 968 553 052. E: elportus@elportus.com

alanrogers.com/ES87520

Set in a secluded south facing bay fringed by mountains, El Portus is a fairly large naturist site enjoying magnificent views and with direct access to a small sand and pebble beach. This part of Spain enjoys almost all-year-round sunshine. There are some 400 pitches, 300 for tourers, ranging from 60-100 sq.m, all but a few having electricity (6A). They are mostly on fairly level, if somewhat stony and barren ground. El Portus has a reasonable amount of shade from established trees and nearly every pitch has a view. Residential units are situated on the hillside above the site.

Facilities

Five acceptable toilet blocks, all unisex, are fully equipped. Opened as required, they are clean and bright. Showers all with hot water. Unit for disabled visitors, key from reception. Washing machines. Motorcaravan services. Well stocked shop. Bar with TV and library. Restaurants. The beach restaurant is closed in low season. Swimming pools (June-Sept). Wellness centre. Play area. Tennis. Pétanque. Yoga. Scuba-diving club (high season). Windsurfing. Spanish lessons. Small boat moorings. Entertainment programme all season. WiFi over site (charged). Off site: Fishing from beach. Golf 28 km.

Open: All year.

Directions

Site is on the coast, 10 km. west of Cartagena. Follow signs to Mazarron then take E22 to Canteras. Site is well signed for 4 km. If approaching through Cartagena, exit the town on N332 following signs for Canteras. Site signed on joining the N332. GPS: 37.585, -1.06717

Charges guide

Per person	€ 7.00
child (3-9 yrs)	€ 5.00
pitch	€ 16.30
pitch incl. 6A electricity	€ 22.20
dog	€ 4.70

Castanares de Rioja

Camping de La Rioja

Ctra de Haro - Sto Domingo de la Calzada, E-26240 Castanares de Rioja (La Rioja) T: 941 300 174.
E: info@campingdelarioja.com **alanrogers.com/ES92250**

This site is situated just beyond the town of Castanares de Rioja. This is a busy site during the peak season with many sporting activities taking place. In low season it becomes rather more quiet with limited facilities available. There are 30 level, grass touring pitches, out of a total of 250, and these are separated by hedges and trees allowing privacy. Each has their own water, drainage and electricity connection. To the rear of the site is the Oja River which is ideal for fishing and there are views of the Obarenes mountains in the distance. Some noise from the main road is possible.

Facilities

The central sanitary facilities are old and traditional in style but clean. Open style washbasins and controllable showers. Laundry and dishwashing facilities. Shop, bar, restaurant, takeaway (on request) all open 20/6-20/9. Outdoor swimming pool (20/6-20/9 supervised). Multisport court. Football. Tennis. River fishing. Riding. Children's cycle circuit. Play area. No individual barbecues. Off site: Town centre 1.5 km. The Guggenheim Museum in Bilbao. City of San Sebastian with beaches and aquarium.

Open: 1 January - 9 December.

Directions

Head west on N120. Turn right onto LR111 signed Castanares de Rioja. Continue through town towards Haro. Site is on left, 800 m. after leaving town speed restriction. GPS: 42.52911, -2.92243

Charges guide

Per person	€ 4.60 - € 5.75
child	€ 4.00 - € 5.00
pitch	€ 10.00 - € 12.50
electricity	€ 3.60

Castelló d'Empúries

Camping Nautic Almata

Ctra GIV- 6216 km 11,6, E-17486 Castelló d'Empúries (Girona) T: 972 454 477. E: info@almata.com

alanrogers.com/ES80300

In the Bay of Roses, south of Empúriabrava and beside the Parc Natural dels Aiguamolls de l'Empordá, this is a high quality site of particular interest to nature lovers (especially birdwatchers). Beautifully laid out, it is arranged around the river and waterways, so will suit those who like to be close to water or who enjoy watersports and boating. It is worth visiting because of its unusual aspects and the feeling of being on the canals, as well as being a superb beachside site. A large site, there are 1,109 well kept, large, numbered pitches, all with electricity and on flat, sandy ground. There are some pitches right on the beach and on the banks of the canal. As you drive through the nature park to the site, watch for the warning signs for frogs and enjoy the wild flamingos alongside the road. The name no doubt derives from the fact that boats can be tied up at the small marina within the site and a slipway also gives access to a river and thence to the sea. Throughout the season there is a varied entertainment programme for children and adults. The facilities on this site are impressive. Some tour operators use the site.

Facilities

Toilet blocks of a high standard include some en-suite showers with basins. Good facilities for disabled visitors. Washing machines. Gas supplies. Excellent supermarket. Restaurants and bar. Two separate bars and snack bar by beach where discos are held in main season. Water-skiing, diving and windsurfing schools. 300 sq.m. swimming pool. New tennis court. Squash. Fronton. Minigolf. Games room. Extensive riding tuition with own stables and stud. New children's play park. Fishing (licence required). Car, motorcycle and bicycle hire. Hairdresser. Internet access and WiFi. ATM. Torches are useful near beach. Off site: Canal trips 18 km. Aquatic Park 20 km.

Open: 14 May - 18 September (with all services).

Directions

Site is signed at 26 km. marker on C252 between Castello d'Empúries and Vildemat, then 7 km. to site. Alternatively, on San Pescador - Castello d'Empuries road head north and site is well signed. GPS: 42.206077, 3.10389

Charges guide

Per unit incl. 2 persons and electricity	€ 28.30 - € 56.60
extra person (over 3 yrs)	€ 2.65 - € 5.30
dog	€ 5.00 - € 6.60
boat or jet ski	€ 9.75 - € 13.00

Castelló d'Empúries

Camping Caravaning La Laguna

Apdo 55, E-17486 Castelló d'Empúries (Girona) T: 972 450 553. E: info@campinglaguna.com

alanrogers.com/ES80150

La Laguna is a relaxed, spacious site on an isthmus within a Catalan national maritime park, on the migratory path of many different birds. It has direct access to an excellent sandy beach and the estuary of the river Muga (also a beach). The owners continue to spend much time and effort on improvements. The double lagoons are a most attractive feature. The 756 pitches (with just 46 mobile homes) are shaded and clearly marked on grass and sand, all with 6/10A electricity. There are also 51 fully serviced pitches. A very attractive bar/restaurant and sitting room overlook the lagoons and there are two swimming pools (one is heated in low season).

Facilities

Five superb toilet blocks, placed to avoid long walks, have solar heated water. Laundry room. Bar, restaurant and takeaway. Comprehensive supermarket. Swimming pools (15/5-31/10). Football. Tennis (free in low seasons). ATM. Minigolf. Windsurfing and sailing schools (July/Aug). Fishing. Miniclub. Play areas. Bicycle hire. Riding. Entertainment programme and competitions. Satellite TV. Internet access. WiFi throughout (charged). Off site: Boat launching. Birdwatching (Ramsar area). Golf 15 km.

Open: 29 March - 24 October.

Directions

Castelló d'Empúries is north of Girona and east of Figueras on the coast. From AP7/E15 take exit 3 south or exit 4 north (note there is no exit 3 north) and then N11 to the C260 towards Roses. At Castelló d'Empúries roundabout (there is only one) follow signs to Depuradora (2 km) and 'camping' for 4 km. on a hard track road to the site. GPS: 42.2374, 3.121

Charges 2012

Per unit incl. 2 persons and electricity	€ 26.25 - € 51.15

Discounts for longer stays and pensioners in low season. No credit cards.

www.almata.com
1ª Cat
N
W
E
S
N 42º.12.45
E 3º 05.10
Camping Nautic Almata
Ctra.Giv-6216
17486 Castelló d'Empuries
Costa Brava-Girona-España
Tel:(34)972 454477
Fax:(34)972 454686
info@almata.com
www.almata.com
F
La Jonquera
Figueres
Castelló d'Empúries
Sant Pere Pescador
Offers on our Website

Castelló d'Empúries

Kawan Village Mas Nou

Mas Nou no. 7, E-17486 Castelló d'Empúries (Girona) T: 972 454 175. E: info@campingmasnou.com

alanrogers.com/ES80120

Some two kilometres from the sea on the Costa Brava, this is a pristine and surprisingly tranquil site in two parts, split by the access road. One part contains the pitches and toilet blocks, the other houses the impressive leisure complex. There are 450 neat, level and marked pitches on grass, a minimum of 70 sq.m. but most 80-100 sq.m, and 300 with electricity (10A). The leisure complex is across the road from reception and features a huge L-shaped swimming pool with a paddling area. A formal restaurant has an adjoining bar/café, pleasant terrace and rotisseria under palms. A barbecue/rotisseria in another part of the site offers takeaway meals (in season). The site owns the large souvenir shop on the entrance road. There are many traditional bargains here and it is worth having a good look around as the prices are extremely good. Lots of time and money goes into the cleanliness of this site and it is very good for families. Ask about the origin of the site coat of arms. The Bay of Roses and the Medes islands have a natural beauty and a visit to Dali's house or the museum (the house is fascinating – book ahead) will prove he was not just a surrealist painter.

Facilities

Three absolutely excellent, fully equipped sanitary blocks include baby baths, good facilities for disabled visitors. Washing machines. Motorcaravan services. Supermarket and other shops. Baker in season. Bar/restaurant, rotisseria and takeaway. Swimming pool with lifeguard (1/5 - 30/9). Tennis. Minigolf. Miniclub (July/Aug). Play areas. Electronic games. Internet access and free WiFi. Car wash. Off site: Public transport 1 km. Riding 1.5 km. Fishing and bicycle hire 2 km. Beach 2.5 km. Aquatic Park. Romanica tour of famous local churches.

Open: 31 March - 30 September.

Directions

From A7 use exit 3. Mas Nou is 2 km. east of Castelló d'Empúries, on the Roses road, 10 km. from Figueras. Do not turn left across the main road but continue to the roundabout and return. Site is clearly marked. GPS: 42.26558, 3.1025

Charges 2012

Per unit incl. 2 persons and electricity	€ 24.20 - € 43.60
extra person	€ 2.60 - € 4.95
child (4-11 yrs)	free - € 3.45

Camping Cheques accepted.

Castrojeriz

Camping Camino de Santiago

Avenida Virgen del Manzano s/n, E-09110 Castrojeriz (Burgos) T: 947 377 255.

E: info@campingcamino.com **alanrogers.com/ES90230**

This tranquil site lies to the west of Burgos on the outskirts of Castrojeriz, in a superb location, almost in the shadow of the ruined castle high on the hillside. The 50 marked pitches are level, grassy and divided by hedges, with electricity (10A). Mature trees provide shade and there is a pretty orchard in one corner of the site. This site is a birdwatchers' paradise – large raptors abound. The owner takes visitors out on birdwatching trips currently on an ad hoc basis but he is considering making it a more formal affair.

Facilities

Older style sanitary block with hot showers, washbasin with cold water and British and Turkish style WCs. No facilities for disabled visitors. Washing machine. Bar/restaurant and takeaway with traditional cuisine. Bicycle hire. Library. WiFi (free). Games room. Tennis. Play area. Barbecue area. Ad hoc guided birdwatching. Off site: Fishing and riding 17 km.

Open: 1 March - 30 November.

Directions

Castrojeriz is 45 km. west of Burgos. From N120/A231 (Leon - Burgos), turn on Bu404 (Villasandino, Castrojeriz). Turn left at crossroads on southwest side of town, then left at site sign. From A62 (Burgos - Valladolid) turn north at Vallaquirán on Bu400/401 to Castrojeriz. Turn sharp right at filling station and as above. GPS: 42.2913, -4.1448

Charges guide

Per unit incl. 2 persons and electricity	€ 19.50 - € 24.00

Ciudad Rodrigo

Camping La Pesquera

Ctra de Caceres - Arrabal, E-37500 Ciudad Rodrigo (Salamanca) T: 923 481 348.

alanrogers.com/ES90190

This modest site has just 54 pitches and is located near the Rio Agueda, looking up to the magnificent fortress ramparts of Ciudad Rodrigo. Entry to the site is through a municipal park with a large play area. Whilst the site is small it can take even the largest units, the centrally located facilities have all been refurbished to a high standard, the pitches are flat and grassy and the roads are well maintained gravel. The pitches are shaded by trees by day and there is site lighting at night although you may find torches useful due to the tree canopy. The reception and a small bar which serves snacks in summer is near the front of the site.

Facilities

Attractive ochre stone sanitary building with British style WCs and free hot showers. Facilities for disabled campers. Washing machine. Basics sold from bar in high season. Bar/snacks (all season). Playground and barbecue area. Torches useful. Off site: River fishing 1 km. Riding 5 km. Superb walking area.

Open: 13 January - 13 December.

Directions

Site is southwest of Salamanca close to Ciudad Rodrigo. From the E80 N260, any direction, take the 526 to Coria. Site is alongside river directly off the road and well signed. GPS: 40.591965, -6.534301

Charges guide

Per unit incl. 2 persons and electricity	€ 13.00 - € 16.40
extra person	€ 3.30
child (up to 12 yrs)	€ 3.10

Colunga

Camping Costa Verde

Playa de la Griega, E-33320 Colunga (Asturias) T: 985 856 373.

alanrogers.com/ES89500

This uncomplicated coastal site has a marked Spanish flavour and is just 1.5 km. from the pleasant town of Colunga. Although little English is spoken, the cheerful owner and his helpful staff will make sure you get a warm welcome. The great advantage for many is that, 200 m. from the gate, is a spacious beach by a low tide lagoon with a recently constructed marine parade, ideal for younger children. Some of the 200 pitches are occupied on a seasonal basis, but 155 are for tourers. These are flat but with little shade, and electricity (6A) is available (long leads needed in places). The site gets very busy in high season.

Facilities

The single toilet block is of a high standard with a mixture of British and Turkish style toilets (all British for ladies), large showers and free hot water throughout. Laundry. Well stocked shop. Bar/restaurant is traditional and friendly. Play area. Torches needed. Off site: Fishing in river alongside site. Nearby towns of Ribadesella, Gijón and Oviedo. Excellent beaches. Bicycle hire 2 km. Sailing 4 km. Golf and riding 18 km.

Open: Easter - 1 October.

Directions

Colunga is 45 km. east of Gijón. Leave the A8 Santander - Oviedo motorway at km. 345 exit and take N632 towards Colunga. In village, turn right on AS257 towards Lastres; site is on right after 1 km. marker. GPS: 43.49662, -5.26447

Charges guide

Per person	€ 4.70
child (over 5 yrs)	€ 4.25
pitch incl. car	€ 8.50 - € 9.85
electricity	€ 3.50 - € 5.20

Conil de la Frontera

Camping Roche

N340 km 19,5, Carril de Pilahito, E-11140 Conil de la Frontera (Cádiz) T: 956 442 216.

E: info@campingroche.com **alanrogers.com/ES88590**

Camping Roche is situated in a pine forest near white sandy beaches in the lovely region of Andalucia. It is a clean, tidy and welcoming site. English is spoken but try your Spanish, German or French as the staff are very helpful. A family site, it offers a variety of facilities including a sports area and swimming pools. The restaurant has good food and a pleasant outlook over the pool. Games are organised for children. A recently built extension provides further pitches, a new toilet block and a tennis court. There are 335 pitches which include 104 bungalows to rent. The touring pitches all have electricity (10A), and 76 also have water and waste water.

Facilities

Three toilet blocks are traditional in style and provide simple, clean facilities. Washbasins have cold water only. Washing machine. Supermarket. Bar and restaurant. Swimming and paddling pools. Sports area. Tennis. Play area. Off site: Bus stops 3 times daily outside gates. Cádiz. Cape Trafalgar. Baelo Claudia archaeological site.

Open: All year.

Directions

From the N340 (Cádiz - Algeciras) turn off to site at km. 19.5 point. From Conil, take El Pradillo road. Keep following signs to site. From CA3208 road turn at km. 1 and site is 1.5 km. down this road on the right. GPS: 36.31089, -6.11268

Charges guide

Per unit incl. 2 persons and electricity	€ 18.81 - € 33.10
extra person	€ 3.71 - € 6.50

Conil de la Frontera

Camping Fuente del Gallo

Apdo 48, E-11149 Conil de la Frontera (Cádiz) T: 956 440 137. E: camping@campingfuentedelgallo.com

alanrogers.com/ES88600

Fuente del Gallo is well maintained with 184 pitches allocated to touring units. Each pitch has 6A electricity and a number of trees create shade to some pitches. Although the actual pitch areas are generally a good size, the majority are long and narrow. This could, in some cases, prevent the erection of an awning and your neighbour may feel close. In low season it is generally accepted to make additional use of an adjoining pitch. The attractive pool, restaurant and bar complex with its large, shaded terrace, are very welcoming in the height of summer. Good beaches are quite near at 300 m.

Facilities

Two modernised and very clean sanitary blocks include excellent services for babies and disabled visitors and hot water at all facilities. Laundry room. Motorcaravan services. Gas supplies. Well stocked shop. Attractive bar and restaurant (breakfast served). Swimming pool (1/6-30/9 with lifeguard) with paddling pool. Play area. TV and games machines in bar area. Safety deposit boxes. Excursions. Torches useful. Picnic area with playground and games. WiFi over site (charged).
Off site: Watersports on beach. Fishing 300 m. Riding 1 km. Bicycle and motor scooter hire 2 km. Golf 5 km.

Open: 23 March - 30 September.

Directions

From the Cadiz - Algeciras road (N340) at km. 23.00, follow signs to Conil de la Frontera town centre, then shortly right to Fuente del Gallo and 'playas', following signs. GPS: 36.2961, -6.1102

Charges 2012

Per unit incl. 2 persons and electricity	€ 24.50 - € 32.50
extra person	€ 5.50 - € 7.00
child (3-10 yrs)	€ 3.50 - € 5.50
dog	€ 3.00

Córdoba

Camping Municipal El Brillante

Avenida del Brillante 50, E-14012 Córdoba (Córdoba) T: 957 403 836. E: elbrillante@campings.net

alanrogers.com/ES90800

Córdoba is one of the hottest places in Europe and the superb pool here is more than welcome. If you really want to stay in the city, then this large site is a good choice. It has 120 neat pitches of gravel and sand, the upper pitches covered by artificial and natural shade but the lower, newer area has little. The site becomes very crowded in high season. The entrance is narrow and may be congested so care must be exercised – there is a lay-by just outside and it is easier to walk in initially. All pitches have electricity (6/10A) plus the newer area has 32 fully serviced pitches and an area for a few large motorcaravans.

Facilities

The toilet blocks include facilities for babies and disabled visitors. Motorcaravan services. Gas supplies. Shop (all year). Bar and restaurant (1/7-15/9). Swimming pool (1/6-10/9). Play area. Off site: Bus service to city centre from outside site. Commercial centre 300 m. (left out of site, right at traffic lights).

Open: All year.

Directions

Site is on the north side of river. From NIV/E25 road from Madrid, take exit at km. 403 (the middle of three exits for Córdoba) and follow signs for Mosque/Cathedral into city centre. Pass it and turn right onto main avenue. Continue and take right fork where road splits, and follow signs for site and/or for district of El Brillante. Site is on right up slight hill on this avenue. GPS: 37.899975, -4.787319

Charges guide

Per unit incl. 2 persons and electricity	€ 25.00 - € 28.00

No credit cards.

Crevillente

Marjal Costa Blanca Eco Resort

AP7. Salida 730 (Catral-Crevillente), E-03330 Crevillente (Alacant) T: 965 484 945.

E: camping@marjalcostablanca.com **alanrogers.com/ES87435**

Marjal Costa Blanca is a brand new site. We will undertake a full inspection in 2012. There will be 1,500 pitches here, ranging in size from 90-180 sq.m. All pitches will have electricity (16A), water and drainage. A number of new mobile homes will also be available. The site is a major new initiative and is sure to become one of the most modern and best equipped campsites in Spain. Leisure amenities will include a tropically themed swimming pool complex and a state-of-the-art wellness centre.

Facilities

Tropical swimming pool complex. Supermarket. Bar, snack bar, restaurant and takeaway food. Play areas. Wellness centre. Hairdresser. Library. Tennis. Football. Entertainment and activity programme. Mobile homes and chalets to rent. Business centre. Car hire service. Pet care facilities. Tourist information. Off site: Nearest beach 15 km. El Honda nature reserve. Terra Mitica theme park. Cycle and walking tracks.

Open: All year.

Directions

Take the southbound A7 coastal motorway until you reach the fork close to Elche - Crevillente. Continue on AP7 towards Cartagena and then take exit 730 (Catral) and follow signs to the site.
GPS: 38.177901, -0.809504

Charges guide

Per unit incl. 2 persons, drainage, TV, WiFi & electricity (plus meter)	€ 25.00 - € 32.00
extra person	€ 4.00

El Escorial

Caravanning El Escorial

Apdo 8, Ctra M600 km 3,5, E-28280 El Escorial (Madrid) T: 902 014 900. E: info@campingelescorial.com

alanrogers.com/ES92000

There is a shortage of good sites in the central regions of Spain, but this is one. El Escorial is very large, there are 1,358 individual pitches of which about 600 are for touring, with the remainder used for permanent or seasonal units, but situated to one side of the site. The pitches are shaded (ask for a pitch without a low tree canopy if you have a 3 m. high motorcaravan). There are another 250 pseudo 'wild' spaces for tourists on open fields, with good shade from mature trees (long cables may be necessary for electricity).

Facilities

One large toilet block for the touring pitches, plus two smart, small blocks for the 'wild' camping area, are all fully equipped with some washbasins in cabins. Baby baths. Facilities for disabled campers. The blocks can be heated. Large supermarket, restaurant/bar and snack bar/takeaway (all year; w/ends only in low season). Disco-bar. Swimming pools (15/5-15/9). Three tennis courts. Two well equipped playgrounds on sand. ATM. Off site: Town 3 km. Riding and golf 7 km.

Open: All year.

Directions

From the south go through town of El Escorial, and follow M600 Guadarrama road. Site is between the 2 and 3 km. markers north of the town on the right. From the north use A6 autopista and exit 47 to M600 towards El Escorial town. Site is on the left. GPS: 40.62400, -4.099

Charges 2012

Per unit incl. 2 persons and electricity	€ 29.80 - € 36.20

No credit cards

El Puerto de Santa Maria

Camping Playa Las Dunas

Paseo Maritimo, Playa de la Puntilla s/n, E-11500 El Puerto de Santa Maria (Cádiz) T: 956 872 210.
E: info@lasdunascamping.com **alanrogers.com/ES88650**

This site lies within the Parque Natural Bahia de Les Dunes and is adjacent to the long and gently sloping golden sands of Puntilla beach. This is a pleasant and peaceful site (though very busy in August) with some 539 separate marked pitches, 260 for tourers, with much natural shade and ample electrical connections (10A). Motorcaravans park in an area called the Oasis which is very pretty. The tent and caravan pitches, under mature trees, are terraced and separated by low walls. This is a spacious site with a tranquil setting and it is popular with people who wish to 'winter over' in peace.

Facilities

Immaculate modern sanitary facilities with separate facilities for disabled campers and a baby room. Laundry facilities are excellent. Gas supplies. Bar/restaurant (all year). Supermarket (high season). Very large swimming pool and paddling pool (1/7-31/8). Night security all year. Barbecues are not permitted 15/5-15/10. WiFi throughout (charged). Off site: Beach 100 m. Fishing 500 m. Bicycle hire, riding and golf 2 km. Municipal sports centre. Local buses for town and city visits and a ferry to Cadiz.

Open: All year.

Directions

Site is 5 km. north of Cadiz off the N443. Take the road to Puerto Santa Maria, site is very well signed throughout the town (small yellow signs high on posts). From south, turn left into town just after large bridge. Keeping sea inlet on your left, follow road for about 1 km. Site on right opposite beach. GPS: 36.5890, -6.2384

Charges 2012

Per unit incl. 2 persons and electricity	€ 21.96 - € 27.11

Empúriabrava

Camping Rubina Resort

Playa de la Rubina, E-17487 Empúriabrava (Girona) T: 972 450 507. E: info@rubinaresort.com

alanrogers.com/ES80200

Situated in the 'Venice of Spain', Empúriabrava is interlaced with inland waterways and canals, where many residents and holidaymakers moor their boats directly outside their expensive homes on the canal banks. Camping Rubina Resort is a large friendly site 200 m. from the wide, sandy beach, which is bordered on the east and west by the waterway canals. It is a surprisingly pretty and hospitable site where people seem to make friends easily and get to know other campers and the staff. The site has 600 touring pitches, most enjoying some shade from strategically placed trees. All have 10A electricity and water connections.

Facilities

Toilet facilities are in five fully equipped blocks. Washing machines. Motorcaravan services. Supermarket, bakery and shop. Restaurant/bar. Disco bar. Takeaway/pizzeria. Watersports with windsurfing school. Organised sports activities, children's programmes and entertainment. Swimming pool (15/4-10/10). Bicycle hire. Playground. Pétanque. Tennis. Very smart Internet café. WiFi over part of site (charged). Dog shower. Apartments. Off site: Beach 200 m. Fishing 300 m. Boat launching 500 m. Riding 1 km.

Open: 1 April - 15 October.

Directions

Empúriabrava is north of Girona and east of Figueras on the coast. From AP7/E15 take exit 3 south or exit 4 north (note there is no exit 3 north) and then N11 to the C260 towards Roses. At Empúriabrava follow 'camping area' signs to site. GPS: 42.25267, 3.1317

Charges 2012

Per person (over 3 yrs)	€ 4.00
pitch incl. electricity and water (85 sq.m)	€ 16.00 - € 36.00

No credit cards.

Espinal

Camping Urrobi

Ctra Pamplona - Valcarlos km 42 N135, E-31694 Espinal (Navarra) T: 948 760 200.
E: info@campingurrobi.com **alanrogers.com/ES90480**

This large site is in a beautiful location with mountain views. At the entrance is a lively bar, a reasonably priced restaurant and a well stocked shop. The site is popular with Spanish families and there are many mobile homes, so it can be busy at holiday times and weekends. However, there is plenty of room on the 150 unmarked grass pitches. All have electricity points (6A) and there are plenty of water taps. Water activities of all types are catered for with both a swimming pool and an area of the river sectioned off for safe bathing and paddling. This is a suitable site for families.

Facilities

Clean sanitary blocks include facilities for disabled visitors (key from reception). Laundry facilities. Motorcaravan service point. Shop, bar and restaurant (all season). Swimming pool. Games room with TV (Spanish). Internet access. Minigolf. Tennis. Playing field. Play area. Off site: Village 1 km. with shops, restaurant and bars. Forest of Irati 15 mins. Bicycle hire 15 km. Golf and riding 40 km. Beach 70 km.

Open: 1 April - 31 October.

Directions

From Pamplona take N135 northeast for 42 km. After village of Auritzberri turn right onto NA172. Site is on the left. GPS: 42.97315, -1.351817

Charges guide

Per unit incl. 2 persons and electricity	€ 24.00 - € 25.50
extra person	€ 5.00
child (2-12 yrs)	€ 4.00

Etxarri-Aranatz

Camping Etxarri

Paraje Dambolintxulo s/n, E-31820 Etxarri-Aranatz (Navarra) T: 948 460 537. E: info@campingetxarri.com
alanrogers.com/ES90420

Situated in the Valle de la Burundi, this site is a peaceful oasis with superb views of the 1,300 m. high San-Donator Mountains. The approach to this improving site is via a road lined by huge 300-year-old oak trees, which are a feature of the site. Reception is housed in the main building beside the pool with a restaurant above (access also by lift). There are 108 pitches of average size on flat ground (50 for tourers) with 6A electricity to all and water to 25. The site is well placed for fascinating walks in unspoilt countryside and is close to three recognised nature walks. The site gets very crowded during the Fiestas de San Fermín (bull-running) in Pamplona early in July. It is essential to make a reservation if you wish to stay. A visit to Pamplona is recommended. Parking is difficult – try to the west of the bullring, then wander down to Plaza de Toros (renamed Plaza Hemingway), to savour the atmosphere. It is common to use dual-naming of places and roads (one in the Spanish language, the other in Basque and it can be confusing) – ask for advice if in doubt.

Facilities

Toilet facilities are good and include a baby bath and facilities for disabled visitors. Laundry. Motorcaravan service point. Gas supplies. Essential supplies kept in high season. Bar (1/4-30/9). Restaurant and takeaway (1/6-15/9). Swimming and paddling pools (15/6-15/9) also open to the public and can get crowded. Bicycle hire. Minigolf. Play area. Entertainment for children in high season. WiFi (charged). Fishing. Tennis and squash courts have been added. No charcoal barbecues. Off site: Buses and trains nearby to Pamplona. Bars, restaurants and shops 2 km. Golf, fishing and riding all 20 km. Pamplona 40 km. Beach 60 km.

Open: 1 April - 3 October.

Directions

Etxarri-Aranatz is 40 km. northwest of Pamplona. From A8 (San Sebastian - Bilbao) take A15 towards Pamplona, then 20 km. northwest of Pamplona, take A10 west towards Vitoria/Gasteix. At km. 19 take NA120 to and through town following site signs. Turn left after crossing railway to site at end of road. GPS: 42.913031, -2.079924

Charges guide

Per unit incl. 2 persons and electricity	€ 23.60 - € 27.60

Eusa

Camping Ezcaba

E-31194 Eusa (Navarra) T: 948 330 315. E: info@campingezcaba.com

alanrogers.com/ES90470

Camping Ezcaba is an all-year site located 5 km. north of Pamplona, near the Ulzama river. Of the 539 pitches, there are just 33 for touring. Pitches are level, grassy and small to moderate in size all with 10A electricity. They are marked by trees which larger units would find difficult to negotiate. A number of mobile homes are available for rent. The majority of the space is specially provided for tents during the very busy Festival of San Fermin in Pamplona and used for youth hostelling the rest of the year. Pamplona is a beautiful city in its own right but is probably more famous for the bull run through the narrow streets during one week in July. Ezcaba is well located for exploring the magnificent Navarra countryside and maybe sample some of its fine wines.

Facilities

Two dated toilet blocks include facilities for disabled visitors. Laundry (not all sinks have hot water). Motorcaravan services. Bar. Large Spanish-style restaurant specialising in local cuisine. Takeaway (high season). Shop (high season). Play area. Swimming pool (high season). Entertainment in peak season. Communal barbecue area. Bicycle hire. WiFi (charged). Off site: Bus stop 500 m. Fishing and golf 5 km. Pamplona 7 km. Walking and cycle trails.

Open: All year.

Directions

From Pamplona take the northbound N121A road towards Irun and the French border. Shortly after leaving the city, turn left to join the NA 4210 and then the NA 4211 to Eusa. Site is clearly signed from here. GPS: 42.85849, -1.62443

Charges guide

Per person	€ 5.20
child	€ 4.50
pitch incl. car and electricity	€ 13.10 - € 17.70

Prices higher during Festival of San Fermin.

Fuente de Piedra

Espacios Rurales Fuente de Piedra

Ctra La Rábita s/n, E-29520 Fuente de Piedra (Málaga) T: 952 735 294. E: info@camping-rural.com

alanrogers.com/ES87900

In a remote area of Andalucia, this tiny campsite with just 30 touring pitches looks over the salty lakes and marshes of the Laguna de Fuente. The average sized pitches are on a sloping, terraced hillside, with some having a view of the lake. With a gravel surface and good shade, many pitches slope so chocks would be useful. There is a separate grassy area for tents near the pool and bungalows (cars are not permitted here). Unusually for a site of this size, there is a pool and an excellent bar, snack bar and huge restaurant which serves delicious Spanish food. Try the excellent, inexpensive 'menu del dia'.

Facilities

Sanitary facilities are in one block and are looking a little tired. Facilities for disabled campers. Washing machines. Shop. Restaurant. Bar with TV. Snack bar. Swimming pool. Pool bar. Electronic games. Bicycle hire.
Off site: Lake with flamingos. Bicycle hire 1 km. Fishing 5 km. Riding 10 km. Golf 40 km. Excursions organised in July/Aug.

Open: All year.

Directions

Site is 20 km. northwest of Antequera. From Antequera take A92 and exit at 132 km. point and follow road to the town. Site is well signed from the town but the signs are small. GPS: 37.1292, -4.7334

Charges guide

Per person	€ 5.40 - € 6.00
child (0-12 yrs)	€ 3.60 - € 4.00
pitch	€ 3.60 - € 8.00
electricity	€ 5.00

Gata

Camping Sierra de Gata

Ctra Ex109 a Gata km 4,100, E-10860 Gata (Cáceres) T: 927 672 168. E: sierradegata@campingsonline.com

alanrogers.com/ES94000

For a taste of the real, rural Spain this very Spanish site (no English was spoken when we visited) is situated just before the tiny village of Sierra de Gata, south of Ciudad Rodrigo and northwest of Plasencia. Situated in beautiful countryside with a small stream alongside the site, the pitches are on grass with plenty of shade from trees. This site is undergoing refurbishment with the addition of 12 beautiful new bungalows to sleep four to six people. A special area with huts for groups of children to stay is positioned in one corner of the site.

Facilities

Two toilet blocks with British style toilets also include child-sized toilets, a laundry room and dishwashing facilities. Medium sized shop for necessities in summer. Smart restaurant/bar complex provides good food. Two swimming pools. Tennis. Play area. Fishing. Riding. Bicycle hire. Off site: Restaurant near site entrance.

Open: 18 March - 3 November.

Directions

Approach ONLY from the southwest from the 109 Ciudad Rodrico - Coria road. Where the 205 meets the 109 take turn 20-30 m. north signed Gata 10. Travel along this road until km. 4. Turn left (near restaurant and small bridge) and site is ahead through gate. GPS: 40.21195, -6.64224

Charges guide

Per person	€ 3.75 - € 4.25
pitch	€ 4.50 - € 8.00
electricity	€ 3.75 - € 4.25

Gavín

Camping Gavín

Ctra N260 km 503, E-22639 Gavín (Huesca) T: 974 485 090. E: info@campinggavin.com

alanrogers.com/ES90640

Camping Gavín is set on a terraced, wooded hillside and you will find a friendly welcome. The site offers 150 pitches of 90 sq.m. in size and with electricity available to all (10A). In some areas the terracing means that some pitches are quite small. The main site buildings have been constructed using natural stone. There are also 13 bungalows and 11 superb, balconied apartments. At about 900 m. the site is surrounded by towering peaks at the portal of the Tena Valley. One can enjoy the natural beauty of the Pyrenees and venture near or far along the great Pyrenean footpaths.

Facilities

Excellent shower and toilet facilities in three main buildings with subtle, tasteful décor include facilities for babies and disabled visitors. Laundry facilities. Bar and snacks. Well stocked supermarket. Swimming pools (15/6-15/9) and paddling pools (all year). Tennis. Playground. Bicycle hire. Barbecues are not permitted at some times of the year. Off site: Windsurfing, rafting, fishing, walking and climbing in the vicinity. Riding 6 km. Golf 15 km. Day excursions to the Monastery of San Juan de la Peña.

Open: All year.

Directions

Site is off the N260, 2 km. from Biescas at km. 503. GPS: 42.61940, -0.30408

Charges guide

Per unit incl. 2 persons and electricity	€ 29.92 - € 37.37
extra person	€ 4.97 - € 6.80

Camping Cheques accepted.

Granada

Camping Suspiro del Moro

Ctra Bailén - Motril km 144, Puerto Suspiro del Moro, E-18630 Granada (Granada) T: 958 555 411.
E: campingsuspirodelmoro@yahoo.es **alanrogers.com/ES92700**

Suspiro del Moro is small family run site with 64 pitches, which packs a big punch with its associated Olympic-sized swimming pool and huge bar and restaurant. It is cool and peaceful with great views from the site perimeter. The flat pitches are shaded by mature trees and there are no statics here. The whole site is neat, clean and well ordered and great for chilling out whilst visiting the area and the famous Alhambra (connecting buses from the gate). The site also has its own small bar and restaurant serving snacks. The large restaurant has an extensive menu with waiter service.

Facilities

Clean and tidy, the small toilet blocks are situated around the camping area with British style WCs and free hot showers. Laundry and dishwashing facilities. Small basic shop. Small simple restaurant/bar (high season). Small play area on gravel. WiFi. Off site: Swimming pool and restaurant adjacent. Sierra Nevada and Granada within reasonable distance to explore. Public transport 50 m. from gate.

Open: All year.

Directions

Leave Granada to Motril road (E902/A44) at exit 144 (from south) or 139 (from north) and follow unnamed campsite signs. At roundabout go towards Suspiro, then left (signed after turn). Site is about 600 m. on right on A4050 beside large restaurant. GPS: 37.0852, -3.6348

Charges guide

Per person	€ 4.00 - € 4.80
child (2-11 yrs)	€ 3.00 - € 3.50
pitch incl. car	€ 9.00 - € 9.50
electricity	€ 3.00 - € 3.30

Granada

Camping Sierra Nevada

Avenida Juan Pablo II no.23, E-18014 Granada (Granada) T: 958 150 062. E: campingmotel@terra.es

alanrogers.com/ES9280

This is a good site either for a night stop or for a stay of a few days while visiting Granada, especially the Alhambra, and for a city site it is surprisingly pleasant. Quite large, it has an open feel and, to encourage you to stay a little longer, a smart, irregular shape pool with a smaller children's pool open in high season. There is some traffic noise around the pool as it is on the road boundary. With 148 pitches for touring units (10/20A electricity), the site is in two connected parts with more mature trees and facilities to the northern end.

Facilities

Two modern sanitary blocks, with good facilities, including cabins, very good facilities for disabled campers and babies. Washing machines. Motorcaravan services. Gas supplies. Shop (15/3-15/10). Swimming pools with lifeguards and charge of € 1.80 (15/6-15/9). Bar/restaurant by pool. Tennis. Pétanque. Large playground. Off site: Supermarket. Bus station 100 m. from site gate. Fishing 10 km. Golf 12 km. Riding 15 km.

Open: 1 March - 31 October.

Directions

Site is just outside the city to north, on road to Jaén and Madrid. From autopista, take Granada North - Almanjayar exit 123 (close to central bus station). Follow road back towards Granada and site is on the right, well signed. From other roads join the motorway to access the correct exit.
GPS: 37.20402, -3.61703

Charges guide

Per unit incl. 2 persons and electricity	€ 30.00
extra person	€ 6.00
child (3-10 yrs)	€ 5.10

Guadalupe

Camping Las Villuercas

Ctra Villanueva, E-10140 Guadalupe (Cáceres) T: 927 367 139

alanrogers.com/ES90280

This rural site nestles in an attractive valley northwest of Guadalupe. The 50 pitches (25 with 10A electricity) are level and of a reasonable size; although large units may experience difficulty in getting into the more central pitches. With an abundance of mature trees most pitches offer some degree of shade. A river runs alongside the site and the ground can be muddy in very wet periods. The site is co-located with hostel accommodation. The restaurant provides excellent food at low prices and leads to a pretty patio with overhead vines and potted plants allowing elevated views of the pools.

Facilities

The single toilet block is older but very clean, with one area for women and one for men, providing British type WCs, washbasins and showers (hot water is from a 40-litre immersion heater which could be overwhelmed in busy periods). Facilities for disabled visitors. Laundry facilities. Restaurant. Bar. Swimming pools. Shop. Tennis. Small playground. Barbecue area. No English spoken. Off site: Riding 2 km. Fishing 3 km.

Open: 1 March - 30 November.

Directions

From NV/E90 Madrid - Mérida exit at Navelmoral de la Mata. Follow south to Guadalupe on CC713 (83 km). Site is 2 km. from Guadalupe (near Monastery). From further southwest take exit 102 off main E90/NV (northeast of Mérida). Follow signs (Guadalupe). Go through a few villages and near 72 km. marker turn left to site, 100 m. on right.
GPS: 39.441228, -5.322

Charges guide

Per person	€ 3.21
child (2-12 yrs)	€ 2.67
pitch	€ 4.28 - € 5.88
electricity	€ 2.67

No credit cards.

Guardamar del Segura

Marjal Camping & Bungalows Resort

Ctra. N332 km 73,4, E-03140 Guardamar del Segura (Alacant) T: **966 727 070.**

E: camping@marjal.com **alanrogers.com/ES87430**

Marjal is located beside the estuary of the Segura river, alongside the pine and eucalyptus forests of the Dunas de Guardamar Natural pPrk. A fine sandy beach can be reached through the forest (800 m). This is a very smart site with a huge tropical lake style pool with bar and a superb sports complex. There are 212 pitches on this award-winning site, 168 for touring with water, electricity (16A), drainage and satellite TV points. The ground is covered with crushed marble, making the pitches clean and pleasant. There is some shade and the site has an open feel with lots of room for manoeuvring. Reception is housed within a delicately coloured building complete with a towering Mirador, topped by a weather vane depicting the 'garza real' (heron) bird which frequents the local area and forms part of the site logo. The large restaurant overlooks the pools and the river that leads to the sea in the near distance. The bar has large terraces fringed by trees, palms and pomegranates. The impressive pool/lagoon complex (1,100 sq.m) has a water cascade, an island bar plus bridge, one part sectioned as a pool for children and a jacuzzi. The extensive sports area is also impressive. No effort has been spared here and facilities are of the highest quality. An extensive programme of entertainment is provided for adults and children in season by a professional team.

Facilities

Three excellent heated toilet blocks have free hot water, elegant separators between sinks, spacious showers and some cabins. Each block has high quality facilities for babies and disabled campers, modern laundry and dishwashing rooms. Motorcaravan service point. Car wash. Well stocked supermarket. Restaurants. Bar. Large outdoor pool complex (1/6-31/10). Heated indoor pool (low season). Jacuzzi. Sauna. Solarium. Beauty salon. Superb well equipped gym. Aerobics. Physiotherapy. All activities discounted for campers. Play room. Minigolf. Floodlit tennis and soccer pitch. Bicycle hire. Car rental. Games room. TV room. Full entertainment programme. Hairdresser. ATM. Business centre. Internet access and free WiFi over site. Caravan storage. Off site: Beach 800 m. Fishing 1 km. Riding and golf 4 km. Parc Natural de las Dunas de GuaRdamar alongside site.

Open: All year.

Directions

On N332 40 km. south of Alicante, site is on the sea side between 73 and 74 km. markers.
GPS: 38.10933, -0.65467

Charges guide

Per unit incl. 2 persons and electricity	€ 38.00 - € 65.00
extra person	€ 7.00 - € 9.00
child (4-12 yrs)	€ 5.00 - € 6.00
dog	€ 2.20 - € 3.20

Low season discounts.

Guardiola de Bergedá

Camping El Bergedá

Ctra B400 a Saldes km 3,5, E-08694 Guardiola de Bergedá (Barcelona) T: **938 227 432.**

E: info@campingbergueda.com **alanrogers.com/ES91390**

The short scenic drive through the mountains to reach the site is breathtakingly beautiful. Situated under trees, this terraced campsite in the area of the Cadi-Moixer Natural Park, is not far from the majestic Pedraforca mountain. A favourite for Catalan climbers and walkers, its amazing rugged peak in the shape of a massive stone fork gives it its name. Access to the site is quite easy for large units. Of the 73 small grass gravel pitches there are 40 for touring, all with 6A electricity. The campsite owners will do all in their power to make your stay here enjoyable.

Facilities

Two clean, well equipped, heated modern toilet blocks. Facilities for campers with disabilities. Three private cabins with washbasin, toilet and bidet. Washing machines and dryer. Small shop, restaurant, bar and takeaway (w/ends only then 1/7-1/9). Outdoor pools (24/6-31/8). Play areas. WiFi over part of site (free). Barbecues are not permitted except in communal area. Off site: Mountain biking. Artigas gardens designed by Gaudi. Picasso Museum. Museum of mines. New adventure park 5 km.

Open: Easter - 30 October.

Directions

Guardiola de Berguedá is 125 km. north of Barcelona. From the C16 Manresa-Berga road 2 km. south of Guardiola de Berguedá turn west towards Saldes. Site is on right after 3.5 km. From France via Puigcerdá take the C16 (Berga/Manresa) to Guardiola de Berguedá, then as above.
GPS: 42.21642, 1.83692

Charges 2012

Per unit incl. 2 persons and electricity	€ 28.45
extra person	€ 5.70
child (1-10 yrs)	€ 4.55

Güejar-Sierra

Camping Las Lomas

Ctra de Sierra Nevada, E-18160 Güejar-Sierra (Granada) T: 958 484 742. E: laslomas@campingsonline.com

alanrogers.com/ES92850

This site is high in the Sierra Nevada Natural Park and looks down on the Patano de Canales reservoir. After a scenic drive to Güejar-Sierra, you are rewarded with a site boasting excellent facilities. It is set on a slope but the pitches have been levelled and are quite private, with high separating hedges and many mature trees giving good shade, (some pitches are fully serviced, with sinks and all but four have electricity). The large bar/restaurant complex and pools have wonderful views over the lake and a grassy sunbathing area runs down to the fence looking over the long drop below. A new feature is private bathrooms for rent, including one with a spa tub which is for hire by the hour. Any infirm visitors may need a car to get around as the inclines are quite steep.

Facilities

Adequate sanitary blocks (heated in winter) provide clean facilities. First class facilities for disabled campers and well equipped baby room (key at reception). Motorcaravan services. Good supermarket. Restaurant/bar. Swimming pool. Play area. Minigolf. Barbecue. WiFi (charged). Torches useful. A no-noise policy (including cars) is strictly enforced midnight-07.00. Off site: Buses to village and Granada (15 km). Bicycle hire 1.5 km. Fishing 3 km. Tours of The Alhambra and GrAnada organised. Useful site for winter skiing. Parascending and skiing nearby.

Open: All year.

Directions

Heading south towards Granada on A44 (E902 Jaén - Motril) take exit 132 onto A395 (Alhamba - Sierra Nevada). After 4 km. marker, exit 5B (Sierra Nevada). At 7 km. marker, exit right onto slip road. At (Cenes de la Vega - Güejar-Sierra) junction turn left. In 200 m. turn right on A4026. In 1.6 km. turn left (Güejar-Sierra). Drive uphill, past dam and site is on right in 2.8 km. GPS: 37.16073, -3.45388

Charges guide

Per person	€ 4.00 - € 6.00
child (2-10 yrs)	€ 3.50 - € 4.50
pitch	€ 12.00 - € 14.00
electricity	€ 3.50

Guils de Cerdanya

Camping Pirineus

Ctra Guils de Cerdanya km 2, E-17528 Guils de Cerdanya (Girona) T: 972 881 062. E: guils@stel.es

alanrogers.com/ES91430

On entering this well organised site close to the French border, high in the Pyrenees, you gain an immediate impression of space, green trees and grass – there is always someone watering and clearing up to maintain the high standards here. The pitches are neat, marked, of average size and organised in rows. Generally flat with some on a gentle incline, a proportion have water at their own sink on the pitch. Many trees offer shade but watch for overhanging branches if you have a high unit. From the restaurant terrace you have fine views of the mountains in the background and the pool in the foreground.

Facilities

One brand new, central and well equipped sanitary block of top quality and decorated with boxes of bright flowers, are kept spotlessly clean and can be heated. Good laundry facilities. Motorcaravan service point. Shop, bar and restaurant (all season). Heated swimming pool and circular paddling pool. Boules. Tennis. Outdoor sports. TV and games room. Snooker. Play area and supervised clubhouse for youngsters. Excursions. Entertainment (high season). WiFi. Dogs not accepted. Off site: Bicycle hire 2 km. Riding 4 km. Golf 6 km. River fishing 7 km.

Open: 22 June - 11 September.

Directions

The site is close to Puigcerdá, just across the border with France at Bourg-Madame. From Perpignan take N116 to Prades and Andorra. Exit at Piugcerdá taking N250 signed Le Seu d'Urgell and almost immediately take second right for Guils de Cerdanya. Follow for 2 km. to site on right. From the south the best road is the C25/C16/N260 from Manresa to Piugcerdá, turning left for Guils de Cerdanya. GPS: 42.44312, 1.90583

Charges 2012

Per unit incl. 2 persons and electricity	€ 35.30 - € 42.80
extra person	€ 6.80
child (3-10 yrs)	€ 5.60

Hospitalet del Infante

Camping-Pension Cala d'Oques

Via Augusta s/n, E-43890 Hospitalet del Infante (Tarragona) T: 977 823 254. E: info@caladoques.com

alanrogers.com/ES85350

This peaceful and delightful, family-run site has a lot going for it: its situation beside the sea with a wide beach of sand and pebbles, its amazing mountain backdrop, the views across the bay to the town and the friendly, relaxed atmosphere created by its owner of 40 years, Elisa Roller, her family and her staff. There are 152 mosty level pitches, some beside the beach, others on wide, informal terracing. Electricity (10A) is available throughout (although long leads may be needed in places). Pine and olive trees are an attractive feature and provide some shade. The restaurant with its homely touches has a good local menu and a reputation extending well outside the site.

Facilities

Toilet facilities are in the central part of the main building. Clean, neat and recently refurbished with a number of en-suite units (shower, washbasin and WC). Hot water to showers by token but free to campers to guard against unauthorised visitors from the beach. New heated unit with toilets and washbasins for winter use. Unit for disabled visitors. Additional small block with toilets and washbasins at the far end of the site. Motorcaravan service point. Restaurant/bar and shop (1/4-30/10). Play area. Kim's kids' club and family entertainment (high season). Fishing. Sailing. Internet access and WiFi. Gas supplies. Torches required in some areas. Mobile home and apartments to rent. Off site: Village facilities, incl. shop and restaurant 1.5 km. Bicycle hire, boat launching, golf and riding 2 km.

Open: All year.

Directions

Hospitalet del Infante is 35 km. southwest of Tarragona, accessed from the A7 (exit 38) or from the N340. From the north take first exit to Hospitalet del Infante at the 1128 km. marker. Follow 'Campings' signs before the village, then signs to site for 1.5 km. GPS: 40.97777, 0.90338

Charges guide

Per unit incl. 2 persons and electricity	€ 24,75 - € 42.95
extra person	€ 4.95 - € 9.50
child (0-10 yrs)	€ 2.50
dog	€ 3.40

Discounts for seniors and for longer stays.
No credit cards.

Isla Plana

Camping Los Madriles

Ctra de la Azohia km 4.5, E-30868 Isla Plana (Murcia) T: 968 152 151. E: camplosmadriles@terra.es

alanrogers.com/ES87480

An exceptional site with super facilities, Los Madriles is run by a hard working team, with constant improvements being made. Twenty kilometres west of Cartagena, the approach to the site and the surrounding area is fairly unremarkable, but the site is not. A fairly steep access road leads to the 313 flat, good to large sized terraced pitches, each having electricity, water and a waste point. Most have shade from large trees with a number benefiting from panoramic views of the sea or behind to the mountains. The site has huge rectangular and lagoon style pools with water sprays and jacuzzis.

Facilities

Four sanitary blocks and one small toilet block provide excellent facilities, including services in one block for disabled campers. Private wash cabins. Washing machines and dryers. Motorcaravan services. Car wash. Supermarket, restaurant/snack bar and bar (all open all season but hours are limited). Swimming pools with jacuzzi. Boules. Play areas. Animals are not accepted. Off site: Town close by. Beach and fishing (licence required, purchase in Puerto Mazarron) 800 m. Boat launching 3 km. Riding and bicycle hire 6 km. Golf 20 km.

Open: All year.

Directions

From E15/A7 take exit 845 and follow RM3 in direction of Cartagena, Fuente Alamo and Mazarron (do not turn into Mazarron). Continue towards Puerto Mazarron and take N332 (Cartagena). On reaching coast continue with N332 (Cartagena and Alicante). At roundabout turn right towards Isla Plana and La Azohia. Site is well signed and on the left in approx. 5 km. GPS: 37.3441N, -1.1147W

Charges guide

Per unit incl. 2 persons and electricity	€ 32.10

Large discounts for longer stays.

Iznate

Camping Iznate

Ctra Benamocarra - Iznate km 2,7, E-29792 Iznate (Málaga) T: 952 535 613. E: info@campingiznate.com

alanrogers.com/ES87850

This new site is situated amid beautiful scenery 1 km. away from the picturesque village of Iznate. It is surrounded by avocado and olive trees and is on the wine route – the region is the centre of Spain's Muscadet production. The site is well thought out and immaculately maintained. The large swimming pool is an ideal spot for cooling off after a walk and the next door restaurant serves excellent food at very reasonable prices. This is a small new site and we would recommend booking during high season. There are wonderful views all round the site and eagles, wild boar and black squirrels can be seen in the surrounding countryside.

Facilities

The modern toilet block has hot showers and facilities for disabled visitors. Laundry facilities under a covered area. Fridge hire. Small shop. Bar/restaurant with terrace adjoining the site. Swimming pool (15/5-15/9). Summer entertainment. Pétanque. Play area. TV room. WiFi. Barbecues not permitted in high season. Off site: Beach 20 mins. drive. Towns of Sayalonga and Frigeliana nearby.

Open: All year.

Directions

From A7/E15 take exit 265 and head towards Cajiz and Iznate. Site is on left after Iznate.
GPS: 36.79219, -4.17131

Charges guide

Per person	€ 4.30
child (2-10 yrs)	€ 3.70
pitch incl. car	€ 8.30 - € 9.30
electricity	€ 3.00 - € 3.50

Jávea

Camping Jávea

Ctra Cami de la Fontana 10, Apdo 83, E-03730 Jávea (Alacant) T: 965 791 070. E: info@camping-javea.com

alanrogers.com/ES87540

The final approach to this site emerges from the bustle of the town and is decorated with palms, orange and pine trees, the latter playing host to a colony of parakeets. English is spoken at reception. The neat, boxed hedges and palms within the site, and its backdrop of hills dotted with villas presents an attractive setting. Three hectares provide space for 214 numbered pitches with 183 for touring units. Flat, level and rectangular in shape, the pitches vary in size 60-80 sq.m. The restaurant provides great food, way above normal campsite standards.

Facilities

Two very clean, fully equipped, sanitary blocks include two children's toilets plus a baby bath. Separate facilities for disabled campers. Two washing machines. Fridge hire. Extensive bar and restaurant with terraces where in high season you purchase bread and milk. Large swimming pool with lifeguard and sunbathing lawns. Play area. Boules. Electronic barriers (deposit for card). Caravan storage. Post. Safes. Five-a-side footaball. Basketball. Tennis. WiFi. Car rental. Off site: Old and New Jávea within easy walking distance with supermarkets and shops catering for all needs. Sandy beach, boat launching, fishing, bicycle hire all 1.5 km. Golf 3 km.

Open: All year.

Directions

Exit N332 for Jávea on A134, continue in direction of Port (road number changes to CV 734). In town the site is well marked with large orange indicators high on posts. Watch carefully for a sudden slip road sign!
GPS: 38.78333, 0.16983

Charges guide

Per unit incl. 2 persons and electricity	€ 28.71 - € 31.40
extra person	€ 5.58 - € 6.20
child	€ 4.68 - € 5.20
dog	€ 1.50 - € 2.00

L'Escala

Camping Neus Tent-Lodge

Cala Montgó, E-17130 L'Escala (Girona) T: 972 770 403. E: info@campingneus.com

alanrogers.com/ES80690

Camping Neus is set on the edges of a forest under mature pines with 190 pitches arranged on sets of terraces, all with 6A electricity. This mature site is being thoughtfully renovated. It is fenced from the road and facilities are mainly close to the reception building. A small pool with a circular paddling pool is welcome after a hot day's sightseeing; other site amenities include a tennis court and small bar/restaurant. A new play area and a volleyball court have been added and gardens planted.

Facilities

Renovated sanitary blocks offer sound and clean facilities along with baby rooms and facilities for disabled campers. Motorcaravan service point. Shop. Bar. Restaurant. Takeaway. Swimming pool. Paddling pool. Tennis. Volleyball. Play area. TV room. Entertainment and activities in peak season. Club for children. WiFi over part of site (free). Bicycle hire. Mobile homes and chalets to rent. Only electric barbecues are permitted. Off site: Resort of Cala Montgó with beach 850 m. Fishing. Kayaking. Diving.

Open: 25 May - 16 September.

Directions

Take exit 5 from the AP7 and the GI623 to L'Escala. Continue to Riells and Montgó. Site is on right just before Cala Montgó. GPS: 42.1049, 3.15816

Charges 2012

Per unit incl. 2 persons and electricity	€ 21.70 - € 44.70
extra person	€ 3.00 - € 5.00
child (4-12 yrs)	€ 1.00 - € 3.50
dog	€ 2.00

L'Estartit

Camping Castell Montgri

Ctra Toroella - l'Estartit km 4,7, E-17258 L'Estartit (Girona) T: **972 751 630.** E: **cmontgri@campingparks.com**

alanrogers.com/ES80070

This is a large, noisy, bustling, expensive site with all the modern paraphernalia of holiday-making. Over 50 per cent of this site is dedicated to catering for tour operators, and obviously so, but there are three designated areas for independent campers. These provide 590 terraced and flat pitches, some shaded but all with electricity. On arrival you are processed by rather impersonal staff. The site could be of interest to families with teenagers, offering the possibility for parents to rest whilst the youngsters enjoy their own type of holiday within the confines of the site. There is a busy, but expensive, bar/restaurant with terraces overlooking a smallish plunge pool with a pair of water slides (one long with attendant and a second small pool). The remainder of the site offers a very wide range of amenities and attractions, including another large pool with restaurant/bar and terrace areas higher on the site.

Facilities

Toilet facilities are adequate, if not that luxurious, each area having its own block. Cleaning is continual (06.00-22.00) but with the numbers on site, queueing and litter can be a problem. Bars and restaurants. Pizzeria. Takeaway. Swimming pools. Supermarket and souvenirs. Tennis. Minigolf. Playground. Large screen TV. Disco. Entertainment programme and excursions. Free bus to L'Estartit. Internet access (expensive) and WiFi (charged). Torches required in some areas. Off site: Riding 500 m. Beach, fishing and bicycle hire 1 km. Golf 5 km.

Open: 15 May - 26 September.

Directions

L'Estartit is on the coast northeast of Girona. Leave the AP7/E15 and take the C66 towards Palamós. Then take the GI642 towards Parlava and the GI643 towards Torroella de Montgri. Site is well signed on the GI 641 Torroella de Montgri - L'Estartit road just north of the town on the left. GPS: 42.0511, 3.1827

Charges guide

Per person	€ 5.00
child (3-10 yrs)	€ 3.50
pitch incl. car and electricity	€ 9.00 - € 56.00
dog	€ 2.35

Discounts in low season.

L'Estartit

Camping Empordá

Ctra Toroella km 4,8, E-17258 L'Estartit (Girona) T: **972 750 649.** E: **info@campingemporda.com**

alanrogers.com/ES80730

Empordá is just 1 km. from the busy town and superb beach of L'Estartit and is a delightful place. When we visited, it had an open feel where the campers all seemed very happy. With just 250 pitches there is a family atmosphere which Francesc, the owner, encourages. The pitches are 80 sq.m. in size and 22 are fully serviced. There is a little shade from young trees and the ground is flat. The great swimming and paddling pools are at the heart of the campsite which has placed all the facilities neatly together. Varied entertainment is provided in high season.

Facilities

Two very clean sanitary blocks, one with facilities for disabled campers and a baby bath. Cabins with hot and cold water, cold water at other basins. Washing machines and dryer. Bar. Restaurant, pizzas and takeaway. Supermarket. Large swimming pool (lifeguard in high season) and paddling pool. Entertainment daily in high season. Miniclub. Disco (high season). Aerobics. Two play areas. Electronic games. TV. Aqua gym. Chalets for rent. WiFi (charged). Off site: Town 1 km. Golf 8 km.

Open: Easter - 12 October.

Directions

From AP7 Figueres - Girona autopista take Palamós exit and then the C66 towards Palamós. Then take the GI642 towards Parlava and the GI643 towards Torroella de Montgri. Lastly take the GI641 towards L'Estartit and the site is well signed shortly before entering the town. GPS: 42.04907, 3.18385

Charges guide

Per unit incl. 2 persons and electricity	€ 14.80 - € 28.60

No credit cards.

L'Estartit

Camping Les Medes

Paratge Camp de L'Arbre, E-17258 L'Estartit (Girona) T: 972 751 805. E: info@campinglesmedes.com

alanrogers.com/ES80720

Les Medes is different from some of the 'all singing, all dancing' sites so popular along this coast, and the friendly family of Pla-Coll are rightly proud of their award-winning site and provide a very warm welcome. With just 170 pitches, the site is small enough for the owners to know their visitors and, being campers themselves, they have been careful in planning their top class facilities and are aware of environmental issues. The level, grassy pitches range in size from 70-80 sq.m. depending on your unit. All have electricity (5/10A) and 155 also have water and drainage. All are clearly marked in rows, but with no separation other than by the deciduous trees which provide summer shade. A cheery children's pool with fountains is behind the unusually shaped pool ringed by palms.

Facilities

Two modern spacious sanitary blocks can be heated and are extremely well maintained. Washbasins in cabins, top class facilities for disabled visitors and baby baths. Washing machines and dryer. Motorcaravan services. Shop. Bar with snacks and pizza (all year). Good value restaurant (1/4-31/10). Swimming and paddling pools (1/5-15/9). Indoor pool with sauna, solarium and massage (15/9-15/6). Play area. TV room. Entertainment, activities and excursions (July/Aug). Diving activities. Multisports area. Boules. Bicycle hire. Internet access and WiFi. Torches are useful. Dogs are not accepted in July/Aug. Off site: Riding 400 m. Nearest beach and fishing 800 m. Medes Natural Reserve 1.5 km. Strait 2 km. Golf 8 km.

Open: All year excl. November.

Directions

Site is signed from the main Torroella de Montgri - L'Estartit road GE641. Turn right after Camping Castel Montgri, at Joc's hamburger/pizzeria and follow signs. GPS: 42.048, 3.1881

Charges 2012

Per unit incl. 2 persons and electricity € 22.80 - € 41.75

Discounts outside high season and special offers for low season longer stays. No credit cards.

L'Escala

Camping Illa Mateua

Avenida de Montgó 260, E-17130 L'Escala (Girona) T: 972 770 200. E: info@campingillamateua.com

alanrogers.com/ES80740

If you prefer a quieter site out of the very busy resort of L'Escala, then this site is an excellent option. This large, family run site has a dynamic owner Marti, who speaks excellent English. The site is divided by the beach access road and has its own private access to the very safe and unspoilt beach. There are 358 pitches in the two parts of the site, all with 10A electricity, some on sloping ground although the pitches in the second part are flat. Established pine trees provide shade for most places with more coverage on the western side. Non-stop improvement and maintenance ensure that all facilities at this site are of a high standard. There are three swimming pools, the largest an 'infinity pool' enjoying an idyllic and most unusual setting on the top of a cliff overlooking the Bay of Roses. A CCTV security system monitors the pools and general security from a purpose built centre. A strong feature of this site is its five-star PADI diving school.

Facilities

Very modern, fully equipped sanitary blocks are kept spotlessly clean by omnipresent cleaners. Brilliant facilities for children and baby baths. Washing machines and dryers. Shop, extensive modern complex of restaurants, bars and takeaways (all open all season). Swimming pools (20/4-12/10). Pool bar. Play areas. Kayak hire. Organised activities for children in high season. Diving school. Sports centre. Internet access and WiFi. ATM. Private access to beach. Off site: Road train service to town centre from outside site. Cala Montgó beach 100 m. with a charming bay of soft sand offering all manner of watersports, pretty restaurants and a disco in season. Fishing 150 m. Riding 2 km. Golf 10 km.

Open: 21 March - 12 October.

Directions

Leave autopista A7 at exit 5 heading for Viladimat, then L'Escala. Site is well signed from town centre. Follow signs for Montgó and site is south of town beside the coast. Site has changed name so some signs may show the old name of Paradis.
GPS: 42.11051, 3.16542

Charges guide

Per unit incl. 2 persons and electricity	€ 22.80 - € 44.00
extra person	€ 3.25 - € 6.00
child (3-10 yrs)	€ 2.30 - € 4.10
dog	€ 2.40 - € 3.80

No credit cards.

La Cabrera

Camping Pico de la Miel

Ctra A1, Salida 57, E-28751 La Cabrera (Madrid) T: 918 688 082. E: info@picodelamiel.com

alanrogers.com/ES92100

Pico de la Miel is a very large site 60 km. north of Madrid. Mainly a long-stay site for Madrid, there are a huge number of very well established, fairly old statics. There is a small separate area with its own toilet block for the 80 touring units, all with electricity (8A Europlug). The pitches are on rather poor, sandy grass, but the articial shade has been removed and trees planted. There are yet more pitches for tents (the ground could be hard for pegs). The noise level from the many Spanish customers is high and you will have a chance to practise your Spanish!

Facilities

Dated but clean tiled toilet block, with some washbasins in cabins. It can be heated. En-suite unit with ramp for disabled visitors. Motorcaravan services. Gas supplies. Shop. Restaurant/bar and takeaway (1/6-30/9 and weekends rest of year). Excellent swimming pool complex (15/6-15/9). Tennis. Playground. WiFi throughout. Off site: Bicycle hire and riding 500 m. Fishing 6 km.

Open: All year.

Directions

Site is well signed from the N1. Going south or north use exit 57 and follow site signs. When at T-junction, facing a hotel, turn left. (Exit 57 is closer to site than exit 60). GPS: 40.85797, -3.6158

Charges guide

Per unit incl. 2 persons	€ 27.10 - € 29.75
extra person	€ 6.20

La Manga del Mar Menor

Caravaning La Manga

Autovia Cartagena-La Manga, Salida 11, E-30386 La Manga (Murcia)
T: 968 563 014. E: lamanga@caravaning.es **alanrogers.com/ES87530**

This is a very large, well equipped, holiday style site with its own beach and both indoor and outdoor pools. With a good number of typical Spanish long stay units, the length of the site is impressive (1 km) and a bicycle is very helpful for getting about. The 1,000 regularly laid out, gravel touring pitches (100 or 110 sq.m) are generally separated by hedges which also provide a degree of shade. Each has 10A electricity supply, water and the possibility of satellite TV reception. La Manga is a 22 km. long narrow strip of land, bordered by the Mediterranean on one side and by the Mar Menor on the other. There are sandy bathing beaches on both sides and considerable development in terms of hotels, apartments, restaurants, night clubs, etc. in between – a little reminiscent of Miami Beach! The very end of the southern part is great for 'getting away from it all' (take a picnic for the beach and be sure to go over the little bridge for privacy). The campsite is situated on the approach to 'the strip', enjoying the benefit of its own semi-private beach with impressive tall palm trees alongside the Mar Menor, which provides shallow warm waters, ideal for families with children. This site's excellent facilities are ideally suited for holidays in the winter when the weather is very pleasantly warm. The November daytime temperatures usually exceed 20°C.

Facilities

Nine clean toilet blocks include washbasins (hot water). Laundry. Gas supplies. Large well stocked supermarket. Restaurant. Bar. Snack bar. Swimming pool complex (April-Sept). Indoor pool, gymnasium (April-Oct), sauna, jacuzzi and massage service. New outdoor fitness course for adults. Open-air family cinema (July/Aug). Pétanque. Minigolf. Play area. Watersports school. Internet café (also WiFi). Winter activities including Spanish classes. Pet washing area. Max. 2 dogs. Off site: Buses to Cartagena and Murcia from outside site. Golf and riding 5 km.

Open: All year.

Directions

Use exit (Salida) 11 from MU312 dual-carriageway towards Cabo de Palos, signed Playa Honda (site signed also). Cross road bridge and double back. Site entrance is visible beside dual carriageway with many flags flying. GPS: 37.62445, -0.74442

Charges guide

Per unit incl. 2 persons and electricity	€ 20.00 - € 35.00
extra person	€ 4.10 - € 5.10

Camping Cheques accepted.

La Marina

Camping Internacional La Marina

Ctra N332 km 76, E-03194 La Marina (Alacant) T: 965 419 200. E: info@campinglamarina.com

alanrogers.com/ES87420

Very efficiently run by a friendly Belgian family, La Marina has 381 pitches of three different types and sizes ranging from 50 sq.m. to 150 sq.m. with electricity (10/16A), TV, water and drainage. Artificial shade is provided and the pitches are extremely well maintained on level, well drained ground with a special area allocated for tents in a small orchard. The huge lagoon swimming pool complex is absolutely fabulous and has something for everyone (with lifeguards). William Le Metayer, the owner, is passionate about La Marina and it shows in his search for perfection. A magnificent new, modern building which uses the latest architectural technology, houses many superb extra amenities. Facilities include a relaxed business centre with Internet access, a tapas bar decorated with amazing ceramics (handmade by the owner's mother) and a quality restaurant with a water fountain feature and great views of the lagoon. There is also a conference centre and an extensive computerised library. The whole of the lower ground floor is dedicated to children with a Marina Park play area and a 'cyber zone' for teenagers. With a further bar and a new soundproofed disco (Anima2), the building is of an exceptional, eco-friendly standard. A superb fitness centre with attentive personal trainers and a covered, heated pool (14x7 m) are incorporated. A pedestrian gate at the rear of the site gives access to the long sandy beach through the coastal pine forest that is a feature of the area. We recommend this site very highly whatever type of holidaying camper you may be. A member of Leading Campings Group.

Facilities

The elegant sanitary blocks offer the very best of modern facilities. Heated in winter, they include private cabins and facilities for disabled visitors and babies. Laundry facilities. Motorcaravan services. Gas. Supermarket. Bars. Restaurant and café (all year). Ice cream kiosk. Swimming pools (1/4-15/10). Indoor pool. Fitness centre. Sauna. Solarium. Jacuzzi. Play rooms. Extensive activity and entertainment programme including barbecues and swimming nights. Sports area. Tennis. Huge playgrounds. Hairdresser. Bicycle hire. Road train to beach. Exclusive area for dogs. Internet café (charged) and free WiFi.
Off site: Fishing 700 m. Boat launching 5 km. Golf 7 km. Riding 15 km. Hourly bus service from outside the gate. Theme parks.

Open: All year.

Directions

Site is 2 km. west of La Marina. Leave the N332 Guardamara de Segura - Santa Pola road at 75 km. marker if travelling north, or 78 km. marker if travelling south. Site is well signed.
GPS: 38.129649, -0.649575

Charges guide

Per unit incl. 2 persons and electricity	€ 33.28 - € 62.61
extra person	€ 5.35 - € 8.00
child (1-10 yrs)	€ 3.75 - € 5.50
dog	free - € 2.14

Good discounts for longer stays in low season.

La Pineda

Camping La Pineda de Salou

Ctra Costa Tarragona - Salou km 5, E-43481 La Pineda (Tarragona) T: 977 373 080.
E: info@campinglapineda.com **alanrogers.com/ES84820**

La Pineda is a clean, neat site north of Salou, just 300 m. from an aquapark and 2.5 km. from Port Aventura, to which there is an hourly bus service from outside the site entrance. There is some noise from the road. The site has two swimming pools; the smaller is heated. A colourful themed paddling pool and outdoor spa are also here, behind tall hedges close to the entrance. A large terrace has sun loungers, and various entertainment aimed at young people is provided in season. The 366 flat pitches (all with 5A electricity) are shaded by mature trees in attractive gardens. La Pineda is a cut above other city sites.

Facilities

Sanitary facilities have been refurbished and are excellent with baby bath, dishwashing and laundry sinks. Facilities for disabled visitors. Washing machines. Gas supplies. Shop (1/7-31/8). Restaurant and snacks (1/7-31/8). Swimming pools, themed paddling pool and outdoor spa (1/7-31/8). Bar (all season). New smart community room with giant satellite TV. Bicycle and road cart hire. Games room. Playground (3-12 yrs). Entertainment (1/7-30/8). Torches may be required. No pets allowed in August. Small wellness centre. WiFi. Bus from gate.

Open: All year.

Directions

From A7 just southwest of Tarragona take exit 35 and follow signs to La Pineda and Port Aventura then campsite signs appear. GPS: 41.08921, 1.1837

Charges guide

Per unit incl. 2 persons and electricity (6A)	€ 29.00 - € 51.50
extra person	€ 5.40 - € 8.30
child (1-10 yrs)	€ 3.70 - € 6.20
dog	€ 3.90 - € 4.00

La Puebla de Castro

Camping Barasona

Ctra N123a km 25, E-22435 La Puebla de Castro (Huesca) T: 974 545 148. E: info@lagobarasona.com
alanrogers.com/ES91250

This site, alongside its associated ten room hotel, is beautifully positioned on terraces across a road from the shores of the Lago de Barasona (a large reservoir), with views of hills and the distant Pyrenees. The very friendly, English-speaking owner is keen to please and has applied very high standards throughout the site. The grassy, fairly level pitches are generally around 100 sq.m. with 35 high quality pitches of 110 sq.m. for larger units. All have electricity (6/10A), many are well shaded and some have great views of the lake and/or hills. Water skiing and other watersports are available in July and August.

Facilities

Two toilet blocks in modern buildings have high standards and hot water throughout including cabins (3 for women, 1 for men). Bar/snack bar and two excellent restaurants (all season). Shop (1/4-30/9). Swimming pools (1/6-30/9). Tennis. Mountain bike hire. Canoe, windsurfing motorboat and pedalo hire. Miniclub (high season). Lake swimming, fishing, canoeing, etc. Walking (maps provided). Money exchange. Mini-disco. WiFi. Wellness centre with sauna, jacuzzi and gym. Off site: Riding 4 km.

Open: All year.

Directions

Site is on the west bank of the lake, near km. 25 on the N123A, 6 km. south of Graus (about 80 km. north of Lleida/Lerida). Travelling from the south, the site is on the left from a newly-built roundabout and slip road. GPS: 42.14163, 0.31525

Charges guide

Per unit incl. 2 persons and electricity	€ 23.00 - € 35.00
extra person	€ 4.50 - € 6.50

Camping Cheques accepted.

Labuerda

Camping Peña Montañesa

Ctra Ainsa - Francia km 2, E-22360 Labuerda (Huesca) T: 974 500 032. E: info@penamontanesa.com
alanrogers.com/ES90600

A large site situated quite high up in the Pyrenees near the Ordesa National Park, Peña Montañesa is easily accessible from Ainsa or from France via the Bielsa Tunnel (steep sections on the French side). The site is essentially divided into three sections opening progressively throughout the season and all have shade. The 288 pitches on fairly level grass are of about 75 sq.m. and 10A electricity is available on virtually all. Grouped near the entrance are the facilities that make the site so attractive, including a fair sized outdoor pool and a glass-covered indoor pool with jacuzzi and sauna.

Facilities

A newer toilet block, heated when necessary, has free hot showers but cold water to open plan washbasins. Facilities for disabled visitors. Small baby room. An older block in the original area has similar provision. Washing machine and dryer. Bar, restaurant, takeaway and supermarket (all 1/1-31/12). Outdoor swimming pool (1/4-31/10). Indoor pool. Playground. Boules. Bicycle hire. Riding. Rafting. Only gas barbecues are permitted. Torches required in some areas. Off site: Fishing 100 m.

Open: All year.

Directions

Site is 2 km. from Ainsa, on the road from Ainsa to France. GPS: 42.4352, 0.13618

Charges guide

Per unit incl. 2 persons and electricity	€ 24.60 - € 33.30

Llafranc

Kim's Camping

Font d'en Xeco 1, E-17211 Llafranc - Palafrugell (Girona) T: 972 301 156. E: info@campingkims.com

alanrogers.com/ES81200

This attractive, terraced site (to which the owner has been welcoming guests for 54 years) is arranged on the wooded slopes of a narrow valley leading to the sea and there are many trees including huge eucalyptus. There are 350 grassy and partly shaded pitches (70-120 sq.m), 240 used for touring units, all with electricity (5A). Many of the larger pitches are on a plateau from which great views can be enjoyed. The terraced pitches are connected by winding drives, narrow in places. This is a pleasant place for holidays where you can enjoy the bustling atmosphere of the village and beach, while staying in a quieter environment. English and Dutch are spoken by the very friendly management and staff.

Facilities

All sanitary facilities are spotlessly clean and include a small new block and excellent toilet facilities for disabled visitors. Laundry facilities. Motorcaravan services. Gas supplies. Well stocked shop. Bar. Bakery and croissanterie. Café/restaurant (15/6-15/9). Swimming pools. Play areas and children's club. TV room. Excursions arranged – bus calls at site. Visits arranged to sub-aqua schools (high season). Torches required. WiFi. Gas only barbecues. Mobile homes to rent. Off site: Beach, sailing and bicycle hire 500 m. Llafranc 1 km. Riding 3.5 km.

Open: Easter - 2 October.

Directions

Llafranc is southeast of Palafrugell. Turn off the Palafrugell - Tamariu road at turn (GIV 6542) signed Llafranc. Site is on right 1 km. further on. GPS: 41.90053, 3.18935

Charges guide

Per unit incl. 2 persons and electricity	€ 18.15 - € 41.20
extra person	€ 2.65 - € 6.55
child (3-10 yrs)	€ 1.00 - € 3.25

Discounts for long stays and for senior citizens.

Lloret de Mar

Camping Tucan

Ctra de Blanes - Lloret, E-17310 Lloret de Mar (Girona) T: 972 369 965. E: info@campingtucan.com

alanrogers.com/ES82100

Situated on the busy Costa Brava near Lloret de Mar, Camping Tucan is well placed to access all the attractions of the area. Views over the mountains are mixed with views of the nearby town. Of the 307 good sized pitches, 48 are fully serviced (60-100 sq.m) and most have electricity (3/6/10A). Laid out in a herringbone pattern, there are areas dedicated to singles, families with young children and couples who enjoy the quiet. Pitches are on terraces, flat surfaced with gravel and many are shaded. Tucan is a lively site with many activities including a programme for children and modest entertainment at night.

Facilities

Two modern toilet blocks include washbasins with hot water and facilities for disabled visitors, although access can be difficult. Washing machines. Gas supplies. Shop. Busy bar and good restaurant. Takeaway. Swimming pools and indoor solarium. Playground and fenced play area for toddlers. TV in bar. Bicycle hire. Entertainment in high season. Miniclub. WiFi (charged). Only charcoal and gas barbecues permitted. Large motorcaravans and twin-axle caravans accepted. Off site: Town with supermarkets 500 m. Nearest beach 600 m. Riding 1 km. Golf 4 km.

Open: 1 April - 25 September.

Directions

From A7/E4, A19 or N11 Girona - Barcelona roads take an exit for Lloret de Mar. Site is 1 km. west of the town, well signed and is at the base of the hill off the roundabout. The entrance can get congested in busy periods. GPS: 41.6972, 2.8217

Charges 2012

Per unit incl. 2 persons and electricity	€ 25.70 - € 55.40

Luarca

Camping Los Cantiles

Ctra N634 km 502,7, E-33700 Luarca (Asturias) T: 985 640 938. E: cantiles@campingloscantiles.com

alanrogers.com/ES89400

Luarca is a picturesque little place with a pretty inner harbour and two sandy beaches, and Los Cantiles is two kilometres to the east of town on a cliff top that juts out into the sea, giving excellent views from some pitches and the sound of the waves to soothe you to sleep. The site is well maintained and is a pleasant place to stop along this under-developed coastline. The 150 pitches, 105 with electricity, are mostly on level grass, divided by huge hedges of hydrangeas and bushes. Some pitches have gravel surfaces. There is a separate area for late arrivals in high season. English is spoken.

Facilities

Two modern, fully equipped sanitary blocks are kept very clean. Facilities for disabled campers and babies. Laundry. Freezer service. Gas supplies. Small shop. Bar with hot snacks (1/7-15/9). Day room for backpackers with tables, chairs and cooking facilities (own gas). Small playing field. Communal barbecue. Torches helpful after midnight. WiFi (charged). Off site: Indoor swimming pool, sauna and fitness centre, plus a bar/restaurant and shop 300 m. Beach and fishing 700 m. Luarca 2 km. Riding 4 km.

Open: All year.

Directions

Luarca is 85 km. west of Gijón. From the A8 Oviedo - La Coruña exit at 467 onto N634 for Luarca. After km. 502 east of Luarca, turn right at petrol station and follow signs to site for 2.5 km. Last 150 m. is narrow. GPS: 43.54998, -6.51665

Charges 2012

Per unit incl. 2 persons and electricity	€ 19.30 - € 21.50
extra person	€ 4.30

No credit cards.

Malpartida de Plasencia

Camping Parque Natural de Monfrague

Ctra Plasencia - Trujillo km 10, E-10680 Malpartida de Plasencia (Cáceres) T: 927 459 233.

E: contacto@campingmonfrague.com alanrogers.com/ES90270

Situated on the edge of the Monfrague National Park, this well managed site owned by the Barrado family, has fine views to the Sierra de Mirabel and delightful surrounding countryside. Many of the 130 good sized grass pitches are on slightly sloping, terraced ground. Scattered trees offer a degree of shade, there are numerous water points and 10A electricity. It would prove difficult to find a more suitable location for those that savour tranquillity. On rare occasions, a goods train travels along the nearby railway line. Created as a national park in 1979, Monfrague is now recognised as one of the best locations in Europe for anyone interested in birdwatching.

Facilities

Large modern toilet blocks, fully equipped, are very clean. Facilities for disabled campers and baby baths. Laundry. Motorcaravan service point. Supermarket/shop. Restaurant, bar and coffee shop. TV room with recreational facilities. Swimming and paddling pools (June-Sept). Play area. Tennis. Entertainment for children in season. Barbecue areas. Free WiFi. Guided safaris into the Park for birdwatching. Off site: Large supermarket at Plasencia. Bicycle hire 2 km. Riding 6 km.

Open: All year.

Directions

On the N630, from the north take EX-208 (previously C524) Plasencia - Trujillo; site on left in 6 km. From the south turn right just south of Plasencia on EX-108 (previously C511) in direction of Malpartida de Plasencia. Right at main junction onto EX-208 to site. GPS: 39.9395, -6.084

Charges 2012

Per unit incl. 2 persons and electricity	€ 20.10 - € 20.40

Camping Cheques accepted.

Marbella

Camping Marbella Playa

Ctra N340 km 192,8, E-29600 Marbella (Málaga) T: 952 833 998. E: recepcion@campingmarbella.com

alanrogers.com/ES88000

This large site is 12 km. east of the internationally famous resort of Marbella with public transport available to the town centre and local attractions. A sandy beach is about 150 metres away with direct access. There are 430 individual pitches of up to 70 sq.m. with natural shade (additional artificial shade is provided to some), and electricity (10/20A) available throughout. Long leads may be required for some pitches, and those next to the road can experience some noise from 18.00 onwards. The site is busy throughout the high season but the high staff/customer ratio and the friendly staff approach ensures a comfortable stay. A large pool complex with a restaurant/bar provides a very attractive feature.

Facilities

Four sanitary blocks of mixed ages, are fully equipped and well maintained. Three modern units for disabled visitors. Laundry service. Large supermarket with butcher and fresh vegetable counter. Bar, restaurant and café (all open all year). Supervised swimming pool (free April-Sept). Playground. Children's activities. WiFi (charged). Torches advised. Off site: Fishing 100 m. Bus service 150 m. Beach 200 m. Golf and bicycle hire 5 km. Riding 10 km.

Open: All year.

Directions

Site is 12 km. east of Marbella with access close to the 193 km. point on the main N340 road. Signed Elviria, then follow camping signs.
GPS: 36.49127, -4.76325

Charges guide

Per person	€ 3.30 - € 5.75
child (1-10 yrs)	€ 2.55 - € 5.06
pitch	€ 4.60 - € 13.70
electricity	€ 4.10 - € 7.05

Marbella

Kawan Village Cabopino

Ctra N340 km 194,7, E-29604 Marbella (Málaga) T: 952 834 373.

E: info@campingcabopino.com alanrogers.com/ES88020

This large, mature site is alongside the main N340/A7 Costa del Sol coast road, 12 km. east of Marbella and 15 km. from Fuengirola. The Costa del Sol is also known as the Costa del Golf and fittingly there is a major golf course alongside the site. The site is set amongst tall pine trees which provide shade for the sandy pitches (there are some huge areas for large units). The 300 touring pitches, a mix of level and sloping (chocks advisable), all have electricity (10A), but long leads may be required for some. There is a separate area on the western side for groups of younger guests.

Facilities

Five mature but very clean sanitary blocks provide hot water throughout (may be under pressure at peak times). Washing machines. Bar/restaurant and takeaway (all year). Shop. Outdoor pool (1/5-15/9) and indoor pool (all year). Play area. Adult exercise equipment. Some evening entertainment. Excursions can be booked. ATM. Torches necessary in the more remote parts of the site. Only gas or electric barbecues are permitted. Off site: Beach and golf 200 m. Fishing, bicycle hire and riding within 1 km.

Open: All year.

Directions

Site is 12 km. from Marbella. Approaching Marbella from the east, leave the N340/A7 at the 194 km. marker (signed Cabopino). Site is off the roundabout at the top of the slip road. GPS: 36.49350, -4.74383

Charges guide

Per unit incl. 2 persons and electricity	€ 23.11 - € 34.82
extra person	€ 4.55 - € 6.97

Camping Cheques accepted.

Marbella

Camping La Buganvilla

Ctra N340 km 188,8, E-29600 Marbella (Málaga) T: 952 831 973. E: info@campingbuganvilla.com

alanrogers.com/ES88030

La Buganvilla is a large, uncomplicated site with mature trees providing shade to some of the 250 touring pitches. They all have 16A electricity and are mostly on terraces so there are some views across to the mountains and hinterland of this coastal area. The terrain is a little rugged in places and the buildings are older and in need of some attention, but all were clean when we visited. A pool complex near the bar and restaurant is ideal for cooling off after a day's sightseeing. This is an acceptable base from which to explore areas of the Costa del Sol and it is an easy drive to the picturesque Ronda Valley.

Facilities

Three painted sanitary blocks are clean and adequate. Laundry facilities (not all sinks have hot water). Outdoor pool (all year). Bar/restaurant with basic food. Well stocked small supermarket. Play area. Tennis (high season). WiFi (charged). Dogs are not accepted in July/Aug. Off site: Bus service close to site entrance. Fishing and watersports 400 m. Bicycle and scooter hire 1 km. Golf 5 km. Resort type entertainment close.

Open: All year.

Directions

Site is between Marbella and Fuengirola off the N340/A7. Access at 188.8 km. marker is only possible when travelling west, i.e. from Fuengirola. From the other direction, continue to the 'cambio de sentido' signed Elviria and turn back over the dual-carriageway. Site is signed. GPS: 36.5023, -4.804

Charges guide

Per unit incl. 2 persons and electricity	€ 22.82 - € 33.82
extra person	€ 5.50 - € 7.50
child (under 10 yrs)	€ 3.00 - € 6.00

Mendigorría

Camping Caravanning Errota el Molino

E-31150 Mendigorría (Navarra) T: 948 340 604. E: info@campingelmolino.com

alanrogers.com/ES90430

This is an extensive site set by an attractive weir near the town of Mendigorría, alongside the river Arga. It takes its name from an old disused water mill (molino) close by. The site is split into separate permanent and touring sections. The touring area is a new development with good-sized flat pitches with electricity and water for tourers, and a separate area for tents. Many trees have been planted around the site but there is still only minimal shade. The friendly owner Anna Beriain will give you a warm welcome. Reception is housed in the lower part of a long building along with the bar/snack bar which has a cool shaded terrace, a separate restaurant and a supermarket. The upper floor of this building is dormitory accommodation for backpackers. The site has a sophisticated dock and boat launching facility and an ambitious watersport competition programme in season with a safety boat present at all times. There are pedaloes and canoes for hire. The site is very busy during the festival of San Fermín (bull running) in July in Pamplona (28 km). Tours of the local bodegas (groups of ten) to sample the fantastic Navarra wines can be organised by reception.

Facilities

The well equipped toilet block is very clean and well maintained, with cold water to washbasins. Facilities for disabled campers. Washing machine. Large restaurant, pleasant bar. Supermarket. Superb new swimming pools for adults and children (1/6-15/9). Bicycle hire. Riverside bar. Weekly entertainment programme (July/Aug) and many sporting activities. Squash courts. Internet access. River walk. Torches useful. Off site: Bus to Pamplona 500 m. Riding 15 km. Golf 35 km.

Open: All year (excl. 23 December - 4 January).

Directions

Mendigorría is 30 km. southwest of Pamplona. From A15 San Sebastian - Zaragoza motorway, leave Pamplona bypass on A12 towards Logon. Leave at km. 23 on NA601 to hilltop town of Mendigorría. At crossroads turn right towards Larraga and down hill to site. GPS: 42.62423, -1.84259

Charges guide

Per person	€ 4.70 - € 5.00
child	€ 3.95 - € 4.22
pitch incl. car and electricity	€ 12.90 - € 13.80

Molinicos

Camping Rio Mundo

Ctra Comarcal 412 km 205, Mesones, E-02449 Molinicos (Albacete) T: 967 433 230.
E: riomundo@campingriomundo.com alanrogers.com/ES90980

This uncomplicated and typically Spanish site is situated in the Sierra de Alcaraz (south of Albacete), just off the scenic route 412 between Elche de la Sierra and Valdepenas. The drive to this site is most enjoyable through beautiful scenery and from the west the main road is winding in some places. Shade is provided by mature trees for the 80 pitches and electricity (6/10A) is supplied to 70 (long leads are useful). It is in a beautiful setting with majestic mountains and wonderful countryside which begs to be explored.

Facilities

One toilet block has been upgraded and provides clean modern facilities. Basic toilet facilities for disabled visitors. Washing machine. Small shop for basics. Outside bar serving snacks with covered seating area. Takeaway (all 15/3-12/10). Another bar by the swimming pool. Playground. Pétanque. WiFi. Only gas and electric barbecues permitted. Off site: Riding 7 km.

Open: 18 March - 12 October.

Directions

Site is just off 412 road which runs west to east between the A30 and 322 roads south of Albacete. Turn at km. 205 on the 412, 5 km. east of Riopar and west of Elche de la Sierra. From here follow signs to site. The road narrows to one lane for a few hundred yards. GPS: 38.48917, -2.34639

Charges guide

Per person	€ 4.30 - € 5.90
pitch incl. car	€ 10.80 - € 14.70
electricity (6/10A)	€ 3.60 - € 5.10

Moncofa

Camping Monmar

Ctra Serratelles s/n, E-12593 Moncofa (Castelló) T: 964 588 592. E: campingmonmar@terra.es
alanrogers.com/ES85900

This purpose built, very neat site is in the small town of Moncofa, just 200 metres from the sea and right beside a water park with pools and slides. There are 170 gravel based pitches arranged in rows off tarmac access roads. The 100 touring pitches all have 6A electricity, water and drainage. Hedges have been planted to separate the pitches but these are still small so there is little shade (canopies can be rented in high season). The site's facilities and amenities are all very modern but small stone reminders of the area's Roman and Arab history are used to decorate corners of the site.

Facilities

Three modern toilet blocks are well placed and provide good, clean facilities. Free hot showers. Facilities and good access for disabled visitors. Laundry facilities. Shop (1/7-31/8). Bar and restaurant (weekends and high season). Swimming pool (all year). Good play area. Boules. New library. Internet (on payment). Animals are not accepted. Off site: Beach 200 m. Water complex. Local amenities within walking distance.

Open: All year.

Directions

Turn off N340 Castellon - Valencia road on CV2250 signed Moncofa. Follow sign for tourist information office in town and then signs for site. Pass supermarket and turn left to site in 600 m. GPS: 39.80884, -0.1281

Charges guide

Per unit incl. 2 persons and electricity	€ 14.00 - € 25.00

Montagut

Camping Montagut

Ctra Montagut - Sadernes km 2, E-17855 Montagut (Girona) T: 972 287 202.
E: info@campingmontagut.com alanrogers.com/ES91220

This is a delightful, small family site where everything is kept in pristine condition. Jordi and Nuria, a brother and sister team, work hard to make you welcome and maintain the superb appearance of the site. Flowers and shrubs abound, with 90 pitches on attractively landscaped and carefully constructed terraces or on flat areas overlooking the pool. All but 10 are for touring units and 5A electricity is available throughout. A tranquil atmosphere pervades the site and it is a delight to enjoy drinks on the pleasant restaurant terrace, or to sample the authentic menu as you enjoy the views over the Alta Garrotxa. There is much to see in the local area between the Pyrenees and the Mediterranean.

Facilities

The modern sanitary block has controllable hot showers, open-style washbasins, a pleasant baby room and an en-suite unit for disabled visitors. Washing and laundry facilities. Motorcaravan services. Supermarket (all season). Restaurant and bar (1/7-28/8, snacks and bar at weekends in low season. Medium sized swimming pool with large sunbathing area and children's pool (1/5-30/9). Playground. Sports field. Pétanque. Barbecue area. WiFi area (free). Torches useful in some areas. Off site: Riding 1 km. Shop, bar and restaurant in village 2 km.

Open: 1 April - 16 October.

Directions

Montagut is 45 km northwest of Girona. From the south on AP7 leave at exit 6 (Girona), take the C66/A26 towards Olot. From north leave AP7 at Figueres, join N11 south and turn west signed Olot to join N260/A26. Take exit 75, turn right towards Montagut. At end of village turn left towards Sadernes and site entrance is on the left in 2 km. GPS: 42.2469, 2.5971

Charges guide

Per unit incl. 2 persons and electricity	€ 20.35 - € 33.00
extra person	€ 5.10 - € 7.10

Montroig

Camping La Torre del Sol

Ctra N340 km 1136, E-43300 Montroig (Tarragona) T: 977 810 486. E: info@latorredelsol.com

alanrogers.com/ES85400

A pleasant banana tree-lined approach road gives way to avenues of palms as you arrive at Torre del Sol. This is a very large site occupying a good position in the south of Catalunya with direct access to the soft sand beach. The site is exceptionally well maintained by a large workforce. There is good shade on a high proportion of the 1,500 individual, numbered pitches. All have electricity and are mostly of about 70-80 sq.m. Strong features here are 800 m. of clean beachfront with a special Mediterranean type of pitch, and the entertainment that is provided all season. Part of the site is between the railway and the sea, so there is some occasional train noise. The cinema doubles as a theatre to stage shows all season. A complex of three pools, thoughtfully laid out with grass sunbathing areas and palms, has a lifeguard. There is wireless Internet access throughout the site. There is usually space for odd nights but for good places between 10/7-16/8 it is best to reserve (only taken for a stay of seven nights or more). We were impressed with the provision of season-long entertainment, giving parents a break whilst children were in the safe hands of the activities team, who ensure they enjoy the novel Happy Camp and various workshops. There is a separate area where the team will take your children to camp overnight in the Indian reservation.

Facilities

Five well maintained, fully equipped, toilet blocks include units for disabled visitors and babies and new facilities for children. Washing machines. Gas supplies. Supermarket, bakery and souvenir shops at entrance, open to public. Full restaurant. Takeaway. Bar with large terrace where entertainment is held daily. Beach bar. Coffee bar and ice cream bar. Pizzeria. Open-roof cinema with permanent seating for 520. 3 TV lounges. Soundproofed disco. Swimming pools (two heated). Solarium. Sauna. Two large jacuzzis. Sports areas. Tennis. Squash. Language school (Spanish). Minigolf. Sub-aqua diving (first dive free!) Bicycle hire. Fishing. Windsurfing school. Sailboards and pedaloes for hire. Playground, crèche and Happy Camp. Fridge hire. Library. Hairdresser. Business centre. WiFi. Car repair and car wash (pressure wash). No animals permitted. No jet skis accepted. Off site: Buses on N340 close to site. Beach fishing. Riding 3 km. Golf 4 km.

Open: 15 March - 31 October.

Directions

Entrance is off main N340 road by 1136 km. marker, about 30 km. from Tarragona towards Valencia. From motorway take Cambrils exit and turn west on N340. GPS: 41.03707, 0.97478

Charges 2012

Per unit incl. 2 persons and electricity	€ 20.30 - € 66.55
extra person	€ 3.35 - € 9.90
child (0-10 yrs)	free - € 7.85

Discounts in low season for longer stays.
Camping Cheques accepted.

Montroig

Playa Montroig Camping Resort

Ctra N340 km 1136, E-43300 Montroig (Tarragona) T: 977 810 637. E: info@playamontroig.com

alanrogers.com/ES85300

What a superb site! Playa Montroig is about 30 kilometres beyond Tarragona set in its own tropical gardens with direct access to a very long, narrow, soft sand beach. The main part of the site lies between the sea, road and railway (as at other sites on this coast, there is some train noise) with a huge underpass. The site is divided into spacious, marked pitches with excellent shade provided by a variety of lush vegetation including very impressive palms set in wide avenues. There are 1,177 pitches, all with electricity and 564 with water and drainage. Some 47 pitches are directly alongside the beach. The site has many outstanding features: there is an excellent pool complex near the entrance, with two pools (one heated for children). A new Espai Grill and bar, with a rock and roll disco and a pretty candlelit patio is just outside the gate. One restaurant serves good food with some Catalan fare (seats 150) and overlooks an entertainment area. A large terrace bar serves drinks or if you yearn for louder music there is a second disco with a smaller bar. There is yet another eating option in a 500-seat restaurant. Above this is the 'Pai-pai' Caribbean cocktail bar where softer music is provided in an intimate atmosphere. Activities for children are very ambitious – there is even a ceramics kiln (multi-lingual carers). 'La Carpa', a spectacular open-air theatre, is an ideal setting for daily keep fit sessions and the professional entertainment provided. Several beach sports are available on the beach. This is an excellent site and there is insufficient space here to describe all the available activities. We recommend it for families with children of all ages, and there is much emphasis on providing activities outside the high season. A member of Leading Campings Group.

Facilities

Very good quality sanitary buildings with washbasins in private cabins and separate WCs. Facilities for disabled campers and for babies. Several launderettes. Motorcaravan services. Good shopping centre. Restaurants and bars. Fitness suite. Hairdressers. TV lounges. Beach bar. Playground. Jogging track. Sports area. Tennis. Minigolf. Organised activities including pottery. Pedalo hire. Boat mooring. Bicycle hire. Gas supplies. Internet café. WiFi in all bars. Dogs are not accepted. Off site: Public transport 100 m. from gate. Riding, golf and boat launching 3 km.

Open: 23 March - 4 November.

Directions

Site entrance is off main N340 nearly 30 km. southwest from Tarragona. From motorway take Cambrils exit and turn west on N340 at 1136 km. marker. GPS: 41.03292, 0.96921

Charges 2012

Per unit incl. 2 persons and electricity	€ 19.00 - € 50.00
extra person	€ 6.00 - € 7.00
child (1-9 yrs)	free - € 5.50

Discounts for longer stays and for pensioners.

Montblanc

Camping Caravaning Montblanc Park

Ctra Prenafeta km 1,8, E-43400 Montblanc (Tarragona) T: 977 862 544. E: montblancpark@franceloc.fr

alanrogers.com/ES85020

Purpose designed, Montblanc Park has 290 terraced pitches of which 160 are ostensibly for touring units, although well over 100 are occupied by permanently-installed seasonal caravans; they are grassless, all have electricity (20A) and vary in size, with hedging and young trees (so little shade). Water taps are scarce. The upper terraces are taken up by 130 wooden chalets for rent. The bar/restaurant and terrace overlook a large, lagoon-style pool with views across the valley, beyond the busy railway-line and the autopista, to the town of Montblanc and the mountains of the Serra del Prades.

Facilities

Two toilet blocks feature en-suite units (WC, washbasin and shower) but no separate WCs or showers, so they must be under considerable pressure in high season. Good unit for disabled visitors. Baby room. Washing machines and dryers. Supermarket (June-Oct). Bar/restaurant and snack bar with takeaway (weekends only in low season). Swimming pool and large paddling pool. Play areas. Games room. Gym. Bicycle hire. Entertainment for children (weekends and main holiday season). Only electric barbecues allowed. Chalets for hire. Free WiFi in leisure area. Off site: Shops, bars and restaurants in town 2 km. Organised mountain activities, including climbing, caving, canyoning and orienteering (pick-up from site). Quad biking and trips by 4x4. Gaudí museum in Reus 25 km. Beach, sailing and sea fishing 38 km. Golf 45 km.

Open: 1 April - 30 November.

Directions

Montblanc is between Barcelona and Lleida on the AP2 motorway. Leave at exit 9 and join the N240 (Reus-Tarragona); take first exit towards Prenafeta and site stands out on the hillside ahead. GPS: 41.3787, 1.1826

Charges guide

Per unit incl. 2 persons and electricity	€ 19.00 - € 34.00
extra person	€ 4.00 - € 6.00
child (0-10 yrs)	free
dog	€ 4.00

Special offer for the 50th anniversary

Plot + 2 pers. from 50 € in high season

**Take this unique opportunity and celebrate with us.
We look forward to see you**

Book online: www.playamontroig.com

50 YEARS
1962 - 2012
PLAYA MONTROIG
CampingResort

Carretera N-340 Km 1.136
E-43300 Montroig
Tarragona - Spain

www.playamontroig.com
info@playamontroig.com
+34 977 810 637
+34 977 811 411

twitter.com/playamontroig
www.facebook.com/playamontroigcampingresort

The Leading Camping & Caravaning Parks of Europe

Moraira

Camping Caravanning Moraira

Camino Paellero 50, E-03724 Moraira-Teulada (Alacant) T: 965 745 249.

E: campingmoraira@campingmoraira.com **alanrogers.com/ES87550**

This neat hillside site with some views over the town and marina is quietly situated in an urban area amongst old pine trees and just 400 metres from a sheltered bay. A striking, stilted and glass-fronted reception building gives great views. Ask about the innovative building features and prepare for pleasant design surprises. Terracing provides shaded pitches of varying sizes, some small (access to some of the upper pitches may be difficult for larger units). There are 17 pitches with full services (6/10A electricity). An attractive irregularly shaped pool with paved sunbathing terrace is below the bar/restaurant and terrace. The pool has large observation windows where you can watch the swimmers and divers as this is used for sub-aqua instruction. The site runs a PADI diving school; the diving here is good and the water warm, even in winter. Buildings here have been designed by the architect owner, giving the site a stylish flair, which is very pleasing and different to mainstream campsites. A glass fronted bar and restaurant are impressive. A sandy beach is 1.5 km. away. A large, painted water tower stands at the top of the site.

Facilities

The high quality toilet blocks, with polished granite floors and marble fittings are built to a unique and ultra-modern design. Facilities for disabled campers. Washing machines and dryers. Motorcaravan services. Bar/restaurant and shop (1/6-30/9). Bread and basics at the bar. Small swimming pool (all year). Sub-aqua with instruction. Tennis. Limited children's entertainment in high season. Torches may be required. WiFi code. Pets welcome.
Off site: Shops, bars and restaurants within walking distance. Beach and fishing 400 m. Gym and ATM 600 m. Bicycle hire 1 km. Golf 8 km.

Open: All year.

Directions

Best approach is from Teulada. From A7 exit 63 take N332 and in 3.5 km. turn right (Teulada and Moraira). In Teulada fork right to Moraira. At junction at town entrance turn right signed Calpe and in 1 km. turn right into road to site on bend immediately after Res. Don Julio. Do not take the first right, as the signs seem to indicate, otherwise you will go round in a loop. GPS: 38.692, 0.14

Charges guide

Per unit incl. 2 persons and electricity	€ 37.00
extra person	€ 7.50
child (4-10 yrs)	€ 5.35

Motril

Camping Don Cactus

Ctra N340 km 343, Playa de Carchuna, E-18730 Carchuna-Motril (Granada) T: 958 623 109.

E: camping@doncactus.com **alanrogers.com/ES92950**

Situated between the main N340 and the beach, this family run campsite is pleasantly surprising with clever planning and ongoing improvements. It is a comfortable site of 320 pitches (280 for touring). The flat pitches vary in size with electricity (5/12A), some providing water and satellite TV connections, and are arranged along avenues with eucalyptus trees for shade. This quieter section of the coast is beautiful with coves and access to larger towns if wished. The friendly reception staff are very helpful with tourist advice and can arrange trips for you if needed.

Facilities

The large toilet block is dated but clean and provides British style WCs, showers and plenty of washbasins. Laundry facilities. Beach showers. Well stocked shop. Bar, restaurant and takeaway (all year). Swimming pool (in high season € 1.50 per day). Tennis. Play area. Summer activities for children. Outdoor fitness centre for adults. Pets corner. ATM. Internet point. WiFi (charged; free in bar). Dogs are not accepted in July/Aug. Barbecues only in special area. Caravan storage. Car wash facility.
Off site: Bus service 500 m.

Open: All year.

Directions

From Motril - Carchuna road (N340/E15) turn towards the sea at km. 343. (site signed, but look at roof level for large green tent on the top of the building!). Travel about 600 m. then turn east to site on left. GPS: 36.70066, -3.44032

Charges guide

Per person	€ 6.96
child (4-10 yrs)	€ 6.60
pitch	€ 15.75
electricity (5A)	€ 4.75

Low season discounts for longer stays.

Mundaka

Camping Portuondo

Ctra Gernika - Bermeo, E-48360 Mundaka (Bizkaia) T: 946 877 701. E: recepcion@campingportuondo.com

alanrogers.com/ES90350

This site has a lovely restaurant, bar and terrace taking full advantage of the wonderful views across the ocean and estuary. Set amongst gardens, the 72 touring pitches are mainly for tents and smaller vans, but there are eight large pitches at the lower levels for caravans and motorcaravans. Access to these is a little difficult as the road is very steep and there is no turning space. The site is mostly terraced, with tent pitches split, one section for your unit, the other for your car and there is some shade. Most are slightly sloping and all have electricity (6A, some may need long leads). It is essential to ring to book your space in July and August.

Facilities

Two toilet blocks include mostly British WCs and a baby room. One new block with facilities for disabled visitors. A reader reports poor cleaning and maintenance during their visit. Washing machines and dryers. Motorcaravan service point. Shop (15/6-15/9). Bar and two restaurants, all open to public (28/1-14/12). Takeaway (15/6-15/9). Swimming pools (15/6-15/9). Free WiFi over part of site. Barbecue area. Torches may be useful. Off site: Fishing 100 m. Buses to Bilbao and Gernika (every 30 mins) 300 m. Surfing on Mundaka beach 500 m. Boat launching and bicycle hire 1 km. Shops, bars and restaurants 2 km.

Open: 23 January - 9 December.

Directions

From A8 (San Sebastián - Bilbao) take exit 18 and follow signs for Gernika on BI635. Continue on BI2235 towards Bermeo. Site is on right as you approach Mundaka. Care is needed as a wide approach may be necessary as this is a sharp right turn with a steep access. Road signs do not permit turning left to site. GPS: 43.39918, -2.69610

Charges 2012

Per unit incl. 2 persons and electricity	€ 30.05 € 34.50
extra person	€ 6.35 - € 8.00

Min. 1 week reservation mid June to end August.

Navajas

Camping Altomira

Ctra CV213 Navajas km 1, E-12470 Navajas (Castelló) T: 964 713 211. E: reservas@campingaltomira.com

alanrogers.com/ES85850

Camping Altomira is a terraced site in a rural, hillside setting, on the outskirts of a quiet village and offers superb views across the valleys and hills. There are 80 touring pitches situated on the higher levels of the site with some shade (artificial awnings are allowed). Due to the nature of this site we would not recommend it for people with mobility problems. Access roads to the gravel pitches are steep with some tight turns. All pitches, although not separated, have electricity and share water points with a neighbour. There are four toilet blocks; the two smaller ones are accessed by stairways from the pitches.

Facilities

Four modern toilet blocks (see above) have showers in cubicles and open style washbasins. The larger block also housing laundry facilities is on the lowest level. Shop. Bar/restaurant with small terrace next to play area. TV room. Outdoor swimming pool. Communal barbecue area. Internet WiFi. Off site: Village has a range of shops bars and restaurants. Lake fishing 2 km. Beach 20 km.

Open: All year.

Directions

From A23 (Sagunto - Teruel) road take exit 33 (Navajas). Follow CV213 to site which is 1 km. north of Navajas. GPS: 39.87471, -0.51051

Charges guide

Per unit incl. 2 persons and electricity	€ 19.56 - € 25.60
extra person	€ 4.70 - € 5.95

Camping Cheques accepted.

Noja

Camping Playa Joyel

Playa de Ris, E-39180 Noja (Cantabria) T: 942 630 081. E: playajoyel@telefonica.net

alanrogers.com/ES90000

This very attractive holiday and touring site is some 40 kilometres from Santander and 80 kilometres from Bilbao. It is a busy, high quality, comprehensively equipped site by a superb beach providing 1,000 well shaded, marked and numbered pitches with 6A electricity available. These include 80 large pitches of 100 sq.m. Some 250 pitches are occupied by tour operators and seasonal units. This well managed site has a lot to offer for family holidays with much going on in high season when it gets crowded. The swimming pool complex (with lifeguard) is free to campers and the superb beaches are cleaned daily mid-June to mid-September.

Facilities

Six excellent toilet blocks include baby baths. Laundry. Motorcaravan services. Gas supplies. Freezer service. Supermarket (all season). General shop. Kiosk. Restaurant and takeaway (1/7-31/8). Bar and snacks (all season). Swimming pools, bathing caps compulsory (20/5-15/9). Entertainment and a soundproofed pub/disco (July/Aug). Gym park. Tennis. Playground. Riding. Fishing. Torches necessary in some areas. Animals are not accepted. WiFi (charged). Off site: Bicycle hire 1 km.

Open: 30 March - 30 September.

Directions

From A8 (Bilbao - Santander) take km. 185 exit and N634 towards Beranga. Almost immediately turn right on CA147 to Noja. In 10 km. turn left at multiple campsite signs and go through town. At beach follow signs to site. GPS: 43.48948, -3.53700

Charges guide

Per unit incl. 2 persons and electricity	€ 28.20 - € 47.40
extra person	€ 4.40 - € 6.70

Oliva

Camping Olé

Partida Aigua Morta s/n, E-46780 Oliva (Valencia) T: 962 857 517. E: campingole@hotmail.com

alanrogers.com/ES86130

Olé is a large, flat seaside holiday site south of Valencia and close to the modern resort of Oliva. Its entrance is only 250 m. from the pleasant sandy beach. For those who do not want to share the busy beach, a large swimming pool is opened in July and August. There are 308 small pitches of compressed gravel and with 6/10A electricity. Many are separated by hedges with pruned trees giving good shade to those away from the beach. A bar and restaurant stand on the dunes overlooking the sea, together with a few unmarked pitches that are ideal for larger units. There are small groups of chalets and a few apartments to rent, all within their own areas.

Facilities

Three clean, well maintained sanitary blocks provide very reasonable facilities. The central one serves most of the touring pitches. Laundry facilities. Fridge rental. Well stocked supermarket (1/3-30/9). Various vending machines. Bar with TV and restaurant with daily menu, drinks and snacks (1/3-15/12). Takeaway. Swimming pool (1/7-1/9). Playground. Entertainment (July/Aug). Fishing off the beach. Off site: Golf 800 m. Bicycle hire. Oliva.

Open: All year.

Directions

From the north on AP7 (Alicante - Valencia) take exit 61 on N332 through Oliva. From the south take exit 62 and turn left for Oliva. Exit at km. 213 (south) or 210 (north) signed 'urbanisation'. At roundabout take third exit following signs to site.
GPS: 38.8943, -0.0536

Charges guide

Per unit incl. 2 persons	€ 29.93 - € 42.85
extra person	€ 6.40

Oliva

Kiko Park Oliva

Ctra Assagador de Carro 2, E-46780 Oliva (Valencia) T: 962 850 905. E: kikopark@kikopark.com

alanrogers.com/ES86150

Kiko Park is a smart site nestling behind protective sand dunes alongside a Blue Flag beach. There are sets of attractively tiled steps over the dunes or a long boardwalk near the beach bar (good for prams and wheelchairs) to take you to the fine white sandy beach and the sea. From the central reception point (where good English is spoken) flat, fine gravel pitches and access roads are divided to the left and right. Backing onto one another, the 180 large pitches all have electricity and the aim is to progressively upgrade all these with full services. There are plenty of flowers, hedging and trees adding shade, privacy and colour. An outdoor pool complex provides a spa, whirlpool, solarium, gym and a pool bar. An award-winning restaurant and a tropical-style beach bar both overlook the marina, beautiful beach and sea. A wide variety of entertainment is provided all year and Spanish lessons are taught along with dance class and aerobics during the winter. The site is run by the second generation of a family involved in camping for 30 years and their experience shows. They are brilliantly supported by a friendly, efficient team who speak many languages. The narrow roads leading to the site can be a little challenging for very large units but it is worth the effort.

Facilities

Four mature, heated sanitary blocks include facilities for babies and for disabled visitors. Laundry facilities. Motorcaravan services. Gas supplies. Supermarket (closed Sundays). Restaurant. Bar with TV. Beach-side bar and restaurant (all year). Swimming pools and gym. New spa with treatments. Playground. Watersports facilities. Diving school (from mid June). Entertainment for children from mid June. Pétanque. WiFi. Bicycle hire.
Off site: 10-minute walk to town. Indoor pool 1 km.

Open: All year.

Directions

From the AP7 take exit 61. From the toll turn right at T-junction and continue to lights. Turn left then at roundabout turn right. At next roundabout (fountains) take third exit signed Platja and Alicante. Follow one way system to next roundabout then site signs.
GPS: 38.9316, -0.0968

Charges guide

Per unit incl. 2 persons	€ 15.20 - € 34.00
extra person	€ 3.20 - € 6.40
electricity (per kWh)	€ 0.40

Palamós

Camping Internacional de Palamós

Apdo 100, E-17230 Palamós (Girona) T: 972 314 736. E: info@internacionalpalamos.com

alanrogers.com/ES81500

This is an uncomplicated, comfortable site which is clean, welcoming and useful for exploring the local area from a peaceful base. Traditional in style, it is open for a long season and has a range of facilities. It might have space when others are full and has over 453 moderate sized pitches. The majority are level and terraced with some less defined under pine trees on a gentle slope. All pitches have a sink and variable shade, with electrical connections (6A) available in most parts. Some access roads are gravel and may suffer in the case of heavy rain.

Facilities

Two refurbished toilet blocks and one smart new one are fully equipped. Some washbasins in cabins. Facilities for disabled campers. Laundry. Small shop. Bar (1/4-29/9). Snack bar serving simple food and takeaway (from 1/6). Swimming pool (36x16 m) with paddling pool. Play area. Car wash. ATM. Torches necessary. Off site: Nearest beach 400 m. Fishing 500 m. Town 1 km. with hourly bus service. Riding 1.5 km.

Open: 30 March - 30 September.

Directions

Central Palamós streets are too narrow for caravans which should turn off C255 road just outside Palamós. Continue north by large garage signed Kings Camping and La Fosca. Turn right just before Kings and follow Camping Internacional Palamós signs (not those for another site close by called Camping Palamós). GPS: 41.85722, 3.13805

Charges guide

Per unit incl. 2 persons and electricity	€ 30.30 - € 47.10

No credit cards.
Camping Cheques accepted.

Pals

Camping-Resort Mas Patoxas Bungalow-Park

Ctra C31 Palafrugell - Pals km 339, E-17256 Pals (Girona) T: 972 636 928.
E: info@campingmaspatoxas.com **alanrogers.com/ES81020**

This is a mature, lush and well laid out site for those who prefer to be apart from, but within easy travelling distance of, the beaches (5 km) and town (1 km). It has a very easy access and is set on a slight slope with wide avenues on level terraces providing 376 grassy pitches of a minimum 72 sq.m. All have 6A electricity and some share water taps. There are some very pleasant views and shade from a variety of mature trees. Both bar and restaurant terraces give views over the pools and distant hills. The air-conditioned restaurant/bar provides both waiter- and self-service meals.

Facilities

Three modern sanitary blocks provide controllable hot showers, some washbasins with hot water. Baby bath and three cabins for children. No specific facilities for disabled campers. Laundry facilities. Fridges for rent. Gas supplies. Supermarket, restaurant/bar, pizzeria and takeaway (all 1/4-30/9). Swimming pool with a new bar (1/5-30/9). Tennis. Entertainment in high season. Fitness area with games. Massage. Bicycle hire. WiFi (charged). Torches useful. Off site: Bus service from site gate. Bicycle hire and riding 2 km. Fishing and golf 4 km.

Open: 13 January - 16 December.

Directions

Site is east of Girona and about 1.5 km. south of Pals at km. 339 on the C31 Figueres - Palamós road, just north of Palafugel. GPS: 41.9568, 3.1573

Charges 2012

Per unit incl. 2 persons and electricity	€ 18.50 - € 52.00
extra person	€ 4.20 - € 7.00
child (1-7 yrs)	€ 3.60 - € 5.00
dog	€ 2.60 - € 4.20

Pechon

Camping Las Arenas-Pechon

Ctra Pechon - Unquera km 2, E-39594 Pechon (Cantabria) T: 942 717 188. E: info@campinglasarenas.com

alanrogers.com/ES89700

This site is in a very quiet, but rather spectacular location bordering the sea and the Tina Mayor estuary, with views to the mountains and access to an attractive little beach. Otherwise, enjoy the pleasant kidney shaped pool that also shares the views. Taking 350 units, half the site has grassy pitches (60 sq.m) in bays or on terraces with stunning sea and mountain views, with electricity available (5A) and connected by asphalted roads. There are some quite steep slopes to tackle – reception is at the top, as are the bar and restaurant; the latter has a terrace with fantastic views of the estuary and the mountains.

Facilities

Clean, well tiled sanitary facilities are in the older, simple style. Various blocks include showers (no divider; add hot water to the cold by pushing a switch). Washing machines. Well stocked supermarket. Restaurant/bar and snack bar (all season). Small playground. Riding arranged (collected from site). River and sea fishing and swimming. Torches helpful. English is spoken. Off site: Shops, bars and restaurants in Pechón, plus a disco/bar 1 km.

Open: 1 June - 30 September.

Directions

Pechón is 70 km. west of Santander. On A8 from Santander, take km. 272 exit for Unquera (N621) at end of motorway section. Take the first exit for the CA380 (Pechón) and site which is 2 km. on left. GPS: 43.39093, -4.5106

Charges guide

Per person	€ 6.25
pitch incl. car	€ 11.00 - € 14.30
electricity	€ 3.60

Peñiscola

Spa Natura Resort

Ptda Villarroyos s/n, AP-7 Salida 43, E-12598 Peñiscola (Castelló) T: 964 475 480.
E: info@spanaturaresort.com **alanrogers.com/ES85590**

Set inland from the popular coastal resort of Peñiscola, Spa Natura Resort is set next to the Sierra de Irta Natura Park and Marine Reserve. This unusual development of residential and holiday park homes, designed and decorated in an environmentally-friendly way, provides 110 level touring pitches, with an increase planned. All pitches have electricity (6/10A) and access to water with wide, gravel roads. Amazingly, most are set on neat, artificial grass. Some shade is provided by young palms, pines and plane trees. The pitches are not separated and large units can be accommodated. Pitches are set between long rows of bungalows and there are very chunky elevated roofs over some. An impressive wellness centre is housed in a towering P&O-style building. A vehicle or bicycle is necessary as the site is rather remote. The sea and a 15 km. stretch of sandy beach are four kilometres away.

Facilities

Two refurbished toilet blocks include showers, open washbasins and separate toilets. Facilities for disabled visitors. Washing machines and dryers. Shop. Bar/restaurant (all year). Small outdoor and indoor swimming pools (Easter-Oct). Spa centre. Gym. Indoor tennis court. Play area. Minigolf. Bicycle hire. Internet access. Activity programme (excursions, Spanish lessons, games, competitions). Dogs are not accepted in July/Aug. Cabins, mobile homes, apartments to rent. WiFi (free).

Open: All year.

Directions

From A7 (Barcelona - Valencia) take exit 43, then the N340 towards Benicarlo. Immediately look for signs at the N340 1040 km marker to Camping Azahar on large boards steering you down a side road. You can see the site with large elevated signs as you come down slip road. GPS: 40.401667, 0.381111

Charges guide

Per unit incl. 2 persons and electricity (10A)	€ 37.00 - € 50.00

Camping Cheques accepted.

Pineda de Mar

Camping Caballo de Mar

Passeig Maritim 52-54, E-08397 Pineda de Mar (Barcelona) T: 937 671 706. E: info@caballodemar.com
alanrogers.com/ES82380

This is definitely a site for lovers of the seaside with its direct access to a lovely, sandy beach. Actually divided into two parts by the railway and dual-carriageway, the main part of the site is neatly arranged off a central access road with plenty of colourful shrubs and trees providing shade. In total there are 450 pitches, 300 taken by seasonal visitors and a few bungalows. On the beach side of the site the pitches are generally smaller (60-70 sq.m), all with shade, but there is a bar, snack bar and a toilet block on this side. All pitches have electricity (5/6A).

Facilities

Two toilet blocks, one in each area, are fully equipped and well maintained. En-suite units to rent with units for disabled visitors. Facilities for babies. Washing machines. Motorcaravan services. Shop and baker (15/6-31/8). Bar and restaurant. Bar and snacks at beach in high season. Swimming pool. Play area. Entertainment organised. Miniclub. Fitness room, massage and UVA machines. Internet access. ATM. Fishing. Off site: Beach activities. Town with bars and restaurants within walking distance or by road train. Bicycle hire 500 m. Riding 3 km. Golf 10 km.

Open: 1 April - 30 September.

Directions

Site is off the N11 coast road, southwest of Pineda de Mar. Leave the C32 at exit 122 and head for Pineda de Mar. Site is well signed off the beach road on the outskirts of the town.
GPS: 41.61664, 2.64997

Charges guide

Per unit incl. 2 persons and electricity	€ 22.25 - € 36.65
extra person	€ 4.60 - € 7.95
child (1-9 yrs)	€ 3.20 - € 5.60

Pitres

Camping El Balcon de Pitres

Ctra Orgiva - Ugijar km 51, E-18414 Pitres (Granada) T: 958 766 111. E: info@balcondepitres.com
alanrogers.com/ES92900

A simple country site perched high in the mountains of Las Alpujarras, on the south side of the Sierra Nevada, El Balcon de Pitres has its own rustic charm. Hundreds of trees planted around the site provide shade. There are stunning views from some of the 175 level grassy pitches (large units may find pitch access difficult). The garden is kept green by spring waters, which you can hear and sometimes see, tinkling away in places. The Lopez family have built this site from barren mountain top to cool oasis in the mountains in just fifteen years.

Facilities

Two toilet blocks provide adequate facilities including some for disabled campers (but the steeply sloping site is unsuitable for people with mobility problems). Bar/snack bar (with TV and pool table). Swimming pools (charged: € 2.40 adult, € 1.50 child). Barbecues are not permitted. Torches useful. WiFi. Off site: Fishing. Canyoning. Trekking. Parascending. Quad bikes. Sports centre.

Open: All year.

Directions

Site is about 30 km. northeast of Motril. Heading south on A44 (E902) exit 164 (Lanjaron) onto E348 towards Orgiva. Fork left at sign (A4132) Pampaneira 8 km. Continue to Pitres (7 km). Site is signed (steep and winding roads). GPS: 36.9323, -3.3334

Charges guide

Per unit incl. 2 persons and electricity	€ 26.75 - € 32.10

Platja d'Aro

Camping Valldaro

Apdo de correos 57, Cami Vell 63, E-17250 Platja d'Aro (Girona) T: 972 817 515.
E: info@valldaro.com alanrogers.com/ES81700

Valldaro is 600 m. back from the sea at Platja d'Aro, a small, bright resort with a long, wide beach and plenty of amusements. It is particularly pleasant during off-peak weeks and is popular with Spanish, Dutch and British visitors. Valldaro has been extended and many pitches have been made larger, bringing them up to 85 sq.m. There are now almost 1,200 pitches with 544 for touring units. The site is flat, with pitches in rows divided up by access roads. You will probably find space here even at the height of the season. The newer section has its own vehicle entrance (the nearest point to the beach) and can be reached via a footbridge; it is brought into use at peak times. It has some shade and its own toilet block, as well as a medium-sized swimming pool of irregular shape with a grassy sunbathing area.

Facilities

Four sanitary blocks are of a good standard and are well maintained. Child sized toilets. Washbasins (no cabins) and adjustable showers (temperature perhaps a bit variable). Two supermarkets and general shops. Two restaurants. Large bar. Swimming pools. New outdoor jacuzzi. Tennis. Minigolf with snack bar. Playgrounds. Sports ground. Children's club. Organised entertainment in season. Hairdresser. Internet. WiFi area (code). Satellite TV. Gas supplies. Off site: Fishing and bicycle hire 1 km. Beach 1.5 km. Riding 4 km. Golf 5 km.

Open: 1 April - 25 September.

Directions

From Girona on the AP7/E15 take exit 7 to Sant Feliu on C65. On C65 at km. 313 take exit to Platja d'Aro (road number changes here to C31). In 200 m. at roundabout take GI662 towards Platja d'Aro. Site is at km. 4. GPS: 41.81427, 3.0437

Charges guide

Per unit incl. 2 persons and electricity	€ 20.00 - € 45.90
extra person	€ 4.10 - € 6.95

No credit cards.
Camping Cheques accepted.

Platja de Pals

Camping Inter-Pals

Avenida Mediterrania, E-17256 Platja de Pals (Girona) T: 972 636 179.
E: interpals@interpals.com alanrogers.com/ES81000

Set on sloping ground with tall pine trees providing shade and about 500 metres from the beach, Inter-Pals has 450 terraced pitches. It is sister site to no. ES81700 Valldaro. Arranged on level terraces, mostly with shade, some of the terraced pitches have views of the sea through the trees. The main entrance and its drive resembles a pretty village street as the bungalows are set on both sides of the street which is lined with traditional lamp posts. Continuing the village theme is a row of shops where you will find most campers' needs. The formal restaurant with good value menu and choice of takeaway overlooks the pools. The site is close to Platja de Pals which is a long sandy unspoilt stretch of beach, a discreet area, reached by a very hard climb, is now an official naturist beach. The pretty town of Pals is close by along with a good golf course. The site will assist with touring plans of the area.

Facilities

Three well maintained toilet blocks have facilities for disabled campers. Motorcaravan service point. Laundry facilities. Gas. Fridge rental. Shops. Restaurant/bar. Pizzeria with dancing and entertainment area. Café/bar by entrance. Swimming pool. Jacuzzi. Playground. Bicycle hire. Organised activities and entertainment in high season. Excursions. Watersports arranged. Mini-adventure park. Medical centre. ATM. Internet access. WiFi. Some breeds of dog are excluded (check with site). Torch useful. Off site: Fishing 200 m. Golf 1 km. Riding 10 km.

Open: 31 March - 25 September.

Directions

Site is on the road leading off the Torroella de Montgri - Bagur road north of Pals and going to Playa de Pals (Pals beach). GPS: 41.97533, 3.19317

Charges 2012

Per unit incl. 2 persons and electricity	€ 29.80 - € 51.80
extra person	€ 4.50 - € 6.90
child (3-12 yrs)	€ 3.30 - € 4.20

No credit cards.
Camping Cheques accepted.

Platja de Pals

Camping Cypsela

Ctra de Pals - Platja de Pals, E-17256 Platja de Pals (Girona) T: 972 667 696. E: info@cypsela.com

alanrogers.com/ES80900

This impressive, deluxe site with lush vegetation and trees is very efficiently run. The main part of the camping area is pinewood, with 688 clearly marked touring pitches of varying categories on sandy gravel, all with electricity and 552 with full facilities. The 267 'élite' pitches of 120 sq.m. are impressive. Cypsela is a busy, well administered site, only 2 km. from the sea, which we can thoroughly recommend, especially for families. The site has good quality fixtures and fittings, all kept clean and maintained to a high standard. All your needs will be catered for here. The site has many striking features, one of which is the sumptuous complex of sports facilities and amenities near the entrance. This provides a fine large swimming pool, playgrounds for children, two excellent squash courts, a tennis court, fitness room, and other entertainment rooms. These include a children's playroom with miniclub and organised entertainment (including video screen), an amusements room and a luxurious, air-conditioned lounge. Les Moreres is a pleasant, al fresco restaurant offering a varied menu plus good wines (it can become very busy). Another air-conditioned indoor restaurant offers a similar excellent service. You have the choice of a smart bar or an air-conditioned cocktail bar. If you wish to travel to the beach there is a regular free bus service from the site. The gates are closed at night. Several tour operators use the site (223 pitches).

Facilities

Four sanitary blocks are of excellent quality with comprehensive cleaning schedules and solar heating. Three have washbasins in cabins and three have amazing children's rooms. Private sanitary facilities to rent. Superb facilities for disabled visitors. Serviced launderette. Supermarket and other shops. Restaurant, caféteria and takeaway. Bar. Hairdresser. Swimming pools. Tennis. Squash. Minigolf. Skating rink. Fitness room. Solarium. Air-conditioned social/TV room. Barbecue and party area. Comprehensive entertainment programme in season. Games room. Bicycle hire. Business centre. WiFi over site (charged). Gas supplies. ATM. Large motorcaravans and twin-axle caravans accepted. Dogs are not accepted. Off site: Shuttle bus. Golf 1 km. Fishing 2 km.

Open: 18 May - 16 September.

Directions

Platja de Pals is southeast of Girona on the coast. From the AP7/E15 at Girona take exit 6 towards Palamós on the C66. This road changes number to the C31 near La Bisbal. 7.5 km. past La Bisbal, exit to Pals on the GI 652. Follow signs for Platja de Pals. At El Masos take the 6502 for 1 km. Main entrance for Cypsela is on the left between the white metal fencing. GPS: 41.98608, 3.18105

Charges 2012

Per unit incl. 2 persons and electricity	€ 36.78 - € 58.12
extra person	€ 6.40
child (2-10 yrs)	€ 4.80

Platja de Pals

Camping Playa Brava

Avenida del Grau 1, E-17256 Platja de Pals (Girona) T: 972 636 894. E: info@playabrava.com

alanrogers.com/ES81010

This is an extremely pleasant site with an open feel, having direct access to an excellent soft sand beach and a freshwater lagoon where you can enjoy watersports and launch your own boat (charged). The ground is level and very grassy with shade provided for many of the 706 spacious touring pitches by a mixture of conifer and broadleaf trees. All the pitches have 10A electricity and about a third have water and drainage. The spaciousness continues around the superb large swimming pool with its huge grass sunbathing areas, the whole being overlooked by the terrace of the restaurant and bar. The restaurant is very pleasant and offers a most reasonable menu of the day including wine. An energetic entertainment programme runs during July and August. There are many interesting things to explore in the area including La Bisbal – famous for ceramics, Dali's museum, the Roman ruins at Empuries Girona and many more. This is a clean, green and pleasant family site.

Facilities

Five modern, fully equipped toilet blocks include facilities for disabled visitors. Washing machines and dryers. Motorcaravan service point. Supermarket. Bar/restaurant. Takeaway. Swimming pool (all season). Tennis. Minigolf. Beach volleyball. Football. Basketball. Play area on grass. Bicycle hire. Watersports on river and beach, including sheltered lagoon for windsurfing novices. New stage show. Internet access. WiFi over site (charged). Satellite TV. Gas supplies. Torches required in some areas. Dogs are not accepted. Off site: Two 18-hole golf courses (50% discount online, 30% through reception), fishing and sailing all 300 m. Riding 6 km. Cycle routes from site. Excursions to Barcelona.

Open: 12 May - 12 September.

Directions

Platja de Pals is southeast of Girona on the coast. From the AP7/E15 at Girona take exit 6 towards Palamós on the C66. 7.5 km. past La Bisbal, exit to Pals on the GIV-6502. Follow signs for Platja de Pals - Golf Platja de Pals. Site is on left just before road ends at beach car park. GPS: 42.001130, 3.193800

Charges 2012

Per unit incl. 2 persons and electricity	€ 32.60 - € 55.80
extra person	€ 2.30 - € 3.40
child (3-9 yrs)	free - € 2.30

Discounts in low season.

Poboleda

Camping Poboleda

Placa de les Casetes s/n, E-43376 Poboleda (Tarragona) T: 977 827 197. E: poboleda@campingsonline.com

alanrogers.com/ES85080

Time stands still at this unique site, watched over by La Morera de Montsant, a peak of the Serra del Montsant. Situated among olive groves, on the edge of the lovely old village of Poboleda, it is an idyllic site for tents, small caravans and motorcaravans. Large units would have problems negotiating the narrow village streets and even small caravans might find it tricky. The 151 averagely sized pitches (70 with 4A electricity) are set on broad grassy terraces under olive and almond trees in a peaceful haven broken only by bird song or the peal of church bells or bird song.

Facilities

One small block, open all year, is fully equipped, as is a larger block open for high season. Shower for children. Facilities for disabled visitors (key). Laundry service. Breakfast to order. Bar. Swimming pool (24/6-11/9). Tennis. Boules. Reception has tourist information, postcards and basic items. WiFi area (free). Off site: Bars, restaurants and shops in village. Bicycle hire 10 km. Fishing and boat launching 12 km. Gaudí Centre in Reus 30 km. Beach and Port Aventura theme park 40 km.

Open: All year.

Directions

Poboleda is best approached from the south. From AP7 at exit 34, take T11 (Reus then Falset) and continue on N420. After Borges del Camp turn north on C242 for 18 km. over Coll d'Alforja. Take the T702 west for 6 km. to Poboleda. Watch for tent signs and follow carefully through narrow streets. Unsuitable for large units. GPS: 41.23231, 0.84316

Charges guide

Per unit incl. 2 persons and electricity	€ 32.32
extra person	€ 6.48

Potes

Camping La Isla Picos de Europa

Picos de Europa, E-39570 Potes-Turieno (Cantabria) T: 942 730 896. E: campicoseuropa@terra.es

alanrogers.com/ES89620

La Isla is beside the road from Potes to Fuente Dé, with many mature trees giving good shade and glimpses of the mountains above. Established for over 25 years, a warm welcome awaits you from the owners (who speak good English) and a most relaxed and peaceful atmosphere exists here. All the campers we spoke to were delighted with the family feeling of the site. The 106 unmarked pitches are arranged around an oval gravel track under a variety of fruit and ornamental trees. Electricity (6A) is available to all pitches, although some need long leads. A brilliant small bar and restaurant are located under dense trees where you can enjoy the relaxing sound of the river which runs through the site.

Facilities

Single, clean and smart sanitary block retains the style of the site. Washbasins with cold water. Washing machine. Gas supplies. Freezer service. Small shop and restaurant/bar (1/4-30/9). Small swimming pool (caps compulsory; 1/5-30/9). Play area. Barbecue area. Fishing. Bicycle hire. Riding. WiFi. Off site: Bus from gate in high season. Shops, bars and restaurants and market (Mon. am) in Potes 2.5 km. Riding 10 km. Fuente Dé and its spectacular cable car ride 18 km. Beach 40 km.

Open: 1 April - 15 October.

Directions

From A8/N634 (Santander - Oviedo) take exit at km. 272 for Unquera (end of motorway section). Take N621 south to Panes and up spectacular gorge (care needed if towing) to Potes. Take CA165 to Fuente Dé and site is on the right, 2.5 km. beyond Potes. GPS: 43.14999, -4.69997

Charges guide

Per person	€ 4.15 - € 4.50
pitch	free - € 11.50
electricity	€ 3.60

Ribera de Cabanes

Camping Torre La Sal 2

Cami l'Atall, E-12595 Ribera de Cabanes (Castelló) T: 964 319 744. E: camping@torrelasal2.com

alanrogers.com/ES85700

Torre La Sal 2 is a very large site divided into two by a quiet road, with a reception on each side with friendly, helpful staff. There are three pool complexes (one can be covered in cooler weather and is heated) all of which are on the west side, whilst the beach (of shingle and sand) is on the east. Both sides have a restaurant – the restaurant on the beach side has two air-conditioned wooden buildings and a terrace. The 530 flat pitches vary in size, some have their own sinks, and most have shade. All have 10A electricity and a few have a partial view of the sea. There are 85 bungalows around the two areas. This is a high quality site offering a great choice to campers.

Facilities

Toilet facilities are of a good standard in both sections, with facilities for disabled campers in both. Baby rooms. Hot water to some sinks. British style toilets. Washing machines. Motorcaravan services. Shop, bars, restaurants and takeaway. Swimming pools (a new pool complex should be ready for the season). Jacuzzi and sauna (winter). Play park. Disco. Sports centre. Tennis. Squash. Two football pitches. Pétanque. Outdoor gym. Games room. Bullring. Activities and entertainment. WiFi.

Open: All year.

Directions

From A7/E15 take exit 45 for Oropesa del Mar on N340. Follow road to Oropesa and then the many clear signs to the site. GPS: 40.127, 0.158

Charges guide

Per unit incl. 2 persons and electricity	€ 36.35
extra person	€ 6.80
child (2-9 yrs)	€ 6.25

Special prices for retired persons 1/9 - 30/6.

Roda de Bará

Kawan Village Stel

Ctra N340 km 1182, E-43883 Roda de Bará (Tarragona) T: 977 802 002. E: rodadebara@stel.es

alanrogers.com/ES84200

Camping Stel is situated between mountains and the sea with direct access to an excellent beach, via a passage under the railway, which runs along the entire coast (so expect some rail noise, especially on the lower pitches). The 800 pitches are generally in rows separated by hedges, all have electricity (5A) and many have individual sinks. In one area, radios and TVs are not allowed. The impressive central area contains a large bar/restaurant with terrace and snack bar overlooking the attractive pool complex, which includes a wonderful fun pool for children, a flume and a pleasant grass area set out with palms.

Facilities

Three clean sanitary blocks provide spacious controllable showers, washbasins in cabins, excellent facilities for children and disabled visitors and four private bathrooms for rent. Baby baths. Launderette. Motorcaravan services. Supermarket and tourist shop. Bar/restaurant and snack bar. Swimming pool (heated in low season), flume and jacuzzi. Sports complex. Tennis courts and Padel court. Gym. Hairdresser. WiFi over site (charged). ATM. Bicycle hire. Miniclub. Chalets for rent. Dogs are not accepted.

Open: Easter - 30 September.

Directions

Roda de Bará is 22 km. east of Tarragona. From east on AP7 leave at exit 31 and take motorway link to join N340 west. From west take exit 32 onto N340 east. Site is at 1182 km. marker on the N340 near Arc de Bará, between Tarragona and Vilanova. GPS: 41.16969, 1.46469

Charges guide

Per unit incl. 2 persons and electricity	€ 23.60 - € 30.60

Camping Cheques accepted.

Roses

Camping Joncar Mar

Ctra Figueres s/n, E-17480 Roses (Girona) T: 972 256 702. E: info@campingjoncarmar.com

alanrogers.com/ES80080

Family owned since 1977, Joncar Mar is a mature, all-year site with variable facilities. Its strength is its location with the beach promenade just outside the gate, and the many resort leisure facilities and local cultural attractions readily available to customers. The site is divided by a minor road and most leisure facilities are positioned on one side of the site. There are no views and the site has some apartment blocks around the periphery. Pitches are small (60 sq.m) with 6A electricity, and the mobile home area in one corner of the site is extremely cramped. Some pitches require long electricity leads. The modest swimming pool has a shallow area at right angles at one end for children, but no barrier separating it from deeper water, so small children will need supervision, especially as there is no lifeguard. The pool is overlooked by a restaurant area offering an uncomplicated 'eat all you can' fixed evening buffet menu, which is open to the street and thus non-camping customers. The site is relatively free from biting insects, which plague some sites hereabouts and has many loyal British customers from 20 years ago. The site offers a very basic, no-frills service which will only appeal to some campers.

Facilities

One refurbished toilet block has very good facilities with good baby room and facilities for disabled campers, the other is adequate; both are well positioned on the main side of the site and the third block on the other side is adequate. One washing machine. Small shop. Small bar and buffet restaurant. Swimming pool. Basic play area. TV in bar. Limited entertainment programme. Internet and WiFi (code). Torches useful. Off site: Nearest beach 50 m. Bicycle hire 100 m. Public transport 600 m. Riding 3 km.

Open: All year.

Directions

Roses is north of Girona and east of Figueres on the coast. From AP7/E15 take exit 3 south or exit 4 north (there is no exit 3 northbound) and then the N11 to the C260 and on to Roses. Site is well signed before you enter the town – follow camping signs initially. GPS: 42.26639, 3.16355

Charges guide

Per person	€ 6.40 - € 6.60
pitch	€ 7.50 - € 13.40
electricity (6A)	€ 4.20 - € 4.35

Ruiloba

Camping El Helguero

Ctra Santillana - Comillas, E-39527 Ruiloba (Cantabria) T: 942 722 124.
E: reservas@campingelhelguero.com **alanrogers.com/ES89610**

This site, in a peaceful location surrounded by tall trees and impressive towering rock formations, caters for 240 units (of which 100 are seasonal) on slightly sloping ground. There are many marked pitches on different levels, all with access to electricity (6A), but with varying amounts of shade. There are also attractive tent and small camper sections set close in to the rocks and 22 site owned chalets. The site gets very crowded in high season, so it is best to arrive early if you have not booked. The reasonably sized swimming pool and children's pool have access lifts for disabled campers.

Facilities

Three well placed toilet blocks, although old, are clean and all include controllable showers and hot and cold water to all basins. Facilities for children and disabled visitors. Washing machines and dryers. Motorcaravan services. Small supermarket (July/Aug). Bar/snack bar plus separate more formal restaurant. Swimming pool (caps compulsory). Playground. Entertainment (high season). ATM. Torches useful in some places. WiFi over site (charged by card). Off site: Bus service 500 m. Bar/restaurants in village (walking distance). Beach, fishing, sailing, golf and riding all 3 km.

Open: 1 April - 30 September.

Directions

From A8 (Santander - Oviedo) take km. 249 exit (Cabezón and Comillas) and turn north on CA135 towards Comillas. At km. 7 turn right on CA359 to Ruilobuca and Barrio la Iglesia. After village turn right up hill on CA358 to site on right (note: signs refer to 'Camping Ruiloba'). GPS: 43.38288, -4.24800

Charges 2012

Per unit incl. 2 persons and electricity	€ 24.10 - € 28.95
extra person	€ 4.55 - € 5.50

Camping Cheques accepted.

Salou

Camping Resort Sanguli Salou

Passeig miramar - Plaça Venus, Apdo 123, E-43840 Salou (Tarragona) T: 977 381 641. E: mail@sanguli.es

alanrogers.com/ES84800

Sanguli is a superb site boasting excellent pools and entertainment. Owned, developed and managed by a local Spanish family, it has something for all the family with everything open when the site is open. There are 1,067 pitches of varying size (75-100 sq.m) and all have electricity. Mobile homes occupy 58 pitches and there are fully equipped bungalows on 147. A wonderful selection of trees, palms and shrubs provides natural shade and an ideal space for children to play. The good sandy beach is little more than 100 metres across the coast road and a small railway crossing. Although large, Sanguli has a pleasant, open feel and maintains a quality family atmosphere due to the efforts of the very keen and efficient staff. There are three very attractive themed pools, one near the entrance with a grassy sunbathing area, a refreshing waterfall and amusing animal figures. The second, deeper pool forms part of the excellent sports complex (with fitness centre, tennis courts, minigolf, crazy golf and football practice area). The third pool is beside the amphitheatre at the top of the site, and includes three further amusing water slides between columns and Roman statues. Located on the promenade near the centre of Salou, the site can offer the attractions of a busy resort while still being private and it is only 3 km. from Port Aventura. This is a large, professional site providing something for all the family, but still capable of providing peace and quiet for those looking for it.

Facilities

The six sanitary blocks are constantly cleaned and are always exceptional, including many individual cabins with en-suite facilities. Improvements are made each year. Some blocks have excellent facilities for babies. Launderette with service. Motorcaravan services. Car wash (charged). Gas supplies. Snack bars. Indoor and outdoor restaurants with takeaway. Swimming pools. Fitness centre. Sports complex. Fitness room (charged). Playgrounds including adventure play area. Miniclub. Minigolf. Multiple Internet options including WiFi (free). Security bracelets. Well equipped medical centre. Off site: Activities on the beach. Bus at gate. Fishing and bicycle hire 100 m. Riding 3 km. Port Aventura 4 km. Aquopolis 5 km. Golf 6 km.

Open: March - November.

Directions

On west side of Salou about 1 km. from the centre, site is well signed from the coast road to Cambrils and from the other town approaches.
GPS: 41.075, 1.116

Charges guide

Per unit incl. 2 persons and electricity	€ 27.00 - € 71.00
extra person	€ 6.00
child (4-12 yrs)	€ 4.00

Reductions outside high season for longer stays. Special long stay offers for senior citizens.

Salou

Camping La Siesta

Calle Norte 37, E-43840 Salou (Tarragona) T: 977 380 852. E: info@campinglasiesta.es

alanrogers.com/ES84700

La Siesta occupies a remarkable location close to the heart of the thriving resort of Salou, yet only two blocks from the fine sandy beach. The 470 pitches, all with 10A electricity, vary in size, some suitable for larger units, others for tents. There is considerable shade from the trees and shrubs that contribute to the site's attractive appearance. Considerable recent investment has seen the creation of a pleasant, grassy play area for children and impressive new sports provision. For 2012, an extensive new leisure pool complex is being built, overlooked by the existing bar/restaurant offering comprehensive and competitively priced menus, and entertainment in high season.

Facilities

Three bright and clean sanitary blocks provide very reasonable facilities including controllable showers and open style washbasins. Unit for disabled visitors. Motorcaravan services. Supermarket. Various vending machines. Self-service restaurant and bar with takeaway. Children's club (June-Aug). Entertainment (July/Aug). New playground. Multisports and short tennis courts. Extensive new leisure pool complex planned for 2012. Medical service daily in season. ATM point. Torches may be required. Off site: Many shops, restaurants and bars nearby. Port Aventura is close. Bicycle hire 200 m. Fishing 500 m. Riding and golf 6 km.

Open: 14 March - 3 November.

Directions

Salou is just 10 km. southwest of Tarragona. Leave AP7 at exit 35 or A7 (toll-free) motorway at exit for Salou. Follow the Tarragona-Salou road (dual-carriageway) until you pass the side of the site on the right. Site is signed (narrow turning). Follow further small signs through the one way system.
GPS: 41.0777, 1.1389

Charges guide

Per unit incl. 2 persons and electricity	€ 27.00 - € 47.00
extra person	€ 5.00 - € 10.00
child (4-9 yrs)	€ 3.60 - € 5.00

Sant Pere Pescador

Camping La Gaviota

Ctra de la Platja s/n, E-17470 Sant Pere Pescador (Girona) T: 972 520 569. E: info@lagaviota.com

alanrogers.com/ES80310

La Gaviota is a delightful, small, family run site at the end of a cul-de-sac with direct beach access. This ensures a peaceful situation with a choice of the pleasant L-shaped pool or the fine clean beach with slowly shelving access to the water. Everything here is clean and smart and the Gil family are very keen that you enjoy your time here. There are 165 touring pitches on flat ground with shade and 8A electricity supply. A lush green feel is given to the site by many palms and other semi-tropical trees and shrubs. The restaurant and bar are very pleasant indeed and have a distinct Spanish flavour. The cuisine is reasonably priced, perfectly prepared and served by friendly staff. All facilities are at the reception end of this rectangular site with extra washing up areas at the far end. The guests here were happy and enjoying themselves when we visited. English is spoken.

Facilities

One smart and very clean toilet block is near reception. All WCs are British style and the showers are excellent. Superb facilities for disabled visitors. Two great family rooms plus two baby rooms. Washing machine. Gas supplies. Supermarket (fresh bread), pleasant bar and small, delightful restaurant (all March-Oct). Swimming pool (May-Oct). Playground. Games room. Limited animation. Beach sports and windsurfing. WiFi over site (charged). Torches useful. ATM. Off site: Boat launching 2 km. Riding 4 km. Sailing 10 km. Golf 15 km. Boat excursions. Cycling routes.

Open: 23 March - 28 October.

Directions

From the AP7/E15 take exit 3 onto the N11 north towards Figueras and then the C260 towards Roses. At Castello d'Empúries take the GIV-6216 and continue to Sant Pere Pescador. Site is well signed in the town. GPS: 42.18901, 3.10843

Charges guide

Per unit incl. 2 persons and electricity	€ 23.95 - € 51.95
extra person	€ 3.50 - € 4.50
child (under 10 yrs)	€ 1.50 - € 3.00
dog	€ 2.00 - € 4.00

No credit cards. Discounts for longer stays.

Sant Pere Pescador

Camping Aquarius

Playa s/n, E-17470 Sant Pere Pescador (Girona) T: 972 520 003. E: camping@aquarius.es

alanrogers.com/ES80500

A smart and efficient family site, Aquarius has direct access to a quiet sandy beach that slopes gently and provides good bathing (the sea is shallow for quite a long way out). Watersports are popular, particularly windsurfing (a school is provided). One third of the site has good shade with a park-like atmosphere. There are 430 touring pitches, all with electricity (6A). Markus Rupp and his wife are keen to make every visitor's experience a happy one and even issue flags to denote the number of years they have stayed at the site. The site is ideal for those who really like sun and sea, with a quiet situation.

Facilities

Attractively tiled, fully equipped toilet blocks provide some cabins for each sex. Good facilities for disabled visitors, plus baths for children. Superb new block has underfloor heating and family cabins with showers and basins. Laundry facilities. Gas supplies. Motorcaravan services. Full size refrigerators. Supermarket. Pleasant restaurant and bar with terrace. Takeaway. Play centre for children (qualified attendant), playground and separate play area for toddlers. TV room. Surf Center. Minigolf. Bicycle hire. Barbecue and dance once weekly when numbers justify. ATM. Internet access. WiFi (charged). Dogs are accepted in one section. (Note: no pool). Off site: Riding 6 km.

Open: 15 March - 31 October.

Directions

Attention: sat nav takes you on a different route, but easier to drive is from AP7 exit 3 (Figueres Nord) direction Roses on C-68. At roundabout Castello d'Empúries take second right to Sant Pere Pescador, cross town and river bridge. From there site is well signed. GPS: 42.18092, 3.09425

Charges 2012

Per person	€ 3.15 - € 4.35
child (under 12 yrs)	free - € 2.90
pitch	€ 9.40 - € 46.90
electricity	€ 3.80

No credit cards.

Sant Pere Pescador

Kawan Village L'Amfora

Avenida Josep Tarradellas, 2, E-17470 Sant Pere Pescador (Girona)

T: 972 520 540. E: info@campingamfora.com alanrogers.com/ES80350

This super, spacious site is family run and friendly. A Greek theme is manifested mainly in the restaurant and around the pool areas. The site is spotlessly clean and well maintained and the owner operates in an environmentally friendly way. There are 830 level, grass pitches (741 for touring units) laid out in a grid system, all with 10A electricity. Attractive trees and shrubs have been planted around each pitch. There is good shade in the more mature areas which include 64 large pitches (180 sq.m), each with an individual sanitary unit (toilet, shower and washbasin). The newer area is more open with less shade and you can choose which you would prefer. Three excellent sanitary blocks (one heated) are fully equipped and offer free hot water, each with staff on almost permanent duty to ensure very high standards are maintained. Access is good for disabled visitors. At the entrance a terraced bar and two restaurants overlook a smart pool complex that includes three pools for children, one with two water slides. In high season (from July) there is ambitious evening entertainment (pub, disco, shows) and an activity programme for children. Alongside the site, the magnificent sandy beach on the Bay of Roses offers good conditions for children and a choice of high season watersport activities.

Facilities

Three main toilet blocks, one heated, provide washbasins in cabins and roomy free showers. Baby rooms. Laundry facilities and laundry service. Motorcaravan services. Supermarket. Terraced bar, self-service and waiter service restaurants. Pizzeria/takeaway. Restaurant and bar on the beach with limited menu (high season). Disco bar. Swimming pools (1/5-30/9). Pétanque. Tennis. Bicycle hire. Minigolf. Play area. Miniclub. Entertainment and activities. Windsurfing. Boat launching and sailing. Fishing. Exchange facilities. Games and TV rooms. Internet room and WiFi. Car wash. Torches required in beach areas. Barbecues are not permitted. Off site: Riding 4 km. Golf 15 km.

Open: 2 April - 29 September.

Directions

Sant Pere Pescador is north of Girona on the coast between Roses and L'Escala. From the north on A17/E15 take exit 3 onto N11 towards Figueres and then shortly onto the C260 towards Roses. At Castello d'Empúries turn right onto the GIV-6216 to Sant Pere. From the south on the A17 use exit 5 (L'Escala) and turn to Sant Pere in Viladamat. Site is well signed in the town towards the beach. GPS: 42.18147, 3.10405

Charges 2012

Per unit incl. 2 persons and electricity	€ 25.00 - € 56.20
extra person	€ 4.50 - € 6.20
child (2-9 yrs)	€ 2.50 - € 4.20
dog	€ 2.60 - € 4.95

Senior citizens specials. Discounts for pensioners for longer stays. No credit cards. Camping Cheques accepted.

Sant Pere Pescador

Camping Las Dunas

Ctra San Marti - Sant Pere, E-17470 Sant Pere Pescador (Girona) T: 972 521 717.
E: info@campinglasdunas.com alanrogers.com/ES80400

Las Dunas is an extremely large, impressive and well organised resort style site with many on-site activities and an ongoing programme of improvements. It has direct access to a superb sandy beach that stretches along the site for nearly a kilometre with a windsurfing school and beach bar. There is also a much used, huge swimming pool, plus a large double pool for children. Las Dunas is very large, with 1,700 individual hedged pitches (1,479 for tourers) of around 100 sq.m. laid out on flat ground in long, regular parallel rows. All have electricity (6/10A) and 180 also have water and drainage. Shade is available in some parts of the site. Pitches are usually available, even in the main season. Much effort has gone into planting palms and new trees here and the results are very attractive. The large restaurant and bar have spacious terraces overlooking the swimming pools or you can enjoy a very pleasant, more secluded, cavern style pub. A magnificent disco club is close by in a soundproofed building (although people returning from this during the night can be a problem for pitches in the central area of the site). With free quality entertainment of all types in season and positive security arrangements, this is a great site for families with teenagers. Everything is provided on site so you don't need to leave it during your stay. A member of Leading Campings Group.

Facilities

Five excellent large toilet blocks with electronic sliding glass doors (resident cleaners 07.00-21.00). British style toilets but no seats, controllable hot showers and washbasins in cabins. Excellent facilities for youngsters, babies and disabled campers. Laundry facilities. Motorcaravan services. Extensive supermarket, boutique and other shops. Large bar with terrace. Large restaurant. Takeaway. Ice cream parlour. Beach bar in main season. Disco club. Swimming pools. Playgrounds. Tennis. Archery. Minigolf. Sailing/windsurfing school and other watersports. Programme of sports, games, excursions and entertainment, partly in English (15/6-31/8). Exchange facilities. ATM. Safety deposit. Internet café. WiFi (charged). Dogs taken in one section. Torches required in some areas. Off site: Resort of L'Escala 5 km. Riding and boat launching 5 km. Water park 10 km. Golf 30 km.

Open: 19 May - 2 September.

Directions

L'Escala is northeast of Girona on the coast between Palamós and Roses. From A7/E15 autostrada take exit 5 towards L'Escala on GI623. Turn north 2 km. before reaching L'Escala towards Sant Marti d'Ampúrias. Site well signed.
GPS: 42.16098, 3.13478

Charges guide

Per unit incl. 2 persons and electricity	€ 21.00 - € 59.20
extra person	€ 3.50 - € 5.75
child (3-10 yrs)	€ 3.00 - € 3.25
dog	€ 3.20 - € 4.50

Santa Cristina d'Aro

Yelloh! Village Mas Sant Josep

Ctra Santa Cristina - Platja d'Aro km 2, E-17246 Santa Cristina d'Aro (Girona) T: 972 835 108.
E: info@campingmassantjosep.com alanrogers.com/ES81750

This is a very large, well appointed, open site in two parts. There are 1025 pitches with 327 for tourers in a separate area, with shade from established trees. These level pitches with some shade are in two sizes, access is good with well maintained gravel and tarmac roads. The main side of the site is centred around charming historic buildings, including a beautiful, but mysterious, locked and long unused chapel. Nearby is a huge, irregular lagoon-style pool with a bridge to a palm decorated island (lifeguards) and an excellent, safe paddling pool. A large complex including a bar, restaurant, takeaway and entertainment areas overlooks the pool.

Facilities

Two sound toilet blocks are here for tourers, ignore the block for the permanent pitches. Very good facilities for disabled visitors and pleasant baby rooms. Washing machines. Dryers. Motorcaravan service point. Large supermarket, bars, restaurant, snack bar and takeaway, swimming pools (all open as site). Safe playgrounds. Huge, well equipped games room. Tennis. Squash. Minigolf. 5-a-side football. Spa room and gym. Entertainment programme. Hairdresser. Internet. WiFi (charged). ATM. Bicycle hire. Torches useful. Dogs only in designated areas. Off site: Riding 1 km. Nearest beach, fishing, boat launching and golf all 5 km.

Open: 6 April - 11 September.

Directions

Site is at Santa Christiana d'Aro, 5 km. from the sea at San Filiu. From AP7 E15 (Girona - Barcelona) take exit 7 and C65 San Filiu road. Site is well signed at the Sant Christina d'Aro roundabout 3 km. from San Filiu. GPS: 41.811167, 3.018217

Charges guide

Per unit incl. 2 persons and electricity	€ 15.00 - € 47.00
extra person (over 7 yrs)	€ 6.00 - € 8.00
child (3-7 yrs)	free - € 8.00
dog	€ 4.00

Discounts for longer stays.

Sant Pere Pescador

Camping La Ballena Alegre

Ctra Sant Marti d'Empuries s/n, E-17470 Sant Pere Pescador (Girona) T: 902 510 520.
E: info@ballena-alegre.com **alanrogers.com/ES80600**

La Ballena Alegre is partly in a lightly wooded setting, partly open, and has almost 2 km. of frontage directly onto an excellent beach of soft golden sand (which is cleaned daily). They claim that none of the 966 touring pitches is more than 100 m. from the beach. The grass pitches are individually numbered and there is a choice of size (up to 120 sq.m). Electrical connections (5/10A) are available in all areas and there are 670 fully serviced pitches. A recent addition is a resort village area within the site with holiday homes and its own small pool and play area. This is a great site for families. There are restaurant and bar areas beside the pleasant terraced pool complex (four pools including a pool for children). For those who wish to drink and snack late there is a pub open until 03.00. The well managed, soundproofed disco is popular with youngsters. A little train ferries people along the length of the site and a road train runs to local villages. Plenty of entertainment and activities are offered, including a well managed watersports centre, with sub-aqua, windsurfing and kite-surfing, where equipment can be hired and lessons taken. You can also use a comprehensive open-air fitness centre near the beach. A full entertainment programme is provided all season. An overflow area across the road provides additional parking and sports activities. The site has won Spanish tourist board awards and is keen on ecological fitness.

Facilities

Seven well maintained toilet blocks are of a very high standard. Facilities for children, babies and disabled campers. Launderette. Motorcaravan services. Gas supplies. Supermarket. 'Linen' restaurant. Self-service restaurant and bar. Takeaway. Pizzeria and beach bar in high season. Swimming pool complex. Jacuzzi. Tennis. Watersports centre. Fitness centre. Bicycle hire. Playgrounds. Soundproofed disco. Dancing twice weekly and organised activities, sports, entertainment, etc. ATM. In high season dogs only allowed in one zone (26/6-22/8). Internet access and WiFi. Torches useful in beach areas. Off site: Go-karting nearby with bus service. Fishing 300 m. Riding 2 km.

Open: 12 May - 24 September.

Directions

From A7 Figueres - Girona autopista take exit 5 to L'Escala GI623 for 18.5 km. At roundabout take sign to Sant Marti d'Empúries and follow site signs.
GPS: 42.15323, 3.11248

Charges 2012

Per unit incl. 2 persons and electricity	€ 25.60 - € 57.00
extra person	€ 4.00 - € 5.00
child (3-10 yrs)	€ 2.80 - € 3.30
dog	€ 2.30 - € 4.80

Discount of 10% on pitch charge for pensioners all season. No credit cards.

Santa Cruz

Camping Los Manzanos

Avenida de Emilia Pardo Bazan, E-15179 Puerto de Santa Cruz (A Coruña) T: **981 614 825.**

E: **informacion@campinglosmanzanos.com** **alanrogers.com/ES89420**

Los Manzanos has a steep access drive down to the site, which is divided by a stream into two sections linked by a bridge. Pitches for larger units are marked and numbered, 85 with electricity (12A) and, in one section, there is a fairly large, unmarked field for tents. Some aircraft noise should be expected as the site is under the flight path to La Coruña (but no aircraft at night). The site impressed us as being very clean, even when full, which it tends to be in high season. Some interesting huge stone sculptures create focal points and conversation pieces.

Facilities

One good toilet block provides modern facilities including free hot showers. Small shop with fresh produce daily (limited outside June-Sept). High quality restaurant/bar (July/Aug). Swimming pool with lifeguard, free to campers (15/6-30/9). Playground. Barbecue area. Bungalows for rent. Off site: Bus service at end of entrance drive. Beach and fishing 800 m. Bicycle hire 2 km. Golf and riding 8 km.

Open: April - 30 September.

Directions

From western end of the AP-9 take exit 3. Site is signed. GPS: 43.34908, -8.33567

Charges guide

Per unit incl. 2 persons and electricity	€ 29.20 - € 29.90
extra person	€ 6.00
child	€ 5.00

Santa Elena

Camping Despeñaperros

Ctra Infanta Elena, E-23213 Santa Elena (Jaén) T: **953 664 192.** E: **info@campingdespenaperros.com**

alanrogers.com/ES90890

This site is on the edge of Santa Elena in a natural park with shade from mature pine trees. This is a good place to stay en-route from Madrid to the Costa del Sol or to just explore the surrounding countryside. The 116 pitches are fully serviced including a satellite TV/Internet link. All rubbish must be taken to large bins outside the site gates (a long walk from the other end of the site). The site is run in a very friendly manner where nothing is too much trouble. Reception has a monitor link with tourist information and access to the region's sites of interest.

Facilities

Two traditional, central sanitary blocks have Turkish style WCs and well equipped showers. One washing machine (launderette in town). Shop. Excellent bar (all year) and charming restaurant (12/3-20/10). Swimming pools (15/6-15/9). Tennis. Caravan storage. Night security. Off site: Walking, riding and mountain sports nearby. The main road gives good access to Jaén and Valdepeñas.

Open: All year.

Directions

Travelling north towards Madrid on A4 (E5) take exit 259 (Santa Elena). Drive through town and site is on right up steep slope (alternative entrance for tall vehicles – ask reception). Travelling south towards Bailén take exit 257 and as above. GPS: 38.34307, -3.53528

Charges guide

Per unit incl. 2 persons and electricity	€ 20.90 - € 23.20
extra person	€ 4.10 - € 4.70
child	€ 3.20 - € 3.90

Santiago de Compostela

Camping As Cancelas

Rue do 25 de Xullo 35, E-15704 Santiago de Compostela (A Coruña) T: **981 580 476.**

E: **info@campingascancelas.com** **alanrogers.com/ES90240**

The beautiful city of Santiago has been the destination for European Christian pilgrims for centuries and they now follow ancient routes to this unique city, the whole of which is a national monument. The As Cancelas campsite is excellent for sharing the experiences of these pilgrims in the city and around the magnificent cathedral. It has 125 marked pitches (60-90 sq.m), arranged in terraces and divided by trees and shrubs. On a hillside overlooking the city, the views are very pleasant, but the site has a steep approach road and access to most of the pitches can be a challenge for large units.

Facilities

Two modern toilet blocks are fully equipped, with ramped access for disabled campers. The quality and cleanliness of the fittings and tiling is good. Laundry with service wash for a small fee. Small shop. Restaurant. Bar with TV. Well kept, unsupervised swimming pool and children's pool. Small playground. Internet access. Off site: Regular bus service into city from near football ground 200 m. Huge commercial centre (open late and handy for off season use) 20 minutes walk downhill (uphill on the return!).

Open: All year.

Directions

From motorway AP9-E1 take exit 67 and follow signs for 'Casco Historico' and 'Centro Ciudad' then follow site signs. GPS: 42.88939, -8.52418

Charges guide

Per person	€ 4.50 - € 5.90
child (up to 12 yrs)	€ 2.70 - € 4.50
pitch	€ 4.50 - € 19.00
electricity	€ 4.10

Sitges

Camping El Garrofer

Ctra 246 km 39, E-08870 Sitges (Barcelona) T: 938 941 780. E: info@garroferpark.com

alanrogers.com/ES83920

This large, pine-covered site beside fields of vines is 900 m. from the beach, close to the pleasant town of Sitges. This is an attractive resort with seaside entertainments and is well worth exploring. The site has over 500 pitches, many of which are occupied by seasonal caravans or chalets. A central area on dusty, baked earth beneath the trees is devoted to touring caravans and a corner of the site has 28 pitches with water mainly used for large motorcaravans. All have electricity (6A). There is an open field for tents. A cosy restaurant with a small terrace offers a varied menu. Next to it are other single-storey buildings including a small supermarket; these are along the site perimeter next to the road, and absorb most of the traffic noise. The restaurant has a good local reputation – the menu of the day is great value. A traditional bar is alongside and from here you can see the pretty mosaic-clad play area. An entertainment programme is organised for children in summer and a variety of family adventure activities and excursions (including a trip to Barcelona) can be organised through reception.

Facilities
One of the three sanitary blocks has been refurbished and provides roomy showers and special bright facilities for children. Separate baby room with bath. Good facilities for disabled campers. Laundry. Bar/restaurant and small supermarket (all season). Saltwater swimming and paddling pools (30/4-31/09). Football pitch. Tennis. Play area for older children and fenced play area for toddlers. Bicycle hire. Boules. WiFi (charged). Off site: Bus from outside site to Barcelona. Golf 500 m. Beach and fishing 900 m. Sailing and boat launching 2 km. Riding 4 km.

Open: 27 January - 16 December.

Directions
40 km. southwest of Barcelona. From north on AP7 leave at exit 29 and take C15/C158 (Sitges) to join C32 motorway east. Leave at exit 26 (Sitges). From Tarragona on AP7 leave at exit 31 to join C32 motorway; continue to exit 26. Follow signs for Sitges and site along C246a to km. 39; site is on right – look for the flags. GPS: 41.23352, 1.78112

Charges guide

Per unit incl. 2 persons and electricity	€ 23.75 - € 35.40
extra person	€ 3.30 - € 5.80

Somiedo

Camping Lagos de Somiedo

Valle de Lago, E-33840 Somiedo (Asturias) T: 985 763 776. E: campinglagosdesomiedo@hotmail.com

alanrogers.com/ES89450

This is a most unusual site in the Parque Natural de Somiedo. Winding narrow roads with challenging rock overhangs, hairpin bends and breathtaking views (for 8 km) finally bring you to the campsite at an elevation of 1,200 m. This is a site for 4x4s, powerful small campervans and cars – not for medium or large motorcaravans, and caravans are not accepted. It is not an approach for the faint hearted! The friendly Lana family make you welcome at their unique site, which is tailored for those who wish to explore the natural and cultural values of the park without the normal campsite amenities. There are 210 pitches (just four with electric hook-up), undefined in two open meadows.

Facilities
There are British style toilets and free hot water to clean hot showers and washbasins. Facilities for babies and children, and for disabled visitors. Washing machine. Combined reception, small restaurant with takeaway food, bar and reference section. Shop for bread, milk and other essentials, plus local produce and crafts. Horses for hire, trekking. Lectures on flora, fauna, history and culture. Fishing (licence required). Barbecue area. Small play area. Gas supplies. Off site: The small village, which maintains the Spanish customs and traditions of this area 500 m.

Open: 1 April - 30 September.

Directions
From N634 via Oviedo turn left at 442 km. marker on AS-15 (Parque Natural de Somiedo). At 9 km. marker past Longoria, turn left on AS-227. At 38 km. marker, turn left into Pol de Somiedo, signed Centro Urbano. Follow signs for Valle de Lago and El Valle; 8 km. of hairpin bends from Pola, passing Urria on the left, brings you to the valley. Site is signed on the right. GPS: 43.072018, -6.198885

Charges guide

Per person	€ 5.35
motorcaravan incl. electricity	€ 11.77

Tarragona

Camping Tamarit Park Resort

N340a km 1172, Tamarit, E-43008 Tarragona (Tarragona) T: 977 650 128. E: resort@tamarit.com

alanrogers.com/ES84830

This is a marvellous, beach-side site, attractively situated at the foot of Tamarit castle at one end of a superb one kilometre long beach of fine sand. Landscaped with lush Mediterranean shrubs and studded with pines and palms, home to mischievous red squirrels. The 470 good sized pitches have 10A electricity (most have water). Fifty are virtually on the beach and are very popular. On hard sand and grass, some are attractively separated by hedging and shaded by trees. The management and staff here are very keen to please and standards are very high.

Facilities

The high quality sanitary blocks (two heated) are modern and tiled. Hot water is available throughout. Private bathrooms to rent. Laundry facilities. Motorcaravan services. Fridge hire. Gas supplies. Supermarket, boutique, bars, restaurant and takeaway. Bakery. Wellness area. Swimming pool. Tennis and Padel courts. Pétanque. Bicycle hire. Minigolf. Playground. Sports zone. Club room with bar. Miniclub. Entertainment programme all season. Fishing. Internet access and WiFi (code). Pets allowed. Gas only barbecues. Off site: Village 1.5 km. along beach. Golf 8 km. Tarragona 9 km. Riding 15 km.

Open: 15 April - 16 October.

Directions

From A7 take exit 32 towards Tarragona and continue for 4.5 km. At roundabout (km. 1172) turn back towards Atafulla/Tamarit and after 200 m. turn right to Tamarit (beside Caledonia Bungalow Park). Take care over railway bridge, then immediately sharp left. Site is on left after 1 km. past another campsite (Trillas Tamarit). GPS: 41.1316, 1.3610

Charges guide

Per unit incl. 2 persons	€ 12.00 - € 80.00
extra person	€ 6.00
child (6-12 yrs)	free - € 4.00

Minimum stay 7 nights 1/7-29/8.

Toledo

Camping El Greco

Ctra CM4000 km 0,7, Puebla de Montalban, E-45004 Toledo (Toledo) T: 925 220 090.

E: campingelgreco@telefonica.net **alanrogers.com/ES90900**

Toledo was the home of the Grecian painter, El Greco, and the site that bears his name boasts a beautiful view of the ancient city from the restaurant, bar and superb pool. The friendly, family owners make you welcome and are proud of their site, which is the only one in Toledo (it can get crowded). The 150 pitches are of 80 sq.m. with electrical connections (5/10A) and shade from strategically planted trees. Most have separating hedges that give privacy, with others in herringbone layouts that make for interesting parking in some areas. The river Tagus stretches alongside the site which is fenced for safety.

Facilities

Two sanitary blocks, both modernised, one with facilities for disabled campers. Everything is of a high standard and kept very clean. Laundry. Motorcaravan services. Swimming pool (15/6-15/9, charged). Restaurant/bar (1/4-30/9) with good menu and fair prices. Small shop in reception. Playgrounds. Ice machine. Off site: Fishing in river. Golf 10 km. Riding 15 km. An hourly air-conditioned bus service runs from the gates to the city centre, touring the outside of the walls first.

Open: All year.

Directions

Site is on C4000 road on the edge of the town, signed towards Puebla de Montelban; site signs also in city centre. From Madrid on N401, turn off right towards Toledo city centre but turn right again at the roundabout at the gates to the old city. Site is signed from the next right turn. GPS: 39.865, -4.047

Charges 2012

Per unit incl. 2 persons and electricity	€ 30.60
extra person	€ 6.65
child (3-10 yrs)	€ 5.75

Tordesillas

Kawan Village Camping El Astral

Camino de Pollos 8, E-47100 Tordesillas (Valladolid) T: 983 770 953.

E: info@campingelastral.es **alanrogers.com/ES90290**

The site is in a prime position alongside the wide River Duero (safely fenced). It is homely and run by a charming man, Eduardo Gutierrez, who has excellent English and is ably assisted by brother Gustavo and sister Lola. The site is generally flat with 154 pitches separated by thin hedges. The 144 touring pitches, 132 with electricity (6/10A), vary in size from 60-200 sq.m. with mature trees providing shade. The new toilet block has been designed with environmental sustainability in mind, including solar heated water. This is a friendly site ideal for exploring the area as you move through Spain.

Facilities

One attractive new sanitary block with fully equipped, modern facilities. Showers for children and baby room. Facilities for disabled campers. Washing machines. Motorcaravan services. Supermarket. Bar and restaurant, frequented by locals, plus a takeaway service all 1/4-30/9. Swimming and paddling pools (1/6-15/9). Playground. Tennis (high season). Minigolf. WiFi throughout (charged). English speaking staff. Local bus service. Torches are useful. No charcoal barbecues.

Open: 1 April - 30 September.

Directions

Tordesillas is 28 km. southwest of Valladolid. From all directions, leave the main road towards Tordesillas and follow signs to campsite or 'Parador' (a hotel opposite the campsite). GPS: 41.495305, -5.005222

Charges 2012

Per unit incl. 2 persons and electricity	€ 21.40 - € 31.30
extra person	€ 4.60 - € 6.85

Camping Cheques accepted.

Torroella de Montgrí

Camping El Delfin Verde

Ctra de Torroella de Montgrí, E-17257 Torroella de Montgrí (Girona) T: 972 758 454.

E: info@eldelfinverde.com **alanrogers.com/ES80800**

A popular and high quality site in a quiet location, El Delfin Verde has its own long beach stretching along its frontage where activities such as scuba diving are organised. A prime feature of this site is an attractive large pool in the shape of a dolphin with a total area of 1,800 sq.m. This is a large site with 1,265 touring pitches and around 6,000 visitors at peak times. It is well managed by friendly staff. Level grass pitches are 100-110 sq.m. and marked, with many separated by small fences and hedging. All have electricity (5/6A) and access to water points. A stream runs through the centre of the site. There is shade in some of the older parts and a particularly pleasant area of pine trees in the centre provides marked but not separated pitches (sandy and not so level). The pool has two island areas, one containing a huge fountain which can be lit at night. In the main season an elevated area with a large bar, full restaurant and a separate takeaway give wonderful views over the huge pool. There is a further restaurant with slightly cheaper, good value food in the main complex with an open-air arena for entertainment. El Delfin Verde is a large and happy holiday site with many good facilities, sports and a free family entertainment programme in season. It is well worth considering for a Costa Brava holiday. Used by British tour operators (60 pitches).

Facilities

Six excellent large and refurbished toilet blocks plus a seventh smaller block, all with resident cleaners, have showers using desalinated water and some washbasins in cabins. Laundry facilities. Motorcaravan services. Supermarket and shops. Swimming pools with lifeguard (from 1/5). Two restaurants, grills and pizzerias. Three bars. 'La Vela' barbecue and party area. Large sports area. 2 km. exercise track. Dancing and entertainment weekly in season. Excursions. Bicycle hire. Minigolf. Extensive new playground. Trampolines. Beach access. Scuba diving. Fishing. Hairdresser. Car servicing. Gas supplies. Internet café. WiFi. Dogs are not accepted in high season (11/7-14/8). Off site: Golf (20% discount) and riding 4 km.

Open: 28 April - 23 September.

Directions

Torroella de Montgri is close to the coast, east of Girona. From A7/E15 take exit 6 and the C66 (Palafrugell). Then the GI642 east to Parlava and turn north on C31 (L'Escala). Cross Ter river and turn east on C31 (Ulla and Torroella de Montgrí). Site signed off the C31 and has a long approach road. Watch for white dolphin marker and flags on the left. GPS: 42.01197, 3.18807

Charges guide

Per unit incl. 2 persons and electricity	€ 30.50 - € 55.00
extra person	€ 4.75 - € 5.50
child (2-9 yrs)	€ 4.00 - € 5.00
dog (excl 10/7-14/8)	€ 4.00

Special offers on long stays in low season.

Vilanova i la Geltrú

Vilanova Park

Ctra de l'Arboc km 2.5, E-08800 Vilanova i la Geltrú (Barcelona)

T: 938 933 402. E: info@vilanovapark.es **alanrogers.com/ES83900**

Sitting on the terrace in front of the restaurant – a beautifully converted Catalan farmhouse dating from 1908 – it is difficult to believe that in 1982 this was still a farm with few trees and known as Mas Roque (Rock Farm). Since then, imaginative planting has led to there being literally thousands of trees and gloriously colourful shrubs making this large campsite most attractive. It has an impressive range of high quality amenities and facilities open all year. There are 336 marked pitches for touring units in separate areas, all with 6/10A electricity, 168 larger pitches also have water and, in some cases, drainage. They are on hard surfaces, on gently sloping ground and with plenty of shade. A further 1,000 or so pitches are mostly occupied by chalets to rent, and by tour operators. The amenities include an excellent pool with water jets and at night time a coloured, floodlit fountain, which complement the dancing and entertainment taking place in the courtyard above. Nearby is a pleasant nature park with picnic tables. A second pool higher up the site has marvellous views across the town to the sea; here also is an indoor pool and wellness complex and in high season a second, more intimate restaurant, for a special romantic dinner overlooking the twinkling evening lights.

Facilities

All toilet blocks are of excellent quality, can be heated and have controllable showers and many washbasins in cabins. Hot water to dishwashing and laundry sinks. Baby rooms. Units for disabled visitors. Serviced and self-service laundry. Motorcaravan services. Supermarket. Souvenir shop. Restaurants. Bar with simple meals and tapas. Outdoor pools (1/4-15/10), indoor pool (all year, charged). Wellness centre including sauna, jacuzzi and gym. Play areas. Sports field. Games room. Excursions and activity and entertainment programme for all ages. Bicycle hire. Tennis. ATM and exchange facilities. WiFi (charged). Caravan storage can be arranged. Off site: Golf and riding 1 km. Fishing, sailing and boat launching 3 km. Shops, restaurants and bars in Vilanova 3 km. (local buses). Excursions arranged to Barcelona, Monserrat and Bodegas Torres (wine-tasting).

Open: All year.

Directions

Vilanova i la Geltrú is 45 km. southwest of Barcelona. Site is 3 km. northwest of town towards L'Arboç (BV2115). From the AP7 from Tarragona take exit 31 onto C32 motorway and leave at exit 16 for Vilanova. Site is on left in 2 km. (use loop on right to cross road). On AP7 from Barcelona take exit 29 onto C15 Vilanova, then C31 west to km. 153, and turn north on BV2115. Site is on right. GPS: 41.23237, 1.69092

Charges guide

Per unit incl. 2 persons and electricity	€ 27.20 - € 46.70
extra person	€ 5.60 - € 10.10
child (4-11 yrs)	€ 3.20 - € 6.10
dog	€ 6.00 - € 12.00

Camping Cheques accepted.

Tossa de Mar

Camping Cala Llevadó

Ctra GI-682 de Tossa a Lloret pk. 18,9, E-17320 Tossa de Mar (Girona) T: **972 340 314.**

E: info@calallevado.com **alanrogers.com/ES82000**

For splendour of position, Cala Llevadó can compare with almost any in this guide. A beautifully situated cliff-side site, enjoying fine views of the sea and coast below. It is shaped something like half a bowl with steep slopes. High up on the site, with a superb aspect, is the attractive restaurant/bar with a large terrace overlooking the pleasant swimming pool directly below. There are terraced, flat areas for tents and caravans (with 10/16A electricity) on the upper levels of the two slopes, with a great many individual pitches for tents scattered around the site. Some of these pitches have fantastic settings and views. The site is unsuitable for campers with disabilities. In some areas cars may be required to park separately.

Facilities

Four very well equipped toilet blocks are immaculately maintained and well spaced around the site. Baby baths. Laundry facilities. Motorcaravan services. Gas supplies. Fridge hire. Large supermarket. Restaurant/bar (5/5-28/9). Swimming and paddling pools. Three play areas. Botanic garden. New amphitheatre (2011) with entertainment for children and adults. Sailing, water skiing and windsurfing school. Fishing. Excursions. Internet access and WiFi. Torches definitely needed in some areas. Off site: Bicycle hire 3 km. Riding 10 km. Large complex adjacent for sports, activities and swimming.

Open: 1 May - 30 September.

Directions

Cala Llevadó is southeast of Girona on the coast. Leave AP7/E15 at exit 7 to the C65 Sant Feliu road, then take C35 southeast to GI681 to Tossa de Mar. Site is signed off the GI682 Lloret - Tossa road at km. 18.9, about 3 km. from Tossa. Route avoids difficult coastal road. GPS: 41.71282, 2.90623

Charges 2012

Per unit incl. 2 persons and electricity (6A)	€ 29.90 - € 49.90
extra person	€ 6.20 - € 8.95
child (4-12 yrs)	€ 3.40 - € 5.30
dog	€ 5.00 - € 5.25

Villargordo del Cabriel

Kiko Park Rural

alan rogers Runner up 2011 Awards

Ctra Embalse Contreras km 3, E-46317 Villargordo del Cabriel (Valencia) T: **962 139 082.**

E: kikoparkrural@kikopark.com **alanrogers.com/ES86250**

Approaching Kiko Park Rural, you will see a small hilltop village appearing in a landscape of mountains, vines and a jewel-like lake. Kiko was a small village and farm and the village now forms the campsite and accommodation. Amenities are contained within the architecturally authentic buildings, some old and some new. The 76 generous pitches (mainly hardstanding and with 6A electricity and water) have high hedges (as does the site) for privacy. Generous plantings have been made which already afford some privacy and hundreds of trees planted in 2003 are now providing shade. The restaurant provides extremely good food in a pleasant, spacious setting overlooking the pools and their surrounding immaculate lawns.

Facilities

Three toilet blocks are well equipped (but have short timers for lighting and showers), including facilities for disabled campers. Motorcaravan services. Gas. Pleasant bar. Excellent restaurant. Takeaway (Easter-Oct). Swimming and paddling pools. Very good playground. Bicycle hire. Entertainment in high season. Many adventurous activities can be arranged, including white-water rafting, gorging, orienteering, trekking, bungee-jumping and riding. Large families and groups catered for. Off site: Fishing, canoeing and windsurfing on the lake. Village 3 km.

Open: All year.

Directions

From autopista A7/E15 on Valencia ring road (near the airport) take A3 (E901) to the west. Villargordo del Cabriel is 80 km. towards Motilla. Take village exit 255 and follow signs through village and over a hill – spot the village on a hill 2 km. away. That is the campsite! GPS: 39.552176, -1.47456

Charges guide

Per unit incl. 2 persons and electricity	€ 20.15 - € 29.95
extra person	€ 5.00 - € 6.25
child (under 10 yrs)	€ 3.80 - € 4.30
dog	€ 0.70

Villoslada de Cameros

Camping Los Cameros

Ctra de la Virgen de Lomos de Orios km 3, E-26125 Villoslada de Cameros (La Rioja) T: **941 747 021.**

E: info@camping-loscameros.com **alanrogers.com/ES92260**

Situated 3 km. from the small town of Villoslada de Cameros, this site is in a quiet location, in a valley surrounded by tree covered mountains. The area provides the opportunity for plenty of hill walking and a footpath from the site takes you into the town. Of the 173 pitches, 146 are available for touring. They are open with some shade and have 5/10A electricity. This is a simple site with limited facilities available but it is well kept and has character; ideal for relaxation. A large playing field allows children to play ball games and bicycles can be hired from reception.

Facilities

One heated sanitary block provides WCs, washbasins with cold water only (one with hot water) and cubicle showers. No facilities for disabled visitors. Cold water only for washing machine and dishwashing. Shop. Bar with games. Restaurant with comprehensive menu and takeaway to order. Playing field and play area. Picnic area. Only gas barbecues permitted on pitches. Off site: Town 3 km. with shops, bars, restaurants and swimming pool.

Open: 20 January - 20 December.

Directions

From Logroño (AP68) turn left onto N111 heading south towards Soria and Madrid. At sign for Villoslada de Cameros turn right, pass the centre and turn left by camping sign (LR448). Site on left in 3 km. Road bumpy and uneven, drive with care and watch for animals. GPS: 42.08068, -2.67723

Charges 2012

Per unit incl. 2 persons and electricity	€ 22.80 - € 25.20
extra person	€ 4.30 - € 4.90
child (under 10 yrs)	€ 3.65 - € 4.15

Zaragoza

Camping Ciudad de Zaragoza

Ctra San Juan Bautista de la Salle s/n, E-50012 Zaragoza (Zaragoza) T: **876 241 495.**

E: info@campingzaragoza.com **alanrogers.com/ES91040**

Zaragoza is a popular en route stop between the ports of Santander and Bilbao and the beaches of the Costa Brava. The city, however, has much more to offer as the former capital of Aragon and now Spain's fifth largest city. Primarily for short stay, transit visitors, this all year site gives impressions of concrete, metal and plastic, although it will soften in time. There are 103 touring pitches with electricity and water, which are mostly of gravel and without shade as yet. A modern bar/restaurant serves good food at reasonable prices, there are good facilities for children and the very pleasant swimming and paddling pools are welcome as it gets very hot here.

Facilities

Modern toilet blocks include good facilities for disabled visitors. Motorcaravan services. Bar and restaurant (all year). Swimming and paddling pools (30/5-30/9). Tennis. Pétanque. Multisports pitch. Play areas. Bungalows for rent. Hostel. Club and TV room. Internet access and free WiFi. Off site: Zaragoza city centre 4 km. (regular bus service 100 m. from gate). Golf 5 km. Many tours available.

Open: All year.

Directions

Follow the Autovia del Nordeste (Zaragoza ring road) southwest to leave at the junction with the N11a. Follow signs to the city centre (Autovia de Madrid) and the site is signed to the right. GPS: 41.63766, -0.94273

Charges guide

Per unit incl. 2 persons and electricity	€ 15.84 - € 25.16
extra person	€ 2.89 - € 4.82
child (0-14 yrs)	€ 2.57 - € 4.28
dog	€ 2.61 - € 2.68

Sweden

With giant lakes and waterways, rich forests, majestic mountains and glaciers, and vast, wide open countryside, Sweden is almost twice the size of the UK but with a fraction of the population.

The beautiful southwest region, otherwise known as the 'Swedish lake and glass country', is easily accessible by ferry or overland from Norway. The area is dominated by two great lakes, Vänern and Vättern, Europe's second and third largest lakes. There are also many fine beaches with picturesque harbours and historic ports such as Gothenburg, Helsingborg and Malmö, which is now linked by a bridge to Copenhagen. Stockholm, the capital, is a delightful place built on fourteen small islands on the eastern coast. It is an attractive, vibrant city, with magnificent architecture, fine museums and historic squares. Moving northwards into central and northern Sweden, you'll discover beautiful forests and around 96,000 lakes, which are perfect for ice skating (in winter!) and you may even see moose and reindeer. Today, Sweden enjoys one of the highest standards of living in the world and a quality of life to go with it.

CAPITAL: Stockholm

Tourist Office
Swedish Travel and Tourism Council
Sweden House, 5 Upper Montagu Street
London W1H 2AG
Tel: 020 7108 6168
Email: info@swetourism.org.uk
Internet: www.visitsweden.com

Population
9 million

Climate
Sweden enjoys a temperate climate thanks to the Gulf Stream. There is generally less rain and more sunshine in the summer than in Britain.

Language
Swedish. English is fairly widely spoken.

Telephone
The country code is 00 46.

Money
Currency: The Krona
Banks: Mon-Fri 09.30-15.00. Some city banks stay open until 17.30/18.00 on Thursdays (regions may vary).

Shops
Mon-Fri 09.00-18.00. Sat 09.00-13.00/16.00. Some department stores remain open until 20.00/22.00.

Public Holidays
New Year; Epiphany; Easter Mon; Labour Day; Ascension; Whit Sun; Constitution Day June 6; Mid-summer Festival; All Saints; Christmas Dec 24-26.

Motoring
Roads are generally much quieter than in the UK. Dipped headlights are obligatory. Away from large towns, petrol stations rarely open 24 hours but most have self-service pumps (with credit card payment). Buy diesel during working hours, it may not be available at self service pumps.

see campsite map 3

Arboga

Herrfallet Camping

S-732 92 Arboga (Västmanlands Län) T: 058 940 110. E: reception@herrfallet.se

alanrogers.com/SW2825

Open all year, Herrfallet Camping is situated on a peninsula and designated nature reserve, on Lake Hjälmaren, one of Sweden's large lakes. There is a 1 km. long sandy beach on the site and the atmosphere is friendly and 'green'. All the 100 touring pitches have electricity hook-ups (10/16A) and the area is neatly laid out overlooking the lake where you can hire boats, canoes, pedal boats and go fishing. Fishing is free. You can explore the beautiful and peaceful surroundings by bicycle, which you can hire at reception. There are 45 large cottages of an excellent standard and five a bit smaller (for two people).

Facilities

Three sanitary blocks, one basic for the summer season, two with central heating. Open washbasins, showers (charged). Provision for disabled visitors. Laundry facilities. Baby room. Motorcaravan service point. Sauna cottage with shower and relaxing room. Lapland hut (Sami style) for barbecue parties. Shop (high season). Restaurant and bar. Takeaway. Pedal car, pedal boat, bicycle, canoe and boat hire. Fishing (free). Minigolf. Football field. Fitness trail. Playground. Internet and WiFi. Off site: Arboga 15 km. Golf 15 km. Julita mansion (old orchard) 30 km.

Open: All year (full services 27/5-28/8).

Directions

Follow signs from the E20/E18. Turn off at Sätra exit towards Arboga and cross the river. Follow signs towards Herrfallet/Västermo. 15 km. from Arboga. GPS: 59.2814, 15.9051

Charges guide

Per unit incl. electricity (10A) SEK 200 - 230

Årjäng

Årjäng Camping & Stugor

Sommarvik, S-672 91 Årjäng (Värmlands Län) T: 057 312 060. E: booking@sommarvik.se

alanrogers.com/SW2750

This is a good site in beautiful surroundings with some of the 350 pitches overlooking the clear waters of the Västra Silen lake in peaceful countryside. The numbered pitches are arranged in terraces on a hillside interspersed with pines and birches, with half set aside for static units and 20 for tents. The remaining touring pitches all have 10A electricity hook-ups and 40 also include water and drainage. The site also has 60 chalets for rent. This site makes an ideal base to explore this scenic region in summer or winter when skiing is an additional attraction.

Facilities

Five sanitary units provide shower cubicles (hot showers on payment), washbasins, toilets, family bathrooms, facilities for disabled visitors and baby changing. All are clean and acceptable but may be stretched in high season. Campers kitchens. Laundry facilities. Motorcaravan services. All activities and amenities are open 1/6-31/8. Small shop (1/5-1/10). Bar, restaurant and takeaway (15/6-20/8). Good play areas. Bicycle hire. Internet access. 'Quick stop' pitches for overnight stays. Youth hostel and conference centre. Off site: Indoor pool complex 3 km. Riding 5 km. Golf 9 km.

Open: All year (full services 19/6-22/8).

Directions

Site is well signed on road 172, 3 km. south of its junction with the E18 close to Årjäng. GPS: 59.36765, 12.13962

Charges guide

Per pitch incl. electricity SEK 200 - 320

Arvidsjaur

Camp Gielas

Järnvägsgatan 111, S-933 34 Arvidsjaur (Norrbottens Län) T: 096 055 600. E: gielas@arvidsjaur.se

alanrogers.com/SW2865

A modern municipal site with excellent sporting facilities on the outskirts of the town, Gielas is well shielded on all sides by trees, providing a very peaceful atmosphere. The 160 pitches, 81 with electricity (16A) and satellite TV connections, are level on sparse grass and accessed by tarmac roadways. The sauna and showers, sporting, gymnasium and Internet facilities at the sports hall are free to campers. Also on site is a snackbar. The lake on the site is suitable for boating, bathing and fishing. There is a swimming pool and a 9-hole golf course nearby, and hunting trips can be arranged.

Facilities

Two modern, heated sanitary units provide controllable hot showers and a unit for disabled visitors. Well equipped kitchens (free). Washing machine and dryer. The unit by the tent area also has facilities for disabled campers and baby changing. Snack bar. Tennis. Minigolf. Play areas. Sauna. Sporting facilities. Boat and canoe hire. Pedal cars. Lake swimming. Fishing. WiFi (free). Bicycle hire. Off site: Golf 200 m. Riding 500 m.

Open: All year.

Directions

Site is on road 95, 3 km. south of town centre. GPS: 65.581798, 19.19024

Charges guide

Per unit incl. 2 persons and electricity SEK 210 - 240

Askim

Lisebergs Camping Askim Strand

Marholmsvägen 124, S-436 45 Askim (Hallands Län) T: **031 840 200.** E: **askim.strand@liseberg.se**

alanrogers.com/SW2706

Within easy reach of the city, this is a very pleasantly located site, close to a long gently sloping beach which is very popular for bathing. As a result the area behind the campsite is populated by many holiday homes and cabins. A very open site with very little shade, it has 200 mostly level, grassy pitches all with 10A electricity (Europlug), and two areas for tents. Many pitches are fairly compact, although there are some larger ones. The key card entry system operates the entrance barrier and access to the buildings and there is a night security guard (June-August).

Facilities

Two heated sanitary buildings, the larger one fairly new, the smaller recently refitted. Both are maintained to a high standard and provide all the usual facilities, including a good suite for small children and a unit for disabled visitors. Laundry. Kitchens with cooking facilities. Hot water is free. Well stocked shop. Motorcaravan services. Snack bar (July). Several playgrounds. TV room. Minigolf. WiFi throughout (free). Sauna (charged). Off site: Beach 300 m. Activity centre, watersports and ball games 500 m. Golf 2 km. City of Göteborg 10 km.

Open: 25 April - 2 September.

Directions

About 10 km. south of Göteborg, take the exit signed Mölndal S and ports (Hamnar). Take the Rv 159 towards Frolunda, and watch for a slip-road to the right. After 200 m. turn left at the roundabout, signed Askim, and follow signs to campsite. GPS: 57.62832, 11.92052

Charges guide

Per pitch	SEK 375

Byxelkrok

Krono Camping Böda Sand

S-380 75 Byxelkrok (Kalmar Län) T: **048 522 200.** E: **bodasand@kronocampingoland.se**

alanrogers.com/SW2690

Krono Camping Böda Sand is beautifully situated at the northern end of the island of Øland and is one of Sweden's largest and most modern campsites. Most of the 1,300 pitches have electricity (10/16A) and TV connections, 130 have water and waste water drainage. The pitches and 123 cabins for rent are spread out in a pine forest, very close to the fabulous 10 km. long, white sand beach. Here you will also find a restaurant, kiosks, toilets and beach showers, and a relaxation centre with an indoor/outdoor pool. The reception, the toilet blocks and the services at this site are excellent and comprehensive.

Facilities

Seven heated sanitary blocks provide a good supply of roomy shower cubicles, washbasins, some washbasin suites and WCs. Facilities for babies and disabled visitors (key at reception). Well equipped laundry rooms. Excellent kitchens with cookers, ovens, microwaves, dishwashers (free) and sinks. Motorcaravan services. Supermarket and bakery. Pizzeria, café, pub and restaurant. Takeaway. Bicycle hire, pedal cars and pedal boat hire. WiFi. Minigolf. 9-hole golf course. Indoor/outdoor swimming pool (on the beach). Trim trails. Family entertainment and activities.

Open: 1 May - 1 October.

Directions

From Kalmar cross the Øland road bridge on road no. 137. On Øland follow road no. 136 towards Borgholm and Byxelkrok. Turn left at the roundabout north of Böda and follow the campsite signs to Krono camping Böda Sand. GPS: 57.27436, 17.04851

Charges guide

Per pitch	SEK 155 - 235
incl. electricity	SEK 195 - 285

Dals Långed

Laxsjöns Camping och Friluftsgård

S-660 10 Dals Långed (Västra Götalands Län) T: **053 130 010.** E: **office@laxsjon.se**

alanrogers.com/SW2740

In the beautiful Dalsland region, Laxsjöns is an all-year-round site, catering for winter sports enthusiasts as well as summer tourists and groups. On the shores of the lake, the site is in two main areas – one flat, near the entrance, with hardstandings and the other on attractive, sloping, grassy areas adjoining. In total there are 180 places for caravans and motorcaravans, 150 with electricity (10/16A), plus more for tents. Leisure facilities on the site include minigolf, trampolines and a playground. A restaurant is at the top of the site with a good range of dishes in high season.

Facilities

The main toilet block has hot showers (on payment), washbasins in cubicles, WCs and a hairdressing cubicle. With a further small block at the top of the site, the provision should be adequate. Facilities for disabled visitors. Laundry with drying rooms for bad weather. Cooking rooms for tenters. Restaurant (high season). Shop. Minigolf. Playground. Lake for swimming, fishing and boating. Off site: Dalslands Aktiviteter, Dalslands kanal.

Open: All year (full services 22/6-15/8).

Directions

From Åmål take road no. 164 towards Bengtfors, then the 172 towards Billingsfors and Dals Långed. Site is signed about 5 km. south of Billingsfors, 1 km. down a good road. From the south, (Uddevalla) take road 172. From the west (Strömstad) take the 164 towards Bengtfors and 5 km. south of Billingsfors turn right towards Långed for 1 km. GPS: 58.95296, 12.25242

Charges guide

Per pitch incl. electricity	SEK 200 - 250

Ed

Gröne Backe Camping & Stugor

Södra Moränvägen, S-668 32 Ed (Västra Götalands Län) T: 053 410 144. E: gronebackecamping@telia.com

alanrogers.com/SW2715

In the heart of the beautiful Dalsland region, this pleasant, well shaded (mostly pine) site is open all year. It is well laid out, mostly overlooking the Lilla Le lake, and there is easy access from road no. 164. There are 180 pitches for caravans and motorcaravans, most with electricity (10/16A) and special areas for tents. Also on the site are 23 cabins for rent and 40 seasonal pitches. A small shop, café and a new restaurant are at the reception building. Canoes, rowing boats and bicycles may be hired. This pleasant, friendly family site is easy to find and the location makes it ideal for a longer stay.

Facilities

Three heated toilet blocks, two in the centre, one at reception, provide washbasins both vanity type and in cubicles. Showers (on payment). Baby rooms. Facilities for disabled visitors. Laundry. Cooking facilities. Motorcaravan services. Small shop. Café and restaurant. Internet and WiFi. Playground. Minigolf. Sports field. Canoes, rowing boats, bicycles and pedal cars for hire. Beach. Sauna raft on the lake. Off site: Village services nearby. Moose ranch. Canodal (large canoe centre). Tresticklan National Park. Dalslands Aktiviteter.

Open: All year.

Directions

Site is on road no. 164 at Ed, and is well signed. GPS: 58.899417, 11.934867

Charges guide

Per pitch incl. electricity	SEK 200 - 230

Färjestaden

Krono Camping Saxnäs

S-386 95 Färjestaden (Kalmar Län) T: 048 535 700. E: info@kcsaxnas.se

alanrogers.com/SW2680

Well placed for touring Sweden's Riviera and the fascinating and beautiful island of Øland, this family run site, part of the Krono group, has 420 marked and numbered touring pitches. Arranged in rows on open, well kept grassland dotted with a few trees, all have electricity (10/16A), 320 have TV connections and 112 also have water. An unmarked area without electricity can accommodate around 60 tents. The site has about 130 long stay units and cabins for rent. The sandy beach slopes very gently and is safe for children. Reception is efficient and friendly with good English spoken. In 2009 an outdoor heated pool and a children's pool were built at the entrance to the site.

Facilities

Three heated sanitary blocks provide a good supply of roomy shower cubicles, washbasins, some washbasin and WC suites and WCs. Facilities for babies and disabled visitors. Laundry room. Kitchen with cookers, microwaves and dishwasher (free), and sinks. Gas supplies. Motorcaravan services. Shop (1/5-30/8). Pizzeria, licensed restaurant and café (all 1/5-30/8). Bar (1/7-31/7). Outdoor heated swimming pool (15/5-22/8). Playgrounds. Bouncy castle. Boules. Canoe hire. Bicycle hire. Minigolf. Family entertainment and activities. Football. Off site: Golf 500 m. Riding 2 km. Fishing 4km.

Open: 16 April - 26 September.

Directions

Cross Øland road bridge from Kalmar on road no. 137. Take exit for Øland Djurpark/Saxnäs, then follow campsite signs. Site is just north of the end of the bridge. GPS: 56.68727, 16.48182

Charges guide

Per unit incl. electricity	SEK 175 - 415

Weekend and weekly rates available.

Göteborg

Lisebergsbyn Karralund

Olbersgatan 9, S-416 55 Göteborg (Västra Götalands Län) T: 031 840 200. E: karralund@liseberg.se

alanrogers.com/SW2705

Well positioned for visiting the city and theme park using the excellent tram system, this busy, well maintained site has 192 marked pitches. Of these, 152 have electricity (10A) and cable TV and there are several areas for tents. Pitches vary in size, 42 are hardstandings, some are fairly compact with no dividing hedges, and consequently units can be rather close together. Additionally there are cabins for rent, a budget hotel and a youth hostel. This makes for a very busy site in the main season, which in this case means June, July and August. An advance telephone call to check for space is advisable.

Facilities

One heated sanitary building is well maintained and clean. It provides all the usual facilities, with controllable hot showers, a suite for small children, kitchens with cooking facilities, and a complete unit for disabled visitors. Laundry facilities near reception. Private cabins available. Shop. Motorcaravan services. Small playground. TV room. WiFi. Off site: City of Göteborg with Liseberg amusement park.

Open: All year (full services 9/5-28/8).

Directions

Site is about 4 km. east of city centre. Follow signs to Lisebergsbyn and campsite symbol from the E20, E6 or Rv40. GPS: 57.70488, 12.02983

Charges guide

Per pitch	SEK 190 - 245
electricity	SEK 50
tent and car	SEK 225

Only pitches with electricity available in high season.

Granna

Grännastrandens Familjecamping

Box 14, S-563 21 Gränna (Jönköpings Län) T: **039 010 706. E: info@grannacamping.se**

alanrogers.com/SW2670

This large, lakeside site with modern facilities and busy continental feel, is set below the old city of Gränna. Flat fields separate Gränna from the shore, one of which is occupied by the 25 acres of Grännastrandens where there are 450 numbered pitches, including a tent area and some seasonal pitches. About 210 pitches have electricity (10A). The site is flat, spacious and very regularly laid out on open ground with only a row of poplars by the lake to provide shelter, so a windbreak may prove useful against any onshore breeze. Part of the lake is walled off to form a swimming area with sandy beaches.

Facilities

Two large, sanitary blocks of a very high standard in the centre of the site have modern, well kept facilities, some with external access, washbasins and free hot showers, some in private cubicles. Laundry facilities. Provision for visitors with disabilities. A further small, older block is by reception. Very good cooking facilities. Motorcaravan services. Shop (15/6-20/8). TV room. Playground. Lake swimming area. Boating and fishing. Off site: Café and restaurant outside site (1/5-31/8) and town restaurants close. Bus stop nearby. Golf 6 km.

Open: 1 May - 30 September.

Directions

Take Gränna exit from E4 motorway (no camping sign) 40 km. north of Jönköping. Site is signed in the centre of the town, towards the harbour and ferry. GPS: 58.02762, 14.45803

Charges guide

Per unit incl. 2 persons	SEK 180 - 260

Hallstahammar

Skantzö Bad & Camping

Sörkvarnsvägen, S-737 27 Hallstahammar (Västmanlands Län) T: **022 024 305.**

E: **skantzo@hallstahammar.se** **alanrogers.com/SW2820**

A very comfortable and pleasant municipal site just off the main E18 motorway from Oslo to Stockholm, this has 200 large marked and numbered pitches, 150 of these with electricity (10A). The terrain is flat and grassy, there is good shade in parts and the site is well fenced. There are 23 alpine style cabins for rent with window boxes of colourful flowers. Reception is very friendly. There is direct access to the towpath of the Strömsholms Kanal and nearby is the Kanal Museum. The site provides hire and transportation of canoes for longer canal tours.

Facilities

Three sanitary blocks are well maintained and equipped to a high standard, including free hot showers (in cubicles with washbasin), facilities for disabled visitors and baby changing. Another unit to the same high standards has been added and both are heated. Good campers' kitchen. Good laundry facilities. Motorcaravan services. Barbecue grill area. Caféteria and shop (27/5-31/8). Swimming pool and waterslide (21/5 -22/8). Minigolf. Tennis. Playground. Bicycle hire. Fishing. Canoe hire. WiFi. Off site: Golf 6 km. Strömsholms Kanal.

Open: 30 April - 26 September.

Directions

Turn off E18 at Hallstahammar and follow road no. 252 to west of town centre and signs to campsite. GPS: 59.61078, 16.21542

Charges guide

Per unit incl. electricity	SEK 200 - 230

Höör

Skånes Djurparks Camping

Jularp, S-243 93 Höör (Skåne Län) T: **041 355 3270. E: info@grottbyn.se**

alanrogers.com/SW2650

This site is probably one of the most unusual we feature. It is next to the Skånes Djurpark – a zoo park with Scandinavian species – and has on site a reconstructed Stone Age Village. The site is located in a sheltered valley and has 110 large, level grassy pitches for caravans and motorcaravans, all with 10A electricity, and a separate area for tents. The most unusual feature of the site is the sanitary block – it is underground! The fully air-conditioned building houses a superb and ample complement of facilities. Well placed for the Copenhagen - Malmo bridge or the ferries.

Facilities

The underground block includes roomy showers, two fully equipped kitchens, laundry and separate drying room and an enormous dining/TV room. Facilities for disabled visitors and baby changing. Cooking facilities. Laundry. There is a new building with a family room and baby bath. New playground. Motorcaravan service point. Small shop and café (15/6-15/8). Small heated family swimming pool (15/6-15/8). Playground. Off site: Fishing 1.8 km. Bicycle hire 5 km. Riding and golf 8 km.

Open: All year (full services 15/6-10/8).

Directions

Turn off no. 23 road 2 km. north of Höör (at roundabout) and follow signs for Skånes Djurpark. Campsite entrance is off the Djurpark car park. GPS: 55.96033, 13.53808

Charges guide

Per unit	SEK 200
electricity	SEK 50

Huddinge

Stockholm Swecamp Flottsbro

Häggstavägen, S-141 32 Huddinge (Stockholms Län) T: 085 353 2700. E: info@flottsbro.se

alanrogers.com/SW2840

Stockholm SweCamp Flottsbro is located at the south entrance to Stockholm, just 20 minutes from Stockholm city centre. The site offers 82 large numbered pitches for caravans and motorcaravans and a separate area for tents. The pitches are arranged on level terraces, 54 with 10A electricity and TV connections. The site itself slopes down to lake Alby and there is a good restaurant at the bottom. Flottsbro is within a large recreation area with hiking trails, beaches and other activities during the summer, and downhill and cross-country skiing during the winter.

Facilities

Two modern sanitary facilities include free showers, a suite for disabled visitors, baby facilities and a family bathroom. Excellent campers' kitchen (inside and outside) with electric cookers, microwaves and sinks with hot water. Washing machine, dryer (charged) and sink. Shop (high season). Restaurant. Minigolf. Frisbee. Jogging tracks. Canoe hire. Playground. Beach volley and sauna raft. Off site: Supermarket and rail station are ten minutes by car from the site. Golf and riding 15 km. Stockholm 15 km.

Open: All year (full services 15/6-15/8).

Directions

Turn off the E4 - E20 at Huddinge onto road no. 259. After 2 km. turn right and follow signs to Flottsbro. GPS: 59.23043, 17.88818

Charges guide

Per unit incl. electricity SEK 190 - 220

Jokkmokk

Jokkmokks Camping Center

Box 75, S-962 22 Jokkmokk (Norrbottens Län) T: 097 112 370. E: campingcenter@jokkmokk.com

alanrogers.com/SW2870

This attractive site is just 8 km. from the Arctic Circle. Large and well organised, it is bordered on one side by the river and with woodland on the other, just 3 km. from the town centre. It has 170 level, grassy pitches, with an area for tents, plus 59 cabins for rent. Electricity (10A) is available to all touring pitches. The site has a heated, open-air pool complex open in summer (no lifeguard). There are opportunities for snow-mobiling, cross-country skiing in spring and ice fishing in winter.

Facilities

Heated sanitary buildings provide mostly open washbasins and controllable showers – some are curtained with a communal changing area, a few are in cubicles with divider and seat. A unit by reception has a baby bathroom, a fully equipped suite for disabled visitors, games room, plus a very well appointed kitchen and launderette. A further unit with WCs, basins, showers plus a steam sauna, is by the pool. Shop, restaurant and bar (in summer). Takeaway (high season). Swimming pools (25x10 m. main pool with water slide, two smaller pools and paddling pool). Sauna. Bicycle hire. Playground and adventure playground. Minigolf. Football field. Games machines. Free fishing. Off site: Riding 2 km.

Open: 15 May - 15 September.

Directions

Site is 3 km. from the centre of Jokkmokk on road 97. GPS: 66.59497, 19.89270

Charges guide

Per unit incl. 2 persons and electricity SEK 235

Jönköping

Jönköping Villa Björkhagen

Friggagatan 31, S-554 54 Jönköping (Jönköpings Län) T: 036 122 863. E: info@villabjorkhagen.se

alanrogers.com/SW2665

Overlooking Lake Vättern, Villa Björkhagen is a good site, useful as a break in the journey across Sweden or visiting the city during a tour of the Lakes. It is on raised ground overlooking the lake, with some shelter in parts. There are 280 pitches on well kept grass which, on one side, slopes away from reception. Some pitches on the other side of reception are flat and there are 200 electrical (10A), 100 cable TV and 40 water connections available. Jönköping is one of Sweden's oldest trading centres with a Charter dating back to 1284 and several outstanding attractions.

Facilities

Heated sanitary facilities were clean when we visited but looking rather tired. They include hot showers on payment (some in private cubicles) and a sauna, plus provision for disabled visitors and babies. Laundry. Motorcaravan services. Gas supplies. Well stocked shop. Bar and restaurant (1/6-16/9). Playground. TV room. Minigolf and bicycle hire. WiFi (free). Off site: Pool complex and fishing 500 m. Beach, golf, sailing and skiing 1 km. Riding 7 km.

Open: All year (full services 1/6-16/9).

Directions

Site is well signed from the E4 road on eastern side of Jönköping. Watch carefully for exit on this fast road. GPS: 57.78702, 14.21795

Charges guide

Per unit incl. 2 persons and electricity € 34.00

Prices may be increased if there is a local exhibition. Camping Cheques accepted.

Kil

Frykenbadens Camping

Stubberud, S-665 91 Kil (Värmlands Län) T: 055 440 940. E: info@frykenbaden.se

alanrogers.com/SW2760

Frykenbadens Camping is in a quiet wooded area on the southern shore of Lake Fryken, taking 200 units on grassy meadows surrounded by trees. One area nearer the lake is gently sloping, the other is flat with numbered pitches arranged in rows, all with electricity (10A). Reception, a good shop, restaurant and takeaway are located in a traditional Swedish house surrounded by lawns sloping down to the shore, with minigolf, a play barn and playground, with pet area also close by. Frykenbadens Camping is a quiet, relaxing place to stay, away from the busier and more famous lakes.

Facilities

The main sanitary block is of good quality and heated in cool weather with showers on payment, open washbasins, a laundry room and room for families or disabled visitors. A further small block has good facilities. Well equipped camper's kitchen. Shop. Snack bar, restaurant and takeaway. Pub. Minigolf. Play barn and playground. Lake swimming. Canoes, rowing boats and bicycles for hire. WiFi (charged). Off site: Golf 1 km. Go-karts, riding, jogging track 4 km.

Open: All year (full services 17/6-13/8).

Directions

Site is signed from the no. 61 Karlstad - Arvika road, then 4 km. towards lake following signs.
GPS: 59.54625, 13.34132

Charges guide

Per unit incl electricity	SEK 220 - 250

Kolmården

First Camp Kolmården

S-618 34 Kolmården (Østergötlands Län) T: 011 398 250. E: kolmarden@firstcamp.se

alanrogers.com/SW2805

This is a family site, located on Bråviken Bay on the Baltic coast 160 km. south of Stockholm. Open all year, the site is just 4 km. from Kolmården Zoo, one of Sweden's most popular family attractions. There are 300 pitches, of which 180 have electrical connections (10A). Some pitches have sea views and there is also a large beautiful wooded area for tents and 99 cabins of various standards for rent. A good range of amenities includes a 120 m. water slide and a children's playground. Adjacent to the site is a handicraft village and the Sjöstugans restaurant.

Facilities

Three sanitary blocks (two heated) provide a good supply of showers, washbasins and toilets. Baby rooms and facilities for disabled visitors. Good kitchen with cookers, microwaves and sinks. Hot water is free throughout. Well equipped laundry rooms. Sauna. Motorcaravan services. Well stocked shop (1/5-15/9). Snack bar. Adjacent licensed restaurant and bar. Takeaway. Playground. Bouncy castle. Water slide. Family entertainment and children's activities (high season). Minigolf. Sea fishing. WiFi. Chalets for rent. Off site: Riding 2 km. Kolmården Zoo 4 km. Golf 18 km. The Göta Canal 30 km.

Open: All year.

Directions

From the E4 motorway take Kolmården exit (no. 126) 23 km. north of Norrköping. Follow signs for Kolmården and site is well signed.
GPS: 58.65972, 16.40065

Charges guide

Per pitch	SEK 145 - 195
electricity	SEK 45

Kramfors

Flogsta Camping

S-872 80 Kramfors (Västernorrlands Län) T: 061 210 005. E: flogsta@basterang.se

alanrogers.com/SW2855

Kramfors lies just to the west of the E4, and travellers may well pass by over the new Höga Kusten bridge (one of the largest in Europe), and miss this friendly little site. This area of Ådalen and the High Coast, reaches as far as Ørnsköldsvik. The attractive garden-like campsite has 50 pitches, 21 with electrical connections (10A), which are arranged on level grassy terraces, separated by shrubs and trees into bays of 2-4 units. All overlook the heated outdoor public swimming pool complex and attractive minigolf course. The non-electric pitches are on an open terrace nearer reception.

Facilities

Sanitary facilities comprise nine bathrooms, each with British style WC, basin with hand dryer, shower. Laundry facilities. More WCs and showers are in the reception building with a free sauna. A new toilet block has a sauna and outside hot tub. A separate building houses a kitchen, with hot-plates, fridge/freezer and TV/dining room (all free). The reception building has a small shop and snack bar. Playground. Snow-mobile hire. Off site: Fishing 10 km. Golf and riding 15 km.

Open: All year.

Directions

Signed from road 90 in the centre of Kramfors, the site lies to the west in a rural location beyond a housing estate and by the Flogsta Bad, a municipal swimming pool complex.
GPS: 62.92562, 17.75642

Charges guide

Per pitch	SEK 100 - 125

Lidköping

Lidköping KronoCamping

Läckögatan, S-531 54 Lidköping (Västra Götalands Län) T: 051 026 804. E: info@kronocamping.com

alanrogers.com/SW2710

This high quality, attractive site provides 413 pitches on flat, well kept grass. It is surrounded by some mature trees, with the lake shore as one boundary and a number of tall pines left to provide shade and shelter. There are 412 pitches with electricity (10A) and TV connections and 90 with water and drainage also, together with 22 cabins for rent. The site takes a fair number of seasonal units. There is a small shop (a shopping centre is very close) and a fully licensed restaurant with conservatory seating area in the reception complex.

Facilities

Excellent, modern, refurbished sanitary facilities are in two blocks with underfloor heating. Hot water is free. Make up and hairdressing areas, baby room and facilities for disabled visitors. Private cabins. Good kitchen with seats, cookers and microwaves and dishwashers. Motorcaravan services. Small shop. Restaurant. Minigolf. Playgrounds. TV room. Games and amusements room. Bicycle hire. Play field. Lake swimming, fishing and watersports. Sauna and jacuzzi. Internet and WiFi. Off site: Swimming pool adjacent. Riding 4 km. Golf 6 km. The castle of Läckö, Kinnekulle, Spiken's fishing harbour. Rörstrand pottery.

Open: All year (full services 1/6-22/8).

Directions

From Lidköping town junctions follow signs towards Läckö then pick up camping signs and continue to site. GPS: 58.513062, 13.13853

Charges guide

Per unit incl. electricity SEK 250 - 370

Linköping

Glyttinge Camping

Berggärdsvägen 6, S-584 37 Linköping (Østergötlands Län) T: 013 174 928. E: glyttinge@nordiccamping.se

alanrogers.com/SW2800

Only five minutes by car from the Ikea shopping mall, Glyttinge is a site with a mix of terrain – some flat, some sloping and some woodland. A site with enthusiastic and friendly management, it is maintained to a good standard, trees and shrubs everywhere create a cosy garden-like atmosphere. There are 116 good sized, mostly level pitches of which 112 have electricity (10A). Children are well catered for – the manager has laid out a fenced and very safe children's play area. The site is also a good stopover place half way between Kolmården and Astrid Lindgren's World.

Facilities

The main, central toilet block (supplemented by additional smaller facilities at reception) is modern, well constructed and well equipped and maintained. It has showers in cubicles, washbasins and WC suites and hand dryers. Separate facilities for disabled visitors. Baby rooms. Laundry. Kitchen and dining/TV room, fully equipped. Motorcaravan services. Small shop (from 20/6). Playground. Off site: Riding and golf 3 km. Fishing 5 km. Linköping old town. Air museum at Malmslätt.

Open: All year.

Directions

Exit E4 Helsingborg - Stockholm motorway north of Linköping at signs for IKEA and site. Turn right at traffic lights and camp sign and follow signs to site. GPS: 58.42135, 15.561522

Charges guide

Per unit incl. electricity SEK 210 - 240

Low season discounts for pensioners.

Mariestad

Ekuddens Camping

Strandbadet, S-542 94 Mariestad (Västra Götalands Län) T: 050 110 637.

E: andrea.appelgren@mariestad.se alanrogers.com/SW2730

Ekuddens occupies a long stretch of the eastern shore of Lake Vänern to the northwest of the town, in a mixed woodland setting, and next door to the municipal complex of heated outdoor pools and sauna. The lake, of course, is also available for swimming and boating and there are bicycles, tandems and canoes for hire at the tourist information office in town. The spacious site can take 300 units, not numbered, and there are 230 electrical hook-ups (10A). Most pitches are under the trees but some at the far end of the site are on more open ground with good views over the lake.

Facilities

There are three sanitary blocks, all clean and well maintained. Free hot showers in cubicles. Facilities for disabled visitors with good access ramps. Baby changing rooms. Excellent kitchen with cooking and dining facilities. Laundry. Shop. Licensed bar. Takeaway (high season). Playground. Minigolf. TV room. Lake swimming, boating and fishing. Entertainment in high season. WiFi around the reception. Off site: Swimming pools adjacent. Bicycle 3 km. Golf 4 km. Riding 7 km.

Open: 1 May - 15 September (full services 15/6-15/8).

Directions

Site is 2.5 km. northwest of the town and well signed at junctions on the ring road. From the E20 motorway take exit for Mariestad S. and follow signs in the direction of Marieholm. GPS: 58.715567, 13.794901

Charges guide

Per unit incl. electricity SEK 190 - 220

Mölle

FirstCamp Mölle

S-260 42 Mölle (Skåne Län) T: 042 347 384. E: molle@firstcamp.se

alanrogers.com/SW2645

FirstCamp Mölle is a family campsite with a fine location at the foot of the Kullaberg, which marks the point where the Atlantic divides into the Kattegatt and Øresund. The site is open all year. There are 250 pitches, generally of a good size and 220 with electrical connections. The nearby Kullaberg Nature Park is dramatic and well worth a visit. The region is also well known for its ceramics and many potters and artists have settled in the area. On-site amenities include a heated paddling pool and water games complex. The nearest beach is 1.5 km. distant and is popular for kayaking and fishing.

Facilities

Two modern sanitary blocks with free hot water and facilities for disabled visitors. Family shower rooms. Laundry with washing machines and dryers. Kitchen with cooking rings and microwave. Motorcaravan services. Restaurant with bar and caféteria. Shop. Minigolf. Sports pitch. Heated paddling pool. Entertainment and children's activity programme (high season). Bicycle hire. TV room. WiFi. Cabins for rent. Off site: Kullaberg Nature Park 1 km. Nearest beach 1.5 km. Kayaking 2 km. Golf 4 km. Mölle lighthouse 6 km. Höganäs ceramics 8 km.

Open: All year.

Directions

From Helsingborg take the E4 north and then join road 111 towards Höganäs. Pass through this town and follow signs to Mölle and site. From the north take exit 33 on E6 towards Höganäs. Follow signs to site. GPS: 56.27086, 12.52996

Charges guide

Per pitch	SEK 150 - 285
electricity	SEK 45
tent pitch	SEK 110 - 240

Mora

Mora Parkens Camping

Box 294, S-792 25 Mora (Dalarnas Län) T: 025 027 600. E: moraparken@mora.se

alanrogers.com/SW2836

Mora, at the northern end of Lake Silijan is surrounded by small localities all steeped in history and culture. On the island of Sollerön, south of Mora, is evidence of a large Viking burial ground. Traditional handicrafts are still alive in the region. Mora is lively, friendly and attractive. The campsite, which is good for family holidays, is only ten minutes walk from the town. The camping area is large, grassy, open and flat. It is bordered by clumps of trees and a stream. The staff are pleasant and helpful.

Facilities

Four fully equipped toilet blocks. Campers' kitchen. Laundry. Shop. Restaurant/bar. Sauna. Fishing. Minigolf. Playground. Canoe hire. Internet access. Off site: Swimming pools. Zorn Museum. Orsa Bear Park. Dalhalla (limestone quarry) musical stage. Nustriäs.

Open: All year.

Directions

Follow signs to centre of town. Campsite is clearly signed from the town centre and is next to Zorngården and Zorn museum. GPS: 618533, 14.531783

Charges guide

Per unit incl. electricity	SEK 180 - 250
tent	SEK 100 - 115

Full services mid-June - mid-August.

Ørebro

Gustavsvik Camping

Sommarrovägen, S-702 30 Ørebro (Ørebro Län) T: 019 196 950. E: camping@gustavsvik.se

alanrogers.com/SW2780

Gustavsvik is one of the most modern and most visited camping and leisure parks in Sweden. It is ideally situated almost half way between Oslo and Stockholm or Gothenburg and Stockholm, at the junction of the E18 and E20 roads. This large campsite provides 675 marked and numbered pitches partly shaded by birch and pine trees, 494 with electrical connections and cable TV, 55 with electricity, water and waste water drainage. There are also three partly shaded areas for tents. The leisure park includes adventure golf, a mini zoo, playgrounds, pools and a water slide and a swimming lake, plus a private fishing lake.

Facilities

Three excellent heated toilet blocks including washbasins with dividers, free hot showers, family rooms, facilities for disabled visitors and children. Make up rooms. Very well equipped kitchens with free hot water. Dining area. Washing machine and dryers. Motorcaravan service points. Shower room for pets. Shop. Restaurant and pub. Takeaway. TV room and playroom. Arcade with games room. Internet. WiFi. Adventure golf. Football. Swimming pool with waterslide. Swimming lake. Fishing lake. Mini zoo. Bicycle hire. Off site: Pool complex adjacent. Golf. Ørebro city centre. Marieberg shopping centre. Karlslund manor house and gardens.

Open: May - October (full services 10/6-14/8).

Directions

Site is 1 km. south of Ørebro town centre. Follow signs from E18/E20 or main road 50/51. GPS: 59.255382, 15.189784

Charges guide

Per unit incl. 2 persons and electricity	SEK 285 - 375

Østersund

Østersunds Camping

Krondikesvagen 95, S-831 46 Østersund (Jämtlands Län) T: 063 144 615.
E: ostersundscamping@ostersund.se alanrogers.com/SW2850

Østersund lies on Lake Storsjön, which is Sweden's Loch Ness, with 200 sightings of the monster dating back to 1635, and more recently captured on video in 1996. Also worthy of a visit is the island of Frösön where settlements can be traced back to prehistoric times. This large site has 254 pitches, electricity (10A) and TV socket available on 131, all served by tarmac roads. There are also 41 tarmac hardstandings available, and over 220 cottages, cabins and rooms for rent. Adjacent to the site are the municipal swimming pool complex with caféteria (indoor and outdoor pools), a Scandic hotel with restaurant, minigolf, and a Statoil filling station.

Facilities
Toilet facilities are in three units, two including controllable hot showers (on payment) with communal changing areas, suites for disabled visitors and baby changing. The third has four family bathrooms each containing WC, basin and shower. Two kitchens, each with full cookers, hobs, fridge/freezers and double sinks (all free of charge), and excellent dining rooms. Washing machines, dryers and free drying cabinet. Very good motorcaravan service point suitable for all types of unit including American RVs. Playground. Off site: Østersund, Frösön.

Open: All year.

Directions
Site is south of the town on the road towards Torvalla. Turn by Statoil station and site entrance is immediately on right. It is well signed from around the town. GPS: 63.15942, 14.67355

Charges guide

Per unit with electricity	€ 22.00 - € 26.00

Ramvik

Snibbens Camping & Stugby och Vandrarhem

Hälledal 527, S-870 16 Ramvik (Västernorrlands Län) T: 061 240 505. E: info@snibbenscamping.com
alanrogers.com/SW2853

Probably you will stop here for one night as you travel the E4 coast road and stay a week. It is a truly beautiful location in the area of 'The High Coast' listed as a World Heritage Site. During high season Snibbens is a busy, popular site but remains quiet and peaceful. Besides 30 bungalows for rent there are 50 touring places, each with 16A electricity, set amongst delightful scenery on the shores of Lake Mörtsjön. The welcoming owners take you to your adequately sized grass pitch set amongst spacious trees. To one end of the campsite there is a beach where the waters are suitable for swimming with a zoned area for young children.

Facilities
Excellent, spotlessly clean facilities include controllable showers and partitioned washbasins. Baby changing facilities. Two kitchens with hot plates, microwaves and a mini oven. Laundry room. Small shop (15/6-20/8). Rowing boats and pedaloes for hire. Minigolf. Free fishing for site guests. Youth hostel. Off site: Small supermarket 800 m. Golf 20 km.

Open: 30 April - 15 September.

Directions
Travelling north on the E4 and immediately prior to Höga Kusten bridge (one of the largest in Europe) take road 90 signed Kramfors. Site is directly off road 90 on left in 3 km, well signed.
GPS: 62.79896, 17.86965

Charges guide

Per pitch	SEK 140
incl. electricity	SEK 155

Röstånga

Röstånga Camping & Bad

Blinkarpsvägen 3, S-268 68 Röstånga (Skåne Län) T: 043 591 064. E: nystrand@msn.com
alanrogers.com/SW2630

Beside the Söderåsen National Park, this scenic campsite has its own fishing lake and many activities for the whole family. There are 180 large, level, grassy pitches with electricity (10A) and a quiet area for tents with a view over the fishing lake. The tent area has its own service building and several barbecue places. A large holiday home and 21 pleasant cabins are available to rent all year round. A pool complex adjacent to the site provides a 50 m. swimming pool, three children's pools and a water slide, all heated during peak season. The friendly staff will be happy to help you to plan interesting excursions in the area.

Facilities
Four good, heated sanitary blocks with free hot water and facilities for babies and disabled visitors. Laundry with washing machines and dryers. Kitchen with cooking rings, oven and microwave. Motorcaravan service point. Small shop at reception. Bar, restaurant and takeaway. Minigolf. Tennis. Fitness trail. Fishing. Canoe hire. Children's club. WiFi (free). Off site: Swimming pool complex adjacent to site (free for campers as is a visit to the zoo). Golf 11 km. Motor racing track at Ring Knutstorp 8 km.

Open: 10 April - 30 September.

Directions
From Malmö: drive towards Lund and follow road no. 108 to Röstånga. From Stockholm: turn off at Østra Ljungby and take road no. 13 to Röstånga. In Röstånga drive through the village on road 108 and follow the signs. GPS: 55.996583, 13.28005

Charges guide

Per unit incl. 2 persons and electricity	€ 25.00 - € 33.00

Skärholmen

Bredäng Camping Stockholm

Stora Sällskapets väg, S-127 31 Skärholmen (Stockholms Län) T: **089 770 71**.
E: **bredangcamping@telia.com** **alanrogers.com/SW2842**

Bredäng is a busy city site, with easy access to Stockholm city centre. Large and fairly level, with very little shade, there are 380 pitches, including 115 with hardstanding and 204 with electricity (10A), and a separate area for tents. Reception is open from 08.00-23.00 in the main season (12/6-20/8), reduced hours in low season, and English is spoken. A Stockholm card is available, or a three-day public transport card from the Tube station. Stockholm has many events and activities, you can take a circular tour on a free sightseeing bus, various boat and bus tours, or view the city from the Kaknäs Tower (155 m). The nearest Tube station is five minutes walk; trains run about every ten minutes between 05.00 and 02.00, and the journey takes about twenty minutes. The local shopping centre is five minutes away and a two minute walk through the woods brings you to a very attractive lake and beach.

Facilities

Four heated sanitary units of a high standard provide British style WCs, controllable hot showers, with some washbasins in cubicles. One has a baby room, a unit for disabled visitors and a first aid room. Cooking and dishwashing facilities are in three units around the site. Laundry facilities. Motorcaravan services and car wash. Well stocked shop, bar, takeaway and fully licensed restaurant (all 1/5-31/8). Sauna. Playground.
Off site: Fishing 500 m.

Open: 18 April - 9 October.

Directions

Site is about 10 km. southwest of city centre. Turn off E4/E20 at Bredängs signpost and follow clearly marked site signs. GPS: 59.29560, 17.92315

Charges guide

Per unit incl. electricity	SEK 280 - 325
1 person tent	SEK 120 - 140

Discounts for pensioners in low season.

Stöllet

Alevi Camping

Fastnäs 53, S-680 51 Stöllet (Värmlands Län) T: **056 386 050**. E: **info@alevi-camping.com**
alanrogers.com/SW2755

Alevi Camping is a small, welcoming site with 60 large pitches and five cabins for hire. Open all year, the site is situated on the bank of the Klarälven river, the longest river in Sweden. With its own beach this is a perfect place for swimming, fishing, canoeing and rafting. The site, which opened in 2006, offers large level pitches all with electricity (4/10A). The county of Värmland is famous for its lakes, rivers and forests. There, if you are lucky, you can see the 'big four' predators of Scandinavia – wolf, bear, wolverine and lynx. Further up the river, at Sysslebäck, you can build your own log raft for a slow journey down the river. The rafts are fully equipped with a tent and whatever you need for a few days on the water. The site owners are happy to help you find the perfect activity for a pleasant stay.

Facilities

One new sanitary block with free hot water. Unisex toilets and showers (charged). Washbasins, both vanity style and in cubicles. Facilities for babies and disabled visitors. Family room. Good campers' kitchen with free hot water. Motorcaravan services. Reception with small shop, restaurant, takeaway. Internet at reception. TV room. Canoes and bicycle hire. River beach. Barbecue area. Sauna. Playground. Fishing. Skiing in winter.
Off site: Supermarket 10 minutes by car. Husky rides and ice fishing in winter.

Open: All year.

Directions

Site is between Ekshärad and Stöllet on road no. 62, 16 km. south of Stöllet. Follow signs.
GPS: 60.285267, 13.406733

Charges guide

Per unit incl. electricity	SEK 100 - 160

Strömstad

Daftö Resort

S-452 97 Strömstad (Västra Götalands Län) T: 052 626 040. E: info@dafto.com

alanrogers.com/SW2735

This extremely high quality, family campsite, with a strong pirate theme, is beautifully situated on the west coast, 5 km. south of Strömstad. A very large site, terraced in parts, has both shady and open areas. In total there are 650 pitches with 310 for touring, all with electrical hook-ups (10A, CEE plugs). In addition, there are 130 modern, very well equipped cabins of various sizes and styles. Daftö Resort has activities for all including boating, beach volleyball, walks and yoga, and all manner of theme-based activities for children including theatre, competitions, treasure hunting and a pirate playground. A member of Leading Campings group.

Facilities

Four toilet blocks of excellent quality with washbasin cubicles, showers, family rooms, a children's bathroom, sunbeds, saunas and makeup rooms. Wellness centre and hairdressers. Units for disabled visitors. Kitchen. Laundry facilities. Shop. Fully licensed restaurant. Heated pool (peak season). Games and TV rooms. Themed minigolf. Bicycle hire. Football field. Children's club. Boat excursions and seal safaris. Internet and WiFi. Motorcaravan services. Conference room. B&B and groups catered for. Off site: Ferry to Norway (Sandefjord) from Strömstad. The Koster islands (ferry from Strömstad). Golf at Strömstad. Aquarium at Tjärnö 6 km.

Open: All year excl. 23 December - 6 January.

Directions

Daftö is 5 km. south of Strömstad on road 176. It is signed. GPS: 58.904267, 11.200117

Charges guide

Per unit incl. electricity and water SEK 200 - 425

Strömsund

Strömsunds Camping

Box 500, S-833 24 Strömsund (Jämtlands Län) T: 067 016 410. E: stromsund.turism@stromsund.se

alanrogers.com/SW2857

A quiet waterside town on the north - south route 45, known as the Inlandsvägen, Strömsund is a good place to begin a journey on the Wilderness Way. This is route 342 which heads northwest towards the mountains at Gäddede and the Norwegian border. Being on the confluence of many waterways, there is a wonderful feeling of space and freedom in Strömsund. The campsite is set on a gentle grassy slope backed by forest. Another part of the site, across the road, overlooks the lake. Cabins are set in circular groups of either six or seven. The site is owned by the town council.

Facilities

Excellent facilities include two toilet blocks, one on each side of the road. Both contain showers, toilets, washbasins with dividers and underfloor heating. Facilities for disabled visitors. Laundry. Large campers' kitchen with cooking rings, microwave and sinks. Motorcaravan service point. Bicycle, canoe, pedalo and boat hire. Play area. Off site: Municipal pool is next to the site. Boat launching 1.5 km. Riding 3 km.

Open: All year.

Directions

Site is 700 m. south of Strömsund on route 45. GPS: 63.846523, 15.534405

Charges 2012

Per unit incl. 2 persons and electricity SEK 180 - 220

Full services mid-June - mid-August.

Sveg

Svegs Camping

Kyrkogränd 1, S-842 32 Sveg (Jämtlands Län) T: 068 013 025. E: info@svegscamping.se

alanrogers.com/SW2845

On the 'Inlandsvägen' route through Sweden, the town centre is only a short walk from this neat, friendly site. Two supermarkets, a café and tourist information office are adjacent. The 80 pitches are in rows, on level grass, divided into bays by tall hedges, and with electricity (10/16A) available to 70. The site has boats, canoes and bicycles for hire, and the river frontage has a barbecue area with covered seating and fishing platforms. Alongside the river with its fountain, and running through the site is a pleasant well lit riverside walk.

Facilities

In the older style, sanitary facilities are functional rather than luxurious, providing stainless steel washing troughs, controllable hot showers with communal changing areas, and a unit for disabled visitors. Although a little short on numbers, facilities will probably suffice at most times as the site is rarely full. Kitchen and dining room with TV, four full cookers and sinks. Laundry facilities. TV room. Minigolf. Canoe, boat and bicycle hire. Fishing.

Open: All year.

Directions

Site is off road 45 behind the tourist information office in Sveg. Site is signed. GPS: 62.03367, 14.37250

Charges guide

Per pitch	SEK 150
electricity	SEK 25

Tidaholm

Tidaholm-Hökensås Semesterby och Camping

Blåhult, S-522 91 Tidaholm (Västra Götalands Län) T: **050 223 053**. E: **info@hokensas.nu**

alanrogers.com/SW2720

Hökensås is located just west of Lake Vättern and south of Tidaholm, in a beautiful nature reserve of wild, unspoiled scenery. This pleasant campsite is part of a holiday complex that includes wooden cabins for rent. It is relaxed and informal, with over 200 pitches either under trees or on a more open area at the far end, divided into rows by wooden rails. These are numbered and electricity (10A) is available on 135. Tents can go on the large grassy open areas by reception. This site is a find for all kinds of people who enjoy outdoor activities.

Facilities

The original sanitary block near reception is supplemented by one in the wooded area, both refurbished. Hot showers in cubicles with communal changing area are free. Separate saunas for each sex and facilities for disabled visitors and babies. Campers' kitchen at each block with cooking, dishwashing and laundry facilities. Small, but well stocked shop. Very good angling shop. Fully licensed restaurant with takeaway. Playground. Minigolf. Lake swimming. Fishing. Boules. Off site: The town of Tidaholm and Lake Hornborga. Fishing 2 km. Riding 10 km. Bicycle hire 15 km.

Open: All year (full services 20/6-11/8).

Directions

Approach site from no. 195 road at Brandstorp, about 40 km. north of Jönköping, turn west at petrol station and camp sign signed Hökensås. Site is about 9 km. up this road. GPS: 58.0982, 14.0746

Charges guide

Per unit	
(more for Midsummer celebrations)	SEK 150 - 160
electricity	SEK 45

Tingsryd

Tingsryds Camping

Mårdslyckesand, S-362 91 Tingsryd (Kronobergs Län) T: **047 710 554**. E: **tingsryd.camping@swipnet.se**

alanrogers.com/SW2655

A pleasant, well managed site by Lake Tiken, Tingsryds Camping is well placed for Sweden's Glass District. The 200 large pitches are arranged in rows divided by trees and shrubs, with some along the edge of a lakeside path (public have access). All have electricity (10/16A) and there is shade in parts. The facilities are housed in buildings near the site entrance, with the reception building having the restaurant, café, bar and a small shop. Adjacent to the site is a small beach, grassy lying out area, playground and lake swimming area and three tennis courts. Hire of canoes, fishing and minigolf are available on site (public access also).

Facilities

Heated sanitary facilities are in two well maintained buildings, one including showers (on payment), mostly with curtains (communal undressing), the other a campers' kitchen with hobs and dining area. Facilities for disabled visitors. Laundry with free ironing. Motorcaravan services. Shop (1/5-15/9). Restaurant and café (1/5-15/9). Minigolf. Playground. Boules. Lake swimming. Canoe hire. Fishing. Bicycle hire. Off site: Golf 15 km.

Open: 5 April - 20 October (full services 24/5-19/8).

Directions

Site is 1 km. from Tingsryd off road no. 120, well signed around the town. GPS: 56.52872, 14.96147

Charges guide

Per unit	SEK 120 - 195
incl. electricity	SEK 160 - 235

Torekov

First Camp Båstad-Torekov

Flymossa Vagen 5, S-260 93 Torekov (Skåne Län) T: **043 136 4525**. E: **torekov@firstcamp.se**

alanrogers.com/SW2640

Part of the First Camp chain, this site is 500 m. from the fishing village of Torekov, 14 km. west of the home of the Swedish tennis WCT Open at Båstad, on the stretch of coastline between Malmö and Göteborg. Useful en route from the most southerly ports, it is a very good site and worthy of a longer stay for relaxation. It has 535 large pitches (390 for touring units), all numbered and marked, mainly in attractive natural woodland, with some on more open ground close to the shore. Of these, 300 have electricity (10A) and cable TV, 77 also having water and drainage.

Facilities

Three very good sanitary blocks with facilities for babies and disabled visitors. Laundry. Cooking facilities and dishwashing. Motorcaravan service point. Bar. Restaurant, pizzeria and snack bar with takeaway (15/6-5/8).
Shop and kiosk. Minigolf. Sports fields. Play areas and adventure park for children. Bicycle hire. TV room. Beach. Fishing. WiFi on all pitches. Off site: Games, music and entertainment in high season. Tennis close by. Golf 1 km. Riding 3 km.

Open: 15 April - 25 September.

Directions

From E6 Malmö - Göteborg road take Torekov/Båstad exit and follow signs for 20 km. towards Torekov. Site is signed 1 km. before village on right. GPS: 56.43097, 12.64055

Charges guide

Per unit incl. 4 persons	
and electricity	SEK 190 - 305

Uddevalla

Hafsten SweCamp Resort

Hafsten 120, S-451 96 Uddevalla (Västra Götalands Län) T: **052 264 4117**. E: **info@hafsten.se**

alanrogers.com/SW2725

This privately owned site on the west coast is situated on a peninsula overlooking the magnificent coastline of Bohuslän. Open all year, it is a lovely, peaceful, terraced site with a beautiful, shallow and child-friendly sandy beach and many nature trails in the vicinity. There are 190 touring pitches, all with electricity (10A), 100 of them with water and drainage. In all, there are 340 pitches including a tent area and 62 cabins of a high standard. There are plenty of activities available ranging from horse riding at the stables on the campsite's own farm to an 86 m. long water chute. Almost any activity can be arranged on the site or elsewhere by the friendly owners if they are given advance notice. Amenities include two clean and well maintained service buildings, a pub, a fully licensed restaurant with wine from their own French vineyard, a well stocked shop and a takeaway. Reception is open and welcoming with natural light used to great effect. This is where the new fitness and wellness facilities can be found. The active area of the site is well away from the main campsite and this means guests can experience a quiet, relaxed holiday while others are busy with the many activities on offer. Hafsten SweCamp Resort also owns and runs the Tånga farm of 250 hectares with horse riding for all ages and abilities.

Facilities

Two heated sanitary buildings provide the usual facilities. Showers are on payment. Kitchen with good cooking facilities. Dining room. Laundry facilities. Units for disabled visitors. Motorcaravan services. Shop. Restaurant, takeaway (1/6-31/8) and pub. Live music evenings. TV room. Relaxation centre with sauna and jacuzzi (charged). Gym. Water slide (charged). WiFi (charged). Riding. Minigolf. Tennis. Boules. Playground. Clay pigeon shooting. Boat hire (canoe, rowing, motor, pedalo). Outside gym and fitness area. Off site: Shopping centre and golf 13 km. Havets hus (marine museum) 30 km. Nordens Ark 40 km.

Open: All year.

Directions

From the E6, north of Uddevalla, at Torpmotet exit take the 161 road towards Lysekil. At the Rotviksbro roundabout take the 160 road towards Orust. The exit to the site is located further on road 2 km. on the left where four flags fly. Follow the signs for 4 km. along a one way road for motorcaravans and caravans. GPS: 58.314683, 11.723333

Charges guide

Per pitch incl. electricity	SEK 230 - 355

Camping Cheques accepted.

Umeå

First Camp Umeå

S-906 54 Umeå (Västerbotens Län) T: **090 702 600**. E: **umea@firstcamp.se**

alanrogers.com/SW2860

An ideal stopover for those travelling the E4 coastal route, or a good base from which to explore the area, this campsite is 6 km. from the centre of this university city. It is almost adjacent to the Nydalsjön Lake, which is ideal for fishing, windsurfing and bathing. There are 450 grassy pitches arranged in bays of 10-20 units, 320 with electricity (10A or 16A), and some are fully serviced. Outside the site, adjacent to the lake, are football pitches, an open-air swimming pool, minigolf, mini-car driving school, beach volleyball and a mini farm.

Facilities

The new large, heated, central sanitary unit includes controllable hot showers with communal changing areas. (Facilities stretched in high season). Kitchen. Large dining room. TV. Laundry facilities. Shop (25/5-21/8). Fully licensed restaurant. WiFi. Walk-on chess. Playgrounds. Bicycle hire. Rowing boat hire. Fishing in the lake. Canoes and pedal cars for hire. Adventure golf. Off site: Riding adjacent. Golf 18 km.

Open: All year (full services 25/5-12/8).

Directions

A camping sign on the E4 at a set of traffic lights 5 km. north of the town directs you to the site. Direction also indicates Holmsund and Vassa. GPS: 63.843333, 20.340556

Charges guide

Per pitch	SEK 160 - 220
incl. electricity	SEK 170 - 260

Västervik

Camping Lysingsbadet

Lysingsvägen, S-593 53 Västervik (Kalmar Län) T: 049 088 920. E: lysingsbadet@vastervik.se

alanrogers.com/SW2675

One of the largest sites in Scandinavia, Lysingsbadet has unrivalled views of the 'Pearl of the East Coast' – Västervik and its fjords and islands. There are around 1,000 large, mostly marked and numbered pitches, spread over a vast area of rocky promontory and set on different plateaux, terraces, in valleys and woodland, or beside the water. It is a very attractive site, and one which never really looks or feels crowded even when busy. There are 83 full service pitches with TV, water and electrical connections, 163 with TV and electricity and 540 with electricity only, the remainder for tents. Reception is smart, efficient and friendly with good English spoken.

Facilities

Ten modern toilet blocks of various ages house a comprehensive mix of showers, basins and WCs. All are kept very clean. Several kitchens with dishwashing sinks and cookers. Four laundry rooms. All facilities and hot water are free. Key cards operate the barriers and gain access to sanitary blocks, pool complex and other facilities. Motorcaravan services. Supermarket (15/5-31/8). Restaurant and café/takeaway (12/6-138). Swimming pool complex (1/6-31/8). Golf. Minigolf. Bicycle and boat hire. Fishing. Entertainment and dances in high season. Playgrounds. Quick Stop service. Bus service.
Off site: Riding 10 km.

Open: All year.

Directions

Turn off E22 for Västervik and follow signs for Lysingsbadet. GPS: 57.738212, 16.668459

Charges guide

Per pitch	SEK 200 - 325
incl. electricity	SEK 250 - 365
incl. electricity, TV	SEK 250 - 385

Switzerland

A small, wealthy country, best known for its outstanding mountainous scenery, fine cheeses, delicious chocolates, Swiss bank accounts and enviable lifestyles. Centrally situated in Europe, it shares its borders with four countries: France, Austria, Germany and Italy, each one having its own cultural influence on Switzerland.

The landscape of Switzerland boasts mountains, valleys, waterfalls and glaciers. The Bernese Oberland is probably the most visited area, with picturesque villages, lakes and awe-inspiring peaks, including the towering Eiger, Mönch and Jungfrau. The highest Alps are those of Valais in the southwest where the small busy resort of Zermatt gives access to the Matterhorn. The southeast of Switzerland has densely forested mountain slopes and the wealthy and glamorous resort of St Moritz. Zurich in the north is a German-speaking city with a wealth of sightseeing, particularly in the old town area with its 16th- and 17th-century houses. Geneva, Montreux and Lausanne on the northern shores of Lake Geneva make up the bulk of French Switzerland, with vineyards that border the lakes and medieval towns. The southernmost canton, Ticino, is home to the Italian-speaking Swiss, with the Mediterranean style lakeside resorts of Lugano and Locarno.

CAPITAL: **Bern**

Tourist Office

Switzerland Tourism
Switzerland Travel Centre,
30 Bedford Street, London WC2E 9ED
Tel: 020 7420 4900 Fax: 020 7845 7699
Email: info.uk@switzerland.com
Internet: www.myswitzerland.com

Population

7.8 million

Climate

Mild and refreshing in the northern plateau. South of the Alps it is warmer, influenced by the Mediterranean. The Valais is noted for its dryness.

Language

German in central and eastern areas, French in the west and Italian in the south. Raeto-Romansch is spoken in the southeast. English is spoken by many.

Telephone

The country code is 00 41.

Money

Currency: Swiss Franc
Banks: Mon-Fri 08.30-16.30. Some close for lunch.

Shops

Mon-Fri 08.00-12.00 and 14.00-18.00.
Sat 08.00-16.00. Often closed Monday mornings.

Public Holidays

New Year; Good Fri; Easter Mon; Ascension; Whit Mon; National Day 1 Aug; Christmas 25 Dec. Other holidays are observed in individual Cantons.

Motoring

The road network is comprehensive and well planned. An annual road tax is levied on all cars using Swiss motorways and the 'Vignette' windscreen sticker must be purchased at the border (credit cards not accepted), or in advance from the Swiss National Tourist Office, plus a separate one for a towed caravan or trailer.

see campsite map 4

Arbon

Camping Buchhorn

Philosophenweg 17, CH-9320 Arbon (Thurgau) T: 071 446 6545. E: info@camping-arbon.ch

alanrogers.com/CH9180

This small site is directly beside Lake Bodensee in the town's parkland. The site has some shade and a few of the touring pitches are by the water's edge. A large, adjoining lawned field is used for tents and also leads to the playground and paddling pool. There are many static caravans but said to be room for 100 tourists. Pitches are on a mixture of gravel and grass, on flat areas on either side of access roads, most with 6-10A electricity. Cars may have to be parked elsewhere. A railway runs directly along one side. A single set of buildings provide all the site's amenities. There are splendid views across this large inland sea and interesting boats ply up and down between Constance and Lindau and Bregenz. This is a beautiful area and the site is well placed for touring around Lake Bodensee.

Facilities

Toilet facilities are clean and modern, and should just about suffice in high season. Washing machine, dryer and drying area. Fridge. Shop (basic supplies, drinks and snacks all season). General room. Playground. Dogs are not accepted. Off site: Tennis 150 m. Town swimming lido 400 m. Watersports and steamer trips are available on the lake, walks and marked cycle tracks around it. Nature reserve nearby.

Open: 1 April - 8 October.

Directions

On Arbon - Konstanz road 13. From Arbon, turn right at the Aldi supermarket. From the A1 take the Arbon West exit and head towards the town. Straight on at the lights and turn left just after the town sign. Turn left again and head towards the warehouses. Turn right, cross the railway line and follow lane to site. GPS: 47.52470, 9.42065

Charges guide

Per person	CHF 8.00
child (6-16 yrs)	CHF 4.00
pitch	CHF 16.00
electricity	CHF 3.00

Bad Ragaz

Camping Giessenpark

CH-7310 Bad Ragaz (St Gallen) T: 081 302 3710. E: giessenpark@bluewin.ch

alanrogers.com/CH9175

The luxury spa resort of Bad Ragaz nestles in the Rhine valley and the municipally owned Giessenpark surrounds this site, which is located in a forest. There are 86 flat, level gravel pitches of which 52 are for touring, all with access to electricity (10A). The Rhine and the extensive park and lake are within a minute's walk and add to the peaceful nature of the site. The local authority swimming pool is close to the site, which is open from mid May to mid September. A restaurant with terrace and a large children's play area are adjacent to the site.

Facilities

Good, modern toilet is well maintained with free showers. Facilities for disabled visitors. Baby room. Sinks with hot water for laundry and dishwashing. Washing machine and dryer. Motorcaravan services. Shop (limited). Restaurant. WiFi (charged). Off site: Bad Ragaz 1 km. Golf and bicycle hire 1 km. Riding 3 km.

Open: All year.

Directions

From the A13 take Bad Ragaz exit and follow Bad Ragaz signs. In town, go over small bridge and turn right immediately, then right again after 300 m. following signs towards the site.
GPS: 47.00516, 9.51266

Charges guide

Per unit incl. 2 persons and electricity	CHF 38.80
extra person	CHF 8.00
child (6-16 yrs)	CHF 3.00
dog	CHF 2.00

Bönigen

TCS Camping Seeblick

Campingstrasse 14, CH-3806 Bönigen (Bern) T: 033 822 1143. E: camping.boenigen@tcs.ch

alanrogers.com/CH9450

This small, quiet site, bordered on two sides by Lake Brienz, is only 1.5 kilometres from the centre of Interlaken and the autoroute exit. It is therefore a useful site, not only to spend time on and enjoy the views, but also as an ideal base to tour this picturesque region, dominated by the Eiger and Jungfrau mountains. Almost all the 119 pitches are available for tourists. On level grassy ground and under tall trees, all have electricity. With magnificent views over the lake, gates give direct access to a footpath and to the lake shores. Interlaken is the tourist centre of the Berner Oberland. This is a region that has a great deal to offer, from sky diving to leisurely boat or train excursions. It is worth spending some time looking through the many tourist brochures available in reception and talking to the site manager Herr Krähenbühl to find activities and places to visit that particularly attract you. Tickets for many excursions are available from the site office. This is a region that has something for everyone.

Facilities

A well maintained, modern sanitary block has free showers and some washbasins in cabins. Facilities for disabled visitors. Baby room. Washing machine and dryer. Motorcaravan service point. Small shop sells gas and provides essentials. Informal bar and snack bar with takeaway food. Small solar heated swimming pool, and paddling pool. Play area. Internet access and WiFi throughout (charged). Off site: Bicycle hire and golf 2 km. Riding 3 km. Boat trips. Cable cars. Paragliding and skydiving.

Open: 4 April - 7 October.

Directions

Site is beside the Brienzersee in the eastern suburbs of Interlaken. From A8 take exit 26 (Interlaken Ost) and follow signs for Bönigen and then site signs. Approaching from Lucerne, take exit 27 (signed Bönigen). GPS: 46.691333, 7.8935

Charges 2012

Per unit incl. 2 persons and electricity	CHF 34.60 - 49.90
extra person	CHF 6.80 - 9.20
child (6-15 yrs)	CHF 3.40 - 4.60
dog	CHF 3.00 - 5.00

Basel

Camping Waldhort

Heideweg 16, CH-4153 Reinach bei Basel (Basel-Land) T: 061 711 6429. E: info@camping-waldhort.ch

alanrogers.com/CH9000

This is a satisfactory site for night halts or for visits to Basel. Although there are almost twice as many static caravan pitches as spaces for tourists, this site, on the edge of a residential district, is within easy reach of the city by tram. It is flat, with 210 level pitches with access from the tarmac road. The grass pitches may become muddy in very wet weather but there are gravel hardstandings for motorcaravans. All pitches have electricity (10A) and young trees give some shade. Owned and run by the Camping and Caravanning Club of Basel, there is usually space available. An extra, separate camping area has been added behind the tennis club which has pleasant pitches but with basic sanitary facilities. There are plans for these to be refurbished.

Facilities

The good quality, fully equipped, central sanitary block includes facilities for babies and disabled visitors. Washing machine and dryer. Kitchen with gas rings. Freezer for ice packs. Motorcaravan services. Small shop with terrace for drinks, snacks and takeaway (all season). Play area with two small pools. No charcoal barbecues. WiFi (free). Outdoor swimming and paddling pool (1/5-30/9).
Off site: Tennis courts next to site. A day ticket for travel on trams and buses throughout the Basel area can be purchased for Sfr 8 (available from reception).

Open: 1 March - 27 October.

Directions

Take Basel - Delémont motorway spur, exit for Reinach-Nord and follow site signs. Do not use the Reinach-Sud exit. GPS: 47.49973, 7.60278

Charges 2012

Per unit incl. 2 persons and electricity	CHF 36.00
extra person	CHF 9.00
child (6-14 yrs)	CHF 5.00
dog	CHF 3.00

Bouveret

Camping Rive-Bleue

Bouveret Plage, CH-1897 Bouveret (Valais) T: 024 481 2161. E: info@camping-rive-bleue.ch

alanrogers.com/CH9600

At the eastern end of Lac Léman with mountain and lakeside views, the main feature of this site is the very pleasant lakeside lido only a short walk of 300 m. from the site, with free entry for campers. It has an excellent pool and paddling pool, with beautiful lawns leading down to the sandy lakeside beach. There are pedalos and canoes for hire, and a sailing school. The site has 220 marked pitches on well tended flat grass, with some shade from young trees and plenty of 8-12A hookups. A pleasant pathway leads to the marina and town. Adjacent is a hotel with a restaurant and snack bar overlooking the pool.

Facilities

Two well equipped toilet blocks offer all the ususal facilities, including spacious rooms for disabled visitors. Washing machine and dryer. Covered area with electric rings, barbecue, sinks, table and chairs, electronic games and a TV. Motorcaravan services (Euro-relais). Shop, restaurant by beach (both all season). Outdoor swimming pool (heated Jun-Aug). Fishing. WiFi. Off site: Bicycle hire (first 2 hours free) 500 m. Boat and train tours in town.

Open: 1 April - 16 October.

Directions

Leave motorway A9/N9, south of Montreux, at exit 16 (Villeneuve) and follow signs for Evian. Just after passing town sign for Le Bouveret, turn right at roundabout and follow Aquaparc and site signs. GPS: 46.38657, 6.86017

Charges guide

Per unit incl. 2 persons and electricity	CHF 33.10 - 40.80
extra person	CHF 8.60 - 10.70
child (6-16 yrs)	CHF 5.90 - 7.10
dog	CHF 3.10

Brienz am See

Camping Aaregg

Seestrasse 28a, CH-3855 Brienz am See (Bern) T: 033 951 1843. E: mail@aaregg.ch

alanrogers.com/CH9510

Brienz, in the Bernese Oberland, is a delightful little town on the lake of the same name and the centre of the Swiss wood carving industry. Camping Aaregg is an excellent site situated on the southern shores of the lake with splendid views across the water to the mountains. There are 65 static caravans occupying their own area and 180 touring pitches, all with electricity (10/16A). Of these, 16 are larger with hardstandings, water and drainage and many of these have good lake views. Pitches fronting the lake have a surcharge. The trees and flowers make an attractive and peaceful environment. An excellent base from which to explore the many attractions of this scenic region, and is a useful night stop when passing from Interlaken to Luzern. Nearby at Ballenberg is the fascinating Freilichtmuseum, a very large open-air park of old Swiss houses which have been brought from all over Switzerland and re-erected in groups. Traditional Swiss crafts are demonstrated in some of these.

Facilities

New, very attractive sanitary facilities built and maintained to first class standards. Showers with washbasins. Washbasins (open style and in cubicles). Children's section. Family shower rooms. Baby changing room. Facilities for disabled visitors. Laundry facilities. Motorcaravan services. Pleasant restaurant with terrace and takeaway in season. Play area. Fishing. Bicycle hire. Boat launching. Lake swimming in clear water (unsupervised). English is spoken. Off site: Frequent train services to Interlaken and Lucerne as well as boat cruises from Brienz to Interlaken and back. Motorboat hire is possible, and waterskiing on the lake.

Open: 1 April - 31 October.

Directions

Site is on road B6/B11 on the east of Brienz. Entrance is just about opposite the Esso filling station, well signed. From the Interlaken-Luzern motorway, take Brienz exit and turn towards Brienz, site then on the left. GPS: 46.7483, 8.04871

Charges guide

Per unit incl. 2 persons and electricity	CHF 39.20 - 56.00
per person	CHF 7.70 - 11.00
child (6-16 yrs)	CHF 4.90 - 7.00
dog	CHF 4.00

Low season less 10%.

Châtel-Saint Denis

Camping Le Bivouac

Route des Paccots 21, CH-1618 Châtel-Saint Denis (Fribourg) T: 021 948 7849. E: info@le-bivouac.ch

alanrogers.com/CH9300

A pleasant little site in the forested mountains above Montreux and Vevey on Lac Léman (Lake Geneva). Le Bivouac has its own small swimming pool and children's pool. Most of the places here are taken by seasonal caravans (130) interspersed with about 30 pitches for tourists. Electrical connections (10A) are available and there are five water points. Due to access difficulties, the site is not open to tourers in winter. The active can take mountain walks in the area, or set off to explore Montreux and the lake. Others will enjoy the peace and quiet of this green hideaway.

Facilities

The good toilet facilities in the main building include free preset hot water in washbasins, showers and sinks for laundry and dishes. Washing machine and dryer. Gas supplies. Shop (1/7-31/8, bread to order). Bar (1/6-30/9). Swimming pool and paddling pool (15/6-15/9). TV. Table football. Fishing in adjacent stream (licence from reception). Internet and WiFi. Off site: Bus to Chatel stops at the gate. Bicycle hire 3 km. Riding 10 km.

Open: 1 May - 30 September.

Directions

From motorway 12/E27 (Bern - Vevey) take Châtel St Denis exit no. 2 and turn towards Les Paccots (1 km). Site is on left up hill. GPS: 46.52513, 6.91828

Charges guide

Per person	CHF 6.50
child (6-16 yrs)	CHF 4.50
pitch	CHF 16.50
electricity	CHF 4.50

No credit cards. Less 10% on showing this guide. Euros are accepted.

Churwalden

Camping Pradafenz

Girabodaweg 34, CH-7075 Churwalden (Graubünden) T: 081 382 1921. E: camping@pradafenz.ch

alanrogers.com/CH9820

In the heart of the village of Churwalden on the Chur - St Moritz road, Pradafenz makes a convenient night stop and being amidst the mountains, is also an excellent base for walking and exploring this scenic area. At first sight, this appears to be a site for static holiday caravans but three large rectangular terraces at the front take 50 touring units. This area has a hardstanding of concrete frets with grass growing through and super pitch facilities of electricity (10A), drainage, gas and TV sockets. A flat meadow is also available for tents or as an overflow for caravans. Although the gravel road which leads to the tourers' terrace is not very steep, the owner will tow caravans there with his tractor if required.

Facilities

New sanitary block is well appointed and heated and includes some washbasins in cabins. Baby room. Another two blocks are in the touring section. Washing machines, dryers and separate drying room. Motorcaravan services. Gas supplies. Small restaurant. WiFi. Off site: Bicycle hire 200 m. Restaurants and shops 300 m. in village. Municipal outdoor pool 500 m. Riding 3.5 km. Fishing 4 km. Golf 5 km.

Open: 1 June - 31 October, 15 December - 10 April.

Directions

Churwalden is 10 km. south of Chur. From Chur take road towards Lenzerheide. It is initially a fairly long, steep climb with one tight hairpin. In centre of Churwalden turn right in front of the tourist office towards the site. GPS: 46.77666, 9.54128

Charges guide

Per unit incl. 2 persons and electricity (winter + meter)	CHF 32.50 - 33.00
extra person	CHF 8.00

Disentis

TCS Camping Fontanivas

Via Fontanivas 9, CH-7180 Disentis (Graubünden) T: 081 947 4422. E: camping.disentis@tcs.ch

alanrogers.com/CH9865

Nestled in the Surselva valley with superb views of the surrounding mountains, this is an attractive site with its own lake. Surrounded by tall pine trees, the site is owned by the Touring Club of Switzerland, the Swiss version of the AA, and provides 110 flat, level pitches, 81 with 13A electricity. There are plenty of opportunities for walks, nature trails and cycle rides, whilst the more adventurous can enjoy canyoning, rafting, hang-gliding or mountain biking. For children, the playground is a challenging combination of water, rocks and bridges. An ideal holiday spot for both sports fans and nature lovers.

Facilities

The excellent sanitary block is well maintained with free showers and hairdryers. Facilities for disabled visitors. Baby room. Washing machine and dryer. Motorcaravan services. Shop. Restaurant/bar. Play room. Bicycle hire. Fishing. Caravans and tent bungalows to rent. WiFi throughout (charged). Off site: Disentis 2 km. Indoor pool.

Open: 20 April - 23 September.

Directions

The site is 2 km. south of Disentis. From Andermatt take the Oberalppass to Disentis. In town at T-junction turn right towards Lukmanier. Site is at bottom of hill on the left, past the droopy power cables. From the East, on arriving in the town, keep left onto the Lukmanier Road. GPS: 46.697, 8.85272

Charges 2012

Per unit incl. 2 persons and electricity	CHF 36.30 - 44.30
extra person	CHF 7.40 - 9.40

Engelberg

Camping Eienwäldli

Wasserfallstrasse 108, CH-6390 Engelberg (Unterwalden) T: 041 637 1949. E: info@eienwaeldli.ch

alanrogers.com/CH9570

This super site has facilities which must make it one of the best in Switzerland. It is situated in a beautiful location 3,500 feet above sea level, surrounded by mountains on the edge of the delightful village of Engelberg. Half of the site is taken up by static caravans which are grouped together at one side. The camping area is in two parts – nearest the entrance there are 57 hardstandings for caravans and motorcaravans, all with electricity (metered) and beyond this is a flat meadow for about 70 tents. Reception can be found in the very modern foyer of the Eienwäldli Hotel which also houses the indoor pool, health complex, shop and café/bar.

Facilities

The main toilet block, heated in cool weather, is situated at the rear of the hotel and has free hot water in washbasins (in cabins) and (charged) showers. A new modern toilet block has been added near the top end of the site. Washing machines and dryers. Shop. Café/bar. Small lounge. Indoor pool complex. Ski facilities including a drying room. Large play area with a rafting pool fed by fresh water from the mountain stream. Torches useful. TV. WiFi. Golf. Off site: Golf driving range and 18-hole course nearby. Fishing and bicycle hire 1 km. Riding 2 km.

Open: All year.

Directions

From N2 Gotthard motorway, leave at exit 33 Stans-Sud and follow signs to Engelberg. Turn right at T-junction on edge of town and follow signs to 'Wasserfall' and site. GPS: 46.80940, 8.42367

Charges guide

Per person	CHF 6.00 - 9.00
child (6-15 yrs)	CHF 3.00 - 4.50
pitch incl. electricity (plus meter)	CHF 10.00 - 17.00
dog	CHF 1.30 - 2.00

Credit cards accepted (surcharge).

Frutigen

Camping Grassi

Grassiweg 60, CH-3714 Frutigen (Bern) T: 033 671 1149. E: campinggrassi@bluewin.ch

alanrogers.com/CH9360

This is a small site with about half the pitches occupied by static caravans, used by their owners for weekends and holidays. The 70 or so places available for tourists are not marked out but it is said that the site is not allowed to become overcrowded. Most places are on level grass with two small terraces at the end of the site. There is little shade but the site is set in a river valley with trees on the hills which enclose the area. Electricity is available for all pitches but long leads may be required in parts. It would make a useful overnight stop en-route for Kandersteg and the railway station where cars can join the train for transportation through the Lotschberg Tunnel to the Rhône Valley and Simplon Pass, or for a longer stay to explore the Bernese Oberland.

Facilities

The well constructed, heated sanitary block is of good quality. Washing machine and dryer. Gas supplies. Motorcaravan services. Communal room with TV. Kiosk (1/7-31/8). Play area and play house. Mountain bike hire. Fishing. Bicycle hire. WiFi. Off site: Shops and restaurants 10 minutes walk away in village. Riding 2 km. Outdoor and indoor pools, tennis and minigolf in Frutigen. A new sauna and wellness centre has recently opened in the village. Skiing and walking.

Open: All year.

Directions

Take Kandersteg road from Spiez and leave at Frutigen Dorf exit from where site is signed.
GPS: 46.58173, 7.64219

Charges guide

Per unit incl. 2 persons and electricity	CHF 25.80 - 32.30
extra person	CHF 6.40
child (1-16 yrs)	CHF 1.50 - 3.20
dog	CHF 1.50

Gampelen

TCS Camping Fanel

Sestrasse 50, CH-3236 Gampelen (Bern) T: 032 313 2333. E: camping.gampelen@tcs.ch

alanrogers.com/CH9055

This Swiss Touring Club site is particularly suited to families with children. From the terrace of a well provisioned self-service restaurant there is a view of the small swimming pool and the large grass area that leads to the gently shelving waters of the lake and a small wooden jetty. The site has 860 pitches (140 for tourists) which means that it becomes quite busy at weekends and holidays. The touring pitches are divided into three sections; one with large service facilities, an open grass area and another among the pine trees with little grass. This quiet site is located in a protected nature area, a habitat for beavers, wild boar and foxes. The site has its own harbour from which boats can be launched and where canoes and paddle boats can be rented.

Facilities

Three modern, well maintained toilet blocks with free showers and some washbasins in cabins. Facilities for disabled visitors. Baby room. Laundry room with washing machines and dryers. Motorcaravan service point. Modern, well appointed self service restaurant with takeaway. Shop. Gas supplies. Internet access. WiFi throughout (charged). Play area. Bicycle hire. Archery. Fishing and boat launching. Canoes and paddle boats for hire. Off site: Boat hire and trips. St. Peter's Island. Erlach and its castle. The Zoo at Seeteufel.

Open: 4 April - 7 October.

Directions

Site is on the northeast shore of Lake Neuchâtel. From A1 exit 29 (Murten) or exit 30 (Kerzers) travel north towards Neuchâtel as far as village of Gampelen where site is well signed.
GPS: 47.001321, 7.040568

Charges guide

Per unit incl. 2 persons and electricity	CHF 35.70 - 53.40
extra person	CHF 7.60 - 9.20
child (6-15 yrs)	CHF 3.80 - 4.60
dog	CHF 3.00 - 5.00

Grindelwald

Camping Gletscherdorf

Gletscherdorf 31, CH-3818 Grindelwald (Bern) T: 033 853 1429. E: info@gletscherdorf.ch

alanrogers.com/CH9480

Set in a flat river valley on the edge of Grindelwald, one of Switzerland's best known winter and summer resorts, Gletscherdorf enjoys wonderful mountain views, particularly of the nearby north face of the Eiger. The site's new owners have a programme of improvements planned for the grounds, pitches and facilities. There are 120 pitches in total, 40 of which are available for touring. Most are marked and have electricity connections (10A), with a few others in an overflow field. This is, above all, a very quiet, friendly site for those who wish to enjoy the peaceful mountain air, walking, climbing and exploring with a mountain climbing school in Grindelwald.

Facilities

Excellent small, heated, fully equipped, sanitary block. Washing machines and dryer. Motorcaravan services. Gas supplies. Small shop for basic food items. Community room. Torches useful. WiFi (free). Dogs are not accepted. Off site: Town shops and restaurants within walking distance. Bicycle hire, indoor pool and golf 1 km.

Open: 1 May - 20 October.

Directions

To reach site, go through the town and turn right at site signs, just by the church, after the town centre. Ignore sat nav instruction to turn before this. The approach road is quite narrow and steep down hill and you should depart by the same route. GPS: 46.62091, 8.04491

Charges guide

Per unit incl. 2 persons and electricity	CHF 30.00 - 36.00
extra person	CHF 7.50 - 8.50

Gwatt

TCS Camping Thunersee

CH-3770 Gwatt (Bern) T: 033 336 4067. E: camping.gwatt@bluewin.ch

alanrogers.com/CH9330

Thunersee is an ideal site for those who wish to explore this part of the Bernese Oberland and who would enjoy staying on a small site in a quiet area, away from the larger sites and town atmosphere of Interlaken. There are 75 numbered, but unmarked pitches for tourists, most with 4A electricity available, and about the same number of static units. There are hard access roads but cars must be parked away from the pitches. Although there are some trees, there is little shade in the main camping area. Direct access to the lake is available for swimming and boating.

Facilities

Single, modern, well constructed sanitary block, fully equipped with hot water provided for washbasins and showers. Facilities should be adequate in high season. Rooms for disabled visitors. Washing machine and dryer. Motorcaravan services. Shop. Good restaurant with terrace. Lake swimming and boating. Bicycle hire. Internet access and WiFi. Off site: Bus stop outside entrance. Municipal play park adjacent. Many cycle tracks. Lakeside walks. Marina and slipway for your own craft.

Open: 1 April - early October.

Directions

From Berne - Thun - Interlaken autoroute, take exit Thun-Süd for Gwatt and follow signs for Gwatt. Site is signed near town centre to the left. Coming from Spiez, the site is signposted on the right, opposite a large TCS signboard. GPS: 46.72749, 7.6276

Charges 2012

Per unit incl. 2 persons and electricity	CHF 35.40 - 52.80
extra person	CHF 7.20 - 9.40
child (6-15 yrs)	CHF 3.60 - 4.70

Hasliberg

Camping Hofstatt-Derfli

Hofstatt, CH-6085 Hasliberg Goldern (Bern) T: 033 971 3707. E: welcome@derfli.ch

alanrogers.com/CH9500

This attractive site has been created by a goldsmith and her husband. Small and family run, with 45 pitches, it is in a quiet location, over 1,000 metres high at the end of a small village in the Berner Oberland. One innovation is the metre-high mushrooms – with their white-dotted red tops they are difficult to miss. They provide the electrical supply points for the 35 touring pitches and site lighting. The grass pitches are level, some with gravel hardstanding for motorcaravans and the gently sloping site is partly surrounded by trees with mountain top views across the valley.

Facilities

Well maintained all the year round, sanitary facilities are housed in the main building. Showers controllable and free, some washbasins in cabins. Baby areas. Kitchen to rent in community room. Laundry facilities. Motorcaravan service point, Small shop. Play area. Bicycle hire. Ski and snowboard room, ski lifts at 1.5 and 2 km. New hot tub. Charcoal barbecues are not permitted. WiFi throughout (charged). Off site: Shop and restaurant 300 m. in village. Lots of scenic walking in the region. Riding 2.5 km. Fishing 15 km.

Open: 15 May - 25 October, 25 December - 15 April.

Directions

Site is 25 km. east-northeast of Interlaken. From A8 exit 30 (Unterbach) follow signs for Luzern and Brünig Pass. At the top Brünig Pass follow signs for Hasliberg (you may spot a dwarf on a swing). Head towards Hasliberg Goldern where site is signed at bottom end of village on the right. GPS: 46.73687, 8.19537

Charges 2012

Per unit incl. 2 persons	CHF 28.00 - 38.00
electricity per kWh	CHF 0.60
extra person	CHF 8.00 - 9.00

No credit cards.

Interlaken

Camping Lazy Rancho 4

Lehnweg 6, CH-3800 Interlaken (Bern) T: 033 822 8716. E: info@lazyrancho.ch

alanrogers.com/CH9430

This super site is in a quiet location with fantastic views of the dramatic mountains of Eiger, Monch and Jungfrau. Neat, orderly and well maintained, the site is situated in a wide valley just 1 km. from Lake Thun and 1.5 km. from Interlaken. The English speaking owners lovingly care for the site and will endeavour to make you feel very welcome. Connected by gravel roads, the 155 pitches, of which 90 are for touring units, are on well tended level grass (some with hardstanding, all with 10A electricity). There are 28 pitches also with water and waste water drainage. This is a quiet friendly site, popular with British visitors. The owners offer advice on day trips out, and how to get the best bargains on the railway.

Facilities

Two good sanitary blocks are both heated with free hot showers, good facilities for disabled campers and a baby room. Laundry. Campers' kitchen with microwave, cooker, fridge and utensils. Motorcaravan service point. Well stocked shop. TV and games room. Play area. Small swimming pool. Bicycle hire (June-Aug). Free WiFi. Free bus in the Interlaken area – bus stop is five minutes walk from site. Off site: Cycle trails and waymarked footpaths. Riding 500 m. Golf and bicycle hire 1 km. Lake Thun for fishing 1.5 km. Boat launching 1.5 km. Interlaken and leisure centre 2 km.

Open: 6 April - 20 October.

Directions

Site is on north side of Lake Thun. From road 8 (Thun - Interlaken) on south side of lake take exit 24 Interlaken West. Follow towards lake at roundabout then follow signs for campings. Lazy Rancho is Camp 4. The last 500 m. is a little narrow but no problem. GPS: 46.68605, 7.830633

Charges 2012

Per unit incl. 2 persons and electricity	CHF 30.50 - 54.50
extra person	CHF 6.00 - 8.00
child (6-15 yrs)	CHF 3.50 - 4.80
dog	free - CHF 3.00

Payment also accepted in euros.

Interlaken

Camping Manor Farm 1

Seestraße 201, CH-3800 Interlaken-Thunersee (Bern) T: 033 822 2264. E: manorfarm1@swisscamps.ch

alanrogers.com/CH9420

Manor Farm has been popular with British visitors for many years, as this is one of the traditional touring areas of Switzerland. The flat terrain is divided into 525 individual, numbered pitches which vary considerably both in size (60-100 sq.m) and price. There is shade in some places. There are 144 pitches equipped with electricity (4/13A), water and drainage, and 55 also have cable TV connections. Reservations can be made, although you should find space, except perhaps in late July/early August when the best places may be taken. Around 40 per cent of the pitches are taken by permanent or letting units and a tour operator.

Facilities

Seven separate toilet blocks are heated. They include free hot water for baths and showers. Twenty private toilet units are for rent. Laundry facilities. Motorcaravan services. Gas supplies. Excellent shop (1/4-15/10). Site-owned restaurant adjoining (1/3-30/10). Snack bar with takeaway (1/7-20/8). TV room. Playground and paddling pool. Minigolf. Bicycle hire. Sailing and windsurfing school. Lake swimming. Boat hire (slipway for your own). Fishing. Activities and entertainment in high season. Excursions. Max. 1 dog. WiFi (charged). Off site: Golf (18 holes) 500 m. (handicap card). Riding 3 km. Cycling and walking.

Open: All year.

Directions

Site is 3 km. west of Interlaken along the road running north of the Thuner See towards Thun. Follow signs for 'Camp 1'. From A8 (bypassing Interlaken) take exit 24 marked 'Gunten, Beatenberg', which is a spur road bringing you out close to site. GPS: 46.68129, 7.81524

Charges guide

Per unit incl. 2 persons and electricity	CHF 37.00 - 63.50
extra person	CHF 10.50
child (6-15 yrs)	CHF 5.00
dog	CHF 4.00

Interlaken

Camping Alpenblick

Seestrasse 130, Unterseen, CH-3800 Interlaken (Bern) T: 033 822 7757. E: info@camping-alpenblick.ch

alanrogers.com/CH9425

Alpenblick is an all-year site, located at the heart of the Bernese Oberland just 100 m. from Lake Thun. Susanne Knecht and George Zehntner took over the site in 2006 and have made a number of improvements, including an excellent new toilet block. There are 80 touring pitches and a further 80 residential pitches. The touring pitches have been re-turfed and all have electrical connections (10A). Some good hardstanding pitches are available for motorcaravans. There are also several teepees available for rent. One of these, complete with bar and indoor barbecue, is used for socialising in the evening and is very popular with campers and local residents.

Facilities

New toilet block. Laundry facilities. Shop with daily delivery of fresh bread, bistro and takeaway (all 1/4-20/10). Teepee with bar and barbecue for socialising and events. Playground. Basketball. Teepees for rent. WiFi. Off site: Nearest lake beach 100 m. Walking and cycle routes. Fishing. Riding. Boat trips on Lake Thun. Neuhaus lakeside restaurant and windsurfing school. Golf.

Open: All year.

Directions

Approaching from Thun and Bern on road no. 8 leave at exit 24 (Interlaken West). Head north towards Neuhaus and follow signs to Camping no. 2. GPS: 46.67999, 7.81728

Charges guide

Per unit incl. 2 persons and electricity	CHF 33.70 - 48.90
extra person	CHF 5.60 - 7.20

No credit cards.

Interlaken

TCS Camping Interlaken Ost

Brienzstrasse 24, CH-3800 Interlaken-Ost (Bern) T: 033 822 4434. E: camping.interlaken@tcs.ch

alanrogers.com/CH9435

Camping Interlaken is a member of the Touring Club Suisse and has a good location alongside River Aar, on the edge of Interlaken and 500 m. from Lake Brienz (a swimming pool is 300 m. away). This is a smart site with 100 grassy, sunny pitches, with some fine views of the Oberland. Around 50 pitches are equipped with 6A electricity. A number of particularly large pitches are available (supplement payable) and one section for motorcaravans has direct riverside access. Fully equipped tents are also available for rent. Canoes, bicycles and electric cycles are all available for rent on site.

Facilities

Modern sanitary facilities include provision for disabled visitors (key access). Direct river access. Canoe and bicycle hire. Boat launching. Small shop. Fishing. Games room. Play area. Tourist information. Occasional activities. Rooms in new chalet complex for rent. Internet access. WiFi throughout (charged). Off site: Swimming pool 300 m. Lake Brienz 500 m. Interlaken Ost station.

Open: 4 April - 7 October.

Directions

Approaching from Bern or Lucerne on A8 motorway take the Ringgenberg exit to the east of Interlaken. Follow signs to Goldswil and signs to camping Number 6. GPS: 46.692434, 7.868652

Charges 2012

Per unit incl. 2 persons and electricity	CHF 33.60 - 48.80
extra person	CHF 6.80 - 8.40

Interlaken

Camping Jungfraublick

Gsteigstrasse 80, Matten, CH-3800 Interlaken (Bern) T: 033 822 4414. E: info@jungfraublick.ch

alanrogers.com/CH9440

The Berner Oberland is one of the most scenic and well known areas of Switzerland with Interlaken probably the best known summer resort. Situated in the village of Matten, Jungfraublick is a delightful, medium sized site with splendid views up the Lauterbrunnen valley to the Jungfrau mountain. The 90 touring pitches (60-90 sq.m) with electricity connections (6A) are in regular rows on level, well cut grass. A number of fruit trees adorn but do not offer much shade. The 30 static caravans are to one side of the tourist area and do not intrude. There is some traffic noise from the main road.

Facilities

The sanitary facilities, although rather dated, are fully equipped and there is provision for disabled visitors. Showers are on payment, as is hot water for dishwashing. Washing machines and dryers. Motorcaravan services. Shop for basics (from 1/6). Small swimming pool (12x8 m) open mid-June-end Aug. according to the weather. Heated communal room with TV and electronic games. Barbecues must be off the ground. Communal barbecue with seating. Internet access and free WiFi. Off site: Buses into Interlaken pass the entrance. Wilderswil train station 10 minutes walk. Bicycle hire 700 m. Town 1 km. Golf, riding and fishing 4 km.

Open: 1 May - 20 September.

Directions

Take the exit Nr. 25 from the N8 motorway, turn towards Interlaken. Site is within 500 m. on left. GPS: 46.67335, 7.86649

Charges guide

Per unit incl. 2 persons and electricity	CHF 26.80 - 51.20
extra person	CHF 7.80 - 9.00
child (4-16 yrs)	CHF 3.80 - 4.50

Kandersteg

Camping Rendez-vous

Hubleweg, CH-3718 Kandersteg (Bern) T: 033 675 1534. E: rendez-vous.camping@bluewin.ch

alanrogers.com/CH9370

Camping Rendez-vous is an all year site located at an altitude of 1,200 m, just outside the delightful mountain village of Kandersteg. There are 60 terraced touring pitches here and a further 20 pitches are occupied by residential caravans. The pitches are grassy and many have fine views over the surrounding mountain scenery. Although there are few amenities on site, Kandersteg is nearby and is an important mountain resort with a good selection of shops and restaurants, as well as a railway station and cable car service. Camping Rendez-vous is an excellent starting point for many of the area's superb walking and mountain biking opportunites, with over 500 km. of marked trails available. The site owners will be pleased to recommend routes. Adjacent to the site is the new Oeschinensee cable car which gives access to a summer toboggan run. During the winter, skiing and other winter sports are possible, with a ski school located nearby.

Facilities

Heated toilet block is adequate. Washing machines and dryers. Small shop, bar, restaurant and takeaway service (all year) at site entrance. WiFi (charged). Off site: Bicycle hire, fishing and riding within 1 km. Kandersteg with wide range of shops, restaurants and bars 1 km. Oeschinensee cable car. Railway station and cable cars. Many walking paths and cycle trails.

Open: All year.

Directions

From the north, take the N6 Bern - Spiez motorway and take the Kandersteg exit. Follow signs to Kandersteg Dorf (25 km) and the site is well signed in the village. GPS: 46.49735, 7.68342

Charges guide

Per unit incl. 2 persons	CHF 22.00 - 36.00
electricity per kWh	CHF 0.70
extra person	CHF 7.00
child (1-16 yrs)	CHF 3.50
dog	CHF 3.00

Krattigen

Camping Stuhlegg

Stueleggstrasse 7, CH-3704 Krattigen (Bern) T: 033 654 2723. E: campstuhlegg@bluewin.ch

alanrogers.com/CH9410

On the outskirts of the village of Krattigen, Camping Stuhlegg is a quiet and attractive site, located well above the lake and with beautiful, wide ranging views over the lake to the mountains beyond. The 60 touring pitches, all with electricity (10/13A Europlug) are arranged on grassy terraced areas, some for motorcaravans having hardstanding. A few young trees provide shade. The friendly bar and bistro is also popular as a meeting point for the villagers, which gives a touch of local colour. This is a site where you can relax and enjoy the fresh mountain air and scenery. The site owner, Herr Schweizer and his partner Frau Gasser speak excellent English.

Facilities

Two modern sanitary facilities, the one near the entrance is heated, the other at the top of the site is for summer use and unheated. They contain all the usual facilities, showers operate with either coins or tokens. Laundry room. Baby bath. Motorcaravan service point. Shop, bar and bistro with takeaway (all open as site). Delightful solar heated natural swimming pool with shallow section for children. TV room. Play area. Internet point. WiFi (free). Off site: Plenty of footpaths in the immediate area. Bicycle hire 800 m. Riding, golf and fishing 4 km. Buses run twice an hour to Spiez, where all manner of watersports and cruises can be arranged.

Open: All year excl. November.

Directions

Site is almost halfway between Spiez and Interlaken on the southern side of the Thunersee. Leave A8 at exit 20 and follow signs for Krattigen. Site is signed at top of village to the right (north).
GPS: 46.657917, 7.717933

Charges guide

Per unit incl. 2 persons and electricity	CHF 28.00 - 37.00
extra person	CHF 6.00 - 7.00
child	CHF 4.60 - 5.00
dog	CHF 3.00

Kreuzlingen

Camping Fischerhaus

Promenadenstrasse 52, CH-8280 Kreuzlingen (Thurgau) T: 071 688 4903.
E: camping.fischerhaus@bluewin.ch **alanrogers.com/CH9185**

Camping Fischerhaus is tucked away behind the town's light industrial area and next to Lake Constance. It provides 250 pitches of which 150 are for tourers, all with 10A electricity supply. These are mainly on grass, with some long hardstandings for larger outfits, and are located towards the back of the site. The seasonal pitches are grouped together near reception and the lakeside. A small toilet block serves the touring area, with full sanitary facilities near reception. The restaurant and bar are pleasantly located by the lakeside. The town of Kreuzlingen is a short walk away along the banks of the lake past a marina.

Facilities

The main sanitary block, near reception, has WCs, showers and facilities for disabled visitors. The second block, near the area used by tourers, just has WCs. Washing machines and dryer. Small shop for basics. Hot and cold snacks available from reception. Indoor and outdoor seating areas. Restaurant and bar overlooking lake. Playground. Fishing. Communal barbecue areas. Dogs are not accepted. Off site: Swimming pool adjacent (free for campers).

Open: 20 March - 26 October.

Directions

Site is at the east side of Kreuzlingen on the banks of Lake Constance. It is well signed from all directions as is the adjoining swimming pool.
GPS: 47.64705, 9.19873

Charges guide

Per person	CHF 9.50
child (6-16 yrs)	CHF 4.50
pitch incl. electricity	CHF 17.00 - 19.50
tent pitch	CHF 8.00 - 16.00

La Fouly

Camping Des Glaciers

CH-1944 La Fouly (Valais) T: 027 783 1826. E: info@camping-glaciers.ch

alanrogers.com/CH9660

Camping des Glaciers is set amidst magnificent mountain scenery in a peaceful location in the beautiful Ferret Valley, 1,600 m. above sea level (care is needed with long units). The site offers some pitches in an open, undulating meadow and the rest are level, individual plots of varying sizes in small clearings, between bushes and shrubs or under tall pines. Most of the 220 pitches have 10A electricity. M. Alain Darbellay has now taken over the reins from his mother, who ran the site for 40 years, and he intends to maintain the strong family interest and friendships built up over the years. Additional land has been added to increase the numbers of pitches available.

Facilities

Three sanitary units of exceptional quality are heated when necessary. The newest unit has super facilities for children and wide access for disabled visitors. Hot water is free in all washbasins (some in cabins), showers and sinks. British style WCs. Washing machines and dryers in each block, one block has a drying room, another a baby room. Gas supplies. Motorcaravan services. Small shop. Recreation room with TV. Playground. WiFi (charged). Torches and long leads may be useful. Off site: Shops and restaurants 500 m. Riding 8 km. Bicycle hire 20 km.

Open: 15 May - 30 September.

Directions

Leave Martigny - Gd St Bernard road (no. 21/E27) to the right where signposted Orsieres/La Fouly. Site is signed on right at end of La Fouly village. Take care along narrow access road. GPS: 45.93347, 7.09367

Charges guide

Per unit incl. 2 persons and electricity	CHF 30.00 - 35.50
extra person	CHF 8.00
child (2-12 yrs)	CHF 4.00
dog	CHF 3.00

Less 20% in May, June and September.

Landquart

TCS Camping Neue Ganda

Ganda 21, CH-7302 Landquart (Graubünden) T: 081 322 3955. E: camping.landquart@tcs.ch

alanrogers.com/CH9850

Situated close to the Klosters - Davos road and the nearby town of Landquart, this deep valley campsite provides a comfortable night stop near the A13 motorway. The 80 touring pitches are not marked or separated but are all on level grass off a central gravel road through the long, narrow wooded site. All pitches have 6/10A electricity. The many static caravans are mostly hidden from view situated in small alcoves. A modern, timber clad building at the entrance houses all the necessary facilities – reception, community room and sanitary facilities. The restaurant/shop adjacent is open all year.

Facilities

The toilet block is extremely well appointed and can be heated. Facilities for disabled visitors. Baby room. Washing machine and dryer. Drying room. Motorcaravan services. Restaurant. Shop. Internet. WiFi throughout (charged). Off site: Tennis, riding and canoeing nearby. Rambling. Cycling tours. Fishing 2 km.

Open: All year excl. 27 February - 15 March and 15 October - 6 December.

Directions

From A13 motorway take Landquart exit 14 and follow road to Davos. 800 m. after crossing large bridge, take the slip road to the right (signed). At the bottom of the slope turn left under the road bridge and follow the signs to the site. Note reception is closed 11.00-16.00. GPS: 46.96900, 9.58933

Charges 2012

Per unit incl. 2 persons and electricity	CHF 35.50 - 41.60
extra person	CHF 7.00 - 8.80

Camping Cheques accepted.

Langwiesen

TCS Camping Rheinwiesen

Haupt Strasse, CH-8246 Langwiesen (Schaffhausen) T: 052 659 3300. E: camping.schaffhausen@tcs.ch

alanrogers.com/CH9160

Rheinwiesen is a friendly site in a very pleasant setting on the banks of the Rhine, with plenty of shade from a variety of tall trees. It is level and grassy, the first half being open lawns and the rest of the touring area wooded, with numbered pitches (mostly small – up to 70 sq.m). There are many day visitors in summer as the site is ideally placed for swimming, canoeing and diving in the Rhine. Whilst here, you would not want to miss the impressive waterfalls at Schaffhausen, 150 m. wide and 25 m. high.

Facilities

For tourers there is an old, but clean, building which might be under pressure at the busiest times. Washing machine and dryer. Bar/snack bar with covered terrace for burgers etc. open daily. Bread to order, some essentials kept. Pool room also used as wet weather rest room. Two shallow paddling pools, with play area close by. Electro-bicycle hire. Dogs are not accepted at any time. Off site: Shop 500 m. Bicycle hire 2 km.

Open: 20 April - 7 October.

Directions

From Schaffhausen head east towards Kreuzlingen (road no. 13) for about 2.5 km. Site is signed just before Langwiesen. If coming from the east, it is a tight turn into the site. GPS: 47.68733, 8.65583

Charges 2012

Per unit incl. 2 persons and electricity	CHF 33.60 - 46.60
extra person	CHF 6.80 - 8.80

Camping Cheques accepted.

Lausanne

Camping De Vidy

Chemin du Camping 3, CH-1007 Lausanne (Vaud) T: 021 622 5000. E: info@clv.ch

alanrogers.com/CH9270

The ancient city of Lausanne spills down the hillside towards Lake Geneva until it meets the peaceful park in which this site is situated. Owned by the city, the managers have enhanced its neat and tidy appearance by planting many flowers and shrubs. Hard access roads separate the site into sections for tents, caravans and motorcaravans, with 10A electrical connections in all parts, except the tent areas. Pitches are on flat grass, numbered but not marked out, with 260 (of 350) for tourers. Some large pitches near the lake are suitable for American type motorhomes. The playground, games and restaurant are all close to the lakeside and do not disturb the majority of campers.

Facilities

Three excellent sanitary blocks, one heated, have mostly British and some Turkish style WCs, hot water in washbasins, sinks and showers with warm, pre-mixed water. Facilities for disabled visitors. Motorcaravan services (Euro-Relais). Gas supplies. Shop and self-service bar/restaurant (1/5-30/9). Takeaway (high season). Playground. Weekend entertainment in high season. Lake swimming. Fishing. Internet point and WiFi (charged). Reception has tourist information on Lausanne.

Off site: Free pass for local transport. Boat excursions on the lake.

Open: All year.

Directions

Site is left of road to Geneva, 500 m. west of La Maladière. Take N1 autobahn Lausanne-Süd, exit no. 3 La Maladière, and at this roundabout almost turn back on yourself following signs for CIO and camping. At traffic lights turn left, then on for site. Take care at La Maladière roundabout (large trolley buses). From the south and east on the N9, exit at J10 and follow signs for CIO (Olympic symbols). Site signed next to CIO HQ. GPS: 46.51600, 6.59900

Charges guide

Per unit incl. 2 persons and electricity	CHF 35.00 - 36.00
extra person	CHF 8.50

Lauterbrunnen

Camping Jungfrau

CH-3822 Lauterbrunnen (Bern) T: 033 856 2010. E: info@camping-jungfrau.ch

alanrogers.com/CH9460

This friendly site has a very imposing and dramatic situation in a steep valley with a fine view of the Jungfrau at the end. It is a popular site and, although you should usually find space, in season do not arrive too late. A fairly extensive area with grass pitches and hardcore access roads. All 391 pitches (250 for touring) have shade in parts, electrical connections (13A) and 50 have water and drainage also. Over 30% of the pitches are taken by seasonal caravans and it is used by two tour operators. Family owned and run by Herr and Frau Fuchs, you can be sure of a warm welcome and English is spoken. You can laze here amid real mountain scenery, though it does lose the sun a little early. There are many active pursuits available in the area, as well as trips on the Jungfrau railway and mountain lifts.

Facilities

Three fully equipped modern sanitary blocks can be heated in winter and one provides facilities for disabled visitors. Baby baths. Laundry facilities. Motorcaravan services. Well equipped campers' kitchen. Excellent shop with photo printing facility. Self-service restaurant with takeaway (May-end Oct). General room with tables and chairs, TV, drink machines, amusements. Playgrounds and covered play area. Excursions and some entertainment in high season. Mountain bike hire. Internet point and WiFi. ATM. Drying room. Ski store. Off site: Free bus to ski station (in winter only).

Open: All year.

Directions

Go through Lauterbrunnen and fork right at far end (look for signpost) before road bends left, 100 m. before church. The final approach is not very wide. GPS: 46.58807, 7.91077

Charges guide

Per person	CHF 9.80 - 11.90
child (6-15 yrs)	CHF 4.80 - 5.50
pitch incl. electricity (plus meter in winter)	CHF 17.00 - 29.50
dog	CHF 3.00

Discounts for camping carnet and for stays over 3 nights outside high season.

Le Landeron

Camping des Pêches

Route du Port, CH-2525 Le Landeron (Neuchâtel) T: **032 751 2900.** E: **info@camping-lelanderon.ch**

alanrogers.com/CH9040

This recently constructed, touring campsite is on the side of Lake Biel and river Thielle, and close to the old town of Le Landeron. The site is divided into two sections, one side of the road for static caravans, and on the other is the modern campsite for tourers. The 180 touring pitches are all on level grass, numbered but not separated; a few have shade, 150 have electricity (10A) and many conveniently placed water points. All the facilities were exceptionally well maintained and in pristine condition during our visit throughout a busy holiday weekend.

Facilities

The spacious, modern sanitary block contains all the usual facilities including a food preparation area with six cooking rings, a large freezer and refrigerator. Payment for showers is by card. Baby room. Facilities for disabled visitors. Laundry. Motorcaravan service point. Shop, restaurant and takeaway (all season). Community room and small café in reception building. Playground. Bicycle hire. TV and general room. WiFi. Off site: Fishing, sailing and swimming pool 300 m. (16/5-1/9; charged). Golf and riding 7 km.

Open: 1 April - 15 October

Directions

Le Landeron is signed from the Neuchâtel - Biel motorway, exit 19 and site is well signed from the town. GPS: 47.05254, 7.06978

Charges guide

Per unit incl. 2 persons and electricity	CHF 33.50 - 41.00
extra person	CHF 9.00
child (6-16 yrs)	CHF 4.00

Le Prese

Camping Cavresc

CH-7746 Le Prese (Graubünden) T: 081 844 0259. E: camping.cavresc@bleuwin.ch

alanrogers.com/CH9855

Le Prese is on the Tirano to St Moritz road, south of the Bernina Pass. Camping Cavresc is on grassy meadows in the Valposchiano valley and, with its southern climate, peaceful ambience and beautiful views, is a very good, newly built site with ultramodern sanitary facilities. For tourers there are 30 flat, level pitches, all with 10A electricity and water, plus a large area for around 50 tents. There is little shade. If the campsite reception is unmanned, walk back into town, as the Sertori family who own the site also run the small well stocked supermarket. Le Prese is close to Italy and the Poschiavo Lake.

Facilities

The excellent toilet block is very well maintained. Showers on payment. Facilities for disabled visitors. Washing machines, dryers and iron. Motorcaravan services. Restaurant/bar (June-Oct). Small shop. Swimming pool (high season). There are plans for outdoor ice-skating to be added. Off site: Le Prese 250 m. Windsurfing, sailing and skiing.

Open: All year.

Directions

Le Prese is 6 km. south of Poschiavo. Coming from Italy on road no. 29, the site is towards the southern end of the town. Turn right towards Pagnoncini/Cantone and site is on right in about 100 m. Go over a humpback bridge at the entrance. GPS: 46.2949, 10.0801

Charges guide

Per unit incl. 2 persons and electricity	CHF 36.00 - 46.00
extra person	CHF 10.00 - 13.00
child (6-16 yrs)	CHF 4.00 - 6.00
dog	CHF 2.00

Les Haudères

Camping de Molignon

route de Molignon, 163, CH-1984 Les Haudères (Valais) T: 027 283 1240. E: info@molignon.ch

alanrogers.com/CH9670

Camping de Molignon, surrounded by mountains, is a peaceful haven 1,450 m. above sea level. The rushing stream at the bottom of the site and the sound of cow bells and birdsong are likely to be the only disturbing factors in summer. The 100 pitches for tourists (75 with 10A electricity) are on well tended terraces leading down to the river. Excellent English is spoken by the owner's son who is now running the site. He is always pleased to give information on all that is available from the campsite. The easy uphill drive from Sion in the Rhône Valley is enhanced by ancient villages and the Pyramids of Euseigne.

Facilities

Two fully equipped sanitary blocks, heated in cool weather, with free hot showers. Baby room. Washing machines and dryer. Kitchen for hikers. Motorcaravan services. Gas supplies. Shop for basic supplies (15/6-15/9). Restaurant. Heated swimming pool with cover for cool weather (6x12 m). Sitting room for games and reading. Playground. Guided walks, climbing, geological museum, winter skiing. Fishing. Off site: Tennis and hang-gliding near. Ski and sports gear hire 1 km. Bicycle hire 1 km. Riding 1.5 km. Langlauf in winter.

Open: All year.

Directions

Leave the motorway at J27 and follow signs southwards from Sion for the Val d'Herens through Evolène to Les Haudères where site is signed on the right at the beginning of the village. GPS: 46.09003, 7.50722

Charges guide

Per unit incl. 2 persons and electricity	CHF 28.30 - 34.40
extra person	CHF 5.80 - 7.20
child (4-16 yrs)	CHF 3.20 - 4.00
dog	CHF 2.55 - 3.20

Less 10% in low season.

Leuk

Camping Bella-Tola

Waldstrasse 57, CH-3952 Susten-Leuk (Valais) T: 027 473 1491. E: info@bella-tola.ch

alanrogers.com/CH9720

An attractive site with good standards, Bella-Tola is on the hillside above Susten (east of Sierre) with good views over the Rhône valley. Extensive terracing has been carried out and most of the pitches are now terraced and flat. All of the 180 individually numbered pitches have electricity connections. The fullest season is 10/7-10/8, but they say that there is usually room somewhere. Used by tour operators (20%). Guests are requested to comply with environmental rules by sorting rubbish as directed. The site boasts a good sized heated swimming pool and children's pool (both free to campers) which, like the restaurant and bar overlooking them, are also open to non-campers and so more crowded at weekends and holidays. In the low rain climate of the Valais the pool is naturally much used.

Facilities

Three good quality modern sanitary blocks should be quite sufficient, with some washbasins in cabins. Free hot water in washbasins, showers and sinks for clothes and dishes, plus baby rooms. Facilities for disabled visitors. Washing machines, dryers and irons. Motorcaravan services. Shop. Newly renovated restaurant/bar. Takeaway (July-Aug). Swimming pool (heated 29/5-20/9). General room with TV. Films and guided walks in July/Aug. Torches advised. WiFi (free). Off site: Riding and tennis. Golf 4 km.

Open: 11 May - 30 September.

Directions

Travelling eastwards from Sierre along main road, small site road is to the right (south) just after entering Susten (site signed).
GPS: 46.29951, 7.63564

Charges 2012

Per unit incl. 2 persons and electricity	CHF 43.48 - 55.95
extra person	CHF 10.95 - 12.05
child (2-16 yrs acc. to age)	CHF 6.54 - 9.65
dog (max. 1)	CHF 2.45 - 2.70

Less 25% on person and pitch fees outside July/Aug.

Leuk

Camping Gemmi Agarn

Briannenstrasse 4, CH-3952 Susten-Leuk (Valais) T: 027 473 1154. E: info@campgemmi.ch

alanrogers.com/CH9730

The Rhône Valley is a popular through route to Italy via the Simplon Pass and a holiday region in its own right. Gemmi is a delightful small, friendly site in a scenic location with 62 level pitches, all with 16A electricity, on grass amidst a variety of trees, some of which offer shade; 41 pitches also have water and drainage. The previous owner maintained high standards and established a campsite mainly for tourers with only a few resident static units. This site is more suitable for the mature camper. Enjoying some of the best climatic conditions in Switzerland, this valley, between two mountain regions, has less rainfall and more hours of sunshine than most of the country. It is an area of vines and fruit trees with mountain walks and the majestic Matterhorn nearby.

Facilities

A modern sanitary block, partly heated, is kept very clean. It includes some washbasins in cabins. Eight private bathrooms for hire on a weekly basis. Washing machines and dryers. Motorcaravan services. Gas supplies. Shop. Small bar/restaurant where snacks and a limited range of local specialities are served. Terrace bar and snack restaurant. Children's playground. TV room. WiFi (charged). Swimming and walking nearby. Off site: Golf 500 m. Fishing, riding and bicycle hire 1.5 km.

Open: 16 April - 16 October.

Directions

From east (Visp), turn left 1 km. after sign for Agarn Feithieren. From west (Sierre), turn right 2 km. after Susten at sign for Camping Torrent and Gemmi.
GPS: 46.29781, 7.65937

Charges guide

Per unit incl. 2 persons and electricity	CHF 36.00 - 41.00
extra person	CHF 8.00 - 9.00
child (1-15 yrs)	CHF 4.00 - 6.50
dog	CHF 3.00

Locarno

Camping Delta

Via Respini 7, CH-6600 Locarno (Ticino) T: 091 751 6081. E: info@campingdelta.com

alanrogers.com/CH9900

Camping Delta is actually within the Locarno town limits, only some 800 m. from the centre. It has a prime position right by the lake, with bathing direct from the site, and is next to the municipal lido and sports field. The site has some moorings on an inlet at one side, with a jetty. It has 300 pitches on flat ground of 50-100 sq.m. of which 240 are available for touring units. They are marked out at the rear but with no other demarcation, giving an informal mix of all kinds of camper. Waterside pitches are premium priced. Campers have access to the municipally owned beach and lakeside gardens.

Facilities

The single toilet block is some distance from the more expensive pitches. Facilities for disabled visitors (key). Washing machine and dryer. Motorcaravan services. Small supermarket. Restaurant/bar with limited menu. Fitness centre. Playgrounds. Babysitting. Badminton. Amusements. Entertainment and excursions. Children's entertainment programme. Bicycle hire. WiFi (charged). Kayaks and electric bikes for hire. Dogs are not accepted. Off site: Golf 2 km. Riding 3.5 km.

Open: 1 March - 31 October.

Directions

From central Locarno follow signs to Camping Delta, Lido or Stadio along the lake. Beware that approaching from south there are also Delta signs which lead you to Albergo Delta in quite the wrong place. GPS: 46.15556, 8.80027

Charges guide

Per unit incl. 2 persons and electricity	CHF 52.00 - 102.00
extra person	CHF 13.00 - 20.00
child (10-15 yrs)	CHF 6.00

Luzern

TCS Camping Steinibachried

Seefeldstrasse, CH-6048 Horw-Luzern (Luzern) T: 041 340 3558. E: camping.horw@tcs.ch

alanrogers.com/CH9115

Situated in the southern suburbs of Luzern and with easy autoroute access, this site is a very convenient base for visiting what is quite deservedly a popular tourist area. The level, grassed site provides 100 touring pitches with electricity, separated into rows by trees and hedges. It is dominated by the Pilatus mountains, over 2,000 metres high. The peaks and mountain top restaurants offer fantastic views and can be reached by cable car on the steepest cog railway in the world from Alpnachstad. Access to the lake from the site is over a wooden walkway which passes through a small protected nature area.

Facilities

Single, well maintained toilet block to one end of touring area (may be stretched with lack of hot water during busy periods). Showers are free, some washbasins in cabins. Facilities for disabled visitors. Baby room. Washing machine and dryer. Motorcaravan service point. Gas supplies. Small shop. Bar with terrace. Convenient self service restaurant with takeaway. New play area. WiFi throughout (charged). Off site: Sports ground and lake adjacent (free use for campers).

Open: 4 April - 7 October.

Directions

Site is 4 km. south of the centre of Luzern and borders the Vierwaldstatter See. Leave motorway 2 at exit 28 Luzern/Horw. Site is signed at roundabout towards Horw-Sud.
GPS: 47.01185, 8.311

Charges 2012

Per unit incl. 2 persons and electricity	CHF 35.70 - 51.20
extra person	CHF 7.60 - 9.60
child (6-15 yrs)	CHF 3.80 - 4.80

No credit cards.

Martigny

TCS Camping les Neuvilles

Rue de Levant 68, CH-1920 Martigny (Valais) T: 027 722 4544. E: camping.martigny@tcs.ch

alanrogers.com/CH9655

Easily accessible from the autoroute (A9) and close to the town centre, this site has a total of 225 pitches. There are 185 for touring units, most with electricity and most on level, grassy ground (some slope slightly). A number of trees provide some shade, although the site is fairly open allowing views of the surrounding mountains. Being close to the autoroute and located in an industrial area, the site can be quite noisy, especially noticeable during the night and mornings. With its ease of access and close proximity to shops, it makes a convenient night stop when travelling along the Rhône Valley for the St. Bernard Pass.

Facilities

Two sanitary buildings, one close to the entrance, the other at the far end. Showers are large and free, some washbasins in cabins, some with only cold water. Facilities for disabled visitors. Baby room. Cooking rings. Washing machines and dryers. Motorcaravan service point. Bar. TV room. Play area and paddling pool. Bouncy castle. Bicycle hire. WiFi throughout (charged). Max. 2 dogs. Off site: Entry to the municipal swimming pool is free. Shop and restaurant nearby. Riding 1 km. Fishing 3 km.

Open: 4 April - 28 October.

Directions

From A9 exit 22 (Martigny) follow signs for Expo. After leaving the autoroute, at first roundabout, site is signed. Follow signs carefully; entrance to site is at the rear, by the cemetery.
GPS: 46.097033, 7.078767

Charges 2012

Per unit incl. 2 persons and electricity	CHF 35.70 - 44.50
extra person	CHF 7.60 - 9.00

Camping Cheques accepted.

Meiringen

Alpencamping

Brünigstrasse 47, CH-3860 Meiringen (Bern) T: 033 971 3676. E: info@alpencamping.ch

alanrogers.com/CH9496

Alpencamping is a small family site located close to Meiringen, an important winter sports resort and hiking centre in the summer with good road and rail links. Opened in 2007, the enthusiastic owners have developed this into a good, all-year site and continue to make improvements. There are 54 touring pitches which are flat and grassy and all have electrical connections. A further 32 pitches are occupied by well maintained residential units. This is a simple site with few amenities but there is a centrally located toilet block and a small shop for essentials. A supermarket is five minutes walk away.

Facilities

Heated toilet block includes facilities for disabled visitors. Washing machine and dryer. Drying area for ski kit. Small shop for essentials with coffee machine. Undercover area with tables, chairs and a microwave for open-air catering. Communal barbecue. Community room with tables, easy chairs, games, TV and books. Winter sauna room. Play area. Max. 2 dogs. Off site: Meiringen with a wide choice of shops, restaurants and bars 500 m. Reichenbach Falls. Brienzersee Lake. Summer and winter skiing.

Open: All year excl. November.

Directions

From Bern take the A6 motorway towards Interlaken and Thun. At Interlaken, join the A8 towards Spiez. Continue on road 11 to Meiringen, from where the site is well signed. GPS: 46.73421, 8.17115

Charges guide

Per unit incl. 2 persons	CHF 27.00 - 34.00
electricity (low season 0.45 per kWh)	CHF 3.50
extra person	CHF 7.00 - 8.00

No credit cards.

Meride

TCS Camping Parco al Sole

CH-6866 Meride (Ticino) T: 091 646 4330. E: camping.meride@tcs.ch

alanrogers.com/CH9970

Meride is a small village in the extreme south of Switzerland close to the Italian border, and not far from the A2/N2 motorway. Parco al Sole is on a slight slope 1 km. from the village, with mountain views. There is space for 64 small units, 40 with electricity connections (13A) available for all. The pitches are not numbered or marked out, but are level on terraces, mostly among tall trees. When the site is busy, units could be crowded, it is therefore requested that towing cars are parked outside. Possibly a little remote for a night stop, but a pleasant, relaxing spot from which to explore as far as Lake Como.

Facilities

A good quality sanitary block with the usual facilities, free hot water and a baby room. Grotto Café with log fire in cool weather serving drinks and simple evening meals. Basic food supplies. Refurbished, heated swimming pool (1/6-30/8) and paddling pool. Playground. Some entertainment is organised in high season. Bouncy castle. WiFi throughout (charged). TV and videos (in café). Off site: Bicycle hire 7 km. Fishing and riding 10 km. Golf 20 km.

Open: 20 April - 23 September.

Directions

From N2/A2 motorway take exit 52 for Mendrisio towards Stabio, Varese. Head to Rancate then Basazio, Arzo and Meride. Site signed (6 km. from motorway exit). Road to site is narrow. GPS: 45.88887, 8.94883

Charges 2012

Per unit incl. 2 persons and electricity	CHF 33.90 - 47.50
extra person	CHF 7.10 0.60
child (6-15 yrs)	CHF 3.70 - 4.80

Camping Cheques accepted.

Montmelon

Camping Tariche

Tariche, Saint Ursanne, CH-2883 Montmelon (Jura) T: 032 433 4619. E: info@tariche.ch

alanrogers.com/CH9015

This lovely site is some 6 km. off the main road along a steep wooded valley, through which flows the Doub on its brief excursion through Switzerland from France. If you're looking for peace and tranquillity then this is a distinct possibility for a short or long stay. A very small friendly site (not suitable for large units), owned and managed by Christine Lodens, there are just 15 touring pitches. It is ideal for walking, fishing or for the more active, the possibility of kayaking along the Doub (the river is not suitable for swimming). Medieval St Ursanne, said to be the most beautiful village in the canton, is some 7 km.

Facilities

The modern, heated toilet block is of a high standard with free showers. Washing machine and dryer. Motorcaravan services. Good kitchen facilities include oven, hob and refrigerator. Restaurant with shaded terrace overlooking the play area so that adults can enjoy a drink and keep watch whilst enjoying the river views. Fishing. WiFi. Off site: St Ursanne 7 km.

Open: 1 March - 31 October.

Directions

From A16 exit St Ursanne (at the end of the tunnel). Turn left towards town and at roundabout turn left and go past first campsite. After 5.6 km. site is on the right next to the restaurant. GPS: 47.33419, 7.14028

Charges guide

Per unit incl. 2 persons and electricity	CHF 32.00 - 42.00
extra person	CHF 9.00
child	CHF 5.00
dog	CHF 3.00

Morges

Camping Le Petit Bois

Promenade du Petit-Bois 15, CH-1110 Morges (Vaud) T: 021 801 1270. E: camping.morges@tcs.ch

alanrogers.com/CH9240

This excellent and busy TCS campsite is on the edge of Morges, a wine-growing centre with a 13th-century castle on Lake Geneva about 8 km. west of Lausanne. Flowers, shrubs and trees adorn the site and the neat, tidy lawns make a most pleasant environment. There are 170 grass pitches for tourists, all with 6/10A electricity and laid out in a regular pattern from wide hard access roads on which cars stand. There are eight larger pitches for motorcaravans with electricity, water and drainage. The friendly manager speaks good English, and will advise on local attractions.

Facilities

Three well built, fully equipped, modern toilet blocks include hot water in half the washbasins, sinks and showers. Separate block with excellent baby room. Facilities for disabled visitors. Laundry facilities. Motorcaravan services. Restaurant and takeaway. Excellent shop. Playground. Boules. Bicycle and scooter hire. Small kitchen with seating. Internet point and WiFi. Children's entertainment (high season). Picnic area. Fishing. Bicycle hire. Off site: Swimming pool adjacent. Small marina. Town centre within walking distance. Tennis.

Open: 1 April - 24 October.

Directions

Leave A1 autoroute (Lausanne - Geneva) at exit 15 (Morges-ouest). Turn towards town and signs for site. GPS: 46.50457, 6.48917

Charges guide

Per unit incl. 2 persons and electricity	CHF 38.90 - 55.30
child (6-15 yrs)	CHF 3.60 - 4.90
extra person	CHF 7.20 - 9.80
dog	CHF 3.00 - 5.00

Muzzano

TCS Camping Piodella

Via alla Force 14, CH-6933 Muzzano (Ticino) T: 091 994 7788. E: camping.muzzano@tcs.ch

alanrogers.com/CH9950

This modernised site, facing south onto Lake Lugano must rank as one of the best in Switzerland for a complete family holiday. There are 250 numbered pitches (200 for touring units) all with 10A electricity and 26 with water and drainage. Trees in most parts of the site offer shade to those who prefer less direct sunshine. Cars must be left in the car park, which makes the site less cluttered and safer for children. The site is a short way from the airport so there will be some aircraft noise. Roads have been re-laid and a marina has been built.

Facilities

The original refurbished toilet block and a splendid new one which includes a baby room and an excellent suite for disabled visitors, are heated in cool weather. Washing machines and dryers. Motorcaravan services. Gas supplies. Shop. Bar/restaurant with pleasant terrace. Swimming pools (May-mid Oct). Day and TV rooms. Playground. Bouncy castle and children's train (in season). Children's games room. One tennis court. Bicycle hire. Fridge hire. Multisports area. Marina. Raft with slide on the lake. WiFi throughout (charged). Off site: Sailing 2 km. Riding 4 km. Golf 5 km. Boat launching 6 km.

Open: All year.

Directions

Piodella is on Bellinzona - Ponte Tresa road; take motorway exit 49 Lugano-Nord for Ponte Tresa and turn left at T-junction in Agno. Follow signs for Piodella or TCS at roundabout. Cross the bridge and turn very sharp right at the Suzuki garage. Site is at south end of the airport. GPS: 45.99592, 8.90838

Charges 2012

Per unit incl. 2 persons and electricity	CHF 44.20 - 62.80
per person	CHF 9.00 - 11.40
child (6-15 yrs)	CHF 4.50 - 5.70
dog	CHF 5.50

Pontresina

Camping Plauns

Morteratsch, CH-7504 Pontresina (Graubünden) T: 081 842 6285. E: plauns@bluewin.ch

alanrogers.com/CH9860

This is a mountain site in splendid scenery near St Moritz. Pontresina is at the mouth of the Bernina Pass road (B29) which runs from Celerina in the Swiss Engadine to Tirano in Italy. Camping Plauns, some 4 km. southeast of Pontresina, is situated in the floor of the valley between fir clad mountains at 1,850 m. above sea level. There are about 250 pitches for tourists in summer, all with electricity, some in small clearings amongst tall trees and some in a larger open space. In winter the number is reduced to 40. They are neither numbered nor marked and size depends on the natural space between the trees.

Facilities

Three fully equipped toilet blocks, one old and two excellent new modern ones, can be heated. Some washbasins in private cabins and showers on payment. Facilities for disabled visitors. Laundry facilities. Shop. Grill/snack bar for drinks or simple meals (July/Aug). TV room. Internet and WiFi. Bicycle hire. Playground. Torch useful. Off site: Restaurant 1 km. Entertainment offered, winter and summer, at nearby Pontresina.

Open: 1 June - 15 October, 15 December - 15 April.

Directions

Site is on B29, the road to Tirano and Bernina Pass, about 4 km. southeast of Pontresina - well signed. GPS: 46.464075, 9.932402

Charges guide

Per person	CHF 10.40
child (6-15 yrs)	CHF 4.00 - 6.50
pitch	CHF 9.00 - 15.00
electricity (6-13A)	CHF 3.00 - 4.50
dog	CHF 3.00

Orbe

TCS Camping Le Signal

CH-1350 Orbe (Vaud) T: **024 441 3857**. E: **camping.orbe@tcs.ch**

alanrogers.com/CH9230

Owned by the Touring Club Suisse, Camping Le Signal is located north of Lausanne, with good access to Lake Geneva and the sandy beaches of Lake Neuchâtel. There are 110 touring pitches here, all with 6A electricity. They are grassy and shaded by conifers – some slope slightly. Three fully equipped tents are available for rent. On-site amenities include a superb swimming pool, 18-hole minigolf (both next door but free to campers), small shop, bar and children's playground. A children's club is organised in July and August. Other entertainment includes sausage evenings, occasional dances and walking excursions in the area. The site has good access to the Swiss motorway network and would be suitable for an en route stop as well as a few days quiet retreat. Orbe is a pleasant small town with a good selection of shops, cafés and restaurants. Its history dates back to the Roman era and a number of mosaics and ruins can be seen. The Gorges de l'Orbe are popular with walkers and the river is also excellent for fly fishing. This is also an important wine producing area and a number of vineyards offer dégustations. The resident wardens are more than helpful.

Facilities

Facilities for disabled visitors. Washing machine and dryer. Shop. Bar/snack bar and takeaway. Swimming pool and minigolf adjacent, both free to campers. Play area. Tourist information. Occasional activities (including a club for children). Bouncy castle. Internet point and WiFi. Tents for rent. Off site: Walking and cycling. Fly fishing. Bicycle hire. Riding.

Open: 4 April - 7 October.

Directions

Approaching from the north or south on A1/N1 motorway take exit 23 to the N9. Exit at J3 towards Orbe. Entering the town, take the left filter lane to Route du Signal – signposted Pool and Campsite. Site is on left at top of hill.
GPS: 46.736239, 6.532343

Charges guide

Per unit incl. 2 persons and electricity	CHF 32.20 - 40.80
extra person	CHF 6.80 - 8.40
child	CHF 3.40 - 4.20
dog	CHF 3.00 - 5.00

Camping Cheques accepted.

Randa

Camping Attermenzen

CH-3928 Randa (Valais) T: 027 967 1379. E: rest.camping@rhone.ch

alanrogers.com/CH9740

Randa, a picturesque Valais village, at 1,409 m. is a beautiful location for a campsite and ideal for those wishing to visit Zermatt only 10 km. away. Reception is open from mid-June to mid-September, otherwise call at the restaurant (closed on Tuesdays). Unmarked pitches are on an uneven field with some areas that are fairly level and 6A electricity is within easy reach. A paradise for walking, mountaineering, climbing and mountain biking and surrounded by famous 4,000 m. peaks, such as the Dom and Weisshorn, this site also offers good modern facilities with a restaurant and bar next door. There is a daily taxi service to Zermatt from the site (CHF 6 per person). The adventurous will try the Cornergrat-Bahn cog railway, which is a little pricey, but well worth it for the 42 minute, 1,470 m. climb. There is also a 9-hole golf course nearby and the Europath from Zermatt to Grächen. The site is open all year depending on the weather. The road from Visp is being significantly improved with new tunnels constructed.

Facilities

The sanitary block is of a good standard and well maintained with free showers. Washing machine. Shop (June-Sept). Gas supplies. Restaurant/bar. Takeaway. WiFi (charged). Off site: Zermatt 10 km.

Open: All year.

Directions

From A9 at Visp turn right at roundabout (Zermatt). Go through the 3.3 km. long tunnel and follow road towards Zermatt. Go through Stalden and turn right at roundabout (Zermatt). Site is about 1 km. after Randa village on the left. GPS: 46.08549, 7.781

Charges guide

Per unit incl. 2 persons and electricity	CHF 26.00 - 28.00
extra person	CHF 6.00
child (6-16 yrs)	CHF 3.00

Reckingen

Camping Augenstern

Postfach 16, CH-3998 Reckingen (Valais) T: 027 973 1395. E: info@campingaugenstern.ch

alanrogers.com/CH9790

The village of Reckingen is about halfway between Brig and the Furka/Grimsel passes. You can still get the train with car and caravan, or motorcaravan from Oberwald to Andermatt to avoid the steep climbs and descents of the Furka Pass, but in doing so you will miss some exhilarating and unforgettable scenery. This family run site, at 1,326 m. provides 100 flat, level pitches for touring units, all with 10A electricity. There is a little shade. Water points are equipped with long hoses. It provides an excellent base for walking, climbing or cycling as well as rafting on the Rhône in the summer or skiing in the winter. Riverside pitches are in great demand, with uninterrupted views of the surrounding forested hills and mountains.

Facilities

The toilet block is good and is well maintained. Showers on payment. Motorcaravan services. Shop for essentials (July/Aug). Restaurant/bar with satellite TV. There are no facilities for campers with disabilities, due to restricted access. WiFi (charged). Off site: Large swimming pool complex 200 m. Bicycle hire 400 m. Reckingen 500 m. Riding 800 m. Local skiing and rafting 1.5 km. Major ski slopes 15 km.

Open: 13 May - 21 October, 15 December - 21 March.

Directions

From the no. 19 road turn south in Reckingen next to church. Go down hill, along one-way street, carefully over railway and covered bridge. Over next bridge and follow the lane past the swimming pool to the site entrance. GPS: 46.46427, 8.24472

Charges guide

Per unit incl. 2 persons and electricity	CHF 38.50 - 48.00
extra person	CHF 9.00 - 11.00

No credit cards.

Saillon

Camping de la Sarvaz

Route de Fully, CH-1913 Saillon (Valais) T: 027 744 1389. E: info@sarvaz.ch

alanrogers.com/CH9640

The Rhône valley in Valais with its terraced vineyards and young orchards provides a beautiful setting for this site. Family owned and run, Camping de la Sarvaz provides excellent facilities and would be a good base for relaxing or, for the more energetic, walking, cycling, climbing or skiing. The focal point of the site is a restaurant/bar with a delightful Chinese style garden. There are 68 level touring pitches all with electricity (16A), 45 of which have water and drainage. Lovely mountain views surround the site and there are 11 chalets to rent. A heated, raised pool is available from May to September.

Facilities

New, heated sanitary facilities are of very high standards, very well maintained. Free showers. Additional toilets on the first floor. Facilities for disabled visitors. Baby room. Washing machine and dryer. Small communal kitchen. Motorcaravan services. First class shop (all season). Restaurant/bar (all season, not Mon/Tues). Excellent games/play areas. Additional children's playroom and games room. Sitting room with TV/DVD and library. Service pitches have TV points. WiFi. Off site: Saillon 2 km. with thermal centre and spa facilities. Bicycle hire in town centre (first 4 hours free).

Open: 6 February - 8 January.

Directions

From the A9 take exit 23 for Saxon/Saillon. Follow signs to Saillon then turn right towards the site, which is 3 km. from the autoroute exit.
GPS: 46.15988, 7.167

Charges 2012

Per unit incl. 2 persons and electricity	CHF 42.00 - 43.00
extra person	CHF 10.00
child (6-16 yrs)	CHF 5.00
dog	CHF 4.00

Sarnen

Camping Seefeld Sarnen

Seestrasse 20, CH-6060 Sarnen (Unterwalden) T: 041 666 5788. E: welcome@seefeldpark.ch

alanrogers.com/CH9540

Sarnen is about 20 km. south of Luzern on the main road to Interlaken and is therefore, ideally placed for skiing in winter and sightseeing in summer. This site was badly damaged by floods in 2006 and re-opened in spring 2011 after an extensive refurbishment and improvement programme, which includes the construction of a new swimming pool complex. The 135 pitches, 94 for tourists with electricity (13A), are 80 sq.m. on grass. There is shade in parts and the location is a quiet one on the edge of the small town. The site is part of the town lido complex with facilities for non-powered boats. The site is on flat ground directly on the lake with lovely views of near and distant mountains. Suitable for long or short stays, it makes an ideal base for this part of Switzerland or for a night stop if passing through. The summit of the well known Mt. Pilatus can be reached by mountain railway (the steepest of its type in the world) from Stansstad, about halfway between Luzern and Sarnen, and steamer trips on Lake Luzern can also be made from here.

Facilities

Good sanitary arrangements, partially heated in cool weather. Facilities for disabled visitors. Washing machines and dryers. Shop, bar, restaurant with large terrace (all year). Swimming pools (1/4-15/9). Playground. Watersports. Tennis. Bicycle hire. WiFi throughout. Off site: Pleasant walk along the lakeside. Luzern. Winter sports

Open: All year.

Directions

Approaching from Luzern (A8), leave at Sarnen's southern junction where town road meets the main road from Interlaken, and follow signs to the site.
GPS: 46.899, 8.266

Charges guide

Per unit incl. 2 persons and electricity	CHF 31.00 - 59.00
dog	CHF 3.00 - 5.00

Sempach

TCS Camping Seeland

Seelandstrasse, CH-6204 Sempach-Stadt (Luzern) T: 041 460 1466. E: camping.sempach@tcs.ch

alanrogers.com/CH9110

Lucerne is a very popular city in the centre of Switzerland and Camping Seeland makes a peaceful base from which to visit the town and explore the surrounding countryside or, being a short way from the main N2 Basel - Chiasso motorway, is a convenient night stop if passing through. This neat, tidy site has 200 grass pitches for tourists, all with electricity (6/13A), a few with gravel hardstanding on either side of hard roads under trees with further places on the perimeter in the open. There are about 235 static caravans. A small river runs through the site with a connecting covered bridge.

Facilities

Four good quality sanitary blocks have the usual facilities including baby rooms and excellent facilities for disabled visitors. Laundry facilities. Hot plates, fridges and freezers. Two motorcaravan service points. Excellent bar/restaurant with terrace overlooking the play area and lake. Shop. Children's paddling pool and playground. Lakeside beach. WiFi (charged). No electric barbecues. Off site: Shops and restaurants in the village. Tennis, boat and bicycle hire, minigolf and golf club. Hot-air ballooning, river rafting and archery can be arranged. Windsurfing school nearby. Adjacent swimming pool. Fishing 300 m.

Open: 4 April - 7 October.

Directions

From the N2 take exit 21 for Sempach and follow signs for Sempach and site.
GPS: 47.12548, 8.18995

Charges guide

Per unit incl. 2 persons and electricity	CHF 35.80 - 54.80
extra person	CHF 7.40 - 9.40
child (6-15 yrs)	CHF 3.70 - 4.70
dog	CHF 3.00 - 5.00

Sent

Camping Sur En

CH-7554 Sur En/Sent (Graubünden) T: 081 866 3544. E: info@sur-en.ch

alanrogers.com/CH9830

Sur En is at the eastern end of the Engadine valley, about 10 km. from the Italian and Austrian borders. The area is perhaps better known as a skiing region, but has summer attractions as well. This level site is in an open valley with little shade. They say there is room for 120 touring units on the meadows where pitches are neither marked nor numbered; there are electricity connections for all (6A). As you approach on road 27 and spot the site way below under the shadow of a steeply rising, wooded mountain, the drop may appear daunting, but becomes less so as you proceed.

Facilities

The modern, heated sanitary block is good with some extra facilities in the main building. Laundry facilities. Motorcaravan services. Shop. Good restaurant with covered terrace. Takeaway (high season). Outdoor heated swimming pool (June-Oct). Bicycle hire. Fishing. Entertainment (July/Aug). A symposium for sculptors is held during the second week in July. Excursions arranged in high season. New adventure ropes course in the forest. WiFi. Off site: Golf 12 km.

Open: All year.

Directions

Sur En is 7 km. east of Scuol. It is signed from the 27 road halfway between Scuol and Ramosch. The road is a steady, winding descent. Cross covered timber bridge (3.8 m. passable height).
GPS: 46.84163, 10.33333

Charges guide

Per unit incl. 2 persons and electricity	CHF 33.00 - 37.00
extra person	CHF 6.50 - 7.50

Sierre

Camping Bois de Finges

CH-3960 Sierre (Valais) T: 027 455 0284. E: camping.sierre@bluewin.ch

alanrogers.com/CH9680

This site is situated in the middle of the Bois des Finges pine forest on a rocky wooded hillside. It is attractive and maintained in sympathy with its natural surroundings. With 100 pitches cut out of the hillside, some are difficult to access but the manager will help. They can take units of up to 7 metres but mainly smaller units and tents in some parts. All pitches are screened by trees and 62 have 4A electricity (long leads useful). Staff are welcoming and helpful but little English is spoken. Useful for an overnight stop. There is weekday noise from a quarry opposite.

Facilities

Two very clean and well maintained wooden toilet blocks are at the top and bottom of the site so a steep walk for some. Freezer, washing machine and dryer. Motorcaravan service point. Well stocked but limited shop and snack bar. Outdoor heated pool (6x12 m) and paddling pool. Well appointed play area. Table tennis. WiFi. Barbecues are not permitted on pitches. Torches and long leads are useful. Off site: Walking and hiking area. Fishing (licence required) 900 m. Sierre 1 km. Golf and riding 3 km.

Open: 15 April - 2 October.

Directions

Leave motorway at exit 29, Sierre East. Follow sign for Sierre. Site is signed on the right (TCS) within 200 m. GPS: 46.29388, 7.55787

Charges guide

Per unit incl. 2 persons and electricity	CHF 35.00 - 41.00
extra person	CHF 7.00 - 8.00
child	CHF 4.00
dog	CHF 5.00

Solothurn

TCS Camping Lido Solothurn

Glutzenhofstrasse 5, CH-4500 Solothurn (Solothurn) T: 032 621 8935. E: camping.solothurn@tcs.ch

alanrogers.com/CH9010

This is one of the most pleasant sites owned by the Swiss Touring Club that we have seen. It is well laid out and beautifully cared for and can be enjoyed as a base for local touring or as a restful stop en route. There are 166 level, grass pitches including 116 for touring units, all with electricity and 12 also have water and drainage. A small marina adjoining the site is under the same ownership. The site is close to the large town of Solothurn, on the banks of the Aare. Situated between the river and farmland, the site enjoys pleasant views of the surrounding hills. An ideal site for visiting the old Baroque city of Solothurn, with its cathedral, castle and street markets, as well as the fascinating old towns of Büren and Aarburg.

Facilities

Two extremely well maintained sanitary blocks. Facilities for disabled visitors. Laundry facilities. Motorcaravan service point. Small shop for basics plus a restaurant overlooking marina (both 3/3-30/11). Playground with bouncy castle in season. Small, unheated children's pool (1/6-15/9). Library. Games room with TV. Internet access. WiFi throughout (charged). Off site: Large municipal swimming pool 200 m. Solothurn and the River Aare. The stork colony at Altreu. River swimming, boating and canoeing. River cruises.

Open: 3 March - 3 December.

Directions

Site is on the western outskirts of Solothurn. From A5 motorway take exit Solothurn West (ouest), then follow Weststadt. The camping site is well signed. GPS: 47.198351, 7.523805

Charges guide

Per unit incl. 2 persons and electricity	CHF 36.90 - 53.90
extra person	CHF 7.20 - 9.20
child (6-15 yrs)	CHF 3.60 - 4.60
dog	CHF 3.00 - 5.00

Camping Cheques accepted.

Tenero

Camping Lido Mappo

Via Mappo, CH-6598 Tenero (Ticino) T: 091 745 1437. E: camping@lidomappo.ch

alanrogers.com/CH9880

Lido Mappo lies on the lakeside at the northeast tip of Lake Maggiore, about 5 km. from Locarno, and has views of the surrounding mountains and hills across the lake. The site is attractively laid out in rows of individual, numbered pitches, half for tents and half for caravans and mostly split up by access roads or hedges. The pitches (357 for touring) vary in size, those by the lake costing more and most are well shaded. Electricity (10-16A) is available on all pitches. With helpful English speaking staff, this is a quiet site with its own narrow, mainly sandy beach. Although reservations are only made for longer stays, there is always a fair chance of finding a vacant place.

Facilities

The five recently renovated toilet blocks can be heated in cool weather and are always well kept. They include individual washbasins, all in cabins for women and some for men. Facilities for disabled visitors. Baby changing area. Washing machines and dryers. Cooking facilities and communal barbecue. Refrigerated compartments for hire. Motorcaravan services. Supermarket. Restaurant/bar. Takeaway. TV room. Large playground. Lake swimming. Fishing. First aid post. Dogs are not accepted. Internet room and WiFi. Off site: Bicycle hire nearby. Riding 3 km. Golf 5 km.

Open: 1 April - 30 October.

Directions

On Bellinzona - Locarno road 13, exit Tenero site is signed at roundabout. From Locarno, enter Tenero and follow signs. There are several campsites, so watch for the names. GPS: 46.17712, 8.84228

Charges guide

Per unit incl. 2 persons and electricity	CHF 36.00 - 93.00

Less 5% for stays over 10 days and 10% over 21 days.

Tenero

Camping Campofelice

Via alle Brere 7, CH-6598 Tenero (Ticino) T: 091 745 1417. E: camping@campofelice.ch

alanrogers.com/CH9890

The largest site in Switzerland, it is bordered on the front by Lake Maggiore and on one side by the Verzasca estuary, where the site has its own marina. Campofelice is divided into rows, with 860 generously sized, individual pitches on flat grass on either side of hard access roads. Mostly well shaded, all pitches have electricity connections (10-13A) and 409 also have water, drainage and TV connections. Pitches near the lake cost more (these are not available for motorcaravans until September) and a special area is reserved for small tents. The sheer quality of this superb site justifies the higher than average prices. Sporting facilities are good and there are cycle paths in the area, including into Locarno. The beach by the lake is sandy, long and wider than the usual lakeside ones. It shelves gently so that bathing is safe for children. Within a demarcated area are floating trampolines and rafts, and a specially marked section for toddlers.

Facilities

The six toilet blocks (three heated) are of exemplary quality. Washing machines and dryers. Motorcaravan services. Gas supplies. Supermarket, restaurant, bar and takeaway (all season). Snack kiosk at beach. Lifeguards on duty. Tennis. Minigolf. Bicycle hire. Canoe and pedalo hire. Boat launching. Playgrounds. Doctor calls. Dogs are not accepted. New chalet for disabled visitors. Camping accessories shop. Car hire. Car wash. WiFi (charged). Off site: Fishing 500 m. Water-skiing and windsurfing 1 km. Riding 5 km. Golf 8 km. Boatyard with maintenance facilities.

Open: 22 March - 31 October.

Directions

On the Bellinzona - Locarno road 13, exit Tenero. Site is signed at roundabout. Coming from the south, enter Tenero and follow signs to site.
GPS: 46.168611, 8.855556

Charges guide

Per unit incl. 2 persons and electricity	CHF 38.00 - 82.00
extra person	CHF 8.00 - 11.00

Some pitches have min. stay regulations.
Discounts for stays over 10 days.

Vésenaz

Camping TCS Pointe à la Bise

Chemin de la Bise, CH-1222 Vésenaz (Genève) T: 022 752 1296. E: camping.geneve@tcs.ch

alanrogers.com/CH9210

Ideal for visiting Geneva, Pointe à la Bise is directly on the lake and has superb views of it and the surrounding mountains, which may well tempt you to stay longer. The 220 pitches for touring units, 140 with electricity (4/10A) are not marked so, although electricity boxes roughly determine where each unit goes, you do not have an exactly defined place which might make for crowding in high season. Tall trees provide some shade. Being away from the main road, this is a quiet site with a relaxed atmosphere. Improvements in recent years have lifted this from a reasonable site to a good one. There are no discos, but occasional light, live music entertainment during high season.

Facilities

The single, fully equipped sanitary block has been refurbished to a high standard. Baby room. Facilities for disabled visitors. Laundry facilities. Motorcaravan services. Gas supplies. Shop. Bar. Restaurant with takeaway. Community room with TV. Children's pool (15/5-15/9). Playground. Lake swimming and watersports. Windsurfing and small boats under 10 h.p. may be used from site. Fishing. Bicycle hire. Activities in July/Aug. WiFi. Off site: Sailing school. Guided walks on the Salève mountain. Open-air cinema (July/Aug). Golf 3 km.

Open: 2 April - 17 October.

Directions

Follow lakeside road from city centre towards Thonon (lake on left hand side) for about 6.5 km. and site is signed. GPS: 46.25000, 6.19569

Charges guide

Per unit incl. 2 persons and electricity	CHF 40.00 - 50.70
extra person	CHF 7.20 - 9.20
child (6-15 yrs)	CHF 3.60 - 4.60
dog	CHF 3.00 - 5.00

Vétroz

Camping du Botza

Route du Camping 1, CH-1963 Vétroz (Valais) T: 027 346 1940. E: info@botza.ch

alanrogers.com/CH9520

Situated in the Rhône Valley at a height of 460 m. and not far from the autoroute, this is a pleasant site with views of the surrounding mountains. It is set in a peaceful wooded location, although there is occasional aircraft noise. There are 125 individual touring pitches, ranging in size (60-155 sq.m) all with 4A electricity, many with some shade and 25 with water and drainage. Considerable investment has taken place in making the site environmentally friendly with solar power used to heat the pool and sanitary blocks and a large recycling facility. A warm welcome is assured from the enthusiastic owner.

Facilities

New sanitary block and another completely renovated. Some private cabins in the heated sanitary block. Washing machines and dryers. Shop. Pizzeria. Takeaway. Swimming pool (15/5-1/9). Playground. Tennis. Basketball. Games/TV room with 3 Internet stations, books in several languages, board games and tourist information. WiFi throughout. Off site: Fitness trail in woods opposite. Walks alongside small streams nearby. Good cycle track. Riding 2 km. Golf and bicycle hire 8 km. Sion 8 km. Football on the FC-Vetros training ground.

Open: All year.

Directions

From the A9/E62 between Sion and Martigny, take exit 25 Conthey/Vétroz and go south towards 'zone industrial', after 200 m. turn right to 'Camping 9.33 Botza' and follow signs. Site is 2.5 km. from autoroute exit. GPS: 46.20583, 7.27807

Charges guide

Per unit incl. 2 persons and electricity	CHF 25.80 - 45.10
extra person	CHF 5.00 - 8.20
child (6-16 yrs)	CHF 2.50 - 4.10

Vitznau

Camping Vitznau

CH-6354 Vitznau (Luzern) T: 041 397 1280. E: info@camping-vitznau.ch

alanrogers.com/CH9130

Camping Vitznau is situated in the small village of the same name, above and overlooking Lake Luzern, with splendid views across the water to the mountains on the other side. It is a small, neat and tidy site very close to the delightful village on the narrow, winding, lakeside road. The 90 touring pitches for caravans or motorcaravans (max length 8 m) have 15A electricity available to most (long leads necessary) and all have fine views. They are on level, grassy terraces with hardstanding for motorcaravans and separated by tarmac roads. There are separate places for tents.

Facilities

The single, well constructed sanitary block provides free hot showers (water heated by solar panels). No facilities for disabled visitors (steep site and access roads). Full laundry facilities. Motorcaravan services. Shop and snack bar. General room for wet weather. Games room. Small heated swimming pool and children's splash pool (1/5-30/9). Off site: Restaurants about five minutes walk. Watersports. Fishing and bicycle hire 1 km. Golf 15 km.

Open: 31 March - 7 October.

Directions

Site is signed from the centre of Vitznau. (Swiss signs show a single black tent on a white background). GPS: 47.006666, 8.486402

Charges guide

Per unit incl. 2 persons and electricity	CHF 40.70 - 59.70
extra person	CHF 10.10 - 12.10
child (4-15 yrs)	CHF 4.00 - 8.50
dog	CHF 4.00 - 5.00

Open All Year

The following sites are understood to accept caravanners and campers all year round. It is always wise to phone the site to check as the facilities available, for example, may be reduced.

Dogs

For the benefit of those who want to take their dogs with them or for people who do not like dogs at the sites they visit, we list here those sites that have indicated to us that they do not accept dogs. If you are, however, planning to take your dog we do advise you to check first – there may be limits on numbers, breeds, etc. or times of the year when they are excluded.

Never – these sites do not accept dogs at any time:

Accepted – certain periods only:

Travelling in Europe

When taking your car (and caravan, tent or trailer tent) or motorcaravan to the continent you do need to plan in advance and to find out as much as possible about driving in the countries you plan to visit. Whilst European harmonisation has eliminated many of the differences between one country and another, it is well worth reading the short notes we provide in the introduction to each country in this guide in addition to this more general summary.

Of course, the main difference from driving in the UK is that in mainland Europe you will need to drive on the right. Without taking extra time and care, especially at busy junctions and conversely when roads are empty, it is easy to forget to drive on the right. Remember that traffic approaching from the right usually has priority unless otherwise indicated by road markings and signs. Harmonisation also means that most (but not all) common road signs are the same in all countries.

Your vehicle

Book your vehicle in for a good service well before your intended departure date. This will lessen the chance of an expensive breakdown. Make sure your brakes are working efficiently and that your tyres have plenty of tread (3 mm. is recommended, particularly if you are undertaking a long journey).

Also make sure that your caravan or trailer is roadworthy and that its tyres are in good order and correctly inflated. Plan your packing and be careful not to overload your vehicle, caravan or trailer – this is unsafe and may well invalidate your insurance cover (it must not be more fully loaded than the kerb weight of the insured vehicle).

CHECK ALL THE FOLLOWING:

- GB sticker. If you do not display a sticker, you may risk an on-the-spot fine as this identifier is compulsory in all countries. Euro-plates are an acceptable alternative within the EU (but not outside). Remember to attach another sticker (or Euro-plate) to caravans and trailers. Only GB stickers (not England, Scotland, Wales or N. Ireland) stickers are valid in the EU.
- Headlights. As you will be driving on the right you must adjust your headlights so that the dipped beam does not dazzle oncoming drivers. Converter kits are readily available for most vehicles, although if your car is fitted with high intensity headlights, you should check with your motor dealer. Check that any planned extra loading does not affect the beam height.
- Seatbelts. Rules for the fitting and wearing of seatbelts throughout Europe are similar to those in the UK, but it is worth checking before you go. Rules for carrying children in the front of vehicles vary from country to country. It is best to plan not to do this if possible.
- Door/wing mirrors. To help with driving on the right, if your vehicle is not fitted with a mirror on the left hand side, we recommend you have one fitted.
- Fuel. Leaded and Lead Replacement petrol is increasingly difficult to find in Northern Europe.

Compulsory additional equipment

The driving laws of the countries of Europe still vary in what you are required to carry in your vehicle, although the consequences of not carrying a required piece of equipment are almost always an on-the-spot fine.

To meet these requirements we suggest that you carry the following:

- FIRE EXTINGUISHER
- BASIC TOOL KIT
- FIRST AID KIT
- SPARE BULBS
- TWO WARNING TRIANGLES – two are required in some countries at all times, and are compulsory in most countries when towing.
- HIGH VISIBILITY VEST – now compulsory in France, Spain, Italy and Austria (and likely to become compulsory throughout the EU) in case you need to walk on a motorway.

Insurance and Motoring Documents

Vehicle insurance

Contact your insurer well before you depart to check that your car insurance policy covers driving outside the UK. Most do, but many policies only provide minimum cover (so if you have an accident your insurance may only cover the cost of damage to the other person's property, with no cover for fire and theft).

To maintain the same level of cover abroad as you enjoy at home you need to tell your vehicle insurer. Some will automatically cover you abroad with no extra cost and no extra paperwork. Some will say you need a Green Card (which is neither green nor on card) but won't charge for it. Some will charge extra for the Green Card. Ideally you should contact your vehicle insurer 3-4 weeks before you set off, and confirm your conversation with them in writing.

Breakdown insurance

Arrange breakdown cover for your trip in good time so that if your vehicle breaks down or is involved in an accident it (and your caravan or trailer) can be repaired or returned to this country. This cover can usually be arranged as part of your travel insurance policy (see below).

Documents you must take with you

You may be asked to show your documents at any time so make sure that they are in order, up-to-date and easily accessible while you travel.

These are what you need to take:

- Passports (you may also need a visa in some countries if you hold either a UK passport not issued in the UK or a passport that was issued outside the EU).
- Motor Insurance Certificate, including Green Card (or Continental Cover clause).
- DVLA Vehicle Registration Document plus, if not your own vehicle, the owner's written authority to drive.
- A full valid Driving Licence (not provisional). The new photo style licence is now mandatory in most European countries.

Personal Holiday insurance

Even though you are just travelling within Europe you must take out travel insurance. Few EU countries pay the full cost of medical treatment even under reciprocal health service arrangements. The first part of a holiday insurance policy covers people. It will include the cost of doctor, ambulance and hospital treatment if needed. If needed the better companies will even pay for English language speaking doctors and nurses and will bring a sick or injured holidaymaker home by air ambulance.

An important part of the insurance, often ignored, is cancellation (and curtailment) cover. Few things are as heartbreaking as having to cancel a holiday because a member of the family falls ill. Cancellation insurance can't take away the disappointment, but it makes sure you don't suffer financially as well. For this reason you should arrange your holiday insurance at least eight weeks before you set off.

Whichever insurance you choose we would advise reading very carefully the policies sold by the High Street travel trade. Whilst they may be good, they may not cover the specific needs of campers, caravanners and motorcaravanners.

Telephone 01580 214000 for a quote for our Camping Travel Insurance with cover arranged through leading leisure insurance providers.

Alternatively visit our website at: alanrogers.com/insurance

European Health Insurance Card (EHIC)

Make sure you apply for your EHIC before travelling in Europe. Eligible travellers from the UK are entitled to receive free or reduced-cost medical care in many European countries on production of an EHIC. This free card is available by completing a form in the booklet 'Health Advice for Travellers' from local Post Offices. One should be completed for each family member. Alternatively visit www.ehic.org.uk and apply on-line. Please allow time to send your application off and have the EHIC returned to you.

The EHIC is valid in all European Community countries plus Iceland, Liechtenstein, Switzerland and Norway. If you or any of your dependants are suddenly taken ill or have an accident during a visit to any of these countries, free or reduced-cost emergency treatment is available – in most cases on production of a valid EHIC.

Only state-provided emergency treatment is covered, and you will receive treatment on the same terms as nationals of the country you are visiting. Private treatment is generally not covered, and state-provided treatment may not cover all of the things that you would expect to receive free of charge from the NHS.

Remember an EHIC does not cover you for all the medical costs that you can incur or for repatriation - it is not an alternative to travel insurance. You will still need appropriate insurance to ensure you are fully covered for all eventualities.

Travelling with children

Most countries in Europe are enforcing strict guidelines when you are travelling with children who are not your own. A minor (under the age of 18) must be accompanied by a parent or legal guardian or must carry a letter of authorisation from a parent or guardian. The letter should name the adult responsible for the minor during his or her stay. Similarly, a minor travelling with just one of his/her parents, must have a letter of authority to leave their home country from the parent staying behind. Full information is available at www.fco.gov.uk

Want independent campsite reviews at your fingertips?

You'll find them here...

Over 3,000 in-depth campsite reviews at

www.alanrogers.com

2012 warms up at ExCeL...
The ONLY SHOW in the spring where the leading caravan and motorhome manufacturers will be displaying their NEW 2012 SEASON MODELS.
The MOTORHOME CARAVAN & CAMPING SHOW
14-19 FEB 2012 · EXCEL LONDON
OFFICIAL PARTNER:
THE CARAVAN CLUB
SUPPORTER:
The Camping and Caravanning Club
The Friendly Club
WWW.MOTORHOMECARAVANANDCAMPING.CO.UK
The NATIONAL SHOW at the NEC where you'll see the NEW 2013 SEASON caravan and motorhome models from all the leading manufacturers.
...and Autumn's looking hot too.
The MOTORHOME & CARAVAN SHOW
16-21 OCT 2012 · NEC BIRMINGHAM
SUPPORTERS:
THE CARAVAN CLUB
The Camping and Caravanning Club
The Friendly Club
WWW.MOTORHOMEANDCARAVANSHOW.CO.UK

Map 1

Belgium, Luxembourg, Netherlands

Please refer to the town index (page 560) for campsite page references

Denmark, Germany

Please refer to the town index (page 560) for campsite page references

Norway, Finland, Sweden

Please refer to the town index (page 560) for campsite page references

Map 4

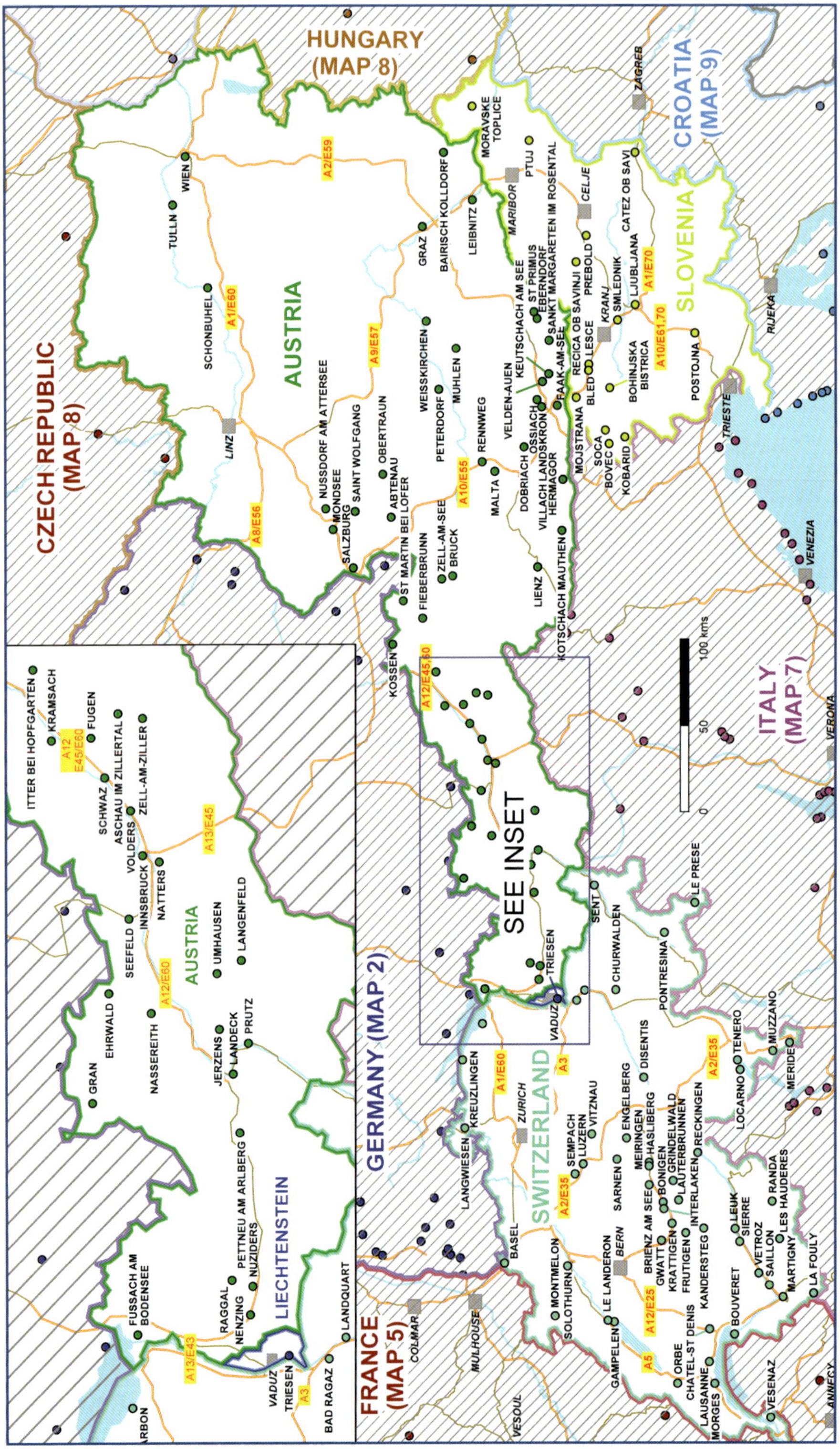

Please refer to the town index (page 560) for campsite page references

Map 5

France (West)

Please refer to the town index (page 560) for campsite page references

France (East)

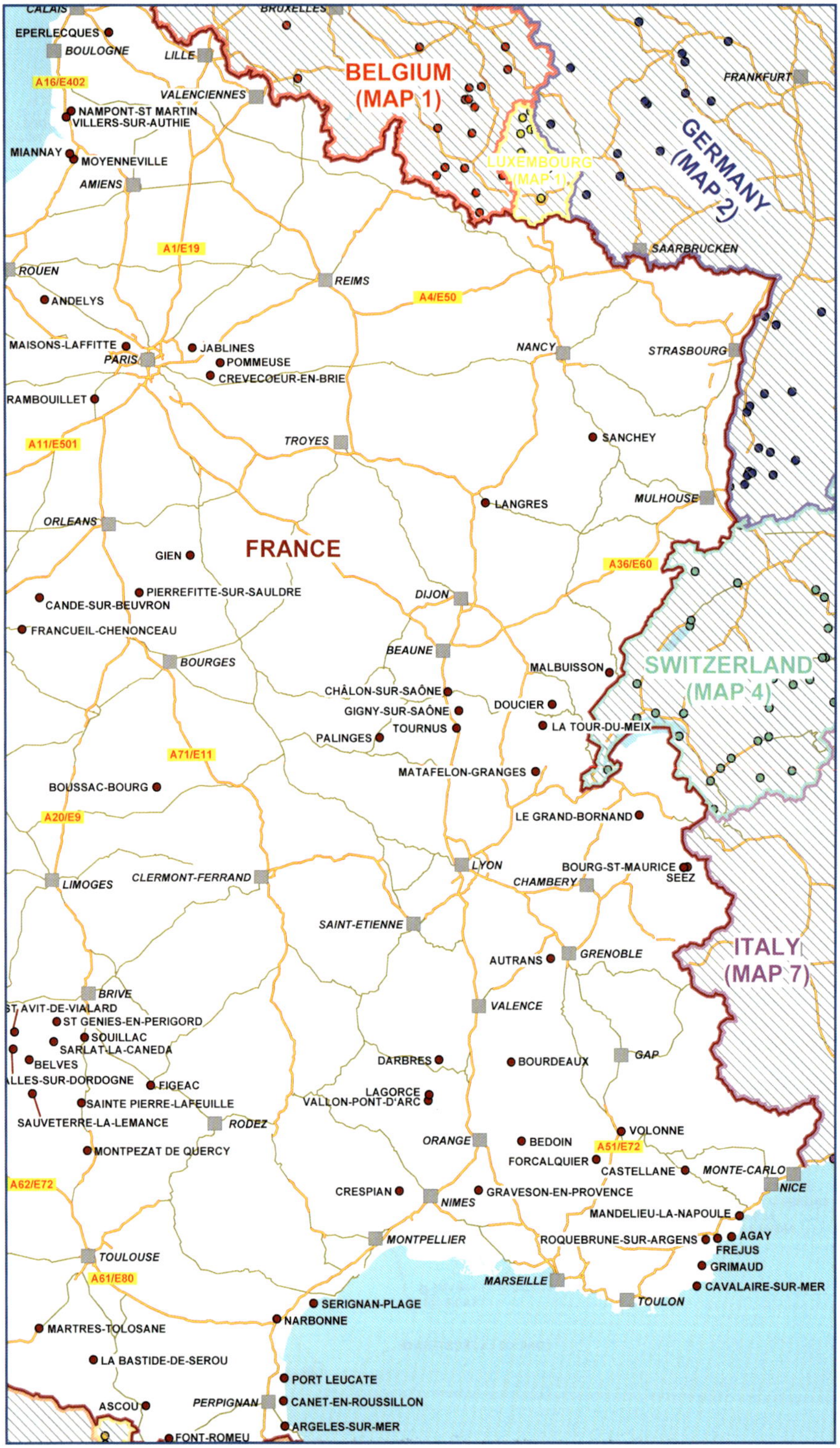

Please refer to the town index (page 560) for campsite page references

Map 7

Italy

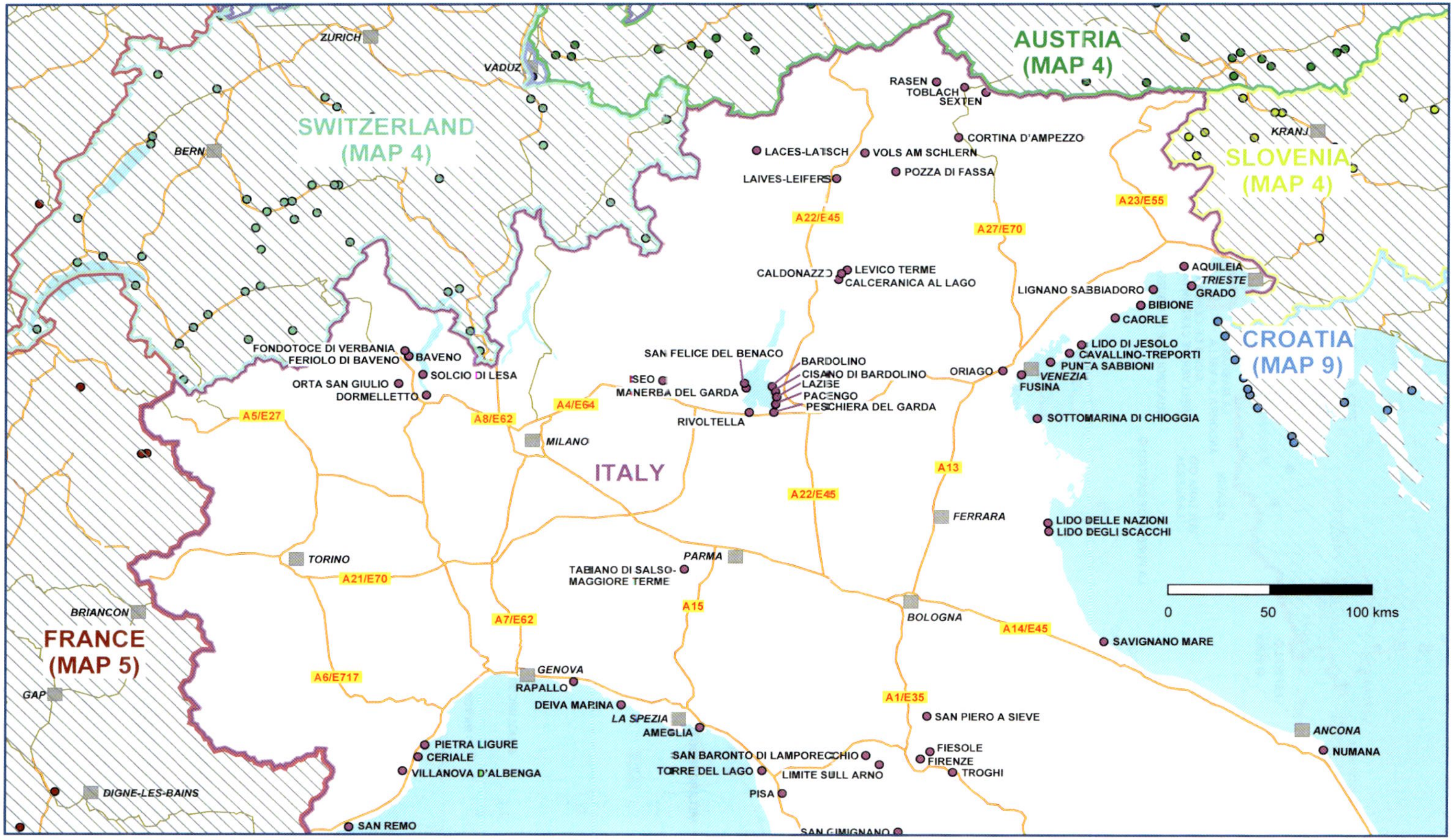

Please refer to the town index (page 560) for campsite page references

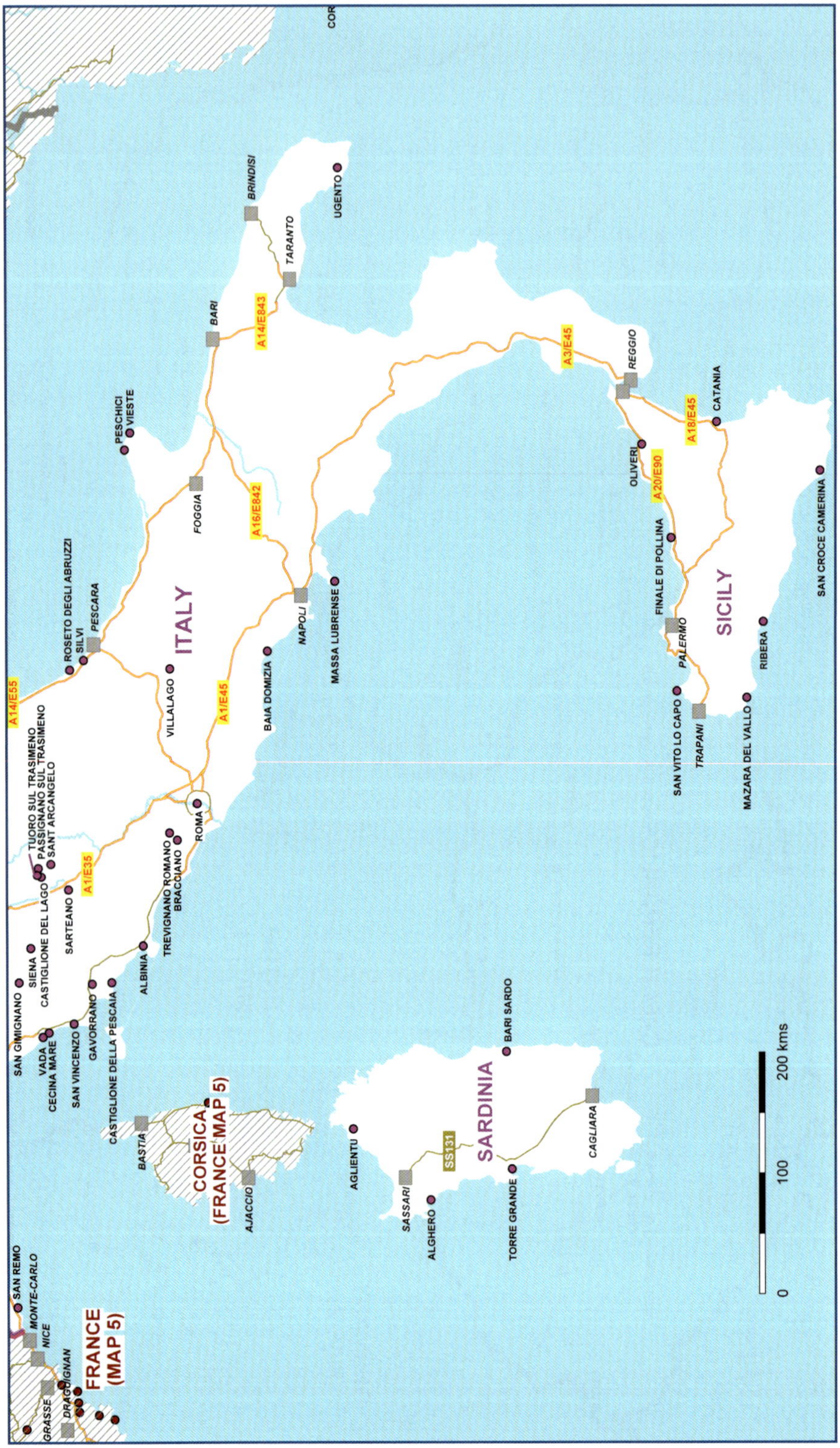

Please refer to the town index (page 560) for campsite page references

Map 8

Czech Republic, Slovakia, Hungary

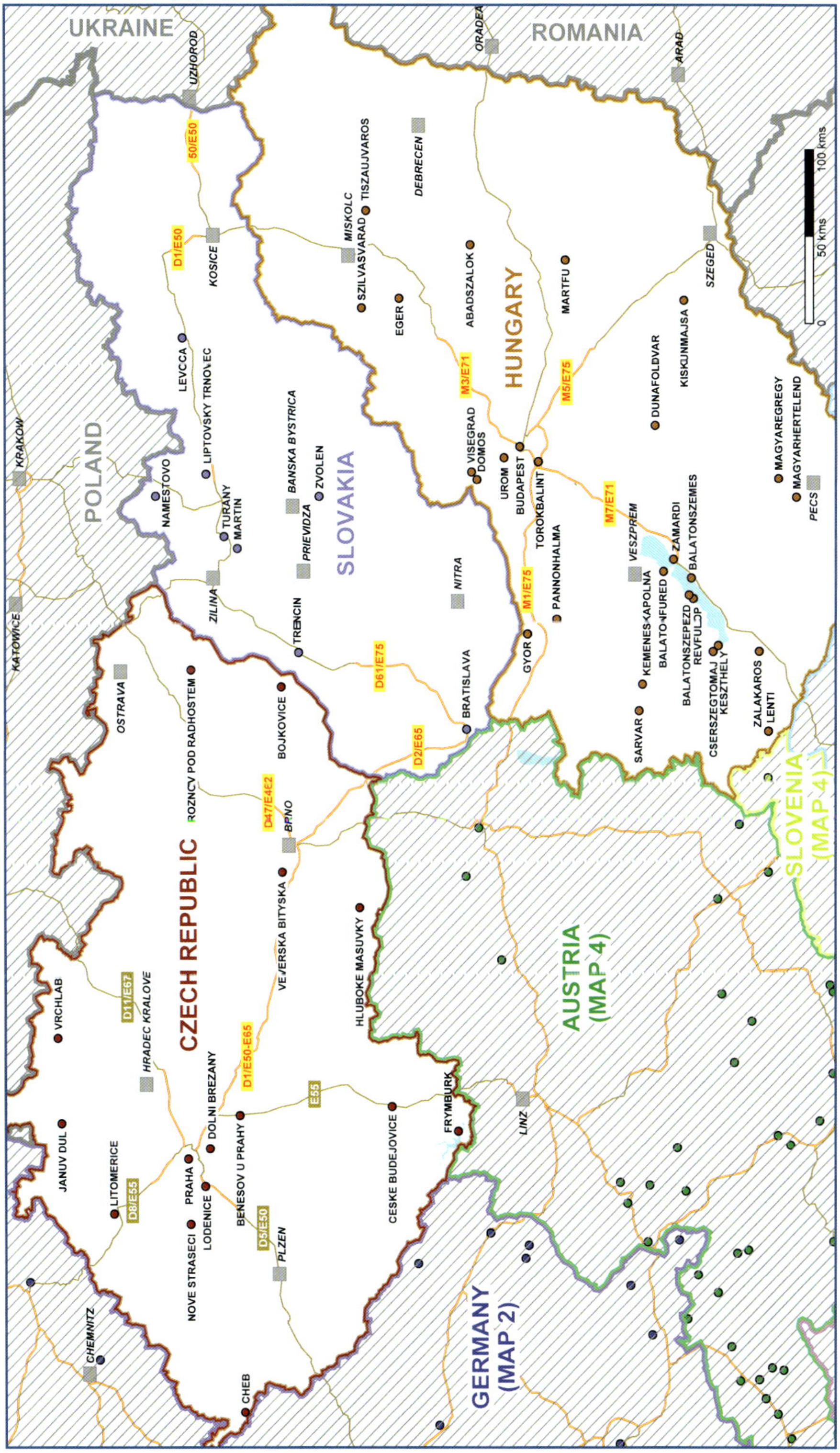

Please refer to the town index (page 560) for campsite page references

Croatia

Greece

Please refer to the town index (page 560) for campsite page references

Town & Village Index

Switzerland

Index by Campsite Number

Andorra

Austria

Belgium

Index - Campsite Number

Germany

Index by Country and Campsite Name